2002
Novel & Short Story Writer's MARKET

Make your publication
DREAMS COME TRUE!

EDITED BY
ANNE BOWLING

ASSISTED BY
VANESSA LYMAN

WRITER'S DIGEST BOOKS
CINCINNATI, OH

If you are a publisher of fiction and would like to be considered for a listing in the next edition of *Novel & Short Story Writer's Market*, send a SASE (or SAE and IRC) with your request for a questionnaire to *Novel & Short Story Writer's Market*—QR, 1507 Dana Ave., Cincinnati OH 45207. Questionnaires received after July 15, 2002, will be held for the 2003 edition.

Editorial Director, Annuals Department: Barbara Kuroff
Managing Editor, Annuals Department: Doug Hubbuch
Production Editor: Vanessa Lyman

Writer's Digest Books website: www.writersdigest.com
Writer's Market website: www.writersmarket.com

International Standard Serial Number 0897-9812
International Standard Book Number 1-58297-073-4

Cover design by Lisa Buchanan. Cover illustration by John Hanley.

Attention Booksellers: This is an annual directory of F&W Publications. Return deadline for this edition is April 30, 2003.

contents at a glance

Contents

RESOURCES

From the Editor

Rafael Montserrat sent me an e-mail about a month ago. A fiction writer from San Rafael, California, he had some questions about how to use *Novel & Short Story Writer's Market* to sell his first novel, *Uncharted Voyage*. I could tell from the e-mail notes we traded and the synopsis he shared that his writing voice was assured, his wit quick, and his sense of timing well-honed. We are still corresponding, and I'm looking forward to the day I hear a publisher has offered him a contract.

About a month before Rafael's e-mail arrived in my mailbox, *The Wall Street Journal* ran an op-ed piece panning "how-to" writing books. Such books, the writer says, "belong in the 'magic' section of the bookstore, next to 'grand illusions' and 'let's pretend.' " She goes on to add that "evidently there exists a widespread belief that the good ol' Yankee can-do spirit—the kind that helps you learn how to puff a soufflé or lay a garden path—extends to an imaginative realm like novel-writing."

It seems to me about once every two years this idea occurs to someone—that books for writers really can't "make" a writer—and they offer it up as though a) it's a new idea and b) it's the whole truth. But there's a lot more to the story: it *is* just that "can-do spirit" that takes unpublished writers to publication. The old butt-in-the-chair, work on your mechanics, perfect your craft approach. You court the idea and coax the muse, draft and revise, draft and revise. There is no how-to book that can instill raw talent where none exists, but there are precious few writers who make it to publication without first mastering that process. And as for talent, I see evidence every day that there's a great deal of it out there.

But don't take my word for it. If you haven't already explored the vast world of online fiction publications, you're in for a real treat. From established literary journals to hypertext to dynamic genre sites, it's an exciting community with thousands of opportunities for fiction writers today. (See our new Online Markets section, page 343). We're also very pleased to bring you a slew of how-to instruction from the best: John Updike, Joyce Carol Oates, Sue Grafton, T.C. Boyle, Linda Lael Miller, Jim Harrison and many more. You'll also find updates to the some 1,700 markets for your work—from book publishers to small presses to zines.

Even with all of today's opportunities, the competition is stiff. It may seem sometimes as though getting your fiction published really does require "magic." But I think magic happens when someone's hard at work behind it, butt in the chair, bringing together that confluence of fresh ideas and technical mastery that results in good fiction. Writers like Rafael and the thousands of others who use *Novel & Short Story Writer's Market* know the work can be demanding, but also that it gives back its rewards, personal and professional. Best wishes for a successful year of writing!

Anne Patterson Bowling
Editor
nsswm@fwpubs.com

With many thanks to Rafael Montserrat and all our community of readers, and to our contributors who have made this edition such a pleasure to put together: writer and production editor Vanessa Lyman, Will Allison, Katie Struckel Brogan, Kelly Milner Halls, Jack Heffron, Kim Kane, Gordon Kirkland, Candi Lace, Val MacEwan, Kelly Nickell, W.E. Reinka, I.J. Schecter, Karen X. Tulchinsky, Brad Vice, Jean Vickers and Lex Williford; and also our Writer's Digest Books staff.

The "Quick-Start" Guide to Publishing Your Fiction

To make the most of *Novel & Short Story Writer's Market* you need to know how to use it. And with more than 600 pages of fiction publishing markets and resources, a writer could easily get lost amid the information. This "quick-start" guide will help you wind your way through the pages of *Novel & Short Story Writer's Market*, as well as the fiction publishing process, and emerge with your dream accomplished—to see your fiction in print.

1. Read, read, read.

Read numerous magazines, fiction collections and novels to determine if your fiction compares favorably with work currently being published. If your fiction is at least the same caliber as that you're reading, then move on to step two. If not, postpone submitting your work and spend your time polishing your fiction. Writing and reading the work of others are the best ways to improve craft.

For help with craft and critique of your work:

- You'll find articles on the craft and business aspects of writing fiction in the Craft & Technique section, beginning on page 32 and in the Getting Published section, beginning on page 54.
- If you're thinking about publishing your work online, see the Electronic Publishing section on page 79.
- If you're a genre writer, you will find information in For Mystery Writers, beginning on page 91, For Romance Writers, beginning on page 105 and For Science Fiction/Fantasy & Horror Writers, beginning on page 121.
- You'll find Conference & Workshop listings beginning on page 552.
- You'll find Organizations for fiction writers on page 598.

2. Analyze your fiction.

Determine the type of fiction you write to best target your submissions to markets most suitable to your work. Do you write literary, genre, mainstream or one of many other categories of fiction? There are magazines and presses seeking specialized work in each of these areas as well as numerous others.

For editors and publishers with specialized interests, see the Category Index beginning on page 618.

3. Learn about the market.

Read *Writer's Digest* magazine (F&W Publications, Inc.), *Poet's & Writers* and *Byline*. Also read *Publishers Weekly*, the trade magazine of the publishing industry, and *Independent Publisher* containing information about small- to medium-sized independent presses. And don't forget the Internet. The number of sites for writers seems to grow daily, and among them you'll find www.writersmarket.com and www.writersdigest.com (see page 610 for Websites of Interest).

4. Find markets for your work.

There are a variety of ways to locate markets for fiction. The periodicals sections of bookstores and libraries are great places to discover new journals and magazines that might be open to your type of short stories. Read writing-related magazines and newsletters for information about new markets and publications seeking fiction submissions. Also, frequently browse bookstore shelves to see what novels and short story collections are being published and by whom. Check acknowledgment pages for names of editors and agents, too. Online journals often have links to the websites of other journals that may publish fiction. And last but certainly not least, read the listings found here in *Novel & Short Story Writer's Market*.

Also, don't forget to utilize the Category Indexes at the back of this book to help you target your fiction to the right market.

5. Send for guidelines.

In the listings in this book, we try to include as much submission information as we can from editors and publishers. Over the course of the year, however, editors' expectations and needs may change. Therefore, it is best to request submission guidelines by sending a self-addressed stamped envelope (SASE). You can also check the websites of magazines and presses which usually contain a page with guideline information. You can find updated guidelines of many of the markets listed here at www.writersdigest.com. And for an even more comprehensive and continually updated online markets list, you can obtain a subscription to www.writersmarket.com by calling 1-800-289-0963.

6. Begin your publishing efforts with journals and contests open to beginners.

If this is your first attempt at publishing your work, your best bet is to begin with local publications or those you know are open to beginning writers. Then, after you have built a publication history, you can try the more prestigious and nationally distributed magazines. For publications and contests most open to beginners, look for the ❑ symbol preceding listing titles. Also, look for the ◨ symbol that identifies markets open to exceptional work from beginners as well as work from experienced, previously published writers.

7. Submit your fiction in a professional manner.

Take the time to show editors that you care about your work and are serious about publishing. By following a publication's or book publisher's submission guidelines and practicing standard submission etiquette, you can better ensure your chances that an editor will want to take the time to read your work and consider it for publication. Remember, first impressions last, and a carelessly assembled submission packet can jeopardize your chances before your story or novel manuscript has had a chance to speak for itself. For help with preparing submissions read The Business of Fiction Writing, beginning on page 70.

8. Keep track of your submissions.

Know when and where you have sent fiction and how long you need to wait before expecting a reply. If an editor does not respond by the time indicated in his market listing or guidelines, wait a few more weeks and then follow up with a letter (and SASE) asking when the editor anticipates making a decision. If you still do not receive a reply from the editor within a reasonable amount of time, send a letter withdrawing your work from consideration and move on to the next market on your list. (See Perfecting Your Submission Process on page 54 for more information.)

9. Learn from rejection.

Rejection is the hardest part of the publication process. Unfortunately, rejection happens to every writer, and every writer needs to learn to deal with the negativity involved. On the other hand, rejection can be valuable when used as a teaching tool rather than a reason to doubt yourself and your work. If an editor offers suggestions with his or her rejection slip, take those comments into consideration. You don't have to automatically agree with an editor's opinion of your work. It may be that the editor has a different perspective on the piece than you do. Or, you may find that the editor's suggestions give you new insight into your work and help you improve your craft.

10. Don't give up.

The best advice for you as you try to get published is be persistent, and always believe in yourself and your work. By continually reading other writers' work, constantly working on the craft of fiction writing and relentlessly submitting your work, you will eventually find that magazine or book publisher that's the perfect match for your fiction. And, *Novel & Short Story Writer's Market* will be here to help you every step of the way.

GUIDE TO LISTING FEATURES

Below you will find an example of the market listings contained in *Novel & Short Story Writer's Market*. Also included are callouts identifying the various format features of the listings. (For an explanation of the symbols used, see the front and back covers of this book.)

ICONS FOR EASY REFERENCING   COMMENTS FROM THE NSSWM EDITOR   WHAT TO SEND   WHO TO CONTACT   PUBLICATION PROFILE

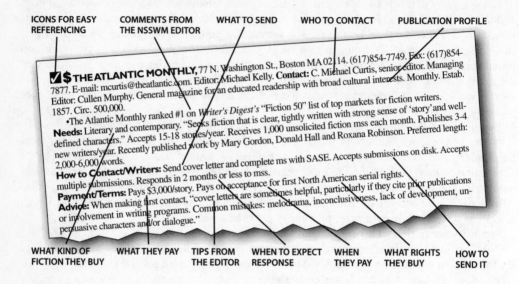

☑ $ **THE ATLANTIC MONTHLY,** 77 N. Washington St., Boston MA 02114. (617)854-7749. Fax: (617)854-7877. E-mail: mcurtis@theatlantic.com. Editor: Michael Kelly. **Contact:** C. Michael Curtis, senior editor. Managing Editor: Cullen Murphy. General magazine for an educated readership with broad cultural interests. Monthly. Estab. 1857. Circ. 500,000.

• The Atlantic Monthly ranked #1 on *Writer's Digest's* "Fiction 50" list of top markets for fiction writers.

Needs: Literary and contemporary. "Seeks fiction that is clear, tightly written with strong sense of 'story' and well-defined characters." Accepts 15-18 stories/year. Receives 1,000 unsolicited fiction mss each month. Publishes 3-4 new writers/year. Recently published work by Mary Gordon, Donald Hall and Roxana Robinson. Preferred length: 2,000-6,000 words.

How to Contact/Writers: Send cover letter and complete ms with SASE. Accepts submissions on disk. Accepts multiple submissions. Responds in 2 months or less to mss.

Payment/Terms: Pays $3,000/story. Pays on acceptance for first North American serial rights.

Advice: When making first contact, "cover letters are sometimes helpful, particularly if they cite prior publications or involvement in writing programs. Common mistakes: melodrama, inconclusiveness, lack of development, unpersuasive characters and/or dialogue."

WHAT KIND OF FICTION THEY BUY   WHAT THEY PAY   TIPS FROM THE EDITOR   WHEN TO EXPECT RESPONSE   WHEN THEY PAY   WHAT RIGHTS THEY BUY   HOW TO SEND IT

Writing Fiction

Dissecting the Short Story: In Class with T.C. Boyle

BY W.E. REINKA

T.C. Boyle likes to tell the story about the time three old ladies in a hotel elevator tried to get him to admit he was a rock star. The more he asserted that he was really a writer and English professor, the more they giggled and begged him to come clean.

Boyle is as likely to sprinkle epigraphs in his fiction quoting Bob Marley or Bruce Springsteen as Herman Melville or Franz Kafka, and he calls rock and roll "the most instructive music of my life." But don't assume he listens to rock and roll when he is working. It turns out Boyle prefers a background of jazz and classical chamber music when he writes. He took to jazz early, heading off to an undergraduate career with his saxophone under his arm, hoping to be a music major. Though he still calls John Coltrane "my god and hero," he flunked his audition and stumbled into creative writing his junior year.

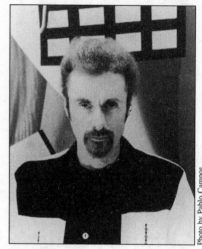

T.C. Boyle

Photo by Pablo Campos

T.C. Boyle's fiction is as impossible to pigeonhole as he is. He often draws on real people past and present in his fiction. Novels like *The Road to Wellville* or *Riven Rock* are based on historical figures. But don't assume he's an historical novelist. His latest novel, *A Friend of the Earth* (Viking), is a futuristic eco-fantasy. "Heart of a Champion," a short story he wrote while still in graduate school, reads like a stand-up comedian's pastiche of the old TV show *Lassie*. In "Greasy Lake" (1981), three 19-year-old punks learn that the disaffected facades they wear like armor are no protection against uncalculated evil. It's terrifying, but not wholly without humor and so beautifully written that its striking images stop readers in mid-sentence. By the time he wrote "56-0" (1992), Boyle was an established name in American letters. At first glance, "56-0" looks like an unabashed romp that hearkens back to "Heart of a Champion," with Boyle aiming his satire at pseudo-values and jocks as heroes. But if a reader gets past first-glance assumptions and delves into that story, it becomes clear that Boyle may remain a stand-up comic, but a comic reared on Twain, Beckett and Barth. It's a complex story about values, honor and futility. In fact, it reads like the perfect story for Boyle and his students to take apart in class.

People aren't always what they seem at first glance. Neither are stories. How apt that a writer who is personally and professionally as complex as T.C. Boyle encourages his writing students to challenge their assumptions. He conducts his writing classes at the University of Southern California primarily by taking stories apart, looking under the hoods of stories, so to speak, to see what works or, conversely, what doesn't work. His workshop method is a good model for

W.E. REINKA *is a fulltime freelance writer of fiction and nonfiction. He is former books editor of the* Berkeley Insider *and the* Berkeley Voice. *He has published reviews, personal essays, profiles, business articles and travel pieces in publications nationwide.*

small writing groups to follow. On a pre-arranged schedule, four stories are passed out for discussion the following week. The students write interpretive comments on them (e.g., What does this mean? This puzzles me. I love this ending. It moved me. I don't understand this.). Boyle reads three anonymous comments aloud to stimulate a class discussion.

"The class approaches the story interpretively as one might discuss a work in a literary class," he tells us. "Part of the discussion is also to see how the story is put together and if that's effective. How does it open? Is that the best way? Why is the author using the present tense here? Is that confusing? Is it effective? The author simply listens to what we have to say. The author doesn't get to stand up and say 'What I really meant was' or 'You guys missed it' or 'Gee, I love you.' Nothing. We are the guinea pigs for the author's experiment in discovering how an audience interprets his or her work."

Boyle also passes back his copy of the story to the student with grammatical notations and refers them to sections of the grammatical handbook they use in class. "I may also sometimes make changes in their phrasing and so on but those are only suggestions. Lastly I write them a note that says what I think is successful and not so successful in the story. The problem with this last part is that my handwriting is so bad that no one can actually read the note." He stares impishly after making the last statement. He often concludes serious with straight-faced humor, challenging his listener to get beyond the surface of the conversation the way he challenges his students to dig into stories.

"Those are only suggestions," exemplifies his approach to teaching. "My job with my students is to be their coach. I just guide them. I want them to be great literary writers in their own way. I try to help them find what that way is and what their voice and direction will be. I think the worst kind of teacher tries to impose their own aesthetic on the students and they wind up making clones of themselves. That does a real disservice to the individual writers."

Fair enough, but beyond that grammatical handbook, aren't there certain basics? Doesn't Boyle tell his students that a good story needs an engaging beginning followed by a distinct middle and end? Or that good stories require resolution and sympathetic characters?

"There are no rules," he says emphatically. "Some writing teachers have certain rules—these things you can and cannot do. I think that is patently absurd because you're working in an art form and you are the only one who can write your own stories, for better or worse. That's one of the miracles of it. In order to do that, you have to find out what your own way is. Any story can break any rule and be great. All you have is an individual work by an individual person. Once that work is complete, you examine it."

That's not to say Boyle and his class might not suggest an individual story might need a more engaging beginning or stronger resolution. "When I say there are no rules, I mean there are no general rules. How could there be because each work is individual? However, I give my opinions about a given work. I may say to the author that perhaps this needs more resolution or perhaps this is confusing or why end here, should this go on to here? In my class, the author also gets 19 other opinions. I emphasize that I may be the pro here but I have my prejudices, too, and I am giving just my opinion on the story and the author can take it or leave it. Unless it's a grammatical change, they are free to do what they want. I cannot impose my will on them. It's not my story; it's their story. I emphasize to them that throughout their careers, no matter who might ask them to change an ending, let's say, that they have to think long and hard and believe that's the case. Otherwise, don't do it. Of course, every writer comes to a point of crisis where an editor for a magazine where they really want to be published says 'I think you ought to change this' with the implication that then they'll publish it. At that point, the author has to do a little soul searching."

Back in the late 1970s when Boyle started the writing program at USC, he taught beginning students. These days he concentrates his personal time on more advanced students who have already shown a talent for writing.

"Writing is not for everybody. If you don't have a talent for it, no amount of teaching will make you a good writer or a great writer. That said, studying writing in depth in the way I would study it with my students, taking it apart and seeing what it is, gives you a great appreciation for it. So even if you don't become a great writer you can know the work from the inside out and appreciate it that way. Many, many people though have a great gift for writing and may not be aware of it. By the time my students come to me, they're aware of it. They've made their choice to pursue it."

As for less advanced writers, Boyle concedes that their work is more apt to suffer from poor mechanics, but he doesn't endorse the typical list of complaints from instructors of beginning writers—inordinate attention to detail, overabundance of modifiers, telling not showing. Rather he bemoans beginners who do not have a foundation in the art form they wish to pursue.

"The biggest problem I find is with students who haven't read much, especially in terms of their contemporaries—who's alive and who's writing today. And so they write in an unsophisticated way and sometimes in an archaic way because the only literature they know they're studying in other classes. They don't know what's current. On the first day in my intermediate class, I ask the students to write down their ten favorite books of fiction and their authors. A lot of them can't name ten. A lot of them fill in with genre writers, thrillers and what not. I say to them, 'I bet you can name ten CDs. I bet you can name fifty! I bet you can name ten movies. I bet you can name ten TV shows.' So they come into this art form presuming or wanting to be artists with the presumption that it just happens. They have no idea that it's an assimilative process and that they have to read in order to produce their own good work. I find beginning writers writing stories that have essentially TV show plots. They have nothing to do with the real world or love of language. Over the years, I have found that better readers invariably prove to be better writers. The only way you can write stories is to have read thousands of them."

As such, part of Boyle's writing class is analyzing the fiction of established writers or "pros," as he likes to call them. He likes to examine the works of these pros not to copy so much as to stimulate the exploration of other possibilities to achieve certain effects. In recent years, the class has focused on such contemporary writers such as Jamaica Kincaid, E. Annie Proulx, Kent Haruf, Stacy Richter, Tobias Wolff and Mary Gaitskill. Back in the 1970s when he attended the Iowa Writers' Workshop, Boyle studied under John Cheever but avoided reading Cheever in favor of then current heroes like Robert Coover, Thomas Pynchon, Donald Barthelme and Gabriel Garcia Marquez. It wasn't until after college that Boyle read Cheever's stories and came to consider the diminutive teacher who wore bow ties to class a masterful short story writer.

Those who didn't grow up with a book under their arm may take heart in Boyle's own history. In an autobiographical essay entitled "This Monkey, My Back," he recalls that it wasn't until college that he first became interested in writing. He began to read in high school but with nowhere near the intensity he developed later on. "Unlike most of my compatriots at the Iowa Writers' Workshop in the '70s, and the majority of my own students now, I didn't develop my addiction in the womb or drink it up with my mother's milk. I wasn't touched by an angel, I didn't wear bottle lenses and braces and hide out in dark corners, my only friend a book."

Boyle also runs contrary to convention in advising writers to write what they don't know. "I love to write fiction and only fiction because it is a process of discovery. I don't know what will come. The old saw with writing is 'write what you know.' I feel just the opposite. 'Write what you don't know and discover something.' That's why it is so exciting for me to continue to write fiction. I never know what will come next."

Sometimes that process of discovery comes slowly. "You just have to think of yourself as a writer and you're going to write and here's the idea and you begin. Maybe it doesn't go so well today. Maybe it doesn't go well for a week. If you keep working, whether you're inspired or not, hopefully you'll break through."

When Boyle attended the Iowa Writers' Workshop, things were pretty loose. It was the hippie era. If he didn't feel like writing, that was fine. But that's not how he conducts his classes. "My students are always under the gun—they must produce work by a given date. I believe in discipline. I don't believe you wait for the creative impulse to hit. I think you make it hit. I think you force it." He pauses like a comedian timing his punch line. "In other words, I don't let my students get away with what I got away with."

Teaching methods aren't the only thing Boyle has adjusted in the last 30 years. "Tom" to friends, his early books list his name as "T. Coraghessan Boyle." He claims his greatest joy is to have his works read. Consistent with that joy, Boyle is a terrific self-promoter as well as a terrific writer. "Coraghessan" would stick with potential readers better than either "Thomas" or "Boyle," even if no one was quite sure exactly how to pronounce "Coraghessan." (On his website, he has posted a *New Yorker* cartoon where a man says to a bookstore clerk, "I'm looking for something by T. What's-His-Face Boyle.") He jokes self-deprecatingly that he changed to "T.C. Boyle" on his book jackets a few years back when his publisher told him they could print his name in bigger letters if he thinned his handle. He may have the distinction of being the only author who writes a single book under two names—his new covers show "T.C. Boyle," the title pages still credit "T. Coraghessan Boyle."

"I find beginning writers writing stories that have essentially TV show plots. They have nothing to do with the real world or love of language. Over the years, I have found that better readers invariably prove to be better writers. The only way you can write stories is to have read thousands of them."

When in front of an audience, Boyle happily discusses how he works. But he questions whether it helps anyone. "People ask how I work as if there's a formula, thinking if they knew how I do it then they could do it, too. I can only tell them how I work which may not be right for them." He works intuitively, trying to shape an idea into the beginning of a story. The first few lines or first page are the hardest part and may take as long as a week as he searches for voice and language and characters slowly form. All the while the story is starting to take shape on an unconscious level. He follows the trail, on the path of that process of discovery.

Likewise, people often ask how writers get their ideas. As far as Boyle is concerned, stories are everywhere, in our own lives, in history books, in the morning papers. "I feel anything can be a story. I write from my own experience or the experience of historical figures. 'The Love of My Life,' about two teenagers who had a baby and dumped it in a bin—that stemmed from a news story." As far as Boyle is concerned, we're all storytellers whether or not we're writers. "We tell each other stories every day. 'You know what happened to me, man? Just yesterday, you won't believe it.' That's a story and that story might involve real people or might be a fantasy or could be any other kind of different story."

Whatever Boyle chooses as his subjects, he considers them as personal and individual as any other aspect of writing. He doesn't want other people's ideas. "I write my books because I write what obsesses and interests me. That's how I relate to the world and that's how I figure out how I feel about things. A story for me is an exercise of the imagination."

While he exercises his imagination, he works single-mindedly—a short story or a novel at a time. Since the publication last fall of *After the Plague*, a collection of 16 new stories, he has put stories aside entirely to spend this year working on his next novel. Once that novel is finished, will he take some well-deserved time off?

Probably not. When he finished *A Friend of the Earth*, Boyle was at a mountain hideaway. His family was back home near sea level ("where they had run to hide"). To commemorate completing the novel he enjoyed a solitary walk in the woods. The next day he started a new story. He had no choice. "Writing is a habit, an addiction, as powerful and overmastering an urge as putting a bottle to your lips or a spike in your arm."

Jim Harrison

Jim Harrison: Literary Shape-Shifter

BY JEAN VICKERS

Shape-shifter: noun; 1887: one that seems able to change form at will.
—Merriam Webster's Collegiate Dictionary

Jim Harrison—novelist, poet, screenwriter, outdoorsman, gourmet cook, world traveler, Zen Buddhist, father, and husband of 40 years—straddles a precarious line. It's one that pretty much all writers struggle with: the line of intimacy you must cross in order to be absorbed by your characters. It's a line that a less devoted writer will never cross. Harrison explains, "You have to temporarily *be* the character in order to understand him. It's sort of what they used to call 'shape-shifting'." His choice of terminology reflects both Harrison's love and respect for Native American teachings, as well as his practice of Zen Buddhism. "Zen is what keeps me alive more than anything," he says. In his essay "Everyday Life, the Question of Zen," Harrison declares, "Without (Zen) I'd be dead as a doornail since I have been a man, at times, of intemperate habits."

Harrison, the Northern Michigan writer who has hitchhiked from one ocean to another, winters in the Arizona desert, and sojourns to France as often as possible, has said that Michigan is the only place he has ever been able to write. Often based in the woods or wide-open spaces of America's heartland, Harrison's stories richly explore the cycles of family relationships, and are earth-dampened, taut with muscle-flexing and vengeance, and crackling with the bygone fires of woodsmen and Native Americans.

Since 1971, Harrison has written 11 novels, four screenplays, nine books of poetry, and innumerable works of nonfiction, including articles for *Sports Illustrated*, *Esquire*, and *Playboy*. Now, of all things, he's also written a children's book titled *The Boy Who Ran to the Woods* (Atlantic Monthly Press, 2000). Harrison, blinded in his left eye from a childhood injury, explains, "I wrote this children's book because my grandson asked me how my eye was hurt, and the only adequate explanation seemed, to me, to be a story where I could tell the whole thing. So *The Boy Who Ran to the Woods* is completely true."

Not only is it completely true, it's also an example of Harrison becoming someone else for the sake of a story. In this case, he became Little Jimmy, the hero of the story and the little boy he used to be. After his tragic injury, Harrison "had become the King of the Wild Boys, which is not something to brag about." He began causing trouble in school and getting poor grades. In an attempt to tame him, his father and uncle took him on a trip deep into the woods. His father said, "you're a wild boy, and this is a good place to be wild." After a few weeks of crazed running through the woods, Jimmy slowed his pace and began to discover some things. He learned that if he crept quietly he wouldn't frighten birds, and could observe them in their nests. He noticed snakes and turtles sunning themselves, and learned how to caw with the crows. He slept outside. He rose at dawn and swam with loons. He learned to use a compass, to fish, and to hunt. He became self-reliant. He also learned that nature would always be there for him

JEAN VICKERS *is a freelance writer living in Southwest Colorado. She has written for newspapers and travel magazines, and wrote the feature story with Canadian singer Hayden for the 2000 edition of* Songwriter's Market. *Jean is currently working on a collection of short fiction inspired by her father who has Alzheimer's, but continues to be "the most blissful man" she has ever known.*

when he needed solace. The woods became the setting for his life.

Nature is also central to his characters' lives. If his characters do end up in a city, they are usually pining for the country—possibly an echo of Harrison's time spent as a university professor. "Universities are in the wrong places," he says. "I like to live in the country, and universities are always in the cities or suburbs. It seems the soul life of an area—to me, at least—resides in its landscape. The Sand Hills of Nebraska, for instance, are like some kind of dream landscape. I mean, we're animals. We're sensual creatures, and it is sights, sounds, and smells that jog our over-intellectualized brains."

To help induce this "jogging," Harrison will get in his car and drive for weeks, with his only destination being "to gather new memories." He mentally collects the aforementioned sensualities of sights, sounds, and smells that he can nurture into stories and characters. For example, he says, "the novel *Farmer* came from the smell of a weed. There's a ground ivy that's in all barnyards. *Dalva* came from that Edward Hopper painting of a girl looking out a window in the evening."

Harrison describes further, "Sometimes you enter some characters more than others." The novels *Dalva* and its sequel *The Road Home* follow the lives of the Northridge family beginning in frontier days. Dalva, the title character, is one that Harrison says he "entered too deeply for real sanity at the time." Not only is Dalva a woman seeking her identity, but "the woman I wanted to be in love with," Harrison says. The transition to a feminine point of view shows Harrison's ability to shape-shift, or as he has described, engage in a Buddhist process in which he will "totally abnegate" his own personality to become the character. That critics had accused Harrison of being a "macho fiction writer" for many years made the successful transition into a woman's point of view particularly satisfying.

Dalva is not the only time Harrison has successfully 'become' a woman. He did so again, as Clare, in the novella *The Woman Lit By Fireflies*, and again as Julip in the novel of the same name. But, he says, "Dalva nearly killed me. Both my eardrums were broken because I had different kinds of flu and viruses, and I ignored them totally until I was about dead. But I guess it was worth it."

"I don't think it matters how fast you write. It's how long you thought about it. I like to think of it as a well filling up. I think about it until the well is full, and then I let go."

Once he has transported himself into his character's world, how exactly does he get the story written? "I don't think it matters how fast you write. It's how long you thought about it. I like to think of it as a well filling up. I think about it until the well is full, and then I let go." For example, at a 1997 lecture Harrison mentioned that he wrote *Legends of the Fall* in only nine days, "but I thought about it for three years." As he said in a 1996 interview, "You have to get it all down before you change your mind. The alternative is not bothering to write at all. That's something you're fighting all the time, what Tom McGuane calls 'the loss of cabin pressure.' "

Of course, at some point a writer must let a character go and shape-shift back to his previous form, a regular person who pays telephone bills and watches television and has to change his socks. When he releases that character he has been for so long, is it like grieving a loss? "I do mourn my characters," Harrison says. "I wrote an essay once where I was sure that far back in a marsh there was a hummock—a little hill of hardwoods—and an old farm house, where all the heroines in my novels lived together with all my beloved dead dogs." He laughs, "I've discussed this with my therapist, naturally. He says it's okay in fair amounts.

"I know actresses and actors who have the same problem. See, they get into the character so completely that it's sometimes hard to get out of the character. Although Jack Nicholson said 'you gotta do something completely different,' and in fact after the finishing of *Brown Dog* it was helpful to go immediately to Paris."

Brown Dog, also known as B.D., is a self-reliant woodsman from, aptly, Northern Michigan. He's a comic hero who appears in three of Harrison's stories, including his 2000 novella *The Beast God Forgot to Invent*. "Brown Dog is my continuing survival mechanism. You know, what I can fall back on. I have a remote cabin and when I'm unhappy with the world I just retreat to that reality. Brown Dog's reality. He's living art in a sense that he's very resilient. He's very similar to a lot of stories about Native American tricksters." (The trickster is often portrayed in Native American stories in the physical form of Coyote, a crafty figure who plays tricks on people or is the butt of other people's jokes.) B.D., like Harrison, is a man fulfilled by the simplest of lives. B.D. states in *The Woman Lit By Fireflies*, "My favorite thing is just walking in the woods. I can do it for days on end without tiring of it." Says Harrison: "Brown Dog gets into horrible situations but he manages to get out. That's why I like him."

Much like Brown Dog, Harrison has suffered horrible situations and gotten out as well. His low points include financial struggles and ensuing depressions early in his writing career. His lowest, most painful point was the sudden death of his father and sister in an automobile accident. "I was 21, and I thought, 'well, if this can happen, you better do what your heart tells you to do, because you just might die for no reason.' " Either as a result of—or in spite of—his personal familiarity with loss, his writing embraces the natural cycles of life, including, of course, death. "It seems to me that in America particularly, we have an unreasonable preoccupation with the idea that we might never get old and die. I heard on the radio that the only way to escape growing old is to die young." The loss of his family members didn't directly nudge him into writing more, "but it's a calling," he says. "And you give your entire heart to your calling. Period."

That's a struggle many writers deal with: balancing "giving your heart to your calling" with giving your heart and time to your family. "Don't do it unless you're going to give your life to it," he says. Yet, he has two daughters, "and I'm still married after 40 years, and hardly anyone is married to the same person after 40 years." He explains how he has managed to give his life to writing and maintain a family life, "Well, what my family always wanted was a small farm, and that's what we've lived on for 30 years. They committed to it. My wife was always a great reader, and so were my daughters, so they knew that that was what was most important. We lived very cheaply for 20 years before I had any kind of success, but it was worth it, you know?"

Indeed. One portion of his success has come from screenwriting. He has written the screenplays for the films *Wolf*, *Legends of the Fall*, *Carried Away*, and *Revenge*. For Harrison, the process of writing for films is different from writing other works of fiction. "When you write for the screen, you have to see it before you write it down. You have to frame. Your imagination is just this frame, like in a movie. That's not hard because I have to see what I write anyway. You know, I imagine it in visual terms. I started out trying to be a painter, actually, when I was a teenager. That's such a large part of my imagination, visual. Things look more interesting in my head."

Does he have any favorite adaptations of his books? "My favorite is the one that nobody's seen, which is *Carried Away*," he says. "I think that one is the most accurate rendition of my work. Dennis Hopper was so perfectly a farmer, even the peculiar way he sort of looks up from underneath the brim of his hat, rather than raise the brim," he laughs. "Hopper was incredible, and so was Amy Irving as Rosalee. She was right on the money." Of his other adaptations, he says, "Nicholson had the character down right in *Wolf*, but I had too many quarrels with the director, changing it too much. They made it too housebroken. Wolf is a wild animal."

A benefit of his success is having the freedom to choose a publishing company for personal reasons. Harrison went with the small publishing company Grove Atlantic for his 1998 release *The Road Home*, and remains with them. "I went with Grove Atlantic because I knew the owner and I want to be with an independent. It's a smaller group of people and I know everybody." He prefers an independent because "they're not part of a big corporation. You know, the most irritating thing about America now is our sense that it's an empire with a capital 'e.' I just prefer more intimate surroundings. I don't want to go into those huge buildings where you can't even hear the elevator."

"Brown Dog is my continuing survival mechanism. You know, what I can fall back on. I have a remote cabin and when I'm unhappy with the world I just retreat to that reality. Brown Dog's reality. He's living art in a sense that he's very resilient. Brown Dog gets into horrible situations but he manages to get out. That's why I like him."

Joyce Carol Oates: A Life of Letters

BY ANNE BOWLING

She is as prolific now as she was when she was first published, nearly 40 years ago. At 61, Joyce Carol Oates is just about the closest thing we have to a living literary icon, but she is not slowing down to luxuriate in her status as grandame. Last spring brought publication of her latest short story collection *Faithless: Tales of Transgression* (Ecco Press), which followed recent appearances of her essays in magazines from *Architectural Digest* to *O*, and the 2000 publication of the 700-page novel based on the life of Marilyn Monroe, titled *Blonde*. And coming up?

"There may be some manuscripts that are set to be published," she says airily. "I have a novel that will come out in October, 2001, called *Middle Age: A Romance*, and then there are some other manuscripts that are sort of in the background, that I've finished, but I'm not sure if I'm going to revise. Most writers have manuscripts in their closets," she adds. "I would imagine Stephen King has like 50 of them."

Photo by Jerry Bauer

Joyce Carol Oates

Once a writer's oeuvre reaches the size of King's or Oates's, most people quit counting. Oates began her life of letters by creating wordless picture books as a girl growing up in the country outside Lockport, New York, before she could read and write. From that early connection with stories, Oates has gone on to become one of the most versatile and well-read writers of her generation: short stories, poetry, essays, plays, librettos, picture books and book reviews. Then of course, there are her novels—41 in all—which range from mystery to romance to more experimental work. Oates's writing is taught in college classrooms, and read to lull fretful children off to sleep. "I'm very happy doing what I do," she says. "I'm really so happy writing, I can be very excited and pleased doing a book review."

While she writes "all over the aesthetic map," as novelist John Barth once commented, geographically Oates has settled not far from where she began. She speaks thoughtfully, with broad, East Coast vowels, from her home in New Jersey. When she's not writing, Oates teaches in Princeton University's creative writing program, and with husband Ray Smith operates a small press, and publishes the literary journal *Ontario Review*. But to Oates, geography may not really matter. Her community is the literary community, she says, "The press and the magazine are supported by my writing and teaching income, so it's like I'm giving back to the culture. My husband is the main person who handles the work of the press, and I'm involved in acquisitions and reading. We talk about all the submissions we get, we design most of our books, because I love the literary culture, and feel very identified with it. I have many, many writer friends and former students out in that world."

ANNE BOWLING *is editor of* Novel & Short Story Writer's Market *and a Cincinnati-based freelance writer. This article originally appeared in* Pages, *and appears here by permission.*

A CLASSIC OATES COLLECTION

Her most recent collection *Faithless* could be called trademark Oates, if there is such a thing. The 22 stories revolve around betrayal, or perceived betrayal, in relationships of high passion, romantic and parental. Critics who have characterized her work as "gothic" will find generous portions of it here. The Pushcart Prize-winning anchor story, "Faithless," is a mystery brought on by a mental image she couldn't shake, Oates says. "I'd been haunted for years by the idea of a story like that, where a mother vanishes from the household and the little children think she's gone away and left them. But in fact it was the husband and the father who killed her. It's a sort of gothic image, I think, where a woman is buried in a shallow grave, right on the property, but the children think she's run away."

The setting for "Faithless" is cold, its tone heavy with foreboding. Oates writes: "That morning. The sisters would never forget that morning. We knew something was wrong, we thought Momma was sick. The night before having heard—what, exactly? Voices. Voices mixed with dreams, and the wind. On that farm, at the brink of a ten-mile descent to the Chautauqua River, it was always windy—on the worst days the wind could literally suck your breath away!—like a ghost, a goblin. An invisible being pushing up close behind you, sometimes even inside the house, even in your bed, pushing his mouth (or muzzle) to yours and sucking out the breath."

Pulling together a collection like *Faithless* takes awhile, Oates says, because she looks for a body of stories that is thematically unified. "It's kind of the way a poet assembles a collection of poems, it's something you do intuitively," she says. "In terms of *Faithless*, sometimes I'm warmly surprised by liking some of the characters so much." But appreciation for the stories that have gone before doesn't cloud her editor's judgment, and if a story doesn't hold up under later scrutiny, Oates will pull it. "I took a couple of stories out of *Faithless*, because one of them I thought had almost too much of a happy ending, and it didn't fit in. Even though I believe in life there are happy endings, this story was just a little too sunny, and there may have been another I thought was too long. So I take things out all the time."

A PRACTICAL FICTION WRITER

It seems a little contradictory, the image of a writer of Oates's stature with little of the usual attending ego. Despite—or maybe because of—the sheer volume of her output, Oates has practical regard for her writing. There is no prima donna posturing about the inviolate nature of her work. Matter-of-factly she'll discuss her most recent novel *Blonde*, which was dramatically cut before publication. Called by *Newsday* "the most important novel of her career" and a finalist for the 2000 National Book Award, *Blonde* was begun as a short novel. But the subject matter held Oates through the transformation of Norma Jean into the feminine icon of Marilyn, and her eventual decline and death. From a 1,400-page manuscript, Oates and her editor trimmed 400 pages, which may have proved painful to less even-tempered authors. But not, apparently, to Oates, who casually mentions of the cuts that "some of the sections have been published or will be published as short stories, because they're very self-contained."

Like *Bellefleur* and *A Bloodsmoor Romance*, which Oates considers her earlier watershed novels, *Blonde* represented chance-taking for the author. Mixing realism and surrealism in a story told posthumously through the point of view of the title character, *Blonde* pushed the boundaries of commercial fiction, Oates says. "There are things about it that are alienating and difficult. I could have told the story in a very simple, realistic prose, in which case it might have sold more, been a bestseller, but it wouldn't interest me. So *Blonde* is as far as I can go in terms of experimentation and expect to be published by a commercial press."

Oates accepts the boundaries of commercial fiction and the limits they impose with customary equanimity. "Among the most experimental writers we have who also sell well are Toni Morrison and Don DeLillo. Toni Morrison is experimental in the William Faulkner tradition—her writing is not easily accessible, so she has a readership who works to read her. It's not like reading something by John Grisham. But there are very few writers who would be given that kind of attention." Are these limitations daunting to Oates? "No," she says, "not really. I've always done so many different things that if one area seemed to not be so rewarding, I would just move to another."

To Oates, awareness of the fiction market is awareness of her readers, and that awareness may be what keeps her working as both a literary and commercial writer. "Art is communication, and it goes out into a community," Oates says. "I think most artists are aware of that, but I also think sometimes there isn't much that one can do about it. For instance, I think James Joyce really would have wanted to have a wide readership, and be read by the peasants and farmers in Ireland. But when most of us look at *Ulysses*, it's arcane, and forbidding, and basically many people can't read it and they don't want to read it. So yes, we try to have a communication with the audience, and we try to communicate clearly, but then something starts to happen when you're working with certain material. It may get more poetic, it may get more private, it may become somewhat strange and dreamlike, so you can't really control it that well."

SWITCHING AUDIENCES

It may be partly her equanimity that makes Oates comfortable treading into previously unex-plored areas of writing. In 1998, at the prompting of a family friend and Ecco Press editor, Oates wrote her first children's book, *Come Meet Muffin*. Based on the editor's daughter Lily and her relationship with her kitten, that story will be followed up by *Who Has Seen Little Reynard?* The title character Reynard is named after Oates's own cat, and will feature a slightly older Lily this time around. Oates found the challenge of writing picture books in the brevity, she says. "You can't have any exposition, really. The story has to move right along, it moves immediately. It's almost like a poem."

From picture books Oates has graduated to writing for the adolescent set, having penned her first young adult novel last summer. "I had never dreamt of writing one, but an editor wrote to me . . . and said she'd always liked my writing for adults, which she had read in college, I guess. She wondered if I'd be interested in writing a young adult novel. So I tried it, and I really, really loved it." *Big Mouth & Ugly Girl* explores an all-consuming friendship between two 16-year-old misfits in high school, and gave Oates the opportunity to write for—and learn about—another audience. "I feel that young people, unlike most adults, change really rapidly. They can be changed for the good, they can be influenced by models—within a year a young person can change," she says. "With my students at Princeton, seeing how much a student can improve in one semester is really amazing. You have a few conferences, you point out what he or she should be doing with his writing . . . and they'll go away and start doing it. It's kind of exhilarating to work with young people."

"WHERE SHE'S GOING, WHERE SHE'S BEEN"

As early as 1975, Oates told a reporter "I am not conscious of working especially hard, or of 'working' at all. Writing and teaching have always been, for me, so richly rewarding that I don't think of them as work in the usual sense of the word." While her output hasn't slackened, her craft has gone through changes that keep fiction writing interesting for her, and keep her readers reading. "I've definitely changed as a writer in that I'm much more experimental," she says. "I would never have considered writing a novel like *Blonde* when I was a younger writer, because I couldn't have conceived of something so massive, that involved different techniques of writing. With *Bellefleur*, I departed from my more realistic novels, and the long novels like *Blonde* and the others demand a lot of planning, where you're spending a lot of time thinking about space, and how chapters relate to one another—it's almost like you're an architect design-ing a spacial structure. When I was a younger writer, I never even thought of that. It was completely beyond me . . . I guess I'm more versatile, and it's more 'how can I limit myself?' Like I have a finite amount of time."

Knopf Editor Ann Close: "An Open Mind Is the Key to Finding Good Books"

BY WILL ALLISON

Thanks to computers and the Internet, Ann Close and her fellow editors at Alfred A. Knopf have instant access to more sales information than ever before. In some ways, though, technology has had little effect on the pace of her work. "It's funny," says Close, a senior editor and recipient of the PEN/Roger Klein Award for editorial excellence. "The time you spend working with a writer, editing a manuscript, getting it published—that has not changed one iota since I've been in publishing."

Fiction comprises about 60 percent of Close's list. But in spite of industry changes, her job is much as it's always been—lots of manuscripts to read, lots of agents and writers to call. The main difference now, she says, is that she has access to so much more information than she did in years past. But that hasn't changed Close's—or Knopf's—basic approach to publishing: "Knopf still takes chances on books we like, whether the numbers work out or not," she says. "We all know the numbers are imaginary anyway."

In her time at Knopf, Close has worked with some of most important authors of the past quarter century. Fiction writers she's edited include Ann Beattie, Sarah Bird, Jay Cantor, Mark Childress, Anita Desai, Mark Helprin, Stephen Harrigan, Mary Hood, James D. Houston, Gish Jen, Brad Leithauser, Richard Marius, Jane Mendelsohn, Alice Munro, Mark O'Donnell, Jayne Anne Phillips, Norman Rush and Mona Simpson.

Close grew up in Savannah, Georgia, and attended Randolph-Macon College in Lynchburg, Virginia. After school, she worked in Cambridge, England for a couple of years, then spent another year in Europe. "At that point I decided I had to get serious about life," she says. "I thought 'What could I do?' And it seemed like I could be an editor. So I came to New York and pursued that."

On a friend's tip, Close applied for a job at Harper & Row in 1965. She started out as an editorial assistant, then she did trade copyediting, then advertising and editing nonfiction trade paperbacks. After five years at Harper & Row, Close was hired to head the copy-editing department at Knopf. Bob Gottlieb was editor-in-chief at the time.

"Bob was not very rigid about people's jobs," she says. "He knew I wanted to be an editor, so I started doing some books about a year after I got there, while I still had the copyediting job."

Her break came in January 1974. "No editors ever want to leave Knopf, but all of a sudden, a couple of people did, and I was made an editor full-time," she says. Close had gotten her start in fiction editing with a book by Richard Marius, which had been signed by Gottlieb. Soon after, she began signing books herself, including an anthology entitled *A Thousand Years of Vietnamese*

WILL ALLISON *is editor-at-large for* Zoetrope: All-Story, *former executive editor of* STORY, *and former editor of* Novel & Short Story Writer's Market. *He is the recipient of an Ohio Arts Council grant for fiction, and has published short stories in* American Short Fiction, *and* Florida Review.

Poetry. ("It's a wonderful book of poetry, actually," says Close. "Listen to me—still pushing it after all these years.") The first book of fiction she acquired was Mark Helprin's debut story collection, *A Dove of the East and Other Stories.* Close went on to sign first books by Jay Cantor, Brad Leithauser, Jane Mendelsohn (*I Was Amelia Earhart*) and Mona Simpson (her national bestseller *Anywhere But Here*). Close also handled Canadian author Alice Munro's first release in the US.

Here Close shares an insider's look at an editor's workday, and her views—based on 30 years in the editor's chair—on what makes a manuscript work.

How have changes in bookselling—the Internet and chain bookstores—affected the way editors work?

I guess it's like anything else: you gain some things, you lose some things. A publisher's recommendations used to carry more weight. We could say to a bookstore, "This writer's new book is much better than his old one; you should take 10 copies instead of the three copies you took last time," and maybe they would. Now in one second they look up sales figures from the author's last book, and if it didn't sell, it's very hard to convince them to order more copies this time around. On the other hand, the minute a books starts to sell, they know it, and they get more copies into the store.

The Internet has really changed the way we market books. *The Gates of the Alamo*, for instance—there were fabulous sites about the Alamo that we were able to link to, so that anybody who was interested in the Alamo was going to learn about our book. The Internet has made it possible to really reach a book's specific audience, which was very difficult in the past. To do the same thing in print—to buy ads in specialty magazines—just wasn't worth it.

Tell us about your average workday. You review agented manuscripts and those that come in over the transom?

First I open my mail and go through my manuscripts. Right away I sort out the ones that are inappropriate, ones that are definitely going back. Some of these you can tell by the cover letter—not because the letter is badly written or anything. Knopf, for instance, doesn't do any genre fiction to speak of. So if I receive a fairly standard piece of science fiction, I know right off the bat that I'm not going to buy it. Agents, in truth, don't usually send me those books, but they do come in over the transom.

I set aside the ones that I will read or ask my assistant to read. If the manuscript is from one of my writers, or if an agent has called me personally to tell me about the book—those are the ones I read. The others I ask my assistant to read first. Anything that makes it through that first screen, I usually read 25 or 50 pages of. I keep going until I know I don't want it, or that I may want it. But in all honesty, I don't do much reading at the office. If I'm really going to read something, I usually take it home.

Also, an absolute ton of time is spent on the phone—either talking to writers or agents, or trying to push people in the house, checking up to see that they're doing the publishing work they should be doing, that a manuscript is moving through copyediting or whatever. And I keep in touch with my writers regularly, the ones I'm publishing, and the ones I'm not publishing, too. I just like to check in on them from time to time. Those can be long conversations.

Aside from unsolicited and agented submissions, how do you acquire manuscripts?

At the beginning of your career, you're hungry for books, so you look for them more assiduously. For instance, Jay Cantor I read in *Triquarterly* and then wrote to him. A lot of my nonfiction writers I've gotten by writing to them.

What about networking? Referrals?

Early on I'd published Mark Helprin. He'd gone to Harvard, so I went up there and I met his writing professors and asked if they had any other promising students, and that's how I got Brad Leithauser. So that often happens. I actually publish a lot of people I've met through Harvard. I've known other editors who got set up with, say, the Iowa Writers Workshop.

What kind of books are you able to publish well?

I am—and I think Knopf is, in general—quite susceptible to literary fiction. It's what we do best. Even our big bestsellers tend to have some kind of interesting turn of mind—a literary element. Michael Crichton, for instance, is a pretty standard writer, but he has got quite an interesting turn of mind. To be honest, popular novels don't work at Knopf unless there is something a little different about them, because the whole industry expects a certain quality from us. Dean Koontz never really worked out for Knopf. I mean, he did all right, but nothing like he'd sold before or after. Everybody's house has its own niche. You learn quickly what your house can do.

What do you look for in a manuscript?

I try to leave myself open. For years, I've never really liked epistolary novels very much, but I recently signed up one that I love. A good writer can convince you to do something that's not your favorite.

If somebody had just called me up and asked if I wanted to do a book on the Donner party, I might not have been too interested. But I actually heard Jim [Houston] read a section of *Snow Mountain Passage*, and right away I knew he'd done something quite different than a straight historical novel. Of course, I'd also read some of his other books and was already interested in him as a writer.

The same with Stephen Harrigan's *The Gates of the Alamo*. That was a kind of historical fiction, too. And if I hadn't read the book, I don't know whether I would have been interested in the idea of a historical book about the Alamo. It's good to stay open, because something you think you might not want turns out to be wonderful.

How would you characterize your approach to editing?

It's hard to say. I think I probably edit by instinct. I had a wonderful English teacher in high school. She totally believed in ear. Although we learned grammar and had to diagram sentences, she always said "Just go ahead and write—trust your ear, trust your instincts." One reason I like Squaw [the Squaw Valley Community of Writers conference] so much is that people actually sit down and talk about plot and openings, and it kind of reminds you to look for all of those things.

I read somewhere that most children know the basic stories of our culture and how stories should work by the time they're four. In a strange way, all writers work off of that basic form of storytelling. A book doesn't work if a writer is following the form too rigidly or too loosely. That's what I think happened to some of the postmodernists: they got too far away from it.

Would you say you edit with a light or heavy hand?

In general, I don't change things unless I think they're wrong. There's an editor I know—one of his writers told me he changes every sentence. That is definitely not my philosophy of editing. More or less, you've got to figure out the author's voice and go with that. Knopf is really lucky because we mostly publish *writers*. Not people who've got a good story and need a lot of help getting it out, but people who are stylists and have a voice. It's the Ludlums of the world who have to have a lot of help, not the Alice Munros.

Are books becoming an endangered species?

E-books kind of hang over our heads, but so far they haven't worked at all. They don't seem to have caught on with anyone except the newspapers, who love to write about them.

Although I've complained as much as anybody else, the '80s and '90s were good for hard-cover books. We sold many, many more than in the previous decade. At the end of the '70s, everybody thought we'd just be publishing trade paperbacks by 1990. Instead, people had a lot of cash, and they bought the hardcover books. It hasn't been an altogether bad time.

Still, the paper producers and the printers have stopped investing. They no longer see book buyers as a growing audience. That could actually be the thing that does us in, rather than people wanting to read e-books.

How have the big book chains affected you?

Barnes & Noble has been strangely very good for fiction and for poetry. First of all, in the store, you know exactly where the fiction and poetry is. They have gone out of their way to support poetry. They actually put poetry books in the window on their own; you don't have to pay for it. The distribution system in Barnes & Noble is amazing, too. You can literally get a book all over the country in about a week. And when something starts selling, they display it well.

What about the role of independent booksellers?

Barnes & Noble has stopped discounting so heavily, as have Amazon and Borders. That's kind of shifting things back toward the independents. And of course, Barnes & Noble can't hand-sell books. When the independents get behind a book, they can make it succeed on a regional level.

How do book reviews affect your work?

The review situation has gotten a lot worse. When newspapers and magazines hit bad times, a lot of them dropped their book reviews. *Time* and *Newsweek* used to review three to five books every week. They don't do that anymore. But in a way, the Internet has taken up the slack. You can get an enormous amount of information about a book on the Barnes & Noble and Amazon sites. *Salon* does a great job on books, too, and a lot of people read their reviews. And so many other websites have started doing book reviews. It's hard to tell how much impact they've had. Nobody has been able to measure it exactly.

What's the most difficult aspect of your job?

Absolutely the toughest thing is reading bad reviews to writers. From the beginning, I felt that I should be the one who did it. Some authors have gotten smart. They don't want to hear the reviews. They just want to know whether they're good or bad.

It's tough, especially with a really good book. There's so much timing and luck involved. With serious authors, it's almost impossible to write a book in less than two or three years. That's a huge chunk of your life gone. And then to have some idiot suddenly trounce it in a major publication—it's very, very difficult. It's very discouraging for the editor, too. You put a lot of work into a book.

What's the most rewarding aspect of your job?

The nicest part is when I get the first finished book. It's a very happy moment. There have been some books I've worked on for ten years, talking them over with the writers, reading them piece by piece. So you really get involved with books, and yet they have an end. When you get that first finished book, the hardcover publishing of it is over, more or less.

Other than that, I would say the most rewarding thing is when you have a terrific manuscript that still has a lot of problems, and you're able to work with the writer or edit it in such a way that it comes to life. It's extremely satisfying. It's amazing. It's like seeing a cake rise, only more exciting.

John Updike's Love Affair With the Written Word Transcends All Genres

BY KELLY NICKELL

Since the release of his first novel, *The Poorhouse Fair*, in 1959, John Updike has published 50 books, written scores of essays, reviews and short stories for the likes of *The New Yorker* and *The New York Times*, received two Pulitzers, and established himself as a living literary legend—not bad for someone who says he "only meant to be a magazine writer."

So, with such an extensive body of work, one can't help but wonder: Does it get easier to sit down with a blank page and turn whiteness to words of power and resilience?

"No, it never gets easier. But, I've written enough now that I wonder if I'm not in danger of having said my say and of repeating myself," he says. "You can't be too worried about that if you're going to be a creative writer—a creative spirit—but yeah, you do, as they say in pitching, lose a little of your fastball."

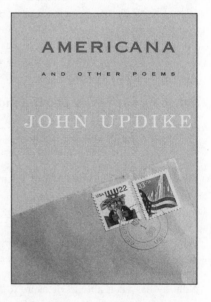

From poetry and book reviews to short stories, novels and a play, there's not much the 69-year-old author hasn't tried his hand at over the years. And each form has presented its own distinct creative satisfaction.

"I must say, when I reread myself, it's the poetry I tend to look at. It's the most exciting to write, and it's over the quickest," says Updike, whose most recent collection of poetry, *Americana*, was released by Knopf last spring. "But they all have their pleasures. The book reviews are perhaps the most lowly of the bunch, but even they have an occasional creative thrill. I like short stories. I'm sorry that I haven't been doing so many lately, but they're very satisfying."

Whatever the form, Updike has made an art of turning life's lost and tormented souls into literary everymen. As he wrote in *The Handbook of Short Story Writing, Volume II*:

"No soul or locale is too humble to be the site of entertaining and instructive fiction. Indeed, all other things being equal, the rich and glamorous are less fertile ground than the poor and plain, and the dusty corners of the world more interesting than its glittering, already sufficiently publicized centers."

He showcases this philosophy in the Pulitzer Prize winning Rabbit series: *Rabbit, Run*; *Rabbit*

KELLY NICKELL *is assistant editor of* Writer's Digest *magazine, and a frequent contributor to* Novel & Short Story Writer's Market. *This interview first appeared in* Writer's Digest *magazine, and is reprinted here with permission.*

John Updike

Redux; *Rabbit Is Rich*; and *Rabbit at Rest*. Through the four novels, Updike employs protagonist Harry "Rabbit" Angstrom to offer his commentary on middle class America: racial tension and sexual freedom, drugs and middle age. And with Rabbit, Updike illustrates that even the flawed and ordinary can become legends given the proper landscape.

"We're past the age of heroes and hero kings," he says. "If we can't make up stories about ordinary people, who can we make them up about? But on the other hand, that's just a theory, and as in America, of course, there's a democracy that's especially tied to that assumption.

"Most of our lives are basically mundane and dull, and it's up to the writer to find ways to make them interesting. It's a rare life so dull that no crisis ever intrude."

Despite saying the Rabbit series was complete with 1990's *Rabbit at Rest*, Updike couldn't resist returning to the storyline one last time in "Rabbit Remembered," a novella appearing along with several short stories in 2000's *Licks of Love*.

"It was like coming home every 10 years and paying a visit," he says. "It was easy because I was at home in that world, and it was a world that I had lived through as a child, and then it was a world that I had made."

The real world Updike created for himself didn't come without a few risks. After graduating from Harvard in 1954, he went on to join the staff of *The New Yorker*. Two years later, with no other job prospects, he left the magazine and moved with his family to Ipswich, Massachusetts, to pursue freelancing fulltime.

"I didn't quite know what I was getting into," he says. "It's possible I might have had to find employment. But I was willing to do journalism and *The New Yorker*'s kind of journalism—I was able to carry some of it with me when I came to New England.

"It was a gamble, but I was young and that was the time to make it . . . when I was young and full of what I had to say."

What felt like a gamble more than 40 years ago now seems an admirable tale of bravery—one man's pursuit of his dream. But even Updike recognizes that in these changing times, his literary start is one not likely duplicated by today's young writers.

"My generation was maybe the last in which you could set up shop as a writer and hope to make a living at it," he says. "I began when print was a lot more glamorous medium than it is now. A beginning fiction writer—Kurt Vonnegut comes to mind—could support himself and a family by selling to magazines. I'm not sure you could do that now."

With the consolidation of major publishing houses and fewer magazines embracing short fiction, up-and-coming authors may find publication even more of a challenge.

"It's harder to make a splash nowadays," he says. "When I was beginning, we weren't getting rock star-type attention, but I think now the buzz seems softer. Publishers are looking for blockbusters—all the world loves a mega-seller. And, there's less readership for fiction that isn't purely escapist."

In 1999, Updike served as editor of *The Best American Short Stories of the Century* (Houghton Mifflin), a compilation of stories selected from the annual volumes of *The Best American Short Stories*. While the book honors a form in which—and about which—Updike has long written, he says there seems to be less of a readership for such work.

"That kind of audience is being trained at universities, but general readers want to sink into longer works, not the stop and start of short stories."

Keeping to his frenetic pace—though he says, "I don't mean to be too overproductive"—the author is currently at work on another novel he hopes to complete by the end of 2001. But, as he writes away the mornings and early afternoons in his Massachusetts home, even Updike is tempted by the same distractions that plague so many others.

"I work at home, upstairs, so it's unfortunately handy to any number of little chores that seem to have attached themselves to the writer's trade . . . answering mail or reading proofs."

Despite the fact that it may not get any easier to start each new book, Updike's long and diverse career now enables him to draw on a wealth of insight inherited from the various forms he's mastered throughout the years.

"Poetry makes you a little more sensitive to the word by word interest of prose, and book reviews make you a little more erudite in some regards . . . probably had I not written so many reviews, I wouldn't have tackled something like *Gertrude and Claudius*, which is a sort of bookish inspiration," he says.

"I'm generally sort of more cautious in the way I write now than I used to be, though. I write slower, try to think a little more."

And to the legions of struggling writers waiting in the wings to make a "splash" of their own, it's perseverance and dedication that Updike advises: "It's never been easy. Books are still produced and sold, and it might as well be you. Try to develop steady work habits, maybe a more modest quota, but keep to it. Don't be thin-skinned or easily discouraged because it's an odds-long proposition; all of the arts are. 'Many are called, few are chosen', but it might be you."

"Keep to it. Don't be thin-skinned or easily discouraged because it's an odds-long proposition, all of the arts are. 'Many are called, few are chosen', but it might be you."

First Bylines

BY VANESSA LYMAN

Frequently, it's the new writers who have the most to teach about writing and publishing. We learn from their mistakes how to correct our own and we learn from their successes how to succeed ourselves. The three writers featured here have recently published their first works of fiction and their experiences are richly instructive. Their paths to publication are vastly different and yet similarities surface. It's the similarities that reveal the nature of their success.

For example, all of the writers are currently working on a new project. This reveals so much about a person as a writer. The writers here know that they need to keep working, because success is ultimately found in the obsessive need to fill up every blank scrap of paper available in the house.

Another shared trait between these three is that they all apprenticed to writing in some way before publishing their book. One was a journalist, another wrote screenplays in Hollywood and another worked as a freelancer.

Sarah Strohmeyer, first time mystery writer and former journalist, says, "It's good to have a job where you write a lot because you get used to writing on deadline. And you don't become a prima donna about your words." There's a lesson there. Keep a journal, write obituaries, do the Sunday crossword or play Mad Libs. It doesn't matter how you apprentice yourself so long as you learn to use words.

SARAH STROHMEYER
Bubbles Unbound, Dutton

"I think I always wanted to be tall, blonde and busty and I wanted men to fall at my feet," says Sarah Strohmeyer. "I'll admit it, I'm not proud." Her first novel, a mystery entitled *Bubbles Unbound*, was published by Dutton in March 2001 as the inaugural book in the Bubbles series. The main character is Bubbles Yablonsky, hairdresser and investigative journalist, tall in high heels, blonder than is natural, thin, busty and subject to men falling at her feet . . . and off bridges . . . and under cars . . . and, *well.*

"I like women who are fun. Bubbles is fun and doesn't take herself too seriously. That's what I like about her." Strohmeyer created her character as a cross between Barbie and the women she'd known in her hometown of Bethlehem, Pennsylvania. "They kind of look soft and fluffy from the outside and on the inside, they're hard as steel."

Strohmeyer, who had worked as a reporter for 20 years, had the opportunity to interview mystery writer Janet Evanovich. "This probably broke all kinds of ethical rules," Strohmeyer admits, "But what the hell." She brought along a parody of Barbie she'd published, called

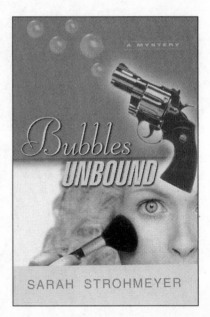

VANESSA LYMAN *is production editor of* Novel & Short Story Writer's Market.

Barbie Unbound, as well as her idea for a mystery series. Evanovich looked it over and suggested Strohmeyer hang on to the Barbie character. "She said, 'You know women like this in Bethlehem,' and she's right. There are all sorts of big-haired, big blonde women in Bethlehem."

Evanovich also advised her not to set the book in Vermont, where Strohmeyer currently lives. "If I had put Bubbles in Vermont, my chances of getting published would have been much less. Pennsylvania has a higher population density. More people are going to be interested in reading the book."

Strohmeyer took Evanovich's advice and set her novel in Lehigh, a fictional steeltown similar to her native Bethlehem. In her breakthrough assignment, Bubbles comes head-to-head with the reigning powers of the steel industry: one hairdresser, just looking for a chip-proof nail polish, is pitted against Lehigh's implacable steel dynasty, the cowed police force, and misogynist, spineless newspaper editors. ("By the way," Strohmeyer adds, "the editors in the publishing world are so nice. They're just so different from these S.O.B.s you find crusting around the table down at the newsrooms.")

Once Strohmeyer had enough material ready to send out, she sent it to an editor at Dutton who had previously considered *Barbie Unbound* and asked if Strohemeyer had anything else to show him. "So I sent him a couple of chapters plus an outline. He got back to me in two weeks and said, 'You know, we really like this and you need to get an agent.' "

The first agent she contacted wasn't so thrilled with the manuscript. "He said, 'Well, as you can imagine, I don't really like it very much and this is why . . .' But his secretary, who's a woman, said, 'I really liked it *a lot*.' I figured there might be some hope so I started contacting other agents. I actually had to choose from agents."

Strohmeyer's agent gave her some good direction for the novel. "I recommend that no one ever finish a novel before they send it out. If you're doing commercial fiction, it's a very good idea to know where the novel is going. And it's a very good idea to have an outline. But I would not ever sit there, write 80,000 words and then send it off. People are going to say 'We don't like three quarters of this book,' unless you're a tremendous writer. And I'm not," says Strohmeyer. "I relied a lot on the direction of my agent and my editors."

Strohmeyer had always intended to continue Bubbles' adventures in a series, though she has learned that isn't the most profitable way to go. "I'm glad Dutton's interested in doing more. I learned a lot from the first one and I'm still learning and I hope I'm getting better," says Strohmeyer. "It's a nice position to be in."

One of the things she's learned from *Bubbles Unbound* that she brought to her second novel in the series, *Bubbles Befuddled*, is the importance of a strong outline. "My editor really hammered it over with me. She had me in her little clutches," Strohmeyer jokes. "And I'm grateful to her for it because plots are hard. Characters are fun and easy to sketch out. The plot, I think, is hard."

Strohmeyer says, "I think you have to have an idea of plot and character. Then you write a little bit and then you need to outline it more." Surprises will arise during the writing and mess up your carefully detailed outline so that you'll need an entirely new one. Minor characters will become more significant or, as in Strohmeyer's case, "I just had a surprise. I'm on page 311, almost done with *Bubbles Befuddled*, and I expected someone completely different to show up in the trunk of Bubbles' car. I was surprised when a different person did and thought, 'You know, this makes more sense and it's better.' I think in those situations, you shouldn't be hampered by your outline. Have a firm structure, but be flexible when it comes to surprises," Strohmeyer says. "It's more fun for you as a writer."

Even if mystery is considered the most plot-dependent genre and even if you outline every possible detail, it might not be enough. "I think the trick [to a good mystery] is to have a really good character. Really put a lot of time and energy into your character."

Above all, don't doubt your own ability. Instead, write. Strohmeyer went to a signing with a woman who'd made millions of dollars writing for ten years. "What I noticed about her was that she had a very positive attitude. Her main piece of advice was just to show up. Every day. By that she means you just write everyday. You don't whine about it, you don't put it off, you don't mope about it, you just do it. And I really liked her positive attitude and that was my attitude about writing mysteries."

MARK FRIEDMAN
Columbus Slaughters Braves, Houghton Mifflin

Mark Friedman was working as a scriptwriter in Los Angeles when he came up with an idea for a screenplay he called "Michael Jordan's Brother." "I just held on to the idea and then I eventually realized it would be very difficult to sell it as a screenplay because I saw it as something a little darker and dramatic. That's a harder sell."

Friedman decided to leave Hollywood behind and go to law school. "I decided to write the novel before I went to law school, sort of as the last thing I was ever going to write before I became a lawyer." The first draft of *Columbus Slaughters Braves* that emerged seven months later told the story of Joe and C.J. Columbus, two brothers locked in a dark, modern Cain and Abel tale. The lyrical novel is narrated by the less successful Joe as he watches C.J.'s rise from talented younger brother to baseball legend and—when diagnosed with leukemia—martyr.

"Unlike screenplays where you can just say 'interior bedroom day,' with a book, you're really accountable for everything in there," says Friedman, "Especially if you're writing about two subjects [like] baseball and cancer. You can't cavalierly throw stuff in there because people are going to notice."

When law school didn't work out, Friedman revised the book, cutting out about 50 pages. "When I first wrote it, I felt the need to describe every object in every room. There was a lot of stuff I was using to try to prove I was capable of writing a novel. It was *obvious* the novel existed because it was sitting right in front of me," Friedman laughs. "That's 300 pages, typed."

The revised book went out to both publishers and movie studios but initially only the movie studios were interested. The movie rights sold but no publishing deal came through, so Friedman enrolled in the Johns Hopkins writing program to work toward his master's degree while he wrote the screenplay for the yet unpublished *Columbus Slaughters Braves.*

It was at Johns Hopkins that Friedman got his break. An editor from Houghton Mifflin wanted to read work from the graduate students and Friedman was asked to turn something in. "I knew that Houghton Mifflin had already passed on my novel so I wasn't enthused about [handing it in]. If I hadn't had a copy, I wouldn't have given it to him. I hadn't thought it worth the trouble of getting one sent from my agent, but I happened to have a copy, so I turned it in." When the editor came to the university to give a talk, he met with Friedman and said he wanted to acquire the novel. Friedman agreed.

Again, major revisions took place. "The editor suggested the book was in the wrong tense. The book was in the present tense and he felt that it should be in past tense. It was a huge amount of work but, once he said it, I didn't argue with him because I knew he was right," says Friedman. "The only reason the story exists is because of the ending. So, that means the ending had to have already happened for [Joe] to be telling it."

Losing the present tense meant that Joe was no longer learning about the situation as it unfolded, an aspect of the manuscript that had been a boon for Friedman during the first writing.

Joe was not an expert on cancer or baseball so as Joe learned, so could Friedman. "I watch baseball and couldn't tell you the difference between a sinker and a slider all the time," says Friedman. "I would love to write a novel where I could spend months hanging out with a baseball player but it wasn't in the cards for how much time I had for the first draft."

Though the revisions were heavy, Friedman didn't find them impossible. In fact, it gave him different perspective on the novel. "I rewrote [Joe's] character and had him reflect on the events that, to *me*, had happened two years before. I had written C.J.'s death in the summer if 1997 and now, two years later, I was revisiting it. I put myself in the mindset to write it in past tense and give the main character a little insight and perspective into what happened." Friedman's experience as a scriptwriter helped in writing and revising. "The size of a project doesn't daunt me," he says. "I knew I had to write five pages a day for sixty days to finish a book. When I first started [screenwriting], the idea of writing something that was one hundred pages long seemed impossible. I've gotten over that. Screenwriting has taught me discipline and how to do the research, but also how to do the homework to get yourself in the mindset to write that kind of thing." Getting in the mindset, Friedman explains, involves overloading on similar projects— either reading books or watching films—before sitting down to write. Friedman also kept a journal of notes and ideas for the novel.

Since its publication, *Columbus Slaughters Braves* was selected for the Barnes & Noble Discover Great New Writers Program and has found a small devoted following. "This is a tough book to market," says Friedman. "It's like a guy book but it's not a Tom Clancy book. I met the woman who runs the [Discover Great New Writers] program and she said, 'It's the kind of book the executives would never pick up on their own, but when they read it, they rave about it.' But then, you've got to get those people to read it." Friedman admits to feeling removed from the book. He's currently working on the screenplay and finds himself answering questions about the novel based on the movie, which he developed in a different direction. Whether or not the movie will be produced isn't certain. "That's one of the good things about the book— the book exists!"

LAURA PRITCHETT

Hell's Bottom, Colorado, **Milkweed Editions**

"I just found my first diary. I wrote my age at the top and had drawn a big picture of a bunny rabbit. On its stomach I had written 'I would like to be a book writer some day.' Writer is spelled r-i-t-e-r. I hopefully learned to spell since then, but it was funny to find that. I hadn't remembered articulating such a wish before," says Laura Pritchett, "But I've always known I wanted to write."

That diary, written while growing up on a small ranch in Eastern Colorado, was the first step in becoming a published author. Pritchett's short story collection, *Hell's Bottom, Colorado*, is as much informed by her childhood home as her desire to write. The style of the writing is simple and rugged, modeled after what Pritchett considers the spirit of the region. The characters that populate these stories are equal to the starkness of the land and the honesty of the prose. They prefer to have "a little Hell swirled in with their Heaven." *Hell's Bottom, Colorado* has just that; stories of salvation are tempered by the truths of survival, and violent hardships are endured with willful strength.

The stories are linked, following one extended family

in intermittent snapshots all out of order. One image carried over enriches the subsequent stories just as one relationship affects another or one act of violence shatters a family only to create another.

"When I first wrote the collection, they were unconnected short stories. I got the advice that I either needed to connect the stories or I needed to differentiate the characters more, because the voices sounded really familiar." Pritchett took the advice to link the stories, creating the jumbled, shuttered effect of the book. "It changed a few of the stories in ways I hadn't originally envisioned. A few of them felt as if they were forced into a shape they weren't meant to be so [the characters] would fit into this particular family," Pritchett admits. "On the other hand, it gave the stories an interesting cohesion. And it was fun to see a family created, all the personalities and relationships come together. I'm glad I did it."

All the revision was worth it. *Hell's Bottom, Colorado* was awarded the Milkweed National Fiction Prize for 2001. "When Emily [Buchwald, Pritchett's publisher] called to tell me the news, I just sat on the phone. There was a long silence because I could not wrap my brain around what she was saying. I just kept trying to form some kind of thank you sentence and it came out as this big, fragmented thing because I was so surprised."

The path to that point involved a lot of writing and many rejections and even two novels that are permanently shelved ("they seem inherently flawed," she says). "After I finished my master's degree, I decided to take one year off to do a lot of writing. I still had to work part time in the afternoons but I wrote every morning for that year. Then that year became three years. I just kept writing and writing."

During that time, Pritchett worked on her novels, her short stories and also did some freelance work. "Anytime a person messes with words and rearranges and looks for the particular right word—any sort of training like that adds to your writing ability. I'm sure [freelancing] helped me become more proficient with language. But if I were independently wealthy, I probably wouldn't have done it just because it takes time away from what I'm interested in," she says. "I cared about the quality but I didn't put my heart and soul in it."

She also submitted her growing number of short stories to various publications and received quite a few rejections. Finally, two short stories were accepted by *The Sun*. "That really helped, not only because it paid something but because it really bolstered my spirits. At the end of those three years and all those rejections, I was getting a little worried that I might have to change dreams. But then they accepted those stories and it really bolstered my spirits and my dedication," says Pritchett. "And I'm sure it helped get my foot in the door because once you can say 'I've been published somewhere,' I think people pay more attention."

When the story collection felt complete, Pritchett sent it out. The manuscript was accepted by a small press but, after only a year and a half, the editor called to inform Pritchett they were ceasing operations. "Luckily, Milkweed Editions picked it up. That was interesting to have it accepted and revised once and then working with Emily Buchwald to re-envision the manuscript. It seemed like a lot of work, a lot of years of work, but it did get stronger and I was really happy to work with Emily.

"For a long time, I hadn't known about small publishers and now I'm such a fan of them. I think they do such great work. I'm so glad there are so many of them— like Milkweed— dedicated to launching new writers. They don't have the bottom line in mind so much, their concerns are completely different."

Regardless of the care Milkweed Editions took in bringing her book to publication, Pritchett has found patience to be a necessary virtue. The process of turning a manuscript into a book is a very long one. "For a while there I was frustrated with it because it felt like it had gone on too long but now it's getting exciting again." Pritchett had just received the advanced reader's copy and was thrilled to see everything come together. "It's materialized into a book. Something I can actually go and pick up. In a bookstore."

Pritchett is already working on a second book, a novel based on an article she'd read about a young mother who left her child in the car while she worked. "She said she had forgotten about her baby and I just wanted to get into the psychology of that. It's awful, but it's understandable, the sorts of pressures that can take you to the brink of acting in totally irrational ways."

The novel's first draft is halfway finished but Pritchett can't depend on a blissfully quiet morning routine to complete it. "Those first three years," Pritchett says, "I wrote every day, every morning for three or four hours. Those were some really productive, writing-intense years. And so now, I've had two children and my life has changed drastically."

Pritchett squeezes in writing time while the children nap or when her husband can free up mornings for her. "It's been a lot more choppy and hectic. In a way that's hard, but in a way that's wonderful because I'm still able to do both and I love being a mother. I feel really lucky that I'm not stuck at some minimum wage job that I hate but I can still balance being a writer and a mother."

Bringing Humor To Your Fiction Writing

BY GORDON KIRKLAND

A couple of years after I took the final step toward becoming a full-time writer, someone told me that nothing was harder to write than humor. Where was he before I started? Just think how much time he could have saved me. Instead of slogging away writing a syndicated humor column, I could have stayed gainfully employed writing reports with titles like *Guide to the Canadian Aquaculture Industry's Trade Potential in Malaysia*, which I am sure has been read by at least 187 people.

Shortly thereafter humor writing got a second, even stronger knock against it. I asked a panel of agents at a writer's conference about the publishing potential for a collection of my columns. One of the agents looked down her nose at me and said, "You'd have to be some kind of a complete idiot to think that any of us up here on the panel would be interested in something like that."

She was right; as I left the room I certainly felt like a complete idiot. I went home and looked at the bookcase in my office. I came to the immediate conclusion that, based on the opinion expressed by that charming agent, Dave Barry, Lewis Grizzard, Erma Bombeck, and Garrison Keillor were all idiots. I decided it was better to be in the company of idiots like them than a client of an agent like her.

While the majority of my writing is in the realm of nonfiction, the same rules (or lack thereof) apply to writing humorous fiction. Humor can be either a genre in its own right, or an important ingredient in many other genres. Shakespeare wrote comedies, tragedies, and romances. Even in the most tragic of his tales, he knew the importance of inserting a humorous scene every so often to bring the audience some comic relief from all the death, deceit, and unrequited love in the rest of the play.

Put simply, writing humor is just a two-step process—think of something funny, and write it down. Most people find that the write-it-down step is much easier than the think-of-something-funny step. Identifying what constitutes humor is nearly impossible. Aristotle tried to define humor. Sigmund Freud tried to identify the purpose of humor. Even Darwin got into the act. None of them could come up with a clear definition of what is and what is not funny. Something that might make a Howard Stern fan laugh might not be considered very funny at all by one of Billy Graham's followers. Therefore, the humorist's first commandment is "Know thy audience."

To many people, humor is synonymous with jokes. While joke writing is a subsection of the genre, and a potentially lucrative one, it would be a mistake to confuse the ability to tell a joke with the ability to write humor. We've all met people who are "quick with a joke." More often than not they are simply repeating, perhaps embellishing, a joke that someone else told them.

GORDON KIRKLAND *is a syndicated humor columnist and author. In the seven years he has been writing the column he has tallied 2,500 publication credits in newspapers, consumer magazines and trade journals. His first book,* Justice Is Blind-And Her Dog Just Peed in My Cornflakes *(Harbour Publishing Co.), received the 2000 Stephen Leacock Award of Merit. Kirkland lives near Vancouver, BC, with his wife Diane and the dumbest dog ever to get lost on a single flight of stairs. They have two grown sons.*

You don't necessarily need a sense of humor to tell a joke. You just need to be good at memorizing short passages and have the ability to recite them with some degree of delivery.

THE THREE MOST IMPORTANT HUMOR WRITING DEVICES

There are three important elements to humor writing. They can be used together or on their own with equal success. They are:

- Playing on incongruities
- Using surprises or unexpected twists
- Creating a sense of superiority

Playing with incongruities and exaggerations

Joining two or more subjects that don't seem to belong together often develops humor. I recently started a column with two seemingly unrelated sentences, "I don't particularly like snakes. I am not a morning person." The connection between the two is pantyhose. They look like a whole herd of pythons through my blurry, first-thing-in-the-morning eyes when my wife leaves them to dry on the shower curtain in our bathroom.

Incongruity might also be achieved by creating a seemingly improbable action such as child-like behavior in an adult. Having a subject display an emotion that's the opposite of what might be expected in the location or setting can also produce humorous results.

Incongruity opens the front door of disbelief. Exaggeration crashes through it. Another way to look at the two devices would be that while exaggeration is definitely fictitious, an incongruous statement might still be within the realm of nonfiction.

Surprise or the unexpected twist

Humor is often built on surprises. When people are asked to recall the funniest thing they ever saw on TV, eventually someone will bring up the final episode of *The Bob Newhart Show*. At the end of the show Newhart woke up in bed with Suzanne Pleshette, who played his wife on a previous TV series, explaining that the entire subsequent six-season series had been some kind of incredible dream. The producers went to great lengths to make sure that no one knew what was going to happen before that episode aired and the result was an incredible surprise for the audience. It remains one of TV's most memorable events.

Closely related to surprise is the use of the unexpected twist. Creating an image in the readers mind, and then completely destroying it with a sudden change in direction is an excellent way to evoke laughter. For example, the following passage is from a piece I wrote about something I had to give up after breaking my spine:

> "I miss the feel of hot, sweaty flesh, pounding rhythmically beneath me, and the sounds of heavy breathing and snorting as I go up and down—at times barely able to avoid falling off. I miss the rush it gave me as it forced adrenaline through my system. It wasn't that I experienced it all that often, and frankly, I wasn't very good at it, but every time I did I had a really good time. Had I known that I'd have to stop doing it, I would have done it a lot more when I could. That's why I find it hard to believe that there are people out there who have no desire to even try it. I'm sure some of you just take doing it for granted. I did, and of course now I wish I hadn't.
>
> Yes, I sure do miss horseback riding."

The first paragraph is ambiguous enough to create the impression that I am talking about another enjoyable activity. By going into a lot of detail, I strung the reader along, even further down the wrong path. The short second paragraph provides an unexpected twist by quickly letting the readers know that what they are thinking is way off base. Had I introduced the idea of horseback riding in the opening, the reader would have created an entirely different image in their minds about the "hot, sweaty flesh, pounding rhythmically beneath me," and the surprise would have been eliminated.

Creating a sense of superiority

A great deal of humor writing is based on creating a sense of superiority, in the reader, the author, or both. Ethnic, racial, and sexist jokes all play on creating a sense of superiority. While political correctness might keep us away from writing that sort of material, it is still possible to use or create a sense of superiority without offending people. Slapstick comedy, practical jokes, and embarrassing the key subject all rely on using the reader or viewer's sense of superiority over the person at the butt of the joke.

One way to create a sense of superiority in the reader is to write autobiographical stories that tend to be a bit self-deprecating. For example, I have used my lack of handyman skills as a basis for several columns. In one I pointed out that my favorite power tool is the eight-inch reciprocating telephone receiver that I use to call people who are handy. By saying that I grant a sense of superiority to anyone who knows the difference between a socket wrench and a pair of pliers.

When I refer to my cocker spaniel as, "the dumbest dog to ever get lost on a single flight of stairs," I am giving a feeling of superiority to anyone with a dog capable of even the most basic cognitive functions.

Creating a sense of superiority in readers gives them permission to laugh at our characters or at us, but with the realization that they are, in fact, laughing with us about these shortcomings or differences. There have been numerous humorists and comedians throughout the years who have played on their ethnic, racial, or religious differences. Occasionally I let my readers and audiences in on a facet of my life that they might have difficulty imagining being humorous. People have a stereotypical image of paraplegics that we are supposed to spend our lives feeling sorry for ourselves. In reality there is humor in my situation. I usually tell my audiences that I ended up this way in a serious golfing accident. That statement is definitely a play for the incongruous element of humor because golf does not seem to be the type of sport that could result in a spinal injury. I go on to explain that my car was rear-ended while I was on my way to the golf course and the accident had a very detrimental effect on my handicap. The element of surprise is created when I juxtapose the golfing term, "handicap" with being physically handicapped. Of course there is a certain amount of politically incorrect language in that statement. With so many new words for being disabled I live in constant fear that I might offend myself.

Playing on my disability creates an involuntary sense of superiority and thankfulness in the reader or audience member that they don't have to be like me. The discomfort that might be created when joking about my situation is substantially reduced by the awareness that I am giving them permission to laugh about it.

FINDING A TOPIC

Finding a humorous topic to write about really only involves looking at the world from the outside of your eyelids forward. Virtually any setting can produce humorous incidents and inspiration. I'm always thankful for that fact, because, as the late *Atlanta Journal-Constitution* columnist Lewis Grizzard once said, "Writing a weekly column is like being married to a nymphomaniac. For the first couple of weeks it's fun, but then you learn that as soon as you are finished it's time to start over again."

The world really is a pretty funny place. Often, when we get caught up in the events of our daily lives, we miss a lot of the humor that surrounds us. Taking a step back and allowing yourself to be a bit more observant will open your eyes to a lot of funny topics. Be careful though. You might become tempted to write about anything and everything that strikes you as funny. Focusing on a selected topic or small group of topics will make it much easier to develop your comedic voice, a specific audience, and a sense of security in your ability to consistently make your readers laugh. I make my living by exploring the funny side of life from the perspective of a husband who is still married to his first wife after nearly 30 years; a father of two sons; and the master of the dumbest dog to ever get lost on a single flight of stairs.

Humorists who focus on family life tend to look closely at the little situations that occur in everyone's life, but that often go unnoticed. Situations that you might find frustrating in your own life might seem quite humorous when someone else writes about facing the same frustration. Parents of teenagers are often exasperated by the quantity of food their offspring can consume, only to return to the kitchen a half an hour later, claiming to be starving. In my weekly column, I've often referred to my sons as my "grocery sucking appetites on legs." Fictitious characters, if they are going to be portrayed as real human beings, are going to run into the same problems, frustrations and foibles as they go through their existence.

In one of my columns about the care and feeding of the teenage male, I said, "You know you're in trouble when you run out of food before you've finished unloading the groceries from the car." That statement uses many of the devices described above. It contains a bit (and believe me, in my family's case, a very little bit) of exaggeration. It also uses surprise, and lets the reader feel a bit superior because, no matter how much their children might eat, they've probably never had it quite that bad.

Obviously, the political arena is filled with opportunities for humorists. Comedians rely heavily on political humor, as do satirists, and commentators. It's topical, anyone who reads a newspaper or watches television will have some knowledge of the subject, and it's filled with incongruities. Politicians seem to have a knack for getting themselves into situations that provide a plethora of material for the humorists who focus on this subject area.

GETTING STARTED

When I teach humor writing at writers' conferences, I ask the participants to write a brief story about their most embarrassing moment. The odds are pretty good that they would have laughed if they had seen the same thing happen to somebody else. Using such an event as the basis for a humorous story gives the writer a great opportunity to make use of elements such as surprise, incongruity, and giving the readers a sense of superiority because it didn't happen to them.

The example that I cite comes from a story I wrote about my son when he was just three years old. He chose his pre-school Christmas pageant to repeat what he had heard me saying the night before while trying to erect the Christmas tree. When he said, "I can't get this freaking tree in the freaking Christmas tree stand," I experienced what has to be my life's most embarrassing moment, especially since neither he nor I used the word "freaking," but rather another slightly similar sounding expletive.

I retold that story in one of my first newspaper columns in 1994. That column has since been reprinted numerous times in newspapers in Canada, the U.S. and abroad. It was also the basis for a magazine article and a radio script.

THE MARKETPLACE FOR HUMOR

Yes Virginia, despite what that agent told me when I was first starting out, there is a market for humor. While most newspapers and some consumer magazines might prefer nonfiction pieces, many still have openings for the occasional bit of fiction other than the promises made by political candidates. Trade magazines tend to shy away from fiction, even if it closely relates to the specific industry they are addressing. Consumer magazines are the best paying potential market for humorous fiction. A great many of the Writers Digest Top 100 magazine markets are looking for humorous material. The 2001 *Writer's Market—The Internet Edition* identified over 120 consumer magazines when I did a search for markets interested in humorous fiction, and it didn't even include the letters section in *Penthouse.*

Fillers

In addition to columns and feature articles, all newspapers and magazines are excellent markets for fillers. A filler is a very short item that the editor can use to fill up a small space left blank at the end of a longer article. Often these pieces are no more than a sentence or two long. For example, one that I have sold and resold is actually a line from a column I wrote about an unpopular article of clothing: "The clothes a man wears can say a lot about his stature. A hospital gown can eliminate any doubt."

Newspapers tend to look for more current or topical fillers, while most magazines are more open to material that isn't as time sensitive.

Greeting cards

If you have a knack for really short pieces that pack a punch, the greeting card market might be right for you. This industry has an almost insatiable demand for new and funny ways of looking at familiar topics like holidays, birthdays, anniversaries, or quadruple bypass surgery.

Other

Other markets for humor include radio and TV shows, stand-up comedians, and even corporations seeking to inject a sense of humor into an otherwise dull and boring speech by the CEO. Some cartoonists use writers to supply the words for their characters in the comics.

GETTING THERE IS HALF THE FUN

The learning process involved in writing humor is an enjoyable one. I recommend that would-be humorists spend a lot of time reading what has already been written, listening carefully to comedians' routines, and observing the passages of time for those unique moments that draw a humorous response.

There are a number of excellent writers who have made humor their primary genre. I am a big fan of the late Lewis Grizzard. Of course, Erma Bombeck was another great inspiration when I was getting started. In addition, I recommend going back and reading everything from Shakespeare's comedies like *Twelfth Night*, to the writings of people like James Thurber and Stephen Leacock. Garrison Keillor created his fictional Lake Wobegon and some of the funniest characters in American literature by focusing on the small, humorous details of daily life in a rural Minnesota community. Even Dave Barry, whose nonfiction is often punctuated with "I am not making this up," has brought his humor to fiction with the publication in 1999 of *Big Trouble* (Putnam Publishing Group.) The mystery writing genre may never be the same. Each of these writers has taught me something about the use of words, timing, and the subtleties of making people laugh with me, at me, and hopefully at themselves.

It is also critical that you keep up to date with current events. I read at least two newspapers each day. Writer's block can hit humorists, too. Small, insignificant items in a newspaper have often triggered the idea for my weekly column. There is no reason your fictitious character can't experience some of the things that occur in the lighter side of the news.

Listening to comedians is another important tool for the humor writer. I've picked up a lot of ideas about timing and how to draw the reader into the story from people like Jay Leno, Jeff Foxworthy, and Tim Allen.

Humor writing contains many of the same elements that are the basis of all good writing. Most colleges and universities offer extension courses in creative writing. I strongly recommend taking as many of them as you can. I'd also recommend attending writers' conferences and critique groups to further hone your style. Conferences have taught me a great deal that has helped me develop as a writer, and I have also learned valuable lessons about dealing with the publishing industry.

Finally, being a humor writer is marvelous therapy. It is really difficult to become depressed when you are focusing your energies on making both yourself and others laugh.

Revision 101: How to Make Good Fiction Better

BY KAREN X. TULCHINSKY

You've finished your story. You've worked hard. You've written a first draft. You've developed your characters. Set the scene. Worked with the plot. Reworked the action. Dug deep inside for emotional complexity. It's a theme you've been thinking about for a long time and it's an important piece of work. But when you read over your manuscript, something is missing. It doesn't sing. It doesn't flow. It sounds awkward. It feels, well, boring. You know it can be better, but you're just not sure how. Or why.

Editors read thousands of manuscripts each year. You need yours to stand out. Don't sweat it if the first, second, even third draft is missing that special quality that will queue you up for the next Pulitzer Prize. Ninety percent of writing is rewriting. A good story becomes great through revision. In a first draft, you strive to capture what's on your mind and in your heart and get it down on the page. It's in the rewriting that your story comes truly alive. Here are seven simple techniques that will help make your good fiction better.

Show, don't tell

Okay, okay. You've probably heard this before. There's a reason: it's the most important technique and is often forgotten by newer writers. It is more effective to show through a character's actions and dialogue than to tell through narrative exposition. This doesn't mean you won't ever use description. Sometimes you need to move the action along quickly, and provide the reader with information. But in general, go through your manuscript and look for scenes where you are telling when you could be showing. Then rewrite and see how much more dynamic the prose becomes.

Here's an example of where the author tells the scene:

> Joe decided finally to phone his father and demand the truth. He was very nervous.

Here's how the author could show the scene:

> Joe's stomach churned. He poured a shot of scotch and knocked it back. The liquor burned his throat on its way down, but the warmth spread quickly through his belly. He took a deep breath, reached for the receiver, and dialed the number. Three rings, then his father's gruff voice on the line. Joe twisted the phone cord around his finger.
> "Hello, Dad?," he began.

Can you see how much more vivid the rewrite is? We 'see' an image of Joe knocking back the scotch, taking a deep breath, twisting the phone cord. This gives the reader so much more than "Joe was very nervous."

Slow the picture down

This is similar to show, don't tell. Often in a first draft we throw away moments that could be exploited for dramatic effect. The more life you can see in a small moment the more power

KAREN X. TULCHINSKY *is the award-winning author of* Love Ruins Everything *and* In Her Nature, *the editor of numerous anthologies of contemporary fiction, and a creative writing instructor.*

and depth the story will have. As a writer, you struggle for depth. And the slower you can move the picture, the more depth you can convey. The trick is, in the rewrite, to go through your manuscript and look for throwaway lines that could be stretched out. You don't want to do this for every single action that occurs in your piece—you want to be choosy. You want to select action to slow down because it reveals something vital about the character or plot.

Here's an example:

> I opened the car door and got out.

That tells the reader something, but not much. Look at how much more vividly the same action reads once the action is slowed down (imagine a movie camera is recording the scene in slow motion):

> I switched off the ignition, took a deep breath and let it out slowly. Gritting my teeth, I reached for the door handle. The metal was cold on my bare fingers. Carefully, I pulled on the latch, pushed at the door with my shoulder and quietly swung it open. Silently, I stepped out, careful not to slip on the icy pavement. Pocketing the key, I eased the door closed without a sound.

Now this tells the reader a whole lot more. It sets the scene, mood and tone. We can see by the character's actions that she is nervous. And she is cautious. She is either sneaking up on someone, or hiding. Note: she opens the door silently, then closes it the same way. You have to try really hard to close a car door silently. You have to do this with intent. Notice not too much has been given away by telling. The reader has not been told why the character is being quiet. Or why she is nervous. Instead, a mystery has been set up. And hopefully, the reader is curious to know why the character is behaving this way.

The five senses

Newer writers often forget that we have five senses; six, if you include intuition and psychic ability. Many writers focus only on what they see. But if, as a writer, you describe a scene using all the senses—what you hear, smell, taste, touch, feel and intuit, as well as see—you will draw your reader right into the scene. They will feel like they are right there with your character. Think of the times when you've heard a song playing from someone's front window as you walked by. Maybe it was an old song, and suddenly you were taken back ten years to your high school prom. You're standing at the back of the gym, with your buddies, in your stiff rented tux, or long strapless gown. The song pulls you back in time instantly and you remember the spiked punch, and the excitement and bittersweet feelings in the air. You are surrounded by the memory just from hearing the opening chords of a song that was popular that year.

Scent can be just as powerful. Have you ever smelled food cooking and instantly been reminded of another time or place? Your neighbor is roasting a turkey, and as the aroma sneaks through the walls of your apartment, you're taken back to Thanksgiving at your grandmother's house. Your mouth begins to water, and your eyes well up with tears because last year your grandmother passed away. You haven't really thought about her in weeks, or months, but just the smell of turkey roasting takes you back to her big oak table, in her airy kitchen, in her farmhouse in New England. And it is not only evoking a memory, but a feeling.

You can create this effect in your readers if you concentrate on writing from all the senses. On a rewrite, go through your manuscript and look for scenes where you can add more sensory detail. Then brainstorm on a separate sheet of paper. Do each sense separately, and push yourself to come up with original ideas.

Let's say your scene is in a coffee shop. In the first draft, you have only described what the character sees: customers sitting at tables; a server behind a counter; a large cappuccino machine; cups and saucers neatly lined up; pastry on shelves; a cash register; a tip jar.

To brainstorm, start with smell. Use a separate sheet of paper as this frees you from worrying about writing beautiful prose. Write down everything you can think of that your character smells while sitting in the coffee shop. Your list might look like this:

- Coffee aroma
- Cigarette smoke
- Women's perfume
- Chocolate icing
- Faint smell of fresh paint

On another separate sheet, work with touch. Your list might look like this:

- Sticky table
- Hard plastic chair seat
- Heat from the coffee mug
- Hard tile floor
- Cold wind blowing in each time the door is opened

Next try sound. Your list might look like this:

- Hiss of the cappuccino machine
- Server shouting out coffee orders
- Baby crying in back of shop
- Man talking loudly at the next table
- Beep of cash register
- Change clattering in tip jar
- Rock music playing softly

Lastly, work on taste. This is a tricky sense to cover in writing, but it's a good idea to try and come up with at least a few items for this list:

- Sweet whipped cream
- Bitter bite of coffee
- Chocolate sprinkles
- Sugar

The trick to remember when brainstorming is never to censor yourself. You're looking for quantity, not quality. And if you let your mind be free and give yourself permission to write down everything that comes up, you may surprise yourself with some very original images.

Once you've completed your brainstorming lists, the next step is to be selective. You won't want to use all of your lists, because there is such a thing as too much sensory detail. Have you ever been reading a book and you come across a section where the author describes the sweeping, bleak, stark, windswept, raw, desolate, dusty, barren, cold, icy, frigid, frozen—you get the idea—and found yourself skipping over several pages out of boredom? The author made two mistakes. First, she wasn't selective. Secondly, she plunked the description into one lump section, instead of evenly spreading it throughout the scene. So first, be selective—use only the most powerful and vivid images you come up with. Secondly, slip the details in here and there, among the action and dialogue. Here's an example of a scene drafted using your lists from above. It needs a little work, but look for your details to appear:

Jack squeezes his long legs under his favorite table at the back, and sets down his steaming cup of mocha cappuccino. Melted whipped cream slides down the sides of the mug over his fingers. He raises it to his lips and licks the sweet cream. Jill's high heels click across the ceramic tile floor toward him. She bumps the table into Jack's knee as she plunks into the chair opposite him.

"Ow," Jack rubs his leg, shifts in his chair.

"I don't see why we have to leave tomorrow," Jill says, lighting a cigarette.

"Honey," Jack waves at the smoke, stifles a cough. "We've been over this a million times."

"Double latte, low-fat milk!" the waiter calls to the cappuccino server.

Jack gulps his coffee too fast, burns his tongue.

"What about your divorce?" Jill stirs her coffee rapidly, her spoon clattering against the glass.

"Honey, please . . ."

"Please what?" She tosses the spoon onto the table, hitting Jack's fingers. A blast of cold air rushes around them as the back door opens.

Melodrama aside, notice how the setting is revealed naturally, within the action and dialogue. This is much more readable than if you had written several paragraphs describing the café, and then begun the dialogue and action.

You can also use sensory detail to convey emotion or foreshadow. A cold blast of air rushes in as the lovers argue. The cold air emphasizes the chilly emotional atmosphere between Jack and Jill and foreshadows the storm to come in their relationship.

Poetic voice

Poetry is the shortest, most economical way to say it. Prose writers, if they are not already also poets, often forget to develop the poetic voice. For some of us, this is a struggle. But it's important to work on your poetic voice, and add some poetry to your prose. You don't need to deviate from your own style, but the poetic voice will help you find the shortest, sharpest way to compress compelling detail, emotion and action into some tight spaces. Poetry is like fine cognac, wine that has been distilled to its finest form. A small snifter of brandy after a meal adds a certain elegance.

To fine-tune your poetic voice, try free writing. On your computer or in a notebook, if you prefer, write for ten minutes. First, close your eyes for a moment and let the essence of your story and your characters float through your mind. Feel what your characters feel. Immerse yourself in your theme. When you're ready, open your eyes and write, stream of consciousness style, with no goal or structure—just get the feelings from your heart on the page.

Free writing is like jumping out of an airplane without a parachute. As you're plunging rapidly toward Earth you are consumed with images and feelings. Write it all down without fear. You're going to die anyway, so you might as well have your say. You will surprise yourself with what you come up with. From this free writing, you may only use one word, or one phrase, several sentences, or none at all. It doesn't always work, but if you keep practicing, you will eventually tap a deeper part of your subconscious where your poetic voice lives. This will strengthen your prose, and like cognac, add elegance to your story.

The beat

Rhythm is important in prose. The best way to check out the rhythm of your piece is to read it out loud. If anything feels awkward in your mouth or to your ears as you read it aloud, circle or underline it. If it sounds awkward, it *is* awkward. Read your piece at least twice, marking it, then go through each phrase or sentence one by one. Sometimes it's a simple matter of shortening the sentence, or rearranging it, or deleting it all together. Pay attention to sentence length. Short sentences move the action along quickly, and are useful in action sequences where you want the reader to feel movement, excitement or fear. Long sentences tend to slow the pace down and are effective when you want the piece to feel slow, lazy, quiet. Make sure to vary sentence length in your piece. Words are your tools—use them conscientiously.

Trim, trim, trim. Sometimes a scene starts too early and goes on too long. It's like the writer is warming up and then winding down. But the important part of the scene was in the middle section. In fact, without the beginning and the end, the scene is more vibrant. It gets right to the point. Go through your manuscript and check for this. See if you can start your scene later and end it earlier. It's hard to chop up your work, but worth it if the end result is stronger, more potent.

This is true for each sentence, as well. Be ruthless. Go through your work several times with a red pen and see if you can trim it down. It can be painful, like chopping off your own arm, but a one-armed character is sometimes more interesting than one with two.

Original words and metaphor

Original language is something we always hear about. Although the best approach is often to tell a story simply, at the same time you want to be sure your language is original. This is where your dictionary and thesaurus come in. Never pull out these reference books in a first draft. Your first draft is time to create. To pound out the story, discover your characters, locate the setting, play within the plot, explore the theme. In the rewriting stage, though, go through your manuscript and circle or underline any word that is boring or unoriginal. You may find bland words, like "walk," all over your manuscript. After you've marked up your piece, pull out the reference books and start searching for original words. Don't go overboard, but stomp, march, glide and saunter are more descriptive than "walk." Also search for repetitions of words and phrases and, unless you're using them deliberately as a device, replace as many as possible.

A note about clichés: Because they have been over-used, they take your reader out of the story. It's okay to throw in some clichés in the first draft, if you can't think of anything else at that moment. You don't want to stop the flow or lose your thought. Just remember to replace them in your rewrite.

To be or not to be

Variations on the verb "to be" are, frankly, boring. Often you can tighten and liven up your prose simply by going through your manuscript and finding "to be" verbs and rewriting the sentence. Here's a simple example:

There are three women living in the house.

Rewrite as this:

Three women live in the house.

See how much simpler, cleaner and more active the rewrite is?

Nobody ever said writing was easy. If it were, everyone would do it. Writing is hard work. And it can be scary. But not as frightening as leaping from an airplane with no parachute. If you revise your work step-by-step using these techniques, rewriting is a little like having a parachute. You plunge free fall, wait till the last second to pull the cord, and then float down to land on your feet.

Revision 102: The "Last" Draft

BY LEX WILLIFORD

How do you know when you've written the "last" draft? Is it when, as Flaubert suggested, you find yourself replacing a period with a comma in the morning, then putting the period back in the same place that afternoon? Or, as Faulkner suggested, when you've slain all your darlings? Or is it only when you're no longer around to revise, like Raymond Carver, who rewrote many stories, then published them in different magazines under different titles—"The Bath," "A Small Good Thing"—then left it to critics to sort it all out in *Studies in Short Fiction*? Or is it, as Pound suggested, that you never really finish anything? You simply abandon it.

I've abandoned this essay four times already, only to return to it again and again with the conviction that it isn't what I meant—not yet. I start again from scratch, cutting two pages of an introduction I've already rewritten from scratch twice—and then abandoned. Like many writers, I have to write enough beginnings to know where to begin, have to write enough to know what I have to write, have to get stuck to get moving. Especially when I'm writing fiction— a far more difficult enterprise, I believe, than writing essays like this—I've come to expect that what I write will (and often *must*) bear little resemblance to what I set out to write, and I'm never sure if I'm done. Caught in that delicate and sometimes frustrating negotiation between the freewheeling imagination and the critical, aesthetic (and too often perfectionist) demands of craft and structure, I've finally accepted that if I have to abandon work, for a short time or for good, I might as well be working on something else, as many projects as I can possibly keep up with. Sometimes, this activity feels a little like juggling five or six chainsaws—the constant fear that at any moment I'm going to lose an arm or my head—but for some reason this is how I work best, how I find joy in working even when the writing is difficult and, at times, downright depressing: a tragic adventure.

There's a moment at the end of Hemingway's "Big Two Hearted River: Part II," when Nick Adams, just back from war in Europe, shell-shocked and trying to regain some balance and quiet by camping and fishing in the north woods wilderness of his youth, decides to stop fishing before he enters a swamp: "Nick did not want to go in there now. He felt a reaction against deep wading with the water deepening under his armpits, to hook big trout in places impossible to land them. In the swamp the banks were bare, the big cedars came together overhead, the sun did not come through, except in patches; in the fast deep water, in the half light, the fishing would be tragic. In the swamp fishing was a tragic adventure. Nick did not want it. He did not want to go down the stream any further today . . . There were plenty of days coming when he could fish the swamp."

The singular discovery I've made about my writing process over the last 20 years is this: I get swamped, stuck, bogged down. A lot. Writing every day, for me, often means getting up the courage to enter a swamp of my own making and then to do what I know is next to impossible— to wade into muck up to my armpits and land a keeper on a flimsy fly rod—and sometimes I have to know when to quit, have to decide to fish the stream a few days more, where the fishing

LEX WILLIFORD *teaches in the MFA creative writing program at the University of Texas at El Paso. His short story collection* Macauley's Thumb *was co-winner of the Iowa Short Fiction Award in 1993. His fiction and nonfiction have appeared in* American Literary Review, Glimmer Train, Quarterly West, Shenandoah *and* Southern Review.

is easier, till my muse is ready to enter that swamp again and again. The writing's better there—deeper, darker, riskier, more unflinchingly honest and difficult—and it's almost impossible to land stories there, scenes, moments of recognition that earn emotion and resonate deeply on an unconscious level. Writing there *is* a tragic adventure, one I look forward to and often dread, something I must wait days, months or even years to return to before I can find the courage to begin, or to begin again.

Writer Ellen Gilchrist once told me she has on her computer hard drive an entire directory of stuck narratives called 'tar babies,' narratives she's gotten helplessly stuck in which she's abandoned then returned to occasionally, only to discover she's come unstuck and is ready to "finish" them. Like Gilchrist and others, I can find no end of ways to get stuck in a narrative: When I ask myself something as simple as, All right, *now* what happens? Or when a character does something utterly baffling and I realize that I don't know the character well enough yet to make that moment credible or inevitable. When I've made an easy move and stopped because I know I'm lying to myself about something important some essential part of me refuses to see. Or when I make a difficult, risky move and realize that I don't have the courage to go on, not yet.

As Annie Dillard writes in *The Writing Life*: "When you are well into writing, and know what comes next, and yet cannot go on; when every morning for a week or a month you enter [your] room and turn your back on [your work]; then the trouble is either of two things. Either the structure has forked, so the narrative, or the logic, has developed a hairline fracture that will shortly split it up the middle-or you are approaching a fatal mistake. What you had planned will not do. If you pursue your present course, the book will explode or collapse, and you do not know about it yet, quite."

"I've come to expect that what I write will bear little resemblance to what I set out to write, and I'm never sure if I'm done. Caught in that delicate and sometimes frustrating negotiation between the freewheeling imagination and the critical, aesthetic demands of craft and structure, I've finally accepted that if I have to abandon work, for a short time or for good, I might as well be working on something else, as many projects as I can possibly keep up with. Sometimes, this activity feels a little like juggling five or six chainsaws—the constant fear that at any moment I'm going to lose an arm or my head."

Many times, I've written toward the ending of a story and, the moment I've gotten there, realized that's not what happened, and no amount of pushing is going to change that fact. One December at Yaddo, the artist colony in Saratoga Springs, New York, I wrote a long story about a Wal-Mart clerk and a chiropractor. I wanted to finish the story, but I was stuck three pages short of the ending. The whole time I struggled with it, there were three feet of pristine snow on the ground outside my studio and a pair of cross country skis leaning against the front porch. I'd never cross-country skied in my life, and I wanted to learn how, wanted to ski in the shadows of giant spruces along the road circling the Trasks' ponds and the turret of Tennessee Williams' famous stone studio, past the Saratoga Race Track, where Carver and Plath and Cheever had all walked, working through some line or scene that had them stuck. But I stayed in my study and suffered through an ending, even when I knew it was a lie. About the time I "finished" and realized this fact, it started to rain, a real downpour, and the next day all the snow was gone.

No matter how much I wanted that ending to come it didn't come until more than eight months later when I sat up in my bed in the middle of the night and realized I'd planted a single needle in the haystack of the story—the sharp pin of a Wal-Mart pocket ID tag—which ended the story as it must. The ending was handed to me. A gift.

"Stuckness," for me, almost always lies at the heart of what stories are *about*, some fear I have to face, some blind spot I have to check and check again, some change I have to make in myself before my character can change and move on (or not change and be fated to repeat the same story again and again). For me, writing stories is about change, stripping away layers of lies till a character is exposed and stunned and utterly changed, and I can only hope that a reader, a bystander of this process, might see and be changed, too. It's damned hard work.

But the process has become less frustrating for me even as my stories have become riskier and more difficult to write. When I was a younger writer, I usually stayed with one project till the end because my critical sensibilities were mostly undeveloped and my capacity for lying to myself and writing from the ego were massive. If writing does anything over many years, it teaches patience and humility. Usually I would push forward until I got to the end and only occasionally got stuck. Then I'd revise the story five or ten times, with several complete over-hauls. Many writers I know work this way, and rarely ever get stuck—an ability I both admire and envy since such writers seem to have so much more confidence and faith than I that they can keep up their forward momentum without having to look back and "fix" anything.

Novelist Valerie Miner once described her writing process to me, and I was fascinated by how differently we wrote: She writes an entire novel draft long hand on a legal pad, then types it into her word processor, and prints up the manuscript. Then she erases her only disk, marks up the typescript, then retypes the entire novel into her word processor again, repeating the process, she says, about seven times. For her, writing a novel is a physical act, a matter of running the words through her fingers until she's reach the "last" draft.

This writing-till-the-end process worked fine for me until I started graduate school, where the demands of craft-consciousness and structure can too often eclipse everything else. For my entire first year in an MFA program, I was blocked (a standard condition if the graduate students I've taught are any indication) until I started revising as I wrote, and even then the writing was slow. Almost glacial.

Several years ago, writer John Keeble described his own writing process to a group of graduate students at the University of Alabama. The diagram he drew on the board described the circular nature of daily writing and revision, each arrow and circle representing an hour's work, a day's, a month's, even a year's, the writer returning to read what she's written the day or month before, then revising and pushing forward through another line or stanza, paragraph, scene, or chapter. Keeble's lucid explanation came to me as a revelation, describing a process I'd struggled with for years, and gave me a kind of permission to write the way I'd been writing all along, but with less frustration. Unfortunately, though, at the time I was also stuck on a long project and realized Keeble had left out the blocks that many writers encounter. When I asked Keeble, "What do you do when you get stuck?" he smiled and said, "Just keep on pushing."

I'd experienced that feeling many times before, when I'd push like Sisyphus shouldering a boulder up a hill, only to watch it roll back down again and again. And I remembered those moments when I'd pushed till, nearing the top, the boulder had gotten lighter and lighter, then lifted me and carried me off: the elation of the breakthrough writers so often work for. Even so, I wasn't being productive and, as I often do when I get stuck, I returned to Rilke's advice to a young poet in 1903: "No one can counsel and help you, no one . . . There is only one single way. Go into yourself . . . Then try, like some first human being, to say what you see and experience and love and lose . . . Leave to your opinions their own quiet undisturbed development, which, like all progress, must come from deep within and cannot be pressed or hurried by anything. *Everything* is gestation and then bringing forth."

Pushing too hard often turns writing—something to do for its own sake alone, for its own intrinsic rewards—into a thankless, depressing chore. Though I write mostly linear stories, I realized, my process is mostly *non*linear. Part of the problem, I knew, from reading about left- and right-brain research and generative heuristics, was the controlling nature of rational linearity itself, having to put one word after another, and how that process was in direct conflict with the spatial and randomly intuitive nature of the imagination. When I worked on just one project, I realized, I often got stuck in obsessive rewriting, like a diamond needle scratching through the looping groove of a vinyl record, then skipping, skipping, skipping, till I'd nudged the needle enough times to get unstuck. But that just wasn't working for me anymore.

Unlike reading, writing is not inherently stuck in its own linearity. Writing is more analogous to a digital process like computer multitasking or a CD set on shuffle so that when one gets stuck one simply moves on to something else, just leaps over to the next track to keep up momentum. To become unstuck, I decided to work on several projects at once: a book of stories, two novels, a screenplay, several essays and an anthology of contemporary short fiction. Not being stuck in the linear groove of working on a single project anymore helped me to stay productive while letting things that had me stuck cook in the unconscious awhile. The point was simply to move beyond stuckness to another project, to let the writing come when it was ready, in its own quiet time.

Since then, for me, writing has become a little like working in a room full of toasters. Whereas before I'd stand around waiting by a single toaster for toast to pop up, my job now is simply to show up every day and feed slices into the slots and, when something pops up, go over and butter it. The problem with such a process is that one may end up stuck with slices of cold, stale bread or charred, inedible toast crumbing the counter everywhere without finishing anything at all, without ever getting fed. But it's a risk I'm willing to take everyday, a hard-won faith that lets things cook in the unconscious longer until they produce more nourishing fare.

In no way would I prescribe this process to anyone. I didn't choose it; it chose me. I'm simply admitting that, because I get stuck a lot, I'm stuck with it. If I could write another way, I would, but accepting this process as a kind of gift rather than a curse, I've increased my productivity and confidence about whether drafts are finished or close to finished, even if I'm never sure I've written the "last" draft.

"For me, writing stories is about change, stripping away layers of lies till a character is exposed and stunned and utterly changed, and I can only hope that a reader, a bystander of this process, might see and be changed, too. It's damned hard work."

How to Create Compelling Characters

BY DONALD MAASS

What do folks remember most about a novel? I have asked this question many times, of all different kinds of people. Your answer is probably the same as that of most readers: the characters. Great characters are the key to great fiction. A high-octane plot is nothing without credible, larger-than-life, highly developed enactors to make it meaningful.

Agents, editors, and novelists alike often speak of character-driven stories. What do they mean by that term? Some are referring to stories in which the main events and narrative thrust are not generated by outside forces but by the inner drives of the main characters. To my way of thinking, though, all stories are character driven. Hot plot devices may propel a protagonist into action, even danger, but how involving is that when the action taken is what anybody would do?

Indeed, it is a common fault of beginning thriller writers to slam an Everyman, your average Joe, into the middle of something big and terrible. Such stories usually feel lackluster because the main character is lackluster. A plot is just a plot. It is the actions of a person that make it memorable or not. Great characters rise to the challenge of great events.

REAL PEOPLE VS. LARGER-THAN-LIFE FIGURES

When people in real life are colorful, outrageous, heroic, highly accomplished, great wits or otherwise memorable, they are said to be "like a character in a novel." When a fictional character exhibits qualities that are out of the ordinary, we say they are "larger-than-life."

Is it any wonder that as readers we are drawn to larger-than-life characters? The greatest characters in our literature are all larger-than-life. But how to construct them? Do you even want to? The whole concept can become a perplexing difficulty if a character with whom you are working is based upon an actual person, or if your purpose is to show your readers that people are the way you observe them to be.

There is nothing wrong with either intention, and in fact I believe it is possible to fashion breakout novels—from the stuff of actual human experience. It just requires identifying what is extraordinary in people who are otherwise ordinary.

I am dismayed that some fiction writers bristle when I make that observation. It is as if deliberately constructing a character is a sin. Some authors feel that if characters are to be credible, then they must be exactly like real people. Others report their characters take on a life of their own: "They tell me what they are going to do! I just write it down!"

There is nothing wrong with these techniques, except that a naturalistic and *laissez-faire* approach may lead too easily to characters who are humdrum, inactive, or uninteresting to read about. Even when they are based in part upon real people, characters always are reflections of

DONALD MAASS, *author of 17 novels, has more than 20 years of experience as a literary agent. Former president of the Association of Authors' Representatives, he speaks at writers conferences throughout the country. This article is excerpted from* Writing the Breakout Novel © 2001 by Donald Maass. Used with permission of Writer's Digest Books, a division of F&W Publications, Inc. For credit card orders phone toll free 1-800-289-0963.

the author's subconscious mind. And the mind can play tricks on the best of us.

For instance, authors who have hit a midcareer crisis are prone to create characters that are dark, depressed, unpleasant—sometimes even repellent. Usually, when I point out the drawbacks of such characters, the authors at first are indignant. "That is what I was going for," they say. "These are the best characters I have ever written! Believe me, there really are people like this out there!"

I am sure. But does anyone really want to read about them? Authors in crisis believe so. They write characters who they feel will win back for them the respect they lost. To bolster their positions, they point to artistic successes like Judith Guest's bestselling *Ordinary People* (1976) or Carolyn Chute's *The Beans of Egypt, Maine* (1985), a harshly detailed picture of rural poverty.

As we shall see later in this chapter, the Jarrett family in Guest's novel may seem ordinary, but their actions are not. The mean-spirited, white trash Beans in Chute's novel are anything but attractive, I will admit. So why did that novel break out?

Chute's characters *are* compelling, but the resistant author generally has not fully worked out how Chute accomplishes that feat. It certainly is not by making her people ugly inside and out. That cannot work. Most of us do not for very long tolerate people who make us feel frustrated, sad, hopeless, or depressed—not in life, not in books. Chute does not try to change our feelings. She is subtle, but as we shall presently see, it does not fly against reader psychology.

Whatever your intentions, whatever the type of people whom you are drawn to write about, certain facts are fundamental to breaking out: The characters in your story will not engross readers unless they are out of the ordinary. How can it be otherwise? In life, ordinary folk do ordinary things every day. How much of that do we remember? Precious little.

In life and in fiction, when people act in ways that are unusual, unexpected, dramatic, decisive, full of consequence and are irreversible, we remember them and talk about them for years. Seemingly ordinary characters can stay with us, too, but usually only when their actions are "out of character."

WHAT MAKES A CHARACTER LARGER-THAN-LIFE?

What does it mean for a character to be larger-than-life? What qualities are we really talking about? Let us dig in and try to get a handle on the stuff of greatness.

Strength

If you look closely, I think you cannot avoid the recognition that what makes breakout characters broadly appealing is not their weaknesses but their strengths, not their defeats but their triumphs. Fiction is not life. It needs to reflect life if it is to be believable, but virtually all readers unconsciously seek out novels for an experience of human life that is admirable, amusing, hopeful, perseverant, positive, inspiring and that ultimately makes us feel whole.

Even a plainly drawn, one-dimensional protagonist can grip the popular imagination if he is a character of strength. James Patterson's psychologist-turned-homicide-detective Alex Cross is no one's idea of a character who is subtle, complex, ambiguous, or deeply developed. He is a plain old hero: straightforward, honest, dedicated, hardworking, and sensitive. He is portrayed with bold, simple strokes. At the beginning of Patterson's 1992 bestseller *Along Came a Spider,* Alex is in the kitchen of his home grabbing a quick bite of breakfast (served up by his rock-solid grandmother, Nana Mama) before rushing to a murder scene:

> "There's been another bad murder over in Langley Terrace. It looks like a thrill killer. I'm afraid that it is," I told her.
>
> "That's too bad," Nana Mama said to me. Her soft brown eyes grabbed mine and held. Her white hair looked like one of the doilies she puts on all our living room chairs. "That's

such a bad part of what the politicians have let become a deplorable city. Sometimes I think we ought to move out of Washington, Alex."

"Sometimes I think the same thing," I said, "but we'll probably tough it out."

"Yes, black people always do. We persevere. We always suffer in silence."

"Not always in silence," I said to her.

Did I mention Alex Cross is black? Cross knows what that costs but does not let it burden him. His priorities are in the right place. The murder turns out to be the mutilation and homicide of a woman and her fourteen-year-old daughter, both of whom worked as prostitutes. Also murdered is the woman's young son. This killing of an innocent is what gets to Alex. When he is yanked from that case to work on the abduction of two rich kids from a private school, Alex angrily confronts his boss, Chief of Detectives Pittman:

"Cross, you just listen to what I have to say," he said as he came over to us. "There's been a kidnapping at this school. It's a major kidnapping—"

"That's a real bad thing," I butted in immediately. "Unfortunately, a killer has also struck Condon Terrace and Langley neighborhoods. The killer's hit two times already. Six people are *dead* so far. Sampson [Cross's partner] and I are the senior people on that case. Basically, we're *it*."

"I'm apprised of the situation in the Condon and Langley projects. I've already made contingencies. It's taken care of," Pittman said.

"Two black women had their breasts sliced off this morning. Their pubic hair was shaved while they were tied up in bed. Were you apprised of that?" I asked him. "A three-year-old boy was murdered, in his pajamas." I was shouting again. I glanced at Sampson and saw him shaking his head.

Patterson's writing is not artful. If his novels offered us only their twisty plots, I am not sure they would hold us. Alex Cross, though, has moral conviction. His determination to do right is a strength that gives Patterson's novels a powerful appeal. Again and again they jump to the top of the bestseller lists. Some authors imagine that Patterson has been "made" by his publishers. Not so. No author can ride atop the lists for so many years without appealing to the public. What has "made" Patterson is Alex Cross.

Think about it: We read fiction not just to see ourselves but also to imagine ourselves as we might be. When we recognize ourselves in the characters of a novel, we are gratified. We identify with them. But that is just the beginning. If self-recognition was all we wanted from fiction, we would be as satisfied with letters, journals, and statistical surveys of the population at large. But we are not satisfied with those things.

We crave stories, particularly the intensely intimate form of story called the novel. That is because a novel, uniquely among art forms, presents powerful points of view, strong conflicts, and a helping of human life that affirms a higher truth. Characters in breakout fiction may seem realistic, even average, but they are bigger than their circumstances. They do not just suffer, but strive. They do not practice patience, but act. They do not merely survive, but endure.

Inner conflict

It is easy to catalog the qualities that we ordinarily associate with greatness: vision, insight, high intelligence, leadership, accomplishment, wisdom, to name a few. If you were to construct a character that embodied all of those qualities, however, you would wind up with someone about whom it is not very interesting to read. Why? Because there is nothing left to discover, nothing unresolved, about such a paragon.

Another way to look at it is this: Accomplishment already accomplished does not hold our attention. Striving to attain the impossible, though, is a struggle from which we cannot take our eyes. Do you watch the Olympics on TV? Who does not? Do you still care what happens to the bronze medal winners a month or two after the closing ceremony? No? Who does?

In a novel, struggle is far more compelling than satisfaction. Conflict is the first principle of plot construction, and it is also the underlying secret of great characters.

I am talking about inner conflicts, those seemingly contradictory sides of people that make them endlessly interesting to think about. Take Scarlett O'Hara: She longs for the solid comfort of Ashley Wilkes, but who is the great love of her life? The roguish Rhett Butler. It is a delicious contradiction; indeed, it has become a paradigm of women's views of men: Ashley or Rhett? The unresolved conflict in Scarlett O'Hara is one of the primary qualities that makes her memorable.

In 1990, Anne Perry published *The Face of a Stranger*, the first in a series of Victorian mystery novels featuring Inspector William Monk. Monk is a police detective who has lost his memory as the result of an accident. His current case remains active, but he knows nothing of it. Or himself. What he discovers disturbs him. He learns that he was a man for whom he does not much care. Why he was so feared by his colleagues on the force is a question that haunts him. The difference between who he was and who he would like to be is a powerful inner conflict. Eleven popular novels later, that conflict is driving Monk still.

Does the protagonist in your current manuscript have a strong inner conflict, or perhaps conflicting sides? If not, why not? Adding aspects of character that cannot easily be reconciled will ensure that your character cannot easily be dismissed. Inner conflict will keep your grip on your reader firm.

Self-regard

A third marker of larger-than-life characters is they are self-conscious. I do not mean socially awkward, but that they have a sense of self-regard. Their emotions matter to them. They do not dismiss what they experience. They embrace life. They wonder about their responses to events and what such responses mean. They take themselves seriously—and, by the way, a sense of humor about oneself is the flip side of the same coin.

Think about your favorite novels: How often does the main character experience a sharp turn of the plot only to remark, "Oh, it doesn't really matter"? A compelling hero does not deny his feelings but instead is immersed in them.

On the first page of Anita Shreve's 1998 novel *The Pilot's Wife*, Kathryn Lyons is awakened at 3:24 A.M. by a knocking on her front door. It would have been sufficient for Shreve simply to get her heroine out of bed, down the stairs and to the door to answer it, but Shreve instead details Kathryn's reactions upon waking:

> The lit room alarmed her, the wrongness of it, like an emergency room at midnight. She thought, in quick succession: Mattie. Then, Jack. Then, Neighbor. Then, car accident. But Mattie was in bed, wasn't she? Kathryn had seen her to bed, had watched her walk down the hall and through a door, the door shutting with a firmness that was just short of a slam, enough to make a statement but not provoke a reprimand. And Jack—where was Jack? She scratched the sides of her head, raking out her sleep-flattened hair. Jack was—where? She tried to remember the schedule: London. Due home around lunchtime. She was certain. Or did she have it wrong and had he forgotten his keys again?

Shreve brings us so deeply inside the pilot's wife's mind that when the knock on the door proves to be the tragic news such a woman dreads—her husband has died in an airplane explosion off the coast of Ireland—we are already intimate with her, involved in her world. Note that Shreve does not merely tell us that Kathryn feels alarm; she *shows* us Kathryn's thought process, her checklist of late-night worries. Through that we come to know what matters to her. We take her measure.

An even more effective application of this principle involves allowing your protagonist to measure himself over time. *How have I changed?* is a good question for your main character to pose. *What do I think has caused that change? Do I long to return to my old way of feeling, or am I determined never to return to that old frame of mind?* The answers will give your readers a sense that your character has altered and grown—or perhaps that he pointedly has not.

Wit and Spontaneity

A fourth characteristic of larger-than-life characters is they do and say things that we ordinary folk would not. Have you ever spit in your father's face? Have you ever driven a car into a ditch just to scare the daylights out of your date? Have you ever slapped a man whom you later slept with? Have you ever told your boss that his ego is showing?

I do not do things like that, either, sad to say. I wish I did. Last summer a play that my wife wrote was presented at an international festival. The venue in which it played was busy. The actors shared a common green room. Preceding my wife's play was a self-indulgent one-woman show, the star of which annoyed one and all. Inexplicably, the woman was nominated for Best Actress at the festival. (So was the female lead of my wife's play.) The obnoxious actress won, and everyone was floored. On the last day of performances, an actor from another company approached her and said, "I just wanted to say congratulations on your award and that you are a total bitch."

Oooh, I wish I had said that!

Like me, I am sure that many times you have thought, too late, of the perfect insult or comeback. Well, guess what? Now is your chance. You are a breakout novelist, and you have characters with mouths to feed. Let loose with the snappy remarks and New York attitude. You gobble that stuff up in other authors' novels, don't you? Your readers will eat it up in yours, too.

DARK PROTAGONISTS

One of the most frequent faults I find in submissions, particularly from midcareer novelists in crisis, is that their main characters are unsympathetic. Ironically, this is often the truest of novelists in crisis who send me their latest manuscripts with the assurance, "This is the best thing I have ever written."

I have to admit when I hear that phrase my heart sinks and too often with good reason. The manuscript in question stands a good chance of being about characters who are dark, tortured, haunted (always by "demons"), angry, depressed, cynical, or in some other way unbearable. When I just as inevitably point out this drawback, the response is usually, "But I like my characters flawed! That is what makes them interesting!"

I long to say, "You mean, *therapeutic*?" But I bite my tongue. Usually it is enough to mention that I grew so weary of the character's unrelenting misery that at some point I set the manuscript down.

Up to a point, those authors are correct: A perfect character is not engaging. Character transformation can be one of the most powerful effects in any story. In fact, it is a fundamental principle in the three-act screenplay form espoused by Robert McKee, whose seminars and book, *Story: Substance, Structure, Style and the Principles of Screenwriting*, are the sermons and bible of the screenwriting business.

But there are tricks to working with dark and flawed characters; tricks that stuck, frustrated, impatient authors generally have not taken the time to master. Such authors sometimes mistakenly imagine that any character misbehavior is entrancing so long as at the end of the story that character is redeemed, changed, reformed, resolved, or has grown.

Not so. The problem with redemption is that it happens only at the end. It ignores the hundreds of pages of wearisome middle in which the flawed protagonist may refuse to see the light. If you have ever found yourself thinking in the middle of a novel, "Oh, come *on!* Grow up! Get a life!" then you know what I mean. Dark protagonists are wearisome.

How can one forestall that reaction and keep readers engaged by a flawed character? In a nutshell, it is this: A character in trouble is engaging if he has sympathetic qualities; for example, he is aware that he is in trouble and tries to change. We can forgive anyone who is trying to be good, even seventy-times-seven like the Bible says. What we cannot tolerate is willful self-destructiveness. There is little sympathy for that behavior.

Earlier I mentioned Judith Guest's *Ordinary People*. Have you read it? It is about the Jarretts, an "ordinary" family shattered by the tragic death of one of two teenage sons in a sailing accident. There are two principle points of view, father and son. The novel opens with the surviving son, Conrad, waking up one school morning and working hard to find the strength and a reason to get out of bed.

Can you imagine a drearier character and a more depressing choice of opening scene? Wait, it gets worse. . . . Guest raises the stakes and simultaneously makes the job of winning sympathy even more difficult by giving Con an even bigger handicap at that moment: He has been home only a month from a psychiatric hospital to which he was sent after a suicide attempt. Every morning he feels overwhelmed by the darkness inside of him. Whoo-boy! Guest has set Con, and herself, quite a task. How tough is it? Pretty tough:

> He rolls onto his stomach, pulling the pillow tight around his head, blocking out the sharp arrows of sun that pierce through the window. Morning is not a good time for him. Too many details crowd his mind. Brush his teeth first? Wash his face? What pants should he wear? What shirt? The small seed of despair cracks open and sends experimental tendrils upward to the fragile skin of calm holding him together. *Are You on the Right Road*?
> Crawford had tried to prepare him for this. "It's all right, Con, to feel anxious. Allow yourself a couple of bad days, now and then, will you?"
> *Sure. How bad? Razor-blade bad*?

Yikes! Are you ready to turn your back on this kid? I do not blame you. However, Guest is too generous to let us, and Con, wallow for too long:

> His father calls to him from the other end of the house. He thrashes to a sitting position, connected at once to sanity and order, calling back: "Yeah! I'm up!" and, miraculously, he *is* up and in the bathroom, taking a leak, washing his hands and face, brushing his teeth. Keep moving, keep busy, everything will fall into place, it always does.

Phew! Just in time! Con strives to break through his darkness, not always successfully but with a good deal of black humor and a healthy dose of self-regard, which surfaces throughout the novel.

In passages like this, Guest lets us know that Con is trying. That makes up for a lot. In fact, I don't know about you, but I found myself pulling hard for Con. I wanted things to come out OK for him.

THE HIGHEST CHARACTER QUALITIES

There are two character qualities that leave a deeper, more lasting and powerful impression of a character than any other: Forgiveness and self-sacrifice.

The Biblical story of the prodigal son is the paradigm of forgiveness. If you recall, not only does the prodigal son leave home and spend all the money his father has given him on worthless pleasures, he stands in contrast to his dutiful brothers who stay home, work hard, and obey their father. Yet when the prodigal son returns, broken and humble, the father loves and celebrates him above the brothers. It seems unfair, at first, but even so the story of the prodigal son's reception is deeply moving. The reason the story moves us is not that the son has repented but that the father has forgiven. Practice forgiveness in your fiction (and in your life!). It is a powerful source of character strength.

As for self-sacrifice, is there a higher form of heroism? It is the ultimate expression of love and as such is about the most powerful action a character can perform. It is as rare in fiction as it is in life. In 1942, Lloyd C. Douglas published an inspirational novel, *The Robe*, that became one of the greatest bestsellers of the twentieth century.

The Robe is the story of a prominent young Roman centurion, Marcellus, who due to a small social gaff is exiled to the remote backwater of Palestine, where he is given command of a rough and undisciplined detachment of soldiers. He wins their respect. Later, though, he winds up overseeing the execution of a local revolutionary, Jesus of Nazareth.

The events around the crucifixion convince Marcellus that Jesus was innocent. Haunted by the injustice of the execution and by the strange power of the robe Jesus wore on the day of his death, Marcellus returns to Rome in a suicidal depression. His father, a powerful senator named Gallio, turns to Marcellus's Greek slave, Demetrius, for help and advice in restoring his son to sanity. Demetrius, a Corinthian captured during war, is warmly portrayed as the equal of Marcellus in all but station. He is a slave, but he is also one of the most memorable characters in epic fiction.

Demetrius explains to Gallio the circumstances that brought on Marcellus's morbid state of mind. They agree that Demetrius should accompany Marcellus to Greece for a rest cure. Their discussion of the arrangements for the coming trip leads to one of the many moments in *The Robe* in which Lloyd C. Douglas powerfully builds his readers' sympathy for a character, using the emotional power of self-sacrifice:

> "Take my son to Athens, Demetrius, and help him recover his mind. But no man should ask a slave to accept such a responsibility." He handed the document to Demetrius. "This is your certificate of manumission. You are a free man."
>
> Demetrius stared at the writing in silence. It was hard for him to realize its full significance. Free! Free as Gallio! He was his own man! Now he could speak—even to Lucia— as a freedman! He was conscious of Gallio's eyes studying him with interest as if attempting to read his thoughts. After a long moment, he slowly shook his head and returned the document to the Senator.
>
> "I appreciate your generosity, sir," he said, in an unsteady voice. "In any other circumstance, I should be overjoyed to accept it. Liberty means a great deal to any man. But I think we would be making a mistake to alter the relationship between my master and his slave."

It is the first of many sacrifices that Demetrius will make for Marcellus. It is a gesture that foreshadows the conversion to Christianity that both men will undergo. Millions of readers have found in Demetrius and Marcellus qualities that make them memorable, sympathetic, and inspiring. Chief among those is the self-sacrificing love of one's fellow man.

DEPTH AND DIFFERENTIATION OF CHARACTER

Just as detailing is the secret of a memorable setting, so depth is the secret of memorable characters. Depth is the degree of detail you bring to your people. Quick brushstrokes are fine in openings, but in the body of the breakout novel, characters can only grow rich if they are examined from many angles. Read just about any breakout novel and you will find its characters are revealed in a number of ways.

One-dimensional characters are flat, simply motivated and always act "in character," that is, predictably. Fully rounded, three-dimensional characters have many sides, complex motives and act in ways that surprise us. Not every type of novel requires depth of characterization; comic novels and pastiches, for instance. Certain plot-driven thrillers also seem to do just fine without fully rounded characters. However, in most novels nothing is lost, and everything is gained, by enriching the inner life of one's cast.

Many time-tested tools are available for character development: backstories, life chronologies, cast diagrams, out-of-story dialogues between author and character, and so on. Find the tools that work for you. Needless to say, the greatest character resource is life itself. Biographies, bar mitzvahs, business meetings . . . we meet "characters" all the time. Developing fictional people is mainly a matter of opening oneself to real people, most of all to ourselves.

By far the most useful technique for character development is a simple principle that Anne Perry, among others, keeps in mind when building characters: "Like them." It is hard to write someone you don't know, harder still if you do not care for them. Eliminate characters whom you do not regard with warmth, to whom you are not drawn. The coldness you feel toward them will show in your writing.

By the way, the same mandate to like your characters may also go for your villain. Don't you find the most interesting villains are the ones whose motives we can understand? The ones who are made evil by circumstances, rather than the ones who simply are born bad? Depth of character in your opposition will make your writing more richly textured.

Character differentiation is the technique of making the characters in your cast different and distinct from one another. Here is where diagrams and charts can help. Contrast is the key. When characters are hard to keep straight, it is often because they are not sufficiently individualized.

One technique frequently employed by novelists is the "tag," a distinct identifier such as an eye patch or a special gesture. I am suspicious of tags. They definitely help me keep characters straight, but they can substitute for real, substantive character development. So can unusual names. While I have become inured to romance hero names like Stone, Cash, and Buck, in other novels gimmick names can be distracting, like an eye tic. True characters do not need tricks.

One of the greatest practitioners of character differentiation is Anne Tyler. Her people are always highly individualized. Who can forget Macon Leary, the travel writer who hates to travel, in Tyler's 1985 triumph *The Accidental Tourist*? When Leary's wife leaves him at the beginning of the novel, his embrace of systems for happy living is not only a comic delight, it is an introduction to an utterly unique character:

> Well, you have to carry on. You have to carry on. He decided to switch his shower from morning to night. This showed adaptability, he felt—some freshness of spirit. While he showered he let the water collect in the tub, and he stalked around in noisy circles, sloshing the day's dirty clothes underfoot . . . At moments—while he was skidding on the mangled clothes in the bathtub or struggling with his body bag on the naked, rust-stained mattress—he realized he might be carrying things too far. He couldn't explain why, either. He'd always had a fondness for method, but not what you would call a mania.

I am sure you have your favorite characters, too. Examine them with an objective eye and you will probably find they are strong, sympathetic, multidimensional, larger-than-life, yet all too human. Their words and actions express the inner conflicts and desires with which we all can identify.

Creating character in the breakout novel is not simple. It involves going deep inside, right to the heart. Breakout characters get to us because they *are* us, only bigger. Build your characters carefully and completely using breakout techniques, and they will spin you a story that we will not soon forget.

Characters in breakout fiction may seem realistic, even average, but they are bigger than their circumstances. They do not just suffer, but strive. They do not practice patience, but act. They do not merely survive, but endure.

Perfecting Your Submission Process: Do You Know Where Your Children Are?

BY I.J. SCHECTER

Sending out stories is like sending your children out into the world. You worry about who's seeing them, how they'll be judged, or whether they'll be noticed at all. You've invested everything you have, and now there's nothing to do but step back and let them fend for themselves. Most of all, you want to keep track of them without being a pest.

The manuscript submission process unfortunately hasn't caught up with the lightning pace of virtually every other industry. Waiting for a response to your story remains a uniquely agonizing process. While you can't control the whims of editors, you *can* increase your chances at publication by following three simple guidelines:

- Keeping a detailed submission log
- Maintaining a constant flow of manuscripts
- Taking advantage of every opportunity

KEEPING A SUBMISSION LOG

With short story manuscripts, the best way to track their progress through the submission maze is to keep a comprehensive log of where they've been and where they're going. Your submission log should look something like the one shown on the next page. Create it on any spreadsheet program with a 'sort' function, so you can sort by date, story title or any other column.

In addition to your overall submission log, start a Top 10 or Priority log. Over time you may develop preferences for certain publications—perhaps those that pay well; maybe those that publish stories you admire; maybe those in which a writer has been published that you'd like to match. (I first started sending stories to *Playboy* because Stephen King had been published in it. They haven't bought anything of mine yet, so I guess he's still winning.) Maintain not only a separate submission log for these magazines or journals—those you've resolved to submit to until they either publish one of your pieces or issue a restraining order—but also subfiles with each publication's detailed contact information. For each publication logged, you should also note the postage rate. Most magazines are not million-dollar enterprises. Making them spend extra change because you attached improper postage is like asking for a rejection slip.

Let's talk a bit more about some of the categories in your submission log, and the basic steps to follow in the process. These will vary slightly from writer to writer, and situation to situation, but I've found the ones shown here work for me.

I.J. SCHECTER *is a Toronto-based freelance writer of fiction and essays. His latest book, a collection of short stories, is titled* The Bottom of the Mug.

Example Submission Log

Name of Piece	Type of Piece	Publication	Date	Submission Method	Expected Response Time	Attention	Result	Date Notified	Notes
The Nature of Phil	Short story	Pinecrest Review	Mar. 3/01	Post	4-6 mos.	Chris Sandler, Ed.	Rejected	Nov. 15/01	
The Nature of Phil	Short story	Willowbrook Journal	Mar. 3/01	Post	6 wks.	Jack Roy, Fict. Ed.	Changes requested	May 12/01	1. Trim by 500 words 2. "Punch up" ending
The Nature of Phil	Short story	Storyteller	Mar. 3/01	Post	3 mos.	Linda Williams, Ed.	Rejected	July 3/01	"Not for us, but please try again."
Fire, Warmth	Short story	Great Lakes Fiction	Mar. 3/01	Post	4-6 mos.	Ken Rolston, Lit. Ed.	Accepted ($25)	June 28/01	
Class of '46	Article	The Toronto Tribune	Mar. 8/01	E-mail	4-6 mos.	Terence Coyles, Ed	Rejected	Aug. 1/01	
The Commute	Personal essay	Ballyhoo Review	Apr. 24/01	Fax	2-3 mos.	Dick Berner, Ed-in-Chief	Magazine closed	June 8/01	
The Commute	Personal essay	Northeastern Review	Apr. 24/01	E-mail	3 mos.	Jeff Kassie, Fict. Ed.	Rejected	Sept. 22/01	
The Commute	Personal essay	Sierra Review	Apr. 24/01	Post	6 wks.	Paul Asper, Exec. Ed.	Rejected	May 21/01	"This one didn't quite work for us, but I like your sense of humour." - Dave Beattie, Fict. Ed.
Fire, Warmth	Short story	Bayview Quarterly	May 15/01	E-mail	6 mos.	Eric Haig, Fict. Ed.	Not accepting mss. until 2003	Dec. 15/01	
Class of '46	Article	Algonquin Monthly	May 16/01	Post	2-6 mos.	Sherry Fawcett, Mng. Ed.	Rejected	Sept. 13/01	

Type of piece

It may seem unnecessary to track this information if you're writing only, say, short stories at the moment. Track it anyway. You never know when a personal essay (or article about writing) might come out—most writers, at some point, decide to branch out and start writing in different styles and forms.

Publication

When addressing any manuscript, cover letter or envelope, get the information right. I know—if you had a nickel for every time you've heard some expert say that a professional-looking submission is your first step toward acceptance, you'd be rich. Those experts are right. Don't let the excitement of getting a manuscript in the mail allow you to miss important details. Get the address and name of the publication correct, to the letter. This goes double for the name of the person to whom you're addressing the manuscript. How much more quickly do you bypass a piece of junk mail that has your name misspelled?

Date sent

Knowing when you've sent a manuscript is vital to your personal sanity and professionalism as an author. I most often view my log by date, since that helps me to quickly observe my submission pattern for a given period and identify zero-submission gaps.

Submission method

Since many publications now accept fax or electronic submissions, tracking this element is more important than ever, especially for determining when to follow up about the status of your manuscript. Read listings carefully to find out which submission methods are preferred.

Expected response time

In general, it's okay to call about the status of a manuscript a month after the expected response time has passed. The hardest part of being a writer, of course, is exercising patience (we've all asked ourselves at least once why a magazine needs *six months* to respond to our 2,500-word story), so take a breath before you make that call. Make sure your tone is polite and professional, not indignant.

It's not unusual to hear, "I don't know what happened to it," or, "We must have sent out a response." If the person truly sounds unsure, send the same manuscript again, noting in the cover letter that you had submitted previously but no record of the manuscript existed when you called. Slush piles are high at any time, and manuscripts do go missing. It's your job to stay on top of the game.

Pay attention to reading periods, especially for magazines published by universities. If a magazine specifies that it only reads manuscripts between October and April, sending them a story in July is going to mark you as a novice or, worse, someone who doesn't consider guidelines important.

Attention

The more specific you can be in your correspondence, the better. It's not good enough just to track which publications you've submitted to. You need to track exactly *whom* you've sent to.

Even if a magazine lists multiple editors, send your manuscript to only one. An important rule of submitting is giving the person at the other end the fewest reasons to reject your work. Addressing your manuscript to two different people gives them both the chance to assume the other is looking at it.

If you aren't certain of the gender of the person you're sending to, either leave the "Mr./Ms." salutation off your letter or call the magazine. I don't want to say I'm put off by letters addressed to Ms. I.J. Schecter, but it doesn't put a big gushy smile on my face.

Result

What is a good success rate? One acceptance out of ten submissions? One out of 20? One out of 100?

The answer is: *It doesn't matter*. Your success rate during a given period depends on the number of submissions a publication is receiving and their needs at the time. Never gauge yourself by your ongoing acceptance rate. If you receive 30 rejections in a row, are you going to stop submitting? Will you retire after three acceptances? No on both counts. So don't worry about it.

It's important to track the specific result of a submission if it is something more than just Accepted or Rejected. This may include items such as "Ceased Publication," "Not Accepting Submissions until January 2003," "Requested Changes," and so on. Was it rejected with an encouraging note? Form letter? Mimeographed letterhead? When you receive a rejection slip, the last thing you want to do is record the details of your rejection, but get them down anyway. It will benefit you when you decide to submit again.

Date notified

Tracking this element tells you over time which magazines always conform to their published guidelines and which routinely take longer to respond than they claim. With these magazines you have two choices: Stop submitting to them, or continue submitting with the understanding that they will always respond later than expected.

MAINTAINING A CONSTANT FLOW OF MANUSCRIPTS

In our ongoing delusions regarding what motivates editors, we convince ourselves, among other things, that there is a "right" time of year to submit. There is no right time. Editors are only looking for one thing at any time: manuscripts that excite them.

The most sensible system, and the one that will keep you the least anxious, is one that involves sending out manuscripts rhythmically. In other words, gaps between sending are never too long, nor are too many ever sent out at once.

First, it makes good practical sense to keep up a regular stream of submissions. Second, it makes good psychological sense to feel that your stuff is always out there, being read by someone, someone who might just be writing you an acceptance note. Once you've begun to submit, you'll find that you feel somehow empty when the 'Result' column on your submission log is filled—nothing going out, nothing coming in. Every writer agrees that it's better to receive a rejection letter than nothing. It's part of what makes us so lovably odd.

A good rule of thumb is always to have ten manuscripts out, whether ten different pieces at different magazines or the same piece at ten different magazines. Whenever you see fewer than ten blank spaces in the 'Result' column, it's time to send out another.

I try to stick to a rule called, "Manuscript in, manuscript out." Whenever I receive a rejection letter, I send a manuscript back out within two days (though not necessarily the same one. In fact, once a given manuscript has been rejected ten times, I won't resubmit it until I've given it a serious reevaluation). This accomplishes two things. First, it doesn't allow me the time to brood over rejections. Second, it forces me to maintain a rhythmic submission flow.

TAKING ADVANTAGE OF EVERY OPPORTUNITY

Whenever you have the chance to make an important contact, build a relationship with an editor, or have a conversation with someone important in the industry, take advantage.

For example, when a rejection slip from an editor is accompanied by a personal note, get another story or article right back to that editor. The difference between a rejection letter on its own and one with a personal note is significant only if you follow up on it. That means resubmitting while your name is fresh. An editor is unlikely to remember who you are six months after sending you an encouraging note, but if he receives something from you two weeks later, your name will have a positive and familiar ring. Beyond that, he'll be impressed by (a) your professionalism (you have another piece appropriate for the market, ready to send), (b) your persistence (you spent no time dwelling on the rejection), and (c) your desire to be published in his magazine (editors have egos just like the rest of us—usually bigger).

Notice in my submission log that I've recorded a note from Dave Beattie, fiction editor at the fictional *Sierra Review*. Though Dave wasn't the person I submitted to, my manuscript found its way to him and he wrote back with a personal note telling me he liked my sense of humor, although he couldn't make room for this particular personal essay. That's my cue to send something else to *Sierra Review* right away, addressed specifically to Dave Beattie. The cover letter will say something like, "Thanks for your kind words in response to my short story called 'The Commute.' I've attached a different piece, a short story called 'The Nature of Phil,' that I hope will better suit your needs."

When corresponding with editors or others who may influence your success, be aware of your tone. It can take time to strike the balance between confidence and arrogance, credibility and overstatement. Before you send a letter, ask someone you trust to read it over. If they tell you it sounds concise and self-assured, send it. If the vibe they get is ingratiating, timid or pompous, back to the drawing board.

Part of your job as a writer is to make it as easy as possible for others to want to print your work. By keeping track of where you send your work, maintaining a constant stream of submissions and capitalizing on every opportunity, you'll never be more than one step away from publication.

Before sending out any manuscript, review this checklist (even if you've already memorized it a hundred times):
- Courier font, 12-point or larger
- Double-spacing
- One-and-a-quarter-inch margins on all sides
- Name, address and phone number in upper left hand corner
- Approximate word count and rights offered in upper right hand corner
- Running header starting on second page in upper right corner, in following format: *Fire, Warmth/Schecter/page #2/(555)797-8888/ijschecter@hotmail.com*

Before submitting, read the magazine's listing at least three times so that you'll:
- Know what rights the magazine buys. Most want first serial or first North American serial rights, but watch for exceptions. If *Novel & Short Story Writer's Market* or another market publication tells you a literary magazine buys first serial rights and you offer reprint rights, not only is an editor likely to reject your work, he will also probably remember your lack of research next time you submit. If you're unsure which rights a magazine buys, call them.
- Know their policy on unsolicited work. If a publisher says they don't accept unsolicited manuscripts, believe it. Don't waste your time, effort and postage submitting something that will likely never be opened. More than one editor has told me that he or she discards any unsolicited material that comes in without looking at it.
- Know their current circulation and years in business. You never want to be caught writing "I'm a long-time fan of your publication . . ." when the magazine is only a year old.

A Note about Cover Letters

Less is more in a cover letter. Always.

Cover letters offer a special challenge because there is so much they need to convey and so little space in which to do it. They must be persuasive but not fawning, succinct but not empty, and professional but not stiff.

They should also be simple and straight-forward—printed on normal white bond paper, standard formatting. Fancy paper or script will annoy editors and bias them against your manuscript. The same goes for tongue-in-cheek humor or exaggerated credentials.

Always mention where you discovered the publication. If you want to add a note about why you wrote the story, make it brief—that means no more than two sentences (my rule is one sentence, and even then only if I think it's truly necessary). Even when an editor writes, "I want to know something about the author and what inspired them to write the story," it doesn't mean, "I want to know every detail of the author's life and a blow-by-blow account of the moment of inspiration." Editors are deluged every day, and brevity is appreciated. Don't be the parent who has to sing his kids' praises. You will likely be surprised at how well the story, like your children, can speak for itself.

The Big Challenges of Publishing in Little Magazines

BY WILL ALLISON

Here's a quiz to help you decide if you're ready to send your short stories to literary magazines. Are you tired of making money from your writing? Do you enjoy waiting months for an editor's reply? Do you thrive on exceedingly long odds? Do you prefer to publish in magazines that most people haven't heard of?

I'm only half-joking when I say that you should be able to answer "yes" to each of these questions if you want to see your short stories in literary magazines. Consider the cold, hard facts: The majority of literary magazines pay in contributor's copies or subscriptions rather than cash, and those that do pay cash sometimes offer as little as five dollars per story. It's not unusual to wait six months for a reply on a submission. At many magazines, more than 99 percent of all manuscripts are rejected. And if you do manage to get published in a top quarterly—say *Epoch* or *The Southern Review*—don't expect your family or coworkers to be impressed. Expect them to say, "That's nice. Could you pass the salt?"

Of course, none of this discourages thousands of short story writers from submitting their work to literary magazines each year. Many of these writers know that so-called "little magazines" perform an important, if unsung, role in the world of letters. In addition to providing a home for cutting-edge fiction that mainstream magazines won't publish, literary magazines are a proving ground for new writers. Your mother or boss may not read them, but agents and book editors do, and many of today's serious writers—the authors who've won Pulitzer Prizes and National Book Awards—got their start in modest quarterlies.

But the real, practical reason that writers submit short stories to literary magazines is because they have few options. These days, only a handful of major magazines (most notably *The New Yorker*, *The Atlantic*, *Harper's*, *GQ*, *Esquire*, and *Playboy*) still publish literary fiction regularly. The sad truth is that there is little demand for short stories—especially literary short stories—outside the realm of little magazines.

They're *magazines*, not markets

When it comes to literary magazines, forget everything you've learned about "the business of fiction writing." Instead, think "labor of love"—a term that applies both to the writers, who are lucky to make a dime from their stories, and to the editors, who are lucky to make a dime from their magazines. If you flip through the listings of literary magazines in this book (page 162), you'll notice that many are affiliated with (and primarily funded by) universities. Many more are funded by grants, private contributions, or by the editors themselves. Few if any literary magazines turn a profit, and, frankly, few are trying to (if they were, they wouldn't be publishing short stories and poetry).

Writers should therefore approach literary magazines with an appreciation for the ways in

WILL ALLISON *is editor at large for* Zoetrope: All-Story, *former executive editor of* Story, *and former editor of* Novel & Short Story Writer's Market. *He is the recipient of an Ohio Arts Council grant for fiction, has published short stories in* American Short Fiction, Florida Review, *and* Kansas Quarterly/Arkansas Review, *and owns an impressive collection of rejection slips.*

which they differ from more commercially oriented publications. For starters, writers ought to refrain from referring to literary magazines as "markets," especially in their cover letters. ("Dear editor: Based on my research, your publication is an appropriate *market* for my fiction.") I do not know a single editor who thinks of his literary magazine as a "market."

The editor is your ally . . .

After you receive your first or tenth or one-hundredth rejection slip from an editor, you may begin to hate that person a little. You may begin to think that he or she doesn't like you, that he enjoys turning down your work, that he doesn't even bother to read your stories. You wonder why it takes him months just to say "no."

Despite the frustrations of the submission process, a levelheaded writer will always bear in mind that editors are allies, not opponents. No editor has ever gotten rich or famous by editing a literary magazine. They choose their jobs for the same reason that you write stories—because they care deeply about fiction. In fact, many editors are writers themselves and know full well how it feels to accumulate a shoebox full of rejection slips.

Rest assured, when an editor reads your story, he wants to fall in love with it. He wants to publish it. He wants readers to clamor for more of your work. He wants the story to win a Pushcart Prize and an O. Henry Award and be chosen for *The Best American Short Stories* and *New Stories from the South*. And if you're unpublished, he *really* wants to love your story, because few things are more satisfying to the editor of a literary magazine than discovering talented new writers.

. . . But the odds are against you

Chances are, however, that your story will be rejected. Editors simply don't have the space, resources, or desire to publish the vast majority of stories they read. For instance, *Zoetrope: All-Story* receives about 6,000 manuscripts each year and publishes only 28 to 30 of those—an acceptance rate of about .5 percent, or 1 in 200. (Compare that to undergraduate admissions at Yale, where the acceptance rate is about 15 percent.)

Depending upon the size of the magazine and the way its staff is organized, your story will likely be screened by one or more editors or readers before reaching—or failing to reach—the editor who actually chooses which stories to publish. Up and down the line, these readers are rooting for your story, but by necessity, they're also "reading to reject," looking for any reason to discard your manuscript and move on to the next.

Most submissions land in a magazine's "slush pile," its stack of unsolicited manuscripts. Such stories are said to have come "over the transom." The majority of submissions are read and rejected at this level. Generally, the way a new (unpublished) writer gets past the slush pile is by writing a great story that catches the eye of an editor who then passes it up the ladder or sets it aside for a closer read. Some lucky stories bypass the slush pile altogether and go directly to higher-ups. These might include solicited stories, stories sent by agents, stories by well-known or well-published writers, and stories by writers with whom the editor has previously corresponded.

How your story is (or isn't) read

How can editors read so many submissions and still have time to publish their magazines, much less eat and sleep? The answer is, most editors don't read most submissions all the way through. This is true for every editor I know (though, to be fair, I once heard of an editor at a small journal who claimed to read every word of every manuscript she received.) Depending upon the story, an editor may read as little as a single line or paragraph, but—based on my experience and on conversations with other editors—I would guess two or three pages, minimum, is the norm.

Cruel as it may seem, such a strategy makes perfect sense. Given the volume of stories they receive, most editors don't begin to have time to read every manuscript from start to finish, and even if they did, it wouldn't be time well spent. An editor need read a story only up to the point at which he loses interest, the point at which he knows he doesn't want to publish it. There is no reason for him to read any further unless perhaps he sees promise in the story and wants to write the author an encouraging note.

But what if the editor stops reading just before the story gets good? What if the story has a great ending, one that the editor would have loved? It doesn't matter. Literary magazines publish stories, not pieces of stories. An editor must love the whole thing, from the first word to the last.

A good editor is in tune with his tastes and has a finely honed sense of when to keep reading and when to stop; a lesser editor stops too soon or reads more than is necessary. A lesser editor is more likely to reject a story that he would have liked had he read it more carefully. Alas, you have no control over an editor's judgment. All you can do is send your work to magazines whose editors' judgment and taste you trust based on the stories they publish.

Not all submissions are created equal

Editors of most literary magazines will tell you quite sincerely that they're looking for the best stories they can find, period, and therefore give equal consideration to all submissions, regardless of outside influences such as an author's publishing credits. Some magazines even employ a blind reading policy in which the editors aren't allowed to see authors' names or cover letters. (For instance, submissions that reach *Zoetrope: All-Story*'s editorial board—the magazine's final round of consideration—are handled in this fashion.)

In practice, however, it's fair to say that outside influences often affect the attention a story receives from an editor. Let's say your cover letter indicates that you've previously published fiction in *The Paris Review*, won *The Missouri Review* Editor's Prize, or attended the Iowa Writer's Workshop. Maybe you're submitting your story on the recommendation of a well-known author or friend of the editor. Maybe you've received favorable feedback from the editor on previous submissions.

None of these factors is going to cause the editor to publish your story. He may, however, be more patient with it. He may give your story an extra two or three pages to catch his interest before setting it aside. No doubt about it, previously unpublished writers are thus at a disadvantage, especially if their work ends up in the hands of an editor who hasn't learned to trust his own taste, who needs outside validation—such as that provided by publishing credits—to make his decisions. Nevertheless, it's safe to say that most editors strive not to be biased, because they know that an open mind increases their chances of recognizing quality work. You don't discover the next Tim Gautreaux or Annie Proulx simply by following the pack.

How to get a fair reading

Every editor owes every submission a fair reading—no more, no less. A fair reading is one that is open-minded and patient (even if it ends with the editor patiently deciding after only one paragraph that the story is unsuitable for his magazine). The good news is, most editors will happily give your story a fair shake, regardless of your credentials. All you have to do is avoid giving them a reason not to.

Start by familiarizing yourself with the conventions of the submissions process. See The Quick-Start Guide to Publishing Your Fiction (page 2); The Business of Fiction Writing, especially the section entitled "Approaching Magazine Markets" (page 70); and the introduction to literary magazine listings (page 162).

Multiple vs. simultaneous submissions

The terms "multiple submission" and "simultaneous submission" are often used interchangeably, but they're two different things. If you send a single story to more than one magazine at a time, you're making a simultaneous submission. If you send more than one story at a time to a single magazine, you're making a multiple submission.

In their writer's guidelines, most magazines clearly state their policy on simultaneous submissions but often don't indicate their position on multiple submissions. Even if a magazine doesn't explicitly prohibit multiple submissions, I recommend that you avoid sending more than one story at a time to a magazine (unless, of course, the editor asks to see several of your stories at once).

"At many magazines, more than 99 percent of all manuscripts are rejected. And if you do manage to get published in a top quarterly—say Epoch *or* The Southern Review*—don't expect your family or coworkers to be impressed. Expect them to say, 'That's nice. Could you pass the salt?' "*

The temptation is understandable. Let's say you've got three stories that you want to send to a particular magazine. Why not send them all at once and save a little money and a lot of time? Three reasons. One, it's selfish. To send three stories at once is like saying to the editor that you deserve three times as much attention and time as those writers who've sent only one story.

Two, you run the risk of shooting yourself in the foot. If the editor dislikes your first story, he may—regardless of his good intentions—be less patient and less open-minded with the next two.

Three, a multiple submission suggests to an editor that you aren't able to gauge the quality of your own work. An editor wants to believe that you're sending him your best story. To send three or five or ten stories is like telling the editor that you haven't learned to separate your wheat from your chaff.

Also, it's wise to wait until you've heard back from an editor before sending him another story. Some writers, dedicated as they are, will mail a new story off to the same magazine every week without waiting for a reply on the last one. Such behavior suggests an emphasis on quantity over quality, and it discourages the editor from initiating correspondence: Why should he bother with a handwritten suggestion if the writer isn't going to read it before sending his next story?

The value of kind words

Writing is a solitary pursuit, but so is editing, especially if you have only a few hundred readers—which is usually the case among literary magazines. A readership of more than one or two thousand is big news. *The Georgia Review* and *Ploughshares* are literary-magazine giants with a circulation of 6,000 each. By comparison, *The New Yorker* boasts a circulation of 750,000.

Like everybody else, editors appreciate feedback. I've heard more than one editor wonder aloud if anybody even reads his magazine. In your cover letter, consider taking time to let the editor know which stories, authors, and issues you've most enjoyed. If you're a subscriber, why not mention that, too? And if you can't find anything nice to say about the magazine, you shouldn't be sending your manuscript there in the first place.

Complimenting the magazine isn't going to make the editor like your story, but it might make him like you, or at least help him to remember your name next time around. Most importantly, it will show him that you've actually read the magazine, which will distinguish you from the vast majority of writers in the slush pile.

On handling rejection

No matter how many years you spend honing your writing, no matter how many stories you send to a magazine, it's possible—in some cases, even likely—that the editor will *never* accept one of your stories. Never! If you're unable to deal with this, you probably shouldn't be sending out your work.

As you begin to build a collection of rejection slips, remember that when your story is turned down, it doesn't mean the editor doesn't want to publish you or your work; it means only that he doesn't want to publish *that particular story*. Don't take rejection personally.

Also, a rejection slip doesn't necessarily mean that your story is unpublishable. Every day, editors reject stories that are snapped up by other editors further along the line. (Often they pass up such stories knowingly. An editor is not obligated to publish every story he finds "acceptable," only those he falls in loves with.) Publishing a short story, then, is a matter of finding the right editor at the right magazine at the right time. In other words, luck is involved.

When you boil it down, all stories are rejected for essentially the same reason: The editor has read (or expects to read) other stories that he likes better than yours. Beyond the words you've put on the page, you have no influence over the editor's decision, so don't waste time stewing. Keep writing and try your luck at the next magazine.

Thank you, sir, may I have another?

Rejection slips are never much fun, but some are better than others. In the process of sending out your stories, you may occasionally receive "good" rejection slips, ones on which the editor has taken the time to write a brief note telling you that he enjoyed the story, inviting you to try again, or offering some suggestion for improvement. Such notes are rare and good things. They mean you're getting closer. You've at least got an editor's attention, if not a "yes."

If you receive a "good" rejection, dash off a quick thank-you note to the editor. This is not brown-nosing, just common courtesy, and the editor will be more likely to remember your name next time around.

Know when to move on

Though editors are by and large fair-minded, hard-working people, inevitably there are some bad eggs—editors who are lazy about getting back to writers, who lose manuscripts, who write rude rejection letters, who don't give every story a fair shake, who publish lousy stories. These editors are not worth your tears and curses. When you come across one, the best thing to do is simply move on. That's one of the beauties of literary magazines. Though editors have different tastes, philosophies, and missions, most are looking for essentially the same thing—the best short stories they can find. As a writer—and a reader—you have plenty of choices.

Northern Exposure: A Writer's Guide to Canadian Publishing

BY I.J. SCHECTER

What do publishing heavy-hitters Michael Ondaatje, Margaret Atwood, Alice Munro, and Carol Shields have in common? They hail from Canada, usually better known for ice hockey, moose, and the Maple Leaf flag (and, of course, really good beer). But literary writing in Canada has a long and rich history (did you know Ernest Hemingway was a reporter for the *Toronto Star*?) and is flourishing today as Canadian writers emerge onto the international stage. Like elsewhere, recent corporate mergers have transformed Canada's publishing industry, but its lifeblood continues to be the small- to medium-sized publishers that turn out high-quality literary fiction year after year.

So what are Canadian publishers and editors looking for in fiction these days? How is the Canadian market different from its U.S. and U.K. counterparts? What sorts of opportunities might fiction writers find? Here, four key industry players gather to share their advice for navigating publishing in the Great White North: **David Kent**, president, HarperCollins Canada (a position he came to eight days prior to this interview, after ten years with Random House); **Iris Tupholme**, editor-in-chief, HarperCollins; **Valerie Hussey**, president, Kids Can Press, a midsize publisher of children's books whose well-known characters include Franklin the Turtle and Elliot Moose; and **Jack David**, publisher, ECW Books, whose eclectic list includes everything from literary fiction to a biography of actress Sarah Jessica Parker.

Is there a secret for breaking into the Canadian market that doesn't apply elsewhere?

Jack David: In general, the same principles apply everywhere. For example, we received a submission from someone in Tulsa. We had listed sports as one of our categories and the author was working on a book about a boxer. We published the book. If you do good research, you're much more likely to get a hit.

Valerie Hussy: The industry here is really just a microcosm of that in the U.S. or the U.K. What makes a book successful here—quality and originality—will make it successful anywhere. A good manuscript will find a home eventually.

David Kent: When someone asks me if a writer—from anywhere—can publish, my answer is simple: If they're good, yes, if they're bad, no. The main difference is that a Canadian writer can now publish at home instead of having to make a beeline for New York. It's no longer just Jack McClelland doing Canadian books.

Do you see a fundamental difference between Canadian and foreign literature? Is there even such a thing as "Canadian" literature, or is it as indefinable as Canadians themselves?

JD: I would say there are regions where you could recognize a Canadian writer. You can read

---

I.J. SCHECTER *is a freelance writer of fiction and essays. His latest book, a collection of short stories, is titled* The Bottom of the Mug. *His nonfiction appears frequently in* Novel & Short Story Writer's Market.

David Adams Richards and say, "That's the Maritime mentality," or Guy Vanderhaeghe and say, "That's the Prairies," or small-town Ontario—"Alice Munro." But I think you could apply the same to the U.S. You'd see recognizably different styles in a Southern writer, an upbeat New York writer, and a writer from Montana. There's closer alignment north-south than east-west. Guy Vanderhaeghe aligns more with North Dakota than downtown Toronto.

VH: I think it's fair to say there is a Canadian sensibility, but it's as individual as the writers themselves. Clearly there are writers who seem to best capture what one might call a national psyche, but no one would say that those individuals are the voice of all Canadians, because the country itself is so varied.

DK: Part of the question is in defining what is a Canadian book. Is a story about the Manhattan homicide squad written by a Canadian a Canadian book? Is a book about a boy growing up in Northern Manitoba corresponding with his mother who works in a movie theater in Toronto, a book filled with Cree Indian poetry and Canadian settings, but written by an American author, Canadian?

JD: I think from the outside people just see quality fiction. People like John Irving have said the bestseller list in Canada is more literary than in the U.S., not Danielle Steele/John Grisham stuff. That perception emerged with Margaret Atwood and Robertson Davies and has grown ever since. Of course, Canadian material is still a difficult sell in the U.S. As the saying goes, stick "Canada" in the title and you're doomed. In the 1930s, Morley Callaghan had to remove all specific references to Toronto from his book before Scribner's would publish it.

Where do you see the Canadian publishing industry right now?

JD: It's a very good time to be writing and finding publishers. That applies to virtually all genres.

VH: I think one must consider the two faces of the Canadian publishing industry—the independent, Canadian-owned companies, and the multinational corporations with editorial offices in Canada. The multinationals have access to resources that the independent publishers don't have. The independents represent an alternative voice, variety, and originality amidst all the sameness. The Canadian industry is not one with deep financial resources, which makes it quite vulnerable and fragile at times. But it's a real success story, one I don't think is going to vanish. The creative talent is here.

DK: The talent was always here, but people have now realized that the talent has to be invested in. A number of things were catalytic in the growth of the industry: Carol Shields' *The Stone Diaries* winning a Pulitzer Prize, the adaptation of Michael Ondaatje's novel *The English Patient* being named Best Picture. As more attention was paid, more people became aware; as more people became aware, more books were bought. And so on. The last ten years have been remarkable.

VH: I don't think we're looking at just a ten-year history of success. It's really been 30 years, maybe more, of a slowly, methodically developing industry that has moved from a very internal industry to an external one. A writer has to look at a Canadian publisher as a publisher for the world.

DK: Looking inward versus outward does have a lot to do with it. There was a time when suddenly South American writers were popular—Julio Cortazar, Gabriel Garcia Marquez, others. It happened with Australian writers, it happened with Indian writers. . . .

JD: I think it begins with centennial year, 1967, when the Canada Council started funding writers. Look at Carol Shields, who published five books before she broke through, or Ondaatje, and how many places he published before hitting it big. Most successful Canadian writers began writing in the '60s, began to flourish in the '70s, and that was pushed along by the Canada Council and the small presses. Take Alice Munro and Mavis Gallant, who both were writing and developing prior to this period. They couldn't develop here because no one was interested. Everyone was leaving—Mavis went to Paris, Mordecai Richler left. When Mordecai came back, that was a sign that you could make a living writing in this country.

DK: I would argue that. I think larger houses have been involved since the beginning. Carol Shields never sold more than 1,500 copies before coming to a larger house because the smaller ones didn't have the resources to develop her. When she came to Random House, they had the economy of scale to really promote her and that's when she began to take off.

VH: The problem is that the big, non-publishing corporations come in and take over thinking bestsellers can be manufactured. They discover you don't create bestsellers the way you do a new brand of soap.

Iris Tupholme: These days, there are new kinds of writers being published, like Andrew Pyper, who are achieving bestsellerdom in Canada but also being purchased internationally. The question now is how far can a Canadian writer go and how big can they be?

Do you look for a range of genres/styles, or just manuscripts that you can't put down?

VH: We're looking for something that catches our eye. If it's good, we'll consider it. We don't want books whose primary purpose is didactic or bibliotherapeutic. Although the Franklin books, as an example, may be viewed as having messages, that is not their first intent. They are first and foremost stories about the life of this little turtle, who is very much Everychild.

JD: We look for two types of books, market-driven and editorial-driven. The first type tend to be subject-oriented—either based on a person who has some kind of celebrity status or on a subject, say a well-known TV show—and have obvious commercial possibilities. The second type are manuscripts that come in and make the hair on the back of our necks stand up.

DK: Which is why there is more than one publisher, and more than one editor per house. All you hope is that, when you read something and get excited, three thousand or three hundred thousand people will feel the same way.

What proportion of your titles are Canadian-authored?

IT: The majority of writers in our Canadian publishing program are Canadian in some way, like Margaret Visser, who was born in South Africa, educated in England, lived here, and now lives in Barcelona and the south of France. We do have some American writers and some British writers.

JD: We do between 40 and 50 books a year, about 80 percent of which are by Canadian writers. The other 20 percent are almost entirely U.S.-authored. I aggressively pursue writers from anywhere. We're always looking to expand our reach.

VH: We publish about 50 books per year, 98 percent of which are Canadian-authored. We're now getting more and more submissions from the U.S. and are beginning to formulate a U.S.-authored program.

What is your policy regarding unsolicited material?

JD: We encourage it. The reason is that we are always finding, if not great publishable material, authors out there we can talk to and work with to develop other projects. Last year, both of our two prize-winning books, *Too Close to the Falls* by Catherine Gildiner and *Code Blue: Crisis in Canada's Health Care System* by David Gratzer, were unsolicited.

VH: We have quite an open policy, but we'd like authors to be familiar with our list before submitting. We prefer strongly structured stories, not just a small concept, which may sound obvious but actually is not.

IT: Most editors don't know where the next big thing is coming from, and for that reason they never want to be the person who didn't return the call or open the envelope. If somebody gets through to me, I'll call back.

How many make it from the unsolicited pile to print?

VH: Less than one percent. We see 3,000 to 4,000 manuscripts per year, and may publish two or three from the unsolicited pile. But we're always looking for the next Franklin or Elliot Moose, both of which came in unsolicited.

JD: Out of the 1,500-2,000 unsolicited submissions we get per year, we probably publish five to eight. Just this morning I was looking at two things that came in—the diary of a high school teacher and a child reminiscence of growing up in Jamaica. You never know. A friend of mine wrote a book called *The Godforsaken Sea*, about a man killed during a round-the-world sailing race. He put together a solid two-page proposal and sent it to 25 publishers. The book was picked up by Knopf Canada and is currently on the bestseller lists. This was one unknown guy with a good idea. The point is that publishers need books. Publishers need good books, and they need them all the time.

DK: And that's why there are 2,000 publishers in Canada.

Does a writer need an agent?

IT: A writer doesn't need an agent, but does need a way in. Either they've called and had a conversation with somebody, or the manuscript has been referred by someone, or, at the very least, they send in the manuscript in the context of other things that are being published. I probably get 10 to 15 manuscripts every week just from agents—whole manuscripts, already vetted. It's a more competitive market.

VH: Which means there has to be some sophistication. The tattered manuscript with handwritten corrections isn't going to cut it.

Why is there such a strict policy against simultaneous submissions?

VH: There shouldn't be. If four different houses stipulate no simultaneous submissions, and their turnaround is three months, you can maybe get four responses in the course of a year. I say screw it. Who's going to know?

DK: The thing about simultaneous submissions is partly for self-protection. The idea of somebody writing a first novel and wanting to send it to Knopf and Random House is a bit like someone finishing their first piano lesson and wanting to go audition for the New York Philharmonic. But by the same token, there are more places to publish that first novel than I can ever remember.

VH: Agreed. We have a high percentage of first-timers on every list, though quality first novels are often harder to spot, because many first novels don't start until page 50. But if the quality of the writing is good, patience can pay off.

IT: True. It can be worth sitting through the beginning of a movie to reach an amazing scene midway through that you might have missed.

What are the most important things developing writers should be aware of?
DK: Learn your chops. Write for the magazines, try a variety of publications. This expectation of overnight stardom is out of whack.

IT: There are lots of overnight success stories—but most after 20 years of unacknowledged hard work.

JD: Do some market research. Are there enough people out there with aquariums to merit doing a book about them? Are these people likely to be book buyers? What other books are out there at the same time?

VH: One—be familiar with a publisher's program. I can't stand when someone sends me something completely out of line with what we publish. Two—the importance of story. If it isn't interesting enough to be read again and again, we won't consider it.

DK: Look around and see who publishes the books you love. Then narrow it down—is there a particular editor who has done your kind of book? Think of sending not so much to houses as to editors. The house is just a building, but what really makes a book is an advocate, a champion for it. Five out of six editors might say we shouldn't do a certain book, but if that one person is adamant about doing it, we will. It isn't majority rule, it's passion.

So a writer is encouraged to mention in a cover letter that he or she has researched other books published by a certain editor at your house?
VH: Absolutely.

DK: I would love that.

JD: I see one line in a cover letter that mentions one of our books, and I'm sold.

IT: Bribes, by the way, do not work. Don't send something that's specially wrapped, or contains items of food. . . .

You've received some . . .creative submissions?
DK: Larry Ashmead, a distinguished editor at HarperCollins, tells the story of getting back to his hotel room in London or Frankfurt and finding a manuscript under his bed sheets. Someone had bribed the chambermaid to get in. He refers to it as the "nocturnal submission."

Is there a misconception that Canadian publishers only look for stories about rural northern communities and harsh prairie winters?
JD: People do still tend to envision Mounties and polar bears and Niagara Falls, but remember, we're an 80 percent urban community.

IT: There is definitely a misconception. Canadians are not only looking to read stories about hockey and winter. There's a whole generation that has grown up in the city. They may drive to the cottage on weekends, but these are people looking for many different stories, not only about Canada but also about other countries and cultures.

What does the irresistible manuscript look like?

JD: I got a proposal last January from a woman in Hamilton I'd never heard of. The idea was compelling, the letter was clear and energetic, and she sent about 20 pages of the first chapter. We did the book. A compelling, well-presented idea from an unknown author, a good letter, a solid proposal, coming in the doldrums of January.

VH: I don't think any one ideal exists, and that's the wonderful thing about creativity—it surprises you.

DK: I agree. There's that indefinable quality. My father, a champion tennis player, could look at a twelve-year-old and say, "This kid's going to be terrific." A basketball coach could have looked at a freshman Michael Jordan and seen that same quality. It's the same with writing.

How much of a manuscript do you have to read before knowing whether it's immediately discardable or breakout material?

DK: For me, it's something you can sense within the first few pages. Does it speak to you or not? Art is so subjective. I mean, somebody told Selznick not to make *Gone With the Wind.*

IT: When you read the number of manuscripts we do, you know which ones are haunting enough to draw you back.

VH: Sometimes you know in the first paragraph. Sometimes the cover letter. My assistant has the responsibility of opening all submissions, reading the cover letter and first page, and then distributing them to the appropriate editor if it's worth reading. Probably 75 percent of what comes in immediately goes back out.

JD: How many get read, of course, is largely a case of big versus small. I look at every single thing that comes in. And the reason is that once or twice a year, I get a book like *Too Close to the Falls.*

DK: Nobody's got all the answers. You don't publish bestsellers. You publish good books and hope others agree with you. We're all asking the same thing about any manuscript—what's special about it?

———————

"Think of sending not so much to houses as to editors. The house is just a building, but what really makes a book is an advocate, a champion for it. Five out of six editors might say we shouldn't do a certain book, but if that one person is adamant about doing it, we will. It isn't majority rule, it's passion."

—David Kent, president, HarperCollins Canada

———————

The Business of Fiction Writing

It's true there are no substitutes for talent and hard work. A writer's first concern must always be attention to craft. No matter how well presented, a poorly written story or novel has little chance of being published. On the other hand, a well-written piece may be equally hard to sell in today's competitive publishing market. Talent alone is just not enough.

To be successful, writers need to study the field and pay careful attention to finding the right market. While the hours spent perfecting your writing are usually hours spent alone, you're not alone when it comes to developing your marketing plan. *Novel & Short Story Writer's Market* provides you with detailed listings containing the essential information you'll need to locate and contact the markets most suitable for your work.

Once you've determined where to send your work, you must turn your attention to presentation. We can help here, too. We've included the basics of manuscript preparation, along with a compilation of information on submission procedures and approaching markets. In addition we provide information on setting up and giving readings. We also include tips on promoting your work. No matter where you're from or what level of experience you have, you'll find useful information here on everything from presentation to mailing to selling rights to promoting your work—the "business" of fiction.

APPROACHING MAGAZINE MARKETS

While it is essential for nonfiction markets, a query letter by itself is usually not needed by most magazine fiction editors. If you are approaching a magazine to find out if fiction is accepted, a query is fine, but editors looking for short fiction want to see *how* you write. A cover letter can be useful as a letter of introduction, but it must be accompanied by the actual piece. Include basic information in your cover letter—name, address, a brief list of previous publications—if you have any—and two or three sentences about the piece (why you are sending it to *this* magazine or how your experience influenced your story). Keep it to one page and remember to include a self-addressed, stamped envelope (SASE) for reply. See the Sample Short Story Cover Letter on page 72.

Agents: Agents are not usually needed for short fiction and most do not handle it unless they already have a working relationship with you. For novels, you may want to consider working with an agent, especially if marketing to publishers who do not look at unsolicited submissions. For more on approaching agents and listings of agents willing to work with beginning and established writers, see our Literary Agents section beginning on page 139. For information on over 500 agents, see *Guide to Literary Agents* (Writer's Digest Books).

APPROACHING BOOK PUBLISHERS

Some book publishers do ask for queries first, but most want a query plus sample chapters or an outline or, occasionally, the complete manuscript. Again, make your letter brief. Include the essentials about yourself—name, address, phone number and publishing experience. Include only the personal information related to your story. Show that you have researched the market with a few sentences about why you chose this publisher. See the Sample Book Query Cover Letter on page 73.

THE SAMPLE COVER LETTER

A successful cover letter is no more than one page (20 lb. bond paper), single spaced with a double space between paragraphs, proofread carefully, and neatly typed in a standard typeface (not script or italic). The writer's name, address and phone number appear at the top, and it is addressed, ideally, to a specific editor. (If the editor's name is unavailable, address to "Fiction Editor.")

The body of a successful cover letter contains the name and word count of the story, the reason you are submitting to this particular publication, a short overview of the story, and some brief biographical information, especially when relevant to your story. Mention that you have enclosed a self-addressed, stamped envelope or postcard for reply. Also let the editor know if you are sending a disposable manuscript that doesn't need to be returned. (More and more editors prefer disposable manuscripts that save them time and save you postage.) When sending a computer disk, identify the program you are using. Remember, however, that even editors who appreciate receiving your story on a disk usually also want a printed copy. Finally, don't forget to thank the editor for considering your story.

BOOK PROPOSALS

A book proposal is a package sent to a publisher that includes a cover letter and one or more of the following: sample chapters, outline, synopsis, author bio, publications list. When asked to send sample chapters, send up to three *consecutive* chapters. An **outline** covers the highlights of your book chapter by chapter. Be sure to include details on main characters, the plot and subplots. Outlines can run up to 30 pages, depending on the length of your novel. The object is to tell what happens in a concise, but clear, manner. A **synopsis** is a very brief description of what happens in the story. Keep it to two or three pages. The terms synopsis and outline are sometimes used interchangeably, so be sure to find out exactly what each publisher wants.

MANUSCRIPT MECHANICS

A professionally presented manuscript will not guarantee publication. But a sloppy, hard-to-read manuscript will not be read—publishers simply do not have the time. Here's a list of suggested submission techniques for polished manuscript presentation:

- **Use white, 8½ × 11 bond paper,** preferably 16 or 20 lb. weight. The paper should be heavy enough so it will not show pages underneath it and strong enough to take handling by several people.
- **Type your manuscript** on a computer using a laser or ink jet printer, or on a typewriter using a new ribbon.
- **Proofread carefully.** An occasional white-out is okay, but don't send a marked-up manuscript with many typos. Keep a dictionary, thesaurus and stylebook handy and use the spellcheck function of your computer.
- **Always double space and leave a 1¼ inch margin** on all sides of the page.
- **For a short story manuscript,** your first page should include your name, address and phone number (single-spaced) in the upper left corner. In the upper right, indicate an approximate word count. Center the name of your story about one-third of the way down, skip two or three lines and center your byline (byline is optional). Skip three lines and begin your story. On subsequent pages, put last name and page number in the upper right hand corner.
- **For book manuscripts,** use a separate cover sheet. Put your name, address and phone number in the upper left corner and word count in the upper right. Some writers list their agent's name and address in the upper right (word count is then placed at the bottom of the page). Center your title and byline about halfway down the page. Start your first chapter on the next page. Center the chapter number and title (if there is one) one-third of the way down the page. Include your last name and page number in the upper right of this page and each page to follow. Start each chapter with a new page.

SAMPLE SHORT STORY COVER LETTER

Jennifer Williamson
8822 Rose Petal Ct.
Norwood OH 45212

January 15, 2002

Rebecca Rossdale
Young Woman Magazine
4234 Market St.
Chicago IL 60606

Dear Ms. Rossdale,

As a teacher and former assistant camp director I have witnessed many a summer romance between teens working at camp. One romance in particular touched me because the young people involved helped each other through a very difficult summer. It inspired me to write the enclosed 8,000-word short story, "Summer Love," a love story about two teens, both from troubled families, who find love and support while working at a camp in upstate New York.

I think the story will fit nicely into your Summer Reading issue. My publishing credits include stories in *Youth Today* and *Sparkle* magazines as well as publications for adults. I am also working on a historical romance.

I look forward to hearing from you.

Sincerely,

Jennifer Williamson
(513)555-5555

Encl.: Manuscript
        SASE

SAMPLE BOOK QUERY COVER LETTER

Bonnie Booth
1453 Nuance Blvd.
Norwood OH 45212

April 12, 2002

Ms. Thelma Collins
Bradford House Publishing
187 72nd St., Fifth Floor
New York NY 10101

Dear Ms. Collins,

I am a published mystery writer whose short stories have appeared in *Modern Mystery* and *Doyle's Mystery Magazine*. I am also a law student and professional hair designer and have brought these interests together in *Only Skin Deep*, my 60,000-word novel set in the glamorous world of beauty care, featuring hair designer to the stars and amateur detective Norma Haines.

In *Only Skin Deep*, Haines is helping put together the state's largest hair design show when she gets a call from a friend at the local police station. The body of famed designer Lynette LaSalle has been found in an Indianapolis motel room. She's been strangled and her legendary blonde mane has been shaved off. Later, when the bodies of two other designers are discovered also with shaven heads, it's clear their shared occupation is more than a coincidence.

Your successful series by Ann Smythe and the bestseller *The Gas Pump Murders*, by Marc Crawford, point to the continued popularity of amateur detectives. *Only Skin Deep* would make a strong addition to your line.

Sincerely,

Bonnie Booth
(513)555-5555

Encl.: three sample chapters
synopsis
SASE

• **Include a word count.** If you work on a computer, chances are your word processing program can give you a word count. If you are using a typewriter, there are a number of ways to count the number of words in your piece. One way is to count the words in five lines and divide that number by five to find an average. Then count the number of lines and multiply to find the total words. For long pieces, you may want to count the words in the first three pages, divide by three and multiply by the number of pages you have.

• **Always keep a copy.** Manuscripts do get lost. To avoid expensive mailing costs, send only what is required. If you are including artwork or photos, but you are not positive they will be used, send photocopies. Artwork is hard to replace.

• **Suggest art where applicable.** Most publishers do not expect you to provide artwork and some insist on selecting their own illustrators, but if you have suggestions, please let them know. Magazine publishers work in a very visual field and are usually open to ideas.

• **Enclose a self-addressed, stamped envelope (SASE)** if you want a reply or if you want your manuscript returned. For most letters, a business-size (#10) envelope will do. Avoid using any envelope too small for an 8½ × 11 sheet of paper. For manuscripts, be sure to include enough postage and an envelope large enough to contain it.

• **Consider sending a disposable manuscript** that saves editors time and saves you money. If you are requesting a sample copy of a magazine or a book publisher's catalog, send an envelope big enough to fit.

• **When sending electronic (disk or modem) submissions,** *contact the publisher first for specific information and follow the directions carefully.* Always include a printed copy with any disk submission. *Fax or e-mail your submissions only with prior approval of the publisher.*

• **Keep accurate records.** This can be done in a number of ways, but be sure to keep track of where your stories are and how long they have been "out." Write down submission dates. If you do not hear about your submission for a long time—about three weeks to one month longer than the reporting time stated in the listing—you may want to contact the publisher. When you do, you will need an accurate record for reference. (See "Perfecting Your Submission Process" on page 54 for tips for an efficient system.)

MAILING TIPS

When mailing short correspondence or short manuscripts:

• Fold manuscripts under five pages into thirds and send in a business-size (#10) envelope.

• Mail manuscripts five pages or more unfolded in a 9 × 12 or 10 × 13 envelope.

• Mark envelopes in all caps, FIRST CLASS MAIL or SPECIAL FOURTH CLASS MANU-SCRIPT RATE.

• For return envelope, fold it in half, address it to yourself and add a stamp or, if going to a foreign country, International Reply Coupons (available at the main branch of your local post office).

• Don't send by certified mail. This is a sign of an amateur and publishers do not appreciate receiving unsolicited manuscripts this way.

• For the most current postage rates, visit the United States Postal Service online at www.usps. gov/.

When mailing book-length manuscripts:

FIRST CLASS MAIL over 11 ounces (@ 65 8½ × 11 20 lb.-weight pages) automatically becomes **PRIORITY MAIL.**

METERED MAIL may be dropped in any post office box, but meter strips on SASEs should not be dated.

The Postal Service provides, free of charge, tape, boxes and envelopes to hold up to two pounds for those using PRIORITY and EXPRESS MAIL.

Requirements for mailing FOURTH CLASS and PARCEL POST have not changed.

Main branches of local banks will cash foreign checks, but keep in mind payment quoted in our listings by publishers in other countries is usually payment in their currency. Also note reporting time is longer in most overseas markets. To save time and money, you may want to include a return postcard (and IRC) with your submission and forgo asking for a manuscript to be returned. If you live in Canada, see Canadian Writers Take Note on page 612.

RIGHTS

Know what rights you are selling. The Copyright Law states that writers are selling one-time rights (in almost all cases) unless they and the publisher have agreed otherwise. A list of various rights follows. Be sure you know exactly what rights you are selling before you agree to the sale.

• **Copyright** is the legal right to exclusive publication, sale or distribution of a literary work. As the writer or creator of a written work, you need simply to include your name, date and the copyright symbol © on your piece in order to copyright it. Be aware, however, that most editors today consider placing the copyright symbol on your work the sign of an amateur and many are even offended by it.

To get specific answers to questions about copyright (but not legal advice), you can call the Copyright Public Information Office at (202)707-5000 weekdays between 8:30 a.m. and 5 p.m. EST. Publications listed in *Novel & Short Story Writer's Market* are copyrighted *unless* otherwise stated. In the case of magazines that are not copyrighted, be sure to keep a copy of your manuscript with your notice printed on it. For more information on copyrighting your work see *The Copyright Handbook: How to Protect and Use Written Works* by Stephen Fishman (Nolo Press, 1992).

Some people are under the mistaken impression that copyright is something they have to send away for, and that their writing is not properly protected until they have "received" their copyright from the government. The fact is, you don't have to register your work with the Copyright Office in order for your work to be copyrighted; any piece of writing is copyrighted the moment it is put to paper. Registration of your work does, however, offer some additional protection (specifically, the possibility of recovering punitive damages in an infringement suit) as well as legal proof of the date of copyright.

Registration is a matter of filling out an application form (for writers, that's generally Form TX) and sending the completed form, a nonreturnable copy of the work in question and a check for $30 to the Library of Congress, Copyright Office, Register of Copyrights, 101 Independence Ave. SE, Washington DC 20540. If the thought of paying $30 each to register every piece you write does not appeal to you, you can cut costs by registering a group of your works with one form, under one title for one $30 fee.

Most magazines are registered with the Copyright Office as single collective entities themselves; that is, the individual works that make up the magazine are *not* copyrighted individually in the names of the authors. You'll need to register your article yourself if you wish to have the additional protection of copyright registration.

For more information, visit the United States Copyright Office, Library of Congress, online at www.loc.gov/copyright/.

• **First Serial Rights**—This means the writer offers a newspaper or magazine the right to publish the article, story or poem for the first time in any periodical. All other rights to the material remain with the writer. The qualifier "North American" is often added to this phrase to specify a geographical limit to the license.

When material is excerpted from a book scheduled to be published and it appears in a magazine or newspaper prior to book publication, this is also called first serial rights.

• **One-time Rights**—A periodical that licenses one-time rights to a work (also known as simultaneous rights) buys the *nonexclusive* right to publish the work once. That is, there is nothing to stop the author from selling the work to other publications at the same time. Simultaneous sales would typically be to periodicals without overlapping audiences.

- **Second Serial (Reprint) Rights**—This gives a newspaper or magazine the opportunity to print an article, poem or story after it has already appeared in another newspaper or magazine. Second serial rights are nonexclusive—that is, they can be licensed to more than one market.
- **All Rights**—This is just what it sounds like. All Rights means a publisher may use the manuscript anywhere and in any form, including movie and book club sales, without further payment to the writer (although such a transfer, or *assignment*, of rights will terminate after 35 years). If you think you'll want to use the material later, you must avoid submitting to such markets or refuse payment and withdraw your material. Ask the editor whether he is willing to buy first rights instead of all rights before you agree to an assignment or sale. Some editors will reassign rights to a writer after a given period, such as one year. It's worth an inquiry in writing.
- **Subsidiary Rights**—These are the rights, other than book publication rights, that should be covered in a book contract. These may include various serial rights; movie, television, audiotape and other electronic rights; translation rights, etc. The book contract should specify who controls these rights (author or publisher) and what percentage of sales from the licensing of these sub rights goes to the author.
- **Dramatic, Television and Motion Picture Rights**—This means the writer is selling his material for use on the stage, in television or in the movies. Often a one-year option to buy such rights is offered (generally for 10% of the total price). The interested party then tries to sell the idea to other people—actors, directors, studios or television networks, etc. Some properties are optioned over and over again, but most fail to become dramatic productions. In such cases, the writer can sell his rights again and again—as long as there is interest in the material. Though dramatic, TV and motion picture rights are more important to the fiction writer than the nonfiction writer, producers today are increasingly interested in nonfiction material; many biographies, topical books and true stories are being dramatized.
- **Electronic Rights**—These rights cover usage in a broad range of electronic media, from online magazines and databases to CD-ROM magazine anthologies and interactive games. The editor should specify in writing if—and which—electronic rights are being requested. The presumption is that unspecified rights are kept by the writer.

Compensation for electronic rights is a major source of conflict between writers and publishers, as many book publishers seek control of them and many magazines routinely include electronic rights in the purchase of print rights, often with no additional payment. Alternative ways of handling this issue include an additional 15% added to the amount to purchase first rights to a royalty system based on the number of times an article is accessed from an electronic database.

PROMOTION TIPS

Everyone agrees writing is hard work whether you are published or not. Yet, once you arrive at the published side of the equation the work changes. Most published authors will tell you the work is still hard but it is different. Now, not only do you continue working on your next project, you must also concern yourself with getting your book into the hands of readers. It becomes time to switch hats from artist to salesperson.

While even bestselling authors whose publishers have committed big bucks to promotion are asked to help in promoting their books, new authors may have to take it upon themselves to plan and initiate some of their own promotion, sometimes dipping into their own pockets. While this does not mean that every author is expected to go on tour, sometimes at their own expense, it does mean authors should be prepared to offer suggestions for promoting their books.

Depending on the time, money and the personal preferences of the author and publisher, a promotional campaign could mean anything from mailing out press releases to setting up book signings to hitting the talk-show circuit. Most writers can contribute to their own promotion by providing contact names—reviewers, home-town newspapers, civic groups, organizations—that might have a special interest in the book or the writer.

Above all, when it comes to promotion, be creative. What is your book about? Try to capitalize

About Our Policies

We occasionally receive letters asking why a certain magazine, publisher or contest is not in the book. Sometimes when we contact a listing, the editor does not want to be listed because they: do not use very much fiction; are overwhelmed with submissions; are having financial difficulty or have been recently sold; use only solicited material; accept work from a select group of writers only; do not have the staff or time for the many unsolicited submissions a listing may bring.

Some of the listings do not appear because we have chosen not to list them. We investigate complaints of unprofessional conduct in editors' dealings with writers and misrepresentation of information provided to us by editors and publishers. If we find these reports to be true, after a thorough investigation, we will delete the listing from future editions. See Important Listing Information on page 137 for more about our listing policies.

If a listing appeared in our book last year but is no longer listed, we list it in the General Index, beginning on page 659, with a code explaining why it is not listed. The key to those codes is given in the introduction to the General Index. Sometimes the listing does not appear because the editor did not respond in time for our press deadline, or it may not appear for any of the reasons previously mentioned above.

There is no charge to the companies that list in this book. Listings appearing in *Novel & Short Story Writer's Market* are compiled from detailed questionnaires, phone interviews and information provided by editors, publishers and awards directors. The publishing industry is volatile and changes of address, editor, policies and needs happen frequently. To keep up with the changes between editors of the book, we suggest you check the monthly Markets columns in *Writer's Digest*. Also check the market information on the *Writer's Market* website at ww.write rsmarket.com, or on the *Writer's Digest* website at www.writersdigest.com.

Club newsletters and small magazines devoted to helping writers also list market information. For those writers with access to online services, several offer writers' bulletin boards, message centers and chat lines with up-to-the-minute changes and happenings in the writing community. Some of these resources are listed in our Websites of Interest (page 610). Many magazine and book publishers offer updated information for writers on their websites. Check individual listtings for those website addresses.

We rely on our readers, as well, for new markets and information about market conditions. Write us if you have any new information or if you have suggestions on how to improve our listings to better suit your writing needs.

on it. For example, if you've written a mystery whose protagonist is a wine connoisseur, you might give a reading at a local wine-tasting or try to set something up at one of the national wine events. For more suggestions on promoting your work see *The Writer's Guide to Promotion & Publicity*, by Elane Feldman (Writer's Digest Books).

Specialized Markets

Online Literary Magazines: A Publishing Renaissance

BY VALERIE HEINOLD MacEWAN

The online literary magazine or "e-zine" is the newest branch in the evolutionary tree of human storytelling. From drawings on cave walls to pixels on a computer screen, humans have created stories to pass on to future generations. The oral tradition transposes itself onto the Internet. It creates unlimited opportunities for publishing the stories of varied cultures and socio-economic groups. Another way to look at it: we've gone from the campfire to the computer.

The instant gratification of the Internet, the ease of creating an online presence, and the low-cost of maintaining a website significantly contribute to the current groundswell of literary fiction e-zines available today. Digital information technology makes it easy to copy and modify information; a website is simply more flexible than a printing press.

Wired Style (HardWired), published in 1996, defines "zine" as a "small, cheap, self-published work; an underground, anarchistic version of a magazine." The e-zine in 1996 had not yet reached any recognizable status, as *Wired* referred to the term "e-zine" as " . . .shorthand for an electronic fanzine . . . not yet recognizable enough to style it without a hyphen." With the speed of an Internet year, e-zine morphed into ezine and the definition became, according to the American Heritage Dictionary, "a magazine that is published electronically, especially on the Internet."

What does this mean for the writer?

An ezine (or e-zine, as it appears still in this publication and others) presents unlimited readership potential and myriad venues offering publication for any style of writing. Writers have the opportunity to learn not only the craft of writing but how to infuse technical knowledge into the piece, thus creating a stronger impression upon the reader. In short, it means that, if you're a writer, there's probably a place for your work in an e-zine. It's a matter of finding the right fit, locating the site with the same philosophy, genre or style found in your writing. In 1993, there were 130 websites, in January 2001—over 120 million. Somebody, somewhere, might just like what you've written and publish it online. Keep looking if you haven't turned them up yet.

Each e-zine defines itself on its own terms, and those terms affect the ability of a search engine to ferret out the website. I tried to get a definitive count of the number of e-zines online today, but came up with varying results. The search for "fiction magazine" resulted in 16,500 listings, but "fiction e-zine" brought up only 635 sites. The keyword "fiction" yielded 7,630,000

VALERIE HEINOLD MacEWAN *grew up under the Garrison Avenue bridge in Fort Smith, Arkansas, where she eeked out a meager living sorting mail for the King of the Gypsies. In 1972, after 10 years of scrimping and saving, she had enough money to buy a portable JC Penney's typewriter. She wrote her way through the next 20 years, returning to graduate work in US history, taking 17 years to complete her BA. She quit college when her thesis topic, "A Conceptual Analysis of the Relevance of Concrete Chickens in the Southern Yard," was rejected by her committee. MacEwan is the editor and architect of the online literary magazine* The Dead Mule School of Southern Literature *[www.deadmule.com]. Her works have been published all over the darn place.*

sites. From there I went to "e-zines," and found 207,000 listings (and when I dropped the "s," the number spiked to 582,000). And to further complicate a search, the metatags on a website as well as the publication's title and opening text determine the search results. If the words "e-zine" or "fiction" or "literary journal" aren't included in the title of the publication or the metatags, chances are the site will be far down the list of sites in your search results. So the answer to the question of how many fiction e-zines are published today is: it's tough to say.

The rise in popularity and the amazing proliferation of literary fiction e-zines creates a bit of a conundrum for the writer. On the positive side: e-zine credits are now acceptable in writers' biographies and are included in the writer's list of publications. This can also create problems. In the early days of literary e-zines, publication online was considered a stepping-stone to "print publication." Writers often submitted their work as original, unpublished pieces when contacting print magazines or journals, despite the piece having been published online. With the rise in e-zine legitimacy, many editors consider online publication as constituting prior publication.

The criteria for acceptance in online publications mirrors that of the print world. The same submission rules apply. You have to read the publication, follow the submission guidelines, check out the masthead, note the editorial style of its publisher. As an editor, I don't have a "slush pile," I have a delete key. When it comes to emailing submissions, use your common sense. You wouldn't send a personal essay about fly-fishing with your grandfather to a science fiction e-zine. Unless, of course, your grandfather was really Commander Zoltar from the planet Lipitron.

Another consideration when submitting to literary e-zines: Very few sites are paying sites. In traditional print literary journals, payment is usually in free copies. Online journals can't offer this. They don't charge for subscriptions. Writers have to be content with seeing their work online and with their name being associated with a particular publication. One thing to remember is that posting an e-zine on the Internet is not free. Computers, modems, Internet connections, web authoring tools and software all cost money. Remember that when you contact an editor. They may not be paying you, but they are footing the cost of posting your work online.

How are literary e-zines categorized?

Michael Neff, editor/publisher of *Web Del Sol* [www.WebDelSol.com], breaks literary e-zines down to three basic categories:
- those begun by hobbyists
- those begun by serious writers and editors
- those begun to complement a national print publication

Alsop Review writer Jeffery Bahr [www.alsopreview.com] considers all literary sites, including fiction e-zines, and comes up with six main categories:
- Mainstream Magazines: websites established to increase exposure and boost readership
- Literary Workshops: sites offering online interaction
- Literary Journals: like the Mainstream Magazines, these sites are designed to increase readership and often serve as archival resources for the journal. There are two subcategories—Commercial Literary Journals and University Literary Publications
- Full-Service Sites: combine literary reviews, structured workshops, conferencing and chat rooms
- Literary Portals: combine the features of all literary sites. The best description of this category is by example—www.WebDelSol.com
- Literary e-zines: accept submissions online and have a periodic publication schedule

What constitutes the legitimacy of a literary fiction e-zine?

As a website architect, I have a different set of standards than I do as an online editor. I consider whether or not the e-zine has its own URL (uniform resource locator) or if it's a free site on Yahoo or AOL. Why? Because, to me, this differentiates a hobbyist from serious editor/

publisher. Registering a URL or domain name, paying server fees for website hosting, the use of an html editor or professional web building software—to me, these signal commitment to an online presence beyond weekend updates. The difference between the technical savvy required to create and truly design a website versus the click-and-post design of a free homepage can signal legitimacy to an e-zine geek like me.

I also look for the frequency of publication. Since the Internet is instant, I want more than issues published biannually. I expect monthly updates at the very least. If the last issue was published in 1998, chances are you don't need to send them a submission. This also shows the commitment of the staff to the publication, even if it's only a staff of one.

One needs to consider who is published in the e-zine. To me, quality is not gauged by the name-brand recognizable writers the site publishes, it is the variety of names in each issue. (Although, I must admit if southern fiction icon Clyde Edgerton wrote a short story for my e-zine, *The Dead Mule School of Southern Literature* [www.deadmule.com], it would be the ulti-mate boost in legitimacy.) When I review an e-zine, I ask myself, is every issue full of writing by the same writers? If so, I consider it a personal website—which is not to be taken as disparag-ing. A personal website is a great way to post a resume, showcase your writing and create an online brochure of your talents and credits. And many successful literary fiction e-zines sprang from one writer posting his work online, emailing writer-friends to solicit more content, and becoming larger than they'd dreamed.

Beauty is in the eye of the downloader. My criteria for legitimacy may not be the consensus. Undoubtedly, many members of the online literary scene enjoy creating template homepages with animated gifs of dancing porpoises, self-loading, browser-crashing music and background images of brick walls with superimposed pale-colored fonts. I'm an html snob, and I don't offer any apologies for it. In a literary journal I want text, quick loading and easy to read. This, to me, is where a literary e-zine differentiates itself from the other categories listed by Bahr.

But, as an online content editor, I look for one basic thing. Quality. Well-written prose. Legitimate writing constitutes a legitimate e-zine. As *Web Del Sol*'s Neff says, "There are far more lit pubs online now than just a few years ago and right now there seem to be more start-ups than ever before. As with anything else, only a small percentage are really good or worth noting." In other words, the cream rises to the top, on the Internet as well as in the dairy.

Why would anyone publish an e-zine?

What motivates someone to independently publish a literary e-zine? I emailed a couple fellow editors and asked their opinion. Here's a sample of their answers. It's interesting to note that, out of 24 editors I contacted, no one mentioned profit.

Mike Storm, founder and managing editor of *MindKites, Perceptions on the Fringe* [www.mindkit es.com], an online magazine published quarterly, says: "I started *MindKites* after a couple attempts to get an actual paper rag put together. I had learned html during slow times at work and saw the Internet as an available and flexible means by which I could at least get a good start. Whether in paper or on the net, the overall idea of *MindKites* was to provide one more medium out there for new writers and artists to be seen, while also promoting our values in free thought and free speech." (Editor's note: At press time, MindKites had discontinued publication.)

Jennifer Burgess created the now defunct *Sweaty Lip Fetish* (SLF) e-zine. She now writes for a new zine, an online music magazine [www.peopletalktooloud.com] which she says is much easier because the burden of the design and coding is on someone else who doesn't view it as a burden, and she can focus on what she liked best about *SLF*, writing. Burgess believes the e-zines that are interactive create a community that revolves around it. Harking back to the old days of the "zine," she says, "It's much harder to do with a Xerox machine and a heavy duty stapler.

"So, I started *SLF* in the summer of 1998," she says. "I had always wanted to make a print zine of some sort, but even the small costs involved in that seemed prohibitive to me. Plus, I didn't have the slightest idea how to do it. Also, I lacked motivation. However, I did have a computer and some free web space, so *SLF* was born. I suppose in a lot of ways the whole reason for staring the site was to get exposure for my own writing. *SLF* was successful in that regard in that my editorials garnered their own following, complete with a couple of psychotic web stalkers. I now run a personal site where I write whenever I want and whatever I want without worrying too much about whether anybody will like it."

John Nettles, book review editor for *PopMatters* [www.popmatters.com] created a literary e-zine, *StaggerPress* and hosted it on Homestead. "I put *Stagger* online because I had the opportunity to do so for free and get the instant gratification I couldn't get from print," Nettles says. The first, print issue of *Stagger* sold six copies—the online version is seen literally around the world, as evidenced by the truly international roster of writers who have appeared on the site. As for why I started it in the first place, the short answer is that I was surrounded by writers whose work really jazzed me, enough that I wanted to create a showcase for them. That's the only criterion for the writing that appears at *Stagger*: I like it. If I read it and say "I wish I'd written that," it's in."

So it appears e-zines are here to stay. Because the Internet is an egalitarian venue with a democratic audience, writers have unlimited opportunities for acceptance and publication. Enjoy.

"The criteria for acceptance in online publications mirrors that of the print world. The same submission rules apply. You have to read the publication, follow the submission guidelines, check out the masthead, note the editorial style of its publisher. As an editor, I don't have a slush pile, I have a delete key."

Electronic Book Publishing: Is It For You?

BY DEBBIE RIDPATH OHI

E-books are just like any other books except for one difference: Rather than being distributed in hardcover or paperback, e-books come in electronic bindings, in a variety of digital formats. Authors are finding new markets for their works because of this development.

Pioneers in this quickly growing market have a variety of methods from which they can choose to realize the publication of their books in digital format—almost a Chinese menu of options—from which authors can choose whichever methods best fit their needs.

Roughly, there are five types of publication available to authors: house, self, subsidy, cooperative, and broker. Though not publishers in the traditional sense of the word, brokers are included in this list so that authors can discern between the differences in services they offer and those of the more traditional publishers.

TYPES OF E-PUBLISHING

House publisher

A house publisher is based most closely on the model of a traditional, royalty-paying publishing company. An author submits a query or a partial submission to the publisher. If the publisher is intrigued by the submission, a complete manuscript is requested. (Some electronic publishers in this category simply request that the full manuscript be sent, most often as a file attached to an e-mail, as the initial submission.)

If the publisher accepts the manuscript and the contract is successfully agreed upon, the house publisher provides most, if not all, of the services normally associated with a traditional, royalty-paying publisher. The manuscript is carefully edited; cover art and back cover information are collected; ARCs (advance review copies or advance reading copies) are sent to reviewers, and initial promotion and marketing is begun. Following publication, the author and the publisher work together to promote the book.

The benefit for the author using this form of publication is that there is little risk involved. The publisher pays for the costs of production and distribution, while the author receives (on average) between 25 percent and 50 percent royalties.

The disadvantage is that, as in the traditional world, final editing and creative control are left with the publisher rather than the author.

Self-publishing

Again, this type is based on the model of self-publishing in traditional print publishing. The exception lies in the process in which the author prepares the book for publication. Rather than visiting a printing press to arrange for print runs, the self-published author either prepares the

DEBBIE RIDPATH OHI *was founder and editor of the award-winning writer's website* Inkspot. *This article was excerpted from* Writer's Online Marketplace, *How and Where to Get Published Online © 2001 by Debbie Ridpath Ohi. Used with permission of Writer's Digest Books, a division of F&W Publications, Inc. For credit card orders phone toll free 1-800-289-0963.*

book himself and converts it into digital format or arranges with an independent contractor to perform the conversions. The other facets of the publication—the cover art, editing, sending of ARCs, and promotion—are also left to the self-published author, as well as the creation of a website (usually with the added convenience of a credit card server) for sales.

The benefits of this form of publication are that the author has complete control of the final presentation of the book and that the author also receives all the proceeds from the sale. The disadvantage of this form of publishing is that the author must promote and market the book without the benefit of the awareness already afforded to established e-publishers. The author is also responsible for the cost of publication, which varies with the level of his computer skills.

Subsidy

Again, subsidy publishing is similar to the traditional model, but does not necessarily carry the associated negative implications. Authors who contract with a subsidy e-publisher choose from a menu of services, each with a separate fee or contained within a "package" deal. The subsidy e-publisher prepares and converts the book as well as provides exposure for it on the publisher's website.

The advantages of subsidy e-publishing are that the author who might not be computer savvy can obtain the services needed more easily and not have to worry about obtaining a credit card server or a website from which to sell his book. The disadvantage is that this form puts the author at financial risk if the book is not successful in sales.

Cooperative publishing

Cooperative publishing is a hybrid form of publishing, rather unique to e-publishing. In this model, the publisher bases its operation on the traditional house model, with the associated book preparation and royalty payment. The cooperative publisher offers the basic editing, cover art, and website preparation, offers the book in its standard formats, and promotes and markets the book. However, if the author wishes to have the book presented in formats not normally offered by the publisher, the publisher will either convert the books, for a fee, or refer the author to a third-party contractor for the conversion. The publisher will then also offer that format for sale from its website. The same is true if the author desires to provide the cover art.

The advantage of cooperative publishing is much the same as for house publishing. However, the disadvantage is that the authors, if they choose, place some money at risk if they decide to obtain conversions or original cover art.

Broker

A broker publisher simply offers the author the opportunity of displaying his book at the broker's website and takes care of the selling and distribution of the book.

The advantage of this sort of publishing lies in the fact that the author need not create a website from which to sell, or worry about selling and distribution. The disadvantage is that the broker normally offers no services such as editing and cover art or promotion. If the broker does offer those types of services, it's usually at a cost in either a fee or in royalty points. Otherwise, this is left to the author, which again puts his capital at risk. This type of publisher normally charges between 25 percent and 75 percent for brokerage of an author's book.

As in any publishing endeavor, it's very important for an author to thoroughly research and investigate every aspect of a publisher before signing a contract.

ELECTRONIC FORMATS

There are a variety of electronic formats in which books are published, including HTML, PDF, PRC, RB, IMP, TXT, RTF, DOC, and WPD. More than just a collection of abbreviations, each of those is a format used in binding e-books. They are called file extensions, and determine the means by which someone reads an e-book.

HTML—hypertext markup language

HTML is the type of electronic file that is read by Internet browsers. There are variations of HTML, but basic HTML is most often used for e-books. The advantage of this type of format is that it allows readers to read the book either online or offline on their computers. Owners of some designated reading devices, such as the Rocket eBook, are also able to import HTML files to read on those devices. Multimedia effects, such as linking to websites, music and video files, and linking internally within a book, are also possible with the HTML format. HTML can also be read by those who have a handheld PDA (personal data assistant) that operates on the Windows CE platform. The disadvantage is that HTML is not usually encrypted and the files offer little security against recopying.

PDF—portable document format

PDF files are very popular in binding e-books. Essentially, when one creates a PDF file, using a special program from Adobe, it "prints" to a file an exact replica of the original document, but adds certain conveniences such as internal linking; linking to audio, video, and graphics files; and linking to external websites. Most information disseminated by the state and federal government agencies as well as manuals and schematics offered by manufacturing companies rely on the PDF format. The advantage is that it is an exact duplication with enhancements. The only disadvantage is that the files tend to be large and can only be viewed on a free reader, also available from Adobe.

PRC

PRC is the file format that can be imported to reading programs for personal, handheld devices operating the Palm™ Pilot platform.

RB and IMP

RB is the file type for Rocket eBook devices and IMP is the file type for SoftBook. Use of these types of files is limited to the devices and requires either a special program (Book Mill for the SoftBook) or specific coding (HTML or OEB, Open E-Book) for the Rocket eBook.

TXT and RTF

TXT and RTF are basic word program file types. There is little formatting that can be accomplished with the basic files. TXT documents or books can also be uploaded to the Rocket eBook device. The advantages of these types of formats are that they are normally universal and can be read on most computers in any word program. Normally, these formats are not used for publishing e-books because there is little or no encryption for security.

DOC and WPD

DOC is the file extension for works created in the Microsoft Word program while WPD is the file extension for works created in the WordPerfect program. Normally, these formats are not used for publishing e-books because there is little or no encryption for security.

Normally, the publisher (or the distributor) delivers these files on diskette or CD or as a download over the Internet.

Often, the question is asked about just how books in electronic bindings will be received in the future. E-books will probably never totally replace traditional bound books. However, writers will see a certain blurring in the distinction between traditional publishers and e-publishers. Inevitably, and it's already occurring with several, traditional publishers will begin to offer books in electronic formats. Likewise, many e-publishers are also beginning to offer books in traditional bindings—both paper and hardcover. Eventually, a publisher will simply be a publisher without any distinction as to the type of bindings in which it presents its books. Of course, the ultimate winner in all of this is the reader, who will have choices in content and delivery as he has never before enjoyed.

HOW TO RESEARCH THE MARKET

You're exploring electronic publishing, but how do you recognize a reputable commercial e-publisher? Thoroughly evaluate and compare e-publishers' sites, guidelines, contracts, and sales before you submit your manuscript.

WEBSITE

Visit the e-publisher's website and look at it from a reader and writer's point of view.

First impressions

• The e-publisher website is a storefront. Is it easy to navigate and organized? Is it neat and professional looking? Does the publisher accept credit cards, and are the transactions secured?
• Look for an "About" page with information about the business itself and the people running it. A good company information page will tell you how old the company is, include real names of the people who work there and ways to contact them, and the business address and phone number. Also look for affiliations and memberships in trade groups such as the Association of Electronic Publishers (AEP) or other publishers' groups.

Authors published

Authors can reveal the size of the company and the caliber of writers who belong. Check that there are more than two authors, indicating the publisher is publishing work other than its own. If there are e-mail addresses for the authors, you could ask about their experiences with that publisher.

Books on the website

• Take a look at the titles offered. Neat web page layout, eye-catching cover art, and reasonable prices are signs the website is designed with the customer in mind.
• Are ISBN numbers assigned to each book? "The acquisition of a publisher prefix (needed to receive ISBN numbers) shows the publisher is serious enough to put their money where their mouth is," says Bonnee Pierson, editor at Dreams Unlimited (www.dreams-unlimited.com). ISBNs also aid booksellers when ordering. Books are not required to have an ISBN, but it greatly increases the sales and marketing options for books.
• Check if the publisher offers out-of-print books. If the majority of books are out of print rather than original new releases, it could affect the level of editing per manuscript.

Final product

• Make sure the e-publisher delivers a professional-looking final product. Buy books and read them; it's the only way to verify the quality of the publisher's editing, book design and layout. Try the free e-book download, if available, but also order a book or two to check the quality of new releases.
• If you have a mystery to submit, buy one or two. Are they similar to your book(s) in quality? Are they well edited? Is the book design easy to read, are page breaks and margins consistent?
• Look at the buying process as a consumer would—was it easy to find the genre, select books, and complete the transaction? How fast was delivery? Is there good customer service?

DOES THE MANUSCRIPT FIT?

Now it's time to determine if your manuscript fits the e-publisher's catalog. Notice the genre breakdowns on the site. Does one fit your manuscript? If your book crosses genre lines, be sure to check for all possible genres. Remember that e-publishers favor nontraditional books, even though the genre listings might look traditional.

• Click to the Submission Guidelines. Here you should find more detailed information about the types of manuscripts that the e-publisher is interested in acquiring. If the guidelines are too general, it could indicate the e-publisher has not defined a target reader market.

• Some guidelines mention "minimal editing." This could mean little more than a spelling and grammar check run on a word processor program. Good editing is essential, and it's important to have a clear understanding of how much editing the e-publisher does on a manuscript. If the guidelines are not specific, ask. Buying one or two of the books is the best way to evaluate the level of editing.

• Check to see if there's a Submission Tracking System available to authors. Many e-publishers have a system that can be accessed by the authors through the publisher's website, telling the manuscript's status.

CONTRACTS AND SALES

You've determined the e-publisher matches your manuscript. Look deeper, at the finer points of contracts and sales. A sample contract is usually on site. If not, ask for a copy. It could be the e-publisher doesn't use a contract, in which case think carefully before proceeding. E-mails are binding, but most advise using a contract; AEP requires its members use contracts. With or without a contract, keep a paper trail at all times.

Royalty rates

• What is the royalty rate? Expect from 25 to 50 percent royalties.

• All royalty packages are not created equal. Because of the deep discounts required by some distributors or booksellers, royalties paid on books sold through them may be less than on books sold directly through the publisher. Is a percentage of royalties given up for using certain distributors or booksellers? For example, if e-books are offered through Amazon.com, do you get less royalty on sales through Amazon.com?

E-rights

E-publishers that publish only electronic editions ask for electronic rights, leaving you free to market the rest of the subsidiary rights such as print and audio.

• Does the e-publisher ask for electronic rights only, electronic and print rights, or all rights?

• If the publisher asks for print rights, is it going to produce print copies?

Contract period

• Is a specific contract period stated? Are there start and end dates?

• Is there an "out" clause if either the author or publisher is not satisfied with the relationship?

Out-of-pocket expenses

The author should not be expected to pay for normal publishing expenses such as editing, cover art, or production expenses. Most e-publishers require the author to pay for registering the copyright. Other items to check include the following:

• If multiple file formats of the e-book are offered, who pays for the file formatting? The e-publisher will pay for the file formats it regularly publishes, but may offer to publish additional formats if the author pays the formatting cost. This is acceptable as long as the publisher pays for formats it regularly offers.

• How many author copies are provided? Are additional copies discounted?

• How many review copies are sent by the e-publisher, and in what format? Some e-publishers send print review copies, increasing the number of reviewers available to review their books.

• Are promotional copies discounted?

• Does the author pay for promotion? What e-publisher promotion is included in the contract? The author shouldn't pay for standard promotion, such as sending the book out for review.
• What advertising is included in the contract? Only advertising and promotion listed in the contract are guaranteed for your book.
• Are there additional costs?

Sales

• Besides your e-publisher's website, where can readers find your e-book? Will it be at barnes andnoble.com, Amazon.com, other online booksellers, or physical bookstores? Don't forget to check if your royalty rates are less on these sales.
• Good e-publishers actively promote their sites, titles, and authors with contests, newsletters, or other interaction to encourage repeat visitors. They also should keep their websites high on the search engines. Use a couple search engines and see where your e-publisher turns up on the list.
• Check whether the e-publisher offer formats compatible with handheld devices, such as the Palm™ Pilot, or formats compatible with dedicated handheld e-book reader devices, such as RocketBook or SoftBook.

NETWORKING

• Ask other writers if they've heard of the e-publisher or have had any experience with it. Ask the published authors about their experiences with promotion and sales support from the publisher. Listservs, either writers' or e-publishing, are good places to ask about e-publishers.
• The E-Pub list was formed November 1, 1998, and is an open forum for discussing the e-publishing industry and the business side of writing. Open to writers (published and unpublished), editors, publishers, and any industry professional interested in electronic publishing. To subscribe, go to www.onelist.com/subscribe/e-pub.
• Subscribe to eBookConnections.com's ePub Market Update for publisher tips and e-publishing industry news for writers (www.onelist.com/subscribe/ebcmktupdate).
• The E-Authors list was formed in the fall of 1999, and is an information source for those interested in e-publishing, and a support group for e-published authors. To subscribe, go to www.onelist.com/subscribe/e-authors.

How to Evaluate Your E-Book Options

BY RICHARD CURTIS AND WILLIAM T. QUICK

Many established print publishers are now beginning very slowly to move into the world of e-publishing, among them atRandom, Random House's e-publishing venture. But there are many more publishers who exist entirely on the Web, and use the Internet as their sole marketing, distribution, and sales tool.

If any of these Web publishers were to develop the same level of customer trust that the print houses have built up over the years, you can see where they might offer a much more powerful outlet for your work than simply putting up your own page on the Web and hoping for the best.

But do they?

The jury is still out. Let's take a look at the usual publication process used by these Web publishing operations, and how it compares, and contrasts, with the print publishers, with an eye to discovering whether they do offer brands as powerful as the longer-established traditional publishers.

First, keep in mind that the print houses buy much less than one percent of all unsolicited manuscripts they receive—estimates run as low as one-tenth of one percent. Obviously, from a writer's perspective, this can be either a good or bad practice. If you're one of the lucky and talented one-tenth of one percent, it probably looks good. But if you fall into the remaining ninety-nine point nine, you will probably view this system with frustration.

Nevertheless, this extreme selectivity on the part of print publishers is the first, and perhaps most major, step in establishing a quality filter. Now, we won't try to convince you that the one-tenth of one percent is selected *solely* on pure literary merit. After all, publishers—and this definitely includes e-publishers—are looking for books of which they can sell a sufficient number to make a profit. Given that public tastes can sometimes incline in the direction of books that could in no way be considered literary masterpieces, we'd be foolish to tell you that profit potential does not on occasion outweigh pure literary merit.

That said, print publishers reject the vast majority of books on issues of basic quality. Manuscripts littered with misspellings, bad grammar and punctuation, or an obvious lack of writing skill or professional-level know-how, are quickly discarded.

Here is how one editor, writing for the website *The Writer's Home* (www.writershome.com/instruction/presenting.htm#spin) in an article titled "A Spin in the Editor's Chair" described the slush-pile process:

RICHARD CURTIS *formed e-reads, a publisher dedicated to reissuing, in e-book and print formats, previously published books in such popular categories as romance, fantasy, science fiction and thrillers. Curtis is also president of Richard Curtis Associates, Inc., a leading New York literary agency which currently represents close to 150 authors in such categories of fiction as romance, westerns, thrillers, science fiction and fantasy.*

WILLIAM T. QUICK *is a futurist, a science fiction author of more than 30 books, a screenwriter and the owner of Iceberg SOHO Systems, a small business network consulting firm.*

This article originally appeared in How to Get Your E-Book Published © *2002 by Richard Curtis and William T. Quick. It appears here with permission of Writer's Digest Books, a division of F&W Publications.*

"First, without even opening them, I can discard the letters that come in small envelopes: too much unfolding, if they are not written on notepaper. If they are, I'm not interested anyway, because undersize sheets get lost in my standard $8\frac{1}{2}\times 11$ files. Next, I can discard all those addressed to an editor who died over a year ago and those addressed to me but misspelling my name.

"Ah, here are three that had postage due, one more in a bright red envelope, two that smell of perfume, and one that says, 'You're gonna love this' on the outside. They can go. Mmmm, four written in pencil, one with an ink smudge, and two from the same guy, both addressed to an editor for another magazine. As the day wears on, others are discarded because they are typed with a pale ribbon, written in longhand or typed in script. Several go right to the shredder because they are not accompanied by SASEs."

Pretty tough. But this winnowing of the slush pile does guarantee that a great deal of bad writing, or at least non-professional writing, never makes it onto the bookshelves or into a dissatisfied reader's hands.

Books accepted for publication by print publishers go through a well-defined process of editing and copyediting designed to improve the work as much as possible (the definition of "improve" is determined in general by the judgments of the publisher and its editors), and eliminate those glitches that slip by even the best of writers. In the end, individual readers may disagree as to the quality of the final product, but in fact most books published by print houses do sell at least a few thousand copies. Somebody out there likes them.

E-publishers vs. print publishers

How well do the online Web publishers function at the same game? Well, if the truth be told, performance can be spotty. Some places we visited offered works indistinguishable in quality from those found in print bookstores, and, in fact, were e-publishing authors who had impressive strings of credits in print publishing.

Others, however, had published works that we can most charitably describe only as marginal. How can you, as a writer interested in making use of branded e-publishing houses, tell the difference?

The best way is simply to go look. Most of these e-publishers allow you to read samples from each book they publish. Put on your reader hat and do so. As you read, ask yourself if what you are reading reaches a level of quality you would pay money for if you found it in a print bookstore. If it does, all e-publishers have instructions on their websites as to the proper method of submitting your manuscript for their consideration.

If the work you read does not meet what you consider to be reasonable standards of quality, then you have to ask yourself if you want *your* work to be associated with the books you've just read.

Remember: just like anybody else, authors too are known by the company they—and their books—keep.

Where to Find Online E-publishers

- eBOOKS-N-BYTES (www.ebooksnbytes.com/epub_list.html).
- eBOOK PALACE (www.ebookpalace.com/cgi-bin/elinks/Ebook_Publishers/).
- WRITERS WRITE (www.writerswrite.com/epublishing/epublishers.htm).
- CROWS NEST BOOKS (www.computercrowsnest.com/greennebula/dir_publishers.htm).
- Association of Electronic Publishers http://members.tripod.com/~BestBooksCom/AEP/aep members.html.

Lawrence Block: Tending the Inner Fire

BY W.E. REINKA

Lawrence Block and his wife, Lynne, collect countries. They've visited about one hundred at last count, some of which most people haven't heard of. Home base to these travel buffs is New York City, which happens also to be home base to most of the characters Block has created in 40 years of writing.

Lawrence Block

Block's fame as a writer of crime fiction extends almost as far as his travels. The French anointed him *Grand Maitre du Roman Noir* and the Japanese presented him with their Maltese Falcon Award. Here in the U.S., his crime fiction kudos include multiple Edgar and Shamus Awards. A few years back, the Mystery Writers of America elected him to the select rank of Grand Master, putting him in the fairly respectable company of Agatha Christie, Graham Greene and John LeCarré.

Block has published somewhere around 50 novels under his own name or acknowledged pseudonyms. For good measure he has edited several anthologies. He has also written a lot about the art of writing fiction, including 14 years worth of monthly columns in *Writer's Digest* and four books on the craft. You would think a longtime *Writer's Digest* columnist who has published four books about craft would offer a long list of fiction writing dos and don'ts. But ask him what makes a good story and he responds, "I have no idea."

He's kidding right? After all, Block has a terrific sense of humor. Pick up one of his "burglar" books—the series which revolves around bookstore owner and burglar Bernie Rhodenbarr—and you're guaranteed a few chuckles in every chapter. In 2000, he had published *Hope to Die* (William Morrow), the latest in his hardboiled series revolving around private eye Matt Scudder. Like its 14 predecessors in the Scudder series, *Hope to Die*'s grittiness is offset by humor. A couple of other books revolve around John Keller (think "Killer"), a professional hit man. Thanks to the wry narrative, even Keller comes across as so darn nice that the reader unabashedly pulls for a character who, let's face it, should be more anti-hero than hero.

But Block doesn't kid around when it comes to writing.

"Let's be clear on one thing—a worldwide shortage of writers is not one of the planet's more threatening problems," he says. "So no one should feel some kind of moral obligation to write, and God knows no one should see it as a sound and logical career choice. Only a very small

W. E. REINKA *is a fulltime freelance writer of fiction and nonfiction. He is former books editor of the* Berkeley Insider *and the* Berkeley Voice. *He has published reviews, personal essays, profiles, business articles and travel pieces in publications nationwide.*

proportion of the people who want to do this will ever be able to make a living at it—and the world of publishing grows smaller and harder to crack every year. If you can get along without doing this, you should. Writing is for people who wouldn't be satisfied doing anything else."

Block characterizes those people who wouldn't be satisfied doing anything else in his book on the writer's craft, *Telling Lies for Fun and Profit* (William Morrow & Co.). He describes them as people fueled by an inner fire that ignites in them the need to write. They're going to write no matter what and they're confident that as they continue to write, they'll improve; perhaps slowly, but improve nevertheless. These same folks believe that if they've had bad luck at publishing, their luck is due to change.

Block has tended his own inner fire, through good times and bad, since back in high school when he decided to be a writer. "I kept writing because I didn't have any choice—it's what I do, it's always been what I do, and I'm not really qualified for anything else."

In an essay entitled "It Takes More than Talent," Block observes: "It seems to me that will is enormously important. There are any number of jobs a person can pretty much fall into, but I don't believe writing is one of them. Every once in a while somebody does become a writer apparently by accident, but such persons rarely remain writers for very long. In order to get into this business and in order to stay in it, you generally have to desire it with a passion bordering on desperation."

That desire helped Block through the time when, after he sold his first novel, he had subsequent novels rejected. Does he recall that period with a woeful "just when I thought I was on my way" tale? No, he says matter-of-factly that "an occasional failure of self-confidence is inevitable for anyone who's paying attention. So what? Do it anyway."

Even though Block does not set himself up as an absolute authority on the writing of fiction ("there is no such thing," he says), his advice on writing and publishing seems almost as lasting as Matt Scudder's fictional exploits. After 15 years, three of his four books on craft remain in print. "If there's an explanation for the ongoing popularity of these books, I think it may lie in the fact that I haven't tried to tell anybody how to do anything. I talk about some of the challenges I've faced at the keyboard and how I've responded, and share some things I've noted in the course of my own reading and writing."

So does he take a firm stand on anything? Only this: that fiction doesn't write itself and one way to learn to write is "by doing it."

That's what he did. After a couple of years at Antioch College, he took a summer job as an associate editor at a literary agency. He dropped out of school to keep the job and though he tried going back to school a year later, he found his focus drifting away from class and toward the fiction he was then starting to sell. He dropped out again. Part of his apprenticeship involved selling softcore sex novels for hire. The pay was low and the deadlines short. But he learned to sit down and write, whether he felt like it or not, and not wait for some mystical muse to whisper narrative in his ear. Except for a brief stint as an editor at Whitman Publishing, he's always been a full-time writer. Now in his early sixties, Block claims not to have missed many meals.

In addition to his "just do it" philosophy, Block offers aspiring writers a second firm suggestion: read and read some more. "It's hard to believe, but there are wannabes who don't like to read, so how do they even know what good is?" Aspiring mystery writers can analyze more than red herrings as they race through the pages to find out whodunnit, he says. "Writing's quite unlike painting or most of the other arts in that the method's self-evident. Look at any piece of writing and you know what the writer did to get the effect—he took those particular words and put them in that particular order. Painters will have interesting conversations with one another about how they did what they did, but such a conversation between writers would be absurd. So, in large measure, you have to be your own instructor."

During his own apprenticeship, Block says, he constantly read and analyzed. Working those nine months at the literary agent's office meant he also read tons of bad prose as he sifted for diamonds in the slush pile. As unpleasant as it may have been at the time, he now says, "There's nothing so instructive as reading bad writing—it teaches you far more than reading good writing."

Sue Grafton: P Is for Persevere

BY JACK HEFFRON

When you write a novel titled *A Is for Alibi* you're making a commitment. At worst, the novel will fail. Next worst: it will succeed. It will be a big hit, and your fans will expect you to write 25 more, all the way to Z. The latter happened to Sue Grafton in 1982, when the first novel in her now-famous mystery series was published, and her private detective Kinsey Milhone won the hearts of many readers.

Twenty years later, Grafton is still working her way through the alphabet. *P Is for Peril* (Putnam), the sixteenth book in the series, is in bookstores and on bestseller lists. And neither the author nor the detective show signs of exhaustion. Instead, reviewers and readers agree that the novels continue to get better. Maintaining that creative edge, however, is a constant challenge for Grafton. One would think a megaselling author doesn't doubt her talent or fear the possibility of writer's block. But one would be wrong.

No writer is immune

"There's always the sense that maybe there aren't any more," she says. "Maybe I'm at the end of the line. I'm out of juice. I've written everything I have to write." Since the series began, she has made a few false starts but has managed to keep the series moving ahead. She has slowed down a bit since 1994, after struggling to complete *K Is for Killer*. During the first four months of that book, K stood for Kidnap, until she scrapped the draft and began again. The yearly deadlines, she admits, were beginning to take their toll. Her days were filled with constant pressure.

"Under those conditions, I don't do well," she says. "I thought, I've got to put a halt to this." Before beginning *L Is for Lawless*, she asked her publisher to extend the deadlines to 18 months. She admits that her request was actually more of a take-it-or-leave-it statement. "I was in a position where I could make that announcement," she says. Given the phenomenal success of the series, the publisher was quick to agree.

"I had a life again," she says. So her fans must wait a little longer for Kinsey's next adventure to arrive, and Grafton maintains a strict regime to be sure they aren't disappointed. "I'm a good Girl Scout," she says. "I meet my deadlines."

Keeping a journal

When she finishes a book, she takes time off, makes regular trips to the grocery store—"a luxury for a writer"—and tries to relax. But after a short while, an idea will strike her, a character will appear. She opens a new journal and begins the next project.

"I do a journal for every book," she explains. "I did it in a rudimentary form in *A Is for Alibi*." The journals are a place for hand-wringing as well as for ideas, a safe place to put those

JACK HEFFRON *is editorial director of* Writer's Digest Books, Story Press, Betterway Books *and* Walking Stick Press. *He is a regular contributor to* Pages *magazine. He also served as associate editor for the literary journal* STORY. *His short fiction has appeared in numerous literary magazines, including* North American Review *and* TriQuarterly, *and has been nominated twice for the Pushcart Prize. His nonfiction has appeared in* Oxford American, Utne Reader *and* ESPN's Total Sports Magazine, *among other publications. He has taught writing at the University of Alabama and the University of Cincinnati. Portions of this article originally appeared in* Pages *magazine.*

feelings of doubt about the current project and a repository for bits of dialogue, character names, and plot possibilities. In her essay "The Use of the Journal in Writing a Private Eye Novel," she writes: "Until I own my worries, I run the risk of self-sabotage or writer's block. The journal serves as a place to off-load anxiety, a verbal repair shop when my internal writing machine breaks down."

The journal also is a way to keep the creative juices flowing, but Grafton admits there is much madness in her method. "These journals are not literary," she says. "They are not readable. They allow me to play. I spitball. I what if. I analyze all the books I've done to be sure what I'm doing this round is not a repeat."

After so many novels in the series, she fears she'll repeat a detail or situation that she has used before. "Some deep lazy part of me would be happy to write the same book over," she said. "The psyche can be very cunning."

Along with her journals, she uses an elaborate chart to outsmart her cunning psyche. On it she writes down the elements of her earlier novels such as the gender of the client and the killer, the killer's motivation, even street and place names. She strives to be consistent with small details from book to book.

"Until I own my worries, I run the risk of self-sabotage or writer's block. The journal serves as a place to off-load anxiety, a verbal repair shop when my internal writing machine breaks down."

Given the number of novels already in the series, consistency can be a problem. Fortunately, Natalie Hevener Kaufman and Carol McGinnis Kay, professors at the University of South Carolina, have compiled all the facts on Kinsey Milhone in a book titled *G Is for Grafton*. When she can't verify a particular detail about her sleuth, Grafton calls the authors and asks them.

Such efforts might seem unnecessary, but Grafton's readers are large in number and fierce in loyalty, and nothing escapes their notice. On her website, they crowd the chatroom to dissect or savor the smallest of details from earlier novels. They speak of Kinsey Milhone as if she were a real person. They fret about Kinsey's poor eating habits, offer her fashion tips, and they hope that someday she'll meet the right man—or at least get a cat. They will notice contradictions and inconsistencies down to the color of Kinsey's shoes. Woe be unto Sue Grafton if a character in one novel returns four novels later a few inches taller. Graftonites will be outraged.

Creating a challenge

Creating a technical challenge is another way to stay fresh, Grafton says. This challenge is not something the reader needs to notice. It's a writerly thing, a strategy involving an element of craft, such as fusing one genre with another or describing settings in a certain way. In *K Is for Killer*, for example, she set most of the scenes at night, even though Kinsey and Grafton are "day people." *N Is for Noose* was written using the stylistic conventions of the western. *M Is for Malice* was her attempt at a ghost story. In *P Is for Peril*, she tried to evoke the film noir atmosphere of 1940s hard-boiled detective movies.

"I love all that art deco, that black-and-white feel," she says. "As much as possible, I stripped the book of color. It was fun to recreate that feel." Through this approach, she also returned to her roots, namely the novels of Raymond Chandler. Beginning a novel with this type of challenge adds another level of interest, for the reader as well as for her, Grafton says. It also makes each book unique as each contains a technical element distinct from the others in the series.

All the way to Z

Despite the doubts and the struggles, Grafton is confident she'll make it through the alphabet. "I think there are 26 stories to be written about murder," she says. "I think I can come up with 26 variations on a theme."

This should make her fans happy, though already they're worried about what happens after Z. "I can tell that after a few more letters I'll have to begin doing some online therapy," says Grafton. "I think it's separation anxiety." Despite her glib tone, it's clear she is sincere when she says, "I love my fans," and she understands their concern about life after Z.

For herself, she is not concerned. She will keep writing. "I'm blessed or cursed with the fact that I'm a writer," she says. "That's what gives my life meaning." More than journals and charts and technical challenges and fans, that's what keeps her going. She's already hard at work on *Q Is for Quarry*. And when she runs out of letters, she believes she may start a new series, but with one important difference: "I'll never do it with linking titles," she says. "I'm too smart for that."

Ridley Pearson: The Heart of Rock-and-Roll is Still Beating

BY KELLY MILNER HALLS

Like most writers, suspense novelist Ridley Pearson (*Middle of Nowhere*, Hyperion) wasn't always a best-selling author. For years, he hungered for salability while working in another field. But here's a twist worthy of popular fiction—Pearson didn't fund his passion with a day job. For 11 years he rocked the City of Angels at night.

Ridley Pearson

"I was a musician in L.A. and I played rock and roll four or five nights a week," Pearson says. "Working musicians don't make much money, so I just barely scraped by. It was hand-to-mouth the whole time. But the blessing was, if I played music at night, I could write all day."

For eight years, Pearson did just that—selling dozens of nonfiction articles, taking an occasional odd job but not yet mastering the fiction he longed to create. "I took it in stride," he says, as his experiences eventually added to the mix. "I was a bartender. I was a dishwasher. I was house cleaner in a hospital, which kept me viscerally connected to the ER." Handy knowledge when suspense is your genre, Pearson points out. "Clean-up guys get real familiar with blood."

When screenwriter Stan Silverman (*Sea Hunt*) and agent Franklin Heller stepped in to mentor Pearson, his luck began to change. "Those two guys taught me how to write," Pearson says. "They could see I was willing to take an edit, that I was taking it seriously, not just writing under some willow tree. I wanted to make a living." Silverman and Heller were willing to show him how.

Selling screenplays wasn't in Pearson's immediate future. "I wrote nine or ten and didn't sell those either," Pearson admits. "But I learned to work with dialogue and tell a story quickly." He also learned how to catch the eye of a literary agent. It was Franklin Heller who suggested Pearson transform one of his screenplays into a paperback original.

"Heller said, 'Are you a longhaired writer, or can you work with editors?' " Pearson recalls. "I said. 'I'm here to learn,' " so the conversion began. Twenty-three publishers turned down that first effort, but under Heller's careful direction Pearson wrote a second. "That one sold," he says. "It was called *Never Look Back*, and it took two-and-a-half years to write."

Released in 1985 and still in print, *Never Look Back* (St. Martin's Press, Inc.) is the story of special agent Andy Clayton and his search for a Russian intelligence spy, the Dragonfly. Each

KELLY MILNER HALLS *is a full-time freelance writer and a frequent contributor to Writer's Digest Books. Her work has been featured in* The Chicago Tribune, Guideposts for Kids, Family Fun, Highlights for Children, U*S* Kids *and* Writer's Digest.

of 16 subsequent titles (including three under pen name Wendell McCall) are also still in print—a measure of success in any writer's book.

What inspires such reader devotion and longevity? "It's a combination of two things," says DeDe Anderson, editor of *MysteryReader.com* (www.mysteryreader.com). "The forensic details in his books are fascinating; but even more importantly, in [his] Lou Boldt [series] Pearson has created a believable protagonist. Lou has money problems and marital problems and work problems with which readers can definitely sympathize."

Research, says Pearson, is the key to dazzling detail. "I do a lot of it on the Internet. I use the search engine Northern Light a lot. And LexisNexis™ is simply the best. If I get a subject bug in my ear, I contact those guys and say give me 70 articles on nesting birds. I pick six of them. What used to take me 18 months takes me 12. When I wrote *Angel Maker*, a book about illegal organ donation, everyone said the topic was just an urban myth. But it wasn't. LexisNexis™ had 40 to 60 articles on it from around the world. I mean, there it was."

Contacts with police and other law enforcement agencies also shape Pearson's fiction. "I think I'm the only guy in America who got a special note on my adoption forms from the FBI," he says of adopting his youngest daughter, Storey. "The person that processed our application knew me from all the research I'd done and took the time to wish us good luck."

"His books are super realistic," agrees Joyce Park, editor of *MysteryGuide.com* (www.mysteryguide.com), "almost like something you'd see on the Discovery Channel, and yet exceptionally imaginative and clever. He gets you to buy into the premise, then hits you with a twist that takes your breath away."

Cable television apparently agrees. "A&E has recently signed with me to bring the Boldt character to life for anywhere from one to seven two-hour films," Pearson said during a recent online chat with cyber-citizens on iUniverse.com. "I am writing the first screenplay now. If we get it off the ground, we're hoping Richard Dreyfuss will star as Boldt."

Considering his recent history with A&E—the cable giant aired an unprecedented documentary on Alcoholics Anonymous scripted by Pearson in June 2000— the Lou Boldt project might well make it into production.

"That experience was fantastic," Pearson says of his Alcoholics Anonymous documentary. "AA has traditionally had a no-promotion policy. But because a friend of mine was part of the managing body of AA for fourteen years, the organization decided if we were set on making the documentary, they might as well cooperate. We were granted access nobody has gotten in sixty-five years. And my friend Lyle Workman, lead guitarist for Beck, did all the music."

Music? Bestselling author or not, it's never far from Pearson's mind. He plays bass guitar and original music with the Toastpoints in his Idaho hometown. And then there are the Rock Bottom Remainders, a group of literary "unlikelies" including authors Stephen King, Dave Barry, Mitch Albom, Amy Tan, and James McBride.

"The Rock Bottom Remainders play 1960s rock and roll—poorly," Pearson says. "But we have a great time, we really get the crowd dancing, and we've raised over $400,000 for children's charities." Most years, the Remainders commit to one show. "But in the fall of 2000," he says, "we played four."

Stops in Boston, Miami, Washington DC, and Denver benefited a children's charity, America Scores. "We are a recreationally linked literacy program serving inner-city kids," says America Scores President Paul Caccamo. "And our reach is expanding, thanks in part to 'rocking' authors like Ridley and the gang."

Pearson's passion for kids doesn't end with his fund-raising efforts with the Rock Bottom Remainders. "I volunteer at the alternative high school in my hometown each year," he says, "and teach the writing class. I love working with those kids. They are amazing."

Adapting his novels for a teenage readership is something Pearson would love to do. "Any of these kids could read my novels. I've talked to my publisher about abridging the novels, removing certain complications and offensive language. I think they'd really appeal to 15- to 18-year-olds.

My publisher isn't opposed to it, but he'd like to wait about a year before we try it."

Pearson is also a devoted father to Paige, age four and Storey, age two. "Storey is a laugh machine—she laughs and squeals almost without provocation. And Paige is so delighted to have a sister. They delight and amaze me. I really am such a lucky father."

Paige and Storey? "OK," Pearson admits, "they are obviously literary references. But both spellings have extra vowels in them so we wouldn't condemn them to that focus for life." Ridley Pearson is nothing if not empathetic.

And that's the point, according to Pearson, whether it comes to writing or life. "It all comes full circle," he says. "When I was a kid, I loved reading. But I remember thinking, 'I'll never be smart enough to be a writer.' People stepped in to help me back then. I feel lucky to have the chance to follow in their footsteps today."

For Pearson, good luck has seldom been lacking. "And that's a good thing," he says. "Because I have endless dreams left to dream, and many, many stories I've yet to write."

———————

"I was a bartender. I was a dishwasher. I was house cleaner in a hospital, which kept me viscerally connected to the ER." Handy knowledge when suspense is your genre, Pearson points out. "Clean-up guys get real familiar with blood."

———————

Leah Stewart: Bringing Back the Plot

BY BRAD VICE

Here is a mystery. How can a person both be commercially successful and keep her artistic integrity? Leah Stewart knows. Her first novel *Body of a Girl* (Viking Press, 2000) has impressed both fans of literary fiction and mystery novels alike. Like the work of Joyce Carol Oates, James Lee Burke, and Tom Franklin, Stewart's first novel is what almost everyone in the publishing world is looking for—a crossover success—fiction that can be praised for its polished style and nuanced understanding of character, but also embraces rather than snubs the entertaining value of plot. "I am no longer interested in character apart from action," Stewart says. "My greatest fear is that someone will pick up something I have written and say, 'this is boring.' "

Leah Stewart

Photo by Miriam Berkley

Body of a Girl is anything but boring, and from the first sentence—"This has been a summer of murders"—the reader is hooked by the author's edgy prose. Using the stark declarative language of a journalist, Stewart's protagonist, Memphis police beat reporter Olivia Dale, takes us to the scene of a gruesome homicide. Kidnapped, bound, and mutilated by tire treads, Allison Avery and the circumstances of her death quickly become more than just another story for the fledgling reporter. Because at first the details of Allison's life seem closely to resemble her own, Olivia becomes obsessed with solving the mystery of the killer's identity. Positive that the murderer is someone close to Allison, Olivia begins interviewing the victim's myriad friends, relatives, and lovers only to find that Allison's own identity is something of an enigma. At one point in the novel, Olivia stops her footwork long enough to look over her notes and wonders how it is possible to discover the motive for killing some who is at once *"Pretty, Hard Worker, Singer, Thief, Slut, Sweet, Young, Churchgoer, Pothead, Drunk, Tease. I wonder what pulls all this together to make a person, if it's only skin and bone."* After a short meditation, Olivia adds another word to her list—"Dead."

The investigative journalist is a mainstay of mystery novels and movies, like a cop or P.I., but I was really impressed with the details of your narrator's occupation. She really seemed to be doing her job, taking notes, weeding out fact from conjecture, even the office politics of the job seem authentic. Do you have a journalism background?

A little. I did a summer internship for the *Commercial Appeal* in Memphis, where the book is set. I made friends with a female intern in Metro, who went on to be a reporter and cover crime, like Olivia. So she was very helpful.

BRAD VICE *has published fiction in* The Atlantic Monthly, The Georgia Review, The Southern Review, Hayden's Ferry, The Greensboro Review, *and* New Stories from the South. *His nonfiction frequently appears in* Writer's Digest, Novel & Short Story Writer's Market, Guide to Literary Agents, *and* The San Francisco Chronicle. *He lives in Russellville, Arkansas, and teaches creative writing at Arkansas Tech University.*

Is that what gave you the idea for the novel? Your novel is one of many successful books that have been touted as a so-called crossover success, a literary mystery. Did you always know the mystery element was going to be there?

Yes and no. When I had the internship I was 19 years old, and it was the first time I had lived alone. I lived in an apartment complex in mid-town Memphis and it was kind of scary. A woman was raped beside a club across the street from my complex. After that I hated to leave the apartment after dark. I wanted to write about the low-level fear that most women experience by virtue of being women, and it made sense to have a narrator who had to look at that every day, because it was her job. Then it made sense to give the narrator a murder victim she could identify with. I never really thought of the book as a *mystery* novel, but I read mystery novels to help me create a convincing plot.

Which books were the most helpful?

Before I started working on the book I hadn't read many mysteries, just a few classics by Chandler and Hammett. When I realized my novel had elements of mystery, I read Edna Buchanan, a mystery writer whose protagonist is a female crime reporter. Other literary crossovers like Kem Nunn's *Tapping the Source*, Jonathan Lethem's *Motherless Brooklyn*, Colson Whitehead's *The Intuitionist*. For a while I was obsessed with James Ellroy's *L.A. Confidential*, both the book and the movie. That story is interesting because it's about character through the lens of crime. You see the three men in transition: Jack Vincennes's celebrity lifestyle is falling down around him, Bud White is learning to use his head instead of his fists, and Ed Exley is learning when not to play by the rules. I wanted my novel to be about Olivia's character in a similar way. She thinks she is simply covering the story, but the story is changing her. Although I knew what kind of character I wanted, I didn't have any idea how to write an extended plot. I watched the movie of *L.A. Confidential* over and over again, first for characterization and mood, and second because it picks the key plot points out of the very complicated narrative of the novel.

I learned something really important reading P.D. James. Mystery novels are based on a question—whodunnit? You're asking your reader to sit through 300 pages to get to the answer. What's going to pull them along? From James I learned to ask and answer smaller questions along the way—Where was the victim's best friend the night of the murder? Where was the victim those three hours after she was last seen? What was her brother doing in her room that night? Creating the plot this way was sort of like writing a poem in form. It gave me structure and propulsion.

The idea of having a crossover hit hopefully means you will appeal to more readers. How was the book received in literary circles versus mystery circles?

When my agent was shopping the book around, one editor said the writing was good but the commercial element wasn't strong enough, another said that the book was too commercial, another wanted me to write a mystery series about Olivia. What all this taught me was that everyone else will feel a need to categorize you, but in the end these categories are meaningless. You just write the best book you can. For me the mystery of identity was always the central question of the book: who am I? Who murdered Allison was secondary. *Body of a Girl* was sometimes reviewed as a literary novel, sometimes as a mystery, sometimes both. Many mystery reviewers liked it, but if they didn't, it was because the novel's ending didn't satisfy their expectations for the genre. Other reviewers concentrated on the questions the novel raises about identity. I've had other writers imply that I sold out—the book was too close to genre and therefore less artistic.

Ultimately, having the book marketed as a mystery opened me up to venues I didn't even know existed, great specialized mystery book stores, like Kate's Mystery Books in Boston or the Mysterious Bookshop in New York. A lot of these stores have book-of-the-month clubs, especially for first-time novelists. Some of them selected my book, so it went out to all of their subscribers. Now I have to see if the people who liked my first book, for whatever reason, will follow me to another.

Your narrator Olivia is always attempting to separate truth from fact. The newspapers only want fact, not truth. Do you think truth belongs to the realm of the novelist?

I guess I was trying to tell the truth by not strictly following genre conventions because eventually they always lead to a sort of secondhand realism. I mean, you don't hear about a lot of reporters solving crimes. Thinking that she can solve the crime on her own is one of Olivia's delusions. Also, I wanted to dispel the notion that journalism is objective. Olivia makes choices about what to reveal to her readers. She keeps a lot of information about Allison secret, so in the eyes of the public she will remain a good girl with bad luck, rather than a bad girl who gets what she deserves. Olivia knows she's in control of the story.

Is your next book another mystery, or do you want to write a different kind of book?

I just finished a new manuscript and it is not a mystery, but it has things in common with *Body of a Girl*. I want to write about women who see the world through their work, and this book is about a young woman who's a secretary. She firmly believes she is destined to do something amazing; she just doesn't know what. I have started fleshing out an idea for another book that involves a war-time army nurse. But whatever I write, I want to keep the narrative structure strong. Maybe it's because I'm a child of TV. Maybe I have a short attention span, but I don't think boring someone in the name of art is justified.

"When my agent was shopping the book around, one editor said the writing was good but the commercial element wasn't strong enough, another said that the book was too commercial, another wanted me to write a mystery series about Olivia. What all this taught me was that everyone else will feel a need to categorize you, but in the end these categories are meaningless. You just write the best book you can."

Mystery Markets
Appearing in This Book

Below is a list of mystery markets appearing in this edition of *Novel & Short Story Writer's Market*. For complete information—including who to contact and how to submit your mystery short story or novel manuscript—turn to the page number provided.

Magazines

Book Publishers

Resources for Mystery Writers

Below is a list of invaluable resources specifically for mystery writers. For more information on the magazines and organizations listed below, check the General Index and the Publications of Interest and Organizations sections of this book. To order any of the Writer's Digest Books titles or to get a consumer book catalog, call 1-800-289-0963. You may also order Writer's Digest Books selections through www.writersdigest.com, Amazon.com, or www.barnesandnoble.com.

MAGAZINES:
- *The Armchair Detective*, P.O. Box 929, Bound Brook NJ 08805-0929.
- *Mystery Readers Journal*, Mystery Readers International, P.O. Box 8116, Berkeley CA 94707.
- *Writer's Digest*, 1507 Dana Ave., Cincinnati OH 45207.

BOOKS:
Howdunit series (Writer's Digest Books):
- *Missing Persons: A Writer's Guide to Finding the Lost, the Abducted and the Escaped*
- *Murder One: A Writer's Guide to Homicide*
- *Armed and Dangerous: A Writer's Guide to Weapons*
- *Deadly Doses: A Writer's Guide to Poisons*
- *Cause of Death: A Writer's Guide to Death, Murder & Forensic Medicine*
- *Scene of the Crime: A Writer's Guide to Crime Scene Investigation*
- *Police Procedural: A Writer's Guide to the Police and How They Work*
- *Body Trauma: A Writer's Guide to Wounds and Injuries*
- *Just the Facts, Ma'am: A Writer's Guide to Investigators and Investigation Techniques*
- *Rip-off: A Writer's Guide to Crimes of Deception*

Other Writer's Digest books for mystery writers:
- *The Criminal Mind, A Writer's Guide to Forensic Psychology*
- *Howdunit*
- *How to Write Mysteries*
- *The Writer's Complete Crime Reference Book*
- *Writing the Modern Mystery*
- *Writing Mysteries: A Handbook by the Mystery Writers of America*
- *Writing the Private Eye Novel: A Handbook by the Private Eye Writers of America*
- *You Can Write a Mystery*

ORGANIZATIONS & ONLINE:
- The Mystery Writers' Forum. Website: www.zott.com/mysforum/default.html.
- Mystery Writers of America, 17 E. 47th St., 6th Floor, New York NY 10017. Website: www.mysterywriters.org.
- The Private Eye Writers of America, 407 W. Third St., Moorestown NJ 08057. Website: www.thrillingdetective.com.
- Sisters in Crime, P.O. Box 442124, Lawrence KS 66044-8933. Website: www.sistersincrime.org.

The Romance Market Today

BY HAROLD LOWRY (aka Leigh Greenwood),
President, Romance Writers of America

Despite the growing difficulties of an increasingly electronic, computerized and digitized world, Romance Writers of America is extremely excited about the growth of the romance market and the appearance of romance writers on the bestselling lists of *The New York Times*, *Publishers Weekly* and *USA Today*. There can be no doubt that romance and romance writers have arrived.

Harold Lowry

To say that romance has historically received no respect is an understatement. We've been vilified, trivialized and pilloried in virtually every TV talk show, newspaper and industry magazine. References to "those little books," "trashy novels" and "lurid covers" are so numerous people have stopped paying attention to them. Even though most commentators prefaced their remarks by stating, "I've never read one of these books, but . . ." audiences would take their word for gospel. It's always amazed me that in a news industry which professed to value accuracy, commentators and reviewers would actually make public value judgments on a genre of books they admitted they hadn't read. It didn't make any difference that millions of these books were being sold. They were trash, and no self-respecting reader would be seen dead with one.

But romance writers are a hardy bunch. We were writing the kind of books we loved, the kind our readers loved, and we were making a living doing what we liked best. Despite questions such as, "When are you going to write a real book?" we ignored the criticism and kept on keeping on.

Then a strange thing happened. One writer, LaVyrle Spencer, became so successful her publisher gave her book *Morning Glory* a non-traditional cover and sold her to the mainstream market. The book was a romance—I read it so I can vouch for that—but the public bought it and liked it so much that LaVyrle became a constant on *The New York Times* bestseller list. Soon after that she went into hardback with sales growing with each book.

But Spencer was just one in a line of romance writers to make their way onto the nation's most revered bestseller lists. The ever-lengthening parade includes some of the biggest names in romance: Catherine Coulter, Judith McNaught, Jude Deveraux, Julie Garwood, Jayne Ann

HAROLD LOWRY *is the current president of the RWA and the first male president in the history of the organization. A former teacher of music, Lowry has written over 30 romances under the name Leigh Greenwood. His award-winning books consistently appear on the* USA Today *bestseller list as well as Waldenbooks, B. Dalton's and Ingram's Most Requested List. Undercover Honeymoon, a Silhouette Special Edition, will be appearing in February 2002 and* CADE: A Texas Homecoming *will be published in March 2002 by Leisure.*

Krentz, Amanda Quick, Barbara Delinsky, Elizabeth Lowell, Iris Johansen, Diana Gabaldon, Tami Hoag, Linda Howard, Janet Evanovich, Heather Graham, Susan Elizabeth Phillips and the phenomenal juggernaut of Nora Roberts (see the interview with her on page 116). In each of my last seven issues of *Publishers Weekly*, RWA members have occupied four or five of the top ten positions on the mass market paperback bestseller list. For the week of July 9th, 2001, they occupied the first four positions. Some still write what is basically a traditional romance, some romantic suspense, and some have moved over into mystery, but all began their careers in romance where they honed their skills writing hundreds of "those little books," or the historicals with the lurid covers. To what do I attribute this astonishing turnaround?

First, these women are superb storytellers who have thoroughly mastered the craft of writing. They wrote two books a year, five books a year, even ten in Nora's case, but they did it over and over again until they could tell a tale that would keep the reader turning pages and could create characters you cared about. And they did it every time because writing those 30, 50 or 75 "little books" had helped them master their craft. Jayne Ann Krentz (Amanda Quick) and Nora Roberts (J.D. Robb) have made the list under two names. Their publishers have packaged the books differently—non-romance covers, hardback, marketing them in other genres—but the stories remain very much the same, and readers are buying them by the millions. Nearly every month brings a new member of RWA to the bestseller lists. Readers may have begun reading these books without knowing they were reading romance, but they know it now and it's not stopping them.

The change is just as exciting for RWA's members as writers as it is for them as readers. Writers can now put as little or as much romance as they want in their books and still sell them. They can step out of the genre entirely and be confident that enough readers will follow them to assure their book's success. They have opened up a new category called Women's Fiction, loosely defined as a relationship book. While these don't have to center around monogamous relationships between men and women (there are parents, children, siblings and friends to be considered), most still include at least one romance at the heart of the story.

During the 1980s, writers of traditional romances began to broaden the range of issues that could be used in a romance. In the 1990s, historicals followed suit. Today's writers are carrying it even further.

RWA is proud to claim these trailblazers as members, but RWA can take credit for some of the genre's success. Established in 1980 by a small group of women looking for emotional and professional support, it has grown into an organization of more than 8,400 members with more than 150 chapters in the United States, Canada and Australia. We support our members at both the national and local levels. We offer a national conference each year in July in a major U.S. city. We offer more than a hundred workshops geared to anyone from the new member and beginning writer up to the multi-published writer thinking of changing genres or looking for career advice. Our conference also offers an opportunity for publishers, editors, and agents to meet our members. On the final night, we hand out the RITAs, our national award that recognizes the best in romance in a dozen categories.

At the local level, our support is more one-on-one with critique groups, craft and hands-on programs or all-day workshops. Many chapters also run contests which provide the entrants with a critique of their entry. At least a dozen chapters have regional conferences with multi-published guest speakers and a smattering of editors or agents. But at all levels, we're working toward the goal of helping our members become published, and making the publishing world more writer friendly. I believe it's essential that RWA have a focus and an agenda that will keep us ahead of the door closing behind us and ready to take advantage of those opening before us. I also believe every organization has a personality of its own. It can do certain things well and can't do others at all. I believe it's essential that we discover that identity so we can use it to grow stronger. Our writers will always be at a disadvantage with publishers. There are simply more books than the market can absorb. So we need to know what we do best and concentrate our efforts.

In the past our efforts have been largely directed toward teaching and support. If you want friends who'll tell you everything they know about writing and sympathize with you every step of the way as you go, from neophyte to multi-published writer, join RWA. We're the warmest, friendliest, most sharing people in the world. But we've pretty much perfected the structure for teaching, networking and support. Now we're moving more into the area of advocacy.

With the proliferation of e-publishers and small print publishers, our members have asked us for guidance in knowing where they'll have the most success in selling their books. E-publishing presents a special challenge because of the ease with which any book can be put on the market either on disk or on a website. In response to this need, RWA has established a list of recognized publishers who have stayed in business at least a year, and who have successfully marketed at least one book. It's up to our members to decide whether or not to use this list.

We've faced several advocacy issues this year. RWA was a signatory to probably the most important issue this year, the *Tasini v. The New York Times* case, which reached the Supreme Court. The Court ruled that publishers may not license to electronic databases any freelancer's work that first appeared in their publications without permission. An even more disturbing case, in my view, is *Random House v. RosettaBooks*. RosettaBooks bought the e-rights to classic novels by William Styron and Kurt Vonnegut, which Random House still maintains on their back list. Random House contends that although the original contracts—which were drafted long before the advent of the Internet—did not specify that Random House retained electronic rights, print publishers "automatically own" all e-rights to the books they publish. A federal judge recently denied Random House's request for a preliminary injunction to stop RosettaBooks from selling e-book editions. They plan to appeal the decision.

Both of these cases illustrate the difficulties and confusion brought about by electronic publishing and the Internet. Organizations such as RWA will have to remain vigilant to protect their rights and livelihoods of our members.

On a more restricted scale, we've approached Amazon on the sale of used books on their site. We had no success with our appeal that Amazon stop selling used books, or at least move the used-book button to another page. As any writer will tell you, neither the writer nor the publisher receives any money for the sale of a used book. So if that book is sold a dozen times, we are paid only on the first sale. Obviously that can have a drastic effect on a writer's ability to earn a living. Because very few romances are on the shelf for more than a month, we asked Amazon to wait three months after the release of a book before they began selling used copies. That would give a writer a fair chance to make a living, but Amazon didn't respond to our letter.

We're in an ongoing discussion with Harlequin over the pseudonym issue. This is more complex than I have space to explain here, but suffice it to say that some writers control their name, whether it is their legal name or a pseudonym, and can take that name to another publisher at any time. This means they're able to take immediate advantage of any career opportunity that might open up. Other writers use a pseudonym which Harlequin controls. They have to ask permission, which is not always granted, before they can use that name for projects with other publishers. Then there's the problem that some writers feel they have to take a pseudonym in order to sell to Harlequin.

This has become an important issue as a consequence of the rapid expansion of the market. With new publishing avenues available and more opening up every day, no writer wants to feel contractually restricted to only one venue. But Harlequin sees this as a way to protect its product and investment in building the author. They also see these names as a company asset. It's not a policy they will abandon without a great deal of consideration.

In all of this, Romance Writers of America is there to help and support its writers. It's a vital and growing organization; our strength lies in the fact that at the local level we stress the individual and at the national level we stress the profession. And we are united in our vision, top to bottom, side to side. Our genre has come a long way in 20 years, and RWA has been responsible for a large part of that success. We look toward an even brighter future.

Linda Lael Miller: Transcending Time and Place in Romance Writing

BY CANDI LACE

Self-proclaimed "barn goddess" Linda Lael Miller certainly hasn't spent most of her life bailing hay, driving Bindlestiff tractors and commanding brush hogs. *The New York Times* bestselling author has produced well over 50 books, earned countless awards, lectured at international forums, and established the Linda Lael Miller Scholarships for Women Foundation. She has been the darling of the *Under the Covers Romance Reviews* for decades, as translations and sales of her Americana and medieval period novels increase each year.

Linda Lael Miller

Photo by Charles William Bush

While a traditional romance novel continues to be the most popular read in the U.S., Miller inteprets the genre on her own terms. Consider some of the scenarios she has equated with "romance": an immortal travels through continents and centuries to feed eternal life into a senator's aide, as in *Forever and the Night* (Berkley Press); an English academic possesses a marshal in a rugged pioneer town, as in *The Women of Primrose Creek: Christy* (Pocket Sonnet); and the proprietor of a boarding house falls in love with a war veteran with dual identities, as in *A Springwater Christmas* (Pocket).

The list of beloved characters goes on and on. "When I write, I am absorbed body and soul in the story, and in my characters—as many as there are," says Miller. "The best part of a romance novel, besides good dialogue, humor, lots of conflict and a bit of danger, is engaging characters—people you *care* about."

Here Miller discusses the increasing appeal of romantic characters, how publishers are working with more first-time authors and the importance of self-promotion.

What changes have you seen in the publishing industry since you began writing romance?

Well, people talk a lot these days about how rough it is for a new author to get started. They were saying that same thing in 1983, when I sold my first historical romance in a market that wasn't buying historical romances. There is, as it happens, *never* a good time to sell a book, but people are out there doing it anyway, every day of the week. Romance writers are changing the face of publishing. Look at Nora Roberts, for instance. Writers Iris Johannson, Linda Howard, Catherine Coulter and Tami Hoag have broken new ground as well.

CANDI LACE *is the production editor and staff writer for* Artist's & Graphic Designer's Market *and* Children's Writer's & Illustrator's Market *(Writer's Digest Books). Her writings have been published in* Clamor, Art Papers, Alternative Cinema, *and* Sojourner: The Women's Forum, *among other venues.*

How has the romance genre expanded in the last 20 years?

The genre has grown and expanded a lot, and I'm beyond thankful for that. Today, heroes and heroines are rational, likeable people with goals, integrity and other admirable traits. In the 1970s, rapes were obligatory in historicals, and "heroes" went around doing things like branding or whipping their heroines. That is *not* romance! That is felonious assault!

As popular as romance novels are in the US, the genre is probably the most misconstrued and publicly reproached. Given your success, how do you feel about this?

Most people who hate romances will admit—if pressed and if they're honest—that they haven't actually read one, either since the 70s when the books truly deserved to be described as bodice rippers, or ever. It is fashionable to slam romances (this phenomenon always reminds me of people who keep lofty tomes on their coffee tables, so people will think they're smart) but the fact is, some of the best writers working today are writing them, and they're damned good books, too.

You've published over 50 novels categorized as "romance." We're speaking of countless sex scenes. How does a romance writer keep the language fresh and explicit?

There are lots of love scenes, and if they are "fresh" and "explicit," it's because the intimate scenes grow out of the particular relationship between the hero and the heroine. It's a subtle thing, hard to explain. Part of the magic and mystery of love is that something as old as humanity can still seem new. Romance writing is composed of many things. Rich though sparing details that make a reader part of the scene are important.

Distinguish Lael St. James from Linda Lael Miller. Why was it necessary to create another pseudonym?

I created the pseudonym partly because I need creative elbow room. I'm prolific and need a place to put other kinds of stories. Some of them are probably more erotic than my romance ones, and they include things that readers of mainstream Linda Lael Miller books might or might not enjoy. Vampire books, for example, and sagas. The main difference is the time period; the first two Lael St. James books, *My Lady Beloved* and *My Lady Wayward*, are set in medieval times.

While describing your recent move to the Arizona desert *Publishers Weekly* quotes you as saying, "I belong in the country with horses." Where does that 'country girl' persona meet that of Linda Lael Miller, author and world traveller? And how does that manifest itself in your writing?

I lived in London on and off for several years, and became fascinated with British history. My favorite writer of all time is Dorothy Dunnett, who writes wonderful historical novels. I love to travel, and it's important for me to explore places for research purposes. Hence, the medieval books were born.

How do you retain the details from your travels to employ in your books?

I keep journals and buy lots of books—especially in museum shops. When I was doing the English stories, I haunted Charing Cross Road. I am also inspired by other novels, and by movies.

How did you meet your publicist, and how has your interaction with her helped your career?

I met my publicist through a good friend. She and I communicate by telephone and e-mail, though we meet in person when we can. She arranges interviews, and sends out promotional material, most of which is designed and produced within her own company. She is an amazingly imaginative woman, with a talented and creative staff.

Do you still advocate self-promotion, in spite of your connections with Pocket and other publishing houses?

Yes, I advocate self-promotion, though I also believe the publishing house should undertake as much advertising as feasible. I've always liked the limelight—I had a police escort when I was born! I like holding contests on my website. Last year, for instance, I flew a reader in for dinner at one of my favorite restaurants, The Roaring Fork, in Scottsdale. She was picked up in a limousine, and I put her up in a nice hotel. We also give away autographed books all the time.

You established the Linda Lael Miller Scholarships for Women program? Can you elaborate on its purpose?

So far, I've given away $15,000 in scholarships to three women. My goal is to build a self-sustaining foundation which will award funds to deserving women in perpetuity. The scholarships can be used for tuition at any college or trade/vocational school, or even for childcare. I care very much about underprivileged children, and firmly believe that if you educate the mother, you educate the entire family.

You obviously feel that the reader-writer relationship is consequential . . .

As far my relationship with my readers, I do my very best to live up to their expectations, and I hope I succeed. I absolutely and always feel an obligation to my readers! This is one of those instances, though, where writers have to keep in mind that you can't please all of the people, all the time . . . no matter what kind of book you write, no matter if you open up a vein and drain the blood out of your soul.

Julia Quinn Chose the Right Career

BY VANESSA LYMAN

Visualize yourself at the pediatrician's reading a romance novel while you wait for your child's appointment. You're willing yourself not to blush as you read a very steamy scene when the pediatrician steps into the lobby. She smiles, stethoscope around her neck, as she looks at the book in you hand. "Why, I wrote that!" she says. And when you flip back to look at the author's photo . . .

Julia Quinn

Well, it could've happened but Julia Quinn, after three months at Yale Medical School, decided that romance was for her. She had already sold two novels to Avon— *Splendid* and *Dancing at Midnight*—and wrote two more—*Minx* and *Everything and the Moon*—before starting medical school.

Since coming to her senses, Quinn has since written six more novels, all of them published by Avon Books. The latest, *An Offer from a Gentleman*, appeared in July 2001 and is the third novel involving the rather large Bridgerton family. *The New York Times* bestselling author is well known for her humorous dialogue, vivid characters and fast-paced plot. She's also considered a bit of an Internet pioneer and has one of the most visited websites in the genre.

Here Quinn discusses the romance industry, writing Regency romances and how the Internet affects romance writers.

Has there been a marked difference in your approach to writing since becoming a full-time romance novelist? How have you evolved as a writer since then?

I wouldn't say there has been much of a difference in my approach to writing. I wasn't disciplined in my work habits then, and sadly, I'm not now. I'm pretty good about getting my butt into my computer chair at the right time, but then I tend to fritter away the minutes surfing the Web and answering e-mail. I *have* removed all the games from my computer, though. That has made a tremendous difference.

I do think I've evolved as a writer. I think all writers must evolve over time, not because the market demands it, but just because you learn a thing or two in the process of writing ten books. I've always been known as a funny romance author, but lately my main editorial goal is to deepen the characterization in my books and to introduce darker themes when appropriate—without losing my humorous voice. I think this blend of light and dark is what has attracted my readership. A funny book is always a wonderful thing, but when you can dig deeper and touch your reader's emotions while still making them laugh—then you've got the makings of a terrific book.

VANESSA LYMAN *is production editor with* Novel & Short Story Writer's Market.

You're cited as saying that the Regency period is "a good time for people who like to write dialogue." What is it about Regency that makes this so? Is this what attracts you to that era?

The Regency is actually a very short period of time: 1811-1820, when King George III was mentally incapacitated, and the Prince of Wales (later George IV) acted as Regent. It is the era in which Jane Austen wrote and was popularized for modern readers by Georgette Heyer, who basically invented the subgenre of the Regency romance. Nowadays there is a distinction between the Regency romance (often called a traditional Regency) and a historical romance set in the regency period. A traditional Regency is shorter, sweeter, and usually has its plot and premise firmly entrenched in the strict societal conventions of the time. A Regency historical is larger in scope and is generally more sensuous. There are clear marketing delineations as well; very few houses publish traditional Regencies any longer.

Whichever type of Regency you write, it is indeed an excellent setting for people like me who excel at dialogue and are weaker in the area of description. People were witty then; conversation was an art. Day to day life wasn't as dangerous as it was in medieval times (another popular era in historical romance), but the Regency still seems old-fashioned to the modern reader, almost fairy-tale-ish.

What is your approach to historical research? Have you made any anachronistic mistakes? Any surprising discoveries?

I've been working within the same time period for many years now, so I'm fairly familiar with the general feel of the era. What this means is that I don't need to research the generalities so much as the small details. So I tend to do my research as I go along, looking things up as I need them.

That said, I should point out that my books are most definitely costume dramas. This means that the politics of the day don't really come into play, and you're not likely to see a real historical figure appear as a character in one of my novels. Some readers want a richer historical tapestry woven into their historical romances, but I myself adore a good costume drama. After all, Jane Austen wrote costume dramas!

As for mistakes and errors, I have definitely made my share of them, as have most authors of historical romance. You won't find a more diligent collection of authors than those of us writing romance, but errors do creep past. Most of the time, you'll find that the errors are with small, insignificant details in the story, rather than something that would affect the entire plot of the book. For example, my biggest error came about quite by accident. I was writing a book set in the 1820s and had a character who mentioned that he had just returned from Paris—a detail which had absolutely no bearing on anything in the story other than the fact that the character had to have just returned from *some*where, given that he had been away for a year. For some reason I can't even recall, I moved the setting of the book back to 1813. Which would be fine, except that puts it right in the middle of the Napoleonic Wars, and it's unlikely that my character, a member of an aristocratic British family, would have traveled to France.

As a romance novelist, what has been your greatest resource?

Without a doubt, the Internet. For research, it is unparalleled. I wanted to put a croquet game in one of my books, and so I turned to the internet to research the history of croquet. Within minutes I had learned that croquet did exist in 1814, but that the rules were slightly different, and it was called Pall Mall, a bastardization of the French *paille-maille*. I don't even want to think about how much time it would have taken me to research that in a library.

But perhaps more importantly, the Internet has enabled writers to chat with their colleagues on a regular basis. People in offices have their water coolers; writers have the Internet. Frankly, I couldn't have been a professional novelist before the Internet age. Writing is lonely, and I'm a social person. With the Internet, I can chat with people who actually know what I'm talking about when I start blabbing on about the craft and business of writing. My favorite group is a listserv composed of about 60 women who write romance or women's fiction for my publishing house. We've developed quite a sisterhood!

What characteristics are absolutely essential for a hero/heroine and how can you add to the character to make him/her special? Do you have any "tricks?"

I think all heroes and heroines need to possess honor and integrity. And a sense of humor and intelligence. After that, you need to dig a little deeper to figure out why Anthony, Viscount Bridgerton, is different from Simon, Duke of Hastings. (And no, not all of my heroes possess aristocratic titles, although all thus far have come from privileged backgrounds.) One thing I always do is come up with one defining experience that is going to shape how the character will behave. Not a characteristic but an experience. I have written a hero who was shunned by his father because he stuttered. A heroine who was orphaned as a young woman and has spent the last few years desperately trying to keep her family together. These are the things that will shape a character's motivation and actions throughout a book. From there, you can flesh it out. Is he stubborn? Is she clumsy? Is he a compulsive list-maker? Does she keep a diary?

If you look at my novels, you can probably see how these methods of characterization play themselves out in my writing, although in truth, moreso in my later books. I guess this is one of those things I've learned along the way!

The "dictionary" in *To Catch an Heiress*, the "guidebook" in *How to Marry a Marquis*, and the gossip column in *The Duke and I* and *The Viscount Who Loved Me*, you frequently use "secondary sources." Why did you choose to write them?

Because they're so much fun! And because they add so much to the story. The first time I employed a literary device within a novel was in *To Catch an Heiress*. In that novel, each chapter begins with a selection from the "personal dictionary" of the heroine. She likes to collect new words, and she writes them down in a little notebook, along with the definition and a sentence using the word in context. Each of the sentences, of course, relates to the story. So for her, this little dictionary becomes a diary of sorts.

The interesting thing is that I didn't start the dictionary until I was well into the book. I was having difficulty getting a grasp of her character. I was sitting there, staring at my computer screen, trying to figure out what made her unique. Her background was different than any other heroine I'd written, but I really felt I needed to know her better. My father had just subscribed me to the A Word a Day listserv, and I was inspired to work a few vocabulary words into the story. But what this really did was allow me to write portions of the story in the first person, which put me a little closer to the essence of the character.

Do you find it important to read within the genre? Outside the genre?

I find it important to read, period. I can't *not* read. I'd feel lost if I didn't have a book somewhere nearby.

I do know of some romance authors who don't like to read within the genre while they are working on a book, but I like to see what other authors are doing. I am inspired by my colleagues. There is a lot of very good writing in the romance field. People tend to dismiss us because we're authors of commercial fiction and we must write within the parameters of our genre (the love story must be the primary plotline in the book; there must be a happy ending). But when you think about it, all genre fiction has parameters and must meet certain reader expectations. Mysteries, for example, must be solved. Can you imagine how disappointed you'd be if you got to the end of an Agatha Christie novel and Hercule Poirot smacked his forehead and said, "That's a stumper!"

Romance writers frequently bemoan the "clinch cover," with the hero and heroine in partial states of undress and bent into unnatural positions. There seems to be a hierarchy of cover design, with clinch cover at the bottom and elegantly designed hardcover on top. Is this, in fact, the case? Do writers have any say about the cover?

I have very mixed feelings about clinch covers. On the one hand, I don't particularly like them and in the days before I was published, I avoided books with clinches like the plague. On the other hand, for a new writer, a clinch cover is often the best way to go. I'm not entirely certain why this is so, but I've seen the sales data to prove it. But clinch covers are like any other covers; some are good and some are bad. A vibrant and eye-catching clinch will do better than a non-clinch that is boring and washed-out.

There is, indeed, a bit of a hierarchy of covers. You won't find the bigger name authors with clinches on their books. As for cover control—I don't personally know anyone who's got it. And that's actually a good thing. Authors generally have no idea of what makes a good cover and what makes a bad one. I'd like to think I'm an exception, but that's just because I've worked in a bookstore and seen what sells.

If you're an aspiring romance author worried about your future covers, don't worry. You may not get control, but you will get input. Publishing houses do routinely ask authors for ideas, and it's a common practice among publishing houses to ask authors for detailed character descriptions so that if you are getting a clinch, whether on the cover or hidden away in a stepback (on the inside front cover) the hair color, etc. will be correct.

You wrote your very first novel before you were sixteen. How did that come about? What happened to it? Was it a romance?

It *was* a romance. A teen romance of the Sweet Dreams variety, if you remember that series. I started it the summer I was 12 years old. All I was doing was sitting around reading teen romance novels, and I guess my father thought I should be reading something a bit more weighty. He told me I could only continue to read the romances if I was benefitting from them in some way. Thinking quickly, I told him it was to expand my vocabulary. He told me to find a vocabulary word in the book I was reading I didn't already know. I couldn't. (I had a pretty big vocabulary by that point.) Then I told him I was reading it for research. I was planning to write my own romance, I boasted.

That very night my dad sat me down in front of his computer and said, "Here you go. Get started." And I did. No one was more surprised —and proud—than he was when, by the end of the week, I had two chapters written. It took me two more summers to finish the book, but I did it! I never did see it published, however. I sent it off to one publishing house with a cover letter revealing my age, and they rejected it without even reading it. I wasn't really sure what to do with it at that point. It's not really right for today's teen market, so it sits and waits in my computer.

You have one of the most visited romance author websites on the Internet. Has this affected your career in any way? Do you think your readership is better for it? One would expect science fiction readers to have a large online fan base. Could you say that of romance readers?

It's hard to measure directly how a website affects sales, but it definitely has an impact. My website contains the first chapter of all of my books, so readers can try before they buy. This is great for attracting new readers. I also have lots of features that will appeal to longtime fans: a monthly contest; a page called "JQ Recommends," on which I recommend other romance novels and "Inside the Story," which contains fun trivia about each book. I think that a vibrant and exciting website makes readers feel more connected to their favorite authors.

Romance readers are *very* active on the Web, perhaps even moreso than science fiction readers. I think that's because romances center on interpersonal relationships, and romance readers tend to like to connect with other people. Also, romance readers are almost exclusively women, and women, in general, are a little more polite to and supportive of each other on the Web. The result is a very busy and often close-knit community of readers.

Romance writers are reputed to have a strong relationship with their readers. Do you think the Internet will become a primary source for that writer/reader connection?

It already has. Ninety-nine percent of my reader mail comes to me electronically. I'm almost surprised when I receive a piece of snail mail these days. Also, the Internet has enabled authors to send out newsletters to readers without incurring printing and postage costs. I send a newsletter to over 1,000 readers whenever I have a new book out. There's a sign-up area on my website for it; we get new subscribers every day.

"All genre fiction has parameters and must meet certain reader expectations. Mysteries, for example, must be solved. Can you imagine how disappointed you'd be if you got to the end of an Agatha Christie novel and Hercule Poirot smacked his forehead and said, 'That's a stumper!'"

Nora Roberts: "Right Down to the Story"

BY KATIE STRUCKEL BROGAN

When Nora Roberts sits down to begin a new romance novel, it's because she has a story to tell.

"The goal would be to tell it as well as I possibly can," she says. "If there's anything else, you can't sit there and think, 'I want to sell x number of copies of this story'—you haven't even written the story yet!" she says. "So, it's like closing the lid on the box. You go into the story, the story's in the box with you, and that's all there is."

Roberts began writing category romance in 1979 when a blizzard forced her to remain housebound. Since that time, Roberts, who also writes under the alias J.D. Robb, has published more than 141 novels. There are 127 million copies of her books in print, another copy selling every four minutes.

In 1986, she became the first author inducted into the Romance Writers of America Hall of Fame. To date, 56 of Roberts' novels have been *New York Times* bestsellers. In 2000 alone, Roberts had 14 titles on *Times* bestseller lists. She admits that there's a secret to her success.

Nora Roberts

"Really, it goes right back down to the story," she says. "I think I do have some advantages, not in story telling, but that I was educated by the nuns. That means I was [raised] with discipline and guilt—they're very wonderful writer's tools."

Roberts goes on to explain that she also has a fast pace and a love of the process of writing. So when she combines those traits, she says, she can produce a lot of books.

In 1981, Roberts published her first novel, *Irish Thoroughbred* (Silhouette Romance). The book became a breakout phenomenon that rocketed her career to the lofty status it enjoys today.

"I just wanted to write the story," she says. "I don't think you can sit down and say, 'I'm going to write a breakout novel.' I think that's not only pompous, it's silly." Rather, Roberts thinks writers should sit down and say, "I want to tell this story."

According to Roberts, if the writer crafts a story that is compelling and he or she puts the time and effort into it, then maybe the author will get lucky. Roberts admits says can't really understand the term "breakout."

"I don't think about stuff like that, I really don't," she says. "And I know that the writing process is very individual, so others who write may think about that because that's part of their process."

For Roberts, the process involves writing daily for eight hours, which allows her to tell the

---

KATIE STRUCKEL BROGAN *is an associate editor with* Writer's Digest *magazine. This article originally appeared in* Writer's Digest, *and is reprinted here with permission.*

story in whatever form she has selected—category romance, contemporary relationship or romantic suspense—or that the story demands, and write it the very best that she can.

Once she has written the story, Roberts says, she relies on other people to market and position the book, and if it becomes a breakout novel, so be it. "My only job is to tell the story," she says. "I think that if writers focused on that, they'd be better off and probably more successful."

She also says that if a writer believes that there is a recipe for writing a bestseller, they're wrong because it just doesn't work that way.

Aside from the story, Roberts says that characters are also important if you want to have a successful book.

"All my books are character driven. Character is key," she says. "Character is plot—character is everything and the story wraps around them." Relationships are the most important element in romance novels, according to Roberts. "It's all about the relationships. If you don't have at least two really interesting, dynamic people at some point in their lives that makes sense—starting into a relationship, developing this relationship with its problems and its complexities and its conflicts—then you don't have a romance. Relationship is what drives the story. Whatever plot there is, whatever outside influences there are, it is all about who these people are and what they're going to bring to each other."

Roberts learned how to use character from her roots in category romance and has to be able to "paint" the characters quickly and clearly in a short period of time.

"Your characters have to jump off the page," she says. "They have to appeal to the reader in some way. If you don't care about the people, then it's all action, and who cares about that if you don't care about who drives the action or who the action happens to?" she says. "It's all about who these people are."

Despite her success and established writing process, Roberts still faces challenges when writing a new novel. It begins at "page one and then page two and so on."

"I start with a situation and 'what if,' and some character types and the canvas," she says. Then, she takes the situation, places it in a variety of settings with different backdrops and character types.

"Then you have to refine that situation into story," she says. However, Roberts makes it clear that she does not refine the story into plot. "I don't plot. I don't sit down and plot a book. It sort of unreels as I write."

So, with each draft she is faced with the challenge of crafting a situation and articulating the story on paper. Within this three- to four-draft process she finds out who her characters are, not just their personality types, but who each is as a person. "It's a challenge every time," she says.

In the end, Roberts says it comes down to having the skill to tell a story. "You have to have the discipline to sit down and tell the story, and the desire to tell a good one."

"Relationship is what drives the story. Whatever plot there is, whatever outside influences there are, it is all about who these people are and what they're going to bring to each other."

Romance Markets Appearing in This Book

Below is a list of romance markets appearing in this edition of *Novel & Short Story Writer's Market*. For complete information—including who to contact and how to submit your romance short story or novel manuscript—turn to the page number provided.

Resources for Romance Writers

Below is a list of invaluable resources specifically for romance writers. For more information on the magazines and organizations listed below, check the General Index and the Publications of Interest and Organizations sections of this book. To order any of the Writer's Digest Books titles or to get a consumer book catalog, call 1-800-289-0963. You may also order Writer's Digest Books selections through www.writersdigest.com, Amazon.com or www.barnesandnoble.com.

MAGAZINES:
- *Romance Writers Report*, Romance Writers of America, 3707 FM 1960 West, Suite 555, Houston TX 77014. (281)440-6885. Fax: (281)440-7510. E-mail: info@rwanational. com.
- *Romantic Times Magazine*, 55 Bergen St., Brooklyn NY 11201. (718)237-1097. Website: www.romantictimes.com.
- *Writer's Digest*, 1507 Dana Ave., Cincinnati OH 45207.

BOOKS:
- *How To Write Romances (Revised and Updated)*, Writer's Digest Books.
- *Keys to Success: A Professional Writer's Career Handbook*, Attention: Handbook, Romance Writers of America, 13700 Veterans Memorial, Suite 315, Houston TX 77014-1023. (281)440-6885, ext. 21. Fax: (281)440-7510. E-mail: info@rwanational.com.
- *Writing Romances: A Handbook by the Romance Writers of America*, Writer's Digest Books.
- *You Can Write a Romance*, Writer's Digest Books.

ORGANIZATIONS & ONLINE
- Romance Writers of America, Inc. (RWA), 3703 FM 1960 West, Suite 555, Houston TX 77068. (281)440-6885, ext. 21. Fax: (281)440-7510. E-mail: info@rwanational.com. Website: www.rwanational.com.
- Romance Writers of America regional chapters. Contact National Office (address above) for information on the chapter nearest you.
- Romance Central website: romance-central.com. Offers workshops and forum where romance writers share ideas and exchange advice about romance writing.
- www.writersmarket.com.
- www.writersdigest.com.

Science Fiction: Building a Believable World

BY DAVID GERROLD

Most science fiction stories are about intelligent folks dealing with an unknown phenomenon. During the course of the story, the reader (if not the hero) discovers the nature of that phenomenon, whatever it is. In that regard, a science fiction story is a lot like a murder mystery. We follow the detective as he figures out who the killer is—only in science fiction, the mystery involves much more than a dead body on the living room floor. The mystery is some facet of the universe that we haven't yet included in our maps.

Here's the good news. You don't have to be a scientist to write effective science fiction, but you do need to be enthused about the adventure of discovery. In science fiction, the sense of wonder comes as an internal *klunk* of recognition.

The bad news. It's not enough to be wonderful, it also has to be believable.

Here's an example. The planet Tatooine, as portrayed in *Star Wars*, is shown as a vast desert, with nothing growing anywhere. It's desolate and dry and uninhabitable. But if nothing grows there, where does the oxygen come from? How do the inhabitants breathe?

And if nothing grows there, how do banthas survive? Those things are as big as elephants. You find elephants on the savanna, on grasslands, in forests, and jungles—where there is plenty of greenery for them to graze. You don't find elephants in deserts. *A bantha is an elephant in a hair shirt. What does it eat?*

(Please don't send me letters explaining how it all works. I can do that exercise myself if I need to. But if you can figure out how to feed a bantha on a desert planet, then you've already learned one of the most important lessons of writing effective science fiction: world-building.)

The first issue in any science fiction story is believability. Because science fiction is rooted in science—*what we actually know about the way the universe works*—the writer has a responsibility to stay consistent with that body of knowledge. Assume the reader is at least as smart as you are. Assume that your audience has just as much experience with the real world. Don't contradict what is already known. You cannot rewrite the laws of physics and expect the reader to believe that your story is possible. (Sometimes you can cheat a little, like Wile E. Coyote, but that's a different discussion.)

Readers come to your story wanting to believe. To create believability, you have to believe in it yourself—because if you don't believe in it, how can anyone else?

If you write about a creature as big as a tank, like a bantha, then let us know what it eats— and what wants to eat it. How does it mate? How do the offspring survive? And if you really want to convince us that you know this creature well, show us the size of its droppings. (Remember the scene with the triceratops in *Jurassic Park*?)

This doesn't mean that you have to explain everything in your story down to the last niggling little detail. Otherwise your hero has to be Murray the Explainer. But whenever you postulate

DAVID GERROLD *is an award-winning writer of science fiction novels, short stories and screenplays. This article was excerpted from Worlds of Wonder © 2001 by David Gerrold. Used with permission of Writer's Digest Books, a division of F&W Publications. For credit card orders phone toll free 1-800-289-0963.*

something in your science fiction world, take a moment to ask a few necessary questions about it.

Theodore Sturgeon used to encourage would-be writers (and everyone else as well) to *ask the next question*. It was one of his best sermons and one of the best lessons a storyteller could learn. He used to wear a medallion of a *Q* with an arrow through it—his symbol for "Ask the next question." He gave that speech almost everywhere he went, and especially anytime anyone asked what the medallion meant.

He used to say, "The writer has to know what is in every nook and cranny of the story. You don't have to write it all down, but if you know what's there, it'll show."

So *after you build it, you have to move into it*. You have to look around, listen, taste, touch, smell, and *feel* what you have created—then report back, so the reader can feel it too. The reader wants to see the scenery, hear the music, taste the spices, pet the critters, smell the air, and most of all, he wants to feel the emotions. This is the *excitement of* science fiction: It gives the reader a chance to be someone else for a while—someone profoundly different; someone in a different universe, facing different challenges.

This is why science fiction and fantasy are sometimes called *escape literature*. They provide escape from reality—but in the hands of a good storyteller, the literature of imagination is also an access to something much more profound. Consider this thought:

Who you think you are is determined by the time and place in which you live.

Context is the largest part of identity—you know who you are by measuring yourself against your surroundings. A person living in a different world is going to have a different sense of who she is and what relationships are possible to her. The stranger the world, the stranger the forces working on the person, and the more bizarre the shape that person's identity will be bent into. And so, too the author of that world:

As you create your story, it takes on a reality of its own—and as you explore its workings, *you* metamorphose. Your thinking changes, your perceptions shift, you become a different person: You become the kind of person who can tell *this* story from the inside. If you succeed, then the way you describe events and places and characters will be as a resident would describe it, and it will feel to the reader as if you've been there yourself.

"There are two parts to a science fiction story. One is science. The other is fiction. The excitement is in the mix."

Consistency Key to Believable Fantasy

BY DAVID GERROLD

Where science fiction has a foundation rooted in the scientific knowledge of the real world, fantasy seems to have no such grounding at all. Fantasy looks like the abandonment of the laws of science. The map says, "Here there be dragons." Meaning: All previous statutes are null and void. They no longer apply. They've been repealed.

That's what it *looks like*.

Dig deeper.

Like science fiction, fantasy also starts out with an *if:*

- *What if* you found a book in the library that taught you how to be a wizard?
- *If* rabbits had a culture, what kind of legends would they have?
- *What if* a hobbit had to throw a magic ring into a volcano to save the world from evil?
- *If* a vampire gave an interview, what kind of story would he tell?
- *What if* a man's best friend was a six-foot-tall invisible rabbit?
- *If* the world was on the back of a giant turtle swimming through space, would NASA be launching spaceships to determine the sex of the turtle?
- *If* a little girl fell into a mirror, what would she find on the other side?
- *What if* the animals had a revolution and kicked all the humans off the farm and ran it themselves?
- *What if* a ghost was still in love with his wife?
- *What if* talking cats had to save New York City from a dimension-hopping evil spirit in the shape of a T. Rex?
- *What if* people started turning into rhinoceroses?
- *What if* people started turning green?
- *What if* people started growing fur all over their bodies?
- *What if* people suddenly started being born with tails?
- *What if* a man woke up one morning and found he had turned into a giant cockroach?
- *What if* a husband and wife could trade bodies, so each could see what the other's life was like?
- *If* human beings could wrap themselves into cocoons like caterpillars, what would they metamorphose into?
- *What if* a little boy fell into Santa's bag of toys?
- *What if* your teddy bear came to life?
- *What if* a talking dog, a telepathic duck, and a psychokinetic rabbit had the winning lotto ticket, but a malicious wizard was determined to turn them all into animal crackers?

Do you notice the difference here between science fiction and fantasy?

There is no limit to what you can postulate in fantasy. You can get pretty silly if you want.

DAVID GERROLD *is an award-winning writer of science fiction novels, short stories and screenplays. This article was excerpted from Worlds of Wonder © 2001 by David Gerrold. Used with permission of Writer's Digest Books, a division of F&W Publications. For credit card orders phone toll free 1-800-289-0963.*

Or you can get poignant, or satirical, or go for sheer epic grandeur. You can do allegory, metaphor, myth, or just sheer absurdity and leave it for the reader to figure out if it means anything.

When you ask a science fiction question, the first thing you have to do is root it in reality; you have to explain to yourself *why* it's possible, so you can believe in it yourself. In a fantasy story, you assume it's already possible, and you don't bother explaining the how or the why. In that respect, fantasy seems to offer much more freedom to the author: *freedom from explaining.* Go ahead, make something up! Anything. After all, this is fantasy, right?

Wrong.

The audience *still* wants to believe in your world—and believability comes from the recognition of an internally consistent system of logic. If things are not consistent, they are (literally!) *unbelievable.*

This is not some arbitrary rule. It's how the human mind works. The mind looks for connections. The mind synthesizes patterns as a key to comprehension. *The mind insists on structure.* Lack of structure is chaos. Without it, the mind flails. And if there is no immediately discernable structure, *the mind makes stuff up*—whatever is convenient, to fill the gap.

Don't take my word for it. *Test it yourself.*

Go out and ask people questions that you know they couldn't possibly know the answer to. "Who really killed Kennedy?" "Why was the third season of the original *Star Trek* so awful?" "When will he write the fifth book?" Out of a hundred people, you will be lucky to find five who are honest enough to say, "I don't know." The rest will make something up. Most people would rather die than admit they don't know something.

Try it. If you ever needed evidence of the mind's desperate need to create structure, it's always right there in front of you. Ask any human being a question that you know he or she can't answer. The human mind cannot stand not knowing something—it would rather have a wrong answer than no answer at all. So it'll grab the first idea it can, no matter how preposterous it might be . . . like a drowning man grabbing for the first anvil he sees.

The result is not information. It is misinformation. It is noise. It does not bring you closer to understanding—it pushes you farther away, because now there is all the made-up stuff you have to disregard before you can find out what's so.

What does this have to do with storytelling?

Simply this: If you don't have answers to the questions that your story engenders, you are casting your readers adrift in a sea of chaos. The reader will not understand what your story is really about or what it is you are trying to accomplish. Your job is to be the vessel, the sails, the compass, and the wind. Your job is to be the sight of land on the horizon. Because—

Fantasy is not the abandonment of logic. It is the reinvention of it. A believable fantasy is the creation of an *alternate* structure of logic. Fantasy is not simply the stuff you make up. Fantasy requires an underlying structure to unify your ideas. Like science, fantasy represents a consistent pattern of knowledge; the difference is that the fantasy map is not designed to map accurately to the real world.

Almost all fantasy relies on *personification*—that is, whatever happens in a fantasy, there is an anthropomorphic reason, *a causative agency:*

> "Who turns out the light in the refrigerator?"
> "A little man who lives inside, called Yehudi."
> "Dammit, why won't this car start?"
> "Gremlins."
> "Say a prayer to the god of parking places, otherwise we'll have to walk from the far end of the lot."
> "Why is Lennie so stupid?"
> "The brain fairy left a quarter under his pillow."
> "Make the stoplight change."

"I can't. It doesn't like you."

"You have to sacrifice a book to the television set, otherwise it'll only show reruns."

Nothing ever happens by accident in the fantasy world. Some phenomenon—supernatural or magic or otherwise—is responsible. *This is the logic of fantasy.* Fantasy is about the assignment of consciousness and reason. In fantasy, everything is conscious, or at least potentially conscious—animals, plants, rocks, machines, the wind. *Everything.*

The logic of fantasy grows out of the surreal logic of the human mind. The human mind is not by nature scientific. Rational thinking is a learned skill. (The front page of your daily newspaper should be regarded as evidence of this. Most minds are still untrained.)

Mind-logic starts as soon as children start learning to talk. As soon as they start associating symbols with things, they start trying to manipulate things by the symbols that connect to them. You teach a child a word, he believes the word has power over the thing. This is called "magical thinking." *If I wish real hard for something, it'll happen. I mustn't wish anything awful or it will happen. Step on a crack and you'll break your mother's back.*

"Magical thinking" presumes that the symbol that represents an object controls it, so what happens to the symbol, happens to the object (e.g., stick a pin in a voodoo doll and your worst enemy gets stabbing pains). This is the kind of logic that the immature mind uses as it tries to grasp some control over the physical universe. It doesn't work, but it takes most people about eight or nine years to figure that out. Some never do.

And because the mind has a great deal of difficulty presuming that anything ever happens without a mind as a causative agent, everything in the universe is therefore either alive or under the control of something alive. *There's a monster living in the closet. There are monsters under my bed. If I pull the covers over my head, they won't find me.* The mind, in becoming aware of itself, presumes that everything else *is also mind.*

As the individual grows, the mind develops other, more sophisticated logics. Some are bizarre, twisted, ugly, dangerous, and psychotic. Others are charming, eccentric, addled, fascinating, mysterious, oblique, and esoteric. There are many different systems of logic, and we step into the ones that serve us best—or that we *think* serve us best.

Most religions are built on self-contained systems of logic. Many human-resource courses present ways to train the mind in the logic of effectiveness. There are whole systems of psychology built around different definitions of mind-logic. But it's *all* mind-logic. *Everything.* (Including this book.) The mind is always trying to figure out how to work the universe, and it's always inventing logical constructions to apply.

It is this need for logic that is the source of all fantasy: "If I go to the bathroom now, the phone will ring." "If I get the car washed, it'll rain." "If I say the right prayers, God will grant my wish." "If I take personal responsibility for this, I can make it happen." The latter statement, at least, has a kernel of power in it.

(To be bluntly pragmatic about the whole thing: To the extent that any system empowers you to produce results, it works; to the extent that it defeats you and keeps you from producing results, it doesn't. If you believe it, it's true for you. If you don't believe it, it's superstition.)

Every great fantasy is built on a perceivable system of logic that—no matter how silly it might seem in the rational world—is still complete and consistent unto itself. If you have talking dogs in your story, then cats probably talk as well. If the wind whispers advice to your hero, then the brook probably babbles madly to itself. If vampires are afraid of crosses, then holy water probably burns them. If death for humans is a human-sized ghostly figure in a black hood carrying a scythe, then death for rats is a rat-sized figure in similar garb. If magic words can make supernatural things happen, then mispronouncing a magic word will have disastrous and dangerous results. If automobiles have souls, then airplanes do too. If the toaster can talk, then so can the vacuum cleaner. If there are no leprechaun nuns, then Paddy kissed a penguin. If Superman came from Krypton, then anyone else coming from Krypton will also have super powers. If Martian wishes can make stoplights change, then Martian wishes can also win a Hugo Award. If the washing machine has a sock-digester, then the dryer has a button-remover. Elevators travel in groups because only one of them knows the way. You'll find it in the last place you look. And never play cards with a man named Doc. If you're a police dog, show me your badge. Fantasy works by its own rules—*but it does have rules.*

You can make up any rules you want for your fantasy story—but once you set those rules, *you are bound by them.* You cannot break them; you cannot change them midway through the book. Doing that betrays the trust of the audience. Remember: If you are creating a world, you are behaving like a god—and gods don't cheat.

Both science fiction and fantasy take you to worlds that don't exist. Both require strict adherence to the rules and structures of believability. The difference is that science fiction is rooted in the logic of the physical universe, and fantasy is rooted in the logic of the personal universe—the logic of the mind. It is the reader's perception of a structure of underlying logic that makes a story credible.

The reader will suspend disbelief—he won't suspend common sense.

------

*"Science fiction is about what's possible.
Fantasy is about what's not. Fantasy is harder."*

What's Left Unsaid: Jean Hanff Korelitz on Psychological Horror

BY SANDRA GURVIS

"I'm very squeamish," admits Jean Hanff Korelitz. Yet *The Sabbathday River* (Farrar, Straus, and Giroux, 1999), her suspense-filled novel of ethical worlds colliding, centers around dead babies and debilitating illness. It opens when Naomi Roth, newly divorced yet desiring a child of her own, discovers the body of a newborn on the banks of the eponymous waterway in her small New Hampshire town.

Both Naomi and Heather Pratt—young, sexy, and openly having an affair with a married man—are considered outsiders, although in vastly different ways. A successful businesswoman and transplanted New Yorker, thirtysomething Naomi employs locals who create handmade rugs and quilts, and Heather is one of her best workers. At first the police suspect Naomi, but after hours of relentless grilling, Heather, rumored to have been pregnant by her lover, confesses to having murdered the child. Unconvinced, Naomi believes there's more to the situation than meets the eye. Another dead baby shows up, and chaos ensues, with accusations, small-town hatreds, and a dramatic trial gushing forth like an swollen stream after a thunderstorm.

In less skilled hands, *The Sabbathday River* could have been a gruesome potboiler, but it's been praised by reviewers and authors ranging from *Booklist* ("intense," and "powerful") to Rosellen Brown ("A rich and satisfying novel . . . fueled by sex, class, mystery, and terrific courtroom theater"). *Interview* weighed in with "scarily well-written," while *Publishers Weekly* concluded, "smart and engrossing, this thriller addresses the complex morality behind its characters' behavior with gravity and deep humanity." It was also a selection of the Book-of-the-Month and Quality Paperback Book Clubs, and along with several foreign editions "there have been some nibbles" with regard to a movie, Korelitz says.

The married mother of a two- and a nine-year-old, Korelitz is also queasy about being labeled a genre writer. "If you don't fit into a particular box—literary, horror, mystery, or whatever—it can be open season on the author. Fortunately, the response to the book has been terrific." Even men, who traditionally shy away from "women's" themes such as childbirth and infertility have recommended *The Sabbathday River* to their wives. It has also become fodder for lively discussion among reading groups.

A New York native who graduated cum laude in English from Dartmouth College and received her Master's from Clare College in Cambridge, England, Korelitz was a poet before attempting fiction. Her first book was a collection of poems, *The Properties of Breath* (Bloodaxe Books/Dufor Editions, 1988), followed by well-received courtroom tale, *A Jury of Her Peers* (Crown, 1996). She's penned (or perhaps more accurately, keyboarded) book reviews for *The New York Times*, *Washington Post*, *Sunday Times* of London and many more, as well as magazine articles for *Newsweek*, *Harper's Bazaar*, Salon.com, *Diversion*, *Seventeen* and others. Here she shares her thoughts about writing, horror, and creativity.

SANDRA GURVIS *is the author of eight nonfiction books, including* Careers for Nonconformists *(Marlowe, 2000), which was a selection of the Quality Paperback Book Club and the upcoming* Where Have All the Flower Children Gone? *(University Press of Mississippi) and* Day Trips from Columbus *(Globe Pequot). Her novel* The Pipe Dreamers *was published by Olmstead Press in 2001.*

Let's talk about the genesis of *The Sabbathday River*. How did you get the idea? What led up to it?

The story was inspired by true events. When I lived in Ireland in the 1980s, there was a bizarre murder case about a dead baby. A woman was arrested for the crime, and then another dead baby turned up. As it turned out, the police had gotten the wrong person, but by then the situation had escalated. The country became obsessed with it, like the O.J. case in the US. The powers-that-be felt they needed to charge the woman with something.

Although she was ultimately proved innocent of the first killing, the exposure tore her life apart. It's my opinion that she killed the second baby, which turned out to be her own child, but nothing was ever substantiated. I even interviewed her for what I hoped would turn out to be a magazine article, but it was a disaster. She seemed to be a completely blank slate, without guile, and I found myself reluctant to ask her whether she was guilty.

But I kept thinking about the incident, especially after I had my first child. It took me 15 years to start the book, but I couldn't get the image of two innocent victims and that unrepentant woman out of my mind.

Did you consciously insert an underlying classical or Biblical theme, so that it ended up being a strong morality tale?

Ireland is a primarily Catholic country, so the press was full of references to Baby Jesus, the Virgin Mary and so on. But that's not my background, which is in Judaism.

I saw it as sort of a Greek tragedy and because the bones of the story deal with religious faith, I was able to extrapolate the basic facts and work from there. From that point on, the novel took on a life of its own—Naomi and her best friend Judith are Jewish, for instance—and became a work of fiction.

How did you do the research?

Mostly I used interviews and newspaper accounts and as well as my own experiences to fill in gaps in the character and plots. I also consulted doctors, pharmacologists, and forensic experts.

Frankly, I dislike looking things up and taking notes or reading 50 books before beginning my own. So I write until I come to the next question and then find someone to answer it. I was lucky with *A Jury of Her Peers*, because lawyers are always willing to share their opinions and observations. With *The Sabbathday River*, I wrote about a third of the book before it really came together. I also created an outline which I never looked at again after I started the actual writing.

Your characters play a large part in creating the novel's Gothic, almost chilling atmosphere. What techniques did you employ to make them into flesh-and-blood people, rather than the "monsters" so often found in horror fiction?

I see a lot of myself in Naomi. I think I might have been like her if I'd made some other choices in my twenties. But she can be very obtuse and I don't always appreciate that. Judith is someone who's retained much of her '60s idealism, which I also admire, but she has done terrible things. Heather is nominally the heroine of the novel, but she makes appalling decisions, and I think my occasional disdain for her is probably apparent. None of my characters were particularly likeable.

Everyone has a not-so-lovely side, and people aren't always what they appear to be. You can hold someone in high regard, and then find out what they've actually done. What are your feelings then? What if you find you can't quite condemn them for their crimes? And what does it say about you if you can't?

How long did it take you to write? Was it a smooth flow or a series of stops and starts? Did you do a lot of rewriting?

I started the novel in 1996 and finished two years later. It was a daily process, and I simply took it one page at a time. There was very little revision, either on my part or the editor's, because

I think I wrote fairly slowly and polished the material as I went along.

But for me, beginning a novel is like pulling teeth. I don't really know if it's going to work until I'm two-thirds of the way through. It's like assuming facts that aren't yet in evidence. Yet the writer must immediately make decisions such as, what color is this person's hair? Then you go back over what you've done later, and say, how could I have described her as a brunette when she was clearly a blonde? But once I had completed the entire manuscript, I did very little revising.

Did you have difficulty finding a publisher? What was the reaction of editors?

At first we gave it to the editor of *A Jury of Her Peers*, who basically wanted a sequel to that book. But I said no, so my agent and I set sail on the rocky seas of publishing. We were turned down by several houses; one editor wanted a whodunit with Naomi as a girl detective. I was tempted by that idea but decided to stick to my original concept.

Then we found a person who loved it and eventually he became the editor. After that, everything was great. We sold the book on the first 100 pages and outline, although the final result was far from the latter.

Did you consider the implications of psychological horror, especially in terms of the vivid descriptions found in the book? Were you ever tempted to present the more graphic violence found in some standard horror novels?

I refuse to write about graphic violence, and am repelled by certain bestselling novelists who do. There's enough brutality in this world and I abhor anything that makes it seem appetizing, intriguing or seductive.

In the case of Naomi, the reader senses beforehand—as does Naomi through flashbacks and other bad memories—that's she's about to find the body of a dead baby. By going into her head and playing upon her worst fears, a scenario is created that is insidious and subtle yet conveys a sense of fear.

What is involved in the skillful execution of psychological horror?

First, you need to realize that whatever lurks in someone's psyche is far more terrifying than anything that might jump out of a closet. A writer needs to learn how to control that fear, and how to release it when the time is right. Consider "The Monkey's Paw," one of the scariest stories ever written. What makes it so powerful is the fact that we never see what's beyond the front door.

How did you come to writing? What drew you to fiction? How did you make the leap from poetry to fiction?

Writing was the only thing I ever wanted to do. I attended the Ethical Culture School in New York City, which was founded by humanists, and it instilled a love of books in me. I saw how they could reach out into the world and touch people's minds and hearts.

At first I only wrote poetry, although I aspired to fiction and had some book reviews and magazine articles published while in college. After I'd married and lived in another country I decided I'd had enough life experience, that I was no longer an empty vessel whose poetic range was limited to one topic—me. Not many people are interested in reading about that!

So I started writing fiction, including two novels which remain unpublished. One was too autobiographical, while the other was wispy and literary. Nor was short fiction my genre: it takes too much effort to create characters who will only live for five or six pages. Once I realized that you can read the paper and find ideas for five novels, I discovered an abundance of fascinating topics to write about. My last two books were sparked by things in the outside world and that's why I think they worked.

Do you have any plans for future books? Do you see yourself becoming drawn more and more to one particular type of story line or plot?

I'm in the very early stages of a new book about a young Jewish woman who comes to believe she's the granddaughter of Hermann Goering. It's set in the 1930s, so it requires a lot of the dreaded research. I don't know where it's going yet exactly, but it does involve some pretty horrible things.

It's difficult to quantify what attracts me to a topic. It begins an idea that niggles at me and won't let go. *A Jury of Her Peers* was sparked by a dream I had of a courthouse, and a jury sitting there, motionless.

Do you have any suggestions for writers who want to hone their skills in psychological horror or simply want to improve their craft?

I've noticed that it's easier to establish an atmosphere of peril than to resolve it. If some evil thing is threatening to take over the world, you need to think of a very plausible way to get rid of it, otherwise you'll have disappointed and angry readers. Having the characters hold hands and visualize world peace or making whatever it is disappear on its own just doesn't cut it.

Writers need to whittle down the menace to a manageable level. For instance, in *Salem's Lot*, Stephen King's malevolent vampire is a finite entity who threatens a small town, person by person, and is extremely real and frightening. Other King novels feature beings which seem omnipotent and undefeatable, and it's far more difficult to convincingly eradicate these. Creating a horror that's both believable and seemingly omnipresent and then making it go away in a convincing manner is of the most difficult challenges a writer of horror can face.

"It's easier to establish an atmosphere of peril than to resolve it. If some evil thing is threatening to take over the world, you need to think of a very plausible way to get rid of it, otherwise you'll have disappointed and angry readers. Creating a horror that's both believable and seemingly omnipresent and then making it go away in a convincing manner is one of the most difficult challenges a writer of horror can face."

Science Fiction/Fantasy & Horror Markets Appearing in This Book

Below is a list of science fiction/fantasy & horror markets appearing in this edition of *Novel & Short Story Writer's Market*. For complete information—including who to contact and how to submit your science fiction/fantasy & horror manuscript—turn to the page number provided.

Magazines (Fantasy)

SCIENCE FICTION/FANTASY & HORROR MARKETS INDEX

Magazines (Science Fiction)

Magazines (Horror)

Book Publishers (Fantasy)

Book Publishers (Science Fiction)

Book Publishers (Horror)

Resources for Science Fiction/ Fantasy & Horror Writers

Below is a list of invaluable resources specifically for science fiction and fantasy writers. For more information on the magazines and organizations listed below, check the General Index and the Publications of Interest and Organizations sections of this book. To order any of the Writer's Digest Books titles or to get a consumer book catalog, call 1-800-289-0963. You may also order Writer's Digest Books selections through www.writersdigest.com, Amazon.com, or www.barnes andnoble.com.

MAGAZINES:
- *Locus*, P.O. Box 13305, Oakland CA 94661. E-mail: locus@locusmag.com.
- *Science Fiction Chronicle*, P.O. Box 022730, Brooklyn NY 11202-0056. (718)643-9011. Fax: (718)522-3308. E-mail: sf_chronicle@compuserve.com.
- *Writer's Digest*, 1507 Dana Ave., Cincinnati OH 45207. Website: www.writersdigest.com.

BOOKS:
Science Fiction Writing series (Writer's Digest Books)
- *Aliens and Alien Societies: A Writer's Guide to Creating Extraterrestrial Life-forms*
- *Space Travel: A Writer's Guide to the Science of Interplanetary and Interstellar Travel*
- *Time Travel: A Writer's Guide to the Real Science of Plausible Time Travel*

Other Writer's Digest books for science fiction & fantasy writers:
- *Worlds of Wonder, How to Write Science Fiction and Fantasy* (Gerrold)
- *How to Write Science Fiction & Fantasy* (Card)
- *The Craft of Writing Science Fiction That Sells*
- *How to Write Tales of Horror, Fantasy & Science Fiction*
- *Science Fiction and Fantasy Writer's Sourcebook, 2nd Edition*
- *The Writer's Complete Fantasy Reference*
- *Writing Horror*

ORGANIZATIONS & ONLINE:
- Science Fiction & Fantasy Writers of America, Inc., P.O. Box 171, Unity ME 04988-0171. E-mail: execdir@sfwa.org. Website: www.sfwa.org/.
- Con-Tour: www.con-tour.com.
- Books and Writing Online: www.interzone.com/Books/books.html.
- www.writersmarket.com.

The Markets

Important Listing Information

- Listings are not advertisements. Although the information here is as accurate as possible, the listings are not endorsed or guaranteed by the editor of *Novel & Short Story Writer's Market*.
- *Novel & Short Story Writer's Market* reserves the right to exclude any listing that does not meet its requirements.

Key to Symbols and Abbreviations

N New listing in all sections
★ Canadian listing
⊕ International listing
A Agented material only
✔ Listing includes change in contact name, address or phone
▣ Online publication
▼ Award-winning publication
$ Market pays money
⊘ Accepts no submissions
◔ Actively seeking beginning writers
◐ Seeking new and established writers
◉ Prefers working with established writers, mostly referrals
◎ Only handles specific types of work
● Comment by editor of *Novel & Short Story Writer's Market*
ms—manuscript; **mss**-manuscripts
b&w—black and white
SASE—self-addressed, stamped envelope
SAE—self-addressed envelope
IRC—International Reply Coupon, for use on reply mail from other countries

(See Glossary for definitions of words and expressions used in writing and publishing.)

Complaint Procedure

If you feel you have not been treated fairly by a listing in *Novel & Short Story Writer's Market*, we advise you to take the following steps:

- First try to contact the listing. Sometimes one phone call or a letter can quickly clear up the matter.
- Document all your correspondence with the listing. When you write to us with a complaint, provide the details of your submission, the date of your first contact with the listing and the nature of your subsequent correspondence.
- We will enter your letter into our files and attempt to contact the listing.
- The number and severity of complaints will be considered in our decision whether or not to delete the listing from the next edition.

Literary Agents

Many publishers are willing to look at unsolicited submissions but most feel having an agent is to the writer's best advantage. In this section we include 60+ agents who specialize in fiction, or publish a significant amount of fiction. These agents were also selected because of their openness to submissions from writers.

The commercial fiction field is intensely competitive. Many publishers have smaller staffs and less time. For that reason, more book publishers are relying on agents for new talent. Some publishers are even relying on agents as "first readers" who must wade through the deluge of submissions from writers to find the very best. For writers, a good agent can be a foot in the door—someone willing to do the necessary work to put your manuscript in the right editor's hands.

It would seem today that finding a good agent is as hard as finding a good publisher. Yet those writers who have agents say they are invaluable. Not only can a good agent help you make your work more marketable, an agent acts as your business manager and adviser, keeping your interests up front during and even after contract negotiations.

Still, finding an agent can be very difficult for a new writer. If you are already published in magazines, you have a better chance than someone with no publishing credits. (Many agents routinely read periodicals searching for new writers.) Although many agents do read queries and manuscripts from unpublished authors without introduction, referrals from their writer clients can be a big help. If you don't know any published authors with agents, you may want to attend a conference as a way of meeting agents. Some agents even set aside time at conferences to meet new writers.

All the agents listed here have said they are open to working with new, previously unpublished writers as well as published writers. Most do not charge a fee to cover the time and effort involved in reviewing a manuscript or a synopsis and chapters.

USING THE LISTINGS

It is especially important when contacting these busy agents that you read individual listings carefully before submitting anything. The first information after the company name includes the address and phone, fax and e-mail address (when available). **Member Agents** gives the names of individual agents working at that company (specific types of fiction an agent handles are indicated in parenthesis after that agent's name). The **Represents:** section lists the types of fiction the agency works with. **Needs** includes any specific types of fiction the agency is currently looking for, as well as what they do not want to see. Reading the **Recent Sales** gives you the names of writers an agent is currently working with and, very importantly, publishers the agent has placed manuscripts with. **Writers' Conferences** identifies conferences an agent attends (and where you might possibly meet that agent). **Tips** presents advice directly from the agent to authors.

THE AHEARN AGENCY, INC., 2021 Pine St., New Orleans LA 70118-5456. (504)861-8395. Fax: (504)866-6434. E-mail: pahearn@aol.com. **Contact:** Pamela G. Ahearn. Estab. 1992. Member of RWA. Represents 25 clients. 20% of clients are new/unpublished writers. Currently handles: 15% nonfiction books; 85% novels.

● Prior to opening her agency, Ms. Ahearn was an agent for eight years and an editor with Bantam Books.

Represents: Nonfiction books; novels; short story collections (if stories previously published). **Considers these fiction areas:** action/adventure; contemporary issues; detective/police/crime; ethnic; family saga; fantasy; feminist; gay/lesbian; glitz; historical; horror; humor/satire; juvenile; literary; mainstream/contemporary; mystery/suspense; psychic/supernatural; regional; romance; science fiction; thriller; westerns/frontier.

O━ This agency specializes in historical romance; also very interested in mysteries and suspense fiction. Does not want to receive category romance.

How to Contact: Query with SASE. Accepts e-mail queries, but no attachments. Considers simultaneous queries. Responds in 1 month to queries; 10 weeks to mss. Obtains most new clients through recommendations from others, solicitations, conferences.

Recent Sales: *Still of the Night*, by Meagan McKinney (Kensington); *A Notorious Love*, by Sabrina Jeffries (Avon); *Black Lotus*, by Laura Joh Rowland (St. Martin's Press).

Terms: Agent receives 15% commission on domestic sales; 20% commission on foreign sales. Offers written contract, binding for 1 year; renewable by mutual consent.

Writers' Conferences: Midwest Writers Workshop; Moonlight & Magnolias; RWA National Conference (Orlando); Virginia Romance Writers (Williamsburg VA); Florida Romance Writers (Ft. Lauderdale FL); Golden Triangle Writers Conference; Bouchercon (Monterey, November).

Tips: "Be professional! Always send in exactly what an agent/editor asks for, no more, no less. Keep query letters brief and to the point, giving your writing credentials and a very brief summary of your book. If one agent rejects you, keep trying—there are a lot of us out there!"

◐ **MIRIAM ALTSHULER LITERARY AGENCY**, 53 Old Post Rd. N., Red Hook NY 12571. (845)758-9408. Fax: (845)758-3118. E-mail: malalit@ulster.net. **Contact:** Miriam Altshuler. Estab. 1994. Member of AAR. Represents 40 clients. Currently handles: 45% nonfiction books; 45% novels; 5% story collections; 5% juvenile books.

• Ms. Altshuler has been an agent since 1982.

Represents: Nonfiction books; novels; short story collections; juvenile books. **Considers these fiction areas:** literary; mainstream/contemporary; multicultural; thriller.

How to Contact: Query with SASE. Prefers to read materials exclusively. No e-mail or fax queries. Considers simultaneous queries. Responds in 2 weeks to queries; 3 weeks to mss. Returns materials only with SASE. Obtains most new clients through recommendations from others.

Terms: Agent receives 15% commission on domestic sales; 20% commission on foreign sales. No written contract. Charges clients for overseas mailing, photocopies, overnight mail when requested by author.

Writers' Conferences: Bread Loaf Writers' Conference (Middlebury VT, August).

◐ **MARCIA AMSTERDAM AGENCY**, 41 W. 82nd St., New York NY 10024-5613. (212)873-4945. **Contact:** Marcia Amsterdam. Estab. 1970. Signatory of WGA. Currently handles: 15% nonfiction books; 70% novels; 5% movie scripts; 10% TV scripts.

• Prior to opening her agency, Ms. Amsterdam was an editor.

Represents: Nonfiction books; novels. **Considers these fiction areas:** action/adventure; detective/police/crime; horror; humor/satire; mainstream/contemporary; mystery/suspense; romance (contemporary, historical); science fiction; thriller; westerns/frontier; young adult.

Also Handles: Feature film; TV movie of the week; sitcom. **Considers these script subject areas:** comedy; mainstream; mystery/suspense; romantic comedy; romantic drama.

How to Contact: Submit outline, 3 sample chapter(s), SASE. Responds in 1 month to queries.

Recent Sales: *Rosey in the Present Tense*, by Louise Hawes (Walker); *Flash Factor*, by William H. Lovejoy (Kensington). *Movie/TV MOW script(s) optioned/sold:* *Mad About You*, by Jenna Bruce (Columbia Tristar TV).

Terms: Agent receives 15% commission on domestic sales; 20% commission on foreign sales; 10% commission on dramatic rights sales. Offers written contract, binding for 1 year. Charges clients for extra office expenses, foreign postage, copying, legal fees (when agreed upon).

Tips: "We are always looking for interesting literary voices."

◐ **APPLESEEDS MANAGEMENT**, 200 E. 30th St., Suite 302, San Bernardino CA 92404. (909)882-1667. **Contact:** S. James Foiles. Estab. 1988. 40% of clients are new/unpublished writers. Currently handles: 15% nonfiction books; 85% novels.

Represents: Nonfiction books; novels. **Considers these fiction areas:** detective/police/crime; mystery/suspense.

How to Contact: Query with SASE. Responds in 2 weeks to queries; 2 months to mss.

Recent Sales: This agency prefers not to share information on specific sales.

Terms: Agent receives 10-15% commission on domestic sales; 20% commission on foreign sales. Offers written contract, binding for 1-7 years.

Tips: "Appleseeds specializes in mysteries with a detective who could be in a continuing series because readership of mysteries is expanding."

N ◙ **PAM BERNSTEIN & ASSOCIATES, INC.**, 790 Madison Ave., Suite 310, New York NY 10021. (212)288-1700. Fax: (212)288-3054. **Contact:** Pam Bernstein or Jonette Suitele. Estab. 1992. Member of AAR. Represents 50 clients. 20% of clients are new/unpublished writers. Currently handles: 50% nonfiction books; 50% novels.
  ● Prior to becoming an agent, Ms. Bernstein served as vice president with the William Morris Agency.
Represents: Nonfiction books; novels. **Considers these fiction areas:** contemporary issues; ethnic; historical; mainstream/contemporary; mystery/suspense; romance (contemporary); thriller.
How to Contact: Query with SASE. Responds in 2 weeks to queries.
Recent Sales: Sold 25 titles in the last year. *Her Daughter's Eyes*, by Jessica Barksdale Inclen; *Canyon Ranch Guide to Living Younger Longer*, (Simon & Schuster).
Terms: Agent receives 15% commission on domestic sales; 20% commission on foreign sales. Offers written contract, binding for 3 years; 30 days notice must be given to terminate contract. 100% of business is derived from commissions on sales. Charges clients for postage and photocopying.

◙ **MEREDITH BERNSTEIN LITERARY AGENCY**, 2112 Broadway, Suite 503A, New York NY 10023. (212)799-1007. Fax: (212)799-1145. Estab. 1981. Member of AAR. Represents 100 clients. 20% of clients are new/unpublished writers. Currently handles: 50% nonfiction books; 50% novels.
  ● Prior to opening her agency, Ms. Bernstein served in another agency for 5 years.
Member Agents: Meredith Bernstein; Elizabeth Cavanaugh
Represents: Nonfiction books; novels. **Considers these fiction areas:** literary; mystery/suspense; romance; women's fiction.
  O→ This agency does not specialize, "very eclectic."
How to Contact: Query with SASE. No e-mail or fax queries. Considers simultaneous queries. Obtains most new clients through recommendations from others, conferences, also develops and packages own ideas.
Recent Sales: *Phatphonics*, by Marion Blanck (Pocher); *7 Steps on the Written Path*, by Nancy Pickard & Lynn Lott (Ballantine).
Terms: Agent receives 15% commission on domestic sales; 20% commission on foreign sales. Charges clients $75 disbursement fee/year.
Writers' Conferences: Southwest Writers Conference (Albuquereque, August); Rocky Moutnain Writers' Conference (Denver, September); Golden Triangle (Beaumont TX, October); Pacific Northwest Writers Conference; Austin League Writers Conference; Willamette Writers Conference (Portland, OR); Lafayette Writers Conference (Lafayette, LA); Surrey Writers Conference (Surrey, BC.); San Diego State University Writers Conference (San Diego, CA).

N **BOOKENDS, LLC**, 136 Long Hill Rd., Gillette NJ 07933. (908)604-2652. E-mail: editor@bookends-inc.com. Website: www.bookends-inc.com. **Contact:** Jessica Faust or Jacky Sach. Estab. 1999. Member of American Book Producers Association. Represents 10 clients. 75% of clients are new/unpublished writers. Currently handles: 50% nonfiction books; 50% novels.
  ● Prior to opening their agency, Ms. Faust and Ms. Sach worked at such publishing houses as Berkley, Macmillan and IDG.
Member Agents: Jessica Faust (romance, relationships, business, finance, pets, general self-help); Jacky Sach (suspense thrillers, mysteries, literary fiction, spirituality, pets, general self-help)
Represents: Nonfiction books; novels. **Considers these fiction areas:** contemporary issues; detective/police/crime; ethnic; family saga; feminist; glitz; historical; literary; mainstream/contemporary; mystery/suspense; romance; thriller; young adult.
  O→ BookEnds specializes in genre fiction and personality driven nonfiction. Actively seeking romance, mystery, women's fiction, literary fiction and suspense thrillers. For nonfiction, relationships, business, general self-help, women's interest, parenting, pets, spirituality, health and psychology. Does not want to receive children's books, screenplays, science fiction, poetry.
How to Contact: Submit outline, 3 sample chapter(s), or submit complete ms. Considers simultaneous queries. Responds in 2 weeks to queries; 6 weeks to mss. Returns materials only with SASE. Obtains most new clients through recommendations from others, solicitations, conferences.
Recent Sales: Sold 10 titles in the last year. *The Complete Idiot's Guide to Women's History*, by Sonia Weiss (Macmillan); *Critical Lives: Che Guevara*, by Eric Luther (Macmillan); *Court TV's You Be the Judge*, by Patrick J. Sauer (Warner).
Terms: Agent receives 15% commission on domestic sales; 20% commission on foreign sales. Offers written contract. Charges clients for photocopying, messenger, cables, overseas postage, long-distance phone calls, copies of the published book when purchases for subsidiary rights submissions. Expenses will not exceed $150.
Writers' Conferences: Harriette Austin Conference (Athens GA, July 2001).
Tips: "When submitting material be sure to include any information that might be helpful to the agent. In your query letter you should include the title of the book, your name, your publishing history and a brief 1 or 2

sentence description of the book. Also be sure to let the agent know if you see this book as part of a series and if you've already begun work on other books. Once an agent has expressed interest in representing you it is crucial to let her know who has seen your book and even supply copies of any correspondence you've had with prospective editors."

⬤ THE JOAN BRANDT AGENCY, 788 Wesley Dr., Atlanta GA 30305-3933. (404)351-8877. **Contact:** Joan Brandt. Estab. 1980. Represents 30 clients. 50% of clients are new/unpublished writers. Currently handles: 45% nonfiction books; 45% novels; 10% juvenile books.
Represents: Nonfiction books; novels; short story collections. **Considers these fiction areas:** contemporary issues; detective/police/crime; family saga; literary; mainstream/contemporary; mystery/suspense; thriller.
How to Contact: Query with SASE. No e-mail or fax queries. Considers simultaneous queries. Returns materials only with SASE. Obtains most new clients through solicitations.
Recent Sales: This agency prefers not to share information on specific sales.
Terms: Agent receives 15% commission on domestic sales; 20% commission on foreign sales. No written contract.

⬤ MARIA CARVAINIS AGENCY, INC., 1350 Avenue of the Americas, Suite 2905, New York NY 10019. (212)245-6365. Fax: (212)245-7196. E-mail: mca@mariacarvainisagency.com. **Contact:** Maria Carvainis, Frances Kuffel. Estab. 1977. Member of AAR, Authors Guild, ABA, MWA, RWA; signatory of WGA. Represents 70 clients. 10% of clients are new/unpublished writers. Currently handles: 34% nonfiction books; 65% novels; 1% poetry.
   ● Prior to opening her agency, Ms. Carvainis spent more than 10 years in the publishing industry as a senior editor with Macmillan Publishing, Basic Books, Avon Books, where she worked closely with Peter Mayer and Crown Publishers. Ms. Carvainis has served as a member of the AAR Board of Directors and AAR Treasurer, as well as serving as chair of the AAR Contracts Committee. She presently serves on the AAR Royalty Committee.
Member Agents: Frances Kuffel (Executive Vice President).
Represents: Nonfiction books; novels. **Considers these fiction areas:** fantasy; historical; literary; mainstream/ contemporary; mystery/suspense; romance; thriller; young adult.
   ⦿╖ Does not want to receive science fiction or children's.
How to Contact: Query with SASE. Responds in 3 weeks to queries; 3 months to mss. Obtains most new clients through recommendations from others, solicitations, conferences, 60% from conferences/referrals; 40% from query letters.
Recent Sales: *The Switch and Envy*, by Sandra Brown (Warner Books); *The Guru Guide to the Knowledge Economy*, by Joseph H. Boyett and Jimmie T. Boyett (John Wiley and Sonts); *Trophy Widow*, by Michael Kahn (TOR/Forge); *Paint It Black*, by P.J. Parrish (Kensington); *Heroin*, by Charlie Smith (W.W. Norton); *Last Breath*, by Peter Stark (Ballantine); *The Devil's Hearth*, by Phillip DePoy (St. Martin's Press); *Private Captain*, by Marty Crisp (Philomel). Other clients include Mary Balogh, David Bottoms, Pam Conrad, Cindy Gerard, Sarah Isidore, Samantha James, Kristine Rolofson, William Sessions, Jose Yglesias, Fred Haefele, D. Anna Love, Fred Willard.
Terms: Agent receives 15% commission on domestic sales; 20% commission on foreign sales. Offers written contract, binding for 2 years. Charges clients for foreign postage, bulk copying.
Writers' Conferences: BEA; Frankfurt Book Fair.

Ⓝ ⬤ RUTH COHEN, INC. LITERARY AGENCY, P.O. Box 2244, La Jolla CA 92038-2244. (858)456-5805. **Contact:** Ruth Cohen. Estab. 1982. Member of AAR, Authors Guild, Sisters in Crime, RWA, SCBWI. Represents 45 clients. 15% of clients are new/unpublished writers. Currently handles: 5% nonfiction books; 60% novels; 35% juvenile books.
   ● Prior to becoming an agent, Ms. Cohen served as directing editor at Scott Foresman & Company (now HarperCollins).
Represents: Novels (adult); juvenile books. **Considers these fiction areas:** ethnic; historical; juvenile; literary; mainstream/contemporary; mystery/suspense; picture books; young adult.
   ⦿╖ This agency specializes in "quality writing in contemporary fiction, women's fiction, mysteries, thrillers and juvenile fiction." Does not want to receive poetry, westerns, film scripts or how-to books.
How to Contact: Submit outline, 1 sample chapter(s). Responds in 3 weeks to queries. Returns materials only with SASE. Obtains most new clients through recommendations from others, solicitations.
Recent Sales: This agency prefers not to share information on specific sales.
Terms: Agent receives 15% commission on domestic sales; 20% commission on foreign sales. Offers written contract, binding for 1 year. Charges for foreign postage, phone calls, photocopying submissions and overnight delivery of mss when appropriate.

Tips: "As the publishing world merges and changes, there seem to be fewer opportunities for new writers to succeed in the work that they love. We urge you to develop the patience, persistence and preseverance that have made this agency so successful. Prepare a well-written and well-crafted manuscript, and our combined best efforts can help advance both our careers."

◎ **CONNOR LITERARY AGENCY**, 2911 W. 71st St., Minneapolis MN 55423. (612)866-1426. Fax: (612)869-4074. E-mail: coolmkc@aol.com. **Contact:** Marlene Connor Lynch. Estab. 1985. Represents 50 clients. 30% of clients are new/unpublished writers. Currently handles: 50% nonfiction books; 50% novels.
• Prior to opening her agency, Ms. Connor served at the Literary Guild of America, Simon and Schuster and Random House. She is author of *What is Cool: Understanding Black Manhood in America* (Crown).
Member Agents: Deborah Coker (children's books); John Lynch (assistant).
Represents: Nonfiction books; novels; juvenile books; especially with a minority slant. **Considers these fiction areas:** horror; literary; mainstream/contemporary; multicultural; mystery/suspense; romance (suspense); thriller; women's.
○┯ This agency specializes in popular fiction and nonfiction.
How to Contact: Query with SASE, outline. Responds in 1 month to queries; 6 weeks to mss. Obtains most new clients through recommendations from others, solicitations, conferences, grapevine.
Recent Sales: *Outrageous Commitments*, by Ronn Elmore (HarperCollins); *Seductions*, by Snow Starborn (Sourcebooks).
Terms: Agent receives 15% commission on domestic sales; 25% commission on foreign sales. Offers written contract, binding for 1 year.
Writers' Conferences: Howard University Publishing Institute; Mid-West Romance Writer's Conference; BEA; Agents, Agents, Agents; Texas Writer's Conference; Detroit Writer's Conference.
Tips: "Seeking previously published writers with good sales records and new writers with real talent."

◎ **CORE CREATIONS, LLC**, 9024 S. Sanderling Way, Littleton CO 80126. (303)683-6792. E-mail: agent@eoncity.com. Website: www.eoncity.com/agent. **Contact:** Calvin Rex. Estab. 1994. Represents 10 clients. 70% of clients are new/unpublished writers. Currently handles: 30% nonfiction books; 60% novels; 5% novellas; 5% games.
• Prior to becoming an agent, Mr. Rex managed a small publishing house.
Member Agents: Calvin Rex.
Represents: Nonfiction books; novels; novellas. **Considers these fiction areas:** detective/police/crime; horror; science fiction.
○┯ This agency specializes in "bold, daring literature." Agency has strong "experience with royalty contracts and licensing agreements."
How to Contact: Query with SASE, proposal package, outline. Responds in 3 weeks to queries; 3 months to mss. Obtains most new clients through recommendations from others, solicitations, through the Internet.
Terms: Agent receives 15% commission on domestic sales; 20% commission on foreign sales. Offers written contract. Charges clients for postage (applicable mailing costs).
Writers' Conferences: Steamboat Springs Writers Group (Colorado, July); Rocky Mountain Fiction Writers Colorado Gold Conference.
Tips: "Have all material proofread. Visit our webpage before sending anything. We want books that dare to be different. Give us a unique angle, a new style of writing, something that stands out from the crowd!"

☑ ◎ **CRAWFORD LITERARY AGENCY**, 94 Evans Rd., Barnstead NH 03218. (603)269-5851. Fax: (603)269-2533. E-mail: CrawfordLit@att.net. **Contact:** Susan Crawford. Estab. 1988. Represents 40 clients. 10% of clients are new/unpublished writers. Currently handles: 50% nonfiction books; 50% novels.
Member Agents: Susan Crawford; Lorne Crawford (commercial fiction); Scott Neister (scientific/techno thrillers); Kristen Hales (parenting, psychology, New Age, self help).
Represents: Nonfiction books; novels (commercial fiction). **Considers these fiction areas:** action/adventure; mystery/suspense; thriller (medical).
○┯ This agency specializes in celebrity and/or media-based books and authors. Actively seeking action/adventure stories, medical thrillers, suspense thrillers, suspense thrillers, celebrity projects, self-help, inspirational, how-to and women's issues. Does not want to receive short stories, poetry.
How to Contact: Query with SASE. No e-mail or fax queries. Responds in 3 weeks to queries. Returns materials only with SASE. Obtains most new clients through recommendations from others, solicitations, conferences.
Recent Sales: Sold 22 titles in the last year. *Krane on Producing*, by Jonathan D. Krane (Renaissance Books); *The John Lennon Affair*, by Robert S. Levinson (Forge Books); *Housebroken*, by Richard Karn and George Mair (HarperCollins); *With Ossie & Ruby*, by Ruby Dee and Ossie Davis (William Morrow); *PSI/Net*, by Billy Dee Williams and Rob MacGregor (TOR/Forge). Other clients include John Travolta, Billy Dee Williams, Producer Jonathan Krane.

Terms: Agent receives 15% commission on domestic sales; 20% commission on foreign sales. Offers written contract, binding for 90 days; 100% of business is derived from commissions on ms sales.

Writers' Conferences: International Film & Writers Workshop (Rockport ME); Maui Writers Conference

N ◑ DARHANSOFF & VERRILL LITERARY AGENTS, 236 W. 26th St., Suite 802, New York NY 10001. (917)305-1300. Fax: (917)305-1400. Estab. 1975. Member of AAR. Represents 100 clients. 10% of clients are new/unpublished writers. Currently handles: 25% nonfiction books; 60% novels; 15% story collections.

Member Agents: Liz Darhansoff; Charles Verrill; Leigh Feldman; Tal Gregory.

Represents: Nonfiction books; novels; short story collections. **Considers these fiction areas:** literary; mystery/suspense.

   O-π Specializes in literary fiction.

How to Contact: Query with SASE. Responds in 2 weeks to queries. Obtains most new clients through recommendations from others.

Recent Sales: *At Home in Mitford*, by Jan Karon (Viking); *Cold Mountain*, by Charles Frazier (Atlantic Monthly Press). Other clients include Arthur Golden.

☑ ◐ ELITE ONLINE, P.O. Box 145, Highspire PA 17034-0145. (717)948-0666. Fax: (717)948-4131. E-mail: DannyBoy_17034@yahoo.com. **Contact:** Daniel M. Kane. Estab. 2000. Represents 10 clients. 40% of clients are new/unpublished writers. Currently handles: 90% novels; 10% story collections.

Member Agents: Daniel M. Kane; Alma Maria Garcia (science fiction).

Represents: Novels; short story collections. **Considers these fiction areas:** action/adventure; feminist; gay/lesbian; horror; humor/satire; psychic/supernatural; science fiction.

   O-π This agency no longer specializes in the placement of e-books, but focuses on print publication almost exclusively. "We offer quick response time whenever possible, and the author never pays reading fees or for editorial assistance. We make an investment of time in each of our authors."

How to Contact: Submit synopsis, with complete ms; include sufficient postage if return is requested. Prefers to read materials exclusively. Electronic copy may be requested at a later time. Responds in under 2 to mss. Obtains most new clients through solicitations.

Recent Sales: This agency prefers not to share information on specific sales.

Terms: Agent receives 15% commission on print sales, 18% on direct electronic sales commission on domestic sales. Offers written contract, binding for 14 months.; 90-day notice must be given to terminate contract. Charges clients prior to sale for photocopying, printing, postage.

Tips: "To paraphrase Clive Barker, no matter how dark or bizarre your imagination, there's probably a market for your work. When in doubt, submit. Include your e-mail address, where most of our correspondence takes place. Our pet peeve is problems with basic grammar/spelling. We represent no one exclusively (unless requested), but rather on a per project basis. When doing gay characters, no stereotypes. No religious material."

◐ ETHAN ELLENBERG LITERARY AGENCY, 548 Broadway, #5-E, New York NY 10012. (212)431-4554. Fax: (212)941-4652. E-mail: agent@ethanellenberg.com. Website: www.ethanellenberg.com. **Contact:** Ethan Ellenberg, Michael Psaltis. Estab. 1983. Represents 80 clients. 10% of clients are new/unpublished writers. Currently handles: 25% nonfiction books; 75% novels.

   ● Prior to opening his agency, Mr. Ellenberg was contracts manager of Berkley/Jove and associate contracts manager for Bantam.

Member Agents: Michael Psaltis (commercial fiction, literary fiction, mysteries, cookbooks, women's fiction, popular science and other unique nonfiction); Ethan Ellenberg.

Represents: Nonfiction books; novels. **Considers these fiction areas:** detective/police/crime; family saga; fantasy; historical; juvenile; literary; mainstream/contemporary; mystery/suspense; picture books; romance; science fiction; thriller; young adult.

   O-π This agency specializes in commercial fiction, especially thrillers and romance/women's fiction. "We also do a lot of children's books." Actively seeking commercial and literary fiction, children's books, break-through nonfiction. Does not want to receive poetry, short stories, westerns, autobiographies.

How to Contact: For fiction: Send introductory letter (with credits, if any), outline, first 3 chapters. For children's books: Send introductory letter (with credits, if any), up to 3 picture book mss, outline and first 3 chapters for longer projects, SASE. No fax queries. Accepts e-mail queries, no attachments. Considers simultaneous queries. Responds in 10 days to queries; 1 month to mss. Returns materials only with SASE.

Recent Sales: Sold 100 in the last 2 years titles in the last year. *Glory Denied*, by Thomas Philpott (Norton); *No Other Option*, by Marcus Wynne (Tor Books); *Hypercane*, by Ben Miller (NAL/Dutton); *Hunters of the Dark Sea*, by Mel Odom (TOR Books).

Terms: Agent receives 15% commission on domestic sales; 10% commission on foreign sales. Offers written contract. Charges clients for "direct expenses only limited to photocopying, postage."

Writers' Conferences: RWA National; Novelists, Inc.; and other regional conferences.

Tips: "We do consider new material from unsolicited authors. Write a good clear letter with a succinct description of your book. We prefer the first three chapters when we consider fiction. For all submissions you must include SASE for return or the material is discarded. It's always hard to break in, but talent will find a home. We continue to see natural storytellers and nonfiction writers with important books."

NICHOLAS ELLISON, INC., affiliated with Sanford J. Greenburger Associates, 55 Fifth Ave., 15th Floor, New York NY 10003. (212)206-6050. Fax: (212)436-8718. **Contact:** Alicka Pistek. Estab. 1983. Represents 70 clients. Currently handles: 25% nonfiction books; 75% novels.
  • Prior to becoming an agent, Mr. Ellison was an editor at Minerva Editions, Harper & Row and editor-in-chief at Delacorte.
Member Agents: Alicka Pistek
Represents: Nonfiction books; novels. **Considers these fiction areas:** literary; mainstream/contemporary.
  O→ Does not want to receive biography or self-help.
How to Contact: Query with SASE. Responds in 6 weeks to queries.
Recent Sales: *The Lion's Game*, by Nelson DeMille (Warner); *Equivocal Death*, by Amy Gutman (Little, Brown). Other clients include Olivia Goldsmith, P.T. Deutermann, James Webb, Nancy Geary.
Terms: Agent receives 15% commission on domestic sales; 20% commission on foreign sales.

ELAINE P. ENGLISH, Graybill & English, LLC, 1920 N. St. NW, Suite 620, Washington DC 20036-1619. (202)861-0106. Fax: (202)457-0662. E-mail: ElaineEngl@aol.com. Website: www.graybillandenglish.com. **Contact:** Elaine English. Member of AAR. Represents 2 clients. 100% of clients are new/unpublished writers. Currently handles: 100% novels.
  • Ms. English is an attorney specializing in media and publishing law.
Member Agents: Elaine English (women's fiction, including romance).
Represents: Novels; women's fiction, including single title romance. **Considers these fiction areas:** historical; mainstream/contemporary; multicultural; romance; women's.
  O→ "While not as an agent, per se, I have been working in publishing for over fifteen years. Also, I'm affiliated with other agents who represent a broad spectrum of projects." Actively seeking women's fiction, including single title romances. Does not want to receive anything other than above.
How to Contact: Submit outline, 3 sample chapter(s), SASE. Accepts e-mail queries. Responds in 3 weeks to queries; 2 months to mss. Returns materials only with SASE. Obtains most new clients through solicitations.
Terms: Agent receives 15% commission on domestic sales; 20% commission on foreign sales. Offers written contract; 30 days notice must be given to terminate contract. Charges only for expenses directly related to sales of manuscript (long distance, postage, copying).
Writers' Conferences: Washington Romance Writers (Harpers Ferry, April); Novelists Inc. (Philadelphia, September).

JAMES FRENKEL & ASSOCIATES, 414 S. Randall Ave., Madison WI 53715. (608)255-7977. Fax: (608)255-5852. E-mail: jfrenkel@panit.com. **Contact:** James Frenkel. Estab. 1987. Represents 35 clients. 20% of clients are new/unpublished writers. Currently handles: 5% nonfiction books; 65% novels; 7% story collections; 2% novellas; 7% juvenile books; 1% scholarly books; 2% movie scripts; 4% media tie-ins/ multimedia; 1% syndicated material; 6% anthologies.
  • Mr. Frenkel has been involved in the publishing industry for 25 years, in positions ranging from editor to publisher.
Member Agents: James Frenkel; Tracy Berg; Jesse Vogel.
Represents: Nonfiction books; novels. **Considers these fiction areas:** contemporary issues; detective/police/crime; ethnic; fantasy; feminist; historical; mainstream/contemporary; mystery/suspense; science fiction; thriller; westerns/frontier; young adult.
  O→ "We welcome and represent a wide variety of material."
How to Contact: Query with SASE, outline, 4 sample chapter(s). Prefers to read materials exclusively. No e-mail or fax queries. Responds in 2 months to queries; 6 months to mss. Obtains most new clients through recommendations from others, conferences.
Recent Sales: Sold 12 titles in the last year. *Veiled Threats, Died to Match*, by Deborah Donnelly (Delacorte/Dell); *The Crucible Trilogy*, by Sarah Douglass (TOR).
Terms: Agent receives 15% commission on domestic sales; 25% commission on foreign sales. Offers written contract, until terminated in writing. Charges clients for office expenses. "Amounts vary from title to title, but photocopying and submission costs are deducted after (and only after) a property sells."
Tips: "If there are markets for short fiction or nonfiction in your field, use them to help establish a name that agents will recognize. Too many times we receive poorly written letters and manuscripts rife with simple spelling errors. This is your work—take the time and effort to put together the best presentation you can."

THE GISLASON AGENCY, 219 Main St. SE, Suite 506, Minneapolis MN 55414-2160. (612)331-8033. Fax: (612)332-8115. E-mail: gislasonbj@aol.com. **Contact:** Barbara J. Gislason. Estab. 1992. Member of Member of Minnesota State Bar Association, Art & Entertainment Law Section (former chair), Internet Committee, Minnesota Intellectual Property Law Association Copyright Committee (former chair).; Also a member of SFWA, MWA, RWA, Sisters in Crime, University Film Society (board member) and Neighborhood Justice (board member). 50% of clients are new/unpublished writers. Currently handles: 25% nonfiction books; 75% novels.

   ● Ms. Gislason became an attorney in 1980, and continues to practice Art & Entertainment Law. She has
   been nationally recognized as a Leading American Attorney and a SuperLawyer.

Member Agents: Deborah Sweeney (fantasy, science fiction); Molly Hennen (partials, nonfiction); Kellie Hultgren (fantasy, science fiction); Adam Kintopf (fantasy, science fiction); Robert E. Ozasky (mystery); Tracy LaChance (romance); Kris Olson (mystery).

Represents: Nonfiction books; novels. **Considers these fiction areas:** fantasy; mystery/suspense; romance; science fiction; thriller (legal).

   ⌐ Do not send personal memoirs, poetry or children's books.

How to Contact: Fiction: Query with synopsis, first 3 chapters and SASE. Responds in 1 month to queries; 3 months to mss. Obtains most new clients through recommendations from others, conferences, *Guide to Literary Agents, Literary Market Place* and other reference books.

Recent Sales: *Historical Romance # 4*, by Linda Cook (Kensington); *Dancing Dead*, by Deborah Woodworth (HarperCollins); *Autumn World*, by Joan Verba, et al (Dragon Stone Press).

Terms: Agent receives 15 commission on domestic sales; 20 commission on foreign sales. Offers written contract, binding for 1 year with option to renew. Charges clients for photocopying and postage.

Writers' Conferences: Romance Writers of America; Midwest Fiction Writers; University of Wisconsin Writer's Institute. Also attend state and regional writers conferences.

Tips: "Cover letter should be well written and include a detailed synopsis (if fiction) or proposal (if nonfiction), the first three chapters and author bio. Appropriate SASE required. We are looking for a great writer with a poetic, lyrical or quirky writing style who can create intriguing ambiguities. We expect a well-researched, imaginative and fresh plot that reflects a familiarity with the applicable genre. If submitting nonfiction work, explain how the submission differs from and adds to previously published works in the field. Scenes with sex and violence must be intrinsic to the plot. Remember to proofread, proofread, proofread. If the work was written with a specific publisher in mind, this should be communicated. In addition to owning an agency, Ms. Gislason practices law in the area of Art and Entertainment and has a broad spectrum of entertainment industry contacts."

GOODMAN-ANDREW-AGENCY, INC., 1275 N. Harper, #7, West Hollywood CA 90046. (323)656-3785. Fax: (323)656-3975. **Contact:** Sasha Goodman. Estab. 1992. Represents 25 clients. 50% of clients are new/unpublished writers. Currently handles: 50% nonfiction books; 50% novels.

Represents: Nonfiction books; novels. **Considers these fiction areas:** contemporary issues; ethnic; gay/lesbian; literary; mainstream/contemporary.

   ⌐ "Not big on genre fiction."

How to Contact: Submit outline, 2 sample chapter(s). Considers simultaneous queries. Responds in 3 weeks to queries; 3 months to mss. Returns materials only with SASE.

Recent Sales: Sold 10 titles in the last year. *Person or Persons Unknown*, by Bruce Alexander (Putnam); *Taking Charge When You're Not in Control*, by Patricia Wiklund, Ph.D. (Ballantine).

Terms: Agent receives 15% commission on domestic sales. Offers written contract. Charges clients for postage.

Writers' Conferences: Pacific Northwest (Seattle, July).

Tips: "Query with 1-page letter, brief synopsis and 2 chapters. Patience, patience, patience. Always enclose return postage/SASE if you want your material returned. Otherwise, say you do not. Remember the agent is receiving dozens of submissions per week so try to understand this, and be patient and courteous."

CARROLL GRACE LITERARY AGENCY, P.O. Box 10938, St. Petersburg FL 33733. (727)865-2099. **Contact:** Pat Jozwiakowski, Sunny Mays. Estab. 1999. Represents 50 clients. 95% of clients are new/unpublished writers. Currently handles: 10% nonfiction books; 90% novels.

Member Agents: Ms. Sunny Mays (acquisitions director/agent); Ms. Pat Jozwiakowski (agent).

Represents: Nonfiction books; novels. **Considers these fiction areas:** action/adventure; detective/police/crime; family saga; fantasy; historical; horror; literary; mainstream/contemporary; mystery/suspense (amateur sleuth, cozy, culinary); psychic/supernatural; romance (contemporary, gothic, historical, regency); thriller; westerns/frontier.

   ⌐ "We understand how difficult it is for a new writer to obtain an agent or a publisher. We want to guide
   careers and encourage our clients to their top potential by offering our experience and knowledge."
   Actively seeking romance, fantasy, mystery/suspense, psychic supernatural, timeswept (romance with
   time travel).

How to Contact: Query with SASE, synopsis, 5 sample chapter(s). No e-mail or fax queries. Considers simultaneous queries. Responds in 6 weeks to queries; 2 months to mss.

Recent Sales: Sold 1 titles in the last year. *Tunnel Vision*, by Rob Marshall (Algora).

Terms: Agent receives 15% commission on domestic sales; 20% commission on foreign sales. Offers written contract, binding for binding time determined on a book-by-book basis.; 90-day notice must be given to terminate contract. notice must be given to terminate contract. Charges clients for photocopying, international and express postage, faxes, postage.

Tips: "Make sure your manuscript is as near to finished as possible—be neat and orderly. Study manuscript formatting, check your manuscript for spelling, grammar and punctuation errors."

N ○ **JILL GROSJEAN LITERARY AGENCY**, 1390 Millstone Rd., Sag Harbor NY 11963-2214. (631)725-7419. Fax: (631)725-8632. E-mail: JILL6981@aol.com. Website: www.hometown.aol.com/JILL6981/myhomepage/index.html. **Contact:** Jill Grosjean. Estab. 1999. Represents 11 clients. 100% of clients are new/unpublished writers. Currently handles: 1% nonfiction books; 99% novels.

- Prior to becoming an agent, Ms. Grosjean was manager of an independent bookstore. She also worked in publishing and advertising.

Represents: Nonfiction books (some); novels (mostly). **Considers these fiction areas:** contemporary issues; historical; humor/satire; literary; mainstream/contemporary; mystery/suspense; regional; romance; thriller.

> ○━ This agency offers some editorial assistance (i.e., line-by-line edits). Actively seeking mysteries, thrillers, suspense novels. Does not want to receive any nonfiction subjects not indicated above.

How to Contact: Query with SASE. Considers simultaneous queries. Responds in 1 week to queries; 1 month to mss. Returns materials only with SASE. Obtains most new clients through recommendations from others, solicitations.

Recent Sales: Sold 4 titles in the last year. *Free Bird*, by Greg Garrett (Kensington); *Two Turtledoves*, by Tony Broadbent (Thomas Dunne).

Terms: Agent receives 15% commission on domestic sales; 20% commission on foreign sales. No written contract. Charges clients for photocopying, mailing expenses; Writers reimbursed for office fees after the sale of ms.

Writers' Conferences: Book Passages Mystery Writer's Conference (Corte Madera CA, July).

✓ ○ **REECE HALSEY NORTH**, 8733 Sunset Blvd., Suite 101, Los Angeles CA 90069. Fax: (310)652-7595 or (310)652-2409. E-mail: bookgirl@worldnet.att.net. Website: www.reecehalseynorth.com or kimberlycameron.com. **Contact:** Kimberly Cameron. Estab. 1995. Member of AAR. Represents 40 clients. 30% of clients are new/unpublished writers. Currently handles: 30% nonfiction books; 70% novels.

Member Agents: Kimberley Cameron (Reece Halsey North); Dorris Halsey (by referral only).

Represents: Nonfiction books; novels. **Considers these fiction areas:** action/adventure; ethnic; historical; literary; mainstream/contemporary; mystery/suspense; science fiction. **Considers these script subject areas:** thriller.

> ○━ This agency specializes in mystery, literary and mainstream fiction, excellent writing. The Reece Halsey Agency has an illustrious client list largely of established writers, including the estate of Aldous Huxley and has represented Upton Sinclair, William Faulkner and Henry Miller. Ms. Cameron has a Northern California office and all queries should be addressed to her at the Tiburon office.

How to Contact: Query with SASE. No e-mail or fax queries. Considers simultaneous queries. Responds in 6 weeks to queries; 3 months to mss. Obtains most new clients through recommendations from others, solicitations.

Recent Sales: *Jinn*, by Matthew Delaney (St. Martin's Press); *Flu Season*, by Earl Merkel (Dutton-NAL).

Terms: Agent receives 15% commission on domestic sales. Offers written contract, binding for 1 year. Requests 6 copies of ms if representing an author.

Writers' Conferences: BEA; Maui Writers Conference.

Reading List: Reads *Glimmer Train*, *The Sun* and *The New Yorker* to find new clients. Looks for "writing that touches the heart."

Tips: "Please send a polite, well-written query and include a SASE with it!"

○ **THE JOY HARRIS LITERARY AGENCY, INC.**, 156 Fifth Ave., Suite 617, New York NY 10010. (212)924-6269. Fax: (212)924-6609. E-mail: gen.office@jhlitagent.com. **Contact:** Joy Harris. Member of AAR. Represents 150 clients. Currently handles: 50% nonfiction books; 50% novels.

Member Agents: Leslie Daniels; Stéphanie Abou.

Represents: Nonfiction books; novels. **Considers these fiction areas:** action/adventure; comic books/cartoon; confession; contemporary issues; detective/police/crime; erotica; ethnic; experimental; family saga; feminist; gay/lesbian; glitz; gothic; hi-lo; historical; horror; humor/satire; literary; mainstream/contemporary; military/war; multicultural; multimedia; mystery/suspense; New Age; occult; picture books; plays; poetry; poetry in translation; psychic/supernatural; regional; religious/inspirational; romance; short story collections; spiritual; sports; thriller; translation; young adult; women's.

> ○━ Does not want to receive screenplays.

How to Contact: Query with outline/proposal, SASE. Considers simultaneous queries. Responds in 2 months to queries. Obtains most new clients through recommendations from clients and editors.

Recent Sales: Sold 15 titles in the last year. This agency prefers not to share information on specific sales.
Terms: Agent receives 15% commission on domestic sales; 20% commission on foreign sales. Charges clients for some office expenses.

✓ ◑ ◎ **HOPKINS LITERARY ASSOCIATES, (Specialized: romance/women's fiction),** 2117 Buffalo Rd., Suite 327, Rochester NY 14624-1507. (716)352-6268. **Contact:** Pam Hopkins. Estab. 1996. Member of AAR, RWA. Represents 30 clients. 5% of clients are new/unpublished writers. Currently handles: 100% novels.
Represents: Novels. **Considers these fiction areas:** historical; mainstream/contemporary; romance; women's.
   O–π This agency specializes in women's fiction, particularly historical, contemporary and category romance as well as mainstream work.
How to Contact: Submit outline, 3 sample chapter(s). No e-mail or fax queries. Considers simultaneous queries. Responds in 2 weeks to queries; 1 month to mss. Returns materials only with SASE. Obtains most new clients through recommendations from others, solicitations, conferences.
Recent Sales: Sold 50 titles in the last year. *The Colonel's Daughter,* by Merline Lovelace (MIRA); *Lord of a Thousand Nights,* by Madeline Hunter (Bantam); *Aphrodite's Kiss,* by Julie Kenner (Dorchester); *Leave It to Max,* by Lori Handeland (Harlequin); *Wedding of the Year,* by Victoria Malvey (Pocket).
Terms: Agent receives 15% commission on domestic sales; 20% commission on foreign sales. No written contract.
Writers' Conferences: Romance Writers of America

◑ **JABBERWOCKY LITERARY AGENCY,** P.O. Box 4558, Sunnyside NY 11104-0558. Phone/fax: (718)392-5985. E-mail: jabagent@aol.com. **Contact:** Joshua Bilmes. Estab. 1994. Member of SFWA. Represents 40 clients. 25% of clients are new/unpublished writers. Currently handles: 25% nonfiction books; 65% novels; 5% scholarly books; 5% other.
Represents: Nonfiction books; novels; scholarly books. **Considers these fiction areas:** action/adventure; comic books/cartoon; contemporary issues; detective/police/crime; ethnic; family saga; fantasy; gay/lesbian; glitz; historical; horror; humor/satire; literary; mainstream/contemporary; psychic/supernatural; regional; science fiction; sports; thriller.
   O–π This agency represents quite a lot of genre fiction and is actively seeking to increase amount of nonfiction projects. It does not handle juvenile or young adult.
How to Contact: Query with SASE. No mss unless requested. No e-mail or fax queries. Considers simultaneous queries. Responds in 2 weeks to queries. Returns materials only with SASE. Obtains most new clients through solicitations, recommendation by current clients.
Recent Sales: Sold 20 titles in the last year. *Shakespeare's Counselor,* by Charlaine Harris (Dell); *Drinking Midnight Wine,* by Simon Green (Roc); *Against the Odds,* by Elizabeth Moon (Baen); *Lupus: Alternate Therapies,* by Sharon Moore (Inner Traditions). Other clients include Tanya Huff, Kristine Smith, Edo van Belkon.
Terms: Agent receives 12.5% commission on domestic sales; 20% commission on foreign sales. Offers written contract, binding for 1 year. Charges clients for book purchases, photocopying, international book/ms mailing, international long distance.
Writers' Conferences: Malice Domestic (Washington DC, May); World SF Convention (San Jose, August); Icon (Stony Brook NY, April).
Reading List: Reads *New Republic, Analog* and various newspapers to find new clients.
Tips: "In approaching with a query, the most important things to me are your credits and your biographical background to the extent it's relevant to your work. I (and most agents) will ignore the adjectives you may choose to describe your own work."

JCA LITERARY AGENCY, 27 W. 20th St., Suite 1103, New York NY 10011. (212)807-0888. Fax: (212)807-0461. **Contact:** Jeff Gerecke, Tony Outhwaite. Estab. 1978. Member of AAR. Represents 100 clients. 10% of clients are new/unpublished writers. Currently handles: 20% nonfiction books; 75% novels; 5% scholarly books.
Member Agents: Jeff Gerecke; Tony Outhwaite; Peter Steinberg.
Represents: Nonfiction books; novels. **Considers these fiction areas:** action/adventure; contemporary issues; detective/police/crime; family saga; historical; literary; mainstream/contemporary; mystery/suspense; sports; thriller.
   O–π Does not want to receive screenplays, poetry, children's books, science fiction/fantasy, genre romance.
How to Contact: Query with SASE. No e-mail or fax queries. Considers simultaneous queries. Responds in 2 weeks to queries; 10 weeks to mss. Returns materials only with SASE. Obtains most new clients through recommendations from others, solicitations, conferences.
Recent Sales: *The Lost Glass Plates of Wilfred Eng,* by Thomas Orton (Counterpoint); *Sharp Shooter,* by David Healey (The Berkley Publishing Group/Jove); *A Healthy Place to Die,* by Peter King (St. Martin's Press). Other clients include Ernest J. Gaines, W.E.B. Griffin, Polly Whitney, David J. Garrow.

Terms: Agent receives 15% commission on domestic sales; 20% commission on foreign sales. No written contract. "We work with our clients on a handshake basis." Charges for postage on overseas submissions, photocopying, mss for submission, books purchased for subrights submission, and bank charges, where applicable. "We deduct the cost from payments received from publishers."

Tips: "We do not ourselves provide legal, accounting, or public relations services for our clients, although some of the advice we give falls somewhat into these realms. In cases where it seems necessary we will recommend obtaining outside advice or assistance in these areas from professionals who are not in any way connected to the agency."

☑ ◑ **CAROLYN JENKS AGENCY**, 24 Concord Ave., Suite 412, Cambridge MA 02138. (617)354-5099. E-mail: cbjenks@att.net. Website: www.carolynjenksagency.com. **Contact:** Carolyn Jenks. Estab. 1990 (re-established after hiatus). Signatory of WGA. 80% of clients are new/unpublished writers. Currently handles: 15% nonfiction books; 75% novels; 5% movie scripts; 5% stage plays. Co-agents for TV in Los Angeles.

- Prior to opening her agency, Ms. Jenks was a managing editor, actor and producer.

Represents: Nonfiction books; novels. **Considers these fiction areas:** contemporary issues; ethnic; gay/lesbian; historical; literary; mainstream/contemporary; mystery/suspense; romance (contemporary, historical); thriller; westerns/frontier.

   O— This agency specializes in "development of promising authors." Actively seeking "exceptionally talented writers committed to work that makes a contribution." Does not want to receive gratuitous violence; drug scenes that are a cliche; war stories unless they transcend; sagas, or cliched coming of age stories."

Also Handles: Feature film; TV movie of the week. **Considers these script subject areas:** contemporary issues; historical; mainstream; mystery/suspense; romantic comedy; romantic drama; thriller.

How to Contact: Query with SASE, author bio. No fax queries. Accepts e-mail queries, no attachments. Responds in 2 weeks to queries; 6 weeks to mss. Returns materials only with SASE.

Recent Sales: Sold 2 scripts in the last year. **Film/TV rights optioned/sold:** *The Red Tent*, by Anita Diamant (now a bestseller) (St. Martin's Press); *White Wings*, by Dan Montague (Japanese); *Hunger*, by Jane Ward (Forge).

Terms: Agent receives 15% commission on domestic sales; 15% commission on dramatic rights sales. Offers written contract.

Tips: "Query first in writing with SASE or to cbjenks@att.net. Do not send samples of writing by e-mail."

◑ **KIDDE, HOYT & PICARD**, 335 E. 51st St., New York NY 10022. (212)755-9461. Fax: (212)223-2501. **Contact:** Katherine Kidde, Zarinah Jones. Estab. 1980. Member of AAR. Represents 80 clients. Currently handles: 15% nonfiction books; 80% novels; 5% juvenile books.

- Prior to becoming an agent, Ms. Kidde was an editor/senior editor at Harcourt Brace, New American Library and Putnam.

Member Agents: Kay Kidde (mainstream fiction, general nonfiction, mysteries, romances, literary fiction); Zarinah Jones(romances, mysteries, literary fiction, general nonfiction).

Represents: Nonfiction books; novels. **Considers these fiction areas:** contemporary issues; detective/police/crime; feminist; gay/lesbian; glitz; historical; humor/satire; literary; mainstream/contemporary; mystery/suspense; romance (contemporary, historical, regency); thriller.

   O— This agency specializes in mainstream fiction and nonfiction. Actively seeking "strong mainstream fiction." Does not want to receive "male adventure, science fiction, juvenile, porn, plays or poetry."

How to Contact: Query with SASE. Considers simultaneous queries. Responds in a few weeks to queries; 1 month to mss. Returns materials only with SASE. Obtains most new clients through recommendations from others, solicitations, "former authors from when I was an editor, listings in LMP, writers' guides."

Recent Sales: Sold 8 titles in the last year. *Sir Francis Drake*, by Michael Cadnum (Viking); *Iceman*, by John Paxson (St. Martin's). Other clients include Virginia Browne, Linda Hawner, Lee Davis, Mark Miano.

Terms: Agent receives 15% commission on domestic sales; 20% commission on foreign sales. Charges clients for photocopying.

Reading List: Reads literary journals and magazines, *Harper's*, *DoubleTake*, etc. to find new clients.

Tips: "We look for beautiful stylistic writing, and that elusive treasure, a good book (mostly fiction). As an editor, I can help launch authors."

HARVEY KLINGER, INC., 301 W. 53rd St., New York NY 10019. (212)581-7068. Fax: (212)315-3823. E-mail: klingerinc@aol.com. **Contact:** Harvey Klinger. Estab. 1977. Member of AAR. Represents 100 clients. 25% of clients are new/unpublished writers. Currently handles: 50% nonfiction books; 50% novels.

Member Agents: David Dunton (popular culture, parenting, home improvement, thrillers/crime); Laurie Liss (literary fiction, human interest, politics, women's issues); Jenny Bent (general nonfiction and women's fiction).

Represents: Nonfiction books; novels. **Considers these fiction areas:** action/adventure; detective/police/crime; family saga; glitz; literary; mainstream/contemporary; mystery/suspense; thriller.

   O— This agency specializes in "big, mainstream contemporary fiction and nonfiction."

How to Contact: Query with SASE. Accepts e-mail queries. No fax queries. Responds in 1 month to queries; 2 months to mss. Obtains most new clients through recommendations from others.

Recent Sales: Sold 30 titles in the last year. *The Music of the Spheres*, by Elizabeth Redfern (Putnam); *The Carousel*, by Richard Paul Evans (Simon & Schuster); *Sacred Ground*, by Barbara Wood (St. Martin's Press). Other clients include Clare Ansberry, Mac Randall.

Terms: Agent receives 15% commission on domestic sales; 25% commission on foreign sales. Offers written contract. Charges for photocopying mss, overseas postage for mss.

THE KNIGHT AGENCY, P.O. Box 550648, Atlanta GA 30355. (404)816-9620. E-mail: deidremk@aol.com. Website: www.knightagency.net. Also: 2407 Matthews St., Atlanta GA 30319. **Contact:** Deidre Knight. Estab. 1996. Member of AAR, RWA, Authors Guild. Represents 45 clients. 40% of clients are new/unpublished writers. Currently handles: 50% nonfiction books; 50% novels.

Member Agents: Deidre Knight (president, agent); Pamela Harty (subsidiary rights director); Lisa Wessling Payne (agency assistant, submissions contact).

Represents: Nonfiction books; novels. **Considers these fiction areas:** ethnic; literary; mainstream/contemporary (commercial); romance (contemporary, historical, inspirational); women's.

> O–π "We are looking for a wide variety of fictions and nonfiction. In the nonfiction area, we're particularly eager to find personal finance, business investment, pop culture, self-help/motivational and popular reference books. In fiction, we're always looking for romance; women's fiction; commercial fiction."

How to Contact: Query with SASE. Considers simultaneous queries. Responds in 2 weeks to queries; 6 weeks to mss.

Recent Sales: Sold 40 titles in the last year. *Kiss of the Highlander*, by Karen Marie Moning (Bantam Dell); *The Friendship Quilt*, by Lauraine Snelling (WaterBrook Press).

Terms: Agent receives 15% commission on domestic sales; 25% commission on foreign sales. Offers written contract, binding for 1 year; 60 days notice must be given to terminate contract. Charges clients for photocopying, postage, overnight courier expenses. "These are deducted from the sale of the work, not billed upfront."

Tips: "At the Knight Agency, a client usually ends up becoming a friend."

✓ ◐ IRENE KRAAS AGENCY, 256 Rancho Alegre Rd., Santa Fe NM 87505. (505)438-7715. Fax: (505)438-7783. Estab. 1990. Represents 30 clients. 75% of clients are new/unpublished writers. Currently handles: 100% novels.

Represents: Novels (adult). **Considers these fiction areas:** action/adventure; detective/police/crime; mystery/suspense; science fiction; thriller (psychological).

> O–π This agency specializes in adult fiction. Actively seeking "books that are well written with commercial potential." Does not want to receive romance, short stories, plays or poetry.

How to Contact: Submit cover letter, first 30 pages, SASE; must include return postage and/or SASE. No e-mail or fax queries. Considers simultaneous queries. Returns materials only with SASE.

Recent Sales: *Night Terror*, by Chandler McGrew (Bantam); *The Fixer*, by Jon Mertz (Kensington); *Acoma Passageway*, by Kimberley Griffiths Little (Knopf). Other clients include Denise Vitola, Duncan Long, Shirley-Raye Redmond, Torry England.

Terms: Agent receives 15% commission on domestic sales. Offers written contract, binding for 1 year. Charges clients for photocopying and postage.

Writers' Conferences: Southwest Writers Conference (Albuquerque); Pacific Northwest Conference (Seattle); Vancouver Writers Conference (Vancouver BC); Austin Writers Workshop; Wilamette Writers' Group.

✓ ◐ DONALD MAASS LITERARY AGENCY, 160 W. 95th St., Suite 1B, New York NY 10025. (212)866-8200. **Contact:** Donald Maass, Jennifer Jackson or Michelle Brummer. Estab. 1980. Member of AAR, SFWA, MWA, RWA. Represents over 100 clients. 5% of clients are new/unpublished writers. Currently handles: 100% novels.

> • Prior to opening his agency, Mr. Maass served as an editor at Dell Publishing (NY) and as a reader at Gollancz (London). He is the current president of AAR.

Member Agents: Donald Maass (mainstream, literary, mystery/suspense, science fiction); Jennifer Jackson (commercial fiction, especially romance, science fiction, fantasy, mystery/suspense); Michelle Brummer (fiction: literary, contemporary, feminist, science fiction, fantasy, romance).

Represents: Novels. **Considers these fiction areas:** detective/police/crime; fantasy; historical; horror; literary; mainstream/contemporary; mystery/suspense; psychic/supernatural; romance (historical, paranormal, time travel); science fiction; thriller; women's.

> O–π This agency specializes in commercial fiction, especially science fiction, fantasy, mystery, romance, suspense. Actively seeking "to expand the literary portion of our list and expand in romance and women's fiction." Does not want to receive nonfiction, children's or poetry.

How to Contact: Query with SASE. Returns material only with SASE. Considers simultaneous queries. Responds in 2 weeks to queries; 3 months to mss.

Recent Sales: Sold over 100 titles in the last year. *Funeral in Blue*, by Anne Perry (Ballantine); *The Lightstone*, by David Zendell (Warner Aspect); *Skin Folk*, by Nalo Hopkinson (Warner Aspect); *Brothers of Cain*, by Miriam Monfredo (Penguin Putnam); *The Pillars of the World*, by Anne Bishop (ROC).

Terms: Agent receives 15% commission on domestic sales; 20% commission on foreign sales. Charges clients for large photocopying orders and book samples "after consultation with author."

Writers' Conferences: Donald Maass: World Science Fiction Convention; Frankfurt Book Fair; Pacific Northwest Writers Conference; Bouchercon and others. Jennifer Jackson: World Science Fiction and Fantasy Convention; RWA National and others. Michelle Brummer: ReaderCon; Luna Con; Frankfurt.

Tips: "We are fiction specialists, also noted for our innovative approach to career planning. Few new clients are accepted, but interested authors should query with SASE. Subagents in all principle foreign countries and Hollywood. No nonfiction or juvenile works considered."

McHUGH LITERARY AGENCY, 1033 Lyon Rd., Moscow ID 83843-9167. (208)882-0107. Fax: (847)628-0146. E-mail: elisabetmch@turbonet.com. **Contact:** Elisabet McHugh. Estab. 1994. Represents 71 clients. 35% of clients are new/unpublished writers. Currently handles: 50% nonfiction books; 50% fiction novels.
   • Prior to opening her agency, Ms. McHugh was a full-time writer for 14 years.

Represents: Nonfiction books; novels. **Considers these fiction areas:** historical; mainstream/contemporary; mystery/suspense; romance; thriller; westerns/frontier.
   O-¬ Does not want to receive children's books, poetry, science fiction, fantasy, horror.

How to Contact: Query by e-mail. Considers simultaneous queries. Returns materials only with SASE.

Recent Sales: *Clark Gable*, (McFarland & Co.); *Hassle-Free Business Travel*, (Ten Speed Press); *Deadly Intent*, (Bantam); *Never Again* (Harlequin).

Terms: Agent receives 15% commission on domestic sales; 20% commission on foreign sales. Does not charge any upfront fees. Offers written contract. "Client must provide all copies of manuscripts needed for submissions."

Tips: "Be professional."

PINDER LANE & GARON-BROOKE ASSOCIATES, LTD., 159 W. 53rd St., Suite 14E, New York NY 10019-6005. (212)489-0880. E-mail: pinderl@interport.com. **Contact:** Robert Thixton. Member of AAR; signatory of WGA. Represents 80 clients. 20% of clients are new/unpublished writers. Currently handles: 25% nonfiction books; 75% novels.

Member Agents: Nancy Coffey (contributing agent); Dick Duane; Robert Thixton.

Represents: Nonfiction books; novels. **Considers these fiction areas:** contemporary issues; detective/police/crime; family saga; fantasy; gay/lesbian; literary; mainstream/contemporary; mystery/suspense; romance; science fiction.
   O-¬ This agency specializes in mainstream fiction and nonfiction. Does not want to receive screenplays, TV series teleplays or dramatic plays.

How to Contact: Query with SASE. Responds in 3 weeks to queries; 2 months to mss. Obtains most new clients through recommendations from others, solicitations.

Recent Sales: Sold 20 titles in the last year. *Nobody's Safe*, by Richard Steinberg (Doubleday); *The Kill Box*, by Chris Stewart (M. Evans); *Return to Christmas*, by Chris Heimerdinger (Ballantine); *Savage Desire*, by Rosemary Rogers (Mira Books).

Terms: Agent receives 15% commission on domestic sales; 30% commission on foreign sales. Offers written contract, binding for 3-5 years.

Tips: "With our literary and media experience, our agency is uniquely positioned for the current and future direction publishing is taking. Send query letter first giving the essence of the ms and a personal or career bio with SASE."

AARON M. PRIEST LITERARY AGENCY, 708 Third Ave., 23rd Floor, New York NY 10017. (212)818-0344. Fax: (212)573-9417. E-mail: lchilds@aaronpriest.com. **Contact:** Aaron Priest or Molly Friedrich. Estab. 1974. Member of AAR. Currently handles: 25% nonfiction books; 75% novels.

Member Agents: Lisa Erbach Vance; Paul Cirone; Aaron Priest; Molly Friedrich; Lucy Childs.

Represents: Nonfiction books; novels.

How to Contact: All unsolicited mss returned unopened. No e-mail or fax queries. Considers simultaneous queries. If interested, will respond within 2 weeks.

Recent Sales: *Bow's Boy*, by Richard Babcock (Scribner); *Of Magic* , by Frances Sherwood (Norton).

Terms: Agent receives 15% commission on domestic sales. Charges for photocopying, foreign postage expenses.

ANGELA RINALDI LITERARY AGENCY, P.O. Box 7877, Beverly Hills CA 90212-7877. (310)842-7665. Fax: (310)837-8143. E-mail: ARinaldilitagcy@aol.com. **Contact:** Angela Rinaldi. Estab. 1994. Member of AAR. Represents 50 clients. Currently handles: 50% nonfiction books; 50% novels.

- Prior to opening her agency, Ms. Rinaldi was an editor at New American Library, Pocket Books and Bantam, and the Manager of Book Development for *The Los Angeles Times*.

Represents: Nonfiction books; novels; TV and motion picture rights for clients only. **Considers these fiction areas:** literary; mainstream/contemporary.

　　O— Actively seeking commercial and literary fiction. Does not want to receive scripts, category romances, children's books, westerns, science fiction/fantasy and cookbooks.

How to Contact: For fiction: Send the first 100 pages, brief synopsis, SASE. Accepts e-mail queries. Considers simultaneous queries. Please advise if this is a multiple submission. Responds in 6 weeks to queries. Returns materials only with SASE.

Recent Sales: *Stepwives*, by Lynne Oxhorn, Louise Oxhorn, and Marjorie Kraus (Simon & Schuster); *Enlightened Golf*, by Dr. Joseph Parent (Doubleday); *Surviving Pregnancy with an Eating Disorder*, by Dr. Paula Bernstein (Berkley); *Who Moved My Cheese?*, by Dr. Spencer Johnson (Putnam). Other clients include Stephanie Kane.

Terms: Agent receives 15% commission on domestic sales; 20% commission on foreign sales. Offers written contract. Charges for photocopying if client doesn't supply copies for submissions.

B.J. ROBBINS LITERARY AGENCY, 5130 Bellaire Ave., North Hollywood CA 91607-2908. (818)760-6602. Fax: (818)760-6616. E-mail: robbinsliterary@aol.com. **Contact:** (Ms.) B.J. Robbins. Estab. 1992. Member of Board of Directors, PEN American Center West. Represents 40 clients. 50% of clients are new/unpublished writers. Currently handles: 50% nonfiction books; 50% novels.

Member Agents: Rob McAndrews (commercial fiction).

Represents: Nonfiction books; novels. **Considers these fiction areas:** contemporary issues; detective/police/crime; ethnic; literary; mainstream/contemporary; mystery/suspense; sports; thriller.

How to Contact: Submit 3 sample chapter(s), outline/proposal, SASE. No e-mail or fax queries. Considers simultaneous queries. Responds in 2 weeks to queries; 6 weeks to mss. Returns materials only with SASE. Obtains most new clients through recommendations from others, conferences.

Recent Sales: Sold 15 titles in the last year. *A Matter of Time*, by John Hough, Jr. (Simon & Schuster/NAL); *The Drums of Quallah Battoo*, by Charles Corn (Dutton).

Terms: Agent receives 15% commission on domestic sales; 20% commission on foreign sales. Offers written contract; 3 months notice must be given to terminate contract. 100% of business is derived from commissions on ms sales. Charges clients for postage and photocopying only. Writers charged for fees only after the sale of ms.

Writers' Conferences: Squaw Valley Fiction Writers Workshop (Squaw Valley CA, August); Maui Writers Conference; SDSU Writers Conference (San Diego CA, January).

JANE ROTROSEN AGENCY LLC, 318 E. 51st St., New York NY 10022. (212)593-4330. Fax: (212)935-6985. E-mail: firstinitiallastname@janerotrosen.com. Estab. 1974. Member of AAR, Authors Guild. Represents over 100 clients. Currently handles: 30% nonfiction books; 70% novels.

Member Agents: Jane Rotrosen; Andrea Cirillo; Ruth Kagle; Annelise Robey; Margaret Ruley.

Represents: Nonfiction books; novels. **Considers these fiction areas:** action/adventure; detective/police/crime; family saga; historical; horror; mainstream/contemporary; mystery/suspense; romance; thriller; women's.

How to Contact: Query with SASE. No e-mail or fax queries. Responds in 2 months to mss. Responds in 2 weeks (to writers who have been referred by a client or colleague). Returns materials only with SASE.

Recent Sales: Sold 120 titles in the last year. This agency prefers not to share information on specific sales.

Terms: Agent receives 15% commission on domestic sales; 20% commission on foreign sales. Offers written contract, binding for 3-5 years; 60-day notice must be given to terminate contract. Charges clients for photocopying, express mail, overseas postage, book purchase.

RUSSELL & VOLKENING, 50 W. 29th St., #7E, New York NY 10001. (212)684-6050. Fax: (212)889-3026. **Contact:** Joseph Regal. Estab. 1940. Member of AAR. Represents 140 clients. 10% of clients are new/unpublished writers. Currently handles: 45% nonfiction books; 50% novels; 3% story collections; 2% novellas.

Member Agents: Timothy Seldes (nonfiction, literary fiction); Joseph Regal (literary fiction, thrillers, nonfiction).

Represents: Nonfiction books; novels; short story collections; novellas. **Considers these fiction areas:** action/adventure; detective/police/crime; ethnic; literary; mainstream/contemporary; mystery/suspense; picture books; sports; thriller.

　　O— This agency specializes in literary fiction and narrative nonfiction.

How to Contact: Query with SASE. Responds in 1 month to queries; 2 months to mss. Obtains most new clients through recommendations from others, occasionally through query letters.

Recent Sales: *The Many Aspects of Mobile Living*, by Martin Clark (Knopf); *The Special Prisoner*, by Jim Lehrer (Random); *The Pick-Up*, by Nadine Gordimer (FSG); *The Beatles in Rishikesh*, by Paul Saltzman (Viking Studio); *Lanterns*, by Marian Wright Edelman (Beacon); *Warriors of God*, by James Reston, Jr. (Doubleday); *The Obituary Writer*, by Porter Shreve (Houghton Mifflin); *Back When We Were Grownups*, by Anne Tyler (Knopf); *Interrogation*, by Thomas H. Cook (Bantam).

Terms: Agent receives 15% commission on domestic sales; 20% commission on foreign sales. Charges clients for "standard office expenses relating to the submission of materials of an author we represent, e.g., photocopying, postage."

Tips: "If the query is cogent, well written, well presented and is the type of book we'd represent, we'll ask to see the manuscript. From there, it depends purely on the quality of the work."

VICTORIA SANDERS & ASSOCIATES LITERARY AGENCY, 241 Avenue of the Americas, New York NY 10014-4822. (212)633-8811. Fax: (212)633-0525. **Contact:** Victoria Sanders or Diane Dickensheid. Estab. 1993. Member of AAR; signatory of WGA. Represents 75 clients. 25% of clients are new/unpublished writers. Currently handles: 50% nonfiction books; 50% novels.

Member Agents: Imani Wilson (assistant literary agent).

Represents: Nonfiction books; novels. **Considers these fiction areas:** action/adventure; contemporary issues; ethnic; family saga; feminist; gay/lesbian; literary; thriller.

How to Contact: Query with SASE. Considers simultaneous queries. Responds in 3 weeks to queries; 1 month to mss. Returns materials only with SASE. Obtains most new clients through recommendations from others, or "I find them through my reading and pursue."

Recent Sales: Sold 15 titles in the last year. *Blindsighted*, by Karin Slaughter (Morrow); *Redemption Song*, by Dr. Bertrice Berry (Doubleday).

Terms: Agent receives 15% commission on domestic sales; 20% commission on foreign sales. Offers written contract. Charges for photocopying, ms, messenger, express mail and extraordinary fees. If in excess of $100, client approval is required.

Tips: "Limit query to letter, no calls, and give it your best shot. A good query is going to get a good response."

SCHERF, INC. LITERARY MANAGEMENT, P.O. Box 80180, Las Vegas NV 89180-0180. (702)243-4895. Fax: (702)243-7460. E-mail: ds@scherf.com. Website: www.scherf.com/literarymanagement.htm. **Contact:** Dietmar Scherf. Estab. 1999. Currently handles: 10% nonfiction books; 85% novels; 5% novellas.

• Prior to opening his agency, Mr. Scherf wrote several nonfiction books, and has been a publisher and editor since 1983.

Member Agents: Mr. Dietmar Scherf (fiction/nonfiction); Ms. Gail Kirby (fiction/nonfiction).

Represents: Nonfiction books; novels; novellas. **Considers these fiction areas:** action/adventure; literary; mainstream/contemporary; mystery/suspense; religious/inspirational; thriller.

0→ This agency specializes in discovering new authors, especially in the highly competitive fiction market. "As much as possible, we want to give every new author with a fresh voice a chance to find a publisher for their work. We also manage literary properties for established writers." Actively seeking well-written contemporary fiction with broad commercial appeal. Does not want to receive gay, lesbian, erotica, or anything with foul language.

How to Contact: Query with SASE. No e-mail or fax queries. Considers simultaneous queries. Responds in 2 months to queries; 3 months to mss. Returns materials only with SASE. Obtains most new clients through recommendations from others, writing contests, unsolicited queries.

Recent Sales: Sold 1 title in the last year. *The Consultant*, by Alec Donzi.

Terms: Agent receives 10-15% commission on domestic sales; 15-20% (depending if new or established author) commission on foreign sales. Offers written contract, binding for variable term; 30-day notice must be given to terminate contract. Charges clients for postage, photocopying. Writers reimbursed for office fees after the sale of ms. May refer new writers to editing service. 0% of business is derived from referrals.

Tips: "Write the best manuscript, and polish it to the max. Write about a story that you love and are enthusiastic about. Learn good writing skills through books, seminars/courses, etc., especially regarding characterization, dialogue, plot, etc. in respect to novels. Know your competition well, and read books from authors that may fall into your category. In nonfiction, do the best research on your subject and be different from your competition with a new approach."

SCHIAVONE LITERARY AGENCY, INC., 236 Trails End, West Palm Beach FL 33413-2135. (561)966-9294. Fax: (561)966-9294. E-mail: profschia@aol.com. Website: www.freeyellow.com/members8/schiavone/ind

ex.html. **Contact:** James Schiavone, Ed.D. Estab. 1996. Member of National Education Association. Represents 40 clients. 2% of clients are new/unpublished writers. Currently handles: 50% nonfiction books; 49% novels; 1% textbooks.

• Prior to opening his agency, Dr. Schiavone was a full professor of development skills at the City University of New York and author of 5 trade books and 3 textbooks.

Member Agents: Diane V. Jacques (film and TV rights; e-mail: JNJSF@aol.com).

Represents: Nonfiction books; novels; juvenile books; scholarly books; textbooks; movie scripts; feature film; TV movie of the week. **Considers these fiction areas:** contemporary issues; ethnic; family saga; historical; horror; humor/satire; juvenile; literary; mainstream/contemporary; science fiction; young adult.

O— This agency specializes in celebrity biography and autobiography. "We have a management division that handles motion picture and TV rights." Actively seeking serious nonfiction, literary fiction and celebrity biography. Does not want to receive poetry.

How to Contact: Query with SASE. Considers one page e-mail queries with no attachments. Does not accept phone or fax queries. Considers simultaneous queries. Responds in 2 weeks to queries; 6 weeks to mss. Returns materials only with SASE. Obtains most new clients through recommendations from others, solicitations, conferences.

Terms: Agent receives 15% commission on domestic sales; 20% commission on foreign sales. Offers written contract, binding for project period; written notice must be given to terminate contract. Charges clients for long distance, photocopying, postage, special handling. Dollar amount varies with each project depending on level of activity.

Writers' Conferences: Key West Literary Seminar (Key West FL, January).

Tips: "I prefer to work with established authors published by major houses in New York. I will consider marketable proposals from new/previously unpublished writers."

SEDGEBAND LITERARY ASSOCIATES, 7312 Martha Lane, Fort Worth TX 76112. (817)496-3652. Fax: (425)952-9518. E-mail: sedgeband@aol.com. Website: members.home.net/sedgeband. **Contact:** David Duperre or Ginger Norton. Estab. 1997. 60% of clients are new/unpublished writers. Currently handles: 40% nonfiction books; 60% fiction novels.

Member Agents: David Duperre (science fiction/fantasy, scripts, mystery, suspense); Ginger Norton (romance, horror, nonfiction, mainstream).

Represents: Nonfiction books; novels; novellas. **Considers these fiction areas:** action/adventure; contemporary issues; ethnic; experimental; fantasy; horror; literary; mainstream/contemporary; mystery/suspense; psychic/supernatural; romance; science fiction.

O— This agency is looking for new writers who have patience and are willing to work hard. Actively seeking all types of material.

How to Contact: Query with SASE or submit synopsis with SASE. No phone queries accepted. Considers simultaneous queries. Responds in 1 month to queries; 3 months to mss. Returns materials only with SASE. Obtains most new clients through queries, the Internet, referrals.

Recent Sales: *Deep in the Woods*, by Edmund Plante (Cora Verlag); *Soulscape*, by John Higgins (America House); *A Dark Magical Place*, by Edmund Plante (Cora Verlag).

Terms: Agent receives 15% commission on domestic sales; 20% commission on foreign sales. Offers written contract, binding for 1 year; written notice must be given to terminate contract. Charges clients for postage, photocopies, long distance calls, "until we make your first sale."

Tips: "Simply put, we care about people and books, not just money. Do not send a rude query—it will get you rejected no matter how good of a writer you might be. And if we ask to review your work, don't wait to send it for several months. Send it as soon as possible. Also, it is better to wait for a contract offer before asking a lot of questions about publication and movie rights."

THE SEYMOUR AGENCY, 475 Miner St., Canton NY 13617. (315)386-1831. Fax: (315)386-1037. E-mail: mseymour@slic.com. Website: www.theseymouragency.com. **Contact:** Mary Sue Seymour. Estab. 1992. Represents 75 clients. 20% of clients are new/unpublished writers. Currently handles: 30% nonfiction books; 50% novels; 10% scholarly books; 10% textbooks.

• Ms. Seymour is a retired New York State certified teacher.

Represents: Nonfiction books; novels. **Considers these fiction areas:** action/adventure; detective/police/crime; ethnic; glitz; historical; horror; humor/satire; mainstream/contemporary; mystery/suspense; religious/inspirational; romance (contemporary, gothic, historical, medieval, regency); westerns/frontier; vampire.

O— Actively seeking nonfiction and well-written novels. Does not want to receive screenplays, short stories, poetry.

How to Contact: Query with SASE, synopsis, first 50 pages. No fax queries. Considers simultaneous queries. Responds in 1 month to queries; 3 months to mss. Returns materials only with SASE.

Recent Sales: Sold 27 titles in the last year. *Black Soldiers, White Wars*, by Betty Alt (Greenwood).

Terms: Agent receives 15% commission on domestic sales; 20% commission on foreign sales. Offers written contract, binding for 1 year.

Tips: "Send query, synopsis and first 50 pages. If you don't hear from us, you didn't send SASE. We are looking for nonfiction and romance—women in jeopardy, suspense, contemporary, historical, some regency and any well-written fiction and nonfiction."

WENDY SHERMAN ASSOCIATES, INC., 450 Seventh Ave., Suite 3004, New York NY 10123. (212)279-9027. Fax: (212)279-8863. E-mail: wendy@wsherman.com. **Contact:** Wendy Sherman. Estab. 1999. Represents 20 clients. 30% of clients are new/unpublished writers. Currently handles: 50% nonfiction books; 50% novels.
- Prior to becoming an agent, Ms. Sherman worked for Aaron Priest agency and was vice president, executive director of Henry Holt, associate publisher, subsidary rights director, sales and marketing director.

Member Agents: Jessica Lichtenstein (romantic suspense); Wendy Sherman.

Represents: Nonfiction books; novels. **Considers these fiction areas:** literary; mystery/suspense; romance.
- "We specialize in developing new writers as well as working with more established writers. My experience as a publisher has proven to be a great asset to my clients."

How to Contact: Query with SASE, or send outline/proposal, 1 sample chapter. All unsolicited mss returned unopened. Considers simultaneous queries. Responds in 1 month to queries. Returns materials only with SASE. Obtains most new clients through recommendations from others.

Recent Sales: Sold 14 titles in the last year. *Massachusetts, California, Timbuktu,* by Stephanie Rosenfeld (Ballantine); *Cliffs of Despair,* by Tom Hunt (Random House); *A Quiet Storm,* by Rachel Hall (Simon & Schuster); *Still With Me,* by Andrea King Collier (Simon & Schuster). Other clients include Alan Eisenstock, Howard Bahr, Lundy Bancroft, Lise Friedman, Tom Schweich.

Terms: Agent receives 15% commission on domestic sales; 20% commission on foreign sales. Offers written contract. Charges for photocopying of ms, messengers, express mail services, etc. (reasonable, standard expenses).

SPECTRUM LITERARY AGENCY, 320 Central Park W., Suite 1-D, New York NY 10025. **Contact:** Eleanor Wood, president. Represents 80 clients. Currently handles: 10% nonfiction books; 90% novels.

Member Agents: Lucienne Diver.

Represents: Nonfiction books; novels. **Considers these fiction areas:** contemporary issues; fantasy; historical; mainstream/contemporary; mystery/suspense; romance; science fiction.

How to Contact: Query with SASE. Responds in 2 months to queries. Obtains most new clients through recommendations from authors and others.

Recent Sales: This agency prefers not to share information on specific sales.

Terms: Agent receives 15% commission on domestic sales. Deducts for photocopying and book orders.

STEELE-PERKINS LITERARY AGENCY, 26 Island Lane, Canandaigua NY 14424. (716)396-9290. Fax: (716)396-3579. E-mail: pattiesp@aol.com. **Contact:** Pattie Steele-Perkins. Member of AAR, RWA. Currently handles: 100% novels.
- Prior to becoming an agent, Ms. Steele-Perkins was a TV producer/writer for 15 years.

Represents: Novels. **Considers these fiction areas:** mainstream/contemporary; multicultural; romance.
- The Steele-Perkins Literary Agency takes an active role in marketing their clients work including preparation for media appearances. They also develop with the author individual career plans. Actively seeking romance, women's fiction and multicultural works.

How to Contact: Submit outline, 3 sample chapter(s), SASE. Considers simultaneous queries. Responds in 6 weeks to queries. Returns materials only with SASE. Obtains most new clients through recommendations from others, solicitations.

Terms: Agent receives 15% commission on domestic sales. Offers written contract, binding for 1 year; 30-day notice must be given to terminate contract.

Writers' Conferences: National Conference of Romance Writer's of America; Book Expo America Writers' Conferences.

Tips: "Be patient. E-mail rather than call. Make sure what you are sending is the best it can be."

STERLING LORD LITERISTIC, INC., 65 Bleecker St., New York NY 10012. (212)780-6050. Fax: (212)780-6095. **Contact:** Peter Matson. Estab. 1952. Signatory of WGA. Represents 600 clients. Currently handles: 50% nonfiction books; 50% novels.

Member Agents: Peter Matson; Sterling Lord; Jody Hotchkiss (film scripts); Philippa Brophy; Chris Calhoun; Charlotte Sheedy; George Nicholson; Neeti Madan; Jim Rutman.

Represents: Nonfiction books; novels; literary value considered first.

How to Contact: Query with SASE. Responds in 1 month to mss. Obtains most new clients through recommendations from others.

Recent Sales: This agency prefers not to share information on specific sales. Other clients include Kent Haruf, Dick Fancis, Mary Gordon, Sen. John McCain, Simon Winchester.

Terms: Agent receives 15% commission on domestic sales; 20% commission on foreign sales. Offers written contract. Charges clients for photocopying.

STERNIG & BYRNE LITERARY AGENCY, 3209 S. 55, Milwaukee WI 53219-4433. (414)328-8034. Fax: (414)328-8034. E-mail: jackbyrne@aol.com. **Contact:** Jack Byrne. Estab. 1950s. Member of SFWA, MWA. Represents 30 clients. 10% of clients are new/unpublished writers. Accepting few new clients. Currently handles: 5% nonfiction books; 65% novels; 35% juvenile books.

Member Agents: Jack Byrne.

Represents: Nonfiction books; novels; juvenile books. **Considers these fiction areas:** action/adventure; fantasy; glitz; horror; juvenile; mystery/suspense; psychic/supernatural; science fiction; thriller; young adult.

> **O—** "We have a small, friendly, personal, hands-on teamwork approach to marketing. Accepting new clients." Actively seeking science fiction/fantasy. Does not want to receive romance, poetry, textbooks, highly specialized nonfiction.

How to Contact: Query with SASE. Responds in 3 weeks to queries; 3 months to mss. Returns materials only with SASE.

Recent Sales: Sold 12 titles in the last year. *The Road to Well*, by Gerard Daniel Houarner (Leisure); *Untitled New Novel*, by Andre Norton (Meisha Merlin). Other clients include Clients include Betty Ren Wright, Lyn McComchie

Terms: Agent receives 15% commission on domestic sales; 20% commission on foreign sales. Offers written contract, binding for open length of time; 60-day notice must be given to terminate contract.

Reading List: Reads *Publishers Weekly, Science Fiction Chronicles*, etc. to find new clients. Looks for "whatever catches my eye."

Tips: "Don't send first drafts; have a professional presentation...including cover letter; know your field. Read what's been done...good and bad."

THE VINES AGENCY, INC., 648 Broadway, Suite 901, New York NY 10012. (212)777-5522. Fax: (212)777-5978. E-mail: jv@vinesagency.com. Website: www.vinesagency.com. **Contact:** James C. Vines, Paul Surdi, Ali Ryan, Gary Neuwirth. Estab. 1995. Member of AAR; signatory of WGA. Represents 52 clients. 20% of clients are new/unpublished writers. Currently handles: 50% nonfiction books; 50% novels.

> • Prior to opening his agency, Mr. Vines served as an agent with the Virginia Barber Literary Agency.

Member Agents: James C. Vines (quality and commercial fiction and nonfiction); Gary Neuwirth; Paul Surdi (women's fiction, ethnic fiction, quality nonfiction); Ali Ryan (women's fiction and nonfiction, mainstream).

Represents: Nonfiction books; novels. **Considers these fiction areas:** action/adventure; contemporary issues; detective/police/crime; ethnic; experimental; family saga; feminist; gay/lesbian; historical; horror; humor/satire; literary; mainstream/contemporary; mystery/suspense; occult; psychic/supernatural; regional; romance (contemporary, historical); science fiction; sports; thriller; westerns/frontier; women's.

> **O—** This agency specializes in mystery, suspense, science fiction, women's fiction, ethnic fiction, mainstream novels, screenplays, teleplays.

Also Handles: Feature film; TV scripts. **Considers these script subject areas:** action/adventure; comedy; detective/police/crime; ethnic; experimental; feminist; gay/lesbian; historical; horror; mainstream; mystery/suspense; romantic comedy; romantic drama; science fiction; teen; thriller; western/frontier.

How to Contact: Submit outline, 3 sample chapter(s), SASE. Accepts e-mail and fax queries. Considers simultaneous queries. Responds in 2 weeks to queries; 1 month to mss. Returns materials only with SASE. Obtains most new clients through query letters, recommendations from others, reading short stories in magazines, soliciting conferences.

Recent Sales: Sold 48 titles and sold 5 scripts in the last year. *America the Beautiful*, by Moon Unit Zappa (Scribner); *The Warmest December*, by Bernice McFadden (Dutton-Plume).

Terms: Agent receives 15% commission on domestic sales; 25% commission on foreign sales. Offers written contract, binding for 1 year; 30 days notice must be given to terminate contract. 100% of business is derived from commissions on ms sales. Charges clients for foreign postage, messenger services, photocopying.

Writers' Conferences: Maui Writer's Conference.

Tips: "Do not follow up on submissions with phone calls to the agency. The agency will read and respond by mail only. Do not pack your manuscript in plastic 'peanuts' that will make us have to vacuum the office after opening the package containing your manuscript. Always enclose return postage."

N ◑ **WITHERSPOON & ASSOCIATES, INC.**, 235 E. 31st St., New York NY 10016. (212)889-8626. **Contact:** David Forrer. Estab. 1990. Represents 150 clients. 20% of clients are new/unpublished writers. Currently handles: 50% nonfiction books; 45% novels; 5% story collections.

● Prior to becoming an agent, Ms. Witherspoon was a writer and magazine consultant.

Member Agents: Maria Massie; Kimberly Witherspoon; David Forrer; Alexis Hurley.

Represents: Nonfiction books; novels. **Considers these fiction areas:** contemporary issues; detective/police/crime; ethnic; family saga; feminist; gay/lesbian; historical; literary; mainstream/contemporary; mystery/suspense; thriller.

How to Contact: Query with SASE. Prefers to read materials exclusively. No unsolicited mss. Responds in 1 month to queries. Obtains most new clients through recommendations from others, solicitations, conferences.

Recent Sales: This agency prefers not to share information on specific sales.

Terms: Agent receives 15% commission on domestic sales; 20% commission on foreign sales. Offers written contract. Office fees are deducted from author's earnings.

Writers' Conferences: BEA (Chicago, June); Frankfurt (Germany, October).

✓ ◑ **ZACHARY SHUSTER HARMSWORTH**, (formerly Zachary Shuster Agency), 729 Boylston St., 5th Floor, Boston MA 02116. (617)262-2400 CA; (212)765-6900 NY. Fax: (617)262-2468 CA ; (212)765-6490 NY. Also: New York Office: 1776 Broadway, Suite 1405, New York, NY 10016. **Contact:** Esmond Harmsworth (CA); Scott Gold (NY). Estab. 1996. Represents 125 clients. 20% of clients are new/unpublished writers. Currently handles: 45% nonfiction books; 45% novels; 5% story collections; 5% scholarly books.

● "Our pricipals include two former publishing and entertainment lawyers, a journalist and an editor/agent." Lane Zachary was an editor at Random House before becoming an agent.

Member Agents: Esmond Harmsworth (commercial and literary fiction, history, science, adventure); Todd Shuster (narrative and prescriptive nonfiction, biography, memoirs); Lane Zachary (biography, memoirs, literary fiction); Jennifer Gates (literary fiction, nonfiction).

Represents: Nonfiction books; novels. **Considers these fiction areas:** contemporary issues; detective/police/crime; ethnic; feminist; gay/lesbian; historical; literary; mainstream/contemporary; mystery/suspense; thriller.

   O→ This agency specializes in journalist-driven narrative nonfiction, literary and commercial fiction. Actively seeking narrative nonfiction, mystery, commercial and literary fiction, memoirs, history, biographies. Does not want to receive poetry.

How to Contact: Query with SASE, submit 50 page sample of ms. Accepts e-mail and fax queries. Considers simultaneous queries. Responds in 3 months to mss. Obtains most new clients through recommendations from others, solicitations, conferences.

Recent Sales: Sold 15 titles in the last year. *The Last River*, by Todd Balf (Crown); *Lay That Trumpet in Our Hands*, by Susan McCarthy (Bantam); *Waiting*, by Ha Jin (Alfred A. Knopf—National Book Award winner); *Le Probleme avec Jane*, by Catherine Jenkins (Simon & Schuster). Other clients include Leslie Epstein, David Mixner.

Terms: Agent receives 15% commission on domestic sales; 20% commission on foreign sales. Offers written contract, binding for 1 work only.; 30 days notice must be given to terminate contract. Charges clients for postage, copying, courier, telephone. "We only charge expenses if the manuscript is sold."

Tips: "We work closely with all our clients on all editorial and promotional aspects of their works."

N ◑ **SUSAN ZECKENDORF ASSOC. INC.**, 171 W. 57th St., New York NY 10019. (212)245-2928. **Contact:** Susan Zeckendorf. Estab. 1979. Member of AAR. Represents 15 clients. 25% of clients are new/unpublished writers. Currently handles: 50% nonfiction books; 50% novels.

● Prior to opening her agency, Ms. Zeckendorf was a counseling psychologist.

Represents: Nonfiction books; novels. **Considers these fiction areas:** detective/police/crime; ethnic; historical; literary; mainstream/contemporary; mystery/suspense; thriller.

   O→ Actively seeking mysteries, literary fiction, mainstream fiction, thrillers, social history, parenting, classical music, biography. Does not want to receive science fiction, romance. "No children's books."

How to Contact: Query with SASE. Considers simultaneous queries. Responds in 10 days to queries; 3 weeks to mss. Returns materials only with SASE.

Recent Sales: *The Key*, by James N. Frey (St. Martin's); *The Hard Scrabble Chronicles*, by Laurie Morrow (Berkley); *The Biography of Bill W.*, by Francis Hartigan (St. Martin's Press).

Terms: Agent receives 15% commission on domestic sales; 20% commission on foreign sales. Charges for photocopying, messenger services.

Writers' Conferences: Central Valley Writers Conference; The Tucson Publishers Association Conference; Writer's Connection; Frontiers in Writing Conference (Amarillo TX); Golden Triangle Writers Conference (Beaumont TX); Oklahoma Festival of Books (Claremont OK); Mary Mount Writers Conference.

Tips: "We are a small agency giving lots of individual attention. We respond quickly to submissions."

Literary Agents Category Index

Agents listed in the preceeding section are indexed below according to the categories of fiction they represent. Use it to find agents who handle the specific kind of fiction you write. Then turn to those listings in the alphabetical Literary Agents section for complete contact and submission information.

Action/Adventure
Ahearn Agency, Inc., The
Amsterdam Agency, Marcia
Crawford Literary Agency
Elite Online
Grace Literary Agency, Carroll
Halsey North, Reece
Harris Literary Agency, Inc., The Joy
Jabberwocky Literary Agency
JCA Literary Agency
Klinger, Inc., Harvey
Kraas Agency, Irene
Rotrosen Agency, LLC, Jane
Russell and Volkening
Sanders & Associates, Victoria
Scherf, Inc., Literary Management
Sedgeband Literary Associates
Seymour Agency, The
Sternig & Byrne Literary Agency
Vines Agency, Inc., The

Cartoon/Comic
Harris Literary Agency, Inc., The Joy
Jabberwocky Literary Agency

Confessional
Harris Literary Agency, Inc., The Joy

Contemporary Issues
Ahearn Agency, Inc., The
Bernstein & Associates, Inc., Pam
BookEnds, LLC
Brandt Agency, The Joan
Frenkel & Associates, James
Goodman-Andrew Agency, Inc.
Grosjean Literary Agency, Jill
Harris Literary Agency, Inc., The Joy
Jabberwocky Literary Agency
JCA Literary Agency
Jenks Agency, Carolyn
Kidde, Hoyt & Picard
Pinder Lane & Garon-Brooke Associates, Ltd.
Robbins Literary Agency, B.J.
Sanders & Associates, Victoria
Schiavone Literary Agency, Inc.
Sedgeband Literary Associates
Spectrum Literary Agency
Vines Agency, Inc., The
Witherspoon & Associates, Inc.

Zachary Shuster Harmsworth

Detective/Police/Crime
Ahearn Agency, Inc., The
Amsterdam Agency, Marcia
Appleseeds Management
BookEnds, LLC
Brandt Agency, The Joan
Core Creations
Ellenberg Literary Agency, Ethan
Frenkel & Associates, James
Grace Literary Agency, Carroll
Harris Literary Agency, Inc., The Joy
Jabberwocky Literary Agency
JCA Literary Agency
Kidde, Hoyt & Picard
Klinger, Inc., Harvey
Kraas Agency, Irene
Maass Literary Agency
Pinder Lane & Garon-Brooke Associates, Ltd.
Robbins Literary Agency, B.J.
Rotrosen Agency, LLC, Jane
Russell and Volkening
Seymour Agency, The
Vines Agency, Inc., The
Witherspoon & Associates, Inc.
Zachary Shuster Harmsworth
Zeckendorf Assoc. Inc., Susan

Erotica
Harris Literary Agency, Inc., The Joy

Ethnic
Ahearn Agency, Inc., The
Bernstein & Associates, Inc., Pam
BookEnds, LLC
Cohen, Inc. Literary Agency, Ruth
Frenkel & Associates, James
Goodman-Andrew Agency, Inc.
Halsey North, Reece
Harris Literary Agency, Inc., The Joy
Jabberwocky Literary Agency
Jenks Agency, Carolyn
Knight Agency, The
Robbins Literary Agency, B.J.
Russell and Volkening
Sanders & Associates, Victoria
Schiavone Literary Agency, Inc.
Sedgeband Literary Associates

Seymour Agency, The
Vines Agency, Inc., The
Witherspoon & Associates, Inc.
Zachary Shuster Harmsworth
Zeckendorf Assoc. Inc., Susan

Experimental
Harris Literary Agency, Inc., The Joy
Sedgeband Literary Associates
Vines Agency, Inc., The

Family Saga
Ahearn Agency, Inc., The
BookEnds, LLC
Brandt Agency, The Joan
Ellenberg Literary Agency, Ethan
Grace Literary Agency, Carroll
Harris Literary Agency, Inc., The Joy
Jabberwocky Literary Agency
JCA Literary Agency
Klinger, Inc., Harvey
Pinder Lane & Garon-Brooke Associates, Ltd.
Rotrosen Agency, LLC, Jane
Sanders & Associates, Victoria
Schiavone Literary Agency, Inc.
Vines Agency, Inc., The
Witherspoon & Associates, Inc.

Fantasy
Ahearn Agency, Inc., The
Carvainis Agency, Inc., Maria
Ellenberg Literary Agency, Ethan
Frenkel & Associates, James
Gislason Agency, The
Grace Literary Agency, Carroll
Jabberwocky Literary Agency
Maass Literary Agency
Pinder Lane & Garon-Brooke Associates, Ltd.
Sedgeband Literary Associates
Spectrum Literary Agency
Sternig & Byrne Literary Agency

Feminist
Ahearn Agency, Inc., The
BookEnds, LLC
Elite Online
Frenkel & Associates, James
Harris Literary Agency, Inc., The Joy
Kidde, Hoyt & Picard
Sanders & Associates, Victoria
Vines Agency, Inc., The
Witherspoon & Associates, Inc.
Zachary Shuster Harmsworth

Glitz
Ahearn Agency, Inc., The
BookEnds, LLC
Harris Literary Agency, Inc., The Joy
Jabberwocky Literary Agency
Kidde, Hoyt & Picard
Klinger, Inc., Harvey
Seymour Agency, The

Sternig & Byrne Literary Agency

Historical
Ahearn Agency, Inc., The
Bernstein & Associates, Inc., Pam
BookEnds, LLC
Carvainis Agency, Inc., Maria
Cohen, Inc. Literary Agency, Ruth
Ellenberg Literary Agency, Ethan
English, Elaine P.
Frenkel & Associates, James
Grace Literary Agency, Carroll
Grosjean Literary Agency, Jill
Halsey North, Reece
Harris Literary Agency, Inc., The Joy
Hopkins Literary Associates
Jabberwocky Literary Agency
JCA Literary Agency
Jenks Agency, Carolyn
Kidde, Hoyt & Picard
Maass Literary Agency
McHugh Literary Agency
Rotrosen Agency, LLC, Jane
Schiavone Literary Agency, Inc.
Seymour Agency, The
Spectrum Literary Agency
Vines Agency, Inc., The
Witherspoon & Associates, Inc.
Zachary Shuster Harmsworth
Zeckendorf Assoc. Inc., Susan

Horror
Ahearn Agency, Inc., The
Amsterdam Agency, Marcia
Connor Literary Agency
Core Creations
Elite Online
Grace Literary Agency, Carroll
Harris Literary Agency, Inc., The Joy
Jabberwocky Literary Agency
Maass Literary Agency
Rotrosen Agency, LLC, Jane
Schiavone Literary Agency, Inc.
Sedgeband Literary Associates
Seymour Agency, The
Sternig & Byrne Literary Agency
Vines Agency, Inc., The

Literary
Ahearn Agency, Inc., The
Altshuler Literary Agency, Miriam
Bernstein Literary Agency, Meredith
BookEnds, LLC
Brandt Agency, The Joan
Carvainis Agency, Inc., Maria
Cohen, Inc. Literary Agency, Ruth
Connor Literary Agency
Darhansoff & Verrill Literary Agency
Ellenberg Literary Agency, Ethan
Ellison, Inc., Nicholas
Goodman-Andrew Agency, Inc.
Grace Literary Agency, Carroll

Halsey North, Reece
JCA Literary Agency
Jenks Agency, Carolyn
Klinger, Inc., Harvey
Knight Agency, The
Maass Literary Agency
Pinder Lane & Garon-Brooke Associates, Ltd.
Rinaldi Literary Agency, Angela
Robbins Literary Agency, B.J.
Russell and Volkening
Sanders & Associates, Victoria
Scherf, Inc., Literary Management
Schiavone Literary Agency, Inc.
Sedgeband Literary Associates
Sherman Associates, Inc., Wendy
Witherspoon & Associates, Inc.
Zachary Shuster Harmsworth
Zeckendorf Assoc. Inc., Susan

Mainstream

Ahearn Agency, Inc., The
Altshuler Literary Agency, Miriam
Bernstein & Associates, Inc., Pam
BookEnds, LLC
Brandt Agency, The Joan
Carvainis Agency, Inc., Maria
Cohen, Inc. Literary Agency, Ruth
Connor Literary Agency
Ellenberg Literary Agency, Ethan
Ellison, Inc., Nicholas
English, Elaine P.
Frenkel & Associates, James
Goodman-Andrew Agency, Inc.
Grace Literary Agency, Carroll
Grosjean Literary Agency, Jill
Halsey North, Reece
Harris Literary Agency, Inc., The Joy
Hopkins Literary Associates
Jabberwocky Literary Agency
JCA Literary Agency
Jenks Agency, Carolyn
Kidde, Hoyt & Picard
Klinger, Inc., Harvey
Knight Agency, The
Maass Literary Agency
McHugh Literary Agency
Pinder Lane & Garon-Brooke Associates, Ltd.
Rinaldi Literary Agency, Angela
Robbins Literary Agency, B.J.
Rotrosen Agency, LLC, Jane
Russell and Volkening
Scherf, Inc., Literary Management
Schiavone Literary Agency, Inc.
Sedgeband Literary Associates
Spectrum Literary Agency
Steele-Perkins Literary Agency
Vines Agency, Inc., The
Witherspoon & Associates, Inc.
Zachary Shuster Harmsworth
Zeckendorf Assoc. Inc., Susan

Mystery/Suspense

Ahearn Agency, Inc., The
Amsterdam Agency, Marcia
Appleseeds Management
Bernstein & Associates, Inc., Pam
Bernstein Literary Agency, Meredith
BookEnds, LLC
Brandt Agency, The Joan
Carvainis Agency, Inc., Maria
Cohen, Inc. Literary Agency, Ruth
Connor Literary Agency
Crawford Literary Agency
Darhansoff & Verrill Literary Agency
Ellenberg Literary Agency, Ethan
Frenkel & Associates, James
Gislason Agency, The
Grace Literary Agency, Carroll
Grosjean Literary Agency, Jill
Halsey North, Reece
Harris Literary Agency, Inc., The Joy
JCA Literary Agency
Jenks Agency, Carolyn
Kidde, Hoyt & Picard
Klinger, Inc., Harvey
Kraas Agency, Irene
Maass Literary Agency
McHugh Literary Agency
Pinder Lane & Garon-Brooke Associates, Ltd.
Robbins Literary Agency, B.J.
Rotrosen Agency, LLC, Jane
Russell and Volkening
Scherf, Inc., Literary Management
Sedgeband Literary Associates
Seymour Agency, The
Sherman Associates, Inc., Wendy
Spectrum Literary Agency
Sternig & Byrne Literary Agency
Vines Agency, Inc., The
Witherspoon & Associates, Inc.
Zachary Shuster Harmsworth
Zeckendorf Assoc. Inc., Susan

Picture Book

Cohen, Inc. Literary Agency, Ruth
Ellenberg Literary Agency, Ethan
Harris Literary Agency, Inc., The Joy
Russell and Volkening

Psychic/Supernatural

Ahearn Agency, Inc., The
Grace Literary Agency, Carroll
Harris Literary Agency, Inc., The Joy
Jabberwocky Literary Agency
Maass Literary Agency
Sedgeband Literary Associates
Sternig & Byrne Literary Agency
Vines Agency, Inc., The

Regional

Ahearn Agency, Inc., The
Grosjean Literary Agency, Jill

Harris Literary Agency, Inc., The Joy
Jabberwocky Literary Agency
Vines Agency, Inc., The

Religious/Inspirational
Harris Literary Agency, Inc., The Joy
Scherf, Inc., Literary Management
Seymour Agency, The

Romance
Ahearn Agency, Inc., The
Amsterdam Agency, Marcia
Bernstein & Associates, Inc., Pam
Bernstein Literary Agency, Meredith
BookEnds, LLC
Carvainis Agency, Inc., Maria
Connor Literary Agency
Ellenberg Literary Agency, Ethan
English, Elaine P.
Gislason Agency, The
Grace Literary Agency, Carroll
Grosjean Literary Agency, Jill
Harris Literary Agency, Inc., The Joy
Hopkins Literary Associates
Jenks Agency, Carolyn
Kidde, Hoyt & Picard
Knight Agency, The
Maass Literary Agency
McHugh Literary Agency
Pinder Lane & Garon-Brooke Associates, Ltd.
Rotrosen Agency, LLC, Jane
Sedgeband Literary Associates
Seymour Agency, The
Sherman Associates, Inc., Wendy
Spectrum Literary Agency
Steele-Perkins Literary Agency
Vines Agency, Inc., The

Sports
Harris Literary Agency, Inc., The Joy
Jabberwocky Literary Agency
JCA Literary Agency
Robbins Literary Agency, B.J.
Russell and Volkening
Vines Agency, Inc., The

Science Fiction
Ahearn Agency, Inc., The
Amsterdam Agency, Marcia
Core Creations
Elite Online
Ellenberg Literary Agency, Ethan
Frenkel & Associates, James
Gislason Agency, The
Halsey North, Reece
Jabberwocky Literary Agency
Kraas Agency, Irene
Maass Literary Agency
Pinder Lane & Garon-Brooke Associates, Ltd.
Schiavone Literary Agency, Inc.

Sedgeband Literary Associates
Spectrum Literary Agency
Sternig & Byrne Literary Agency
Vines Agency, Inc., The

Thriller/Espionage
Ahearn Agency, Inc., The
Altshuler Literary Agency, Miriam
Amsterdam Agency, Marcia
Bernstein & Associates, Inc., Pam
BookEnds, LLC
Brandt Agency, The Joan
Carvainis Agency, Inc., Maria
Connor Literary Agency
Crawford Literary Agency
Ellenberg Literary Agency, Ethan
Frenkel & Associates, James
Gislason Agency, The
Grace Literary Agency, Carroll
Grosjean Literary Agency, Jill
Harris Literary Agency, Inc., The Joy
Jabberwocky Literary Agency
JCA Literary Agency
Jenks Agency, Carolyn
Kidde, Hoyt & Picard
Klinger, Inc., Harvey
Kraas Agency, Irene
Maass Literary Agency
McHugh Literary Agency
Robbins Literary Agency, B.J.
Rotrosen Agency, LLC, Jane
Russell and Volkening
Sanders & Associates, Victoria
Scherf, Inc., Literary Management
Sternig & Byrne Literary Agency
Vines Agency, Inc., The
Witherspoon & Associates, Inc.
Zachary Shuster Harmsworth
Zeckendorf Assoc. Inc., Susan

Westerns/Frontier
Ahearn Agency, Inc., The
Amsterdam Agency, Marcia
Frenkel & Associates, James
Grace Literary Agency, Carroll
Jenks Agency, Carolyn
McHugh Literary Agency
Seymour Agency, The
Vines Agency, Inc., The

Young Adult
Amsterdam Agency, Marcia
BookEnds, LLC
Carvainis Agency, Inc., Maria
Cohen, Inc. Literary Agency, Ruth
Ellenberg Literary Agency, Ethan
Frenkel & Associates, James
Harris Literary Agency, Inc., The Joy
Schiavone Literary Agency, Inc.
Sternig & Byrne Literary Agency

Literary Magazines

This section contains markets for your literary short fiction. Although definitions of what constitutes "literary" writing vary, editors of literary journals agree they want to publish the "best" fiction they can acquire. Qualities they look for in fiction include creativity, style, flawless mechanics, and careful attention to detail in content and manuscript preparation. Most of the authors writing such fiction are well-read and well-educated, and many are students and graduates of university creative writing programs.

Please also review our new Online Markets section, page 343, for electronic literary magazines. At a time when paper and publishing costs rise while funding to university presses continues to be cut or eliminated, electronic literary magazines are helping generate a publishing renaissance for experimental as well as more traditional literary fiction. These electronic outlets for literary fiction also benefit writers by eliminating copying and postage costs and providing the opportunity for much quicker responses to submissions. Also notice that some magazines with websites give specific information about what they offer on their websites, including updated writer's guidelines and sample fiction from their publications.

STEPPING STONES TO RECOGNITION

Some well-established literary journals pay several hundred or even several thousand dollars for a short story. Most, though, can only pay with contributor's copies or a subscription to their publication. However, being published in literary journals offers the important benefits of experience, exposure, and prestige. Agents and major book publishers regularly read literary magazines in search of new writers. Work from among these journals is also selected for inclusion in annual prize anthologies such as *The Best American Short Stories*, *Prize Stories: The O. Henry Awards*, *Pushcart Prize: Best of the Small Presses*, and *New Stories from the South: The Year's Best*.

You'll find most of the well-known prestigious literary journals listed here. Many, including *Carolina Quarterly* and *Ploughshares*, are associated with universities, while others such as *The Paris Review* are independently published.

SELECTING THE RIGHT LITERARY JOURNAL

Once you have browsed through this section and have a list of journals you might like to submit to, read those listings again, carefully. Remember that this is information editors present to help you in submitting work that fits their needs. The "Quick Start" Guide to Publishing Your Fiction, starting on page 2, will guide you through the process of finding markets for your fiction.

This is the only section in which you will find magazines that do not read submissions all year long. Whether limited reading periods are tied to a university schedule or meant to accommodate the capabilities of a very small staff, those periods are noted within listings. The staffs of university journals are usually made up of student editors and a managing editor who is also a faculty member. These staffs often change every year. Whenever possible, we indicate this in listings and give the name of the current editor and the length of that editor's term. Also be aware that the schedule of a university journal usually coincides with that university's academic year, meaning that the editors of most university publications are difficult or impossible to reach during the summer.

FURTHERING YOUR SEARCH

It cannot be stressed enough that reading the listings for literary journals is only the first part of developing your marketing plan. The second part, equally important, is to obtain fiction guidelines and read the actual journal you'd like to submit to with great care. Reading copies of these journals helps you determine the fine points of each magazine's publishing style and sensibility. There is no substitute for this type of hands-on research.

Unlike commercial periodicals available at most newsstands and bookstores, it requires a little more effort to obtain some of the magazines listed here. The new super chain bookstores are doing a better job these days of stocking literaries and you can find some in independent and college bookstores, especially those published in your area. You may, however, need to send for a sample copy. We include sample copy prices in the listings whenever possible. In addition to reading your sample copies, pay close attention to the **Advice** section of each listing. There you'll often find a very specific description of the style of fiction editors at that publication prefer.

Another way to find out more about literary magazines is to check out the various prize anthologies and take note of journals whose fiction is being selected for publication there. Studying prize anthologies not only lets you know which magazines are publishing award-winning work, but it also provides a valuable overview of what is considered to be the best fiction published today. Those anthologies include:

• *Best American Short Stories*, published by Houghton Mifflin, 222 Berkeley St., Boston MA 02116.
• *New Stories from the South: The Year's Best*, published by Algonquin Books of Chapel Hill, P.O. Box 2225, Chapel Hill NC 27515.
• *Prize Stories: The O. Henry Awards*, published by Doubleday/Anchor, 1540 Broadway, New York NY 10036.
• *Pushcart Prize: Best of the Small Presses*, published by Pushcart Press, Box 380, Wainscott NY 11975.

At the beginnings of listings, we include symbols to help you in narrowing your search. Keys to those symbols can be found on the inside front and back covers of this book.

✓ ◖ ACM, (ANOTHER CHICAGO MAGAZINE), Left Field Press, P.O. Box 180017, Chicago IL 60618. E-mail: editors@anotherchicagomag.com. Website: www.anotherchicagomag.com (includes guidelines, contest information, subscription information). Editor: Barry Silesky. **Contact:** Sharon Solwitz, fiction editor. Magazine: 5½×8½; 200-220 pages; "art folio each issue." Estab. 1977.
Needs: Contemporary, ethnic, experimental, feminist, gay, lesbian, literary, prose poem and translations. No religious, strictly genre or editorial. Receives 300 unsolicited fiction mss each month. **Publishes 10 new writers/ year.** Recently published work by Robin Hemley, Alyce Miller, Bill Roorbach, Michael Mortone and Lidia Yuknavitch. Also publishes creative nonfiction.
How to Contact: Unsolicited mss acceptable with SASE. "Send only one story (unless you work short, less than five pgs.) then we'll read two. We encourage cover letters." Publishes ms 6-12 months after acceptance. Sample copies are available for $8 ppd. Responds in 5 months. Receives small press collections.
Payment/Terms: Pays small honorarium when possible, contributor's copies and 1 year subscription. Acquires first North American serial rights.
Advice: "Support literary publishing by subscribing to at least one literary journal—if not ours another. Get used to rejection slips, and don't get discouraged. Keep introductory letters short. Make sure manuscript has name and address on every page, and that it is clean, neat and proofread. We are looking for stories with freshness and originality in subject angle and style, and work that encounters the world and is not stuck in its own navel."

◎ ▼ THE ACORN, a Journal of the Western Sierra, Hot Pepper Press, P.O. Box 1266, El Dorado CA 95623-1266. Phone/fax: (530)642-9265. E-mail: theacorn@visto.com or kirkcolvin@visto.com. Editor: Kirk Colvin. **Contact:** Fiction Editor. Magazine: 8½×5½; 44 pages. *The Acorn* primarily publishes work about the "western slope of Sierra Nevada and rural lifestyle, but encourages the submission of any and all good writing." Quarterly. Estab. 1993. Circ. 200.
• A work from *The Acorn* received first place for Best Western Short Fiction from the Western Writers of America.

Needs: Adventure, historical, humor/satire, literary, mainstream/contemporary, regional, senior citizen/retirement. "No porn or erotica. We usually try to choose subjects or topics that fit the season. Historical fiction is attractive to us, but we like to see all forms of fiction." Receives 75-100 unsolicited mss/month. Accepts 5-6 mss/issue; 24 mss/year. Publishes ms 1 month after acceptance. **Publishes 5 new writers/year.** Published work by Taylor Graham, Kirk Colvin, Margaret S. Burns and Virgil Suarez. Length: 4,000 words maximum. Publishes short shorts. Also publishes literary essays and poetry. Often comments on rejected mss. Sponsors contest; send SASE for information.

How to Contact: Send complete ms with a cover letter. Include 1-paragraph bio and list of publications. Accepts queries/mss by e-mail. Responds in 4 months to mss. Send SASE for reply, return of ms or send a disposable copy of ms. No simultaneous submissions; accepts reprints. Electronic submissions encouraged. Sample copy for $4. Guidelines for #10 SASE.

Payment/Terms: Pays 2 contributor's copies; additional copies for $3.75. Pays on publication for one-time rights.

Advice: Looks for "memorable work that captures the flavor of our region—its history, landforms and wildlife and rural lifestyle. Good writing helps too. If we remember a story the next day, if we find ourselves thinking about the story or a character while driving around in our car, you've struck a nerve and taken a huge first step. Proper formatting will at least get your story read—fancy fonts, italics and clip art are distracting and a short cut to rejection. We encourage electronic submissions of manuscripts. Since we use an editorial board approach and have 5-6 editors reviewing each submission, electronic submissions allow us to save time and money, as well as accelerating the review process."

$ **ADRIFT, Writing: Irish, Irish American and . . .**, 46 E. First St. #3D, New York NY 10003. **Contact:** Thomas McGonigle, editor. Magazine: 8×11; 32 pages; 60 lb. paper stock; 65 lb. cover stock; illustrations; photos. "Irish-Irish American as a basis—though we are interested in advanced writing from anywhere." Semiannual. Estab. 1983. Circ. 1,000.

Needs: Contemporary, erotica, ethnic, experimental, feminist, gay, lesbian, literary, translations. Receives 40 unsolicited mss/month. Accepts 3 mss/issue. **Published new writers within the last year.** Published work by Francis Stuart. Length: open. Also publishes literary criticism. Sometimes critiques rejected mss.

How to Contact: Send complete ms. Responds as soon as possible. SASE for return of ms. Sample copy for $5. Reviews novels or short story collections.

Payment/Terms: Pays $7.50-300. Pays on publication for first rights.

Advice: "The writing should argue with, among others, James Joyce, Flann O'Brien, Juan Goytisolo, Ingeborg Bachmann, E.M. Cioran, Max Stirner and Patrick Kavanagh."

N **$** **ADVENTURES OF SWORD & SORCERY**, Double Star Press, P.O. Box 807, Xenia OH 45385. E-mail: double_star@yahoo.com. **Contact:** Randy Dannenfelser, editor. Magazine: 8½×11; 80 pages; slick cover stock; illustrations. "We publish sword and sorcery, heroic and high fantasy fiction." Quarterly. Estab. 1995. Circ. 7,000.

Needs: Sword and sorcery, heroic and high fantasy fiction. "We want fiction with an emphasis on action and adventure, but still cognizant of the struggles within as they play against the struggles without. Include sexual content only as required by the story, but not excessive/porn." Receives approximately 250 unsolicited mss/month. Accepts 9 mss/issue; 36 mss/year. Publishes ms 1 year after acceptance. Agented fiction 5%. **Publishes 8 new writers/year.** Published work by Mike Resnick, Stephen Baxter and Darrell Schweitzer. Length: 1,000-20,000 words; average length: 5,000 words. Also publishes literary criticism and book reviews (only solicited). Always comments on rejected mss.

How to Contact: Send complete ms with a cover letter. Include estimated word count, Social Security number, list of publications, phone number and e-mail address. Responds in 1 month to queries; 2 months to mss. Send SASE for reply, return of ms. No simultaneous submissions. Accepts electronic submissions (e-mail, disk or modem). Sample copy $6. Guidelines for #10 SASE. Reviews novels and short story collections.

Payment/Terms: Pays 3-6¢/word and 3 contributor's copies; additional copies 40% discount plus shipping. Pays on acceptance for first North American serial rights. Sends galleys to author.

Advice: "Recently we are looking for more adventuresome work with settings other than generic medieval Europe. We look for real emotion in the prose. Think about the audience we are targeted at, and send us appropriate stories."

ADVOCATE, PKA'S PUBLICATION, PKA Publications, 301A Rolling Hills Park, Prattsville NY 12468. (518)299-3103. Tabloid: 9⅜×12¼; 32 pages; newsprint paper; line drawings; b&w photographs. "Eclectic for a general audience." Bimonthly. Estab. 1987. Publishes 12,000 copies.

Needs: Adventure, contemporary, ethnic, experimental, fantasy, feminist, historical, humor/satire, juvenile (5-9 years), literary, mainstream, mystery/suspense, prose poem, regional, romance, science fiction, senior citizen/retirement, sports, western, young adult/teen (10-18 years). "Currently looking for equine (horses) stories, poetry, art, photos and cartoons. The *Gaited Horse Newsletter* is currently published within the pages of *PKA's Advocate*." Nothing religious, pornographic, violent, erotic, pro-drug or anti-environment. Receives 60 unsolicited mss/ month. Accepts 6-8 mss/issue; 36-48 mss/year. Publishes ms 4 months to 1 year after acceptance. Length: 1,000 words preferred; 1,500 words maximum. Sometimes critiques rejected mss.

How to Contact: Send complete ms with cover letter. Responds in 2 weeks to queries; 2 months to mss. SASE. No simultaneous submissions. Sample copy for $4 (US currency for inside US; $5.25 US currency for Canada). Writers guidelines for SASE.

Payment/Terms: Pays contributor's copies. Acquires first rights.

Advice: "The highest criterion in selecting a work is its entertainment value. It must first be enjoyable reading. It must, of course, be original. To stand out, it must be thought provoking or strongly emotive, or very cleverly plotted. Will consider only previously unpublished works by writers who do not earn their living principally through writing."

AETHLON, East Tennessee State University, Box 70, 683, Johnson City TN 37614-0683. (423)439-5994. E-mail: morefiel@etsu.edu. **Contact:** John Morefield, fiction editor. Magazine: 6×9; 180-240 pages; photos. "Theme: Literary treatment of sport. We publish articles on that theme, critical studies of author's treatment of sport and original fiction and poetry with sport themes. Most of our readers are academics." Biannual. Estab. 1983. Circ. 800.

Needs: Sport. No fantasy, science fiction, mystery, nostalgia, "trick endings," novel excerpts or horror. "Stories must have a sport-related theme and subject; otherwise, we're wide open. No personal memoirs, mystery, sci-fi, horror, 'trick ending,' etc." Receives 15-20 fiction mss/month. Accepts 6-10 fiction mss/issue; 12-20 fiction mss/ year. Publishes ms "about 1 year" after acceptance. **Publishes 2-3 new writers/year.** Recently published work by James Hinton, Michael Hollister, Leonard Blumenschine and a translation of a story by the Uruguayan writer Juan Carlos Onneti. Length: 500-7,500; average length: 2,500-5,000 words. Also publishes literary essays, literary criticism, poetry. Sometimes critiques rejected mss.

How to Contact: Send complete ms and brief cover letter with 1-2 lines for a contributor's note. Responds in 6 months. SASE in size to fit ms. No simultaneous or electronic submissions. Final copy must be submitted on disk (WordPerfect). Sample copy for $12.50. Reviews novels and short story collections. Send books to Prof. Joe Dewey, Dept. of English, University of Pittsburgh-Johnstown, Johnstown PA 15601.

Payment/Terms: Pays 1 contributor's copy and 5 offprints.

Advice: "We are looking for well-written, insightful stories. The only criterion is literary excellence. A story should begin immediately to develop tension or conflict. It should have strong characters and a well-drawn setting. Don't be afraid to be experimental. Take more care with your manuscript. Please send a legible manuscript free of grammatical errors. Be willing to revise."

$ ⬤ AFRICAN AMERICAN REVIEW, Indiana State University, Department of English, Root Hall A220, Terre Haute IN 47809. (812)237-2968. Fax: (812)237-3156. E-mail: ascleco@amber.indstate.edu. **Contact:** Joe Weixlmann, editor. Magazine: 7×10; 176 pages; 60 lb., acid-free paper; 100 lb. skid stock cover; illustrations; photos. "*African American Review* publishes stories and poetry by African American writers, and essays about African American literature and culture." Quarterly. Estab. 1967. Circ. 4,200.

● *African American Review* is the official publication of the Division of Black American Literature and Culture of the Modern Language Association. The magazine received American Literary Magazine Awards in 1994 and 1995.

Needs: Ethnic/Multicultural: experimental, feminist, literary, mainstream/contemporary. "No children's/juvenile/young adult/teen." Receives 50 unsolicited mss/month. Accepts 40 mss/year. Publishes ms 1 year after acceptance. Agented fiction 10%. Published work by Clarence Major, Ann Allen Shockley, Ishmael Reed. Length: 3,000 words average. Also publishes literary essays, literary criticism, poetry. Sometimes comments on rejected mss.

How to Contact: Send complete ms with a cover letter. Responds in 2 weeks to queries; 3 months to mss. Send SASE for reply, return of ms or send a disposable copy of ms. Sample copy for $6. Guidelines for #10 SASE. Reviews novels and short story collections. Send books to Keneth Kinnamon, Dept. of English, Univ. of Arkansas, Fayetteville, AR 72701.

Payment/Terms: Pays $25-100 and 10 contributor's copies. Pays on publication for first North American serial rights. Sends galleys to author.

$ ⬤ ⬤ AGNI, Creative Writing Program, Boston University, 236 Bay State Rd., Boston MA 02215. (617)353-7135. Fax: (617)353-7134. E-mail: agni@bu.edu. Website: www.bu.edu/Agni (includes names of editors, short fiction, poetry and interviews with authors). **Contact:** Askold Melnyczuk, editor. Magazine: 5½×8½; 250 pages; 55 lb. booktext paper; recycled cover stock; occasional art portfolios. "Eclectic literary magazine publishing first-rate poems and stories." Biannual. Estab. 1972.

● Editor Melnyczuk won the Pens 2001 Nora Magid Award for Literary Editing; work from *Agni* has been selected regularly for inclusion in both *Pushcart Prize* and *Best American Short Stories* anthologies. Jhumpa Lahiri, published in Agni 47, won the Pulitzer Prize in fiction; Ha Jin was runnerup. *Agni* ranked #39 on the *Writer's Digest* "Fiction 50" list of top markets.

Needs: Stories, excerpted novels, prose poems and translations. No science fiction or romance. Receives more than 250 unsolicited fiction mss/month. Accepts 4-7 mss/issue, 8-12 mss/year. Reading period October 1 through February 15 only. Due to the volume of previous submissions, *Agni* cannot begin reading again until October 2002. **Publishes 30 new writers/year.** Recently published work by Jhumpa Lihiri, Ha Jin, Ilan Stavane, Frederick Busch and Thom Kennedy.

How to Contact: When reading period reopens, send complete ms with SASE and cover letter listing previous publications. Accepts simultaneous and electronic (disk) submissions. Responds in 5 months. Sample copy for $9.

Payment/Terms: Pays $10/page up to $150, 2 contributor's copies and one-year subscription. Pays on publication for first North American serial rights. Sends galleys to author.

Advice: "Read *Agni* carefully to understand the kinds of stories we publish. Read—everything, classics, literary journals, bestsellers. People need to read and subscribe to the magazines before sending their work. It's important for artists to support the arts."

$ ☑ THE AGUILAR EXPRESSION, 1329 Gilmore Ave., Donora PA 15033. (724)379-8019. **Contact:** Xavier F. Aguilar, editor. Magazine: 8½×11; 10-16 pages; 20 lb. bond paper; illustrations. "We are open to all writers of a general theme—something that may appeal to everyone." Semiannual. Estab. 1989. Circ. 150.

Needs: Adventure, ethnic/multicultural, experimental, horror, mainstream/contemporary, mystery/suspense (romantic suspense), romance (contemporary). No religious, erotic or first-person stories. Want more current social issues. Receives 15 unsolicited mss/month. Accepts 1-2 mss/issue; 2-4 mss/year. Publishes ms 1 month to 1 year after acceptance. **Publishes 2-4 new writers/year (90% of works published are by new writers).** Recently published work by Ken Bennet. Length: 750-1,500 words; average length: 1,000 words. Also publishes poetry.

How to Contact: Send complete ms with cover letter. Responds to queries in 1 week; mss in 1 month. Send SASE for reply to a query or send a disposable copy of ms. No simultaneous submissions. Sample copy for $6. Guidelines for first class stamp.

Payment/Terms: Pays $10 and 1 contributor's copy for lead story; additional copies at a reduced rate of $3. Acquires one-time rights. Not copyrighted. Write to publication for details on contests, awards or grants.

Advice: "Clean, clear copy makes a manuscript stand out."

$ ☑ ☷ ALASKA QUARTERLY REVIEW, University of Alaska—Anchorage, 3211 Providence Dr., Anchorage AK 99508. (907)786-6916. E-mail: ayaqr@uaa.alaska.edu. Website: www.uaa.alaska.edu/aqr. **Contact:** Ronald Spatz, fiction editor. Magazine: 6×9; 260 pages; 60 lb. Glatfelter paper; 12 pt. C15 black ink varnish cover stock; photos on cover only. *AQR* "publishes fiction, poetry, literary nonfiction and short plays in traditional and experimental styles." Semiannual. Estab. 1982. Circ. 2,200.

● Work appearing in the *Alaska Quarterly Review* has been selected for the *Prize Stories: The O. Henry Awards*, *Best American Essays*, *Best American Poetry*, *Beacon Best* and *Pushcart Prize* anthologies. *The Washington Post* calls the *Alaska Quarterly Review*, "one of the nation's best literary magazines."

Needs: Contemporary, experimental, literary, prose poem, translations. "If the works published in *Alaska Quarterly Review* have certain characteristics, they are these: freshness, honesty, and a compelling subject. What makes a piece stand out from the multitude of other submissions? The voice of the piece must be strong—idiosyncratic enough to create a unique persona. We look for the demonstration of craft, making the situation palpable and putting it in a form where it becomes emotionally and intellectually complex. One could look through our pages over time and see that many of the pieces published in *Alaska Quarterly Review* concern everyday life. We're not asking our writers to go outside themselves and their experiences to the absolute exotic to catch our interest. We look for the experiential and revelatory qualities of the work. We will, without hesitation, champion a piece that may be less polished or stylistically sophisticated, if it engages me, surprises me, and resonates for me. The joy in reading such a work is in discovering something true. Moreover, in keeping with our mission to publish new writers, we are looking for voices our readers do not know, voices that may not always be reflected in the dominant culture and that, in all instances, have something important to convey." Receives 200 unsolicited fiction mss/month. Accepts 7-13 mss/issue, 15-24 mss/year. Does not read mss May 15-August 15. Length: not exceeding 90 pages. **Publishes 6 new writers/year.** Recently published work by Ben Brooks, Nicholas Montemarano, Edna Ziesk and Pedro Ponce. Publishes short shorts.

How to Contact: Send complete mss with SASE. Accepts queries by e-mail. Simultaneous submissions "undesirable, but will accept if indicated." Responds in 2-3 months "but during peak periods a reply may take up to 6 months." Publishes ms 6 months to 1 year after acceptance. Sample copy for $6.

Payment/Terms: Pays 1 contributor's copy and a year's subscription. Pays $50-200 honorarium when grant funding permits. Acquires first rights.

Advice: "Professionalism, patience, and persistence are essential. One needs to do one's homework and know the market. The competition is very intense, and funding for the front-line journals is generally inadequate, so staffing is low. It takes times to get a response, and rejections are a fact of life. It is important not to take the rejections personally, and also to know that editors make decisions for better or worse, and they make mistakes too. Fortunately there are many gatekeepers. *Alaska Quarterly Review* has published many pieces that had been turned down by other journals—including pieces that then went on to win national awards. We also know of instances in which pieces *Alaska Quarterly Review* rejected later appeared in other magazines. We haven't regretted that we didn't take those pieces. Rather, we're happy that the authors have made a good match. Disappointment should *never* stop anyone. Will counts as much as talent, and new writers need to have confidence in themselves and stick to it."

ALGONQUIN ROUNDTABLE REVIEW, Algonquin College, B122d-1385 Woodroffe Ave., Nepean, Ontario K2Y 1V8 Canada. (613)727-4723, ext. 7028. Fax: (613)727-7601. E-mail: roundtable_review@algonquincollege.com. Website: www.algonquincollege.com/roundtable_review (includes mandate, call for submissions, submission guidelines). **Contact:** Dan Doyle and Nicholas Strachan, editors. Magazine: 8½×11; 82 pages; Plainfield Plus (120M) paper; Cornwall cover coated one side (eight point); illustrations; photos. "We are based on the idea of inclusion: a group with equal status, equal voices, sitting around a table, telling stories, reciting poetry, arguing a point, telling jokes, reading from a script, showing off photographs or graphics." Annual. Estab. 1999. Circ. 1,000.

Needs: Ethnic/multicultural, experimental, feminist, humor satire, literary, translations. "No clichéd stories, undue violence, or sexual/racial stereotypes. No moralizing or sentimentality either." See website for upcoming themes. Receives 15-20 unsolicited mss/month. Accepts 10-15 mss/issue. Publishes ms 4-6 months after acceptance. **Publishes 6-8 new writers/year.** Recently published work by Mark Molnar, Nichole McGill, Marnie Woodrow and Jeffrey Ross. Length: 1,000-4,000 words; average length: 2,500 words. Publishes short shorts. Average length: 600 words. Also publishes literary essays, literary criticism, poetry, photography and graphics.

How to Contact: Send complete ms with a cover letter. Accepts submissions by e-mail. Include estimated word count, brief bio and list of publications. Responds in 2 weeks to queries; 6 months to mss. Online queries preferred. Send a disposable copy of ms and #10 SASE for reply only. Accepts multiple submissions. Sample copy for $8 (Canadian). Guidelines by e-mail or visit website.

Payment/Terms: Pays 1 contributor's copy; additional copies $8. Acquires first rights.

Advice: "We prefer electronic submissions in ASCII, Rich Text format or WordPerfect (avoid macros, headers, footers and page numbers). Write something you'd like to have read fifty years from now. (Write commercials if you want money.)"

THE ALLEGHENY REVIEW, A National Journal of Undergraduate Literature, Thomson-Shore, Inc., 7300 W. Joy Rd., Dexter MI 48130-9701. (734)426-3939. Fax: (800)706-4545. Website: www.review.allegheny.edu (includes poem of the week, staff info, guidelines, award winners, latest issue's journal content, ordering info). **Contact:** Beata M. Gomulak, senior editor. Magazine: 6×9; 100 pages; illustrations; photos. "*The Allegheny Review* is one of America's only nationwide literary magazines exclusively for undergraduate works of poetry, fiction, and nonfiction. Our intended audience is persons interested in quality literature." Annual. Estab. 1983.

● "There is an entry fee of $5/year for submission that includes a one year subscription."

Needs: Adventure, ethnic/multicultural, experimental, family saga, fantasy, feminist, gay, historical, horror, humor/satire, lesbian, literary, mainstream, military/war, mystery/suspense, New Age, psychic/supernatural/occult, religious (general), romance, science fiction, western. "We will consider anything catering to an intellectual audience." No "fiction not written by undergraduates—we accept nothing but fiction written by currently enrolled undergraduate students." Receives 50 unsolicited mss/month. Accepts 3 mss/issue. Publishes ms 2 months after deadline. "Most—around 90%—of the authors in *Allegheny Review* are previously unpublished. Recently published work by Dianne Paige, Monica Stahl and DJ Kinney. Length: 20 pages maximum; average length: varies. Publishes short shorts. Average length: varies. Also publishes literary essays, literary criticism and poetry. Sometimes comments on rejected mss.

How to Contact: Send complete ms with a cover letter. Accepts submissions on disk. Include estimated word count, brief bio and list of publications. Responds in 2 weeks to queries; 4 months to mss. Send disposable copy of ms and #10 SASE for reply only. Accepts multiple submissions. Sample copy for $4. Guidelines for SASE, by e-mail or on website.

Payment/Terms: Pays 1 contributor's copy; additional copies $2. Acquires all rights. Sponsors contest. "Please visit our website or write/e-mail for information."

Advice: "We look for quality work that has been thoroughly revised. What stands out include: unique voice, interesting topic, and playfulness with the English language. Revise, revise, revise! And be careful how you send it—the cover letter says a lot. We definitely look for diversity in the pieces we publish."

N **⊕** **$** **AMBIT, Poetry/Art/Short Fiction**, 17 Priory Gardens, London, N6 5QY, United Kingdom. Phone: 0181 3403566. Website: www.AMBIT.CO.UK (includes writer's guidelines, names of editors, short fiction, subscription info). Editor: Martin Bax. **Contact:** Geoff Nicholson, J.G. Ballard, fiction editors. Magazine: 240cm × 170cm; 100 pages; removable cover; illustrations; photos. Publishes "avant-garde material; short stories only, no novels." Quarterly. Estab. 1959. Circ. 3,000.

Needs: Erotica, ethnic/multicultural, experimental, contemporary, translations. No fantasy/horror/science fiction. No genre fiction. Receives 80 unsolicited mss/month. Accepts 5 mss/issue; 20 mss/year. Publishes ms up to 1 year after acceptance. Agented fiction under 1%. **Publishes 10 new fiction writers/year.** Recently published works by Victor Anant, John Berger, Heather Reyes and Sophie Frank. Length: 1,000-5,000 words; average length: 3,000 words. Also publishes poetry.

How to Contact: Send 1-2 stories. Accepts mss on disk. Responds in 3 months. "No crits given." Send SASE with UK stamps or IRCs for reply, return of ms. Sample copy for $16. Guidelines free.

Payment/Terms: Pays approximately £5/printed page and 2 contributor's copies; additional copies $12. Acknowledgment if reprinted. Pays on publication. Not copyrighted.

Advice: Chooses a ms for publication "if it involves you straight away—if it makes you ask questions of it and look for answers. Know how to edit your own work and remember your readers are not patient and do not know you."

✓ **◐** **AMERICAN LITERARY REVIEW**, University of North Texas, P.O. Box 311307, Denton TX 76203-1307. (940)565-2755. Fax: (940)565-4355. Website: www.engl.unt.edu/alr/ (includes excerpts, subscription information, writer's guidelines, contest details). **Contact:** Barb Rodman, editor. Magazine: 7 × 10; 128 pages; 70 lb. Mohawk paper; 67 lb. Wausau Vellum cover. "Publishes quality, contemporary poems and stories." Semiannual. Estab. 1990. Circ. 900.

Needs: Mainstream and literary only. No genre works. Receives 50-75 unsolicited fiction mss/month. Accepts 4-8 mss/issue; 8-16 mss/year. Reading period: September 1-May 1. Publishes ms within 2 years after acceptance. Recently published work by Marianna Wright, William Tester, Tenaya Darlington and John Fulton. Length: less than 7,500 words. Critiques or comments on rejected mss when possible. Also accepts poetry and essays.

How to Contact: Send complete ms with cover letter. Responds in 2-3 months. SASE. Accepts simultaneous submissions. Sample copy for $8. Guidelines free.

Payment/Terms: Pays in contributor's copies. Acquires one-time rights.

Advice: "We like to see stories that illuminate the various layers of characters and their situations with great artistry. Give us distinctive character-driven stories that explore the complexities of human existance." Looks for "the small moments that contain more than at first appears possible, that surprise us with more truth than we thought we had a right to expect."

✓ **◐** **AMERICAN WRITING; A Magazine**, Nierika Editions, 4343 Manayunk Ave., Philadelphia PA 19128. E-mail: amwr@concentric.net. **Contact:** Alexandra Grilikhes, editor. Magazine: 8½ × 5½; 96 pages; matte paper and cover stock; photos. "We publish new writing that takes risks with form, point of view, language, ways of perceiving. We are interested in the voice of the loner, the artist as shaman, the powers of intuition, exceptional work of all kinds." Semiannual. Estab. 1990. Circ. 2,500.

Needs: Contemporary, excerpted novel, ethnic/multicultural, experimental, feminist, gay, lesbian, literary, translations. "We're looking for more literary, experimental, contemporary writing—writing that drives you to write it." No mainstream, romance, genre fiction, stories about sports. Receives 350 unsolicited mss/month. Accepts 4-5 mss/issue; 25 mss/year. Does not read mss June, December, January. Publishes ms 6-12 months after acceptance. Agented fiction less than 1%. **Publishes 4-6 new writers/year.** Recently published work by Cris Mazza, Pam Ryder, Saikat Mazumdor, Anne Spollen. Length: 5,000 words maximum; average length: 3,500 words. Publishes short shorts. Also publishes literary essays, personal essays, literary criticism, poetry. Critiques or comments on rejected mss "when there is time."

How to Contact: Send complete ms with a brief cover letter. Include brief bio and list of publications if applicable. "No full-length books. Send one ms at a time." Responds in 4 months. Send SASE for reply, return of ms or send a disposable copy of ms. Accepts simultaneous submissions. Sample copy for $6; guidelines for #10 SASE.

Payment/Terms: Pays 2 contributor's copies. Acquires first or one-time rights.

Advice: "We look for intensity, vision, voice, imaginative use of language, freshness, craft, sophistication; stories that delve. Read not just current stuff, but the old masters—Dostoyevsky, Chekhov and Hesse. Learn about subtlety and depth. Reading helps you to know who you are as a writer, writing makes you more that person, if you're lucky. Read one or two issues of the magazine *carefully.*"

❧ **✓** **◐** **THE AMETHYST REVIEW**, Marcasite Press, 23 Riverside Ave., Truro, Nova Scotia B2N 4G2 Canada. (902)895-1345. E-mail: amethyst@auracom.com. Website: www.auracom.com/~amethyst (includes guidelines, samples of poetry and fiction, names of editors, links, etc.). **Contact:** Penny Ferguson, editor. Magazine: 8×5¼; 84 pages; book weight paper; card stock cover; illustrations. "We publish quality contemporary fiction and poetry of interest to the literary reader." Semiannual. Estab. 1993. Circ. 150-210.

● *The Amethyst Review* has received grants from the Nova Scotia Department of Education and Culture.

Needs: Literary. No erotica. Receives 25 unsolicited mss/month. Accepts 2-3 mss/issue; 4-6 mss/year. Publishes ms maximum 6 months after acceptance, "usually much sooner." **Publishes 10% new writers/year.** Recently published work by Jan Houston, J.P. Jones and Lori Hahnel. Length: 5,000 words maximum. Publishes short shorts. Also publishes poetry.

How to Contact: Send complete ms with cover letter. Include estimated word count, a 50-word bio and list of publications. Responds in up to 7 months to mss. Send SASE or SAE and IRCs for reply, return of mss or send a disposable copy of ms. Sample copy for $7 (current) or $5 (back issues). Guidelines for SASE or SAE and IRCs. "Please do not send American stamps! We are no longer replying to submissions without adequate return postage." Reviews novels and short story collections "only by people we have published."

Payment/Terms: Pays 1 contributor's copy; additional copies $7. Pays on publication for first North American serial rights. Sponsors contest; send SASE for information.

Advice: "For us, a story must be memorable because it touches the reader's heart or imagination. Quality is our criterion. Try to delight us with originality and craft. Send for guidelines and sample. We don't look for a specific type of story. We publish the *best* of what we receive. We are seeking literary quality and accessibility. A story that stands out gives the reader a 'tingle' and stays in your mind for days to come. Pay attention to detail, don't be sloppy. Care about your subjects because if you don't neither will the reader. Dazzle us with quality instead of trying to shock us!"

✓ $ ◖ ◎ ⊻ **ANTIETAM REVIEW**, Washington County Arts Council, 41 S. Potomac St., Hagerstown MD 21740-5512. Phone/fax: (301)791-3132. **Contact:** Winnie Wagaman, managing editor. Magazine: 8½×11; 54-68 pages; glossy paper; light card cover; photos. A literary journal of short fiction, poetry and black-and-white photographs. "Our audience is primarily in the six state region. Urban, suburban and rural writers and readers, but copies are purchased nationwide, both by libraries as well as individuals. Sales and submissions increase yearly." Annual. Estab. 1982. Circ. 1,800.

● Work published in *Antietam Review* has been included in the *Pushcart Prize* anthology and *Best American Short Stories*. The magazine also received a grant from the Maryland State Arts Council and Washington County Arts Council.

Needs: Condensed/excerpted novel, contemporary, ethnic, experimental, feminist, literary and prose poem. Wants more contemporary, ethnic, experimental. "We read manuscripts from our region only—Delaware, Maryland, Pennsylvania, Virginia, West Virginia and Washington D.C. We read from September 1 through February 1." No horror, romance, inspirational, pornography. Receives about 100 unsolicited mss/month. Buys 8-10 stories/year. Publishes ms 2-3 months after acceptance. **Publishes 2-3 new writers/year.** Published work by Marc Bookman, Tom Glenn, Richard Plant, Shirley G. Cochran, Kevin Stewart, Judy Wilson and Jamie Holland. Length: 3,000 words average. Also publishes poetry.

How to Contact: "Send ms and SASE with a cover letter. Let us know if you have published before and where." Accepts queries by e-mail. Include estimated word count, 1-paragraph bio and list of publications. Responds in 2-4 months. "If we hold a story, we let the writer know. Occasionally we critique returned ms or ask for rewrites." Sample copy for $6.30. Back issue $5.25. Guidelines for legal-size SAE.

Payment/Terms: "We believe it is a matter of dignity that writers and poets be paid. We have been able to give $50-100 a story and $25 a poem, but this depends on funding. Also 2 copies." Buys first North American serial rights. Sends galleys to author if requested.

Advice: "We seek high quality, well-crafted work with significant character development and shift. We seek no specific theme. We look for work that is interesting, involves the reader, and teaches us a new way to view the world. A manuscript stands out because of its energy and flow. Most of our submissions reflect the times (i.e., the news, current events) more than industry trends. We also seek a compelling voice, originality, magic. We now require *accepted* stories to be put on disk by the author to cut down on printing costs. We are seeing an increase of first person narrative stories."

◪ ✓ $◖ **THE ANTIGONISH REVIEW**, St. Francis Xavier University, P.O. Box 5000, Antigonish, Nova Scotia B2G 2W5 Canada. (902)867-3962. Fax: (902)867-5563. E-mail: TAR@stfx.ca. Website: www.antigonishreview.com. **Contact:** Allan Quigley, editor. Literary magazine for educated and creative readers. Quarterly. Estab. 1970. Circ. 800.

Needs: Literary, contemporary, prose poem, translations. No erotic or political material. Accepts 6 mss/issue. Receives 50 unsolicited fiction mss each month. **Published new writers within the last year.** Published work by Arnold Bloch, Richard Butts and Helen Barolini. Length: 1,000-6,000 words. Sometimes comments briefly on rejected mss.

How to Contact: Send complete ms, double spaced with bio, SAE and IRC and cover letter. SASE ("U.S. postage not acceptable"). No simultaneous submissions. Accepts electronic (disk compatible with WordPerfect/IBM and Windows or e-mail) submissions. Prefers hard copy with disk submission. Responds in 3 months. Publishes ms 4-8 months after acceptance. Sample copy for $4. Guidelines free.

Payment/Terms: Pays $50 for stories. Authors retain copyright. Pays on publication for first serial rights.

Advice: "Learn the fundamentals and do not deluge an editor."

☑ $ ⌻ **ANTIOCH REVIEW**, Box 148, Yellow Springs OH 45387-0148. (937)769-1365. Website: www.antioch.edu/review (includes guidelines, awards, authors, titles and excerpts of current and upcoming issue, history of the Review, subscription info). Editor: Robert S. Fogarty. Associate Editor: Nolan Miller. **Contact:** Fiction Editor. Magazine: 6×9; 128 pages; 50 lb. book offset paper; coated cover stock; illustrations "seldom." "Literary and cultural review of contemporary issues, and literature for general readership." Quarterly. Published special fiction issue last year; plans another. Estab. 1941. Circ. 5,100.

Needs: Literary, contemporary, experimental, translations. No children's, science fiction or popular market. Accepts 5-6 mss/issue, 20-24 mss/year. Receives approximately 275 unsolicited fiction mss each month. Does not read mss June 1-September 1. Approximately 1-2% of fiction agented. **Publishes 1-2 new writers/year.** Published work by Gordon Lish, Jean Ross Justice, Peter LaSalle, Sylvia Foley, Josie Milliken, Teresa Svoboda, Joseph Caldwell, Richard Stern, Emily Cerf and Carolyn Osborn. Length: generally under 8,000 words.

How to Contact: Send complete ms with SASE, preferably mailed flat. Responds in 2 months. Publishes ms 6-9 months after acceptance. Sample copy for $6. Guidelines for SASE.

Payment/Terms: Pays $10/page and 2 contributor's copies; $3.90 for extras. Pays on publication for first and one-time rights (rights returned to author on request).

Advice: "Our best advice, always, is to *read* the *Antioch Review* to see what type of material we publish. Quality fiction requires an engagement of the reader's intellectual interest supported by mature emotional relevance, written in a style that is rich and rewarding without being freaky. The great number of stories submitted to us indicates that fiction still has great appeal. We assume that if so many are writing fiction, many must be reading it."

⌻ **APOSTROPHE: University of South Carolina Beaufort Journal of the Arts**, 801 Carteret St., Beaufort SC 29902. (843)521-4100. Fax: (843)522-9733. E-mail: sjtombe@gwm.sc.edu. Editor: Sheila Tombe. **Contact:** Ellen Malphrus, fiction editor. Magazine: 8×5; 70 pages. Annual. Estab. 1996. Circ. 250-300.

Needs: Literary. Does not want anything "poorly written" or "in bad taste." Receives 3 unsolicited mss/month. Accepts 3-4 mss/issue. Does not read mss "during semester." Publishes ms 1-2 months after acceptance. **Publishes 3 new writers/year.** Recently published work by Evan Balkan, Mary Stewart Atwell and Mike Wilson. Publishes short shorts. Also publishes literary essays, literary criticism, poetry. Sometimes comments on rejected mss.

How to Contact: Send complete ms with a cover letter. Include short bio. Responds in 2 weeks to queries; 10 months to mss. Send SASE for reply, return of ms or send a disposable copy of ms. Accepts simultaneous submissions and reprints. Sample copy for $3, 8×5 SAE and 2 first-class stamps. Guidelines free for letter-size SASE.

Payment/Terms: Pays 2 contributor's copies; additional copies $5. Not copyrighted.

Advice: Looks for "excellent prose style; nothing trite or clichéd; nothing 'crafted' à la college fiction writing course. Don't be afraid to ignore your writing instructors, when appropriate. We prefer thoughtful construction; artful phrasing; maturity. Don't rely on anyone to teach you. Write to learn."

Ⓝ ⌻ ◎ **ARBA SICULA**, St John's University, Jamaica NY 11439. **Contact:** Gaetano Cipolla, editor. Magazine: 5½×8½; 85 pages; top-grade paper; good quality cover stock; illustrations; photos. Bilingual ethnic literary review (Sicilian-English) dedicated to the dissemination of Sicilian culture. Published twice a year. Plans special fiction issue. Estab. 1979. Circ. 2,500.

Needs: Accepts ethnic literary material consisting of various forms of folklore, stories both contemporary and classical, regional, romance (contemporary, historical, young adult) and senior citizen. Material submitted must be in the Sicilian language, with English translation desirable or in English on Sicilian topics. **Published new writers within the last year.** Critiques rejected mss when there is time. Sometimes recommends other markets.

How to Contact: Send complete ms with SASE and bio. Responds in 2 months. Publishes ms 1-3 years after acceptance. Accepts simultaneous submissions and reprints. Sample copy for $8 with 8½×11 SAE and 90¢ postage.

READ "THE BUSINESS OF FICTION WRITING" section for information on manuscript preparation, mailing tips, rights and more.

Payment/Terms: Pays 5 free author's copies; $4 for extra copies. Acquires all rights.
Advice: "This review is a must for those who nurture a love of the Sicilian language."

☑ ◉ **ARKANSAS REVIEW, A Journal of Delta Studies**, Department of English and Philosophy, P.O. Box 1890, Arkansas State University, State University AR 72467-1890. (501)972-3043. Fax: (501)972-3045. E-mail: delta@astate.edu. Website: www.clt.astate.edu/arkreview (includes guidelines, names of editors, ordering information, tables of contents). Editor: William M. Clements. **Contact:** Norman Stafford, fiction editor. Magazine: 8¼×11; 64-100 pages; coated, matte paper; matte, 4-color cover stock; illustrations; photos. Publishes articles, fiction, poetry, essays, interviews, reviews, visual art evocative of or responsive to the Mississippi River Delta. Triannual. Estab. 1996. Circ. 700.
Needs: Regional short stories, literary essays, literary criticism. "No genre fiction. Must have a Delta focus." Receives 30-50 unsolicited mss/month. Accepts 2-3 mss/issue; 5-7 mss/year. Publishes ms 6-12 months after acceptance. Agented fiction 1%. **Publishes 3-4 new writers/year.** Published work by Chalana Oueles, Deborah Elliott Deutschmann, Mark Sindecuse and Craig Black. Also publishes literary essays and poetry. Always comments on rejected mss.
How to Contact: Send complete ms with cover letter. Accepts queries/mss by e-mail and fax. Include bio. Responds in 1 week to queries; 4 months to mss. Send SASE for reply, return of ms or send a disposable copy of ms. Sample copy for $7.50. Guidelines free for #10 SASE.
Payment/Terms: Pays 5 contributor's copies; additional copies for $5. Acquires first North American serial rights.
Advice: "We publish new writers in every issue. We look for distinguished, mature writing, surprises, a perfect ending and a story that means more than merely what went on in it. We don't like recognizable imitations of currently fashionable writers."

◉ **THE ARMCHAIR AESTHETE**, Pickle Gas Press, 31 Rolling Meadows Way, Penfield NY 14526. (716)388-6968. E-mail: bypaul@netacc.net. **Contact:** Paul Agosto, editor. Magazine: 5½×8½; 40-65 pages; 20 lb. paper; 110 lb. card stock color cover. *The Armchair Aesthete* seeks quality writing that enlightens and entertains a thoughtful audience (ages 9-90) with a "good read." Quarterly. Estab. 1996. Circ. 100.
Needs: Adventure, fantasy (science fantasy, sword and sorcery), historical (general), horror, humor/satire, mainstream/contemporary, mystery/suspense (amateur sleuth, cozy, police procedural, private eye/hardboiled, romantic suspense), science fiction (soft/sociological), westerns (frontier, traditional). No racist, pornographic, advert gore; no religious or material intended for or written by children. Plans to publish special fiction issue. Receives 90 unsolicited mss/month. Accepts 13-18 mss/issue; 60-80 mss/year. Publishes ms 3-9 months after acceptance. Agented fiction less than 5%. **Publishes 10-15 new writers/year.** Recently published work by Sam Meader, Tom Pachelo, Joseph Segriff and Don Stockard. Length: 3,000 words maximum; average length: 2,000 words. Publishes short shorts. Also publishes poetry. Sometimes comments on rejected mss.
How to Contact: Send complete ms with a cover letter. Include estimated word count, 50-100 word bio and list of publications. Responds in 2-3 weeks to queries; 1-3 months to mss. Send SASE for reply, return of ms or send a disposable copy of ms. Accepts simultaneous, multiple, reprint and electronic submissions. Sample copy for $3 and 2 first-class stamps. Guidelines free for #10 SASE. Reviews novels and short story collections.
Payment/Terms: Pays 1 contributor's copy; additional copies for $3 (pay to P. Agosto, editor). Pays on publication for one-time rights.
Advice: "Clever, compelling storytelling has a good chance here. We look for a clever plot, thought-out characters, something that surprises or catches us off guard. Write on innovative subjects and situations. Submissions should be professionally presented and technically sound."

Ⓝ ◉ ◎ **ARNAZELLA**, English Department, Bellevue Community College, 3000 Landerholm Circle SE, Bellevue WA 98007. (206)603-4032. Fax: (425)643-2690. E-mail: arnazella@prostar.com. Website: www.bcc.ctc.edu/english/arnazella.html. **Contact:** Woody West, advisor. Magazine: 10×9; 104 pages, 70 lb. paper; heavy coated cover; illustrations; photos. "For those interested in quality fiction." Annual. Estab. 1976. Circ. 500.
Needs: Adventure, contemporary, ethnic, experimental, fantasy, feminist, gay, historical, humor/satire, lesbian, literary, mainstream, mystery/suspense, regional. Submit Sept. 1-Dec. 31 for issue published in spring. **Publishes 25 new writers/year.** Recently published work by Mary Lou Sanelli, Mary Winters and Virgil Suárez. Publishes short shorts. Also publishes literary essays, poetry.
How to Contact: Send complete ms with cover letter. "We accept submissions September through December only." Responds to mss in spring. SASE. Accepts multiple submissions. Sample copy for $5. Guidelines for SASE.
Payment/Terms: Pays in contributor's copies. Acquires first rights.
Advice: "Read this and similar magazines, reading critically and analytically. Since *Arnazella* does not edit for anything other than very minor problems, we need pieces that are technically sound."

☑ $ ⬙ **ARTFUL DODGE**, Dept. of English, College of Wooster, Wooster OH 44691. (330)263-2332. Website: www.wooster.edu/artfuldodge (includes writer's guidelines, editors' bios, interviews with authors, subscription information, history of the magazine). Editor-in-Chief: Daniel Bourne. **Contact:** Ron Antonucci, fiction editor. Magazine: 100 pages; illustrations; photos. "There is no theme in this magazine, except literary power. We also have an ongoing interest in translations from Central/Eastern Europe and elsewhere." Biannual. Estab. 1979. Circ. 1,000.

Needs: Experimental, literary, prose poem, translations. "We judge by literary quality, not by genre. We are especially interested in fine English translations of significant contemporary prose writers. Translations should be submitted with original texts." Receives 40 unsolicited fiction mss/month. Accepts 5 mss/year. Published fiction by Edward Kleinschmidt, Robert Mooney, David Surface, Leslie Pietrzyk and Zbigniew Herbert; and interviews with Tim O'Brien, Lee Smith, Michael Dorris and Stuart Dybek. **Published 1 new writer within the last year.** Length: 10,000 words maximum; 2,500 words average. Also publishes literary essays, literary criticism, poetry. Occasionally critiques rejected mss.

How to Contact: Send complete ms with SASE. Do not send more than 30 pages at a time. Responds in 1 week to 8 months. No simultaneous or reprint submissions. Sample copies are $5 for older issues; $7 for current issues. Guidelines for #10 SASE.

Payment/Terms: Pays 2 contributor's copies and honorarium of $5/page, "thanks to funding from the Ohio Arts Council." Acquires first North American serial rights.

Advice: "If we take time to offer criticism, do not subsequently flood us with other stories no better than the first. If starting out, get as many *good* readers as possible. Above all, read contemporary fiction and the magazine you are trying to publish in."

⬚ ◯ ⬙ **ARTISAN, a journal of craft**, P.O. Box 157, Wilmette IL 60091. (847)673-7246. E-mail: artisanjn l@aol.com. **Editor:** Joan Daugherty. Tabloid: 8½ × 11; 36 pages. "The philosophy behind *artisan* is that anyone who strives to express themselves through their craft is an artist and artists of all genres can learn from each other." For artists and the general public. Quarterly. Estab. 1995. Circ. 200.

Needs: "We love to see 'literary' stories that can still appeal to a general audience—stories that are well-written and sophisticated without being stuffy. Nothing sexually or violently graphic with foul language unless it clearly contributes to the story." Receives 50 unsolicited mss/month. Accepts 6-8 mss/issue; 25 mss/year. Publishes ms 4-8 months after acceptance. Recently published work by Amy Branson, Laura Durnell, Arthur Franz and Gregory Wolos. Length: 4,000 words maximum; average length: 2,000 words. Publishes short shorts. Also publishes literary essays, literary criticism, poetry. Sometimes comments on rejected mss.

How to Contact: Send complete ms with brief cover letter. Include estimated word count. Responds in 1 month to queries; up to 8 months to mss. SASE for reply and send a disposable copy of ms. Accepts electronic submissions (e-mail or ASCII). Sample copy for $6. Subscription: $18. Guidelines for #10 SASE. Guidelines also posted on the Internet at members.aol.com/artisanjnl. Will sponsor annual short fiction competition: $200 1st prize; $100 2nd prize. Send SASE for guidelines. Contest deadline is July 31.

Payment/Terms: Pays 2 contributor's copies; additional copies $5. Acquires first rights.

Advice: "There are very few, if any, original stories left to tell. The difference is how you choose to tell them. Show us fresh use of language, character and story line. Make it personal."

☑ $ **ARTS & LETTERS**, Journal of Contemporary Culture, Georgia College & State University, Campus Box 89, Milledgeville GA 31061. E-mail: al@gcsu.edu. Website: http://al.gcsu.edu (includes cover art, guidelines, editorial staff, contents of previous issues, brief introduction to *Arts & Letters*, competition guidelines and more). **Contact:** Kellie Wells, fiction editor. Literary magazine: 7 × 10; 200 pages; 60 lb. joy white; some photos. "*Arts & Letters* publishes poetry, fiction, creative nonfiction and commentary on contemporary culture. The journal features the mentors interview series, the world of poetry translation series, and color reproductions of original artistic prints. Also it is the only journal nationwide to feature authors and artists that represent such an eclectic range of creative work. Our audience is those people who make a reasoned distinction between contemporary culture and popular culture." Semiannual. Estab. 1999. Circ. 1,500.

Needs: Literary. No genre fiction. Receives 50 unsolicited mss/month. Accepts 3 mss/issue; 6 mss/year. Publishes ms 6-12 months after acceptance. **Publishes 1-2 new writers/year.** Recently published work by Bret Lott, Heather Sellers, Edith Pearlman and Austin Ratner. Length: 3,000-7,500 words; average length: 6,000 words. Sometimes comments on rejected mss.

How to Contact: Send complete ms with cover letter. Include estimated word count, brief bio and list of publications. Responds in 4 months to mss. Send disposable copy of ms and #10 SASE for reply only. Sample copy for $5 plus $1 for postage. Guidelines for SASE, e-mail or website.

Payment/Terms: Pays $50 or $10 per printed page, 1 contributor's copy and one-year subscription; additional copies $5. Pays on publication for first North American serial rights. Sends galleys to author.

Advice: "An obvious, but not gimmicky, attention to and fresh usage of language. A solid grasp of the craft of story writing. Fully realized work."

☑ ◐ ◎ **ASIAN PACIFIC AMERICAN JOURNAL**, The Asian American Writers' Workshop, 16 W. 32nd St., 10th Floor, New York NY 10001. (212)494-0061. Fax: (212)494-0062. E-mail: desk@aaww.org. Website: www.aaww.org. **Contact:** Hanya Yanagihara, editor. Magazine: 5½×8½; 250 pages; illustrations. "We are interested in publishing works by writers from all segments of the Asian Pacific American community. The journal appeals to all interested in Asian-American literature and culture." Semiannual. Estab. 1992. Circ. 1,500.

Needs: Condensed/excerpted novel, erotica, ethnic/multicultural, experimental, feminist, gay, graphic novels, historical (general), humor/satire, lesbian, literary, mainstream/contemporary, regional, serialized novel, translations, Asian-American themes. "We are interested in anything related to the Asian American community." Receives 120 unsolicited mss/month. Accepts 15 mss/issue; 30 mss/year. Publishes ms 4-6 months after acceptance. Agented fiction 5%. Recently published work by David Henry Hwang, Chitra Banerjee Divakarvni, Kimiko Hahn, Bino A. Realuyo and Rahna Rizzuto. Length: 3,000 words average. Publishes short shorts. Also publishes literary essays, poetry.

How to Contact: Send SASE for guidelines. Should include estimated word count, 3-5 sentence bio, list of publications. Responds in 1 month to queries; 4 months to mss. SASE for reply or send 4 disposable copies of ms. Accepts simultaneous, reprint, electronic (disk, Macintosh or IBM, preferably Microsoft Word 5 for Mac) submissions. Sample copy for $10. Guidelines for SASE.

Payment/Terms: Pays 2 contributor's copies; additional copies at 40% discount. Acquires one-time rights. Sponsors contests, awards or grants for fiction writers. "Send query with SASE."

Ⓝ ◐ **AXE FACTORY REVIEW**, Cynic Press, P.O. Box 40691, Philadelphia PA 19107. **Contact:** Joseph Farley, editor. Magazine: 11×17 folded to 8½×11; 30-60 pages; 20 lb. stock paper; 70 lb. stock cover; illustrations; photos on occasion. "We firmly believe that literature is a form of (and/or expression/manifestations of) madness. We seek to spread the disease called literature. We will look at any genre. But, we search for the quirky, the off-center, the offensive, the annoying, but always the well-written story, poem, essay." Biannual. Estab. 1986. Circ. 100.

Needs: Adventure, comics/graphic novels, erotica, ethnic/multicultural (Asian), experimental, fantasy (space fantasy, sword and sorcery), feminist, gay, historical, horror (dark fantasy, futuristic, psychological, supernatural), humor/satire, lesbian, literary, mainstream, military/war, mystery/suspense, New Age, psychic/supernatural/occult, regional (Philadelphia area), religious (general religious, inspirational, religious mystery/suspense), romance, science fiction (hard science/technological, soft/sociological, cross genre), thriller/espionage, translations, western (frontier saga, traditional). "No genteel professional gibberish." Receives 20 unsolicited mss/month. Accepts 1-2 mss/issue; 3 mss/year. Publishes ms 6 months after acceptance. Length: 500-5,000 words; average length: 3,000 words. Publishes short shorts. Also publishes literary essays, literary criticism and poetry. Often comments on rejected mss.

How to Contact: Send complete ms with a cover letter. Include brief bio, list of publications and discuss why you write/philosophy. Responds in 6 weeks to queries and mss. Send SASE (or IRC) for return of ms. Accepts simultaneous, previously published and multiple submissions. Sample copy for $8. Reviews novels, short story collections and nonfiction books of interest to writers. Send review copies to Joseph Farley.

Payment/Terms: Pays 1-2 contributor's copies; additional copies $8. Pays on publication for one-time and anthology rights.

Advice: "It must be typed. Crayon will not do. I must like it on the first read and still like it on the second read. Read a few issues."

◐ ◎ **THE AZOREAN EXPRESS**, Seven Buffaloes Press, Box 249, Big Timber MT 59011. **Contact:** Art Coelho, editor. Magazine: 6¾×8¼; 32 pages; 60 lb. book paper; 3-6 illustrations/issue; photos rarely. "My overall theme is rural; I also focus on working people (the sweating professions); the American Indian and Hobo; the Dustbowl era; and I am also trying to expand with non-rural material. For rural and library and professor/student, blue collar workers, etc." Semiannual. Estab. 1985. Circ. 600.

Needs: Contemporary, ethnic, experimental, humor/satire, literary, regional, western, rural, working people. Receives 10-20 unsolicited mss/month. Accepts 2-3 mss/issue; 4-6 mss/year. Publishes ms 1-6 months after acceptance. Length: 1,000-3,000 words. Also publishes short shorts, 500-1,000 words. "I take what I like; length sometimes does not matter, even when longer than usual. I'm flexible."

How to Contact: "Send cover letter with ms; general information, but it can be personal, more in line with the submitted story. Not long rambling letters." Responds in 1-4 weeks. SASE. Sample copy for $7.75 postpaid. Guidelines for SASE.

Payment/Terms: Pays in contributor's copies. "Depends on the amount of support author gives my press." Acquires first North American serial rights. "If I decide to use material in anthology form later, I have that right." Sends galleys to the author upon request.

Advice: "There would not be magazines like mine if I was not optimistic. But literary optimism is a two-way street. Without young fiction writers supporting fiction magazines the future is bleak because the commercial magazines allow only formula or name writers within their pages. My own publications receive no grants. Sole support is from writers, libraries and individuals."

THE BALTIMORE REVIEW, Baltimore Writers' Alliance, P.O. Box 410, Riderwood MD 21139. (410)377-5265. Fax: (410)377-4325. E-mail: hdiehl@bcpl.net. Website: www.baltimorewriters.org (includes guidelines, info about Baltimore Writers' Alliance, and subscription and sample copy information). Editor: Barbara Diehl. **Contact:** Fiction Editor. Magazine: 6×9; 128 pages; 60 lb. paper; 10 pt. CS1 gloss film cover. Showcase for the best short stories and poetry by writers in the Baltimore area and beyond. Semiannual. Estab. 1996.

Needs: Ethnic/multicultural, experimental, literary, mainstream/contemporary. No science fiction, westerns, children's, romance, etc. Accepts 8-12 mss/issue; 16-24 mss/year. Publishes ms 1-9 months after acceptance. **Publishes "at least a few" new writers/year.** Recently published work by Roberta Murphy, Pearl Canick Solomon and Tristan Davies. Length: short shorts to 6,000 words maximum; average length: 3,000 words. Also publishes poetry.

How to Contact: Send complete ms with a cover letter. Include estimated word count, brief bio and list of publications. Responds in 1-3 months. Send SASE for reply, return of ms or send a disposable copy of ms. Accepts simultaneous submissions. No e-mail or fax submissions.

Payment/Terms: Pays 2 contributor's copies. Pays on publication for first North American serial rights.

Advice: "We look for compelling stories and a masterful use of the English language. We want to feel that we have never heard this story, or this voice, before. Read the kinds of publications you want your work to appear in. Make your reader believe, and care."

BARBARIC YAWP, Bone World Publishing, 3700 County Rt. 24, Russell NY 13684-3198. (315)347-2609. Editor: John Berbrich. **Contact:** Nancy Berbrich, fiction editor. Magazine: digest-size; 60 pages; 24 lb. paper; matte cover stock. "We are not preachers of any particular poetic or literary school. We publish any type of quality material appropriate for our intelligent and wide-awake audience." Quarterly. Estab. 1997. Circ. 120.

Needs: Adventure, experimental, fantasy (science, sword and sorcery), historical, horror, humor/satire, literary, mainstream/contemporary, psychic/supernatural/occult, regional, religious/inspirational, science fiction (hard, soft/sociological). Wants more humor, satire and adventure. "We don't want any pornography, gratuitous violence or whining." Receives 30-40 unsolicited mss/month. Accepts 10-12 mss/issue; 40-48 mss/year. Publishes ms within 6 months after acceptance. **Publishes 6 new writers/year.** Published work by Mark Spitzer, Errol Miller and Jeff Grimshaw. Length: 1,200 words maximum; average length: 600 words. Publishes short shorts. Also publishes literary essays, literary criticism, poetry. Often comments on rejected mss.

How to Contact: Send complete ms with a cover letter. Include estimated word count, brief bio and list of publications. Responds in 2 weeks to queries; 4 months to mss. Send SASE for reply, return of ms or send a disposable copy of ms. Accepts simultaneous submissions and reprints. Sample copy for $3. Guidelines for #10 SASE.

Payment and Terms: Pays 1 contributor's copy; additional copies $3. Acquires one-time rights.

Advice: "We are primarily concerned with work that means something to the author, but which is able to transcend the personal into the larger world. Send whatever is important to you. We will use Yin and Yang. Work must hold my interest and be well-crafted. Read, read, read; write, write, write—then send us your best. Don't get discouraged. Believe in yourself. Take risks. Do not fear rejection."

BATHTUB GIN, Pathwise Press, P.O. Box 2392, Bloomington IN 47402. (812)339-7298. E-mail: charter@bluemarble.net. Website: www.bluemarble.net/~charter/btgin.htm (includes guidelines, news, links and catalogue). Editor: Chris Harter. **Contact:** Fiction Editor. Magazine: 8½×5½; 60 pages; recycled 20-lb. paper; 80-lb. card cover; illustrations; photos. "*Bathtub Gin* is looking for work that has some kick to it. We are very eclectic and publish a wide range of styles. Audience is anyone interested in new writing and art that is not being presented in larger magazines." Semiannual. Estab. 1997. Circ. 150.

Needs: Condensed/excerpted novel, experimental, humor/satire, literary. "No horror, science fiction, historical unless they go beyond the usual formula." Want more experimental fiction. Receives 20 unsolicited mss/month. Accepts 2-3 mss/issue. Does not read mss September 15-December 1 and March 15-July 1; "we publish in mid-October and mid-April." **Publishes 10 new writers/year.** Recently published work by Melissa Frederick and Allen Purdy. Length: 10 double-spaced pages maximum. Publishes short shorts. Also publishes literary essays, literary criticism, poetry. Often comments on rejected ms.

How to Contact: Send complete ms with a cover letter. Include estimated word count, 3-5 line bio. Accepts queries by e-mail. Responds in 1-2 months. Send SASE for reply, return of ms or send a disposable copy of ms. Accepts simultaneous, reprint and electronic submissions (modem). Sample copy for $5 with 6×9 SAE and 4 first-class stamps. Guidelines for #10 SASE. Reviews novels and short story collections.

Payment/Terms: Pays 1 contributor's copy; discount on additional copies. Rights revert to author upon publication.

Advice: "We are looking for writing that contains strong imagery, is complex, and is willing to take a chance with form and structure. Query first and obtain a sample of a magazine to see what it is looking for and if you really want to be published there."

◑ BEACON STREET REVIEW, 100 Beacon St., Emerson College, Boston MA 02116. (617)824-8750. E-mail: beaconstreetreview@hotmail.com. **Contact:** Prose Editor. Editors change each year. Magazine: 5½×8½; 100 pages; 60 lb. paper. The *Beacon Street Review*, a journal of new prose and poetry, is published twice a year by students in the graduate writing, literature and publishing department of Emerson College. Biannual. Estab. 1986. Circ. 1,500.

Needs: Literary. Receives 120 mss/year. Accepts 5-10 mss/issue; 10-20 mss/year. Does not read mss in the summer. Publishes ms 1-2 months after acceptance. **Publishes 8 new writers/year.** Recently published work by Matthew Goodman, Keith Regan and D.M. Gordon. Length: 25 pages maximum. Publishes short shorts. Also publishes literary essays and poetry. Sometimes comments on rejected mss.

How to Contact: Send complete ms with a cover letter. Accepts submissions by e-mail. Include estimated word count and bio. Responds in 2 weeks to queries; 2 months to mss. Send disposable copy of ms. Accepts simultaneous submissions with notification. Sample copy for $3 with 6×9 SAE. Guidelines free. Reviews novels, short story collections and nonfiction books of interest to writers.

Payment/Terms: Pays 3 contributor's copies; additional copies $1.50. Pays on publication for one-time rights. Sponsors Editor's Choice Award. One piece is selected from every two issues for a $75 award judged by an established local author.

☑ $◑ THE BELLINGHAM REVIEW, Western Washington University, MS9053, Bellingham WA 98225-9053. (360)650-4863. E-mail: bhreview@cc.wwu.edu. Website: www.wwu.edu/~bhreview (includes guidelines, contest information, staff, sample writing, links). Editor: Brenda Miller. **Contact:** Fiction Editor. Magazine: 6×8¾; 150 pages; 60 lb. white paper; four color cover. "A literary magazine featuring original prose and poetry of palpable quality." Semiannual. Estab. 1977. Circ. 1,600.

● The editors are actively seeking submissions of creative nonfiction, as well as stories that push the boundaries of the form. The Tobias Wolff Award in Fiction Contest runs December 1-March 15; see website for guidelines or send SASE.

Needs: All genres/subjects considered. Accepts 3-4 mss/issue. Does not read mss February 2-September 30. Publishes short shorts. **Publishes 3-4 new writers/year.** Recently published work by Christie Hodgen, Robert Van Wagoner and Joan Leegeant. Length: 9,000 words or less. Also publishes poetry.

How to Contact: Send complete ms. Responds in 3 months. Publishes ms an average of 1 year after acceptance. Sample copy for $7. Reviews novels and short story collections.

Payment/Terms: Pays as funds permit, and one-year subscription, gift subscription, 2 contributor's copies and discount on additional copies. Acquires first North American serial rights.

Advice: "We look for work that is ambitious, vital, and challenging both to the spirit and the intellect."

◑ ☑ BELLOWING ARK, A Literary Tabloid, P.O. Box 5564, Shoreline WA 98155. (206)440-0791. Editor: R.R. Ward. **Contact:** Fiction Editor. Tabloid: 11½×17½; 28 pages; electro-brite paper and cover stock; illustrations; photos. "We publish material which we feel addresses the human situation in an affirmative way. We do not publish academic fiction." Bimonthly. Estab. 1984. Circ. 650.

● Work from *Bellowing Ark* appeared in the *Pushcart Prize* anthology. The editor says he's using much more short fiction and prefers positive, life-affirming work. Remember, he likes a traditional, narrative approach and "abhors" minimalist and post-modern work.

Needs: Contemporary, literary, mainstream, serialized/excerpted novel. No science fiction or fantasy. Receives 600-800 unsolicited fiction mss/year. Accepts 2-5 mss/issue; 10-20 mss/year. Time varies, but publishes ms not longer than 6 months after acceptance. **Published 10-50 new writers/year.** Recently published work by Robin Sterns, Shelley Uva, Tanyo Ravicz, Susan Montag and E.R. Romaine. Length: 3,000-5,000 words average ("but no length restriction"). Publishes short shorts. Also publishes literary essays, literary criticism, poetry. Sometimes critiques rejected mss.

How to Contact: No queries. Send complete ms with cover letter and short bio. "Prefer cover letters that tell something about the writer. Listing credits doesn't help." No simultaneous submissions. Responds in 6 weeks to mss. SASE. Sample copy for $3, 9×12 SAE and $1.21 postage.

Payment/Terms: Pays in contributor's copies. Acquires all rights, reverts on request.

Advice: "*Bellowing Ark* began as (and remains) an alternative to the despair and negativity of the Workshop/Academic literary scene; we believe that life has meaning and is worth living—the work we publish reflects that belief. Learn how to tell a story before submitting. Avoid 'trick' endings—they have all been done before and better. *Bellowing Ark* is interested in publishing writers who will develop with the magazine, as in an extended community. We find *good* writers and stick with them. This is why the magazine has grown from 12 to 28 pages."

BELOIT FICTION JOURNAL, Box 11, 700 College St., Beloit College WI 53511. (608)363-2577. E-mail: darlingr@beloit.edu. **Contact:** Clint McCown, editor-in-chief; Heather Skyler, managing editor. Magazine: 6×9; 250 pages; 60 lb. paper; 10 pt. C1S cover stock; illustrations; photos on cover. "We are interested in publishing the best contemporary fiction and are open to all themes except those involving pornographic, religiously dogmatic or politically propagandistic representations. Our magazine is for general readership, though most of our readers will probably have a specific interest in literary magazines." Annual. Estab. 1985.
● Work first appearing in *Beloit Fiction Journal* has been reprinted in award-winning collections, including the *Flannery O'Connor* and the *Milkweed Fiction Prize* collections and has won the Iowa Short Fiction award.
Needs: Contemporary, literary, mainstream, prose poem, spiritual and sports. Wants more experimental and short shorts. No pornography, religious dogma, science fiction, horror, political propaganda. Receives 400 unsolicited fiction mss/month. Accepts 20 mss/year. Replies take longer in summer. Reads mss August 1-December 1. Publishes ms within 9 months after acceptance. **Publishes 3 new writers/year.** Recently published work by Rick Bass, A. Manette Ansay and David Milofsky. Length: 250 words-10,000 words; average length: 5,000 words. Sometimes critiques rejected mss and recommends other markets.
How to Contact: Send complete ms with cover letter. Responds in 1 week to queries; 2 months to mss. SASE for ms. Accepts simultaneous submissions if identified as such. Sample copy for $14; back issues $7. Guidelines for #10 SASE.
Advice: "We're looking for a strong opening paragraph, interesting narrative line, compelling voice and unusual subject matter. Many of our contributors are writers whose work we have previously rejected. Don't let one rejection slip turn you away from our—or any—magazine."

BERKELEY FICTION REVIEW, 10 Eshleman Hall, University of California, Berkeley CA 94720. (510)642-2892. E-mail: nmwright@uclink4.berkeley.edu. Website: www.OCF.Berkeley.EDU/~bfr/ (includes guidelines, contest info and short fiction). **Contact:** Natalie Wright and Elisha Cohen, editors. Magazine: 5½×8½; 180 pages; perfect-bound; glossy cover; some b&w art; photographs. "The mission of *Berkeley Fiction Review* is to provide a forum for new and emerging writers as well as writers already established. We publish a wide variety of contemporary short fiction for a literary audience." Annual. Estab. 1981. Circ. 1,000.
Needs: Contemporary/mainstream, literary, experimental. "Quality, inventive short fiction. No poetry or formula fiction." Receives 60 unsolicited mss/month. Accepts 10-20 mss/issue. **Publishes work by 5-10 new writers/ year.** Recently published work by Donna Storey, Ruthanne Wiley and Steve Tomasula. Also publishes short shorts. Occasionally comments on rejected mss.
How to Contact: Send complete ms to "Editor" with very brief cover letter and SASE. Accepts mss by e-mail and disk. Usually reports in 3-4 months, longer in summer. Accepts simultaneous and multiple submissions. Sample copy for $9.50. Guidelines for SASE.
Payment/Terms: Pays 1 contributor's copy. Acquires first rights. Sponsors short story contest with $100 first prize. Entry fee: $6. Send SASE for guidelines.
Advice: "Our criteria is fiction that resonates. Voices that are strong and move a reader. Clear, powerful prose (either voice or rendering of subject) with a point. Unique ways of telling stories—these capture the editors. Work hard, don't give up. Don't let your friends or family critique your work. Get someone honest to point out your writing weaknesses, and then work on them. Don't submit thinly veiled autobiographical stories—it's been done before—and better. With the proliferation of computers, everyone thinks they're a writer. Not true, unfortunately. The plus side though is ease of transmission and layout and the diversity and range of new work."

BIBLIOPHILOS, A Journal for Literati, Savants, Bibliophiles, Amantes Artium, and Those Who Love Animals, 200 Security Building, Fairmont WV 26554-2834. (304)366-8107. Editor: Gerald J. Bobango, Ph.D. **Contact:** Fiction Editor. Literary magazine: 5½×8; 68-72 pages; white glossy paper; illustrations; photos. Magazine "for literate persons who are academically and scholastically oriented, focused on the liberal arts, one-third fiction. Nonfiction includes criticism, history, art, music, theology, philosophy, economics. In fiction we look for that which shows the absurdity of our slavish devotion to technology and all-encompassing big government; that which is not politically correct; that which exposes the egregious dumbing down of education; traditional pre-1960 American values." Estab. 1981. Circ. 300.
● Brown University Library has purchased a complete file of *Bibliophilos* for its American Serials collection.
Needs: Adventure, ethnic, family saga, historical (general, US, Eastern Europe), horror (psychological, supernatural), humor/satire, literary, mainstream/contemporary, military/war, mystery/suspense (police procedural, private eye/hardboiled, courtroom), regional (New England, Middle Atlantic), romance (gothic, historical, regency pe-

riod), short story collections, thriller/espionage, translations, western (frontier saga, traditional), Civil War, US ethnic history, immigration, 19th century politics. "No science fiction, high tech, Erma Bombeck material, 'how I found Jesus and it changed my life.' " Receives 15 unsolicited mss/month. Accepts 2 mss/issue; 6-7 mss/year. Publishes ms up to 1 year after acceptance. **Publishes 2-3 new writers/year.** Published work by Johnnie Mae Hawkins, Lenore McComas Caberly, George R. Higinbotham and Robert Walter. Length: 1,500-3,000 words. Also publishes literary essays, literary criticism and poetry. Often comments on rejected ms.

How to Contact: Query with clips of published work. Include bio, SASE and $5 for sample issue. Responds in 2 weeks to queries. Accepts simultaneous and reprint submissions. Sample copy for $5. Guidelines for SASE. Reviews novels, short story collections and nonfiction books of interest to writers. Send books to editor.

Payment/Terms: Pays subscription to magazine and 3 contributor's copies; additional copies $5. Acquires first North American serial rights.

Advice: "Use correct English, correctly written and punctuated. No jargon, cant, or short-cut language. Type the manuscript on a typewriter, not on a word-processor or computer and you'll have an advantage over other contributors from the start. Scholarly magazines and journals are becoming a rarity. If you use 'feel' rather than 'think' as your verb of choice, better look elsewhere."

BLACK JACK, Seven Buffaloes Press, Box 249, Big Timber MT 59011. **Contact:** Art Coelho, editor. "Main theme: Rural. Publishes material on the American Indian, farm and ranch, American hobo, the common working man, folklore, the Southwest, Okies, Montana, humor, Central California, etc. for people who make their living off the land. The writers write about their roots, experiences and values they receive from the American soil." Annual. Estab. 1973. Circ. 750.

Needs: Literary, contemporary, western, adventure, humor, American Indian, American hobo, and parts of novels and long short stories. "Anything that strikes me as being amateurish, without depth, without craft, I refuse. Actually, I'm not opposed to any kind of writing if the author is genuine and has spent his lifetime dedicated to the written word." Receives approximately 10-15 unsolicited fiction mss/month. Accepts 5-10 mss/year. Length: 3,500-5,000 words (there can be exceptions).

How to Contact: Query for current theme with SASE. Responds in 1 month to queries and mss. Sample copy for $7.75 postpaid.

Payment/Terms: Pays 1-2 contributor's copies. Acquires first North American serial rights and reserves the right to reprint material in an anthology or future *Black Jack* publications. Rights revert to author after publication.

Advice: "Enthusiasm should be matched with skill as a craftsman. That's not saying that we don't continue to learn, but every writer must have enough command of the language to compete with other proven writers. Save postage by writing first to find out the editor's needs. A small press magazine always has specific needs at any given time. I sometimes accept material from writers that aren't that good at punctuation and grammar but make up for it with life's experience. This is not a highbrow publication; it belongs to the salt-of-the-earth people."

☑ ◻ ◎ **BLACK LACE**, BLK Publishing Co., P.O. Box 83912, Los Angeles CA 90083-0912. (310)410-0808. Fax: (310)410-9250. E-mail: newsroom@blk.com. Website: www.blacklace.org. Editor: Alycee Lane. **Contact:** Fiction Editor. Magazine: 8⅛ × 10⅞; 48 pages; book stock; color glossy cover; illustrations; photos. "*Black Lace* is a lifestyle magazine for African-American lesbians. Published quarterly, its content ranges from erotic imagery to political commentary." Estab. 1991.
● Member, COSMEP. The editor would like to see more full-length erotic fiction, politically-focused articles on lesbians and the African-American community as a whole, and nostalgia and humor pieces.

Needs: Ethnic/multicultural, lesbian. "Avoid interracial stories or idealized pornography." Accepts 4 mss/year. Published work by Nicole King, Wanda Thompson, Lynn K. Pannell, Sheree Ann Slaughter, Lyn Lifshin, JoJo and Drew Alise Timmens. Publishes short shorts. Also publishes literary essays, literary criticism, poetry.

How to Contact: Query first with clips of published work or send complete ms with a cover letter. Should include bio (3 sentences). Send a disposable copy of ms. No simultaneous submissions. Accepts electronic submissions. Sample copy for $7. Guidelines free.

Payment/Terms: Pays 2 contributor's copies. Acquires first North American serial rights and right to anthologize.

Advice: *Black Lace* seeks erotic material of the highest quality. The most important thing is that the work be erotic and that it feature black lesbians or themes. Study the magazine to see what we do and how we do it. Some fiction is very romantic, other is highly sexual. Most articles in *Black Lace* cater to black lesbians between these two extremes."

🅽 ● ◪ **THE BLACK MOUNTAIN REVIEW**, Black Mountain Press, P.O. Box 9, Ballycrare, Co. Antrim BT390JW N. Ireland. E-mail: bmreview@totalise.co.uk. **Contact:** Editor. Magazine: A5; approximately 100 pages. "We publish short fiction with a contemporary flavour for an international audience." Semiannual. Estab. 1999.

Needs: Ethnic/multicultural (general), experimental, historical (literary), literary, regional (Irish), religious (general religious, inspirational), romance (literary), science fiction (literary), translations. Publishes ms up to 5 months after acceptance. **Publishes many new writers/year.** Recently published work by Cathal Ó Searcaigh, Michael Longley and Brian Keenan. Length: up to 3,000 words maximum; average length: 1,500-2,000 words. Publishes short shorts. Average length: 500-1,000 words. Also publishes literary essays, literary criticism and poetry. Sometimes comments on rejected mss.

How to Contact: Send complete ms with disk/e-mail in Word .txt format. Include estimated word count, brief bio and list of publications. Responds in 2 months to queries; 4 months to mss. Send SASE (or IRC) for return of ms or send a disposable copy of ms and #10 SASE for reply only. Accepts multiple submissions. Sample copy for $4.50. Guidelines for SASE or by e-mail. Reviews novels, short story collections and nonfiction books of interest to writers. Send review copies to the editor.

Payment/Terms: Pays 1 contributor's copy; additional copies $4.50. Pays on publication for one-time rights.

Advice: "We look for literary quality. Write well."

✓ $ 🖉 ⛉ BLACK WARRIOR REVIEW, Box 862936, Tuscaloosa AL 35486-0027. (205)348-4518. E-mail: bwr@ua.edu. Website: webdelsol.com/bwr (includes writer's guidelines, names of editors, samples, contributor index and online ordering). Editor-in-Chief: Ander Monson. **Contact:** Tommy Zurhellen, fiction editor. Magazine: 6×9; 200 pages; illustrations; photos. "We publish contemporary fiction, poetry, reviews, essays, photography and interviews for a literary audience. We strive to publish the most compelling, best written work that we can find." Semiannual. Estab. 1974. Circ. 2,000.

● Work that appeared in the *Black Warrior Review* has been included in the *Pushcart Prize* anthology, *The Year's Best Fantasy & Horror*, *Harper's Magazine*, *Best American Short Stories*, *Best American Poetry* and in *New Short Stories from the South*.

Needs: Contemporary, literary, short and short-short fiction. Want "work that is conscious of form, good experimental writing, short-short fiction, writing that is more than competent—that sings." No genre fiction please. Receives 200 unsolicited fiction mss/month. Accepts 5 mss/issue, 10 mss/year. Approximately 5% of fiction is agented. **Publishes 5 new writers/year.** Recently published work by Cynthia Riede, John Russell, Drew Perry and Rick Bass. Length: 7,500 words maximum; average length: 2,000-5,000 words. Occasionally critiques rejected mss. Unsolicited novel excerpts are not considered unless the novel is already contracted for publication.

How to Contact: Send complete ms with SASE (1 story per submission). Accepts simultaneous submissions if noted. Responds in 4 months. Publishes ms 2-5 months after acceptance. Sample copy for $8. Guidelines for SASE. Reviews novels and short story collections. "We read year-round."

Payment/Terms: Pays up to $100 per story and 2 contributor's copies. Pays on publication.

Advice: "We look for attention to the language, freshness, honesty, a convincing and sharp voice. Also, send us a clean, well-printed, typo-free manuscript. Become familiar with the magazine prior to submission. We're increasingly interested in considering good experimental writing and in reading short-short fiction."

✓ ◯ ◎ THE BLUE SKUNK COMPANION, The Blue Skunk Society Inc., P.O. Box 8400, CSU 173, Mankato MN 56002-8400. Editor: Jessica Gunderson. **Contact:** Fiction Editor. Magazine: 5×8; 60-70 pages; illustrations; photos. "We publish fiction, poetry, nonfiction and essays that are inspired by life, not by classic literature, periods or styles. We intend to reach readers who wish to be entertained and moved no matter their age, race or culture." Semiannual. Estab. 1997. Circ. 100-500.

Needs: Adventure, condensed/excerpted novel, ethnic/multicultural, experimental, fantasy (contemporary), historical (general), horror, humor/satire, literary, mainstream/contemporary, psychic/supernatural/occult, regional, romance (contemporary), science fiction (contemporary), translations. "We do not want fiction/prose that falls into clichés." Receives 10-20 unsolicited mss/month. Accepts 5-7 mss/issue; 10-14 mss/year. Publishes ms 4-6 months after acceptance. Published work by Roger Sheffer, Brian Batt, Samuel Dollar and Kevin Langton. Length: 1,000-7,000 words; average length: 1,000-4,000 words. Also publishes literary essays, literary criticism, poetry.

How to Contact: Send complete ms with a cover letter. Include estimated word count, ½-1-page bio and list of publications. Responds in 1 month to queries; 6 months to mss. SASE. Accepts simultaneous submissions. Sample copy for $5 and 6×9 SAE with 6 first-class stamps. Guidelines for 4×12 SASE. Reviews novels and short story collections.

Payment/Terms: Pays free subscription to the magazine; additional copies for $5. Pays on publication for first rights. Not copyrighted.

Advice: "We look for a voice that sounds like a 'person' and not like a 'writer.' Good use of language as function, taste and art; not a boastful vocabulary. Try to avoid genre until you have a good grasp of mainstream and contemporary prose. Once that has been achieved, your genre fiction will be much better. Always be fresh with ideas and themes. We feel that good fiction/prose can be found on the back shelves of bookstores and not on the bestsellers list."

☑ ◪ ◉ **BLUELINE**, English Dept., SUNY, Potsdam NY 13676. (315)267-2043. E-mail: blueline@potsda m.edu. Website: www.potsdam.edu/engl/bluelinedefault.html (includes calls, tables of contents for previous is- sues). Editor: Rick Henry. **Contact:** Fiction Editor. Magazine: 6×9; 200 pages; 70 lb. white stock paper; 65 lb. smooth cover stock; illustrations; photos. "*Blueline* is interested in quality writing about the Adirondacks or other places similar in geography and spirit. We publish fiction, poetry, personal essays, book reviews and oral history for those interested in the Adirondacks, nature in general, and well-crafted writing." Annual. Estab. 1979. Circ. 400.

Needs: Adventure, contemporary, humor/satire, literary, prose poem, regional, reminiscences, oral history, na- ture/outdoors. No urban stories or erotica. Receives 8-10 unsolicited fiction mss/month. Accepts 6-8 mss/issue. Does not read January-August. Publishes ms 3-6 months after acceptance. **Publishes 2 new writers/year.** Re- cently published work by Joan Connor, Laura Rodley and Ann Mohin. Length: 500-3,000 words; average length: 2,500 words. Also publishes literary essays, poetry. Occasionally critiques rejected mss.

How to Contact: Send complete ms with SASE, word count and brief bio. Accepts submissions by e-mail. Submit mss September through November 30. Responds in January. Accepts simultaneous submissions. Sample copy for $6. Guidelines for 5×10 SASE.

Payment/Terms: Pays 1 contributor's copy; charges $7 each for 3 or more extra copies. Acquires first rights.

Advice: "We look for concise, clear, concrete prose that tells a story and touches upon a universal theme or situation. We prefer realism to romanticism but will consider nostalgia if well done. Pay attention to grammar and syntax. Avoid murky language, sentimentality, cuteness or folksiness. We would like to see more good fiction related to the Adirondacks and more literary fiction and prose poems. If manuscript has potential, we work with author to improve and reconsider for publication. Our readers prefer fiction to poetry (in general) or reviews. Write from your own experience, be specific and factual (within the bounds of your story) and if you write about universal features such as love, death, change, etc., write about them in a fresh way. Triteness and mediocrity are the hallmarks of the majority of stories seen today."

◪ **BOGG, A Magazine of British & North American Writing**, Bogg Publications, 422 N. Cleveland St., Arlington VA 22201-1424. (703)243-6019. **Contact:** John Elsberg, US editor. Magazine: 6×9; 68-72 pages; 70 lb. white paper; 70 lb. cover stock; line illustrations. "American and British poetry, prose poems, experimental short 'fictions,' reviews, and essays on small press." Published "two or three times a year." Estab. 1968. Circ. 850.

Needs: Very short experimental fiction and prose poems. "We are always looking for work with British/Com- monwealth themes and/or references." Receives 25 unsolicited fiction mss/month. Accepts 1-2 mss/issue; 3-6 mss/year. Publishes ms 3-18 months after acceptance. **Published 25-50 new fiction and poetry writers within the last year.** Published work by Dan Lenihan, Harriet Zinnes, Laurel Speer and Brian Johnson. Length: 300- 500 words. Also publishes literary essays, literary criticism, poetry. Occasionally critiques rejected mss.

How to Contact: Query first or send ms (2-6 pieces) with SASE. Accepts submissions on disk. Responds in 1 week to queries; 2 weeks to mss. Sample copy for $3.50 or $4.50 (current issue). Reviews novels and short story collections.

Payment/Terms: Pays 2 contributor's copies; reduced charge for extras. Acquires one-time rights.

Advice: "We look for voice and originality. Read magazine first. We are most interested in prose work of experimental or wry nature to supplement poetry, and are always looking for innovative/imaginative uses of British themes and references."

◪ **BOOKPRESS, The Newspaper of the Literary Arts**, The Bookery, 215 N. Cayuga St., Ithaca NY 14850. (607)277-2254. Fax: (607)275-9221. E-mail: bookpress@thebookery.com. Website: www.thebookery. com/bookpress (includes current issue, credits and archives). **Contact:** Jack Goldman, editor-in-chief. Newspaper: 12-16 pages; newsprint; illustrations and photos. Contains book reviews, analysis, fiction and excerpts from published work. Monthly. Estab. 1991. Circ. 12,000.

Needs: Condensed/excerpted novel, feminist, gay, historical, lesbian, literary, regional. No new age. Publishes special fiction issues or anthologies. Receives 10-12 unsolicited mss/month. Accepts 0-2 mss/issue. Does not read during the summer. Publishes ms 1-3 months after acceptance. **Publishes 5-10 new writers/year.** Published work by J. Robert Lennon, Brian Hall and Robert Sward. Length: 4,000 words maximum; average length: 2,000 words. Also publishes literary essays, literary criticism and poetry.

How to Contact: Send complete ms with a cover letter. Also include on disk in Microsoft Word or .rif format. Submissions accepted via e-mail. Include 3-sentence bio. Responds in 1 month to mss. Send SASE for return of ms. Accepts simultaneous submissions. Sample copy and guidelines free. Reviews novels or short story collec- tions. Send books to editor.

Payment/Terms: Pays free subscription to newspaper.

Advice: "Send a brief, concise cover letter. No overwriting or overly cerebral academic work. The author's genuine interest and passion for the topic makes for good work."

☑ $◑ ☯ **BOULEVARD**, Opojaz Inc., PMB 332, 4579 Laclede Ave., St. Louis MO 63108-2103. (314)361-2986. Website: www.richardburgin.com (includes writer's guidelines, sample contents, writing contest information, excerpts from the magazine, etc.). **Contact:** Richard Burgin, editor. Magazine: 5½×8½; 150-225 pages; excellent paper; high-quality cover stock; illustrations; photos. "We strive to publish the best contemporary fiction and other forms of literature regardless of the writer's particular aesthetics. We are open to many kinds of writing excellence and believe there is only one school that counts—the school of talent." Published 3 times/ year. Estab. 1986. Circ. about 3,500.

● *Boulevard* ranked #15 on the *Writer's Digest* "Fiction 50" list of top markets.

Needs: Contemporary, experimental, literary. Does not want to see "anything whose first purpose is not literary." No science fiction, erotica, westerns, horror, romance. Receives over 600 mss/month. Accepts about 10 mss/ issue. Does not accept manuscripts between April 1 and October 1. Publishes ms less than 1 year after acceptance. Agented fiction ⅓-¼. Length: 8,000 words maximum; average length: 5,000 words. Publishes short shorts. **Publishes 10 new writers/year.** Recently published work by Melissa Pritchard, Peter LaSalle, Joyce Carol Oates and Robert Phillips. Also publishes literary essays, literary criticism, poetry. Sometimes critiques rejected mss and recommends other markets.

How to Contact: Send complete ms with cover letter. Accepts mss on disk. Responds in 2 weeks to queries; 2 months to mss. SASE for reply. Accepts simultaneous and multiple submissions. Sample copy for $8 and SAE with 5 first-class stamps.

Payment/Terms: Pays $150-300 and contributor's copies; charges for extras. Acquires first North American serial rights. Does not send galleys to author unless requested.

Advice: "We pick the stories that move us the most emotionally, stimulate us the most intellectually, are the best written and thought out. Don't write to get published—write to express your experience and vision of the world."

☑ ◑ ☯ **THE BRIAR CLIFF REVIEW**, Briar Cliff University, 3303 Rebecca St., Sioux City IA 51104-0100. (712)279-5477. E-mail: currans@briarcliff.edu. Website: www.briarcliff.edu/bcreview (includes writer's guidelines, contest guidelines, previous contest winners and their winning poems/short stories and cover artwork). Managing Editor: Tricia Currans-Sheehan. **Contact:** Phil Hey, fiction editor. Magazine: 8½×11; 80 pages; 70 lb. Finch Opaque cover stock; illustrations; photos. "*The Briar Cliff Review* is an eclectic literary and cultural magazine focusing on (but not limited to) Siouxland writers and subjects. We are happy to proclaim ourselves a regional publication. It doesn't diminish us; it enhances us." Annual. Estab. 1989. Circ. 750.

● *The Briar Cliff Review* has received The Gold Crown and Silver Crown awards from the Columbia Scholastic Press Association and the National Pacemaker Award from the Associated Collegiate Press.

Needs: Ethnic/multicultural, feminist, historical, humor/satire, literary, mainstream/contemporary, regional. No romance, horror or alien stories. Accepts 5 mss/year. Reads mss only between August 1 and November 1. Publishes ms 3-4 months after acceptance. **Publishes 10-14 new writers/year.** Recently published work by J. Annie MacLeod, Christine Phillips, John Lofy, Ken Wheaton, Jacob Appel, Laura Wilson, Cynthia Gregory and Josip Nova Kovich. Length: 2,500-4,000 words; average length: 3,000 words. Also publishes literary essays, literary criticism and poetry. Sometimes comments on rejected mss.

How to Contact: Send complete ms with a cover letter. Include estimated word count, bio and list of publications. Responds in 4-5 months to mss. Send a SASE for return of ms. Accepts electronic submissions (disk). Accepts simultaneous submissions. Sample copy for $10 and 9×12 SAE. Guidelines free for #10 SASE. Reviews novels and short story collections.

Payment/Terms: Pays 2 contributor's copies; additional copies available for $5. Acquires first rights

Advice: "So many stories are just telling. We want some action. It has to move. We prefer stories in which there is no gimmick, no mechanical turn of events, no moral except the one we would draw privately."

◑ **BRILLIANT CORNERS, A Journal of Jazz & Literature**, Lycoming College, Williamsport PA 17701. (570)321-4279. Fax: (570)321-4090. E-mail: feinstei@lycoming.edu. **Contact:** Sascha Feinstein, editor. Journal: 6×9; 100 pages; 70 lb. Cougar opaque, vellum, natural paper; photographs. "We publish jazz-related literature— fiction, poetry and nonfiction." Semiannual. Estab. 1996. Circ. 1,200.

Needs: Condensed/excerpted novel, ethnic/multicultural, experimental, literary, mainstream/contemporary, romance (contemporary). Receives 10-15 unsolicited mss/month. Accepts 1-2 mss/issue; 2-3 mss/year. Does not read mss May 15-September 1. Publishes ms 4-12 months after acceptance. Very little agented fiction. Publishes short shorts. Also publishes literary essays, literary criticism and poetry. Rarely comments on rejected mss.

How to Contact: Send complete ms with a cover letter. Include 1-paragraph bio and list of publications. Responds in 2 weeks to queries; 1-2 months to mss. SASE for return of ms or send a disposable copy of ms. Accepts unpublished work only. Sample copy for $7. Reviews novels and short story collections. Send books to editor.

Payment/Terms: Pays 2 contributor's copies. Acquires first North American serial rights. Sends galleys to author when possible.

Advice: "We look for clear, moving prose that demonstrates a love of both writing and jazz. We primarily publish established writers, but we read all submissions carefully and welcome work by outstanding young writers."

☑ ◑ **BUTTON, New England's Tiniest Magazine of Poetry, Fiction & Gracious Living**, P.O. Box 26, Lunenburg MA 01462. E-mail: buttonx26@aol.com. Website: www.moonsigns.net (includes history of magazine, honor roll of contributors). Editor: S. Cragin. **Contact:** W.M. Davies, fiction editor. Magazine: 4×5; 34 pages; bond paper; color cardstock cover; illustrations; photos. "*Button*'s designed as a vehicle of gracious living. *Button* attempts to reflect a world you'd want to live in." Annual. Estab. 1993. Circ. 1,500.

Needs: Literary. No genre fiction, science fiction, techno-thriller. Wants more of "anything Herman Melville, Henry James or Betty MacDonald would like to read." Receives 20-40 unsolicited mss/month. Accepts 1-2 mss/issue; 3-5 mss/year. Publishes ms 3-9 months after acceptance. Recently published work by Ralph Lombreglia, Michele Chalfoun, Arctic Traveller and Lawrence Millman. Length: 500-2,500 words. Also publishes literary essays, poetry. Sometimes comments on rejected ms "if it shows promise."

How to Contact: Request guidelines. Send ms with bio, list of publications and advise how you found magazine. Responds in 1 month to queries; 2-4 months to mss. SASE. Sample copy for $2. Guidelines for SASE. Reviews novels and short story collections. Send book to editor. Sponsors poetry contest, for more info send SASE.

Payment/Terms: Pays honorarium and multiple free subscriptions to the magazine. Pays on publication for first North American serial rights. Sends galleys to author if there are editorial changes. "Chats up your brilliance to a wide and varied circle of acquaintances."

Advice: "What makes a manuscript stand out? Flannery O'Connor once said, 'Don't get subtle till the fourth page,' and I agree. We look for interesting, sympathetic, believable characters and careful setting. I'm really tired of stories that start strong and then devolve into dialogue uninterrupted by further exposition. Also, no stories from a mad person's POV unless it's really tricky and skillful. Advice to prospective writers: continue to read at least ten times as much as you write. Read the best, and read intelligent criticism if you can find it. *No beginners please.* Please don't submit more than once a year—it's more important that you work on your craft rather than machine-gunning publications with samples, and don't submit more than 3 poems in a batch (this advice goes for other places, you'll find . . .)."

☑ $ ◑ **BYLINE**, Box 130596, Edmond OK 73013-0001. (405)348-5591. E-mail: mpreston@bylinemag. com. Website: www.bylinemag.com (includes writer's guidelines, names of editors, contest list and rules, ad rates and sample article from magazine). Editor-in-Chief: Marcia Preston. **Contact:** Carolyn Wall, fiction editor. Monthly magazine "aimed at encouraging and motivating all writers toward success, with special information to help new writers. Articles center on how to write better, market smarter, sell your work." Estab. 1981.

● Byline ranked #13 on *Writer's Digest*'s Fiction 50 list of top markets for fiction writers.

Needs: Literary, genre, general fiction. Receives 100-200 unsolicited fiction mss/month. Does not want to see erotica or explicit graphic content. No science fiction or fantasy. Accepts 1 ms/issue; 11 mss/year. **Published many new writers within the last year.** Recently published work by Julie Weary and Virginia Reiser. Length: 2,000-4,000 words. Also publishes poetry and articles.

How to Contact: Send complete ms with SASE. Accepts simultaneous submissions, "if notified. For us, no cover letter is needed." Responds in 6-12 weeks. Publishes ms an average of 3 months after acceptance. Sample copy for $4. Guidelines for #10 SASE.

Payment/Terms: Pays $100 and 3 contributor's copies. Pays on acceptance for first North American rights.

Advice: "We look for good writing that draws the reader in; conflict and character movement by story's end. We're very open to new writers. Submit a well-written, professionally prepared ms with SASE. No erotica or senseless violence; otherwise, we'll consider most any theme. We also sponsor short story and poetry contests. Read what's being published. Find a good story, not just a narrative reflection. Keep submitting."

☑ ◑ ◎ ▼ **CALLALOO, A Journal of African-American and African Diaspora Arts and Letters**, Dept. of English, P.O. Box 400121, University of Virginia, Charlottesville VA 22904-4121. (434)982-5798. Fax: (434)924-6472. E-mail: callaloo@virginia.edu. Website: www.people.virginia.edu/~callaloo (includes links to *Callaloo* online, writer's guidelines, sample issues, copyright information and editorial information). Editor: Charles H. Rowell. **Contact:** Ginger Thornton, managing editor. Magazine: 7×10; 250 pages. Quarterly. "Devoted to publishing fiction, poetry, drama of the African diaspora, including North, Central and South America, the Caribbean, Europe and Africa. Visually beautiful and well-edited, the journal publishes 3-5 short stories in all forms and styles in each issue." Estab. 1976. Circ. 2,000.

● One of the leading voices in African-American literature, *Callaloo* has received NEA literature grants. Several pieces every year are chosen for collections of year's best stories (*Beacon's Best*, for example). John Wideman's "Weight" from *Callaloo* won the 2000 O'Henry Award.

Needs: Contemporary, ethnic (black culture), feminist, historical, humor/satire, literary, prose poem, regional, science fiction, serialized/excerpted novel, translations. Also publishes poetry and drama. "Would like to see more experimental fiction, science fiction and well-crafted literary fiction particularly dealing with the black middle class, immigrant communities and/or the black South." No romance, confessional. Accepts 3-5 mss/issue; 10-20 mss/year. Length: 50 pages maximum. **Publishes 5-10 new writers/year.** Recently published work by Randall Kenan, Gloria Naylor, Julia Alvarez, Janet Diaz and Samuel Delany.

How to Contact: Submit complete ms in triplicate and cover letter with name, mailing address, e-mail address, if possible and loose stamps. Accepts submissions on disk with hard copy. Accepts queries by e-mail and fax. Responds to queries in 2 weeks; 6 months to mss. Accepts multiple submissions (maximum 2). Previously published work accepted "only as part of a special issue or if solicited." Sample copy for $10.

Payment/Terms: Pays in contributor's copies. Acquires all rights. Sends galleys to author.

Advice: "We look for fresh perspective, vividness of writing. We strongly recommend looking at the journal before submitting."

CALYX, A Journal of Art & Literature by Women, Calyx, Inc., P.O. Box B, Corvallis OR 97339. (541)753-9384. Fax: (541)753-0515. E-mail: calyx@proaxis.com. Director: Margarita Donnelly. **Contact:** Beverly McFarland, senior editor. Magazine: 6×8; 128 pages per single issue; 60 lb. coated matte stock paper; 10 pt. chrome coat cover; original art. Publishes prose, poetry, art, essays, interviews and critical and review articles. "*Calyx* exists to publish women's literary and artistic work and is committed to publishing the work of all women, including women of color, older women, working class women, and other voices that need to be heard. We are committed to nurturing beginning writers." Biannual. Estab. 1976. Circ. 6,000.

Needs: Receives approximately 1,000 unsolicited prose and poetry mss when open. Accepts 4-8 prose mss/issue, 9-15 mss/year. Reads mss October 1-December 15; submit only during this period. Mss received when not reading will be returned. **Publishes 10-20 new writers/year.** Recently published work by M. Evelina Galang, Chitrita Banerji, Diana Ma and Catherine Brady. Length: 5,000 words maximum. Also publishes literary essays, literary criticism, poetry.

How to Contact: Send ms with SASE and bio. Accepts requests for guidelines by e-mail. Accepts simultaneous submissions. Responds in 8 months to mss. Publishes ms an average of 8 months after acceptance. Sample copy for $9.50 plus $2 postage. Guidelines available for SASE. Reviews novels, short story collections, poetry and essays.

Payment/Terms: "Combination of payment, free issues and 1 volume subscription."

Advice: Most mss are rejected because "the writers are not familiar with *Calyx*—writers should read *Calyx* and be familiar with the publication. We look for good writing, imagination and important/interesting subject matter."

CAMBRENSIS, 41 Heol Fach, Cornelly, Bridgend, Mid-Glamorgan, CF33 4LN Wales. Editor: Arthur Smith. **Contact:** Fiction Editor. Quarterly. Circ. 500.

Needs: "Devoted solely to the short story form, featuring short stories by writers born or resident in Wales or with some Welsh connection; receives grants from the Welsh Arts' Council and the Welsh Writers' Trust; uses artwork—cartoons, line-drawings, sketches etc." Length: 2,500 words maximum.

How to Contact: Writer has to have some connection with Wales. SAE and IRCs or similar should be enclosed with "air mail" postage to avoid long delay.

Payment/Terms: Writers receive 3 copies of magazine. Send IRCs for a sample copy. Subscriptions via Blackwell's Periodicals, P.O. Box 40, Hythe Bridge Street, Oxford, OX1 2EU, UK or Swets & Zeitlinger B V, P.O. Box 800, 2160 S Z Lisse, Holland.

CAPERS AWEIGH, Cape Breton Poetry & Fiction, Capers Aweigh Press, 19 Cliff St., Glace Bay, Nova Scotia B1A 1B3 Canada. (902)849-0822. E-mail: capersaweigh@hotmail.com. Editor: John MacNeil. **Contact:** Fiction Editor. Magazine: 5×8; 80 pages; bond paper; Cornwall-coated cover. "*Capers Aweigh* publishes poetry and fiction of, by and for Cape Bretoners." Publication frequency varies. Estab. 1992. Circ. 500.

Needs: Adventure, ethnic/multicultural, fantasy, feminist, historical, humor/satire, literary, mainstream, contemporary, mystery/suspense, psychic/supernatural/occult, regional, science fiction. List of upcoming themes available for SASE. Receives 2 unsolicited mss/month. Accepts 30 mss/issue. Publishes ms 9 months after acceptance. Published work by C. Fairn Kennedy and Shirley Kiju Kawi. Length: 2,500 words. Publishes short shorts. Also publishes literary criticism, poetry. Sponsors contests only to Cape Bretoners fiction writers.

How to Contact: Query first. Send SASE for reply or send a disposable copy of ms. Accepts electronic submissions (IBM). Sample copy for $4.95 and 6×10 SAE.

Payment/Terms: Pays free subscription to the magazine and 1 contributor's copy; additional copies for $4.95. Acquires first North American serial rights. Sends galleys to author.

THE CAPILANO REVIEW, 2055 Purcell Way, North Vancouver, British Columbia V7J 3H5 Canada. (604)984-1712. E-mail: tcr@capcollege.bc.ca. Website: www.capcollege.bc.ca/dept/TCR (includes guidelines, excerpts and complete bibliography of 25 years worth of contributors). **Contact:** Ryan Knighton, editor. Magazine: 6×9; 90-120 pages; book paper; glossy cover; perfect-bound; illustrations; photos. Magazine of "fresh, innovative art and literature for literary/artistic audience." Triannual. Estab. 1972. Circ. 900.

Needs: Experimental, literary and drama. Receives 80 unsolicited mss/month. Accepts 1 ms/issue; 3-5 mss/year. **Published new writers within the last year.** Recently published work by Anne Stone and Michael Turner. Length: 4,000 words average. Also publishes literary essays, poetry.

How to Contact: Send complete ms with cover letter and SASE or IRC. Include 2- to 3-sentence bio and brief list of publications. Responds to mss in 2-4 months. Send SASE or IRCs for return of ms. Sample copy for $9 (Canadian). "No U.S. postage please—we cannot use it."

Payment/Terms: Pays $50-200, 2 contributor's copies and one-year subscription. Pays on publication for first North American serial rights.

Advice: "We are looking for exceptional, original style; strong thematic content; innovation and quality writing. We would like to see more postmodern; cross-genre fiction. Read several issues before submitting and make sure your work is technically perfect."

THE CARIBBEAN WRITER, The University of the Virgin Islands, RR 02, Box 10,000—Kingshill, St. Croix, Virgin Islands 00850. (340)692-4152. Fax: (340)692-4026. E-mail: qmars@uvi.edu. Website: www.TheCaribbeanWriter.com (includes writer's guidelines and excerpts from past publications). Editor: Erika J. Waters. **Contact:** Quilin B. Mars, managing editor. Magazine: 6×9; 304 pages; 60 lb. paper; glossy cover stock; illustrations; photos. "*The Caribbean Writer* is an international magazine with a Caribbean focus. The Caribbean should be central to the work, or the work should reflect a Caribbean heritage, experience or perspective." Annual. Estab. 1987. Circ. 1,500.

• *The Caribbean Writer* has received a Pushcart Prize and Quenepon Award.

Needs: Contemporary, historical (general), humor/satire, literary, mainstream and prose poem. Receives 800 unsolicited mss/year. Accepts 60 mss/issue. Also accepts poetry, essays, translations, plays. **Publishes approximately 20% new writers/year.** Recently published work by Maria Lemus, Cyril Dabydeen, Eugenia O'Neal and Dionne Jackson Miller.

How to Contact: Send complete ms with cover letter. Accepts queries/mss by e-mail. "Blind submissions only. Send name, address and title of manuscript on separate sheet. Title only on manuscript. Manuscripts will not be returned unless this procedure is followed." SASE (or IRC). Accepts simultaneous and multiple submissions. Sample copy for $7 and $2 postage.

Payment/Terms: Pays 2 contributor's copies. Acquires one-time rights. Annual prizes for best story ($400); for best poem ($300); $200 for first publication; best work by Caribbean author ($500); best work by Virgin Islands author ($100).

Advice: Looks for "work which reflects a Caribbean heritage, experience or perspective."

CAROLINA QUARTERLY, Greenlaw Hall CB #3520, University of North Carolina, Chapel Hill NC 27599-3520. (919)962-0244. Fax: (919)962-3520. E-mail: cquarter@unc.edu. Website: www.unc.edu/depts/cqonline (includes writer's guidelines, current contents, index to past contributors). **Contact:** Chad Trevitte, editor-in-chief. Literary journal: 70-90 pages; illustrations. Publishes fiction for a "general literary audience." Triannual. Estab. 1948. Circ. 1,400.

• Work published in *Carolina Quarterly* has been selected for inclusion in *Best American Short Stories*, in *New Stories from the South: The Year's Best*, and *Best of the South*. *Carolina Quarterly* received a special mention in 1999 *Pushcart Prize* stories.

Needs: Literary. "We would like to see more short/micro-fiction and more stories by minority/ethnic writers." Receives 150-200 unsolicited fiction mss/month. Accepts 4-5 mss/issue; 14-16 mss/year. Does not read mss June-August. Publishes ms an average of 4 months after acceptance. **Publishes 1-2 new writers/year.** Published work by Clyde Edgerton, Barry Hannah and Doris Betts. Length: 7,000 words maximum; no minimum. Also publishes short shorts, literary essays, poetry. Occasionally critiques rejected mss.

How to Contact: Send complete ms with cover letter and SASE to fiction editor. Accepts queries by phone, fax and e-mail. No simultaneous submissions. Responds in 2-4 months. Sample copy for $5; writer's guidelines for SASE.

Payment/Terms: Pays in contributor's copies. Acquires first rights.

MARKET CONDITIONS are constantly changing! If you're still using this book and it is 2003 or later, buy the newest edition of *Novel & Short Story Writer's Market* at your favorite bookstore or order from Writer's Digest Books by calling 1-800-289-0963.

N **⊘** **CENTER: A Journal of the Literary Arts**, University of Missouri, 202 Tate Hall, Columbia MO 65211. (573)884-7775. E-mail: bsw88f@mizzou.edu. Website: www.web.missouri.edu/~cwp. **Contact:** Jean Braithwaite. Magazine: 5×9; 125-200 pages; 60 lb. paper; 80 lb. dull cover; illustrations. "*Center*'s goal is to publish the best in literary fiction, poetry and creative nonfiction by previously unpublished and emerging writers, as well as more established writers." Semiannual. Estab. 2000. Circ. 500.

Needs: Ethnic/multicultural, experimental, humor/satire, literary, genre-crossing multimedia. Receives 30-50 unsolicited mss/month. Accepts 2-3 mss/issue; 3-5 mss/year. Publishes ms 6 months after acceptance. **Publishes 25% new writers/year.** Recently published work by Lisa Glatt and Robert Root. Length: 10,000 words maximum. Publishes short shorts. Average length: 1,000 words. Also publishes literary essays and poetry. Sometimes comments on rejected mss.

How to Contact: Send complete ms with a cover letter. Include brief bio. Responds in 2 months to queries; 6 months to mss. Send SASE (or IRC) for return of ms or send a disposable copy of ms and #10 SASE for reply only. Accepts simultaneous and multiple submissions. Sample copy for $3. Guidelines for SASE. Reviews novels, short story collections and nonfiction books of interest to writers. Send review copies to Stephanie Powell Watts.

Payment/Terms: Pays 2 contributor's copies; additional copies $3. Pays on publication for one-time rights. Sends galleys to author.

⊕ **✓** **$** **CHAPMAN**, 4 Broughton Place, Edinburgh EH1 3RX Scotland. **Contact:** Joy Hendry, fiction editor. Phone: (+44)131 557 2207. Fax: (+44)131 556 9565. E-mail: editor@chapman-pub.co.uk. Website: www.chapman-pub.co.uk (includes samples from current issues, guidelines, catalog). "*Chapman*, Scotland's quality literary magazine, is a dynamic force in Scotland, publishing poetry, fiction, criticism, reviews; articles on theatre, politics, language and the arts. Our philosophy is to publish new work, from known and unknown writers, mainly Scottish, but also worldwide." Quarterly. Circ. 2,000. Publishes 4-6 stories/issue. Estab. 1970.

Needs: No horror, science fiction. **Publishes 25 new writers/year.** Published work by Quim Monzo, Dilys Rose, Leslie Schenck. Length: 1,000-6,000 words.

How to Contact: Include SAE and return postage (or IRC) with submissions.

Payment/Terms: Pays by negotiation. Sample copy available for £5 (includes postage).

Tips: "We seek challenging work which attempts to explore difficult/new territory in content and form, but lighter work, if original enough, is welcome."

$ **⊘** **THE CHARITON REVIEW**, Truman State University, Kirksville MO 63552. (816)785-4499. Fax: (816)785-7486. Editor: Jim Barnes. **Contact:** Fiction Editor. Magazine: 6×9; approximately 100 pages; 60 lb. paper; 65 lb. cover stock; photographs on cover. "We demand only excellence in fiction and fiction translation for a general and college readership." Semiannual. Estab. 1975. Circ. 700.

Needs: Literary, contemporary, experimental, translations. Accepts 3-5 mss/issue; 6-10 mss/year. **Published new writers within the last year.** Published work by Ann Townsend, Glenn DelGrosso, Paul Ruffin and X.J. Kennedy. Length: 3,000-6,000 words. Also publishes literary essays, poetry. Critiques rejected mss when there is time.

How to Contact: Send complete ms with SASE. No book-length mss. No simultaneous submissions. Responds in less than 1 month to mss. Publishes ms an average of 6 months after acceptance. Sample copy for $5 with SASE. Reviews novels and short story collections.

Payment/Terms: Pays $5/page up to $50 maximum and contributor's copy on publication; additional copies for $5.50. Acquires first North American serial rights; rights returned on request.

Advice: "Do not ask us for guidelines: the only guidelines are excellence in all matters. Write well and study the publication you are submitting to. We are interested only in the very best fiction and fiction translation. We are not interested in slick material. We do not read photocopies, dot-matrix, or carbon copies. Know the simple mechanics of submission—SASE, no paper clips, no odd-sized SASE, etc. Know the genre (short story, novella, etc.). Know the unwritten laws. There is too much manufactured fiction; assembly-lined, ego-centered personal essays offered as fiction."

✓ **$** **⊘** **♈** **THE CHATTAHOOCHEE REVIEW**, Georgia Perimeter College, 2101 Womack Rd., Dunwoody GA 30338-4497. (770)551-3019. Website: www.chattahoochee-review.org. Editor: Lawrence Hetrick. Managing Editor: Jo Ann Yeager Adkins. **Contact:** Fiction Editor. Magazine: 6×9; 150 pages; 70 lb. paper; 80 lb. cover stock; illustrations; photos. Quarterly. Estab. 1980. Circ. 1,250.

● Fiction from *The Chattahoochee Review* has been included in *Best New Stories of the South*.

Needs: Literary, mainstream. No juvenile, romance, science fiction. Receives 900 unsolicited mss/year. Accepts 5 mss/issue. **Published new writers within the last year.** Published work by Merrill Joan Gerber, Mary Ann Taylor-Hall, Anthony Grooms and Greg Johnson. Length: 2,500 words average. Also publishes creative nonfiction, interviews with writers, poetry reviews, poetry. Sometimes critiques rejected mss.

How to Contact: Send complete ms with cover letter, which should include sufficient bio for notes on contributors' page. Responds in 2-4 months. SASE. May consider simultaneous submission "reluctantly." Sample copy for $6. Fiction and poetry guidelines available on request. Reviews novels and short story collections.
Payment/Terms: Pays $20/page fiction; $15/page nonfiction; $50/poem. Acquires first rights.
Advice: "Arrange to read magazine before you submit to it." Known for publishing Southern regional fiction.

N **CHICAGO QUARTERLY REVIEW**, Monadnock Group Publishers, 517 Sherman Ave., Evanston IL 60202. **Contact:** Brian Skinner and Syed Haider. editors. Magazine: 8½×11; 48 pages; 60 lb. paper; 80 lb. cover stock; illustrations; photos. "*CQR* was begun by a group of writers who felt there were too few venues for quality work that did not conform to preordained criteria. We continue to publish examples of solid writing not in thrall to any particular school of thought or aesthetics." Quarterly. Estab. 1994. Circ. 300.
Needs: Literary. Does not want "any work that is easily categorized, academic, obtuse or self-impressed." Receives 10-12 unsolicited mss/month. Accepts 2-3 mss/issue; 4-8 mss/year. Publishes ms up to 1 year after acceptance. Agented fiction 10%. **Publishes 1-2 new writers/year.** Recently published work by Chris Fountain, Elizabeth McKenzie, Richard Kostelanetz and Barbara Cranford. Length: 5,000 words maximum; average length: 2,500 words. Publishes short shorts. Average length: 1,000 words. Also publishes literary essays and poetry. Sometimes comments on rejected mss.
How to Contact: Send complete ms with a cover letter. Include estimated word count and brief bio. Responds in 2 months to queries; 6 months to mss. Send a disposable copy of ms and #10 SASE for reply only. Accepts simultaneous and previously published submissions. Sample copy for $6.50. Guidelines for SASE.
Payment/Terms: Pays 1 contributor's copy; additional copies $5. Pays on publication for one-time rights.
Advice: "We look for work that does not require a secret decoder ring to figure out. The writer's voice ought to be clear and unique, and should explain something of what it means to be human. Best of all is that rare piece that makes us forget we are reading fiction. Good writing is a result of inspiration, passion, skill, and assiduous, even ruthless editing. Publication should be an afterthought to this process, a way to share one's work, not merely to garner recognition."

$ **CHICAGO REVIEW**, 5801 S. Kenwood Ave., Chicago IL 60637. (773)702-0887. E-mail: chicago-review@uchicago.edu. Website: humanities.uchicago.edu (includes guidelines, editors' names, subscription information). **Contact:** William Martin, fiction editor. Magazine for a highly literate general audience: 6×9; 128 pages; offset white 60 lb. paper; illustrations; photos. Quarterly. Estab. 1946. Circ. 3,500.
● The *Chicago Review* has won two *Pushcart* prizes and an Illinois Arts Council Award.
Needs: Literary, contemporary and experimental. Accepts up to 5 mss/issue; 20 mss/year. Receives 80-100 unsolicited fiction mss each week. **Publishes 2 new writers/year.** Published work by Hollis Seamon, Tom House, Rachel Klein and Doris Dörrie. No preferred length, except will not accept book-length mss. Also publishes literary essays, literary criticism, poetry. Sometimes recommends other markets.
How to Contact: Send complete ms with cover letter. Accepts queries/mss by e-mail. SASE. No simultaneous submissions. Responds in 4-5 months to mss. Sample copy for $8. Guidelines via website or with SASE. Reviews novels and short story collections. Send books to Book Review Editor.
Payment/Terms: Pays 3 contributor's copies and subscription.
Advice: "We look with interest at fiction that addresses subjects inventively, work that steers clear of clichéd treatments of themes. We're always eager to read writing that experiments with language, whether it be with characters' viewpoints, tone or style. We like a strong voice capable of rejecting gimmicks in favor of subtleties. We are most impressed by writers who have read both deeply and broadly, but display their own inventiveness. However, we have been receiving more submissions and are becoming more selective."

CHIRON REVIEW, 702 N. Prairie, St. John KS 67576-1516. (620)786-4955. E-mail: chironreview@hotmail.com. Website: www.geocities.com/SoHo/Nook/1748 (includes writer's guidelines, names of editors, chat line, sample poems and contest info). Editor: Michael Hathaway. **Contact:** Ray Zepeda, fiction editor. Tabloid: 10×13; minimum 24 pages; newsprint; illustrations; photos. Publishes "all types of material, no particular theme; traditional and off-beat, no taboos." Quarterly. Estab. 1982. Circ. 1,200.
Needs: Contemporary, experimental, humor/satire, literary. No didactic, religious or overtly political writing. Receives 100 mss/month. Accepts 1-6 ms/issue; 6-24 mss/year. Publishes ms within 6-18 months of acceptance. **Publishes 100 new writers and poets/year.** Published work by Janice Eidus, David Newman, Craig Curtis, Jay Marvin and Ad Hudler. Length: 3,500 words maximum. Publishes short shorts. Sometimes recommends other markets to writers of rejected mss.
How to Contact: Responds in up to 2 months. SASE. No simultaneous or reprint submissions. Deadlines: November 1 (Winter), February 1 (Spring), May 1 (Summer), August 1 (Autumn). Sample copy for $5 ($10 overseas). Guidelines for #10 SASE.
Payment/Terms: Pays 1 contributor's copy; extra copies at 50% discount. Acquires first rights.
Advice: "Research markets thoroughly."

$◐ CHRYSALIS READER, Journal of the Swedenborg Foundation, The Swedenborg Foundation, 320 N. Church St., West Chester PA 19380-3213. (610)430-3222. Send mss to: Rt. 1, Box 4510, Dillwyn VA 23936. (804)983-3021. **Editor:** Carol S. Lawson. Book series: 7½×10; 192 pages; archival paper; coated cover stock; illustrations; photos. "A literary magazine centered around one theme per issue. Publishes fiction, essays and poetry for intellectually curious readers interested in spiritual topics." Biannual. Estab. 1985. Circ. 3,000.

Needs: Fiction (leading to insight), contemporary, experimental, historical, literary, mainstream, mystery/suspense, science fiction, spiritual, sports. No religious, juvenile, preschool. Upcoming theme: "Spiritual Wellness" (October 2002). Receives 50 mss/month. Accepts 15-20 mss/issue; 20-40 mss/year. Publishes ms within 2 years of acceptance. Published work by Robert Bly, Larry Dossey and John Hitchcock. Length: 2,000-3,500 words. Also publishes literary essays, literary criticism, chapters of novels, poetry. Sometimes critiques rejected mss and recommends other markets.

How to Contact: Query first and send SASE for guidelines. Responds in 2 months. SASE. No simultaneous, reprinted or in-press material. Sample copy for $10. Guidelines for #10 SASE.

Payment/Terms: Pays $75-250 and 5 contributor's copies. Pays on publication for one-time rights. Sends galleys to author.

Advice: Looking for "1. *Quality*; 2. appeal for our audience; 3. relevance to/illumination of an issue's theme."

☑ $CICADA, Carus Publishing Company, 315 Fifth St., Peru IL 61354. (815)224-6656. Fax: (815)224-6615. E-mail: mmiklavcic@caruspub.com. Website: www.cricketmag.com or www.cicadamag.com. **Contact:** Deborah Vetter, executive editor. Associate Editor: Tracy Schoenle. Literary magazine: 128 pages; some illustrations. Bimonthly. Estab. 1998. Circ. 14,500.

Needs: Young adult/teen (adventure, fantasy/science fiction, historical, mystery/suspense, romance, sports, western, humor). "Our readership is age 14-21. Submissions should be tailored for high-school and college-age audience, not junior high or younger." Accepts 10 mss/issue; 60 mss/year. Publishes 1 year after acceptance. Length: 3,000-15,000 words; average length: 5,000 words. Also publishes poetry. Sometimes comments on rejected mss.

How to Contact: Send complete ms with cover letter. Include estimated word count and brief bio. Responds in 3 months to mss. Send SASE for return of ms or send disposable copy of ms and #10 SASE for reply only. Accepts simultaneous and multiple submissions. (Prefers original mss if ms is tagged as simultaneous submission.) Sample copy for $8.50. Guidelines for SASE or on website. Reviews novels "geared toward our teen readership."

Payment/Terms: Fiction and articles pay 25¢/word and 2 contributor's copies. Poems: up to $3/line and 2 contributor's copies; additional copies $4. Pays on publication. Sends edited ms for author approval. "For stories and poems previously unpublished, *CICADA* purchases first publication rights in the English language as well as additional rights options. *CICADA* also requests the rights to reprint the work in any volume or anthology published by Carus Publishing Company upon payment of half the original fee. For stories and poems previously published, *CICADA* purchases second North American publication rights. Fees vary, but are generally less than fees for first publication rights. For recurring features, *CICADA* purchases the material outright. The work becomes the property of *CICADA*, and is copyrighted in the name of Carus Publishing Company. A flat fee per feature is usually negotiated. For commissioned artwork, first publication rights plus promotional rights (promotions, advertising, or any other form not offered for sale), subject to the terms outlined: Physical art remains the property of the illustrator; payment is made within 45 days of acceptance; *CICADA* retains the additional, nonexclusive right to reprint the work in any volume or anthology published by *CICADA* subject to pro-rata share of 7% royalty of net sales."

Advice: "Quality writing, good literary style, genuine teen sensibility, depth, humor, good character development, avoidance of stereotypes. Read several issues to familiarize yourself with our style."

☑ $◐ CIMARRON REVIEW, Oklahoma State University, 205 Morrill Hall, Stillwater OK 74074-0135. (405)744-9476. E-mail: cimarronreview@hotmail.com. Website: cimarronreview.okstate.edu. **Contact:** Toni Graham, Andrea Koenig, fiction editors. Magazine: 6×9; 120 pages. "Poetry and fiction on contemporary themes; personal essay on contemporary issues that cope with life in the 20th century, for educated literary readers. We work hard to reflect quality. We are eager to receive manuscripts from both established and less experienced writers that intrigue us by their unusual perspective, language, imagery and character." Quarterly. Estab. 1967. Circ. 500.

Needs: Literary and contemporary. "Would like to see more language-aware writing that gets away from the crutch of first person." No collegiate reminiscences, science fiction or juvenilia. Accepts 5-6 mss/issue, 20-24 mss/year. **Publishes 8 new writers/year.** Published work by Jose Saramago, Adam Braver, Jonathan Ames and Robert Olen Butler. Also publishes literary essays, literary criticism, poetry.

How to Contact: Send complete ms with SASE. "Short cover letters are appropriate but not essential, except for providing *CR* with the most recent mailing address available." No simultaneous submissions. Responds in 3 months to mss. Publishes ms within 1 year after acceptance. Sample copy with SASE and $7. Reviews novels, short story collections, and poetry collections.

Payment/Terms: Pays $50 for each prose piece. Acquires first North American serial rights only.

Advice: "Don't try to pass personal essays off as fiction. Short fiction is a genre uniquely suited to the modern world. *CR* seeks an individual, innovative style that focuses on contemporary themes."

CITY PRIMEVAL: Narratives of Urban Reality, P.O. Box 30064, Seattle WA 98103. (206)440-0791. Editor: David Ross. **Contact:** Fiction Editor. Magazine: 6×9; 72 pages; 60 lb. paper; card cover stock; illustrations; photos. *City Primeval* "features work in the new genre: urban narrative." Quarterly. Estab. 1995. Circ. 200.

Needs: Adventure, literary, military/war, mystery/suspense, thriller/espionage. Receives 75-150 unsolicited mss/ month. Accepts 6-10 mss/issue; 36-60 mss/year. Publishes ms 3-6 months after acceptance. **Publishes 6-10 new writers/year.** Published work by Robin Sterns, Robert R. Ward, P.F. Allen, Susan Montag and Diane Trzcinski. Length: 5,000 words average; 10,000 words maximum. Publishes short shorts. Also publishes literary essays and poetry. Sometimes comments on or critiques rejected ms.

How to Contact: Send complete ms with a cover letter. Include 6-12 line bio. Responds to mss in 6 weeks. Send SASE for return of ms. No simultaneous submissions. Sample copy for $5. Guidelines for SASE.

Payment/Terms: Pays 1 contributor's copy. Pays on publication for first North American serial rights.

Advice: "Must meet editorial requirements—request guidelines before submitting. Know the market."

THE CLIMBING ART, 6390 E. Floyd Dr., Denver CO 80222-7638. Phone/fax: (303)757-0541. E-mail: rmorrow@dnvr.uswest.net. Editor: Ron Morrow. **Contact:** Fiction Editor. Magazine: 5½×8½; 150 pages; illustrations; photos. "*The Climbing Art* publishes literature, poetry and art for and about the spirit of climbing." Semiannual. Estab. 1986. Circ. 1,200.

Needs: Adventure, condensed/excerpted novel, ethnic/multicultural, experimental, fantasy, historical, literary, mainstream/contemporary, mystery/suspense, regional, science fiction, sports, translations. "No religious, rhyming, or non-climbing related." Receives 50 unsolicited mss/month. Accepts 4-6 mss/issue; 10-15 mss/year. Publishes ms up to 1 year after acceptance. Agented fiction 10%. **Publishes 25-30 new writers/year.** Published work by Reg Saner, Robert Walton and Gary Every. Length: 500-10,000 words. Publishes short shorts. Also publishes literary essays, literary criticism, poetry. Sometimes comments on rejected mss. Sometimes sponsors contests.

How to Contact: Send complete ms with a cover letter. Include estimated word count, 1-paragraph bio and list of publications. Accepts queries/mss by fax or e-mail. Responds in 1 month to queries; 2-8 weeks to mss. SASE. Accepts simultaneous and electronic submissions. Sample copy $7. Reviews novels and short story collections.

Payment/Terms: Pays free subscription and 2 contributor's copies; additional copies for $4. Acquires one-time rights.

Advice: Looks for knowledge of subject matter and love of the sport of climbing. "Read several issues first and make certain the material is related to climbing and the spirit of climbing. We have not seen enough literary excellence."

$ COLORADO REVIEW, English Department, Colorado State University, Fort Collins CO 80523. (970)491-5449. E-mail: creview@colostate.edu. Website: www.coloradoreview.com. Editor: David Milofsky. **Contact:** Fiction Editor. Literary journal: 200 pages; 20 lb. book weight paper. Triquarterly. Estab. 1966. Circ. 1,300.

Needs: Contemporary, ethnic, experimental, literary, mainstream, translations. No genre fiction. Receives 600 unsolicited fiction mss/month. Accepts 3-4 mss/issue. **Published new writers within the last year.** Published work by T. Alan Broughton, Elizabeth Gaffney, Ann Hood and Robert Boswell. Length: under 6,000 words. Does not read mss May-August. Also publishes literary essays, book reviews, poetry. Occasionally critiques rejected mss.

How to Contact: Send complete ms with SASE (or IRC) and brief bio with previous publications. Responds in 3 months. Publishes ms 6-12 months after acceptance. Sample copy for $10. Reviews novels or short story collections.

Payment/Terms: Pays $5/printed page for fiction; 2 contributor's copies; extras for $6. Pays on publication for first North American serial rights. "We assign copyright to author on request." Sends galleys to author.

Advice: "We are interested in manuscripts that show craft, imagination, and a convincing voice. If a story has reached a level of technical competence, we are receptive to the fiction working on its own terms. The oldest advice is still the best: persistence. Approach every aspect of the writing process with pride, conscientiousness— from word choice to manuscript appearance."

☑ ◙ **CONDUIT**, Conduit, Inc., 510 Eighth Ave. NE, Minneapolis MN 55413. (612)362-0995. E-mail: conduit@bitstream.net. Website: www.conduit.org. Editor: William Waltz. **Contact:** Brett Astor, fiction editor. Magazine: 5×10; 64 pages; letterpress cover; illustrations; photos. "*Conduit* is primarily a poetry magazine, but we're eager to include lively fiction. *Conduit* publishes work that is intelligent, serious, irreverent and daring." Biannual. Estab. 1993. Circ. 1,000.

Needs: Experimental, literary, translations. Receives 100 unsolicited mss/month. Accepts 4 mss/issue; 12 mss/year. Publishes ms 3-6 months after acceptance. Length: 1,500-3,000 words maximum. Publishes short shorts. Also publishes poetry.

How to Contact: Send complete ms with a cover letter. Responds in 6-24 weeks. Send SASE for reply, return of ms or send a disposable copy of ms. Sample copy for $6, postage/envelope included. Guidelines free for SASE.

Payment/Terms: Pays 3 contributor's copies. Acquires first North American serial rights.

Advice: "Write and send work that feels like it is absolutely essential, but avoid the leg-hold traps of self-importance and affectation."

$ ☐ ☒ **CONFRONTATION**, English Dept., C.W. Post of Long Island University, Brookville NY 11548. (516)299-2720. Fax: (516)299-2735. **Contact:** Martin Tucker, editor. Associate Editor: Jonna Semeiks. Magazine: 6×9; 250-350 pages; 70 lb. paper; 80 lb. cover; illustrations; photos. "We like to have a 'range' of subjects, form and style in each issue and are open to all forms. Quality is our major concern. Our audience is made up of literate, thinking people; formally or self-educated." Semiannual. Estab. 1968. Circ. 2,000.

● *Confrontation* has garnered a long list of awards and honors, including the Editor's Award for Distinguished Achievement from CCLP and NEA grants. Work from the magazine has appeared in numerous anthologies including the *Pushcart Prize, Best Short Stories* and *O. Henry Prize Stories. Confrontation* was ranked #30 on *Writer's Digest*'s Fiction 50 list of top markets for fiction writers.

Needs: Literary, contemporary, prose poem, regional and translations. No "proseletyzing" literature or genre fiction. Accepts 30 mss/issue; 60 mss/year. Receives 400 unsolicited fiction mss each month. Does not read June-September. Approximately 10-15% of fiction is agented. **Publishes 20-30 new writers/year.** Recently published work by Nadine Gordimer, David Ray, Peter Orner, Carole Hebald and Dorothea Straus. Length: 500-4,000 words. Publishes short shorts. Also publishes literary essays, poetry. Critiques rejected mss when there is time. Sometimes recommends other markets.

How to Contact: Send complete ms with SASE. "Cover letters acceptable, not necessary. We accept simultaneous submissions but do not prefer them." Accepts diskettes if accompanied by computer printout submissions. Responds in up to 2 months to mss. Publishes ms 6-12 months after acceptance. Sample copy for $3. Reviews novels, short story collections, poetry and literary criticism.

Payment/Terms: Pays $20-250 and 1 contributor's copy; half price for extras. Pays on publication for all rights "with transfer on request to author."

Advice: "Keep trying."

Ⓝ ◙ ☒ **CONNECTICUT REVIEW**, Connecticut State University System, SCSU 501 Crescent St., New Haven CT 06515. (203)392-6737. Fax: (203)392-5748. **Contact:** Dr. Vivian Shipley, editor. Magazine: 6×9; 202 pages; white/heavy paper; glossy/heavy cover; illustrations; photos. "*Connecticut Review* presents a wide range of cultural interests that cross disciplinary lines. The editors invite the submission of academic articles of general interest, thesis-oriented essays, translations, short stories, plays, poems, and interviews." Semiannual. Estab. 1968. Circ. 4,000. Member, CELJ, CLMJ.

● Work published in *Connecticut Review* has won the Pushcart Prize and inclusion in *Best American Short Stories 2000. CR* has also received the Phoenix Award for Significant Editorial Achievement, and National Public Radio's Award for Literary Excellence.

Needs: Literary. "Content must be suitable for circulation to libraries and high schools." Receives 250 unsolicited mss/month. Accepts 6 mss/issue; 12 mss/year. Does not read mss June-August. Publishes ms 1 year after acceptance. **Publishes 3 new writers/year.** Recently published work by John Searles, Marc Fitch, Meghann England and Paul Ruffin. Length: 2,000-4,000 words. Publishes short shorts. Also publishes literary essays and poetry.

How to Contact: Send complete ms with a cover letter. Include estimated word count, brief bio, list of publications and 2 copies of mss. Responds in 4 months to queries. Send a disposable copy of ms and #10 SASE for reply only. Accepts simultaneous submissions. Sample copy for $6. Guidelines for SASE.

Payment/Terms: Pays 2 contributor's copies; additional copies $6. Pays on publication for first rights. Sends galleys to author.

☑ ◙ **COTTONWOOD**, Box J, 400 Kansas Union, University of Kansas, Lawrence KS 66045-2115. (785)864-2516. Fax: (785)864-4298. E-mail: tlorenz@ukans.edu. **Contact:** Tom Lorenz, fiction editor. Magazine:

6×9; 100 pages; illustrations; photos. "*Cottonwood* publishes high quality prose, poetry and artwork and is aimed at an audience that appreciates the same. We have a national scope and reputation while maintaining a strong regional flavor." Semiannual. Estab. 1965. Circ. 500.

Needs: "We publish only literary prose and poetry." Receives 25-50 unsolicited mss/month. Accepts 5-6 mss/ issue; 10-12 mss/year. Publishes ms 6-18 months after acceptance. Agented fiction 10%. **Publishes 1-3 new writers/year.** Published work by Connie May Fowler, Oakley Hall and Cris Mazza. Length: 1,000-8,000 words; average length: 2,000-5,000 words. Publishes short shorts. Length: 1,000 words. Sometimes publishes literary essays; publishes literary criticism, poetry.

How to Contact: Send complete ms with a cover letter or submit through agent. Include 4-5 line bio and brief list of publications. Responds in up to 6 months. SASE for return of ms. Accepts simultaneous submissions. Sample copy for $8.50, 9×12 SAE and $1.90. Reviews novels and short story collections. Send books to review editor at our Cottonwood address.

Payment/Terms: Pays 1 contributor's copy; additional copies $6.50. Pays on publication for one-time rights.

Advice: "We're looking for depth and/or originality of subject matter, engaging voice and style, emotional honesty, command of the material and the structure. *Cottonwood* publishes high quality literary fiction, but we are very open to the work of talented new writers. Write something honest and that you care about and write it as well as you can. Don't hesitate to keep trying us. We sometimes take a piece from a writer we've rejected a number of times. We generally don't like clever, gimmicky writing. The style should be engaging but not claim all the attention for itself."

☑ ⊘ **CRAB CREEK REVIEW**, P.O. Box 840, Vashon WA 98070. (206)463-5668. Website: www.crabcreek review.org. **Contact:** Eleanor Lee, Harris Levinson, Laura Sinai and Terri Stone, editors. Magazine: 6×9 paperbound; 80-112 pgs., line drawings. "Magazine publishing poetry, short stories, and cover art for an audience interested in literary, visual and dramatic arts and in politics." Published twice yearly. Estab. 1983. Circ. 450.

Needs: Contemporary, humor/satire, literary and translations. No confession, erotica, horror, juvenile, preschool, religious/inspirational, romance or young adult. Receives 100 unsolicited mss/month. **Published new writers within the last year.** Recently published work by Andrea Dupree, Max Ruback, Joseph Powell and Julie Odell. Length: 1,200-6,000 words; average length: 3,000 words. Publishes short shorts.

How to Contact: Send complete ms with short list of credits. Responds in 2-4 months. SASE. No simultaneous submissions. Sample copy for $5. *Anniversary Anthology* $3.

Payment/Terms: Pays 2 contributor's copies; $4 charge for extras. Acquires first rights. Rarely buys reprints.

Advice: "We appreciate 'sudden fictions.' Type name and address on each piece. Enclose SASE. Send no more than one story in a packet (except for short shorts—no more than three, ten pages total). Know what you want to say and say it in an honest, clear, confident voice."

$ ⊘ ☒ **CRAB ORCHARD REVIEW, A Journal of Creative Works**, Southern Illinois University at Carbondale, English Department, Faner Hall, Carbondale IL 62901-4503. (618)453-6833. Fax: (618)453-8224. Website: www.siu.edu/~crborchd (includes contest information and guidelines). Prose Editor: Carolyn Alessio. **Contact:** Jon Tribble, managing editor. Magazine: $5\frac{1}{2} \times 8\frac{1}{2}$; 275 pages; 55 lb. recycled paper, card cover; photo on cover. "We are a general interest literary journal published twice/year. We strive to be a journal that writers admire and readers enjoy. We publish fiction, poetry, creative nonfiction, fiction translations, interviews and reviews." Estab. 1995. Circ. 1,800.

● Crab Orchard Review has won an Illinois Arts Council Literary Award for prose fiction by Ricardo Cortez Cruz (2001).

Needs: Excerpted novel, ethnic/multicultural, literary, translations. No science fiction, romance, western, horror, gothic or children's. Wants more novel excerpts that also work as stand alone pieces. List of upcoming themes available on website. Receives 300 unsolicited mss/month. Accepts 5-10 mss/issue, 10-18 mss/year. Does not read during the summer. Publishes ms 9-12 months after acceptance. Agented fiction 1%. Published work by Tim Parrish, Gordon Weaver, Ellen Slezak and Gina Ochsner. **Publishes 1 new writer/year.** Length: 1,000-6,500 words; average length: 2,500 words. Also publishes literary essays and poetry. Rarely comments on rejected mss.

How to Contact: Send complete ms with a cover letter. "No queries necessary." Include brief bio and list of publications. Responds in 3 weeks to queries; up to 9 months to mss. Send SASE for reply, return of ms. Accepts simultaneous submissions. Sample copy for $6. Guidelines for #10 SASE. Reviews books, small press and university press anthologies and story collections only. Reviews done in house by staff only. No outside reviews. Send review copies to Managing Editor Jon Tribble.

Payment/Terms: Pays $100 minimum; $10/page maximum, 2 contributor's copies and a year's subscription. Acquires first North American serial rights.

Advice: "We look for well-written, provocative, fully realized fiction that seeks to engage both the reader's senses and intellect. Don't submit too often to the same market, and don't send manuscripts that you haven't read over carefully. Writers can't rely on spell checkers to catch all errors. Always include a SASE. Read and support the journals you admire so they can continue to survive."

N ◯ **CRANIAL TEMPEST**, Canned Phlegm Press, 410 El Dorado St., Vallejo CA 94590. E-mail: cranialte mpest@hotmail.com. **Contact:** Jeff Fleming, editor. Magazine: 5½ × 8½; 28 pages; one-color card cover; illustrations; photos. "I love newcomers and oldtimers alike. I love when the printed word comes alive." Publishes every 6 weeks. Estab. 2000. Circ. 150.

Needs: Adventure, ethnic/multicultural, experimental, family saga, fantasy, feminist, gay, historical (general), horror (dark fantasy, futuristic, psychological, supernatural), humor/satire, lesbian, literary, mainstream, military/war, mystery/suspense, psychic/supernatural/occult, regional, science fiction (hard science/technological, soft, sociological), thriller/espionage, translations, western. Receives 20 unsolicited mss/month. Accepts 2-4 mss/issue; 18-36 mss/year. Publishes ms 3 weeks after acceptance. **Publishes 10 new writers/year.** Recently published work by Jennifer Norwood, John Grey, Normal, Michael Brownstein and Ed Galing. Length: 20-3,500 words; average length: 1,500 words. Publishes short shorts. Average length: 900 words. Also publishes poetry. Sometimes comments on rejected mss.

How to Contact: Send complete ms with a cover letter. Include estimated word count and brief bio. Responds in 2 weeks to queries; 2 months to mss. Send SASE (or IRC) for return of ms or send a disposable copy of ms and #10 SASE for reply only. Accepts simultaneous, previously published and multiple submissions. Sample copy for $2. Guidelines for SASE or by e-mail. Reviews novels, short story collections and nonfiction books of interest to writers. Send review copies to Jeff Fleming.

Payment/Terms: Pays 1 contributor's copy; additional copies $2. Pays on publication for one-time rights. Sponsors contest.

N **CRAZYHORSE**, College of Charleston, Dept. of English, 66 George St., Charleston SC 29424. (843)953-7740. Email: crazyhorse@cofc.edu. **Contact:** Editors. Literary magazine: 8½ × 7; 150 pages; illustrations; photos. "Crazyhorse publishes writing of fine quality regardless of style, predilection, subject. Editors are especially interested in original writing that engages in the work of honest communication." Semiannual. Estab. 1961. Circ. 1,000. Raymond Carver called Crazyhorse "an indispensable literary magazine of the first order."

Needs: All fiction of fine quality. Receives 10-15 unsolicited mss/month. Accepts 2-4 mss/issue; 4-8 mss/year. Publishes ms 6-12 months after acceptance. Recently published work by Andrew Hudgins, Paul Zimmer and Lisa Burnell. Length: 35 pages; average length: 15 pages. Publishes short shorts. Also publishes literary essays and poetry.

How to Contact: Send complete ms with cover letter. Include brief bio and list of publications. Responds in 1 week to queries; 5 weeks to mss. Send SASE for return of ms or disposable copy of ms and #10 SASE for reply only. Accepts simultaneous submissions. Sample copy for $7. Guidelines for SASE or by e-mail.

Payment/Terms: Pays 2 contributor's copies; additional copies $5. Acquires first North American serial rights. Sends galleys to author. Sponsors contest; guidelines available for e-mail.

Advice: "Write to explore subjects you care about. Clarity of language; subject is one in which something is at stake."

✓ ◯ **THE CREAM CITY REVIEW**, University of Wisconsin-Milwaukee, Box 413, Milwaukee WI 53201. (414)229-4708. E-mail: creamcity@csd.uwm.edu. Website: www.uwm.edu:80/Dept/English/CCR (includes writer's guidelines, names of editors, table of contents from past issues, cover art scanned and magazine's history). Editor-in-Chief: Karen Auvenin. **Contact:** Steve Nelson, fiction editor. Editors rotate. Magazine: 5½ × 8½; 200-300 pages; 70 lb. offset/perfect-bound paper; 80 lb. cover stock; illustrations; photos. "General literary publication—an eclectic and electric selection of the best we receive." Semiannual. Estab. 1975. Circ. 2,000.

Needs: Ethnic, experimental, literary, prose poem, regional, translations. "Would like to see more international writings, intranational writing." Does not want to see horror, formulaic, racist, sexist, pornographic, homophobic, science fiction, romance. Receives approximately 300 unsolicited fiction mss each month. Accepts 6-10 mss/issue. Does not read fiction or poetry May 1-August 31. **Publishes 10 new writers/year.** Published work by Pete Fromm. Length: 1,000-10,000 words. Publishes short shorts. Also publishes literary essays, literary criticism, poetry.

How to Contact: Send complete ms with SASE. Accepts simultaneous and multiple submissions if notified and submissions on disk. Responds in 6 months. Sample copy for $5 (back issue), $7 (current issue). Reviews novels and short story collections.

Payment/Terms: Pays in copies. Acquires first rights. Sends galleys to author. Rights revert to author after publication.

Advice: "The best stories are those in which the reader doesn't know what is going to happen or what the writer is trying to do. Avoid formulas."

✓ ◯ **THE CRESCENT REVIEW**, The Crescent Review, Inc., P.O. Box 7959, Shallotte NC 28470-7959. E-mail: review@mindspring.com. Website: www.crescentreview.org (includes essays, interviews, guidelines, and more). Editor: J.T. Holland. **Contact:** Editor. Magazine: 6 × 9; 160 pages. Triannual. Estab. 1982.

• Work appearing in *The Crescent Review* has been included in *O. Henry Prize Stories*, *Best American Short Stories*, *Pushcart Prize*, *Sudden Fiction* and *Black Southern Writers* anthologies and in the *New Stories from the South*.

Needs: "Well-crafted stories." Wants shorter-length pieces (though will publish stories in the 6,000-8,000 word range). Wants stories where choice has consequences. Recently published work by Madison Smartt Bell, Melinda Haynes and Julia Slavin. Conducts two annual writers contests: The Renwick-Sumerwell Award (exclusively for new unpublished writers) and the Chekhov Award for Fine Storytelling. Does not read submissions May-June and November-December.

How to Contact: Responds in up to 6 months. SASE. Please visit website for guidelines prior to submitting. Also, see website for sample stories—one from current issue and one from past issue. Sample issue for $9.40 plus postage.

Payment/Terms: Pays 2 contributor's copies; discount for contributors. Acquires first North American serial rights.

⊕ $⃝ CRIMEWAVE, TTA Press, 5 Martins Lane, Witcham, Ely, Cambs CB6 2LB England. E-mail: ttapress@aol.com. Website: www.tta-press.freewire.co.uk (includes news, biographies, secure credit card transaction facility). **Contact:** Andy Cox, fiction editor. Magazine: 128 pages; lithographed, color; perfect bound. Magazine publishes "modern crime fiction from across the waterfront, from the misnamed cozy to the deceptively subtle hardboiled." Biannual. Published in June and December.

Needs: Mystery (amateur sleuth, cozy, police procedural, private eye/hardboiled), suspense, thriller, etc. Accepts 15 mss/issue. Recently published work by Chaz Brenchley, Ian Rankin, James Lovegrove and Christopher Fowler.

How to Contact: Send complete ms with a cover letter. "Send one story at a time plus adequate return postage, or disposable ms plus 2 IRC's or e-mail address—but no e-mail submissions. No reprints." Query by e-mail. Sample copy: $12 US or for 4 issues: $40.

Payment/Terms: "Relatively modest flat fee, but constantly increasing." Contract on acceptance, payment on publication.

⃝ CROSSCONNECT, P.O. Box 2317, Philadelphia PA 19103. (215)898-5324. Fax: (215)898-9348. E-mail: xconnect@ccat.sas.upenn.edu. Website: ccat.sas.upenn.edu/xconnect. **Editor:** David Deifer. "*CrossConnect* publishes tri-annually on the World Wide Web and annually in print, with the best of our Web issues, plus nominated work from editors in the digital literary community. *xconnect: writers of the information age* is a nationally distributed, full color, journal sized book." 5½×8½; trade paper; 200 pages.

Needs: Literary and experimental fiction. "Our mission—like our name—is one of connection. *CrossConnect* seeks to promote and document the emergent creative artists as well as established artists who have made the transition to the new technologies of the Information Age." **Publishes 25 new writers/year.**Recently published work by Bob Perelman, Paul Hoover and Yusef Komunyakaa.

How to Contact: Electronic and traditional submissions accepted. "We prefer your submissions be cut and pasted into your mail readers and sent to us. No attached files unless requested." Send complete ms (up to three stories) with cover letter and short bio. Accepts previously published and simultaneous submission. Rarely comments on rejections.

Payment/Terms: Pays 1 contributor's copy for use in print version. Author retains all rights. Regularly sends prepublication galleys.

Advice: "Persistence."

⃝ CRUCIBLE, English Dept., Barton College, College Station, Wilson NC 27893. (252)399-6456. Editor: Terrence L. Grimes. **Contact:** Fiction Editor. Magazine of fiction and poetry for a general, literary audience. Annual. Estab. 1964. Circ. 500.

Needs: Contemporary, ethnic, experimental, feminist, literary, regional. Would like to see more short shorts. Receives 20 unsolicited mss/month. Accepts 5-6 mss/year. Publishes ms 4-5 months after acceptance. Does not normally read mss from April 30 to December 1. **Publishes 5 new writers/year.** Recently published work by Sally Buckner. Length: 8,000 words maximum.

How to Contact: Send 3 complete copies of ms unsigned with cover letter which should include a brief biography, "in case we publish." Responds in 6 weeks to queries; 4 months to mss (by July 1). SASE. Sample copy for $6. Guidelines free.

Payment/Terms: Pays contributor's copies. Acquires first rights.

Advice: "Write about what you know. Experimentation is fine as long as the experiences portrayed come across as authentic, that is to say, plausible."

⃝ CUTBANK, English Dept., University of Montana, Missoula MT 59812. (406)243-6156. E-mail: cutbank@ selway.umt.edu. Website: www.umt.edu/cutbank (includes writer's guidelines, names of editors, interviews with authors and excerpts). **Contact:** Fiction Editor. Editors change each year. Magazine: 5½×8½; 115-130 pages. "Publishes serious-minded and innovative fiction and poetry from both well known and up-and-coming authors." Semiannual. Estab. 1973. Circ. 600.

Needs: "Innovative, challenging, experimental material." No "science fiction, fantasy or unproofed manuscripts." Receives 200 unsolicited mss/month. Accepts 6-12 mss/year. Does not read mss April 1-August 15. Publishes ms up to 6 months after acceptance. **Publishes 4 new writers/year.** Recently published work by Dan Barden and Todd Pierce. Length: 40 pages maximum. Also publishes literary essays, literary criticism, poetry. Occasionally critiques rejected mss.

How to Contact: Send complete ms with cover letter, which should include "name, address, publications." Responds in 4 months to mss. SASE. Accepts simultaneous submissions. Sample copy for $4 (current issue $6.95). Guidelines for SASE. Reviews novels and short story collections. Send books to fiction editor.

Payment/Terms: Pays 2 contributor's copies. Rights revert to author upon publication, with provision that *Cutbank* receives publication credit.

Advice: "Strongly suggest contributors read an issue. We have published stories by Kevin Canty, Chris Offutt and Pam Houston in recent issues, and like to feature new writers alongside more well-known names. Send only your best work."

THE DALHOUSIE REVIEW, Dalhousie University, Halifax, Nova Scotia B3H 3J5 Canada. (902)494-2541. Fax: (902)494-3561. E-mail: dalhousie.review@dal.ca. Website: www.dal.ca/~dalrev (includes guidelines, subscription information, journal history and excerpts). **Contact:** Dr. Ronald Huebert, editor. Magazine: 15cm×23cm; approximately 140 pages; photographs sometimes. Publishes articles, book reviews, short stories and poetry. Published 3 times a year. Circ. 400.

Needs: Literary. Length: 5,000 words maximum. Also publishes essays on history, philosophy, etc., and poetry. Recently published work by Melissa Hardy, Kim Bridgford, Eugene Dubnov and Shalom Camenietzki.

How to Contact: Send complete ms with cover letter. SASE (Canadian stamps or IRCs). Sample copy for $10 (Canadian) including postage. Occasionally reviews novels and short story collections.

DAN RIVER ANTHOLOGY, P.O. Box 298, S. Thomaston ME 04861. (207)354-0998. Fax: (207)354-8953. E-mail: cal@americanletters.org. Website: www.americanletters.org (includes writer's guidelines, catalogue). **Contact:** R. S. Danbury III, editor. Book: 5½×8½; 180 pages; 60 lb. paper; gloss 65 lb. full-color cover; b&w illustrations. For general/adult audience. Annual. Estab. 1984. Circ. 800.

● The *Dan River Anthology* ranked #27 on *Writer's Digest*'s Fiction 50 list of top markets for fiction writers.

Needs: Adventure, contemporary, ethnic, experimental, fantasy, historical, horror, humor/satire, literary, mainstream, prose poem, psychic/supernatural, regional, romance (contemporary and historical), science fiction, senior citizen/retirement, suspense/mystery and western. "Would like to see more first-person adventure." No "evangelical Christian, pornography or sentimentality." Receives 150 unsolicited fiction mss each submission period (January 1 through March 31). "We generally publish 12-15 pieces of fiction." Reads "mostly in April." Length: 800-2,500 words; average length: 2,000-2,400 words. Also publishes poetry.

How to Contact: *Charges reading fee: $1 for poetry; $3 for prose* (cash only, no checks). Send complete ms with SASE. Responds by May 15 each year. No simultaneous submissions. Sample copy for $13.95 paperback, $59.95 cloth, plus $3.25 shipping. Guidelines for #10 SASE or on website.

Payment/Terms: Pays approximately $4/page, minimum *cash advance on acceptance* against royalties of 10% of all sales attributable to writer's influence: readings, mailings, autograph parties, etc., plus up to 50% discount on copies, plus other discounts to make total as high as 73%. Acquires first rights.

Advice: "Know your market. Don't submit without reading guidelines."

DENVER QUARTERLY, University of Denver, Denver CO 80208. (303)871-2892. **Contact:** Bin Ramke, editor. Magazine: 6×9; 144-160 pages; occasional illustrations. "We publish fiction, articles and poetry for a generally well-educated audience, primarily interested in literature and the literary experience. They read *DQ* to find something a little different from a strictly academic quarterly or a creative writing outlet." Quarterly. Estab. 1966. Circ. 2,000.

● *Denver Quarterly* received an Honorable Mention for Content from the American Literary Magazine Awards and selections have been anthologized in the *Pushcart Prize* anthologies.

Needs: "We are interested in experimental fiction (minimalism, magic realism, etc.) as well as in realistic fiction and in writing about fiction. No sentimental, science fiction, romance or spy thrillers. No stories longer than 15 pages!" **Published 5 new writers within the last year.** Published work by Frederick Busch, Judith E. Johnson, Stephen Alter and Harriet Zinnes. Also publishes poetry.

How to Contact: Send complete ms and brief cover letter with SASE. Does not read mss May-September 15. Do not query. Responds in 3 months to mss. Publishes ms within a year after acceptance. Accepts simultaneous submissions. Sample copy $6.

Payment/Terms: Pays $5/page for fiction and poetry and 2 contributor's copies. Acquires for first North American serial rights.

Advice: "We look for serious, realistic and experimental fiction; stories which appeal to intelligent, demanding readers who are not themselves fiction writers. Nothing so quickly disqualifies a manuscript as sloppy proofreading and mechanics. Read the magazine before submitting to it. We try to remain eclectic, but the odds for beginners are bound to be small considering the fact that we receive nearly 10,000 mss per year and publish only about ten short stories."

DESCANT, Descant Arts & Letters Foundation, P.O. Box 314, Station P, Toronto, Ontario M5S 2K9. (416)593-2557. Fax: (416)593-9362. E-mail: descant@web.net. Website: www.descant.on.ca (includes guidelines, editors' names, excerpts and subscription information). **Contact:** Karen Mulhallen, editor. Quarterly literary journal. Estab. 1970. Circ. 1,200. Member, CMPA.

• *Descant* has received the Canadian National Magazine Award in various categories, including fiction.

Needs: Ethnic/multicultural, experimental, feminist, gay, historical, humor/satire, lesbian, literary. No gothic, religious, beat. **Publishes 14 new writers/year.** Recently published work by Andrew Pyper, Douglas Gloner and Judith McCormack. Also publishes poetry and literary essays. Submit seasonal material 4 months in advance.

How to Contact: Send complete ms with cover letter. Sample copy for $8.50. Guidelines for SASE.

Payment/Terms: Pays $100 (Canadian); additional copies $8. Pays on publication.

Advice: "Familiarize yourself with our magazine before submitting."

DOUBLETAKE, 55 Davis Square, Somerville MA 02144-2908. (617)591-9389. E-mail: dtmag@doubltakemagazine.org. Website: www.doubletakemagazine.org (includes guidelines, limited contents, links to DoubleTake Summer Documentary Institute and other related things). **Contact:** Albert LaFarge, deputy editor. "We strive to present storytelling in its many guises—visual and in words."

Needs: "Realistic fiction in all of its variety; it's very unlikely we'd ever publish science fiction or gothic horror, for example. "We would like to see more fiction distinguished by literary excellence and a rare voice." Recently published work by David Leavitt, Charles Baxter, Richard Bausch and Jose Saramago. **Publishes more than 10 new writers/year.** Buys 12 mss/year. Length: 3,000-8,000 words.

How to Contact: Send complete ms with cover letter. Accepts simultaneous submissions. Responds in 3 months to mss. Sample copy for $12. Guidelines for #10 SASE.

Payment/Terms: Pays "competitively." Pays on publication for worldwide first rights.

Advice: "Use a strong, developed narrative voice. Don't attempt too much."

DOWNSTATE STORY, 1825 Maple Ridge, Peoria IL 61614. (309)688-1409. E-mail: ehopkins@prairienet.org. Website: www.wiu.edu/users/mfgeh/dss (includes guidelines, names of editors, short fiction and reviews). **Contact:** Elaine Hopkins, editor. Magazine: includes illustrations. "Short fiction—some connection with Illinois or the Midwest." Annual. Estab. 1992. Circ. 500.

Needs: Adventure, ethnic/multicultural, experimental, historical, horror, humor/satire, literary, mainstream/contemporary, mystery/suspense, psychic/supernatural/occult, regional, romance, science fiction, westerns. No porn. Wants more political fiction. Accepts 10 mss/issue. Publishes ms up to 1 year after acceptance. Length: 300-2,000 words. Publishes short shorts. Also publishes literary essays.

How to Contact: Send complete ms with a cover letter. Responds "ASAP." SASE for return of ms. Accepts simultaneous submissions. Sample copy for $8. Guidelines for SASE.

Payment/Terms: Pays $50 maximum. Pays on acceptance for first rights.

THE EDGE CITY REVIEW, Reston Review, Inc., 10912 Harpers Square Court, Reston VA 20191. Fax: (703)716-5752. E-mail: terryp17@aol.com. Website: www.edge-city.com. **Contact:** T.L. Ponick, editor. Magazine: 8½×11; 44-52 pages; 60 lb. paper; 65 lb. color cover. "We publish Formalist poetry, well-plotted artistic or literary fiction, literary essays and book reviews. Our editorial philosophy is right of center." Triannual. Estab. 1994. Circ. 500.

Needs: Humor/satire, literary, regional, serialized novel. "We see too much fiction that's riddled with four-letter words and needless vulgarity." Receives 20 unsolicited mss/month. Accepts 1-2 mss/issue; 3-6 mss/year. Publishes ms 6-8 months after acceptance. Length: 1,500-3,000 words; average length: 2,000 words. Also publishes literary essays, literary criticism, poetry. Sometimes comments on rejected ms.

CHECK THE CATEGORY INDEXES, located at the back of the book, for publishers interested in specific fiction subjects.

How to Contact: Send complete ms with a cover letter. Include estimated word count, 25-50 word bio, list of publications. Responds in 1 month to queries; 3-5 months to mss. Send SASE for reply, return of ms or send a disposable copy of ms. Accepts electronic submissions (disk or modem). Sample copy for $4. Reviews novels and short story collections. "No 'chapbooks' or self-published, please."

Payment/Terms: Pays 2 contributor's copies; additional copies $4. Acquires first North American serial rights. Sponsors contest; watch for announcements in major publications.

Advice: "We are looking for character-based fiction. Most fiction we receive does not grow out of its characters—but finely wrought characters, fully realized, are what we want to see."

✓ 🌐 ◎ **ELYSIAN FIELDS QUARTERLY: The Baseball Review**, P.O. Box 14385, St. Paul MN 55114-0385. (651)644-8558. Fax: (651)644-8086. E-mail: info@efqreview.com. Website: www.efqreview.com (includes ordering capabilities, back issues, affiliated products, sample stories, distribution information, e-mail addresses of staff and links). **Contact:** Tom Goldstein, editor. Magazine: 6×9; 96 pages; 60 lb. paper; gloss/varnish cover; illustrations; and photos. *Elysian Fields Quarterly* is "unique because nobody covers baseball the way that we do, with such an offbeat, irreverent manner and yet with full appreciation for the game." Quarterly. Estab. 1992. Circ. 1,300.

Needs: "Any fiction piece about baseball will be considered. We do not want to see general fiction that tries to be a baseball story by making tangential connections to baseball, but in reality is not a fiction piece about baseball." Receives 3-5 unsolicited mss/month. Accepts 2-3 mss/issue; 10-15/year. Publishes ms 3-9 months after acceptance. **Publishes 10-12 new writers/year.** Published work by W.P. Kinsella, Donald Dewey, Rick Wilber, Lynn Rigney Schott, William McGill and George Bowering. Word length: 2,000-3,000 words average; 1,000 words minimum; 4,000 words maximum. Does not generally publish short shorts "but we don't rule out any good writing." Length: 750 words. Also publishes literary essays, literary criticism and poetry. Very rarely comments on or critiques rejected ms.

How to Contact: Send complete ms with a cover letter. Accepts inquiries by e-mail. "E-mail submissions should be properly formatted in readable attachments." Include 50 word bio. Responds in 4 months. Send SASE for reply, return of ms or send a disposable copy of ms. "Will occasionally consider" simultaneous and reprint submissions. Sample copy for $7.50. Guidelines free. "We review baseball books and novels of interest to our readership."

Payment/Terms: Pays 4 contributor's copies; additional copies $5. Acquires one-time rights and the right to reprint in any anthologies. Sponsors contest: Dave Moore Award for the "most important baseball book."

Advice: "Originality, creativity, believability—is it truly a baseball story? We do not pay attention to industry trends; we just try to publish good writing, irrespective of what is being published elsewhere."

🍁 ✓ ⊘ **EMPLOI PLUS**, DGR Publication, 1256 Principale North St., #203, L'Annonciation, Quebec J0T 1T0 Canada. Phone/fax: (819)275-3293. Website: www.publishingonline.com. **Contact:** Daniel G. Reid, fiction editor. Magazine: 7×8½; 12 pages; illustrations; photos. Bilingual (French/English) magazine publishing Canadian and American authors. Every 2 or 3 years. Estab. 1990. Circ. 500.

Needs: Serialized novel. Published work by Robert Biro and D.G. Reid. Also publishes poetry.

How to Contact: *Closed to unsolicited submissions.* Sample copy free.

$ ◐ 🏆 **EPOCH MAGAZINE**, 251 Goldwin Smith Hall, Cornell University, Ithaca NY 14853-3201. (607)255-3385. Fax: (607)255-6661. **Contact:** Michael Koch, editor. (Submissions should be sent to Michael Koch). Magazine: 6×9; 128 pages; good quality paper; good cover stock. "Top level fiction and poetry for people who are interested in good literature." Published 3 times a year. Estab. 1947. Circ. 1,000.

● Work originally appearing in this quality literary journal has appeared in numerous anthologies including *Best American Short Stories*, *Best American Poetry*, *Pushcart Prize*, *The O. Henry Prize Stories*, *Best of the West* and *New Stories from the South*. *Epoch* was ranked #38 on *Writer's Digest*'s Fiction 50 list of top markets for fiction writers.

Needs: Literary, contemporary and ethnic. No science fiction. Accepts 15-20 mss/issue. Receives 500 unsolicited fiction mss each month. Does not read in summer (April 15-September 15). **Publishes 3-4 new writers/year.** Recently published work by Jill McCorkle, Dan Chaon, Heidi Jon Schmidt and Jhumpa Lahiri. Length: no limit. Also publishes literary essays, poetry. Critiques rejected mss when there is time. Sometimes recommends other markets.

How to Contact: Send complete ms with SASE. No simultaneous submissions. Responds in 1 month to mss. Publishes ms an average of 6 months after acceptance. Sample copy for $5.

Payment/Terms: Pays $5-10/printed page and contributor's copies. Pays on publication for first North American serial rights.

Advice: "Read the journals you're sending work to."

✓ ◑ **EUREKA LITERARY MAGAZINE**, 300 E. College Ave., Eureka College, Eureka IL 61530-1500. (309)467-6336. E-mail: llogsdon@eureka.edu. Editor: Loren Logsdon. **Contact:** Jane S. Groeper, fiction editor. Magazine: 6×9; 120 pages; 70 lb. white offset paper; 80 lb. gloss cover; photographs (occasionally). "We seek to be open to the best stories that are submitted to us. We do not want to be narrow in a political sense of the word. Our audience is a combination of professors/writers and general readers." Semiannual. Estab. 1992. Circ. 500.

Needs: Adventure, ethnic/multicultural, experimental, fantasy (science), feminist, historical, humor/satire, literary, mainstream/contemporary, mystery/suspense (private eye/hardboiled, romantic), psychic/supernatural/occult, regional, romance (historical), science fiction (soft/sociological), translations. "We try to achieve a balance between the traditional and the experimental. We do favor the traditional, though. We look for the well-crafted story, but essentially any type of story that has depth and substance to it—any story that expands us as human beings and celebrates the mystery and miracle of the creation. Make sure you have a good beginning and ending, a strong voice, excellent use of language, good insight into the human condition, narrative skill, humor—if it is appropriate to the subject. No drug stories of any kind, stories with gratuitous violence or stories with heavy propaganda." Receives 30 unsolicited mss/month. Accepts 4 mss/issue; 8-9 mss/year. Does not read mss mainly in late summer (August). **Publishes 5-6 new writers/year.** Recently published work by B.Z. Niditch, Laura Treacy Bentley, Jane Guill, Patty Dickson Pieczka and Natalia Nebel. Length: 7,000-8,000 words; average length: 4,500 words. Publishes short shorts. Also publishes poetry.

How to Contact: Send complete ms with a cover letter. Should include estimated word count and bio (short paragraph). Responds in 1 week to queries; 4 months to mss. Send SASE for reply, return of ms or send a disposable copy of ms. Accepts simultaneous submissions and multiple submissions. Sample copy for $7.50.

Payment/Terms: Pays free subscription to the magazine and 2 contributor's copies. Acquires first rights or one-time rights.

Advice: "Send manuscripts that are neat and easy to read. Do not send a manuscript that appears to have been in circulation for 20 years. That is a sure tip-off to an editor that this story has been rejected several times. Be sure to include an SASE. If an editor's name is gender neutral, do not address the editor as Ms. or Mr., hoping that you guessed correctly. Instead, address the editor by the full name or by title: Chris Carpenter or Editor Carpenter or Editor. It is not necessary for a writer to give a plot summary of a short story or a long list of credits. Each story must stand on its own merits. Thus make the cover letter brief. It is acceptable for a writer to ask for helpful critical comments on poems or stories, but most editors these days are overwhelmed with submissions and cannot accommodate such a request. Please do not expect an editor to praise a story that is rejected to ease the rejection. There is really no way for an editor to say no in a way that is soothing or nice. Also, please realize that there may be several reasons for a rejection—in addition to the possibility that the story is not good. Also, realize that editors may be wrong in their judgment of a story. Please do not give up after one rejection. I have noticed that the general quality of fiction that we are receiving has improved dramatically. We are rejecting many good stories these days because we do not have room for them, stories that we would have accepted five years ago. We look for effective use of language and a story that offers good insight into the human condition."

◑ **EVANSVILLE REVIEW**, University of Evansville, 1800 Lincoln Ave., Evansville IN 47722. (812)488-1114. E-mail: evansvillereview@yahoo.com. **Contact:** Erica Schmidt, editor. Editors change every 1-2 years. Magazine: 6×9; 180 pages; 70 lb. white paper; glossy full color cover; perfect bound. Annual. Estab. 1990. Circ. 2,500.

Needs: "We're open to all creativity. No discrimination. All fiction, screenplays, nonfiction, poetry, interviews, photo essays and anything in between." No children or young adult. List of upcoming themes available for SASE. Receives 1,000 unsolicited mss/year. Does not read mss February-August. Agented fiction 2%. **Publishes 15 new writers/year.** Recently published work by Arthur Miller, Christopher Bigsby, Julia Kasdorf, Vivian Shipley, Dale Ray Phillips and Reginald Gibbons. Also publishes literary essays, poetry.

How to Contact: Send complete ms with a cover letter, e-mail or fax. Include 150 word or less bio and list of publications. Responds in 2 weeks to queries; 3 months to mss. Send SASE for reply, return of ms or send a disposable copy of ms. Accepts simultaneous and reprint submissions. Sample copy for $5. Guidelines free.

Payment/Terms: Pays 2 contributor's copies. Pays on publication for one-time rights. Sends galleys to author if requested. Not copyrighted.

Advice: "Because editorial staffs roll over every 1-2 years, the journal always has a new flavor."

🌺 ✓ $ ◑ ▼ **EVENT**, Douglas College, Box 2503, New Westminster, British Columbia V3L 5B2 Canada. Fax: (604)527-5095. E-mail: event@douglas.ba.ca. Website: http://event.douglas.bc.ca/event (includes guidelines, contest information, contents and author information, names of editors). Editor: Cathy Stonehouse. **Contact:** Christine Dewar, fiction editor. Assistant Editor: Ian Cockfield. Magazine: 6×9; 136 pages; quality paper and cover stock. "Primarily a literary magazine, publishing poetry, fiction, reviews, creative nonfiction; for creative writers, artists, anyone interested in contemporary literature." Triannual. Estab. 1971. Circ. 1,250.

● Fiction originally published in *Event* has been included in *Best Canadian Stories*, and the publication was nominated for a Western Magazine Award in 2000.

Needs: Literary, contemporary, feminist, humor, regional. "No technically poor or unoriginal pieces." Receives approximately 100 unsolicited fiction mss/month. Accepts 6-8 mss/issue. **Publishes 2-3 new writers/year.** Recently published work by Leon Rouke, Bill Gaston and Annabel Lyon. Length: 5,000 words maximum. Also publishes poetry and creative nonfiction.

How to Contact: Send complete ms, bio and SAE with Canadian postage or IRC. Responds in 1-4 months to mss. Publishes ms 6-12 months after acceptance. Sample copy for $5.

Payment/Terms: Pays $22/page and 2 contributor's copies. Pays on publication for first North American serial rights.

Advice: "We're looking for a strong, effective point of view; well-handled and engaging characters, attention to language and strong details."

N ◯ ⬤ **FAT TUESDAY**, 560 Manada Gap Rd., Grantville PA 17028. (717)469-7517. E-mail: cotolo@excite.com. Editors: B. Lyle Tabor (emeritus) and Thom Savion. Associate Editors: Lionel Stevroid and Kristen vonOehrke. **Contact:** F.M. Cotolo, editor-in-chief. Journal: 8½×11 or 5×8; 27-36 pages; bond paper; heavy cover stock; saddle-stitched; b&w illustrations; photos. "Generally, we are an eclectic journal of fiction, poetry and visual treats. Our issues to date have featured artists like Patrick Kelly, Charles Bukowski, Gerald Locklin, Chuck Taylor and many more who have focused on an individualistic nature with fiery elements. We are a literary mardi gras—as the title indicates—and irreverancy is as acceptable to us as profundity as long as there is fire! Our audience is anyone who can praise literature and condemn it at the same time. Anyone too serious about it on either level will not like *Fat Tuesday*." Annual. Estab. 1981. Circ. 700.

Needs: Comics, erotica, experimental, humor/satire, literary, prose poem, psychic/supernatural/occult, serialized/excerpted novel and dada. "Although we list categories, we are open to feeling out various fields if they are delivered with the mark of an individual and not just in the format of the particular field." Does not want to see sci-fi, romance, mystery, mainstream in general. Receives 20 unsolicited fiction mss/month. Accepts 4-5 mss/issue. **Publishes new writers.** Length: 1,000 words maximum. Publishes short shorts. Occasionally critiques rejected mss and usually responds with a personal note or letter.

How to Contact: Send complete ms with SASE. Accepts submissions by e-mail. "No previously published material considered." No simultaneous submissions. Responds in 1 month. Publishes ms 3-10 months after acceptance. Sample copy (in print or audio) for $5.

Payment/Terms: Pays 1 contributor's copy. Acquires one-time rights.

Advice: "As *Fat Tuesday* crawls through its second decade, we find publishing small press editions more difficult than ever. Money remains a problem, mostly because small press seems to play to the very people who wish to be published in it. In other words, the cast is the audience, and more people want to be in *Fat Tuesday* than want to buy it. It is through sales that our magazine supports itself. This is why we emphasize buying a sample issue ($5) before submitting. Please specify in-print or audio issue. As far as what we want to publish—send us shorter works that are 'crystals of thought and emotion which reflect your individual experiences—dig into your guts and pull out pieces of yourself. Your work is your signature; like time itself, it should emerge from the penetralia of your being and recede into the infinite region of the cosmos,' to coin a phrase, and remember *Fat Tuesday* is mardi gras—so fill up before you fast. Bon soir."

⬤ ◎ **FEMINIST STUDIES**, Department of Women's Studies, University of Maryland, College Park MD 20742. (301)405-7415. Fax: (301)314-9190. E-mail: femstud@umail.umd.edu. Website: www.inform.umd.edu/femstud. Editor: Claire G. Moses. **Contact:** Shirley Lim, fiction editor. Magazine: journal-sized; about 200 pages; photographs. "Scholarly manuscripts, fiction, book review essays for professors, graduate/doctoral students; scholarly interdisciplinary feminist journal." Triannual. Estab. 1974. Circ. 7,500.

Needs: Contemporary, ethnic, feminist, gay, lesbian. Receives about 15 poetry and short story mss/month. Accepts 2-3 mss/issue. "We review fiction twice a year. Deadline dates are May 1 and December 1. Authors will receive notice of the board's decision by June 30 and January 30, respectively." Published work by Bell Chevigny, Betsy Gould Gibson and Joan Jacobson. Sometimes comments on rejected mss.

**FOR EXPLANATIONS OF THESE SYMBOLS,
SEE THE INSIDE FRONT AND BACK COVERS OF THIS BOOK.**

How to Contact: Send complete ms with cover letter. No simultaneous submissions. Sample copy for $15. Guidelines free.

Payment/Terms: Pays 2 contributor's copies and 10 tearsheets. Sends galleys to authors.

☑ $⊘ ⍩ **FICTION**, % Dept. of English, City College, 138th St. & Convent Ave., New York NY 10031. (212)650-6319/650-6317. E-mail: fiction@fictioninc.com. Website: www.fictioninc.com. **Contact:** Mark J. Mirsky, editor. Managing Editor: Kathy Fowler. Magazine: 6×9; 150-250 pages; illustrations; occasionally photos. "As the name implies, we publish *only* fiction; we are looking for the best new writing available, leaning toward the unconventional. *Fiction* has traditionally attempted to make accessible the unaccessible, to bring the experimental to a broader audience." Biannual. Estab. 1972. Circ. 4,000.

● Stories first published in *Fiction* have been selected for inclusion in the *Pushcart Prize* and *Best of the Small Presses* anthologies.

Needs: Contemporary, experimental, humor/satire, literary and translations. No romance, science-fiction, etc. Receives 200 unsolicited mss/month. Accepts 12-20 mss/issue; 24-40 mss/year. Does not read mss June-August. Publishes ms up to 1 year after acceptance. Agented fiction 10-20%. Recently published work by Joyce Carol Oates, Robert Musil and Romulus Linney. Length: 5,000 words maximum. Publishes short shorts. Sometimes critiques rejected mss and recommends other markets.

How to Contact: Send complete ms with cover letter. Responds in approximately 3 months to mss. SASE. Accepts simultaneous submissions, but please advise. Sample copy for $5. Guidelines for SASE.

Payment/Terms: Minimum payment per contributor is $114. Acquires first rights.

Advice: "The guiding principle of *Fiction* has always been to go to terra incognita in the writing of the imagination and to ask that modern fiction set itself serious questions, if often in absurd and comic voices, interrogating the nature of the real and the fantastic. It represents no particular school of fiction, except the innovative. Its pages have often been a harbor for writers at odds with each other. As a result of its willingness to publish the difficult, experimental, unusual, while not excluding the well known, *Fiction* has a unique reputation in the U.S. and abroad as a journal of future directions."

🍁 ☑ $⊘ **THE FIDDLEHEAD**, University of New Brunswick, Campus House, Box 4400, Fredericton, New Brunswick E3B 5A3 Canada. (506)453-3501. Website: www.lib.unb.ca/texts/fiddlehead. Editor: Ross Leckie. **Contact:** Mark A. Jarman, fiction editor. Magazine: 6×9; 104-128 pages; ink illustrations; photos. "No criteria for publication except quality. For a general audience, including many poets and writers." Quarterly. Estab. 1945. Circ. 1,000.

Needs: Literary. No non-literary fiction. Receives 100-150 unsolicited mss/month. Buys 4-5 mss/issue; 20-40 mss/year. Publishes ms up to 1 year after acceptance. Small percent agented fiction. **Publishes 30 new writers/ year.** Published work by Eric Miller, Tony Steele and A.F. Moritz. Length: 50-3,000 words average. Publishes short shorts. Occasionally critiques rejected mss.

How to Contact: Send complete ms with cover letter. Send SASE and *Canadian* stamps or IRCs for return of mss. No simultaneous submissions. Responds in 6 months. Sample copy for $10 (US). Reviews novels and short story collections—*Canadian only*.

Payment/Terms: Pays $20 (Canadian)/published page and 1 contributor's copy. Pays on publication for first or one-time rights.

Advice: "Less than 5% of the material received is published."

☑ ⊘ **FIRST CLASS, Four-Sep Publications**, P.O. Box 12434, Milwaukee WI 53212. E-mail: christopher m@four-sep.com. Website: www.four-sep.com (includes all information regarding Four-Sep Publications). **Contact:** Christopher M, editor. Magazine: 8½×11; 48-56 pages; 24 lb./60 lb. offset paper; craft cover; illustrations; photos. "*First Class* features short fiction and poetics from the cream of the small press and killer unknowns— mingling before your very hungry eyes. I publish plays, too." Triannual. Estab. 1995. Circ. 200-400.

Needs: Erotica, literary, mainstream, science fiction (soft/sociological), short story collections, post-modern. "No religious or traditional poetry, or 'boomer angst'—therapy-driven self loathing." Receives 20-30 unsolicited mss/month. Accepts 3-4 mss/issue; 10-12 mss/year. Publishes ms 2-3 months after acceptance. **Publishes 5-6 new writers/year.** Published work by Gerald Locklin, John Bennett and B.Z. Niditch. Length: 5,000-8,000 words; average length: 2,000-3,000 words. Publishes short shorts. Length: 500 words. Also publishes poetry. Sometimes comments on rejected mss.

How to Contact: Send complete ms with a cover letter. Accepts queries by e-mail. Include 1 page bio and SASE. Responds in 1 week to queries; 2 weeks to mss. Send SASE for reply, return of ms or send a disposable copy of ms. Accepts simultaneous submissions and reprints. Sample copy for $6. Guidelines free for #10 SASE. Reviews novels and short story collections. Send books to Christopher M.

Payment/Terms: Pays 1 contributor's copy; additional copies $5. Pays on publication for one-time rights.

Advice: "Don't bore me with puppy dogs and the morose/sappy feelings you have about death. Belt out a good, short, thought-provoking, graphic, uncommon piece."

☑ **$** ⊘ ☒ **FIVE POINTS: A Journal of Literature and Art**, Georgia State University, University Plaza, Atlanta GA 30303-3083. (404)651-0071. Fax: (404)651-3167. E-mail: msexton@gsu.edu. Website: www. webdelsol.com/fivepoints (includes excerpts from issue, guidelines, announcements and links). **Contact:** David Bottoms, editor. Magazine: 6×9; 200 pages; cotton paper; glossy cover; and photos. *Five Points* is "committed to publishing work that compels the imagination through the use of fresh and convincing language." Triannual. Estab. 1996. Circ. 2,000.

● *Five Points* won the CELJ award for Best New Journal.

Needs: List of upcoming themes available for SASE. Receives more than 250 unsolicited mss/month. Accepts 4 mss/issue; 15-20 mss/year. Does not read mss April 30-September 1. Publishes ms up to 6 months after acceptance. Publishes 1 new writer/year. Recently published work by Frederick Busch, Ursula Hegi and Melanie Rae Thon. Word length: 7,500 words average. Publishes short shorts. Also publishes literary essays and poetry. Sometimes comments on or critiques rejected ms.

How to Contact: Send complete ms with a cover letter. Include 3-4 line bio and list of publications. Send SASE for reply to query. No simultaneous submissions. Sample copy $7. Guidelines free on website.

Payment/Terms: Pays $15/page minimum; $250 maximum, free subscription to magazine and 2 contributor's copies; additional copies $4. Acquires first North American serial rights. Sends galleys to author. Sponsors contest: Paul Bowles Prize, annual award for fiction published in *Five Points*.

Advice: "We place no limitations on style or content. Our only criterion is excellence. If your writing has an original voice, substance, and significance, send it to us. We will publish distinctive, intelligent writing that has something to say and says it in a way that captures and maintains our attention."

Ⓝ ⊘ ◎ **FLINT HILLS REVIEW**, Dept. of English, Box 4019, Emporia State University, Emporia KS 66801-5087. (316)341-5216. Fax: (316)341-5547. E-mail: webbamy@emporia.edu. Website: www.emporia. edu/fhr/index.htm (includes submission and subscription information). **Contact:** Amy Webb or Philip Heldrich, managing editors. Magazine: 9×6; 115 pages; 60 lb. paper; glossy cover; illustrations; photos. "*FHR* seeks to be the flagship journal for the state of Kansas, showcasing writing by Kansas and Great Plains writers, and writing about that region. Includes work by beginning and established writers from other regions as well. Prefers writing with strong sense of place/regional focus." Annual. Estab. 1996. Circ. 500. Member, CLMP.

Needs: Ethnic/multicultural, gay, historical, regional (Plains), translations. "No religious, genre, young adult." List of upcoming themes available online. Receives 5-15 unsolicited mss/month. Accepts 2-5 mss/issue; 2-5 mss/year. Does not read mss April-December. Publishes ms up to 4 months after acceptance. **Publishes 2-5 new writers/year.** Recently published work by Thomas Fox Averill, George Looney, Kristine Sommerville, Virgil Suarez, Jeff Knorr, L.R. Berger, Helen Trubek Glenn, Anna Moon Bradley, Hiram Lucke, Lanessa Poulton, Meagan Baalman and Timothy Johnson. Length: 1 page-5,000 words; average length: 3,000 words. Publishes short shorts. Average length: 1,500 words. Also publishes literary essays, literary criticism and poetry.

How to Contact: Send complete ms with a cover letter. Accepts submissions by e-mail, fax and disk. Include brief bio. Responds in 5 weeks to queries; 6 months to mss. Send a disposable copy of ms and #10 SASE for reply only. Accepts simultaneous and multiple submissions. Sample copy for $5.50. Guidelines for SASE, by e-mail, fax or on website. Reviews novels, short story collections and nonfiction books of interest to writers. Send review copies to Amy Sage Webb.

Payment/Terms: Pays 2 contributor's copies; additional copies $5.50. Pays on publication for one-time rights.

Advice: "We look for a strong sense of place informing the work, writing of literary quality, accomplished use of language, depth of character development, sense of how place or region informs the piece or characters within it. We are attempting to re-define region, especially as the 'regional' applies to Kansas and the Great Plains (region as fidelity to place, as work informed by place, but not region as colloquial). We do not seek to revive a literary tradition of region, but to create a new one in our region. We seek new images of the midwest, especially Kansas and the Plains to contradict existing stereotypes and images of the region."

⊘ ☒ **THE FLORIDA REVIEW**, Dept. of English, University of Central Florida, Orlando FL 32816. (407)823-2038. Fax: (407)823-6582. Website: pegasus.cc.ucf.edu/~english/floridareview/home.htm (includes writer's guidelines, contest information and covers and table of contents of the six most recent issues. **Contact:** Pat Rushin. Magazine: 6×9; 144 pages; semigloss full-color cover; perfect-bound. "We publish fiction of high 'literary' quality—stories that delight, instruct and aren't afraid to take risks. Our audience consists of avid readers of contemporary fiction, poetry and personal essay." Semiannual. Estab. 1972. Circ. 1,000.

● *The Florida Review* was ranked #49 on *Writer's Digest*'s Fiction 50 list of top markets for fiction writers.

Needs: Contemporary, experimental and literary. "We welcome experimental fiction, so long as it doesn't make us feel lost or stupid. We aren't especially interested in genre fiction (science fiction, romance, adventure, etc.), though a good story can transcend any genre." Receives 200 mss/month. Accepts 4-6 mss/issue;

8-12 mss/year. Publishes ms within 3-6 months of acceptance. **Publishes 2-4 new writers/year.** Published work by Richard Wirick, Daniel Ort and Debbie Lee Wesselmann. Also publishes literary criticism, poetry and essays.

How to Contact: Send complete ms with cover letter. Responds in 4 months. SASE required. Accepts simultaneous submissions. Sample copy for $6. Guidelines for SASE. Reviews novels and short story collections.

Payment/Terms: Pays in contributor's copies. Small honorarium occasionally available. "Copyright held by U.C.F.; reverts to author after publication. (In cases of reprints, we ask that a credit line indicate that the work first appeared in the *F.R.*)"

Tips: "We're looking for writers with fresh voices who are not afraid to take risks. Read contemporary writers/ literary magazines."

⬤ **FLYWAY, A Literary Review,** Iowa State University, 206 Ross Hall, Ames IA 50011. (515)294-8273. Fax: (515)294-6814. E-mail: flyway@iastate.edu. Website: www.engl.istate.edu/main/flyway/flyway.html. **Contact:** Stephen Pett, editor. Literary magazine: 8½×11; 64 pages; quality paper; cover stock; some illustrations; photos. "We publish quality fiction. Our stories are accompanied by brief commentaries by their authors, the sort of thing a writer might say introducing a piece at a reading." Triannual. Estab. 1995. Circ. 500.

Needs: Literary. Receives 50 unsolicited mss/month. Accepts 2-5 mss/issue; 10-12 mss/year. Publishes mss 5 months after acceptance. **Publishes 7-10 new writers/year.** Published work by Duane Niatum, Christina D. Allen-Yazzie, Jacob Appel. Length: 5,000 words; average length: 3,500 words. Publishes short shorts; average length: 500 words. Often comments on rejected mss.

How to Contact: Send complete ms with cover letter. Send SASE. Sample copy for $8. Guidelines for SASE.

Payment/Terms: Pays 1 contributor's copy; additional copies $6. Pays on publication for one-time rights.

Advice: "Quality, originality, voice, drama, tension. Make it as strong as you can."

☑ ⬤ **FOLIO: A LITERARY JOURNAL,** %American University Department of Literature, 4400 Massachusetts Ave. NW, Washington DC 20016. (202)885-2990. Editor changes yearly. **Contact:** Editor. Magazine: 6×9; 64 pages. "Fiction is published if it is well written. We look for fresh language, engaging plot and character development." Semiannual. Estab. 1984.

Needs: Contemporary, literary, mainstream, prose poem, translations, essay, b&w art or photography. No pornography. Occasional theme-based issues. See guidelines for info. Receives 150 unsolicited mss/month. Accepts 3-5 mss/issue; 6-40 mss/year. Does not read mss March-August. **Publishes new writers.** Published work by Henry Taylor, Kermit Moyer, Linda Pastan. Length: 4,500 words maximum; average length: 2,500 words. Publishes short shorts. Occasionally critiques rejected mss.

How to Contact: Send complete ms with cover letter. Include a brief bio. Responds in 2 months. SASE. Accepts simultaneous and reprint submissions (if noted). Sample copy for $5. Guidelines for #10 SASE.

Payment/Terms: Pays in contributor's copies. Acquires first North American rights. "$100 award for best fiction, poetry and art. Query for guidelines."

ℕ ⬤ **FOURTEEN HILLS: The SFSU Review,** Dept. of Creative Writing, San Francisco State University, 1600 Holloway Ave., San Francisco CA 94132. (415)338-3083. E-mail: hills@sfsu.edu. Website: mercury.sfsu. edu/~hills/14hills.html. Editors change each year. Magazine: 6×9; 160 pages; 60 lb. paper; 10 point C15 cover. "*Fourteen Hills* publishes the highest quality innovative fiction and poetry for a literary audience." Semiannual. Estab. 1994. Circ. 700.

Needs: Ethnic/multicultural, gay, humor/satire, lesbian, literary, mainstream/contemporary, translations. "No sexist or racist work, and no stories in which the plot has been chosen for its shock value. No genre fiction, please." Receives 100 unsolicited mss/month. Accepts 8-10 mss/issue; 16-20 mss/year. Does not usually read mss during the summer. Publishes ms 2-4 months after acceptance. **Publishes 6 new writers/year.** Published work by Terese Svoboda, Peter Rock and Stephen Dixon. Length: 7,000 words maximum. Publishes short shorts. Also publishes literary essays, poetry. Sometimes comments on rejected mss.

How to Contact: Send complete ms with a cover letter. Include brief bio and list of publications. Responds in 5 months to mss. SASE for return of ms. Sample copy for $7. Guidelines for #10 SASE.

Payment/Terms: Pays 2 contributor's copies. Pays on publication for one-time rights. Sends galleys to author.

Advice: "Please read an issue of *Fourteen Hills* before submitting."

⬤ $ **FRANK, An International Journal of Contemporary Writing and Art,** 32 rue Edouard Vaillant, 93100 Montreuil, France. **Editor:** David Applefield. "Semiannual journal edited and published in Paris in English." Circ. 3,000. Publishes 20 stories/issue. "At *Frank*, we publish fiction, poetry, literary and art interviews, and translations. We like work that falls between existing genres and has social or political consciousness." Send IRC or $5 cash. Must be previously unpublished in English (world). Pays 2 copies and $10 (US)/printed page. "Send your most daring and original work. At *Frank*, we like work that is not too parochial or insular, however, don't try to write for a 'French' market." Sample copy $10 (US/air mail included), $38 for 4 issues; guidelines available upon request. Subscriptions, inquiries, and an online edition of *Frank* available at www.paris-anglo.com/frank.

N ✂ $ ☉ FREEFALL MAGAZINE, The Alexandra Writers' Centre Society, 922 Ninth Ave. SE, Calgary, Alberta T2G 0S4 Canada. Phone/fax: (403)264-4730. E-mail: awcsawrittenword.org. Website: www.written word.org/awcs (includes editors, guidelines, subscription form). **Contact:** Barbara Howard, editor. Magazine: 8½×11; 40 pages; bond paper; bond stock; illustrations; photos. "*FreeFall* features the best of new, emerging writers and gives them the chance to get into print along with established writers. Now in its tenth year, *FreeFall* seeks to attract readers looking for well-crafted stories, poetry, and artwork." Semiannual. Estab. 1990. Circ. under 500. Member, Alberta Magazine Publishers Association (AMPA).
Needs: Literary. Accepts 3-5 mss/issue; 6-10 mss/year. Does not read mss January-February, June-August. Publishes ms 6 months after acceptance. **Publishes 40% new writers/year.** Recently published work by Jan Beecher, Marie Huston, John Ballem and Sebastian Bell. Length: 500-3,000 words; average length: 2,500 words. Publishes short shorts. Average length: 500 words. Also publishes poetry. Sometimes comments on rejected mss.
How to Contact: Send complete ms with a cover letter. Include estimated word count, brief bio, e-mail address. Responds in 3 months to mss. Send SASE (or IRC) for return of ms or send a disposable copy of ms and #10 SASE for reply only. Accepts previously published submissions. Sample copy for $6 (US). Guidelines for SASE, e-mail or on website.
Payment/Terms: Pays $5 (Canadian)/printed page and 1 contributor's copy; additional copies $6 (US). Pays on publication for first North American serial rights.
Advice: "We look for thoughtful word usage that conveys clear images and encourages further exploration of the story's ideas and neat, clean presentation of work. Carefully read *FreeFall* guidelines before submitting. Do not fold manuscript and submit in 9×11 envelope. Include SASE/IRC for reply and/or return of manuscript. You may contact us by e-mail after initial hardcopy submission. For accepted pieces a request is made for disk or e-mail copy. Web presence attracts submissions from writers all over the world."

N ✂ ◐ ◎ FRONT & CENTRE, Black Bile Press, 136-A Billings Ave., Ottawa, Ontario K1H 5K9 Canada. (613)731-6161. E-mail: firth@istar.ca. **Contact:** Matthew Firth. editor. Magazine: letter-size; 50-60 pages; illustration; photos. "We look for new fiction from Canadian and international writers—bold, aggressive work that does not compromise quality." Semiannual. Estab. 1998. Circ. 500.
Needs: Literary, "contemporary realism/gritty urban. No science fiction, horror, mainstream, romance or religious." Receives 30-40 unsolicited mss/month. Accepts 10-12 mss/issue; 20-25 mss/year. Publishes ms 6 months after acceptance. Agented fiction 10%. **Publishes 1-2 new writers/year.** Recently published work by Kenneth J. Harvey, David Rose, Laura Hird, Gregorio Santo Arena and Lindsey Tipping. Length: 50-4,000 words; average length: 2,500 words. Publishes short shorts. Average length: 200 words. Always comments on rejected mss.
How to Contact: Send complete ms with a cover letter. Include estimated word count, brief bio and list of publications. Responds in 2 weeks to queries; 4 months to mss. Send SASE (or IRC) for return of ms or send a disposable copy of ms and #10 SASE for reply only. Accepts multiple submissions. Sample copy for $5. Guidelines for SASE or by e-mail. Reviews novels, short story collections and nonfiction books of interest to writers. Send review copies to Matthew Firth.
Payment/Terms: Pays 2 contributor's copies; additional copies $5. Pays on publication for first rights. Not copyrighted.
Advice: "We look for attention to detail; unique voice; not overtly derivative; bold writing; not pretentious. We would like to see more realism. Read the magazine first—simple as that!"

◐ FRONTIERS: A Journal of Women Studies, Washington State University, Frontiers, Women's Studies, Box 644007, Pullman WA 99164-4007. E-mail: frontier@wsu.edu. **Contact:** Fiction Editor. Magazine: 6×9; 200 pages; photos. "Women studies; academic articles in all disciplines; criticism; exceptional creative work (art, short fiction, photography, poetry)."
Needs: Feminist, multicultural, lesbian. "We want to see fiction that deals with women's lives and experience from a feminist perspective." Receives 15 unsolicited mss/month. Accepts 7-12 mss/issue. Publishes ms 6-12 months after acceptance. **Publishes 2 new writers/year.** Published work by Elizabeth Bell, Nadine Chapman, Tricia Currans-Sheehan and Alethea Eason.
How to Contact: Send 3 copies of complete ms with cover letter. Responds in 1 month to queries; up to 6 months to mss. SASE. Writer's guidelines for #10 SASE. Sample copy for $15.
Payment/Terms: Pays 2 contributor's copies. Acquires first North American serial rights.
Advice: "We are a *feminist* journal. *Frontiers* aims to make scholarship in women studies, and *exceptional* creative work, accessible to a cross-disciplinary audience inside and outside academia. Read short fiction in *Frontiers* before submitting."

☑ $☐ **FUGUE, Literary Digest of the University of Idaho**, English Dept., Rm. 200, Brink Hall, University of Idaho, Moscow ID 83844-1102. (208)885-6156. Fax: (208)885-5944. E-mail: witt931@novell.uida ho.edu. Website: www.uidaho.edu/LS/Eng/Fugue (includes writer's guidelines, names of editors, short fiction). **Contact:** Managing Editor. Magazine: 6×9; 60-100 pages; 20 lb. stock paper. "We are interested in all classifications of fiction—we are not interested in pretentious 'literary' stylizations. We expect stories to be written in a manner engaging for anyone, not just academics and literati. If we could put together an 'ideal' issue, we would probably have 6 or 7 pieces of fiction, each of which would run no more than 10 pages (printed—probably 15 or 16 manuscript pages), a modest essay, and maybe 10 or a dozen poems. The fiction would include a couple of solid 'mainstream/literary' stories, at least one 'regional/local' story (preferably by a writer from the inland Northwest), at least one story by an ethnic writer (Chicano, Native American, Asian-American, African-American), at least one story that had some sort of international or cosmopolitan angle (set, perhaps, in Hong Kong or Quito and written by someone who really knew what he or she was doing), and at least one story that would be 'experimental' (including postmodernism, fantasy, surrealism . . .). Wit and humor are always welcome." Semiannual. Estab. 1990. Circ. 300.

Needs: Adventure, ethnic/multicultural, experimental, fantasy, historical, humor/satire, literary, mainstream/contemporary, regional. "We're looking for good ethnic fiction by ethnic writers; work with a cosmopolitan/international flavor from writers who know what they're doing; and intelligent and sophisticated mainstream and postmodern work." Does not want to see Dungeons & Dragons, Sword & Sorcery, Harlequin, "Cowboy Adventure Stories," True Confessions, etc. No genre fiction. Receives 100 unsolicited mss/month. Accepts 4-8 mss/issue; 8-16 mss/year. Publishes ms 1 year after acceptance. **Publishes 6-7 new writers/year.** Recently published work by Matt Sullivan, Mildred Morris, Anna Harrington and Ryan G. Van Cleave. Length: 500-6,000 words; average length: 3,000 words. Publishes short shorts. Also publishes literary essays and poetry. Sometimes comments on rejected mss.

How to Contact: Send complete ms with cover letter. "Obtain guidelines first." Include estimated word count and list of publications. Responds in 2 weeks to queries; 3 months to mss. SASE for a reply to a query or return of ms. No simultaneous submissions. Sample copy for $5. Guidelines for #10 SASE.

Payment/Terms: Pays $10-20 and contributor's copy; extra copies available at a discount. Pays on publication for first North American serial rights.

Advice: Looks for "competent writing, clarity and consideration for the reader; also stylistic flair/energy. Here are what we consider the characteristics of a 'good' story: distinct voice; the quality of strangeness; engaging, dynamic characters; engaging language, style, craftsmanship; emotional resonance ('snap'); and an un-put-down-ability. Be original and inventive. Take chances, but present your work as a professional. Proper manuscript format is essential."

☑ $☐☑ **FUTURES MAGAZINE for writers and artists**, 3039 38th Ave. S, Minneapolis MN 55406-2140. (612)724-4023. E-mail: babs@suspenseunlimited.net. Website: www.futuresforstorylovers.com (includes excerpts, writer's guidelines, names of editors, interviews with authors, fiction not included in print version, contests, cover art, color posters and greeting cards for writers for sale). **Contact:** Earl Staggs, senior fiction editor. Magazine: 8½×11; 100 pages; illustrations; photos. "We are multi-genre as well as literary—we offer inspiration and guidance and we're fun! We help writers—entering and nominating for Edgars, Derringer Award, Pushcart Prize, New Century Award and more." Bimonthly. Estab. 1998. Circ. 2,000.

● Publisher Babs Lakey received a Derringer Award from the Short Mystery Fiction Society.

Needs: Comics/graphic novels, ethnic/multicultural, experimental, feminist, gay, glitz, horror, humor/satire, lesbian, literary, mainstream, mystery/suspense (amateur sleuth, cozy, police procedural, private eye/hardboiled), psychic/supernatural/occult, romance, science fiction, thriller/espionage, western, young adult/teen. "We would like to see more thrillers, also family mainstream." No erotica or pornography. List of upcoming themes available for SASE. Receives 80-120 unsolicited mss/month. Accepts 35-40 mss/issue; 250 mss/year. Publishes ms 3-8 months after acceptance. **Publishes at least 15 new writers/year.** Recently published work by Henry Slesar, David Harford, Ashok Banker and Elizabeth Serini. Length: up to 12,000 words maximum; average length: 2,500 words. Publishes short shorts. Average length: 300-1,000 words. Also publishes literary essays, literary criticism and poetry. Sometimes comments on rejected mss.

How to Contact: Send complete ms with a cover letter. Accepts submissions by e-mail. "Send e-mail; paste inside the e-mail with name, address, word count, genre, bio. No snail mail unless there is no way you can e-mail to us." Responds in 1 week to queries; 2 months to mss. Send SASE (or IRC) for return of ms or send a disposable copy of ms and #10 SASE for reply only. Accepts simultaneous and multiple submissions, but put each in a separate e-mail. Sample copy for $6. Guidelines for SASE or by e-mail.

Payment/Terms: Pays $10-25 and many awards (2 publishers choices in each issue receive additional fee and award); additional copies $5. Acquires first rights. Sponsors contests. Visit website for details.

Advice: "The Internet makes us want, and used to getting, instant gratification. People are getting published without editing their works. We are attempting to keep up with today while still hanging on to the values of solid good creative works. Please make the effort to read a copy before you submit."

GARGOYLE, % Atticus Books. (703)548-7580. Website: www.atticusbooks.com. **Contact**: Richard Peabody and Lucinda Ebersole, editors. Literary magazine: 6×9; 350 pages; illustrations; photos. "*Gargoyle* is a literary magazine for poets and writers who actually read and care about what their peers are writing." Annual. Estab. 1976. Circ. 3,000.

● At press time, *Gargoyle* was moving. Please visit their website for the street address update for submissions.

Needs: Erotica, ethnic/multicultural, experimental, gay, lesbian, literary, mainstream/contemporary, translations, "good short stories with sports and music backgrounds." No romance, horror, science fiction. Receives 50-200 unsolicited mss/month. Accepts 15 mss/issue. Reads in summer (June, July, August). Publishes ms 6-12 months after acceptance. Agented fiction 5%. **Publishes 5-6 new writers/year.** Recently published work by Kim Addonizio, Mary Caponegro, Billy Childish, Helen Schulman and Curtis White. Length: 30 pages maximum; average length: 5-10 pages. Publishes short shorts. Length: 2-3 pages. Also publishes literary essays, criticism and poetry. Sometimes comments on rejected ms.

How to Contact: Send complete ms. Responds in 2 weeks to queries; 3 months to mss. Send SASE for reply, return of ms or send a disposable copy of ms. Accepts simultaneous submissions. Sample copy for $12.

Payment/Terms: Pays 1 contributor's copy; additional copies for ½ price. Acquires first rights, first North American rights or first British rights. Sends prepublication galleys to author.

Advice: "Read a copy. Our favorite living writers are Paul Bowles and Jeanette Winterson. That should give you a clue. We are, as far as I can tell, one of the few magazines that likes both realism and experimental work. Both poles are welcome."

✓ $ ⊘ ▼ THE GEORGIA REVIEW, The University of Georgia, Athens GA 30602-9009. (706)542-3481. Fax: (706)542-0047. E-mail: garev@arches.uga.edu. Website: www.uga.edu/~garev (includes writer's guidelines, names of editors, order/subscription info, guestbook, current issue contents and more). **Contact:** T.R. Hummer, editor. Associate Editor: Stephen Corey. Journal: 7×10; 208 pages (average); 50 lb. woven old-style paper; 80 lb. cover stock; illustrations; photos. "*The Georgia Review* is a journal of arts and letters, featuring a blend of the best in contemporary thought and literature—essays, fiction, poetry, visual art and book reviews for the intelligent nonspecialist as well as the specialist reader. We seek material that appeals across disciplinary lines by drawing from a wide range of interests." Quarterly. Estab. 1947. Circ. 5,000.

● Stories first published in *The Georgia Review* have been anthologized in *Best American Short Stories, Best American Mystery Stories, Best Stories from the South* and the *Pushcart Prize Collection. The Georgia Review* was a finalist for the National Magazine Award in Fiction in 2000.

Needs: Experimental and literary. "We're looking for the highest quality fiction—work that is capable of sustaining subsequent readings, not throw-away pulp magazine entertainment. Nothing that fits too easily into a 'category.' " Receives about 300 unsolicited fiction mss/month. Accepts 3-4 mss/issue; 12-15 mss/year. Does not read unsolicited mss May 15-August 15. Would prefer *not* to see novel excerpts. **Published new writers within the last year.** Recently published work by Mary Hood, Barry Lopez, James Tate and Kent Nelson. Length: Open. Also publishes literary essays, literary criticism, poetry. Occasionally critiques rejected mss.

How to Contact: Send complete ms (one story) with SASE. No multiple submissions. Usually responds in 3 months. Sample copy for $7; guidelines for #10 SASE. Reviews short story collections.

Payment/Terms: Pays $40/printed page, 1 year complimentary subscription and 1 contributor's copy; reduced charge for additional copies. Pays on publication for first North American serial rights. Sends galleys to author.

✓ ⊘ GERTRUDE: A Journal of Voice & Vision, P.O. Box 270814, Ft. Collins CO 80527-0814. (970)491-5957. E-mail: editor@gertrudejournal.com. Website: www.gertrudejournal.com (includes writer's guidelines, excerpts, subscription info, events, links). **Contact:** Eric Delehoy, editor. Magazine: 5×8½, 36-48 pages; 60 lb. paper; glossy card cover; illustrations; photos. *Gertrude* is a "biannual publication featuring the voices and visions of the gay, lesbian, bisexual, transgender and supportive community." Estab. 1999. Circ. 550.

Needs: Ethnic/multicultural, feminist, gay, humor/satire, lesbian, literary, mainstream. No romance, pornography or science fiction. Wants more humorous and multicultural fiction. "We'd like to publish more humor and positive portrayals of gays—steer away from victim roles, pity." Receives 3-5 unsolicited mss/month. Accepts 2-3 mss/issue; 4-6 mss/year. Publishes ms 1-2 months after acceptance. **Publishes 5-7 new writers/year.** Recently pub-

---

MARKET CONDITIONS are constantly changing! If you're still using this book and it is 2003 or later, buy the newest edition of *Novel & Short Story Writer's Market* at your favorite bookstore or order from Writer's Digest Books by calling 1-800-289-0963.

lished work by Kendal Ericson, Demrie Alonzo, Elisabeth Tyler-James and Elizabeth Howkins. Length: 200-2,000 words; average length: 1,500 words. Publishes short shorts. Length: 200-500 words. Also publishes poetry. Often comments on or critiques rejected ms.

How to Contact: Send complete ms with a cover letter. Include estimated word count, 1 paragraph bio and list of publications. Responds in 4 months to mss. Send SASE for reply to query and a disposable copy of ms. No simultaneous submissions. Accepts multiple submissions (no more than two). Sample copy for $5, 6×9 SAE and 3 1st class stamps. Guidelines for #10 SASE.

Payment/Terms: Pays 1-2 contributor's copies; additional copies $4. Payment on publication. Author retains rights upon publication. Not copyrighted.

Advice: "We look for strong characterization, imagery and new, unique ways of writing about universal experiences. Follow the construction of your work until the ending. Many stories start out with zest, then flipper and die. Show us, don't tell us."

$ ◯ ⊻ THE GETTYSBURG REVIEW, Gettysburg College, Gettysburg PA 17325. (717)337-6770. Fax: (717)337-6775. Website: www.gettysburgreview.com (includes writer's guidelines, staff biographies and excerpts from the most recent issues). Editor: Peter Stitt. **Contact:** Mark Drew, assistant editor. Magazine: 6¾×10; 170 pages; acid free paper; full color illustrations. "Quality of writing is our only criterion; we publish fiction, poetry, and essays." Quarterly. Estab. 1988. Circ. 4,500.

● Work appearing in *The Gettysburg Review* has also been included in *Prize Stories: The O. Henry Awards*, the *Pushcart Prize* anthology, *Best American Fiction, Best American Poetry, New Stories from the South, Harper's* and elsewhere. It is also the recipient of a Lila Wallace-Reader's Digest grant and NEA grants.

Needs: Contemporary, experimental, historical, humor/satire, literary, mainstream, regional and serialized novel. "We require that fiction be intelligent, and aesthetically written." Receives 350 mss/month. Accepts 4-6 mss/issue; 16-24 mss/year. Publishes ms within 1 year of acceptance. **Publishes 1-5 new writers/year.** Published work by Robert Olen Butler, Joyce Carol Oates, Naeem Murr, Tom Perrotta, Alison Baker and Peter Baida. Length: 1,000-20,000 words; average length: 3,000 words. Occasionally publishes short shorts. Also publishes literary essays, some literary criticism, poetry. Sometimes critiques rejected mss.

How to Contact: Send complete ms with cover letter September through May. Responds in up to 6 months. SASE. No simultaneous submissions. Sample copy for $7 (postage paid). Does not review books per se. "We do essay-reviews, treating several books around a central theme." Send review copies to editor.

Payment/Terms: Pays $25/printed page, subscription to magazine and contributor's copy; charge for extra copies. Pays on publication for first North American serial rights.

Advice: "Reporting time can take more than three months. It is helpful to look at a sample copy of *The Gettysburg Review* to see what kinds of fiction we publish before submitting."

◯ ◎ GINOSKO, between literary vision and spiritual realities, P.O. Box 246, Fairfax CA 94978. (415)460-8436. E-mail: RobertPaulCesaretti@hotmail.com. **Contact:** Robert Cesaretti, editor. Magazine: 4×6; 50-60 pages; standard paper; card cover; illustrations; photos. Published "when material permits."

Needs: Experimental, literary, stylized; "consider 'Pagan Night' by Kate Braverman, 'Driving the Heart' by Jason Brown, 'Customs of the Country' by Madison Smartt Bell." Does not want conventional work. Wants more work like Kate Braverman. Receives 15-20 unsolicited mss/month. Length: 500-15,000.

How to Contact: Send complete ms with a cover letter. Responds in 3 months to mss. SASE for return of ms. Accepts simultaneous and reprint submissions.

Payment/Terms: Pays 1 contributor's copy. Acquires one-time rights.

Advice: "I am looking for a style that conveys spiritual hunger and depth yet avoids religiosity and convention—*Between literary vision and spiritual realities*."

Ⓝ ◯ GLASS TESSERACT, Glass Tesseract, P.O. Box 702, Agoura Hills CA 91376. E-mail: glass_tesseract@email.com or editor@glasstesseract.com. Website: www.glasstesseract.com (includes excerpts, guidelines, names of editors, price). **Contact:** Michael Chester, editor. Magazine: 5½×8½; 48-96 pages; 24 lb. ivory linen paper; cardstock cover. "Addressed to a literary readership, *Glass Tesseract* is versatile, publishing stories that range in style and treatment from traditional to wide-open experimental. The purpose of the magazine is to help bring works of art into the world." Semiannual. Estab. 2001.

Needs: Experimental, literary, mainstream. "No sentimental, moralizing, devotional, cute, coy, or happy-face stories." Publishes ms 6 months after acceptance. Recently published work by Dick Wimmer, Thomas Neuburger, Isabelle Hannich and Arshur Marin. Length: 200-3,000 words; average length: 1,500 words. Publishes short shorts. Average length: 700 words. Also publishes poetry. Always comments on rejected mss.

How to Contact: Send complete ms with or without a cover letter. Accepts submissions by e-mail. Include estimated word count and list of publications. Responds in up to 3 months to mss. Send SASE (or IRC) for return of ms or send a disposable copy of ms and #10 SASE (or IRC) for reply only. Accepts simultaneous, previously published and multiple submissions (up to 3 stories). Sample copy for $5. Guidelines for SASE, by e-mail or on website.

Payment/Terms: Pays 2 contributor's copies; additional copies $5. Pays on publication for one-time rights. Sometimes sends galleys to author.

Advice: "We look for a style of language that, whether lean or rich, is artfully constructed without being pretentious, strained, or laden with clichés. We want characters who have dimensionality, not fitting into standard all-good, all-bad, all-wise, or all-innocent molds. We want story lines that emerge naturally (if not inevitably) from the nature of the characters and the language. Read the stories we have published. Send e-mail (or standard mail with SASE) to the editor with any questions. Most of all (no matter where you are going to send your stories), steep yourself in the best literature you can find—then go your own way."

$ ⬛ ⬛ **GLIMMER TRAIN STORIES**, Glimmer Train Press, 710 SW Madison St., Suite 504, Portland OR 97205. (503)221-0836. Website: www.glimmertrain.com (includes writer's guidelines, story excerpts and a Q&A section for writers). **Editors:** Susan Burmeister-Brown and Linda Burmeister Davies. Magazine: 6¾×9¼; 160 pages; recycled, acid-free paper; 20 illustrations; 12 photographs. Quarterly. Estab. 1990. Circ. 13,000.
   • *Glimmer Train* was ranked #18 on *Writer's Digest's* "Fiction 50" list of top markets for fiction writers. The magazine also sponsors an annual short story contest for new writers and a very short fiction contest.

Needs: Literary. Receives 4,000 unsolicited mss/month. Accepts 10 mss/issue; 40 mss/year. Reads in January, April, July, October. Publishes ms up to 2 years after acceptance. Agented fiction 20%. **Publishes "about 8" new writers/year.** Published work by Judy Budnitz, Brian Champeau, Ellen Cooney, Andre Dubus III, Thomas Kennedy, Chris Offutt, Alberto Rios and Monica Wood. Length: up to 12,000 words.

How to Contact: Submit work online at www.glimmertrain.com. Accepted work published in *Glimmer Train Stories*. Sample copy for $10. Guidelines provided online.

Payment/Terms: Pays $500 and 10 contributor's copies. Pays on acceptance for first rights.

Advice: "If you're excited about a story you've written, send it to us! If you're not very excited about it, wait and send one that you are excited about. When a story stays with us after the first reading, it gets another reading. Those stories that simply don't let us set them aside, get published. Read good fiction. It will often improve the quality of your own writing."

🍁 ✅ **$** ⬛ ⬛ **GRAIN**, Saskatchewan Writers' Guild, Box 1154, Regina, Saskatchewan S4P 3B4 Canada. (306)244-2828. Fax: (306)244-0255. E-mail: grain.mag@sk.sympatico.ca. Website: www.skwriter.com/grain (includes history, news, subscription and contest information). **Editor:** Elizabeth Philips. **Contact:** Dianne Warren, fiction editor. Literary magazine: 6×9; 128 pages; Chinook offset printing; chrome-coated stock; some photos. Quarterly. Estab. 1973. Circ. 1,700.
   • *Grain* won magazine of the year-Saskatchewan at the Western Magazine awards and was ranked #22 on *Writer's Digest's* Fiction 50 list of top markets for fiction writers.

Needs: Contemporary, experimental, literary, mainstream and prose poem. Want to see more magic realism. "No propaganda—only artistic/literary writing." No genre fiction. No mss "that stay *within* the limits of conventions such as women's magazine type stories, science fiction; none that push a message." Receives 80 unsolicited fiction mss/month. Accepts 8-12 mss/issue; 32-48 mss/year. Recently published work by Marcus Youssef, Bill Stenson, Valerie Compton and Marina Endicott. Length: "No more than 30 pages." Also publishes poetry and creative nonfiction. Occasionally critiques rejected mss.

How to Contact: Send complete ms with SASE (or IRC) and brief letter. Accepts queries by e-mail or fax. No simultaneous submissions. Responds within 4 months to mss. Publishes ms an average of 4 months after acceptance. Sample copy for $7.95 plus postage. No e-mail submissions.

Payment/Terms: Pays $40/page up to $175 and 2 contributor's copies. Pays on publication for first Canadian serial rights. "We expect acknowledgment if the piece is republished elsewhere."

Advice: "Submit a story to us that will deepen the imaginative experience of our readers. *Grain* has established itself as a first-class magazine of serious fiction. We receive submissions from around the world. If Canada is a foreign country to you, we ask that you *do not* use U.S. postage stamps on your return envelope. If you live outside Canada and neglect the International Reply Coupons, we *will not* read or reply to your submission. We look for attention to detail, credibility, lucid use of language and metaphor and a confident, convincing voice. Sweat the small stuff. Make sure you have researched your piece, that the literal and metaphorical support one another."

✅ **$** ⬛ ⬛ ▭ **GRAND STREET**, 214 Sullivan St., Suite 6C, New York NY 10012. (212)533-2944. Fax (212)533-2737. Website: www.grandstreet.com. Editor: Jean Stein. **Contact:** David Grosz, associate editor. Magazine: 7¾×9½; 240-270 pages; illustrations; art portfolios. "We publish new fiction and nonfiction of all types." Quarterly. Estab. 1981. Circ. 7,000.
   • Work published in *Grand Street* has been included in the *Best American Short Stories*.

Needs: Poetry, essays, translations. Agented fiction 90%. Published work by Durs Grunbëin, José Saramago, Ozren Kebo, Jorge Luis Borges and Mike Davis. Length: 9,000 words maximum; average length: 4,000 words.
How to Contact: *Not accepting unsolicited fiction mss.* Sample copy for $15; $18 overseas and Canada.
Payment/Terms: Pays $250-1,000 and 2 contributor's copies. Pays on publication for first North American serial rights. Sends galleys to author.

☐ ✓ $ GRANTA, The Magazine of New Writing, 2-3 Hanover Yard, Noel Rd., London N1 8BE England. Phone: 0207 704 9776. Fax: 0171 704 0474. E-mail: editorial@granta.com. Website: www.granta.com. Editor: Ian Jack. **Contact:** Fatema Ahmed, editorial assistant. Magazine: paperback, 256 pages approx.; photos. "*Granta* magazine publishes fiction, reportage, biography and autobiography, history, travel and documentary photography. It rarely publishes 'writing about writing.' The realistic narrative—the story—is its primary form." Quarterly. Estab. 1979. Circ. 80,000.
Needs: Literary. "No fantasy, science fiction, romance, historical, occult or other 'genre' fiction." Themes decided as deadline approaches. Receives 100 unsolicited mss/month. Accepts 0-1 ms/issue; 1-2 mss/year. Percentage of agented fiction varies. **Publishes 1-2 new writers/year.** Length: open.
How to Contact: Responds in 3 months to mss. Send SAE and IRCs for reply, return of ms or send a disposable copy of ms. Accepts simultaneous submissions. Sample copy £9.95.
Payment/Terms: Pays £75-5,000 and 3 contributor's copies. Acquires variable rights. Sends galleys to author.
Advice: "We are looking for the best in realistic stories; originality of voice; without jargon, connivance or self-conscious 'performance'—writing that endures."

✓ ◑ GRASSLANDS REVIEW, P.O. Box 626, Berea OH 44017-0626. E-mail: grasslandsreview@aol.com. Website: hometown.aol.com/glreview/prof/index.htm (includes guidelines, contest information, sample text, table of contents for latest issue). **Contact:** Laura B. Kennelly, editor. Magazine: 6×9; 80 pages. *Grasslands Review* prints creative writing of all types; poetry, fiction, essays for a general audience. "Designed as a place for new writers to publish." Semiannual. Estab. 1989. Circ. 300.
Needs: Contemporary, ethnic, experimental, fantasy, horror, humor/satire, literary, prose poem, regional, science fiction and western. Nothing pornographic or overtly political or religious. Accepts 1-3 mss/issue. Reads only in October and March. Publishes ms 6 months after acceptance. **Publishes 5 new writers/year.** Recently published work by Catherine Ferguson and Charles Edward Brooks. Length: 100-3,500 words; average length: 1,500 words. Publishes short shorts (100-150 words). Also publishes poetry. Sometimes critiques rejected mss and recommends other markets.
How to Contact: Send complete ms in October or March *only* with cover letter. No simultaneous submissions. Responds in 3 months to mss. SASE. Sample copy for $4.
Payment/Terms: Pays in contributor's copies. Acquires one-time rights. Publication not copyrighted.
Advice: "A fresh approach, imagined by a reader for other readers, pleases our audience. We are looking for fiction which leaves a strong feeling or impression—or a new perspective on life. The *Review* began as an in-class exercise to allow experienced creative writing students to learn how a little magazine is produced. It now serves as an independent publication, attracting authors from as far away as the Ivory Coast, but its primary mission is to give unknown writers a start."

◑ THE GREEN HILLS LITERARY LANTERN, Published by North Central Missouri College and co-published by The North Central Missouri Writer's Guild, P.O. Box 375, Trenton MO 64683. (660)359-3948, ext. 324. Fax: (660)359-3202. E-mail: jsmith@mail.ncmc.cc.mo.us. Website: www.ncmc.cc.mo.us. (includes writer's guidelines, excerpts from current issue, subscription information). Editor: Jack Smith. **Contact:** Sara King, fiction editor. Magazine: 6×9; 200 pages; good quality paper with glossy 4-color cover. "The mission of *GHLL* is to provide a literary market for quality fiction writers, both established and beginners, and to provide quality literature for readers from diverse backgrounds. We also see ourselves as a cultural resource for North Central Missouri. Our publication works to publish the highest quality fiction—dense, layered, subtle, and, at the same time, fiction which grabs the ordinary reader. We tend to publish traditional short stories, but we are open to experimental forms." Annual. Estab. 1990. Circ. 500.
Needs: Ethnic/multicultural, experimental, feminist, humor/satire, literary, mainstream/contemporary and regional. "Fairly traditional short stories but we are open to experimental. Our main requirement is literary merit. Wants more quality fiction about rural culture." No adventure, crime, erotica, horror, inspirational, mystery/suspense, romance. Receives 40 unsolicited mss/month. Accepts 7-10 mss/issue. Publishes ms 6-12 months after acceptance. Recently published work by Ian MacMillan, Walter Cummins, Karl Harshbarger, and Robert Garner McBrearty. **Publishes 0-1 new writer/year.** Length: 7,000 words maximum; average length: 3,000 words. Publishes short shorts. Also publishes poetry. Sometimes comments on rejected mss.
How to Contact: Send complete ms with a cover letter. Include bio (50-100 words) with list of publications. Accepts queries (only) by e-mail. Responds in 4 months to mss. SASE for return of ms. Accepts simultaneous submissions and multiple submissions (2-3). Sample copy for $7 (includes envelope and postage).

Payment/Terms: Pays 2 contributor's copies. Acquires one-time rights. Sends galleys to author.

Advice: "We look for strong character development, substantive plot and theme, visual and forceful language within a multilayered story. Make sure your work has the flavor of life—a sense of reality. A good story, well-crafted, will eventually get published. Find the right market for it, and above all, don't give up."

$ ⊘ ✿ GREEN MOUNTAINS REVIEW, Johnson State College, Box A-58, Johnson VT 05656. (802)635-1350. Editor-in-Chief: Neil Shepard. **Contact:** Tony Whedon, fiction editor. Magazine: digest-sized; 160-200 pages. Semiannual. Estab. 1975 (new series, 1987). Circ. 1,700.

• *Green Mountain Review* has received a Pushcart Prize and Editors Choice Award.

Needs: Adventure, contemporary, experimental, humor/satire, literary, mainstream, serialized/excerpted novel, translations. Receives 80 unsolicited mss/month. Accepts 6 mss/issue; 12 mss/year. Publishes ms 6-12 months after acceptance. Reads mss September 1 through March 1. **Publishes 0-4 new writers/year.** Recently published work by Howard Norman, Debra Spark, Valerie Miner and Peter LaSalle. Length: 25 pages maximum. Publishes short shorts. Also publishes literary criticism, poetry. Sometimes critiques rejected mss.

How to Contact: Send complete ms with cover letter. "Manuscripts will not be read and will be returned between March 1 and September 1." Responds in 1 month to queries; 6 months to mss. SASE. Accepts simultaneous submissions (if advised). Sample copy for $5.

Payment/Terms: Pays contributor's copies, 1-year subscription and small honorarium, depending on grants. Acquires first North American serial rights. Rights revert to author upon request. Sends galleys to author upon request.

Advice: "We're looking for more rich, textured, original fiction with cross-cultural themes. The editors are open to a wide spectrum of styles and subject matter as is apparent from a look at the list of fiction writers who have published in its pages. One issue was devoted to Vermont fiction, and another issue filled with new writing from the People's Republic of China, and a recent issue devoted to literary ethnography."

✿ ⊘ GREEN'S MAGAZINE, Fiction for the Family, Green's Educational Publications, Box 3236, Regina, Saskatchewan S4P 3H1 Canada. **Contact:** David Green, editor. Magazine: 5¼×8½; 96 pages; 20 lb. bond paper; matte cover stock; line illustrations. Publishes "solid short fiction suitable for family reading." Quarterly. Estab. 1972.

Needs: Adventure, fantasy, humor/satire, literary, mainstream, mystery/suspense and science fiction. No erotic or sexually explicit fiction. Receives 20-30 mss/month. Accepts 10-12 mss/issue; 40-50 mss/year. Publishes ms usually within 3-6 months of acceptance. Agented fiction 2%. **Publishes 6 new writers/year.** Recently published work by Gerald Standley, Jim Sullivan and Mary Wallace. Length: 1,500-4,000 words; 2,500 words preferred. Also publishes poetry. Sometimes critiques rejected mss.

How to Contact: Send complete ms. "Cover letters welcome but not necessary." Responds in 2 months. SASE (in Canada), SAE and IRC (for US and overseas). Accepts multiple submissions. Sample copy for $5. Guidelines for #10 SASE (IRC). Reviews novels and short story collections.

Payment/Terms: Pays in contributor's copies. Acquires first North American serial rights.

Advice: "No topic is taboo, but we avoid sexuality for its own sake, and dislike material that is needlessly explicit or obscene. We look for strongly written stories that explore their characters through a subtle blending of conflicts. Plots should be appropriate, rather than overly ingenious or reliant on some *deus ex machina*. It must be a compression of experience or thoughts, in a form that is both challenging and rewarding to the reader. We have no form rejection slip. If we cannot use a submission, we try to offer constructive criticism in our personal reply. Often, such effort is rewarded with reports from our writers that following our suggestions has led to placement of the story or poem elsewhere."

⊘ ✿ THE GREENSBORO REVIEW, English Dept., 134 McIver Bldg., UNC Greensboro, P.O. Box 26170, Greensboro NC 27402-6170. (336)334-5459. E-mail: jlclark@uncg.edu. Website: www.uncg.edu/eng/mfa (includes writer's guidelines, literary awards guidelines, address, deadlines, subscription information, sample work). **Contact:** Jim Clark, editor. Fiction editor changes each year. Send mss to the editor. Magazine: 6×9; approximately 128 pages; 60 lb. paper; 65 lb. cover. Literary magazine featuring fiction and poetry for readers interested in contemporary literature. Semiannual. Circ. 800.

• Stories from *The Greensboro Review* have been included in *The Best American Short Stories, Prize Stories: The O. Henry Awards, New Stories from the South*, and *Pushcart Prize*.

Needs: Contemporary and experimental. Accepts 6-8 mss/issue, 12-16 mss/year. **10% of all work published is by previously unpublished authors.** Published work by Robert Morgan, George Singleton, Robert Olmstead, Jean Ross Justice, Dale Ray Phillips and Kelly Cherry. Length: 7,500 words maximum.

How to Contact: Send complete ms with SASE. Accepts multiple submissions. No simultaneous submissions or previously published works. Unsolicited manuscripts must arrive by September 15 to be considered for the spring issue and by February 15 to be considered for the fall issue. Manuscripts arriving after those dates may be held for the next consideration. Responds in 4 months. Sample copy for $5.

Payment/Terms: Pays in contributor's copies. Acquires first North American serial rights.
Advice: "We want to see the best being written regardless of theme, subject or style."

THE GRIFFIN, Gwynedd-Mercy College, P.O. Box 901, 1325 Sumneytown Pike, Gwynedd Valley PA 19437-0901. (215)646-7300. Fax: (215)923-3060. E-mail: z31w@aol.com or kaleraol.gmc.edu. **Contact:** Anne K. Kaler, Ph.D., editor. Editor: Susan E. Wagner. Literary magazine: 8½×5½; 112 pages. "*The Griffin* is a literary journal sponsored by Gwynedd-Mercy College. Its mission is to enrich society by nurturing and promoting creative writing that demonstrates a unique and intelligent voice. We seek writing which accurately reflects the human condition with all its intellectual, emotional, and ethical challenges." Semiannual. Estab. 1999. Circ. 500.
Needs: Adventure, ethnic/multicultural (general), family saga, fantasy, feminist, historical, horror, humor/satire, literary, mainstream, mystery/suspense, religious (general), romance, science fiction, thriller/espionage, western. "No slasher, graphic violence or sex." Receives 2-3 unsolicited mss/month. Accepts mss depending on the quality of work submitted. Publishes ms 3-6 months after acceptance. **Publishes 10-15 new writers/year.** Recently published work by Pat Carr, Linda Wisniewski and Michael McGregor. Length: 2,500 words; average length: 2,000 words. Publishes short shorts; average length: 1,000 words. Also publishes literary essays and poetry.
How to Contact: Send complete ms with cover letter. Accepts submissions by e-mail, fax and disk. Include estimated word count and brief bio. Responds in 1 month to queries; 6 months to mss. Send SASE for return of ms or send disposable copy of ms and #10 SASE for reply only. Accepts simultaneous submissions "if notified." Sample copy for $6. Guidelines for SASE or e-mail.
Payment/Terms: Pays in 2 contributor's copies; additional copies for $6. Pays on publication for one-time rights.
Advice: "Looking for well-constructed works that explore universal qualities, respect for the individual and community, justice and integrity. Check our description and criteria. Rewrite until you're sure every word counts. We publish the best work we find regardless of industry trends."

$ GULF COAST, A Journal of Literature & Fine Arts, Dept. of English, University of Houston, Houston TX 77204-3012. (713)743-3223. Fax: (713)743-3215. Website: www.gulfcoast.uh.edu. **Contact:** Miah Arnold, fiction editor. Editors change each year. Magazine: 6×9; 144 pages; stock paper, gloss cover; illustrations; photos. "Innovative fiction for the literary-minded." Estab. 1984. Circ. 1,500.
● Work published in *Gulf Coast* has been selected for inclusion in the *Pushcart Prize* anthology and *Best American Short Stories.*
Needs: Contemporary, ethnic, experimental, literary, regional, translations. Wants more "cutting-edge, experimental" fiction. No children's, genre, religious/inspirational. Receives 150 unsolicited mss/month. Accepts 8-10 mss/issue; 16-20 mss/year. Publishes ms 6 months-1 year after acceptance. Agented fiction 5%. Published work by Amy Storrow, Beverly Lowry, Diana Joseph, Karen Mary Penn and J. David Stevens. Length: no limit. Publishes short shorts. Sometimes critiques rejected mss.
How to Contact: Send complete ms with brief cover letter. "List previous publications; please notify us if the submission is being considered elsewhere." Responds in 6 months. Accepts simultaneous submissions. Back issue for $6, 7×10 SAE and 4 first-class stamps. Guidelines on website or for #10 SASE.
Payment/Terms: Pays contributor's copies and *small* honorariam for one-time rights.
Advice: "Rotating editorship, so please be patient with replies. As always, please send one story at a time."

GULF STREAM MAGAZINE, Florida International University, English Dept., Biscayne Bay Campus, 3000 N.E. 151st St., N. Miami FL 33181-3000. (305)919-5599. Editors: Lynne Barrett and John Dufresne. **Contact:** Fiction Editor. Editors change every 1-2 years. Magazine: 5½×8½; 96 pages; recycled paper; 80 lb. glossy cover; cover illustrations. "We publish *good quality*—fiction, nonfiction and poetry for a predominately literary market." Semiannual. Estab. 1989. Circ. 600.
Needs: Contemporary, literary, mainstream. Receives 250 unsolicited mss/month. Accepts 5 mss/issue; 10 mss/year. Does not read mss during the summer. Publishes ms 3-6 months after acceptance. **Publishes 2-5 new writers/year.** Recently published work by Jane McCafferty, Maya Sonenberg, Christopher Kelly, Lisa Stolley and Lydia Webster. Length: 7,500 words maximum; average length: 5,000 words. "Usually longer stories do not get accepted. There are exceptions, however." Publishes short shorts. Also publishes poetry. Sometimes critiques rejected mss.

 A BULLET INTRODUCES COMMENTS by the editor of *Novel & Short Story Writer's Market* indicating special information about the listing.

How to Contact: Send complete manuscript with cover letter including list of previous publications and a short bio. Responds in 3 months. SASE. Accepts simultaneous submissions "if noted." Sample copy for $5. Guidelines for SASE.

Payment/Terms: Pays in gift subscriptions and contributor's copies. Acquires first North American serial rights.

Advice: "Looks for good concise writing—well plotted with interesting characters."

$ ⬤ HAPPY, The Happy Organization, 240 E. 35th St., 11A, New York NY 10016. (212)689-3142. E-mail: bayardx@aol.com. Editor: Bayard. **Contact:** Fiction Editor. Magazine: 5½×8; 150-200 pages; 60 lb. text paper; 150 lb. cover; perfect-bound; illustrations; photos. Quarterly. Estab. 1995. Circ. 500.
   ● *Happy* was ranked #16 on *Writer's Digest*'s "Fiction 50" list of top markets for fiction writers.

Needs: Erotica, ethnic/multicultural, experimental, fantasy, feminist, gay, horror, humor/satire, lesbian, literary, psychic/supernatural/occult, science fiction. No "television rehash or religious nonsense." Want more work that is "strong, angry, empowering, intelligent, God-like, expressive." Receives 300-500 unsolicited mss/month. Accepts 30-40 mss/issue; 100-150 mss/year. **30-50% of work published is by new writers.** Publishes ms 6-12 months after acceptance. Length: 6,000 words maximum; average length: 1,000-3,500 words. Publishes short shorts. Often comments on rejected mss.

How to Contact: Send complete ms with a cover letter. Include estimated word count. Accepts queries by e-mail. Responds in 1 week to mss. Send SASE for reply, return of ms or send a disposable copy of ms. Accepts simultaneous submissions. Sample copy for $15.

Payment/Terms: Pays average of 1¢/word, minimum $10 and 1 contributor's copy. Pays on publication for one-time rights.

Advice: "Excite me!"

[N] ⬤ ◎ HARD ROW TO HOE, Potato Eyes Foundation, P.O. Box 541-I, Healdsburg CA 95448. (707)433-9786. **Contact:** Joe E. Armstrong, editor. Magazine: 8½×11; 12 pages; 60 lb. white paper; illustrations; photos. "We look for literature of rural life, including environmental and Native American subjects. Book reviews, short story, poetry and a regular column. So far as we know, we are the only literary newsletter that features rural subjects." Triannual. Estab. 1982. Circ. 200.

Needs: "Rural, environmental, Native American. Receives 5-10 unsolicited mss/month. Accepts 2-3 mss/issue; 6-8 mss/year. Publishes ms 10 months after acceptance. **Publishes 2-3 new writers/year.** Recently published work by Margaret Karmazin, Daniel Curtaina, Dorothy L. Bussemer and Michael Leslie. Length: 2,000 words maximum; average length: 1,200 words. Publishes short shorts. Average length: 600 words. Also publishes literary essays and poetry. Often comments on rejected mss.

How to Contact: Send complete ms with a cover letter. Include brief bio. Responds in 2 weeks to queries; 6 weeks to mss. Send SASE for return of ms or send a disposable copy of ms and #10 SASE for reply only. Accepts multiple submissions. Sample copy for $2. Guidelines for SASE. Reviews novels, short story collections and nonfiction books (of rural subjects). Send review copies to editor.

Payment/Terms: Pays 2 contributor's copies; additional copies $2. Pays on publication for one-time rights.

Advice: "Work must exhibit authenticity of rural subjects."

[N] $ ⬤ HARPUR PALATE at Binghamton University, Dept. of English, Binghamton University, P.O. Box 6000, Binghamton NY 13902-6000. (607)355-4761. Website: http://go.to/hpjournal.com (includes guideline and contest information, editors' contact information, subscription information, and sample fiction and poetry content from current and past issues). **Contact:** Fiction Editor. Magazine: 5½×8; 80-120 pages; coated or uncoated paper; 80 lb. coated or uncoated cover; illustrations; photos. "We believe writers should explore different genres to tell their stories. *Harpur Palate* accepts pieces regardless of genre, as long as the works pay attention to craft, structure, language, and the story is well told." Semiannual. Estab. 2001. Circ. 400.

Needs: Adventure, ethnic/multicultural, experimental, fantasy, historical, horror, humor/satire, literary, mainstream, mystery/suspense, science fiction. "Also magical realism, metafiction, slipstream, fiction blurring genre boundaries that might have trouble finding a home somewhere else. No solipsistic or self-centered/pretentious fiction, erotica, pornography, excessive profanity, or shock value for shock value's sake. No fiction that reads like autobiography." Receives 50 unsolicited mss/month. Accepts 5-10 mss/issue; 10-20 mss/year. Does not read mss March 16-July 31 and October 16-December 31. Publishes ms 2 months after acceptance. **Publishes 20% new writers/year.** Recently published work by Ilsa J. Bick, Candi Chu, Jarret Keene, Leigh Kirkland and Josh November. Length: 250-8,000 words; average length: 2,000-4,000 words. Publishes short shorts. Average length: 500-750 words. Also publishes poetry. Sometimes comments on rejected mss.

How to Contact: Send complete ms with a cover letter. "Include e-mail address on cover if have one. We don't accept e-mail submissions yet; this may change soon. Submitters should check our guideline information on the website." Include estimated word count, brief bio, list of publications (OK if don't have any). Responds in 2 weeks to queries; 3 months (hopefully sooner) to mss. Send SASE for return of ms or send a disposable copy of ms and #10 SASE for reply only. Accepts simultaneous submissions (please note this in cover letter), multiple submissions (sent in separate envelopes) and short shorts (up to 1,500 words). Sample copy for $7.50. Guidelines for SASE, by e-mail or on website.

Payment/Terms: Pays $5-20 (when funding is available) and 2 contributor's copies; additional copies $5. Pays on publication for first North American serial and electronic rights. Sponsors contest: John Gardner Memorial Prize for Fiction. $500 prize and publication in summer issue of *Harpur Palate*. See the listing in Contests section, page 503.

Advice: "There's nothing new under the sun, but we're looking for stories that do inventive things with fiction. We don't try to define what 'art' is or put limitations on what 'art' can be, and we try to have an eclectic mix of genre, mainstream, and experimental works in every issue. The editorial board chooses manuscripts during final selection meetings after the reading period deadlines. Most of us are writers and know what it's like to wait for editorial responses to arrive in the mailbox. If we would like to hold your fiction manuscript for final selection, we will inform you. Always send a professionally written cover letter and a clean manuscript with no typos or grammatical errors. No matter how good the story, sloppy presentation always makes a terrible first impression. We are always interested in seeing literary speculative fiction and literary mystery/suspense as well as more mainstream stories."

🖼✅ $⊘ THE HARPWEAVER, Harpweaver, Brock University, St. Catherines, Ontario L2S 3A1 Canada. Phone: (905)688-5550, ext. 3472. Fax: (905)688-4461. E-mail: harpweav@spartan.or.brocku.ca. **Contact:** Co-editor. Magazine: 5½×8½; 100-128 pages; illustrations; photos. Publishes short fiction, reviews, poetry and visual arts for a general, literate audience. Semiannual. Estab. 1996. Circ. 700.

Needs: Welcomes all categories and styles of fiction. Receives 10-15 mss/month. Accepts 2-3 mss/issue; 4-6 mss/year. Publishes ms 3 months after acceptance. **Publishes 5-6 new writers/year.** Recently published work by Nonalesia Earle, Joy Howit Nann, Richard Scarsbrook. Length: 5,000 words maximum. Publishes short shorts. Also publishes poetry.

How to Contact: Send complete ms with a cover letter. Accepts submissions by e-mail or on disk. Include estimated word count, brief bio and list of publications. Responds in 2 months to mss. Send SASE. Accepts multiple submissions. Sample copy for $4. Guidelines by e-mail. Reviews novels, short story collections and nonfiction books of interest to writers.

Payment/Terms: Pays $10 minimum. Pays on publication for one-time rights. Not copyrighted.

🅽 ⊘ HAWAII PACIFIC REVIEW, Hawaii Pacific University, 1060 Bishop St., Honolulu HI 96813. (808)544-0262. Fax: (808)544-0862. E-mail: pwilson@hpu.edu. Website: www.hpu.edu. **Contact:** Patrice M. Wilson, editor. Magazine: 6×9; 100 pages; glossy coated cover. "*Hawaii Pacific Review* is looking for poetry, short fiction, and personal essays that speak with a powerful and unique voice. We encourage experimental narrative techniques and poetic styles, and we welcome works in translation." Annual.

Needs: Ethnic/multicultural (general), experimental, fantasy, feminist, historical (general), humor/satire, literary, mainstream, regional (Pacific), translations. "Open to all types as long as they're well done. Our audience is adults, so nothing for children/teens." Receives 25-40 unsolicited mss/month. Accepts 5-10 mss/year. Does not read mss January-August each year. Publishes ms 10 months after acceptance. **Publishes 1-2 new writers/year.** Recently published work by Rosemary Edghill, D. Prinzo and Stephen Dixon. Length: 250-5,000 words. Publishes short shorts. Also publishes literary essays and poetry. Sometimes comments on rejected mss.

How to Contact: Send complete ms with a cover letter. Include estimated word count, brief bio and list of publications. Responds in 2 weeks to queries; up to 15 weeks to mss. Send SASE for return of ms or send a disposable copy of ms and #10 SASE for reply only. Accepts simultaneous submissions (must be cited in the cover letter). Sample copy for $5.

Payment/Terms: Pays 2 contributor's copies; additional copies $4. Pays on publication for first North American serial rights.

Advice: "We look for the unusual or original plot; prose with the texture and nuance of poetry. Character development or portrayal must be unusual/original; humanity shown in an original insightful way (or characters); sense of humor where applicable. Be sure it's a draft that has gone through substantial changes, with supervision from a more experienced writer if you're a beginner."

✅ $⊘ 🏆 HAYDEN'S FERRY REVIEW, NSSWM Box 871502, Arizona State University, Tempe AZ 85287-1502. (480)965-1243. Fax: (480)965-2229. E-mail: hfr@asu.edu. Website: www.haydensferryreview.org. **Contact:** Fiction Editor. Editors change every 1-2 years. Magazine: 6×9; 128 pages; fine paper; illustrations; photos. "Contemporary material by new and established writers for a varied audience." Semiannual. Estab. 1986. Circ. 1,300.

● Work from *Hayden's Ferry Review* has been selected for inclusion in *Pushcart Prize* anthologies. *Hayden's Ferry Review* was ranked #47 on *Writer's Digest*'s Fiction 50 list of top markets for fiction writers.

Needs: Contemporary, experimental, literary, prose poem, regional. Possible special fiction issue. Receives 250 unsolicited mss/month. Accepts 5 mss/issue; 10 mss/year. Publishes mss 3-4 months after acceptance. Published work by T.C. Boyle, Raymond Carver, Ken Kesey, Rita Dove, Chuck Rosenthal and Rick Bass. Length: No preference. Publishes short shorts. Also publishes literary essays.
How to Contact: Send complete ms with cover letter. Responds in up to 5 months from deadline to mss. SASE. Sample copy for $6. Guidelines for SAE. "Please, no electronic submissions."
Payment/Terms: Pays $25/page with a maximum of $100 and 2 contributor's copies. Acquires first North American serial rights. Sends page proofs to author.

⚑ HEArt, Human Equity Through Art, HEArt, P.O. Box 81038, Pittsburgh PA 15217-0538. (412)244-0122. Fax: (412)244-0210. E-mail: dhmorrow@ix.netcom.com. Website: www.trfn.clpgh.org/heart/. **Contact:** Daniel H. Morrow, fiction editor. Literary magazine: 7½×5; 80 pages; 60 lb. offset paper, 80 lb. cardstock cover, illustrations; photos. "HEArt is the nation's only journal of contemporary literature and art devoted to confronting discrimination and promoting social justice." Triannual. Estab. 1997. Circ. 1,000. Member, CLMP.
Needs: Ethnic (general), feminist, gay, lesbian, activist literature. Receives 6 unsolicited mss/month. Accepts 0-1 mss/issue; 2-3 mss/year. Publishes ms 3 months after acceptance. Recently published work by Daryl Glenn and C.M. Largey. Length: 7,000 words; average length: 2,500. Publishes short shorts. Average length: 500 words. Also publishes literary essays, literary criticism and poetry.
How to Contact: Send complete ms with cover letter. Accepts mss by e-mail, fax and disk. Include estimated word count and brief bio with submission. Responds in 2 months. Send SASE for return of ms or disposable copy of ms and #10 SASE for reply only. Accepts simultaneous and multiple submissions. Sample copy for $8. Reviews novels, short story collections and nonfiction books.
Payment/Terms: Pays $40 and 2 contributor's copies; additional copies for $5. Payment on publication for first North American serial rights. Sponsors contest: see website or write with SASE for contest guidelines.

☑ ◐ $ ◎ THE HEARTLANDS TODAY, The Firelands Writing Center, Firelands College of BGSU, Huron OH 44839. (419)433-5560. Website: www.theheartlandstoday.net. Editors: Larry Smith, Nancy Dunham, Connie W. Everett, David Shevin and Zita Sodeika. **Contact:** Fiction Editor. Magazine: 6×9; 160 pages; b&w illustrations; 15 photos. *Material must be set in the Midwest.* "We prefer material that reveals life in the Midwest today for a general, literate audience." Annual. Estab. 1991.
Needs: Ethnic, humor, literary, mainstream, regional (Midwest). Receives 15 unsolicited mss/month. Accepts 6 mss/issue. Does not read mss August-December. "We edit between January 1 and June 5. Submit then." 2002 theme is "A Life's Work"; 2003 theme is "Our Natural World." Publishes ms 6 months after acceptance. Published work of Wendell Mayo, Tony Tomassi, Gloria Bowman. Length: 4,500 words maximum. Also publishes literary essays, poetry. Sometimes critiques rejected mss.
How to Contact: Send complete ms with cover letter. Responds in 2 months to mss. Send SASE for ms, not needed for query. Accepts simultaneous submissions, if noted. Sample copy for $5. "We edit January to June. June 5th deadline."
Payment/Terms: Pays $10-20 and 2 contributor's copies. Pays on publication for first rights.
Advice: "We look for writing that connects on a human level, that moves us with its truth and opens our vision of the world. If writing is a great escape for you, don't bother with us. We're in it for the joy, beauty or truth of the art. We look for a straight, honest voice dealing with human experiences. We do not define the Midwest, we hope to be a document of the Midwest. If you feel you are writing from the Midwest, send your work to us. We look first at the quality of the writing."

◐ ◎ HEAVEN BONE, Heaven Bone Press, Box 486, Chester NY 10918. (914)469-9018. E-mail: heavenbone@aol.com. **Contact:** Steven Hirsch and Kirpal Gordon, editors. Magazine: 8½×11; 96-116 pages; 60 lb. recycled offset paper; full color cover; computer clip art, graphics, line art, cartoons, halftones and photos scanned in tiff format. "Expansive, fine surrealist and experimental literary, earth and nature, spiritual path. We use current reviews, essays on spiritual and esoteric topics, creative stories. Also: reviews of current poetry releases and expansive literature." Readers are "scholars, surrealists, poets, artists, musicians, students." Annual. Estab. 1987. Circ. 2,500.
Needs: Esoteric/scholarly, experimental, fantasy, psychic/supernatural/occult, regional, spiritual. "No violent, thoughtless, exploitive or religious fiction." Receives 45-110 unsolicited mss/month. Accepts 5-15 mss/issue; 12-30 mss/year. Publishes ms 2 weeks-10 months after acceptance. **Publishes 3-4 new writers/year.** Published work by Keith Abbott and Stephen-Paul Martin. Length: 1,200-5,000 words; average length: 3,500 words. Publishes short shorts. Also publishes literary essays, literary criticism, poetry. Sometimes critiques rejected mss.
How to Contact: Query first; send complete ms with cover letter. Include short bio of recent activities. Responds in 3 weeks to queries; up to 10 months to mss. Send SASE for reply or return of ms. Accepts reprint submissions. Accepts electronic submissions via "Apple Mac versions of Macwrite, Microsoft Word or Writenow 3.0." Sample copy for $10. Guidelines for SASE. Reviews novels and short story collections.

Payment/Terms: Pays in contributor's copies; charges for extras. Acquires first North American serial rights. Sends galleys to author, if requested.

Advice: "Read a sample issue first. Our fiction needs are temperamental, so please query first before submitting. We prefer shorter fiction. Do not send first drafts to test them on us. Please refine and polish your work before sending. Always include SASE. We are looking for the unique, unusual and excellent."

N HICK AND THE BLACKMAN, H.B. Press, 213 Country Club Dr., Cape Girardeau MO 53701. Website: www.geocities.com/Blackhick2000/intro.com. **Contact:** Dan Crocker and Dave Taylor, editors. Literary magazine: 40 pages; cardstock cover; illustrations; photos. "We like humor that subverts stereotypes." Quarterly. Estab. 2000. Circ. 200.

Needs: Erotica, ethnic, experimental, gay, horror (psychological), humor satire, lesbian, literary. "No racist or homophobic fictions." Receives 20 unsolicited mss/month. Accepts 2 mss/issue; 8 mss/year. Publishes ms 6 months after acceptance. **Publishes 4 new writers/year.** Recently published work by Gerald Locklin, Hugh Fox and Nate Graziano. Average length: 6,000 words. Publishes short shorts. Average length: 500 words. Also publishes literary essays, literary criticism and poetry. Sometimes comments on rejected mss.

How to Contact: Send complete ms with cover letter. Include brief bio with submission. Responds in 2 months. Send SASE for return of ms or disposable copy of ms and #10 SASE for reply only. Accepts simultaneous, previously published and multiple submissions. Sample copy for free with SASE (8×10 SASE with $1.01 postage). Guidelines for SASE. Reviews novels, short story collections and nonfiction books.

Payment/Terms: Pays 1 contributor's copy; send SASE for additional copies. Acquires one-time rights. Not copyrighted.

Advice: "Fiction should have a voice of its own. Be bold. We do not pay attention to trends."

○ THE HIGGINSVILLE READER, The Higginsville Writers, P.O. Box 141, Three Bridges NJ 08887. (908)788-0514. E-mail: hgvreader@yahoo.com. **Contact:** Frank Magalhaes, Amy Finkenaur and Kathe Palka, editors. Magazine: 7×7½; 16 pages; 20 lb. white paper; illustrations; photos. "*HR* is a literary quarterly geared to a general adult audience. Though small, our distribution is national as are our contributors. We print the best short fiction, essays and poetry culled from the submissions received. We have eclectic tastes and print a broad range of styles." Quarterly. Estab. 1991. Circ. 200.

Needs: Humor/satire, literary, mainstream, translations. "No young adult/teen, children's/juvenile, senior citizen/retirement." Receives 3-10 unsolicited mss/month. Accepts 2 mss/issue; 6-8 mss/year. Publishes ms 1 year after acceptance. **Publishes 1 new writer/year.** Recently published work by Jim Meirose, Barbara F. Lefcowitz, Jorge Zentner translated by Mark Ostrowski, and Mark Levy. Length: 3,500 words maximum; average length: 1,500-2,500 words. Publishes short shorts. Also publishes creative nonfiction, memoir and poetry. Sometimes comments on rejected mss.

How to Contact: Send complete ms with a cover letter. Accepts submissions by e-mail. Include estimated word count and brief bio. Responds in 2 weeks to queries; 3 months to mss. Send SASE for return of ms or send a disposable copy of ms and #10 SASE for reply only. Accepts simultaneous submissions and previously published work but requires that both paper as well as Internet and electronic publishing history be disclosed. "Accepts multiple submissions but no more than 3 works at a time. Require notification on simultaneous submissions." Sample copy for $1.50 plus 75¢ foreign postage. Guidelines for SASE or by e-mail.

Payment/Terms: Pays 1 contributor's copy; additional copies $1.50 or 8 copies for $10, 20 copies for $20. Pays on publication for one-time rights. Not copyrighted.

Advice: "Read the best writers of today. Learn to edit and refine your work ruthlessly, and without remorse. Be familiar with an editor's tastes before submitting."

$○ HIGH PLAINS LITERARY REVIEW, 180 Adams St., Suite 250, Denver CO 80206. Phone/fax: (303)320-6828. Editor-in-Chief: Robert O. Greer, Jr. **Contact:** Fiction Editor. Magazine: 6×9; 135 pages; 70 lb. paper; heavy cover stock. "The *High Plains Literary Review* publishes poetry, fiction, essays, book reviews and interviews. The publication is designed to bridge the gap between high-caliber academic quarterlies and successful commercial reviews." Triannually. Estab. 1986. Circ. 2,200.

Needs: Most pressing need: outstanding essays, serious fiction, contemporary, humor/satire, literary, mainstream, regional. No true confessions, romance, pornographic, excessive violence. Receives approximately 400 unsolicited mss/month. Accepts 4-6 mss/issue; 12-18 mss/year. Publishes ms usually 6 months after acceptance. **Published new writers within the last year.** Published work by Naton Leslie, Tony Ardizzone, Cris Mazza and Gordon Weaver. Length: 1,500-8,000 words; average length: 4,200 words; prefers 3,000-6,000 words. Also publishes literary essays, literary criticism, poetry. Occasionally critiques rejected mss.

How to Contact: Send complete ms with cover letter. Include brief publishing history. Responds in 4 months. Send SASE for reply or return of ms. Accepts simultaneous submissions. Sample copy for $4.

Payment/Terms: Pays $5/page for prose and 2 contributor's copies. Pays on publication for first North American serial rights. "Copyright reverts to author upon publication." Sends copy-edited proofs to the author.

Advice: "*HPLR* publishes *quality* writing. Send us your very best material. We will read it carefully and either accept it promptly, recommend changes or return it promptly. Do not start submitting your work until you learn the basic tenets of the game including some general knowledge about how to develop characters and plot and how to submit a manuscript. I think the most important thing for any new writer interested in the short story form is to have a voracious appetite for short fiction, to see who and what is being published, and to develop a personal style."

HILL AND HOLLER: Southern Appalachian Mountains, Seven Buffaloes Press, P.O. Box 249, Big Timber MT 59011. **Editor:** Art Coelho. Magazine: 5½×8½; 80 pages; 70 lb. offset paper; 80 lb. cover stock; illustrations; photos rarely. "I use mostly rural Appalachian material: poems and stories, and some folklore and humor. I am interested in heritage, especially in connection with the farm." Annual. Published special fiction issue. Estab. 1983. Circ. 750.
Needs: Contemporary, ethnic, humor/satire, literary, regional, rural America farm. "I don't have any prejudices in style, but I don't like sentimental slant. Deep feelings in literature are fine, but they should be portrayed with tact and skill." Receives 10 unsolicited mss/month. Accepts 4-6 mss/issue. Publishes ms 6 months-1 year after acceptance. Length: 2,000-3,000 words average. Also publishes short shorts of 500-1,000 words.
How to Contact: Query first. Responds in 1 month to queries. SASE. Sample copy for $7.75 postpaid.
Payment/Terms: Pays in contributor's copies. Acquires first North American serial rights "and permission to reprint if my press publishes a special anthology." Sometimes sends galleys to author.
Advice: "In this Southern Appalachian rural series I can be optimistic about fiction. Appalachians are very responsive to their region's literature. I have taken work by beginners that had not been previously published. Be sure to send a double-spaced clean manuscript and SASE. I have the only rural press in North America; maybe even in the world. So perhaps we have a bond in common if your roots are rural."

HINDSIGHT, A journal of short stories and essays, Maple Leaf Press, P.O. Box 313, Piscataway NJ 08855-0313. E-mail: mapleleafpress@aol.com. **Contact:** Lawrence J. Imboden, editor. Magazine: 5½×8½; 96 pages; 20 lb. paper; cardstock cover. "*Hindsight* publishes short stories and essays, preferably by new, unpublished/underpublished writers of all ages—college students, senior citizens who have written for years but have never attempted to be published. It publishes unknown writers of talent trying to establish their writing careers. It gives new talents a chance to be heard, a chance the large, well-established fiction magazines seldom offer. And it distributes the magazine to bookstores free." Annual. Estab. 2002.
Needs: Family saga, literary, mainstream, young adult/teen (easy-to-read, problem novels, sports, coming of age). "No action/adventure, children's stories, erotica, gothic, romance, science fiction, vampire stories." Accepts 6-12 mss/issue. Publishes ms up to 1 year after acceptance. **Publishes 6-10 new writers/year.** Length: 1,500-7,000 words; average length: 4,000 words. Also publishes literary essays. Often comments on rejected mss.
How to Contact: Send complete ms with a cover letter. Include estimated word count and brief bio. Responds in 1 month to queries; 4 months to mss. SASE. Sample copy for 10×13 SASE. Guidelines for SASE. Reviews short story collections. Send review copies to Lawrence Imboden, editor.
Payment/Terms: Pays up to $25 and 1-3 contributor's copies. Pays on publication for first North American serial rights.
Advice: "There must be a clear conflict/goal, a major decision to be made by the protagonist, or a significant change in attitude/behavior. Strong, sympathetic, active protagonist a must—realistic dialogue. Write the kind of stories that you enjoy reading. Submit stories that mean something to you. The readers will feel your passion. Go to bookstores and read the other fiction anthologies/magazines. Learn the value of patience, of resting your story for a month and rereading it. Too many publications reject quality stories because of a restrictive word count policy. *Hindsight* will publish any short story of quality regardless of its size, never rejecting a powerful work because it won't fit, nor will we ask a writer to make major cuts to make it fit. New writers with talent but no publications to their credit are not published enough. *Hindsight* will help correct this for the new writers."

THE HUNTED NEWS, The Subourban Press, P.O. Box 9101, Warwick RI 02889-9101. (401)826-7307. **Contact:** Mike Wood, editor. Magazine: 8½×11; 30-35 pages; photocopied paper. "I am looking for good writers in the hope that I can help their voices be heard. Like most in the small press scene, I just wanted to create another option for writers who otherwise might not be heard." Annual. Estab. 1991. Circ. 200.
Needs: Experimental, historical, horror, literary, mainstream/contemporary, regional, religious/inspirational, translations. "No self-impressed work, shock or experimentation for its own sake." Would like to see more religious/spiritual fiction. Receives 50-60 unsolicited mss/month. Accepts 3 mss/issue. Publishes ms within 3-4 months after acceptance. **Publishes 5 new writers/year.** Published work by Alfred Schwaid, Steve Richmond, Darryl Smyers and Charles Bukowski. Length: 700 words maximum. Publishes short shorts. Also publishes literary essays, literary criticism and poetry. Often comments on rejected mss.

How to Contact: Send complete ms with cover letter. Responds in 1 month. Send SASE for return of ms. Accepts simultaneous and reprint submissions. Sample copy for 8½ × 11 SAE and 3 first-class stamps. Guidelines free. Reviews novels or short story collections.

Payment/Terms: Pays 3-5 contributor's copies. Acquires one-time rights.

Advice: "I look for an obvious love of language and a sense that there is something at stake in the story, a story that somehow needs to be told. Write what you need to write, say what you think you need to say, no matter the subject, and take a chance and send it to me. A writer will always find an audience if the work is true."

$ ☑ **THE ICONOCLAST**, 1675 Amazon Rd., Mohegan Lake NY 10547-1804. **Contact:** Phil Wagner, editor. Journal. 8½ × 5½; 40-64 pages; 20 lb. white paper; 50 lb. cover stock; illustrations. "*The Iconoclast* is a self-supporting, independent, unaffiliated general interest magazine with an appreciation of the profound, absurd and joyful in life. Material is limited only by *its* quality and *our* space. We want readers and writers who are open-minded, unafraid to think, and actively engaged with the world." Published 6 times/year. Estab. 1992. Circ. 1,000-3,000 (special issues).

Needs: Adventure, ethnic/multicultural, humor/satire, literary, mainstream/contemporary, science fiction. Wants to see more "literary fiction with plots. Nothing militant, solipsistic, or silly. No slice of life, character studies." Receives 150 unsolicited mss/month. Accepts 3-6 mss/issue; 25-30 mss/year. Publishes ms 9-12 months after acceptance. **Publishes 8-10 new writers/year.** Recently published work by R.D.T. Byrd, Efrem Sigel and Ben Satterfield. Length: 100 words minimum; occasionally longer; 2,000-2,500 words preferred. Publishes short shorts. Also publishes essays, poetry. Sometimes comments on rejected mss.

How to Contact: Send complete ms. Responds in 1 month. Send SASE for reply, return of ms or send a disposable copy of the ms labeled as such. Sample copy for $2.50. Reviews novels and short story collections.

Payment/Terms: Pays 1¢/word and 2-5 contributor's copies; additional copies $1.50 (40% discount). Pays on acceptance for one-time rights.

Advice: "We like fiction that has something to say (and not about its author). We hope for work that is observant, intense and multi-leveled. Follow Pound's advice—'make it new.' Write what you want in whatever style you want without being gross, sensational, or needlessly explicit—then pray there's someone who can appreciate your sensibility. Read good fiction. It's as fundamental as learning how to hit, throw and catch is to baseball. With the increasing American disinclination towards literature, stories must insist on being heard. Read what is being published—then write something better—and different. Do all rewrites before sending a story out. Few editors have time to work with writers on promising stories; only polished."

☑ ☑ ☑ **THE IDAHO REVIEW**, Boise State University, English Dept., 1910 University Dr., Boise ID 83725. (208)426-1002. Fax: (208)426-5426. E-mail: mwieland@boisestate.edu. **Contact:** Mitch Wieland, editor. Magazine: 6 × 9; 180-200 pages; acid-free accent opaque paper; coated cover stock; photos. "A literary journal for anyone who enjoys good fiction." Annual. Estab. 1998. Circ. 1,000. Member, C.L.M.P.

• A story from *The Idaho Review* was reprinted in *The Pushcart Prize* anthology.

Needs: Experimental, literary. No genre fiction of any type. Receives 150 unsolicited mss/month. Accepts 5-7 mss/issue; 5-7 mss/year. "We do not read from December 16-August 31." Publishes ms 1 year after acceptance. Agented fiction 5%. **Publishes 1 new writer/year.** Recently published work by Madison Smartt Bell, Brett Lott, David Huddle and Stuart Dybek. Length: open; average length: 7,000 words. Publishes short shorts. Average length: 750 words. Also publishes literary essays and poetry. Sometimes comments on rejected mss.

How to Contact: Send complete ms with a cover letter. Include estimated word count, brief bio and list of publications. Responds in 5 months to mss. Send SASE for return of ms or send a disposable copy of ms and #10 SASE for reply only. Accepts simultaneous and multiple submissions. Sample copy for $8.95. Guidelines for SASE. Reviews novels, short story collections and nonfiction books of interest to writers.

Payment/Terms: Pays free subscription to the magazine and 5 contributor's copies; additional copies $5. Pays on publication for first North American serial rights. Sends galleys to author.

Advice: "We look for strongly crafted work that tells a story that needs to be told. We demand vision and intelligence and mystery in the fiction we publish."

N: ☑ **ILLUMINATIONS: An International Magazine of Contemporary Writing**, c/o Dept. of English, College of Charleston, 66 George St., Charleston SC 29424-0001. (843)953-1993. Fax: (843)953-3180. E-mail: lewiss@cofc.edu. Website: www.cofc.edu/Illuminations (includes writer's guidelines and information on back issues). **Contact:** Simon Lewis, editor. Magazine: 5 × 8; 80 pages; illustrations. "*Illuminations* is one of the most challengingly eclectic little literary magazines around, having featured writers from the United States, Britain and Romania as well as Southern Africa." Annual. Estab. 1982. Circ. 400.

Needs: Literary. Receives 2 unsolicited mss/month. Accepts 2 mss/year. **Publishes 1 new writer/year.** Recently published work by Klaus de Albuquerque. Length: 400-1,500. Mainly publishes poetry. Sometimes comments on or critiques rejected ms.

How to Contact: Send complete ms with a cover letter. Accepts inquiries by e-mail, fax and on disk. Include estimated word count and 50 word bio. Responds in 2 weeks to queries; 2 months to mss. Send SASE for reply, return of ms or send a disposable copy of ms. No simultaneous submissions. Sample copy for $10 and a 6×9 envelope. Guidelines free.

Payment/Terms: Pays 2 contributor's copies of current issue; 1 of subsequent issue. Acquires one-time rights.

☑ ◯ **ILLYA'S HONEY**, The Dallas Poets Community, P.O. Box 225435, Dallas TX 75222-5435. Website: www.dallaspoets.org (website is for Dallas Poets Community. *Illya's Honey* is a link). **Contact:** Ann Howells or Meghan Ehrlich, editors. Magazine: 5½×8½; 34 pages; 24 lb. paper; glossy cover; photos. "We publish poetry and flash fiction. We try to present quality work by writers who take time to learn technique—aimed at anyone who appreciates good literature." Quarterly. Estab. 1994. Circ. 125.

Needs: Ethnic/multicultural, experimental, feminist, gay, historical, humor/satire, lesbian, literary, mainstream, regional, flash fiction. Receives 10 unsolicited mss/month. Accepts 2-8 mss/year. Publishes ms 3-5 months after acceptance. **Publishes 2-3 new writers/year.** Recently published work by Paul Sampson, Susanne Bowers and Denworthy. "We accept only flash (also known as micro) fiction." Length: 200 words or less. Also publishes poetry. Sometimes comments on rejected mss.

How to Contact: Send complete ms with a cover letter. Include estimated word count and brief bio. Responds in 6 months. Send SASE for return of ms or send a disposable copy of ms and #10 SASE for reply only. Sample copy for $4. Guidelines for SASE.

Payment/Terms: Pays 1 contributor's copy; additional copies $6. Pays on publication for first North American serial rights.

Advice: "We would like to see more character studies, humor."

⊡ ⊕ $ **IMAGO**, Creative Writing & Cultural Studies, Faculty of Creative Industries, QUT, GPO Box 2434, Brisbane 4001 Australia. Phone: (07)3289 1068. Fax: (07)3864 1810. E-mail: h.horton@qut.edu.au. Website: www.imago.qut.edu.au. **Contact:** Dr. Philip Neilsen or Helen Horton. Published 3 times/year. Circ. 750. 30-50% fiction. *Imago* is a literary magazine publishing short stories, poetry, articles, interviews and book reviews.

Needs: "While content of articles and interviews should have some relevance either to Queensland or to writing, stories and poems may be on any subject. The main requirement is good writing." Length: 1,000-3,000 words; average length: 3,000 words; 2,000 words preferred.

How to Contact: "Contributions should be typed double-spaced on one side of the paper, each page bearing the title, page number and author's name. Name and address of the writer should appear on a cover page of longer mss, or on the back, or bottom, of single page submissions. A SAE and IRCs with sufficient postage to cover the contents should be sent for the return of ms or for notification of acceptance or rejection. No responsibility is assumed for the loss of or damage to unsolicited manuscripts." Accepts queries/mss by e-mail, fax. Accepts multiple submissions "but not too many." Sample copy available for $A9. Guidelines, as above, available on request.

Payment/Terms: Pays on publication at editor's discretion and depending on funding. Also provides contributor's copy.

☑ $ ◯ ⍟ **INDIANA REVIEW**, Ballantine Hall 465, 1020 E. Kirkwood Ave., Bloomington IN 47405-7103. (812)855-3439. Fax: (812)855-4253. E-mail: inreview@indiana.edu. Website: www.indiana.edu/~inrev iew/ir.html (includes writer's guidelines, excerpts from publication, back issues, subscription/back issue order form, current news, staff, supporters). **Contact:** Shannon Gibney, fiction editor. Editors change yearly. Magazine: 6×9; 160 pages; 50 lb. paper; Glatfelter cover stock. *Indiana Review* is a nonprofit literary magazine dedicated to showcasing the talents of emerging and established writers. Our mission is to offer the highest quality writing within a wide aesthetic." Semiannual. Estab. 1976. Circ. 2,000.

● *Indiana Review* received a Pushcart Prize (2001) and work published in *Indiana Review* was included in *Best New American Voices* (2001). *IR* also received an Indiana Arts Council Grant.

Needs: Ethnic, literary, regional, translations. Also considers novel excerpts. No genre fiction. "We look for stories which integrate theme, language, character and form. We like mature, sophisticated fiction which has consequence beyond the world of its narrator." Receives 200 unsolicited mss each month. Accepts 7-9 prose mss/issue. **Publishes 6-8 new writers/year.** Recently published work by Josh Pryor, Melanie Abrams, James Foley and Tim Westmoreland. Length: 1-35 magazine pages. An issue featuring the work of writers of color is scheduled for publication in May 2002 (submission deadline: December 2001). Also publishes literary essays, poetry and reviews.

How to Contact: Send complete ms with cover letter. Cover letters should be *brief* and demonstrate specific familiarity with the content of a recent issue of *Indiana Review*. SASE. Accepts simultaneous submissions (if notified *immediately* of other publication). Responds in 3 months. Publishes ms an average of 3-6 months after acceptance. Does not read mss mid-December-mid-January. Sample copy for $8. Sponsors annual $1,000 fiction and poetry contests. SASE for guidelines.

Payment/Terms: Pays $5/page and 2 contributor's copies. Acquires first North American serial rights.

Advice: "Because our editors change each year, so do our literary preferences. It's important that potential contributors are familiar with the most recent issue of *Indiana Review* via library, sample copy or subscription. Beyond that, we look for prose that is well crafted and socially relevant. Dig deep. Don't accept you first choice descriptions when you are revising. Cliché and easy images sink 90% of the stories we reject. Understand the magazines you send to—investigate!"

INTERBANG: Dedicated to perfection in the art of writing, P.O. Box 1574, Venice CA 90294. (310)450-6372. E-mail: heather@interbang.net. Website: www.interbang.net (includes back issues and writer's guide). **Contact:** Heather Hoffman, editor. Magazine: 8½×7, 30 pages; 60 lb. paper; card cover stock; illustrations; photos. Quarterly. Estab. 1995. Circ. 2,000.

Needs: Adventure, ethnic/multicultural, experimental, family saga, fantasy (space fantasy, sword and sorcery), feminist, gay, glitz, historical (general), horror (dark fantasy, futuristic, psychological, supernatural), humor/satire, lesbian, literary, mainstream, military/war, mystery/suspense (amateur sleuth, cozy, police procedural, private eye/hardboiled), New Age, psychic/supernatural/occult, regional, science fiction (hard science/technological, soft/sociological), short story collections, thriller/espionage, translations. No travel or children's. Wants to see more historical fiction, science fiction/fantasy." Receives 50 unsolicited mss/month. Accepts 5 mss/issue; 25 mss/year. Publishes ms 1 month after acceptance. Agented fiction 5%. **Publishes 50 new writers/year.** Recently published work by Sharon Mesmer, Ron Bloom, L. Fitzgerald Sjöberg. Length: 2,500 words average. Publishes short shorts. Also publishes literary essays. Sometimes comments on or critiques rejected ms.

How to Contact: Send complete ms with a cover letter. Accepts inquiries by e-mail. Include estimated word count and bio. Responds in 2 weeks to queries; 3 months to mss. Send SASE for reply, return of ms or send a disposable copy of ms. Accepts simultaneous submissions. Sample copy free. Reviews novels, short story collections and nonfiction books. Send books to editor.

Payment/Terms: Pays free subscription to the magazine, an *Interbang* T-shirt and 5 contributor's copies. Pays on publication for one-time rights.

Advice: "We're looking for well-written stories with strong, vivid descriptions, well-developed characters and complex themes. Focus on a consistent narrative style. We do not publish stories that read like a TV show. We want stories with style and depth."

$ THE IOWA REVIEW, University of Iowa, 308 EPB, Iowa City IA 52242. (319)335-0462. E-mail: iowa-review@uiowa.edu. Website: www.uiowa.edu/~iareview. Editor: David Hamilton. **Contact:** Fiction Editor. Magazine: 6×9; 200 pages; first-grade offset paper; Carolina CS1 10-pt. cover stock. "Stories, essays, poems for a general readership interested in contemporary literature." Triannual. Estab. 1970. Circ. 2,000.

Needs: "We are open to a range of styles and voices and always hope to be surprised by work we then feel we need." Receives 600 unsolicited fiction mss/month. Agented fiction less than 2%. Accepts 4-6 mss/issue, 12-18 mss/year. Does not read mss April-August. "We discourage simultaneous submissions. **Published new writers within the last year.** Recently published work by Joshua Harmon, Katherine Vaz, Mary Helen Stefaniak and Steve Tomasula. Also publishes literary essays, literary criticism, poetry.

How to Contact: Send complete ms with cover letter. "Don't bother with queries." SASE for return of ms. Responds in 4 months to mss. Publishes ms an average of 12-18 months after acceptance. Sample copy for $6. Guidelines for SASE. Reviews novels and short story collections (3-6 books/year).

Payment/Terms: Pays $10/page and 2 contributor's copies; additional copies 30% off cover price. Pays on publication for first North American serial rights.

Advice: "We have no set guidelines as to content or length; we look for what we consider to be the best writing available to us and are pleased when writers we believe we have discovered catch on with a wider range of readers. It is never a bad idea to look through an issue or two of the magazine prior to a submission."

IRIS: A Journal About Women, P.O. Box 800588, University of Virginia, Charlottesville VA 22908. (434)924-4500. E-mail: iris@virginia.edu. Coordinating Editor: Kim Roberts. **Contact:** Fiction Editor. Magazine: 8½×11; 80 pages; glossy paper; heavy cover; illustrations; artwork; photos. "Material of particular interest to women. For a feminist audience, college educated and above." Semiannual. Estab. 1980. Circ. 3,500.

Needs: Experimental, feminist, lesbian, literary, mainstream. "I don't think what we're looking for particularly falls into the 'mainstream' category—we're just looking for well-written stories of interest to women (particularly feminist women)." Receives 300 unsolicited mss/year. Accepts 5 mss/year. Publishes ms within 1 year after acceptance. **Publishes 1-2 new writers/year.** Recently published work by Sheila Thorne, Marsha Recknagel and Denise Laughlin. Length: 2,500-4,000 words average. Sometimes critiques rejected mss.

How to Contact: Send complete ms with cover letter. Include "previous publications, vocation, other points that pertain. Make it brief!" Accepts queries by e-mail. Responds in 3 months to mss. SASE. Accepts simultaneous submissions. Accepts electronic submissions via disk or e-mail. Sample copy for $5. Guidelines with SASE. Label: Fiction Editor.

Payment/Terms: Pays in contributor's copies and 1 year subscription. Acquires one-time rights.

Advice: "I select mss which are lively imagistically as well as in the here-and-now; I select for writing which challenges the reader. My major complaint is with stories that don't elevate the language above the bland sameness we hear on the television and everyday. Read the work of the outstanding women writers, such as Alice Munro and Louise Erdrich."

☑ $ ◫ ◎ **IRREANTUM, Exploring Mormon Literature**, The Association for Mormon Letters, P.O. Box 51364, Provo UT 84605. (801)714-1326. E-mail: irreantum2@cs.com. Website: www.xmission.com/~aml/ irreantum.htm (includes basic information, names of editors). **Contact:** Tory Anderson. Magazine or Zine: 8½×5½; 68-100 pages; 20 lb. paper; 20 lb. color cover; illustrations; photos. "While focused on Mormonism, *Irreantum* is a cultural, humanities-oriented magazine, not a religious magazine. Our guiding principle is that Mormonism is grounded in a sufficiently unusual, cohesive and extended historical and cultural experience that it has become like a nation, an ethnic culture. We can speak of a Mormon literature at least as surely as we can of a Jewish or Southern literature. *Irreantum* publishes stories, one-act dramas, stand-alone novel and drama excerpts, and poetry by, for or about Mormons (as well as author interviews, essays and reviews). The magazine's audience includes readers of any or no religious faith who are interested in literary exploration of the Mormon culture, mindset and worldview through Mormon themes and characters. *Irreantum* is currently the only magazine devoted to Mormon literature." Quarterly. Estab. 1999. Circ. 400.

Needs: Adventure, ethnic/multicultural (Mormon), experimental, family saga, fantasy, feminist, historical, horror, humor/satire, literary, mainstream, mystery/suspense, New Age, psychic/supernatural/occult, regional (Western USA/Mormon), religious, romance, science fiction, thriller/espionage, translations, young adult/teen. Receives 5 unsolicited mss/month. Accepts 3 mss/issue; 12 mss/year. Publishes ms 3-12 months after acceptance. **Publishes 6 new writers/year.** Recently published work by Ed Snow, Benson Parkinson, John Bennion and Marilyn Brown. Length: 1,000-7,000 words; average length: 5,000 words. Publishes short shorts. Also publishes literary essays, literary criticism and poetry. Sometimes comments on rejected mss.

How to Contact: Send complete ms with a cover letter. Accepts submissions by e-mail and disk. "Note: Submissions by other than e-mail or floppy are strongly discouraged." Include brief bio and list of publications. Responds in 2 weeks to queries; 2 months to mss. Send a disposable copy of ms and #10 SASE for reply only. Accepts simultaneous submissions, previously published work and multiple submissions. Sample copy for $5. Guidelines for e-mail. Reviews novels, short story collections and nonfiction books of interest to writers. Send review copies to AML, P.O. Box 51364, Provo UT 84605.

Payment/Terms: Pays $0-100 and 2 contributor's copies; additional copies $3. Pays on publication for one-time and electronic rights.

Advice: "*Irreantum* is not interested in didactic or polemnical fiction that primarily attempts to prove or disprove Mormon doctrine, history or corporate policy. We encourage beginning writers to focus on human elements first, with Mormon elements introduced only as natural and organic to the story. Readers can tell if you are honestly trying to explore the human experience or if you are writing with a propagandistic agenda either for or against Mormonism. For conservative, orthodox Mormon writers, beware of sentimentalism, simplistic resolutions, and foregone conclusions."

Ⓝ ⊕ $ **ISLAND**, P.O. Box 210, Sandy Bay 7006 Australia. 03 6226 2325. Fax: 03 6226 2765. E-mail: island@tassie.net.au. Website: www.islandmag.com (includes recent issue, subscription information, poetry contest). **Contact:** David Owen, editor. "*Island* seeks quality fiction, poetry, essays, articles. Our philosophy is general, with some emphasis on environment." Quarterly. Circ. 1,000.

Needs: "*Island* is a quarterly of ideas, criticism, fiction and poetry." **Publishes 10 new writers/year.** Length: 4,000 words maximum.

How to Contact: Send laser print copy where possible. Accepts mss by e-mail, fax and disk. Include a brief cover letter and SASE (or IRC). Accepts inquiries by fax and e-mail.

Payment/Terms: Pays $100 (Australian) minimum and 2 contributor's copies; additional copies free. Acquires one-time rights. Sample copy available for $8.95 (Australian), back issues $5 plus postage.

☑ $ ◫ ◎ **JAPANOPHILE**, Box 7977, Ann Arbor MI 48107. (734)930-1553. Fax: (734)930-9968. E-mail: japanophile@aol.com. Website: www.japanophile.com (includes writer's guidelines, sample fiction). **Contact:** Susan Lapp, Madeleine Vala and Jason Bredle, editors. Magazine: 5¼×8½; 58 pages; illustrations; photos. Magazine of "articles, photos, poetry, humor, short stories about Japanese culture, not necessarily set in Japan, for an adult audience, most with a college background and who like to travel." Quarterly. Estab. 1974. Circ. 800.

● Most of the work included in *Japanophile* is set in recent times, but the magazine will accept material set back as far as pre-WWII.

Needs: Adventure, historical, humor/satire, literary, mainstream, and mystery/suspense. No erotica, science fiction or horror. Published special fiction issue last year; plans another. Receives 40-100 unsolicited fiction mss/month. Accepts 12 ms/issue, 15-20 mss/year. Published work by Suzanne Kamata, Amy Chavez and Matt Malcomson. Publishes 12 previously unpublished writers/year. Length: 2,000-6,000 words; average length: 3,200 words. Also publishes essays, book reviews, literary criticism and poetry.

How to Contact: Send complete ms with SASE, cover letter, bio and information about story. Accepts queries/mss by e-mail and fax. Accepts simultaneous and reprint submissions. Responds in 2 months to mss. Sample copy for $4; guidelines for #10 SASE.

Payment/Terms: Pays $20. Pays on publication for all rights, first North American serial rights or one-time rights (depends on situation). Stories submitted to the magazine may be entered in the annual contest. *A $5 entry fee must accompany each submission* to enter contest. Prizes include $100 plus publication for the best short story. Deadline: December 31.

Advice: "We look for originality and sensitivity to cultural detail. Clarity and directness of expression make manuscripts stand out. Short stories usually involve Japanese and 'foreign' (non-Japanese) characters in a way that contributes to understanding of Japanese culture and the Japanese people. However, a *good* story dealing with Japan or Japanese cultural aspects anywhere in the world will be considered, even if it does not involve this encounter or meeting of Japanese and foreign characters. Some stories may also be published in an anthology with approval of the author and additional payment."

N **◘** **JEOPARDY, Literary Arts Magazine**, CH 132, Western Washington University, Bellingham WA 98225. (360)650-3118. E-mail: jeopardy@cc.wwu.edu. Website: jeopardy.wwu.edu (includes writer's guidelines, names of editors, short fiction, artwork, poetry, links to other online mags). **Contact:** Carter Hasegawa. Editors change every year. Magazine: 5×7; 192 pages; 70 lb. paper; glossy cover stock; illustrations; photos. "*Jeopardy Magazine*'s intended audience is an intelligent readership which enjoys risks, surprises and subtlety. Our philosophy is that reputation is nothing and words/images are everything. We focus on the best work published by local student writers coupled with the best work by established national writers." Annual. Estab. 1965. Circ. 1,500.

Needs: Contemporary, ethnic, gay, historical, lesbian, literary. No long stories. "We are not interested in conventional narratives, plot-driven fiction or formulaic genre fiction." Receives 50-100 unsolicited mss/month. Accepts 5-10 mss/year. Reading period: September 15-April 15. Publishes ms 3 months after acceptance. **Publishes 30 new writers/year.** Recently published work by Brenda Miller, Sheila Fox and J.C. Schmidt. Length: 250-5,000 words; average length: 1,500 words. Also publishes literary essays, poetry.

How to Contact: Send complete ms with cover letter and 50-word bio. SASE and disposable copy of the ms. Does not return mss. Accepts simultaneous and multiple submissions. Responds in 6 months. Sample copy for $5. Guidelines for #10 SASE.

Payment/Terms: Pays 2 contributor's copies. Acquires one-time rights.

Advice: "A clear, insightful voice and style are major considerations. Things that will get your manuscript recycled: tired representations of sex and/or death and/or angst. We like writers who take risks! Know your characters thoroughly—know why someone else would want to read about what they think or do. Then, submit your work and don't give up at initial failures. Don't send us stories about being a writer/artist and/or a college student/professor. We would like to see more fiction pieces which involve unique or unexpected situations and characters. We look for a strong voice, a willingness to take risks, and writers who are willing to push the boundaries of what's been done. Have something to say and say it well. Proofreading helps."

◎ **THE JOURNAL OF AFRICAN TRAVEL-WRITING**, P.O. Box 346, Chapel Hill NC 27514-0346. (919)929-0419. E-mail: ottotwo@email.unc.edu. Website: www.unc.edu/~ottotwo/ (includes guidelines, selected texts, table of contents). **Contact:** Amber Vogel, editor. Magazine: 7×10; 192 pages; 50 lb. paper. "*The Journal of African Travel-Writing* presents materials in a variety of genres that explore Africa as a site of narrative." Annual. Estab. 1996. Circ. 600.

● Sponsors annual award for best piece published in the journal.

Needs: Literary, translations. Accepts 1-4 mss/issue. Publishes ms up to 1 year after acceptance. Published work by Eileen Drew, Lisa Fugard and Sandra Jackson-Opoku. Also publishes literary essays, literary criticism and poetry. Sometimes comments on rejected mss.

How to Contact: Send complete ms with a cover letter. Sample copy for $6. Reviews novels and short story collections. Send books to editor.

Payment/Terms: Pays 5 contributor's copies for first rights. Sends galleys to author.

SENDING TO A COUNTRY other than your own? Be sure to send International Reply Coupons (IRC) instead of stamps for replies or return of your manuscript.

✓ $◑ **THE JOURNAL**, Dept of English, Ohio State University, 164 W. 17th St., Columbus OH 43210. (614)292-4076. Website: www.cohums.ohio-state.edu/english/journals/the_journal. **Contact:** Kathy Fagan (poetry); Michelle Herman (fiction), editors. Magazine: 6×9; 150 pages. "We are open to all forms of quality fiction and poetry." For an educated, general adult audience. Semiannual. Estab. 1973. Circ. 1,500.

Needs: No romance, science fiction or religious/devotional. Accepts 2 mss/issue. Receives approximately 100 unsolicited fiction mss/month. Usually publishes ms within 1 year of acceptance. Agented fiction 10%. **Published new writers within the last year.** Published work by Stephen Dixon, Norma Rosen, Mark Jacobs and Liza Wieland. Length: Open. Critiques rejected mss when there is time.

How to Contact: Send complete ms with cover letter. Responds within 3 months. SASE. Sample copy for $7; guidelines for SASE.

Payment/Terms: Pays $30 stipend when funds are available and contributor's copies; $7 charge for extras.

Terms: Acquires first North American serial rights. Sends galleys to author.

Advice: Mss are rejected because of "lack of understanding of the short story form, shallow plots, undeveloped characters. Cure: read as much well-written fiction as possible. Our readers prefer 'psychological' fiction rather than stories with intricate plots. Take care to present a clean, well-typed submission."

$◑ ◎ 🛇 **KALEIDOSCOPE: Exploring the Experience of Disability through Literature and the Fine Arts**, 701 S. Main St., Akron OH 44311-1019. (330)762-9755. Fax: (330)762-0912. E-mail: mshiplett @udsakron.org. Website: www.udsakron.org (includes guidelines, upcoming themes and names of editors). Editor-in-Chief: Darshan Perusek, Ph.D. Senior Editor: Gail Willmott. **Contact:** Fiction Editor. Magazine: 8½×11; 56-64 pages; non-coated paper; coated cover stock; illustrations (all media); photos. "*Kaleidoscope* Magazine explores the experiences of disability through literature and the fine arts. Unique in the field of disability studies, it is not an advocacy, rehabilitation, or independent living journal but expresses the experiences of disability from the perspective of individuals, families, healthcare professionals, and society as a whole. Each issue explores a specific theme which deals with disability. Readers include people with and without disabilities." Semiannual. Estab. 1979. Circ. 1,000.

● *Kaleidoscope* has received awards from the American Heart Association, the Great Lakes Awards Competition and Ohio Public Images.

Needs: "We look for well-developed plots, engaging characters and realistic dialogue. We lean toward fiction that emphasizes character and emotions rather than action-oriented narratives." Upcoming themes: "Disability: Mythology/Folklore" (deadline March 2002) and "Disability and the Road Less Traveled" (deadline August 2002). No fiction that is stereotypical, patronizing, sentimental, erotic, or maudlin. No romance, religious or dogmatic fiction; no children's literature. Receives 20-25 unsolicited fiction mss/month. Accepts 10 mss/year. Approximately 1% of fiction is agented. **Publishes 1 new writer/year.** Recently published work by H.H. Morris, Beverly Sheresh, John A. Broussard, Keith H. Hansen and Marcia Calhoun Forecki. Length: 5,000 words maximum. Also publishes poetry.

How to Contact: Query first or send complete ms and cover letter. Accepts queries by fax. Include author's educational and writing background and if author has a disability, how it has influenced the writing. Accepts simultaneous, previously published and multiple submissions. Responds in 1 month to queries; 6 months to mss. Sample copy for $5. Guidelines for #10 SASE.

Payment/Terms: Pays $10-125 and 2 contributor's copies; additional copies $6. Pays on publication for first rights. Reprints permitted with credit given to original publication.

Advice: "Read the magazine and get submission guidelines. We prefer that writers with a disability offer original perspectives about their experiences; writers without disabilities should limit themselves to our focus in order to solidify a connection to our magazine's purpose. Do not use stereotypical, patronizing and sentimental attitudes about disability."

◑ 🛇 **KALLIOPE, A Journal of Women's Literature & Art**, Florida Community College at Jacksonville, 3939 Roosevelt Blvd., Jacksonville FL 32205. (904)381-3511. Website: www.fccj.org/kalliope (includes guidelines, subscription information, contents of current issue, contests, cassette information, back issues, events, history and post address). Editor: Mary Sue Koeppel. **Contact:** Fiction Editor. Magazine: 7¼×8¼; 120 pages; 70 lb. coated matte paper; Bristol cover; 16-18 halftones per issue. "A literary and visual arts journal for women, *Kalliope* celebrates women in the arts by publishing their work and by providing a forum for their ideas and opinions." Short stories, short shorts, poems, plays, essays, reviews and visual art. Biannual. Estab. 1978. Circ. 1,550.

● *Kalliope* has received the Frances Buck Sherman Award from the local branch of the National League of Pen Women. The magazine has also received awards and grants for its poetry, grants from the Florida Department of Cultural Affairs and the Jacksonville Club Gallery of Superb Printing Award. Claudia Smith Brinson received an O. Henry award for "Einstein's Daughters," originally published in *Kalliope*.

Needs: "Quality short fiction by women writers." No science fiction. Accepts up to 7 mss/issue depending on length. Receives approximately 100 unsolicited fiction mss each month. **Publishes 3 new writers/year.** Recently published work by Edith Pearlman, Janice Daugharety, Susan Hubbard and Marey Gardner. Preferred length: 750-2,000 words, but occasionally publishes longer (and shorter) pieces. Also publishes poetry and short shorts. "We dedicated an entire issue to short shorts and it was very successful." Critiques rejected mss "when there is time and if requested."

How to Contact: Send complete ms with SASE and short contributor's note. No simultaneous submissions. Responds in 3 months on ms. Publishes ms an average of 1-3 months after acceptance. Sample copy: $9 for current issue; $7 for issues from '89-2001; $4 for issues from '78-'88. Reviews short story collections and novels.

Payment/Terms: Pays 2 contributor's copies or 1-years subscription. Acquires first rights. Discount for extras. "We accept only unpublished work. Copyright returned to author upon request."

Advice: "Read our magazine. The work we consider for publication will be well written and the characters and dialogue will be convincing. We like a fresh approach and are interested in new or unusual forms. Make us believe your characters; give readers an insight which they might not have had if they had not read you. We would like to publish more work by minority writers." Manuscripts are rejected because "1) nothing *happens*!, 2) it is thinly disguised autobiography (richly disguised autobiography is OK), 3) ending is either too pat or else just trails off, 4) characterization is not developed, and 5) point of view falters."

KARAMU, English Department, Eastern Illinois University, 600 Lincoln Ave., Charleston IL 61920. (217)581-6297. Editor: Olga Abella. **Contact:** Fiction Editor. Literary magazine: 5×8; 132-136 pages; illustrations; photos. "*Karamu* is a literary magazine of ideas and artistic expression independently produced by the faculty members and associates of Eastern Illinois University. Contributions of essays, fiction, poetry and artwork of interest to a broadly educated audience are welcome." Annual. Estab. 1969. Circ. 400.
• A short story published in *Karamu* received an Illinois Arts Council Award.

Needs: Adventure, ethnic/multicultural, experimental, feminist, gay, historical, humor/satire, lesbian, literary, mainstream/contemporary, regional. No pornographic, religious, or moralistic work. List of upcoming editorial themes available for SASE. Receives 60-70 unsolicited mss/month. Accepts 7-10 fiction mss/issue. Does not read mss March 1-September 1. Publishes ms 1 year after acceptance. **Publishes 3-6 new writers/year.** Recently published work by Thaddeus Rutkowski, Jan Leary, Diane Farrington and Meg Moceri. Length: 3,500 words maximum. Publishes short shorts, poetry and essays. Sometimes comments on rejected ms.

How to Contact: Query first. Include estimated word count, 1-paragraph bio and list of publications. Responds in 1 week to queries. Send SASE for reply. Accepts simultaneous submissions. Sample copy for $7.50 or $6 for back issues. Guidelines for SASE.

Payment/Terms: Pays 1 contributor's copy; additional copies at discount. Acquires one-time rights.

Advice: Looks for "development of characters, strong voice and original story line."

THE KARITOS REVIEW, Karitos Christian Arts Festival, 35689 N. Helendale Rd., Ingleside IL 60041. (847)587-9111. E-mail: robuserid@prodigy.net or bob@intersurfer.com. Website: www.karitos.com (includes writer's guidelines and information about our writer's conference). **Contact:** Gina Merritt, fiction editor. Magazine: 8½×5½; 48 pages; illustrations. "The *Karitos Review* publishes poetry, fiction and essays. Our audience is multicultural, mostly evangelical Christians involved in the arts. Though we are evangelical, not everything we publish is religious. We are especially interested in receiving material from writers whose work falls between the Christian and secular markets." Annual. Estab. 1999. Circ. 150.

Needs: Ethnic/multicultural, experimental, fantasy, historical, humor/satire, literary, mainstream, psychic/supernatural/occult, religious (general, inspirational, fantasy, mystery/suspense, thriller), science fiction, translations, western. No romance, graphic sex and nothing with anti-Christian bias. No religious stereotypes. No formulaic Christian fiction. Would like to see more "realistic, literary quality stories. Would like to see some fantasy, too." List of upcoming themes available online. Accepts 4-5 mss/issue; 4-5 mss/year. Does not read mss over the summer. Recently published work by Chris Wave, John Desjarlais and Dr. Phillip Barnhart. Length: 2,500 words maximum; average length: 1,000-1,500 words. Publishes short shorts. Also publishes literary essays and poetry. Sometimes comments on rejected mss.

How to Contact: Send complete ms with a cover letter. Accepts submissions by e-mail. Include estimated word count, brief bio, list of publications, phone number and/or e-mail address. Responds in 2 weeks to queries; 4 months to mss. Send SASE for return of ms or send a disposable copy of ms and #10 SASE for reply only. Accepts simultaneous, previously published and multiple submissions. Sample copy for $2 plus 6×9 SASE with 77¢ postage. Guidelines on website.

Payment/Terms: Pays 2-3 contributor's copies; additional copies $2. Pays on publication for one-time and first rights.

Advice: "We want quality material written from a Christian worldview—spiritual depth without didacticism. Read a sample copy. Much material that is appropriate for other Christian publications does not fit our style."

☑ ◪ ◎ **KELSEY REVIEW**, Mercer County College, P.O. Box B, Trenton NJ 08690. (609)586-4800, ext. 3326. Fax: (609)586-2318. E-mail: kelsey.review@mccc.edu. Website: www.mccc.edu (includes deadlines and writer's guidelines). **Contact:** Robin Schore, editor-in-chief. Magazine: 7 × 14; 98 pages; glossy paper; soft cover. "Must live or work in Mercer County, NJ." Annual. Estab. 1988. Circ. 1,750.

Needs: Open. Regional (Mercer County only). Receives 120 unsolicited mss/year. Accepts 24 mss/issue. Reads mss only in May. Publishes ms 1-2 months after acceptance. **Publishes 8 new writers/year.** Recently published work by Beatrice Cohen, Janet Kirk and Robert Motley. Length: 2,000 words maximum. Publishes short shorts. Also publishes literary essays, literary criticism and poetry. Always comments on rejected mss.

How to Contact: Send complete ms with cover letter. SASE for return of ms. Accepts queries/mss by e-mail. Accepts multiple submissions. Responds in 2 months. Sample copy free.

Payment/Terms: Pays 5 contributor's copies. Rights revert to author on publication.

Advice: Looks for "quality, intellect, grace and guts. Avoid sentimentality, overwriting and self-indulgence. Work on clarity, depth and originality."

$ ◪ ☑ **THE KENYON REVIEW**, Kenyon College, Gambier OH 43022. (740)427-5208. Fax: (740)427-5417. E-mail: kenyonreview@kenyon.edu. Website: www.kenyonreview.org (includes excerpts, advertising information, issue highlights, writer's guidelines, summer programs and author bios and photos). Editor: David H. Lynn. **Contact:** Fiction Editor. "Our mission is to publish best contemporary writing by established and emerging writers alike. Our audience is anyone who appreciates fine writing and literature." Triannual. Estab. 1939. Circ. 5,000.

● Work published in the *Kenyon Review* has been selected for inclusion in *Pushcart Prize* anthologies and Best American Short Stories.

Needs: Condensed/excerpted novel, contemporary, ethnic, experimental, feminist, gay, historical, humor/satire, lesbian, literary, mainstream, translations. Receives 400 unsolicited mss/month. Unsolicited mss typically read only from September 1 through March 31. Publishes ms 12-18 months after acceptance. Recently published work by Patrick White, Anesa Miller, Yvonne Jackson and Michael Dahlie. Length: 3-15 typeset pages preferred.

How to Contact: Send complete ms with cover letter. Responds to mss in 4 months. SASE. No simultaneous or electronic submissions. Sample copy for $9.

Payment/Terms: Pays $10-15/page. Pays on publication for first-time rights. Sends copyedited version to author for approval.

Advice: "We look for strong voice, unusual perspective, and power in the writing."

◎ **KEREM, Creative Explorations in Judaism**, Jewish Study Center Press, Inc., 3035 Porter St. NW, Washington DC 20008. (202)364-3006. Fax: (202)364-3806. Website: www.kerem.com. **Contact:** Sara R. Horowitz and Gilah Langner, editors. Magazine: 6 × 9; 128 pages; 60 lb. offset paper; glossy cover; illustrations; photos. "*Kerem* publishes Jewish religious, creative, literary material—short stories, poetry, personal reflections, text study, prayers, rituals, etc." Annual. Estab. 1992. Circ. 2,000

Needs: Jewish: feminist, humor/satire, literary, religious/inspirational. Receives 10-12 unsolicited mss/month. Accepts 1-2 mss/issue. Publishes ms 2-10 months after acceptance. Recently published work by Marge Piercy, William Novak and Anita Diamant. Length: 6,000 words maximum. Also publishes literary essays, poetry.

How to Contact: Send complete ms with a cover letter. Should include 1-2 line bio. Responds in 2 months to queries; 5 months to mss. Send SASE for reply, return of ms or send a disposable copy of ms. Accepts simultaneous submissions. Sample copy for $8.50.

Payment/Terms: Pays free subscription and 2-10 contributor's copies. Acquires one-time rights.

Advice: "Should have a strong Jewish content. We want to be moved by reading the manuscript!"

KESTREL, A Journal of Literature and Art, Division of Language and Literature, Fairmont State College, 1201 Locust Ave., Fairmont WV 26554-2470. (304)367-4815. Fax: (304)367-4896. E-mail: kestrel@mail.fscwv.edu. Website: www.fscwv.edu/pubs/kestrel/kestrel.html (includes issue contents, contests, guidelines, subscription forms, festival itinerary). Editor: Mary Dillow Stewart. **Contact:** Fiction Editor. Magazine: 6 × 9; 100 pages; 60 lb. paper; glossy cover; photographs. "An eclectic journal publishing the best fiction, poetry, creative nonfiction and artwork for a literate audience. We strive to present contributors' work in depth." Semiannual. Estab. 1993. Circ. 500.

Needs: Condensed/excerpted novel, literary, translations. "No pornography, children's literature, romance fiction, pulp science fiction—formula fiction in general." Upcoming themes: French/Louisiana Writers/Spring 2002; Latin Writers/Fall 2002; Writing Couples/Spring 2003. Receives 100-150 unsolicited mss/month. Acquires 10-20 mss/issue; 20-40 mss/year. Publishes ms 3-12 months after acceptance. Recently published work by Cáit R. Coogan, Sharon Dilworth, Peter Paul Sweeney and John Maher. Length: 1,500-6,000 words. Publishes short shorts. Also publishes literary essays and poetry. Sometimes comments on rejected mss.

How To Contact: Send complete ms with "short but specific" cover letter. Include list of publications. Responds in 3-6 months to mss. SASE for return of ms or disposable copy of ms. No simultaneous submissions. Accepts electronic (disk) submissions. Sample copy for $6.

Payment/Terms: Pays 5 contributor's copies. Rights revert to contributor on publication.

Advice: Looks for "maturity, grace and verve . . . whether you're 21 or 81 years old. Live with a story for a year or more before you send it anywhere, not just *Kestrel*."

✓ $ Ⓛ KIDS' HIGHWAY, Oo! What a Ride!, P.O. Box 6275, Bryan TX 77805-6275. E-mail: kidshighway@earthlink.net. Website: http://home.earthlink.net/~kidshighway/index.html (includes mission statement, updated table of contents, contest winners, contest information, writer's guidelines, short fiction, e-mail address and subscription information). Editor: Miranda Garza. **Contact:** Hector Cole Garza, fiction editor. Magazine: 8½ × 11; 22 pages; illustrations. "*Kids' Highway* is a literary magazine that has something for everyone. It has fiction for kids and a tear-out section for adults. We do publish nonfiction." Published 5 times/year. Estab. 1999.

Needs: Adventure, children's/juvenile (adventure, animal, fantasy, mystery, series), mystery/suspense (amateur sleuth, cozy), young adult/teen (adventure, fantasy/science fiction, mystery/suspense, series, western). "We are looking for young writers as well as new ones. No ghosts, magic, occult, horror, religious, political, experimental, problem novels, gay or lesbian." Accepts 5-6 mss/issue; 25-30 mss/year. Publishes ms up to 6 months after acceptance. **Publishes many new writers/year.** Recently published work by Guy Bellerant, Pamela Garza and Jill Williams. Length: children's stories, 1,200 words maximum; adult stories, 900-2,200 words. Publishes short shorts. Length: 50-400 words. Also publishes poetry. Often comments on rejected mss.

How to Contact: Send complete ms with a cover letter. "Send SASE for reply. Send disposable copy of manuscript or send adequate postage for return of manuscript." Accepts queries/mss by e-mail. Include estimated word count, 100 word maximum bio. "If student, include age in cover letter or on manuscript." Responds in 2 months. Send SASE for reply, return of ms or send a disposable copy of ms. Accepts simultaneous and multiple submissions and reprints. Sample copy for $3, 9 × 12 SAE and 3 first-class stamps. Guidelines free for #10 SASE. Reviews novels and short story collections. Send books to Miranda Garza (children's novels and juvenile fiction).

Payment/Terms: Pays ¼-½¢/word. Pays on publication for one-time, reprint rights and electronic rights. Sends galleys to author "upon request and with SASE."

Advice: "We detect enthusiasm from a writer. We love it. Leave us with a smile of warmth, fun, humor, reflection or satisfaction. Have fun!"

Ⓝ Ⓛ ▣ KIMERA: A JOURNAL OF FINE WRITING, N. 1316 Hollis, Spokane WA 99201. E-mail: kimera@js.spokane.wa.us. Website: www.js.spokane.wa.us/kimera. **Contact:** Jan Strever, editor. Electronic and print magazine. "*Kimera* attempts to meet John Locke's challenge: Where is the head with no chimeras? We seek fiction that pushes the edge in terms of language use and craft." Semiannual online; annual print version. Estab. 1995. Circ. 2,000 (online), 300 (print).

Needs: Eclectic, energetic fiction. "Nothing badly conceived; attention to the muscularity of language." No erotica. Receives 50 mss/month. Accepts 5 mss/issue. Publishes mss up to 1 year after acceptance. **Publishes new writers.** Published work by L. Lynch and G. Thomas. Publishes short shorts. Also publishes literary essays and poetry. Sometimes comments on rejected mss.

How to Contact: Send complete ms with a cover letter. Accepts mss by e-mail. Include bio. Responds in 3 weeks to queries; 3 months to mss. Send SASE for return of ms, SASE for reply only, or disposable copy of ms. Accepts simultaneous submissions. Sample copy: $5. Guidelines free.

Payment/Terms: Pays 1 contributor's copy. Pays on publication for first rights. Sponsors contest: visit website for details.

Advice: "We look for clarity of language. Read other writers and previous issues."

Ⓛ KIOSK, English Department, S.U.N.Y. at Buffalo, 306 Clemens Hall, Buffalo NY 14260. (716)645-2575. E-mail: ed-kiosk@acsu.buffalo.edu. Website: wings.buffalo.edu/kiosk (includes writer's guidelines, names of editors, representative fiction and poetry from issues). **Contact:** Kevin Grauke, editor-in-chief. Magazine: 5½ × 8½; 150 pages; 80 lb. cover; illustrations. "We seek innovative, non-formula fiction and poetry." Annual. Estab. 1986. Circ. 500.

Needs: Literary. "While we subscribe to no particular orthodoxy, we are most hospitable to stories with a strong sense of voice, narrative direction and craftsmanship." No genre fiction. Wants more experimental fiction. Receives 50 mss/month. Accepts 10-20 mss/issue. Publishes ms within 6 months of acceptance. **Published new writers within the last year.** Recently published work by Mark Jacobs, Jay Atkinson and Richard Russo. Length: 7,500 words maximum; 3,000 words preferred. Publishes short shorts, "the shorter the better." Also publishes poetry. Sometimes critiques rejected mss.

How to Contact: Send complete mss with cover letter. Accepts queries/mss by e-mail. Does not read mss June-August. Responds in 4 months to mss. SASE. Accepts simultaneous and reprint submissions. Sample copy for $5. Guidelines for SASE.

Payment/Terms: Pays in contributor's copies. Acquires one-time rights.

Advice: "First and foremost, *Kiosk* is interested in sharp writing. Make it new, but also make it worth the reader's effort. Demand our attention with the first paragraph and maintain it to the end. Read as many different journals as possible. See what people are writing and publishing."

LA KANCERKLINIKO, 162 rue Paradis, 13006 Marseille France. Phone/fax: 2-48-61-81-98. E-mail: a.lazarus-1.septier@wanadoo.fr. **Contact:** Laurent Septier, fiction editor. "An Esperanto magazine which appears 4 times annually. Each issue contains 32 pages. *La Kancerkliniko* is a political and cultural magazine." Quarterly. Circ. 300.

Needs: Science fiction. Short stories or very short novels. "The short story (or the very short novel) must be written only in esperanto, either original or translation from any other language." Wants more science fiction. **Publishes 2-3 new writers/year.** Recently published work by Mao Zifu, Manuel de Sabrea, Peter Brown and Aldo de'Giorgi. Length: 15,000 words maximum.

How to Contact: Accepts queries/mss by e-mail, fax and disk. Accepts multiple submissions.

Payment/Terms: Pays in contributor's copies. Sample copy on request with 3 IRCs from Universal Postal Union.

THE LAMPLIGHT, Beggar's Press, 8110 N. 38 St., Omaha NE 68112. (402)455-2615. E-mail: beggars press@yahoo.com. **Contact:** Richard R. Carey, publisher. Magazine: 8½×11; 60 pages; 20 lb. bond paper; 65 lb. stock cover; some illustrations; a few photos. "Our purpose is to establish a new literature drawn from the past. We relish foreign settings in the 19th century when human passions transcended computers and fax machines. We are literary but appeal to the common intellect and the mass soul of humanity." Semiannual.

Needs: Historical (general), humor/satire, literary, mystery/suspense (literary). "Settings in the past. Psychological stories. Would like to see more historical humor." Receives 120-140 unsolicited mss/month. Accepts 15 mss/issue; 30 mss/year. Publishes ms 4-12 months after acceptance. **Publishes 3 new writers/year.** Published work by James Scoffield, Fred Zydek and Ulla Pironi. Length: 500-3,500 words; 2,000 words preferred. Publishes short shorts. Length: 300 words. Also publishes literary criticism and poetry. Critiques or comments on rejected mss.

How to Contact: Send complete ms with cover letter. Include estimated word count, bio (a paragraph or two) and list of publications. Responds in 1 month to queries; 2½ months to mss. SASE. Accepts simultaneous and reprint submissions. Sample copy for $10.95, 9×12 SAE. Guidelines for #10 SASE. Reviews novels and short story collections.

Payment/Terms: Pays 1 contributor's copy. Acquires first North American serial rights.

Advice: "We deal in classical masterpieces. Every piece must be timeless. It must live for five centuries or more. We judge on this basis. These are not easy to come by. But we want to stretch authors to their fullest capacity. They will have to dig deeper for us, and develop a style that is different from what is commonly read in today's market. We promote our writers after publication."

THE LAMP-POST, of the Southern California C.S. Lewis Society, 29562 Westmont Ct., San Juan Capistrano CA 92675. (949)347-1255. E-mail: lamppost@ix.netcom.com. **Contact:** David G. Clark, editor. Magazine: 5½×8½; 34 pages; 7 lb. paper; 8 lb. cover; illustrations. "We are a literary review focused on C.S. Lewis and like writers." Quarterly. Estab. 1977. Circ. 200.

● C.S. Lewis was an English novelist and essayist known for his science fiction and fantasy featuring Christian themes. He is especially well-known for his children's fantasy, *The Chronicles of Narnia*. So far, the magazine has found little fiction suitable to its focus, although they remain open.

Needs: "Literary fantasy and science fiction for children to adults." Publishes ms 9 months after acceptance. **Publishes 3-5 new writers/year.** Recently published work by Rita Quinton and DJ Kolacki. Length: 1,000-5,000 words; average length: 2,500 words. Also publishes literary essays, literary criticism and poetry. Sometimes comments on rejected mss.

How to Contact: Query first or send complete ms with a cover letter. Accepts queries/mss by e-mail. Include 50-word bio. Responds in 2 months. Send SASE for reply, return of ms or send a disposable copy of ms. No simultaneous submissions. Accepts reprints and electronic (disk) submissions. Sample copy for $3. Guidelines for #10 SASE. Reviews fiction or criticism having to do with Lewis or in his vein. Send books to: Dr. David W. Landrum, book review editor, Cornerstone College, 1001 E. Beltline, NE, Grand Rapids MI 49525.

Payment/Terms: Pays 3 contributor's copies; additional copies $3. Acquires first North American serial rights or one-time rights.

Advice: "We look for fiction with the supernatural, mythic feel of the fiction of C.S. Lewis and Charles Williams. Our slant is Christian but we want work of literary quality. No inspirational. Is it the sort of thing Lewis, Tolkien and Williams would like—subtle, crafted fiction? If so, send it. Don't be too obvious or facile. Our readers aren't stupid."

$ 🖉 ◎ LARCOM REVIEW, The Arts and Literature of New England, The Larcom Press, P.O. Box 161, Prides Crossing MA 01965. (978)927-8707. Fax: (978)927-8904. E-mail: amp@larcompress.com. Website: www.larcompress.com. **Contact:** Susan Oleksiw, editor. Magazine: 8½×11; 160-200 pages; acid free paper; 10 pt. CIS cover; illustrations; photos. "We showcase contemporary work by writers and artists of New England as well as exploring work of earlier times. We are interested in all aspects of the six states of this region. Our audience is targeted towards New Englanders but not limited to them." Semiannual. Estab. 1999. Circ. 100. Member, American Booksellers Association.

Needs: Family saga, literary, mainstream, inspirational. "No violence, sexual themes." Receives 200-300 unsolicited mss/month. Accepts 6-10 mss/issue; 15-30 mss/year. Publishes ms 2-3 months after acceptance. **Publishes 1-2 new writers/year.** Recently published work by Susan Barrie, Kelly Brennan and Dorothy Stephens. Length: 3,000 words maximum; average length: 1,500-2,500 words. Publishes short shorts. Also publishes literary essays, literary criticism and poetry. Often comments on rejected mss.

How to Contact: Send complete ms with a cover letter or query first with article. Accepts submissions by e-mail, fax and disk. Include an estimated word count, brief bio and telephone number. Must send SASE (or IRC) for return of ms. Accepts simultaneous submissions and no more than 2 multiple submissions. Sample copy for $7. Guidelines for SASE. Reviews novels, short story collections and nonfiction books of interest to writers.

Payment/Terms: Pays $25-300 and 1 contributor's copy; additional copies discounted 50%. Pays on publication for first North American serial rights. Sends galleys to author.

[N] 💟 THE LAUREL REVIEW, Northwest Missouri State University, Dept. of English, Maryville MO 64468. (660)562-1739. E-mail: abenson@mail.nwmissouri.edu. **Contact:** Amy Benson, William Trowbridge, David Slater, Catie Rosemorgy and Beth Richards, co-editors. Associate Editors: Leigh Allison Wilson, Ann Cummins, Jim Simmerman, Jeff Mock, Randall R. Freisinger. Reviewer: Peter Makuck. Magazine: 6×9; 124-128 pages; good quality paper. "We publish poetry and fiction of high quality, from the traditional to the avant-garde. We are eclectic, open and flexible. Good writing is all we seek." Biannual. Estab. 1960. Circ. 900.

Needs: Literary and contemporary. No genre or politically polemical fiction. Accepts 3-5 mss/issue, 6-10 mss/year. Receives approximately 120 unsolicited fiction mss each month. Approximately 1% of fiction is agented. **Publishes 1-2 new writers/year.** Recently published work by Christine Sneed, Judith Kitchen and James Doyle. Length: 2,000-10,000 words. Sometimes publishes literary essays; also publishes poetry.

How to Contact: Send complete ms with SASE. No simultaneous submissions. Reading period: September 1-May 1. Responds in 4 months to mss. Publishes ms an average of 1-12 months after acceptance. Sample copy for $3.50.

Payment/Terms: Pays 2 contributor's copies and 1 year subscription. Acquires first rights. Copyright reverts to author upon request.

Advice: "Nothing really matters to us except our perception that the story presents something powerfully felt by the writer and communicated intensely to a serious reader. (We believe, incidentally, that comedy is just as serious a matter as tragedy, and we don't mind a bit if something makes us laugh out loud; we get too little that makes us laugh, in fact). We try to reply promptly, though we don't always manage that. In short, we want good poems and good stories. We hope to be able to recognize them, and we print what we believe to be the best work submitted."

○ LEAPINGS LITERARY MAGAZINE, 2455 Pinercrest Dr., Santa Rosa CA 95403-8946. (707)544-4861. Fax: (707)568-7531. E-mail: editserv@compuserve.com. Website: home.inreach.com/editserv/leapings.html (includes writer's guidelines). Editor: S.A. Warner. **Contact:** Fiction Editor. Magazine: 5×8; 40 pages; 20 lb. paper; glossy cover; illustrations; photos. "Eclectic magazine emphasizing diversity." Semiannual. Estab. 1998. Circ. 200.

Needs: Adventure, ethnic/multicultural, experimental, fantasy, feminist, humor satire, literary, mainstream, mystery/suspense, science fiction. No romance. Receives 30 unsolicited mss/month. Accepts 2 mss/issue; 4 mss/year. Publishes ms 6 months after acceptance. Less than 10% of fiction accepted is agented. **Publishes 5 new writers/year.** Publishes short shorts. Also publishes literary essays, literary criticism, poetry. Sometimes comments on rejected mss.

How to Contact: Send complete ms with a cover letter. Include estimated word count. Responds in 6 weeks. Send SASE for reply, return of ms or send a disposable copy of ms. No simultaneous submissions. Sample copy for $5. Guidelines free for #10 SASE. Reviews novels and short story collections. Send books to S.A. Warner.

Payment/Terms: Pays 2 contributor's copies; additional copies $5. Pays on publication for first rights.

Advice: Looks for "good presentation and sound writing showing the writer has worked at his/her craft. Write and rewrite and only submit it when you've made the work as crisp and clear as possible."

☑ ◑ **THE LICKING RIVER REVIEW**, University Center, Northern Kentucky University, Highland Heights KY 41099. (859)572-5812. E-mail: lrr@nku.edu. **Contact:** Andrew Miller, faculty advisor. Magazine: 7×11; 96 pages; photos. Annual. Estab. 1991. Circ. 1,500.
Needs: Experimental, literary, mainstream/contemporary. No erotica. Wants more experimental. Receives 40 unsolicited mss/month. Accepts 7-9 mss/year. Does not read mss January-August. Publishes ms 6 months after acceptance. **Publishes 2-3 new writers/year.** Recently published work by Linda Arnest, dayna mari, Judith Sroufe, Charles Edward Brooks and J.W.M. Morgan. Length: 5,000 words maximum. Publishes short shorts. Also publishes poetry.
How to Contact: Send complete ms with a cover letter. Accepts queries by e-mail. Include list of publications. Responds in 6 months to mss. SASE for return of manuscript or send disposable copy of ms. No simultaneous submissions. Sample copy for $5.
Payment/Terms: Pays 2 contributor's copies. Pays on publication.
Advice: "We look for good writing and an interesting, well-told story. Read a sample copy first. Don't do what everyone else is doing. Be fresh, original. Write what you like—it will show. Tell a story you care about and work on it every day until you love it before sending it out."

☑ ◑ **LIGHT QUARTERLY**, P.O. Box 7500, Chicago IL 60680. Website: www.lightquarterly.com. Editor: John Mella. **Contact:** Fiction Editor. Magazine: 6×9; 64 pages; Finch opaque (60 lb.) paper; 65 lb. color cover; illustrations. "Light and satiric verse and prose, witty but not sentimental. Audience: intelligent, educated, usually 'professional.' " Quarterly. Estab. 1992. Circ. 1,000.
Needs: Humor/satire, literary. Receives 10-40 unsolicited fiction mss/month. Accepts 2-4 mss/issue. Publishes ms 6-24 months after acceptance. Published work by X.J. Kennedy, J.F. Nims and John Updike. Length: 600-2,000 words; 1,200 words preferred. Publishes short shorts. Also publishes literary essays, literary criticism and poetry. Sometimes comments on rejected mss.
How to Contact: Query first. Include estimated word count and list of publications. Responds in 1 month to queries; 4 months to mss. Send SASE for reply, return of ms or send a disposable copy of ms. No simultaneous submissions. Accepts electronic submissions (disk only). Sample copy for $6 (plus $2 for 1st class). Guidelines for #10 SASE. Reviews novels and short story collections. Send review copies to review editor.
Payment/Terms: Pays contributor's copies (2 for domestic; 1 for foreign). Acquires first North American serial rights. Sends galleys to author.
Advice: Looks for "high literary quality; wit, allusiveness, a distinct (and distinctive) style. Read guidelines or issue first."

$◻ **LITERAL LATTÉ, Mind Stimulating Stories, Poems & Essays**, Word Sci, Inc., 61 E. Eighth St., Suite 240, New York NY 10003. (212)260-5532. E-mail: litlatte@aol.com. Website: www.literal-latte.com (includes excerpts, writer's guidelines, names of editors, interviews with authors, fiction not included in print version). **Contact:** Jenine & Jeff Bockman, editors. Magazine: 11×17; 24 pages; newsprint paper; 50 lb. cover; illustrations; photos. "Publishes great writing in many flavors and styles. *Literal Latté* expands the readership for literary magazines by offering free copies in New York coffeehouses and bookstores." Bimonthly. Estab. 1994. Circ. 25,000. Member, CLMP.
Needs: Experimental, fantasy, literary, science fiction. Receives 4,000 mss/month. Accepts 5-8 mss/issue; 40 mss/year. Publishes ms 6 months after acceptance. Agented fiction 5%. **Publishes 6 new writers/year.** Length: 500-6,000 words; average length: 4,000 words. Publishes short shorts. Often comments on rejected mss.
How to Contact: Send complete ms with a cover letter. Include estimated word count and brief bio. Responds in 6 months to mss. Send SASE for return of mss or send a disposable copy of ms and #10 SASE for reply only or e-mail for reply only. Accepts simultaneous and multiple submissions. Sample copy for $3. Guidelines for SASE, e-mail or check website. Reviews novels, short story collections and nonfiction books of interest to writers.
Payment/Terms: Pays 10 contributor's copies, a free subscription to the magazine and 2 gift certificates; additional copies $1. Pays on publication for first and one-time rights. Sponsors contest; guidelines for SASE, e-mail or on website.
Advice: "Words make a manuscript stand out, words beautifully woven together in striking and memorable patterns."

◑ ☑ **THE LITERARY REVIEW, An International Journal of Contemporary Writing**, Fairleigh Dickinson University, 285 Madison Ave., Madison NJ 07940. (973)443-8564. Fax: (973)443-8364. E-mail: tlr@fd u.edu. Website: www.webdelsol.com/tlr/ (includes subscription information, writer's guidelines, names of editors, chapbooks and selections from printed issues). **Contact:** Walter Cummins, editor-in-chief. Magazine: 6×9; 140

pages; professionally printed on textpaper; semigloss card cover; perfect-bound. "Literary magazine specializing in fiction, poetry, and essays with an international focus." Our audience is general with a leaning toward scholars, libraries and schools." Quarterly. Estab. 1957. Circ. 2,300.

- Work published in *The Literary Review* has been included in *Editor's Choice*, *Best American Short Stories* and *Pushcart Prize* anthologies.

Needs: Works of high literary quality only. Does not want to see "overused subject matter or pat resolutions to conflicts." Receives 50-60 unsolicited fiction mss/month. Approximately 1-2% of fiction is agented. **Publishes 80% new writers/year.** Recently published work by Irvin Faust, Todd James Pierce, Joshua Shapiro and Susan Schwartz Senstadt. Length: 5,000 words maximum. Acquires 15-20 mss/year. Does not read submissions during June, July and August. Also publishes literary essays, literary criticism, poetry. Occasionally critiques rejected mss.

How to Contact: Send 1 complete ms with SASE. "Cover letter should include publication credits." Responds in 3 months to mss. Publishes ms an average of 1½-2 years after acceptance. Considers multiple submissions. Sample copy for $5; guidelines for SASE. Reviews novels and short story collections.

Payment/Terms: Pays 2 contributor's copies; 25% discount for extras. Acquires first rights.

Advice: "We want original dramatic situations with complex moral and intellectual resonance and vivid prose. We don't want versions of familiar plots and relationships. Too much of what we are seeing today is openly derivative in subject, plot and prose style. We pride ourselves on spotting new writers with fresh insight and approach."

N ◐ ▣ **LITRAG, A magazine of poetry, fiction, art & essay**, P.O. Box 21066, Seattle WA 98111. E-mail: litrag@hotmail.com. Website: www.litrag.com. **Contact:** Derrick Hachey, editor. Magazine: 8½ × 11; 40 pages; illustrations; photos. "We publish the finest work received." Triannual. Estab. 1997. Circ. 500.

Needs: Literary. Receives 20 unsolicited mss/month. Accepts 1-2 mss/issue; 3-6 mss/year. Publishes ms 3 months after acceptance. Agented fiction 5%. **Publishes 5 new writers/year.** Recently published work by J. Robert Lennon, Rob Carney and Laura Cuthbert. Publishes short shorts. Also publishes literary essays, literary criticism and poetry.

How to Contact: Send complete ms with a cover letter. Accepts submissions by e-mail. Include list of publications. Responds in 2 weeks to queries; 1 month to mss. Send SASE. Accepts simultaneous submissions. Sample copy for $3. Guidelines for SASE. Reviews novels, short story collections and nonfiction books of interest to writers. Send review copies to James Gorley.

Payment/Terms: Pays 4 contributor's copies; additional copies $3. Pays on publication for first North American serial rights.

Advice: "Read an issue before submitting. Always send a SASE."

✔ ◐ **THE LONG STORY**, 18 Eaton St., Lawrence MA 01843. (978)686-7638. E-mail: rpbtls@aol.com. **Contact:** R.P. Burnham, editor. Magazine: 5½ × 8½; 150-200 pages; 60 lb. paper; 65 lb. cover stock; illustrations (b&w graphics). For serious, educated, literary people. No science fiction, adventure, romance, etc. "We publish high literary quality of any kind, but especially look for stories that have difficulty getting published elsewhere— committed fiction, working class settings, left-wing themes, etc." Annual. Estab. 1983. Circ. 1,200.

Needs: Contemporary, ethnic, feminist and literary. Receives 30-40 unsolicited mss/month. Accepts 6-7 mss/ issue. **50% of writers published are new.** Length: 8,000-20,000 words. Best length: 8,000-12,000 words.

How to Contact: Send complete ms with a brief cover letter. Responds in 2 months. Publishes ms an average of 3 months to 1 year after acceptance. SASE. May accept simultaneous submissions ("but not wild about it"). Sample copy for $6.

Payment/Terms: Pays 2 contributor's copies; $5 charge for extras. Acquires first rights.

Advice: "Read us first and make sure submitted material is the kind we're interested in. Send clear, legible manuscripts. We're not interested in commercial success; rather we want to provide a place for long stories, the most difficult literary form to publish in our country."

✔ ◐ ◎ **LONZIE'S FRIED CHICKEN®, A journal of accessible southern fiction & poetry**, Southern Escarpment Company, P.O. Box 189, Lynn NC 28750. E-mail: lonziesfriedchic@teleplex.net. Website: www.l onziesfriedchicken.com (includes thumbnail photos of each issue, editors notes and list of contributor's from each issue, bookstore list & writers' guidelines, subscription and ordering info, story behind the name). **Contact:** E.H. Goree, editor/publisher. Literary magazine: 5½ × 8½; about 100 pages; 65 lb. paper; cardstock cover stock; photos for cover only. "*Lonzie's Fried Chicken* publishes the best work by regional writers and poets. Our focus is to promote both new and established writers. Our growing subscribers' list contains readers from all parts of the US, from all walks of life. *Lonzie's* is an independent publication, funded by subscriptions and bookstore sales." Semiannual. Estab. 1998. Circ. 1,000.

Needs: Historical (general), humor/satire, literary, mainstream, regional (southern US themes). "No gore, hate, erotica, fantasy, science fiction, no essays about your great aunt's funeral." Receives 150 unsolicited mss/month.

Accepts 10-15 mss/issue; 20-30 mss/year. Publishes ms 1-6 months after acceptance. **Publishes 25 new writers/ year.** Recently published work by Beth Boswell Jacks, Charles Price, Keith Flynn and Leslie Bourke. Length: 1,000-4,000 words; average length: 2,500 words. Publishes short shorts; average length: 200 words. Also publishes poetry. Only comments on rejected ms upon request and if time permits.

How to Contact: Send complete ms with cover letter. Submit by regular mail only. Responds in 4 months to mss. Send SASE for return of ms or send disposable copy of ms and #10 SASE for reply only. Accepts simultaneous submissions if notified and multiple submissions. Sample copy for $6. Guidelines for SASE.

Payment/Terms: Pays 3 contributor's copies; additional copies $6. Pays on publication for first rights and anthology.

Advice: "We look for subtlety and humor, rejecting the quaint and too-cute. We want your well-written short and short-short stories and novel excerpts with a feel for the region. Writers don't have to live in or be from the South; some of our favorite pieces were written by transplants, some by folks who merely drove through the South! We are interested in work by all writers who write southern-style pieces. Send only your best work."

LOST AND FOUND TIMES, Luna Bisonte Prods, 137 Leland Ave., Columbus OH 43214. (614)846-4126. **Contact:** John M. Bennett, editor. Magazine: 5½×8½; 56 pages; good quality paper; good cover stock; illustrations; photos. Theme: experimental, avant-garde and folk literature, art. Published irregularly (twice yearly). Estab. 1975. Circ. 375.

Needs: Contemporary, experimental, literary, prose poem. Prefers short pieces. The editor would like to see more short, extremely experimental pieces. "No 'creative writing' workshop stories." Also publishes poetry. Accepts approximately 2 mss/issue. **Published new writers within the last year.** Published work by Spryszak, Steve McComas, Willie Smith, Rupert Wondolowski, Al Ackerman.

How to Contact: Query with clips of published work. SASE. No simultaneous submissions. Responds in 1 week to queries, 2 weeks to mss. Sample copy for $6.

Payment/Terms: Pays 1 contributor's copy. Rights revert to authors.

LOUISIANA LITERATURE, A Review of Literature and Humanities, Southeastern Louisiana University, SLU 792, Hammond LA 70402. (504)549-5783. Fax: (504)549-5021. E-mail: ngerman@selu.edu. Website: www.selu.edu. Editor: Jack Bedell. **Contact:** Norman German, fiction editor. Magazine: 6¾×9¾; 150 pages; 70 lb. paper; card cover; illustrations. "Essays should be about Louisiana material; preference is given to fiction and poetry with Louisiana and Southern themes, but creative work can be set anywhere." Semiannual. Estab. 1984. Circ. 400 paid; 500-700 printed.

Needs: Literary, mainstream, regional. "No sloppy, ungrammatical manuscripts." Receives 100 unsolicited fiction mss/month. Accepts mss related to special topics issues. May not read mss June through July. Publishes ms 6-12 months maximum after acceptance. **Publishes 4 new writers/year.** Recently published work by Anthony Bukowski, Tim Parrish, Robert Phillips and Andrew Otis Haschemeyer. Length: 1,000-6,000 words; 3,500 words preferred. Also publishes literary essays (Louisiana themes), literary criticism, poetry. Sometimes comments on rejected mss.

How to Contact: Send complete ms. Responds in 3 months to mss. SASE. Sample copy for $8. Reviews novels and short story collections (mainly those by Louisiana authors).

Payment/Terms: Pays usually in contributor's copies. Acquires one-time rights.

Advice: "Cut out everything that is not a functioning part of the story. Make sure your manuscript is professionally presented. Use relevant specific detail in every scene. We love detail, local color, voice and craft. Any professional manuscript stands out."

THE LOUISIANA REVIEW, % Division of Liberal Arts, Louisiana State University at Eunice, P.O. Box 1129, Eunice LA 70535. (337)550-1328. E-mail: mgage@lsue.edu. **Contact:** Dr. Maura Gage and Ms. Barbara Deger, editors. Magazine: 7½×11; 124 pages; glossy cover; illustrations; photos. "While we will accept some of the better works submitted by our own students, we prefer excellent work by Louisiana writers as well as those outside the state who tell us their connection to it." Annual. Estab. 1999. Circ. 500-700.

Needs: Ethnic/multicultural (Cajun or Louisiana culture), historical (Louisiana-related or setting), regional (Louisiana), romance (gothic). Receives 25 unsolicited mss/month. Accepts 5-7 mss/issue. Does not read mss April-December. Publishes ms up to 11 months after acceptance. Recently published work by Roberto Ferrar, David Palling and Susan LeJeune. Length: 1,000-3,000 words; average length: 2,000 words. Publishes short shorts. Also publishes poetry. Sometimes comments on rejected mss.

How to Contact: Send complete ms with a cover letter. Accepts submissions by disk (with a hard copy attached, Microsoft Word only). Include letter stating connection to Louisiana. Responds in 5 weeks to queries; 10 weeks to mss. Send SASE (or IRC) for return of ms. Accepts simultaneous submissions, previously published work and multiple submissions. Sample copy for $3. Reviews novels, short story collections and nonfiction books of interest to writers.

Payment/Terms: Pays 1-2 contributor's copies; additional copies $3. Pays on publication for one-time rights. Not copyrighted (but has an ISSN #).
Advice: "We do like to have fiction play out visually as a film would rather than static and undramatred."

☑ ◉ **THE LOUISVILLE REVIEW**, College of Arts and Sciences, Spalding University, 851 S. Fourth St., Louisville KY 40203. (502)585-9911, ext. 2767. E-mail: louisvillereview@spalding.edu. Website: www.louisville review.org. **Contact:** Sera Jeter Naslund, editor. Literary magazine. "We are a literary journal seeking original stories with fresh imagery and vivid language." Semiannual. Estab. 1976.
Needs: Literary. Receives 25-30 unsolicited mss/month. Accepts 4-6 mss/issue; 8-12 mss/year. Publishes ms 6 months after acceptance. **Publishes 2-4 new writers/year.** Recently published work by Maura Stanton, Ursula Hegi, Robin Lippincott, Jhumpa Lahiri. Publishes short shorts. Also publishes literary essays and poetry. Sometimes comments on rejected mss.
How to Contact: Send complete ms with cover letter. Include estimated word count, brief bio and list of publications. Accepts multiple submissions. Responds in 6 months to queries and mss. Send SASE for return of ms or send disposable copy of ms and #10 SASE for reply only.
Payment/Terms: Pays 2 contributor's copies.

☑ $◉ **LYNX EYE**, ScribbleFest Literary Group, 542 Mitchell Dr., Los Osos CA 93402. (805)528-8146. Fax: (805)528-7676. E-mail: pamccully@aol.com. **Contact:** Pam McCully, co-editor. Magazine: 5½×8½; 120 pages; 60 lb. book paper; varied cover stock. "*Lynx Eye* is dedicated to showcasing visionary writers and artists, particularly new voices." Quarterly. Estab. 1994. Circ. 500.
Needs: Adventure, condensed/excerpted novel, erotica, ethnic/multicultural, experimental, fantasy (science), feminist, gay, historical, horror, humor/satire, lesbian, literary, mainstream/contemporary, mystery/suspense, romance, science fiction, serialized novel, translations, westerns. No horror with gratuitous violence or YA stories. Receives 500 unsolicited mss/month. Accepts 30 mss/issue; 120 mss/year. Publishes ms approximately 3 months after acceptance (contract guarantees publication within 12 months or rights revert and payment is kept by author). **Publishes 30 new writers/year.** Published work by Anjali Banerjee, Jean Ryan, Karen Wendy Gilbert, Jack Random and Robert R. Gass. Length: 500-5,000 words; average length: 2,500 words. Also publishes artwork, literary essays, poetry.
How to Contact: Send complete ms with a cover letter. Include name and address on page one; name on *all* other pages. Responds in 3 months. Send SASE for reply, return of ms or send a disposable copy of ms. Accepts multiple submissions. Sample copy for $7.95. Guidelines for #10 SASE.
Payment/Terms: Pays $10 and 3 contributor's copies; additional copies $3.95. Pays on acceptance for first North American serial rights.
Advice: "We consider any well-written manuscript. Characters who speak naturally and who act or are acted upon are greatly appreciated. Your high school English teacher was correct. Basics matter. Imaginative, interesting ideas are sabotaged by lack of good grammar, spelling and punctuation skills. Most submissions are contemporary/ mainstream. We could use some variety. Please do not confuse confessional autobiographies with fiction."

◉ **THE MACGUFFIN**, Schoolcraft College, Department of English, 18600 Haggerty Rd., Livonia MI 48152-2696. (734)462-4400, ext. 5292 or 5327. Fax: (734)462-4679. E-mail: macguffin@schoolcraft.cc.mi.us. Website: www.macguffin.org (includes guidelines, contests and special issues). Editor: Arthur J. Lindenberg. **Contact:** Elizabeth Kircos, fiction editor. Magazine: 6×9; 164 pages; 60 lb. paper; 110 lb. cover; b&w illustrations; photos. "*The MacGuffin* is a literary magazine which publishes a range of material including poetry, nonfiction and fiction. Material ranges from traditional to experimental. We hope our periodical attracts a variety of people with many different interests." Triannual. Quality fiction a special need. Estab. 1984. Circ. 600.
Needs: Adventure, contemporary, ethnic, experimental, fantasy, historical (general), humor/satire, literary, mainstream, prose poem, psychic/supernatural/occult, science fiction, translations. No religious, inspirational, juvenile, romance, horror, pornography. Upcoming themes: "Speaking of Freedom." The issue focuses on all the varied forms of freedom. This will be published in June, 2002. We will consider works until March 15, 2002. Receives 25-40 unsolicited mss/month. Accepts 5-10 mss/issue; 10-30 mss/year. Does not read mss between July 1-August 15. Publishes ms 6 months to 2 years after acceptance. Agented fiction: 10-15%. **Published 30 new writers within the last year.** Recently published work by Virgil Suarez, Lora Volkert and Karen Rosenberg. Length: 100-5,000 words; average length: 2,000-2,500 words. Publishes short shorts. Also publishes literary essays. Occasionally critiques rejected mss and recommends other markets.
How to Contact: Send complete ms with cover letter, which should include: "1. *brief*, 50-word biographical information; 2. note that this *is not* a simultaneous submission." Responds in 3 months. SASE. Accepts reprint and electronic (disk) submissions. Sample copy for $7; current issue for $8. Guidelines free.
Payment/Terms: Pays 2 contributor's copies. Acquires one-time rights.
Advice: "We want to give promising new fiction writers the opportunity to publish alongside recognized writers. Be persistent. If a story is rejected, try to send it somewhere else. When we reject a story, we may accept the

next one you send us. When we make suggestions for a rewrite, we may accept the revision. There seems to be a great number of good authors of fiction, but there are far too few places for publication. However, I think this is changing. Make your characters come to life. Even the most ordinary people become fascinating if they live for your readers."

✓ Ⓓ **THE MADISON REVIEW**, Department of English, Helen C. White Hall, 600 N. Park St., University of Wisconsin, Madison WI 53706. (608)263-0566. E-mail: madreview@mail.student.wisc.edu. Website: http://mendota.english.wisc.edu/~madrev (includes contact information, magazine's history, publishing and prize guidelines, fiction [short story, poetry]). **Contact:** Jason Harklerode and Hillary Schroeder, fiction editors. Magazine: 6×9; 180 pages. "Magazine of fiction and poetry with special emphasis on literary stories and some emphasis on Midwestern writers." Semiannual. Estab. 1978. Circ. 1,000.
Needs: Experimental and literary stories, prose poems, novel excerpts and stories in translation. "We would like to see more contemporary fiction; however, we accept fiction of any creative form and content." No historical fiction. Receives 10-50 unsolicited fiction mss/month. Acquires approximately 6 mss/issue. Does not read mss May-September. Publishes ms an average of 4 months after acceptance. **Publishes 4 new writers/year.** Recently published work by Maurice Glenn Taylor and John McNally. Length: 4,000 words average. Also publishes poetry.
How to Contact: Send complete ms with cover letter and SASE. Accepts submissions on disk. Include estimated word count, 1-page bio and list of publications. "The letter should give one or two sentences of relevant information about the writer—just enough to provide a context for the work." Responds in 4 months to mss. Accepts multiple submissions. Sample copy for $3 via postal service or e-mail.
Payment/Terms: Pays 2 contributor's copies; $2.50 charge for extras. Acquires first North American serial rights.

Ⓝ Ⓓ **MAELSTROM**, Hey Baby! Productions, P.O. Box 7, Tranquility NJ 07879. E-mail: imaelstrom@aol.com. Website: www.geocities.com/~readmaelstrom. **Contact:** Christine L. Reed, editor. Magazine: 8½×7; 48 pages; full color photo cover; illustrations; photos. "*Maelstrom* likes short fiction with a twist that engages the reader." Quarterly. Estab. 1997. Circ. 500.
Needs: Comics/graphic novels, experimental, horror (futuristic, psychological, supernatural), humor/satire, literary, flash fiction. Receives 5 unsolicited mss/month. Accepts 1-2 mss/issue; 8 mss/year. Publishes ms 6 months after acceptance. **Publishes 10 new writers/year.** Recently published work by Barbara Lefcowitz, Rob Hill and Grace Cavalieri. Length: 3,000 words maximum; average length: 2,000 words. Publishes short shorts. Average length: 500 words. Also publishes literary essays and poetry.
How to Contact: Send complete ms with a cover letter. Accepts submissions by e-mail and disk. Include estimated word count and brief bio. Responds in 1 month to queries; 3 months to mss. Send SASE for return of ms or send a disposable copy of ms and #10 SASE for reply only. Accepts simultaneous and multiple submissions. Sample copy for $4. Guidelines for SASE, by e-mail or on website. Reviews short story collections.
Payment/Terms: Pays 1 contributor's copy; additional copies $4. Acquires one-time rights.
Advice: "We are looking for skill with language, dialogue and suspense. The story has to grab the reader in the first paragraph. Use natural language in your writing. Most work from beginning writers seems stilted or choppy."

⤴ $ Ⓓ Ⓨ **MALAHAT REVIEW**, University of Victoria, P.O. Box 1700, STN CSC, Victoria, British Columbia V8W 2Y2 Canada. (250)721-8524. Website: web.uvic.ca/malahat (includes guidelines, contest info, names of editors and recent contributors). E-mail: malahat@uvic.ca (for queries only). **Contact:** Marlene Cookshaw, editor. Quarterly. Circ. 1,200.
   ● *The Malahat Review* has received the National Magazine Award for poetry and fiction. *Malahat Review* ranked #31 on *Writer's Digest*'s "Fiction 50" list of top markets.
Needs: "General fiction and poetry." Publishes 3-4 stories/issue. **Publishes 4-5 new writers/year.** Published work by Niki Singh, Mark Anthony Jarman, Elizabeth Moret Ross, Andrew Pyper and Chris Fink. Length: 10,000 words maximum.
How to Contact: "Enclose proper postage on the SASE." Responds in 3 months. No simultaneous submissions. Sample copy: $11 available through the mail; guidelines available upon request or on the web.
Payment/Terms: Pays $30/printed page and contributor's copies.
Advice: "We do encourage new writers to submit. Read the magazines you want to be published in, ask for their guidelines and follow them. Write for information on *Malahat*'s novella competitions."

Ⓝ **MANDRAKE POETRY REVIEW**, Mandrake Press, P.O. Box 792, Larkspur CA 94977-0792. **Contact:** D. Castleman, editor. Literary magazine: illustrations; photos. "As much as we may, we ignore the dictates of time and fashion. "We focus on an inadvertent originality and a deliberate facility. We are proud and we are playful, and appreciate the real." Semiannual. Estab. 1994. Circ. 300.
Needs: Ethnic, experimental, fantasy, feminist, horror (psychological, supernatural), literary, mainstream, religious (religious fantasy), science fiction. "No conscientious slovenliness." Receives 4 unsolicited mss/month.

Accepts 2 mss/issue; 8 mss/year. Publishes ms months after acceptance. **Publishes 10 new writers/year.** Length: 100-20,000 words; average length: 1,000 words. Publishes short shorts. Also publishes literary essays, literary criticism and poetry. Sometimes comments on rejected mss.

How to Contact: Send complete ms with cover letter. Include brief bio with submission. Send SASE (or IRC) for return of ms. Accepts simultaneous, multiple and previously published submissions. Sample copy for $5 or free with SASE. Guidelines for SASE. Reviews novels, short story collections and nonfiction books.

Payment/Terms: Pays contributor's copies; additional copies $5. Pays on publication for one-time rights. Sends galleys to author.

Advice: "Serendipity makes a manuscript stand out. Unplug your television. Explore a variety of centuries and peoples."

$ ◐ ▼ MANOA, A Pacific Journal of International Writing, English Dept., University of Hawaii, Honolulu HI 96822. (808)956-3070. Fax: (808)956-7808. E-mail: mjournal-1@hawaii.edu. Website: www.hawaii.edu/mjournal (includes writer's guidelines, names of editors, short fiction and poetry). Editor: Frank Stewart. **Contact:** Ian MacMillan, fiction editor. Magazine: 7×10; 240 pages. "An American literary magazine, emphasis on top US fiction and poetry, but each issue has a major guest-edited translated feature of recent writings from an Asian/Pacific country." Semiannual. Estab. 1989.

• *Manoa* has received numerous awards, and work published in the magazine has been selected for prize anthologies.

Needs: Contemporary, excerpted novel, literary, mainstream and translation (from US and nations in or bordering on the Pacific). "Part of our purpose is to present top U.S. fiction from throughout the U.S., not only to U.S. readers, but to readers in Asian and Pacific countries. We are not limited to stories related to or set in the Pacific." Accepts 8-10 mss/issue; 16-20/year. Publishes ms 6-24 months after acceptance. Agented fiction 10%. **Publishes 1-2 new writers/year.** Published work by Robert Olen Butler, Monica Wood and Barry Lopez. Publishes short fiction. Also publishes essays, book reviews, poetry.

How to Contact: Send complete ms with cover letter or through agent. Responds in 6 months. SASE. Accepts simultaneous submissions; query before sending e-mail. Sample copy for $10. Reviews novels and short story collections. Send books or reviews to Reviews Editor.

Payment/Terms: Pays "competitive rates," and contributor's copies. Acquires first North American serial rights and one-time reprint rights. Sends galleys to author.

☑ ◐ ▼ MANY MOUNTAINS MOVING, a literary journal of diverse contemporary voices, 420 22nd St., Boulder CO 80302-7909. (303)545-9942. Fax: (303)444-6510. E-mail: mmm@mmminc.org. Website: www.mmminc.org (includes guidelines for submission, contest guidelines). **Contact:** Naomi Horii, editor. Magazine: 6×8¾; 300 pages; recycled paper; color/heavy cover; illustrations; photos. "We publish fiction, poetry, general-interest essays and art. We try to seek contributors from all cultures." Semiannual. Estab. 1994. Circ. 2,500.

• Work from *Many Mountains Moving* has been reprinted in *Pushcart* anthology and *Best American Poetry*.

Needs: Ethnic/multicultural, experimental, feminist, gay, historical, humor/satire, lesbian, literary, mainstream/contemporary, translations. No genre fiction. Plans special fiction issue or anthology. Receives 400 unsolicited mss/month. Accepts 4-6 mss/issue; 12-18 mss/year. Publishes ms 2-8 months after acceptance. Agented fiction 1%. Recently published work by Stephen Dobyns, Steven Huff, Rahna Reiko Rizzuto and Mathew Chacko. **"We try to publish at least one new writer per issue; more when possible."** Length: 3,000-10,000 words average. Publishes short shorts. Also publishes literary essays, poetry. Sometimes comments on rejected mss.

How to Contact: Send complete ms with a cover letter. Include estimated word count, list of publications. Responds in 2 weeks to queries; 3 months to mss. Send SASE for reply, return of ms or send a disposable copy of ms. Accepts simultaneous submissions. Sample copy for $6.50 and enough IRCs for 1 pound of airmail/printed matter. Guidelines for #10 SASE.

Payment/Terms: Pays 3 contributor's copies; additional copies for $3. Acquires first North American serial rights. Sends galleys to author "if requested." Sponsors a contest, $200 prize. Send SASE for guidelines. Deadline: December 31.

Advice: "We look for top-quality fiction with fresh voices and verve. We would like to see more humorous literary stories. Read at least one issue of our journal to get a feel for what kind of fiction we generally publish."

◐ ▼ THE MARLBORO REVIEW, The Marlboro Review Inc., P.O. Box 243, Marlboro VT 05344-0243. (802)254-4938. E-mail: marlboro@marlbororeview.com. Website: www.marlbororeview.com (includes excerpts, guidelines, subscription forms, short reviews, more). **Contact:** Helen Fremont, fiction editor. Magazine: 6×9; 80-120 pages; 60 lb. paper; photos. "We are interested in cultural, philosophical, scientific and literary issues. Approached from a writer's sensibility. Our only criterion for publication is strength of work." Semiannual. Estab. 1996. Circ. 300. Member, CLMP, AWP

• Works published in *The Marlboro Review* have received Pushcart Prizes.

Needs: Literary, translations. Receives 150 unsolicited mss/month. Accepts 2-3 mss/issue; 4-6 mss/year. "Accepts manuscripts June through September." Publishes ms 1 year after acceptance. Published work by Jenny Browne, Kathleen Lester, Nancy Eimers and Alberto Rios. Length: 500-12,000 words; average length: 7,000 words. Publishes short shorts. Average length: 1,000 words. Also publishes literary essays, literary criticism and poetry.

How to Contact: Send complete ms with a brief cover letter (short bio, publication history if appropriate). Responds in 3 months to queries; 4 months to mss. Send SASE for return of ms or send a disposable copy of ms and #10 SASE for reply only. Accepts simultaneous and multiple submissions. Sample copy for $8.75. Guidelines for SASE or on website. Reviews novels, short story collections and nonfiction books of interest to writers. Send review copies to Ellen Dudley, editor.

Payment/Terms: Pays 2 contributor's copies; additional copies $5. Pays on publication. All rights revert to author on publication. Sometimes sends galleys to author.

Advice: "We're looking for work with a strong voice and sense of control. Do your apprenticeship first. The minimalist impulse seems to be passing and for that we are grateful. We love to see great, sprawling, musical, chance-taking fiction. *The God of Small Things* is the favorite of more than one editor here."

☑ $⊘ ☒ **THE MASSACHUSETTS REVIEW**, South College, University of Massachusetts, Amherst MA 01003. (413)545-2689. Fax: (413)577-0740. E-mail: massrev@external.umass.edu. Website: www.massreview.org (includes general overview, information on editors, excerpts, guidelines). Editors: Mary Heath, Jules Chametzky, Paul Jenkins, David Lenson. **Contact:** Fiction Editor. Magazine: 6×9; 172 pages; 52 lb. paper; 65 lb. vellum cover; illustrations; photos. Quarterly. Estab. 1959. Circ. 1,200.

• Stories from the *Massachusetts Review* have been anthologized in the *100 Best American Short Stories of the Century* and the *Pushcart Prize* anthology. This magazine ranked #26 on *Writer's Digest's* Fiction 50 list of top markets for fiction writers.

Needs: Short stories. Wants more prose less than 30 pages. No mystery or science fiction. Does not read fiction mss June 1-October 1. **Publishes 3-5 new writers/year.** Recently published work by Vern Rutsala, Peter Love and Neal Durando. Approximately 5% of fiction is agented. Also accepts poetry. Critiques rejected mss when time permits.

How to Contact: Send complete ms. No ms returned without SASE. Accepts simultaneous submissions, if noted. Responds in 2 months. Publishes ms an average of 9-12 months after acceptance. Sample copy for $8. Guidelines available for SASE or on website.

Payment/Terms: Pays $50 maximum. Pays on publication for first North American serial rights.

Advice: "Shorter rather than longer stories preferred (up to 28-30 pages)." Looks for works that "stop us in our tracks." Manuscripts that stand out use "unexpected language, idiosyncrasy of outlook and are the opposite or ordinary."

☑ ⊘ **MATRIARCH'S WAY; JOURNAL OF FEMALE SUPREMACY**, Artemis Creations, 3395 Nostrand Ave., 2J, Brooklyn NY 11229-4053. Phone/fax: (718)648-8215. E-mail: artemispub@metconnect.com. Website: www.artemiscreations.com (includes contest news, subscription info, purpose). Editor: Shirley Oliveira. **Contact:** Fiction Editor. Magazine: 5½×8½; illustrations; photos. *Matriarch's Way* is a "matriarchal feminist" publication. Biannual. Estab. 1996.

Needs: Condensed/excerpted novel, erotica (quality), ethnic/multicultural, experimental, fantasy (science, sword and sorcery), feminist (radical), horror, humor/satire, literary, psychic/supernatural/occult, religious/inspirational, romance (futuristic/time travel, gothic, historical), science fiction (soft/sociological), serialized novel. "No Christian anything." Want more "femme dominant erotica and sci-fi." Upcoming themes: "Science of Matriarchy" and "What it Means to be a Female 'Other.'" Receives 10 unsolicited mss/week. Often comments on rejected mss. **50% of work published is by new writers.**

How to Contact: Query first, query with clips of published work or query with synopsis plus 1-3 chapters of novel. Accepts queries/mss by e-mail and disk. Include estimated word count, bio and list of publications with submission. Responds in 1 week to queries; 6 weeks to mss. SASE for reply or send a disposable copy of ms. Sample copy for $10. Reviews novels and short story collections and excerpts "We need book reviewers, original or reprints. We supply books."

Payment/Terms: Pays 1 copy of published issue. Acquires one-time rights.

Advice: Looks for "a knowledge of subject, originality and good writing style. If you can best Camille Paglia, you're on your way!" Looks for "professional writing—equates with our purpose/vision—brave and outspoken."

INTERESTED IN A PARTICULAR GENRE? Check our sections for: **Mystery/Suspense**, page 91; **Romance**, page 105; **Science Fiction & Fantasy**, page 121.

N 🗓 **MEDICINAL PURPOSES, Literary Review**, Poet to Poet Inc., 86-37 120 St., #2D, % Catterson, Richmond Hill NY 11418. (718)847-2150, (718)847-2150. **Contact:** Thomas M. Catterson, editor. Magazine: 8½×5½; 80 pages; illustrations. "*Medicinal Purposes* publishes quality work that will benefit the world, though not necessarily through obvious means." Biannual. Estab. 1995. Circ. 1,000.

Needs: Adventure, erotica, ethnic/multicultural, experimental, fantasy, feminist, gay, historical, horror, humor/satire, lesbian, literary, mainstream/contemporary, mystery/suspense, psychic/supernatural/occult, regional, romance, science fiction, senior citizen/retirement, sports, westerns, young adult/teen. "Please no pornography, or hatemongering." Receives 15 unsolicited mss/month. Accepts 2-3 mss/issue; 8 mss/year. Publishes ms up to four issues after acceptance. **Publishes 24 new writers/year.** Recently published work by Charles E. Brooks and Bernadette Miller. Length: 50-3,000 words; average length: 2,000 words. "We prefer maximum of 10 double-spaced pages." Publishes short shorts. Also publishes literary essays, literary criticism, poetry. Sometimes comments on rejected mss.

How to Contact: Send complete ms with a cover letter. Include estimated word count, brief bio, Social Security number. Responds in 6 weeks to queries; 8 weeks to mss. SASE. Sample copy for $9, 6×9 SAE and 4 first-class stamps. Guidelines free for #10 SASE.

Payment/Terms: Pays 2 contributor's copies. Acquires first rights.

Advice: "Writers should know how to write. This occurs less often than you expect. Try to be entertaining, and write a story that was worth the effort in the first place."

🗓 🗓 **MERIDIAN, The Semiannual from the University of Virginia**, University of Virginia, P.O. Box 400121, Charlottesville VA 22904-4121. (804)924-3354. Fax: (804)924-1478. E-mail: meridian@virginia.edu. Website: www.engl.virginia.edu/meridian (includes excerpts, cover, guidelines, contact info). **Contact:** Fiction Editor. Literary magazine: 6×9; 160 pages; some illustrations. "Produced in affiliation with the University of Virginia's M.F.A. Program in Creative Writing, *Meridian* seeks to publish the best fiction, poetry, and other writing from established and emerging writers." Semiannual. Estab. 1998. Circ. 500.

● Three stories from *Meridian* were included in *New Stories From the South 2001*, and work appearing in *Meridian* was also included in the Pushcart Prize anthology.

Needs: "We are open to all literary short fiction, of any reasonable theme or length." Receives 40-80 unsolicited mss/month. Accepts 3 mss/issue; 6 mss/year. Publishes ms 3-6 months after acceptance. Agented fiction 15%. **Publishes 3 new writers/year.** Recently published work by Ben Miller, Percival Everett, Christie Hodgen and Siobhan Fallon. Length: any; average length: 6,000 words. Publishes short shorts. Also publishes literary essays, literary criticism and poetry. Rarely comments on rejected mss.

How to Contact: Send complete ms with cover letter. Include estimated word count, brief bio, list of publications and e-mail address. Responds in up to 4 months to mss. Send SASE for return of ms or send disposable copy of ms and #10 SASE for reply only. Accepts simultaneous and multiple submissions. Sample copy for $7. Guidelines for SASE or on website.

Payment/Terms: Pays in 2 contributor's copies; additional copies $3.50. Acquires first North American serial rights. Sends galleys to author.

Advice: "Strong action, vivid characters, dynamic language. Keep cover letters brief and factual."

$ ◎ 🗓 **MERLYN'S PEN: Fiction, Essays and Poems by America's Teens, Grades 6-12**, Box 1058, East Greenwich RI 02818. (401)885-5775. Fax: (401)885-5222. E-mail: merlynspen@aol.com. Website: www.merlynspen.com (includes writer's guidelines, the first page of most stories that appear in our anthology collection: *The American Teen Writer Series*). **Contact:** R. Jim Stahl, publisher. Magazine: 8⅜×10⅞; 100 pages; 70 lb. paper; 12 pt. gloss cover; illustrations; photos. Student writing only (grades 6 through 12) for libraries, homes and English classrooms. Annual (each November). Estab. 1985. Circ. 6,000.

● At press time, *Merlyn's Pen* was not accepting unsolicited submissions. Please see their website for updates.

$ 🗓 **MICHIGAN QUARTERLY REVIEW**, University of Michigan, 3032 Rackham, Ann Arbor MI 48109-1070. (734)764-9265. E-mail: mqr@umich.edu. Website: www.umich.edu/~mqr (includes history and description of magazine; information on current and forthcoming issues, subscription information). Editor: Laurence Goldstein. **Contact:** Fiction Editor. "An interdisciplinary journal which publishes mainly essays and reviews, with some high-quality fiction and poetry, for an intellectual, widely read audience." Quarterly. Estab. 1962. Circ. 1,800.

● Stories from *Michigan Quarterly Review* have been selected for inclusion in *The Best American Short Stories*, *O. Henry* and *Pushcart Prize* volumes.

Needs: Literary. No "genre" fiction written for a "market." "Would like to see more fiction about social, political, cultural matters, not just centered on a love relationship or dysfunctional family." Receives 200 unsolicited fiction mss/month. Accepts 2 mss/issue; 8 mss/year. **Publishes 1-2 new writers/year.** Published work by Nicholas Delbanco, Elizabeth Searle, Marian Thurm and Lucy Ferriss. Length: 1,500-7,000 words; average length: 5,000 words. Also publishes poetry, literary essays.

How to Contact: Send complete ms with cover letter. "I like to know if a writer is at the beginning, or further along, in his or her career. Don't offer plot summaries of the story, though a background comment is welcome." Responds in 2 months. SASE. No simultaneous submissions. Sample copy for $2.50 and 2 first-class stamps.

Payment/Terms: Pays $8-10/printed page. Pays on publication for first rights. Awards the Lawrence Foundation Prize of $1,000 for best story in *MQR* previous year.

Advice: "There's no beating a good plot and interesting characters, and a fresh use of the English language. (Most stories fail because they're written in such a bland manner, or in TV-speak.) Be ambitious, try to involve the social world in the personal one, be aware of what the best writing of today is doing, don't be satisfied with a small slice of life narrative but think how to go beyond the ordinary."

$ 🖊 📖 MID-AMERICAN REVIEW, Department of English, Bowling Green State University, Bowling Green OH 43403. (419)372-2725. Website: www.bgsu.edu/midamericanreview (includes submission guidelines, sample work and contest info). **Contact:** Michael Czyzniejewski, fiction editor. Magazine: 6×9; 176 pages; 60 lb. bond paper; coated cover stock. "We try to put the best possible work in front of the biggest possible audience. We publish serious fiction and poetry, as well as critical studies in contemporary literature, translations and book reviews." Biannual. Estab. 1981.

● Work published in *Mid-American Review* has received the Pushcart Prize.

Needs: Experimental, literary, memoir, prose poem, traditional and translations. "No genre fiction. Would like to see more short shorts." Receives about 150 unsolicited fiction mss/month. Accepts 6-8 mss/issue. Approximately 5% of fiction is agented. **Publishes 4-8 new writers/year.** Recently published work by Aimee Bender, Steve Almond, Alvin Greenberg and Melanie Rae Thon. Length: 25 pages maximum. Also publishes essays and poetry. Occasionally critiques rejected mss. Sponsors the Sherwood Anderson Short Fiction Award.

How to Contact: Send complete ms with SASE. Responds in about 4 months. Publishes ms an average of 6 months after acceptance. Sample copy for $5. Reviews novels and short story collections. Send books to editor-in-chief.

Payment/Terms: Pays $10/page, up to $50 and 2 contributor's copies; charges for additional copies. Acquires first North American serial rights.

Advice: "We look for well-written stories that make the reader want to read on past the first line and page. Clichéd themes and sloppy writing turn us off immediately. Read literary journals to see what's being published in today's market. We tend to publish work that is more non-traditional in style and form, but are open to all literary non-genre submissions."

📖 THE MIDDAY MOON, Essays, Fiction, Poetry, Other Things of That Sort, Montag Publishing, P.O. Box 368, Waite Park MN 56387. (320)656-5473. **Contact:** Susan Montag, editor. Magazine: 8½×11; 24 pages; 80 lb. Number 3 Gloss enamel text paper; self cover; illustrations; photos. "*The Midday Moon* is a literary magazine for those not interested in gloom and depression. We want to appeal to open-minded people who want to 'think smart, feel good and laugh at humor their coworkers don't get.' We have a unique section called 'What the Writers Read', a book review section." Estab. 2000. Circ. 300.

Needs: Literary, mainstream. "No romance, erotica, western, horror." Receives about 50 unsolicited mss/month. Accepts 2-3 mss/issue; 8-12 mss/year. Publishes ms 2 months after acceptance. **Publishes 10 new writers/year.** Length: 6,000 words maximum; average length: 3-5,000 words. Publishes short shorts. Also publishes literary essays and poetry. Sometimes comments on rejected mss.

How to Contact: Send complete ms with a cover letter. Include estimated word count, brief bio and list of publications. Responds in 3 months to queries and mss. Send SASE (or IRC) for return of ms or send a disposable copy of ms and #10 SASE for reply only. Accepts simultaneous submissions, previously published work and multiple submissions. Sample copy for $4.50. Guidelines for SASE.

Payment/Terms: Pays 2 contributor's copies; additional copies $3.50. Pays on publication.

Advice: "We look for fiction that is concise and thought provoking. The story should begin with the first sentence. We like to be amused. Research the market and send for sample copies."

📷 MINAS TIRITH EVENING-STAR, W.W. Publications, Box 7871, Flint MI 48507. **Contact:** Philip Helms, editor. Magazine: 5½×8½; 24 pages; typewriter paper; black ink illustrations; photos. Magazine of J.R.R. Tolkien and fantasy—fiction, poetry, reviews, etc. for general audience. Quarterly. Published special fiction issue; plans another. Estab. 1967. Circ. 500.

Needs: "Fantasy and Tolkien." Receives 5 unsolicited mss/month. Accepts 1 ms/issue; 5 mss/year. **Published new writers within the last year.** Length: 5,000 words maximum; 1,000-1,200 words preferred. Publishes short shorts. Also publishes literary essays, literary criticism, poetry. Occasionally critiques rejected mss.

How to Contact: Send complete ms and bio. Responds in 2 months. SASE. No simultaneous submissions. Accepts reprint submissions. Sample copy for $2. Reviews novels and short story collections.

Terms: Acquires first rights.

Advice: Goal is "to expand knowledge and enjoyment of J.R.R. Tolkien's and his son Christopher Tolkien's works and their worlds."

MINDPRINTS, A Literary Journal, Disabled Student Programs and Services, Allan Hancock College, 800 S. College Dr., Santa Maria CA 93454-6399. (805)922-6966, ext. 3274. Fax: (805)922-3556. E-mail: htcdsps @sbceo.org. **Contact:** Paul Fahey, editor. Magazine: 6×9; 125-150 pages; 50 lb. white offset paper; glossy cover; illustrations; photos. "*Mindprints, A Literary Journal* is one of a very few college publications created as a forum for writers and artists with disabilities or for those with an interest in the field. The emphasis on flash fiction and the fact that we are a national journal as well puts us on the cutting edge of today's market." Annual. Estab. fall 2000. Circ. 500.

Needs: Literary, mainstream. Receives 20-30 unsolicited mss/month. Accepts 60 mss/year. Does not read mss June-August. Publishes ms 6 months after acceptance. **Publishes 25-30 new writers/year.** Published work by Catherine Ryan Hyde, Ingrid Reti, Wendy Whitaker and Denize Lavoie Cain. Length: 250-750 words; average length: 500 words. Publishes short shorts. Average length: 400-500 words. Also publishes poetry. Often comments on rejected mss.

How to Contact: Send complete ms with a cover letter. No e-mail submissions unless writer resides outside US. Include estimated word count, brief bio, list of publications and "reasons why you are submitting to *Mindprints*; your interest in the disability field, etc." Responds in 1 week to queries; 4 months to mss. Send a disposable copy of ms and #10 SASE for reply only. Accepts simultaneous, previously published and multiple (2 shorts/ memoirs) submissions. Sample copy for $5 and $2 postage or IRCs. Guidelines for SASE, by e-mail or fax.

Payment/Terms: Pays 1 contributor's copy; additional copies $5. Pays on publication for one-time rights. Not copyrighted.

Advice: "We look for a great hook; a story that grabs us from the beginning; fiction and memoir with a strong voice and unusual themes; stories with a narrowness of focus yet broad in their appeal. We would like to see more flash or very short fiction. Read and study the flash fiction genre. *Flash Fiction* by Thomas, Thomas and Hazuka is highly recommended. Revise, revise, revise. Do not send manuscripts that have not been proofed. Our mission is to showcase as many voices and world views as possible. We want our readers to sample creative talent from a national and international group of published and unpublished writers and artists."

THE MINNESOTA REVIEW, A Journal of Committed Writing, Dept. of English, University of Missouri, Columbia MO 65211. (573)882-3059. Fax: (573)882-5785. **Contact:** Jeffrey Williams, editor. Magazine: 5¼×7½; approximately 200 pages; some illustrations; occasional photos. "We emphasize socially and politically engaged work." Semiannual. Estab. 1960. Circ. 1,500.

Needs: Experimental, feminist, gay, historical, lesbian, literary. Receives 50-75 mss/month. Accepts 3-4 mss/ issue; 6-8 mss/year. Publishes ms within 6-12 months after acceptance. Recently published work by E. Shaskan Bumas, Carlos Fuentes, Maggie Jaffe and Laura Nixon Dawson. Length: 1,500-6,000 words preferred. Publishes short shorts. Also publishes literary essays, literary criticism, poetry. Occasionally critiques rejected mss and recommends other markets.

How to Contact: Send complete ms with optional cover letter. Responds in 3 weeks to queries; 3 months to mss. SASE. Accepts simultaneous submissions. Reviews novels and short story collections. Send books to book review editor.

Payment/Terms: Pays in contributor's copies. Charge for additional copies. Acquires first rights.

Advice: "We look for socially and politically engaged work, particularly short, striking work that stretches boundaries."

THE MISSING FEZ, A Quarterly Publication of Unconventional and Otherwise Abnormal Literature, Red Felt Publishing, P.O. Box 57310, Tucson AZ 85711. (520)323-1486. E-mail: missingfez@h otmail.com. Website: www.missingfez.com. **Contact:** Eleanor Horner, fiction editor. Magazine: 8½×7; 36-40 pages; semigloss paper; glossy cover. "We strive to publish fiction of high quality which for some reason falls outside the traditional literary spectrum." Quarterly. Estab. 2000. Circ. 1,000.

Needs: Erotica, experimental, fantasy (space fantasy), feminist, gay, horror, humor/satire, literary, mainstream, mystery/suspense (private eye/hardboiled), psychic/supernatural/occult, science fiction, thriller/espionage. Would like to see more humor, satire, experimentation. "Please do not send anecdotes or lessons of morality." Receives 30 unsolicited mss/month. Accepts 4-5 mss/issue; 16-20 mss/year. Publishes ms 6 months after acceptance. Agented fiction 20%. **Publishes 10-15 new writers/year.** Recently published work by Joanna Kosowsky, Peter Hoffman and Alice Whittenburg. Length: 10-8,000 words; average length: 5,000 words. Publishes short shorts. Average length: 1,000 words. Also publishes poetry. Always comments on rejected mss.

How to Contact: Send complete ms with a cover letter and $3 reading fee payable to: Red Felt Publishing. Include estimated word count and list of publications. Responds in 6 weeks to mss. Send a disposable copy of ms and #10 SASE for reply only. Accepts simultaneous submissions. Sample copy for $3. Guidelines for SASE or by e-mail.

Payment/Terms: Pays $25 and 1 contributor's copy; additional copies $3. Pays on acceptance for first rights. Sponsors contest. Send SASE for guidelines. Visit website for sample pieces and upcoming contest info.

Advice: "We get a lot of stories about morality and doing the right thing—we would like to see less of this."

✓ ☑ ▣ **MISSISSIPPI REVIEW**, University of Southern Mississippi, Box 5144, Hattiesburg MS 39406-5144. (601)266-4321. Fax: (601)266-5757. E-mail: fb@netdoor.com. Website: http://sushi.st.usm.edu/mrw/. (The website publishes new work, independent of the print edition. It is open for electronic submissions. Check the site for current reading editors.) **Contact:** Rie Fortenberry, managing editor. "Literary publication for those interested in contemporary literature—writers, editors who read to be in touch with current modes." Semiannual. Estab. 1972. Circ. 1,500.

Needs: Literary, contemporary, fantasy, humor, translations, experimental, avant-garde and "art" fiction. Quality writing. No juvenile or genre fiction. Theme issues for the print edition are solicited; theme issues for the web version are listed on the site and are open to unsolicited submissions. Buys varied amount of mss/issue. Does not read mss in summer. **Publishes 10-20 new writers/year.** Published work by Jason Brown, Terese Svoboda and Barry Hannah. Length: 30 pages maximum.

How to Contact: Not currently reading unsolicited work. Submit work via e-mail to our World Wide Web publication, which is a monthly (except August) and publishes more new work than we are able to in the print version. Send submissions to fb@netdoor.com as ASCII files in the text of your e-mail message, or as Microsoft Word or WordPerfect attachments to your message. Sample copy for $8.

Payment/Terms: Pays in contributor's copies. Acquires first North American serial rights.

$ ☑ ☒ **THE MISSOURI REVIEW**, 1507 Hillcrest Hall, University of Missouri—Columbia, Columbia MO 65211. (573)882-4474. Fax: (573)884-4671. Website: www.missourireview.org (includes guidelines, contest information, staff photos, editorial column, short fiction, poetry, essays, interviews, features and book reviews). **Contact:** Speer Morgan, editor. Magazine: 6×9; 212 pages. Theme: fiction, poetry, essays, reviews, interviews, cartoons, "all with a distinctly contemporary orientation. For writers, and the general reader with broad literary interests. We present nonestablished as well as established writers of excellence. The *Review* often runs feature sections or special issues dedicated to particular topics frequently related to fiction." Published 3 times/academic year. Estab. 1977. Circ. 6,800.

● This magazine had stories anthologized in the *Pushcart Prize Anthology, Best American Short Stories, Best American Erotica* and *New Stories From the South.*

Needs: Condensed/excerpted novel, ethnic/multicultural, humor/satire, literary, contemporary. "No genre or flash fictions; no children's." Receives approximately 400 unsolicited fiction mss each month. Accepts 5-6 mss/issue; 15-20 mss/year. **Publishes 6-10 new writers/year.** Recently published work by Lucy Ferriss and Paul LaFarge. No preferred length. Also publishes personal essays, poetry. Often critiques rejected mss.

How to Contact: Send complete ms with SASE. May include brief bio and list of publications. Responds in 10 weeks. Send SASE for reply, return of ms or send disposable copy of ms. Sample copy for $8.

Payment/Terms: Pays $30/printed page minimum on signed contract for all rights. Awards William Peden Prize in fiction; $1,000 to best story published in *Missouri Review* in a given year. Also sponsors Editors' Prize Contest with a prize of $2,000 for fiction, $1,500 for essays and the Larry Levis Editors' Prize for poetry, with a prize of $2,000; and the Tom McAfee Discovery Prize in poetry for poets who have not yet published a book.

✓ ◎ **THE MUSING PLACE, The Literary & Arts Magazine of Chicago's Mental Health Community**, The Thresholds, 2700 N. Lakeview, Chicago IL 60614. (773)281-3800, ext. 2465. Fax: (773)281-8790. E-mail: sford@thn.thresholds.org. **Contact:** Shannon Ford, editor. Magazine: 8½×11; 36 pages; 60 lb. paper; glossy cover; illustrations. "We are mostly a poetry magazine by and for mental health consumers. We want to give a voice to those who are often not heard. All material is composed by mental health consumers. The only requirement for consideration of publication is having a history of mental illness." Semiannual. Estab. 1986. Circ. 1,000.

Needs: Adventure, condensed/excerpted novel, ethnic/multicultural, experimental, fantasy (science fantasy, sword and sorcery), feminist, gay, historical (general), horror, humor/satire, lesbian, literary, mainstream/contemporary, mystery/suspense, regional, romance, science fiction and serialized novel. Publishes ms up to 6 months after acceptance. Published work by Allen McNair, Donna Willey and Mark Gonciarz. Length: 700 words maximum; average length: 500 words. Length: 500 words. Also publishes poetry.

How to Contact: Send complete ms with a cover letter. Include bio (paragraph) and statement of having a history of mental illness. Responds in 6 months. Send a disposable copy of ms. Accepts simultaneous and reprint submissions. Sample copy $3.

Payment/Terms: Pays contributor's copies. Acquires one-time rights.

N **◐** **NASSAU REVIEW**, Nassau Community College, State University of New York, 1 Education Dr., Garden City NY 11530-6793. (516)272-7792. **Contact:** Editorial Board. Magazine: 6½×9½; 200 pages; heavy stock paper and cover; illustrations; photos. "Looking for high-level, professionally talented fiction on any subject matter. Not geared to college students or others of that age who have not yet reached professional competency." Annual. Estab. 1964. Circ. 1,200. Member, Council of Literary Magazines & Presses.
Needs: Historical (general), humor/satire, literary, mainstream, mystery/suspense (amateur sleuth, cozy). No science fiction. Receives 20-25 unsolicited mss/month. Accepts 1 ms/issue; 7-10 mss/year. Does not read mss April-September. Publishes ms 6 months after acceptance. **Publishes 1 new writer/year.** Published work by Louis Phillips, Dick Wimmer, Norbert Petsch and Mike Lipstock. Length: 2,000-6,000 words; average length: 3,000-4,000 words. Publishes short shorts. Average length: 1,200 words. Also publishes literary essays, literary criticism and poetry.
How to Contact: Send complete ms with a cover letter. Include brief bio and list of publications. No simultaneous submissions. Responds in 2 weeks to queries; up to 6 months to mss. Send a disposable copy of ms and #10 SASE for reply only. Sample copy free.
Payment/Terms: Pays contributor's copies. Acquires one-time rights. Sponsors contest.
Advice: "We look for narrative drive, perceptive characterization and professional competence."

◐ **NEBO, A Literary Journal**, Arkansas Tech University, Dept. of English, Russellville AR 72801. (501)968-0256. Editors change each year. **Contact:** Dr. Michael Karl Ritchie, editor. Literary, fiction and poetry magazine: 5×8; 50-60 pages. For a general, academic audience. Annual. Estab. 1983. Circ. 500.
Needs: Literary, mainstream, reviews. Upcoming theme: pop icon fiction and poetry (fiction and poetry that plays with the roles of pop icons). Receives 20-30 unsolicited fiction mss/month. Accepts 2 mss/issue; 6-10 mss/year. Does not read mss May 1-September 1. **Published new writers within the last year.** Published work by Steven Sherrill, J.B. Bernstein, Jameson Currier, Tricia Lande and Joseph Nicholson. Length: 3,000 words maximum. Also publishes literary essays, literary criticism, poetry. Occasionally critiques rejected mss.
How to Contact: Send complete ms with SASE and cover letter with bio. No simultaneous submissions. Responds in 3 months to mss. Publishes ms an average of 6 months after acceptance. Sample copy for $6. "Submission deadlines for all work are November 15 and January 15 of each year." Reviews novels and short story collections.
Payment/Terms: Pays 1 contributor's copy. Acquires one-time rights.
Advice: "A writer should carefully edit his short story before submitting it. Write from the heart and put everything on the line. Don't write from a phony or fake perspective. Frankly, many of the manuscripts we receive should be publishable with a little polishing. Manuscripts should *never* be submitted with misspelled words or on 'onion skin' or colored paper."

◐ **Y** **THE NEBRASKA REVIEW**, University of Nebraska at Omaha, Omaha NE 68182-0324. (402)554-3159. E-mail: jreed@unomaha.edu. **Contact:** James Reed, fiction editor. Magazine: 5½×8½; 108 pages; 60 lb. text paper; chrome coat cover stock. "*TNR* attempts to publish the finest available contemporary fiction, poetry and creative nonfiction for college and literary audiences." Publishes 2 issues/year. Estab. 1973. Circ. 1,000.
   • Work published in *The Nebraska Review* was reprinted in *New Stories From the South* and the *Pushcart Prize Anthology*.
Needs: Contemporary, humor/satire, literary and mainstream. No genre fiction. Receives 40 unsolicited fiction mss/month. Accepts 4-5 mss/issue, 8-10 mss/year. Reads for the *Nebraska Review* Awards in Fiction and Poetry and Creative Nonfiction September 1 through November 30. Open to submissions January 1-April 30; does not read May 1-August 31. **Publishes 2-3 new writers/year.** Published work by Cris Mazza, Mark Wisniewski, Stewart O'Nan, Elaine Ford and Tom Franklin. Length: 5,000-6,000 words average. Also publishes poetry and creative nonfiction.
How to Contact: Send complete ms with SASE. Responds in 6 months. Publishes ms an average of 6-12 months after acceptance. Sample copy for $4.50.
Payment/Terms: Pays 2 contributor's copies and 1 year subscription; additional copies $4. Acquires first North American serial rights.
Advice: "Write stories in which the lives of your characters are the primary reason for writing and techniques of craft serve to illuminate, not overshadow, the textures of those lives. Sponsors a $500 award/year—write for rules."

✓ **◐** **Y** **NEOTROPE**, Broken Boulder Press, P.O. Box 6305, Santa Barbara CA 93160. E-mail: apowell10 @hotmail.com. Website: www.brokenboulder.com (includes submission guidelines, ordering information and addresses, samples of published work, and general information about press). Editors: Adam Powell, Paul Silvia.
Contact: Fiction Editor. Magazine: 5½×8½; 160 pages; perfect-bound; illustrations; photos. "We view *Neotrope*

as a deprogramming tool for refugees from MPW programs and fiction workshops. We are seeking aggressively experimental fiction. We publish new and progressive forms of fiction writing, stories that are experimental in structure, style, subject matter and execution. We don't target any specific groups, but trust our audience to define itself." Published annually in October. Estab. 1998. Circ. 1,000.

• *Neotrope* received The Tumbrel Prize in March 2000, given by webwritersworkshop.com. *Neotrope* was ranked #33 on *Writer's Digest's* Fiction 50 list of top markets for writers.

Needs: Experimental fiction and drama. "No genre fiction, erotica, gothic, inspirational, nothing traditional." Receives 60-100 unsolicited mss/month. Accepts 12-15 mss/issue. Publishes ms up to 1 year after acceptance. **Publishes 1-5 new writers/year.** Recently published works by Jim Meirose, Norman Lock, Richard Peabody, Pamela Gay and Bill DiMichele. Length: open. Publishes short shorts. Always comments on rejected ms.

How to Contact: Send complete ms with a cover letter and SASE. Responds in 2 weeks. Accepts multiple submissions. Sample copy for $5 postpaid. Guidelines free.

Payment/Terms: Pays 2 contributor's copies; additional copies at cost. Acquires one-time rights. Sometimes sends galleys to author.

Advice: "If it reminds me of something I've seen before, it's not ready for *Neotrope*. You can never take too much time to develop your art. I despise this unwritten code of honor among editors which prohibits all but the most general and impersonal replies with returned manuscripts. Most editors don't even bother to sign their names to a xeroxed rejection slip. Those people who are confident enough to set themselves up as the caretakers of contemporary literature have an obligation to prove their worth by helping other writers along."

NERVE COWBOY, Liquid Paper Press, P.O. Box 4973, Austin TX 78765. Editors: Joseph Shields and Jerry Hagins. **Contact:** Fiction Editor. Magazine: 7 × 8½; 60-64 pages; 20 lb. paper; card stock cover; illustrations. "*Nerve Cowboy* publishes adventurous, comical, disturbing, thought-provoking, accessible poetry and fiction. We like to see work sensitive enough to make the hardest hard-ass cry, funny enough to make the most hopeless brooder laugh and disturbing enough to make us all glad we're not the author of the piece." Semiannual. Estab. 1996. Circ. 250.

• Sponsors an annual chapbook contest for fiction or poetry. Deadline January 15. Send SASE for details.

Needs: Literary. No "racist, sexist or overly offensive" work. Wants more "unusual stories with rich description and enough twists and turns that leaves the reader thinking." Receives 40 unsolicited mss/month. Accepts 2-3 mss/issue; 4-6 mss/year. Publishes ms 6-12 months after acceptance. **Publishes 5-10 new writers/year.** Published work by Albert Huffstickler, Celeste Bowman, Catfish McDaris, Laurel Speer, Brian Prioleau, Marcy Shapiro, Susanne R. Bowers and Adam Gurvitch. Length: 1,500 words maximum; average length: 750-1,000 words. Publishes short shorts. Also publishes poetry.

How to Contact: Send complete ms with a cover letter. Include bio and list of publications. Responds in 2 weeks to queries; 2 months to mss. Send SASE for reply, return of ms or send disposable copy of ms. No simultaneous submissions. Accepts reprints. Sample copy for $5. Guidelines for #10 SASE.

Payment/Terms: Pays 1 contributor's copy. Acquires one-time rights.

Advice: "We look for writing which is very direct and elicits a visceral reaction in the reader. Read magazines you submit to in order to get a feel for what the editors are looking for. Write simply and from the gut."

$ ☑ NEW ENGLAND REVIEW, Middlebury College, Middlebury VT 05753. (802)443-5075. E-mail: nereview@mail.middlebury.edu. Website: www.middlebury.edu/~nereview (includes guidelines, staff, ordering information, sample works from current and back issues). **Contact:** Stephen Donadio, editor. Magazine: 7 × 10; 180 pages; 50 lb paper; coated cover stock. A literary quarterly publishing fiction, poetry and essays with special emphasis on contemporary cultural issues, both in the US and abroad. For general readers and professional writers. Quarterly. Estab. 1977. Circ. 2,000.

Needs: Literary. Receives 250 unsolicited fiction mss/month. Accepts 5 mss/issue; 20 mss/year. Does not read mss June-August. **Publishes 1-2 new writers/year.** Recently published work by Madison Smart Bell, Robert Cohen, Carolyn Cooke and Chuck Kinder. Publishes ms 3-9 months after acceptance. Agented fiction: less than 5%. Prose length: 10,000 words maximum, double spaced. Novellas: 30,000 words maximum. Publishes short shorts occasionally. Sometimes critiques rejected mss.

How to Contact: Send complete ms with cover letter. "Cover letters that demonstrate that the writer knows the magazine are the ones we want to read. We don't want hype, or hard-sell, or summaries of the author's intentions. Will consider simultaneous submissions, but must be stated as such." Responds in 15 weeks to mss. SASE.

Payment/Terms: Pays $10/page, $20 minimum and 2 contributor's copies; charge for extras. Pays on publication for first rights and reprint rights. Sends galleys to author.

Advice: "It's best to send one story at a time, and wait until you hear back from us to try again."

☑ NEW LAUREL REVIEW, New Orleans Poetry Forum/New Laurel Review, P.O. Box 770257, New Orleans LA 70112. Phone/fax: (504)947-6001. **Editor:** Lee Meitzen Grue. Poetry Editor: Lenny Emmanuel. Magazine:

6½×8; 125 pages; 60 lb. white paper; illustrations; photos. Journal of poetry, fiction, critical articles and reviews. "We have published such internationally known writers as James Nolan, Tomris Uyar and Yevgeny Yevtushenko." Readership: "Literate, adult audiences as well as anyone interested in writing with significance, human interest, vitality, subtlety, etc." Published irregularly. Estab. 1970. Circ. 500. Member, Council of Editors of Learned Journals.

Needs: Literary, ethnic/multicultural, excerpted novel, translations, "cutting edge." No "dogmatic, excessively inspirational or political" material. No science fiction. Want more classic short story and experimental short story. Acquires 1-2 fiction mss/issue. Receives approximately 25 unsolicited fiction mss each month. Does not read mss during summer months and December. Agented fiction 10%. **Publishes 5 new writers/year.** Length: about 10 printed pages. Publishes short shorts. Also publishes literary essays and poetry. Critiques rejected mss when there is time.

How to Contact: Send complete ms with a cover letter. Include bio and list of publications. Responds in 3 months. Send SASE for reply or return of ms. No simultaneous submissions. Sample copy for $10. "Authors need to look at sample copy before submitting."

Payment/Terms: Pays 1 contributor's copy; additional copies $10, discounted. Acquires first rights.

Advice: "We are interested in fresh, original work that keeps a reader reading. Send a finished manuscript: clean."

✓ $ ⬙ ⬚ **NEW LETTERS MAGAZINE,** University of Missouri-Kansas City, University House, 5101 Rockhill Rd., Kansas City MO 64110. (816)235-1120. Fax: (816)235-2611. E-mail: mckinleyj@umkc.edu. Website: www.umkc.edu/newletters (includes writer's and awards guidelines, back issue availability, samples from magazine, staff information). **Contact:** James McKinley, editor. Magazine: 14 lb. cream paper; illustrations. Quarterly. Estab. 1971 (continuation of *University Review*, founded 1935). Circ. 2,500.

● *New Letters Magazine* received a Pushcart prize for fiction. The magazine was ranked #29 on *Writer's Digest*'s Fiction 50 list of top markets for writers.

Needs: Contemporary, ethnic, experimental, humor/satire, literary, mainstream, translations. "Generally don't publish straight genre fiction." **Publishes 5-10 new writers/year.** Recently published work by Robin Becker, Maxine Kumin, Alan Cheuse and Anton Chekov. Agented fiction: 10%. Also publishes short shorts. Rarely critiques rejected mss.

How to Contact: Send complete ms with cover letter. Does not read mss May 15-October 15. Responds in 3 weeks to queries; up to 18 weeks to mss. SASE for ms. No simultaneous or multiple submissions. Sample copy $5.50 or on website.

Payment/Terms: Pays honorarium—depends on grant/award money; 2 contributor's copies. Sends galleys to author.

Advice: "Seek publication of representative chapters in high-quality magazines as a way to the book contract. Try literary magazines first."

Ⓝ ◯ **NEW MIRAGE QUARTERLY,** Good Samaritan Press, P.O. Box 803282, Santa Clarita CA 91380. (661)799-0694. E-mail: adorxyz@aol.com. **Contact:** Jorita Lee, senior editor. Magazine: 5×8; 16 pages; illustrations. "We are issued by the Mirage Group of Southern California, a writers association. Much of the material we publish is the work of our members." Quarterly. Estab. 1997. Circ. 100.

Needs: Fantasy, literary, mainstream, religious, romance, science fiction. "We would like to see more Christian literature, science fiction, romance." Receives 1 unsolicited ms/month. Publishes ms 6 months after acceptance. **Publishes 7 new writers/year.** Recently published work by Eugenia Hairston. Publishes short shorts. Also publishes literary criticism and poetry. Sometimes comments on rejected mss.

How to Contact: Send complete ms with a cover letter. Accepts submissions by e-mail. Responds in 6 weeks to queries. Send SASE for return of ms. Accepts simultaneous, previously published and multiple submissions. Sample copy for $7. Reviews novels, short story collections and nonfiction books of interest to writers.

Payment/Terms: Pays 1 contributor's copy; additional copies $26. Pays on publication. Sends galleys to author. Not copyrighted. Sponsors contest. "Send SASE for standards."

Advice: "The basics are important—organization, clarity, spelling, plot, etc. We recommend working with a writers association."

✓ ◯ ⬚ **NEW ORLEANS REVIEW,** Box 195, Loyola University, New Orleans LA 70118. (504)865-2295. Fax: (504)865-2294. E-mail: noreview@loyno.edu. Website: www.loyno.edu/~noreview/ (includes current issue, table of contents, cover, subscription form, submission guidelines, links, masthead, back issues (covers/table of contents). **Contact:** Chris Chambers, editor. Journal: 6×9; perfect bound; 125-160 pages; photos. "Publishes poetry, fiction, translations, photographs, nonfiction on literature and film. Readership: those interested in current culture, literature." Biannually. Estab. 1968. Circ. 1,300.

● Work from the *New Orleans Review* has been anthologized in *Best American Short Stories*.

Needs: "Storytelling between traditional and experimental." No romance. Want more experimental fiction. **Publishes 6-8 new writers/year.** Recently published work by Gordon Lish, Mark Halliday, Rob Trucks and Madeleine Marcotte.

How to Contact: Send complete ms with SASE. Accepts queries/mss by fax. Accepts simultaneous submissions (if we are notified immediately upon acceptance elsewhere). No electronic submissions. Responds in 3 months. Sample copy for $7.

Payment/Terms: "Inquire." Most payment in copies. Pays on publication for first North American serial rights.

Advice: "We're looking for dynamic writing that demonstrates attention to the language, and a sense of the medium, writing that engages, surprises, moves us. We're not looking for genre fiction, or academic articles. We subscribe to the belief that in order to truly write well, one must first master the rudiments: grammar and syntax, punctuation, the sentence, the paragraph, the line, the stanza. We receive about 3,000 manuscripts a year, and publish about 5% of them. Check out a recent issue, send us your best, proofread your work, be patient, be persistent."

N **⟲** **⌀** **THE NEW ORPHIC REVIEW**, New Orphic Publishers, 706 Mill St., Nelson, British Columbia V1L 4S5 Canada. (250)354-0494. Fax: (250)352-0743. **Contact:** Ernest Hekkanen, editor-in-chief. Magazine: 5½×8½; 120 pages; common paper; 100 lb. color cover. "In the traditional *Orphic* fashion, our magazine accepts a wide range of styles and approaches—from naturalism to the surreal, but, please, get to the essence of the narrative, emotion, conflict, state of being, whatever." Semiannual. Estab. 1998. Circ. 300.

Needs: Ethnic/multicultural, experimental, fantasy, historical (general), literary, mainstream. "No detective stories." Upcoming themes: Special Swiss Issue (May), deadline March 31, 2002. List of upcoming themes available for SASE. Receives 20 unsolicited mss/month. Accepts 10 mss/issue; 22 mss/year. Publishes ms up to 1 year after acceptance. **Publishes 6-8 new writers/year.** Recently published work by Jack Cady, W.P. Kinsella, Michael Bullock and Sandra Filippelli. Length: 2,000-10,000 words; average length: 3,500 words. Publishes short shorts. Average length: 3,500 words. Also publishes literary essays, literary criticism and poetry. Sometimes comments on rejected mss.

How to Contact: Send complete ms with a cover letter. Include estimated word count, brief bio and list of publications. Responds in 1 month to queries; 4 months to mss. Send SASE (or IRC) for return of ms or send a disposable copy of ms and #10 SASE for reply only. Accepts simultaneous submissions. Sample copy for $15. Guidelines for SASE. Reviews novels, short story collections and nonfiction books of interest to writers. Send review copies to Margrith Schraner.

Payment/Terms: Pays 1 contributor's copy; additional copies $12. Pays on publication for first North American serial rights. Sponsors contest: New Orphic Short Story Contest. Deadline: April 1. 1st Prize: $300, 2nd Prize: $100, 3rd Prize: $50.

Advice: "I like fiction that deals with issues, accounts for every motive, has conflict, is well-written and tackles something that is substantive. Don't be mundane; try for more, not less."

N **the new renaissance, An international magazine of ideas & opinions, emphasizing literature and the arts,** The Friends of "the new renaissance", 26 Heath Rd., #11, Arlington MA 02474-3645. E-mail: wmichaud@gwi.net. **Contact:** Michal Anne Kucharski, co-editor. Magazine: 6×9; 144-4182 pages; 70 lb. matte white paper; 4-color cover; illustrations; photos; artwork: 80 lb. dull glossy. "*tnr* is dedicated to publishing a diverse magazine, with a variety of styles, statements and tones for a sophisticated general literature audience. We publish assorted long & short fiction, including bilingual fiction (Italian, German, French, Danish, Russian [Cyrillic], etc . . .), and Indian fiction in translation." Semiannual. Estab. 1968. Circ. 1,300.

Needs: Ethnic (general), experimental, horror (psychological, supernatural), humor satire, literary, regional (general), translation. "We do not want to see strictly commercial or popular fiction. Within the last two years we have been receiving quasi-naturalistic fiction and we would like to see less of that." Receives 50-70 unsolicited mss/month (January-February); 20-35 mss/month (September 1-October 31). Accepts 3-5 mss/issue; 6-10 mss/year. Does not read mss in July-August or November-December. Publishes ms 10-18 months after acceptance. Agented fiction 5-8%. **Publishes 1-2 new writers/year.** Recently published work by Lucille Bellucci, Mitch Evich, and Kurt Tucholsky. Length: 250-10,500 words. Also publishes literary essays, literary criticism and poetry. Often comments on rejected mss.

How to Contact: All fiction and poetry submissions are tied to our awards programs and require a $16.50 entry fee (U.S.) for non subscribers; $11.50 for subscribers; add $3 foreign. Send complete ms with cover letter. Include estimated word count with submission. Responds in 1 month to queries; 8 months to mss. Send SASE (or IRC) for return of ms or send disposable copy of ms and #10 SASE for reply only. Accepts multiple submissions if the mss are 4 pages or less, absolutely." Guidelines for SASE or e-mail. Reviews novels, short story collections and nonfiction books. Send to fiction, poetry or nonfiction editors.

Payment/Terms: Pays $48-80 and 1 contributor's copy (under 30 pages), 2 copies 31-36 pages. Offers discount for additional copies. Acquires all rights; after publication, rights returned to writer. Sponsors contests: After the third issue of each volume is published, we have independent judges (one for fiction, one for poetry) decide on the best work in a volume. Send ms with $16.50 (U.S., foreign add $1.50 U.S. dollars). Writers will receive, their choice, two back issues or one recent issue.

Advice: "We're looking for the individual voice, in both style and vision. We prefer density in characterization or/and dialogue, atmosphere, etc. We're not as interested in the "Who Cares?" stories. We like a story to offer something memorable; we leave the particulars of what that something is to the individual writer. We feel that the first person narration is becoming an all too predictable commonplace."

NEW SHETLANDER, Shetland Council of Social Service, 11 Mounthodly St., Lerwick, Shetland Scotland 2E1 0BJ United Kingdom. Phone: 01595 693816. Fax: 01595 696787. E-mail: shetlandcss@zetnet.co. uk. **Contact:** John Hunter or Alex Cluness. Magazine: A4/A5; 34 pages; glossy paper; illustrations; photos. Quarterly. Estab. 1947. Circ. 2,000.

Needs: Literary. Receives 20 unsolicited mss/month. Accepts 2 mss/issue; 8 mss/year. Publishes ms 2-3 months after acceptance. **Publishes 10-20 new writers/year.** Length: 1,700 words maximum; average length: 1,000 words. Publishes short shorts. Average length: 700-1,000 words. Also publishes literary essays, literary criticism and poetry. Sometimes comments on rejected mss.

How to Contact: Send complete ms with a cover letter. Accepts submissions by e-mail, fax and disk. Include estimated word count and brief bio. Responds in 4 months to queries. Send SASE (or IRC) for return of ms or send a disposable copy of ms and #10 SASE for reply only. Accepts previously published work and multiple submissions. Sample copy free. Reviews novels, short story collections and nonfiction books of interest to writers.

Payment/Terms: Pays contributor's copies; additional copies £1-80. Not copyrighted.

Advice: "Editorial committee select manuscripts."

NEW STONE CIRCLE, New Stone Circle, 1185 E. 1900 North Rd., White Heath IL 61884. **Contact:** Mary Hays, fiction editor. Magazine: 8½×5½; 40-58 pages; illustrations; photos. Annual. Estab. 1994. Circ. 100.

• *New Stone Circle* has won Pipistrelle Award for Best Literary Magazine.

Needs: "No racist or misogynist work." Receives 30 unsolicited mss/month. Accepts 4-5 mss/issue; 4-10 mss/year. Publishes ms 1 year after acceptance. Agented fiction 1%. **Publishes 1-2 new writers/year.** Recently published work by Christine Chiu, Cris Mazza, Elizabeth Weiser and Jessica Inclan. Publishes short shorts.

How to Contact: Send complete ms with a cover letter. Accepts submissions by disk (Mac compatible). Include brief bio and list of publications. Responds in 2 months to queries; 6 months to mss. Send SASE for return of ms or send a disposable copy of ms and #10 SASE for reply only. Accepts simultaneous submissions, previously published work and multiple submissions. Sample copy for $4.50. Guidelines for SASE. Reviews novels and short story collections.

Payment/Terms: Pays 1 contributor's copy; additional copies $3.50. Pays on publication for one-time rights. Sends galleys to author. Sponsors contest. Send SASE for guidelines.

Advice: "Show fresh imagery. As a reader, I want to be transported to the fictional world. Keep reading, keep writing, keep sending your work out."

NEW VIRGINIA REVIEW, 2A, 1306 E. Cary St., Richmond VA 23219. (804)782-1043. Editor: Mary Flinn. Magazine: 6½×10; 180 pages; high quality paper; coated, color cover stock. "Authors are serious writers of contemporary fiction." Published January, May and October. Estab. 1978. Circ. 2,000.

Needs: Contemporary, experimental, literary, mainstream, serialized/excerpted novel. No blue, science fiction, romance, children's. Receives 50-100 unsolicited fiction mss/month. Accepts an average of 15 mss/issue. Does not read mss April 1-September 1. Publishes ms an average of 6-9 months after acceptance. Length: no minimum; 8,000 words maximum; average length: 5,000-6,500 words. Also publishes poetry. Sometimes critiques rejected mss.

How to Contact: Send complete ms with cover letter, name, address, telephone number, brief biographical comment. Responds in 6 weeks to queries; up to 6 months to mss. "Will answer questions on status of ms." SASE (or IRC). Sample copy for $7 and 9×12 SAE with 5 first-class stamps.

Payment/Terms: Pays $10/printed page and contributor's copies; charge for extras, ½ cover price.

Terms: Pays on publication for first North American serial rights. Sponsors contests and awards for Virginia writers only.

Advice: "Try to write good strong fiction, stick to it, and try again with another editor."

THE NEW WRITER, P.O. Box 60, Cranbrook TN17 2ZR United Kingdom. 01580 212626. Fax: 01580 212041. E-mail: editor@thenewwriter.com. Website: www.thenewwriter.com (includes editorials, guidelines, extracts, links, etc.) **Contact:** Suzanne Ruthven, editor. Magazine: A4; 48 pages; illustrations; photos.

Contemporary writing magazine which publishes "the best in fact, fiction and poetry." Publishes 10 issues per annum. Estab. 1996. Circ. 1,500. "We consider short stories from subscribers only but we may also commission guest writers."

Needs: "We will consider most categories apart from stories written for children." No horror, erotic or cosy fiction. Accepts 4 mss/issue; 40 mss/year. Publishes ms up to 1 year after acceptance. Agented fiction 5%. **Majority of work is by previously unpublished writers.** Recently published work by Alan Dunn, Annabel Lamb, Laureen Vonnegut and Stephen Finucan. Length: 2,000-5,000 words; average length: 3,500 words. Publishes short shorts. Average length: 1,500 words. Also publishes literary essays, literary criticism and poetry. Often comments on rejected mss.

How to Contact: Query with clips of published work. Accepts queries but not mss by e-mail and fax. Include estimated word count, brief bio and list of publications. Responds in 4 months to queries; 8 months to mss. Send SASE (or IRC) for return of ms or send a disposable copy of ms and #10 SASE for reply only. Accepts simultaneous submissions. Sample copy for SASE and A4 SAE with IRCs only. Guidelines for SASE. Reviews novels, short story collections and nonfiction books of interest to writers.

Payment/Terms: Pays £10 per story by credit voucher; additional copies £1.50. Pays on publication for first rights. Sponsors contest, prose and poetry prizes (entry via website).

Advice: "Hone it—always be prepared to improve the story. It's a competitive market."

$⊘ NEW YORK STORIES, English Dept., LaGuardia Community College, E-103, 31-10 Thomson Ave., Long Island City NY 11101. (718)482-5673. **Contact:** Daniel Caplice Lynch, editor. Magazine: 9×11; 48 pages; photos. Quarterly. Estab. 1998.

Needs: Ethnic/multicultural, experimental, feminist, gay, humor/satire, lesbian, literary, mainstream/contemporary, regional. Receives 300 unsolicited mss/month. Accepts 5-10 mss/issue; 20-40 mss/year. Does not read mss June-August. Publishes ms 6 months after acceptance. Agented fiction 5%. **Publishes 2 new writers/year.** Length: 100 words minimum; average length: 2,500-3,000 words. Publishes short shorts. Also publishes literary essays, especially about New York. Sometimes comments on rejected mss.

How to Contact: Send complete ms with a cover letter. Include 1-paragraph bio and e-mail address. Responds in 2 months to queries; 3 months to mss. Send SASE for return of ms or send disposable copy of ms. Accepts simultaneous submissions and reprints. Guidelines for #10 SASE or by e-mail.

Payment/Terms: Pays $100-$1,000. Pays on publication.

Advice: "Fresh angles of vision, dark humor and psychological complexity are hallmarks of our short stories. Present characters who are 'alive.' Let them breathe. To achieve this, revise, revise, revise. Lately, the industry of publishing fiction seems to be playing it safe. We want your best—no matter what."

⊘◎ NIGHTFIRE, Camel's Back Books, P.O. Box 181126, Boston MA 02118. (617)825-5866. Fax: (617)282-5749. E-mail: nightfir10@aol.com. **Contact:** Michael Dubson, editor. Magazine: 6×9; 60-80 pages; 50 lb. uncoated book stock; colored cover stock/tape binding. "The theme of *Nightfire* is that there is much to celebrate in the lives of gay men, our primary target audience, and to survive in this culture is a triumph. To thrive and excel is a miracle. *Nightfire* will honor and exhault this phenomena in our work, and give gay authors a chance to express ideas not likely to be found in commercial, mainstream gay magazines." Quarterly. Estab. 2000. Small Publishers of North America, Publishers Marketing Association.

Needs: Adventure, experimental, family saga, gay, humor satire, literary, mainstream, mystery/suspense, New Age, psychic/supernatural/occult, romance, science fiction, all with an emphasis on the erotic. "Must be for and about gay men. Nothing that promotes or glorifies violence, particularly male-to-male violence. Homophobia must be portrayed as bad/harmful. Nothing dry or academic. Let passion—in all its forms—drive your writing." Accepts 7-10 mss/issue; 28-40 mss/year. Publishes ms 6 months after acceptance. Length: 1,000-5,000 words; average length: 2,500 words. Publishes short shorts. Average length: 1,250 words. Also publishes literary essays—personal experience or philosophical discussions of sexual and gender dynamics and societal norms.

How to Contact: Send complete ms with a cover letter or fax. Do not e-mail initial submissions, although authors of accepted pieces may be asked to e-mail. Include estimated word count and brief bio. Responds in 1

**FOR EXPLANATIONS OF THESE SYMBOLS,
SEE THE INSIDE FRONT AND BACK COVERS OF THIS BOOK.**

month to queries; 3 months to mss. Send SASE (or IRC) for return of ms or send a disposable copy of ms and #10 SASE for reply only. Accepts simultaneous submissions and multiple submissions. Sample copy for $8. Guidelines for SASE, by e-mail or fax.

Payment/Terms: Pays 2 contributor's copies. Pays on publication for first rights.

Advice: "We're looking for strong characters who are survivors—able to stand up against all adversaries—internal, external, societal, etc. Stories may end sadly or badly; but the power and strength of the character must always be clear. Write from the heart—what are the things, the people, the experiences you really care about? Make these the material of your stories. Make your goal as a writer to make your reader and editor feel. Gay publications are growing in both number and in size and we want *Nightfire* to be a part of that trend, but we also want it to challenge and counter some of the main streaming that goes on. We also want to find and give voice to new writers."

$⃞ NIMROD, International Journal of Prose and Poetry, University of Tulsa, 600 S. College Ave., Tulsa OK 74104-3126. (918)631-3080. Fax: (918)631-3033. E-mail: nimrod@utulsa.edu. Website: www.utulsa. edu/nimrod/ (includes writer's guidelines, excerpts from published work, contest rules, theme issue announcements, ed-in-chief name and subscription/sample issue order form). **Contact:** Gerry McLoud, fiction editor. Magazine: 6×9; 192 pages; 60 lb. white paper; illustrations; photos. "We publish one thematic issue and one awards issue each year. A recent theme was "Islands in the Sea and of the Mind," a compilation of poetry and prose from all over the world. We seek vigorous, imaginative, quality writing. Our mission is to discover new writers and publish experimental writers who have not yet found a 'home' for their work." Semiannual. Estab. 1956. Circ. 3,000.

Needs: "We accept contemporary poetry and/or prose. May submit adventure, ethnic, experimental, prose poem or translations." No science fiction or romance. Upcoming theme: "Making Language II," a translation issue. Submit by January 2002. Issue will be published in the summer of 2002. Receives 120 unsolicited fiction mss/month. **Published 5-10 new writers within the last year.** Recently published work by Felicia Ward, Ellen Bass, Kimberly Meyer and Linda Mannheim. Length: 7,500 words maximum. Also publishes poetry.

How to Contact: SASE for return of ms. Accepts queries by e-mail. No mss by e-mail except for writers living overseas. Accepts simultaneous and multiple submissions. Responds in 5 months. Sample copy: "to see what *Nimrod* is all about, send $10 for a back issue."

Payment/Terms: Pays 2 contributor's copies.

Advice: "We have not changed our fiction needs: quality, vigor, distinctive voice. We have, however, increased the number of stories we print. See current issues. We look for fiction that is fresh, vigorous, distinctive, serious and humorous, seriously-humorous, unflinchingly serious, ironic—whatever. Just so it is quality. Strongly encourage writers to send #10 SASE for brochure for annual literary contest with prizes of $1,000 and $2,000."

☑ ⃞ 96 Inc., P.O. Box 15559, Boston MA 02215-0011. (617)267-0543. Fax: (617)262-3568. E-mail: to96inc @ici.net. **Contact:** Vera Gold or Nancy Mehegan, editors. Magazine: 8½×11; 50 pages; 20 lb. paper; matte cover; illustrations; photos. "*96 Inc.* promotes the process; integrates beginning/young with established writers; reaches out to audiences of all ages and backgrounds." Annual. Estab. 1992. Circ. 3,000.

Needs: All types, styles and subjects. Receives 200 unsolicited mss/month. Accepts 12-15 mss/issue; 30 mss/year. Agented fiction 10%. **Publishes 2-10 new writers/year.** Recently published work by Rose Moss, Alene Bricken, Harlyn Aizley, Sharon Stratts and Judith Stitzel. Length: 1,000-7,000 words. Publishes short shorts. Also publishes literary essays, literary criticism and poetry. Sometimes comments on rejected mss.

How to Contact: Query first. Accepts mss on disk. Include estimated word count, bio (100 words) and list of publications. Responds in 3 weeks to queries; up to 1 year to mss. Send SASE for reply, return of ms or send a disposable copy of ms. Accepts simultaneous and multiple submissions. Sample copy for $7.50. Guidelines for #10 SASE. Reviews novels and short story collections on occasion.

Payment/Terms: Pays modest sum if funds are available, not depending on length or merit, free subscription and 4 contributor's copies. Pays on publication for one-time rights.

Advice: Looks for "good writing in any style. Pays attention to the process. Read at least one issue. Be patient—it takes a very long time for readers to go through the thousands of manuscripts."

☑ $THE NORTH AMERICAN REVIEW, University of Northern Iowa, Cedar Falls IA 50614-0516. (319)273-6455. Fax: (319)273-4326. E-mail: nar@uni.edu. Website: http://webdelsol.com/NorthAmReview/ NAR. Editor: Vince Gotera. **Contact:** Grant Tracey, fiction editor. "The NAR is the oldest literary magazine in America and one of the most respected; though we have no prejudices about the subject matter of material sent to us, our first concern is quality." Bimonthly. Estab. 1815. Circ. 4,000.

Needs: Open (literary). Reads fiction mss from January 1 to April 1 only.

How to Contact: Send complete ms with SASE. No simultaneous submissions. Sample copy for $5.

Payment/Terms: Pays $5 per 350 words of prose, $20 minimum and 2 contributor's copies; additional copies $4.50. Pays on publication for first North American serial rights.

Advice: "We are interested in high-quality fiction on any subject, but we are especially interested in work that addresses contemporary North American concerns and issues, particularly the environment, gender, race, ethnicity and class. We like stories that start quickly and have a strong narrative arc. We'd also like to see more stories engaged with wonder and humor."

NORTH DAKOTA QUARTERLY, University of North Dakota, Box 7209, University Station, Grand Forks ND 58202. (701)777-3322. Fax: (701)777-3650. E-mail: ndq@sage.und.nodak.edu. Website: www.1 92.41.6.160/ndq (includes editors, samples of published work and covers). Editor: Robert W. Lewis. **Contact:** William Borden, fiction editor. Poetry Editor: Jay Meek. Magazine: 6×9; 200 pages; bond paper; illustrations; photos. Magazine publishing "essays in humanities; some short stories; some poetry." University audience. Quarterly. Estab. 1911. Circ. 700.

● Work published in *North Dakota Quarterly* was selected for inclusion in *The O. Henry Awards* anthology. The editors are especially interested in work by Native American writers.

Needs: Contemporary, ethnic, experimental, feminist, historical, humor/satire, literary. Receives 100-120 unsolicited mss/month. Accepts 4 mss/issue; 16 mss/year. **Publishes 4-5 new writers/year.** Published work by Debra Marquort, Andrew Dillon, Richard Broderick, Robert Wrigley, Phillip Dacey, Adrian C. Louis and Nancy L. Walker. Length: 3,000-4,000 words average. Also publishes literary essays, literary criticism, poetry. Sometimes comments on or critiques rejected ms.

How to Contact: Send complete ms with cover letter. Include one-paragraph bio. "But it need not be much more than hello; please read this story; I've published (if so, best examples) . . ." SASE. Responds in 3 months. Publishes ms an average of 1 year after acceptance. Sample copy for $8. Reviews novels and short story collections.

Payment/Terms: Pays 2-4 contributor's copies; 30% discount for extras. Acquires one-time rights. Sends galleys to author.

NORTHEAST ARTS MAGAZINE, P.O. Box 4363, Portland ME 04101. **Contact:** Mr. Leigh Donaldson, publisher. Magazine: 6½×9½; 32-40 pages; matte finish paper; card stock cover; illustrations; photos. Bimonthly. Estab. 1990. Circ. 750.

Needs: Ethnic, gay, historical, literary, mystery/suspense (private eye), prose poem (under 2,000 words). No obscenity, racism, sexism, etc. Receives 50 unsolicited mss/month. Accepts 1-2 mss/issue; 5-7 mss/year. Publishes ms 2-4 months after acceptance. Agented fiction 20%. Length: 750 words preferred. Publishes short shorts. Sometimes critiques rejected mss.

How to Contact: Send complete ms with cover letter. Include short bio. Responds in 1 month to queries; 4 months to mss. SASE. Accepts simultaneous submissions. Sample copy for $4.50, SAE and 75¢ postage. Guidelines free.

Payment/Terms: Pays 2 contributor's copies. Acquires first North American serial rights.

Advice: Looks for "creative/innovative use of language and style. Unusual themes and topics."

NORTHWEST REVIEW, 369 PLC, University of Oregon, Eugene OR 97403. (503)346-3957. Website: darkwing.uoregon.edu/~engl/deptinfo/NWR.html. Editor: John Witte. **Contact:** Janice MacCrae, fiction editor. Magazine: 6×9; 140-160 pages; high quality cover stock; illustrations; photos. "A general literary review featuring poems, stories, essays and reviews, circulated nationally and internationally. For a literate audience in avant-garde as well as traditional literary forms; interested in the important writers who have not yet achieved their readership." Triannual. Estab. 1957. Circ. 1,200.

● *Northwest Review* received the Oregon Governor's Award for the Arts.

Needs: Contemporary, experimental, feminist, literary and translations. Accepts 4-5 mss/issue, 12-15 mss/year. Receives approximately 100 unsolicited fiction mss each month. **Published new writers within the last year.** Published work by Diana Abu-Jaber, Madison Smartt Bell, Maria Flook and Charles Marvin. Length: "Mss longer than 40 pages are at a disadvantage." Also publishes literary essays, literary criticism, poetry. Critiques rejected mss when there is time. Sometimes recommends other markets.

How to Contact: Send complete ms with SASE. "No simultaneous submissions are considered." Responds in 4 months. Sample copy for $4. Reviews novels and short story collections. Send books to John Witte.

Payment/Terms: Pays 3 contributor's copies and one-year subscription; 40% discount on extras. Acquires first rights.

$ NORTHWOODS JOURNAL, A Magazine for Writers, Conservatory of American Letters, P.O. Box 298, Thomaston ME 04861. (207)354-0998. Fax: (207)354-8953. E-mail: cal@americanletters.org. Website: www.americanletters.org (includes guidelines and catalogue). Editor: R.W. Olmsted. **Contact:** Ken Sieben, fiction editor (submit fiction to Ken Sieben, 253 Ocean Ave., Sea Bright NJ 07760). Magazine: 5½×8½; 32-64 pages; white paper; 70 lb. text cover; offset printing; some illustrations; photos. "No theme, no philosophy—for writers and for people who read for entertainment." Quarterly. Estab. 1993. Circ. 500.

Needs: Adventure, experimental, fantasy (science fantasy, sword and sorcery), literary, mainstream/contemporary, mystery/suspense (amateur sleuth, police procedural, private eye/hard-boiled, romantic suspense), psychic/supernatural/occult, regional, romance (gothic, historical), science fiction (hard science, soft/sociological), sports, westerns (frontier, traditional). Publishes special fiction issue or anthology. "Would like to see more first-person adventure." No porn or evangelical. Receives 20 unsolicited mss/month. Accepts 12-15 mss/year. **Publishes 15 new writers/year.** Published work by Paul A. Jurvie, Richard Vaughn, Bryn C. Gray and Sandra Thompson. Length: 2,500 words maximum. Also publishes literary essays, literary criticism and poetry.

How to Contact: *Charges $3 reading fee per 2,500 words.* Read guidelines *before* submitting. Send complete ms with a cover letter. Include word count and list of publications. There is a $3 fee per story (make checks payable to Ken Sieben. The magazine gets none of the reading fee). Responds in 2 days to queries; by next deadline plus 5 days to mss. Send SASE for reply, return of ms or send a disposable copy of ms. No simultaneous submissions. No electronic submissions. Sample copies: $5.50 next issue, $8.75 current issue, $12.50 back issue (if available), all postage paid. Guidelines for #10 SASE. Reviews novels, short story collections and poetry.

Payment/Terms: Varies, "minimum $3/published page." Pays on acceptance for first North American serial rights.

Advice: "Read guidelines, read the things we've published. Know your market."

$ ⊘ NOTRE DAME REVIEW, University of Notre Dame, English Department, Creative Writing, Notre Dame IN 46556. (219)631-6952. Fax: (219)631-8209. E-mail: english.ndreview.1@nd.edu. Website: www.nd.edu/~ndr/review.htm (includes guidelines, editors, additional poetry, fiction, book reviews, art, audio clips of authors and photos). Senior editor: Steve Tomasula. Editor: John Matthias. **Contact:** William O'Rourke, fiction editor. Literary magazine: 6×9; 115 pages; 50 lb. smooth paper; illustrations; photos. "The *Notre Dame Review* is an independent, non-commercial magazine of contemporary American and international fiction, poetry, criticism and art. We are especially interested in work that takes on big issues by making the invisible seen, that gives voice to the voiceless. In addition to showcasing celebrated authors like Seamus Heaney and Czelaw Milosz, the *Notre Dame Review* introduces readers to authors they may have never encountered before, but who are doing innovative and important work. In conjunction with the *Notre Dame Review*, the on-line companion to the printed magazine, the *Notre Dame Re-view* engages readers as a community centered in literary rather than commercial concerns, a community we reach out to through critique and commentary as well as aesthetic experience." Semiannual. Estab. 1995. Circ. 2,000.

Needs: "We're eclectic." No genre fiction. Upcoming theme issues planned. List of upcoming themes or editorial calendar available for SASE. Receives 75 unsolicited fiction mss/month. Accepts 4-5 mss/issue; 10 mss/year. Does not read mss May-August. Publishes ms 6 months after acceptance. **Publishes 1 new writer/year.** Published work by Ed Falco, Jarda Cerverka and David Green. Length: 3,000 words maximum. Publishes short shorts. Also publishes literary criticism and poetry. Sometimes comments on rejected ms.

How to Contact: Send complete ms with cover letter. Include 4-sentence bio. Responds in 4 months. Send SASE for response, return of ms, or send a disposable copy of ms. Accepts simultaneous submissions. Sample copy for $6.

Payment/Terms: Pays $5-25 and contributor's copies. Pays on publication for first North American serial rights.

Advice: "We're looking for high quality work that takes on big issues in a literary way. Please read our back issues before submitting."

☑ $ ◎ NOW & THEN, Center for Appalachian Studies and Services, East Tennessee State University, Box 70556, Johnson City TN 37614-1707. (423)439-6173. E-mail: woodsidj@etsu.edu. Website: http://cass.etsu.edu/n~t. **Contact:** Jane Woodside, editor. Magazine: 8½×11; 44-48 pages; coated paper and cover stock; illustrations; photos. Publication focuses on Appalachian culture, present and past. Readers are mostly people in the region involved with Appalachian issues, literature, education." Triannual. Estab. 1984. Circ. 1,250.

Needs: Ethnic, literary, regional, excerpted novel, prose poem. "Absolutely has to relate to Appalachian theme. Can be about adjustment to new environment, themes of leaving and returning, for instance. Nothing unrelated to region." Upcoming themes: Natural Resources, Appalachia & the World and First Person Appalachia (first person fiction and essays). Buys 2-3 mss/issue. Publishes ms 3-4 months after acceptance. **Published new writers within the last year.** Published work by Lee Smith, Pinckney Benedict, Gurney Norman, George Ella Lyon, Fred Chappell and Robert Morgan. Length: 3,000 words maximum. Publishes short shorts. Also publishes literary essays, poetry.

How to Contact: Send complete ms with cover letter. Responds in 6 months. Include "information we can use for contributor's note." SASE (or IRC). Accepts simultaneous submissions, "but let us know when it has been accepted elsewhere right away." Sample copy for $7. Publishes reviews of novels or short story collections. Send books to: Marianne Worthington, Dept. of Communications & Theatre Arts, Cumberland College, 6000 College Station Dr., Williamsburg KY 40769.

Payment/Terms: Pays up to $75 per story, contributor's copies.

Terms: Holds copyright.

Advice: "Keep in mind that *Now & Then* only publishes fiction related to the Appalachian region (all of West Virginia and parts of 12 other states from southern New York to northern Mississippi, Alabama and Georgia). Plus we only publish fiction that has some plausible connection to a specific issues themes. Get the guidelines. We like to offer first-time publication to promising writers."

N ⊕ OASIS, Oasis Books, 12 Stevenage Rd., London SW6 6ES United Kingdom. **Editor:** Ian Robinson. Published 3 times/year. Circ. 400. Publishes usually 1 story/issue.

Needs: "Innovative, experimental fiction. No science fiction, fantasy, surreal. Wants non-standard, 'experimental' short stories." Published work by Eugenio de Andrade (Portugal), Sheila E. Murphy (USA), Henrikas Radauskas (Lithuania), D.F. Lewis (UK), Jay Woodman (S. Africa), Neil Leadbeater (Scotland) and Michael Wilding (Australia). Length: 1,800 words maximum.

Payment/Terms: Pays in copies. Sample copy available for $3.50 check (made payable to Robert Vas Dias) and 4 IRCs.

Advice: "Have a look at a copy of the magazine before submitting. We look for originality of thought and expression, and a willingness to take risks."

$ ⊘ OASIS, A Literary Magazine, P.O. Box 626, Largo FL 33779-0626. (727)449-2186. E-mail: oasislit@ aol.com. Editor: Neal Storrs. **Contact:** Fiction Editor. Magazine: 70 pages. "Literary magazine first, last and always—looking for styles that delight and amaze, that are polished and poised. Next to that, content considerations relatively unimportant—open to all." Quarterly. Estab. 1992. Circ. 500.

● *Oasis* was ranked #43 on *Writer's Digest*'s Fiction 50 list of top markets for writers.

Needs: High-quality writing. Also publishes translations. Receives 150 unsolicited mss/month. Accepts 6 mss/ issue; 24 mss/year. Publishes ms 4-6 months after acceptance. **Publishes 2 new writers/year.** Recently published work by Wendell Mayo, Al Masarik and Mark Wisniewski. Length: no minimum or maximum. Also publishes literary essays and poetry. Occasionally comments on rejected mss.

How to Contact: Send complete ms with or without a cover letter. Accepts queries/mss by e-mail. Usually reports same day. Send SASE for reply, return of ms or send a disposable copy of ms. Accepts simultaneous, multiple, reprint and electronic (e-mail) submissions. Sample copy for $7.50. Guidelines for #10 SASE.

Payment/Terms: Pays $15-30 and 1 contributor's copy. Pays on publication for first rights.

Advice: "If you want to write good stories, read good stories. Cultivate the critical ability to recognize what makes a story original and true to itself."

✓ ⊘ THE OHIO REVIEW, 344 Scott Quad, Ohio University, Athens OH 45701-2979. (740)593-1900. Fax: (740)597-2967. Website: www.ohiou.edu/theohioreview/.

● *The Ohio Review* has ceased publication with release of its 30th anniversary *New & Selected* edition. Please see the website for a complete listing of back issues.

⊘ OPEN SPACES QUARTERLY, PMB 134, 6327 C SW Capitol Hwy., Portland OR 97201-1937. (503)227-5764. Fax: (503)227-3401. E-mail: info@open-spaces.com. Website: www.open-spaces.com (includes overview, contents of current and back issues, sample articles and creative writing, submission guidelines, contact information). Editor: Penny Harrison. **Contact:** A. Bradley, fiction editor. Magazine: 64 pages; illustrations; photos. "We are a high-quality, general-interest publication with an intelligent, well-educated readership appreciative of well-written, insightful work." Quarterly. Estab. 1997.

Needs: "Excellence is the issue—not subject matter." Accepts 2 mss/issue; 8 mss/year. Published work by William Kittredge, Terence O'Donnell, Pattiann Rogers and David James Duncan. Publishes short shorts. Also publishes literary essays and poetry. Sometimes comments on rejected mss.

How to Contact: Send complete ms with a cover letter. Accepts queries/mss by fax. Include short bio, social security number and list of publications. SASE for return of ms or send a disposable copy of ms. Sample copy for $10. Guidelines free for SASE.

Payment/Terms: Pays on publication.

Advice: "The surest way for a writer to determine whether his or her material is right for us is to read the magazine."

⚑ ✓ $ ⊘ OTHER VOICES, Other Voices Publishing Society, Garneau, P.O. Box 52059, 8210-109 St., Edmonton, Alberta T6G 2T5 Canada. (780)424-5059. E-mail: editor@othervoices.ab.ca. Website: www.othervoic es.ab.ca (includes excerpts, upcoming issues, names of editors, newsletter). **Contact:** Jannie Edwards, fiction editor. Magazine: 4¼×5½; 150 pages; illustrations; photos. "While our magazine is not limited to the publication of women artists, we encourage, in particular, work by women speaking from diverse cultural, sexual and regional perspectives. *Other Voices* is committed to helping underrepresented voices find the space to be heard." Biannual. Estab. 1987. Circ. 400. Member, Alberta Magazine Publisher's Association, Canadian Magazine Publishers' Association.

Needs: Erotica, ethnic/multicultural, experimental, family saga, feminist, gay, historical, humor satire, lesbian, literary, New Age. No genre fiction or excessive sexuality, crudity. Receives 30 unsolicited mss/month. Accepts 6 mss/issue; 12 mss/year. Publishes ms 3 weeks after acceptance. **Publishes 4 new writers/year.** Recently published work by Patricia Young, Ken Rivard and Virgil Suarez. Length: 2,500-5,000 words; average length: 3,000 words. Publishes short shorts. Average length: 500 words. Also publishes literary essays and poetry. Sometimes comments on rejected mss.

How to Contact: Send complete ms with a cover letter. Include estimated word count, brief bio and list of publications. Responds in 3 weeks to queries; 4 months to mss. Send SASE (or IRC) for return of ms or send a disposable copy of ms and #10 SASE for reply only. Accepts multiple submissions. Sample copy for $12 (US); $10 (Canadian). Guidelines for SASE or by e-mail. Reviews novels, short story collections and nonfiction books of interest to writers.

Payment/Terms: Pays $30; additional copies $8 (Canadian). Pays on publication for electronic rights (we will ask individual authors if we wish to publish on our website). Not copyrighted. Sponsors annual contest with prizes of $500 (poetry, fiction).

Advice: "Our magazine has expanded from publishing exclusively women's writing to publishing other voices more generally. We provide a space for both emerging and established writers who might otherwise not have the space to be heard."

☑ ◑ ☯ OTHER VOICES, The University of Illinois at Chicago, Dept. of English (M/C 162), 601 S. Morgan St., Chicago IL 60607. (312)413-2209. Website: www.othervoicesmagazine.org (includes writer's guidelines, names of editors, e-mail address and subscription information). Editors: Lois Hauselman and Gina Frangello. **Contact:** Lois Hauselman or Gina Frangello. Magazine: 5⅞×9; 168-205 pages; 60 lb. paper; coated cover stock; occasional photos. "Original, fresh, diverse stories and novel excerpts" for literate adults. Semiannual. Estab. 1985. Circ. 1,500.

- *Other Voices* ranked #32 on *Writer's Digest*'s "Fiction 50" list of top markets for fiction writers. Work from *OV* was included in *Best American Short Stories of the Century* and *Pushcart Best of the Small Presses 2000*. *Other Voices* has received 18 Illinois Arts Council Awards since it began.

Needs: Fiction only. Contemporary, excerpted novel, experimental, humor/satire and literary. No taboos, except ineptitude and murkiness. No science fiction, romance, horror. Would like to see more one-act plays and experimental literary stories. Receives 300 unsolicited fiction mss/month. Accepts 17-20 mss/issue. **Publishes 6 new writers/year. Publishes new writers.** Recently published work by Aimee Bender, Wanda Coleman, Cris Mazza and Dan Chaon. Length: 5,000 words maximum; average length: 4,000 words.

How to Contact: Send ms with SASE October 1 to April 1 only. No e-mail submissions. No multiple submissions. Mss received during non-reading period are returned unread. Cover letters "should be brief and list previous publications. Also, list title of submission. Most beginners' letters try to 'explain' the story—a big mistake." Accepts simultaneous submissions. Responds in 3 months to mss. Sample copy for $7 (includes postage). Guidelines for #10 SASE.

Payment/Terms: Pays in contributor's copies and modest cash gratuity. Acquires one-time rights.

Advice: "There are so *few* markets for *quality* fiction! By publishing up to 40 stories a year, we provide new and established writers a forum for their work. Send us your best voice, your best work, your best best."

$ ◑ ◎ THE OXFORD AMERICAN, The Southern Magazine of Good Writing, P.O. Box 1156, Oxford MS 38655. (662)236-1836. Website: www.oxfordamericanmag.com. **Contact:** Marc Smirnoff, editor. Magazine: 8½×11; 100 pages; glossy paper; glossy cover; illustrations; photos. Quarterly. Estab. 1992. Circ. 40,000.

Needs: Regional (Southern); stories set in the South. Published work by Lewis Nordan, Donna Tartt, Florence King and Tony Earley. Also publishes literary essays and poetry. Sometimes comments on rejected mss.

How to Contact: Send complete ms. Send SASE for reply, return of ms or send a disposable copy of ms. No simultaneous submissions without indicating as such. No e-mail or faxed submissions. "No further guidelines available than those stated here." Sample copy for $5.95. "We review Southern novels or short story collections only."

Payment/Terms: Pays $100 minimum. Pays on publication for first rights; prices vary.

Advice: "I know you've heard it before—but we appreciate those writers who try to get into the spirit of the magazine which they can best accomplish by being familiar with it."

[N] ◑ OXYGEN, A Literary Magazine, Oxygen Editions, 537 Jones St., PMB 999, San Francisco CA 94102. E-mail: oxygen@slip.net. Website: www.oxygeneditions.net (includes excerpts, guidelines, quotations, drawings). **Contact:** Richard Hack, editor. Magazine: 5½×8½; 130 pages; 60 lb. vellum paper; 110 lb. laminated cover; illustrations; photos. "We are San Francisco's best literary magazine, as various prize-winning authors have noted. We continue a West Coast tradition of trying new things, promoting visions of beauty, truth and communal spirit. We like work both innovative and traditional, religious or secular, pleasure-seeking. We have an unusually broad range of work and points-of-view." Annual. Estab. 1991. Circ. 500.

Needs: "We look at almost any type or subject matter. Liveliness, depth, style, originality and economy are main considerations for selection. Please, no genre or formula fiction." Receives 50 unsolicited mss/month. Accepts 3-6 mss/issue; 3-6 mss/year. Publishes ms 4 months after acceptance. **Publishes 3-4 new writers/year.** Length: 250-5,000 words; average length: 1,750 words. Publishes short shorts. Average length: 750 words. Also publishes literary essays, literary criticism and poetry.

How to Contact: Send complete ms with a cover letter. Include brief bio. Responds in up to 4 months to mss (We recommend simultaneous submissions.) Accepts simultaneous, previously published and multiple submissions (if in smaller venue or chapbook). Sample copy for $5. Guidelines for SASE.

Payment/Terms: Pays 2 contributor's copies; additional copies $4 plus postage. Pays on publication. All rights revert to authors. Sends galleys to author.

✔ ◪ ☑ ▣ **OYSTER BOY REVIEW OF FICTION AND POETRY**, P.O. Box 77842, San Francisco CA 94107-0842. E-mail: fiction@oysterboyreview.com. Website: www.oysterboyreview.com (includes full text of print issues, all back issues, submission and subscription information, staff, author index, related links). **Contact:** Damon Sauve, publisher, fiction editor. Electronic and print magazine. "We publish kick-ass, teeth-cracking stories."

• *Oyster Boy* was *Writer's Digest* Best Poetry Zine 2000. Work from *Oyster Boy* was selected for the *Pushcart Prize 1999* anthology.

Needs: "Fiction that revolves around characters in conflict with themselves or each other; a plot that has a beginning, a middle, and an end; a narrative with a strong moral center (not necessarily 'moralistic'); a story with a satisfying resolution to the conflict; and an ethereal something that contributes to the mystery of a question, but does not necessarily seek or contrive to answer it." No genre fiction. **Publishes 4 new writers/year.** "We would like to see longer stories—5,000 or more words." Recently published work by Tod Goldberg, Ken Wainio, Elisha Porat and Kevin McGowin.

How to Contact: Electronic and traditional submissions accepted. "E-mail submissions should be sent as the body-text of the e-mail message, or as an attached ASCII-text file. Accepts multiple submissions.

Advice: "Keep writing, keep submitting, keep revising."

✔ ◪ **PACIFIC COAST JOURNAL**, French Bread Publications, P.O. Box 56, Carlsbad CA 92018. E-mail: paccoastj@frenchbreadpublications.com. Website: www.frenchbreadpublications.com/pcj (includes guidelines, contest information, past published work). Editor: Stillson Graham. **Contact:** Stephanie Kylkis, fiction editor. Magazine: 5½×8½; 40 pages; 20 lb. paper; 67 lb. cover; illustrations; b&w photos. "Slight focus toward Western North America/Pacific Rim." Quarterly (or "whenever we have enough money"). Estab. 1992. Circ. 200.

Needs: Ethnic/multicultural, experimental, feminist, historical, humor/satire, literary, science fiction (soft/socio-logical, magical realism). No children. Receives 30-40 unsolicited mss/month. Accepts 3-4 mss/issue; 10-12 mss/year. Publishes ms 6-18 months after acceptance. **Publishes 3-5 new writers/year.** Published work by Tamara Jane, Lisa Garrigues and Charles Ordine. Length: 4,000 words maximum; 2,500 words preferred. Publishes short shorts. Also publishes literary essays and poetry. Sometimes comments on rejected mss. Sponsors contest. Send SASE for details.

How to Contact: Send complete ms with a cover letter. Include 3 other publication titles that are recommended as good for writers. Responds in 6 months. Send SASE for reply, return of ms or send a disposable copy of ms. Accepts simultaneous, reprint and electronic submissions (Mac or IBM disks). Sample copy for $2.50, 6×9 SASE. Reviews novels and short story collections.

Payment/Terms: Pays 1 contributor's copy. Acquires one-time rights.

Advice: "We tend to comment more on a story not accepted for publication when an e-mail address is provided as the SASE. There are very few quality literary magazines that are not backed by big institutions. We don't have those kinds of resources so publishing anything is a struggle. We have to make each issue count."

✔ ◪ ▣ **PACIFIC ENTERPRISE, A Magazine for Enterprising Filipinos and Friends**, P.O. Box 1907, Fond du Lac WI 54936-1907. (920)922-9218. E-mail: rudyled@vbe.com. Website: www.penpacific.com. **Contact:** Rudy Ledesma, editor. Magazine: 8½×11; 36-44 pages; 35 lb. stock newsprint paper; coated enamel cover; illustrations; photos. "*Pacific Enterprise* welcomes submissions of unpublished works from emerging and established writers. Although our primary audience is Filipino Americans, we welcome submissions from every-one. Our aim is to publish the best work we can find regardless of the author's country of origin." Published "once or twice a year." Estab. 1998. Circ. 3,000.

• *Pacific Enterprise* has converted to an electronic publication with selected pieces to be included in periodic print editions.

Needs: Literary. "No fantasy, juvenile, western, romance, horror, science fiction." Receives about 3 unsolicited mss/month. Accepts 0-3 mss/issue; 2-3 mss/year. Publishes ms 6-12 months after acceptance. Recently published work by Val Vallejo and Holly Lalena Day. Length: 700-5,000 words. Publishes short shorts. Length: 500 words. Also publishes literary essays, literary criticism, poetry. Sometimes comments on rejected mss.

How to Contact: Send complete ms by e-mail (in body or as Word attachment). Include estimated word count, 4-5 sentence bio and list of publications. Responds in 6 months "or longer." Send a disposable copy of ms. Accepts simultaneous submissions. Sample copy for $4, 9×12 SAE and 3 first-class stamps. Guidelines free and on website. Reviews novels and short story collections. Send books to the editor at above address.

Payment/Terms: Pays 2 contributor's copies "if the work appears in printed format." Pays on publication for first North American serial rights. Sends galleys to author.

Advice: "We're looking for a strong command of language; something happening in the story; a story that surprises us. Request a sample copy and send in your work."

PALO ALTO REVIEW, A Journal of Ideas, Palo Alto College, 1400 W. Villaret, San Antonio TX 78224. (210)921-5021. Fax: (210)921-5008. E-mail: eshull@accd.edu. **Contact:** Bob Richmond and Ellen Shull, editors. Magazine: 8½×11; 60 pages; 60 lb. natural white paper (50% recycled); illustrations; photos. "Not too experimental nor excessively avant-garde, just good stories (for fiction). Ideas are what we are after. We are interested in connecting the college and the community. We would hope that those who attempt these connections will choose startling topics and interesting angles with which to investigate the length and breadth of the teaching/learning spectrum, life itself." Semiannual (spring and fall). Estab. 1992. Circ. 500-600.

  • *Palo Alto Review* was awarded the Pushcart Prize for 2001.

Needs: Adventure, ethnic/multicultural, experimental, fantasy, feminist, historical, humor/satire, literary, mainstream/contemporary, mystery/suspense, regional, romance, science fiction, translations, westerns. Upcoming themes available for SASE. Receives 100-150 unsolicited mss/month. Accepts 2-4 mss/issue; 4-8 mss/year. Does not read mss March-April and October-November when putting out each issue. Publishes ms 2-15 months after acceptance. **Publishes 30 new writers/year.** Published work by Layle Silbert, Naomi Chase, Kenneth Emberly, C.J. Hannah, Tom Juvik, Kassie Fleisher and Paul Perry. Length: 5,000 words maximum. Publishes short shorts. Also publishes articles, interviews, literary essays, literary criticism, poetry. Always comments on rejected mss.

How to Contact: Send complete ms with a cover letter. "Request sample copy and guidelines." Accepts queries by e-mail. Include brief bio and brief list of publications. Responds in 4 months. Send SASE for reply, return of ms or send a disposable copy of ms. Accepts simultaneous and electronic (Macintosh disk) submissions. Sample copy for $5. Guidelines for #10 SASE.

Payment/Terms: Pays 2 contributor's copies; additional copies for $5. Acquires first North American serial rights.

Advice: "Good short stories have interesting characters confronted by a dilemma working toward a solution. So often what we get is 'a moment in time,' not a story. Generally, characters are interesting because readers can identify with them. Edit judiciously. Cut out extraneous verbiage. Set up a choice that has to be made. Then create tension—who wants what and why they can't have it."

PANGOLIN PAPERS, Turtle Press, P.O. Box 241, Nordland WA 98358. (360)385-3626. E-mail: trtlbluf@olympus.net. **Contact:** Pat Britt, managing editor. Magazine: 5½×8½; 120 pages; 24 lb. paper; 80 lb. cover. "Best quality literary fiction for an informed audience." Triannual. Estab. 1994. Circ. 500.

Needs: Condensed/excerpted novel, experimental, humor/satire, literary, translations. "We would like to see more funny but literate stories." No "genre such as romance or science fiction." Plans to publish special fiction issues or anthologies in the future. Receives 30 unsolicited mss/month. Accepts 7-10 mss/issue; 20-30 mss/year. Publishes ms 4-12 months after acceptance. Agented fiction 10%. **Publishes 3-4 new writers/year.** Published work by Jack Nisbet and Barry Gifford. Length: 100-7,000 words; average length: 3,500 words. Publishes short shorts. Length: 400 words. Also publishes literary essays. Sometimes comments on rejected mss.

How to Contact: Send complete ms with a cover letter. Include estimated word count and short bio. Accepts mss on disk. Responds in 2 months to mss. Send SASE for reply, return of ms or send a disposable copy of ms. No simultaneous submissions. Sample copy for $6 and $1.50 postage. Guidelines for #10 SAE.

Payment/Terms: Pays 2 contributor's copies. Offers annual $200 prize for best story. Acquires first North American serial rights. Sends galleys to author.

Advice: "We are looking for original voices; good story, tight writing. Follow the rules and be honest in your work."

$ THE PARIS REVIEW, P.O. Box 1557, New York NY 10113-1557 (*business office only, send mss to address below*). (212)861-0016. Fax: (212)861-4504. Website: www.parisreview.com (includes history, excerpts from the magazine, masthead, audio clips). **Contact:** George A. Plimpton, editor. Magazine: 5¼×8½; about 260 pages; illustrations; photos (unsolicited artwork not accepted). "Fiction and poetry of superlative quality, whatever the genre, style or mode. Our contributors include prominent, as well as less well-known and previously unpublished writers. Writers at Work interview series includes important contemporary writers discussing their own work and the craft of writing." Quarterly.

• Work published in *The Paris Review* received five Pushcart awards. It ranked #5 on *Writer's Digest*'s Fiction 50 list of top markets for writers.

Needs: Literary. Receives about 1,000 unsolicited fiction mss each month. **Publishes 5 new writers/year.** Recently publisher work by Thomas Wolfe, Denis Johnson, Melissa Pritchard, Robert Cording and Jeff Dolven. No preferred length. Also publishes literary essays, poetry.

How to Contact: *Send complete ms with SASE to Fiction Editor, 541 E. 72nd St., New York NY 10021.* Responds in 8 months. Accepts simultaneous and multiple submissions. Sample copy for $12. Writer's guidelines for #10 SASE (from *The Paris Review,* 45-39 171st Place, Flushing NY 11358). Sponsors annual Aga Khan Fiction Contest award of $1,000.

Payment/Terms: Pays up to $1,000. Pays on publication for all rights. Sends galleys to author.

PARTING GIFTS, 3413 Wilshire, Greensboro NC 27408-2923. E-mail: rbixby@aol.com. Website: users.aol.com/marchst (includes guidelines, samples, free websites and newsletter). **Contact:** Robert Bixby, editor. Magazine: 5×7; 60 pages. "High-quality insightful fiction, very brief and on any theme." Semiannual. Estab. 1988.

Needs: "Brevity is the second most important criterion behind literary quality." Publishes ms within one year of acceptance. Recently published work by Ray Miller, Katherine Taylor, Curtis Smith and William Snyder, Jr. Length: 250-1,000 words. Also publishes poetry. Sometimes critiques rejected mss.

How to Contact: Send complete ms with cover letter. Accepts submissions by e-mail. Responds in 1 day to queries; 1 week to mss. Accepts simultaneous and multiple submissions. SASE.

Payment/Terms: Pays in contributor's copies. Acquires one-time rights.

Advice: "Read the works of Amy Hempel, Jim Harrison, Kelly Cherry, C.K. Williams and Janet Kauffman, all excellent writers who epitomize the writing *Parting Gifts* strives to promote. I need more than ever for my authors to be better read. I sense that many unaccepted writers have not put in the hours reading."

$ **PARTISAN REVIEW,** 236 Bay State Rd., Boston MA 02215. (617)353-4260. Fax: (617)353-7444. E-mail: partisan@bu.edu. Website: www.partisanreview.com (includes excerpts, writer's guidelines and subscription information). Editor-in-Chief: William Phillips. Editor: Edith Kurzweil. **Contact:** Fiction Editor. Magazine: 6×9; 160 pages; 40 lb. paper; 60 lb. cover stock. "Theme is of world literature and contemporary culture: fiction, essays and poetry with emphasis on the arts and political and social commentary, for the general intellectual public and scholars." Quarterly. Estab. 1934. Circ. 8,000.

Needs: Contemporary, experimental, literary, prose poem, regional and translations. Receives 100 unsolicited fiction mss/month. Buys 1-2 mss/issue; 4-8 mss/year. Published work by Leonard Michaels, Muriel Spark and Doris Lessing. Length: open.

How to Contact: Send complete ms with SASE and cover letter listing past credits. No simultaneous submissions. Responds in 4 months to mss. Sample copy for $6 and $1.50 postage.

Payment/Terms: Pays $25-200 and 2 contributor's copies. Pays on publication for first rights.

Advice: "Please research the type of fiction we publish. Often we receive manuscripts which are entirely inappropriate for our journal. Sample copies are available for sale and this is a good way to determine audience."

✔ **PASSAGES NORTH,** Northern Michigan University, Department of English, 1401 Presque Isle Ave., Marquette MI 49855-5363. (906)227-1795. Fax: (906)227-1096. E-mail: khanson@nmu.edu. Editor: Kate Myers Hanson. **Contact:** John Smolens, fiction editor. Poetry Editor: Austin Hummell. Magazine: 8×5½; 80 lb. paper. "*Passages North* publishes quality fiction, poetry and creative nonfiction by emerging and established writers." Readership: General and literary. Annual. Estab. 1979. Circ. 1,000.

Needs: Ethnic/multicultural, literary, mainstream/contemporary, regional. "Seeking more multicultural work." No genre fiction, science fiction, "typical commercial press work." Receives 100-200 mss/month. Accepts 20 fiction mss/year. Does not read May-August. **25% of mss published are from new writers.** Recently published works by W.P. Kinsella, Jack Gantos, Bonnie Campbell, Anthony Bukoski and Peter Orner. Length: 5,000 words maximum. Critiques returned mss when there is time. Also publishes interviews with authors.

How to Contact: Send complete ms with SASE and estimated word count. No electronic or fax submissions. Responds in 2 months. Accepts simultaneous submissions. Sample copy for $7. Guidelines free.

Payment/Terms: Pays 2 contributor's copies. Rights revert to author on request.

Tips: "We look for voice, energetic prose, writers who take risks. Revise, revise. Read what we publish."

Ⓝ **THE PATERSON LITERARY REVIEW,** Passaic County Community College, One College Blvd., Paterson NJ 07505. (973)684-6555. Fax: (973)523-6085. E-mail: mgillan@pccc.cc.nj.us. **Contact:** Maria Mazziotti Gillan, editor. Magazine: 6×9; 336 pages; 60 lb. paper; 70 lb. cover; illustrations; photos. Annual.

• Work from *PLR* has been included in the *Pushcart Prize* anthology.

Needs: Contemporary, ethnic, literary. "We are interested in quality short stories, with no taboos on subject matter." Receives about 60 unsolicited mss/month. Publishes ms about 6 months to 1 year after acceptance. **5% of work published is by new writers.** Published work by Robert Mooney. Length: 1,500 words maximum. Also publishes literary essays, literary criticism, poetry.

How to Contact: Submit no more than 1 story at a time. Submission deadline: March 1. Send SASE for reply or return of ms. "Indicate whether you want story returned." Accepts simultaneous submissions. Sample copy for $12. Reviews novels and short story collections.

Payment/Terms: Pays in contributor's copies. Acquires first North American rights.

Advice: Looks for "clear, moving and specific work."

☑ ◑ ◎ **PEARL, A Literary Magazine**, Pearl, 3030 E. Second St., Long Beach CA 90803-5163. Phone/ Fax: (562)434-4523. E-mail: mjohn5150@aol.com. Website: www.pearlmag.com (includes writer's guidelines, contest guidelines, subscription information, books, current issue, about the editors). **Contact:** Marilyn Johnson, editor. Magazine: 5½×8½; 96 pages; 60 lb. recycled, acid-free paper; perfect-bound; coated cover; b&w drawings and graphics. "We are primarily a poetry magazine, but we do publish some *very short* fiction and nonfiction. We are interested in lively, readable prose that speaks to *real* people in direct, living language; for a general literary audience." Biannual. Estab. 1974. Circ. 600.

Needs: Contemporary, humor/satire, literary, mainstream, prose poem. "We will only consider short-short stories up to 1,200 words. Longer stories (up to 4,000 words) may only be submitted to our short story contest. All contest entries are considered for publication. Although we have no taboos stylistically or subject-wise, obscure, predictable, sentimental, or cliché-ridden stories are a turn-off." Publishes an all fiction issue each year. Receives 10-20 unsolicited mss/month. Accepts 1-10 mss/issue; 12-15 mss/year. Submissions accepted September-May *only*. Publishes ms 6 months to 1 year after acceptance. **Publishes 1-5 new writers/year.** Recently published work by John Brantingham, Suzanne Greenberg, Gina Ochsner, Helena Maria Viramontes, Lisa Glatt and Gerald Locklin. Length: 500-1,200 words; average length: 1,000 words. Accepts multiple submissions. Also publishes poetry. Sponsors an annual short story contest. Send SASE for complete guidelines.

How to Contact: Send complete ms with cover letter including publishing credits and brief bio. Accepts simultaneous submissions. Responds in 2 months to mss. SASE. Sample copy for $7 (postpaid). Guidelines for #10 SASE.

Payment/Terms: Pays 1 contributor's copy. Acquires first North American serial rights. Sends galleys to author.

Advice: "We look for vivid, *dramatized* situations and characters, stories written in an original 'voice,' that make sense and follow a clear narrative line. What makes a manuscript stand out is more elusive, though—more to do with feeling and imagination than anything else . . ."

☑ ◑ **PEMBROKE MAGAZINE**, Box 1510, University of North Carolina at Pembroke, Pembroke NC 28372. (910)521-6358. Website: www.uncp/pembrokemagazine.edu. Editor: Shelby Stephenson. **Contact:** Tina Emanuel, managing editor. Magazine: 6×9; approximately 200 pages; illustrations; photos. Magazine of poems and stories plus literary essays. Annual. Estab. 1969. Circ. 500.

Needs: Open. Receives 120 unsolicited mss/month. Publishes short shorts. **Published new writers within the last year.** Published work by Fred Chappell, Robert Morgan. Length: open. Occasionally critiques rejected mss and recommends other markets.

How to Contact: Send complete ms. No simultaneous submissions. Responds in up to 3 months. SASE. Sample copy for $8 and 9×10 SAE.

Payment/Terms: Pays 1 contributor's copy.

Advice: "Write with an end for *writing*, not publication."

⊕ ☑ $◑ **PENINSULAR, Literary Magazine**, Cherrybite Publications, Linden Cottage, 45 Burton Rd., Little Neston, Cheshire CH64 4AE England. Phone: 0151 353 0967. Fax: 0870 165 6282. E-mail: helicon@gl obalnet.co.uk. Website: www.cherrybite.co.uk (includes guidelines, brief magazine description, competition rules). **Contact:** Shelagh Nugent, editor. Magazine: 80 pages; card cover. "We're looking for brilliant short fiction to make the reader think/laugh/cry. A lively, up and coming quality magazine." Quarterly. Estab. 1985. Circ. 400. "We ask only that a potential writer buy at least one copy. Subscribing is not essential."

Needs: Adventure, ethnic/multicultural (general), fantasy (space fantasy), gay, historical (general), horror (futuristic, psychological, supernatural), humor/satire, lesbian, literary, New Age, psychic/supernatural/occult, science fiction (soft/sociological). Wants to see more science fiction, historical, adventure. "I'll read anything but avoid animals telling the story and clichés. No pornography or children's fiction. Also avoid purple prose." Receives 50 unsolicited mss/month. Accepts 10 mss/issue; 40 mss/year. Publishes ms 3-6 months after acceptance. **Publishes 4-5 new writers/year.** Recently published work by Alex Keegan, Sarah Klerbart, PDR Lindsay and Leigh Eduardo. Length: 1,000-4,000 words; average length: 3,000 words. Publishes short shorts. Average length: 1,000 words. Often comments on rejected mss.

How to Contact: Send for guidelines. Prefers hard copy for submissions. Include estimated word count. Responds in 1 week to queries; 2 weeks to mss. "I often write comments on the manuscript." Accepts simultaneous submissions and previously published work. Sample copy for $5. Guidelines for SASE with 2 IRCs or by e-mail.

Payment/Terms: Pays £5 sterling per 1,000 words or can pay in copies and subscriptions; additional copies £5 sterling or equivalent in dollars cash. Pays on publication for one-time rights. Sponsors contest. "Send IRCs for current competition details."

Advice: "We look for impeccable presentation and grammar, outstanding prose, original story line and the element of difference that forbids me to put the story down. A good opening paragraph usually grabs me. Read one or two copies and study the guidelines. A beginning writer should read as much as possible. The trend seems to be for stories written in first person/present tense and for stories without end leaving the reader thinking 'so what?' Stories not following this trend stand more chance of being published by me!"

PENNSYLVANIA ENGLISH, Penn State DuBois, College Place, DuBois PA 15801. (814)375-4814. Fax: (814)375-4784. E-mail: ajv2@psu.edu. **Contact:** Antonio Vallone, editor. Magazine: 5½×8½; up to 180 pages; perfect bound; full color cover featuring the artwork of a Pennsylvania artist. "Our philosophy is quality. We publish literary fiction (and poetry and nonfiction). Our intended audience is literate, college-educated people." Annual. Estab. 1985. Circ. 300.

Needs: Short shorts, literary, contemporary mainstream. No genre fiction or romance. Publishes ms within 12 months after acceptance. **Publishes 4-6 new writers/year.** Recently published work by Dave Kress, Dan Leone and Paul West. Length: "no maximum or minimum." Publishes short shorts. Also publishes literary essays, literary criticism, poetry. Sometimes critiques rejected mss.

How to Contact: Send complete ms with cover letter. No e-mail submissions. Responds in 2 months. SASE. Accepts simultaneous submissions.

Payment/Terms: Pays in 3 contributor's copies. Acquires first North American serial rights.

Advice: "Quality of the writing is our only measure. We're not impressed by long-winded cover letters or résumés detailing awards and publications we've never heard of. Beginners and professionals have the same chance with us. We receive stacks of competently written but boring fiction. For a story to rise out of the rejection pile, it takes more than basic competence."

PEREGRINE, published by Amherst Writers & Artists Press, P.O. Box 1076, Amherst MA 01004-1076. (413)253-3307. Fax: (413)253-7764. Website: www.amherstwriters.com (includes writer's guidelines, names of editors, excerpts from publication and interviews with authors). **Contact:** Nancy Rose, assistant editor. Magazine: 6×9; 120 pages; 60 lb. white offset paper; glossy cover. "*Peregrine* has provided a forum for national and international writers for over 20 years, and is committed to finding excellent work by new writers as well as established authors. We publish what we love, knowing that all editorial decisions are subjective, and that all work has a home somewhere." Annual.

Needs: Poetry and prose—short stories, short short. No previously published work. No children's stories. "We welcome work reflecting diversity of voice." Accepts 6-12 fiction mss/issue. Publishes ms an average of 4 months after acceptance. **Published 7-10 new writers/year.** Recently published work by Virgil Suarez, Penelope Scambly Schott, G.E. Cogshall, Cheryl Hellner, Frank Johnson, Clifford Browder and Margaret Hoehn. "We like to be surprised. We look for writing that is honest, unpretentious, and memorable." Length: 3,000 words maximum. Short pieces have a better chance of publication.

How to Contact: Send #10 SASE to "Peregrine Guidelines" or visit website for writer's guidelines. Send ms with cover letter; include 40-word (maximum) biographical note, prior publications and word count. Accepts simultaneous submissions. Enclose sufficiently stamped SASE for return of ms; if disposable copy, enclose #10 SASE for response. Deadline for submission: April 1, 2002. Read October-April. Sample copy $10.

Payment/Terms: Pays contributor's copies. All rights return to writer upon publication.

Advice: "We look for heart and soul as well as technical expertise. Trust your own voice. Familiarize yourself with *Peregrine*." Every ms is read by several readers; all decisions are made by editors.

PHOEBE, An Interdisciplinary Journal of Feminist Scholarship, Theory and Aesthetics, Women's Studies Department, State University of New York, College at Oneonta, Oneonta NY 13820-4015. (607)436-2014. Fax: (607)436-2656. E-mail: omarakk@oneonta.edu. **Contact:** Kathleen O'Mara, editor. Journal: 7×9; 140 pages; 80 lb. paper; illustrations; photos. "Feminist material for feminist scholars and readers." Semiannual. Estab. 1989. Circ. 400.

Needs: Feminist: ethnic, experimental, gay, humor/satire, lesbian, literary, translations. Receives 25 unsolicited mss/month. Wants to see more experimental fiction. "One-third to one-half of each issue is short fiction and poetry." Does not read mss in summer. Publishes ms 3-4 months after acceptance. **Publishes 4-6 new writers/ year.** Published work by Elaine Hatfield, Betty A. Wilder, Jenny Potts, Kristan Ruona and Sylvia Van Nooten. Length: 1,500-2,500 words preferred. Publishes short shorts. Sometimes critiques rejected mss and recommends other markets.

How to Contact: Send complete ms with cover letter. Responds in 1 month to queries; 15 weeks to mss. Accepts electronic (WordPerfect/Microsoft Word disk, e-mail) submissions. Sample copy for $7.50. Guidelines free.

Payment/Terms: Pays in contributor's copies. Acquires one-time rights.

Advice: "We look for writing with a feminist perspective. *Phoebe* was founded to provide a forum for cross-cultural feminist analysis, debate and exchange. The editors are committed to providing space for all disciplines and new areas of research, criticism and theory in feminist scholarship and aesthetics. *Phoebe* is not committed to any one conception of feminism. All work that is not sexist, racist, homophobic, or otherwise discriminatory, will be welcome. *Phoebe* is particularly committed to publishing work informed by a theoretical perspective which will enrich critical thinking."

PHOEBE, A Journal of Literary Arts, George Mason University, MSN 2D6, 4400 University Dr., Fairfax VA 22030. (703)993-2915. E-mail: phoebe@gmu.edu. Website: www.gmu.edu/pubs/phoebe (includes writer's guidelines, fiction and poetry contest guidelines, subscription information, past issue descriptions, etc.). **Contact:** Michael Pabich, fiction editor. Editors change each year. Magazine: 6×9; 116 pages; 80 lb. paper; 0-5 illustrations; 0-10 photos. "We publish mainly fiction and poetry with occasional visual art." Published 2 times/year. Estab. 1972. Circ. 3,000.

Needs: "Looking for a broad range of fiction and poetry. We encourage writers and poets to experiment, to stretch the boundaries of genre." No romance, western, juvenile, erotica. Receives 30 mss/month. Accepts 3-5 mss/issue. Does not read mss in summer. Publishes ms 3-6 months after acceptance. **Publishes 9 new writers/ year.** Recently published work by Gina Ochsner, W.P. Osborn and Ralph Tyler. Length: no more than 35 pages of fiction, no more than 15 pages of poetry.

How to Contact: Send complete ms with cover letter. Include "name, address, phone. Brief bio." SASE. Accepts simultaneous submissions. Sample copy for $6.

Payment/Terms: Pays 2 contributor's copies. Acquires one-time rights. All rights revert to author.

Advice: "We are interested in a variety of fiction and poetry. We suggest potential contributors study previous issues. Each year *Phoebe* sponsors fiction and poetry contests, with $500 awarded to the winning short story and poem. The deadline for both the Greg Grummer Award in Poetry and the Phoebe Fiction Prize is December 15. E-mail or send SASE for complete contest guidelines."

PIKEVILLE REVIEW, Pikeville College, Sycamore St., Pikeville KY 41501. (606)218-5002. Fax: (606)218-5225. E-mail: eward@pc.edu. Website: www.pc.edu (includes writer's guidelines, names of editors, short fiction). Editor: Elgin M. Ward. **Contact:** Fiction Editor. Magazine: 8½×6; 120 pages; illustrations; photos. "Literate audience interested in well-crafted poetry, fiction, essays and reviews." Annual. Estab. 1987. Circ. 500.

Needs: Ethnic/multicultural, experimental, feminist, humor/satire, literary, mainstream/contemporary, regional, translations. Receives 60-80 unsolicited mss/month. Accepts 3-4 mss/issue. Does not read mss in the summer. Publishes ms 6-8 months after acceptance. **Publishes 20 new writers/year.** Recently published work by Jim Wayne Miller and Robert Morgan. Length: 15,000 words maximum; average length: 5,000 words. Publishes short shorts. Also publishes literary essays and poetry. Often critiques rejected mss. Sponsors occasional fiction award: $50.

How to Contact: Send complete ms with cover letter. Include estimated word count. Send SASE for reply, return of ms or send a disposable copy of ms. Accepts simultaneous submissions. Sample copy for $4. Reviews novels and short story collections.

Payment/Terms: Pays 5 contributor's copies; additional copies for $3. Acquires first rights.

Advice: "Send a clean manuscript with well-developed characters."

$ PLANET-THE WELSH INTERNATIONALIST, P.O. Box 44, Aberystwyth, Ceredigion, SY23 3ZZ Cymru/ Wales UK. Phone: 01970-611255. Fax: 01970-611197. E-mail: planet.enquiries@planetmagazine.or g.uk. Website: www.planetmagazine.org.uk (includes details of staff; excepts from current and past issues; details of *Planet*'s aims and interests). **Contact:** John Barnie, fiction editor. Bimonthly. Circ. 1,400. Publishes 1-2 stories/ issue.

Needs: "A literary/cultural/political journal centered on Welsh affairs but with a strong interest in minority cultures in Europe and elsewhere." No magical realism, horror, science fiction. Would like to see more "inventive, imaginative fiction that pays attention to language and experiments with form." Recently published work by Harriet Richards, Katie O'Reilly and Guy Vanderhaeghe. Length: 1,500-4,000 words maximum.

How to Contact: No submissions returned unless accompanied by an SAE. Writers submitting from abroad should send at least 3 IRCs for return of typescript; 1 IRC for reply only.

Payment/Terms: Writers receive 1 contributor's copy. Payment is at the rate of £40 per 1,000 words for prose; a minimum of £25 per poem (in the currency of the relevant country if the author lives outside the UK). Sample copy: cost (to USA & Canada) £2.87. Writers' guidelines for SAE.

Advice: "We do not look for fiction which necessarily has a 'Welsh' connection, which some writers assume from our title. We try to publish a broad range of fiction and our main criterion is quality. Try to read copies of any magazine you submit to. Don't write out of the blue to a magazine which might be completely inappropriate to your work. Recognize that you are likely to have a high rejection rate, as magazines tend to favor writers from their own countries."

$⬭🗑 PLEIADES, Department of English & Philosophy, Central Missouri State University, Martin 336, Warrensburg MO 64093-5046. (660)543-4425. Fax: (660)543-8544. E-mail: rmk8708@cmsu2.cmsu.edu. Website: www.cmsu.edu/englphil/pleiades.htm (includes guidelines, editors, sample poetry or prose). Editor: R.M. Kinder. **Contact:** Susan Strinberg, fiction editor. Poetry: Kevin Prufer. Magazine: 5½×8½; 150 pages; 60 lb. paper; perfect-bound; 8 pt. color cover. Sponsored in part by Missouri Arts Council. "*Pleiades* emphasizes cultural diversity, publishes poetry, fiction, essays, occasional drama, interviews and reviews for a general educated audience." Semiannual. Estab. 1939. Circ. 2,000.

● A story first published in *Pleiades* was recently awarded a Pushcart Prize.

Needs: Ethnic/multicultural, experimental, especially cross-genre, feminist, gay, humor/satire, literary, mainstream/contemporary, regional, translations. "No westerns, romance, mystery, etc. Nothing pretentious, didactic or overly sentimental." Receives 100 unsolicited mss/month. Accepts 8 mss/issue; 16 mss/year. "We're slower at reading manuscripts in the summer." Publishes ms 6-12 months after acceptance. **Publishes 3-4 new writers/year.** Recently published work by Sherman Alexie, Richard Foerster and Ingeborg Bachmann. Length: 800-8,000 words; average length: 3,000-6,000 words. Also publishes literary essays, literary criticism and poetry. Sometimes comments on rejected mss.

How to Contact: Send complete ms with a cover letter. Accepts queries by e-mail but not submissions. Include 75-100 bio, Social Security number and list of publications. Responds in 3 weeks to queries; 4 months to mss. Send SASE for reply, return of ms or send a disposable copy of ms. Accepts simultaneous submissions. Sample copy (including guidelines) for $6.

Payment/Terms: Pays $10 or subscription and 1 contributor's copy. Pays on publication for first North American serial rights.

Advice: Looks for "a blend of language and subject matter that entices from beginning to end. Send us your best work. Don't send us formula stories. While we appreciate and publish well-crafted traditional pieces, we constantly seek the story that risks, that breaks form and expectations and wins us over anyhow."

☑ $⬭🗑 PLOUGHSHARES, Emerson College, 120 Boylston St., Boston MA 02116. (617)824-8753. Website: www.plough.org. Editor: Don Lee. **Contact:** Fiction Editor. "Our mission is to present dynamic, contrasting views on what is valid and important in contemporary literature, and to discover and advance significant literary talent. Each issue is guest-edited by a different writer. We no longer structure issues around preconceived themes." Triquarterly. Estab. 1971. Circ. 6,000.

● Work published in *Ploughshares* has been selected regularly for inclusion in the *Best American Short Stories* and *O. Henry Prize* anthologies. In fact the magazine has the honor of having the most stories selected from a single issue (three) to be included in *B.A.S.S.* Guest editors have included Richard Ford, Tim O'Brien and Ann Beattie. *Ploughshares* ranked #45 on *Writer's Digest*'s "Fiction 50" list of top markets for fiction writers.

Needs: Literary. "No genre (science fiction, detective, gothic, adventure, etc.), popular formula or commercial fiction whose purpose is to entertain rather than to illuminate." Buys 30 mss/year. Receives 1,000 unsolicited fiction mss each month. **Published new writers within the last year.** Published work by Rick Bass, Joy Williams and Andre Dubus. Length: 300-6,000 words.

How to Contact: Reading period: postmarked August 1 to March 31. Cover letter should include "previous pubs." SASE. Responds in 5 months to mss. Sample copy for $8. (Please specify fiction issue sample.) Current issue for $9.95. Guidelines for #10 SASE.

Payment/Terms: Pays $25/page, $50 minimum; $250 maximum, copies and a subscription. Pays on publication for first North American serial rights. Offers 50% kill fee for assigned ms not published.

Advice: "Be familiar with our fiction issues, fiction by our writers and by our various editors (e.g., Sue Miller, Tobias Wolff, Rosellen Brown, Richard Ford, Jayne Anne Phillips, James Alan McPherson) and more generally acquaint yourself with the best short fiction currently appearing in the literary quarterlies, and the annual prize anthologies (*Pushcart Prize, O. Henry Awards, Best American Short Stories*). Also realistically consider whether the work you are submitting is as good as or better than—in your own opinion—the work appearing in the magazine you're sending to. What is the level of competition? And what is its volume? Never send 'blindly' to a magazine, or without carefully weighing your prospect there against those elsewhere. Always keep a log and a copy of the work you submit."

N ◯ POETRY & PROSE ANNUAL, Golden Mean, P.O. Box 541, Manzanita OR 97130. (503)717-0112. E-mail: poetry@poetryproseannual.com. Website: www.poetryproseannual.com (includes writer's guidelines, names of editors, extracts, photographs, prose not necessarily included in print version). **Contact:** Sandra Foushée, editor. Magazine: 7×8½; 88 pages; semi-gloss paper; glossy cover; illustrations; photos. "*Poetry & Prose Annual* is organized and edited to be read as a whole, as a book, the prose (both fiction and nonfiction) and poetry directed to an enlightened intelligence with a positive perspective on the world." Annual. Estab. 1997. Circ. 1,000.
- There is a $20 entry fee for the contest for the Gold Pen Award. The entry fee includes a subscription at $15 and a $5 reading fee.

Needs: Adventure, ethnic/multicultural, experimental, family saga, feminist, historical, humor/satire, literary, mainstream, mystery/suspense (amateur sleuth, cozy), New Age, psychic/supernatural/occult, regional, romance (contemporary, futuristic/time travel, historical, regency period, romantic suspense). Accepts 20-30 mss/issue; 20-30 mss/year. **Publishes 40% new writers/year.** Recently published work by Mark Christopher Eades, June Stromberg, Robin Reid and Kay Kinnear. Length: 2,500 words maximum; average length: 1,200 words. Publishes short shorts. Average length: 500 words. Also publishes literary essays and poetry. Sometimes comments on rejected mss.

How to Contact: Send complete ms with a cover letter. Accepts submissions by e-mail and disk. Include estimated word count, brief bio and list of publications. Responds in 5 months to mss. Send a disposable copy of ms and #10 SASE for reply only. Accepts simultaneous (with notification if the piece is accepted elsewhere), previously published (if author has retained copyright) and multiple submissions. Sample copy for $10. Guidelines for SASE or on website.

Payment/Terms: Pays 2 contributor's copies and subscription to magazine; additional copies $8. Pays on publication for one-time and electronic rights. Sends galleys to author. Sponsors contest: Gold Pen Award. With the submission, writer is automatically a participant.

Advice: "We look for substantive and enlightening ideas, a writing style with clarity and ingenuity, an awareness of emotional, intellectual, and physical consciousness. Follow the submission guidelines completely and enclose all the required elements. Familiarize yourself with the editorial intent of the *Annual*. The trend toward short short stories fits our format well, but we are open to longer prose, both fiction and nonfiction."

☑ ◯ POETRY FORUM SHORT STORIES, Poetry Forum, 5713 Larchmont Dr., Erie PA 16509. Phone/fax: (814)866-2543 (fax hours 8-10 a.m., 5-8 p.m.). E-mail: 75562.670@compuserve.com. Website: www.thepoetryforum.com. **Contact:** Gunvor Skogsholm, editor. Newspaper: 7×8½; 34 pages; card cover; illustrations. "Human interest themes (no sexually explicit or racially biased or blasphemous material) for the general public—from the grassroot to the intellectual." Quarterly. Estab. 1989. Circ. 400.

Needs: Confession, contemporary, ethnic, experimental, fantasy, feminist, historical, literary, mainstream, mystery/suspense, prose poem, religious/inspirational, romance, science fiction, senior citizen/retirement, young adult/teen. "No blasphemous, sexually explicit material." Publishes annual special fiction issue. Receives 50 unsolicited mss/month. Accepts 12 mss/issue; 40 mss/year. Publishes ms 6 months after acceptance. Agented fiction less than 1%. **80% of work published is by new writers.** Recently published work by Scott Fields and Frank Bland. Length: 500-5,000 words; average length: 2,000 words. Also publishes literary essays, literary criticism, poetry.

How to Contact: *This magazine charges a "professional members" fee of $36 and prefers to work with subscribers.* The fee entitles you to publication of a maximum of 3,000 words. Send complete ms with cover letter. Accepts queries/mss by e-mail and fax. Responds in up to 2 months to mss. SASE. Accepts simultaneous and reprint submissions. "Accepts electronic submissions via disk gladly." Sample copy for $3. Guidelines for SASE. Reviews novels and short story collections.

Payment/Terms: Preference given to submissions by subscribers. Acquires one-time rights.

Advice: "Tell your story with no padding as if telling it to a person standing with one hand on the door ready to run out to a meeting. Have a good lead. This is the 'alpha & omega' of all good story writing. Don't start with 'This is a story about a boy and a girl.' Avoid writing how life 'ought to be,' rather write how life is."

VISIT THE WRITER'S MARKET WEBSITE at www.writersmarket.com for hot new markets, daily market updates, writers' guidelines and much more.

N: ☑ **THE POINTED CIRCLE**, Portland Community College-Cascade, 705 N. Killingsworth St., Portland OR 97217. (503)978-5087. Fax: (503)978-5050. E-mail: ckimball@pcc.edu. Student editorial staff, editors. **Contact:** Cynthia Kimball, English instructor, faculty advisor. Magazine: 80 pages; b&w illustrations; photos. "Anything of interest to educationally/culturally mixed audience." Annual. Estab. 1980.
Needs: Contemporary, ethnic, literary, prose poem, regional. "We will read whatever is sent, but encourage writers to remember we are a quality literary/arts magazine intended to promote the arts in the community." No pornography. Acquires 3-7 mss/year. Accepts submissions only December 1-February 15, for July 1 issue. **Publishes 10 new writers/year.** Recently published work by Dan Raphael, Stephanie Dickinson and Vera Schwarcz. Length: 3,000 words maximum.
How to Contact: Send complete ms with cover letter and brief bio, #10 SASE. Accepts submissions by e-mail, fax and disk. "The editors consider all submissions without knowing the identities of the contributors, so please do not put your name on the works themselves." Accepts multiple submissions. Sample copy for $4.50. Entry guidelines, send #10 SASE. Submitted materials will not be returned; SASE for notification only.
Payment/Terms: Pays 1 copy. Acquires one-time rights.
Advice: "Looks for quality—topicality—nothing trite. The author cares about language and acts responsibly toward the reader, honors the reader's investment of time and piques the reader's interest."

☑ **PORCUPINE LITERARY ARTS MAGAZINE**, P.O. Box 259, Cedarburg WI 53012-0259. (262)375-3128. E-mail: ppine259@aol.com. Website: members.aol.com/ppine259 (includes writer's guidelines, cover art, interviews, excerpts, subscription information, table of contents). Editor: W.A. Reed. **Contact:** Chris Skoczynski, fiction editor. Magazine: 5×8½; 125 pages; glossy color cover stock; art work and photos. Publishes "primarily poetry and short fiction. Novel excerpts are acceptable if self-contained. No restrictions as to theme or style." Semiannual. Estab. 1996. Circ. 1,500.
Needs: Condensed/excerpted novel, ethnic/multicultural, literary, mainstream/contemporary. No pornographic or religious. Receives 30 unsolicited mss/month. Accepts 3 mss/issue; 6 mss/year. Publishes ms within 1 year of acceptance. **Publishes 4-6 new writers/year.** Recently published work by Judith Ford, Holly Day, Yang Huang and Jeffrey Perso. Length: 2,000-7,500 words; average length: 3,500 words. Publishes literary essays and poetry. Sometimes comments on rejected mss.
How to Contact: Send complete ms with a cover letter. Accepts queries/mss by e-mail. Include estimated word count, 5-line bio and list of publications. Responds in 2 weeks to queries; 2 months to mss. Send SASE for reply, return of ms or send a disposable copy of ms. No simultaneous submissions. Sample copy for $5. Guidelines for #10 SASE.
Payment/Terms: Pays 1 contributor's copy; additional copies for $8.95. Pays on publication for one-time rights.
Advice: Looks for "believable dialogue and a narrator I can see and hear and smell. Form or join a writers' group. Read aloud. Rewrite extensively."

☑ ☑ **PORTLAND REVIEW**, Portland State University, Box 347, Portland OR 97207-0347. (503)725-4533. Fax: (503)725-4534. E-mail: review@vanguard.vg.pdx.edu. Website: www.angelfire.com/in/portlandreview.com (includes writer's guidelines, e-mail and links to other journals). Editor: Ryan Spear. **Contact:** Haley Hach, editor. Magazine: 9×6; 100 pages; b&w art and photos. "We seek to publish fiction in which content takes precedence over style." Quarterly. Estab. 1954. Circ. 300.
● The editors say they are looking for experimental work "dealing with the human condition."
Needs: Adventure, ethnic/multicultural, experimental, fantasy (science), feminist, gay, historical, humor/satire, lesbian, literary, mainstream/contemporary, mystery/suspense, regional, science fiction. Wants more humor. Receives about 100 mss each month. Accepts 4-6 mss/issue; 10-12 mss/year. Also publishes critical essays, poetry, drama, interviews and reviews. Published work by Ian McMillan, Heather King and Benjamin Chambers.
How to Contact: Submit complete ms with short bio. Accepts queries/mss by e-mail and fax. Manuscripts returned only if SASE is supplied. Accepts simultaneous and electronic submissions (if noted). Responds in "several" months. Sample copy for $6 plus $1 postage.
Payment/Terms: Pays contributor's copies. Acquires one-time rights.
Advice: "Our editors, and thus our tastes/biases change annually, so keep trying us."

☑ ☑ **POTOMAC REVIEW, The Journal of Arts & Humanities**, 1186 N. Pitt St., Alexandria VA 22314. (703)549-6167. Fax: (703)836-6029. E-mail: wattrsedge@aol.com. Website: www.meral.com/potomac (includes editor's note, contents page, contact information, submission guidelines, some sampling of stories, poems). Editor: Eli Flam. **Contact:** Managing Editor. Magazine: 5½×8½; 128-160 pages; 50 lb. paper; 65 lb. cover; illustrations. *Potomac Review* "explores the inner and outer terrain of the Mid-Atlantic and beyond via a challenging diversity of prose, poetry and b&w artwork." Estab. 1994. Circ. 2,000.
Needs: "Stories with a vivid, individual quality that get at 'the concealed side' of life." Special section opens each issue, e.g., upcoming "Pulling the Strings: Puppetry in Action," "Native Americans: Home Ground."

Receives about 75 unsolicited mss/month. Accepts 20-30 mss/issue. Publishes ms within 1 year after acceptance. Agented fiction under 5%. **Publishes up to 20 new writers/year.** Recently published work by Sharon Barrett, Sam Smith, Merrill Leffler, Helen Chappell, Barbara Hurd and Lisa Couturier. Length: up to 3,000 words; average length: 2,000 words. Publishes short shorts from 250 words. Humor (plus essays, cogent nonfiction of all sorts) welcome.

How to Contact: Send complete ms with a cover letter. Include estimated word count, 2-3 sentence bio and SASE. Responds in 3 weeks to queries; 3 months to mss. Send SASE for reply, return of ms or send a disposable copy of ms. Accepts simultaneous and occasional reprint submissions. Sample copy for $5. Submission guidelines for #10 SASE or see website. Reviews novels, short story collections, other books.

Payment/Terms: Pays 1 or more contributor's copy; additional copies for a 40% discount.

Advice: "Have something to say in an original voice; check the magazine first; rewriting often trumps the original."

POTPOURRI, P.O. Box 8278, Prairie Village KS 66208. (913)642-1503. Fax: (913)642-3128. E-mail: editor@potpourri.org. Website: www.potpourri.com (includes guidelines, contents, reprints of fiction, author profiles, contests). Senior Editor: Polly W. Swafford. **Contact:** John Weber, fiction editor. Magazine: 8×11; 76 pages; glossy cover. "Literary magazine: short stories, verse, essays, travel, prose poetry for a general adult audience." Quarterly. Estab. 1989. Circ. 4,500.

Needs: Adventure, contemporary, ethnic, experimental, fantasy, historical (general), humor/satire, literary, mainstream, suspense, prose poem, romance (contemporary, historical, romantic suspense), science fiction (soft/sociological), western (frontier stories). "*Potpourri* accepts a broad genre; hence its name. No religious, confessional, racial, political, erotic, abusive, or sexual preference materials unless fictional and necessary to plot or characterization." Receives 75 unsolicited fiction mss/month. Accepts 10-12 fiction mss/issue; 60-80 prose mss/year. Publishes ms 10-12 months after acceptance. Agented fiction 1%. **Publishes 3-4 new writers/year.** Recently published work by Thomas E. Kennedy, Richard Moore, David Ray and Deborah Shouse. Length: 3,500 words maximum. Also publishes poetry and literary essays. Sometimes critiques rejected mss. *Potpourri* offers annual awards (of $100 each) for best of volume in fiction and poetry, more depending on grants received, and sponsors the Annual Council on National Literatures Award. "Manuscripts must celebrate our multicultural and/or historic background." Reading fee: $5 per story. Send SASE for guidelines.

How to Contact: Send complete ms with cover letter. Accepts queries by e-mail and fax. Include "complete name, address, phone number, e-mail address, brief summary statement about submission, short author bio." Responds in 4 months. SASE. Accepts simultaneous submissions when advised at time of submission. Sample copy for $4.95 with 9×12 envelope. Guidelines for #10 SASE.

Payment/Terms: Pays contributor's copies. Acquires first rights.

Advice: "We look for well-crafted stories of literary value and stories with reader appeal. First, does the manuscript spark immediate interest and the introduction create the effect that will dominate? Second, does the action in dialogue or narration tell the story? Third, does the conclusion leave something with the reader to be long remembered? We look for the story with an original idea and an unusual twist. We are weary of excessive violence and depressing themes in fiction and are looking for originality in plots and some humorous pieces."

POTTERSFIELD PORTFOLIO, P.O. Box 40, Station A, Sydney, Nova Scotia B1P 6G9 Canada. E-mail: pportfolio@seascape.ns.ca. **Contact:** Douglas Arthur Brown, editor. Magazine: 8×11; 60 pages; illustrations. "Literary magazine interested in well-written fiction and poetry. No specific thematic interests or biases." Triannual. Estab. 1979. Circ. 2,000.

Needs: Receives 40-50 fiction mss/month. Buys 4-5 fiction mss/issue. Recently published work by David Adams Richards, Vivette Kady and M.J. Hull. Length: 4,000 words maximum. Sometimes comments on rejected mss.

How to Contact: Send complete ms with SASE and cover letter. Include estimated word count and 50-word bio. No simultaneous submissions. No fax or e-mail submissions. Responds in 3 months. SASE. Sample copy for $7.95 (US).

Payment/Terms: Pays contributor's copy and $10 Canadian/printed page to a maximum of $50. Pays on publication for first Canadian serial rights.

Advice: "Provide us with a clean, proofread copy of your story. Include a brief cover letter with biographical note, but don't try to sell the story to us. *Always* include a SASE with sufficient *Canadian* postage, or IRCs, for return of the manuscript or a reply from the editors."

THE PRAIRIE JOURNAL OF CANADIAN LITERATURE, Prairie Journal Press, Box 61203, Brentwood Postal Services, Calgary, Alberta T2L 2K6 Canada. E-mail: prairiejournal@yahoo.com. Website: www.geocities.com/prairiejournal/ (includes guidelines, poems of the month, news and reviews). **Contact:** A.E. Burke, editor. Journal: 7×8½; 50-60 pages; white bond paper; Cadillac cover stock; cover illustrations. Journal of creative writing and scholarly essays, reviews for literary audience. Semiannual. Published special fiction issue last year. Estab. 1983.

Needs: Contemporary, literary, prose poem, regional, excerpted novel, novella, double-spaced. Canadian authors given preference. Publishes "a variety of types of fiction—fantasy, psychological, character-driven, feminist, etc. We publish authors at all stages of their careers from well-known to first publication." No romance, erotica, pulp, westerns. Publishes anthology series open to submissions: *Prairie Journal Poetry II* and *Prairie Journal Fiction III*. Receives 50 unsolicited mss each month. Accepts 10-15 mss/issue; 20-30 mss/year. Suggests sample issue before submitting ms. **Publishes 10 new writers/year.** Recently published work by Robert Clark and Christopher Blais. Length: 100-3,000 words; average length: 2,500 words. Suggested deadlines: April 1 for spring/summer issue; October 1 for fall/winter. Also publishes literary essays, literary criticism, poetry. Sometimes critiques rejected mss and recommends other markets.

How to Contact: Send complete ms. Responds in 1 month. SASE (IRC). Sample copy for $8 (Canadian) and SAE with $1.10 for postage or IRC. Include cover letter of past credits, if any. Reply to queries for SAE with 55¢ for postage or IRC. No American stamps. Reviews excerpts from novels and short story collections. Send only 1 story.

Payment/Terms: Pays contributor's copies and modest honoraria. Acquires first North American serial rights. In Canada author retains copyright with acknowledgement appreciated.

Advice: "We like character-driven rather than plot-centered fiction." Interested in "innovational work of quality. Beginning writers welcome! There is no point in simply republishing known authors or conventional, predictable plots. Of the genres we receive fiction is most often of the highest calibre. It is a very competitive field. Be proud of what you send. You're worth it."

PRAIRIE SCHOONER, University of Nebraska, English Department, 201 Andrews Hall, Lincoln NE 68588-0334. (402)472-0911. Fax: (402)472-9771. E-mail: eflanaga@unlnotes.unl.edu. Website: www.unl.edu/schooner/psmain.htm (includes guidelines, editors, table of contents and excerpts of current issue). **Contact:** Hilda Raz, editor. Magazine: 6×9; 200 pages; good stock paper; heavy cover stock. "A fine literary quarterly of stories, poems, essays and reviews for a general audience that reads for pleasure." Quarterly. Estab. 1926. Circ. 3,200.
   ● *Prairie Schooner*, one of the oldest publications in this book, has garnered several awards and honors over the years. Work appearing in the magazine has been selected for anthologies including *Pushcart Prizes* and *Best American Short Stories*. *Prairie Schooner* ranked #42 on *Writer's Digest*'s "Fiction 50" list of top fiction markets.

Needs: Good fiction (literary). Accepts 4-5 mss/issue. Receives approximately 500 unsolicited fiction and poetry mss each month. Mss are read September through May only. **Published new writers within the last year.** Recently published work by Joyce Carol Oates, Judith Ortiz Coter, Chitra Divakaruni, Daniel Stern and Janet Burroway. Length: varies. Also publishes poetry. Offers annual prize of $1,000 for best fiction, $1,000 for excellence in writing, $500 for best new writer (poetry or fiction), two $500 awards for best poetry (for work published in the magazine in the previous year).

How to Contact: Send complete ms with SASE and cover letter listing previous publications—where, when. Does not accept mss by e-mail or fax. Responds in 4 months. Sample copy for $5. Reviews novels, poetry, short story and essay collections.

Payment/Terms: Pays in contributor's copies and prize money awarded. Acquires all rights. Will reassign rights upon request after publication.

Advice: "*Prairie Schooner* is eager to see fiction from beginning and established writers. Be tenacious. Accept rejection as a temporary setback and send out rejected stories to other magazines. *Prairie Schooner* is not a magazine with a program. We look for good fiction in traditional narrative modes as well as experimental, meta-fiction or any other form or fashion a writer might try. Create striking detail, well-developed characters, fresh dialogue; let the images and the situations evoke the stories' themes. Too much explication kills a lot of otherwise good stories. Be persistent. Keep writing and sending out new work. Be familiar with the tastes of the magazines where you're sending. We are receiving record numbers of submissions. Prospective contributors must sometimes wait longer to receive our reply."

prechelonian, a literary & fine art magazine, blue night press, 1003 Lakeway, Kalamazoo MI 49001. (616)552-9349. E-mail: Jadhbat@aol.com. **Contact:** Danielle Trussoni, fiction editor. Magazine: 5½×8½; 25-30 pages; archival, acid-free paper; 80 lb. card cover. "We publish quality experimental fiction and poetry from emerging and established writers. The editors at blue night press place a great deal of emphasis on structural experimentation and formal exploration—work that successfully moves beyond the mere craft of writing and seeks to enter into dialogue with theory is, essentially, what they are after." Semiannual. Estab. 1991. Circ. 250-300.

Needs: Erotica, ethnic/multicultural (general), experimental, feminist, gay, historical (general), humor/satire, lesbian, literary, western (frontier saga, traditional). "No adventure, fantasy, horror, New Age, romance, mystery/suspense." Receives 10-20 unsolicited mss/month. Publishes ms 6 months after acceptance. Agented fiction 10%.

Recently published work by Brandon LaBelle, William Lee, Chad Allen and Matt Dube. Length: 100-2,500 words. Publishes short shorts. Also publishes literary essays, literary criticism and poetry. Often comments on rejected mss.

How to Contact: Send complete ms with a cover letter. Responds in 2 weeks to queries; 1 month to mss. Send SASE (or IRC) for return of ms or send a disposable copy of ms and #10 SASE for reply only. Accepts simultaneous, previously published and multiple submissions. Sample copy for $4. Guidelines for SASE. Reviews novels, short story collections and nonfiction books of interest to writers. Send review copies to Derek Pollard, editor.

Payment/Terms: Pays 2 contributor's copies. Pays on publication.

Advice: "We look for work with a focal combination of both the parts and the whole. The writing must be done in earnest. Manuscripts must be well-written and intuitively sound. Have conviction in your work; be able to go toe-to-toe over it, otherwise we're not interested."

PRISM INTERNATIONAL, Buch E462-1866 Main Mall, University of British Columbia, Vancouver, British Columbia V6T 1Z1 Canada. (604)822-2514. Fax: (604)822-3616. E-mail: prism@intercha nge.ubc.ca. Website: www.arts.ubc.ca/prism/ (includes entire year of issues, writer's guidelines, contest information, PRISM news and e-mail address). Executive Editor: Michael Kissinger. **Contact:** Abigail Kinch, editor. Magazine: 6×9; 72-80 pages; Zephyr book paper; Cornwall, coated one side cover; artwork on cover. "An international journal of contemporary writing—fiction, poetry, drama, creative nonfiction and translation." Readership: "public and university libraries, individual subscriptions, bookstores—a world-wide audience concerned with the contemporary in literature." Quarterly. Estab. 1959. Circ. 1,200.

● *PRISM international* has won numerous magazine awards and stories first published in *PRISM* have been included in the *Journey Prize Anthology* every year since 1991. Cynthia Flood's "Religious Knowledge" published in 38.4 won a gold medal for fiction at the National Magazine Awards. *Prism* ranked #48 on *Writer's Digest*'s "Fiction 50" list of top fiction markets.

Needs: New writing that is contemporary and literary. Short stories and self-contained novel excerpts. Works of translation are eagerly sought and should be accompanied by a copy of the original. Would like to see more translations. No gothic, confession, religious, romance, pornography, or sci-fi. Also looking for creative nonfiction that is literary, not journalistic, in scope and tone. Buys approximately 70 mss/year. Receives over 100 fiction unsolicited mss each month. "*PRISM* publishes both new and established writers; our contributors have included Franz Kafka, Gabriel Garcia Marquez, Michael Ondaatje, Margaret Laurence, Mark Anthony Jarman, Gail Anderson-Dargatz and Eden Robinson." **Publishes 7 new writers/year.** Recently published works by Mark Anthony Jarman, Matt Cohen and Cynthia Flood. Submissions should not exceed 5,000 words "though flexible for outstanding work" (only one long story per submission, please). Publishes short shorts. Also publishes poetry and drama. Sponsors annual short fiction contest with $2,000 (Canadian) grand prize: send SASE (IRC) for details.

How to Contact: Send complete ms with SASE or SAE, IRC and cover letter with bio, information and publications list. "Keep it simple. U.S. contributors take note: Do note send U.S. stamps, they are not valid in Canada. Send International Reply Coupons instead." Responds in 6 months. Sample copy for $5 (U.S./Canadian).

Payment/Terms: Pays $20 (Canadian)/printed page and 1 year's subscription. Pays on publication for first North American serial rights. Selected authors are paid an additional $10/page for digital rights.

Advice: "Read several issues of our magazine before submitting. We are committed to publishing outstanding literary work. We look for strong, believeable characters; real voices; attention to language; interesting ideas and plots. Send us fresh, innovative work which also shows a mastery of the basics of good prose writing. Poorly constructed or sloppy pieces will not receive serious consideration. We welcome e-mail submissions and are proud to be one of few print literary journals who offer additional payment to select writers for digital publication. Too many e-mail submissions, however, come to us unpolished and unprepared to be published. Writers should craft their work for e-mail submission as carefully as they would for submissions through traditional methods. They should send one piece at a time and wait for our reply before they send another."

PROVINCETOWN ARTS, Provincetown Arts, Inc., 650 Commercial St., P.O. Box 35, Provincetown MA 02657. (508)487-3167. Fax: (508)487-8634. E-mail: www.capecodaccess.com. **Contact:** Christopher Busa, editor. Magazine: 9×12; 184 pages; 60 lb. coated paper; 12 pcs. cover; illustrations; photos. "*PA* focuses broadly on the artists, writers and theater of America's oldest continuous art colony." Annual. Estab. 1985. Circ. 8,000.

● *Provincetown Arts* is a recipient of a CLMP seed grant. Provincetown Arts Press has an award-winning poetry series.

Needs: Plans special fiction issue. Receives 300 unsolicited mss/year. Buys 5 mss/issue. Publishes ms 3 months after acceptance. Published work by Carole Maso and Hilary Masters. Length: 1,500-8,000 words; average length: 3,000 words. Publishes short shorts. Also publishes literary essays, literary criticism, poetry. Sometimes critiques rejected mss and recommends other markets.

How to Contact: Send complete ms with cover letter including previous publications. No simultaneous submissions. Responds in 2 weeks to queries; 3 months to mss. SASE. Sample copy for $7.50. Reviews novels and short story collections.

Payment/Terms: Pays $75-300. Pays on publication for first rights. Sends galleys to author.

☑ ◐ **PUCKERBRUSH REVIEW**, Puckerbrush Press, 76 Main St., Orono ME 04473. (207)866-4868/581-3832. **Contact:** Constance Hunting, editor/publisher. Magazine: 9×12; 80-100 pages; illustrations. "We publish mostly new Maine writers; interviews, fiction, reviews, poetry for a literary audience." Semiannual. Estab. 1979. Circ. approx. 500.

Needs: Belles-lettres, experimental, gay (occasionally), literary. "Wants to see more original, quirky and well-written fiction." No genre fiction. "Nothing cliché." Receives 30 unsolicited mss/month. Accepts 6 mss/issue; 12 mss/year. Publishes ms 1 year after acceptance. **Publishes 24 new writers/year.** Recently published work by Farnham Blair, David Rosen and Heather Carson. Sometimes publishes short shorts. Also publishes literary essays, literary criticism, poetry. Sometimes critiques rejected mss.

How to Contact: Send complete ms with cover letter. "No disks please!" Responds in 2 months. SASE. Accepts simultaneous and multiple submissions. Sample copy for $2. Guidelines for SASE. Sometimes reviews novels and short story collections.

Payment/Terms: Pays in contributor's copies.

Advice: "I don't want to see tired plots or treatments. I want to see respect for language—the right words. Be true to yourself, don't follow fashion."

☑ ○ **PUERTO DEL SOL**, New Mexico State University, Box 3E, Las Cruces NM 88003-0001. (505)646-3931. Fax: (505)646-2345. E-mail: PUERTO@nmsu.edu. **Contact:** Kevin McIlvoy, editor-in-chief and fiction editor. Poetry Editor: Kathleene West. Magazine: 6×9; 200 pages; 60 lb. paper; 70 lb. cover stock; photos sometimes. "We publish quality material from anyone. Poetry, fiction, art, photos, interviews, reviews, parts-of-novels, long poems." Semiannual. Estab. 1961. Circ. 1,500.

Needs: Contemporary, ethnic, experimental, literary, mainstream, prose poem, excerpted novel and translations. Receives varied number of unsolicited fiction mss/month. Acquires 8-10 mss/issue; 12-15 mss/year. Does not read mss March-August. **Publishes 8-10 new writers/year.** Published work by Dagobeuto Gilb, Wendell Mayo and William H. Cobb. Also publishes poetry. Occasionally critiques rejected mss.

How to Contact: Send complete ms with SASE. Accepts multiple submissions. Responds in 3 months. Sample copy for $7.

Payment/Terms: Pays 2 contributor's copies. Acquires one-time rights (rights revert to author).

Advice: "We are open to all forms of fiction, from the conventional to the wildly experimental, as long as they have integrity and are well written. Too often we receive very impressively 'polished' mss that will dazzle readers with their sheen but offer no character/reader experience of lasting value."

☑ ◐ ◎ **QUARTER AFTER EIGHT, A Journal of Prose and Commentary**, QAE, Ellis Hall, Ohio University, Athens OH 45701. (740)593-2827. Website: www.quarteraftereight.com (includes guidelines, sample submissions, table of contents and links). **Contact:** Thom Conroy, editor-in-chief. Magazine: 6×9; 310 pages; 20 lb. glossy cover stock; photos. "We look to publish work which challenges boundaries of genre, style, idea, and voice." Annual.

Needs: Condensed/excerpted novel, erotica, ethnic/multicultural, experimental, gay, humor/satire, lesbian, literary, mainstream/contemporary, translations. Send SASE for list of upcoming themes. Receives 150-200 unsolicited mss/month. Accepts 40-50 mss/issue. Does not read mss mid-March-mid-September. Publishes ms 6-12 months after acceptance. Agented fiction 15%. **Publishes 10-15 new writers/year.** Recently published work by Sandra Alcosser, David Baratier, Joan Connor, Colette Inez, Jane Miller and Maureen Seaton. Length: 10,000 words maximum; average length: 3,000 words. Publishes short shorts. Also publishes literary essays, literary criticism, prose poetry. Also sponsors an annual prose contest: $300 award. Sometimes comments on rejected ms.

How to Contact: Send complete ms with a cover letter. Include short bio and list of publications. Responds in 3 months. Send SASE for return of ms or send a disposable copy of ms. Accepts simultaneous submissions and multiple submissions (up to 5 short works and 2 longer works). Sample copy for $10, 8×11 SAE and $1.60 postage. Guidelines for #10 SASE. Reviews novels and short story collections. Send books to Book Review Editor, Patrick Madden.

Payment/Terms: Pays 2 contributor's copies; additional copies $10. Acquires first North American serial rights. Rights revert to author upon publication. Sponsors contest. Send SASE for guidelines.

Advice: "We're interested in seeing more stories that push language and the traditional form to their limits."

☑ $ ○ ♥ **QUARTERLY WEST**, University of Utah, 200 S. Central Campus Dr., Room 317, Salt Lake City UT 84112-9109. (801)581-3938. Fax: (801)585-5167. Website: www.utah.edu/quarterlywest (includes novella guidelines, submission guidelines, recent issues with samples of contributors' work). Editor: David Hawkins. **Contact:** Steve Tuttle, fiction editor. Magazine: 6 × 9; 224 pages; 60 lb. paper; 5-color cover stock; illustrations; photos rarely. "We try to publish a variety of fiction and poetry from all over the country based not so much on the submitting author's reputation but on the merit of each piece. Our publication is aimed primarily at an educated audience interested in contemporary literature and criticism." Semiannual. "We sponsor a biennial novella competition." (Next competition held in 2000). Estab. 1976. Circ. 1,800.

● *Quarterly West* was awarded First Place for Editorial Content from the American Literary Magazine Awards. Work published in the magazine has been selected for inclusion in the *Pushcart Prize* anthology and *The Best American Short Stories* anthology.

Needs: Literary, contemporary, experimental, translations. No detective, science fiction or romance. Accepts 6-10 mss/issue, 12-20 mss/year. Receives 300 unsolicited fiction mss each month. **Publishes 3 new writers/year.** Recently published work by Catherine Ryan Hyde, David Shields, James Tate and David Roderick. No preferred length; interested in longer, "fuller" short stories, as well as short shorts.

How to Contact: Send complete ms. Brief cover letters welcome. Send SASE for reply or return of ms. No fax or e-mail submissions. Accepts simultaneous submissions with notification. Responds in up to 8 months; "sooner, if possible." Sample copy for $7.50.

Payment/Terms: Pays $15-50 and 2 contributor's copies. Pays on publication for all rights (negotiable).

Advice: "We publish a special section of short shorts every issue, and we also sponsor a biennial novella contest. We are open to experimental work—potential contributors should read the magazine! We solicit occasionally, but tend more toward the surprises—unsolicited. Don't send more than one story per submission, and wait until you've heard about the first before submitting another."

⊞ ✓ ◖ **$ QWF (QUALITY WOMEN'S FICTION), Breaking the Boundaries of Women's Fiction**, P.O. Box 1768, Rugby, Warks CVZ1 4ZA United Kingdom. 01788 334302. Fax: 01788 334702. E-mail: jo@qwfmagazine.co.uk. **Contact:** Jo Good, editor. Magazine: A5; 80-90 pages; glossy paper. "*QWF* gets under the skin of the female experience and exposes emotional truth." Bimonthly. Estab. 1994. Circ. 2,000.

Needs: Erotica, ethnic/multicultural, experimental, fantasy, feminist, gay, horror (psychological, supernatural), humor/satire, lesbian, literary, New Age, psychic/supernatural/occult, science fiction (soft/sociological), translations. Receives 30-50 unsolicited mss/month. Accepts 12 mss/issue; 72 mss/year. Does not read mss June-August. Publishes ms up to 18 months after acceptance. **Publishes 20 new writers/year.** Published work by Julia Darling, Sally Zigmond and Diana Forrester. Length: 1,000-4,500 words; average length: 2,500 words. Publishes short shorts. Average length: 900 words. Also publishes literary criticism. Always comments on rejected mss.

How to Contact: Send complete ms, cover letter. Accepts submissions by disk. Include estimated word count, brief bio, list of publications and IRCs or stamps. Responds in 2 weeks to queries; 3 months to mss. Send SASE (or IRC) for return of ms or send a disposable copy of ms and #10 SASE (or IRC) for reply only. Accepts previously published work. Guidelines for SASE (or IRC), by e-mail or fax. Reviews novels, short story collections and nonfiction books of interest to writers.

Payment/Terms: Pays £10 sterling maximum. Pays on publication for first British serial rights. Sponsors contest. SASE or IRC for details.

Advice: "Take risks with subject matter. Study at least one copy of *QWF*. Ensure story is technically sound."

✓ ◯ **THE RABBIT HOLE PRESS**, 2 Huntingwood Crescent, Brampton, Ontario L6S 1S6 Canada. E-mail: rabbitholepress@hotmail.com. **Contact:** A. Cobham, editor. Magazine: digest sized; saddle stitched; desktop published; illustrations; photos. "Rabbit Hole Press is a one-person operation on a part-time basis. We publish original poetry, short fiction, essays, art and photography by new and unpublished writers/editors. We seek to provide a forum for beginning writers." Quarterly. Estab. 1999. Circ. 500.

Needs: Adventure, erotica, ethnic/multicultural, experimental, fantasy (space fantasy, sword and sorcery), feminist, gay, historical, horror (dark fantasy, futuristic, psychological, supernatural), humor satire, lesbian, literary, mainstream, military/war, mystery/suspense, New Age, psychic/supernatural/occult, regional, romance, science fiction, thriller/espionage. Publishes ms 6-9 months after acceptance.

How to Contact: Send complete ms with a cover letter. Accepts submissions by e-mail. Include estimated word count and brief bio. Responds in 3 months to queries; 6 months to mss. Send SASE (or IRC) for return of ms or send a disposable copy of ms and #10 SASE for reply only. Accepts simultaneous submissions. Sample copy for $5 (US).

Payment/Terms: Pays 1 copy.

Advice: "We want eclectic, provocative, culturally diverse, metaphysical, philosophical, imaginative, radical, 'how deep is the rabbit hole?' submissions."

✓ **$◖ RAIN CROW**, (formerly 32 Pages), P.O. Box 11013, Chicago IL 60611-0013. E-mail: submissions @rain-crow.com. Website: http://rain-crow.com/ (includes writer's guidelines, sample issue, back issue sales, contest news, author news, advertising rates). **Contact:** Michael S. Manley, editor. Magazine/journal: 8½ × 5½;

144-160 pages; white bond paper; glossy cover; illustrations; photos. "*Rain Crow* publishes new and experienced writers in many styles and genres. I look for eclectic, well-crafted, entertaining fiction aimed at those who enjoy literature for its pleasures." Triannual. Estab. 1997. Circ. 300. Member, CLMP.

Needs: Erotica, experimental, literary, mainstream, speculative fiction, translations. "No propaganda, pornographic, juvenile, or formulaic fiction. No poetry." Receives 120-150 unsolicited mss/month. Accepts 10-12 mss/issue; 30 mss/year. Publishes ms within 6 months after acceptance. **Publishes several new writers/year.** Published work by Susan Neville, Peter Johnson, Paul Maliszewski, Peter Hynes, Carolyn Allesio and Laura Denham. Length: 250-8,000 words; average length: 3,500 words. Publishes short shorts. Also publishes novellas, creative nonfiction, short shorts. No poetry. Sometimes comments on rejected mss.

How to Contact: Send complete ms with a cover letter. May also e-mail submissions. Include list of publications. Responds in 5 months. Send SASE for reply, return of ms or send a disposable copy of ms. Accepts simultaneous submissions, reprints and electronic submissions. Sample copy for $7. Guidelines for #10 SASE (1 IRC) or on website.

Payment/Terms: Pays $5 per page, free subscription to magazine and 2 contributor's copies; additional copies for 20% discount. Pays on publication for one-time rights. Sends galleys to author. "Watch for announcements in writer's publications and on our website for contests."

Advice: "I look for attention to craft: voice, language, character and plot working together to maximum effect. I look for stories that deserve rereading and that I would gladly recommend others read. Send your best work. Present your work professionally. Unique, credible settings and situations that entertain get the most attention."

✔ ◑ **RASKOLNIKOV'S CELLAR**, The Beggars's Press, 8110 N. 38th St., Omaha NE 68112-2018. (402)455-2615. **Contact:** Richard Carey, publisher. Fiction Editor: Danielle Staton. Magazine: 8½×12; 60-150 pages; 20 lb. bond paper; 12pt soft cover. "We want to revive good writing of past eras. Period pieces are welcome—but be authentic. Our readers are sophisticated." Semiannual. Estab. 1952. Circ. 1,200.

• Member, International Association of Independent Publishers and the Federation of Literary Publishers.

Needs: Historical, horror, humor/satire, literary, serialized novels, translations. No "religious, sentimental, folksy, science fiction or ultra modern." Would like to see more "short but powerful pieces, and stark realism." Publishes special fiction issue or anthologies. Receives 135 unsolicited mss/month. Accepts 15 mss/issue; 30-45 mss/year. Publishes ms 2-6 months after acceptance. Agented fiction 5%. **Publishes 4 new writers/year.** Published work by James Scoffield, Richard Davignon and Philip Sparacino. Length: 50-3,000 words; average length: 1,500-2,000 words. Publishes short shorts. Also publishes literary essays, literary criticism and poetry.

How to Contact: Send complete ms with a cover letter. Include estimated word count and 1 page bio. Responds in 2 months to queries and mss. Accepts simultaneous and multiple submissions. Sample copy for $10 plus 9×12 SAE with 2 first-class stamps. Guidelines for #10 SAE with 2 first-class stamps. Reviews novels or short story collections. Send books to Danielle Staton.

Payment/Terms: Pays 1 contributor's copy. Acquires first North American serial rights.

Advice: "First of all learn your craft thoroughly. Be persistent when dealing with a publisher. Keep in touch even when rejected. Make your name known with the editors. In our bustling modern age, start your story with a direct opening or you will lose the editor at once. Interest him in the first couple of sentences. Promise something in the story and fulfill that promise. Most of all, be original. Before sending out material, consult guidelines or buy a magazine. Small press magazines keep writers abreast of the currents of literature. Don't forget the SASE."

✔ ◑ **RATTAPALLAX**, Rattapallax Press, 532 La Guardia Place, Suite 353, New York NY 10012. (212)560-7459. E-mail: rattapallax@hotmail.com. Website: www.rattapallax.com. **Contact:** Alan Cheuse, fiction editor. Literary magazine: 6×9; 128 pages; bound; some illustrations; photos. "General readership. Our stories must be character driven with strong conflict. All accepted stories are edited by our staff and the writer before publication to ensure a well-crafted and written work." Semiannual. Estab. 1999. Circ. 2,000.

Needs: Literary. Receives 15 unsolicited mss/month. Accepts 3 mss/issue; 6 mss/year. Publishes ms 3-6 months after acceptance. Agented fiction 15%. **Publishes 5-10 new writers/year.** Recently published work by Stuart Dybeth, Dana Gioia and Williaim P.H. Root. Length: 1,000-10,000 words; average length: 5,000 words. Publishes short shorts; average length: 1,000 words. Also publishes poetry. Often comments on rejected mss.

How to Contact: Send complete ms with cover letter. Reports in 3 months to queries and mss. Send SASE for return of ms. Sample copy for $7.95. Guidelines for SASE or on website.

Payment/Terms: Pays 2 contributor's copies; additional copies $7.95. Pays on publication for first North American serial rights. Sends galleys to author.

Advice: "Character driven, well-crafted, strong conflict."

ℕ ◑ **RE:AL, The Journal of Liberal Arts**, Stephen F. Austin State University, P.O. Box 13007, Nacogdoches TX 75962-3007. (409)468-2059. Fax: (409)468-2614. E-mail: f_real@titansfasu.edu. Website: http://libweb.sfasu.edu/real/default.htm. (includes complete interactive-version or printed journal). **Contact:** W. Dale Hearell, editor. Academic journal: 6×10; perfect-bound; 175-225 pages; "top" stock. Editorial content: 30% fiction,

30% poetry, 30% scholarly essays and criticism; book reviews (assigned after query) and interviews. "Work is reviewed based on the intrinsic merit of the scholarship and creative work and its appeal to a sophisticated international readership (U.S., Canada, Great Britain, Ireland, Brazil, Puerto Rico, Italy)." Semiannual. Estab. 1968. Circ. 400.

Needs: Adventure, contemporary, genre, science fiction, historical, experimental, regional. No pornographic material, romance or juvenile fiction. Want more speculative, experimental, feminist and contemporary. Receives 1,400-1,600 unsolicited mss/2 issues. Accepts 5-10 fiction mss/issue. Publishes ms 1-12 months after acceptance. **Publishes 20 new writers/year.** Published work by Holly Kulak, Cyd Adams, John Dublin and Salem Pflueger. Length: 1,000-5,000 words. Occasionally critiques rejected mss and conditionally accepts on basis of critiques and changes.

How to Contact: Send 2 copies of ms with cover letter. No simultaneous submissions. Accepts multiple submissions (up to 2). Responds in 2 weeks to queries; 1 month to mss. SASE. Sample copy and writer's guidelines for $15. Guidelines for SASE.

Payment/Terms: Pays 2 contributor's copies; charges for extras. Rights revert to author.

Advice: "Please study an issue. *RE:AL* seeks finely crafted stories that include individualistic ideas and approaches, allowing and encouraging deeper repeated readings. Have your work checked by a well-published writer—who is not a good friend. Also proofread for grammatical and typographical errors. A manuscript must show that the writer is conscious of what he or she is attempting to accomplish in plot, character and theme. A short story isn't written but constructed; the ability to manipulate certain aspects of a story is the sign of a conscious storyteller."

N: ☑ REASONING NOVEL MAGAZINE, Forward Book Co., Room 106, 1/F, New Treasure Centre, 10 NG Fong St., San Po Kong, KLN Hong Kong 852. Phone: (852)235-35856. Fax: (852)23296585. E-mail: forward@hkauthors.com. Website: www.hkauthors.com.hk. **Contact:** Cheng Ey Shem, publisher. Magazine: 5½×8¼; 192 pages; illustrations; photos. "The only reasoning novel magazine in China and Hong Kong. Our intended audience is students and teenagers." Bimonthly. Estab. 1996. Circ. 10,000. Member, Hong Kong Writer Association.

• *Reasoning Novel Magazine* received the 2nd National Reasoning Novel Awards of China.

Needs: Literary. Receives 30 unsolicited mss/month. Accepts 20 mss/issue; 120 mss/year. Publishes ms 2 months after acceptance. Agented fiction 60%. **Publishes 2-3 new writers/year.** Length: 100,000-600,000 words; average length: 20,000 words. Publishes short shorts. Average length: 2,000 words. Also publishes literary essays and literary criticism.

How to Contact: Send complete ms with cover letter. Accepts mss by e-mail. Include estimated word count, brief bio and list of publications with submission. Responds in 1 month to queries; 2 months to mss. No simultaneous and multiple submissions. Sample copy for $20. Guidelines by e-mail.

Payment/Terms: Pays on publication for all rights. Sends galleys to author.

Advice: "Submissions should have good content."

☑ ◐ RED ROCK REVIEW, Community College of Southern Nevada, 3200 E. Cheyenne Ave., N. Las Vegas NV 89030. E-mail: rich_logsdon@ccsn.nevada.edu. Website: www.ccsn.nevada.edu/english/redrock review/index/htm. **Contact:** Dr. Richard Logsdon, senior editor. Magazine: 5×8; 125 pages. "We're looking for the very best literature. Stories need to be tightly crafted, strong in character development, built around conflict. Poems need to be tightly crafted, characterized by expert use of language." Semiannual. Estab. 1995. Circ. 250. Member, CLMP.

Needs: Experimental, literary, mainstream. Receives 125 unsolicited mss/month. Accepts 5-7 mss/issue; 10-14 mss/year. Does not read mss during summer. Publishes ms 3-5 months after acceptance. **Publishes 5-10 new writers/year.** Recently published work by Kari Brooks, Robert Thomas, Shaun Griffin and David Lee. Length: 1,500-5,000 words; average length: 3,500 words. Publishes short shorts. Average length: 3,500 words. Also publishes literary essays, literary criticism and poetry. Sometimes comments on rejected mss.

How to Contact: Send complete ms with a cover letter. Accepts submissions by e-mail and disk. Include brief bio and list of publications. Responds in 2 weeks to queries; 2 months to mss. Send SASE (or IRC) for return of ms. Accepts simultaneous submissions and multiple submissions. Sample copy for $5.50. Guidelines for SASE, by e-mail or on website.

Payment/Terms: Pays 2 contributor's copies. Pays on acceptance for first rights.

☑ ◐ RED WHEELBARROW, De Anza College, 21250 Stevens Creek Blvd., Cupertino CA 95014-5702. (408)864-8600. E-mail: splitterrandolph@fhda.edu. Website: www.deanza.fhda.edu/redwheelbarrow (includes guidelines, names of editors, short fiction, authors, links). **Contact:** Randolph Splitter, editor-in-chief. Magazine: 6×9; 100-140 pages; photos. "Contemporary poetry, fiction, creative nonfiction, b&w graphics, comics and photos." Annual. Estab. 1976 as *Bottomfish*; 2000 as *Red Wheelbarrow*. Circ. 250-500.

Needs: "Careful, thoughtful, personal writing. We welcome submissions of all kinds, and we seek to publish a diverse range of styles and voices from around the country and the world." Receives 50-100 unsolicited fiction mss/month. Accepts 8-10 mss/issue. Agented fiction 1%. Publishes mss an average of 3 months after acceptance. **Publishes 0-2 new writers/year.** Recently published work by Michael Bourne, Joonseong Park and James D. Houston. Length: 4,000 words maximum; average length: 2,500 words. Publishes short shorts; average length: 400 words. Also publishes poetry.

How to Contact: Reads mss September through December. Submission deadline: December 31; publication date: April. Accepts queries by e-mail (no mss). Submit 1 short story or up to 3 short shorts with cover letter, brief bio, list of publications and SASE. "Sorry, we cannot return manuscripts." Writer's guidelines for SASE. Responds in 6 months. No reprints. Accepts simultaneous submissions. Sample copy for $5.

Payment/Terms: Pays 2 contributor's copies. Acquires first North American serial rights.

Advice: "Write freely, rewrite carefully. Move beyond clichés and stereotypes."

◓ ◎ **REFLECT**, 1317-D Eagles Trace Path, Chesapeake VA 23320-3033. (757)547-4464. **Contact:** W.S. Kennedy, editor. Magazine: 5½×8½; 48 pages; pen & ink illustrations. "Spiral Mode fiction and poetry for writers and poets—professional and amateur." Quarterly. Estab. 1979.

Needs: Spiral fiction. "The four rules to the Spiral Mode fiction form are: (1) The story a situation or condition. (2) The outlining of the situation in the opening paragraphs. The story being told at once, the author is not overly-involved with dialogue and plot development, may concentrate on *sound*, *style*, *color*—the superior elements in art. (3) The use of a concise style with euphonic wording. Good poets may have the advantage here. (4) The involvement of Spiral Fiction themes—as opposed to Spiral Poetry themes—with love, and presented with the mystical overtones of the Mode." Would like to see more mystical fiction. No "smut, bad taste, socialist." Accepts 2-6 mss/issue; 8-24 mss/year. Publishes ms 3 months after acceptance. **Publishes 4-6 new writers/year.** Recently published work by Joan P. Kincaid, BZ Niditch, Ruth Wildes Schuler and Dr. Elaine Hatfield. Length: 2,000 words maximum; average length: 1,500 words. Publishes short shorts. Sometimes critiques rejected mss.

How to Contact: Send complete ms with cover letter. Responds in 2 months to mss. SASE. No simultaneous submissions. Sample copy for $2. (Make checks payable to W.S. Kennedy.) Guidelines in each issue of *Reflect*.

Payment/Terms: Pays contributor's copies. Acquires one-time rights. Publication not copyrighted.

Advice: "Subject matter usually is not relevant to the successful writing of Spiral Fiction, as long as there is some element or type of *love* in the story, and provided that there are mystical references. (Though a dream-like style may qualify as 'mystical.')"

$ ◓ **THE REJECTED QUARTERLY, A Journal of Quality Literature Rejected at Least Five Times**, Black Plankton Press, P.O. Box 1351, Cobb CA 95426. E-mail: bplankton@juno.com. Editor: Daniel Weiss. **Contact:** Daniel Weiss, Jeff Ludecke, fiction editors. Magazine: 8½×11; 40 pages; 60 lb. paper; 10 pt. coated cover stock; illustrations. "We want the best literature possible, regardless of genre. We do, however, have a bias toward the unusual and toward speculative fiction. We aim for a literate, educated audience. *The Rejected Quarterly* believes in publishing the highest quality rejected fiction and other writing that doesn't fit anywhere else. We strive to be different, but will go for quality every time, whether conventional or not." Quarterly. Estab. 1998.

Needs: Experimental, fantasy, historical, humor/satire, literary, mainstream/contemporary, mystery/suspense, romance (futuristic/time travel only), science fiction (soft/sociological), sports. Receives 30 unsolicited mss/month. Accepts 4-6 mss/issue; 16-24 mss/year. Publishes ms 1-12 months after acceptance. **Publishes 1-2 new writers/year.** Recently published work by Vera Searles, Steve Cooke and Lenora K. Rogers. Length: 8,000 words maximum; average length: 5,000 words. Publishes short shorts. Also publishes literary essays, literary criticism, poetry. Often comments on rejected ms.

How to Contact: Send complete ms with a cover letter and 5 rejection slips. Include estimated word count, 1-paragraph bio and list of publications. Accepts queries by e-mail. Responds in 2 weeks to queries; up to 9 months to mss. Send SASE for reply, return of ms or send a disposable copy of ms. Accepts reprint submissions. Sample copy $6 (IRCs for foreign requests). Reviews novels, short story collections and nonfiction.

Payment/Terms: Pays $5 and 1 contributor's copy; additional copies, one at cost, others $5. Pays on acceptance for first rights. Sends galleys to author if possible.

Advice: "We are looking for high-quality writing that tells a story or expresses a coherent idea. We want unique stories, original viewpoints and unusual slants. We are getting far too many inappropriate submissions. Please be familiar with the magazine. Be sure to include your rejection slips! Send out quality rather than quantity. Work on one piece until it is as close to a masterpiece in your own eyes as you can get it. Find the right place for it. Be selective in ordering samples, but do be familiar with where you're sending your work."

✔ ◓ ♆ **RHINO**, The Poetry Forum, P.O. Box 554, Winnetka IL 60093. Website: www.rhinopoetry.org (includes guidelines, events, and excerpts). **Contact:** Alice George, co-editor. Magazine: 5½×7½; 90-120 pages; glossy cover stock; illustrations; photos. "An eclectic magazine looking for strong voices and risk-taking." Annual. Estab. 1976.

• *Rhino* short fiction has received three Illinois literary awards.

Needs: Ethnic/multicultural, experimental, feminist, humor/satire, literary, mainstream/contemporary, regional. "No long stories—we only print short-shorts/flash fiction." Receives 60 unsolicited fiction mss/month. Accepts 1-2 mss/issue. Publishes ms up to 9 months after acceptance. **Publishes 4 new writers/year.** Recently published work by Barry Silesky and S.I. Weisenberg. Length: flash fiction/short shorts (under 500 words) only. Also publishes literary essays. Sometimes comments on rejected ms.

How to Contact: Send complete ms with a cover letter. Include bio. Responds in 1 month to queries; 3 months to mss. Send SASE for reply, return of ms or send a disposable copy of ms. Accepts simultaneous and multiple submissions. Current issue $10; back issues $5. Guidelines free.

Payment/Terms: Pays 2 contributor's copies; additional copies $3.50. Acquires one-time rights. Sends galleys to author.

☑ ◑ RIO GRANDE REVIEW, UT El Paso's literary magazine, Student publications, 105 E. Union, University of Texas at El Paso, El Paso TX 79968-0062. (915)747-5161. Fax: (915)747-8031. E-mail: rgr@utep.e du. Website: www.utep.edu/proscmine/rgr/. Editor: Adriana Chavez. Editors change each year. **Contact:** Fiction Editor. Magazine: 6×9; approximately 200 pages; 70 lb. paper; 85 lb. cover stock; illustrations; photos. "We publish any work that challenges writing and reading audiences alike. The intended audience isn't any one sect in particular; rather, the work forcing readers to think as opposed to couch reading is encouraged." Semiannual. Estab. 1981. Circ. 1,000.

Needs: Experimental, feminist, gay, humor/satire, lesbian, mainstream/contemporary, flash fiction, short drama, short fiction. No regional, "anything exclusionarily academic." Receives 40-45 unsolicited mss/month. Accepts 3-4 mss/issue; 6-8 mss/year. Publishes ms approximately 2 months after acceptance. **Publishes 5 new writers/ year.** Published work by Lawrence Dunning, James J. O'Keeffe and Carole Bubash. Length: 1,100-2,000 words; average length: 1,750 words. Publishes short shorts. Also publishes poetry. Sometimes comments on rejected mss.

How to Contact: Send complete ms with a cover letter. Include estimated word count, 40-word bio and list of publications. Responds in 3 months to queries; 4 months to mss. Send SASE for reply and disposable copy of ms. Accepts electronic submissions. Sample copy for $8.

Payment/Terms: Pays 2 contributor's copies; additional copies for $6. Pays on publication for "one-time rights that revert back to the author but the *Rio Grande Review* must be mentioned."

Advice: "Be patient. If the beginning fiction writer doesn't make it into the edition the first time, re-submit. Be persistent. One huge category that the *RGR* is branching into is flash fiction. Because the attention span of the nation is dwindling, thereby turning to such no-brain activities as television and movies, literature must change to accommodate as well."

☑ $ ◑ ♉ RIVER STYX, Big River Association, 634 N. Grand Blvd., 12th Floor, St. Louis MO 63103-1218. (314)533-4541. Fax: (314)533-3345. E-mail: r-t-newman@hotmail.com. Website: www.riverstyx.org (includes writer's guidelines, names of editors, contest and theme issue information, excerpts and art from publication). **Contact:** Richard Newman, editor. Magazine: 6×9; 100 pages; color card cover; perfect-bound; b&w visual art. "No theme restrictions; only high quality, intelligent work." Triannual. Estab. 1975.

• *River Styx* has twice received the Stanley Hanks Award, and has had stories appear in *Best Stories of the South.*

Needs: Excerpted novel chapter, contemporary, ethnic, experimental, feminist, gay, satire, lesbian, literary, mainstream, prose poem, translations. No genre fiction, "less thinly veiled autobiography, or science fiction." Receives 150-200 unsolicited mss/month. Accepts 1-3 mss/issue; 3-8 mss/year. Reads only May through November. **Publishes 20 new writers/year.** Recently published work by Julianna Baggott, Naomi Shihab Nye, Molly Peacock and Pattiann Rogers. Length: no more than 20-30 manuscript pages. Publishes short shorts. Also publishes poetry. Sometimes critiques rejected mss and recommends other markets.

How to Contact: Send complete ms with name and address on every page. SASE required. Responds in 5 months to mss. Accepts simultaneous submissions, "if a note is enclosed with your work and if we are notified immediately upon acceptance elsewhere." Sample copy for $7.

Payment/Terms: Pays 2 contributor's copies, 1-year subscription and $8/page "if funds available." Acquires first North American serial rights.

Advice: "We want high-powered stories with well-developed characters. We like strong plots, usually with at least three memorable scenes, and a subplot often helps. No thin, flimsy fiction with merely serviceable language. Short stories shouldn't be any different than poetry–every single word should count. One could argue every word counts more since we're being asked to read 10 to 30 pages."

☑ ◑ ROANOKE REVIEW, Roanoke College, 221 College Lane, Salem VA 24153-3794. (540)375-2380. **Contact:** Paul Hanstedt, editor. Magazine: 6×9; 200 pages; 60 lb. paper; 70 lb. cover. "We're looking for fresh, thoughtful material that will appeal to a broader as well as literary audience. Humor encouraged." Annual. Estab. 1964. Circ. 500.

Needs: Erotica, feminist, gay, humor/satire, lesbian, literary, mainstream, regional. No pornography, science fiction or horror. Receives 50 unsolicited mss/month. Accepts 5-10 mss/year. Does not read mss April 15-September 1. Publishes ms 6 months after acceptance. Agented fiction 5%. **Publishes 4-5 new writers/year.** Recently published work by Ruth Latta, Adrianne Marcus and Arthur Powers. Length: 1,000-6,000 words; average length: 1,500 words. Publishes short shorts. Also publishes poetry. Sometimes comments on rejected mss.

How to Contact: Send complete ms with a cover letter. Include brief bio. Responds in 1 month to queries; 6 months to mss. Send SASE for return of ms or send a disposable copy of ms and #10 SASE for reply only. Accepts simultaneous and multiple submissions. Sample copy for 8 × 11 SAE with $2 postage. Guidelines for SASE.

Payment/Terms: Pays 2 contributor's copies; additional copies $5. Pays on publication for one-time rights.

Advice: "Pay attention to sentence-level writing—verbs, metaphors, concrete images. Don't forget, though, that plot and character keep us reading. We're looking for stuff that breaks the MFA story style."

✅ $⊘ ROCKET PRESS, P.O. Box 672, Water Mill NY 11976-0672. E-mail: rocketpress@hotmail.com. Website: www.people.delphi.com/rocketusa. **Contact:** Darren Johnson, editor. 16-page newspaper. "A Rocket is a transcendental, celestial traveler—innovative and intelligent fiction and poetry aimed at opening minds—even into the next century." Biannual. Estab. 1993. Circ. 500-2,000.

Needs: Erotica, experimental, humor/satire, literary, special interests (prose poetry). "No historical, romance, academic." Publishes annual special fiction issue or anthology. Receives 20 unsolicited mss/month. Accepts 2-4 mss/issue; 8-16 mss/year. Recently published work by Chris Woods, Roger Lee Kenvin and Ben Ohmart. Publishes 1 new writer/year. Length: 500-2,000 words; average length: 1,000 words. Publishes short shorts. Length: 400 words. Also publishes poetry. Sometimes comments on rejected mss.

How to Contact: "We now only accept fiction manuscripts (under 2,000 words) via e-mail." Accepts simultaneous submissions. Responds in 3 months. Current issue $2, past issue $1.

Payment/Terms: Pays 1¢/word. Acquires one-time rights.

Advice: "Your first paragraph is crucial. Editors are swamped with submissions, so a plain or clumsy lead will send your manuscript to the recycling bin. Also, too many writers come off as self-important. When writing a cover letter really try to talk to the editor—don't just rattle off a list of publications you've been in."

🌐 ⃠ ◎ $ ROOM OF ONE'S OWN, P.O. Box 46160, Suite D, Vancouver, British Columbia V6J 5G5 Canada. Website: www.islandnet.com/Room/enter (includes selected works from current issue). **Contact:** Growing Room Collective. Magazine: 112 pages; illustrations; photos. Quarterly. Estab. 1975.

Needs: Feminist, literary. "No humor, science fiction, romance." Receives 60-100 unsolicited mss/month. Accepts 18-20 mss/issue; 75-80 mss/year. Publishes ms 1 year after acceptance. **Publishes 15-20 new writers/year.** Length: 5,000 words maximum. Publishes short shorts. Also publishes poetry.

How to Contact: Send complete ms with a cover letter. Include estimated word count and brief bio. Send a disposable copy of ms and #10 SASE or IRC for reply only. Reviews novels, short story collections and nonfiction books of interest to writers. Send review copies to Virginia Aulin.

Payment/Terms: Pays $35 Canadian, free subscription to the magazine and 2 contributor's copies. Pays on publication for first North American serial rights.

🆕 ⃠ 🏆 ▦ THE ROSE & THORN LITERARY E-ZINE, Showcasing Emerging and Established Writers and A Writer's Resource. E-mail: raven763@aol.com or amaznbella@aol.com. Website: members. aol/Raven763/index.html (includes writer's resources, current issue, submissions guidelines and staff information). Editor: Jasmin Randick. **Fiction Editor:** Barbara Quinn. E-zine specializing in literary works of fiction, poetry and essays: 35-40 pages; illustrations; photos. "We created *The Rose & Thorn Literary E-zine* for readers and writers alike. We offer inspiration from eclectic works of distinction and provide a forum for emerging and established voices. We blend contemporary writing with traditional prose and poetry in an effort to promote the literary arts and expand the venue of standard publishing." Quarterly. Estab. 1998. Circ. 12,000.

  • *The Rose & Thorn Literary E-zine* has received the Page One Award For Literary Contribution (1998), Scars Publications Editor's Choice Award (1998), The Original Cool Site of the Day Award (1998) and the Home and Hearth Award of Excellence (1998).

Needs: Adventure, ethnic/multicultural (general), experimental, fantasy (space fantasy, sword and sorcery), historical, horror (dark fantasy, futuristic, psychological, supernatural), humor satire, literary, mainstream, mystery/suspense, New Age, regional, religious (inspirational, religious fantasy, religious mystery/suspense, religious thriller, religious romance), romance (contemporary, futuristic/time travel, gothic, historical, regency period, romantic suspense), science fiction (hard science/technological, soft/sociological, thriller/espionage, western. Receives "several hundred" unsolicited mss/month. Accepts 8-10 mss/issue; 40-50 mss/year. "We are very open to unpublished writers and encourage submissions by both emerging and established writers. About 50% of accepted manuscripts are by unpublished writers." Recently published work by Ibarionex R. Perello and Anjana Basu. Length: 250-2,000 words. Publishes short shorts. Length: 250-750 words. Also publishes literary essays and poetry. Sometimes comments on rejected mss.

How to Contact: Send queries/mss by e-mail to Jasmin Randick, managing editor at raven763@aol.com or Barbara Quinn, co-managing editor at amaznbella@aol.com. Include estimated word count, 150 word bio, list of publications and authors byline. Responds in 1 week to queries; 1 month to mss. Accepts simultaneous submissions and reprints. Sample copy and guidelines free. Reviews novels and short story collections. Send books to Jasmin Randick, managing editor at raven763@aol.com.

Payment/Terms: "No payment except feedback from visitors and subscribers to the site. Writer retains all rights—our goal is to showcase exceptional writers." Sends galleys to author.

Advice: "Clarity, control of the language, evocative stories that tug at the heart and make their mark on the reader long after it's been read. We look for uniqueness in voice, style and characterization. New twists on old themes are always welcome. Use all aspects of good writing in your stories, including dynamic characters, strong, narrative voice and a riveting and original plot. We have eclectic tastes so go ahead and give us a shot. Read the publication and other quality, literary journals to see if your work would fit with our style. Always check your spelling and grammar before submitting. Reread your submission with a critical eye and ask yourself, does it evoke an emotional response? Have I completely captured my reader? Check your submission for 'it' and 'was' and see if you can come up with a better way to express yourself. Be unique."

SALMAGUNDI, Skidmore College, Saratoga Springs NY 12866. Fax: (518)580-5188. **Contact:** Peg Boyers, editor. Magazine: 8×5; 200-300 pages; illustrations; photos. "*Salmagundi* publishes an eclectic variety of materials, ranging from short short fiction to novellas from the surreal to the realistic. Authors include Nadine Gordimer, Russell Banks, Steven Millhauser, Gordon Lish, Clark Blaise, Mary Gordon, Joyce Carol Oates and Cynthia Ozick. Our audience is a generally literate population of people who read for pleasure." Quarterly. Estab. 1965. Circ. 4,800. Member, CLMP.

● *Salmagundi* authors are regularly represented in Pushcart collections and *Best American Short Story* collections.

Needs: Ethnic/multicultural (general), experimental, family saga, gay, historical (general), literary. Receives 50-70 unsolicited mss/month. Accepts 2 mss/year. Does not read mss May 1-October 15. Publishes ms up to 2 years after acceptance. Agented fiction 10%. Publishes short shorts. Also publishes literary essays, literary criticism and poetry.

How to Contact: Send complete ms with a cover letter or submit through agent. Include brief bio, list of publications and how they heard about *Salmagundi*. Responds in 6 months to queries and mss. Send SASE for return of ms or send a disposable copy of ms and #10 SASE for reply only. Sample copy for $5. Guidelines for SASE. Reviews novels, short story collections and nonfiction books of interest to writers. Send review copies to Peg Boyers.

Payment/Terms: Pays 6-10 contributor's copies and subscription to magazine; additional copies $3. Pays on publication for first and electronic rights.

Advice: "I look for excellence and a very unpredictable ability to appeal to the interests and tastes of the editors. Be brave. Don't be discouraged by rejection. Keep stories in circulation. Of course, it goes without saying: work hard on the writing. Revise tirelessly. Study magazines and send only to those whose sensibility matches yours."

SAMSARA, The Magazine of Suffering, P.O. Box 367, College Park MD 20741-0367. E-mail: rdfgoalie@aol.com. Website: http://samsara.cjb.net (includes writer's guidelines, reading periods and tips for writers). **Contact:** R. David Fulcher, editor. Magazine: 8½×11; 50-80 pages; Xerox paper; poster stock cover; illustrations. "*Samsara* publishes only stories or poems relating to the theme of suffering/healing." Semiannual. Estab. 1994. Circ. 250.

Needs: Condensed/excerpted novel, erotica, experimental, fantasy (science fantasy, sword and sorcery), horror, literary, mainstream/contemporary, science fiction (hard science, soft/sociological). Would like to see more fantasy and science fiction relating to suffering/healing. Receives 80 unsolicited mss/month. Accepts 17-20 mss/issue; 40 mss/year. "*Samsara* closes to submission after the publication of each issue. However, this schedule is not fixed." Publishes ms 4 months after acceptance. **Publishes 20 new writers/year.** Published work by D.F. Lewis, D. Ceder and Christopher Hivner. Average length: 2,000 words. Publishes short shorts. Also publishes poetry. Sometimes comments on rejected ms.

TO RECEIVE REGULAR TIPS AND UPDATES about writing and Writer's Digest publications via e-mail, send an e-mail with "SUBSCRIBE NEWSLETTER" in the body of the message to newsletter-request@writersdigest.com.

How to Contact: Send complete ms with a cover letter. Accepts mss on disk. Include estimated word count, 1-page bio and list of publications. Responds in 6 months to queries. Send SASE for reply, return of ms or send a disposable copy of ms. Accepts simultaneous, multiple and reprint submissions. Sample copy for $5.50. Guidelines for #10 SASE.

Payment/Terms: Pays 1 contributor's copy. Acquires first North American serial rights and reprint rights.

Advice: "We seek out writers who make use of imagery and avoid over-writing. Symbolism and myth really make a manuscript stand out. Read a sample copy. Too many writers send work which does not pertain to the guidelines. Writers should avoid sending us splatter-punk or gore stories."

N $ □ SAN DIEGO WRITERS' MONTHLY, 3910 Chapman St., San Diego CA 92101. (619)266-0896. E-mail: mcarthy@sandiego-online.com. Website: www.sandiego-online.com/entertainment/sdwm. **Contact:** Michael T. MacCarthy, editor. Literary magazine: 8×10; 32 pages; 60 lb. paper; illustrations; photos. "A publication dedicated to the San Diego writing community, *San Diego Writers' Monthly* will cross all genres and include columns, interviews, essays, feature, reviews, fiction and poetry written by San Diego County residents." Monthly. Estab. 1991. Circ. 500.

Needs: Adventure, ethnic/multicultural (general), family saga, fantasy (space fantasy), historical (general), horror (psychological), humor/satire, literary, mainstream/contemporary, mystery/suspense (police procedural, private eye/hardboiled), New Age/mystic/spiritual, regional (south west US), religious (inspirational), romance (contemporary, futuristic/time travel, gothic, historical, romantic suspense), science fiction (soft/sociological), thriller/espionage, western (traditional), young adult/teen (adventure, fantasy/science fiction, historical, horror, mystery/suspense, western). No children's/juvenile, erotica, occult, translations. Receives 25-100 unsolicited mss/month. Accepts 2 mss/issue; 24 mss/year. Recently published work by Philip Goldberg, Ida Voss and Dale Fetherling. **Publishes 12-15 new writers/year.** Length: 2,500-4,000 words. Also publishes literary essays, criticism and poetry. Sometimes comments on rejected ms.

How to Contact: Send complete ms with a cover letter. Accepts mss by mail, e-mail (short) and disk. Include estimated word count, 25-50 word bio, list of publications. Send SASE for reply and a disposable copy of ms. Accepts reprint and multiple submissions. Sample copy for $4. Guidelines for SASE. Reviews novels, short story collections or nonfiction books of interest to writers. Send books to editor.

Payment/Terms: Pays $15-25 and 1 contributor's copy. Pays on publication for one-time rights.

Advice: Looks for "good, tight, entertaining writing. Follow the guidelines."

☑ ⊘ ♈ SANSKRIT, Literary Arts Magazine of UNC Charlotte, University of North Carolina at Charlotte, Highway 49, Charlotte NC 28223-0001. (704)547-2326. Fax: (704)547-3394. E-mail: sanskrit@email. uncc.edu. Website: www.uncc.edu/life/sanskrit (includes 1999, 2000 editions). **Contact:** Jason Keath, literary editor. Magazine: 9×12, 64 pages. "*Sanskrit* is an award-winning magazine produced with two goals in mind: service to the student staff and student body, and the promotion of unpublished and beginning artists. Our intended audience is the literary/arts community of UNCC, Charlotte, other schools and contributors and specifically individuals who might never have read a literary magazine before." Annual. Estab. 1968.

● *Sanskrit* has received the Pacemaker Award, Associated College Press, Gold Crown Award and Columbia Scholastic Press Award.

Needs: "Not looking for any specific category—just good writing." Receives 50 unsolicited mss/month. Acquires 2-3 mss/issue. Publishes in late March. Deadline: first Friday in November. Published work by Bayard. Length: 250-3,500 words. Publishes short shorts. Also publishes poetry. Seldom critiques rejected mss.

How to Contact: Send complete manuscript with cover letter. Accepts queries/mss by e-mail. SASE. Accepts simultaneous submissions. Sample copy for $10; additional copies $7. Guidelines for #10 SAE.

Payment/Terms: Pays contributor's copy. Acquires one-time rights. Publication not previously copyrighted.

Advice: "Remember that you are entering a market often saturated with mediocrity—an abundance of cute words and phrases held together by clichés simply will not do."

⊘ SANTA MONICA REVIEW, Santa Monica College, 1900 Pico Blvd., Santa Monica CA 90405. (310)434-4242. **Contact:** Andrew Tonkovich, editor. Magazine: 250 pages. "The editors are committed to fostering new talent as well as presenting new work by established writers. There is also a special emphasis on presenting and promoting writers who make their home in Southern California." Estab. 1989. Circ. 1,500.

Needs: Literary, experimental. No "genre writing, no TV, no clichés, no gimmicks." Want more "self-conscious, smart, political, humorous, digressive, meta-fiction." Publishes special fiction issues or anthologies. Receives 250 unsolicited mss/month. Accepts 10 mss/issue; 20 mss/year. Agented fiction 10%. **Publishes 3-4 new writers/year.** Published work by Jim Krusoe, Aimee Bender, Gregg Bills, Judith Grossman and Amy Gerstler. Also publishes literary essays, memoirs and novel chapters.

How to Contact: Send complete ms with a cover letter. Responds in 3 months. Send a disposable copy of ms. Accepts simultaneous submissions. Sample copy for $7.

insider report

The accidental editor furnishes his "House of Fiction"

As a graduate of the MFA program at University of California-Irvine, Andrew Tonkovich once hoped to publish his fiction in the *Santa Monica Review*. Instead, he ended up the magazine's editor.

Andrew Tonkovich

Former editor Lee Montgomery had left *SMR* after the spring 1998 issue, and founding editor Jim Krusoe, a creative writing professor at Santa Monica College, was searching for a replacement. That search led him to Tonkovich, a former student and fellow faculty member.

"I'd been rejected regularly by *SMR*, probably justifiably," Tonkovich says. "Then Jim sat down with me and asked me to edit the journal. I honestly thought he was joking around. I went home and sent another story to *SMR*. I saw Jim the next week. He complimented my story, and I thought, 'finally I'll get published.' "

Instead, Krusoe "sort of insisted" that Tonkovich become the magazine's editor. "I still haven't been published in one of my favorite journals," Tonkovich said. "Maybe that's right."

When not editing and teaching, Tonkovich continues to hone his craft: "Nothing is lost on a writer, said Henry James, I think," he says. "I'm still sort of a beginning writer myself, but as a reader and editor, I like to think I see and am able to jump on good work, that nothing is lost on me. It's a wonderful job, really, kind of like furnishing a little house—maybe the 'house of fiction?' "

Here, Tonkovich talks about what makes a manuscript jump out of the slush pile, common mistakes writers should avoid, and how he furnishes his "house of fiction."

How would you characterize the fiction in *SMR*?

When I became editor, Jim Krusoe told me to "be eccentric," to establish a profile, a recognizable taste. He also advised me that "immortality" was the standard by which I should select work for the magazine. He was only half-joking.

I think the stories in *SMR* fall into two broad categories. First there are stories that succeed almost entirely on the strength of voice and language. Writers like Krusoe, Ben Slotky, Diane Lefer, Eva Wilson, Ben Weissman, Michelle Latiolais, or Janice Shapiro are incredibly good at creating a narrative presence that pretty much overwhelms plot.

I also publish more traditional writers like Carolyn Allport, Oakley Hall, Gary Soto, Rhoda Huffey, and Frances Kerridge, who fully use the short-story form, being careful and thorough and doing that thing where you experience the "suspension of disbelief."

I confess I print a lot more of the former, perhaps because so many writers do the latter badly.

How do you go about gathering material for *SMR?*

I receive nearly 50 manuscripts a week in my little P.O. box at Santa Monica College. We print less than one percent of what we get. Lisa Alvarez, my editorial assistant (a writer, teacher, co-director of the fiction program at Squaw Valley Community of Writers, and my wife) helps me to immediately locate and return work that is obviously not right: strictly genre fiction, very beginner stuff, poor writing. Also, I aggressively solicit writers whose work I admire. I'm sort of a geek that way, a real honest fan.

How do you know when to give up on a manuscript?

I'm probably too generous with my time, but I'd rather give people who submit to *SMR* the benefit of the doubt. Typically I'll drop a lousy story, but I'll slog through a marginal story, hoping, hoping. At least I feel confident that I've been fair to serious writers, people who are working on craft.

What qualities do you look for in a short story that might distinguish your taste from that of another editor?

I can only guess, but I'd like to think that my tastes aren't so different from the editors of magazines I esteem—*Ploughshares, Witness,* the recent issues of *Sundog,* the now dormant *Story, Quarterly West, Doubletake, Threepenny Review, Zyzzyva.*

You once said that you aim to publish "stories of consequence." What did you mean?

A consequential story leaves the reader smarter or happier or emotionally affected or contented or even angry. I hate fatalism, politically and personally. I think a too-typical story is one that presents a so-called "alienated" character facing a too familiar, too stereotypical problem (guns, death, TV stuff) with an ending that does little more than punish the character—an ending that basically says "life is difficult because this character is unhappy." Yikes. There must be consequences, not just endless "situations," right? The writers of these stories haven't yet found the reasons for the conflict, for the (God help us) gun or the missing spouse or whatever. They haven't read *The New York Times* or the local paper lately (try the police log!) or actually listened to people with real problems.

What are the three most common mistakes you see among unsolicited submissions?

That's easy. 1) The writer has no idea what the magazine is about. 2) The story doesn't actually begin until at least halfway through. 3) The story has the kind of clichéd plot you see in pop movies or TV, or it is ideologically fatalistic or trivial or inconsequential.

To what extent do your politics influence *SMR?*

My political consciousness is, I think, fairly typical among serous writers. I am a socialist with anarchist tendencies, a member of the Green Party and DSA. [Tonkovich also team-teaches a radical sociology class called "Theory and Practice of Nonviolence" that reflects his interests as a peace and justice activist.] I think the really engaging writers are involved in constructing critiques of the world. I have no idea how Margaret Atwood, Penelope Lively, Jim Crace, or my other favorites vote, but I know that they know what's at stake, what's important, that they have a worldview. Of course, I do know about Joy Williams, Grace Paley, James Baldwin, E.L. Doctorow, Toni Morrison, Alice Walker. They're activists, too, and personal heroes of mine—they don't just write "about" ethnicity or class or history; they engage.

Aside from publishing first-rate work, what are your goals for SMR?

I'd like to attract traditional readers of literary magazines, but I'd also like to engage people who might never pick up the old *Story*, or *Ploughshares*. I'd like to get wider national distribution, and—I've never said this out loud—I'd like for the Best American and Pushcart folks to choose the work I've nominated! Meanwhile, I'm quite happy with the list of writers whose recently published books include the words "first appeared in *Santa Monica Review*": Gary Soto, Judith Grossman, Oakley Hall, Rhoda Huffey, Alan Cheuse, Greg Bills, and Charles Champlin, longtime film critic of *The Los Angeles Times*.

If it seems I'm plugging writers, I am. I'm proud of the folks who appear in the *SMR*. I'm committed to them. That's my job as editor: to find them, to encourage them, to talk them up.

—Will Allison

Payment/Terms: Pays 2 contributor's copies. Acquires first North American serial rights. Sends galleys to author.

N M O SCRIVENER CREATIVE REVIEW, 853 Sherbrooke St. W., Montreal, Quebec H3A 2T6 Canada. (514)398-6588. E-mail: scrivenermag@hotmail.com. **Contacts:** Alyssa Raushbaum and Zachary Lerner, fiction editors. Coordinating Editors: Elizabeth MacInnis and Phillip Todd. Magazine: 8×9; 100 pages; matte paper; illustrations; b&w photos. "*Scrivener* is a creative journal publishing fiction, poetry, graphics, photography, reviews, interviews and scholarly articles. We encourage new and emerging talent; our audience comprises primarily university-aged students." Annual. Estab. 1980. Circ. 500.
Needs: Open, "good writing." Would like to see "fewer relationship stories;" no hate stories; wants more experimental submissions. Receives 10 unsolicited mss/month. Accepts 20 mss/year. Does not read mss May 1-Sept 1. Publishes ms 2 months after acceptance. **Publishes 2-3 new writers/year.** Published work by Lisa Propst and Martine Fournier. Length: 20 pages maximum. Occasionally publishes short shorts. Also publishes literary essays, literary criticism, poetry. Often critiques rejected mss.
How to Contact: Send complete ms with a cover letter and SASE (IRC). Include "critical statements; where we can reach you; 50-100 word bio; education; previous publications." Accepts queries/mss by e-mail and on disk. Accepts multiple submissions. Responds in 4 months to queries and mss. Sample copy for $7 (US in USA; Canadian in Canada). Guidelines for SAE/IRC. Reviews novels and short story collections. Send books to Nonfiction Editor.
Payment/Terms: Pays contributor's copies; charges for extras. Rights retained by the author.
Advice: "Fiction we accept must stand out from the others in terms of interesting content and style. We look for writing that is innovative, vibrant, image-laden, crafted and compelling. It must not be more than 20 pages double-spaced."

$ O THE SEATTLE REVIEW, Padelford Hall Box 354330, University of Washington, Seattle WA 98195. (206)543-9865. E-mail: seaview@english.washington.edu. Website: http://depts.washington.edu/engl/seaview1.h tml (includes short fiction, guidelines, list of back issues, mission statement and visuals of covers). **Contact:** Colleen J. McElroy, editor. Magazine: 6×9. "Includes general fiction, poetry, craft essays on writing, and one interview per issue with a Northwest writer." Semiannual. Published special fiction issue. Estab. 1978. Circ. 1,000.
Needs: Contemporary, ethnic, experimental, fantasy, feminist, gay, historical, horror, humor/satire, lesbian, literary, mainstream, prose poem, psychic/supernatural/occult, regional, science fiction, excerpted novel, mystery/suspense, translations, western. Wants more creative nonfiction. "We also publish a series called Writers and their Craft, which deals with aspects of writing fiction (also poetry)—point of view, characterization, etc., rather than literary criticism, each issue." Does not want to see "anything in bad taste (porn, racist, etc.)." Receives about 100 unsolicited mss/month. Buys about 3-6 mss/issue; about 4-10 mss/year. Does not read mss June-September. Agented fiction 25%. **Published new writers within the last year.** Recently published work by

Daniel Orozco, Frederick Busch, Peter Bacho, Jewell Parker Rhodes and David Guterson. Length: 500-10,000 words; average length: 3,500 words. Publishes short shorts. Sometimes critiques rejected mss. Occasionally recommends other markets.

How to Contact: Send complete ms. Responds in 8 months. SASE. Sample copy "half-price if older than one year." Current issue for $6; some special issues $8.

Payment/Terms: Pays 0-$100, 2 contributor's copies; charge for extras. Pays on publication for first North American serial rights. Copyright reverts to writer on publication; "please request release of rights and cite *SR* in reprint publications." Sends galleys to author.

Advice: "Beginners do well in our magazine if they send clean, well-written manuscripts. We've published a lot of 'first stories' from all over the country and take pleasure in discovery."

⬤ SEEMS, Lakeland College, Box 359, Sheboygan WI 53082-0359. (920)565-1276. Fax: (920)565-1206. E-mail: kelder@excel.net. **Contact:** Karl Elder, editor. Magazine: 7×8½; 40 pages. "We publish fiction and poetry for an audience which tends to be highly literate. People read the publication, I suspect, for the sake of reading it." Published irregularly. Estab. 1971. Circ. 300.

Needs: Literary. "We would like to see more quick fiction—that which straddles the boundaries between prose and poetry." Accepts 4 mss/issue. Receives 12 unsolicited fiction mss each month. **Publishes 1-2 new writers/ year.** Recently published work by Charles Edward Brooks, Holly Holdman and Hugh Schulze. Length: 5,000 words maximum. Publishes short shorts. Also publishes poetry. Critiques rejected mss when there is time.

How to Contact: Send complete ms with SASE. Responds in 2 months to mss. Accepts multiple submissions. Publishes ms an average of 1-2 years after acceptance. Sample copy for $4.

Payment/Terms: Pays 1 contributor's copy; $4 charge for extras. Rights revert to author.

Advice: "Send clear, clean copies. Read the magazine in order to help determine the taste of the editor. The story must invoke the imagination, the setting must become visible, the piece needs to be original or at least unusual in some manner, and the prose must be economical—above all else it must be economical. Good fiction contains all of the essential elements of poetry; study poetry and apply those elements to fiction. Our interest is shifting to story poems, the grey area between genres."

$⬤ THE SEWANEE REVIEW, University of the South, 735 University Ave., Sewanee TN 37383-1000. (931)598-1246. E-mail: rjones@sewanee.edu. Website: www.sewanee.edu/sreview/home.html (includes extracts from recent and back issues, magazine's history, writers' guidelines, links to other literary sites). Editor: George Core. **Contact:** Fiction Editor. Magazine: 6×9; 192 pages. "A literary quarterly, publishing original fiction, poetry, essays on literary and related subjects, book reviews and book notices for well-educated readers who appreciate good American and English literature." Quarterly. Estab. 1892. Circ. 3,500.

Needs: Literary, contemporary. No erotica, science fiction, fantasy or excessively violent or profane material. Editor prefers stories that have a plot. Buys 10-15 mss/year. Receives 100 unsolicited fiction mss each month. Does not read mss June 1-August 31. **Publishes 2-3 new writers/year.** Recently published work by Marlin Barton, Paul Brodeur, William Hoffman and Mitch Weiland. Length: 6,000-7,500 words. Critiques rejected mss "when there is time." Sometimes recommends other markets.

How to Contact: Send complete ms with SASE and cover letter stating previous publications, if any. Responds in 6 weeks to mss. Sample copy for $7.25. Writer's guidelines for SASE.

Payment/Terms: Pays $10-12/printed page; 2 contributor's copies; $4.25 charge for extras. Pays on publication for first North American serial rights and second serial rights by agreement.

Advice: "Send only one story at a time, with a serious and sensible cover letter. We think fiction is of greater general interest than any other literary mode."

✓ ⬤ ▼ SHADES OF DECEMBER, Box 244, Selden NY 11784. (631)736-4155. E-mail: fiction@shades ofdecember.com. Website: www.shadesofdecember.com (includes guidelines, reviews, sample work, upcoming themes). **Contact:** Brandy Danner, editor. Magazine: 8½×5½; 84 pages. "Good writing comes in all forms and should not be limited to overly specific or standard genres. Our intended audience is one that is varied in taste and open to the unorthodox." Quarterly. Estab. 1998. Circ. 200-300.

• Shades of December won an honorable mention in *Writer's Digest*'s zine competition.

Needs: Experimental, humor/satire, literary, mainstream/contemporary. "We are not limited in the categories of writing that we will consider for publication." Accepts 1-4 mss/issue; 8-16 mss/year. Publishes ms 1-6 months after acceptance. **Publishes 2-6 new writers/year.** Recently published work by Katherine Arline, Marzena Adriana Czarnecka and Angela Lam. Length: 4,000 words maximum. Prefers 2,800. Publishes short shorts. Also publishes scripts, poetry. Sometimes comments on rejected ms.

How to Contact: Send complete ms with a cover letter. Include bio (75 words or less). Responds in 1-3 months. Send SASE for reply, return of ms or send a disposable copy of ms. Accepts simultaneous submissions. Electronic submissions preferred. Make checks payable to Alexander Danner. Sample copy $7. Guidelines for #10 SASE.

Payment/Terms: Pays 2 contributor's copies. Acquires first serial rights.

Advice: "We like to see work that strays from the conventional. While we print good writing in any form, we prefer to see work that takes risks."

☑ ◐ **SHATTERED WIG REVIEW**, Shattered Wig Productions, 425 E. 31st, Baltimore MD 21218. (410)243-6888. Website: www.normals.com/wig.html. **Contact:** Collective, editor. Attn: Sonny Bodkin. Magazine: 8½×8½; 70 pages; "average" paper; cardstock cover; illustrations; photos. "Open forum for the discussion of the absurdo-miserablist aspects of everyday life. Fiction, poetry, graphics, essays, photos." Semiannual. Estab. 1988. Circ. 500.
Needs: Confession, contemporary, erotica, ethnic, experimental, feminist, gay, humor/satire, lesbian, literary, prose poem, psychic/supernatural/occult, regional. Does not want "anything by Ann Beattie or John Irving." Receives 15-20 unsolicited mss/month. Publishes ms 2-4 months after acceptance. **Published new writers within the last year.** Published work by Al Ackerman, Kim Harrison and Mok Hossfeld. Publishes short shorts. Also publishes literary criticism, poetry. Sometimes critiques rejected mss and recommends other markets.
How to Contact: Send complete ms with cover letter. *No electronic submissions, please!* Responds in 2 months. Send SASE for return of ms. Accepts simultaneous and reprint submissions. Sample copy for $4.
Payment/Terms: Pays in contributor's copies. Acquires one-time rights.
Advice: "The arts have been reduced to imploding pus with the only material rewards reserved for vapid stylists and collegiate pod suckers. The only writing that counts has no barriers between imagination and reality, thought and action. Send us at least three pieces so we have a choice."

☑ $ ◐ **SHENANDOAH, The Washington and Lee Review**, 2nd Floor, Troubadour Theater, Lexington VA 24450-0303. (540)463-8765. Fax: (540)463-8461. Website: http://shenandoah.wLu.edu (includes samples, guidelines and contents). Editor: R.T. Smith. **Contact:** Fiction Editor. Magazine: 6×9; 124 pages. "We are a literary journal devoted to excellence." Quarterly. Estab. 1950. Circ. 2,000.
Needs: Literary. Receives 400-500 unsolicited fiction mss/month. Accepts 5 mss/issue; 20 mss/year. Does not read mss during summer. Publishes ms 6-12 months after acceptance. **Publishes 2 new writers/year.** Published work by Kent Nelson, Barry Gifford, Nicholas Delbanco and Reynolds Price. Publishes short shorts. Also publishes literary essays, literary criticism and poetry.
How to Contact: Send complete ms with cover letter. Include a 3-sentence bio and list of publications ("just the highlights"). Responds in 10 weeks to mss. Send a disposable copy of ms. Sample copy for $8. Guidelines for #10 SASE or on website. Reviews novels and short story collections.
Payment/Terms: Pays $25/page, $2.50/line (poetry) and free subscription to the magazine on publication. Acquires first North American serial rights. Sends galleys to author. Sponsors contest.
Advice: Looks for "thrift, precision, originality. As Frank O'Connor said, 'Get black on white.' "

☑ $ ◐ **SHORT STUFF MAGAZINE FOR GROWN-UPS**, Bowman Publications, 712 W. Tenth St., Loveland CO 80537. (970)669-9139. E-mail: shortstf89@aol.com. **Contact:** Donna Bowman, editor. Magazine: 8½×11; 40 pages; bond paper; enamel cover; b&w illustrations; photos. "Nonfiction is regional—Colorado and adjacent states. Fiction and humor must be tasteful, but can be any genre, any subject. We are designed to be a 'Reader's Digest' of fiction. We are found in professional waiting rooms, etc." Publishes 6 issues/year.
 • *Short Stuff for Grown-ups* ranked #44 on *Writer's Digest*'s Fiction 50 list of top markets for writers.
Needs: Adventure, contemporary, historical, humor/satire, mainstream, mystery/suspense (amateur sleuth, English cozy, police procedural, private eye, romantic suspense), regional, romance (contemporary, gothic, historical), western (frontier). No erotica; nothing morbid or pornographic. "We want to see more humor—not essay format—real stories with humor; 1,000-word mysteries, modern lifestyles. The 1,000-word pieces have the best chance of publication." We use holiday themes. Need 3 month lead time. Issues are Valentine (February/March); Easter and St. Patrick's Day (April/May); Mom's and Dad's (June/July); Americana (August/September); Halloween (October/November); and Holiday (December/January). Receives 500 unsolicited mss/month. Accepts 9-12 mss/issue; 76 mss/year. **90% of stories published are written by new writers.** Recently published work by Bill Hallstead, Eleanor Sherman, Dede Hammond and Skye Gibbons. Length: 1,500 words maximum; average length: 1,000 words.
How to Contact: Send complete ms with cover letter. SASE. Responds in 6 months. Sample copies for $1.50 and 9×12 SAE with $1.65 postage. Guidelines for SASE.
Payment/Terms: Pays $10-50 "at our discretion" and subscription to magazine. $1-5 for fillers (less than 500 words). "We do not pay for single jokes or poetry, but do give free subscription if published." Pays on publication for first North American serial rights.
Advice: "We seek a potpourri of subjects each issue. A new slant, a different approach, fresh viewpoints—all of these excite us. We don't like gore, salacious humor or perverted tales. Prefer third person, past tense. Be sure it is a story with a beginning, middle and end. It must have dialogue. Many beginners do not know an essay from a short story. Essays frequently used if *humorous*. We'd like to see more young (25 and over) humor; 'clean' humor is hard to come by. Length is a big factor. Writers who can tell a good story in a thousand words are true

artists and their work is highly prized by our readers. Stick to the guidelines. We get manuscripts of up to 10,000 words because the story is 'unique and deserving.' We don't even read these. Too many writers fail to include SASE. These submissions are not considered."

✓ $ 🖉 🍷 **SIDE SHOW, Short Story Anthology,** Somersault Press, P.O. Box 1428, El Cerrito CA 94530-1428. E-mail: jisom@atdial.net. **Contact:** Shelley Anderson and Marjorie K. Jacobs, editors. Book (paperback): 5½×8½; 300 pages; 50 lb. paper; semigloss card cover with color illustration; perfect-bound. "Quality short stories for a general, literary audience." Estab. 1991. Circ. 3,000.
- Previously published as an annual anthology, *Side Show* will now publish a book once they have the requisite number of publishable stories (approximately 20-25). There is no longer a yearly deadline. Stories are accepted year round. Work published in *Side Show* has been selected for inclusion in the *Pushcart Prize* anthology.

Needs: Contemporary, ethnic, feminist, gay, humor/satire, literary, mainstream. Nothing genre, religious, pornographic; no essays, novels, memoirs. Receives 50-60 unsolicited mss/month. Accepts 25-30 mss/issue. Publishes ms up to 9 months after acceptance. **Publishes 5-10 new writers/per book.** Published work by George Harrar, Elisa Jenkins and Miguel Rios. 25% of fiction by previously unpublished writers. Length: Open. Critiques rejected mss, if requested.

How to Contact: Accepts queries by e-mail. All submissions entered in contest. *$10 entry fee* (includes copy of latest *Side Show*). No guidelines. Send complete ms with cover letter and entry fee. Responds in 6 weeks to mss with SASE. Accepts simultaneous submissions. Multiple submissions encouraged (entry fee covers all submissions mailed in same envelope). Sample copy for $10 and $2 postage and handling ($.83 sales tax CA residents).

Payment/Terms: Pays $5/printed page. Pays on publication for first North American serial rights. Sends galleys to author. All submissions entered in our contest for cash prizes of $200 (1st), $100 (2nd) and $75 (3rd).

Advice: Looks for "readability, vividness of characterization, coherence, inspiration, interesting subject matter, imagination, point of view, originality, plausibility. If your fiction isn't inspired, you probably won't be published by us (i.e., style and craft alone won't do it)."

✓ $ 🖉 🍷 **THE SILVER WEB, A Magazine of the Surreal,** Buzzcity Press, Box 38190, Tallahassee FL 32315. (850)385-8948. Fax: (850)385-4063. E-mail: buzzcity@yourvillage.com. **Contact:** Ann Kennedy, editor. Magazine: 8½×11; 80 pages; 20 lb. paper; full color; perfect bound; glossy cover; b&w illustrations; photos. "Looking for unique character-based stories that are off-beat, off-center and strange, but not inaccessible." Semiannual. Estab. 1989. Circ. 2,000.
- Work published in *The Silver Web* has appeared in *The Year's Best Fantasy and Horror* (DAW Books) and *The Year's Best Fantastic Fiction*.

Needs: Experimental, horror, science fiction (soft/sociological). No "traditional storylines, monsters, vampires, werewolves, etc. *The Silver Web* publishes surrealistic fiction and poetry. Work too bizarre for mainstream, but perhaps too literary for genre. This is not a straight horror/sci-fi magazine. No typical storylines." Receives 500 unsolicited mss/month. Accepts 8-10 mss/issue; 16-20 mss/year. Does not read mss September-December. Publishes ms 6-12 months after acceptance. Published work by Brian Evenson, Jack Ketchum and Joel Lane. Length: 100-8,000 words; average length: 6,000 words. Publishes short shorts. Also publishes poetry. Sometimes critiques rejected ms.

How to Contact: Send complete ms with a cover letter. Include estimated word count. Responds in 1 week to queries; 2 months to mss. Send SASE for reply, return of ms or send a disposable copy of ms plus SASE for reply. Accepts simultaneous and reprint submissions. Sample copy for $7.20. Guidelines for #10 SASE. Reviews novels and short story collections.

Payment/Terms: Pays 2-3¢/word and 2 contributor's copies; additional copies for $4. Acquires first North American serial rights, reprint rights or one-time rights.

Advice: "I have a reputation for publishing excellent fiction from newcomers next to talented, established writers, and for publishing cross-genre fiction. No traditional, standard storylines. I'm looking for beautiful writing with plots that are character-based. Tell a good story; tell it with beautiful words. I see too many writers writing for the marketplace and this fiction just doesn't ring true. I'd rather read fiction that comes straight from the heart of the writer." Read a copy of the magazine, at least get the writer's guidelines.

✓ 🔲 ◎ **SINISTER WISDOM, A Journal for the Lesbian Imagination in the Arts and Politics,** Sinister Widsom, Inc., Box 3252, Berkeley CA 94703. (510)595-7331. Website: www.sinisterwisdom.org (includes guidelines, upcoming themes and subscription information). Magazine: 5½×8½; 128-144 pages; 55 lb. stock; 10 pt C1S cover; illustrations; photos. Lesbian-feminist journal, providing fiction, poetry, drama, essays, journals and artwork. Triannual. Past issues included "Lesbians of Color," "Old Lesbians/Dykes" and "Lesbians and Religion." Estab. 1976. Circ. 2,000.

Needs: Lesbian: erotica, ethnic, experimental. No heterosexual or male-oriented fiction; no 70s amazon adventures; nothing that stereotypes or degrades women. List of upcoming themes available for SASE and on website. Receives 30 unsolicited mss/month. Accepts 6 mss/issue; 24 mss/year. Publishes ms 3 months to 1 year after acceptance. **Published new writers within the last year.** Published work by Jacqueline Miranda, Amanda Esteva and Sharon Bridgeforth; Length: 500-4,000 words; average length: 2,000 words. Publishes short shorts. Also publishes literary essays, literary criticism, poetry. Sometimes critiques rejected mss.

How to Contact: Send 1 copy of complete ms with cover letter, which should include a brief author's bio to be published when the work is published. Accepts submissions on disk. Responds in 6 months. Accepts simultaneous and multiple submissions, if noted. SASE. Sample copy for $7.50. Guidelines for #10 SASE. Reviews novels and short story collections. Send books to "Attn: Book Review."

Payment/Terms: Pays 2 contributor's copies. Acquires one-time rights.

Advice: *Sinister Wisdom* is "a multicultural lesbian journal reflecting the art, writing and politics of our communities."

☑ ◑ SKYLARK, Purdue University Calumet, 2200 169th St., Hammond IN 46323-2094. (219)989-2273. Fax: (219)989-2165. E-mail: poetpam49@yahoo.com. **Contact:** Pamela Hunter, editor-in-chief. Magazine: 8½ × 11; 100 pages; illustrations; photos. "*Skylark* presents short stories, essays and poetry which capture a positive outlook on life through vivid imagery, well-developed characterization and effective, well-thought-out plots. We publish adults, both beginners and professionals, and young authors side by side to complement the points of view of writers of all ages." Annual. Estab. 1971. Circ. 1,000.

Needs: Contemporary, ethnic, experimental, feminist, humor/satire, literary, mainstream and prose poem. Wants to see more experimental and avant garde fiction. No erotica, science fiction, overly-religious stories. Upcoming theme: "Holidays" (submit by April 2002). Receives 25 mss/month. Accepts 10 mss/issue. **Publishes 7-10 new writers/year.** Recently published work by Norm Forer, Sandra Goldsmith, Sarah Mills-Dirlam and Janet Moran. Length: 4,000 words maximum. Also publishes essays and poetry.

How to Contact: Send complete ms. Send SASE for return of ms. Accepts queries/mss by fax. Responds in 4 months. No simultaneous submissions. Sample copy for $8; back issue for $6.

Payment/Terms: Pays 3 contributor's copies. Acquires first rights. Copyright reverts to author.

Advice: "We seek fiction that presents effective imagery, strong plot, and well-developed characterization. Graphic passages concerning sex or violence are unacceptable. We're looking for dramatic, closely edited short stories. Manuscript must require little editing both for content and syntax. Author must be sincere in the treatment of plot, characters and tone. Please state in your cover letter that the story is not being considered elsewhere. We live in one of the most industrialized sections of the country. We are looking for stories set in steel mills and refractories, etc. We especially need well-wrought stories set in these areas."

☑ ◑ ◎ SLIPSTREAM, Box 2071, New Market Station, Niagara Falls NY 14301. (716)282-2616. E-mail: editors@slipstreampress.org. Website: www.slipstreampress.org (includes guidelines, editors, current needs, info on current and past releases, sample poems, contest info). **Contact:** Dan Sicoli, editor. Magazine: 7 × 8½; 80-100 pages; high quality paper; card cover; illustrations; photos. "We use poetry and short fiction with a contemporary urban feel." Estab. 1981. Circ. 500.

Needs: Contemporary, erotica, ethnic, experimental, humor/satire, literary, mainstream and prose poem. No religious, juvenile, young adult or romance. Occasionally publishes theme issues; query for information. Receives over 25 unsolicited mss/month. Accepts 2-4 mss/issue; 6 mss/year. Recently published work by E.R. Baxter III and Rosemary Kothg. Length: under 15 pages. Publishes short shorts. Rarely critiques rejected mss. Sometimes recommends other markets.

How to Contact: "Query before submitting." Responds within 2 months. Send SASE for reply or return of ms. Sample copy for $6. Guidelines for #10 SASE. No electronic submissions.

Payment/Terms: Pays 2 contributor's copies. Acquires one-time rights.

Advice: "Writing should be honest, fresh; develop your own style. Check out a sample issue first. Don't write for the sake of writing, write from the gut as if it were a biological need. Write from experience and mean what you say, but say it in the fewest number of words."

◑ THE SMALL POND MAGAZINE, Box 664, Stratford CT 06615. (203)378-4066. Editor: Napoleon St. Cyr. **Contact:** Fiction Editor. Magazine: 5½ × 8½; 42 pages; 60 lb. offset paper; 65 lb. cover stock; illustrations (art). "Features contemporary poetry, the salt of the earth, peppered with short prose pieces of various kinds. The college educated and erudite read it for good poetry, prose and pleasure." Triannual. Estab. 1964. Circ. 300.

Needs: "Rarely use the formula stories you'd find in *Cosmo*, *Redbook*, *Ladies Home Journal*, etc. Philosophy: Highest criteria, originality, even a bit quirky is OK. Don't mind O. Henry endings but better be exceptional. Readership: College grads, and college staff, ⅓ of subscribers are college and university libraries." No science fiction, children's. Accepts 10-12 mss/year. Longer response time in July and August. Receives approximately

40 unsolicited fiction mss each month. **Publishes 1-2 new writers/year.** Recently published work by Judah Jacobowitz, Charles Rammelcamp, Joshua R. Pahigian and Ruth Innes. Length: 200-2,500 words. Critiques rejected mss when there is time. Sometimes recommends other markets.

How to Contact: Send complete ms with SASE and short vita. Responds in up to 3 months. Publishes ms an average of 2-18 months after acceptance. Sample copy for $4; $3 for back issues.

Payment/Terms: Pays 2 contributor's copies; $3/copy charge for extras, postage paid. Acquires all rights.

Advice: "Send for a sample copy first. All mss must be typed. Name and address and story title on front page, name of story on succeeding pages and paginated. I look for polished, smooth progression—no clumsy paragraphs or structures where you know the author didn't edit closely. Also, no poor grammar. Beginning and even established poets read and learn from reading lots of other's verse. Not a bad idea for fiction writers, in their genre, short or long fiction."

✓ ☑ **SNAKE NATION REVIEW**, Snake Nation Press, Inc., #2 West Force St., 110, Valdosta GA 31601. (912)244-0752. Fax: (912)253-9125 (call first). E-mail: jeana@snakenationpress.org. Website: www.snakenation press.org. **Contact:** Jean Arambula, editor. 6×9; 110 pages; acid free 70 lb. paper; 90 lb. cover; illustrations; photos. "We are interested in all types of stories for an educated, discerning, sophisticated audience." Quarterly. Estab. 1989. Circ. 2,000.

• *Snake Nation Review* receives funding from the Georgia Council of the Arts, the Georgia Humanities Council and the Porter/Fleming Foundation for Literature. *Snake Nation Review* ranked #34 on *Writer's Digest's* Fiction 50 list of top markets for writers.

Needs: "Short stories of 5,000 words or less, poems (any length), art work that will be returned after use." Condensed/excerpted novel, contemporary, erotica, ethnic, experimental, fantasy, feminist, gay, horror, humor/satire, lesbian, literary, mainstream, mystery/suspense, prose poem, psychic/supernatural/occult, regional, science fiction, senior citizen/retirement. "We want our writers to have a voice, a story to tell, not a flat rendition of a slice of life." Plans annual anthology. Receives 50 unsolicited mss/month. Buys 8-10 mss/issue; 40 mss/year. Publishes ms 6 months after acceptance. Agented fiction 1%. Published work by Robert Earl Price and O. Victor Miller. Length: 300-5,500 words; average length: 3,500 words. Publishes short shorts. Length: 500 words. Also publishes literary essays, poetry. Reviews novels and short story collections. Sometimes critiques rejected mss and recommends other markets.

How to Contact: Send complete ms with cover letter. Responds to queries in 3 months. SASE. Sample copy for $6, 8×10 SAE and 90¢ postage. Guidelines for SASE.

Payment/Terms: Pays 2 contributor's copies. Acquires one-time rights. Sends galleys to author.

Advice: "Looks for clean, legible copy and an interesting, unique voice that pulls the reader into the work." Spring contest: short stories (5,000 words); $300 first prize, $200 second prize, $100 third prize; entry fee: $5 for stories, $1 for poems. Contest Issue with every $5 fee.

$ ☑ **SNOWY EGRET**, P.O. Box 9, Bowling Green IN 47833. Publisher: Karl Barnebey. Editor: Philip Repp. **Contact:** Fiction Editor. Magazine: 8½×11; 50 pages; text paper; heavier cover; illustrations. "*Snowy Egret* explores the range of human involvement, particularly psychological, with the natural world. Its fiction depicts characters who identify strongly with nature, either positively or negatively, and who grow in their understanding of themselves and the world of plants, animals and landscape." Semiannual. Estab. 1922. Circ. 500.

Needs: Nature writing, including 'true' stories, eye-witness accounts, descriptive sketches and traditional fiction. "We are interested in penetrating psychological and spiritual journeys of characters who have strong ties to or identifications with the natural world. No works written for popular genres: horror, science fiction, romance, detective, western, etc." Receives 25 unsolicited mss/month. Accepts up to 6 mss/issue; up to 12 mss/year. Publishes ms 6-12 months after acceptance. **Publishes 4-6 new writers/year.** Recently published work by James Hinton, Marion Blue, Alice Cross and Maeve Mullin Ellis. Length: 500-10,000 words; 1,000-3,000 words preferred. Publishes short shorts. Length: 400-500 words. Sometimes critiques rejected mss.

How to Contact: Send complete ms with cover letter. "Cover letter optional: do not query." Responds in 2 months. SASE. Accepts simultaneous (if noted) submissions. Sample back issues for $8 and 9×12 SAE. Send #10 SASE for writer's guidelines.

Payment/Terms: Pays $2/page and 2 contributor's copies; charge for extras. Pays on publication for first North American serial rights and reprint rights. Sends galleys to author.

Advice: Looks for "honest, freshly detailed pieces with plenty of description and/or dialogue which will allow the reader to identify with the characters and step into the setting; characters who relate strongly to nature, either positively or negatively, and who, during the course of the story, grow in their understanding of themselves and the world around them."

☑ **SONGS OF INNOCENCE**, Pengradonian Publications, P.O. Box 719, New York NY 10101-0719. E-mail: mmpendragon@aol.com. Editor: Michael Pendragon. **Contact:** Fiction Editor. Literary magazine/journal:

9×6; 175 pages; perfect bound; illustrations. "A literary publication which celebrates the nobler aspects of humankind and the human experience. Along with sister-publication, *Penny Dreadful*, *Songs* seeks to provide a forum for poetry and fiction in the 19th century/Romantic/Victorian tradition." Triannual. Circ. estimated 200.
Needs: Fantasy, historical (19th century or earlier), literary, New Age, psychic/supernatural/occult. No "children's/young adult; modern tales; Christian (or anything dogmatic)." Receives 100 unsolicited mss/month. Accepts 15 mss/issue; 30 mss/year. Publishes ms up to 2 years after acceptance. Length: 500-5,000 words. Publishes short shorts. Also publishes literary essays, literary criticism, poetry. Often comments on rejected mss. Published works by John Berbrich, John B. Ford, Ann Kucera and Jason E. Schlismann.
How to Contact: Send complete ms with a cover letter. Include estimated word count, 1 page or less bio and list of publications. Accepts mss by e-mail or disk. Responds in 3 weeks to queries; 6-12 months to mss. SASE for reply and send a disposable copy of ms. Accepts simultaneous submissions and reprints. Sample copy for $10, 9×6 SAE. Guidelines for SASE.
Payment/Terms: Pays 1 contributor's copy; additional copies $10 each. Pays on publication for one-time rights. Sends galleys to author.
Advice: "We prefer tales set in 1910 or earlier (preferably earlier). We prefer prose in the 19th century/Victorian style. We do not like the terse, modern, post-Hemingway 'see Dick run' style. Tales should transcend genres and include a spiritual supernatural element (without becoming fantasy). Avoid strong language, sex, etc. Include name and address on the title page. Include word count on title page. Double space, 12-pt. Times/Courier font, etc. (usual professional format). We select stories/poems that appeal to us and do not base selection on whether one has been published elsewhere."

✓⬤ SOUTH CAROLINA REVIEW, Strode Tower, Clemson University, Clemson SC 29634-1503. (864)656-3543. Fax: (864)656-1345. E-mail: cwayne@clemson.edu. Website: www.clemson.edu/caah/cedp (includes introduction page/background, editorial and publication policy, tables of contents for all issues, subscription page). Editor: Wayne Chapman. **Contact:** Keith Morris, associate editor/fiction. Magazine: 6×9; 200 pages; 60 lb. cream white vellum paper; 65 lb. cream white vellum cover stock. Semiannual. Estab. 1967. Circ. 700.
Needs: Literary and contemporary fiction, poetry, essays, reviews. Receives 50-60 unsolicited fiction mss each month. Does not read mss June-August or December. **Published new writers within the last year.** Published work by Joyce Carol Oates, Rosanne Coggeshall and Stephen Dixon. Rarely critiques rejected mss.
How to Contact: Send complete ms with SASE. Requires text on disk upon acceptance in WordPerfect or Microsoft Word format. Responds in 4 months to mss. "No unsolicited reviews." Sample copy for $5.
Payment/Terms: Pays in contributor's copies.

✓⬤ SOUTH DAKOTA REVIEW, University of South Dakota, Box 111, University Exchange, Vermillion SD 57069. (605)677-5184. Fax: (605)677-5298. E-mail: sdreview@usd.edu. Website: www.usd.edu/engl/SDR/index.html (includes masthead page with editors' names and submission/subscription guidelines, sample covers, sample story and essay excerpts and poems). Editor: Brian Bedard. **Contact:** Fiction Editor. Magazine: 6×9; 140-170 pages; book paper; glossy cover stock; illustrations sometimes; photos on cover. "Literary magazine for university and college audiences and their equivalent. Emphasis is often on the American West and its writers, but will accept mss from anywhere. Issues are generally personal essay, fiction, and poetry with some literary essays." Quarterly. Estab. 1963. Circ. 500.
Needs: Literary, contemporary, ethnic, regional. "We like very well-written, thematically ambitious, character-centered short fiction. Contemporary Western American setting appeals, but not necessary. No formula stories, horror, or adolescent 'I' narrator." Receives 40 unsolicited fiction mss/month. Accepts about 40 mss/year. Summer editor accepts mss in April through June. Agented fiction 5%. Publishes short shorts of 5 pages double-spaced typescript. **Publishes 3-5 new writers/year.** Recently published work by Jon Hassler, Stephanie Dickinson and Marie Argeris. Length: 1,000-6,000 words. (Has made exceptions, up to novella length.) Sometimes recommends other markets.
How to Contact: Send complete ms with SASE. "We like cover letters that are not boastful and do not attempt to sell the stories but rather provide some personal information about the writer which can be used for a contributor's note." Responds in 10 weeks. Publishes ms an average of 1-6 months after acceptance. Sample copy for $5.
Payment/Terms: Pays 1-year subscription and 2 contributor's copies. Acquires first and reprint rights.
Advice: Rejects mss because of "careless writing; often careless typing; stories too personal ('I' confessional); aimlessness of plot, unclear or unresolved conflicts; subject matter that editor finds clichéd, sensationalized, pretentious or trivial. We are trying to use more fiction and more variety."

⬤ ◎ SOUTHERN HUMANITIES REVIEW, Auburn University, 9088 Haley Center, Auburn University AL 36849. Website: www.auburn.edu/english/shr/home.htm. Co-editors: Dan R. Latimer and Virginia M. Kouidis. **Contact:** Fiction Editor. Magazine: 6×9; 100 pages; 60 lb. neutral pH, natural paper; 65 lb. neutral pH med.

coated cover stock; occasional illustrations; photos. "We publish essays, poetry, fiction and reviews. Our fiction has ranged from very traditional in form and content to very experimental. Literate, college-educated audience. We hope they read our journal for both enlightenment and pleasure." Quarterly. Estab. 1967. Circ. 800.

Needs: Serious fiction, fantasy, feminist, humor and regional. Receives approximately 25 unsolicited fiction mss each month. Accepts 1-2 mss/issue, 4-6 mss/year. Slower reading time in summer. **Published new writers within the last year.** Published work by Anne Brashler, Heimito von Doderer and Ivo Andric. Length: 3,500-15,000 words. Also publishes literary essays, literary criticism, poetry. Critiques rejected mss when there is time. Sometimes recommends other markets.

How to Contact: Send complete ms (one at a time) with SASE and cover letter with an explanation of topic chosen—"special, certain book, etc., a little about author if he/she has never submitted." Responds in 3 months. Sample copy for $5. Reviews novel and short story collections.

Payment/Terms: Pays 2 contributor's copies; $5 charge for extras. Rights revert to author upon publication. Sends galleys to author.

Advice: "Send us the ms with SASE. If we like it, we'll take it or we'll recommend changes. If we don't like it, we'll send it back as promptly as possible. Read the journal. Send typewritten, clean copy carefully proofread. We also award annually the Hoepfner Prize of $100 for the best published essay or short story of the year. Let someone whose opinion you respect read your story and give you an honest appraisal. Rewrite, if necessary, to get the most from your story."

✅ $🚫 ☑ **THE SOUTHERN REVIEW**, Louisiana State University, 43 Allen Hall, Baton Rouge LA 70803-5005. (225)578-5108. Fax: (225)578-5098. E-mail: mgriffi@lsu.edu. Website: www.lsu.edu/thesouthernreview (includes subscription information, staff, guidelines, table of contents, current issue). **Contact:** Michael Griffith, associate editor. Magazine: 6¾×10; 240 pages; 50 lb. Glatfelter paper; 65 lb. #1 grade cover stock. "A literary quarterly publishing critical essays, poetry and fiction for a highly intellectual audience." Quarterly. Estab. 1935. Circ. 3,100.

   ● *The Southern Review* ranked #40 on *Writer's Digest*'s "Fiction 50" list of top fiction markets. Several stories published in *The Southern Review* were Pushcart Prize selections.

Needs: Literary. "We emphasize style and substantial content. No mystery, fantasy or religious mss." Accepts 4-5 mss/issue. Receives approximately 300 unsolicited fiction mss each month. Does not read mss June-August. Publishes ms 6-9 months after acceptance. Agented fiction 1%. **Publishes 4-6 new writers/year.** Recently published work by William Gay, Romulus Linney, Richard Bausch and Ingrid Hill. Length: 2,000-10,000 words. Also publishes literary essays, literary criticism, poetry. Sponsors annual contest for best first collection of short stories published during the calendar year.

How to Contact: Send complete ms with cover letter and SASE. "Prefer brief letters giving information on author concerning where he/she has been published before, biographical info and what he/she is doing now." Responds in 2 months to mss. Sample copy for $8. Guidelines free for SAE. Reviews novels and short story collections.

Payment/Terms: Pays $12/printed page and 2 contributor's copies. Pays on publication for first North American serial rights. Sends galleys to author.

Advice: "Develop a careful, clear style. Although willing to publish experimental writing that appears to have a valid artistic purpose, *The Southern Review* avoids extremism and sensationalism."

🚫 **SOUTHWEST REVIEW**, P.O. Box 750374, 307 Fondren Library West, Southern Methodist University, Dallas TX 75275-0374. (214)768-1037. Fax: (214)768-1408. E-mail: swr@mail.smu.edu. Editor: Willard Spiegelman. **Contact:** Elizabeth Mills, senior editor. Magazine: 6×9; 144 pages. "The majority of our readers are college-educated adults who wish to stay abreast of the latest and best in contemporary fiction, poetry, literary criticism and books in all but the most specialized disciplines." Quarterly. Estab. 1915. Circ. 1,600.

Needs: "High literary quality; no specific requirements as to subject matter, but cannot use sentimental, religious, western, poor science fiction, pornographic, true confession, mystery, juvenile or serialized or condensed novels." Receives approximately 200 unsolicited fiction mss each month. Published work by Bruce Berger, Thomas Larsen, Alice Hoffman, Matthew Sharpe, Floyd Skloot, Daniel Harris and Daniel Stern. Length: prefers 3,000-5,000 words. Also publishes literary essays and poetry. Occasionally critiques rejected mss.

How to Contact: Send complete ms with SASE. Responds in 6 months to mss. Publishes ms 6-12 months after acceptance. Sample copy for $6. Guidelines for SASE.

Payment/Terms: Payment varies; writers receive 3 contributor's copies. Pays on publication for first North American serial rights. Sends galleys to author.

SENDING TO A COUNTRY other than your own? Be sure to send International Reply Coupons (IRC) instead of stamps for replies or return of your manuscript.

Advice: "We have become less regional. A lot of time would be saved for us and for the writer if he or she looked at a copy of the *Southwest Review* before submitting. We like to receive a cover letter because it is some reassurance that the author has taken the time to check a current directory for the editor's name. When there isn't a cover letter, we wonder whether the same story is on 20 other desks around the country."

☑ ◑ ◎ ☒ **SOUTHWESTERN AMERICAN LITERATURE**, Center for the Study of the Southwest, Southwest Texas State University, 601 University Dr., San Marcos TX 78666. (512)245-2232. Fax: (512)245-7462. E-mail: mb13@swt.edu. Website: http://wp29.english.swt.edu/css/cssindex.htm. Editor: Mark Busby, D.M. Heaberlin. **Contact:** Elka Karl, fiction editor. Magazine: 6×9; 125 pages; 80 lb. cover stock. "We publish fiction, nonfiction, poetry, literary criticism and book reviews. Generally speaking, we want material concerning the Greater Southwest, or material written by southwestern writers." Semiannual. Estab. 1971. Circ. 300.

• A poem published in *Southwestern American Literature* was selected for the anthology, *Best Texas Writing 2*.

Needs: Ethnic/multicultural, literary, mainstream/contemporary, regional. No science fiction or romance. Receives 10-15 unsolicited mss/month. Accepts 1-2 mss/issue; 4-5 mss/year. Publishes ms up to 6 months after acceptance. **Publishes 1-2 new writers/year.** Published work by Jerry Craven, Paul Ruffin, Robert Flynn and Philip Heldrich. Length: 6,250 words maximum; average length: 6,000 words. Publishes short shorts. Also publishes literary essays, literary criticism, poetry. Sometimes comments on rejected ms.

How to Contact: Send complete ms with a cover letter. Include estimated word count, 20-word bio and list of publications. Accepts queries by e-mail. Responds in 2 months. SASE for return of ms. Accepts simultaneous submissions. Sample copy $7. Guidelines free. Reviews novels and short story collections. Send books to Mark Busby.

Payment/Terms: Pays 2 contributor's copies; additional copies $7. Acquires first rights.

Advice: "We look for crisp language, interesting approach to material; regional emphasis is desired but not required. Read widely, write often, revise carefully. We are looking for stories that probe the relationship between the tradition of Southwestern American literature and the writer's own imagination in creative ways. We seek stories that move beyond stereotype and approach the larger defining elements of regional literature with three qualities: originality, supple language, and humanity. We want stories with regional elements and also ones that, as William Faulkner noted in his Nobel Prize acceptance speech, treat subjects central to good literature—the old verities of the human heart such as honor and courage and pity and suffering, fear and humor, love and sorrow."

◖ **SPEAK UP**, Speak Up Press, P.O. Box 100506, Denver CO 80250. (303)715-0837. Fax: (303)715-0793. E-mail: SpeakUPres@aol.com. Website: www.speakuppress.org. **Contact:** Gretchen Bryant, senior editor. Magazine: 5½×8½; 128 pages; 55 lb. Glat. Supple Opaque Recycled Natural paper; 12 pt. CIS cover; illustrations; photos. "*Speak Up* features the original fiction, nonfiction, poetry, plays, photography and artwork of young people 13-19 years old. *Speak Up* provides a place for teens to be creative, honest and expressive in an uncensored environment." Annual. Estab. 1999. Circ. 2,900.

Needs: Teen writers. Receives 30 unsolicited mss/month. Accepts 30 mss/issue; 30 mss/year. Publishes ms 3-12 months after acceptance. **Publishes 20 new writers/year.** Length: 5,000 words maximum; average length: 500 words. Publishes short shorts. Also publishes literary essays and poetry.

How to Contact: Send complete ms with a cover letter. Accepts submissions by e-mail and fax. Responds in 3 months to queries. Send SASE for return of ms. Accepts simultaneous submissions, previously published work and multiple submissions. Sample copy free. Guidelines for SASE, by e-mail, fax or on website.

Payment/Terms: Pays 2 contributor's copies. Pays on publication for all, first North American serial or one-time rights.

☑ ◑ ☒ **SPINDRIFT**, Shoreline Community College, 16101 Greenwood Ave. North, Seattle WA 98133. (206)546-5864. **Contact:** Gary Parks, editor. Magazine: 140 pages; quality paper; photographs; b&w artwork. "We look for fresh, original work that is not forced or 'straining' to be literary." Annual. Estab. around 1967. Circ. 500.

• *Spindrift* has received awards for "Best Literary Magazine" from the Community College Humanities Association both locally and nationally and awards from the Pacific Printing Industries.

Needs: Contemporary, ethnic, experimental, historical (general), prose poem, regional, science fiction, serialized/excerpted novel, translations. No romance, religious/inspirational. Receives up to 150 mss/year. Accepts up to 20 mss/issue. Does not read during spring/summer. Publishes ms 3-4 months after acceptance. **Published new writers within the last year.** Published work by David Halpern and Jana Harris. Length: 250-4,500 words maximum. Publishes short shorts.

How to Contact: Send complete ms, and "bio, name, address, phone and list of titles submitted." Responds in up to 1 month to queries; juries after February 1 and responds by March 15 with SASE. Sample copy for $7, 8×10 SAE and $1 postage.

Payment/Terms: Pays in contributor's copies; charge for extras. Acquires first rights. Publication not copyrighted.

Advice: "The tighter the story the better. The more lyric values in the narrative the better. Read the magazine, keep working on craft. Submit by February 1."

☑ ◉ **SPINNING JENNY**, Black Dress Press, P.O. Box 1373, New York NY 10276. E-mail: submissions@ blackdresspress.com. Website: www.blackdresspress.com (includes guidelines, subscription information, catalog). **Contact:** C.E. Harrison. Magazine: 60 lb. paper; offset printed; perfect bound; illustrations. Literary magazine publishing short stories and novel excerpts. Estab. 1994. Member, CLMP. **Publishes 3 new writers/year.**

Needs: Experimental, literary. Publishes ms less than 1 year after acceptance.

How to Contact: Send complete ms with a cover letter. Accepts submissions by e-mail. Responds in 2 months. Send SASE for return of ms or send a disposable copy of ms and #10 SASE for reply only. Accepts electronic submissions. Guidelines for SASE or on website.

Payment/Terms: Pays 5 contributor's copies.

⟦N⟧ ◯ ◎ **SPITBALL**, 5560 Fox Rd., Cincinnati OH 45239. (513)385-2268. **Editor:** Mike Shannon. Magazine: 5½ × 8½; 96 pages; 55 lb. Glatfelter Natural, neutral pH paper; 10 pt. CS1 cover stock; illustrations; photos. Magazine publishing "fiction and poetry about *baseball* exclusively for an educated, literary segment of the baseball fan population." Biannually. Estab. 1981. Circ. 2,000.

Needs: Confession, contemporary, experimental, historical, literary, mainstream and suspense. "We're looking for literary fiction about baseball *exclusively*! If it ain't about baseball, don't send it! This goes for you too, Lynn Lifshin." Receives 100 unsolicited fiction mss/year. Accepts 16-20 mss/year. **Published new writers within the last year.** Published work by Dallas Wiebe, Michael Gilmartin and W.P. Kinsella. Length: 20 typed double-spaced pages. "The longer it is, the better it has to be."

How to Contact: Send complete ms with cover letter and SASE. Include brief bio about author. Reporting time varies. Publishes ms an average of 3 months after acceptance. *First-time submitters are required to purchase a sample copy for $6.*

Payment/Terms: "No monetary payment at present. We may offer nominal payment in the near future." Pays 2 free contributor's copies per issue in which work appears. Acquires first North American serial rights.

Advice: "Our audience is mostly college educated and knowledgeable about baseball. The stories we have published so far have been very well written and displayed a firm grasp of the baseball world and its people. In short, audience response has been great because the stories are simply good as stories. Thus, mere use of baseball as subject is no guarantee of acceptance. We are always seeking submissions. Unlike many literary magazines, we have no backlog of accepted material. Also, don't forget to *tell a story*. Devise a plot, make something *happen*!"

$◯ ◎ ⟦Y⟧ **STONE SOUP, The Magazine By Young Writers and Artists**, Children's Art Foundation, Box 83, Santa Cruz CA 95063. (831)426-5557. E-mail: gmandel@stonesoup.com. Website: www.stonesoup.com (includes writer's guidelines, sample copy, links, projects, international children's art). **Contact:** Ms. Gerry Mandel, editor. Magazine: 7 × 10; 48 pages; high quality paper; photos. Stories, poems, book reviews and art by children through age 13. Readership: children, librarians, educators. Published 6 times/year. Estab. 1973. Circ. 20,000.

● This is known as "the literary journal for children." *Stone Soup* has previously won the Ed Press Golden Lamp Honor Award and the Parent's Choice Award.

Needs: Fiction by children on themes based on their own experiences, observations or special interests. Also, some fantasy, mystery, adventure. No clichés, no formulas, no writing exercises; original work only. Receives approximately 1,000 unsolicited fiction mss each month. Accepts approximately 15 mss/issue. **Published new writers within the last year.** Length: 150-2,500 words. Also publishes literary essays and poetry. Critiques rejected mss upon request.

How to Contact: Send complete ms with cover letter. "We like to learn a little about our young writers, why they like to write, and how they came to write the story they are submitting." SASE. No simultaneous submissions. Responds in 1 month to mss. Does not respond to mss that are not accompanied by an SASE. Publishes ms an average of 3-6 months after acceptance. Sample copy for $4. Guidelines for SASE. Reviews children's books.

Payment/Terms: Pays $35 and 2 contributor's copies; $2.75 charge for extras. Buys all rights. Subscription: $33/year.

Advice: Mss are rejected because they are "derivatives of movies, TV, comic books; or classroom assignments or other formulas. Go to our website, where you can see many examples of the kind of work we publish."

☑ ◉ ⟦Y⟧ **STORYQUARTERLY**, 431 Sheridan Rd., Kenilworth IL 60043-1220. (847)256-6998. Fax: (847)256-6997. E-mail: storyquarterly@hotmail.com. Website: www.storyquarterly.com (includes contents of each issue, links to individual stories changing each month, submission guidelines, subscription information, coming events). Editor: M.M.M. Hayes. **Contact:** Fiction Editors. Magazine: 6×9; 400 pages; good quality paper; an all-story magazine, committed to a full range of styles and forms. "We publish contemporary American and international fiction of high quality, in a full range of styles and forms, outstanding writing and fresh insights; we need great humor and serious literary stories of any type or style (nothing gimmicky), of no preferred length, stories that break your heart and make you laugh, that explore others and deepen understanding. Short-shorts as well as fully rendered work, memoir and novel excerpts with a sense of closure." Annual. Estab. 1975. Circ. 4,500.

● *StoryQuarterly* ranked #37 in *Writer's Digest*'s "Fiction 50" list of top markets. *StoryQuarterly* received honorable mentions in *O. Henry Prize Stories*, *Best American Stories*. *O'Leary Prize Essays* and *Pushcart Prize Collection* in the last 2 years. The publication also won Illinois Arts Council Awards, two apiece in the last 2 years, as well as the Dan Curley Award from the Illinois Arts Council in 2000, for the best story submitted to the Arts Council that year.

Needs: "Great humor, serious and well-written stories that get up and run from the first page. No genre stories. Receives 400 unsolicited fiction mss/month. Accepts 35-40 mss/issue. **Publishes new writers in every issue.** Recently published work by J.M. Coetzee, Stuart Dybek, Reginald Gibbons, Gail Godwin, Charles Johnson, Romulus Linney, Jim McManus and Askold Melnyczuk.

How to Contact: Send complete ms. E-mail preferred or regular mail with SASE. Responds in 3 months to mss. Sample copy for $7. Guidelines on website.

Payment/Terms: Pays 10 contributor's copies and a life subscription (value $200). Acquires first North American serial rights. Copyright reverts to author after publication. Electronic publishing agreement available.

Advice: "Send one manuscript at a time, subscribe to the magazine, send SASE with hard copy submissions. Fiction selected based on command and use of the language, originality of material, sense of a larger world outside the hermitage of the story. A sense of humor goes a very long way, as long as it's not simply ridicule. Literary magazines (even the independents) deal with reality in ways the industry trends do not. Smashing openings, middles that build and create tension, and well-earned and surprising endings all figure in the composition of an outstanding story."

✓ ◐ STOVEPIPE, A Journal of Little Literary Value, P.O. Box 1076, Georgetown KY 40324. (502)868-6573. Fax: (502)868-6566. E-mail: troyteegarden@worldradio.org. Website: www.undergroundpoets.org. Editor: Troy Teegarden. **Contact:** Fiction Editor. Magazine: 8½×5½; 30-60 pages; 70 lb. paper; card stock cover; illustrations. "We like to have a good time with what we read. We publish fiction, nonfiction, poetry and black-and-white art." Quarterly. Estab. 1995. Circ. 250.

Needs: Comics/graphic novels, experimental, humor/satire, literary, short story collections. No religious, fantasy. Want more experimental, humor and fringe. Receives 50 unsolicited mss/month. Accepts 1-2 mss/issue; 4-8 mss/year. Publishes ms 1-3 months after acceptance. **Publishes 4-8 new writers/year.** Recently published work by Michael Fowler and Benjamin Newell. Length: 3,500 words maximum. Publishes short shorts. "We really dig short short stories." Also publishes poetry. Often comments on rejected ms.

How to Contact: Send complete ms with a cover letter. Accepts queries by e-mail. Include estimated word count, short but informative bio and list of publications. Responds in 2 weeks to queries; 1 month to mss. Send SASE for reply, return of ms. Sample copy $2 or send 5½×8½ SAE with 78¢ postage. Guidelines for #10 SASE.

Payment/Terms: Pays 1 year subscription; additional copies $2. Acquires one-time rights.

Advice: "Stories must be interesting and new and they must offer something original to the reader. We don't see much fiction but would like to publish more. We look for originality, creativity, strong characters and unique perspectives. Write for yourself. Just because we don't publish it doesn't mean it's not good. We are very particular."

✓ ◐ STRUGGLE, A Magazine of Proletarian Revolutionary Literature, Box 13261, Detroit MI 48213-0261. (213)273-9039. E-mail: timhall@yahoo.com. **Contact:** Tim Hall, editor. Magazine: 5½×8½; 36-72 pages; 20 lb. white bond paper; colored cover; illustrations; occasional photos. Publishes material related to "the struggle of the working class and all progressive people against the rule of the rich—including their war policies, racism, exploitation of the workers, oppression of women and general culture, etc." Quarterly. Estab. 1985.

Needs: Contemporary, ethnic, experimental, feminist, historical (general), humor/satire, literary, prose poem, regional, science fiction, senior citizen/retirement, translations, young adult/teen (10-18). "The theme can be approached in many ways, including plenty of categories not listed here. Readers would like fiction about the anti-globalization movement, the fight against racism, prison conditions. Would also like to see more fiction that depicts the life, work and struggle of the working class of every background; also the struggles of the 1930s and 60s illustrated and brought to life." No romance, psychic, mystery, western, erotica, religious. Receives 10-12 unsolicited fiction mss/month. Publishes ms 6 months or less after acceptance. **Published new writers within the last year.** Recently published work by Carl Dimitri, Saint Solomon and Lisa McDaniel. Length: 4,000 words maximum; average length: 1,000-3,000 words. Publishes short shorts. Normally critiques rejected mss.

How to Contact: Send complete ms; cover letter optional. "Tries to" report in 3-4 months. SASE. Accepts e-mail, simultaneous, multiple and reprint submissions. Sample copy for $2.50. Make checks payable to Tim Hall-Special Account.

Payment/Terms: Pays 2 contributor's copies. No rights acquired. Publication not copyrighted.

Advice: "Write about the oppression of the working people, the poor, the minorities, women, and if possible, their rebellion against it—we are not interested in anything which accepts the status quo. We are not too worried about plot and advanced technique (fine if we get them!)—we would probably accept things others would call sketches, provided they have life and struggle. For new writers: just describe for us a situation in which some real people confront some problem of oppression, however seemingly minor. Observe and put down the real facts. Experienced writers: try your 'committed'/experimental fiction on us. We get poetry all the time. We have increased our fiction portion of our content in the last few years. The quality of fiction that we have published has continued to improve. If your work raises an interesting issue of literature and politics, it may get discussed in letters and in my editorial. I suggest ordering a sample."

N ☑ **THE STYLES**, P.O. Box 7171, Madison WI 53707. E-mail: thestylesorg@yahoo.com. Website: www.thestyles.org (includes writer's guidelines, names of staff, about our publication, contributors, subscription information). **Contact:** Sophia Estante or Amara Dante Verona, editors. Magazine: 8×8; 104 pages; 60 lb. white perfect-bound matte lamination; 10 point cover. "*The Styles* is a publication of eclectic content with emphasis on artistic excellence in experimental fiction and nonfiction. We publish short stories, short plays, and poetry. We encourage literary essays, prose poetry and short-shorts." Semiannual. Estab. 2001. Circ. 1,000.

Needs: Experimental, literary, humor. "No genre fiction." Publishes ms 3 months after acceptance. Length: 6,000 words maximum. Publishes short shorts. Also publishes literary essays and poetry. Often comments on rejected mss.

How to Contact: Send complete ms with a cover letter or query. Include brief bio. Responds in 2 weeks to queries; 2 months to mss. Send SASE for return of ms or send a disposable copy of ms and #10 SASE for reply only. Accepts simultaneous and multiple submissions. Sample copy for $8. Guidelines for SASE or on website.

Payment/Terms: Pays $3 and 1 contributor's copy. Pays on acceptance for first North American serial rights. "Sometimes sends prepublication galleys to author."

Advice: "*The Styles* publishes ambitious original and creative writing. We publish pieces that create their own ideas and standards of what writing should be. *The Styles* encourages new ideas about how writing should be written, read, evaluated and what it should accomplish."

☑ **SULPHUR RIVER LITERARY REVIEW**, P.O. Box 19228, Austin TX 78760-9228. (512)292-9456. **Contact:** James Michael Robbins, editor. Magazine: 5½×8½; 145 pages; illustrations; photos. "*SRLR* publishes literature of quality—poetry and short fiction with appeal that transcends time. Audience includes a broad spectrum of readers, mostly educated, many of whom are writers, artists and educators." Semiannual. Estab. 1978. Circ. 400.

Needs: Ethnic/multicultural, experimental, feminist, humor/satire, literary, mainstream/contemporary and translations. Would like to see more experimental, surreal and unique fiction. No "religious, juvenile, teen, sports, romance or mystery." Receives 30-40 unsolicited mss/month. Accepts 4-5 mss/issue; 8-10 mss/year. Publishes ms 1-2 years after acceptance. **Publishes few new writers/year.** Recently published work by Hugh Fox, Arnold Sabatelli, Russell Thorburn and Theresa A. Williams. Publishes short shorts. Also publishes literary essays, literary criticism and poetry. Critiques or comments on rejected mss when requested.

How to Contact: Send complete ms with a cover letter. Include short bio and list of publications. Responds in 1 week to queries; 1 month to mss. Send SASE for reply, return of ms or send a disposable copy of ms. No simultaneous submissions. Sample copy for $7.

Payment/Terms: Pays 2 contributor's copies; additional copies for $7. Acquires first North American serial rights.

Advice: Looks for "Quality. Imagination served perfectly by masterful control of language."

N ☑ **A SUMMER'S READING**, 409 Lakeview Dr., Sherman IL 62684-9432. (217)496-3012. E-mail: t_morrissey@hotmail.com. **Contact:** Ted Morrissey, publisher/editor. Magazine: 8½×5½; 75 pages; 20 lb paper; card cover; full color cover, b&w inside; illustrations; photos. "Unlike the majority of literary magazines, our primary reading time is the summer. We want to provide one more attractive, well-edited outlet for new, emerging and established writers and artists." Annual. Estab. 1997. Circ. 200.

Needs: Experimental, literary, translations, narrative essays, prose poetry. "No genre." Receives 60 unsolicited mss/month. Accepts 3-6 mss/issue; 3-6 mss/year. "Reading is slow during 'academic' year." Publishes ms up to 1 year after acceptance. **Publishes 1 new writer/year.** Recently published work by William Jackson, Rachel B. Perkes, Christine Zilius and Mark Wisniewski. Length: 500-8,000 words; average length: 3,000-5,000 words. Publishes short shorts. Also publishes poetry. Often comments on rejected mss.

How to Contact: Send complete ms with a cover letter. Include estimated word count, brief bio, list of publications and e-mail address. Responds in up to 1 year to mss. Send SASE (or IRC) for return of ms or send a disposable copy of ms and #10 SASE for reply only. Accepts simultaneous, previously published "if noted" and multiple submissions "if very short." Sample copy for $5. Guidelines for SASE or by e-mail. Reviews novels, short story collections "if space allows." Send review copies to publisher.

Payment/Terms: Pays 2 contributor's copies; additional copies $4.50. Pays on publication for one-time rights. Sends galleys to author.

Advice: "We look for a combination of a plot which keeps us turning the pages and a practiced writing style. We will be fair. Your work has a better chance of getting published if it's on our desk instead of yours. Not being university affiliated, it is difficult to find reliable readers—thus reporting time is slower than we prefer."

☑ ◉ SUNDOG: THE SOUTHEAST REVIEW, English Department, Florida State University, Tallahassee FL 32306-1036. (850)644-2640. E-mail: sundog@english.fsu.edu. Website: www.english.fsu.edu/sundog/ (includes names of editors and writer's guidelines). **Contact:** Todd Pierce, editor. Magazine: 6×9; 60-100 pages; 70 lb. paper; 10 pt. Krome Kote cover; illustrations; photos. Biannual. Estab. 1979. Circ. 2,000.

Needs: "We want stories (under 3,000 words) with striking images, fresh language, and a consistent voice." Would like to see more literary fiction. No genre or formula fiction. **Publishes 4-6 new writers/year.** "We receive approximately 180 submissions per month; we accept less than 5%. We will comment briefly on rejected mss when time permits." Published work by G. Travis Regier, Rita Ciresi, Stephen Dixon, Susan Hubbard, Pat Rushin and Tracy Daugherty.

How to Contact: Send complete ms with SASE and a brief cover letter. Responds in 2 months. Publishes ms an average of 2-6 months after acceptance. Sample copy for $5. Subscriptions for $9.

Payment/Terms: Pays 2 contributor's copies. Acquires first North American serial rights which then revert to author.

Advice: "Avoid trendy experimentation for its own sake (present-tense narration, observation that isn't also revelation). Fresh stories, moving, interesting characters and a sensitivity to language are still fiction mainstays. Also publishes winner and runners-up of the World's Best Short Short Story Contest sponsored by the Florida State University English Department."

☑ ◎ ♀ SYCAMORE REVIEW, Department of English, Purdue University, West Lafayette IN 47907. (765)494-3783. Fax: (765)494-3780. E-mail: sycamore@expert.cc.purdue.edu. Website: www.sla.purdue.edu/academic/engl/sycamore (includes back and current issues, index, submission guidelines, subscription information, journal library). Editor-in-Chief: Paul D. Reich. Editors change every two years. **Contact:** Fiction Editor. Magazine: 5½×8½; 150-200 pages; heavy, textured, uncoated paper; heavy laminated cover. "Journal devoted to contemporary literature. We publish both traditional and experimental fiction, personal essay, poetry, interviews, drama and graphic art. Novel excerpts welcome if they stand alone as a story." Semiannual. Estab. 1989. Circ. 1,000.

● Work published in *Sycamore Review* has been selected for inclusion in the *Pushcart Prize* anthology.
The magazine was also named "The Best Magazine from Indiana" by the *Clockwatch Review*.

Needs: Contemporary, experimental, humor/satire, literary, mainstream, regional, translations. "We generally avoid genre literature, but maintain no formal restrictions on style or subject matter. No science fiction, romance, children's." Would like to see more experimental fiction. Publishes ms 3 months to 1 year after acceptance. **10% of material published is by new writers.** Recently published work by Lucia Perillo, June Armstrong, W.P. Osborn and William Giraldi. Length: 250 words minimum; 3,750 words preferred. Also publishes poetry, "this most recently included Billy Collins, Thomas Lux, Kathleen Peirce and Vandana Khanna." Sometimes critiques rejected mss and recommends other markets.

How to Contact: Send complete ms with cover letter. Cover letter should include previous publications and address changes. Only reads mss September through March 31. Responds in 4 months. SASE. Accepts simultaneous submissions. Sample copy for $7. Guidelines for #10 SASE.

Payment/Terms: Pays in contributor's copies; charge for extras. Acquires one-time rights.

Advice: "We publish both new and experienced authors but we're always looking for stories with strong emotional appeal, vivid characterization and a distinctive narrative voice; fiction that breaks new ground while still telling an interesting and significant story. Avoid gimmicks and trite, predictable outcomes. Write stories that have a ring of truth, the impact of felt emotion. Don't be afraid to submit, send your best."

🌐 ☑ $ TAKAHE, P.O. Box 13-335, Christchurch, 8001, New Zealand. (03)382-1813. E-mail: isamoyn@ihug.co.nz. Website: www.nzwriters.co.nz (includes writer's guidelines and the names of editors). **Contact:** Mark Johnstone, administrator. "A literary magazine which appears three or four times a year, and publishes short stories and poetry by both established and emerging writers. The publisher is the Takahe Collective Trust, a charitable trust formed by established writers to help new writers and get them into print."

Needs: Publishes 25 new writers/year. Recently published work by Nick Edlin, Hannah Collins and Jenna Sauers.

How to Contact: Send complete ms with bio. SASE with IRCs for overseas submissions. No e-mail submissions.

Payment/Terms: "There is a small payment for work published. $NZ30 ($US12) to each writer/poet appearing in a particular issue regardless of number/length of items, but the amount is subject to change according to circumstaces. Editorials and literary commentaries are by invitation only and not being covered by our grant, are not paid for. All contributors receive two copies of the issue in which theirwork appears. Copyright reverts to the author on publication."

Advice: "While insisting on correct British spelling (or recognised spellings in foreign languages), smart quotes, and at least internally-consistent punctuation, we, nonetheless, try to allow some latitude in presentation. Any use of foreign languages must be accompanied by an English translation."

☑ ⊘ TALKING RIVER REVIEW, Lewis-Clark State College, Division of Literature and Languages, 500 8th Ave., Lewiston ID 83501. (208)792-2307. Fax: (208)792-2324. **Contact:** Dennis Held, editor. Magazine: 6×9; 150 pages; 60 lb. paper; coated, color cover; illustrations; photos. "We look for new voices with something to say to a discerning general audience." Semiannual. Estab. 1994. Circ. 500.

Needs: Condensed/excerpted novel, ethnic/multicultural, feminist, historical, humor/satire, literary, mainstream/contemporary, regional. "Wants more well-written, character-driven stories that surprise and delight the reader with fresh, arresting yet unself-conscious language, imagery, metaphor, revelation." No stories that are sexist, racist, homophobic, erotic for shock value, romance. Receives 200 unsolicited mss/month. Accepts 5-8 mss/issue; 10-15 mss/year. Reads mss September 1-May 1 only. Publishes ms up to 1 year after acceptance. Agented fiction 10%. **Publishes 10-15 new writers/year.** Recently published work by Gary Gildner, Al Sim and David Long. Length: 7,500 words maximum; average length: 3,000 words. Also publishes literary essays and poetry. Sometimes comments on rejected mss.

How to Contact: Send complete manuscript with a cover letter. Include estimated word count, 2-sentence bio and list of publications. Responds in 3 months to mss. Send SASE for reply, return of ms or send disposable copy of ms. Accepts simultaneous submissions if indicated. Sample copy for $6. Guidelines for #10 SASE. Subscription: $14/year.

Payment/Terms: Pays 2 contributor's copies and a year's subscription; additional copies $4. Acquires one-time rights.

Advice: "We look for the strong, the unique; we reject clichéd images and predictable climaxes."

$⊘ TAMEME, New Writing from North America/Nueva literatura de Norteamérica, Tameme, Inc., 199 First St., Los Altos CA 94022. (650)941-2037. Fax: (650)941-5338. E-mail: editor@tameme.org. Website: www.tameme.org (includes editor, contributors, writer's guidelines, staff, index of magazine). Editor: C.M. Mayo. **Contact:** Fiction Editor. Magazine: 6×9; 220 pages; good quality paper; heavy cover stock; illustrations; photos. "*Tameme* is an annual fully bilingual magazine dedicated to publishing new writing from North America in side-by-side English-Spanish format. *Tameme*'s goals are to play an instrumental role in introducing important new writing from Canada and the United States to Mexico, and vice versa, and to provide a forum for the art of literary translation." Estab. 1996. Circ. 1,000. Member, Council of Literary Magazines and Presses (CLMP).

Needs: Ethnic/multicultural, literary, translations. No genre fiction. Plans special fiction issue or anthology. Receives 10-15 unsolicited mss/month. No romance, mystery or western. Accepts 3-4 mss/issue; 6-8 mss/year. Publishes ms 1 year after acceptance. Agented fiction 5%. **Publishes 1-3 new writers/year.** Published work by Fabio Morábito, Margaret Atwood, Juan Villoro, Jaime Sabines, Edwidge Danticat, A. Manette Ansay, Douglas Glover and Marianne Toussaint. Publishes short shorts. Also publishes literary essays and poetry.

How to Contact: Send complete ms with a cover letter. Translators query or submit mss with cover letter, curriculum vita and samples of previous work. Include 1-paragraph bio and list of publications. Responds in 6 weeks to queries; 3 months to mss. Send SASE for reply, return of ms or send a disposable copy of ms. Accepts simultaneous submissions. Sample copy for $14.95. Guidelines for SASE and on website.

Payment/Terms: Pays 3 contributor's copies to writers; $20 per double-spaced WordPerfect page to translators. Pays on publication for one-time rights. Sends galleys to author.

Advice: "We're looking for whatever makes us want to stand up and shout YES! Read the magazine, send for guidelines (with SASE), then send only your best, with SASE. No electronic submissions please."

☑ $⊘ TAMPA REVIEW, 401 W. Kennedy Blvd., Box 19F, University of Tampa, Tampa FL 33606-1490. (813)253-6266. Fax: (813)258-7593. E-mail: utpress@ut.edu. Website: www.tampareview.utampa.edu. Editor: Richard Mathews. **Contact:** Lisa Birnbaum, Kathleen Ochshorn, fiction editors. Magazine: 7½×10½; hardback; approximately 100 pages; acid-free paper; visual art; photos. "Interested in fiction of distinctive literary quality." Semiannual. Estab. 1988.

Needs: Contemporary, ethnic, experimental, fantasy, historical, literary, mainstream, prose poem, translations. "We are far more interested in quality than in genre. Nothing sentimental as opposed to genuinely moving, nor self-conscious style at the expense of human truth." Buys 4-5 mss/issue. Publishes ms within 7 months-1 year of acceptance. Agented fiction 60%. Published work by Elizabeth Spencer, Lee K. Abbott, Lorrie Moore, Gordon Weaver and Tim O'Brien. Length: 250-10,000 words. Publishes short shorts "if the story is good enough." Also publishes literary essays (must be labeled nonfiction), poetry.

How to Contact: Send complete ms with cover letter. Include brief bio. No simultaneous submissions. SASE. Reads September through December; reports January through March. Sample copy for $5 (includes postage) and 9×12 SAE. Guidelines on website or for #10 SASE.

Payment/Terms: Pays $10/printed page. Pays on publication for first North American serial rights. Sends galleys to author upon request.

Advice: "There are more good writers publishing in magazines today than there have been in many decades. Unfortunately, there are even more bad ones. In T. Gertler's *Elbowing the Seducer*, an editor advises a young writer that he wants to hear her voice completely, to tell (he means 'show') him in a story the truest thing she knows. We concur. Rather than a trendy workshop story or a minimalism that actually stems from not having much to say, we would like to see stories that make us believe they mattered to the writer and, more importantly, will matter to a reader. Trim until only the essential is left, and don't give up belief in yourself. And it might help to attend a good writers' conference, e.g. Wesleyan or Bennington."

N ◐ TAPROOT LITERARY REVIEW, Taproot Writer's Workshop, Inc., Box 204, Ambridge PA 15003. (724)266-8476. E-mail: taproot10@aol.com. **Contact:** Tikvah Feinstein, editor. Magazine: 5½×8½; 93 pages; #20 paper; hard cover; attractively printed; saddle-stitched. "We select on quality, not topic. Variety and quality are our appealing features." Annual. Estab. 1987. Circ. 500.

Needs: Literary. No pornography, religious, popular, romance fiction. "Want more multicultural-displaced people living among others in new places." The majority of mss published are received through their annual contest. Receives 20 unsolicited mss/month. Accepts 6 fiction mss/issue. **Publishes 2-4 new writers/year.** Recently published work by Laura Hogan, Kathleen Downey and Susan Williams. Length: 250-3,000 words maximum (no longer than 10 pages, double-spaced maximum); 2,000 words preferred. Publishes short shorts. Length: 300 words preferred. Sometimes comments on rejected mss. Also publishes poetry. Sponsors annual contest. Entry fee: $15/story. Deadline: December 31. Send SASE for details.

How to Contact: Send for guidelines first. Send complete ms with a cover letter. Accepts queries by e-mail, mss by e-mail and disk. Include estimated word count and bio. Responds in 6 months. Send SASE for return of ms or send a disposable copy of ms. No simultaneous submissions. Sample copy for $5, 6×12 SAE and 5 first-class stamps. Guidelines for #10 SASE.

Payment/Terms: Awards $25 in prize money for first place fiction and poetry winners each issue; certificate for 2nd and 3rd place; 1 contributor's copy. Acquires first rights.

Advice: "*Taproot* is getting more fiction submissions and everyone is read entirely. This takes time, so response can be delayed at busy times of year. Our contest is a good way to start publishing. Send for a sample copy and read it through. Ask for a critique and follow suggestions. Don't be offended by any suggestions—just take them or leave them and keep writing. Looks for a story that speaks in its unique voice, told in a well-crafted and complete, memorable style, a style of signature to the author. Follow writer's guidelines. Research markets. Send cover letter. Don't give up."

⊕ $◐ TEARS IN THE FENCE, 38 Hod View, Stourpaine, Nr. Blandford Forum, Dorset DT11 8TN England. Phone: 01258-456803. Fax: 01258-454026. E-mail: poets@wanderingdog.co.uk. Editor: David Caddy. **Contact:** Fiction Editor. Three issues per annum.

● *Tears in the Fence* has expanded to 112 pages and is accepting more prose and prose poems.

Needs: A magazine of poetry, fiction, criticism and reviews, open to a variety of contemporary voices from around the world. Upcoming themes: "Minding the Gap" (June 2002). **Publishes 1-2 new writers/year.** Recently published work by K.M. Dersley, Hazel Stewart, Brian George, Gerald Locklin, Helen Kitson, Joyce Finn and Simon Howells. Publishes short and long fiction. Publishes 4-5 stories/issue.

Payment/Terms: Pays £7.50 per story and complimentary copy of the magazine. Sample copy for $5 (US).

Advice: "Look for firm narrative control with an economical style that takes the reader far beyond the obvious and inconsequential. Explore the market by buying sample copies."

✓ ◐ THE TEXAS REVIEW, Texas Review Press at Sam Houston State University, P.O. Box 2146, Huntsville TX 77341-2146. (936)294-1992. Fax: (936)294-3070 (inquiries only). Website: www.shsu.edu. **Contact:** Paul Ruffin, editor. Magazine: 6×9; 148-190 pages; best quality paper; 70 lb. cover stock; illustrations; photos. "We publish top quality poetry, fiction, articles, interviews and reviews for a general audience." A member of the Texas A&M University Press consortium. Semiannual. Estab. 1976. Circ. 1,200.

Needs: Literary and contemporary fiction. "We are eager enough to consider fiction of quality, no matter what its theme or subject matter. No juvenile fiction." Accepts 4 mss/issue. Receives approximately 40-60 unsolicited fiction mss each month. Does not read June-August. **Published new writers within the last year.** Published work by George Garrett, Ellen Gilchrist and Fred Chappell. Length: 500-10,000 words. Critiques rejected mss "when there is time." Recommends other markets.

How to Contact: Send complete ms, cover letter optional. SASE. No mss accepted via fax. Responds in 3 months to mss. Sample copy for $5.

Payment/Terms: Pays contributor's copies and one year subscription. Acquires first North American serial rights. Sends galleys to author.

✓ $ ⊘ ▼ **THEMA**, Box 8747, Metairie LA 70011-8747. (504)887-1263. E-mail: thema@home.com. Website: http://members.home.net/thema (includes guidelines, list of upcoming themes, table of contents of recent issues and subscription information). **Contact:** Virginia Howard, editor. Magazine: 5½×8½; 200 pages; Grandee Strathmore cover stock; b&w illustrations. "Different specified theme for each issue—short stories, poems, b&w artwork must relate to that theme." Triannual. Estab. 1988.

● Ranked #24 on *Writer's Digest*'s "Fiction 50" list of top markets for fiction writers. *Thema* received a Certificate for Excellence in the Arts from the Arts Council of New Orleans.

Needs: Adventure, contemporary, experimental, humor/satire, literary, mainstream, mystery/suspense, prose poem, psychic/supernatural/occult, regional, science fiction, sports, western. "Each issue is based on a specified premise—a different unique theme for each issue. Many types of fiction acceptable, but must fit the premise. No pornographic, scatologic, erotic fiction." Upcoming themes (deadlines for submission in 2002): "Paper Tigers" (March 1); "Lost in Translation" (July 1); and "An Unlikely Alliance" (November 1). Publishes ms within 6 months of acceptance. **Publishes 8 new writers/year.** Recently published work by Marilyn Johnston, Jack Foster, Kemp Pheley and Ben Satterfield. Length: fewer than 6,000 words preferred. Also publishes poetry. Sometimes critiques rejected mss and recommends other markets.

How to Contact: Send complete ms with cover letter, include "name and address, brief introduction, specifying the intended target issue for the mss." Accepts queries by e-mail. Responds in 1 week to queries; 5 months after deadline for specified issue. Accepts simultaneous and multiple submissions. SASE. Sample copy for $8. Guidelines available on website or for SASE.

Payment/Terms: Pays $25; $10 for short shorts. Pays on acceptance for one-time rights.

Advice: "Do not submit a manuscript unless you have written it for a specified premise. If you don't know the upcoming themes, send for guidelines first, before sending a story. We need more stories told in the Mark Twain/ O. Henry tradition in magazine fiction."

⊕ ✓ ◯ **THE THIRD ALTERNATIVE**, TTA Press, 5 Martins Lane, Witcham, Ely, Cambs CB6 2LB England. E-mail: ttapress@aol.com. Website: www.tta.press.freewire.co.uk (includes news, art, interviews, stories, links, contributor's guidelines, secret credit card ordering facility). **Contact:** Andy Cox, fiction editor. Quarterly. Publishes 8 stories/issue. A4, 68 pages, lithographed, color, laminated.

Needs: "Modern fiction: no mainstream or genre clichés. Innovative, quality science fiction/fantasy/horror and slipstream material (cross-genre)." Recently published M. John Harrison, Michael Marshall Smith and Muriel Gray. Length: No minimum; no maximum (no serials).

How to Contact: Only send one story at a time, mailed flat or folded no more than once. USA stamps are not acceptable as return postage (UK stamps, 2 IRCs or an e-mail address—but no submissions via e-mail). "A covering letter is appreciated." Standard ms format and SAE (overseas: disposable ms and 2 IRCs or an e-mail address). No simultaneous submissions. No reprints.

Payment/Terms: Payment is £30 per 1,000 words. $7 sample copy, $36 6-issue subscription. US checks acceptable, payable to TTA Press.

✓ ⊘ ▼ **THIRD COAST**, Dept. of English, Western Michigan University, Kalamazoo MI 49008-5092. (616)387-2675. Fax: (616)387-2562. Website: www.wmich.edu/thirdcoast (includes guidelines, editors names and samples of past fiction we have published are all available on the website). Managing Editor: Shanda Blue. **Contact:** Lisa Lishman and Libbie Searcy, fiction editors. Magazine: 6×9; 150 pages. "We will consider many different types of fiction and favor that exhibiting a freshness of vision and approach." Semiannual. Estab. 1995. Circ. 600.

● *Third Coast* has received *Pushcart Prize* nominations. The editors of this publication change with the university year.

Needs: Literary. "While we don't want to see formulaic genre fiction, we will consider material that plays with or challenges generic forms." Receives approximately 100 unsolicited mss/month. Accepts 6-8 mss/issue; 15 mss/year. Publishes ms 3-6 months after acceptance. Recently published work by Peter Ho Davies, Sharon Dilworth, Trudy Lewis and Mark Winegardner. Length: no preference. Publishes short shorts. Also publishes literary essays, poetry and interviews. Sometimes comments on rejected mss.

How to Contact: Send complete ms with a cover letter. Include list of publications. Responds in 2 months to queries; 5 months to mss. Send SASE for reply or return of ms. No simultaneous submissions. Sample copy for $6. Guidelines for #10 SASE.
Payment/Terms: Pays 2 contributor's copies as well as 1 year subscription to the publication; additional copies for $4. Acquires first North American serial rights.
Advice: "Of course, the writing itself must be of the highest quality. We love to see work that explores non-western contexts, as well as fiction from all walks of American (and other) experience."

THE THIRD HALF MAGAZINE, "Amikeco," 16, Fane Close, Stamford, Lincolnshire PE9 1HG England. Phone: (01780)754193. **Contact:** Kevin Troop, fiction editor.
Needs: *"The Third Half* literary magazine publishes mostly poetry, but editorial policy is to publish as much *short* short story writing as possible in separate books." **Publishes 2 new writers/year.** Recently published work by Michael Bangerter, Idris Caffrey, John Light and Mario Petrucci. Length: 2,000 words maximum.
Payment/Terms: Pays in contributor's copies. Sample copy £4.95; £5.50 by post in England; £10 overseas.

THORNY LOCUST, TL Press, P.O. Box 32631, Kansas City MO 64171-5631. (816)756-5096. E-mail: thornylocust@netscape.net. **Contact:** Silvia Kofler. Magazine: 32 pages; illustrations; photos. *"Thorny Locust* is a literary quarterly produced in a dusty corner of the publisher's hermitage. We are interested in poetry, fiction, and artwork with some 'bite'—e.g., satire, epigrams, well-structured tirades, black humor, and bleeding-heart cynicism. Absolutely no natural or artificial sweeteners, unless they're the sugar-coating on a strychnine tablet. We are not interested in polemics, gratuitous grotesques, somber surrealism, weeping melancholy, or hate-mongering. To rewrite Jack Conroy, 'We prefer polished vigor to crude banality.' " Estab. 1993. Circ. 200.
Needs: Ethnic/multicultural (general), experimental, humor/satire, literary. Receives 4-5 unsolicited mss/month. Accepts 1 ms/issue; 2-3 mss/year. Publishes ms up to 2 months after acceptance. Length: 250-2,000 words; average length: 1,500 words. Publishes short shorts. Average length: 500 words. Also publishes poetry. Rarely comments on rejected mss.
How to Contact: Send complete ms with a cover letter. Include brief bio. Responds in 3 months to queries. Send SASE (or IRC) for return of ms or send a disposable copy of ms and #10 SASE for reply only. Accepts simultaneous submissions. Sample copy for $3. Guidelines for SASE or by e-mail.
Payment/Terms: Pays 1 contributor's copy. Acquires one-time rights.
Advice: "We look for work that is witty and original. Edit your work carefully."

THE THREEPENNY REVIEW, P.O. Box 9131, Berkeley CA 94709. (510)849-4545. Website: www.threepennyreview.com. **Contact:** Wendy Lesser, editor. Tabloid: 10×17; 40 pages; Electrobrite paper; white book cover; illustrations. "Serious fiction." Quarterly. Estab. 1980. Circ. 9,000.
- *The Threepenny Review* ranked #20 on *Writer's Digest's* "Fiction 50" list of top markets for fiction writers, and has received GE Writers Awards, CLMP Editor's Awards, NEA grants, Lila Wallace grants and inclusion of work in the *Pushcart Prize Anthology.*
Needs: Literary. "Nothing 'experimental' (ungrammatical)." Receives 300-400 mss/month. Accepts 3 mss/issue; 12 mss/year. Does *not* read mss June through August. Publishes 6-12 months after acceptance. Agented fiction 5%. Published Sigrid Nunez, Dagoberto Gilb, Gina Berriault and Leonard Michaels. Length: 5,000 words maximum. Publishes short shorts. Also publishes literary essays, literary criticism, poetry.
How to Contact: Send complete ms with a cover letter. *Does not accept e-mail or faxed submissions.* Responds in 1 month to queries; 2 months to mss. Send SASE for reply, return of ms or send a disposable copy of the ms. No simultaneous submissions. Sample copy for $10. Guidelines for #10 SASE or on website. Reviews novels and short story collections.
Payment/Terms: Pays $200 and free subscription to the magazine; additional copies at half price. Pays on acceptance for first North American serial rights. Sends galleys to author.

TICKLED BY THUNDER, Helping Writers Get Published Since 1990, Tickled By Thunder Publishing Co., 14076 86A Ave, Surrey British Columbia V3W 0V9 Canada. (604)951-6095. E-mail: thunder@istar.ca. Website: www.home.istar.ca/~thunder. **Contact:** Larry Lindner, publisher. Magazine: digest-sized; 24 pages; bond pages; bond cover stock; illustrations; photos. "Tickled By Thunder is designed to encourage beginning writers of fiction, poetry and nonfiction." Quarterly. Estab. 1990. Circ. 1,000.
Needs: Fantasy, humor/satire, literary, mainstream, mystery/suspense, science fiction, western. "No overly indulgent horror, sex, profanity or religious material." Receives 25 unsolicited ms/month. Accepts 3 mss/issue; 12 mss/year. Publishes ms 3-9 months after acceptance. **Publishes 10 new writers/year.** Recently published work by Rick Cook and Jerry Shane. Length: 2,000 words maximum; 1,500 words average. Publishes short shorts: average length 300 words. Also publishes literary essays, literary criticism and poetry.
How to Contact: Send complete ms with cover letter. Include estimated word count and brief bio. Responds in 3 months to queries; 6 months to mss. Send SASE (or IRC) for return of ms; or send disposable copy of ms

and #10 return SASE for reply only. Accepts simultaneous, multiple and previously published submissions. Sample copy for $2.50. Guidelines for SASE, via e-mail, or on website. Reviews novels, short story collections and nonfiction books of interest to writers. Send material to Larry Lindner.

Payment/Terms: Pays on publication for first and reprint rights.

Advice: "Make your characters breathe on their own. Use description mixed with action."

N: $ ◙ TIMBER CREEK REVIEW, 3283 UNCG Station, Greensboro NC 27413. (336)334-6970. E-mail: timber_creek_Review@hoopsmail.com. **Editor:** J.M. Freiermuth. Associate Editor: Celestine Woo. Newsletter: 5½×8½; 76-84 pages; copy paper; some illustrations; photos. Quarterly. Circ. 150.

Needs: Adventure, contemporary, ethnic, feminist, historical, humor/satire, literary, mainstream, mystery/suspense (cozy, private eye), regional, western (adult, frontier, traditional). No religion, children's, gay, romance. Receives 40-60 unsolicited mss/month. Accepts 15-20 mss/issue; 70-75 mss/year. Publishes ms 3-12 months after acceptance. **Publishes 0-3 new writers/year.** Recently published work by J. Michael Blue, Delray Dvoracek, Tod Golberg, Karl Nilsson, Catherine Uroff and Roslyn Willett. Length: 2,500-10,000 words; average length: 3,500 words. Sometimes critiques rejected mss. "If you don't like to hear the slightest bad news, mention that in your cover letter and I won't bother."

How to Contact: Send complete ms and/or DOS disk (uses MS Word). Cover letter required. "There are no automatons here, so don't treat us like machines. We recognize the names of a couple hundred writers on sight, but if you are not a dead white guy, we may not recognize your name at the top of the manuscript. A few lines about you break the ice. The names of three or four magazines that have published you in the last year would show your reality. A bio blurb of 37 +/- words including the names of two or three of the magazines you send the occasional subscription check (where you aspire to be?) could help. If you are not sending a check to some little magazine that is supported by subscriptions and the blood sweat and tears of the editors, why would you send your work to any of them and expect to receive a warm welcome? No requirement to subscribe or buy a sample, but they are available at $4.25 and encouraged. There are no phony contests and never a reading fee. Read all year long, but may take one to six months to respond." Accepts simultaneous and multiple submissions but no reprints.

Payment/Terms: Pays $10-35. Pays subscription to magazine for first publication and contributor's copies for subsequent publications. Acquires one-time rights. Publication not copyrighted.

Advice: "Stop watching TV and read that book of stories your last manuscript appeared in. If you are not reading other people's stories, they are probably not reading yours either. If no one reads this stuff, was it worth wasting the tree? If your story has a spark of life or a degree of humor that brings a smile to my face, you may have a chance here. Most stories lack these ingredients. Write new stories. If you have 20 stories circulating, you have a better chance of having one published."

✓ $ ◙ TIN HOUSE, P.O. Box 10500, Portland OR 97296-0500. (503)274-4393. Fax: (503)222-1154. E-mail: tinhouse@europa.com. Website: www.tinhouse.com. Editor: Win McCormack. **Contact:** Rob Spillman and Elissa Schappell, fiction editors. Literary magazine: 7×9; 200 pages, 50 lb. paper; glossy cover stock; illustrations and photos. Quarterly.

Needs: Experimental, literary. Accepts 3-4 mss/issue. Publishes ms up to one year after acceptance. Length: 2,000-5,000 words; average length: 3,500 words. Publishes short shorts. Also publishes literary essays, literary criticism and poetry.

How to Contact: Send complete ms with a cover letter or submit through an agent. Include estimated word count. Responds in 6 weeks to mss. Send SASE for return of ms. Accepts simultaneous submissions. Sample copy for $16. Guidelines for $2.

Payment/Terms: Pays $100-800 and 2 contributor's copies; additional copies $16. Acquires first North American serial and Anthology rights.

Advice: "Our criteria are boldness of concept, intense level of emotion and energy, precision of observation, deployment of imagination, grace of style. Any sentence read at random is impeccable and as good as any other in the work. Do not send anything that does not make you feel like laughing or crying, or both, when you read it yourself."

N: ◙ TOUCHSTONE LITERARY JOURNAL, P.O. Box 8308, Spring TX 77387-8308. E-mail: panthercreek3@hotmail.com. Website: www.panthercreekpress.com. Editor/Publisher: William Laufer. Managing Editor: Guida Jackson. **Contact:** Julia Gomez-Rigas, fiction editor. Magazine: 5½×8½; 56 pages; linen paper; kramkote cover; perfect bound; b&w illustrations; occasional photos. "Literary and mainstream fiction, but enjoy experimental work and multicultural. Audience middle-class, heavily academic. We are eclectic and given to whims—i.e., two years ago we devoted a 104-page issue to West African women writers." Annual (with occasional special supplements). Estab. 1976. Circ. 1,000.

● Touchstone Press also publishes a chapbook series. Send a SASE for guidelines.

Needs: Humor/satire, literary, translations. No erotica, religious, juvenile, "stories written in creative writing programs that all sound alike." List of upcoming themes available for SASE. Publishes special fiction issue or anthology. Receives 20-30 mss/month. Accepts 3-4 mss/issue. Does not read mss in December. Publishes ms within the year after acceptance. Published work by Ann Alejandro, Lynn Bradley, Roy Fish and Julia Mercedes Castilla. Length: 250-5,000 words; 2,500 words preferred. Publishes short shorts. Length: 300 words. Also publishes literary essays, literary criticism and poetry. Sometimes comments on rejected mss.

How to Contact: Send complete ms with a cover letter. Include estimated word count and 3-sentence bio. Responds in 6 weeks. Send SASE for return of ms. Accepts multiple submissions. Guidelines for #10 SASE.

Payment/Terms: Pays 2 contributor's copies; additional copies $7. Acquires one-time rights. Sends galleys to author (unless submitted on disk).

Advice: "We like to see fiction that doesn't read as if it had been composed in a creative writing class. If you can entertain, edify, or touch the reader, polish your story and send it in. Don't worry if it doesn't read like our other fiction."

N ⊘ TRADESMAN MAGAZINE, Trademan magazine, P.O. Box 3462, Ann Arbor MI 48106-3462. **Contact:** K. Walker, editor. Magazine: digest-sized; about 40 pages; card stock cover; 24 lb. bond inside pages. "There aren't many magazines that specialize in publishing gay erotic fiction, especially ones that are open to gay 'humanistic' fiction, as well as genre types such as science fiction and fantasy (which have gay characters)." Triannual. Estab. 2001. Circ. 250.

Needs: Erotica, gay, lesbian. "We do not want anything that does not have a gay angle, or a gay character. We're interested in seeing what writers can do with categories or genres such as sci-fi, fantasy and others." Accepts 4 mss/issue; 12 mss/year. Publishes ms 2 months after acceptance. Length: 1,500-3,000 words; average length: 2,500 words. Publishes short shorts. Also publishes poetry. Sometimes comments on rejected mss.

How to Contact: "Send a complete manuscript; query if unsure." Include estimated word count and brief bio. Responds in 1 month to queries; 3 months to mss. Send SASE for return of ms. Accepts simultaneous and multiple submissions. "Response time would be a little longer for multiple submissions." Sample copy for $5.

Payment/Terms: Pays 2 contributor's copies; additional copies $5. Pays on publication for first North American serial rights.

Advice: "We look for good writing, and work that is professionally submitted. Anything you send in should either be gay-themed or have a major character who the reader knows is gay. We're open to lesbian characters too."

⊘ ◎ ⛛ TRANSITION, An International Review, Duke University Press, 69 Dunster St., Cambridge MA 02138. (617)496-2845. Fax: (617)496-2877. E-mail: transition@fas.harvard.edu. Website: http://web-dubois. fas.harvard.edu/transition (includes contents of all issues, abstracts, editorial history and current info, purchasing and subscription info). **Contact:** Michael Vazquez, executive editor. Magazine: 9½×6½; 150-175 pages; 70 lb. Finch Opaque paper; 100 lb. white Warren Lustro dull cover; illustrations; photos. "*Transition* magazine is a quarterly, international review known for compelling and controversial writing on race, ethnicity, culture and politics. This prestigious magazine is edited at Harvard University, and editorial board members include heavy-hitters such as Toni Morrison, Jamaica Kincaid and bell hooks. The magazine also attracts famous contributors such as Spike Lee, Philip Gourevitch and Carlos Fuentes." Quarterly. Estab. 1961. Circ. 3,500.

● Winner of Alternative Press Award for international reporting 2000, 1999, 1995; finalist in the 2000 National Magazine Award in General Excellence category; American Association of University Publishers Outstanding Design 1997, 1995.

Needs: Ethnic/multicultural (general), historical, humor satire, literary, regional (Africa diaspora, India, Third World, etc.) Receives 10 unsolicited mss/month. Accepts 4-6 mss/year. Publishes ms 3-4 months after acceptance. Agented fiction 30-40%. **Publishes 1 new writer/year.** Recently published work by George Makana Clark, Paul Beatty and Victor D. LaValle. Length: 4,000-8,000 words; average length: 7,000 words. Also publishes literary essays and literary criticism. Sometimes comments on rejected mss.

How to Contact: Send complete ms with a cover letter or query with clips of published work. Include brief bio and list of publications. Responds in 2 months to queries; 4 months to mss. Send disposable copy of ms and #10 SASE for reply only. Accepts simultaneous submissions and previously published work. Sample copy for $8.99 through website. Guidelines for SASE. Reviews novels, short story collections and nonfiction books of interest to writers.

Payment/Terms: Pays 3 contributor's copies. Rights negotiable. Sends galleys to author.

Advice: "We look for a non-white, alternative perspective, dealing with issues of race, ethnicity in an unpredictable, provocative way, but not exclusively."

✓ ⊘ ⛛ TRIQUARTERLY, Northwestern University, 2020 Ridge Ave., Evanston IL 60208-4302. (847)491-3490. **Contact:** Susan Hahn, editor. Magazine: 6×9¼; 240-272 pages; 60 lb. paper; heavy cover stock;

illustration; photos. "A general literary quarterly. We publish short stories, novellas or excerpts from novels, by American and foreign writers. Genre or style is not a primary consideration. We aim for the general but serious and sophisticated reader. Many of our readers are also writers." Triannual. Estab. 1964. Circ. 5,000.

 • Stories from *Triquarterly* have been reprinted in *The Best American Short Stories*, *Pushcart Prizes* and *O. Henry Prize* Anthologies.

Needs: Literary, contemporary and translations. "No prejudices or preconceptions against anything *except* genre fiction (romance, science fiction, etc.)." Accepts 10 mss/issue, 30 mss/year. Receives approximately 500 unsolicited fiction mss each month. Will begin reading October 1, 2001. Agented fiction 10%. **Publishes 1-5 new writers/year.** Published work by John Barth, Chaim Potok, Joyce Carol Oates, Hélène Cixous, Charles Baxter, Margot Livesey and Robert Girardi. Length: no requirement. Publishes short shorts.

How to Contact: Send complete ms with SASE. No simultaneous submissions. Responds in 4 months to mss. Publishes ms an average of 6-12 months after acceptance. Sample copy for $5.

Payment/Terms: Pays 2 contributor's copies; cover price less 40% discount for extras. Pays on publication for first North American serial rights. Sends galleys to author. Honoraria vary, depending on grant support.

TUCUMCARI LITERARY REVIEW, 3108 W. Bellevue Ave., Los Angeles CA 90026. **Contact:** Troxey Kemper, editor. Magazine: 5½×8½; about 40 pages; 20 lb. bond paper; 67 lb. cover stock; few illustrations; photocopied photos. "Old-fashioned fiction that can be read and reread for pleasure; no weird, strange pipe dreams and no it-was-all-a-dream endings." Bimonthly. Estab. 1988. Circ. small.

Needs: Adventure, contemporary, ethnic, historical, humor/satire, literary, mainstream, mystery/suspense, regional (southwest USA), senior citizen/retirement, western (frontier stories). No "sci-fi, occult, violence, liquor, tobacco, sex sex sex, dirty language for no reason, or romance. Would like to see more Western, mystery and O. Henry endings." No drugs/acid rock, occult, pornography, horror, martial arts or children's stories. Accepts 6 or 8 mss/issue; 35-40 mss/year. Publishes ms 2-6 months after acceptance. **Publishes 30 new writers/year.** Published work by Wilma Elizabeth McDaniel, Ruth Daniels, Andy Peterson, Robert Richeson and Bobby Rivera. Length: 400-1,200 words preferred. Also publishes rhyming poetry.

How to Contact: Send complete ms with or without cover letter. Responds in 2 weeks. SASE. Accepts simultaneous and reprint submissions. Sample copy for $2. Guidelines for #10 SASE.

Payment/Terms: Pays in contributor's copies. Acquires one-time rights. Publication not copyrighted.

Advice: "Computers/printers are 'nice' but sometimes handwritten work on 3-hole lined notebook paper is interesting, too. We are often overstocked, but if a piece is good, I'll find room for it."

N **UNBOUND**, Suny Potsdam, Dept. of English and Communication, Morey Hall, Potsdam NY 13676. (315)267-2043. E-mail: unbound@potsdam.edu. **Contact:** Rick Henry, editor. Magazine. "*Unbound* seeks fiction that exceeds the page. We are interested in collage, avant-garde, experimental, new media, multimedia fiction that maintains a strong narrative thread." Annual. Estab. 2002.

Needs: Experimental. "No genre fiction." Does not read mss March-August. Publishes short shorts.

How to Contact: Send complete ms with a cover letter. Include brief bio. Responds in 2 months to queries; 10 weeks to mss (or by February). Send SASE for return of ms or send a disposable copy of ms and #10 SASE for reply only. Accepts multiple submissions. Guidelines for SASE or by e-mail.

Payment/Terms: Pays 1 contributor's copy; additional copies $5. Pays on publication for first North American serial rights.

Advice: "We look for an intelligent relationship between a fiction's form and content. Fiction need not be limited by the borders of 8½×11 sheets of paper."

N **THE UNKNOWN WRITER**, P.O. Box 698, Ramsey NJ 07446. E-mail: unknown_writer_2000@yah oo.com. Website: www.munno.net/unknownwriter (includes guidelines, selections from previous issues and current issue, staff bios). **Contact:** Rick Maffei or Janell Robisch, fiction editors. Magazine: 6×9; 40-60 pages; cardstock cover; illustrations; photos. "We exist to give new writers a place to publish their quality writing. We want writers with no or limited publishing credits who have a strong, detailed, compelling story to tell. We publish short fiction, poetry, and art that strives to make a direct connection with the reader in a fresh, intelligent way. Our first and foremost goal is to entertain, but we prefer to publish selections that will make readers continue to think after they finish reading the piece. Our intended audience is readers of all ages that prefer original, intelligent fiction and poetry and wish to escape the mediocrity of mainstream publications and authors." Quarterly. Estab. 1995.

Needs: Adventure, ethnic/multicultural (general), experimental, fantasy, feminist, gay, historical, horror, lesbian, literary, mainstream, military/war, mystery/suspense, New Age, psychic/supernatural/occult, romance, science fiction, thriller/espionage, western. "No erotic, vulgar or graphic violence." **Publishes 2-4 new writers/year.** Accepts 3-5 mss/issue; 12-20 mss/year. Publishes ms up to 6 months after acceptance. Length: 5-5,000 words. Publishes short shorts. Average length: 500-1,000 words. Also publishes poetry. Sometimes comments on rejected mss.

How to Contact: Send complete ms with a cover letter. Accepts submissions by e-mail. Include estimated word count. Responds in 3 weeks to queries; 4 months to mss. Send SASE for return of ms or send a disposable copy of ms and #10 SASE for reply only. Accepts simultaneous and multiple submissions. Guidelines for SASE, by e-mail or on website.

Payment/Terms: Pays 2 contributor's copies. Pays on publication for first rights.

Advice: "We look for strong characters, storyline, readability and entertainment value as well as a clear conflict and reasonable but not predictable resolution. Your manuscript should be clean and free of spelling and grammatical errors. Make sure you work on a strong plot, not creating something for shock value. Use creative but realistic detail and dialogue to help bring your story to life when possible."

UNMUZZLED OX, Unmuzzled Ox Foundation Ltd., 105 Hudson St., New York NY 10013. (212)226-7170. E-mail: mandreox@aol.com. **Contact:** Michael Andre, editor. Magazine: 5½ × 8½. "Magazine about life for an intelligent audience." Published irregularly. Estab. 1971. Circ. 7,000.

- Recent issues of this magazine have included poetry, essays and art only. Check before sending submissions.

Needs: Contemporary, literary, prose poem and translations. No commercial material. Receives 20-25 unsolicited mss/month. Also publishes poetry. Occasionally critiques rejected mss.

How to Contact: "Please no phone calls and no e-mail submissions. Correspondence by mail *only*. Cover letter is significant." Responds in 1 month. SASE. Sample copy for $10.

Payment/Terms: Pays in contributor's copies.

Advice: "You may want to check out a copy of the magazine before you submit."

$ 🖊 ◎ THE URBANITE, Surreal & Lively & Bizarre, Urban Legend Press, P.O. Box 4737, Davenport IA 52808. Website: members.tripod.com/theurbanite/ (includes information on current and upcoming issues and also features a fiction showcase). **Editor:** Mark McLaughlin. Magazine: 8½ × 11; 52-80 pages; bond paper; coated cover; saddle-stitched; illustrations. "We look for quality fiction with a surrealistic tone. We publish character-oriented, sophisticated fiction that expands the boundaries of the speculative genres. Our readers appreciate the best in imaginative fiction." Each issue includes a featured writer, a featured poet and a featured artist. Published three times a year. Estab. 1991. Circ. 500-1,000.

- *The Urbanite* ranked as #8 on the *Writer's Digest* "Fiction 50" list of top markets.

Needs: Experimental, fantasy (dark fantasy), horror, humor/satire, literary, psychic/supernatural/occult, science fiction (soft/sociological). "We love horror, but please, no tired, gore-ridden horror plots. Horror submissions must be subtle and sly. Want more unusual, stylish stories with a sense of 'voice.' Also, more bizarre humor." Upcoming themes: "The Zodiac" and "All Horror" issue. List of upcoming themes available for SASE. Receives over 800 unsolicited mss/month. Accepts 15 mss/issue; 45 mss/year. Publishes ms 6 months after acceptance. **Publishes at least 2-3 new writers/year.** Published work by Basil Copper, Wilum Pugmire, Hertzan Chimera, Marni Scofidio Griffin, Alexa de Monterice and Thomas Ligotti. Length: 500-3,000 words; 2,000 words preferred. Publishes short shorts. Length: 350 words preferred. Also publishes poetry. Sometimes comments on rejected mss.

How to Contact: Include estimated word count, 4- to 5-sentence bio, Social Security number and list of publications. Responds in 1 month to queries; 4 months to mss. Send large SASE for reply and return of ms, or send a stamped, self-addressed business-size envelope and a disposable copy of ms. Sample copy for $5. Guidelines for #10 SASE.

Payment/Terms: Pays 2-3¢/word and 2 contributor's copies. Featured authors receive 3¢/word, 6 contributor's copies and a lifetime subscription to the magazine. Authors of stories in our website's fiction showcase receive $25. Acquires first North American serial rights and nonexclusive rights for public readings.

Advice: "The tone of our magazine is unique, and we strongly encourage writers to read an issue to ascertain the sort of material we accept. The number one reason we reject many stories is because they are inappropriate for our publication: in these cases, it is obvious that the writer is not familiar with *The Urbanite*. We are known for publishing quality horror—work from *The Urbanite* has been reprinted in *Year's Best Fantasy & Horror, The Year's Best Fantastic Fiction*, England's *Best New Horror*, volumes 7 and 8, and on the *Masters of Terror Website*. We want to see more bizarre (yet urbane and thought-provoking) humor. Excellence is priority number one. We simply want stories that are well-written, compelling and unique. Find your own 'voice.' Put your own style and personality into your work!"

INTERESTED IN A PARTICULAR GENRE? Check our sections for: **Mystery/Suspense**, page 91; **Romance**, page 105; **Science Fiction & Fantasy**, page 121.

USI WORKSHEETS, % US1 Poet's Cooperative, P.O. Box 127, Kingston NJ 08528-0127. Editor: Rotating board. **Contact:** Fiction Editor. Magazine: 5½×8½; 72 pages. Publishes poetry and fiction. Annual. Estab. 1973.

Needs: "No restrictions on subject matter or style. Good storytelling or character delineation appreciated. Audience does not include children." **Publishes 1-2 new writers/year.** Recently published work by Alicia Ostriker, Joan Baranow, Lois Marie Harrod, Frederick Tibbetts and Rod Tulloss. Publishes short shorts. Word limit for prose: 2,000 words.

How to Contact: Query first "or send a SAE postcard for reading dates. We read only once a year." Responds to queries "as soon as possible." SASE. Sample copy for $4.

Payment/Terms: Pays in contributor's copies. Acquires one-time rights. Copyright "reverts to author."

VALLEY GRAPEVINE, Seven Buffaloes Press, Box 249, Big Timber MT 59011. Editor/Publisher: Art Coelho. Theme: "poems, stories, history, folklore, photographs, ink drawings or anything native to the Great Central Valley of California, which includes the San Joaquin and Sacramento valleys. Focus is on land and people and the oil fields, farms, orchards, Okies, small town life, hobos." Readership: "rural and small town audience, the common man with a rural background, salt-of-the-earth. The working man reads *Valley Grapevine* because it's his personal history recorded." Annual. Estab. 1978. Circ. 500.

Needs: Literary, contemporary, ethnic (Arkie, Okie), regional and western. No academic, religious (unless natural to theme), or supernatural material. Receives approximately 4-5 unsolicited fiction mss each month. Length: 2,500-10,000 (prefers 5,000) words.

How to Contact: Query. SASE for query, ms. Responds in 1 week. Sample copy available to writers for $7.75.

Payment/Terms: Pays 1-2 contributor's copies. Acquires first North American serial rights. Returns rights to author after publication, but reserves the right to reprint in an anthology or any future special collection of Seven Buffaloes Press.

Advice: "Buy a copy to get a feel of the professional quality of the writing. Know the theme of a particular issue. Some contributors have 30 years experience as writers, most 15 years. Age does not matter; quality does."

$ THE VINCENT BROTHERS REVIEW, The Vincent Brothers Company, 4566 Northern Circle, Riverside OH 45424-5733. **Editor:** Kimberly Willardson. Magazine: 5½×8¼; 88-100 perfect-bound pages; 60 lb. white coated paper; 60 lb. Oxford (matte) cover; b&w illustrations; photos. "We publish at least two theme issues per year. Writers must send SASE for information about upcoming theme issues. Each issue of *TVBR* contains poetry, b&w art, at least six short stories and usually one nonfiction piece. For a mainstream audience looking for an alternative to the slicks." Triannual. Estab. 1988. Circ. 400.

● *TVBR* was ranked #12 in the *Writer's Digest*'s "Fiction 50." It has received grants from the Ohio Arts Council for the last six years. Also received grant from the Montgomery County Regional Arts and Cultural District of Ohio for 1998. Won Special Merit Award in 1996 American Literary Magazine Awards sponsored by *Poet* Magazine and Cooper House Publishing. The magazine sponsors a fall fiction contest; deadline in October. Contact them for details.

Needs: Adventure, condensed/excerpted novel, contemporary, ethnic, experimental, feminist, historical, humor/satire, literary, mainstream, mystery/suspense (amateur sleuth, cozy, private eye), prose poem, regional, science fiction (soft/sociological), senior citizen/retirement, serialized novel, translations, western (adult, frontier, traditional). "We focus on the way the story is presented rather than the genre of the story. No racist, sexist, fascist, etc. work." Receives 200-250 unsolicited mss/month. Buys 6-10 mss/issue; 30 mss/year. Publishes ms 2-4 months after acceptance. **Publishes 8-12 new writers/year.** Published work by Gordon C. Wilson, Tom D. Ellison, Nikolaus Maack, Laurel Jenkins-Crowe and Ariel Smart. Length: 250-7,000 words; average length: 2,500 words. Maximum 10,000 words for novel condensations. Publishes short shorts. Length: 250-1,000 words. Also publishes literary essays, literary criticism, poetry. Often critiques rejected mss and sometimes recommends other markets.

How to Contact: "Send query letter *before* sending novel excerpts or condensations! *Send only one short story at a time*—unless sending short shorts." Send complete ms. Accepts simultaneous submissions, but not preferred. Responds in 1 month to queries; 3 months to mss with SASE. Sample copy for $6.50; back issues for $4.50. Guidelines for #10 SASE. Reviews novels and short story collections.

Payment/Terms: Pays $15-250. Pays on acceptance for first North American serial rights. $200 first place; $100 second; $50 third for annual short story contest. Charge (discounted) for extras.

Advice: "The best way to discover what *TVBR* editors are seeking in fiction is to read at least a couple issues of the magazine. We are typical readers—we want to be grabbed by the first words of a story and rendered unable to put it down until we've read the last word of it. We want stories that we'll want to read again. This doesn't necessarily mean we seek stories that grab the reader via shock tactics; gross-out factors; surface titillation; or emotional manipulation. Good writers know the difference. Research the markets. Read good writing. Dig deep to find original and compelling narrative voices. It's amazing how many dozens and dozens of stories we receive sound/read so very much alike. We've noticed a marked increase in violent and/or socially ill/deviant-themed stories. Hmm. Is this art imitating life or life imitating art or is it just writers desperate to shock the reader into believing this now passes for originality? Incest stories have been done and done well, but that doesn't mean everyone should write one. Same goes for divorce, death-watch, I-killed-my-boss (spouse, etc.) and got-away-with-it stories."

☑ $ **VIRGINIA ADVERSARIA**, Empire Publishing Inc., P.O. Box 2349, Poquoson VA 23662. (757)868-6595. E-mail: empirepub@hotmail.com. **Contact:** Bill Glose, editor. Literary magazine: 7×10; 64 pages; some illustrations; photos. Quarterly. Estab. 2000. Circ. 2,500.
Needs: Adventure, ethnic/multicultural, family saga, historical, humor/satire, literary, mainstream, mystery/suspense, regional, romance, thriller/espionage. No erotica or horror. Would like more well-written humor. Receives 75 unsolicited mss/month. Accepts 10-15 mss/issue; 50-60 mss/year. Publishes ms 4-7 months after acceptance. **Publishes 12 new writers/year.** Recently published work by Isak Romun, John Broussard and Virginia O'Keefe. Length: up to 6,000 words; average length: 3,000 words. Publishes short shorts. Also publishes literary essays and poetry. Often comments on rejected mss.
How to Contact: Send complete ms with cover letter. Include estimated word count, brief bio and social security number. Responds in 1 month to queries and mss. Send SASE for return of ms. Accepts simultaneous, previously published and multiple submissions. Sample copy for $4.95. Guidelines for SASE.
Payment/Terms: Pays 1¢/word and 1 contributor's copy; additional copies for $3. Pays on publication for one-time rights. Sends galleys to author.
Advice: "We accept powerful and emotional pieces. If the manuscript doesn't make us laugh, cry or feel touched in some way, it won't stand out against the many other manuscripts we receive. Move us with your words and you stand a good chance of being published. Create strong characters and a plot that has purpose. Know where you're taking the reader instead of ambling to a weak ending."

◑ **WAR, LITERATURE & THE ARTS: An International Journal of the Humanities**, Dept. of English & Fine Arts, United States Air Force Academy, 2354 Fairchild Dr., Suite 6D45, USAF Academy CO 80840-6242. (719)333-3930. Fax: (719)333-3932. E-mail: donald.anderson@usafa.af.mil. Website: www.usafa.edu/dfeng/wla. **Contact:** Donald Anderson, editor. Magazine: 6×9; 200 pages; illustrations; photos. "*WLA* seeks artistic depictions of war from all periods and cultures. From time immemorial, war and art have reflected one another. It is the intersection of war and art that *WLA* seeks to illuminate." Semiannual. Estab. 1989. Circ. 500. Member, Council of Editors of Learned Journals, CLMP.
Needs: No fantasy, science fiction. Accepts 2 mss/issue; 4 mss/year. Publishes ms 1 year after acceptance. Agented fiction 50%. **Publishes 2 new writers/year.** Published work by Paul West, Philip Caputo, Robert Morgan and Philip Appleman. Publishes short shorts. Also publishes literary essays, literary criticism and poetry. Sometimes comments on rejected mss.
How to Contact: Send complete ms with a cover letter. Include brief bio and list of publications. Responds in 6 weeks to queries; 6 months to mss. Send a disposable copy of ms and #10 SASE for reply only. Accepts simultaneous submissions "if told." Sample copy for $5. Guidelines on website. Reviews novels, short story collections and nonfiction books of interest to writers. Send review copies to the editor.
Payment/Terms: Pays 2 contributor's copies; additional copies $5. Pays on publication for first North American serial and electronic rights. Sends galleys to author.
Advice: "Our only criterion is literary excellence and fresh language. Our current writer's guidelines are 'Make the world new.'"

❂ ☑ ◐ $ **WASCANA REVIEW OF CONTEMPORARY POETRY AND SHORT FICTION**, University of Regina, Regina, Saskatchewan S4S 0A2 Canada. (306)585-4302. Fax: (306)585-4827. E-mail: michael.trussler@uregina.ca. Website: www.uregina.ca/english/wrhome.htm (includes excerpts from publication, description of journal and its mandate). Editor: Dr. Kathleen Wall. **Contact:** Dr. Michael Trussler, fiction editor. "Literary criticism, fiction and poetry for readers of serious fiction." Semiannual. Estab. 1966. Circ. 500.
Needs: Literary and humor. "No fiction that's predictable, that lacks an original voice. Frankly, we're also tired of coming-of-age stories, particularly macho ones." Check website for upcoming themes. Buys 8-10 mss/year. Receives approximately 20 unsolicited fiction mss/month. Agented fiction 5%. **Publishes 2-3 new writers/year.** Length: 2,000-6,000 words. Occasionally recommends other markets.
How to Contact: Accepts queries by e-mail. Send complete ms with SASE. Responds in 2 months to mss. Publishes ms an average of 6 months after acceptance. Sample copy for $5. Guidelines with SASE.
Payment/Terms: Pays $3/page for prose; $10/page for poetry; 2 contributor's copies. Pays on publication for first North American rights.
Advice: "Stories we receive are often technically incompetent or deal with trite subjects. Usually stories are longer than necessary by about one-third. Be more ruthless in cutting back on unnecessary verbiage. All approaches to fiction are welcomed by the *Review* editors—but we continue to seek the best in terms of style and technical expertise. As our calls for submission state, the *Wascana Review* continues to seek "short fiction that combines craft with risk, pressure with grace.""

N **THE WASHINGTON REVIEW OF THE ARTS**, Friends of the Washington Review of the Arts, P.O. Box 50132, Washington DC 20091-0132. **Contact:** Jamie Brown, associate literary fiction editor. Literary magazine specializing in art and performance. Bimonthly.

Needs: Experimental, literary. "No pet stores, dead pet stories, true love, young, love or tales of recovery which have no point other than therapy for the author!" Receives 100-150 unsolicited mss/month. Accepts 1 mss/issue; 6-7 mss/year. Publishes ms 2-8 months after acceptance. **Publishes 2-3 new writers/year.** Publishes short shorts. Often comments on rejected mss.

How to Contact: Send complete ms with cover letter. Include estimated word count, brief bio, list of publications, hard copy on clean paper plus 3.5" floppy with Word Perfect 4.5 compatible formatting with submission. Send SASE for return of ms or disposable copy of ms and #10 SASE for reply only. Accepts simultaneous and multiple submissions.

Payment/Terms: Pays 2 contributor's copies. Pays on publication. Sponsors contest: annual awards for short story and best poetry to have appeared in the previous year.

Advice: "A sense of style that is not merely stylistic and a story which is important enough to be told to people other than family members. Keep your ego out of it."

✓ ☯ WASHINGTON SQUARE, Literary Review of New York University's Creative Writing Program, NYU Creative Writing Program, 19 University Place, 3rd Floor, Room 310, New York NY 10003-4556. (212)992-9685. Fax: (212)427-7285. E-mail: wsmgr@hotmail.com. Website: www.nyu.edu/gsas/program/cwp/wsr.htm (includes writer's guidelines, excerpts from recent issues, editor's names). **Contact:** Michelle Mortimer, fiction editor. Editors change each year. Magazine: 5½×8½; 144 pages; photographs. "*Washington Square* is the literary review produced by New York University's Graduate Creative Writing Program. We publish outstanding works of fiction and poetry by the students and faculty of NYU as well as the work of writers across the country." Semiannual. Estab. 1996 (we were previously called *Ark/Angel Review*, estab. 1987). Circ. 1,000. Member, CLMP.

Needs: Condensed/excerpted novel, ethnic/multicultural, experimental, humor, literary, mainstream/contemporary. No adventure, children's, erotica, horror, fantasy. Would like to see more contemporary, experimental, humor, short-shorts. Receives 75 unsolicited mss/month. Accepts 5 mss/issue; 10 mss/year. Publishes ms 3-5 months after acceptance. Agented fiction 20%. **Publishes 2 new writers/year.** Recently published work by Arthur Japin, Ron Carlson, Elizabeth Stuckey-French and Mark Jarman. Length: 7,000 words maximum; average length: 5,000 words. Publishes short shorts. Also publishes poetry. Sometimes comments on rejected mss.

How to Contact: Send complete ms with a cover letter. Include estimated word count (only put name on first page). Responds in 2 weeks to queries; up to 5 months to mss. Send SASE for reply, return of ms or send a disposable copy of ms. Accepts simultaneous submissions. Sample copy for $6.

Payment/Terms: Pays 3 contributor's copies and 2-year subscription; additional copies for $6. Acquires first North American serial rights. "Each fall we sponsor a short story contest. Send SASE for more info."

Advice: "We look for work that is polished and challenging; stories that, for whatever reason, stand out from other stories. We welcome and seek work that takes risks in both form and content, but the risk needs to be balanced with a careful attention to craft. Above all, send us stories that you're excited about."

M $ ☯ WEST COAST LINE, A Journal of Contemporary Writing & Criticism, 2027 E. Academic Annex, Simon Fraser University, Burnaby, British Columbia V5A 1S6 Canada. (604)291-4287. Fax: (604)291-4622. E-mail: wcl@sfu.ca. Website: www.sfu.ca/west-coast-line. **Contact:** Roger Farr, managing editor. Magazine: 6×9; 128-144 pages. "Poetry, fiction, criticism—modern and contemporary, North American, experimental, avant-garde, cross-cultural. Readers include academics, writers, students." Triannual. Estab. 1990. Circ. 600.

Needs: Experimental, ethnic/multicultural, feminist, gay, literary. "We do not publish journalistic writing or strictly representational narrative." Receives 30-40 unsolicited mss/month. Accepts 2-3 mss/issue; 3-6 mss/year. Publishes ms 2-10 months after acceptance. **Publishes 3 new writers/year.** Recently published work by Rita Wong, Bruce Andrews, Lisa Robertson, Dodie Bellemy and Dan Ferrell. Length: 3,000-4,000 words. Publishes short shorts. Length: 250-400 words. Also publishes literary essays and literary criticism.

How to Contact: Send complete ms with a cover letter. "We supply an information form for contributors." Responds in 3 months. Send SAE with IRCs, not US postage, for return of ms. No simultaneous submissions. Sample copy for $10. Guidelines free.

Payment/Terms: Pays $3-8/page (Canadian); subscription; 2 contributor copies; additional copies for $6-8/copy, depending on quantity ordered. Pays on publication for one-time rights.

Advice: "Special concern for contemporary writers who are experimenting with, or expanding the boundaries of conventional forms of poetry, fiction and criticism; also interested in criticism and scholarship on Canadian and American modernist writers who are important sources for current writing. We recommend that potential contributors send a letter of enquiry or read back issues before submitting a manuscript."

N ◯ **WEST WIND REVIEW**, 1250 Siskiyou Blvd., Ashland OR 97520. (503)552-6518. E-mail: westwind @tao.sou.edu. **Contact:** Dottie Lou Taylor, editor. Editors change each year. Magazine: 5¾×8½; 150-250 pages; illustrations; photos. "Literary journal publishing prose/poetry/art. Encourages new writers, accepts established writers as well, with an audience of people who like to read challenging fiction." Annual. Estab. 1980. Circ. 500.

Needs: Adventure, ethnic/multicultural, experimental, historical (general), humor/satire, literary, mainstream/ contemporary, mystery/suspense, regional, romance, senior citizen/retirement, sports, translations—"just about anything." No pornography. "Would like to see more fiction that flows from character rather than plot. Would like to see more fiction that takes stylistic risks." Receives 6-60 unsolicited mss/month. Accepts 15-20 mss/ issue. Publishes ms almost immediately after acceptance. **Publishes 5-10 new writers/year.** Recently published work by Virgil Suarez. Length: 3,000 words maximum. Publishes short shorts. Also publishes poetry. Sometimes comments on rejected ms.

How to Contact: Send complete ms with a cover letter. Include estimated word count and short bio. Responds by March 1 to mss. Send SASE for reply, return of ms or send a disposable copy of ms. No simultaneous submissions. For guidelines send SASE.

Payment/Terms: Accepted authors receive 1 free copy. Authors retain all rights.

Advice: "Good writing stands out. Content is important but style is essential. Clearly finished pieces with subtle action, reaction and transformation are what we like."

N ⊕ **$ WESTERLY**, English Dept., University of Western Australia, Crauley, 6009 Australia. 08 9380 2101. Fax: 08 9380 1030. E-mail: westerly@arts.uwa.edu.au. Website: www.arts.uwa.edu.au/westerly (includes details of current issue, past issues, forthcoming issues and information about subscribing and contributing). **Contact:** Monica Anderson, administrator. Annual. Circ. 1,000.

Needs: "An annual of poetry, prose and articles of a literary and cultural kind, giving special attention to Australia and Southeast Asia." No romance, children's, science fiction.

How to Contact: Accepts queries by e-mail.

Payment/Terms: Pays $40 (AUS) minimum and 1 contributor's copy. Sample copy for $8 (AUS) plus postage.

◯ **WESTVIEW, A Journal of Western Oklahoma**, Southwestern Oklahoma State University, 100 Campus Dr., Weatherford OK 73096-3098. (580)774-3168. Editor: Fred Alsberg. **Contact:** Fiction Editor. Magazine: 8½×11; 64 pages; 24 lb. paper; slick color cover; illustrations; photos. Semiannual. Estab. 1981. Circ. 400.

Needs: Contemporary, ethnic (especially Native American), humor, literary, prose poem. No pornography, violence, or gore. No overly sentimental. "We are particularly interested in writers of the Southwest; however, we accept work of quality from elsewhere." Receives 20 unsolicited mss/month. Accepts 5 mss/issue; 10 mss/year. Publishes ms 3-12 months after acceptance. Published work by Diane Glancy, Wendell Mayo, Jack Matthews and Mark Spencer. Length: 2,000 words average. Also publishes literary essays, literary criticism, poetry. Occasionally critiques rejected mss.

How to Contact: Accepts simultaneous submissions. Send complete ms with SASE. Responds in 2 months. "We welcome submissions on a 3.5 disk formatted for WordPerfect 5.0, IBM or Macintosh. Please include a hard copy printout of your submission."

Payment/Terms: Pays contributor's copy. Acquires first rights.

✔ ◯ **WHETSTONE**, Barrington Area Arts Council, P.O. Box 1266, Barrington IL 60011. (847)382-5626. **Contact:** Dale Griffith, editor. Magazine: 9×6; 130 pages; heavy cover stock. "We try to publish the best quality nonfiction, fiction and poetry for the educated reader." Annual. Estab. 1984. Circ. 700. Member, CLMP.

● *Whetstone* has received numerous Illinois Arts Council Awards.

Needs: Humor/satire, literary, mainstream/contemporary. "No genre, formula or plot driven fiction." Receives 100 unsolicited mss/month. Accepts 8-10 mss/year. Publishes ms by April 1 of the year following acceptance. Recently published work by Barbara Croft, Ann Joslin Will, James Reed, Leslie Pietzyk and Scott Blackwood. **Publishes 1-2 new writers/year.** Length: 3,000 words average; 6,000 words maximum. Also publishes poetry. Sometimes comments on rejected mss "depending on the work. We often write out the readers' responses if they are helpful. A work gets a minimum of two readers and up to four or five."

How to Contact Send complete ms with a cover letter. Include a 50-word bio. Responds 6 months on mss "or sooner depending on the time of the year." Send SASE for return of ms or reply only. Simultaneous submissions OK. Sample copy (including guidelines) for $5.

Payment/Terms: Pays a variable amount and 2 contributor's copies. Pays on publication for first North American serial rights. Sends galleys to author. "We frequently work with writers on their pieces. All works selected for publication are considered for the $500 Whetstone Prize and the $250 McGrath Award."

Advice: "We like strong characterization and a vivid use of language and, of course, a coherent plot. We like texture and a story which resonates. Read the journal and other small literary journals. Study good writing wherever you find it. Learn from editorial comments. Read. Read. Read, but do it as a writer reads."

N ◐ **WIND MAGAZINE**, P.O. Box 24548, Lexington KY 40524. (859)227-6849. E-mail: wind@wind.org. **Contact:** Chris Green, editor. Magazine: 6×9; 100 pages. "Eclectic literary journal with stories, poems, book reviews from small presses, essays. Readership is students, professors, housewives, literary folk, adults." Semiannually. Estab. 1971. Circ. 450.

Needs: Literary, mainstream/contemporary, translations. Accepts 2 fiction mss/issue; 6 mss/year. Publishes ms less than 1 year after acceptance. Recently published work by Normandi Ellis, Graham Shelby and B.Z. Niditch. Length: 9,000 words maximum. Publishes short shorts, length: 300-400 words. Also publishes literary essays, literary criticism and poetry. Sometimes comments on rejected mss.

How to Contact: Send complete ms with a cover letter. Include estimated word count and 50-word bio. No e-mail submissions accepted. Responds in 2 weeks to queries; 4 months to mss. Send SASE for reply, return of ms or send a disposable copy of ms. No simultaneous submissions. Sample copy for $4.50. Reviews novels and short story collections from small presses.

Payment/Terms: Pays 1 contributor's copy; additional copies for $3.50. Acquires first North American serial rights and anthology reprint rights.

Advice: "Successful fiction works as powerful language, dynamic characters and strong plot. It builds a world the reader keeps living within."

◻ **WINDHOVER: A Journal of Christian Literature**, University of Mary Hardin-Baylor, P.O. Box 8008, Belton TX 76513. (254)295-4564. E-mail: dwnixon@umhb.edu. Website: www.uclj.com (includes excerpts, writer's guidelines, names of editors). **Contact:** Donna Walker-Nixon, editor. Magazine: 6×9; white bond paper. "We want to publish literary fiction by writers of faith." Annual. Estab. 1997. Circ. 500.

Needs: Ethnic/multicultural (general), experimental, family saga, fantasy, historical (general), humor/satire, literary. "No erotica." Receives 30 unsolicited mss/month. Accepts 5 mss/issue; 5 mss/year. Publishes ms 1 year after acceptance. **Publishes 5 new writers/year.** Published work by Walt McDonald, James Schaap, Jeanne Murray Walker and David Hopes. Length: 1,500-4,000 words; average length: 3,000 words. Publishes short shorts. Average length: 150 words. Also publishes literary essays and poetry. Sometimes comments on rejected mss.

How to Contact: Send complete ms by e-mail to windhover2001@yahoo.com. Include estimated word count, brief bio and list of publications. Responds in 3 weeks to queries; 4 months to mss. Send SASE for return of ms or send a disposable copy of ms and #10 SASE for reply only. Accepts simultaneous submissions. Sample copy for $6. Guidelines by e-mail.

Payment/Terms: Pays 2 contributor's copies; additional copies $8. Pays on publication for first rights.

Advice: "Be patient. We have an editorial board and sometimes replies take longer than I like. We particularly look for convincing plot and character development."

N **■** **$**◐ **WINDSOR REVIEW, A Journal of the Arts**, Dept. of English, University of Windsor, Windsor, Ontario N9B 3P4 Canada. (519)253-3000, ext. 2332. Fax: (519)973-7050. E-mail: uwrevu@uwindsor.ca. Website: www.uwrevu@uwindsor.ca. Editor: Katherine Quinsey. **Contact:** Alistair MacLeod, fiction editor. Magazine/perfect bound book: 6×9; 110 pages; illustrations; photos. "We try to offer a balance of fiction and poetry distinguished by excellence." Semiannual. Estab. 1965. Circ. 250.

Needs: Literary. No genre fiction (science fiction, romance), "but would consider if writing is good enough." Publishes ms 6-9 months after acceptance. Accepts 1-4 unsolicited mss/issue. Publishes ms 6 months after acceptance. Recently published work by Rosemary Sullivan and Tom Wayman. Length: 1,000-5,000 words. Also publishes poetry. Sometimes comments on rejected mss.

How to Contact: Send complete ms with a cover letter. Accepts queries/mss by e-mail. Include estimated word count, bio, Social Security number and list of publications. Responds in 1 month to queries; 6 weeks to mss. Send SASE for reply, return of ms or send a disposable copy of ms. No simultaneous submissions. Sample copy for $7 (US). Guidelines free.

Payment/Terms: Pays $50 and 1 contributor's copy; additional copies available for $10. Pays on publication for one-time rights.

Advice: "Good writing, strong characters, experimentational fiction is appreciated."

☑ ◐ ▼ **WISCONSIN REVIEW**, University of Wisconsin, Box 158, Radford Hall, Oshkosh WI 54901. (920)424-2267. E-mail: wireview@yahoo.com. **Contact:** Andrew Osborne, senior editor. "The publication is for an adult contemporary audience. Fiction including fantastic imagery and fresh voices is published. We seek to publish quality not quantity." Magazine: 6×9; 60-100 pages; illustrations. Literary prose and poetry. Estab. 1966. Circ. 2,000.

• *Wisconsin Review* received the Pippistrelle Best of the Small Press Award #13.

Needs: Literary and experimental. Receives 30 unsolicited fiction mss each month. **Publishes 3 new writers/ year.** Recently published work by Brian Ames, Wendy Herbert, John Addiego and Silas Zobel. Length: up to 5,000 words. Publishes short shorts.

How to Contact: Send complete ms with SASE and cover letter with bio notes. Accepts simultaneous submissions. Responds in 6 months. Publishes ms an average of 1-3 months after acceptance. Sample copy for $4.
Payment/Terms: Pays 2 contributor's copies. Acquires first rights.
Advice: "We accept fiction that displays strong characterization, dialogue that provides pertinent information and transports the story, vivid imagery, and unique plots and themes."

THE WORCESTER REVIEW, Worcester Country Poetry Association, Inc., 6 Chatham St., Worcester MA 01609. (508)797-4770. Website: www.geocities.com/Paris/LeftBank/6433. Editor: Rodger Martin. **Contact:** Fiction Editor. Magazine: 6×9; 100 pages; 60 lb. white offset paper; 10 pt. CS1 cover stock; illustrations; photos. "We like high quality, creative poetry, artwork and fiction. Critical articles should be connected to New England." Annual. Estab. 1972. Circ. 1,000.
Needs: Literary, prose poem. "We encourage New England writers in the hopes we will publish at least 30% New England but want the other 70% to show the best of writing from across the US." Receives 20-30 unsolicited fiction mss/month. Accepts 2-4 mss/issue. Publishes ms an average of 6 months to 1 year after acceptance. Agented fiction less than 10%. Published work by Robert Pinsky, Marge Piercy, Wes McNoir and Deborah Diggeso. Length: 1,000-4,000 words; average length: 2,000 words. Publishes short shorts. Also publishes literary essays, literary criticism, poetry. Sometimes critiques rejected mss and recommends other markets.
How to Contact: Send complete ms with cover letter. Responds in 9 months to mss. SASE. Accepts simultaneous submissions if other markets are clearly identified. Sample copy for $6; guidelines free.
Payment/Terms: Pays 2 contributor's copies and honorarium if possible. Acquires one-time rights.
Advice: "Send only one short story—reading editors do not like to read two by the same author at the same time. We will use only one. We generally look for creative work with a blend of craftsmanship, insight and empathy. This does not exclude humor. We won't print work that is shoddy in any of these areas."

WORDS OF WISDOM, 8689 UNCG Station, Greensboro NC 27413-1031. (336)334-6970. E-mail: wowmail@hoopsmail.com. **Contact:** Mikhammad Abdel Ishara, editor. Associate Editor: Celestine Woo. Newsletter: 5½×8½; 72-88 pages; computer generated on copy paper; saddle-stapled with 40 lb. colored paper cover; some illustrations. "Fiction, satire/humor, poetry and travel for a general audience." Estab. 1981. Circ. 150-160.
Needs: Adventure, contemporary, ethnic, feminist, historical, humor/satire, literary, mainstream, mystery/suspense (cozy, private eye), regional, western. No religion, children's, gay or romance. Fall 2000 issue to feature travel stories in foreign lands. Receives 500-600 unsolicited mss/year. Accepts 67-75 mss/year. Publishes ms 2-6 months after acceptance. **Publishes 0-5 new writers/year.** Published work by Paul Agosto, Joyce S. Zaritsky, Toby Tucker Hecht, D.L. Nelson, Geoff Uark, Patricia Prime and Joseph S. Salemi. Length: 1,200-6,000 words; average length: 3,000 words. Publishes short shorts.
How to Contact: Cover letter required. "There are no automatons here, so don't treat us like machines. We may not recognize your name at the top of the manuscript. A few lines about yourself breaks the ice, the names of three or four magazines that have published you in the last year would show your reality, and a bio blurb of 37 +/- words including the names of two or three of the magazines you send the occasional subscription check (where you aspire to be?) could help. If you are not sending a check to some little magazine that is supported by subscriptions and the blood, sweat and tears of the editors, why would you send your manuscript to any of them and expect to receive a warm welcome? No requirement to subscribe or buy a sample, but they are available at $4 and encouraged. There are no phony contests and never a reading fee. Read all year long, but may take one to six months to respond." Seldom comments on rejections. Accepts simultaneous submissions but no reprints. Reviews short story collections.
Payment/Terms: Pays subscription to magazine for first story published. Acquires one-time rights. Publication not copyrighted.
Advice: "Stop watching TV and read that book of stories where your last manuscript appeared."

WRITING FOR OUR LIVES, Running Deer Press, 647 N. Santa Cruz Ave., Annex, Los Gatos CA 95030-4350. (408)354-8604. **Contact:** Janet M. McEwan, editor. Magazine: 5¼×8¼; 80 pages; 70 lb. recycled white paper; 80 lb. recycled cover. "*Writing For Our Lives* is a periodical which serves as a vessel for poems, short fiction, stories, letters, autobiographies, and journal excerpts from the life stories, experiences and spiritual journeys of women. Audience is women and friends of women." Annual. Estab. 1992. Circ. 600.
Needs: Ethnic/multicultural, experimental, feminist, humor/satire, lesbian, literary, translations, "autobiographical, breaking personal or historical silence on any concerns of women's lives. *Women writers only, please.* We have no preannounced themes." Receives 15-20 unsolicited mss/month. Accepts 10 mss/issue; 20 mss/year. Publishes ms 2-24 months after acceptance. **Publishes 3-5 new writers/year.** Recently published work by Sabah Akbar, Anjali Banerjee, Debra Kay Vest, Lisa M. Ortiz and Luci Yamamoto. Length: 2,100 words maximum. Publishes short shorts. Also publishes poetry. Rarely comments on rejected mss.

How to Contact: Send complete ms and bio with a cover letter. "Publication date is October. Closing date for mss is August 15. Initial report immediate; next report, if any, in 1-18 months." Send 2 SASE's for reply, and one of them must be sufficient for return of ms if desired. Accepts simultaneous, multiple and reprint submissions. Sample copy for $6-8 (in California add 8% sales tax), $9-11 overseas. Guidelines for #10 SASE.

Payment/Terms: Pays 2 contributor's copies; additional copies for 50% discount and 2 issue subscription at 50% discount. Acquires one-time rights in case of reprints and first worldwide English language serial rights.

Advice: "It is in our own personal stories that the real herstory of our time is told. This periodical is a place for exploring the boundaries of our empowerment to break long historical and personal silences. While honoring the writing which still needs to be held close to our hearts, we can begin to send some of our heartfelt words out into a wider circle."

⊘ WV, The magazine of Emerging Writers, The Writers Voice of the West Side YMCA, 5 W. 63rd St., New York NY 10023. (212)875-4124. E-mail: wswritersvoice@ymcanyc.org. Website: www.ymcanyc.org (includes full information about our workshops, readings, contests, magazine). Magazine: 8½×11; 64 pages; coated paper; glossy cover; illustrations. "*WV* is for writers who are coming into their own. We specifically look for writers who are on the cusp of publishing and also look for non-mainstream writers doing outstanding work." Semiannual. Estab. 1998. Circ. 1,000. Member, CLMP.

• *WV* is currently on hiatus and will not be accepting any submissions.

Needs: Comics/graphic novels, erotica, experimental, feminist, gay, lesbian, literary. Receives 30 unsolicited mss/month. Accepts 10-12 mss/issue; 20-25 mss/year. Publishes ms 2-6 months after acceptance. **Publishes 15-20 new writers/year.** Recently published work by Gerry Gomez Pearlberg, Caroline Koeppel and Essence Mason. Length: 5,000 words maximum; average length: 3,000-5,000 words. Publishes short shorts. Average length: 500-1,000 words. Also publishes poetry. Sometimes comments on rejected mss.

How to Contact: Sample copy for $5. Guidelines for SASE, by e-mail or on website.

Payment/Terms: Pays 5 contributor's copies and free subscription to the magazine. Pays on publication for one-time rights. Not copyrighted. Sponsors contest. "The Writer's Voice awards are part of our literary arts center. Award winners may be considered for *WV*."

Advice: "We are seeing pieces that straddle the line between fiction and memoir—usually not successfully. Please seriously consider what genre a piece is, and work to the requirements of that form."

⊘ XAVIER REVIEW, Xavier University, 1 Drexel Dr., New Orleans LA 70125-1098. (504)485-7944. Fax: (504)485-7197. E-mail: rnlcoll@bellsouth.net (correspondence only—no mss). **Contact:** Thomas Bonner, Jr., editor. Managing Editor: Robert E. Skinner. Associate Editor: Richard Collins. Assistant Editor: Patrice Melnick. Production Consultant: Mark Whitaker. Magazine: 6×9; 75 pages; 50 lb. paper; 12 pt. CS1 cover; photographs. Magazine of "poetry/fiction/nonfiction/reviews (contemporary literature) for professional writers/libraries/colleges/universities." Semiannual. Estab. 1980. Circ. 500.

Needs: Contemporary, ethnic, experimental, historical (general), literary, Latin American, prose poem, Southern, religious, serialized/excerpted novel, translations. Receives 100 unsolicited fiction mss/month. Accepts 2 mss/issue; 4 mss/year. Does not read mss during the summer months. **Publishes 2-3 new writers/year.** Published work by Randall Ivey, Rita Porteau, John Goldfine and Christine Wiltz. Length: 10-15 pages. Publishes literary criticism, literary essays, books of creative writing and poetry. Occasionally critiques rejected mss.

How to Contact: Send complete ms. Include 2-3 sentence bio. SASE. Responds in 10 weeks. Sample copy for $5.

Payment/Terms: Pays 2 contributor's copies.

$ ⊘ THE YALE REVIEW, Yale University/Blackwell Publishers Inc., P.O. Box 208243, New Haven CT 06520-8243. (203)432-0499. Fax: (203)432-0510. Editor: J.D. McClatchy. **Contact:** Susan Bianconi, fiction editor. Magazine: 9¼×6; 180-190 pages; book stock paper; glossy cover; illustrations; photos. "*The Yale Review* is meant for the well-read general reader interested in a variety of topics in the arts and letters, in history, and in current affairs." Quarterly. Estab. 1911. Circ. 7,000.

Needs: Mainstream/contemporary. Receives 80-100 unsolicited mss/month. Accepts 1-3 mss/issue; 7-12 mss/year. Publishes ms 3 months after acceptance. Agented fiction 25%. Published work by Steven Millhauser, Deborah Eisenberg, Jeffrey Eugenides, Sheila Kohler, Joe Ashby Porter, Julie Orringer, John Barth and James McCourt. Publishes short shorts (but not frequently). Also publishes literary essays, poetry.

How to Contact: Send complete ms with a cover letter. Include estimated word count and list of publications. Responds in 1 month to queries; 2 months to mss. Send SASE for reply, return of ms or send a disposable copy of ms. Always include SASE. No simultaneous submissions. Reviews novels and short story collections. Send books to the editors.

Payment/Terms: Pays $300-400 and 2 contributor's copies; additional copies for $8.50. Pays on publication. Sends galleys to author. "Awards by the editors; cannot be applied for."

Advice: "We find that the most accomplished young writers seem to be people who keep their ears open to other voices; who read widely."

☑ ◨ ▼ **YEMASSEE, The literary journal of the University of South Carolina**, Department of English, University of South Carolina, Columbia SC 29208. (803)777-2085. Fax: (803)777-9064. E-mail: yemassee@gwm.sc.edu. Website: www.cla.sc.edu/ENGL/yemassee/index.htm (includes cover of latest issue, origin of name and subscription info). **Contact:** Corinna McLeod, editor. Magazine: 5½ × 8½; 60-80 pages; 60 lb. natural paper; 65 lb. cover; cover illustration. "We are open to a variety of subjects and writing styles. *Yemassee* publishes primarily fiction and poetry, but we are also interested in one-act plays, brief excerpts of novels, essays, reviews and interviews with literary figures. Our essential consideration for acceptance is the quality of the work." Semiannual. Estab. 1993. Circ. 375.

● Stories from *Yemassee* have been selected for publication in *Best New Stories of the South*.

Needs: Condensed/excerpted novel, ethnic/multicultural, experimental, feminist, gay, historical, humor/satire, lesbian, literary, regional. No romance, religious/inspirational, young adult/teen, children's/juvenile, erotica. Wants more experimental. Receives 30 unsolicited mss/month. Accepts 1-3 mss/issue; 2-6 mss/year. "We hold manuscripts until our reading periods—October 1 to November 15 and March 15 to April 30." Publishes ms 2-4 months after acceptance. **Publishes 6 new writers/year.** Published work by Robert Coover, Chris Railey, Virgil Suarez, Susan Ludvigson and Kwame Dawes. Length: 4,000 words or less. Publishes short shorts. Also publishes literary essays and poetry.

How to Contact: Send complete ms with a cover letter. Include estimated word count, brief bio, Social Security number and list of publications. Responds in 2 weeks to queries, 4 months after deadlines to mss. Send SASE for reply, return of ms or send disposable copy of ms. Accepts simultaneous submissions. Sample copy for $5. Guidelines for #10 SASE.

Payment/Terms: Pays 2 contributor's copies; additional copies $3. All submissions are considered for the *Yemassee* awards—$200 each for the best poetry and fiction in each issue when funding permits. Acquires first rights

Advice: "Our criteria are based on what we perceive as quality. Generally that is work that is literary. We are interested in subtlety and originality, interesting or beautiful language; craft and precision. Read more, write more and revise more. Read our journal and any other journal before you submit to see if your work seems appropriate. Send for guidelines and make sure you follow them."

☑ ◎ **ZAUM, the literary review of Sonoma State University**, Sonoma State University/English Department, 1801 E. Cotati Ave., Rohnert Park CA 94928. E-mail: gillian.Conoley@sonoma.edu. Website: www.sonoma.edu/English/Zaum. **Contact:** Gillian Conoley, faculty advisor. Magazine: perfect bound. "Our journal concentrates on undergraduate and graduate writing that pushes traditional boundaries, is well-crafted, leaning towards avant-garde. All writers must be enrolled as a graduate or undergraduate student at the time of submission." Annual. Estab. 1996. Circ. 500.

Needs: Erotica, experimental, slice-of-life vignettes. No religious work. Accepts 5-7 mss/issue. Publishes ms 6-8 months after acceptance. Length: 2,500 words maximum.

How to Contact: Send complete ms with a cover letter. Accepts submissions by e-mail. Include brief bio. Responds in 2 weeks to queries; 3 months to mss. Guidelines for #10 SASE.

Payment/Terms: Pays 1 contributor's copy. Pays on publication for first North American serial rights.

☑ $ ◨ ▼ **ZOETROPE: All-Story**, AZX Publications, 1350 Avenue of the Americas, 24th Floor, New York NY 10019. (212)708-0400. Fax: (212)708-0475. E-mail: info@all-story.com. Website: www.all-story.com (includes information on short story contests, online writer's workshop, upcoming events, etc.) **Contact:** Adrienne Brodeur, editor-in-chief. Magazine: 10½ × 14; 60 pages; illustrations; photos. Quarterly. "Winner of the 2001 National Magazine Award for Fiction, *Zoetrope: All-Story* presents a new generation of classic stories. Inspired by the Coppala heritage of independence and creativity, the magazine is at once innovative and deeply traditional. It explores the intersection of fiction and film and anticipates some of its stories becoming memorable films." Estab. 1997. Circ. 40,000.

● Library Journal named *Zoetrope: All-Story* one of the ten best new magazines. Stories from *Zoetrope* have received the O. Henry Prize, the Pushcart Prize and have been reprinted in *New Stories from the South* and received honorable mentions in *Best American Short Stories*. *Zoetrope: All-Story* was ranked #2 on the *Writer's Digest*'s "Fiction 50" list of top markets for fiction writers.

Needs: Literary, mainstream/contemporary, one act plays. No genre fiction or excerpts from larger works. Receives 500 unsolicited mss/month. Accepts 5-7 mss/issue; 32-40 mss/year. Publishes ms approximately 6 months after acceptance. Agented fiction 15%. **Publishes 4-6 new writers/year.** Recently published work by Melissa Bank, Rick Moody, Stacey Richter, Robert Olen Butler and David Schickler.

How to Contact: Send complete manuscript (no more than 2) with a cover letter. Accepts queries by mail. Include estimated word count and list of publications. Accepts simultaneous submissions. Sample copy for $5.95 and 9×12 SAE and $1.70 postage. Guidelines for #10 SASE. *No unsolicited submissions from June 1-August 31.*

Payment/Terms: Pays $1,500 for first serial rights and 2 year option on movie rights for unsolicited submissions; $5,000 for commissioned works. Sponsors contest.

Advice: "We like fiction that really tells a full story. Voices that we haven't heard before and solid prose help a story stand out."

☑ $◨ ◎ ▼ **ZYZZYVA, the last word: west coast writers & artists**, POB 590069, San Francisco CA 94159-0069. (415)752-4393. Fax: (415)752-4391. E-mail: editor@zyzzyva.org. Website: www.zyzzyva.org (includes guidelines, names of editors, selections from current issues, editor's note). **Contact:** Howard Junker, editor. Magazine: 6×9; 208 pages; graphics; photos. "Literate" magazine featuring West Coast writers and artists. Triquarterly. Estab. 1985. Circ. 4,000.

● *ZYZZYVA* ranked #21 on *Writer's Digest*'s "Fiction 50" list of top markets for fiction writers.

Needs: Contemporary, experimental, literary, prose poem. West Coast US writers only. Receives 400 unsolicited mss/month. Accepts 8 fiction mss/issue; 24 mss/year. Agented fiction: 10%. **Publishes 20 new writers/year.** Recently published work by Robert Glück, Joy Harjo and F.X. Toole. Length: varies. Also publishes literary essays.

How to Contact: Send complete ms. "Cover letters are of minimal importance." Accepts submissions by e-mail and disk. Responds in 2 weeks to mss. SASE. No simultaneous or reprint submissions. Sample copy for $6. Guidelines on masthead page.

Payment/Terms: Pays $50. Pays on acceptance for first North American serial rights.

Advice: "Keep the faith."

Small Circulation Magazines

This section of *Novel & Short Story Writer's Market* contains general interest, special interest, regional and genre magazines with circulations of under 10,000. Although these magazines vary greatly in size, theme, format and management, the editors are all looking for short stories. Their specific fiction needs present writers of all degrees of expertise and interests with an abundance of publishing opportunities.

Although not as high-paying as the large-circulation consumer magazines, you'll find some of the publications listed here do pay writers 1-5¢/word or more. Also, unlike the big consumer magazines, these markets are very open to new writers and relatively easy to break into. Their only criteria is that your story be well written, well presented, and suitable for their particular readership.

DIVERSITY IN OPPORTUNITY

Among the diverse publications in this section are magazines devoted to almost every topic, every level of writing and every type of writer. Some of the markets listed here publish fiction about a particular geographic area or by authors who live in that locale. Even more specialized editorial needs than genre and regional fiction include *Moxie* and *Italian Americana*.

SELECTING THE RIGHT MARKET

First, zero in on those markets most likely to be interested in your work. If you write genre fiction, check out specific sections for lists of magazines publishing in that genre (mystery, page 91; romance, page 105; science fiction/fantasy & horror, page 121). For other types of fiction, begin by looking at the Category Index starting on page 618. If your work is more general—or conversely, very specialized—you may wish to browse through the listings, perhaps looking up those magazines published in your state or region. Also check the Zine and Online Markets sections for other specialized and genre publications.

In addition to browsing through the listings and using the Category Index, check the ranking codes at the beginning of listings to find those most likely to be receptive to your work. This is especially true for beginning writers, who should look for magazines that say they are especially open to new writers (☐) and for those giving equal weight to both new and established writers (◙). For more explanation about these codes, see the inside front and back covers of this book.

Once you have a list of magazines you might like to try, read their listings carefully. Much of the material within each listing carries clues that tell you more about the magazine. The "Quick Start" Guide to Publishing Your Fiction starting on page 2 describes in detail the listing information common to all the markets in our book.

The physical description appearing near the beginning of the listings can give you clues about the size and financial commitment to the publication. This is not always an indication of quality, but chances are a publication with expensive paper and four-color artwork on the cover has more prestige than a photocopied publication featuring a clip art self-cover. For more information on some of the paper, binding and printing terms used in these descriptions, see Printing and Production Terms Defined on page 613.

FURTHERING YOUR SEARCH

It cannot be stressed enough that reading the listing is only the first part of developing your marketing plan. The second part, equally important, is to obtain fiction guidelines and read the actual magazine. Reading copies of a magazine helps you determine the fine points of the magazine's publishing style and philosophy. There is no substitute for this type of hands-on research.

Unlike commercial magazines available at most newsstands and bookstores, it requires a little more effort to obtain some of the magazines listed here. You may need to send for a sample copy. We include sample copy prices in the listings whenever possible. See The Business of Fiction Writing on page 70 for the specific mechanics of manuscript submission. Above all, editors appreciate a professional presentation. Include a brief cover letter and send a self-addressed envelope for a reply or a self-addressed envelope in a size large enough to accommodate your manuscript, if you would like it returned. Be sure to include enough stamps or International Reply Coupons (for replies from countries other than your own) to cover your manuscript's return. Many publishers today appreciate receiving a disposable manuscript, eliminating the cost to writers of return postage and saving editors the effort of repackaging manuscripts for return.

Most of the magazines listed here are published in the US. You will also find some English-speaking markets from around the world. These foreign publications are denoted with a ⊕ symbol at the beginning of listings. To make it easier to find Canadian markets, we include a ⬛ symbol at the start of those listings.

N ⊕ ⬒ ⬔ ⬛ ALBEDO ONE, The Irish Magazine of Science Fiction, Fantasy and Horror, Albedo One, 2 Post Rd., Lusk, Co Dublin Ireland. Phone: (+353)1-8730177. E-mail: bobn@eircom.net. Website: www.yellowbrickroad.ie/albedo. **Contact:** Editor, *Albedo One*. Magazine: A4; 44 pages. "We hope to publish interesting and unusual fiction by new and established writers. We will consider anything, as long as it is well-written and entertaining, though our definitions of both may not be exactly mainstream. We like stories with plot and characters that live on the page. Most of our audience are probably committed genre fans, but we try to appeal to a broad spectrum of readers—the narrow focus of our readership is due to the public-at-large's unwillingness to experiment with their reading/magazine purchasing rather than any desire on our part to be exclusive." Triannual. Estab. 1993. Circ. 900.

● Albedo One was awarded European SF magazine of the year, 1997; European small press of the year, 1997; and European SF publisher of the year, 1999.

Needs: Comics/graphic novels, experimental, fantasy, horror, literary, science fiction. Receives more than 20 unsolicited mss/month. Accepts 15-18 mss/year. Publishes ms 1 year after acceptance. **Publishes 4 new writers/ year.** Length: 2,000-5,000 words; average length: 4,000 words. Also publishes literary criticism. Sometimes comments on rejected mss.

How to Contact: Send complete ms with a cover letter. Accepts submissions by fax and disk. Responds in 4 months to mss. Send a disposable copy of ms and #10 SASE for reply only. Sample copy for $9. Guidelines available by e-mail or on website. Reviews novels, short story collections and nonfiction books of interest to writers.

Payment/Terms: Pays 1 contributor's copy; additional copies £3.25 plus p&p. Pays on publication for first rights.

Advice: "We look for good writing, good plot, good characters. Read the magazine, and don't give up."

⬛ ◯ ALEMBIC, Singularity Rising Press, P.O. Box 28416, Philadelphia PA 19149. (215)743-4927. E-mail: alembic33@aol.com. **Contact:** Larry Farrell, editor. Magazine: 8½×11; 64 pages; bond paper; illustrations. "*Alembic* is a literary endeavor magically bordering intersecting continua." The magazine publishes poems, stories and art. Quarterly. Estab. 1999. Circ. 100.

Needs: Fantasy (space fantasy, sword and sorcery), horror (dark fantasy, futuristic, psychological, supernatural), literary, mystery/suspense (amateur sleuth, cozy, police procedural, private eye/hardboiled), science fiction (hard science/technological, soft/sociological), thriller/espionage. No children's, religious, romance. Would like to see more mystery. Receives 15 unsolicited mss/month. Accepts 6 mss/issue; 24 mss/year. Publishes ms 9-18 months after acceptance. **Publishes 15 new writers/year.** Recently published work by William S. Frankl and Bill Glose. Length: 1,000-5,000 words; average length: 3,000 words. Publishes short shorts. Average length: 1,000 words. Also publishes poetry. Often comments on rejected mss if requested.

How to Contact: Send complete ms with a cover letter. Include estimated word count, brief bio and list of publications. Responds in up to 6 months to mss. Accepts multiple submissions. Sample copy for $5. Guidelines for SASE or by e-mail. Reviews novels, short story collections and nonfiction books of interest to writers.

Payment/Terms: Pays 1 contributor's copy; additional copies $3.50. Pays on publication for first North American serial rights. Sends galleys to author. Not copyrighted. Sponsors contest. Send for guidelines.

Advice: "Fiction we publish has to grab me and make me care what will or won't happen to the characters. Write, rewrite and rewrite again. After all that, keep on submitting. A rejection never killed anyone."

☑ ◪ **ANTHOLOGY**, P.O. Box 4411, Mesa AZ 85211-4411. (480)461-8200. E-mail: lisa@anthologymagazi ne.com. Website: www.anthologymagazine.com (includes guidelines and links to literary sites). **Contact:** Elissa Harris, prose editor. Magazine: 8½×11; 20-28 pages; 20 lb. paper; 60-100 lb. cover stock; illustrations; photos. "Our intended audience is anyone who likes to read good fiction." Bimonthly. Estab. 1994. Circ. 500-1,000.
Needs: Adventure, children's/juvenile (5-9 and 10-12 years); fantasy (science fantasy, sword and sorcery), humor/satire, literary, mystery/suspense (amateur sleuth, police procedural, private eye/hardboiled), science fiction (hard science, soft/sociological). No erotica or graphic horror. Receives 20-30 unsolicited mss/month. Accepts 2-3 mss/issue; 12-18 mss/year. Publishes ms 6-12 months after acceptance. **Publishes 8-10 new writers/year.** Recently published work by Elisha Porat, Kent Robinson and Sarah Mlynowski. Length: 3,000-6,000 words average. Publishes short shorts. Also publishes poetry.
How to Contact: Send complete ms with a cover letter. Include estimated word count. Responds in 1 month to queries; 2 months to mss. Send SASE for reply, return of ms or send disposable copy of ms. Accepts simultaneous submissions. Sample copy for $3.95. Guidelines for 4½×9½ SASE. Reviews chapbooks and audio books.
Payment/Terms: Pays 1 contributor's copy; additional copies $2. Acquires one-time rights.
Advice: "Is there passion in the writing? Is there forethought? Will the story make an emotional connection to the reader? Send for guidelines and a sample issue. If you see that your work would not only fit into, but add something to *Anthology*, then send it."

$ ◪ **ARCHAEOLOGY**, P.O. Box 1264, Huntington WV 25714. **Contact:** fiction editor. Magazine: 8½×11; 24 pages; illustrations; photos. Authors are "archaeology writers who have a message for children and young adults." Quarterly. Estab. 1993. Circ. 10,000.
Needs: Children's/juvenile (adventure, historical, mystery, preschool, series), historical, mystery/suspense (procedural), young adult/teen (adventure, historical, mystery/suspense, series, western), archaeology. No science fiction. Receives 25 unsolicited mss/month. Accepts 1-2 mss/issue; 12-16 mss/year. Publishes ms 1-3 months after acceptance. Published work by Linda Lyons and Rocky Nivison. Length: 500 words minimum. Also publishes literary essays, criticism and poetry. Always comments on rejected ms.
How to Contact: Send complete ms with a cover letter. Include estimated word count, bio and list of publications. Responds in 1 month to queries; 2 months to mss. Send SASE for reply, return of ms or send disposable copy of ms. Accepts simultaneous, multiple and reprint submissions. Sample copy for $10. Guidelines free.
Payment/Terms: Pays 2-5¢/word maximum and 2 contributor's copies. Pays on acceptance for first rights. Sends prepublication galleys to author.
Advice: "Guidelines are the best reference to knowing if a manuscript or filler is acceptable for a magazine. Writers' time and resources can be saved by submitting their work to publications that need their style of writing. Guidelines for *Archaeology* are sent for a SASE."

$ ◪ ◩ **ARTEMIS MAGAZINE, Science and Fiction for a Space-Faring Age**, 1380 East 17th St., Suite 201, Brooklyn NY 11230-6011. E-mail: magazine@lrcpubs.com. Website: www.lrcpublications.com (includes writer's guidelines, names of editors, reviews, author information, letters, news, etc.). **Contact:** Ian Randal Strock, editor. Magazine: 8½×11; 64 pages; glossy cover; illustrations. "The magazine is an even mix of science and fiction. We are a proud sponsor of the Artemis Project, which is constructing a commercial, manned moon base. We publish science articles for the intelligent layman, and near-term, near-Earth hard science fiction stories." Quarterly. Estab. 1999.
    ● Short stories published in *Artemis* have been nominated for Hugo and Nebula awards, and have been named to the Year's Best Science Fiction 6.
Needs: Adventure, science fiction, thriller/espionage. No fantasy, inspirational. Receives 200 unsolicited mss/month. Accepts 4-7 mss/issue. Publishes ms 3-12 months after acceptance. **Publishes 4 new writers/year.** Recently published work by Joseph J. Lazzaro, Fred Lerner, Ron Collins, Linda Dunn, Stanley Schmidt and Jack Williamson. Length: 1-15,000 words; average length: 2,000-8,000 words. Publishes short shorts. Also publishes poetry. Often comments on rejected ms.
How to Contact: Send complete ms with a cover letter. Include estimated word count, 1-3-paragraph bio, Social Security number, list of publications. Responds in 1 month to mss. Send SASE for reply, return of ms or send a disposable copy of ms. Sample copy for $5 and a 9×12 SAE with 4 first-class stamps. Guidelines for SASE. Reviews novels, short story collections and nonfiction books of interest to writers and readers. Send books to editor.
Payment/Terms: Pays 3-5¢/word and 3 contributor's copies. Pays on acceptance for first rights. Sends prepublication galleys to author.
Advice: "Write the best possible story you can. Read a lot of fiction that you like, and reread it a few times (if it doesn't hold up to rereading, it might not be so great. And don't give me any rip-offs of current television shows, video or role-playing games, or movies.) Then go over your story again, and make it even better. Remember that neatness counts when you prepare your manuscript (also, knowledge of the English language and grammar, and the concepts of fiction). Then send it to the magazine that publishes fiction most like the story you've written.

Remember that you're up against many hundreds of manuscripts for a very few slots in the magazine. Make your story absolutely fantastic. In my case, a science fiction story must contain both science and fiction. Remember that, to be interesting to the reader, your story will probably be about the most important moment or event in the character's life."

$ ⬚ ◎ ⬚ **THE BARK, The Modern Dog Culture Magazine**, The Bark, Inc., 2810 Eighth, Berkeley CA 94710. (510)704-0827. Fax: (510)704-0933. E-mail: editor@thebark.com. Website: www.thebark.com. **Contact:** Claudia Kawczynska, editor-in-chief. Magazine: 8×10; 88 pages; matte gloss paper; illustrations; photos. "We are the only cultural/literary arts publication for the modern dog lover. We explore the unique bond between ourselves and our dogs." Quarterly. Estab. 1997. Circ. 75,000. Member, IPA.
  ● *The Bark* has received an *Utne Reader* Alternative Press award in lifestyle coverage.
Needs: Adventure, children's/juvenile (adventure, animal), comics/graphic novels, feminist, gay, humor/satire, literary, short story collections. Would like to see more fiction which deals with "dogs as an archetype—not breed-specific." Receives 15 unsolicited mss/month. Publishes ms 6 months after acceptance. **Publishes 10 new writers/year.** Recently published work by Ann Patchett, Rick Bass and Maeve Brennan. Length: 500-2,000 words; average length: 1,200 words. Publishes short shorts. Also publishes literary essays and poetry.
How to Contact: Query with clips of published work. Include estimated word count, brief bio, Social Security number and list of publications. Responds in 6 months to queries and mss. Send a disposable copy of ms and #10 SASE for reply only. Accepts simultaneous submissions, previously published work and multiple submissions. Sample copy for $5. Guidelines for SASE or by e-mail. Reviews novels, short story collections and nonfiction books of interest to writers.
Payment/Terms: Compensation varies by word count. Also pays free subscription to the magazine and contributor's copies. Pays on publication for first rights.

$ ⬚ **BASEBALL**, P.O. Box 1264, Huntington WV 25714. Magazine: 8½×11; illustrations; photos. Quarterly. Estab. 1998. Circ. 10,000.
Needs: Children's/juvenile (sports), young adult/teen (sports), baseball. No pornography or violence. Would like to see more history. **Publishes 12 new writers/year.** Length: 500 words minimum. Also publishes literary essays, criticism and poetry. Often comments on rejected ms.
How to Contact: Send complete ms with a cover letter. Include estimated word count, bio and list of publications. Responds in 1 month to queries; 2 months to mss. Send SASE for reply, return of ms or send disposable copy of ms. Accepts simultaneous and reprint submissions. Sample copy for $10. Guidelines free.
Payment/Terms: Pays 2-5¢/word maximum and contributor's copies. Pays on acceptance for first rights. Sends prepublication galleys to author.

☑ **BEGINNINGS, A Magazine for the Novice Writer**, Beginnings Publishing, P.O. Box 92-N, Shirley NY 11967. (614)924-7824. E-mail: scbeginnings@juno.com. Website: www.scbeginnings.com (includes guidelines, subscriptions, reader's reviews, bulletin board for posting work for critiquing). **Contact:** Jenine Boisits, editor. Magazine: 8½×11; 54 pages; matte; glossy cover; some photos. "We are a magazine dedicated to the novice writer. We only publish work by beginners. We do accept articles by professionals pertaining to the craft of writing. We have had many new writers go on to be published elsewhere after being featured in our magazine." Semiannual. Estab. 1998. Circ. 1,000.
Needs: Adventure, family saga, mystery/suspense (amateur sleuth), romance (contemporary), science fiction (soft/sociological). No erotica or horror. Receives 125 unsolicited mss/month. Accepts 9 mss/issue; 18-20 mss/year. Publishes ms 3-4 months after acceptance. **Publishes 100% new writers/year.** Recently published work by Ann F. Shalaski, Patricia Woo, Lois Peterson. Length: 3,000 words; average length: 2,500. Publishes short shorts. Average length: 900 words. Also publishes poetry. Often comments on rejected mss.
How to Contact: Send complete ms with cover letter. Accepts submissions by e-mail. Include estimated word count and brief bio. Responds in 6 weeks to mss. Send disposable copy of ms and #10 SASE for reply only; however, will accept SASE for return of ms. Accepts simultaneous submissions and previously published submissions. Sample copy for $4. Guidelines for SASE, e-mail or on website.
Payment/Terms: Pays 1 contributor's copy; additional copies $3. Pays on publication for first North American serial rights.

READ "THE BUSINESS OF FICTION WRITING" section for information on manuscript preparation, mailing tips, rights and more.

Advice: "Originality, presentation, proper grammar and spelling a must. Non-predictable endings. Many new writers confuse showing vs. telling. Writers who have that mastered stand out. Study the magazine. Check and double check your work. Original storylines, well thought-out, keep up a good pace. Presentation is important, too! Rewrite, rewrite!"

$ ◑ ⓨ BOY'S QUEST, The Bluffton News Publishing & Printing Co., P.O. Box 227, Bluffton OH 45817-0227. (419)358-4610. Fax: (419)358-5027. Website: www.boysquest.com (includes samples of magazine content, order form). **Contact:** Marilyn Edwards, editor. Magazine: 7×9; 50 pages; enamel paper; illustrations; photos. "Magazine for boys 5-13, wholesome, encouraging kindness, helping others, etc." Bimonthly. Estab. 1994.

• *Boy's Quest* received an EDPRESS Distinguished Achievement Award for Excellence in Educational Journalism, and a Silver Award-Gallery of Superb Printing.

Needs: Children's/juvenile (5-9 years, 10-13 years) adventure, ethnic/multicultural, historical, sports. No violence, romance, fads. "We would like to see more wholesome adventure and humorous stories." Upcoming themes: disasters, achievers, racing, water, inventions, bugs, horses, space, flying, boats, and turtles, snakes. List of upcoming themes available for SASE. Receives 300-400 unsolicited mss/month. Accepts 20-40 mss/year. Agented fiction 2%. **Publishes 40 new writers/year.** Recently published work by Eve Marar, John Hillman, Marcie Tichenor, John Thomas Waite, Carolyn Mott Ford and Robert Redding. Length: 500 words maximum; average length: 300-500 words. Publishes short shorts. Length: 250-400 words. Also publishes poetry. Always comments on rejected mss.

How to Contact: Send complete ms with a cover letter. Include estimated word count, 1 page bio, Social Security number, list of publications. Responds in 2-4 weeks to queries; 6-10 weeks to mss. Accepts simultaneous, multiple and reprint submissions. Sample copy for $4. Guidelines for #10 SASE. Reviews novels and short story collections.

Payment/Terms: Pays 5¢/word and 1 contributor's copy; additional copies $4, $2.50 for 10 or more. Pays on publication for first North American serial rights.

◑ $ BRAIN, CHILD, The Magazine for Thinking Mothers, March Press, P.O. Box 1161, Harrisonburg VA 22801. (540)574-2379. E-mail: editor@brainchildmag.com. Website: www.brainchildmag.com (includes excerpts, guidelines, mission statement, editorial staff info, subscription info). **Contact:** Jennifer Niesslein and Stephanie Wilkinson, co-editors. Magazine: 7¾×10; 60-100 pages; 80 lb matte cover; illustrations; photos. "*Brain, Child* is a new quarterly magazine spotlighting women's own experience of motherhood. Instead of focusing on childrearing tips and techniques, like most parenting publications, our writers explore the more personal transformations that motherhood brings. Each issue is packed with essays, in-depth features, humor, reviews, news and fiction, plus superb art, photography, cartoons and more." Quarterly. Estab. 2000. Circ. 8,000. Member, IPA.

• *Brain, Child* was nominated for *Utne Reader*'s "Best of the Alternative Press" award in 2000

Needs: Literary, mainstream. Receives less than 20 unsolicited mss/month. Accepts 1 ms/issue; 4 mss/year. Publishes ms 6 months after acceptance. Recently published work by Anne Tyler, Barbara Lucy Stevens and Jane Smiley. Length: 1,000-5,000 words; average length: 2,500 words. Will consider short shorts but prefer longer pieces. Also publishes literary essays. Sometimes comments on rejected mss.

How to Contact: Send complete ms with a cover letter. Accepts submissions by e-mail (be sure to copy and paste the ms into the body of the e-mail). Include estimated word count, brief bio and list of publications. Responds in 6 weeks to queries; 10 weeks to mss. Send SASE (or IRC) for return of ms or send a disposable copy of ms and #10 SASE for reply only. Accepts previously published work and multiple submissions (no more than 2 at once). Sample copy for $5. Guidelines for SASE or on website. Reviews novels, short story collections and nonfiction books of interest to mothers.

Payment/Terms: "Our fees vary, depending on a number of considerations. In general, though, payment is modest for now." Pays on publication for electronic rights and the right to include the piece in a *Brain, Child/* March Press anthology, should one ever happen. Sends galleys to author.

Advice: "Since much of *Brain, Child* is made of personal essays, we have to walk a straight line between fiction and fact (i.e., stories should read like stories, not essays). We look for strongly developed characters in fiction. We're open to myriad subjects, but are most interested in literary stories that resonate with women as mothers and individuals."

$ ◑ BRIDAL GUIDES, P.O. Box 1264, Huntington WV 25714. **Contact:** fiction editor. Magazine: 8½×11; illustrations; photos. "*Bridal Guides* emphasis is on wedding planning, primarily for Christians of any denomination. We provide free material for Christian writers' groups on request." Quarterly. Estab. 1993. Circ. 10,000.

Needs: Children's/juvenile, romance, young adult/teen (romance); the emphasis is on weddings. Would like to see more romance for Christians and children's Christian stories. Receives 25 unsolicited mss/month. Accepts 1-4 mss/issue; 24-30 mss/year. Publishes ms 1-3 months after acceptance. **Publishes 12 new writers/year.** Length: 500 words minimum. Also publishes poetry. Always comments on rejected ms.

How to Contact: Send complete ms with a cover letter. Include estimated word count, bio and list of publications. Responds in 1 month to queries; 2 months to mss. Send SASE for reply, return of ms or send disposable copy of ms. Accepts simultaneous and reprint submissions. Sample copy for $10. Guidelines free.

Payment/Terms: Pays 2-5¢/word and 2 contributor's copies. Pays on acceptance for first rights. Sends prepublication galleys to author.

N **⚑** **$◻** **CHALLENGING DESTINY, New Fantasy & Science Fiction**, Crystalline Sphere Publishing, R.R. #6, St. Marys Ontario N4X 1C8 Canada. E-mail: csp@golden.net. Website: home.golden.net/~csp/ (includes previews of published and upcoming magazines, writer's guidelines, interviews with authors, reviews of books, movies, soundtracks and games, links to other websites). **Contact:** David M. Switzer, editor. Magazine: 8×5¼; 120 pages; Kallima 10 pt cover; illustrations. "We publish all kinds of science fiction and fantasy short stories." Quarterly. Estab. 1997. Circ. 300.

Needs: Fantasy, science fiction. No horror, short short stories. Receives 40 unsolicited mss/month. Accepts 6 mss/issue, 24 mss/year. Publishes ms 1-3 months after acceptance. **Publishes 6 new writers/year.** Recently published work by Hugh Cook, Rudy Kremberg and D.K. Latta. Length: 2,000-10,000 words; average length: 6,000 words. Often comments on rejected mss.

How to Contact: Send complete ms with a cover letter. Include estimated word count. Responds in 1 month to queries; 2 months to mss. Send SAE and IRC for reply, return of ms or send disposable copy of ms. Accepts simultaneous submissions. Sample copy for $6.50. Guidelines for 1 IRC. Reviews novels and short story collections. Send books to James Schellenberg.

Payment/Terms: Pays 1¢/word plus 2 contributor's copies. Acquires first North American serial rights. Sends galleys to author.

Advice: "Manuscripts with a good story and interesting characters stand out. We look for fiction that entertains and makes you think. If you're going to write short fiction, you need to read lots of it. Don't reinvent the wheel. Use your own voice."

N **◎** **CHILDREN FAR AND WIDE**, CAFECR.org, N. 507 Sullivan Rd., Suite A-6, Veradale WA 99037-8531. (509)777-0064. Fax: (509)928-2392. E-mail: info@childrenfarandwide.com. Website: www.childrenfarand wide.com. **Contact:** Managing editor. Magazine: 8½×11; 112 pages; b&w plus four color ink on Bristol; full cover; illustrations. "Children, parenting, foster and other children stories; themes around children issues; abused and neglected children; stories about the outcome of children (in various settings in life)." Quarterly. Estab. 2002. Circ. 5,000-10,000. Member, PMA.

Needs: Adventure, children/juvenile (adventure, animal, easy-to-read, fantasy, historical, mystery, preschool, series, sports), family saga, historical (children), humor satire, regional, translation, young adult/teen (adventure, historical). Upcoming themes available online. Receives 20 unsolicited mss/month. Accepts 10-15 mss/issue. Publishes ms 2-3 months after acceptance. **Publishes 20 new writers/year.** Length: 700-4,000 words. Publishes short shorts. Also publishes poetry. Sometimes comments on rejected mss.

How to Contact: Send complete copy of ms with cover letter. Accepts mss by e-mail and on disk. Include estimated word count with submission. Responds in 3 months to queries. Send disposable copy of ms and #10 SASE for reply only. Accepts simultaneous, multiple and previously published submissions. Sample copy free. Guidelines for SASE, e-mail and on website.

Payment/Terms: Pays 10 contributor's copies and free subscription to the magazine; additional copies $5. Pays on publication for first rights. Sponsors contests: see guidelines.

Advice: "We look for creative fiction appropriate to our magazine. Send your best work that matches the theme for our magazine. We are open to new writers who can produce quality short stories with our theme."

⚑ **$◻** **◎** **CHRISTIAN COURIER,** Reformed Faith Witness, Unit 4, 261 Martindale Rd., St. Catharines, Ontario L2W 1A1 Canada. (905)682-8311. Fax: (905)682-8313. E-mail: cceditor@aol.com. **Contact:** Harry Der Nederlander, editor. Tabloid: 11½×14; 20 pages; newsprint; illustrations; photos. Biweekly. Estab. 1945. Circ. 4,000.

Needs: Historical, religious/inspirational, senior citizen/retirement, sports. No "sentimental 'religious' stuff; superficial moralizing." Receives 5-10 unsolicited mss/month. Accepts 12 mss/year. Does not read mss from the end of July through early August. Publishes ms within a month after acceptance. Length: no minimum; 2,000 words maximum; average length: 1,200 words. Publishes short shorts. Also publishes literary essays (if not too technical), literary criticism and poetry.

How to Contact: Send complete ms with a cover letter. Include word count and bio (100 words maximum). Responds in 6 weeks to mss. Send a disposable copy of ms. Accepts simultaneous, reprint and electronic submissions. Sample copy free. Guidelines for SASE.

Payment/Terms: Pays $25-60 and 1 contributor's copy (on request). Pays on publication for one-time rights.

Advice: Looks for work "geared to a Christian audience but reflecting the real world, real dilemmas, without pat resolutions—written in an engaging, clear manner."

⬤ **THE CIRCLE MAGAZINE**, Circle Publications, 1325 S. Cocalico Rd., Denver PA 17517. Phone/fax: (610)670-7017. E-mail: circlemag@aol.com. Website: www.circlemagazine.com (includes guidelines, poetry and fiction not in print issue, links, etc.) **Contact:** Penny Talbert, editor. Magazine: 8½×5½; 40-48 pages; white offset paper; illustrations; photos. "*The Circle* is an eclectic mix of culture and subculture. Our goal is to provide the reader with thought-provoking reading that they remember." Quarterly.

Needs: Adventure, experimental, humor/satire, literary, mainstream, mystery/suspense, New Age, psychic/supernatural/occult, romance, science fiction, thriller/espionage. No religious fiction. Receives 100 unsolicited mss/month. Accepts 3-5 mss/issue; 12-20 mss/year. Publishes ms 1-4 months after acceptance. Recently published work by David McDaniel, Bart Stewart, Ace Boggess and Stephen Forney. Length: 2,000-6,000 words; average length: 3,500 words. Publishes short shorts. Average length: 1,200 words. Also publishes literary essays, literary criticism and poetry. Sometimes comments on rejected mss.

How to Contact: Send complete ms with a cover letter. Accepts submissions by e-mail, fax and disk. E-mail submissions should be in body of text or attached as a text file. Include estimated word count, brief bio and list of publications. Responds in 1 month to queries; 4 months to mss. Send SASE (or IRC) for return of ms or send a disposable copy of ms and #10 SASE for reply only. Accepts simultaneous submissions, previously published work and multiple submissions. Sample copy for $4. Guidelines on website.

Payment/Terms: Pays 1 contributor's copy; additional copies $4. Pays on publication for one-time and electronic rights.

Advice: "The most important thing is that submitted fiction keeps our attention and interest. The most typical reason for rejection: bad endings! Proofread your work and send it in compliance with our guidelines."

⬤ **COCHRAN'S CORNER**, 1003 Tyler Court, Waldorf MD 20602-2964. Phone/fax: (301)870-1664. President: Ada Cochran. **Contact:** Jeanie Saunders, editor. Magazine: 5½×8; 52 pages. "We publish fiction, nonfiction and poetry. Our only requirement is no strong language." For a "family" audience. Quarterly magazine. Estab. 1986. Circ. 500.

Needs: Adventure, children's/juvenile, historical, horror, humor/satire, mystery/suspense, religious/inspirational, romance, science fiction, young adult/teen (10-18 years). Would like to see more mystery and romance fiction. "Mss must be free from language you wouldn't want your/our children to read." Plans a special fiction issue. Receives 50 mss/month. Accepts 4 mss/issue; 8 mss/year. Publishes ms by the next issue after acceptance. **Publishes approximately 30 new writers/year.** Published work by James Hughes, Ellen Sandry, James Bennet, Susan Lee and Judy Demers. Length: 300-1,000 words; 500 words preferred. Also publishes literary essays, literary criticism, poetry.

How to Contact: "Right now we are forced to limit acceptance to *subscribers only.*" Send complete ms with cover letter. Responds in 3 weeks to queries; 6-8 weeks to mss. SASE for manuscript. Accepts simultaneous and reprint submissions. Sample copy for $5, 9×12 SAE and 90¢ postage. Guidelines for #10 SASE.

Payment/Terms: Pays in contributor's copies. Acquires one-time rights.

Advice: "I feel the quality of fiction is getting better. The public is demanding a good read, instead of having sex or violence carry the story. I predict that fiction has a good future. We like to print the story as the writer submits it if possible. This way writers can compare their work with their peers and take the necessary steps to improve and go on to sell to bigger magazines. Stories from the heart desire a place to be published. We try to fill that need. Be willing to edit yourself. Polish your manuscript before submitting to editors."

⬤ **THE COZY DETECTIVE, Mystery Magazine**, Meager Ink Publishing, 686 Jakes Ct., McMinnville OR 97128. Phone/fax: (503)472-4896. E-mail: papercapers@yahoo.com. Editor: David Workman. **Contact:** Charlie Bradley, fiction editor. Magazine: 8½×5½; 80 pages; illustrations; photos. Publishes mystery/suspense fiction and true crime stories for mystery buffs. Quarterly. Estab. 1994. Circ. 2,000.

Needs: Condensed/excerpted novel, mystery/suspense (amateur sleuth, cozy, police procedural, private eye/hardboiled), science fiction (mystery), serialized novel, young adult (mystery). No "sex, violence or vulgarity." Publishes special fiction issues or anthologies. Receives 15-25 unsolicited mss/month. Accepts 5 mss/issue; 20 mss/year. Does not read mss June-August. Recently published work by Kris Neri, Wendy Dager, Ruth Latta, James Geisert, C. Lester Bradley and Robert W. Kreps. Length: 6,000 words maximum; will consider longer stories for two-part series. Publishes short shorts. Also publishes poetry. Sometimes comments on rejected ms.

How to Contact: Send complete ms with a cover letter. Include 1-paragraph bio and estimated word count. Responds in 2 months to queries; 6 months to mss. Send SASE for reply, return of ms or send disposable copy of ms. Accepts simultaneous, reprint and electronic submissions. Sample copy for $2.95. Guidelines for #10 SASE. Reviews novels and short story collections. Send books to "Review Editor."

Payment/Terms: Pays 2 contributor's copies; additional copies $1.50. Acquires first North American serial rights.

Advice: "Do your best work—don't rush. Try to make your plot secondary to characters in the story. We look for action, crisp dialogue and original use of old ideas. We love a good mystery."

$☑ DANCE, P.O. Box 1264, Huntington WV 25714. **Contact:** fiction editor. "*Dance* features stories with a multicultural or ethnic flavor that deliver a positive message." Magazine: 8½ × 11; illustrations; photos. Quarterly. Estab. 1993. Circ. 10,000.

Needs: Children's/juvenile, young adult/teen, dance. Receives 25 unsolicited mss/month. Accepts 1-2 mss/issue; 12-16 mss/year. Publishes ms 1-3 months after acceptance. **Publishes 12 new writers/year.** Length: 500 words minimum. Also publishes literary essays, criticism and poetry. Always comments on rejected ms.

How to Contact: Send complete ms with a cover letter. Include estimated word count, bio and list of publications. Responds in 1 month to queries; 2 months to mss. Send SASE for reply, return of ms or send disposable copy of ms. Accepts simultaneous and reprint submissions. Sample copy for $10. Guidelines free.

Payment/Terms: Pays 2-5¢/word and contributor's copies. Pays on acceptance for first rights. Sends prepublication galleys to author.

☑ ◎ DREAM INTERNATIONAL/QUARTERLY, U.S. Address: Charles I. Jones, #H-1, 411 14th St., Ramona CA 92065-2769. (760)789-1020. **Contact:** Charles I. Jones, editor-in-chief. Magazine: 8½ × 11; 143 pages; Xerox paper; parchment cover stock; some illustrations; photos. "Publishes fiction and nonfiction that is dream-related or clearly inspired by a dream. Also dream-related fantasy and poetry." Quarterly. Estab. 1981. Circ. 65-100.

Needs: Confession, erotica (soft), fantasy (dream), historical, horror, humor/satire, literary, prose poem, psychic/supernatural/occult, science fiction, young adult/teen (10-18). "We would like to see submissions that deal with dreams that have an influence on the person's daily waking life. Suggestions for making dreams beneficial to the dreamer in his/her waking life. We would also like to see more submissions dealing with lucid dreaming." Receives 35-40 unsolicited mss/month. Accepts 20 mss/issue; 50-55 mss/year. Publishes ms 8 months to 3 years after acceptance. Agented fiction 1%. **Publishes 20-30 new writers/year.** Recently published work by Jeffrey Lewis, Dave Merrill and Michele Mitchell-Weal. Length: 1,000-1,500 words. Publishes short shorts. Also publishes literary essays, poetry (poetry submissions to Carmen M. Pursifull, 809 W. Maple St., Champaign IL 61820-2810. Hard copy only for poetry. No electronic submissions please! Send SASE for poetry guidelines).

How to Contact: Submit ms. Responds in 6 weeks to queries; 3 months to mss. SASE. Accepts simultaneous and reprint submissions. Sample copy for $13. Guidelines $2 with SAE and 2 first-class stamps. Subscription: $56 (1-year); $112 (2-year). "Accepted mss will not be returned unless requested at time of submission."

Payment/Terms: Pays in contributor's copy (contributors must pay $4 for postage and handling). Acquires first North American serial and electronic rights. Sends prepublication galleys to author on request.

Advice: "Write about what you know. Make the reader 'stand up and take notice.' Avoid rambling and stay away from chichés in your writing unless, of course, it is of a humorous nature and is purposefully done to make a point."

◼ $☑ DREAMS & VISIONS, New Frontiers in Christian Fiction, Skysong Press, 35 Peter St. S., Orillia, Ontario L3V 5AB Canada. Website: www.bconnex.net/~skysong. **Contact:** Steve Stanton, editor. Magazine: 5½ × 8½; 56 pages; 20 lb. bond paper; glossy cover. "Contemporary Christian fiction in a variety of styles for adult Christians." Triannual. Estab. 1989. Circ. 200.

Needs: Contemporary, experimental, fantasy, humor/satire, literary, religious/inspirational, science fiction (soft/sociological). "All stories should portray a Christian world view or expand upon Biblical themes or ethics in an entertaining or enlightening manner." Receives 20 unsolicited mss/month. Accepts 7 mss/issue; 21 mss/year. Publishes ms 2-6 months after acceptance. Length: 2,000-6,000 words; average length: 2,500 words.

How to Contact: Send complete ms with cover letter. "Bio is optional: degrees held and in what specialties, publishing credits, service in the church, etc." Responds in 1 month to queries; 4 months to mss. SASE. Accepts simultaneous submissions. Sample copy for $4.95. Guidelines for SASE or on website.

Payment/Terms: Pays ½¢/word and contributor's copy. Acquires first North American serial rights and one-time, non-exclusive reprint rights.

Advice: "In general we look for work that has some literary value, that is in some way unique and relevant to Christian readers today. Our first priority is technical adequacy, though we will occasionally work with a beginning writer to polish a manuscript. Ultimately, we look for stories that glorify the Lord Jesus Christ, stories that build up rather than tear down, that exalt the sanctity of life, the holiness of God, and the value of the family."

⊕ ☑ $◎ ▼ EIDOLON, The Journal of Australian Science Fiction and Fantasy, P.O. Box 225, North Perth, Western Australia 6906. E-mail: jeremy@eidolon.net. Website: www.eidolon.net (includes general news on Australia science fiction and fantasy, original fiction, reviews and articles). **Contact:** Jeremy Byrne, editor. Magazine: A5 size; 124 pages; gloss cover; illustrations; photos. "We publish "quality genre fiction by Australians for an international audience." Primarily Australian science fiction, fantasy and horror magazine. Quarterly. Estab. 1990. Circ. 350.

• *Eidolon* published two Ditmer Awards and one Aurealis Award-winning stories.

Needs: Fantasy, psychic/supernatural/occult, romance (futuristic/time travel), science fiction, young adult/teen (horror, science fiction). Receives 25 unsolicited mss/month. Accepts 6 mss/issue; 25 mss/year. Publishes ms up to 1 year after acceptance. Agented fiction less than 1%. **Publishes 2 new writers/year.** Recently published work by Terry Dowling, Sean Williams, Simon Brown, Jack Dann, Damien Broderick, Stephen Dedman. Length: 10,000 words maximum; average length: 4,000 words. Publishes short shorts.

How to Contact: Send complete ms with a cover letter. Include estimated word count, 100-word bio, list of publications and e-mail address. Send SASE for reply and a disposable copy of ms. Accepts multiple submissions. Publishes fiction by Australians only. Sample copy for $8 Aus. Guidelines for #10 SASE or SAE with 1 IRC.

Payment/Terms: Pays $20 and 1 contributor's copy. Acquires first Australian rights and optional electronic reproduction rights. Sends galleys to author.

Advice: Looks for "sophisticated, original explorations of fantastic themes, surprising plots and intelligent characterization. Proof carefully, work hard on dialogue. Make sure you know the field you're writing in well to avoid rehashing old themes. We expect writers to avoid stereotypical, sexist, racist or otherwise socially unacceptable themes and styles."

N ○ **ELEMENTS MAGAZINE**, Oliver Press Printing Co., 2820 Houston St., Alexandria LA 71301-4329. (318)445-5055. **Contact:** Bernard Washington, editor. Magazine: 8½ × 11; 50 pages; bonded paper; illustrations; photos. "Our audience comprises all who want a new perspective about current events, literature and the arts. We publish items from new and unpublished authors in every issue." Bimonthly. Circ. 500. Member, The Small Press Review.

Needs: Children's/juvenile (adventure, animal, easy-to-read, historical, sports), ethnic/multicultural, family saga, feminist, gay, historical (general), horror (futuristic), humor/satire, lesbian, literary, mainstream, mystery/suspense, religious (general, inspirational, religious romance), romance (contemporary, futuristic/time travel, historical, romantic suspense), science fiction (soft/sociological), western (frontier saga, traditional), young adult/teen (adventure, easy-to-read, historical, problem novels, sports, western). No child pornography. Receives 3 unsolicited mss/month. Accepts 3 mss/issue; 36 mss/year. Publishes ms 2 months after acceptance. **Publishes 15 new writers/year.** Recently published work by Albert Russo, B.Z. Niditch, William Dauenhauer and Lorraine Toliver. Length: 500-1,000 words; average length: 800 words. Publishes short shorts. Average length: 1,500 words. Also publishes literary essays, literary criticism and poetry. Sometimes comments on rejected mss.

How to Contact: Send complete ms with a cover letter. Include estimated word count, brief bio and list of publications. Responds in 3 weeks to queries; 1 month to mss. Send SASE (or IRC) for return of ms or send a disposable copy of ms and #10 SASE for reply only. Accepts simultaneous, previously published and multiple submissions. Sample copy for 9 × 12 SAE with $2 postage. Guidelines for SASE. Reviews novels, short story collections and nonfiction books of interest to writers. Send review copies to Bernard Washington.

Payment/Terms: Pays 1-2 contributor's copies; additional copies $7. Pays on publication for one-time rights.

Advice: "Fiction must be written well and entertaining. A manuscript stands out for its clarity and style. Be original and write well—write something everyday and keep a positive attitude."

N ◑ ◎ **THE ELOQUENT UMBRELLA**, Linn-Benton Community College, 6500 SW Pacific Blvd., Albany OR 97321-3779. (541)753-3335. E-mail: terrance@peak.org. **Contact:** Terrance Millet. Magazine: illustrations; photos. "*The Eloquent Umbrella*'s purpose is to showcase art, photography, poetry and prose of Linn and Benton Counties in Oregon." Annually. Estab. 1990. Circ. 500.

Needs: Regional. "No slander, pornography or other material unsuitable for community reading." Accepts 50-100 mss/issue. Deadline January 15 each year. Reads mss during winter term only; publishes in spring. Length: 2,000 words maximum. Publishes short shorts. Also publishes literary essays, literary criticism and poetry.

How to Contact: Send complete ms with cover letter. Include 1- to 5-line bio. Responds in 6 weeks to mss. SASE for return of ms or send a disposable copy of ms. Accepts simultaneous and multiple submissions. Sample copy for $2 and 8½ × 11 SAE.

Payment/Terms: Rights remain with author.

Advice: "The magazine is created by a collective editorial board and production team in a literary publication class."

○ **ENIGMA**, Audacious/Bottle Press, 402 South 25 St., Philadelphia PA 19146. (215)545-8694. E-mail: sydx@ att.net. **Contact:** Syd Bradford, publisher. Magazine: 8½ × 11; 100 pages; 24 lb. white paper; illustrations; photos. "Everything is done—except printing—by me, the publisher. No editors, etc. Eclectic—I publish articles, fiction, poetry." Quarterly. Estab. 1989. Circ. 70.

Needs: Adventure, experimental, fantasy, historical, horror, humor/satire. "No sentimental or religious fiction." Accepts 30 mss/issue. Publishes ms 3 months after acceptance. **Publishes 20 new writers/year.** Recently published work by Richard A. Robbins, Eleanor Leslie and Diana K. Rubin. Length: 1,000-3,000 words; average length: 1,500 words. Publishes short shorts. Also publishes literary essays, literary criticism and poetry.

How to Contact: Send complete ms with a cover letter. Accepts submissions by e-mail. Include brief bio. Send SASE (or IRC) for return of ms. Sample copy for $6. Guidelines for SASE. Reviews novels, short story collections and nonfiction books of interest to writers.

Payment/Terms: Pays 1 contributor's copy; additional copies $6, plus $1.30 postage. Sends galleys to author.

Advice: "I look for imaginative writing, excellent movement, fine imagery, stunning characters."

EYES, 3610 North Doncaster Ct., Apt. X7, Saginaw MI 48603-1862. (517)498-4112. E-mail: fjm3eyes@aol. com. Website: http://members.aol.com/eyeonweb/index.html (includes guidelines, contact information, stories and reviews). **Contact:** Frank J. Mueller, III, editor. Magazine: 8½×11; 40+ pages. "No specific theme. Speculative fiction and surrealism most welcome. For a general, educated, not necessarily literary audience." Estab. 1991.

Needs: Contemporary, horror (psychological), mainstream, ghost story. "Especially looking for speculative fiction and surrealism. Would like to see more ghost stories, student writing. Dark fantasy OK, but not preferred." No sword/sorcery, overt science fiction, pornography, preachiness or children's fiction. Accepts 5-9 mss/issue. Publishes ms up to 1 year or longer after acceptance. **Publishes 15-20 writers/year.** Length: 6,000 words maximum. Sometimes comments on rejected mss.

How to Contact: Query first or send complete ms. A short bio is optional. Responds in 1 month to queries; 3 months or longer to mss. SASE. No simultaneous submissions. Sample copy for $6; extras $4. Subscriptions $20/4 issues. (Checks to Frank J. Mueller III.) Guidelines for #10 SASE.

Payment/Terms: Pays 1 contributor's copy. Acquires one-time rights.

Advice: "Pay attention to character. A strong plot, while important, may not be enough alone to get you in *Eyes*. Atmosphere and mood are also important. Please proofread. If you have a manuscript you like enough to see in *Eyes*, send it to me. Above all, don't let rejections discourage you. I would encourage the purchase of a sample to get an idea of what I'm looking for. Read stories by authors such as Algernon Blackwood, Nathaniel Hawthorne, Shirley Jackson, Henry James and Poe. Also, please write for information concerning chapbooks."

$ FLESH & BLOOD, Quiet Tales of Horror & Dark Fantasy, Flesh & Blood Press, 121 Joseph St., Bayville NJ 08721. E-mail: HorrorJack@aol.com. Website: www.geocities.com/soho/lofts/3459/fnb.html (includes news, updates, guidelines, sales, releases). **Contact:** Jack Fisher, senior editor/publisher. Magazine: digest sized; 44-52 pages; 60 lb. paper; thick/glossy cover; illustrations. "We publish fiction with heavy emphasis on the supernatural, fantastic and bizarre." Triannual. Estab. 1997. Circ. 500.

Needs: Fantasy (light), horror (dark fantasy, supernatural). "We love unique ghost stories. "No psychological, revenge, old-storyline stories." Receives 250 unsolicited mss/month. Accepts 6-8 mss/issue; 18-24 mss/year. Publishes ms 6-10 months after acceptance. Agented fiction 1%. **Publishes 4-6 new writers/year.** Recently published work by Wendy Rathbone. Length: 500-4,000 words; average length: 2,000 words. Publishes short shorts. Average length: 100-500 words. Also publishes poetry. Often comments on rejected mss.

How to Contact: Send complete ms with a cover letter. Accepts submissions by e-mail. Include brief bio and list of publications. Responds in 2 weeks to queries; 3 months to mss. Send SASE (or IRC) for return of ms. Accepts previously published work. Sample copy for $4. Guidelines free for SASE or by e-mail.

Payment/Terms: Pays $5-80 plus 1 contributor's copy. Pays within 3 months after acceptance for first North American serial rights.

Advice: "Too many fiction submissions today are cliché, rushed and sloppy. Offer new, original ideas and present them properly and professionally."

$ FREE FOCUS/OSTENTATIOUS MIND, Wagner Press, Bowbridge Press, P.O. Box 7415, JAF Station, New York NY 10116-7415. **Contact:** Patricia Denise Coscia, editor. Editors change each year. Magazine: 8×14; 10 pages; recycled paper; illustrations; photos. "*Free Focus* is a small-press magazine which focuses on the educated women of today, and *Ostentatious Mind* is designed to encourage the intense writer, the cutting reality." Bimonthly. Estab. 1985 and 1987. Circ. 100 each.

Needs: Experimental, feminist, humor/satire, literary, mainstream/contemporary, mystery/suspense (romantic), psychic/supernatural/occult, westerns (traditional), young adult/teen (adventure). "X-rated fiction is not accepted." List of upcoming themes available for SASE. Plans future special fiction issue or anthology. Receives 1,000 unsolicited mss/month. Does not read mss February to August. Publishes ms 3-6 months after acceptance. **Publishes 200 new writers/year.** Published work by Edward Janz. Length: 1,000 words maximum; average length: 500 words. Publishes short shorts. Also publishes literary essays, literary criticism and poetry. Always comments on rejected mss. Sponsors contest for work submitted to *Free Focus*.

INTERESTED IN A PARTICULAR GENRE? Check our sections for: **Mystery/ Suspense**, page 91; **Romance**, page 105; **Science Fiction & Fantasy**, page 121.

How to Contact: Query with clips of published work or send complete ms with a cover letter. Should include 100-word bio and list of publications. Responds in 3 months. Send SASE for reply. Accepts simultaneous submissions. Sample copy for $3, #10 SAE and $1 postage. Guidelines for #10 SAE and $1 postage. Reviews novels and short story collections.

Payment/Terms: Pays $2.50-5 and 2 contributor's copies; additional copies $2. Pays on publication for all rights. Sends galleys to author.

Advice: "This publication is for beginning writers. Do not get discouraged; submit your writing. We look for imagination and creativity; no x-rated writing."

N ◎ GAITED HORSE INTERNATIONAL MAGAZINE, N. 507 Sullivan Rd., Suite A-3, Veradale WA 99037. (509)232-2698. Fax: (509)232-2665. E-mail: info@gaitedhorsemagazine.com. Website: www.gaitedhorse magazine.com. **Contact:** Managing editor. Magazine: 8½×11; 112 pages; b&w plus four color ink on Bristol; full cover; illustrations. "Gaited Horses, breeding, owning, training, history and care." Quarterly. Estab. 2002. Circ. 5,000-10,000.

Needs: Adventure, children/juvenile (adventure, animal, preschool, series, sports), historical (gaited horses), humor satire, regional, translation, young adult/teen (adventure, historical). Upcoming themes available online. Receives 20 unsolicited mss/month. Accepts 10-15 mss/issue. Publishes ms 2-3 months after acceptance. **Publishes 10 new writers/year.** Length: 700-4,000 words. Publishes short shorts. Also publishes poetry. Sometimes comments on rejected mss.

How to Contact: Send complete copy of ms with cover letter. Accepts mss by e-mail and disk. Include estimated word count with submission. Responds in 3 months to queries. Send disposable copy of ms and #10 SASE for reply only. Accepts simultaneous, multiple and previously published (with permission only) submissions. Sample copy free. Guidelines for SASE, e-mail and on website.

Payment/Terms: Pays 10 contributor's copies and free subscription to magazine; additional copies $5. Pays on publication for first rights. Sponsors contests: see guidelines.

Advice: "We seek creative fiction appropriate to our magazine. Send your best work that matches the theme for our magazine."

$◎ GHOST TOWN, P.O. Box 1264, Huntington WV 25714. **Contact:** fiction editor. Magazine: 8½×11; illustrations; photos. Quarterly. Estab. 1999.

Needs: Children's/juvenile (historical), historical (ghost towns), western, young adult/teen (historical). No science fiction. Wants to see more "westerns set in true-to-life ghost towns." Receives 50 unsolicited mss/month. Accepts 1-2 mss/issue; 12-16 mss/year. Publishes ms 1-3 months after acceptance. **Publishes 12 new writers/ year.** Length: 500 words minimum. Also publishes poetry. Always comments on rejected ms.

How to Contact: Send complete ms with a cover letter. Include estimated word count, bio and list of publications. Responds in 1 month to queries; 2 months to mss. Send SASE for reply, return of ms or send disposable copy of ms. Accepts simultaneous and reprint submissions. Sample copy for $10. Guidelines free.

Payment/Terms: Pays 2-5¢/word and contributor's copies. Pays on acceptance for first rights. Sends prepublication galleys to author.

Advice: "Photographs with ms are a plus."

N ⊕ ◎ GLOBAL TAPESTRY JOURNAL, BB Books, 1 Spring Bank, Longsight Rd., Copster Green, Blackburn, Lancashire BB1 9EU England. **Contact:** Dave Cunliffe, editor. Global Tapestry Journal is a manifestation of exciting creativity." Magazine. Limited press run: 1,000-1,500/issue.

Needs: "Post-underground with avant-garde, experimental, alternative, counterculture, psychedelic, mystical, anarchist etc. fiction for a bohemian and counterculture audience." No genre. **Publishes 20-50 new writers/ year.** Published fiction by Lain Sinclair, Chris Challis, John Power and Jeff Cloves.

How to Contact: Accepts unsolicited mss. SAE, IRCs. Responds in 2-6 weeks.

Payment/Terms: Pays contributor's copy. Sample copy for $4 (Sterling Cheque, British Money Order or dollar currency).

◎ HARD ROW TO HOE, Potato Eyes Foundation, P.O. Box 541-I, Healdsburg CA 95448. (707)433-9786. **Contact:** Joe Armstrong, editor. Newsletter: 8½×11; 12 pages; 60 lb. white paper; illustrations; photos. "Book reviews, short story and poetry of rural USA including environmental and nature subjects." Triannually. Estab. 1982. Circ. 150.

• *Hard Row to Hoe* was called "one of ten best literary newsletters in the U.S." by *Small Press* magazine.

Needs: Rural America. "No urban material or stories of pets. Would like to see stories that depict organic farming." Receives 8-10 unsolicited mss/month. Acquires 1 ms/issue; 3-4 mss/year. Publishes ms 6-9 months after acceptance. **Publishes 1-2 new writers/year.** Recently published work by Deborah Rowland Stambul and Karen Richardson Kettner. Length: 2,000-2,200 words; average length: 1,500 words. Publishes short shorts. Sometimes critiques rejected mss.

How to Contact: Send complete ms with cover letter. Responds in 1 month to mss. SASE. Accepts multiple submissions. Sample copy for $2. Guidelines for legal-size SASE.

Payment/Terms: Pays 2 contributor's copies. Acquires one-time rights.

Advice: "Be certain the subject fits the special need."

$ ◐ **HARDBOILED,** Gryphon Books, P.O. Box 209, Brooklyn NY 11228-0209. **Contact:** Gary Lovisi, editor. Magazine: Digest-sized; 100 pages; offset paper; color cover; illustrations. Publishes "cutting edge, hard, noir fiction with impact! Query on nonfiction and reviews." Quarterly. Estab. 1988.

Needs: Mystery/suspense (private eye, police procedural, noir). Receives 40-60 mss/month. Accepts 10-20 mss/year. Publishes ms within 6 months-2 years of acceptance. **Published many new writers within the last year.** Published work by Andrew Vachss, Joe Lansdale, Bill Nolan, Richard Lupoff, Bill Pronzini and Eugene Izzi. Length: 2,000-3,000 words. Sometimes comments on rejected mss and recommends other markets.

How to Contact: Query first or send complete ms with cover letter. Query with SASE only on anything over 3,000 words. No full-length novels. Responds in 1 month to queries; 2 months to mss. SASE. Accepts simultaneous submissions, but query first. Sample copy for $8. Subscriptions are 5 issues $35.

Payment/Terms: Pays $5-50 and 2 contributor's copies. Pays on publication for first North American serial rights. Copyright reverts to author.

Advice: By "hardboiled" the editor does not mean rehashing of pulp detective fiction from the 1940s and 1950s but, rather, realistic, gritty material. Lovisi could be called a pulp fiction "afficionado," however. He also publishes *Paperback Parade* and holds an annual vintage paperback fiction convention each year.

N ◉ ◐ ▼ **HEIST MAGAZINE,** P.O. Box 2, Newcastle University Union, Callaghan NSW 2308 Australia. 0419-31-MOCK. E-mail: heist@mockfrog.com. Website: www.mockfrog.com/heist (includes writer's guidelines). **Contact:** Matthew Ward, editor. Magazine: 32 pages; bond 80 gsm paper; 150 gsm cover; illustrations; photos. "*Heist Magazine* aims to capture the essense of male-dom through writing and art." Quarterly. Estab. 1998. Circ. 1,000.

● *Heist* has received the Jethro Californian Memorial Prize for Short Stories, 2000. Considers work by men only.

Needs: Adventure, erotica, experimental, family saga, fantasy (space fantasy, sword and sorcery), historical (general), horror (dark fantasy, futuristic, psychological, supernatural), humor satire, literary, mainstream, military/war, mystery/suspense (amateur sleuth, police procedural, private eye/hardboiled, Bindaburra), short story collections, thriller/espionage, western (frontier saga, traditional), men. "We do not want chapters from unpublished novels. We want short stories in their entirety. Anything that captures the essence of what it is like to be a man. And that does not have to mean tales of guys going into the woods, standing around a roaring fire and rubbing bear fat into their stomachs." Receives 50 unsolicited mss/month. Accepts 15 mss/issue; 60 mss/year. Publishes ms 3 months after acceptance. **50% of works published are by new writers.** Recently published work by Rick Mager, Dick Robin and Daniel S. Irwin. Length: 500-2,000 words. Also publishes poetry. Sometimes comments on rejected mss.

How to Contact: Send complete ms with a cover letter. Accepts queries/mss by e-mail. Include estimated word count, 50 word bio, list of publications, SASE. Responds in 2 weeks to queries; 2 months to mss. Send SASE for reply, return of ms or send a disposable copy of ms. Accepts simultaneous submissions. Sample copy for $5, A4 envelope and IRCs. Guidelines available on website.

Payment/Terms: Pays 1 contributor's copy; additional copies $5. Pays on publication for first rights. Sometimes sends galleys to author.

Advice: Looks for work "accessible to most readers, not too obscure. Enjoyable. *Heist* is a fiction mag. We usually get too much poetry, so send fiction. Don't send a chapter from that (as yet) unpublished novel. Try to send a slice of life! Read as many of other people's short stories as you can (try Chandler, Carver et al)."

$ ◐ ▼ **HOPSCOTCH: THE MAGAZINE FOR GIRLS,** The Bluffton News Publishing & Printing Co., P.O. Box 164, Bluffton OH 45817-0164. (419)358-4610. Fax: (419)358-5027. Website: hopscotchmagazine.com (includes samples of articles and order info). **Contact:** Marilyn Edwards, editor. Magazine: 7×9; 50 pages; enamel paper; pen & ink illustrations; photos. Publishes stories for and about girls ages 5-13. "We are trying to produce a wholesome magazine for girls 5-13, encouraging childhood. There is nothing on makeup, boyfriends, fads, clothing, etc." Bimonthly. Estab. 1989. Circ. 9,000.

● *Hopscotch* is indexed in the *Children's Magazine Guide* and *EdPress* and has received a Parents' Choice Gold Medal Award and EdPress Awards.

Needs: Children's/juvenile (5-9, 10-13 years): adventure, ethnic/multicultural, historical (general), sports. No fantasy, science fiction, romance. "We would like to see more stories that rhyme and stories that have a subtle moral." Upcoming themes: Names; The Circus; Zoo Animals; Hats; Women of Courage; Ballet; That's Entertainment; Weather; Astronomy; Water Creatures; It's a Mystery. "All writers should consult the theme list before sending in articles." Current theme list available for SASE. Receives 300-400 unsolicited mss/month. Accepts

20-40 mss/year. Agented fiction 2%. Published work by Lois Grambling, Betty Killion, John Thomas Waite, Kelly Musselman, Marilyn Helmer and Joyce Styron Madsen. Length: 300-750 words; 500-750 words preferred. Publishes short shorts. Length: 250-400 words. Also publishes poetry, puzzles, hidden pictures and crafts. Always comments on rejected mss.

How to Contact: Send complete ms with cover letter. Include estimated word count, 1-page bio, Social Security number and list of publications. Responds in 1 month to queries; 10 weeks to mss. Send SASE for reply, return of ms or send disposable copy of the ms. Accepts simultaneous, multiple and reprint submissions. Sample copy for $4. Guidelines for #10 SASE. Reviews novels and short story collections.

Payment/Terms: Pays 5¢/word (extra for usable photos or illustrations) and 1 contributor's copy; additional copies $4; $2.50 for 10 or more. Pays before publication for first North American serial rights

Advice: "Make sure you have studied copies of our magazine to see what we like. Follow our theme list. We are looking for wholesome stories. This is what our publication is all about."

☑ ◑ HURRICANE ALICE, A Feminist Quarterly, Hurricane Alice Fn., Inc., Dept. of English, Rhode Island College, Providence RI 02908. (401)456-8377. E-mail: mreddy@ric.edu. **Contact:** Maureen Reddy, executive editor. Fiction is collectively edited. Tabloid: 11×17; 12-16 pages; newsprint stock; illustrations; photos. "We look for feminist fictions with a certain analytic snap, for serious readers, seriously interested in emerging forms of feminist art/artists." Quarterly. Estab. 1983. Circ. 600-700.

Needs: Experimental, feminist, gay, humor/satire, lesbian, science fiction, translations, work by young women. "No coming-out stories, defloration stories, abortion stories, dreary realism. Would like to see more speculative and experimental fiction." Receives 30 unsolicited mss/month. Publishes 8-10 stories annually. Publishes mss up to 1 year after acceptance. **Publishes 4-5 new writers/year.** Published work by Vickie Nelson, Mary Sharratt and Kathryn Duhamel. Length: up to 3,500 words maximum. Publishes short shorts. Occasionally comments on rejected mss.

How to Contact: Send complete ms with cover letter. "A brief biographical statement is never amiss. Writers should be sure to tell us if a piece was commissioned by one of the editors." Responds in 9 months. SASE for response. Accepts simultaneous submissions, but must be identified as such. Sample copy for $2.50, 11×14 SAE and 2 first-class stamps.

Payment/Terms: Pays 6 contributor's copies. Acquires one-time rights.

Advice: "Fiction is a craft. Just because something happened, it isn't a story; it becomes a story when you transform it through your art, your craft."

◑ HYBOLICS, Da Literature and Culture of Hawaii, Hybolics, Inc., P.O. Box 3016, Aiea HI 96701. (808)366-1272. E-mail: hybolics@lava.net. Website: www.hybolics.com (includes writer's guidelines and back issue ordering information). **Contact:** Lee Tonouchi, co-editor. Magazine: 8½×11; 80 pages; 80 lb. coated paper; cardstock cover; illustrations; photos. "We publish da kine creative and critical work dat get some kine connection to Hawaii." Annual. Estab. 1999. Circ. 1,000.

Needs: Comics/graphic novels, ethnic/multicultural, experimental, humor/satire, literary. "No genre fiction. Wants to see more sudden fiction." Receives 5 unsolicited mss/month. Accepts 10 mss/year. Publishes ms 1 year after acceptance. **Publishes 3 new writers/year.** Recently published work by Darrell Lum, Rodney Morales, Lee Cataluna and Lisa Kanae. Length: 1,000-8,000 words; average length: 4,000 words. Publishes short shorts. Also publishes literary essays, literary criticism and poetry.

How to Contact: Send complete ms with a cover letter. Include estimated word count, brief bio and list of publications. Responds in 5 weeks to queries; 5 months to mss. Send SASE (or IRC) for return of ms or send a disposable copy of ms and #10 SASE for reply only. Sample copy for $13.35. Guidelines for SASE.

Payment/Terms: Pays 2 contributor's copies; additional copies $7.25. Pays on publication for first rights.

[N] ◎ ICELANDIC SHEEPDOG INTERNATIONAL MAGAZINE, N. 507 Sullivan Rd., Suite A-3, Veradale WA 99037. (509)232-2698. Fax: (509)232-2665. E-mail: info@icelandicsheepdog.com. Website: www.icelandicsheepdogmagazine.com. **Contact:** Managing editor. Magazine: 8½×11; 112 pages; b&w plus four color ink on Bristol; full cover; illustrations. "Sheepdog and nature. Iceland, care and registries of sheepdogs." Quarterly. Estab. 2002. Circ. 5,000-10,000.

Needs: Adventure, children/juvenile (adventure, animal, preschool, series, sports), historical (Icelandic sheepdogs), humor satire, regional, translation, young adult/teen (adventure, historical). Upcoming themes available online. Receives 20 unsolicited mss/month. Accepts 10-15 mss/issue. Publishes ms 2-3 months after acceptance. **Publishes 10 new writers/year.** Length: 700-4,000 words. Publishes short shorts. Also publishes poetry. Sometimes comments on rejected mss.

How to Contact: Send complete copy of ms with cover letter. Accepts mss by e-mail and on disk. Include estimated word count with submission. Responds in 3 months to queries. Send disposable copy of ms and #10 SASE for reply only. Accepts simultaneous, multiple and previously published (with permission only) submissions. Sample copy free. Guidelines for SASE, e-mail and on website.

Payment/Terms: Pays 10 contributor's copies and free subscription to magazine; additional copies $5. Pays on publication for first rights. Sponsors contests: see guidelines.

Advice: "Creative fiction appropriate to our magazine. Send your best work that matches the theme for our magazine. We are open to new writer's who can produce quality short stories with our theme. These fiction stories can be international themed and settings as well as any creative ideas from the writer."

✓ $ ⊘ ◎ ▼ IN THE FAMILY, The Magazine for Queer People and Their Loved Ones, P.O. Box 5387, Takoma Park MD 20913. (301)270-4771. Fax: (301)270-4660. E-mail: lmarkowitz@aol.com. Website: www.inthefamily.com (includes writer's guidelines, bulletin board, overview of magazine content and back issue themes). Editor: Laura Markowitz. **Contact:** Helena Lipstadt, fiction editor. Magazine: 8½×11, 32 pages; coated paper; coated cover; illustrations; photos. "We use a therapy lens to explore the diverse relationships and families of lesbians, gays, bisexuals and their straight relations." Quarterly. Estab. 1995. Circ. 2,000.

- Received 1997 Excellence in Media Award from the American Association for Marriage and Family Therapy. Member of IPA.

Needs: Ethnic/multicultural, feminist, gay, humor/satire, lesbian. No erotica or science fiction. Would like to see more short stories. List of upcoming themes available for SASE. Receives 25 unsolicited mss/month. Accepts 1 ms/issue; 4 mss/year. Publishes ms 3-6 months after acceptance. **Publishes 6 new writers/year.** Recently published work by Greg Pokarney and Kristin Gonzalez. Length: 2,500 words maximum; average length: 2,000 words. Publishes short shorts. Also publishes literary essays and poetry. Sometimes comments on rejected mss.

How to Contact: Send complete ms with a cover letter. Include estimated word count and 40-word bio. Responds in 6 weeks to queries and mss. Send SASE for reply, return of ms or send disposable copy of ms. Accepts multiple submissions. Sample copy for $5.50. Guidelines free. Reviews novels and short story collections. Send books to Book Review Editor.

Payment/Terms: Pays $25-50, free subscription to magazine and 5 contributor's copies. Acquires first rights.

Advice: "We're looking for beautiful writing relevant to our magazine's theme. Story must relate to our theme of gay/lesbian/bi relationships and family in some way. Read a few issues and get a sense for what we publish. Shorter is better."

◩ $ ☉ ▼ INDIAN LIFE, Intertribal Christian Communications, P.O. Box 3765, RPO Redwood Centre, Winnepeg, Manitoba R2W 3R6 Canada. (204)661-9333. Fax: (204)661-3982. E-mail: jim.editor@indianlife.org. Website: www.indianlife.org. **Contact:** Jim Uttley, editor. Religious tabloid: 11×17; 16 pages; newsprint paper; illustrations; photos. "*Indian Life* is an Aboriginal newspaper which seeks to present positive news stories of Native Americans and deals with social issues facing Aboriginal people. It is our mission to bring hope, healing and honor to Native Americans." Bimonthly. Estab. 1968. Circ. 32,000. Member, Evangelical Press Association, Native American Journalists Association.

- *Indian Life* won the Award of Excellence from EPA (1997, 1998).

Needs: Adventure, children's/juvenile (adventure, animal, easy-to-read, historical), comics/graphic novels, ethnic/multicultural (Native American), historical, religious (children's religious, general religious, inspirational), western (frontier saga, traditional). "No writing which berates or puts down Native Americans. Writers must write from Native perspective." Please contact editor by phone for upcoming themes. Receives 4 unsolicited mss/month. Accepts 1 ms/issue; 6 mss/year. Publishes ms 2 months after acceptance. Agented fiction 1%. **Publishes 3 new writers/year.** Length: 500-2,000 words; average length: 800-1,500 words. Publishes short shorts. Average length: 800 words. Also publishes literary essays, literary criticism and poetry. Often comments on rejected mss.

How to Contact: Query first. Accepts submissions by e-mail, fax and disk. Include estimated word count and brief bio. Responds in 1 month to queries; 2 months to mss. Send a disposable copy of ms and #10 SASE for reply only. Accepts simultaneous submissions, previously published work and multiple submissions. Sample copy for SASE with $2 postage. Guidelines for SASE, by e-mail, fax or on website. Reviews novels, short story collections and nonfiction books of interest to writers.

Payment/Terms: Pays $50-100 (Canadian) and 3 contributor's copies; additional copies 25¢. Pays on publication for first rights. Plans to sponsor contest.

Advice: "Research, research, research. Do everything you can to get heart for Native Americans."

✓ INKY TRAIL NEWS, Inky Trail News, 70 Macomb Place, #226, Mt. Clemens MI 48043. E-mail: wendy@inkytrails.com. Website: www.inkytrails.com. **Contact:** Wendy Fisher, editor. Tabloid newspaper: 24-28 pages; newsprint; some illustrations; photos. "Friendship newsletter for women/seniors, penpals, journaling, memories, crafts and more." Bimonthly. Estab. 1993. Circ. 500.

Needs: Historical (general memories), mainstream, women penpals, new writers, homelife, personal journals, gardening, seniors, crafts. Receives 2-3 unsolicited mss/month. Accepts 2-3 mss/issue. Publishes 3-4 months after acceptance. **Publishes 60-100 new writers/year.** Recently published work by Martha Green, Janice Caldwell and Bonnie Patterson. Length: 600 words; average length: 600-800 words. Publishes short shorts.

How to Contact: Send complete ms with cover letter. Accepts submissions by e-mail or on disk. Responds to queries and ms within days (if submitted by e-mail). Send SASE for return of ms or send a disposable copy of ms and #10 SASE for reply only. Accepts simultaneous submissions, previously published work and multiple submissions. Sample copy for $3. Guidelines for SASE, e-mail or on website.

Payment/Terms: Pays 6 contributor's copies or free subscription to magazine; additional copies $1. Pays on for publication for one-time and electronic rights.

Advice: "Use our topics."

✓ ◐ ◎ ITALIAN AMERICANA, URI/CCE 80 Washington St., Providence RI 02903-1803. (617)864-6427. Fax: (401)277-5100. Website: www.uri.edu/prov/italian/italian.html (includes writer's guidelines, names of editors). **Contact:** Carol Bonomo Albright and John Paul Russo, editors. Poetry Editor: Dana Gioia. Magazine: 6×9; 200 pages; varnished cover; perfect-bound; photos. "*Italian Americana* contains historical articles, fiction, poetry and memoirs, all concerning the Italian experience in the Americas." Semiannual. Estab. 1974. Circ. 1,200.

Needs: Italian American: literary. No nostalgia. Wants to see more fiction featuring "individualized characters." Receives 10 mss/month. Accepts 3 mss/issue; 6-7 mss/year. Publishes up to 1 year after acceptance. Agented fiction 5%. **Publishes 2-4 new writers/year.** Recently published work by Salvatore La Pume. Length: 20 double-spaced pages. Publishes short stories. Also publishes literary essays, literary criticism, poetry. Sometimes comments on rejected mss. Sponsors $500-1,000 literature prize annually.

How to Contact: Send complete ms (in triplicate) with a cover letter. Accepts queries/mss by fax. Include 3-5 line bio, list of publications. Responds in 1 month to queries; 2 months to mss. Send SASE for reply, return of ms or send a disposable copy of ms. No simultaneous submissions. Sample copy for $7. Guidelines for SASE. Reviews novels and short story collections. Send books to Professor John Paul Russo, English Dept., Univ. of Miami, Coral Gables, FL 33124.

Payment/Terms: Awards two $250 prizes to best fiction of year and 1 contributor's copy; additional copies $7. Acquires first North American serial rights.

Advice: "Please individualize characters, instead of presenting types (i.e., lovable uncle, etc.). No nostalgia."

◎ JEWISH CURRENTS MAGAZINE, 22 E. 17th St., New York NY 10003-1919. (212)924-5740. Fax: (212)414-2227. Magazine: 8½×11; 36 pages. "We are a secular, progressive, independent Jewish monthly, pro-Israel though not Zionist, printing fiction, poetry articles and reviews on Jewish politics and history, Holocaust/Resistance; mideast peace process, Black-Jewish relations, labor struggles, women's issues. Audience is secular, left/progressive, Jewish, mostly urban." Monthly. Estab. 1946. Circ. 2,000.

● This magazine may be slow to respond. They continue to be backlogged.

Needs: Contemporary, ethnic, feminist, historical, humor/satire, literary, senior citizen/retirement, translations. "Must be well written! We are interested in *authentic* experience and readable prose; humanistic orientation. Must have Jewish theme. Could use more humor; short, smart, emotional and intellectual impact. No religious, sectarian; no porn or hard sex, no escapist stuff. Go easy on experimentation, but we're interested." Upcoming themes (submit at least 3 months in advance): "Black-Jewish Relations" (February); "International Women's Day" (March); "Holocaust/Resistance, Passover" (April); "Israel" (May); "Jews in the USSR & Ex-USSR" (July-August); Jewish Book Month" (November); "Hanuka" (December). Receives 6-10 unsolicited fiction mss/month. Accepts 0-1 ms/issue; 8-10 mss/year. Published work by Galina Vromen, Michael Book, Michael Gould-Wartofsky, Beverly Nieves. Length: 1,000-3,000 words; average length: 1,800 words. Also publishes literary essays, literary criticism, poetry.

How to Contact: Send complete ms with cover letter. "Writers should include brief biographical information, especially their publishing histories." SASE. Responds in 2 months to mss. Publishes ms 2-24 months after acceptance. No mss by fax, e-mail or disk. Sample copy for $3 with SAE and 3 first-class stamps. Reviews novels and short story collections.

Payment/Terms: Pays complimentary one-year subscription and 6 contributor's copies. "We readily give reprint permission at no charge." Sends galleys to author.

Advice: Noted for "stories with Jewish content and personal Jewish experience—e.g., immigrant or Holocaust memories, assimilation dilemmas, dealing with Jewish conflicts OK. Space is increasingly a problem. Be intelligent, imaginative, intuitive and absolutely honest. Have a musical ear, and an ear for people: how they sound when they talk, and also hear what they don't say."

◖ JOURNAL OF POLYMORPHOUS PERVERSITY Wry-Bred Press, Inc., 10 Waterside Plaza, Suite 20-B, New York NY 10010. (212)689-5473. Fax: (212)689-6859. E-mail: info@psychhumor.com. Website: www.psychhumor.com (includes excerpts). **Contact:** Glenn Ellenbogen, editor. Magazine: 6¾×10; 24 pages; 60 lb. paper; antique india cover stock; illustrations with some articles. "*JPP* is a humorous and satirical journal of psychology, psychiatry, and the closely allied mental health disciplines." For "psychologists, psychiatrists, social workers, psychiatric nurses, *and* the psychologically sophisticated layman." Semiannal. Estab. 1984.

Needs: Humor/satire. "We only consider materials that are funny or that relate to psychology *or* behavior." Receives 50 unsolicited mss/month. Accepts 8 mss/issue; 16 mss/year. Most writers published last year were previously unpublished writers. Length: 4,000 words maximum; average length: 1,500 words. Comments on rejected mss.

How to Contact: Send complete ms *in triplicate*. Include cover letter and SASE. Responds in 3 months to mss. SASE. Accepts multiple submissions. Sample copy for $7. Guidelines for #10 SASE.

Payment/Terms: Pays 2 contributor's copies; additional copies $7.

Advice: "We will *not* look at poetry. We only want to see intelligent spoofs of scholarly psychology and psychiatry articles written in scholarly scientific language. Take a look at *real* journals of psychology and try to lampoon their *style* as much as their content. There are few places to showcase satire of the social sciences, thus we provide one vehicle for injecting a dose of humor into this often too serious area. Occasionally, we will accept a piece of creative writing written in the first person, e.g. 'A Subjective Assessment of the Oral Doctoral Defense Process: I Don't Want to Talk About It, If You Want to Know the Truth' (the latter being a piece in which Holden Caulfield shares his experiences relating to obtaining his Ph.D. in Psychology). Other creative pieces have involved a psychodiagnostic evaluation of The Little Prince (as a psychiatric patient) and God being refused tenure (after having created the world) because of insufficient publications and teaching experience."

KRAX MAGAZINE, 63 Dixon Lane, Leeds LS12 4RR, Yorkshire, Britain, U.K. **Contact:** Andy Robson, fiction editor. "*Krax* publishes lighthearted, humorous and whimsical writing. It is for anyone seeking light relief at a gentle pace." Appears 1-2 times/year.

Needs: "We publish mostly poetry of a lighthearted nature but use comic or spoof fiction, witty and humorous essays." Accepts 1 ms/issue. Recently published work by Jim Sullivan. Length: 2,000 words maximum.

How to Contact: No specific guidelines.

Payment/Terms: Pays contributor's copies. Sample copy for $2 direct from editor.

Advice: "Don't spend too long on scene-setting or character construction as this inevitably produces an anti-climax in a short piece. Send IRCs or currency notes for return postal costs."

LEFT CURVE, P.O. Box 472, Oakland CA 94604-0472. (510)763-7193. E-mail: leftcurv@wco.com. Website: www.ncal.verio.com/~leftcurv. **Contact:** Csaba Polony, editor. Magazine: 8½×11; 144 pages; 60 lb. paper; 100 pt. C1S Durosheen cover; illustrations; photos. "*Left Curve* is an artist-produced journal addressing the problem(s) of cultural forms emerging from the crises of modernity that strive to be independent from the control of dominant institutions, based on the recognition of the destructiveness of commodity (capitalist) systems to all life." Published irregularly. Estab. 1974. Circ. 2,000.

Needs: Contemporary, ethnic, experimental, historical, literary, prose poem, regional, science fiction, translations, political. "No topical satire, religion-based pieces, melodrama. We publish critical, open, social/political-conscious writing." Receives approximately 12 unsolicited fiction mss/month. Accepts approximately 1 ms/issue. Publishes ms a maximum of 12 months after acceptance. Published work by Pēter Lengyel and Michael Filas. Length: 500-2,500 words; average length: 1,200 words. Publishes short shorts. Sometimes comments on rejected mss.

How to Contact: Send complete ms with cover letter. Include "statement of writer's intent, brief bio and reason for submitting to *Left Curve*." Accepts electronic submissions; "prefer 3½ disk and hard copy, though we do accept e-mail submissions." Responds in 6 months. SASE. Sample copy for $10, 9×12 SAE and $1.24 postage. Guidelines for 1 first-class stamp.

Payment/Terms: Pays in contributor's copies. Rights revert to author.

Advice: "We look for continuity, adequate descriptive passages, endings that are not simply abandoned (in both meanings). Dig deep; no superficial personalisms, no corny satire. Be honest, realistic and gorge out the truth you wish to say. Understand yourself and the world. Have writing be a means to achieve or realize what is real."

MAJESTIC BOOKS P.O. Box 19097A, Johnston RI 02919-0097. E-mail: majesticbk@aol.com. **Contact:** Cindy MacDonald, fiction editor. Bound softcover short story anthologies; 5½×8½; 224 pages; 50 lb. paper; C1S cover stock. "Majestic Books is a small press which was formed to give children an outlet for their work. We publish softcover bound anthologies of fictional stories by children, for children and adults who enjoy the work of children." Triannual. Estab. 1993. Circ. 250.

Needs: Stories written on any subject by children (under 18) only. Children's/juvenile (10-12 years), young adult (13-18 years). Receives 50 unsolicited mss/month. Accepts 100 mss/year. Publishes ms 1 year maximum after acceptance. **Publishes 95 new writers/year.** Recently published work by Ellen Green and Emily Breyfogle. Length: 2,000 words maximum. Publishes short shorts. Also publishes literary essays.

How to Contact: Send complete ms with a cover letter. Include estimated word count and author's age. Accepts submissions by e-mail and disk. Responds in 3 weeks. Send SASE for reply. Accepts simultaneous and multiple submissions. Sample copy for $5. Guidelines for #10 SASE.

Payment/Terms: Pays 10% royalty for all books sold due to the author's inclusion.

Advice: "We love stories that will keep a reader thinking long after they have read the last word. Be original. We have received some manuscripts of shows we have seen on television or books we have read. Write from inside you and you'll be surprised at how much better your writing will be. Use *your* imagination."

☑ $ ◎ **MINDSPARKS, The Magazine of Science and Science Fiction**, Molecudyne Research, P.O. Box 1302, Laurel MD 20725-1302. E-mail: asaro@sff.net. Website: www.sff.net/people/asaro/ (includes interviews, reviews, information on the Skolian Empire/Ruby Dynasty books, science articles). **Contact:** Catherine Asaro, editor. Magazine: 8½×11; 44 pages; 20 lb. white paper; 60 lb. cover; illustrations; photos. "We publish science fiction and science articles." Published on a varied schedule. Estab. 1993. Circ. 1,000.
  • *Mindsparks* is in the process of changing from a paper magazine to an electronic publication. For more information, either write the above editorial address or check the website. At publication, *Mindsparks* was closed to unsolicited submissions.
Needs: Science fiction (hard science, soft/sociological), young adult (science fiction). "No pornography." Receives 50 unsolicited submissions/month. Accepts 2-4 mss/issue; 12-14 mss/year. Publishes ms 1-24 months after acceptance. **Publishes an average of 10 new writers/year.** Published work by Hal Clement, G. David Nordley, Lois Gresh and Paul Levinson. Length: 8,000 words maximum; average length: 4,000 words. Publishes short shorts. Also publishes literary essays, literary criticism and poetry. Often comments on rejected mss.
How to Contact: Send complete ms with a cover letter. Include estimated word count and list of publications. "Prefers initial contact be made by mail." Responds in 3 months. Send SASE for reply, return of ms or send a disposable copy of ms. Accepts simultaneous submissions. Sample copy for $4.50, 8½×11 SAE and $1 postage or 2 IRCs. Guidelines for #10 SASE. Reviews novels and short story collections.
Payment/Terms: Pays 2¢/word. Pays on publication for first North American serial rights. Sends galleys to author.
Advice: Looks for "well-written, well-researched, interesting science ideas with good characterization and good plot. Read a copy of the magazine. We receive many submissions that don't fit the intent of *Mindsparks*."

☑ $ ◎ **THE MIRACULOUS MEDAL**, The Central Association of the Miraculous Medal, 475 E. Chelten Ave., Philadelphia PA 19144-5785. (215)848-1010. Website: www.cmphila.org/camm/. Editor: Rev. William J. O'Brien, C.M. **Contact:** Charles Kelly, general manager. Magazine. Quarterly.
Needs: Religious/inspirational. Receives 25 unsolicited fiction mss/month. Accepts 2 mss/issue; 8 mss/year. Publishes ms up to 2 years or more after acceptance.
How to Contact: Query first with SASE. Sample copy and fiction guidelines free.
Payment/Terms: Pays 2¢/word minimum. Pays on acceptance for first rights.

☒ ◯ **MOUNTAIN LUMINARY**, P.O. Box 1187, Mountain View AR 72560-1187. (870)585-2260. Fax: (870)269-4110. E-mail: ecomtn@mvtel.net. **Contact:** Anne Thiel, editor. Magazine; photos. "*Mountain Luminary* is dedicated to bringing information to people about the Aquarian Age; how to grow with its new and evolutionary energies and how to work with the resultant changes in spirituality, relationships, environment and the planet. *Mountain Luminary* provides a vehicle for people to share ideas, philosophies and experiences that deepen understanding of this evolutionary process and humankind's journey on Earth." International quarterly. Estab. 1985.
Needs: Humor/satire, metaphor/inspirational/Aquarian-Age topics. Accepts 8-10 mss/year. Publishes ms 6 months after acceptance. **Publishes 2 new writers/year.** Recently published work by Alex Bledson and Sakie Brown.
How to Contact: Query with clips of published work. SASE for return of ms. Accepts queries/mss by fax and e-mail. Accepts simultaneous submissions. Sample copy and writer's guidelines free.
Payment/Terms: Pays 1 contributor's copy. "We may offer advertising space as payment." Acquires first rights.
Advice: "We look for stories with a moral—those with insight to problems on the path which raise the reader's awareness. Topical interests include: New Age/Aquarian Age, astrology, crystals, cultural and ethnic concerns, dreams, ecosystems, the environment, extraterrestrials, feminism, folklore, healing and health, holistic and natural health, inspiration, juvenile and teen issues, lifestyle, meditation, men's issues, metaphysics, mysticism, nutrition, parallel dimensions, prayer, psychic phenomenon, self-help, spirituality and women's issues."

$ ◙ ◎ **MOXIE, For the Woman Who Dares**, Moxie, 1230 Glen Ave., Berkeley CA 94708. (510)540-5510. Fax: (510)540-8595. E-mail: emily@moxiemag.com. Website: www.moxiemag.com (includes entirely original content, no overlap with print edition—articles, short stories, book reviews and poems). **Contact:** Emily Hancock, editor. Magazine: 8¼×10¾; 56 pages; illustrations; photos. "Our audience is smart, gutsy women who want something more than fashion, sex and beauty in a magazine." Annual. Estab. 1998. Circ. under 10,000. Member, IPA.

Needs: Essays, family saga, feminist, adventure, profiles. Upcoming theme: Family/Friends/Lovers. List of upcoming themes available for SASE. Receives 90-100 unsolicited mss/month. Accepts 90-100 mss/year. **Publishes 80 new writers/year.** Recently published work by dgk goldberg, Danya Ruttenberg and Jessica Leigh Lebos. Length: 750-4,000 words; average length: 1,500-2,000 words. Publishes short shorts. Average length: 750 words. Also publishes literary essays, literary criticism and poetry. Often comments on rejected mss.

How to Contact: Send complete ms with a cover letter by e-mail only. Include estimated word count and e-mail address. Responds in 3 weeks to mss. Accepts simultaneous submissions and previously published work. Sample copy for $6. Guidelines free or by e-mail. Accepts reviews of novels, short story collections and nonfiction books of interest to writers.

Payment/Terms: Pays $10-25 and 3 contributor's copies; additional copies $5. Pays on publication. Sends galleys to author.

Advice: "Does it have a beginning, middle and end?"

✓ ⊕ MSLEXIA, For Women Who Write, Mslexia Publications Ltd., P.O. Box 656, Newcastle Upon Tyne NE99-2RP United Kingdom. Phone: (00)44-191-2616656. Fax: (00)44-191-2616636. E-mail: lisa@mslexia .demon.co.uk. Website: www.mslexia.co.uk. **Contact:** Lisa Matthews, marketing manager. Magazine: A4; 60 pages; some illustrations; photos. "*Mslexia* is for women who write, who want to write, who have a specialist interest in women's writing of who teach creative writing. *Mslexia* is a blend of features, articles, advice, listings, and original prose & poetry. Many parts of the magazine are open to submission from any women. Please request contributors guidelines prior to sending in work." Quarterly. Estab. 1999. Circ. 6,000.

Needs: Each issue is to a specific theme. Themes for SASE. Some themes included erotica, death writing from a male perspective & body image. No work of men. Receives 100-200 unsolicited mss/month. Accepts 5-6 mss/ issue; 20-25 mss/year. Publishes ms 3-4 months after acceptance. **Publishes 10-15 new writers/year.** Length: 2,000 words; average length: 1,000-2,000 words. Publishes short shorts. Average length: 1,000-2,000 words. Also publishes poetry.

How to Contact: Query first. Accepts submissions by e-mail. Responds in 2 weeks to queries; 3 months to mss. Send disposable copy of ms and #10 for reply only. Sample copy for £4.95 (sterling). Guidelines for SASE, e-mail, fax or on website.

Payment/Terms: Pays in contributors copies.

Advice: "Prose—An unusual slant on the theme. Well structured, short pieces. Also intelligent, humorous, or with a strong sense of voice. Poetry—Innovative diction use/syntax, free verse or intelligent subversion of form, well crafted structrued. Consider the theme and all obvious interpretations of it. Try to think of a new angle/ slant. Dare to be different. Make sure the piece is strong on craft as well as content."

$☐ ☑ MYSTERY TIME, An Anthology of Short Stories, Hutton Publications, P.O. Box 2907, Decatur IL 62524-2907. **Contact:** Linda Hutton, editor. Booklet: 5½×8½; 52 pages; bond paper. "Semiannual collection of short stories with a suspense or mystery theme for mystery buffs, with an emphasis on women writers and women protagonists. We focus on older women, both as characters and as authors. It is our goal to encourage middle-aged and older females by presenting a positive, up-beat picture of them and their lives." Estab. 1983.

● *Mystery Time* ranked #23 on *Writer's Digest*'s Fiction 50 list of top markets.

Needs: Mystery/suspense only. "No true crime or brutal gore. Would like to see more protagonists like Miss Marple, with a touch of humor." Receives 10-15 unsolicited fiction mss/month. Accepts 20-24 mss/year. **Published 10-12 new writers/year.** Recently published work by Jane E. Allen, Linda Kerslake and Thomas Millstead. Length: 1,500 words maximum. Occasionally comments on rejected mss and recommends other markets.

How to Contact: Send complete ms with SASE. "No cover letters." Accepts simultaneous, multiple and previously published submissions. Responds in 1 month to mss. Publishes ms an average of 6-8 months after acceptance. Sample copy for $4. Guidelines for #10 SASE. Reviews mysteries and women's studies books. Send galleys or book with SASE.

Payment/Terms: Pays ¼-1¢/word and 1 contributor's copy; additional copies $2.50. Pays on acceptance for one-time rights.

Advice: "Study a sample copy and the guidelines. Too many amateurs mark themselves as amateurs by submitting blindly."

✓ $⊘ NEW ENGLAND WRITERS' NETWORK, P.O. Box 483, Hudson MA 01749-0483. (978)562-2946. E-mail: NEWNmag@aol.com. Editor: Glenda Baker. **Contact:** Liz Aleshire, fiction editor. Poetry Editor: Judy Adourian. Magazine: 8½×11; 24 pages; coated cover. "We are devoted to helping new writers get published and to teaching through example and content. We are looking for well-written stories that grab us from the opening paragraph." Quarterly. Estab. 1994. Circ. 200.

● *New England Writers' Network* has a new feature called First Fiction. A story by a previously unpublished fiction writer is spotlighted under the heading First Fiction.

Needs: Adventure, condensed/excerpted novel, ethnic/multicultural, humor/satire, literary, mainstream/contemporary, mystery/suspense, religious/inspirational, romance. "We will consider anything except pornography or extreme violence." Accepts 5 mss/issue; 20 mss/year. Reads mss only from June 1 through September 1. Publishes ms 4-12 months after acceptance. **Publishes 10-12 new writers/year.** Recently published work by Laura Pedersen, Esther Holt and Pat Car. Length: 2,000 words maximum. Publishes short shorts. Also publishes poetry and 3-4 personal essays per issue. Always comments on rejected mss.

How to Contact: Send complete ms with a cover letter. Include estimated word count. Bio on acceptance. Responds in 4 months. SASE for return of ms. No simultaneous submissions. Sample copy for $5.50. Guidelines free. "We do not review story collections or novels. We do publish 2,000-word (maximum) novel excerpts. Writer picks the excerpt—do not send novel."

Payment/Terms: Pays $10 for fiction, $5 for personal essays, $3 per poem and 1 contributor's copy. Pays on publication for first North American serial rights.

Advice: "We are devoted to helping new writers get published and to teaching through example and content. Give us a try! Please send for guidelines and a sample."

$⊘ ▼ NIGHT TERRORS, 1202 W. Market St., Orrville OH 44667-1710. (330)683-0338. E-mail: dedavidson@night-terrors-publications.com. Website: www.night-terrors-publications.com (includes updated guidelines, bios of the editor and writers, short fiction, order info, links to other sites of interest to writers and readers of horror). **Contact:** D.E. Davidson, editor/publisher. Magazine: 8½×11; 52 pages; 80 lb. glossy cover; illustrations; photos. "*Night Terrors* publishes quality, thought-provoking horror fiction for literate adults." Quarterly. Estab. 1996. Circ. 1,000.

• *Night Terrors* has had 22 stories listed in the Honorable Mention section of *The Year's Best Fantasy and Horror, Annual Collections.*

Needs: Horror, psychic/supernatural/occult. "Night Terrors does not accept stories involving abuse, sexual mutilation or stories with children as main characters. We publish traditional supernatural/psychological horror for a mature audience. Our emphasis is on literate work with a chill." Wants to see more psychological horror. Receives 50 unsolicited mss/month. Accepts 12 mss/issue; 46 mss/year. Does not read mss June-August. Publishes ms 2-6 months after acceptance. **Publishes 16 new writers/year.** Published work by John M. Clay, Ken Goldman, and Barbara Rosen. Length: 2,000-5,000 words; average length: 3,000 words. Often comments on rejected mss.

How to Contact: Send complete ms with a cover letter. Include estimated word count, 50-word bio and list of publications. Responds in 1 week to queries; 3 months to mss. Send SASE for reply, return of ms or send a disposable copy of ms. Accepts simultaneous submissions. Sample copy for $6 (make checks to Night Terrors Publications). Guidelines free for #10 SASE.

Payment/Terms: Pays up to $100 and 1-2 contributor's copy; additional copies for $4.50. Pays on publication for first North American serial rights. Sends galleys to author.

Advice: "I publish what I like. I like stories which involve me with the viewpoint character and leave me with the feeling that his/her fate could have or might be mine. Act professionally. Check your work for typos, spelling, grammar, punctuation, format. Send your work flat. And if you must, paper clip it, don't staple. Include a brief, to-the-point cover letter."

Ｎ ◯ THE NOCTURNAL LYRIC, Journal of the Bizarre, The Nocturnal Lyric, P.O. Box 542, Astoria OR 97103. E-mail: nocturnallyric@melodymail.com. Website: www.angelfire.com/ca/nocturnallyric (includes guidelines, poetry, names of upcoming writers, specials on back issues. **Contact:** Susan Moon, editor. Magazine: 8½×5½; 40 pages; illustrations. "Fiction and poetry submitted should have a bizarre horror theme. Our audience encompasses people who stand proudly outside of the mainstream of society." Quarterly. Estab. 1987. Circ. 400.

Needs: Horror (dark fantasy, futuristic, psychological, supernatural, satirical). "No sexually graphic material—it's too overdone in the horror genre lately." Receives 25-30 unsolicited mss/month. Accepts 8-9 mss/issue; 30 mss/year. Publishes ms 1 year after acceptance. **Publishes 20 new writers/year.** Recently published work by Jeffrey Valka, Brad Maier, D. Harlan Wilson and Hanna K. Lee. Length: 2,000 words maximum; average length: 1,500 words. Publishes short shorts. Average length: 500 words. Also publishes literary essays and poetry. Rarely comments on rejected mss.

How to Contact: Send complete ms with a cover letter. Include estimated word count and "your philosophy on life." Responds in 1 month to queries; 8 months to mss. Send SASE (or IRC) for return of ms. Accepts simultaneous, previously published and multiple submissions. Sample copy for $2 (back issue); $3 (current issue). Guidelines for SASE or on website. Reviews novels, short story collections and nonfiction books of interest to writers. Send review copies to the editor.

Payment/Terms: Pays with discounts on subscription and copies of issue. Pays on acceptance for one-time rights. Not copyrighted.

Advice: "A manuscript stands out when the story has a very original theme and the ending is not predictable. Don't be afraid to be adventurous with your story. Mainstream horror can be boring. Surreal, satirical horror is what true nightmares are all about."

THE OAK, 1530 Seventh St., Rock Island IL 61201. (309)788-3980. **Contact:** Betty Mowery, editor. Magazine: 8½×11; 8-10 pages. "To provide a showcase for new authors while showing the work of established authors as well; to publish wholesome work, something with a message." Bimonthly. Estab. 1991. Circ. 300.
Needs: Adventure, contemporary, experimental, fantasy, humor, mainstream, prose poem. No erotica or love poetry. Receives 25 mss/month. Accepts up to 12 mss/issue. Publishes ms within 3 months of acceptance. **Publishes 25 new writers/year. Publishes 10 new writers/year.** Length: 500 words maximum.
How to Contact: Send complete ms. Responds in 1 week. SASE. Accepts simultaneous, multiple and reprint submissions. Sample copy for $3. Subscription $10 for 4 issues.
Payment/Terms: None, but not necessary to buy a copy in order to be published. Acquires first rights.
Advice: "I do not want erotica, extreme violence or killing of humans or animals for the sake of killing. Just be yourself when you write. Please include SASE or manuscripts will be destroyed. Be sure name and address are on the manuscript. Study the markets for length of manuscript and what type of material is wanted."

$☉ ON SPEC, Box 4727, Edmonton, Alberta T6E 5G6 Canada. (780)413-0215. Fax: (780)413-1538. E-mail: onspec@earthling.net. Website: www.icomm.ca/onspec (includes writer's guidelines, past editorials, excerpts from published fiction, links to writer's Internet resources). **Contact:** The Editors. Magazine: 5¼×8; 112 pages; illustrations. "Provides a venue for Canadian speculative writing—science fiction, fantasy, horror, magic realism." Quarterly. Estab. 1989. Circ. 2,000.
Needs: Fantasy and science fiction. No condensed or excerpted novels, no religious/inspirational stories. "We would like to see more horror, fantasy, science fiction—well-developed stories with complex characters and strong plots." Receives 50 mss/month. Accepts 10 mss/issue; 40 mss/year. "We read manuscripts during the month after each deadline: February 28/May 31/August 31/November 30." Publishes ms 6-18 months after acceptance. **Publishes new writers, number varies.** Length: 1,000-6,000 words; average length: 4,000 words. Also publishes poetry. Often comments on rejected mss.
How to Contact: Send complete ms with a cover letter. No submissions by e-mail or fax. Include estimated word count, 2-sentence bio and phone number. Responds in 5 months to mss. SASE for return of ms or send a disposable copy of ms plus #10 SASE for response. Include Canadian postage or IRCs. Accepts simultaneous submissions. Sample copy for $7. Guidelines for #10 SASE.
Payment/Terms: Pays $40-180 and 2 contributor's copies; additional copies for $7. Pays on acceptance for first North American serial rights.
Advice: "We're looking for original ideas with a strong SF element, excellent dialogue, and characters who are so believable, our readers will really care about them."

N ☺ PARADOXISM, Anti-literary Journal, University of New Mexico, Gallup NM 87301. Fax: (505)863-7532 (Attn. Dr. Smarandache). E-mail: smarand@unm.edu. Website: www.gallup.unm.edu/~smaranda che/. **Contact:** Florentin Smarandache, editor. Magazine: 8½×11; 100 pages; illustrations. "The paradoxism is an avant-garde movement set up by the editor in the 1980s in Romania, based on excessive use of antithesis, antimonies, contradictions, paradoxes in the creation. It tries to generalize the art, to make the unliterary become literary." Annually. Estab. 1993. Circ. 500.
Needs: "Crazy, uncommon, experimental, avant-garde"; also ethnic/multicultural. Plans specific themes in the next year. Publishes annual special fiction issue or anthology. Receives 3-4 unsolicited mss/month. Accepts 10 mss/issue. Published work by Dan Topa and Anatol Ciocanu. Length: 500-1,000 words. Publishes short shorts. Also publishes literary essays, literary criticism and poetry. Focus on new literary terms such as paradoxist distich, tautological distich, dual distich
How to Contact: Query with clips of unpublished work. Responds in 2 months to mss. Send a disposable copy of ms. Sample copy for $19.95 and 8½×11 SASE.
Payment/Terms: Pays 1 contributor's copy. Not copyrighted.
Advice: "The Basic Thesis of the paradoxism: everything has a meaning and a non-meaning in a harmony each other. The Essence of the paradoxism: a) the sense has a non-sense, and reciprocally b) the non-sense has a sense. The Motto of the paradoxism: 'All is possible, the impossible too!' The Symbol of the paradoxism: (a spiral—optic illusion, or vicious circle)."

☉ ☺ THE PIPE SMOKER'S EPHEMERIS, The Universal Coterie of Pipe Smokers, 20-37 120 St., College Point NY 11356-2128. **Contact:** Tom Dunn, editor. Magazine: 8½×11; 84-116 pages; offset paper and cover; illustrations; photos. Pipe smoking and tobacco theme for general and professional audience. Irregular quarterly. Estab. 1964.
Needs: Pipe smoking related: historical, humor/satire, literary. Publishes ms up to 1 year after acceptance. Length: 5,000 words maximum; average length: 2,500 words. Also publishes short shorts. Occasionally critiques rejected mss.
How to Contact: Send complete ms with cover letter. Responds in 2 weeks to mss. Accepts simultaneous submissions and reprints. Sample copy for 8½×11 SAE and 6 first-class stamps.

Payment/Terms: Acquires one-time rights.

⬤ ◎ **POSKISNOLT PRESS, Yesterday's Press,** Yesterday's Press, JAF Station, Box 7415, New York NY 10116-4630. **Contact:** Patricia D. Coscia, editor. Magazine: 7×8½; 20 pages; regular typing paper. Estab. 1989. Circ. 100.

Needs: Contemporary, erotica, ethnic, experimental, fantasy, feminist, gay, humor/satire, lesbian, literary, mainstream, prose poem, psychic/supernatural/occult, romance, senior citizen/retirement, western, young adult/teen (10-18 years). "X-rated material is not accepted!" Plans to publish a special fiction issue or anthology in the future. Receives 50 unsolicited mss/month. Accepts 30 mss/issue; 100 mss/year. Publishes ms 6 months after acceptance. Length: 100-500 words; average length: 200 words. Publishes short shorts. Length: 100-500 words. Sometimes comments on rejected mss and recommends other markets.

How to Contact: Query first with clips of published work or send complete ms with cover letter. Responds in 1 week to queries; 6 months to mss. SASE. Accepts simultaneous submissions. Sample copy for $5 with #10 SAE and $2 postage. Guidelines for #10 SAE and $2 postage.

Payment/Terms: Pays with subscription to magazine or contributor's copies; charges for extras. Acquires all rights, first rights or one-time rights.

✓ $⬤ **THE POST,** Publishers Syndication International, P.O. Box 6218, Charlottesville VA 22906-6218. Fax: (434)964-0096. E-mail: asam@firstra.com. Website: www.publisherssyndication.com/. **Contact:** A.P. Samuels, editor. Magazine: 8½×11; 32 pages. Monthly. Estab. 1988.

Needs: Adventure, mystery/suspense (private eye), romance (romantic suspense, historical, contemporary), western (traditional). "No explicit sex, gore, weird themes, extreme violence or bad language." Receives 35 unsolicited mss/month. Accepts 1 ms/issue; 12 mss/year. Time between acceptance and publication varies. Agented fiction 10%. **Publishes 1-3 new writers/year.** Length: 10,000 words average.

How to Contact: Send complete ms with cover letter. Responds to mss in 5 weeks. Guidelines for #10 SASE.

Payment/Terms: Pays ½-4¢/word. Pays on acceptance for all rights.

Advice: "Manuscripts must be for a general audience."

✓ ○ **PRAYERWORKS, Encouraging, God's people to do the real work of ministry—intercessory prayer,** The Master's Work, P.O. Box 301363, Portland OR 97294-9363. (503)761-2072. Fax: (503)760-1184. E-mail: vannmi@aol.com. **Contact:** V. Ann Mandeville, editor. Newsletter: 5½×8; 4 pages; bond paper. "Our intended audience is 70% retired Christians and 30% families. We publish 350-500 word devotional material— fiction, nonfiction, biographical poetry, clean quips and quotes. Our philosophy is evangelical Christian serving the body of Christ in the area of prayer." Estab. 1988. Circ. 1,000.

Needs: Religious/inspirational. "Subject matter may include anything which will build relationship with the Lord—prayer, ways to pray, stories of answered prayer, teaching on a Scripture portion, articles that will build faith, or poems will all work. We even use a series occasionally." Publishes 2-6 months after acceptance. **Publishes 30 new writers/year.** Recently published work by Sue Milholen and Petey Prater. Length: 350-500 words; average length: 350-500 words. Publishes short shorts. Also publishes poetry. Often comments on rejected mss.

How to Contact: Send complete ms with a cover letter. Include estimated word count and a very short bio. Responds in 1 month. Send SASE for reply, return of ms or send a disposable copy of ms. Accepts simultaneous submissions and reprints. Sample copy and guidelines for #10 SASE.

Payment/Terms: Pays free subscription to the magazine and contributor's copies. Pays on publication. Writer retains all rights. Not copyrighted.

Advice: Stories "must have a great take-away—no preaching; teach through action. Be thrifty with words— make them count."

✓ $⬤ **PSI,** P.O. Box 6218, Charlottesville VA 22906-6218. Fax: (804)964-0096. E-mail: asam@firstva.com. Website: www.publisherssyndication.com. **Contact:** A.P. Samuels, editor. Magazine: 8½×11; 32 pages; bond paper; self cover. "Mystery and romance." Bimonthly. Estab. 1987.

Needs: Adventure, romance (contemporary, historical, young adult), mystery/suspense (private eye), western (traditional). No ghoulish, sex, violence. Wants to see more believable stories. Receives 35 unsolicited mss/month. Accepts 1-2 mss/issue. **Publishes 1-3 new writers/year.** Length: 10,000 (stories) and 30,000 (novelettes) words average. Comments on rejected mss "only on a rare occasion."

How to Contact: Send complete ms with cover letter. Responds in 2 weeks to queries; 6 weeks to mss. SASE. Accepts electronic submissions via disk.

Payment/Terms: Pays 1-4¢/word plus royalty. Pays on acceptance for all rights.

Advice: "Manuscripts must be for a general audience. Just good plain story telling (make it compelling). No explicit sex or ghoulish violence."

✅ $ **THE PSYCHIC RADIO**, 1111 Elmwood Ave., Rochester NY 14620-3005. (716)241-1200, ext. 1288. **Contact:** Lester Billips Jr., editor. Magazine: full size; 32-64 pages; 70 lb. text gloss; 100 lb. text gloss card cover. "My magazine is to periodicals, what 'alternative rock' is to music. *Psychic Radio* offers straight talk about problems long kept in the dark. My intended audience is anyone concerned with the moral fiber of our country." Quarterly. Estab. 2001.

Needs: Fantasy (sword and sorcery), horror (futuristic, psychological, supernatural), new age, psychic/supernatural/occult, religious (general, inspirational, religious fantasy), science fiction (soft/sociological). Accepts 5-10 mss/issue; 20-25 mss/year. Publishes in 3-4 months after acceptance. Publishes short shorts. Also publishes literary essays and poetry. Sometimes comments on rejected mss.

How to Contact: Send complete ms with cover letter. Include estimated word count and brief bio. Responds in 1 month to queries and mss. Send SASE for return of ms or send a disposable copy of ms and #10 SASE for reply only. Accepts simultaneous submissions, previously published work and multiple submissions. Sample copy for $2.50. Guidelines for SASE.

Payment/Terms: Pays $20-50 and contributor's copies; additional copies $2.50. Pays on acceptance for one-time rights.

Advice: "I look for work with relevance to the growing psychic problem in America today. Be honest and be urgent."

✅ 🄾 **QUEEN OF ALL HEARTS,** Queen Magazine, Montfort Missionaries, 26 S. Saxon Ave., Bay Shore NY 11706-8993. (631)665-0726. Fax: (631)665-4349. E-mail: rogercharest@worldnet.att.net. **Contact:** Roger M. Charest, S.M.M., managing editor Magazine: 7¾×10¾; 48 pages; self cover stock; illustrations; photos. Magazine of "stories, articles and features on the Mother of God by explaining the Scriptural basis and traditional teaching of the Catholic Church concerning the Mother of Jesus, her influence in fields of history, literature, art, music, poetry, etc." Bimonthly. Estab. 1950. Circ. 2,500.

 • *Queen of All Hearts* received a Catholic Press Award for General Excellence (third place) and a Prayer and Spirituality Journalism Award.

Needs: Religious/inspirational. "No mss not about Our Lady, the Mother of God, the Mother of Jesus." **Publishes 6 new writers/year.** Published work by Richard O'Donnell and Jackie Clements-Marenda. Length: 1,500-2,000 words. Sometimes recommends other markets.

How to Contact: Send complete ms with SASE. Accepts queries/mss by e-mail and fax (mss by permission only). Responds in 1 month to mss. Publishes ms 6-12 months after acceptance. Sample copy for $2.50 with 9×12 SAE.

Payment/Terms: Varies. Pays 6 contributor's copies.

Advice: "We are publishing stories with a Marian theme."

🄼 $ 🄾 🄼 **QUEEN'S QUARTERLY, A Canadian Review**, Queen's University, Kingston, Ontario K7L 3N6 Canada. Phone/fax: (613)533-2667. Fax: (613)533-6822. E-mail: qquarter@post.queensu.ca. Website: info.q ueensu.ca./quarterly. **Contact:** Boris Castel, editor. Magazine: 6×9; 800 pages/year; illustrations. "A general interest intellectual review, featuring articles on science, politics, humanities, arts and letters. Book reviews, poetry and fiction." Quarterly. Estab. 1893. Circ. 3,000.

Needs: Contemporary, historical, literary, mainstream, women's. "*Special emphasis on work by Canadian writers.*" Accepts 2 mss/issue; 8 mss/year. **Published new writers within the last year.** Published work by Gail Anderson-Dargatz, Mark Jarman, Rick Bowers and Dennis Bock. Length: 2,000-3,000 words. Also publishes literary essays, literary criticism, poetry.

How to Contact: "Send complete ms with SASE and/or IRC. No reply with insufficient postage." Accepts submissions by e-mail. Responds within 3 months. Sample copy for $6.50. Reviews novels and short story collections.

Payment/Terms: Pays $100-300 for fiction, 2 contributor's copies and 1-year subscription; additional copies $5. Pays on publication for first North American serial rights. Sends galleys to author.

🄾 **REFLECTIONS, Literary Journal**, Piedmont Community College, P.O. Box 1197, Roxboro NC 27573. (336)599-1181. E-mail: thrasht@piedmont.cc.nc.us. **Contact:** Tami Sloane Thrasher, editor. Magazine: 128 pages. "We publish work which addresses and transcends humanity and cultures." Annual. Estab. 1999. Circ. 500.

FOR EXPLANATIONS OF THESE SYMBOLS,
SEE THE INSIDE FRONT AND BACK COVERS OF THIS BOOK.

Needs: Literary, translations. Receives 30 unsolicited mss/month. Accepts 5 mss/issue. Publishes ms 4 months after acceptance. **Publishes 2 new writers/year.** Recently published work by Lynn Veach Sadler, H.G. Myers and Emily A. Kern. Length: 5,000 words maximum; average length: 2,500 words. Publishes short shorts. Also publishes poetry.

How to Contact: Send complete ms with a cover letter. Include estimated word count, brief bio and SASE. Send SASE (or IRC) for return of ms or send a disposable copy of ms and #10 SASE for reply only. Accepts multiple submissions. Sample copy for $6. Guidelines for SASE or by e-mail. "Note that our annual deadline is December 31. We make our selections in February; therefore, writers submitting in January or February will have a one-year wait before being notified of acceptance or rejection."

Payment/Terms: Pays 1 contributor's copy; additional copies $6 pre-publication; $7 post-publication. Pays on publication for first North American serial rights. Writers are automatically considered for $50 annual Editor's Choice Award for best fiction.

Advice: "We look for good writing with a flair, which captivates an educated lay audience. Must speak to the human condition."

N **⬛** **◎** **RFD, A Country Journal for Gay Men Everywhere,** Short Mountain Collective, P.O. Box 68, Liberty TN 37095. (615)536-5176. E-mail: mail@rfdmag.org. Website: www.rfdmag.org. **Contact:** Fred Lowe, fiction editor. Magazine: 8½×11; 64-80 pages. "Focus on radical faeries, gay men's spirituality—country living." Quarterly. Estab. 1974. Circ. 2,500.

Needs: Gay: Erotica, ethnic/multicultural, experimental, fantasy, feminist, humor/satire, literary, mainstream/ contemporary, mystery/suspense, psychic/supernatural/occult, regional, romance. Receives 10 unsolicited mss/ month. Accepts 3 mss/issue; 12 mss/year. Length: open. Publishes short shorts. Also publishes literary essays, literary criticism and poetry.

How to Contact: Send complete ms with cover letter and estimated word count. Accepts e-mail and disk submissions. Accepts multiple submissions. Usually reports in 6-9 months. Send SASE for reply, return of ms or send disposable copy of ms. Sample copy for $7.75. Free guidelines.

Payment/Terms: Pays 1-2 contributor's copies. Not copyrighted.

$ **⬛** **ROSEBUD**™, **For People Who Enjoy Good Writing,** P.O. Box 459, Cambridge WI 53523. Phone/ fax: (608)423-9609. Website: www.hyperionstudio.com/rosebud (includes writer's guidelines, contests, preview, *Rosebud* bulletin board, teachers guide to current issue, outreach programs and advertising rates). **Editor:** Roderick Clark. Magazine: 7×10; 136 pages; 60 lb. matte; 100 lb. cover; illustrations. Quarterly. Estab. 1993. Circ. 11,000.

Needs: Adventure, condensed/excerpted novel, ethnic/multicultural, experimental, historical (general), humor/ satire, literary, mainstream/contemporary, psychic/supernatural/occult, regional, romance (contemporary), science fiction (soft/sociological), serialized novel, translations. Each submission must fit loosely into one of the following categories to qualify: City and Shadow (urban settings), Songs of Suburbia (suburban themes), These Green Hills (nature and nostalgia), En Route (any type of travel), Mothers, Daughters, Wives (relationships), Ulysses' Bow (manhood), Paper, Scissors, Rock (childhood, middle age, old age), The Jeweled Prize (concerning love), Lost and Found (loss and discovery), Voices in Other Rooms (historic or of other culture), Overtime (involving work), Anything Goes (humor), I Hear Music (music), Season to Taste (food), Word Jazz (wordplay), Apples to Oranges (miscellaneous, excerpts, profiles). Publishes annual special fiction issue or anthology. Receives 1,200 unsolicited mss/month. Accepts 16 mss/issue; 64 mss/year. Publishes ms 1-3 months after acceptance. **70% of work published is by new writers.** Published work by Seamus Heany, Louis Simpson, Allen Ginsberg and Philip Levine. Length: 1,200-1,800 words average. Occasionally uses longer pieces and novel excerpts (prepublished). Publishes short shorts. Also publishes literary essays. Often comments on rejected mss.

How to Contact: Send complete ms with a cover letter. Include estimated word count and list of publications. Responds in 3 months to mss. SASE for return of ms. Accepts simultaneous and reprints submissions. Sample copy for $6.95. Guidelines for legal SASE.

Payment/Terms: Pays $15 and 3 contributor's copies; additional copies $4.40. Pays on publication for one-time rights.

Advice: "Each issue will have six or seven flexible departments (selected from a total of sixteen departments that will rotate). We are seeking stories, articles, profiles, and poems of: love, alienation, travel, humor, nostalgia and unexpected revelation. Something has to 'happen' in the pieces we choose, but what happens inside characters is much more interesting to us than plot manipulation. We like good storytelling, real emotion and authentic voice."

⬛ **⬛** **SKIPPING STONES: A Multicultural Children's Magazine,** P.O. Box 3939, Eugene OR 97403-0939. (541)342-4956. E-mail: skipping@efn.org. Website: www.efn.org/~skipping (includes writer's guidelines).

Contact: Arun N. Toké, executive editor. Magazine: 8½×11; 36 pages; recycled 50 lb. halopaque paper; 100 lb. text cover; illustrations; photos. *"Skipping Stones* is a multicultural, international, nature awareness magazine for children 8-16, and their parents and teachers." Published 5 times a year. Estab. 1988. Circ. 2,500.

• *Skipping Stones* has received EdPress and NAME awards.

Needs: Children's/juvenile (8-16 years): ethnic/multicultural, feminist, religious/inspirational, young adult/teen, international, nature. No simplistic, fiction for the sake of fiction, mystery, violent/abusive language or science fiction. "We want more authentic pieces based on truly multicultural/intercultural/international living experiences of authors. We welcome works by people of color." Upcoming themes: "Living Abroad," "Crosscultural Communications," "Challenging Disabililty," "Celebrations," "Folktales," "Turning Points in Life . . ." List of upcoming themes available for SASE. Receives 50 mss/month. Accepts 5-8 mss/issue; 20-25 mss/year. Publishes ms 3-6 months after acceptance. **Publishes up to 15 new writers/year.** Recently published work by Jon Bush, Kathleen Ahrens and Linda Raczek. Length: 250-1,000 words; average length: 750 words. Publishes short shorts. Also publishes literary essays and poetry (by youth under 18). Often comments on rejected mss. Sponsors contests and awards for writers under 17 years of age.

How to Contact: Send complete ms with a cover letter. Accepts queries/mss by e-mail. Include 50- to 100-word bio with background, international or intercultural experiences. Responds in 1 month to queries; 4 months to mss. Send SASE for reply, return of ms or send a disposable copy of ms. Accepts simultaneous submissions. Sample copy for $5, and 4 first-class stamps. Guidelines for #10 SASE.

Payment/Terms: Pays 1-4 contributor's copies; additional copies for $3. Acquires first North American serial rights and nonexclusive reprint rights.

Advice: Looking for stories with "multicultural/multiethnic theme. Realistic and suitable for 8- to 16-year-olds (with use of other languages when appropriate). Promoting social and nature awareness. In addition to encouraging children's creativity, we also invite adults to submit their own writing and artwork for publication in *Skipping Stones*. Writings and artwork by adults should challenge readers to think and learn, cooperate and create."

☑ STEPPING OUT OF THE DARKNESS, Puritan/Jewish Newsletter, P.O. Box 712, Hingham MA 02043. (781)878-5531. E-mail: ThePuritanLight@aol.com. Website: www.members.tripod.com/puritan55 (includes excerpts, writers' guidelines). **Contact:** Editor. Newsletter/magazine: 9-12 pages. "Our main focus is on New England in earlier centuries. We uncover lost spiritual truths in Holy living (with the help of such great figures as Richard Baxter, Gov. John Winthrop, Cotton Mather and many more.) We also print current concerns, poetry and inspirational fiction. We like to see work from children and teens as well as adults. Our publication is read by Christians and also those who are unsure about God. We also print Jewish stories." Monthly. Estab. 1998. Circ. 50.

Needs: Children's/juvenile, family saga, historical (general), religious (children's, general, inspirational, religious thriller), young adult/teen (adventure, historical), general family, Jewish stories. No fantasy. Accepts 1 mss/issue; 12 mss/year. Publishes ms 2-4 months after acceptance. Length: 500-1,400 words; average length: 900. Publishes short shorts; average length: 700 words. Also publishes poetry. Always comments on rejected mss.

How to Contact: Send complete ms with cover letter. Include estimated word count and brief bio. Responds in 2 months to queries; 2 months to mss. Send disposable copy of ms and #10 SASE for reply only. Accepts multiple submissions. Sample package for $3. Guidelines for SASE.

Payment/Terms: Pays 2 contributor's copies. Acquires one-time rights.

Advice: "Fiction must be biblically accurate, well-written, and have a great message."

STORY DIGEST, The Magazine for Writers, Shaun Lockhart Communications, P.O. Box 744, Louisville KY 40201-0744. (502)635-5453. Fax: (502)635-7072. E-mail: storydigest@aol.com. Website: www.storydigest. com (includes links, magazine description, editors' names, guidelines). **Contact:** Shaun Lockhart, editor. Estab. 1996. Quarterly. Circ. 5,000. Magazine: 5½×8½; 64-72 pages; glossy cover; illustrations; photos. *"Story Digest* is a writer's guide to networking and freelancing opportunities. This magazine infuses life and imagination into news, features, reports, fiction and poetry, all dealing with writing. We aim to inspire, enlighten and entertain writers who have an interest in expanding their careers. *Story Digest* publishes a wide range of material, as long as it relates to the writer or writer's craft.

Needs: "We are looking for interesting stories in all forms that relate to writing or writers. These stories can be in the form of mystery, horror, thriller, and so on. Please do not send stories that do not adhere to our criteria." List of themes available with SASE. Receives 30 unsolicited mss/month. Accepts 10 mss/issue; 60-70 mss/year. Publishes ms 2 months after acceptance. Agented fiction less than 5%. **Publishes 15-20 new writers/year.** Recently published work by Kalintu Wilson, LaVon Rice and Michael Ray. Length: 4,000 words maximum. Also publishes literary essays, poetry, criticism, nonfiction. Often comments on rejected mss; "sometimes we will comment and ask writers to resubmit."

How to Contact: Send complete ms or query with ms by e-mail. Include estimated word count, brief bio, photo or art suggestions. Responds in 2 months to mss. SASE. Simultaneous submissions and reprints okay. Sample copy for $5. Also reviews novels, short story collections, and nonfiction books of interest to writers.

Payment/Terms: Pays 3 contributors copies; additional copies for $5. Acquires first or reprint rights.

Advice: "We look at fiction writing to first make sure it fits our criteria. Afterwards, we ask how the piece can inspire, enlighten or entertain our readers. Does this piece offer a glimpse into the life of a writer? How so? The best tip we can offer beginning writers is to simply write. Before submitting to our publication or any other, understand the format and structure. Editors are sometimes not sympathetic to you as a beginning writer when they have tons of work to do."

◯ THE STORYTELLER, A Writers Magazine, 2441 Washington Rd., Maynard AR 72444. (870)647-2137. Fax: (870)647-2137. E-mail: storyteller1@cox-internet.com. **Contact:** Regina Cook Williams, editor. Tabloid: 8½×11; 64 pages; typing paper; glossy cover; illustrations. "This magazine is open to all new writers regardless of age. I will accept short stories in any genre and poetry in any type. Please keep in mind, this is a family publication." Quarterly. Estab. 1996.

• *Note:* nonsubscribers must pay reading fee: $1/poem, $2/short story.

Needs: Adventure, historical, humor/satire, literary, mainstream/contemporary, mystery/suspense, regional, religious/inspirational, romance, senior citizen/retirement, sports, westerns, young adult/teen. "I will not accept pornography, erotica, science fiction, new age, foul language, horror or graphic violence." Wants more well-plotted mysteries. Publishes ms 3-9 months after acceptance. **Publishes 30-40 new writers/year.** Published work by Randy Offner, Frank McKinley, Dusty Richards, and Tony Hillerman. Length: 200-1,500 words. Publishes short shorts. Also publishes literary essays and poetry. Sometimes comments on rejected mss.

How to Contact: Send complete ms with a cover letter. Include estimated word count and 5-line bio. Responds in 1 month to queries; 2 months to mss. Send SASE for reply, return of ms or send a disposable copy of ms. Accepts simultaneous and reprint submissions. "*Must* tell where and when it was first published." Sample copy for $6. Guidelines for #10 SASE.

Payment/Terms: "Readers vote quarterly for their favorites in all categories. Winning authors receive certificate of merit and free copy of issue in which their story or poem appeared."

Advice: "Follow the guidelines. No matter how many times this has been said, writers still ignore this basic and most important rule." Looks for "professionalism, good plots and unique characters. Purchase a sample copy so you know the kind of material we look for. Even though this is for unpublished writers, don't send us something you would not send to paying markets." Would like more "well-plotted mysteries and suspense and a few traditional westerns. Avoid sending anything that children or young adults would not (or could not) read, such as really bad language."

☑ $ THE STRAND MAGAZINE, Box 1418, Birmingham, MI 48012-1418. (800)300-6657. Fax: (248)874-1046. E-mail: strandmag@worldnet.att.net. **Contact:** A. F. Gulli, editor. Quarterly mystery magazine. Estab. 1998. "After an absence of nearly half a century, the magazine known to millions for bringing Sir Arthur Conan Doyle's ingenious detective, Sherlock Holmes, to the world has once again appeared on the literary scene. First launched in 1891, *The Strand* included in its pages the works of some of the greatest writers of the 20th century: Agatha Christie, Dorothy Sayers, Margery Allingham, W. Somerset Maugham, Graham Greene, P.G. Wodehouse, H.G. Wells, Aldous Huxley and many others. In 1950, economic difficulties in England caused a drop in circulation which forced the magazine to cease publication."

Needs: Mysteries, detective stories, tales of terror and the supernatural "written in the classic tradition of this century's great authors. Stories can be set in any time or place, provided they are well written and the plots interesting and well thought out. We are NOT interested in submissions with any sexual content." Length: 2,000-6,000 words, "however, we may occasionally publish short shorts of 1,000 words or sometimes go as long as a short novella."

How to Contact: Send complete ms, typed, double-spaced on one side of each page. SASE (IRCs if outside the US). Responds in 4 months.

Payment/Terms: Pays $50-175. Pays on acceptance for first North American serial rights.

⊕ ◖ STUDIO: A JOURNAL OF CHRISTIANS WRITING, 727 Peel St., Albury 2640 Australia. Phone/fax: (+61)26021-1135. E-mail: pgrover@bigpond.com. **Contact:** Paul Grover, managing editor. Quarterly. Circ. 300.

Needs: "*Studio* publishes prose and poetry of literary merit, offers a venue for new and aspiring writers, and seeks to create a sense of community among Christians writing." Accepts 30-40 mss/year. **Publishes 40 new writers/year.** Recently published work by Andrew Lansdown and Benjamin Gilmour. Length: 500-5,000 words.

How to Contact: Send SASE. "Overseas contributors must use International postal coupons in place of stamped envelope." Responds in 1 month to ms. Sample copy for $8 (Aus).

Payment/Terms: Pays in copies; additional copies are discounted. "Copyright of individual published pieces remains with the author, while each edition as a whole is copyright to studio." Subscription $48 (Australian) for 4 issues (1 year). International draft in Australian dollars and IRC required, or Visa or MasterCard facilities available.

$ ⊘ TALEBONES, Fiction on the Dark Edge, Fairwood Press, 5203 Quincy Ave. SE, Auburn WA 98092-8723. (253)735-6552. E-mail: talebones@nventure.com. Website: www.fairwoodpress.com (includes guidelines, submission requirements, excerpts, news about the magazine, bios). **Contact:** Patrick and Honna Swenson, editors. Magazine: digest size; 84 pages; standard paper; glossy cover stock; illustrations; photos. "We like stories that have punch, but still entertain. We like dark science fiction and dark fantasy, humor, psychological and experimental works." Quarterly. Estab. 1995. Circ. 600.

Needs: Fantasy (dark), humor/satire, science fiction (hard science, soft/sociological, dark). "No straight slash and hack horror. No cat stories or stories told by young adults. Would like to see more science fiction." Receives 200 mss/month. Accepts 6-7 mss/issue; 24-28 mss/year. Publishes ms 3-4 months after acceptance. **Publishes 2-3 new writers/year.** Recently published work by Mary Soon Lee, Leslie What and Steve Rasnic Tem. Length: 1,000-6,000 words; average length: 3,000-4,000 words. Publishes short shorts. Length: 1,000 words. Also publishes poetry.

How to Contact: Send complete ms with a cover letter. Accepts queries/submissions by e-mail and on disk. Include estimated word count and 1-paragraph bio. Responds in 1 week to queries; 1 month to mss. Send SASE for reply, return of ms or send a disposable copy of ms. Sample copy for $5. Guidelines for SASE. Reviews novels and short story collections.

Payment/Terms: Pays $10-100 and 1 contributor's copy; additional copies $3. Pays on acceptance for first North American serial rights. Sends galleys to author.

Advice: "The story must be entertaining, but should blur the boundary between science fiction and horror. Most of our stories have a dark edge to them, but often are humorous or psychological. Be polite and know how to properly present a manuscript. Include a cover letter, but keep it short and to the point."

☑ $ ⊘ ⚑ TERRA INCOGNITA, A New Generation of Science Fiction, 52 Windermere Ave., Lansdowne PA 19050-1812. E-mail: terraincognita@writeme.com. Website: www.voicenet.com/~incognit (includes writer's guidelines, names of editors, excerpts from previous issues, advice for writers, subscription information). **Contact:** Jan Berrien Berends, editor/publisher. Magazine: 64 pages; e-brite paper; full-color glossy cover; illustrations; photos. "*Terra Incognita* is devoted to Earth-based science fiction stories and relevant nonfiction articles. Readers of quality fiction—even those who are not science fiction fans—enjoy *TI*. Audience ranges from ages 18 and upward. We encourage feminist and socially conscious submissions." Quarterly. Estab. 1996.

● A story published in *Terra Incognito* was included in the sixteenth annual collection of *The Year's Best Science Fiction*, edited by Gardner Dozois. Another was short listed for the James Tiptree Jr. Memorial Award in 2000.

Needs: Science fiction (hard science, soft/sociological). "No horror, fantasy, pornography. No sexism and gratuitous sex and violence, racism or bias; avoid prose poems and vignettes. We prefer character-driven stories with protagonists and plots." Receives 200-300 unsolicited mss/month. Accepts 6-10 mss/issue; 25-35 mss/year. Publishes ms 3 months to 1 year after acceptance. **Publishes 10 new writers/year.** Published work by L. Timmel Duchamp, Mary Soon Lee, Terry McGarry, Darrell Schweitzer, W. Gregory Stewart, Sally Caves, Don D'Ammassa. Length: 100-15,000 words; average length: 5,000 words. Publishes short shorts. Also publishes literary essays, literary criticism and poetry.

How to Contact: Send complete ms with cover letter. Include estimated word count and anything you think might be interesting in a cover letter. Accepts multiple submissions "but each must have its own SASE." Responds in 2 weeks to queries; 3 months to mss. Send SASE for reply, return of ms or send a disposable copy of ms. "A cover letter is optional; an SASE is not." Sample copy for $6; $8 overseas. Fiction guidelines for #10 SASE. Reviews novels and short story collections.

Payment/Terms: Pays at least 3¢/word and 2 contributor's copies; additional copies $6. Pays on acceptance for first North American serial rights.

Advice: Looks for "good writing and literary merit; a story that grabs our interest and holds it straight through to the end. Write as well as you can (which means—don't overwrite, but do use the words themselves to advance your story), and tell us a story—preferably one we haven't heard before. Don't get your great idea rejected on account of lousy grammar or poor manuscript format. We take all submissions seriously."

⊘ THE THRESHOLD, Crossover Press, P.O. Box 101362, Pittsburgh PA 15237. E-mail: threshmag@aol.com. Website: www.thresholdmagazine.com (includes fiction, meet the editors, excerpts from magazine, subscriber information, activities page and guestbook). **Contact:** Don H. Laird and Michael Carricato, editors. Magazine: 8½×11; 48 pages; colored bond paper; glossy cover; illustrations. "*The Threshold* is a journal that promotes new and established writers. Our goal is to provide the best in new short fiction while illuminating each story with unique black and white line illustrations and graphic flourishes." Quarterly. Estab. 1996. Circ. 1,000.

Needs: Adventure, experimental, fantasy, horror, mystery/suspense, psychic/supernatural/occult, romance (contemporary, futuristic/time travel/gothic), serialized novel. No slice of life vignettes. Publishes special fiction issues or anthologies. Receives 80 unsolicited mss/month. Accepts 6-8 mss/issue, 24-32 mss/year. Publishes ms up to 5 months after acceptance. **Publishes 8-10 new writers/year.** Recently published work by Michael Kent, Renne Carter Hall, Sherrie Brown, Edward Hunter, Steve Burt. Length: 8,000 words maximum; average length: 3,000-5,000 words. Also publishes poetry.

How to Contact: Send complete ms. Include estimated word count and 2-paragraph bio. Responds in 2 weeks to queries; 6 months to mss. Send SASE for reply, return of ms or send disposable copy of ms. Accepts simultaneous submissions. Sample copy for $5.95. Guidelines for #10 SASE.

Payment/Terms: Pays 1 contributor's copy and up to $25 under special arrangement with publisher. Acquires one-time rights.

Advice: "Good writers are a dime a dozen. Good storytellers are priceless. Most publications print stories, we illuminate them. To better understand this unique approach, however, we highly recommend reading an issue or two before submitting your work."

THRESHOLDS QUARTERLY, School of Metaphysics Associates Journal, SOM Publishing, School of Metaphysics World Headquarters, 163 Moon Valley Rd., Windyville MO 65783. (417)345-8411. Fax: (417)345-6668 (call first, computerized). Website: www.som.org. **Contact:** Dr. Barbara Condron, editor. Senior Editor: Dr. Laurel Clark. Magazine: 7×10; 32 pages; line drawings and b&w photos. "The School of Metaphysics is a nonprofit educational and service organization invested in education and research in the expansion of human consciousness and spiritual evolution of humanity. For all ages and backgrounds. Themes: dreams, healing, science fiction, personal insight, morality tales, fables, humor, spiritual insight, mystic experiences, religious articles, creative writing with universal themes." Quarterly. Estab. 1975. Circ. 5,000.

Needs: Adventure, fantasy, humor, psychic/supernatural, religious/inspirational, science fiction. Upcoming themes: "Dreams, Visions, and Creative Imagination" (February); "Health and Wholeness" (May); "Intuitive Arts" (August); "Man's Spiritual Consciousness" (November). Receives 5 unsolicited mss/month. Length: 4-6 double-spaced typed pages. Publishes short shorts. Also publishes literary essays and poetry. Often comments on rejected mss.

How to Contact: Query with outline; will accept unsolicited ms with cover letter; no guarantee on time length to respond. Include bio (1-2 paragraphs). Send SASE for reply, return of ms or send a disposable copy of ms. Sample copy for 9×12 SAE and $1.50 postage. Guidelines for #10 SASE.

Payment/Terms: Pays up to 5 contributor's copies. Acquires all rights.

Advice: "We encourage works that have one or more of the following attributes: uplifting, educational, inspirational, entertaining, informative and innovative."

UP DARE?, la Pierna Tierna Press, P.O. Box 100, Shartlesville PA 19554. (610)488-6894. **Contact:** Mary M. Towne and Loring D. Emery, editors. "The only requirement is that all submitted material must pertain to folks with physical or psychological handicaps." Magazine: digest-sized; 48 pages; illustrations. Bimonthly. Estab. 1997.

Needs: Fiction and poetry. Looks for "honesty, plain language and message." No smut. Published work by Dan Buck, Karen Elkins, Sylvia Mais-Harak, Betty June Silconas, Vanda One and Denise Corrigan. Length: 2,000 words maximum.

How to Contact: "We will take single-spaced and even double-sided submissions so long as they are legible. We prefer to optically scan all material to avoid typos. We will not insist on an SASE if you truly have financial limitations. We're trying to make it as easy as possible. We will take short (250 words or less) pieces in Braille." Sample copy for $2.50. Guidelines for #10 SASE.

Advice: "We will not use euphemisms—a chair with a leg missing is a 'three-legged chair,' not a 'challenged seat.' We would like to hear from folks who are handicapped, but we aren't closing the door to others who understand and help or just have opinions to share. We will take reprints if the original appearance is identified."

$ VIRGINIA QUARTERLY REVIEW, One West Range, P.O. Box 400223, Charlottesville VA 22904-4223. (804)924-3124. Fax: (804)924-1397. **Contact:** Staige Blackford, editor. "A national magazine of literature and discussion. A lay, intellectual audience; people who are not out-and-out scholars but who are interested in ideas and literature." Quarterly. Estab. 1925. Circ. 4,000.

Needs: Adventure, contemporary, ethnic, feminist, humor, literary, romance, serialized novels (excerpts) and translations. "No pornography." Buys 3 mss/issue, 20 mss/year. Length: 3,000-7,000 words.

How to Contact: Query or send complete ms. SASE. Responds in 2 weeks to queries, 2 months to mss. Sample copy for $5.

Payment/Terms: Pays $10/printed page. Pays on publication for all rights. "Will transfer upon request." Offers Emily Clark Balch Award for best published short story of the year.

Advice: Looks for "stories with a somewhat Southern dialect and/or setting. Humor is welcome; stories involving cancer and geriatrics are not."

☑ $ 🖊 ◎ **WEBER STUDIES: Vices and Viewpoints of the Contemporary West**, 1214 University Circle, Ogden UT 84408-1214. (801)626-6473. E-mail: blroghaar@weber.edu. Website: http://weberstudies.webe r.edu (includes full web edition of journal). **Contact:** Brad L. Roghaar, editor. Magazine: 7½×10; 120-140 pages; coated paper; 4-color cover; illustrations; photos. "We seek the following themes: preservation of and access to wilderness, environmental cooperation, insight derived from living in the West, cultural diversity, changing federal involvement in the region, women and the West, implications of population growth, a sense of place, etc. We love good writing that reveals human nature as well as the natural environment." Triannual "with occasional 4th issues." Estab. 1984. Circ. 1,000.

Needs: Adventure, comics/graphic novels, ethnic/multicultural, experimental, fantasy (space fantasy), feminist, gay, historical, humor satire, lesbian, literary, mainstream, military/war, mystery/suspense, New Age, psychic/supernatural/occult, regional (contemporary western US), science fiction, short story collections, translations, western (frontier saga, traditional, contemporary). No children's/juvenile, erotica, religious or young adult/teen. Receives 50 unsolicited mss/month. Accepts 3-6 mss/issue; 9-18 mss/year. Publishes ms up to 18 months after acceptance. **Publishes "few" new writers/year.** Recently published work by Rex Burns, Steven Beeber and Gerald Vizenor. Length: 5,000 words maximum. Publishes short shorts. Also publishes critical essays, poetry and personal narrative. Sometimes comments on rejected ms.

How to Contact: Send complete ms with a cover letter. Include estimated word count, bio (not necessary), and list of publications (not necessary). Responds to mss in 3 months. Send SASE for return of ms or disposable copy of ms. Accepts multiple submissions. Sample copy for $10.

Payment/Terms: Pays $70-150, free subscription to the magazine and 1 contributor's copy. Pays on publication for first serial rights, electronic edition rights and requests electronic archive permission. Sends galleys to author.

Advice: "Is it true? Is it new? Is it interesting? Will the story appeal to educated readers who are concerned with the contemporary western United States? Declining public interest in reading generally is of concern. We publish both in print media and electronic media because we believe the future will expect both options."

$ 🖊 **WEIRD TALES**, Terminus Publishing Co., Inc., 123 Crooked Lane, King of Prussia PA 19406-2570. (610)275-4463. E-mail: owlswick@netaxs.com. **Contact:** George H. Seithers and Darrell Schweitzer, editors. Magazine: 8½×11; 68 pages; white, non-glossy paper; glossy 4-color cover; illustrations. "We publish fantastic fiction, supernatural horror for an adult audience." Quarterly. Estab. 1923. Circ. 10,000.

Needs: Fantasy (sword and sorcery), horror, supernatural/occult, translations. "We want to see a wide range of fantasy, from sword and sorcery to supernatural horror. We can use some unclassifiables." No hard science fiction or non-fantasy. Receives 400 unsolicited mss/month. Accepts 8 mss/issue; 32 mss/year. Publishes ms 6-18 months after acceptance. Agented fiction 10%. **Publishes 6 new writers/year.** Published work by Tanith Lee, Thomas Ligotti, Ian Watson and Lord Dunsany. Length: 10,000 words maximum (very few over 8,000); average length: 4,000 words. "No effective minimum. Shortest we ever published was about 100 words." Publishes short shorts. Also publishes poetry. Always comments on rejected mss.

How to Contact: Send complete ms. Include estimated word count. Responds in 2-3 weeks to mss. Send SASE for reply, return of ms or send a disposable copy of ms with SASE. Accepts multiple submissions. No simultaneous submissions. No reprint submissions, "but will buy first North American rights to stories published overseas." Sample copy for $4.95. Guidelines for #10 SASE. Reviews novels and short story collections relevant to the horror/fantasy field.

Payment/Terms: Pays 3¢/word minimum and 2 contributor's copies. Acquires first North American serial rights plus anthology option. Sends galleys to author.

Advice: "We look for imagination and vivid writing. Read the magazine. Get a good grounding in the contemporary horror and fantasy field through the various 'best of the year' anthologies. Avoid the obvious cliches of technicalities of the hereafter, the mechanics of vampirism, generic Tolkien-clone fantasy. In general, it is better to be honest and emotionally moving rather than clever. Avoid stories which have nothing of interest save for the allegedly 'surprise' ending."

☑ 🖊 **THE WHITE CROW**, Osric Publishing, P.O. Box 4501, Ann Arbor MI 48106-4501. E-mail: chris@os ric.com. Website: www.wcrow.com (includes writer's guidelines, staff contact list, excerpts from publication). **Contact:** Christopher Herdt, editor. Zine: 5½×8; 32 pages; 20 lb. white paper; 60 lb. cover stock; illustrations; photos. "We seek solid literary works which will appeal to an intelligent but not necessarily literary audience." Quarterly. Estab. 1994. Circ. 200.

Needs: Ethnic/multicultural, experimental, humor/satire, literary, translations. No erotica, horror. "Wants to see more satire, and more decent character fiction." Receives 6 mss/month. Accepts 1-2 mss/issue; 6 mss/year. Publishes ms up to 4 months after acceptance. **Publishes 1 new writer/year.** Recently published work by Mary Spangler and Jas Isle. Length: 300-3,000 words; average length: 2,500 words. Publishes short shorts. Also publishes literary essays and poetry. Often comments on rejected mss.

How to Contact: Send complete ms with cover letter. Include estimated word count and a 30-word bio. Responds in 6 months. Send SASE for return of ms. Accepts simultaneous submissions and reprints. Sample copy for $2.

Payment/Terms: Pays 1 contributor's copy; additional copies for $1. Acquires one-time rights. Not copyrighted.

Advice: "Is the story focused? Is it driven by a coherent, meaningful idea that can be grasped by an intelligent (but not literary) reader? We're here to edit a publication, not your writing, so please proofread your ms. Running spell check is a fabulous idea too."

N $◻ XODDITY, A Magazine of Speculative Fiction, P.O. Box 61736, Boulder City NV 89006. (702)293-3039. E-mail: xoddity@aol.com. Website: www.agoldmine.com (includes writer's guidelines, names of editors, short fiction, products). **Editors**: Carol C. MacLeod & M. Cathy Strachan. Magazine: $5\frac{1}{2} \times 8\frac{1}{2}$; 40-70 pages; white offset paper; slick cover; illustrations; photos. Bimonthly science fiction magazine. Estab. 1998. Circ. 200.

Needs: Fantasy (space fantasy, sword and sorcery, cross genre), horror (dark fantasy, futuristic, psychological, supernatural), romance (futuristic/time travel), science fiction (hard science/technological, soft/sociological). "Try us with things that may seem off the wall. Horror and romance should be mainly science fiction and fantasy." List of upcoming themes available for SASE. Receives 100-150 unsolicited mss/month. Accepts 4-6 mss/issue; 36 mss/year. Publishes ms 2-6 months after acceptance. **Publishes 75% new writers/year.** Recently published work by T. Lynn Neal, Kelly Ferjutz, Louise Feaver Crawford, Paul E. Martens, Elizabeth Pearl and Cynthia Ward. Length: 100-5,000 words; average length: 3,500 words. Publishes short shorts. Length: 250 words. Also publishes literary essays, literary criticism and poetry. Always comments on rejected ms.

How to Contact: Send complete ms with a cover letter. Include estimated word count, bio, social security number and list of publications. Responds in 6 weeks to queries; 3 months to mss. Send SASE for reply, return of ms or send a disposable copy of ms. Sample copy for $4 and 6×9 SAE with 78¢ postage. Guidelines for SASE. Reviews novel, short story collections and nonfiction books of interest to writers. Send books to editor.

Payment/Terms: Pays $5-75. Pays on publication for first North American serial rights. Sometimes buys electronic rights. Sends prepublication galleys to author.

Advice: "Our criteria are straightforward—a professional looking manuscript written well in the genre of our magazine. The writing must grab us on page one and compel us to read more. Please read our magazine first. Get our guidelines. We've had to reject a lot of great writing recently because the author hadn't read our guidelines."

N ⊕ THE ZONE, Pigasus Press, 13 Hazely Combe, Arreton, Isle of Wight, PO30 3AJ England. E-mail: pigasus.press@virgin.net. Website: http://website.lineone.net/~pigasus.press/index.html. **Contact:** Tony Lee, editor. Magazine. "A magazine of quality science fiction plus articles and reviews." Publishes up to 6 stories/issue. Biannually.

Needs: Science fiction (hard, contemporary science fiction/fantasy). No sword and sorcery, supernatural horror. Length: 1,000-5,000 words.

How to Contact: "Study recent issues of the magazine. Unsolicited submissions are always welcome but writers must enclose SAE/IRC for reply, plus adequate postage to return ms if unsuitable."

Payment/Terms: Pays in copies. "Token payment for stories and articles of 2,000 words and over." Sample copies available for $9 (cash, US dollars) or 9 IRCs; for UK, £3.20; EC countries, £5 (cheques/eurocheques, should be made payable to Tony Lee).

◎ ZOPILOTE, Oldie Publications, 824 S. Mill Ave., Suite 219, Tempe AZ 85281. (480)557-7195. Fax: (480)838-7264. E-mail: zopilote@inficad.com. Website: www.zopilote.com. **Contact:** Marco Albarrán, publisher. Magazine: $8\frac{1}{2} \times 11$; 26 pages; illustrations; photos. "*Zopilote* magazine is one of the few cultural magazines that promotes indigenous and Latino cultures in the U.S. We publish material pertinent to the history, ways of life, philosophies, traditions and changes taking place right now." Bimonthly. Estab. 1993. Circ. 5,000. Member, Council of Literary Magazines and Presses.

Needs: Comics/graphic novels, ethnic/multicultural (indigenous Latino), historical (indigenous Latino), literary, science fiction (ancient science of the Americas), western (indigenous Latino). "No religious, romance, erotica." Receives 5-10 unsolicited mss/month. Accepts 3 mss/issue; 18-20 mss/year. Publishes ms 3-5 months after acceptance. **Publishes 60-70% new writers/year.** Recently published work by Roberto Rodriquez, Cristina Gonzalez and Carmen Vaxones Martinez. Length: 150-500 words; average length: 300 words. Publishes short shorts. Also publishes literary essays, literary criticism and poetry. Sometimes comments on rejected mss.

How to Contact: Send complete ms with a cover letter. Accepts submissions by e-mail. Include estimated word count, brief bio and list of publications. Responds in 6 weeks. Send a disposable copy of ms and #10 SASE for reply only. Accepts simultaneous submissions, previously published work and multiple submissions. Sample copy free for $8\frac{1}{2} \times 11$ SAE and $3 postage. Guidelines by e-mail. Reviews novels, short story collections and nonfiction books of interest to writers.

Payment/Terms: Pays 5 contributor's copies; additional copies $3.50.

Zines

The zine market is nearly unparalleled in dynamism and opportunity. Vastly different from one another in appearance and content, the common source of zines seems to be a need to voice opinions. Although they've always been around, it was not until the '70s, and possibly beginning with the social upheaval of the '60s, that the availability of photocopiers and computers provided an easy, cheap way to produce the self-published and usually self-written "zines." And now, with the cyberspace explosion, an overwhelming number of "e-zines" are springing up in an electronic format every day (See the Online Markets section, page 343, for Internet-only zines).

SELF-EXPRESSION AND ARTISTIC FREEDOM

The editorial content of zines runs the gamut from traditional and genre fiction to personal rants and highly experimental work. Artistic freedom, however, is a characteristic of all zines. Although zine editors are open to a wide range of fiction that more conventional editors might not consider, don't make the mistake of thinking they expect any less from writers than the editors of other types of publications. Zine editors look for work that is creative and well presented and that shows the writer has taken time to become familiar with the market. And since most zines are highly specialized, familiarity with the niche markets they offer is extremely important.

Some of the zines listed here have been published since the early '80s, but many are relatively new and some were just starting publication as they filled out the questionnaire to be included in this edition of *Novel & Short Story Writer's Market*. Unfortunately, due to the waning energy and shrinking funds of their publishers (and often a lack of material), few last for more than several issues. Fortunately, though, some have been around since the late '70s and early '80s, and hundreds of new ones are launched every day.

While zines represent one of the most volatile groups of publications in *Novel & Short Story Writer's Market*, they are also the most open to submissions by beginning writers. As mentioned above, the editors of zines are often writers themselves and welcome the opportunity to give others a chance at publication.

SELECTING THE RIGHT MARKET

Zero in on the zines most likely to be interested in your work by browsing through the listings. This is especially important since zines are the most diverse and specialized markets listed in this book. If you write genre fiction, check out the specific sections for lists of magazines publishing in that genre (mystery, page 91; romance, page 105; science fiction/fantasy & horror, page 121). For other types of fiction, check the Category Index (starting on page 618) for the appropriate subject heading.

In addition to browsing through the listings and using the Category Index, check the ranking codes at the beginning of listings to find those most likely to be receptive to your work. Most all zines are open to new writers (☐) or to both new and established writers (◪). For more explanation about these codes, see the inside front and back covers of this book.

Once you have a list of zines you might like to try, read their listings carefully. Zines vary greatly in appearance as well as content. Some paper zines are photocopies published whenever the editor has material and money, while others feature offset printing and regular distribution schedules. And a few have evolved into four-color, commercial-looking, very slick publications. The physical description appearing near the beginning of the listings gives you clues about the size and financial commitment to the publication. This is not always an indication of quality, but chances are a publication with expensive paper and four-color artwork on the cover has more prestige than a photocopied publication featuring a clip art self-cover. If you're a new writer or your work is considered avant garde, however, you may be more interested in the photocopied zine or one of the electronic zines. For more information on some of the paper, binding and printing terms used in these descriptions, see Printing and Production Terms Defined on page 613. Also, The "Quick Start" Guide to Publishing Your Fiction, starting on page 2, describes in detail the listing information common to all markets in our book.

FURTHERING YOUR SEARCH

Reading the listings is only the first part of developing your marketing plan. The second part, equally important, is to obtain fiction guidelines and a copy of the actual zine. Reading copies of the publication helps you determine the fine points of the zine's publishing style and philosophy. Especially since zines tend to be highly specialized, there is no substitute for this hands-on, eyes-on research.

Unlike commercial periodicals available at most newsstands and bookstores, it requires a little more effort to obtain most of the paper zines listed here. You will probably need to send for a sample copy. We include sample copy prices in the listings whenever possible.

✓ 🖸 **AFFABLE NEIGHBOR**, P.O. Box 3635, Ann Arbor MI 48106-3635. E-mail: affableneighbor@hotmail.com. Editor: Joel Henry-Fisher. **Contact:** Joel Henry-Fisher, Leigh Chalmers, fiction editors. Zine: size/pages vary; usually photocopy paper and cover stock; illustrations; photos. "Counter-culture zine publishing high and low art and experimentation of all forms, advocating the Affable Neighbor Worldview®." Estab. 1994. Circ. under 500.
Needs: Adventure, comics/graphic novels, erotica, ethnic/multicultural, experimental, fantasy, feminist, gay, glitz, historical, horror, humor/satire, lesbian, literary, psychic/supernatural/occult, romance ("kamp/sleaze perhaps"), science fiction, short story collections, translations, collage/text. "No pro-religious—unless, perhaps, fringe related; no tired, formulaic writings." Receives 30 unsolicited mss/month. Accepts 1-2 mss/issue. **Publishes 6 new writers/year.** Recently published work by Marshall Stanley, Scott Hoye, Steve G. Toth and Geoff Daily. Length: short. Publishes short shorts (under 500 words). Also publishes literary essays, literary criticism, poetry. Sometimes comments on rejected ms.
How to Contact: Send complete ms with a cover letter. Responds in approximately 1 week. Send SASE for reply, return of ms or send a disposable copy of ms. Accepts simultaneous and reprint submissions. Sample copy for 3 first-class stamps, if available. Reviews novels, short story collections and nonfiction books of interest. Send books to Leigh Chalmers, Assistant Editor, Affable Neighbor, 729 E. Burnside #210, Portland OR 97214. Send disposable copies or SASE.
Payment/Terms: Payment negotiable. Pays free subscription if requested and contributor's copies. Not copyrighted.
Advice: "We like interesting and exciting works—experimental, brash, and sometimes dead-serious."

✓ 🖸 **ART:MAG**, P.O. Box 70896, Las Vegas NV 89170-0896. (702)734-8121. E-mail: magman@iopener.net. **Contact:** Peter Magliocco, editor. Zine: 7×8½×8½, 8½×14, also 8½×11; 70-90 pages; 20 lb. bond paper; b&w pen and ink illustrations; photos. Publishes "irreverent, literary-minded work by committed writers," for "small press, 'quasi-art-oriented'" audience. Annual. Estab. 1984. Circ. under 500.
Needs: Condensed/excerpted novel, confession, contemporary, erotica, ethnic, experimental, fantasy, feminist, gay, historical (general), horror, humor/satire, lesbian, literary, mainstream, mystery/suspense, prose poem, psychic/supernatural/occult, regional, science fiction, translations and arts. Wants to see more "daring and thought-provoking" fiction. No "slick-oriented stuff published by major magazines." Receives 1 plus ms/month. Accepts 1-2 mss/year. Does not read mss July-October. Publishes ms within 3-6 months of acceptance. **Publishes 1-2 new writers/year.** Recently published work by Jeff Weddle. Length: 250-3,000 words; 2,000 words preferred. Also publishes literary essays "if relevant to aesthetic preferences," literary criticism "occasionally," poetry. Sometimes comments on rejected mss.
How to Contact: Send complete ms with cover letter. Responds in 3 months. SASE. Accepts simultaneous submissions. Sample copy for $5, 6×9 SAE and 79¢ postage. Two-year subscription for $10. Guidelines for #10 SASE.
Payment/Terms: Pays contributor's copies. Acquires one-time rights.
Advice: "Seeking more novel and quality-oriented work, usually from solicited authors. Magazine fiction today needs to be concerned with the issues of fiction writing itself—not just with a desire to publish or please the largest audience. Think about things in the fine art world as well as the literary one and keep the hard core of life in between."

☑ ◑ **babysue**, P.O. Box 33369, Decatur GA 30033. (404)320-1178. Websites: www.babysue.com and www. LMNOP.com (includes comics, poetry, fiction and a wealth of music reviews). **Contact:** Don W. Seven, editor. Zine: 8½×11; 32 pages; illustrations; photos. "*babysue* is a collection of music reviews, poetry, short fiction and cartoons for anyone who can think and is not easily offended." Biannual. Estab. 1983. Circ. 5,000.

• Sometimes funny, very often perverse, this 'zine featuring mostly cartoons and "comix" definitely is not for the easily offended.

Needs: Erotica, experimental and humor/satire. Receives 5-10 mss/month. Accepts 3-4 mss/year. Publishes ms within 3 months of acceptance. Published work by Daniel Lanette, Massy Baw, Andrew Taylor and Barbara Rimshaw. Publishes short shorts. Length: 1-2 single-spaced pages.

How to Contact: Query with clips of published work. SASE. Accepts simultaneous submissions. No submissions via e-mail.

Payment/Terms: Pays 1 contributor's copy.

Advice: "Create out of the love of creating, not to see your work in print!"

◑ **THE BITTER OLEANDER**, 4983 Tall Oaks Dr., Fayetteville NY 13066-9776. (315)637-3047. Fax: (315)637-5056. E-mail: bones44@ix.netcom.com. Website: www.bitteroleander.com. **Contact:** Paul B. Roth, editor. Zine specializing in poetry and fiction: 6×9; 128 pages; 55 lb. paper; 12 pt. CIS cover stock; photos. "We're interested in the surreal; deep image; particularization of natural experiences." Semiannual. Estab. 1974. Circ. 1,500.

Needs: Experimental, new age/mystic/spiritual, translations. "No pornography; no confessional; no romance." Receives 100 unsolicited mss/month. Accepts 1-2 mss/issue; 2-4 mss/year. Does not read mss in July. Publishes ms 4-6 months after acceptance. Recently published work by Isabella Ripota, T.R. Healy and John Shepley. Publishes short shorts. Length: 2,500 words. Also publishes literary essays, poetry. Always comments on rejected ms.

How to Contact: Send complete ms with a cover letter. Include estimated word count, 50-word bio and list of publications. Responds in 1 week to queries; 1 month to mss. Send SASE for reply, return of ms. Sample copy for $8, 7×10 SAE with 4 first-class stamps. Guidelines for #10 SASE.

Payment/Terms: Pays 1 contributor's copy; additional copies $8. Acquires first rights.

Advice: "If within the first 100 words my mind drifts, the rest rarely makes it. Be yourself and listen to no one but yourself."

☑ ◑ **BLACK PETALS**, Fossil Publications, 11627 Taft, Wichita KS 67209-1036. E-mail: blackptls@aol.com. Website: www.blackpetals.com (includes writer's guidelines, subscription information, addresses, editors' names, sample story). **Contact:** Kenneth James Crist, editor. Zine specializing in horror/science fiction: digest size; perfect-bound; over 88 pages; photocopied; illustrations. "A little something special for those special readers of oddity and terror. *Black Petals* is about the dark side of science fiction and the bizarre and unusual in horror—mature audience *only*." Quarterly. Estab. 1997. Circ. 200.

Needs: Experimental, horror, psychic/supernatural; science fiction (soft/sociological). Wants more hard core horror. No children's or romance, "Star Trek," vampires, stories from "beyond the grave. We don't get nearly enough science fiction that is based on current scientific fact—or even scientific speculation. We look for original ideas, strong characters, emotional involvement, good, vivid background." Receives over 10-15 unsolicited mss/month. Accepts 14-20 mss/issue. **Publishes 3-5 new writers/year.** Recently published work by Lee Clark, D.F. Lewis and Scott Urban. Length: no minimum; 3,500 words maximum; average length: 1,500 words. Publishes short shorts. Also publishes poetry. Always comments on rejected mss.

How to Contact: Send complete ms. Include estimated word count and list of publications. Responds in 2-4 weeks to queries and mss. "Disposable copies please. No e-mail submissions, query first." Accepts simultaneous and multiple submissions and reprints. Sample copy for $4. Guidelines for #10 SASE.

Payment/Terms: Pays contributor's copies; additional copies $4.

Advice: "My best advice—submit! How do you know if you'll get published unless you submit! Also, obtain a sample copy, follow guidelines and don't watch the mailbox. New unpublished writers are high on my list. If I have time I'll even help edit a manuscript. If I reject a manuscript, I encourage writers to send something else. Don't ever be discouraged, and don't wallpaper your office with rejection notes—toss them!"

⊕ ☑ ◑ **THE BROBDINGNAGIAN TIMES**, 96 Albert Rd., Cork, Ireland. Phone: (21)4311227. **Contact:** Giovanni Malito, editor. Zine specializing in short international work: 6×8½; 8 pages; 80 gramme paper; illustrations. "There are no obvious editorial slants. We are interested in any prose from anyone anywhere provided it is short (700 words maximum)." Quarterly. Estab. 1996. Circ. 250.

Needs: Ethnic/multicultural, experimental, horror, humor/satire, literary, romance (contemporary), science fiction (hard science/technological, soft/sociological). "No ghost stories/dysfunctional family stories/first sex stories." Receives 4-6 unsolicited mss/month. Accepts 2 mss/issue; 8 mss/year. Publishes ms in next issue after

acceptance. **Publishes 2-3 new writers/year.** Published work by D.F. Lewis, Christopher Woods, Michael Wynne, Laura Lush, Ruba Neda and Jon Rourke. Length: 50-1,000 words; average length: 600 words. Publishes short shorts. Average length: 500 words. Also publishes literary essays, poetry. Always comments on rejected ms.
How to Contact: Send complete ms with a cover letter. Include estimated word count. Responds in 1 week to queries; 3 weeks to mss. Send SASE (IRCs) for reply, return of ms or send a disposable copy of ms. Accepts simultaneous and reprint submissions. Sample copy for #10 SAE and 2 IRCs. Guidelines for #10 SAE and 1 IRC.
Payment/Terms: Pays 2 contributor's copies; additional copies for postage. Acquires one-time rights for Ireland/U.K. Sends galleys to author if required. Copyrighted Ireland/U.K.
Advice: "Crisp language. Economy of language. These are important, otherwise almost anything goes."

☑ ◖ BURNING SKY: Adventures in Science Fiction Terror, Thievin' Kitty Publications, P.O. Box 341, Marion MA 02738. E-mail: theedge@capecod.net. Website: http://beam.to/thievinkitty (includes guidelines, current and back issue information, cover art, ordering information, information on editors). **Contact:** Greg F. Gifune, editor. Associate editors: Carla Gifune and Chuck Deude. Zine specializing in science fiction horror: digest; 30-40 pages; white bond; glossy card cover. *Burning Sky* publishes "sci/fi horror blends ONLY." Triannual. Estab. 1998. Circ. 500.
Needs: Horror and science fiction blends. Receives more than 100 unsolicited mss/month. Accepts 5-6 mss/issue; 15-18 mss/year. Does not read January, May and September. Publishes ms 1-4 months after acceptance. Agented fiction 1-2%. **Publishes 1-3 new writers/year.** Published work by D. F. Lewis, Michael Laimo, Suzanne Donahue, Christopher Stires, Denis Kirk and Stephen van Maanen. Length: 500-3,500 words; average length: 2,000-3,000 words. Also publishes literary criticism. Often comments on rejected ms.
How to Contact: Send complete ms with a cover letter. Accepts queries by e-mail, but no mss. Include estimated word count, bio, list of publications and cover letter. Responds in 1 week to queries; 2 months to mss. Send SASE for reply, return of ms or send a disposable copy of ms. Sample copy for $4 in US, $5 elsewhere. Reviews novels, short story collections and nonfiction books of interest to writers. Send books to editor.
Payment/Terms: Pays 1 contributor's copy; additional copies $4. Pays on publication. Sends galleys to author on request.
Advice: "We like strong, concise, lean writing, stories that follow our very specific guidelines of blending sci-fi and horror, stories with an 'edge of your seat' quality. Thought-provoking, tension filled and genuinely frightening stories with realistic dialogue and a gritty style. Do not send straight sci-fi or horror stories. We need elements of both. Read a copy. *Burning Sky* is a very particular market, but we are proud to have published three first stories in our first three issues, along with more established writers. Send us a well written story in proper manuscript format that fits our guidelines. We don't want highly technical or introverted ramblings—we want exciting, highly entertaining and frightening stories."

☑ ▣ CHILDREN, CHURCHES AND DADDIES LITERARY MAGAZINE, the un-religious, non-family oriented publication, Scars Publications and Design, 829 Briar Court, Gurnee IL 60031-3155. E-mail: ccandd96@aol.com. Website: http://scars.tv (includes all issues, writings, guidelines). **Contact:** Janet Kuypers, editor-in-chief. E-zine and literary magazine: laser paper; cmyk color cover stock; some illustrations; photos. "We look for detail oriented writing that makes a gripping sense of action is still realism." Estab. 1993.
Needs: Ethnic/multicultural, feminist, gay, horror (futuristic, psychological, supernatural), lesbian, literary, mainstream, mystery/suspense, psychic/supernatural/occult. No religious, romantic or children's writings. Accepts 25-45 mss/issue; 25-45 mss/year. Publishes ms 1 year after acceptance. Agented fiction 60-80%. **Publishes 75% new writers/year.** Recently published work by Gabriel Athens, Marina Arturo, Alexandria Rend and Acon Logan. Publishes short shorts. Also publishes poetry.
How to Contact: Send complete ms with cover letter by e-mail. Include e-mail address. Responds in 1 month to queries; 2 months to mss. Send SASE for return of ms or send a disposable copy of the ms and #10 SASE for reply only. Sample copy free on website. Guidelines for SASE, e-mail, or on website.
Payment/Terms: Acquires one-time and electronic rights.
Advice: "Use descriptive detail, gripping logic and reason. We want to feel like we are living in a scene we are reading about. View our issues and guidelines online and enter our contest."

◖ CLARK STREET REVIEW, P.O. Box 1377, Berthoud CO 80513-2377. (970)669-5175. E-mail: clarkreview@earthlink.net. Website: http://home.earthlink.net/~clarkreview/ (includes guidelines only). **Contact:** Ray

CHECK THE CATEGORY INDEXES, located at the back of the book, for publishers interested in specific fiction subjects.

Foreman, editor. Zine specializing in poetry and short fiction: $5\frac{1}{2} \times 8\frac{1}{2}$; 20 pages; 20 lb. paper; 20 lb. cover stock. "We publish only narrative poetry and short shorts with communicable content tuned to the spoken language and distinguished by clarity and humanity. We are small enough not to bore a reader and publish often enough to make him know we are alive and stamping our feet." Bimonthly. Estab. 1998. Circ. 100.

Needs: Mainstream. No children's and "dull, my-vacation stories." Receives 10 unsolicited mss/month. Accepts 20-40 mss/year. Publishes ms 6 months after acceptance. Recently published work by Errol Miller, T.J. Spina, Laurel Speer. Length: 800 words maximum; average length: 400-700 words. Also publishes literary essays, literary criticism and poetry.

How to Contact: Send complete ms with a cover letter. Include estimated word count. Responds in 1 month. Send a disposable copy of ms and #10 SASE for reply only. Accepts simultaneous submissions, previously published work and multiple submissions. Sample copy for $2. Guidelines for SASE or by e-mail.

Payment/Terms: Pays 1 contributor's copy.

Advice: "Read good, and a lot of, short stories. And read some poor stuff from beginners and discover the difference."

A COMPANION IN ZEOR, 1622B Swallow Crest Dr., Edgewood MD 21040-1751. Fax: (410)676-0164. E-mail: klitman323@aol.com or karenlitman@juno.com. Website: www.simegen.com/sgfandom/rimonslibrary/cz. (includes guidelines, back issue flyers, etc.). **Contact:** Karen MacLeod, editor. Fanzine: $8\frac{1}{2} \times 11$; 60 pages; "letter" paper; heavy blue cover; b&w line illustrations; occasional b&w photos. Publishes science fiction based on the various Universe creations of Jacqueline Lichtenberg. Occasional features on Star Trek, and other interests, convention reports, reviews of movies and books, recordings, etc. Published irregularly. Estab. 1978. Circ. 300.

● *Companion in Zeor* is one fanzine devoted to the work and characters of Jacqueline Lichtenberg. Lichtenberg's work includes several future world, alien and group culture novels and series including the Sime/Gen Series and The Dushau trilogy. She's also penned two books on her own vampire character and she co-authored *Star Trek Lives*.

Needs: Fantasy, humor/satire, prose poem, science fiction. "No vicious satire. Nothing X-rated. Homosexuality prohibited unless *essential* in story. Occasionally receives one manuscript a month." Publication of an accepted ms "goes to website posting." Occasionally comments on rejected mss and recommends other markets.

How to Contact: Query first or send complete ms with cover letter. "Prefer cover letters about any writing experience prior, or related interests toward writing aims." Responds in 1 month. SASE. Accepts simultaneous submissions. Sample copy price depends on individual circumstances. Guidelines for #10 SASE. "I write individual letters to all queries. No form letter at present." SASE for guidelines or can be sent by e-mail. Reviews science fiction/fantasy collections or titles. "We can accept e-mail queries and manuscripts through AOL providers."

Payment/Terms: Pays in contributor's copies. Acquires first and electronic rights.

Advice: "Send concise cover letter asking what the author would like me to do for them if the manuscript cannot be used by my publication. They should follow guidelines of the type of material I use, which is often not done. I have had many submissions I cannot use as they are general fiction. Ask for guidelines before submitting to a publication. Write to the best of your ability and work with your editor to develop your work to a higher point than your present skill level. Take constructive criticism and learn from it. Electronic publishing seems the way the industry is heading. Receipt of manuscripts can only be through klitman323@aol.com. Juno cannot handle attachments. People can learn more through the domain—www.simegen.com/index.html."

CURRICULUM VITAE, Simpson Publications, Grove City Factory Stores, P.O. Box 1309, Grove City PA 16127. (661)825-9550. E-mail: simpub@hotmail.com. Website: www.dittman.homestead.com (includes guidelines, contacts, fiction, interviews). **Contact:** Michael Dittman, editor. Zine: digest-sized; 75-100 pages; standard paper; card cover stock; illustrations. "We are dedicated to new, exciting writers. We like essays, travelogues and short stories filled with wonderful, tense, funny work by writers who just happen to be underpublished or beginners. Our audience is young and overeducated." Quarterly. Estab. 1995. Circ. 2,000.

Needs: Condensed/excerpted novel, erotica, ethnic/multicultural, experimental, humor/satire, literary, mainstream/contemporary, serialized novel, sports, translations. Wants to see more hyper realism, magic realism and translations. "No sentimental 'weepers' or Bukowski-esque material." Publishes special fiction issues or anthologies. Receives 45 unsolicited mss/month. Accepts 7 mss/issue; 28 mss/year. Publishes mss 12 months after acceptance. **Publishes 25 new writers/year.** Published work by Amber Meadow Adams and Carl Hoffman. Publishes short shorts. Also publishes literary essays, literary criticism, poetry. Often comments on rejected mss.

How to Contact: Send complete ms with cover letter. Accepts queries/mss by e-mail. Responds in 1 month to queries and mss. Send SASE for reply, return of ms or send a disposable copy of ms. Accepts simultaneous, reprint and electronic submissions. Sample copy for $3. Guidelines for #10 SASE. Reviews novels and short story collections. Send books to Amy Dittman.

Payment/Terms: Pays minimum 2 contributor's copies to $125 maximum. Pays on publication for one-time rights.

Advice: "Looks for quality of writing, a knowledge of past works of literature and a willingness to work with our editors. Submit often and take criticism with a grain of salt."

N **O** **DEVIL BLOSSOMS**, Asterius Press, P.O. Box 5122, Seabrook NJ 08302-3511. E-mail: theeditor@asteriuspress.com. Website: www.asteriuspress.com (includes guidelines, online bookstore, interviews, articles, etc.). **Contact:** John C. Erianne, publisher/editor. Zine specializing in fiction and poetry: 7×10; 24 pages; 20-30 lb. paper; card stock cover. "This is a publication for radical free-thinking geniuses—Twain, De Sade, Swift, Dostoyevsky, etc. would have found a home here. If you are in this tradition, you too may find a home." Semiannual. Estab. 1998. Circ. 750-1,000.

Needs: Erotica, experimental, horror (psychological), humor/satire, literary, science fiction (soft/sociological). "No romance, inspirational, New Age, supernatural horror." Receives 200 unsolicited mss/month. Accepts 3-4 mss/issue; 6-8 mss/year. Publishes ms 6 months after acceptance. **Publishes 1-2 new writers/year.** Recently published work by Ehren Bivens, Jim Sullivan and Brendan Connell. Length: 300-2,500 words; average length: 1,500 words. Publishes short shorts. Average length: 750 words. Also publishes poetry. Sometimes comments on rejected mss.

How to Contact: Send complete ms with a cover letter. Accepts submissions by e-mail. Include estimated word count and address in the upper left-hand corner. Responds in 1 week to queries; 3 weeks to mss. Send SASE (or IRC) for return of ms or send a disposable copy of ms and #10 SASE for reply only. Accepts simultaneous submissions. Sample copy for $3. Guidelines for SASE or on website.

Payment/Terms: Pays 1 contributor's copy; additional copies $3. Pays on publication for first and non-exclusive one-time reprint (anthology) rights.

Advice: "I look for originality, interesting characters and tales that take risks. Safe, boring, middle-of-the-road crap has no place here. Present yourself in a professional manner, follow the guidelines, leave your ego at home, have talent, but most of all remember that it is not my job to impress you."

✓ **♥** **THE EDGE, TALES OF SUSPENSE**, Thievin' Kitty Publications, P.O. Box 341, Marion MA 02738. E-mail: theedge@capecod.net. Website: http://beam.to/thievinkitty (includes guidelines, samples, and updates. **Contact:** Greg F. Gifune, editor. Associate Editors: Carla S. Gifune, Chuck A. Deude. Zine specializing in varied genre suspense: digest-sized; 80-88 pages; heavy stock paper; heavy card cover. "We publish a broad range of genres, subjects and styles. While not an easy magazine to break into, we offer thrilling, 'edge of your seat' fiction from both seasoned and newer writers. We focus on the writing, not illustrations or distracting bells and whistles. Our goal is to present a quality, entertaining publication." Triannual. Estab. 1998. Circ. 1,000.

Needs: Adventure, erotica, gay, horror, lesbian, mystery/suspense (police procedural, private eye/hardboiled, noir), psychic/supernatural/occult, westerns with supernatural or horror element only. "Emphasis is on horror, crime and blends." No children's, young adult, romance, humor. Receives over 100 unsolicited mss/month. Accepts 10-12 mss/issue; 30-36 mss/year. Publishes ms 1-4 months after acceptance. Agented fiction 1-2%. **Publishes 1-6 new writers/year.** Published work by Ken Goldman, John Roux, Scott Urban, Stefano Donati, Suzanne Donahue, Robert Dunbar and Michael Laimo. Length: 700-8,000 words; average length: 2,500-4,500 words. Also publishes poetry. Always comments on rejected ms.

How to Contact: Send complete ms with a cover letter. Include estimated word count, brief bio and list of publications. Responds in 8 weeks. Send SASE for reply, return of ms or send a disposable copy of ms. Accepts simultaneous submissions but not preferred. Sample copy for $6 U.S., $7 elsewhere (includes postage). Guidelines for #10 SASE. No e-mail submissions.

Payment/Terms: Pays 1 contributor's copy; additional copies $5. Acquires one-time rights.

Advice: "We look for taut, tense thrillers with realistic dialogue, engaging characters, strong plots and endings that are both powerful and memorable. Graphic violence, sex and profanity all have their place but do not have to be gratuitous. We will not accept anything racist, sexist, sacrilegious, or stories that depict children or animals in violent or sexual situations!"

$ **O** **ENCOUNTER, meeting God Face-to-Face**, Standard Publishing, 8121 Hamilton Ave., Cincinnati OH 45231. (513)931-4050. Fax: (513)931-0950. E-mail: kcarr@standardpub.com. Website: www.standardpub.com (includes lists of Standard Publishing's products and how to order them). **Contact:** Kelly Carr, editor. Zine specializing in Christian teens: 8½×11; 8 pages; glossy paper; illustrations; photos. "We seek to cause teens to look at their relationship with God in a new light and encourage them to live out their faith." Weekly. Estab. 1951. Circ. 35,000.

Needs: Religious, young adult/teen. Short stories that have Christian principles. "No non-religious fiction." Upcoming themes: friendships, peer pressure, loneliness, respecting authority, dealing with anger. List of upcoming themes available for SASE. Receives 35 unsolicited mss/month. Accepts 2 mss/issue; 45 mss/year. Publishes ms 1 year after acceptance. Length: 500-1,100 words. Always comments on rejected mss.

How to Contact: Send complete ms with a cover letter. Include estimated word count and Social Security number. Responds in 3 months. Send SASE (or IRC) for return of ms or send a disposable copy of ms and #10 SASE for reply only. Accepts simultaneous submissions, previously published work and multiple submissions. Sample copy free for 11×13 SASE. Guidelines for SASE.

Payment/Terms: Pays 6-8¢/word and 5 contributor's copies. Pays on acceptance.

Advice: "We look for realistic teenagers with up-to-date dialogue who cope with modern-day problems."

N $ THE FUNNY PAPER, F/J Writers Service, P.O. Box 22557, Kansas City MO 64113-0557. E-mail: felix22557@aol.com. Website: www.angelfire.com/biz/funnypaper. **Contact:** F.H. Fellhauer, editor. Zine specializing in humor, contest and poetry: 8½×11; 10 pages. Published 4 times/year. No summer or Christmas. Estab. 1985.

Needs: Children/juvenile, humor satire, literary. "No controversial fiction." Length: 1,000 words. Publishes short shorts. Average length: 4,000. Also publishes poetry. Sometimes comments on rejected mss.

How to Contact: Send for guidelines. Accepts mss by e-mail. Include estimated word count with submission. Send disposable copy of ms and #10 SASE for reply only. Accepts simultaneous submissions. Sample copy for $2. Guidelines for SASE, e-mail or on website.

Payment/Terms: Prizes for stories, jokes and poems for $5-100 (humor, inspirational, fillers). No fee. Additional copies $2. Pays on publication for one-time rights.

Advice: "Do your best work, no trash. We try to keep abreast of online publishing and provide information."

$ THE FUNNY TIMES, 2176 Lee Rd., Cleveland Heights OH 44118. (216)371-8600. E-mail: ft@funnytimes.com. Website: www.funnytimes.com (includes information about *The Funny Times*, cartoon of the week and laugh links). **Contact:** Ray Lesser and Susan Wolpert, editors. Zine specializing in humor: tabloid; 24 pages; newsprint; illustrations. *The Funny Times* is a "liberal-left monthly humor review." Estab. 1985. Circ. 60,000.

Needs: "Anything funny." Receives hundreds of unsolicited mss/month. Accepts 5 mss/issue; 60 mss/year. Publishes ms 1-6 months after acceptance. Agented fiction 10%. **Publishes 10 new writers/year.** Length: 500-700 words average. Publishes short shorts.

How to Contact: Send complete ms with a cover letter. Include list of publications. Responds in 3 months. Send SASE for return of ms or disposable copy of ms. Accepts simultaneous and reprint submissions. Sample copy for $3, 11×14 SAE and 77¢ 1st class postage. Guidelines for #10 SASE.

Payment/Terms: Pays $50, free subscription to the zine and 5 contributor's copies. Pays on publication for one-time rights.

Advice: "It must be funny."

N $ HADROSAUR TALES, Hadrosaur Productions, P.O. Box 8468, Las Cruces NM 88006-8468. (505)527-4163. E-mail: hadrosaur.productions@verizon.net. Website: www.hadrosaur.com (includes news, ordering information, publication updates, guidelines, links to author websites). **Contact:** David L. Summers, editor. Zine specializing in science fiction: 5½×8½; 100-125 pages; 50 lb. white stock; 80 lb. cover. "*Hadrosaur Tales* publishes science fiction and fantasy with a literary slant. We want to see new ideas explored with engaging characters and drama. The magazine is read by people of all ages." Triannual. Estab. 1995. Circ. 100.

Needs: Fantasy (space fantasy, sword and sorcery), science fiction (hard science/technological, soft/sociological). "No graphic violence. No graphic/explicit sex. I do not want to see fiction with no science fiction/fantasy/mythic elements." Receives 15 unsolicited mss/month. Accepts 7-10 mss/issue; 21-30 mss/year. Does not read mss January 1-April 30 and June 15-October 31. Publishes ms 1 year after acceptance. **Publishes 15 new writers/ year.** Recently published work by Gary Every, Robert Collins, Neal Asher, Rebecca Inch-Partridge and Cliff Pliml. Length: 1,000-6,000 words; average length: 4,000 words. Publishes short shorts. Average length: 1,200 words. Also publishes poetry. Always comments on rejected mss.

How to Contact: Send complete ms with a cover letter. Accepts submissions by e-mail. Include estimated word count, brief bio and list of publications. Responds in 1 month to queries; 4 months to mss. Send SASE (or IRC) for return of ms or send a disposable copy of ms and #10 SASE for reply only. Sample copy for $6.95. Guidelines for SASE or on website.

Payment/Terms: Pays $6 and 2 contributor's copies; additional copies $4.76. Pays on acceptance for one-time rights.

Advice: "First and foremost, I look for engaging drama and believable characters. With those characters and situation, I want you to take me someplace I've never been before. The story I'll buy is the one set in a new world or where the unexpected happens—but I cannot help but believe in the situation because it feels real. Let your imagination soar to its greatest heights and write down the results. Start with a character you believe in and take them into a fantastic circumstance or a plausible future. Don't limit yourself to 'conventions' of science fiction and fantasy. Sometimes folklore and your own experiences are the very best places to start."

☒ ◎ ◩ ▣ HOLOGRAM TALES. (0181)649-8148. E-mail: short@sfcrowsnest.com. Website: www.sfcr owsnest.com or www.crowsnestbooks.com. **Contact:** Stephen Hunt, publisher. Electronic magazine. Publishes science fiction and fantasy including short fiction, film/tv reviews, book reviews, author interviews and convention reports.

● Hologram Tales was named science fiction website of the year in 1999, and won Topica's Best Contest Award for 2000.

Needs: Science fiction and fantasy (sword and sorcery). Would like to see more space opera and high adventure. No horror. **Publishes "hundreds" of new writers/year.** Recently published work by Stephen King, Geoff Willmetts, Greg Bear, William Gibson and David Eddings.

How to Contact: Electronic submissions only. Send mss by e-mail.

Advice: "Make sure you have read the publication before you submit to it. We're looking for imagination, good craftsmanship and realistic dialogue."

☒ ◐ JACK MACKEREL MAGAZINE, Rowhouse Press, P.O. Box 23134, Seattle WA 98102-0434. **Contact:** Greg Bachar, editor. Zine: 5½ × 8½; 40-60 pages; Xerox bond paper; glossy card cover stock; b&w illustrations; photos. "We enjoy simple literary fiction that explores big ideas. We publish unconventional art, poetry and fiction." Quarterly. Estab. 1993. Circ. 1,000.

Needs: Condensed/excerpted novel, literary, surreal. No genre fiction. Publishes occasional chapbooks and anthologies. Receives 20-100 unsolicited mss/month. Accepts 10-20 mss/issue; 40-75 mss/year. Published work by William Waltz, Brett Astor and Jenny Sheppard. Length: 250-5,000 words. Publishes short shorts. Also publishes literary essays, literary criticism and poetry.

How to Contact: Send complete ms with a cover letter. Include bio with submission. Accepts submissions on disk and multiple submissions. Send SASE for reply, return of ms or send a disposable copy of ms. Sample copy for $5 (make checks or money order out to Greg Bachar).

Payment/Terms: Pays in contributor's copies.

☒ ◐ KIDS' WORLD, The Magazine That's All Kids!, Stone Lightning Press, 1300 Kicker Rd., Tuscaloosa AL 35404. (205)553-2284. Editor: Lillian Kopaska-Merkel. Zine: digest size; 16-24 pages; standard white Xerox paper; card stock cover; illustrations. Publishes stories written by children under 17: "fantasy and 'kid stuff'—themes by kids, about kids and for kids." Quarterly. Estab. 1992. Circ. 60-80.

Needs: Children's/juvenile (4-12 years): adventure, fantasy (children's), mystery/suspense (amateur sleuth), science fiction (hard science, soft/sociological); young adult/teen (adventure, mystery, science fiction). No horror or romance. Receives 18-24 unsolicited mss/month. Accepts 30 mss/issue; 70-100 mss/year. Publishes ms from 1-24 months after acceptance. Recently published work by Brianne Butler, Betsy Champagne, McKay Talley and Michelle Tran. Length: 75-500 words; average length: 300 words. Publishes short shorts. Length: 150-200 words. Also publishes poetry.

How to Contact: Send complete ms with a cover letter including your age. Responds in 3 months to mss. Send SASE for reply, return of ms or send a disposable copy of ms. Sample copy for $2. Guidelines for SASE.

Payment/Terms: Pays 1 contributor's copy. Acquires first North American serial rights.

Advice: "Stories must be appropriate for kids. Have an adult check spelling, grammar and punctuation."

$ ◐ LADY CHURCHILL'S ROSEBUD WRISTLET, An Occasional Outburst, Gleek It, Inc., 106 Warren St., Brighton MA 02115. (617)266-7746. E-mail: lcrw@hotmail.com. Website: www.netcolony.com/arts/lcrw (includes guidelines, contents and occasional extras not in the zine). **Contact:** Gavin Grant, editor. Zine: half legal size; 40 pages; 60 lb. paper; cardstock cover; illustrations; photos. Semiannual. Estab. 1996. Circ. 200.

Needs: Comics/graphic novels, experimental, fantasy, feminist, literary, science fiction, short story collections, translations. Receives 1 unsolicited ms/month. Accepts 4-6 mss/issue; 8-12 mss/year. Publishes ms 6 months after acceptance. **Publishes 2-4 new writers/year.** Recently published work by Kelly Link, Lucy Snyder, Margaret Muirhead and Stuart Davies. Length: 200-7,000 words; average length: 3,500 words. Publishes short shorts. Average length: 500 words. Also publishes literary essays and poetry. Sometimes comments on rejected mss.

How to Contact: Send complete ms with a cover letter. Accepts submissions by e-mail and disk. Include estimated word count. Responds in 2 weeks to queries; 1 month to mss. Send SASE (or IRC) for return of ms or send a disposable copy of ms and #10 SASE for reply only. Accepts simultaneous submissions, previously published work and multiple submissions. Sample copy for $3. Guidelines by e-mail. Reviews novels, short story collections and nonfiction books of interest to writers.

Payment/Terms: Pays $5-10 and 2 contributor's copies; additional copies $3. Pays on publication for first or one-time rights.

Advice: "I like fiction that tends toward the speculative."

☑ $ THE LEADING EDGE, Magazine of Science Fiction and Fantasy, TLE Press, 3163 JKHB, Provo UT 84602. (801)378-4455. E-mail: tle@byu.edu. Website: http://tle.clubs.byu.edu (includes excerpts, writer's, artist's, advertising guidelines, previews, subscription information). **Contact:** Ellen Lund, fiction director. Zine specializing in science fiction; 5½×8½; 120 pages; card stock; some illustrations. "*The Leading Edge* is dedicated to helping new writers make their way into publishing. We send critiques back with every story. We don't print anything with heavy swearing, violence that is too graphic, or explicit sex. We have an audience that is about 50% Latter Day Saints." Semiannual. Estab. 1981. Circ. 400.

Needs: Fantasy (space fantasy, sword/sorcery), science fiction (hard science/technological, soft/sociological). Receives 60 unsolicited mss/month. Accepts 6 mss/issue; 12 mss/year. Publishes ms 1-6 months after acceptance. **Publishes 9-10 new writers/year.** Recently published work by Orson Scott Card, Dan Wells and Dave Wolverton. Length: 12,000 words; average length 7,000 words. Publishes short shorts. Average length: 1,200 words. Also publishes poetry. Always comments on rejected mss.

How to Contact: Send complete ms with cover letter. Include estimated word count, brief bio and list of publications. Responds in 5 months on mss. Send disposable copy of ms and #10 SASE for reply only. Accepts multiple submissions. Sample copy for $4.50. Guidelines for SASE. Review novels, short story collections and nonfiction books of interest.

Payment/Terms: Pays 1¢/word; $100 maximum and 2 contributor's copies; additional copies $3.95. Pays on publication for first North American serial rights. Sends galleys to author.

Advice: "Don't base your story on your favorite TV show, book or game. Be original, creative and current. Base science fiction on recent science, not 50s horror flicks."

☑ ◯ **LIQUID OHIO, Voice of the Unheard**, Grab Odd Dreams Press, P.O. Box 60265, Bakersfield CA 93386-0265. (805)871-0586. E-mail: liquidchrista@hotmail.com. Website: www.liquidohio.net. **Contact:** Christa Hart, fiction editor. Magazine: 8×11; 32 pages; newsprint; illustrations; photos. Quarterly. Estab. 1995. Circ. 500.

Needs: Experimental, humor/satire, literary. Receives 15-20 unsolicited mss/month. Accepts 2 mss/issue; 24-30 mss/year. Publishes ms 1-3 months after acceptance. **Publishes 15 new writers/year.** Recently published work by Marvin Pinkis, Richard Robbins and Hillary Wentworth. Length: 2,500-3,000 words; average length: 1,500-1,800 words. Publishes short shorts. Also publishes literary essays, literary criticism, poetry.

How to Contact: Send complete ms with a cover letter. Should include estimated word count. Responds in 1 month to queries; 3 months to mss. Send SASE for reply, return of ms or send a disposable copy of ms. Accepts simultaneous, multiple, submissions, reprint and electronic submissions. Sample copy for $4, 11×14 SAE and 3 first-class stamps. Guidelines for #10 SASE.

Payment/Terms: Pays 3 contributor's copies. Acquires one-time rights.

Advice: "We like things that are different, but not too abstract or 'artsy' that one goes away saying, 'huh?' Write what you feel, not necessarily what sounds deep or meaningful—it will probably be that naturally if it's real. Send in anything you've got—live on the edge. Stories that are relatable, that deal with those of us trying to find a creative train in the world. We also love stories that are extremely unique, e.g., talking pickles, etc."

☑ $◯ ◎ **LITERALLY HORSES, Poetry, Fiction, Nonfiction & Other Expressions of the Horse**, Equestrienne Ltd., 208 Cherry Hill St., Kalamazoo MI 49006. (616)345-5915. E-mail: literallyhorses@aol.com. **Contact:** Laurie A. Cerny, publisher/editor. Zine specializing in horse/cowboy-related fiction/poetry: 5¼×8½; 28 pages; 20 lb. paper; 20 lb. cover stock; illustrations; photos. "We showcase poetry/fiction that has a horse/cowboy, western lifestyle theme. Most of the mainstream horse publications, as well as ones that publish western history, ignore these genres. I'm very interested in subject material geared toward the English riding discipline of the horse industry, as well as horse racing, driving. etc." Biannual. Estab. 1999. Circ. 1,000. Member, American Horse Publications, Western Writers of America.

Needs: Adult fiction, children's/juvenile (horse; ages 7-13), comics/graphic novels, western (frontier saga, traditional, cowboy/rodeo related). "No horror, gay, erotica." Receives 25 unsolicited mss/month. Accepts 8 mss/year. Publishes ms 6 months after acceptance. **Publishes 50 new writers/year.** Recently published work by Kim Marie Wood, Wally Badgett and John R. Erickson. Length: 1,500-2,500 words; average length: 1,500 words. Publishes short shorts. Average length: 500 words. Also publishes literary criticism and poetry. Sometimes comments on rejected mss.

How to Contact: Send complete ms with a cover letter. Include brief bio. Responds in 6 weeks to mss. Send a disposable copy of ms and #10 SASE for reply only. Accepts simultaneous submissions, previously published work and multiple submissions. Sample copy for $2.25. Guidelines for SASE. Reviews novels, short story collections and nonfiction books of interest to writers.

Payment/Terms: Pays $3/poem, $12/short story and 2 contributor's copies; additional copies $2. Pays on publication for one-time rights. Not copyrighted. Sponsors annual contest. Deadline is July 15 of each year. SASE for rules.

Advice: "Right now many other mainstream literary publications seem to be interested in very dark, disturbed fiction. I'm focusing on fiction that is positive (it still may deal with hard issues) and spiritual. A reader should come away feeling good and not depressed after reading the fiction in *Literally Horses.*"

$  **MUSHROOM DREAMS**, 14537 Longworth Ave., Norwalk CA 90650-4724. **Contact:** Jim Reagan, editor. Magazine: 8½×5½; 32 pages; 20 lb. paper; heavy cover stock; illustrations. "Eclectic content with emphasis on literary quality." Semiannually. Estab. 1997. Circ. 100.

Needs: Realistic or naturalistic fiction. No gay, lesbian, fantasy. Receives 10-15 unsolicited mss/month. Accepts 3 mss/issue; 6 mss/year. Publishes ms 6-12 months after acceptance. Recently published work by William E. Meyer, Jr., John Taylor, Bayard and Edward M. Turner. Length: 250-1,800 words; average length: 800 words. Publishes short shorts. Length: 250 words. Also publishes poetry. Often comments on rejected ms.

How to Contact: Send complete ms with a cover letter. Include estimated word count, short paragraph bio. Responds in 1 week to queries; 6 weeks to mss. Send SASE for reply or return of ms. Accepts simultaneous and reprint submissions. Sample copy $1. Guidelines free.

Payment/Terms: Pays $5-10 and 2 contributor's copies; additional copies $1. Pays on publication for first rights.

N **NEGATIVE CAPABILITY**, The Zine You Can Believe In, Lurky Co. Worldwide, P.O. Box 225338, San Francisco CA 94122-5338. Phone/Fax: (415)430-2160, ext. 9006. E-mail: negcap@yahoo.com. Website: www.negcap.com. **Contact:** Josh Saitz, publisher. Zine specializing in humor and anger: 8½×11; 48-64 pages; 60 lb. bright white; 10pt c1s cover; illustrations; photos. "*Negative Capability* is a funny, daring and complex magazine that aims to force people to confront the ugly truths of life. It is vicious and obnoxious but always aims for the last laugh." Semiannual. Estab. 1997. Circ. 3,000. Member, ULA, Underground Literary Alliance and the Zine syndicate.

• 1997 Best New Zine at the Royal Fest; 1998 Zine of the Year; 2001 1st place *Writer's Digest* Zine Contest.

Needs: Humor satire. "Does not accept anything that is for kids, religious, genre, romance, new age, western or historical. Must be very funny or very angry only." Receives 5 unsolicited mss/month. Publishes ms 6-9 months after acceptance. Recently published work by Natasha Vlahovic, Juli Hunsucker and Lurky Saitz. Length: 2,000 words. Rarely comments on rejected mss.

How to Contact: Query first. Include list of publications with submission. Responds in 6 weeks to queries; 2 months to mss. Send disposable copy of ms and #10 SASE for reply only. Sample copy for $3. Guidelines on website.

Payment/Terms: Pays 5 contributor's copies; additional copies $3. Pays on publication for first and electronic rights.

Advice: "Submissions must make me laugh out loud, unique in style and tone and must offend someone, even me. Find your own voice. Take chances and risks. Do not be afraid to fail."

$ **NOVA SCIENCE FICTION MAGAZINE**, Nova Publishing Company, 17983 Paseo Del Sol, Chino Hills CA 91709-3947. (909)393-0806. **Contact:** Wesley Kawato, editor. Zine specializing in evangelical Christian science fiction: 8½×5½; 64 pages; cardstock cover. "We publish religious science fiction short stories, no fantasy or horror. One story slot per issue will be reserved for a story written from an evangelical Christian viewpoint. We also plan to carry one article per issue dealing with science fiction wargaming." Quarterly. Estab. 1999. Circ. 25.

Needs: Science fiction (hard science/technological, soft/sociological, religious). "No stories where the villain is a religious fanatic and stories that assume the truth of evolution." Accepts 3 mss/issue; 12 mss/year. Publishes ms 3 months after acceptance. **Publishes 3 new writers/year.** Recently published work by Wesley Kawato, Tom Cron, Robert Alley, Ellen Straw, Megan James, Steve Lofton and Brad Linaweaver. Length: 250-7,000 words; average length: 4,000 words. Publishes short shorts. Average length: 250 words. Sometimes comments on rejected mss.

How to Contact: Query first. Include estimated word count and list of publications. Responds in 3 months to queries and mss. Send SASE (or IRC) for return of ms. Accepts previously published work and multiple submissions. Sample copy for $6. Guidelines free for SASE.

Payment/Terms: Pays $1.25-35. Pays on publication for first North American serial rights. Not copyrighted.

Advice: "Make sure your plot is believable and describe your characters well enough so I can visualize them. If I like it, I buy it. I like happy endings and heroes with a strong sense of faith."

✓ **NUTHOUSE, Essays, Stories and Other Amusements**, Twin Rivers Press, P.O. Box 119, Ellenton FL 34222. E-mail: nuthouse449@aol.com. Website: http://hometown.aol.com/Nuthous499/index2.html (in-

---

● **A BULLET INTRODUCES COMMENTS** by the editor of *Novel & Short Story Writer's Market* indicating special information about the listing.

cludes writer's guidelines, readers' letters, excerpts). **Contact:** Dr. Ludwig "Needles" Von Quirk, chief of staff. Zine: digest-sized; 12-16 pages; bond paper; illustrations; photos. "Humor of all genres for an adult readership that is not easily offended." Published every 6 weeks. Estab. 1993. Circ. 100.

Needs: Humor/satire: erotica, experimental, fantasy, feminist, historical (general), horror, literary, main-stream/contemporary, mystery/suspense, psychic/supernatural/occult, romance, science fiction and westerns. Plans annual "Halloween Party" issue featuring humorous verse and fiction with a horror theme. Deadline: July 31. Receives 30-50 unsolicited mss/month. Accepts 5-10 mss/issue; 50-60 mss/year. Publishes ms 6-12 months after acceptance. **Publishes 10-15 new writers/year.** Recently published work by Dale Andrew White, Michael Fowler and Tim Myers. Length: 100-1,000 words; average length: 500 words. Publishes short shorts. Length: 100-250 words. Also publishes literary essays, literary criticism and poetry. Often comments on rejected mss.

How to Contact: Send complete ms with a cover letter. Include estimated word count, bio (paragraph) and list of publications. Responds in 1 month to mss. SASE for return of ms or send disposable copy of ms. Accepts simultaneous and reprint submissions. Sample copy for $1.25 (payable to Twin Rivers Press). Guidelines for #10 SASE.

Payment/Terms: Pays 1 contributor's copy. Acquires one-time rights. Not copyrighted.

Advice: Looks for "laugh-out-loud prose. Strive for original ideas; read the great humorists—Saki, Woody Allen, Robert Benchley, Garrison Keillor, John Irving—and learn from them. We are turned off by sophomoric attempts at humor built on a single, tired, overworked gag or pun; give us a story with a beginning, middle and end."

$ ⬛ ◎ **OF UNICORNS AND SPACE STATIONS**, %Gene Davis, P.O. Box 200, Bountiful UT 84011-0200. Website: www.genedavis.com. **Contact:** Gene Davis, senior editor. Zine: 5½×8½; 60 pages; 20 lb. white paper; card cover stock; illustrations. "We want science fiction and fantasy of a positive nature, that gives us ideas, that warns us about the future and gives potential answers. It should be for adults, though graphic sex, violence and offensive language are not considered." Biannual. Estab. 1994. Circ. 100.

Needs: Fantasy (science fantasy, sword and sorcery), science fiction (hard science, soft/sociological, utopian). Wants "clear writing that is easy to follow." Receives 20 unsolicited mss/month. Accepts 9-13 mss/issue; approximtely 25 mss/year. Publishes ms 6-12 months after acceptance. **Publishes approximately 4 new writers/year.** Recently published work by Gordon Ross Lanser and Jackie Shank. Length: 3,000 words average. Publishes short shorts. Also publishes poetry. Sometimes comments on rejected mss.

How to Contact: Send complete ms (clean, well-written, not stapled) with a cover letter. Include estimated word count, bio (75 words or less) and writer's classification of the piece (science fiction, fantasy, poetry). Responds in 3 months. Send SASE for reply, return of ms or send a disposable copy of ms. Accepts simultaneous, reprint and electronic (disk only) submissions. If a subscriber, e-mail submissions OK. Sample copy for $4. Guidelines for #10 SASE.

Payment/Terms: Pays 5¢/word and 1 contributor's copy for stories; $5/poem and 1 contributor's copy for poetry; additional copies for $4. Acquires one-time rights.

Advice: "Keep trying. It may take several tries to get published. Most stories I see are good. You just need to find an editor that goes ga-ga over your style."

ℕ ◎ **ONCE UPON A WORLD**, 1881 W. Alexander #1046, North Las Vegas NV 89032. E-mail: 107753.2 174@compuserve.com. **Contact:** Emily Alward, editor. Zine: 8½×11; 80-100 pages; white paper; card stock cover; pen & ink illustrations. "A science fiction and fantasy zine with emphasis on alternate-world cultures and stories of idea, character and interaction. Also publishes book reviews and poems for an adult audience, primarily readers of science fiction and fantasy. We're known for science fiction and fantasy stories with excellent wordbuilding and a humanistic emphasis." Annually. Estab. 1988. Circ. 150.

Needs: Fantasy, science fiction. No realistic "stories in contemporary settings"; horror; stories using Star Trek or other media characters; stories with completely negative endings. Wants to see more "stories set in worlds with alternate political, economic or family arrangements." List of upcoming themes available for SASE. Receives 20 unsolicited mss/month. Accepts 8-12 mss/issue; per year "varies, depending on backlog." Publishes ms from 2 months to 1½ years after acceptance. **Publishes 4 new writers/year.** Recently published work by Jon C. Picciuolo, Tamela Viglione and Patricia Mathews. Length: 400-10,000 words; average length: 3,000 words. Publishes short shorts. Also publishes poetry. Sometimes comments on rejected mss and recommends other markets.

How to Contact: Send complete manuscript. Responds in 2-4 weeks to queries; 2-16 weeks to mss. SASE. "Reluctantly" accepts simultaneous submissions. Sample copy for $9. Make checks payable to Emily Alward. Guidelines for #10 SASE. Reviews novels and short story collections.

Payment/Terms: Pays contributor's copies. Acquires first rights. "Stories copyrighted in author's name; copyrights not registered."

Advice: "Create your own unique universe, and then show its texture and how it 'works' in the story. This is a good way to try out a world that you're building for a novel. But, don't forget to also give us interesting characters with believable problems. Submit widely, but pay attention to editors' needs and guidelines—don't scattershot.

Take on new challenges—i.e., never say 'I only write science fiction, romance, or even fiction in general—you never know where your 'sideline' work is going to impress an editor. We aim to fill some niches not necessarily well-covered by larger publishers currently: science fantasy; cross-genre; SF love stories; and non-cyber centered futures. Also, we see too many stories with generic, medieval-type world settings and premises."

N ⊕ $ ◎ ORB, Speculative Fiction, ORB Publications, P.O. Box 1621, West Preston, Melbourne, Victoria, Australia 3072. Phone: (+61) 03 94719270. E-mail: kendacot@vicnet.net.au. Website: www.home.vicnet .net.au/~kendacot/Orb. **Contact:** Sarah Endacott, editor. Zine specializing in speculative fiction: A5; 196 pages; 90gsm white; 200gsm full color cover; illustrations. "An Australian speculative fiction magazine that publishes Australian authors, artwork, reviews, interviews and articles." Biannual. Estab. 1999. Circ. 400.

• *Orb* was nominated for two Ditmars in 1999 and 2 Aurealis Awards in 2000.

Needs: Children/juvenile (fantasy), fantasy (space fantasy, sword and sorcery), horror, psychic/supernatural/ occult, religious (religious fantasy), romance (futuristic/time travel), science fiction (hard science/technological, soft/sociological), young adult/teen (fantasy/science fiction). "Fiction must be from Australian writers and have some speculative content." Receives 20 unsolicited mss/month. Accepts 10-12 mss/issue; 20-30 mss/year. **Publishes 4 new writers/year.** Length: 100-10,000 words; average length: 3,000. Publishes short shorts. Average length: 300 words. Also publishes literary essays and literary criticism. Often comments on rejected mss.

How to Contact: Send complete copy of ms with cover letter. Include estimated word count and brief bio with submission. Responds in 3 weeks to queries; 3 months to mss. Send SASE (or IRC) for return of the ms or disposable copy of ms and #10 SASE for reply only. Accepts simultaneous and multiple submissions. Sample copy for $16 (Australian dollars). Guidelines for SASE and on website. Reviews novels, short story collections and nonfiction books.

Payment/Terms: Pays $30 (Australian) and 1 contributor's copy; additional copies $16 (Australian). Pays on publication for first rights. Sends galleys to author.

Advice: "Challenging, controversial concepts make manuscript/stories stand out. This must accompany solid plot and characterization and clear, proficient writing style. Read widely in the genre."

◑ ⚑ OUTER DARKNESS, Where Nightmares Roam Unleashed, Outer Darkness Press, 1312 N. Delaware Place, Tulsa OK 74110. **Contact:** Dennis Kirk, editor. Zine: 8½×5½; 60-80 pages; 20 lb. paper; 90 lb. glossy cover; illustrations. Specializes in imaginative literature. "Variety is something I strive for in *Outer Darkness*. In each issue we present readers with great tales of science fiction and horror along with poetry, cartoons and interviews/essays. I seek to provide readers with a magazine which, overall, is fun to read. My readers range in age from 16 to 70." Quarterly. Estab. 1994. Circ. 500.

• Fiction published in *Outer Darkness* has received honorable mention in *The Year's Best Fantasy and Horror.*

Needs: Fantasy (science), horror, mystery/suspense (with horror slant), psychic/supernatural/occult, romance (gothic), science fiction (hard science, soft/sociological). No straight mystery, pure fantasy—works which do not incorporate elements of science fiction and/or horror. Also, no slasher horror with violence, gore, sex instead of plot. Wants more "character driven tales—especially in the genre of science fiction. I do not publish works with children in sexual situations and graphic language should be kept to a minimum." Receives 50-75 unsolicited mss/month. Accepts 7-9 mss/issue; 20-50 mss/year. **Publishes 3-5 new writers/year.** Recently published work by David Lindschmidt, Suzanne Donahue and Jeffrey Thomas. Length: 1,000-5,000 words; average length: 3,000 words. Also publishes literary essays and poetry. Always comments on rejected mss.

How to Contact: Send complete ms with a cover letter. Include estimated word count, 50- to 75-word bio, list of publications and "any awards, honors you have received." Responds in 2 weeks to queries; 3 months to mss. Send SASE for reply, return of ms or send a disposable copy of ms. Accepts simultaneous and multiple submissions. Sample copy for $3.95. Guidelines for #10 SASE.

Payment/Terms: Pays 3 contributor's copies for fiction, 2 for poetry and art. Pays on publication for one-time rights.

Advice: "Suspense is one thing I look for in stories. I want stories which grab the reader early on . . . and don't let go. I want stories which start off on either an interesting or suspenseful note. Read the works of Alan Dean Foster, Robert Bloch, William Greenleaf and Richard Matheson. Don't be discouraged by rejections. The best writers have received their share of rejection slips. Be patient. Take time to polish your work. Produce the best work you can and continue to submit, regardless of rejections. New writers now have more markets than ever before. I believe readers are searching for more 'traditional' works and that's what I strive to feature."

☑ ◑ ◎ ⚑ PENNY DREADFUL, Tales & Poems of Fantastic Terror, Pendragonian Publications, P.O. Box 719, New York NY 10101-0719. E-mail: mmpendragon@aol.com. Website: www.pennydreadful.org.

Contact: Michael Pendragon, editor. Zine specializing in horror: 9×6; 175 pages; illustrations; photos. Publication to "celebrate the darker aspects of man, the world and their creator. We seek to address a highly literate audience who appreciate horror as a literary art form." Biannual. Estab. 1996. Circ. 200.

● *Penny Dreadful* won several Honorable Mentions in St. Martin's Press's *The Year's Best Fantasy and Horror* competition.

Needs: Fantasy (dark symbolist), horror, psychic/supernatural/occult. Wants more "tales set in and in the style of the 19th century." No modern settings "constantly referring to 20th century persons, events, products, etc." List of upcoming themes available for SASE. Receives 100 unsolicited mss/month. Accepts 10 mss/issue; 30 mss/year. "*Penny Dreadful* reads all year until we have accepted enough submissions to fill more than one year's worth of issues." **Publishes 1-3 new writers/year.** Recently published work by James S. Dorr, Scott Thomas, John B. Ford, Susan E. Abramski, Paul Bradshaw and John Light. Length: 500-5,000 words. Publishes short shorts. Also publishes poetry. Always comments on rejected mss.

How to Contact: Send complete ms with a cover letter. Include estimated word count, bio and list of publications. Responds in up to 1 year to queries and mss. Send SASE for reply, return of ms or send disposable copy of ms. Accepts simultaneous submissions and reprints. Sample copy for $10. Subscription for $25. Guidelines for #10 SASE.

Payment/Terms: Pays 1 contributor copy. Acquires one-time rights. Sends galleys to author. Not copyrighted.

Advice: Whenever possible, try to submit to independent zines specializing in your genre. Be prepared to spend significant amounts of time and money. Expect only one copy as payment. Over time—if you're exceptionally talented and/or lucky—you may begin to build a small following."

N PINDELDYBOZ, Pindeldyboz, 25-53 36th St., Astoria NY 11103. Website: www.pindeldyboz.com or www.pboz.net. **Contact:** Whitney Pastorek, senior editor. Literary magazine: 8½×11; 272 pages; matte cover; illustrations. "Fiction by the contemporary authors you love to read and those you'd love if you only knew them. We have an unique philosophy and will not create something you will not absolutely love." Semiannual. Estab. 2001.

Needs: Comics/graphic novels, experimental, family saga, fantasy (sword and sorcery), humor satire, literary, translation. Upcoming themes available online. Receives 25 unsolicited mss/month. Accepts 16 print mss/issue; 32 print mss/year; 5 web mss/year; 110 web mss/year. Publishes ms 3 months after acceptance. **Publishes 25-30 new writers/year.** Recently published work by Neal Polloch, Dan Kennedy, Bryce Newhart, Corey Mesler, Rob Maiton. Length: 250+ words; average length: 2,000. Publishes short shorts. Average length: 500 words. Also publishes literary essays and poetry. Sometimes comments on rejected mss.

How to Contact: Send complete copy of ms with cover letter. Accepts mss by e-mail and disk. Include brief bio, list of publications and phone number with submission. Responds in 2 weeks to queries; 3 months to mss. Send SASE (or IRC) for return of the ms and disposable copy of ms and #10 SASE for reply only. Accepts simultaneous and multiple submissions. Sample copy for $10. Guidelines on website.

Payment/Terms: Pays 1 contributor's copy; additional copies $10. Pays on publication for one-time rights.

Advice: "We look for good grammar. Bad grammar stands out but in a bad way. Make us laugh. Make us smile. Make us peanut butter and jelly sandwiches."

○ BERN PORTER COSMOGRAPHIC, 50 Salmond St., Belfast ME 04915. (207)338-4303. E-mail: bpinter national@hotmail.com. **Contact:** Natasha Bernstein and Sheila Holtz, editors. Magazine: 8½×11; 8 pages; illustrations; photos. "Experimental prose and poetry at the edge of established literary forms." Monthly. Estab. 1997.

Needs: Experimental, literary, prose poem, translations, international. "No long conventional narratives. Want more short vignettes and surreal prose-poems." Receives 30-50 unsolicited mss/month. Publishes ms immediately after acceptance. **Publishes 12 new writers/year.** Published work by Stephen Jama, Natasha Bernstein, C.A. Conrad, T. Anders Carson and Anne Welsh. Length: 2 pages maximum. Publishes short shorts.

How to Contact: Query first. Accepts queries by e-mail. Responds in 1 week. Accepts simultaneous and reprint submissions. Sample copy $2. Guidelines free.

Payment/Terms: Pays in copies.

Advice: "Do not compromise your style and vision for the sake of the market. Megamarketing of authors by big mega publishers sucks. We seek to counter this trend by giving voice to authors who would not be heard in that world."

N ▼ PROSE AX, doses of prose, poetry, visual and audio art, P.O. Box 22643, Honolulu HI 96823-2643. E-mail: prose_ax@att.net. Website: www.proseax.com (includes all writings that appear in print version. Many photos and much artwork that appears in print does not appear on website). **Contact:** J. Calma, editor. Zine and online magazine specializing in prose, poetry and art: 8½×7; 24-30 pages; 20 lb. paper; illustrations; photos. "We are a literary journal that publishes stimulating, fresh prose and poetry. We are committed to publishing new and ethic writers or ethnic themes. The style of our website and print version is very visual, very stylish, and I think this makes our publication different. We present fresh voices in a fresh way." Quarterly. Estab. 2000. Circ. 450-500 print; 50 unique visitors average per day to website.

● Prose Ax won a *Writer's Digest* 2000 Zine Competition honorable mention.

Needs: Ethnic/multicultural (general), experimental, fantasy (fantastic realism), horror (dark fantasy), literary, novel excerpts that work well alone, flash fiction. "No genre, especially romance and mystery." Receives 30-50 unsolicited mss/month. Accepts 3-7 mss/issue. Publishes ms 1-3 months after acceptance. **Publishes 30 new writers/year.** Length: 50-5,000 words; average length: 1,000. Publishes short shorts. Average length: 500 words. Recently published work by Eric Paul Shafer, Ken Goldman, Jasmine Orr, Jason D. Smith, K.J. Stevens and Kenneth Champeon. Also publishes literary essays and poetry. Often comments on rejected mss.

How to Contact: Send complete copy of ms with cover letter. Accepts mss by e-mail. Include estimated word count with submission. Responds in 1-2 months. Send disposable copy of ms and #10 SASE for reply only. Accepts simultaneous, multiple and previously published submissions. Sample copy free with SASE (8×12 SAE and $1.50 postage or IRC) if available. Guidelines send SASE, e-mail or on website. Reviews novels, short story collections and nonfiction books.

Payment/Terms: Pays 2 contributor's copies; additional copies send SASE. Pays on publication for one-time and electronic rights. Sends galleys to author. Sponsors contest: All accepted pieces eligible to win Potent Prose Ax Award. Pays $10 for most potent fiction; $5 for most potent poetry.

Advice: "A good story has good details and descriptions. Read our zine first to see if what you write will fit in with the tone and style of Prose Ax. Write a little 'hello' to us instead of sending only your mss."

QECE, Question Everything Challenge Everything, 406 Main St. #3C, Collegeville PA 19426. E-mail: qece@yahoo.com. Website: www.geocities.com/qece. **Contact:** Larry Nocella, editor. Zine: 5½× 8½; 60 pages; copy paper; copy paper cover; illustrations; photos; color artwork centerfold. Zine "seeking to inspire free thought and action by encouraging a more questioning mentality. Intended for dreamers and laidback rebels." Biannual. Estab. 1996. Circ. 300.

● QECE was listed among *Maximumrocknroll's Zine Top Ten* and won an honorable mention in *Writer's Digest* zine publishing competition 2000.

Needs: Experimental. "Anything that inspires others to question and challenge conventions of fiction. Aggressive, compelling, short, fun is OK too. No lame stuff. Be wary of anything too literary. Would like to see more innovation, less pretentiousness." No genre fiction, no formulas. Receives 15 unsolicited mss/month. Accepts 1 ms/issue; 3 mss/year. Publishes ms 6 months after acceptance. **Publishes 6 new writers/year.** Recently published work by Andy Rant, Candi Lace and Colin Develin. Length: 1,000 words average. Publishes short shorts. Always comments on rejected mss.

How to Contact: Send complete ms with a cover letter. Include estimated word count and 25 words or less bio. Responds in 4 months. Send SASE for reply, return of ms or send a disposable copy of ms. Accepts simultaneous and e-mail submissions. Sample copy for $3. Guidelines free for #10 SASE.

Payment/Terms: Pays 2 contributor's copies; additional copies for $3. Money-orders made out to "Larry Nocella" or cash. No personal checks, please. Acquires one-time rights.

Advice: "Ignore 'trends'; be yourself as much as possible and you'll create something unique. Be as timeless as possible. Avoid obscure, trendy references. Tie comments about a current trend to timeless observation. If it's in the 'news' chances are it won't be in QECE, The 'news' is a joke. Tell me something I need to know. Favor anecdotes and philosophy over intense political opinions. I'd prefer to hear about personal experiences and emotions everyone can relate to. Criticism is welcome, though. QECE can be negative, but remember it is positive too. Just go for it! Send away and let me decide! Get busy!"

STARSHIP EARTH, Black Moon Publishing, P.O. Box 484, Bellaire OH 43906. (740)676-5659. E-mail: shadowhorse@earthlink.net. Editor: Kirin Lee. **Contact:** Ms. Silver Shadowhorse, fiction editor. Zine specializing in the sci-fi universe: 8½×11; 60 pages; glossy paper and cover; illustrations; photos. "We are mostly non-fiction with one piece of fiction per month." Monthly. Estab. 1995. Circ. 30,000.

● Sponsors contest. Send SASE for details.

Needs: Fantasy (science fantasy), science fiction (hard science, soft/sociological, historical). Wants more hard science fiction. No "sword and sorcery, religious, mystery, erotica or comedy." Would like to see more "hard science fiction." Publishes special fiction issues or anthologies. Receives 100-200 unsolicited mss/month. Accepts

---

SENDING TO A COUNTRY other than your own? Be sure to send International Reply Coupons (IRC) instead of stamps for replies or return of your manuscript.

1 ms/issue; 12 mss/year. Publishes ms 16-18 months after acceptance. **Publishes 10 new writers/year.** Recently published work by Jackson Frazier and Sean Kennedy. Length: 3,000 words maximum; average length: 2,000-3,000 words. Publishes short shorts. Sometimes comments on rejected mss.

How to Contact: Query or send complete ms with a cover letter. Include estimated word count, short bio and list of publications. Responds in 3 weeks to queries; 3-4 months to mss. Send SASE for reply, return of ms or send disposable copy of ms. Guidelines for #10 SASE. Reviews novels and short story collections. Send books to Jenna Dawson.

Payment/Terms: Pays 1¢/word minimum; 3¢/word maximum and 1 contributor's copy. Acquires first rights.

Advice: "Get our guidelines. Submit in the correct format. Send typed or computer printed manuscripts only. Avoid bad language, explicit sex and violence. Do not include any religious content. Manuscripts stand out when they are professionally presented."

◑ TRANSCENDENT VISIONS, Toxic Evolution Press, 251 S. Olds Blvd., 84-E, Fairless Hills PA 19030-3426. (215)547-7159. **Contact:** David Kime, editor. Zine: letter size; 24 pages; xerox paper; illustrations. *"Transcendent Visions* is a literary zine by and for people who have been labeled mentally ill. Our purpose is to illustrate how creative and articulate mental patients are." Quarterly. Estab. 1992. Circ. 200.

● *Transcendent Visions* has received excellent reviews in many underground publications.

Needs: Experimental, feminist, gay, humor/satire, lesbian. Especially interested in material dealing with mental illness. "I do not like stuff one would find in a mainstream publication. No porn." Would like to see more "quirky, nonmainstream fiction." Receives 5 unsolicited mss/month. Accepts 7 mss/issue; 20 mss/year. Publishes ms 3-4 months after acceptance. Recently published work by D. Harlan Wilson, Jim Sullivan and Robert Layden. Length: under 10 pages typed, double-spaced. Publishes short shorts. Also publishes poetry.

How to Contact: Send complete ms with cover letter. Include half-page bio. Responds in 2 weeks to queries; 1 month to mss. Send disposable copy of ms. Accepts simultaneous submissions and reprints. Sample copy for $2.

Payment/Terms: Pays 1 contributor's copy. Pays on publication for one-time rights.

Advice: "We like unusual stories that are quirky. We like shorter pieces. Please do not go on and on about what zines you have been published in or awards you have won, etc. We just want to read your material, not know your life story. Please don't swamp me with tons of submissions. Send up to five stories. Please print or type your name and address."

Ⓝ ▣ TROUT. E-mail: editor@troutmag.org. Website: www.troutmag.org. **Editor:** Robin Parkinson. E-zine. *Trout* is "slightly fishy, but never coarse."

Needs: "We publish humorous fiction, with a strong British slant. Our material ranges from themed collections of one-liners to a novel-length multi-threaded serial. The intended audience is composed of intelligent, articulate, literate people with a sense of humor and enough understanding of British culture to follow the jokes. No non-humorous fiction." Would like to see more "humorous short stories." **Publishes 3-4 new writers/year.** Recently published work by Joann L. Dominik, Ric Craig, Andy Gittins, Elly Kelly, Steve Lewin, Sue McCoan and Alexander MacDonald.

How to Contact: "*Trout* does not accept unsolicited manuscripts, manuscript fragments or synopses. Writers who might wish to contribute to *Trout* should contact the editor by e-mail and be prepared to show a sample of their work."

Payment/Terms: "*Trout* is entirely noncommercial. We receive no payment so we have none to pass on."

Advice: "Read us. If you find what you read amusing and feel that you are capable of writing material in a similar vein then talk to us. However, if you don't understand what we're getting at, we would not recommend that you attempt to 'slant' your material to fit what you perceive *Trout*'s philosophy to be. We are interested in writers whose natural 'voice' matches what we are doing."

Online Markets

As production and distribution costs go up and subscribers numbers fall, more and more magazines are giving up print publication and moving online. Relatively inexpensive to maintain and quicker to accept and post submissions, online fiction sites are growing fast in numbers and legitimacy. Says Robert L. Ward, director of the *Dana Literary Society Online Journal*: "This electronic medium is quickly overtaking Mr. Gutenberg."

Writers exploring online opportunities for publication will find a rich and diverse community of voices. Genre sites are strong, in particular those for science fiction/fantasy and horror (see the award-winning *Cyber Age Adventures*, *Scifi.com* and *Twilight Showcase*). Mainstream short fiction markets are also growing exponentially (see *American Feed Magazine*, *collectedstories.com*, *Cenotaph* and *Intertext*, among many others). Online literary journals range from the traditional (*The Barcelona Review*, *Paumonok Review*) to those with a decidedly more quirky, regional bent (*The Dead Mule School of Southern Literature*, *Big Country Peacock Chronicle*). Writers will also find here more highly experimental work that could exist no where else than in cyberspace, such as the hypertext fiction found on Scott Rettberg's *Alt-X* site.

Online journals are gaining respect for the writers who appear on their sites. As Jill Adams, publisher and editor of *The Barcelona Review*, says: "We see our Internet review, like the small independent publishing houses, as a means of counterbalancing the big-business mentality of the multi-national publishing houses. At the same time, we want to see our writers 'make it big.' Last year we heard from more and more big houses asking about some of our new writers, wanting contact information, etc. So I see a healthy trend in that big houses are, finally—after being skeptical and confused—looking at it seriously and scouting online."

While the medium of online publication is different, the traditional rules of publishing apply to submissions. Writers should research the site and archives carefully, looking for a match in sensibility for their work among the varied sites publishing. They should then follow submission guidelines exactly, and submit courteously. True, these sites aren't bound by traditional print schedules, so your work theoretically may be published more quickly. But that doesn't mean a larger staff, so do exercise patience with editors considering your manuscript.

Also, while reviewing the listings in this market section, notice they are grouped differently from other market listings. In our literary magazines section, for example, you'll find primarily only publications searching for literary short fiction. But Online Markets are grouped by medium, so you'll find publishers of mystery short stories listed next to those looking for horror next to those specializing in flash fiction, so review with care. In addition, those online markets with print counterparts, such as *North American Review*, you will find listed in the print markets sections.

A final note about online publication: like literary journals, the majority of these markets are either nonpaying or very low paying. In addition, writers will not receive print copies of the publications because of the medium. So in most cases, do not expect to be paid for your exposure.

THE ABSINTHE LITERARY REVIEW, P.O. Box 328, Spring Green WI 53588. E-mail: staff@absinthe-literary-review.com. Website: www.absinthe-literary-review.com. **Contact:** Charles Allen Wyman, editor. Electronic literary magazine. "We publish short stories, novel excerpts, poems and occasionally essays. Our target audience is the literate individual who enjoys creative language use, character-driven fiction and the clashing of worlds—real and surreal, poetic and prosaic, archaic and modern."

Needs: "*ALR* has a special affection for the blending of archaic materials with modern subjects. Elements of myth, archetype or symbolism should figure heavily in most submissions. We favor the surrealist, the poet and the philosopher over the storyteller even in our fiction choices. We also desire submissions from highly educated writers whose work is too dense, florid or learned for other markets. At the very least, your work should show an odd turn or a disaffected viewpoint. We abhor minimalist fiction simply because of its abundance in the present marketplace, but we can still appreciate a spare, well-done piece. Any genre work must substantially transcend traditional limitations of the form to be considered. Plot based fiction should be significantly odd." No mainstream storytellers; "Oprah" fiction, high school or beginner fiction, poetry or fiction that contains no capital letters or punctuation, "hot" trends, genre and utterly normal prose or poetry, first, second or third drafts, pieces that exceed our stated word count by thousands of words, writers who do not read and follow submissions guidelines." **Publishes 5-10 new writers/year.** Recently published work by Gerard Varni and Norman Lock. Length: 4,000-5,000 words. Reviews novels, short story collections and nonfiction works of interest to writers.

How to Contact: "Send fiction submissions to fiction@absinthe-literary-review.com. Though we now accept snail mail submissions, *we prefer e-mail*."

Payment/Terms: "We believe that writers should be paid for their work and will attempt to remit a small gratuity upon publication (usually in the $5-10 range) when funds are available. There is, however, no guarantee of payment. We are a nonprofit organization."

Advice: "Be erudite but daring in your writing. Draw from the past to drag meaning from the present. Kill cliché. Invest your work with layers of meaning that subtly reveal multiple realities. Do not submit pieces that are riddled with spelling errors and grammatical snafus. Be professional. For those of you who don't understand what this means, please send your manuscripts elsewhere until you have experienced the necessary epiphany."

N ◑ AMERICAN FEED MAGAZINE, American Feed Magazine, RR #1, Box 2177, Kingfield ME 04947. (207)235-2345. E-mail: editor@americanfeedmagazine.com. Website: www.Americanfeedmagazine.com. **Contact:** Shaw Izikson, editor. Online magazine: illustrations; photos. "We like to give a place for new voices to be heard, as well as established voices a place to get a wider audience for their work." Estab. 1994.

Needs: Adventure, comics/graphic novels, ethnic/multicultural, experimental, family saga, fantasy, feminist, glitz, historical, horror, humor/satire, literary, mainstream, mystery/suspense, New Age, psychic/supernatural/occult, science fiction, thriller/espionage. Receives 100 unsolicited mss/month. Accepts 15 mss/issue. Publishes ms 2 months after acceptance. **Publishes 15 new writers/year.** Recently published work by Joshua Farber and Daniel LaFavbre. Average length: 1,500. Publishes short shorts. Also publishes literary essays, literary criticism and poetry. Always comments on rejected mss.

How to Contact: Send complete ms with a cover letter. Accepts submissions on disk. Include estimated word count and brief bio. Responds in 2 months to queries and mss. Send SASE (or IRC) for return of ms or send a disposable copy of ms and #10 SASE for reply only. Accepts simultaneous, previously published and multiple submissions. Guidelines by e-mail or on website. Reviews novels, short story collections and nonfiction books of interest to writers. Send review copies to Shaw Izikson.

Payment/Terms: Acquires one-time rights.

Advice: "Make sure the story flows naturally, not in a forced way. You don't need a vivid imagination to write fiction, poetry or anything. Just look around you, because life is usually the best inspiration."

✓ $◑ ANOTHEREALM, 1560 W. Dempster #110, Mt. Prospect IL 60056. (847)718-0528. E-mail: gmark ette@aol.com. Website: www.anotherealm.com. **Contact:** Gary A. Markette, senior editor. "*Anotherrealm* publishes speculative fiction dealing with science fiction, fantasy, and horror themes. We strive for excellence. Our audience is anyone who enjoys good stories that are well written." Weekly. Estab. 1998. Member, Zine Guild.

Needs: Fantasy (space fantasy, sword and sorcery), horror (dark fantasy, futuristic, psychological, supernatural), science fiction (hard science/technological, soft/sociological). No pornography, westerns (unless science fiction, fantasy or horror-themed), romances (unless ditto), historical fiction (unless . . . you get the idea). Receives 100 unsolicited mss/month. Accepts 104 mss/year. Reads only during October, "although submissions are accepted year-round." Publishes ms 3 months after acceptance. **Publishes 80% new writers/year.** Length: 5,000 words maximum. Often comments on rejected ms.

How to Contact: Send complete ms with a cover letter pasted as part of e-mail. Include estimated word count. Responds to mss in 2 months. Accepts previously published work and multiple submissions. Sample copy and guidelines free on website.

Payment/Terms: Pays $10. Pays on acceptance for electronic rights.

Advice: "We look for the same as everyone else—editor's prejudiced view of 'the best.' Read Jean Goldstrum's book *How to Write Creatively for Internet Magazines*."

◑ ARCHIPELAGO, An International Journal On-Line of Literature, Art and Opinion, Box 2485, Charlottesville VA 22902-2485. (804)979-5292. E-mail: editor@archipelago.org. Website: www.archipelago.org. **Contact:** Katherine McNamara, editor. Electronic magazine: 90-100 pages in download (PDF) edition, available from website. "Literary (print-based, in spirit) work, meaning well-formed, fine writing, on diverse subjects and in various genres with an international tone. Readership is educated, well-read, international." Quarterly. Estab. 1997. Circ. 23 countries, 100,000 hits/month.

Needs: Literary. "No academic, self-involved, 'hip' fiction." Receives several unsolicited mss/month. Accepts 1 ms/issue. Does not read mss in the month before publication. Usually publishes ms in next issue after acceptance. Recently published work by Benjamin Cheever and Anna Maria Ortese. Publishes short shorts. Also publishes literary essays, literary criticism, translations, poetry (in translation and in original language). Sometimes comments on rejected ms if requested.

How to Contact: Query first. Accepts queries by e-mail only. Include brief bio. Responds in 2 months to queries; 4 months to mss. Electronic submissions read only if requested by editor. No unsolicited mss. Reviews novels, short story collections and nonfiction books of interest to readers.

Payment/Terms: No payment. Acquires first serial and first serial electronic rights. Sends galleys to author. Copyright reverts to author on publication.

Advice: "We look for superb writing; engaged, adult imagination. As big publishing becomes more and more part of the entertainment industry, I look for writers deeply read, thoughtful, uncontaminated by pop culture and commercial plot-lines."

N ✹ ○ ASCENT, Aspirations For Artists, Ascent, 1560 Arbutus Dr., Nanoose Bay, British Columbia C9P 9C8 Canada. E-mail: ascent@bcsupernet.com. Website: www.bcsupernet.com/users/ascent. **Contact:** David Fraser, editor. E-zine specializing in short fiction (all genres) and poetry, essays, visual art: 40 electronic pages; illustrations; photos. "*Ascent* is a quality electronic publication dedicated to promotions and encouraging aspiring writers of any genre. The focus however is toward interesting experimental writing in dark mainstream, literary, science fiction, fantasy and horror. Poetry can be on any theme. Essays need to be unique, current and have social, philosophical commentary." Quarterly. Estab. 1997.

Needs: Erotica, experimental, fantasy (space fantasy, sword and sorcery), feminist, horror (dark fantasy, futuristic, psychological, supernatural), literary, mainstream, mystery/suspense, New Age, psychic/supernatural/occult, science fiction (hard science/technological, soft/sociological). List of upcoming themes available online. Receives 20-30 unsolicited mss/month. Accepts 5 mss/issue; 20 mss/year. Publishes ms 3 months after acceptance. **Publishes 5-10 new writers/year.** Recently published work by Taylor Graham, Janet Buck and Travis Ray. Length: 500-4,000 words; average length: 2,000 words. Publishes short shorts. Average length: 2,000 words. Also publishes literary essays, literary criticism and poetry. Sometimes comments on rejected mss.

How to Contact: "Query by e-mail with word attachment." Accepts submissions by e-mail. Include estimated word count, brief bio and list of publications. Responds in 1 week to queries; 3 months to mss. Accepts simultaneous, previously published and multiple submissions. Guidelines by e-mail or on website. Reviews novels, short story collections and nonfiction books of interest to writers.

Payment/Terms: "No payment at this time. Rights remain with author."

Advice: "Short fiction should first of all tell a good story, take the reader to new and interesting imaginary or real places. Short fiction should use language lyrically and effectively, be experimental in either form or content and take the reader into realms where they can analyze and think about the human condition. Write with passion for your material, be concise and economical and let the reader work to unravel your story. In terms of editing, always proofread to the point where what you submit is the best it possible can be. Never be discouraged if your work is not accepted; it may be just not the right fit for a current publication."

BABEL, the Multilingual, Multicultural Online Journal of Arts and Ideas, E-mail: malcolm@towerofbabel.com. Website: www.towerofbabel.com. **Contact:** Malcolm Lawrence, editor-in-chief. Electronic zine. Publishes "regional reports from international stringers all over the planet, as well as features round table discussions, fiction, columns, poetry, erotica, travelogues, reviews of all the arts and editorials. We are an online community involving an extensive group of over 50 artists, writers and programmers, and over 150 translators representing (so far) 35 of the world's languages."

Needs: "There are no specific categories of fiction that we are not interested in. Possible exceptions: lawyers/vampires, different genders hailing from different planets, cold war military scenarios and things that go bump in the suburban night." Recently published work by Nicholas P. Snoek, Yves Jaques, Doug Williamson, A.L. Fern, Laura Feister, Denzel J. Hankinson, Pete Hanson and Malcolm Lawrence.

How to Contact: Send queries/mss by e-mail. "Please send submissions with a résumé/cv or biography, as Microsoft Word attached to e-mail." Reviews novels and short story collections.

Advice: "We would like to see more fiction with first-person male characters written by female authors as well as more fiction with first-person female characters written by male authors. The best advice we could give to writers wanting to be published in our publication is simply to know what you're writing about and to write passionately about it. We should also mention that the phrase 'dead white men' will only hurt your chances. The Internet is the most important invention since the printing press and will change the world in the same way. One look at *Babel* and you'll see our predictions for the future of electronic publishing."

⊕ ◑ ☯ THE BARCELONA REVIEW, Correu Vell 12 - 2, 08002 Barcelona, Spain. Phone/fax: (00) 34 93 319 15 96. E-mail: editor@barcelonareview.com. Website: www.barcelonareview.com. **Contact:** Jill Adams, editor. "*TBR* is an international review of contemporary, cutting-edge fiction published in English, Spanish and Catalan. Our aim is to bring both new and established writers to the attention of a larger audience. Well-known writers such as Alicia Erian in the U.S., Michael Faber in the U.K., Carlos Gardini in Argentina, and Andrés Ibàñez in Spain, for example, were not known outside their countries until appearing in *TBR*. Our multilingual format increases the audience all the more. Internationally-known writers, such as Irvine Welsh and Douglas Coupland, have contributed stories that ran in small press anthologies available in only one country. We try to keep abreast of what's happening internationally and to present the best finds every two months. Our intended audience is anyone interested in contemporary, cutting-edge fiction; we assume that our readers are well read and familiar with contemporary fiction in general."

● *The Barcelona Review* ranked #19 *Writer's Digest*'s Fiction 50 list of top markets for fiction writers. *TBR* has also been named "Best Online Only Literary Review" by Nan A. Talese/Doubleday.

Needs: Short fiction. Length: 4,000 words maximum. Also publishes articles and essays, book reviews and author interviews. "Most, but not all of our fiction lies somewhere out of the mainstream. Our bias is towards potent and powerful cutting-edge material; given that general criteria we are open to all styles and techniques and all genres. No slice-of-life stories, vignettes or sentimental writing, and nothing that does not measure up, in your opinion, to the quality of work in our review, which we expect submitters to be familiar with." **Published 20 new writers in 2000.** "That number will increase as the quality of writing presents itself." Recently published work by Pagan Kennedy, Pinckney Benedict, A.M. Home, George Saunders, Alicia Grian and Jess Mowry. Length: 4,000 words maximum.

How to Contact: Send submissions by e-mail as an attached file. Hard copies accepted but cannot be returned. No simultaneous submissions.

Payment/Terms: "In lieu of pay we offer a highly professional Spanish translation to English language writers and vice versa to Spanish writers."

Advice: "Send top drawer material that has been drafted two, three, four times—whatever it takes. Then sit on it for a while and look at it afresh. Keep the text tight (rewrite until every unnecessary word is eliminated). Grab the reader in the first paragraph and don't let go. Keep in mind that a perfectly crafted story that lacks a punch of some sort won't cut it. Make it new, make it different. Surprise the reader in some way. Read the best of the short fiction available in your area of writing to see how yours measures up. Don't send anything off until you feel it's ready and then familiarize yourself with the content of the review/magazine to which you are submitting."

N $ ▣ ▽ BAY FOREST ONLINE READER, Bay Forest Publishing, P.O. Box 61688, Phoenix AZ 85082-1688. (602)625-3402. Fax: (305)489-8086. E-mail: infodesk@bayforest.com. Website: www.bayforest. com (includes full text fiction/nonfiction and poetry, writer's guidelines, member services page and book sales are available). E-zine specializing in fiction/nonfiction and poetry. "The *Bay Forest Online Reader* is an online magazine containing a wide variety of literary genres and styles from both new and established writers of today. Unlike a quarterly or monthly publication, *The Online Reader* is a 'continuous update' publication, meaning we publish our stories as soon as they complete the editing process. Through continuous update we can provide readers access to the latest selections while providing writers the opportunity to see their work in print much more rapidly." Estab. 1998. Circ. 45,000.

● The *Bay Forest Online Reader* won one honorable mention in *Writer's Digest*'s zine competition, 2001.

Needs: Adventure, fantasy (space fantasy, sword and sorcery), horror (dark fantasy, futuristic, psychological, supernatural), humor/satire, mystery/suspense (amateur sleuth, cozy, police procedural, private eye/hardboiled), psychic/supernatural/occult, romance (contemporary, futuristic/time travel, gothic, historical, regency period, romantic suspense), science fiction (hard science/technological, soft/sociological), thriller/espionage, western (frontier saga, traditional) young adult/teen (adventure, easy-to-read, fantasy/science fiction, historical, horror, mystery/suspense, problem novels, romance, series, sports, western). "No religion, politics, erotic, offensive language, hate speech or other inflammatory language." Receives 20-25 unsolicited mss/month. Publishes ms 90 days after acceptance. **Publishes 80-90 new writers/year.** Recently published work by Kay Vetter, Marc Toso, Lars Thorson and Ronald Sefchick. Length: 500-15,000 words; average length: 3,000 words. Publishes short shorts. Average length: 1,200 words. Also publishes poetry. Always comments on rejected mss.

FOR EXPLANATIONS OF THESE SYMBOLS,
SEE THE INSIDE FRONT AND BACK COVERS OF THIS BOOK.

How to Contact: Send complete ms with a cover letter. Accepts submissions by e-mail and disk. Include estimated word count, brief bio, Social Security number, genre. Responds in 3 weeks to queries; 6 weeks to mss. Send SASE (or IRC) for return of ms or send a disposable copy of ms and #10 SASE for reply only. Accepts simultaneous, previously published and multiple submissions. Guidelines for SASE, by e-mail or on website.

Payment/Terms: Pays $7.50. Pays on publication for first rights. Sends galleys to author.

Advice: "The most important tip—read and adhere to the writer's guidelines. The *Bay Forest* editors are looking for well written, entertaining manuscripts. Special consideration is given for those manuscripts that show obvious signs of writer diligence, such as consistent character names and gender, limited spelling and grammar errors, and appropriate plot developments. Take your time. If you are in a hurry to complete your manuscript, it will be very obvious to the editors. If an editor requests that you rewrite and resubmit, take advantage of their input and advice. Too many beginning writers simply submit to another publisher."

N ◯ Ⓥ BIG COUNTRY PEACOCK CHRONICLE, Online Magazine, RR1, Box 89K-112, Aspermont TX 79502. (806)254-2322. E-mail: publisher@peacockchronicle.com. Website: www.peacockchronicle.com. **Contact:** Audrey Yoeckel, owner/publisher. Online magazine. "We publish articles, commentaries, reviews, interviews, short stories, serialized novels and novellas, poetry, essays, humor and anecdotes. Due to the nature of Internet publication, guidelines for lengths of written works are flexible and acceptance is based more on content. Content must be family friendly. Writings that promote hatred or violence will not be accepted. *The Big Country Peacock Chronicle* is dedicated to the preservation of community values and American folk cultures. In today's society, we are too often deprived of a solid feeling of community which is so vital to our security and well-being. It is our attempt to keep the best parts of our culture intact. We are always on the lookout for items and sites that promote fellowship and solid community values. Our goal is to build a place for individuals, no matter the skill level, to test their talents and get feedback from others in a non-threatening, friendly environment. The original concept for the magazine was to open the door to talented writers by providing not only a publishing medium for their work but support and feedback as well. It was created along the lines of a smalltown publication in order to remove some of the anxiety about submitting works for first time publication." Monthly. Estab. 2000.

● *Big Country Peacock Chronicle* was named the Heartland Heartbeat Featured Site for February, 2001.

Needs: Adventure, children's/juvenile (adventure, animal, easy-to-read, fantasy, historical, mystery, preschool, series, sports), ethnic/multicultural (general), family saga, fantasy (space fantasy, sword and sorcery), gay, historical (general), horror (futuristic, psychological, supernatural), humor/satire, literary, military/war, mystery/suspense (amateur sleuth, police procedural, private eye/hardboiled), psychic/supernatural/occult, regional, religious (children's religious), romance (gothic, historical, romantic suspense), science fiction (soft/sociological), thriller/espionage, translations, western (frontier saga, traditional). "While the genre of the writing or the style does not matter, excessive or gratuitous violence, foul language, and sexually explicit material is not acceptable." Accepts 2-3 mss/issue (depending on length). Publishes ms 2 months after acceptance. Recently published work by Meredith Weber and Julie Alexander. Length: 3,500 words maximum; average length: 2,500 words. Publishes short shorts. Average length: fewer than 1,500 words. Also publishes literary essays, literary criticism and poetry. Always comments on rejected mss.

How to Contact: Send cover letter and entire item for submission if under 1,500 words or 1,500 word clip of longer pieces. Accepts submissions by e-mail. Include estimated word count, brief bio, list of publications and Internet contact information, i.e., e-mail, website address. Responds in 3 weeks to queries; 6 weeks to mss. Send SASE (or IRC) for return of ms or send a disposable copy of ms and #10 SASE for reply only. Accepts simultaneous, previously published and multiple submissions. Guidelines by e-mail or on website. Reviews novels, short story collections and nonfiction books of interest to writers. Send review copies to Audrey Yoeckel, publisher@peacockchronicle.com.

Payment/Terms: Acquires electronic rights. Sends galleys to author. "While the authors and artists retain sole copyright to the material they submit to the *Peacock Chronicle*, the submission of that material constitutes permission for nonexclusive, perpetual rights for the free electronic distribution of archived material unless otherwise negotiated."

Advice: "We look for writing that promotes community and traditional values regardless of genre. If the story takes place on Mars or in the Old West, or is about relationships, history, adventure, etc., it must contain an identifiable positive attitude toward societal interaction. We look for continuity and coherence. The work should be clean with a minimum of typographical errors. The advantage to submitting works to us is the feedback and support. We work closely with our writers, offering promotion, resource information, moral support and general help to achieve success as writers. While we recommend doing business with us via the Internet, we have also published writers who do not have access. For those new to the Internet, we also provide assistance with the best ways to use it as a medium for achieving success in the field."

☑ ⬤ **THE BLUE MOON REVIEW**, 14313 Winter Ridge Lane, Midlothian VA 23113. E-mail: editor@thebl uemoon.com; fiction@thebluemoon.com. Website: www.TheBlueMoon.com. **Contact:** Doug Lawson, editor. Electronic magazine: Illustrations and photos. Quarterly. Estab. 1994. Circ. 16,000.

Needs: Experimental, feminist, gay, lesbian, literary, mainstream/contemporary, regional, translations. No genre fiction or condensed novels. Receives 40-70 unsolicited mss/month. Accepts 7-10 mss/issue; 51-60 mss/year. Publishes ms up to 9 months after acceptance. Published work by Edward Falco, Deborah Eisenberg, Robert Sward and Aldo Alvarez. Length: 3,000 words maximum. Publishes short shorts. Also publishes literary essays, literary criticism, poetry. Sometimes comments on rejected mss.

How to Contact: Send complete ms with a cover letter via e-mail. Only accepts electronic submissions. Include a brief bio, list of publications and e-mail address if available. Responds in 2 months to mss. Accepts simultaneous and electronic submissions. Sample copy and guidelines available at above website.

Payment/Terms: Acquires first North American serial and one-time anthology rights. Rights revert to author upon request.

Advice: "We look for strong use of language or strong characterization. Manuscripts stand out by their ability to engage a reader on an intellectual or emotional level. Present characters with depth regardless of age and introduce intelligent concepts that have resonance and relevance."

☑ $ **BLUE MURDER MAGAZINE**, Blue Murder, Ltd., 225 SW Broadway, Suite 300, Portland OR 97205. (503)292-6987, ext. 259. Fax: (503)296-0945. E-mail: info@bluemurder.com. Website: www.bluemurder.com (includes the entire magazine). **Contact:** Elise Lyons. Online e-zine specializing in crime noir fiction; 75 pages. "*Blue Murder* features hardboiled, crime noir fiction. Our magazine was the first of its kind on the web. Our audience, (worldwide) enjoys reading crime/mystery fiction." Bimonthly. Estab. 1998.

Needs: Mystery/suspense (police procedural, private eye/hardboiled crime). No romantic mysteries, horror, gothic, cozy or cat mysteries. Receives 400-500 mss/month. Accepts 12-15 mss/issue; 70-100 mss/year. Publishes ms 1-6 months after acceptance. Agented fiction 10%. **Publishes 2-5 new writers/year.** Recently published work by Gina Gallo, Andrew Vachss and Kris Neri. Length: 250-3,000 words; average length: 3,000. Publishes short shorts. Average length: 3,000. Also publishes literary essays and literary criticism. Accepts submissions by e-mail. Include estimated word count and brief bio. Responds in 1 week to queries and mss. Online submissions only. Accepts simultaneous submissions and multiple submissions. Sample copy free upon request. Guidelines for e-mail and website. Reviews novels, short story collections and nonfiction books of interest. Contact: David Firks.

Payment/Terms: Pays $20-100. Pays on publication for one-time rights and electronic rights.

Advice: "A manuscript should have voice, be unique. The first two paragraphs are very important. The short story should move the reader at lightening pace. Read as much as you can, everything you can. Know what crime noir fiction is about. Read our back issues."

⌷N⌷ ⬤ **BULK HEAD, Laxative of the Literary Mind**, Bridge Burner's Publishing, P.O. Box 5255, Mankato MN 56002-5255. (507)385-0635. E-mail: editor@bulkhead.org. Website: www.bulkhead.org. **Contact:** Curtis Meyer, editor. Online magazine: illustrations; photos. "We are an online literary magazine specializing in short fiction. Most of the work we publish is humorous, angry, sarcastic, experimental and energetic." Quarterly. Estab. 2000.

Needs: Comics/graphic novels, erotica, ethnic/multicultural (general), experimental, feminist, gay, humor/satire, lesbian, literary, mainstream, New Age, psychic/supernatural/occult, regional. "We do not publish hardcore genre stories. We do not publish religious material." Receives 15 unsolicited mss/month. Accepts 2-3 mss/issue; 6-12 mss/year. Publishes ms 3 months after acceptance. **Publishes 6-10 new writers/year.** Recently published work by Neil Harrison, Bruce Nelson, Charles Frank Roethel, Jay Marvin, Tessa Derksen, John Lee Clark, Neil Stanoff and Paul Dilsaver. Length: 50-3,500 words; average length: 2,000 words. Publishes short shorts. Average length: 900 words. Also publishes literary essays and poetry. Rarely comments on rejected mss.

How to Contact: Send complete ms with a cover letter. Accepts submissions by e-mail and disk. Include estimated word count, brief bio and list of publications. Responds in 3 months to queries; 6 months to mss. Send SASE (or IRC) for return of ms or send a disposable copy of ms and #10 SASE for reply only. Accepts multiple submissions. Sample copy free. Guidelines on website.

Payment/Terms: Acquires first rights. Sponsors contest.

Advice: "Shorter is better for our publication. We like experimentation and spunk. We especially like to see work that has angst and ignores the 'rules.' We loath formulated fiction. We also like great scenes. Give us short fiction, not stories. There is a difference. Don't wrap it up with a bow. Throw away the recipe cards. Action. Action. Action. Cut any similes and metaphors. Attention spans are shorter today—our readers are www addicted and hyper-caffeinated. We look for short, sweet explosions. If your story lacks action and dialogue, send it elsewhere."

☑ $⃞ ◉ ◪ **THE CAFE IRREAL, International Imagination**. E-mail: editors@cafeirreal.com. Website: www.cafeirreal.com. **Contact:** Alice Whittenburg, G.S. Evans, editors. E-zine; illustrations. *"The Cafe Irreal* is a webzine focusing on short stories and short shorts of an irreal nature." Semiannually.

• *The Cafe Irreal* was listed as one of the top 50 Internet Markets by *Writer's Digest*.

Needs: Experimental, fantasy (literary), science fiction (literary), translations. "No horror or 'slice-of-life' stories; no genre or mainstream science fiction or fantasy." Accepts 10-15 mss/issue; 20-30 mss/year. Publishes mss 6 months after acceptance. Recently published translations of works by Anna Maria Shua and Edwald Murrer. Length: no minimum; 2,000 words maximum (excerpts from longer works accepted). Publishes short shorts. Also publishes literary essays, literary criticism. Often comments on rejected ms.

How to Contact: Electronic submissions only. No attachments; include submission in body of e-mail. Include estimated word count. Responds in 2 months to mss. Accepts reprint submissions if indicated as such. See website for sample copy and guidelines.

Payment/Terms: Pays 1¢/word, $2 minimum. Pays on publication for first rights, one-time rights. Sends galleys (the html document via e-mail) to author.

Advice: "Forget formulas. Write about what you *don't* know, take me places I couldn't *possibly* go, don't try to make me care about the characters. Read short fiction by writers such as Kafka, Kobo Abe, Julio Cortazar, Leonara Carrington and Stanislaw Lem. Also read our website and guidelines."

☑ ◉ **CARVE MAGAZINE**, Mild Horse Press, P.O. Box 72231, Davis CA 95617. E-mail: editor@carvezine. com. Website: www.carvezine.com. **Contact:** Melvin Sterne, managing editor. Bimonthly online journal with annual printed "best of" anthology. Estab. 2000. Online circ. 3,000-5,000 per edition and growing. *Carve Magazine* nominates deserving authors for the Pushcart Prize Anthology. Member, Council of Literary Magazines and Presses.

Needs: We publish short stories only. Literary fiction. No genre, poetry or nonfiction. Publishes 50-70 stories/ year. As a web publication we are read in more than 40 countries worldwide and publish a mix of US and foreign authors, established and new writers. **Publishes 10-20 new writers/year.** Recently published work by Nan Leslie, Tanya Egan Gibson, XuXi, Robin Parks and Richard Messer. Hosts the Raymond Carver Short Story Award at *Carve Magazine*.

How to Contact: Electronic submissions only. Visit our website at www.carvezine.com for guidelines and to submit. Length: 10,000 words maximum. Accepts simultaneous submissions if identified (except for contest). Responds in 2 months. Occasionally critiques mss.

Advice: "We look for stories with strong characterization, conflict, and tightly written prose. Do you know what a fictive moment is? We generally dislike gimmicky and experimental fiction. If you tell a good story, we'll read it."

☑ **CENOTAPH, Fiction for the New Millennium**, Cayuse Press, P.O. Box 66003, Burien WA 98166-0003. E-mail: editor@cenotaph.net. Website: www.cenotaph.net (includes submission guidelines, features, writer's resources and two writers forums). **Contact:** Paul Tylor, editor. Electronic literary journal. "Published quarterly, *Cenotaph* is fiction for the new millennium, and seeks innovative fiction, shimmering with vision and originality for a literate audience." Estab. 1999.

Needs: Adventure, ethnic/multicultural (general), fantasy, historical, literary, mainstream, mystery/suspense, thriller/espionage, translations, cross-genre, science fiction, surrealism, magic realism, speculative. Romance (of any orientation) is acceptable if not sexually graphic. No children's, young adult, excessive violence, pro-drug or erotica. Wants to see more mystery, cross-genre, historical, surrealism. Receives 30 unsolicited mss/month. Publishes 10-12 mss/issue; 40-48 mss/year. Publishes ms 2-6 months after acceptance. **Willing to publish new writers.** Recently published work by Paul Taylor, Mary Chandler, Teresa White. Length: 800-2,500 words; average length: 1,500 words; prefers 2,000 words. Sometimes comments on rejected mss.

How to Contact: Send complete ms with a cover letter by e-mail only. No attachments will be accepted. Include estimated word count, 100-200 word bio and list of publications. Responds in 2 months after deadline to mss. Accepts multiple submissions. Prefers unpublished work, but will consider previously published, with proper documentation. Writer retains copyright. Guidelines and deadlines available on website or by return e-mail to guidelines@cenotaph.net. We will also no longer accept postal submissions unless accompanied by a valid e-mail address. No postal mss will be returned.

Payment/Terms: Acquires one-time rights.

Advice: "Read and study the guidelines, then follow them when submitting. We are always looking for new voices and original stories. Short works best on the Internet—we are interested in good writing, period. All styles will be considered, but your work won't make the short list if it exhibits sloppy mechanics. We're more attracted to stories under 1,000 words. We look forward to working with you."

▨ ◉ **CHRONICLES OF DISORDER**, 20 Edie Rd., Saratoga Springs NY 12866. **Contact:** Thomas Christian, editor. Estab. 1996.

● *"Chronicles of Disorder* is undergoing a transformation that will present future editions online. An annual 'best of' edition (culled from the online edition) will be published in a traditional paper format. We are hopeful that this will occur sometime in 2002. For more information, contact us at the above address."

Needs: Erotica, experimental, literary.

N $ **C/OASIS, New Writing for a New World**, Sun Oasis Publishing, 491 Moraga Way, Orinda CA 94563. (925)258-9026. Fax: (603)971-5013. E-mail: eide491@earthlink.net. Website: www.sunoasis.com/oasis.html. **Contact:** David Eide, editor. Online magazine. "We look for excellent fiction by experienced writers who have some publication under their belt. Writers from India, Australia, England as well as the USA have been published." Monthly. Estab. 1998. Circ. 3,000 unique visitors/month.

Needs: Literary. "No romance, religious, young adult." Receives 3-5 unsolicited mss/month. Accepts 1 ms/issue; 9-10 mss/year. Publishes ms 1-2 months after acceptance. Recently published work by Ahmed Khan and Michael Hanson. Length: 1,000-4,000 words; average length: 2,000 words. Publishes short shorts. Average length: 1,000 words. Also publishes literary essays and poetry. Sometimes comments on rejected mss.

How to Contact: Query with clips of published work. Accepts submissions by e-mail. Responds in 1 month to queries; 5 months to mss. Accepts previously published submissions. Guidelines by e-mail ("in the subject line write submission/Oasis") or on website. Reviews novels, short story collections and nonfiction books of interest to writers. Send review copies to David Eide.

Payment/Terms: Pays $15-20. Pays on publication for one-time and reprint rights.

Advice: "Tell your own story in your own way."

N **collectedstories.com, spin a yarn, weave a story**, collectedstories.com, Columbia U. Station, P.O. Box 250626, New York NY 10025. (212)696-7997. E-mail: info@collectedstories.com. Website: www.collected stories.com (includes short fiction, offering original stories, books, author interviews, excerpts and reports on upcoming releases, deals, contests and other news related to the form). **Contact:** Dara Albanese and Wendy Ball, co-publishers. Online magazine: photos. "An online magazine devoted exclusively to short fiction, *collectedstories.com* considers itself unique in that it not only publishes original short stories but also reports on various aspects related to the short form—features on upcoming releases, author interviews, news on short story book deals, etc. The founders strive to provide the short form with a quality venue of its own." Bimonthly. Estab. 2000.

Needs: Literary. "No young adult or children's fiction." Receives 40 unsolicited mss/month. Accepts 4 mss/issue; 24 mss/year. Publishes ms 1 month after acceptance. **Publishes 7 new writers/year.** Recently published work by David Fickett, Amy Halloran, James Iredell and Rawn M. James, Jr. Length: 500-5,000 words; average length: 1,800 words. Publishes short shorts. Average length: 900 words.

How to Contact: Submit mss via online form. Accepts submissions by e-mail. Include information from contact form. Responds in 1 week to queries; 3 months to mss. Accepts previously published and multiple submissions. Sample copy online. Guidelines by e-mail or on website. Reviews novels, short story collections and nonfiction books of interest to writers. Send review copies to Dara Albanese.

Payment/Terms: Writer retains copyright. Sends galleys to author.

Advice: "Since stories are accepted on a revolving basis at *collectedstories.com,* criteria may vary in that a story is up against the best of only that particular batch under consideration for the next issue at that particular time. We select the most readable stories, that is, stories that are original, compelling or witty and stories that show a command for structure, a sense of character, and evidence of talent (or promise of talent) with prose. Writers should become familiar with a publication before submission, develop a strong hold on grammar and thereby submit only clean, finished works for consideration."

N **CONSPIRE, a journal of literary art**, CanAm, 201 Astor Ave., Lansing MI 48910. E-mail: editor@c onspire.org. Website: www.conspire.org. **Contact:** CK Tower, editor. Online magazine specializing in poetry and prose. Quarterly. Estab. 1996. Circ. 700 visitors/month average. Member, ILEF—Internet Literary Editor's Fellowship.

Needs: Adventure, children's/juvenile (adventure, animal, fantasy), ethnic/multicultural, experimental, family saga, fantasy, feminist, gay, glitz, historical, horror (dark fantasy, futuristic, psychological, supernatural), humor/satire, lesbian, literary, mainstream, military/war, mystery/suspense, New Age, regional, science fiction (soft/sociological), thriller/espionage, translations, young adult/teen. "No pornography, religious or erotic." Upcoming themes: Every February we publish a women's issue. List of upcoming themes available online. Receives 10-15 unsolicited mss/month. Accepts up to 10 mss/issue; 25-40 mss/year. "Generally, we don't read manuscripts 2-3 weeks prior to the release of a new issue." Publishes ms within 3 months after acceptance. **Publishes 5-10 new writers/year.** Recently published work by Daniela Gioseffi, Elish Porat, Walter Cummins and Jason Gurley. Length: 500-2,000 words. Publishes short shorts. Also publishes literary essays, literary criticism and poetry.

How to Contact: Send complete ms with a cover letter. Accepts submissions by e-mail. Include estimated word count and brief bio. Responds in 3 month to queries and mss. Accepts simultaneous, previously published and multiple submissions. Guidelines on website. Reviews novels, short story collections and nonfiction books of interest to writers. Send review copies to thealu@en.com.
Payment/Terms: Payment is publication.
Advice: "We look for fiction that is well-crafted and innovative, and shows diversity, creative language, imagistic power and continuity."

N $ CONVERSELY, Conversely, Inc., PMB #121, 3053 Fillmore St., San Francisco CA 94123-4009. E-mail: writers@conversely.com. Website: www.conversely.com. "We are a webszine, all our content is online."
Contact: Alejandro Gutierrez, editor. Online magazine specializing in relationships between men and women. Illustrations; photos. "*Conversely* is dedicated to exploring relationships between women and men, every stage, every aspect, through different forms of writing, essays, memoirs, and fiction. Our audience is both female and male, mostly between 18-35 age range. We look for writing that is intelligent, provocative, and witty; we prefer topics that are original and appealing to our readers." Monthly, some sections are published weekly. Estab. 2000.
Needs: Literary, "must be about relationships between women and men." No erotica, gothic, science fiction, romance. Receives 300 unsolicited mss/month. Accepts 1-2 mss/issue; 12-18 mss/year. Publishes ms 3 months after acceptance. **Publishes 1-2 new writers/year.** Recently published work by Tod Goldberg, Stephanie Aulenback and Jim Nichols. Length: 500-3,000 words; average length: 2,500 words. Publishes short shorts.
How to Contact: Send complete ms with cover letter. Accepts submissions by e-mail. "We much prefer e-mail over regular mail." Include estimated work count, brief bio, list of publications and notice if ms is simultaneous or previously published. Responds in 2 weeks to queries; 2 months to mss. Send disposable copy of ms and #10 SASE for reply only (include e-mail and phone number if sending by regular mail). Accepts simultaneous submissions and previously published submissions. Guidelines for e-mail on website.
Payment/Terms: Pays $50-100. Pays on publication for electronic rights (90 days exclusive, non-exclusive there after). Sends galleys to author.
Advice: "We look for stories that hold attention from start to finish, that cover original topics or use a fresh approach, that have a compelling narrative voice. We prefer stories that deal with relationships in a manner that is complex and insightful, honest, and that surprise by revealing more about a character than was expected. Keep in mind our target audience. Know when to start and know where to end, what to leave out and what to keep in."

N ◍ THE COPPERFIELD REVIEW, A Journal for Readers and Writers of Historical Fiction, Meredith Allard, Publisher, P.O. Box 11091, Canoga Park CA 91309. E-mail: info@copperfieldreview.com. Website: www.copperfieldreview.com (includes the journal: historical fiction and essays, reviews and interviews related to historical fiction). **Contact:** Meredith Allard, editor-in-chief. "*The Copperfield Review* is an online literary journal that publishes historical fiction and articles, reviews and interviews related to historical fiction. We believe that by understanding the lessons from our past through historical fiction we can gain better insight into the nature of our society today, as well as a better understanding of ourselves." Quarterly. Estab. 2000.
Needs: Historical (general), romance (historical), western (frontier saga, traditional). "We will consider submissions in most fiction categories, but the setting must be historical in nature." Does not want to see "anything not related to historical fiction." Receives 30 unsolicited mss/month. Accepts 7-10 mss/issue; 28-40 mss/year. Publishes ms 3 months after acceptance. **"Between 30-50% of our authors are first time."** Recently published work by RD Larson, Aidan Baker, Anthony Arthur, Lad Moore and Anu Kumar. Length: 500-3,000 words; average length: 1,500 words. Publishes short shorts. Average length: 500 words. Also publishes literary essays, literary criticism and poetry. Often comments on rejected mss.
How to Contact: Send complete ms with a cover letter. Accepts submissions by e-mail, fax and disk. Include estimated word count and brief bio. Name and e-mail address should appear on the first page of the submission. Send e-mail submissions to info@copperfieldreview.com. Responds in 6 weeks to queries and mss. Send SASE (or IRC) for return of ms or send a disposable copy of ms and #10 SASE for reply only. Accepts simultaneous, previously published and multiple submissions. Sample copy available online. Guidelines on website. Reviews novels, short story collections and nonfiction books of interest to writers. Send review copies to Meredith Allard, editor-in-chief.
Payment/Terms: Acquires one-time rights. Sponsors contest. Guidelines will be posted on *Copperfield*.
Advice: "*The Copperfield Review* wishes to showcase the very best in literary historical fiction. Stories that use historical periods and details to illuminate universal truths will immediately stand out. We are thrilled to receive thoughtful work that is polished, poised, and written from the heart. Be professional, and only submit your very best work. Be certain to adhere to a publication's submission guidelines, and always treat your e-mail submissions with the same care you would use with traditional publishers. Above all, be strong and be true to your calling as a writer. It is a difficult, frustrating, but wonderful journey."

CRIMSON, Night Terrors Publications, 1202 W. Market St., Orrville OH 44667-1710. (330)683-0338. E-mail: dedavidson@nt-publications.com. Website: www.NIGHT-TERRORS-PUBLICATIONS.com (includes excerpts, writer's guidelines, editor bio, free reading, articles, links of interest to readers and writers, writer bios, NT screen saver, etc.). **Contact:** D. E. Davidson, editor/publisher. E-zine specializing in dark works: equivalent to 8½×5½; equivalent to 35-60 pages; 50 lb. cover. "*Crimson* publishes stories submitted to *Night Terrors Magazine* which the editor finds to have merit but which do not fit the concept for *Night Terrors Magazine*. Genre doesn't matter and the magazine is free." Estab. 1999. Circ. 700.

Needs: "*Crimson* publishes any story of sufficient quality which was submitted to *Night Terrors Magazine* but for various reasons was not appropriate for that publications. This could include science fiction, horror, religious, literary, erotica, fantasy or most other adult categories of fiction. "No graphic sex or violence toward children and women. No stories written specifically for *Crimson*. Please read the *Night Terrors* guidelines and write with the goal of publication there." Receives 100 unsolicited mss/month. Accepts 4 mss/issue; 24 mss/year. Publishes ms 4 months after acceptance. **Publishes 10 new writers/year.** Recently published work by A. R. Morlan, Ezra Claverie, Vera Searles and Craig Maull. Length: 2,000-5,000 words; average length: 3,000 words. Sometimes comments on rejected mss.

How to Contact: Send complete ms with cover letter. Include estimated word count, brief bio and list of publications with submission. Responds December 3. Send disposable copy of ms and #10 SASE for reply only. Accepts simultaneous submissions. Sample copy and guidelines free on website.

Payment/Terms: Pays 1 contributor's copy; all back issues on CD. Pays on publication for one-time electronic and one-time print rights. Sends galleys to author. Not copyrighted.

Advice: "Please read our guidelines before submitting. These are available on our website. Be professional. Do not submit stories which are less than 2,000 words or longer than 5,000 words. Do not submit stories folded. Send stories only in a 9×12 envelope. Do not use small type. Please use 12pt New Roman or Courier or equivalent. Proof your work. Use appropriate ms format and always include SASE. Send only one at a time."

CYBER AGE ADVENTURES, The future of superheroes, Cyber Age Adventures, Inc., 2403 NW 27th Ave., Boynton Beach FL 33436. (561)742-3634. E-mail: Editor@cyberageadventures.com. Website: www.cyberageadventures.com. "Our website is home to our award-winning online magazine, as well as an online store where visitors may purchase print anthologies of our stories. The site is also home to other goodies such as t-shirts, coffee mugs, free wallpaper, writer's guidelines and helpful tutorials." **Contact:** Tom Waltz, submissions editor. E-zine: illustrations. "Cyber Age Adventures is not a comic book. You'll find no sequential art on our pages. It's not fan-fiction, either, though many of our writers are certainly fans of the comic book medium. What we are is a universe of extraordinary stories, brought to an ever-growing audience through a vast array of meda. One of our main goals is to dispel the misconception that superheroes and comic books are synonymous. The masked men and women who safeguard our lives have predated the advent of the comic book by decades, exploding into the public eye (or ear, as the case may be) with radio serials created and aired for an adult market. We present our stories the way we do because we believe that there are a great many people who love superheroes, but who might not be willing to make a monthly trip to a comic book store to read about them. We believe there is a whole untapped market of people who read novels, but feel that they've outgrown the superhero tales they once loved so much. In the end, we believe in *Cyber Age Adventures* because we know that if we continue to tell great stories, people will come back. And they'll bring their friends." Monthly. Estab. 1999. Circ. 30,000.

● *Cyber Age Adventures* is a multiple-award winning e-zine, and has received awards for fiction and art each year since its inception. In 2000, *Cyber Age Adventures* won Best Pro Zine in the Electronic Runes Poll, and was the Grand Prize winner of *Writer's Digest*'s zine competition.

Needs: Adventure, fantasy, horror, literary, mystery/suspense, romance (contemporary, gothic), science fiction. "*Cyber Age Adventures* publishes superhero fiction. Despite common conceptions, superheroes aren't a genre unto themselves. They're like deep space or underwater. Certain rules and conventions must be adhered to, but beyond that, any story can be told, be it horror, a setting, romance or adventure." "While we occasionally publish humor pieces, we will not publish parody, anything that pokes fun at superheroes, or harps on the absurd that comic books have made of them." Receives 20 unsolicited mss/month. Accepts up to 12 mss/year. Agented fiction 10%. **Publishes approximately 40% new writers/year.** Recently published work by Sean Taylor, Tom Waltz, Jade Walker and Daniel Bishop. Length: 1,000-3,000 words; average length: 3,000 words. Publishes short shorts. Average length: 1,000 words. Also publishes literary essays, literary criticism and poetry. Sometimes comments on rejected mss.

How to Contact: Send complete ms with a cover letter. Accepts submissions by e-mail. Include estimated word count, brief bio and list of publications. Responds in 2 weeks to queries; 6 weeks to mss. Accepts previously published and multiple submissions. Sample copy free. Guidelines by e-mail or on website.

Payment/Terms: Pays 4-7¢/printed word. Pays on publication for one-time rights for the e-zine, print anthology and its e-book counterpart.

Advice: "Not to state the obvious, but a clean manuscript always puts a smile on our face. Spell-checked, proofed for grammar and punctuation. . . the usual. Beyond that deliver an outstanding story about people and make the fantastic elements believable. First of all, forget what you think you know about superheroes. We don't cater to the adolescent male fantasy here. No idiotic fights for no reason. No female characters (or any characters for that matter) that just stand around to look good in their costumes. We tell stories about people. They just happen to be people with powers."

N **$** **◐** **DANA LITERARY SOCIETY ONLINE JOURNAL**, Dana Literary Society, P.O. Box 3362, Dana Point CA 92629-8362. Website: www.danaliterary.org (includes fiction, nonfiction and poetry. Also included: editorial commentary and writer's guidelines. All details can be viewed on website). **Contact:** Robert L. Ward, director. Online journal. "Fiction we publish must be well-crafted and thought-provoking. We particularly desire humor/satire and stories with a message or moral to reach a thinking audience." Monthly. Estab. 2000. Approximately 8,000 visitors to website monthly.
Needs: Humor/satire. Also stories with a message or moral. "Most categories are acceptable if work is mindful of a thinking audience. No romance, children/juvenile, religion/inspirational, pornographic, excessively violent or profane work. Would like to see more humor/satire, suspense/intrigue, and above all stories that accurately reflect the human condition." Receives 30 unsolicited mss/month. Accepts 3 mss/issue; 36 mss/year. Publishes ms 3 months after acceptance. **Publishes 15 new writers/year.** Recently published work by Kate Smith, Hai T. Nguyen and A.B. Jacobs. Length: 800-2,500 words; average length: 2,000 words. Also publishes literary essays and poetry. Often comments on rejected mss.
How to Contact: "Submissions should be clearly legible, preferably typed, either single or double-spaced, and include your name, mailing address, and e-mail address on the first page. They should be snail-mailed to Dana Literary Society, P.O. Box 3362, Dana Point CA 92629-8362, along with a self-addressed stamped #10 envelope. No cover letter is required. Each work must be the original creation of the submitter. Both unpublished and previously published works are welcome." Responds in 2 weeks to mss. Send a disposable copy of ms and #10 SASE for reply only. Accepts simultaneous and previously published submissions. Guidelines on website.
Payment/Terms: Pays $50 for each short story accepted. Pays on online publication for right to display in online journal for 1 month. Not copyrighted.
Advice: "Success requires two qualities: ability and tenacity. Perfect your technique through educational resources, expansion of your scope of interests and regular reevaluation and as required, revision of your works. Profit by a wide exposure to the writings of others. Submit works systematically and persistently, keeping accurate records so you know what went where and when. Take to heart responses and suggestions and plan your follow-up accordingly."

◐ **DARGONZINE**. E-mail: dargon@shore.net. Website: www.dargonzine.org. **Contact**: Ornoth D.A. Liscomb, editor. Electronic zine specializing in fantasy. "*DargonZine* is a collaborative anthology, designed to give aspiring amatuer writers the opportunity to interact with a live readership as well as other writers. Our goal is to write fantasy fiction that is mature, emotionally compelling and professional."
Needs: Fantasy. "We only accept fantasy fiction that is developed within our common milieu. We would like to see more fantasy stories with characters who are easy to identify with, which offer the reader an emotionally compelling experience, and restore a sense of wonder that modern fantasy has lost. Membership in the Dargon Project is a requirement for publication." **Publishes 6-10 new writers/year.**
How to Contact: Guidelines available on website.
Payment/Terms: "Authors retain all rights to their stories, and our only compensation is the growth and satisfaction that comes with working with other writers through peer review and close collaboration."
Advice: "Start by reading our Readers' and Writers' FAQs on our website. We have a strong idea of what makes good fantasy fiction, and we live with certain restrictions as a part of our collaborative milieu. Furthermore, writing for *DargonZine* requires a nontrivial commitment of time."

N **◐** **DARK PLANET, A Webzine of Science Fiction, Modern Fantasy, Poetry, and Related Non-fiction**, Columbus OH. Website: www.sfsite.com/darkplanet/ (includes all the magazine's content). **Contact:** Lucy A. Snyder, editor. E-zine. "*Dark Planet* is a free, noncommercial web magazine that publishes a wide range of speculative fiction, poetry, and nonfiction from new and established authors." Semiannual. Estab. May 1995. 2,000 front-page visitors per month.
Needs: Fantasy (space fantasy, slipstream, magic realism), horror (dark fantasy, futuristic, psychological, supernatural), science fiction (hard science/technological, soft/sociological, erotica). Receives 30-60 unsolicited mss/month. Accepts 15 mss/issue; 30-40 mss/year. "We are closed to submissions from December 1 to February 28 and from June 1 to August 31 each year. We publish everything we accept during a given reading period in the next semiannual update; thus, the publication delay ranges from six days to six months." **Publishes 15% new writers/year.** Recently published work by Gary A. Braunbeck, Redena Hobbs, Ron Horsley, Michael Mayhew,

Tim Waggoner, Steve Beai, G.W. Thomas and Jenise Aminoff. Length: 500-15,000 words; average length: 5,000 words. Publishes short shorts. Average length: 1,000 words. Also publishes literary essays, literary criticism and poetry. Often comments on rejected mss.

How to Contact: "We only accept e-mail submissions, and we do not accept Word attachments. Please send stories as RTF or Word Perfect attachments or plain text. Read our guidelines for more information." Accepts submissions by e-mail. Include list of publications. Responds in up to 1 week to queries; up to 3 months to mss. Accepts simultaneous, previously published and multiple submissions. Guidelines by e-mail or on website. "Send a query via e-mail first."

Payment/Terms: We ask for 6 months of web-exclusive rights to a story. Sends galleys to author.

Advice: "The single best way to know what we publish is to visit the site, read what we've published, and read the online writers' guidelines (we are closed to submissions for a good part of the year, so you need to find out when we are accepting work). We get too many submissions from people who clearly haven't bothered to visit the site."

THE DEAD MULE. E-mail: editor@deadmule.com. Submissions e-mail: newmule@deadmule.com. Website: www.deadmule.com. **Contact:** Valerie MacEwan, editor. "*The Dead Mule* is an online literary magazine featuring Southern fiction, articles, poetry and essays, and is proud to claim a long heritage of Southern literary excellence. We consider any writing with a Southern slant. By that we mean the author needs either Southern roots or the writing must be Southern in subject matter. We've been online since early 1996. In Internet years, that's a century." Estab. 1996.

Needs: Literary. Also reviews novels, short story collections and nonfiction of interest to writers. Send reviews of Southern literature (old and new) to Southernbooks@deadmule.com. Go to http://southernbooks.deadmule.com for information.

How to Contact: See website for complete details. Send complete ms by e-mail. Do not send attachments—copy and paste your submission into the body of the e-mail. Length: 2,500 words maximum.

Payment/Terms: Acquires first electronic rights. All rights revert to the author on publication. "Works distributed by *The Dead Mule* may not be republished for profit in any form without the express consent of the author and notification of the editor. Any specific works published in *The Dead Mule* may not be entered into any database without the express permission of the author and *The Dead Mule*."

Advice: "What we want are writers. Pure and simple. Folks who write about the South. While long lists of previously published works are impressive, they don't matter much around here. That's why we don't include that type of information. We don't think anyone is less of a writer because their list is short. You're a writer because you say you are. Also, you've worked hard on whatever it is you wrote. Don't blow it all by not submitting correctly. If you're thinking about submitting, remember to tell us why, if it's not obvious from the content, you should be admitted to The Dead Mule School of Southern Literature. Before we read the submission, we need to know why you think you're 'Southern.' No good Southern fiction is complete without a dead mule."

DEATHLINGS.COM, Dark Fiction for the Discerning Reader, 130 E. Williamette Ave., Colorado Springs CO 80903-1112. (719)636-1006. E-mail: cvgelvin@aol.com. Website: www.DeathLings.com. Short stories are dark in tone: 4 issues/year; 3-4 stories/issue. **Contact:** C. V. Gelvin, editor. E-zine specializing in dark fiction. "Our wonderfully quirky themes for the short story contests include "Frozen Smiles" (dolls), "Burbian Horrors", and "Love Gone Wrong." Quarterly. Estab. 2000.

• 1st Place Genre Fiction in *Writer's Digest* E-zine contest in July 2001.

Needs: Erotica, horror, (dark fantasy, futuristic, psychological, supernatural). "No children's, poetry and romance." List of upcoming themes available on website. Receives 10-15 unsolicited mss/month. Accepts 3-4 mss/issue. Publishes ms 1-2 months after acceptance. **Publishes 3-6 new writers/year.** Recently published work by David Ballard, Fiona Curnow, Denise Dumars, Jason, d.g.k. Goldberg, C.V. Gelvin. Length: 4,000 words; average length: 3,000 words. Publishes short shorts. Average length: 1,500. Sometimes comments on rejected mss.

How to Contact: Send complete ms with cover letter. Accepts mss by e-mail. Include estimated word count, brief bio and list of publications with submission. Responds in 1 month to mss. No queries. Send disposable copy of ms and #10 SASE for reply only. Accepts simultaneous, multiple and previously published submissions. Guidelines free by e-mail or on website.

Payment/Terms: Pays 3¢/word. Pays on publication for electronic rights. Sponsors contest: Every issue features a short story contest with a different theme.

DEEP OUTSIDE SFFH, 6549 Mission Gorge Rd., PMB 260, San Diego CA 92120. E-mail: johncullen@candcpublishers.com. Website: www.clocktowerbooks.com. **Contact:** John Cullen or Brian Callahan, editors. Web-only magazine. "*Outside* is a paying professional magazine of SF and dark imaginative fiction, aimed at people who love to read well-plotted, character-driven genre fiction. We are interested in fiction that transcends the limitations and ventures outside the stereotypes of genre fiction." Monthly. Estab. 1998. Circ. 3,000+

Needs: Fantasy (dark), horror (dark fantasy, futuristic, psychological), science fiction (hard science/technological, soft/sociological). No pornography, excessive gore, "or vulgarity unless it directly furthers the story (sparingly, at that)." No sword and sorcery, elves, high fantasy, cookie-cutter space opera. Receives 100-150 unsolicited mss/month. Accepts 1 ms/issue; 12 mss/year. Publishes ms 1-3 months after acceptance. **Publishes 1-2 new writers/year.** Recently published work by Pat York, Melanie Tem, and Joe Murphy. Length: 2,000-4,000 words. Often comments on rejected ms.

How to Contact: Send complete ms with a cover letter. "Manuscripts must be sent by postal mail only." Include estimated word count; list of publications. Responds in 3 months. Send disposable copy of ms and SASE for reply.

Payment/Terms: Pays 3¢/word. Pays on acceptance for first rights. Sends prepublication galleys to author.

Advice: "We look for the best quality story. Genre comes second. We look for polished, first-rate, professional fiction. It is most important to grab us from the first three paragraphs—not only as a common standard but because that's how we lead with both the monthly newsletter and the main page of the magazine. Please read the tips and guidelines at the magazine's website for up-to-the-moment details. Do not send envelopes asking for guidelines, please—all the info is online at our website."

N $ © ▼ DRAGONLAUGH, Possum Press, P.O. Box 1031, Madison MS 39130-1031. E-mail: editor@ dragonlaugh.com. Website: www.dragonlaugh.com. **Contact:** Mark Johnson, editor. Online magazine. "Dragonlaugh is the only zine on the web devoted only to humorous sword and sorcery fiction and artwork." Triannual. Estab. 1999. Member, The Zine Guild.
  • Awards include 1999 Cyber Platinum Award, 1999-2000 Golden Web Award and 2001 *Writer's Digest* "50 Best Places to be Published Online."

Needs: Fantasy (sword and sorcery, humor only). "Nothing outside the narrow sub-genre." Receives 10 unsolicited mss/month. Accepts 4-7 mss/issue; 12-21 mss/year. Publishes ms 3 months after acceptance. **Publishes 2-3 new writers/year.** Recently published work by Lyn McConchie, Nora M. Mulligan and Nick Aires. Length: 500-5,000 words; average length: 3,000 words. Publishes short shorts. Average length: 750 words. Sometimes comments on rejected mss.

How to Contact: Send complete ms with cover letter. Accepts mss by e-mail or on disk. Include estimated word count and brief bio with submission. Responds in 2 months to mss. No queries. Send SASE (or IRC) for return of ms or disposable copy of ms and #10 SASE for reply only. Accepts simultaneous and previously published (in print only; no online reprints) submissions. Guidelines send SASE, e-mail or on website.

Payment/Terms: Pays $5. Pays on acceptance for first electronic and one-time print anthology rights.

Advice: "It must be funny and have some connection to a medieval setting. Sword and sorcery preferred but the amount of medieval tie-in is flexible. Read the guidelines and a few of the stories we've published. Sending material that does not fit the guidelines wastes the author's time and mine."

N DROUGHT, A Literary Review, P.O. Box 338, South Beloit IL 61080-0338. E-mail: drought_review@ya hoo.com. Website: www.geocities.com/drought_review/. Online magazine. "Drought is interested in verse and short prose with the intensity of unforgiving weather." Triannual. Estab. 2001.

Needs: Literary, regional. Receives 1-3 unsolicited mss/month. Publishes 1-3 mss/issue; 6 mss/year. Publishes ms 1-4 months after acceptance. Length: 1,000-2,000 words. Publishes short shorts. Also publishes literary essays, poetry. Sometimes comments on rejected mss.

How to Contact: E-mail complete mss per online guidelines (see website). Include estimated word count, brief bio, social security number, land mail address. Responds in 4 months. Accepts multiple submissions. Sample copy free online. Reviews novels, short story collections, nonfiction of interest to writers. Query by e-mail.

Payment/Terms: Acquires one-time electronic rights, nonexclusive electronic reprint rights. Sends prepublication galleys to author. "Work appears under author's copyright."

Advice: "I look for how finely tuned the writer's eye and ear are for both the internal and the external world of the dramatic situation. I also look at whether the story keeps my interest, surprises me, reveals the overlooked or denied, documents a time, world or kind of life. Familiarize yourself with the fiction we publish by reading the work on our website."

N $ DRUNKEN BOAT, An Online Journal of Arts & Literature, Drunken Boat, 233 Park Place #27, Brooklyn NY 11238. (718)398-5822. E-mail: editors@drunkenboat.com. Website: www.drunkenboat.com. **Contact:** Ravi Shankas, editor. Online magazine. "Drunkenboat.com is dedicated to creating an arena where works of art endemic to the medium of the web (hypertext, digital animation, music) can coexist with works of more traditional print forms of representation (poetry, critical and fictive prose, photography). It is our conviction that while digital technology will not, in the near future, supplant the print publishing industry, opportunities exist on the web to create new communities of artists and readers that are more egalitarian in terms of accessibility and less narrow in the scope of potential genre than those offered by the conventional print journal. We believe in the kind of creative cross-pollination that includes on the same site, for example, a poem and the oral recording of a thespian's monologue or a collection of short films alongside a collaboratively evolving work of fiction. Drunken Boat was intended from the outset to be a non-profit venture that exists exclusively online and includes a diverse group of newly emerging and well-established artists." Semiannual. Estab. 1999. Circ. 10,000.

Needs: "We don't want to see inarticulate stories with poorly developed plots and/or characters." Accepts 5 mss/year. Publishes ms 6 months after acceptance. Length: 10-10,000 words. Also publishes literary essays, literary criticism and poetry.

How to Contact: Send complete ms with a cover letter.

Payment/Terms: Pays $100.

Advice: "At *Drunken Boat* we are especially interested in work that utilizes the web in a dynamic way. Think of the medium of representation as an integral park of aesthetic expression. We are also looking for the highest quality work: thoughtful, provocative, musical work that evinces a knowledge of literary tradition alongside a recognition of the modern moment."

DUCT TAPE PRESS. E-mail: ducttapepress@yahoo.com. Website: www.io.com/~crberry/DuctTape (includes all zine content). **Contact:** Josh Wardrip, editor. Electronic zine. "We seek writing that is perhaps riskier than what mainstream journals typically publish but we also demand the writing be very well crafted."

Needs: Experimental, literary. "No genre fiction that fails to challenge the conventions of the given genre." **Publishes 25-35 new writers/year.** Recently published work by Norman Lock, Michael Salinger and Travis Mader. Also publishes poetry.

How to Contact: Send queries/mss by e-mail.

Advice: Looks for "daring, envelope-pushing writing that displays intelligence, attention to craft and imagination. We see a lot of writing that combines a few of these attributes, but rarely all of them. Familiarize yourself with the publication. A casual perusal should give you a general indication of the kind of material we favor. Don't assume that because we are a non-paying electronic zine we set lower standards than print publications. Please send your best work."

ANTONIN DVORAK'S NOCTURNE HORIZONS, ADVORAK.COM, P.O. Box 251, Painted Post NY 14870. E-mail: visitingwriters@advorak.com. Website: www.ADVORAK.com. E-zine: www.advorak.com/Horizons/Flaindex.html. **Contact:** Ms. Rebecca A. Raiche. E-zine specializing in fantasy, science fiction and horror. Photos. "Our publication is hosted by a writer for his audience. If you want to share Dvorak's readership, and you write similar work, submit!" Quarterly. Estab. 2001. Circ. 1,000.

Needs: Adventure, fantasy (supernatural), horror (dark fantasy, futuristic, psychological, supernatural), psychic/supernatural/occult, romance (supernatural), science fiction (hard science/technological, soft/sociological), thriller/espionage. "No religious, erotica, children's juvenile, gay or feminist." Receives 20 unsolicited mss/month. Accepts 3-5 mss/issue; 12-20 mss/year. Publishes ms 2 months after acceptance. **Publishes 7 new writers/year.** Length: 1,000-10,000 words; average length: 6,000. Publishes short shorts. Average length: 1,000 words. Also publishes poetry. Sometimes comments on rejected mss.

How to Contact: Send complete ms with cover letter by e-mail. Accepts mss by e-mail or on disk. Include estimated word count, brief bio and list of publications with submission. Responds in 4-6 weeks. Send SASE (or IRC) for return of ms or disposable copy of ms and #10 SASE for reply only. Accepts simultaneous and multiple submissions. Guidelines on website.

Payment/Terms: Acquires first electronic rights. Sends galleys to author. Not copyrighted. Sponsor contests: First Fiction Contest will be hosted and begin April 1, 2002.

Advice: "We love to read a good story. Grammar and writing style can always be polished. Without a compelling story, there is nothing to polish. Write, write, and write some more. Writing is a talent, but also a skill. E-zines are popping up all over the internet. We pride ourselves on standing out. We provide a cutting edge design and fill it with cutting edge work."

ENTERZONE, hyper web text media zine art, Borderless Publishing, 1017 Bay View Ave., Oakland CA 94610-4032. (510)532-7573. E-mail: query@ezone.org. Website: www.ezone.org. **Contact:** Briggs Nisbet, editor. E-zine. "Live on the web since 1994, *Enterzone* tries to subvert the byways of commerce and predigested 'experience' by sneaking poetry, stories, art, genre bending, and 'what is it?' to those who happen by. We are easily findable, well linked, adequately exposed (recognized by *The New Yorker* in 1995) and committed to breaking new ground." Quarterly. Estab. 1994. Circ. 30,000.

Needs: Comics/graphic novels, ethnic/multicultural, experimental, family saga, feminist, gay, historical, humor/satire, lesbian, literary, regional, translations. "We are averse to genre fiction, with rare exceptions." Receives

10 unsolicited mss/month. Accepts 2 mss/issue; 8 mss/year. Publishes ms 1 week after acceptance. Agented fiction 5%. **Publishes 2 new writers/year.** "*Enterzone* was on hiatus during the last year." Length: 1-10,000 words; average length: 5,000 words. Publishes short shorts. Average length: 1,000 words. Also publishes literary essays, literary criticism and poetry. Often comments on rejected mss.

How to Contact: Query first. Accepts submissions by e-mail. Include estimated word count, brief bio and list of publications. Responds in 1 month to queries; 6 months to mss. Send SASE (or IRC) for return of ms or send a disposable copy of ms and #10 SASE for reply only. Accepts simultaneous and previously published submissions. Guidelines by e-mail. Reviews novels, short story collections and nonfiction books of interest to writers. Send review copies to reviews@ezone.org.

Payment/Terms: Acquires first, first North American serial, one-time and electronic rights.

Advice: "We look for originality, voice, tone, confidence. Fiction should 'swing.' Use your best stuff right away, but boil it down."

EWGPRESENTS, 406 Shady Lane, Cayce SC 29033. (803)794-8869. E-mail: EWGBet@aol.com. Website: www.ewgpresents.com. **Contact:** EWGBet@aol.com, fiction editor. Electronic zine. "A contemporary journal of literary quality by new and established writers. *EWGPresents* continues to provide an online forum for writers to present their works internationally, and to usher literature into the digital age."

Needs: Literary. "No pornography or excessive violence and gore beyond the legitimate needs of a story. When in doubt, leave it out." **Publishes 50-60 new writers/year.** Recently published work by Tessa Nardi, L.C. Mohr, Mary Gordon, Jeffrey L. Jackson and Vasilis Afxentiou.

How to Contact: Send queries/mss by e-mail only. No attachments. Submissions should be directed to specific departments with work on the body of the e-mail. Read and adhere to guidelines provided at the zine.

Advice: "We seek well-written, professionally executed fiction, with attention to basics—grammar, punctuation, usage. Be professional. Be creative. And above all, be yourself. We have the means to reach a universal audience by the click of a mouse. Writers are gifted with a new medium of exposure and the future demands taking advantage of this format."

FAILBETTER.COM, Failbetter, 63 Eighth Ave., #3A, Brooklyn NY 11217. E-mail: editor@failbetter.com. Website: www.failbetter.com (includes total publication, contact and submission information). **Contact:** Thom Didato or David Mclendon, editors. Webzine specializing in literary fiction, poetry and art. "*failbetter.com* is a quarterly webzine in the spirit of a traditional literary journal—dedicated to publishing quality fiction, poetry and artwork. While the web plays host to hundreds, if not thousands, a genre-related literary sights (i.e., sci fi and horror—many of which have merit) *failbetter.com* is not one of them." Quarterly. Estab. 2000. Circ. 20,000.

Needs: Literary. "No genre fiction—romance, fantasy or science fiction." Would like to see "more character driven literary fiction where something happens!" Receives 25-50 unsolicited mss/month. Accepts 3-5 mss/issue; 12-20 mss/year. Publishes ms 4 months after acceptance. **Publishes 4-6 new writers/year; at least 1/issue.** Recently published work by Martha Cooley, Lisa Shea, Peter Markus, David Hollander and Jim Zervanos. Publishes short shorts. Average length: 1,500 words. Often comments on rejected mss.

How to Contact: Send complete ms with a cover letter or send e-mail to submissions@failbetter.com. Accepts submissions by e-mail and disk. "Please send all submissions in the body of the e-mail—do not send attachments. If you wish to send a Word attachment, please query first." Responds in 2 weeks to queries; 1 month to mss. Send a disposable copy of ms and #10 SASE for reply only. Accepts simultaneous submissions. Guidelines on website.

Payment/Terms: Acquires one-time rights.

Advice: "*failbetter.com* places a high degree of importance on originality, believing that even in this age of trends it is still possible. *failbetter.com* is not looking for what is current or momentary. We are not concerned with length: one good sentence may find a home here; as the bulk of mediocrity will not. Most importantly, know that what you are saying could only come from you. When you are sure of this, please feel free to submit."

THE FAIRFIELD REVIEW, 1 Kings Highway N., Westport CT 06880. (203)255-1199. Fax: (203)256-1970. E-mail: FairfieldReview@hpmd.com. Website: www.fairfieldreview.org. **Editors:** Edward and Janet Granger-Happ. Electronic magazine. "Our mission is to provide an outlet for poetry, short stories and essays, from both new and established writers and students, which are accessible to the general public."

Needs: Short stories, poetry, essays. Would like to see more stories "rich in lyrical imagery and those that are more humorous." **Publishes over 20 new writers/year.** Published work by Rowan Wolf and Kristen Huston. "We encourage students and first-time writers to submit their work."

How to Contact: Electronic submissions preferred. Fax submissions accepted.

Advice: "In addition to the submission guidelines found in each issue on our website, we recommend reading the essay *Writing Qualities to Keep in Mind* from our Editors and Authors page on the website. Keep to small, directly experienced themes; write crisply using creative, poetic images; avoid the trite expression."

N **◎** **FEMINISTA!, the online journal of feminist construction**, Feminista!, 1388 Haight St., PMB 30, San Francisco CA 94117. E-mail: editor@feminista.com. Website: www.feminista.com. **Contact:** Cat Canyon, assistant editor. E-zine specializing in feminist issues. "*Feminista!* aspires to be an online journal of such quality that we are known regionally, nationally and internationally for our content and networking capacity. *Feminista!* is a journal of art, literature, social commentary, philosophy, wit, humor, and respect, and is currently published on the first of each month." Monthly. Estab. 1997. Circ. 25,000.

Needs: Adventure, ethnic/multicultural, feminist, gay, historical (feminism), lesbian, literary, mystery/suspense, science fiction (feminist). "No pornography, erotica or horror." Receives 30 unsolicited mss/month. Accepts 2-4 mss/issue; 24-48 mss/year. Publishes ms 2 months after acceptance. **Publishes 24 new writers/year.** Recently published work by Susan Brownmiller, Lydia Cutler and Adriene Sere. Length: 5,000 words maximum. Publishes short shorts. Also publishes literary essays, literary criticism and poetry. Sometimes comments on rejected mss.

How to Contact: Send complete ms with a cover letter. Accepts submissions by e-mail. Include brief bio. Responds in 3 weeks to queries; 2 months to mss. Accepts simultaneous, previously published and multiple submissions. Sample copy free. Guidelines by e-mail or on website. Reviews novels, short story collections and nonfiction books of interest to writers. Send review copies to Juliette Cutler Page.

Payment/Terms: Acquires "only right to include mss in anthology within 1 year of publication."

N **◻** **FICTION FUNHOUSE.** Website: www.FictionFunhouse.com (includes all of our previously published material, as well as submission guidelines are available on the website. "We are strongly considering producing our first print edition in 2002". **Contact:** Peter Vaeth and Steven Bucaro, editors. Online magazine. "*Fiction Funhouse* is a biweekly online magazine dedicated—as much as we can be dedicated to anything—to the self conscious refraction of ourselves and our culture as we perceive it. In addition to fiction, essays, and poetry, we regularly publish humor, online Mad Libs, columns, and music reviews. We have a wide-ranging audience. Readers come for the music reviews and humor, and stay for the prose and opinions, or vice versa." Biweekly. Estab. 2000. Circ. 1,500-2,000 visitors/month.

Needs: Experimental, humor/satire, literary, mainstream, meta-fiction, short shorts. Receives 20 unsolicited mss/month. Accepts 1-2 mss/issue; 20-25 mss/year. Publishes ms 1 month after acceptance. **Publishes 15-25 new writers/year.** Recently published work by Daniel G. Fitzgerald, Laura Bork and Brian Tochterman. Length: 300-3,000 words; average length: 1,500 words. Publishes short shorts. Average length: 1,000 words. Also publishes literary essays and poetry. Always comments on rejected mss.

How to Contact: E-mail or submit through our website. Accepts submissions by e-mail. Include brief bio. Accepts simultaneous and previously published submissions. Guidelines by e-mail or on website.

Advice: "We like fiction that provokes. Make us laugh. Make us cringe. Make us feel. Make us think. Taking chances with style, form and structure, questioning the authority and purpose of fiction—these things we admire. Read our website. All of our previously published material is available for reading. If you have something that fits, take a chance. We like to laugh. We like to be provoked or moved. And we like people who actually read and follow our guidelines. More than anything, we encourage new authors to just let it rip."

N **5-TROPE.** E-mail: 5trope@webdelsol.com. Website: www.webdelsol.com/5-trope. **Contact:** Chad Johnson, senior fiction editor. Online literary journal. "*5-Trope* aims to publish the new and original in fiction, poetry and new media. We hope to appeal to writers and readers with a seriousness about playing with language and form." Bimonthly. Estab. 1999. Circ. 5,000.

Needs: Comics/graphic novels, experimental, literary. "No religious, horror, fantasy, espionage." Receives 50 unsolicited fiction mss/month. Publishes 6 mss/issue, 30 mss/year. Publishes mss one month after acceptance. **Publishes 5 previously unpublished writers/year.** Recently published work by Gary Lutz, Maile Chapman and Sarah Levine. Length: 250-5,000 words; average length 2,500 words. Publishes short shorts. Average length: 100 words. Also publishes poetry. Sometimes comments on rejected mss.

How to Contact: Send complete ms with cover letter. Accepts submissions by e-mail. Include brief bio. Responds in 1 week to queries; 5 weeks to mss. Accepts simultaneous and multiple submissions. Sample copy free on website. Guidelines on website.

Payment/Terms: Acquires first rights. Sends prepublication galleys to author.

Advice: "We look for originality in language and form, coupled with a strong authorial presence. The first thing a writer should do before submitting is to read several issues of *5-Trope* to get a feel for what we're looking for."

N **◑** **flashquake, An Online Journal of Flash Literature**, River Road Studios, P.O. Box 2154, Albany NY 12220-0154. E-mail: dorton@flashquake.org. Website: www.flashquake.org. "Our website is our publication. We do create a CD version of the site as a contributor's copy and may eventually offer the publication PDF or hardcopy to subscribers. Included on the website are fiction, nonfiction, plays, poetry, artwork, submission guidelines and a submission form." **Contact:** Debi Orton, publisher. Ezine specializing in flash literature. "*flashquake* is a new quarterly online literary journal specifically centered around flash literature—flash fiction, flash memoir, flash plays and poetry. Our goal is to create a literary venue for all things flash. Send us your best flash, works that leave your readers thinking. Although we define flash as works less than 1,000 words, shorter pieces will impress us; poetry can be up to 35 lines. Plays should be no more than 10 minutes in length when performed. We want to read the best story you have to tell us in the fewest words you need to do it! Move us, engage us, give us a complete story that only you could have written."

- "There is a $2 reading fee required for fiction, nonfiction, poetry and plays. The fee goes toward monetary awards for some authors whose work is accepted for publication and to defray expenses associated with the publication. There is no review fee for artwork or photography since there is no payment currently being made for artwork or photography. All contributors will receive copies."

Needs: Ethnic/multicultural (general), experimental, literary, flash literature of all types. "Flash fiction, flash memoir, flash plays, poetry and artwork. Themed and open submissions sought. We admire brevity and will receive shorter works favorably. Not interested in romance or work of a religious nature." Upcoming themes: Spring issue (March 1, 2002); Weapons (submissions accepted December 15, 2001-February 1, 2002); Summer issue (June 1, 2002); Confession (submissions accepted March 15-May 1). List of upcoming themes available on website. Accepts 20-25 mss/issue; 80-100 mss/year. Publishes ms 1 month after acceptance. Length: 1,000 maximum words; average length: 500-750 words. Publishes short shorts. Average length: 500-750 words. Also publishes literary essays and literary criticism. Sometimes comments on rejected mss.

How to Contact: Accepts submissions by website's submission form, postal mail and disk. Include estimated word count, brief bio and e-mail address. Guidelines on website.

Payment/Terms: Pays 1 contributor's copy on CD. Pays on acceptance for electronic rights. Sponsors contests. Each quarterly issue has a theme; contributors of fiction, nonfiction, poetry and plays which include the theme are eligible for payment. First Prize: $25; Second Prize: $10; Third Prize: $5.

Advice: "Read our submission guidelines before submitting. Then, send us your best flash, works that leave your readers thinking. Proof your work thoroughly. Typographical and grammatical errors may disqualify your submission, and will certainly make a less than favorable impression on our editors. Give us characters and emotions we can recognize without describing them in minute detail."

FULLOSIA PRESS, Rockaway Park Philosophical Society, 299-9 Hawkins Ave., Suite 865, Ronkonkoma NY 11779. Fax: (631)588-9428. E-mail: deanofrpps@aol.com. Website: www.angelfire.com/bc2/FullosiaPress/. **Contact:** J.D. Collins, editor. E-zine. "One-person, part-time. Publishes fiction and nonfiction. Our publication is right wing and conservative but amenable to the opposition's point of view. We promote an independent America. We are anti-global, anti-UN. Collects unusual news from former British or American provinces. Fiction interests include military, police, private detective, courthouse stories." Monthly. Estab. 1999. Circ. 100.

Needs: Historical (American), military/war, mystery/suspense, thriller/espionage. List of upcoming themes for SASE. Publishes ms 1 week after acceptance. Recently published work by Grant DeMan and HM Pax. Length: 500-2,000 words; average length: 750 words. Publishes short shorts. Also publishes literary essays. Always comments on rejected mss.

How to Contact: Query first. Accepts submissions by e-mail, fax and disk. Include brief bio and list of publications. Responds in 1 week to queries; 1 month to mss. Send SASE (or IRC) for return of ms. Accepts simultaneous, previously published work and multiple submissions. Guidelines for SASE. Reviews novels, short story collections and nonfiction.

Payment/Terms: No payment. Acquires electronic rights.

Advice: "Make your point quickly. If you haven't done so, after five pages, everybody hates you and your characters."

THE GREEN TRICYCLE: "The fun-to-read lit mag!" Cayuse Press, P.O. Box 66003, Burien WA 98166-0003. E-mail: editor@greentricycle.com. Website: http://greentricycle.com ("The website offers everything writers need for publication in the *Green Tricycle*. You'll find guidelines, themes, deadlines, current and archived issues, tools and tips for writers, freebies, and access to the five forums open to all writers.") **Contact:** B. Benepe, editor. "*The Green Tricycle* is an online thematic literary journal, with three themes per issue. Each piece is limited to 200 words. We accept poetry, micro-fiction, mini-essays, letters, and drama, as long as it addresses the theme in an original manner." Quarterly. Estab. 1999.

Needs: Literary. Wants more mystery, literary and cross-genre. "No erotica, horror, or occult—too much of that is on the Internet already." List of upcoming themes available on website. Receives 40-100 unsolicited mss/month. Accepts 2-5 mss/issue; 8-10 mss/year. Publishes ms 1-3 months after acceptance. Agented fiction 10%. **Publishes 10 new writers/year.** Recently published work by Ron Gibson, Jr. and Diane Schuller. Word length: 175 words average; 100 words minimum; 200 words maximum. Also publishes literary essays and poetry. Sometimes comments on or critiques rejected ms.

How to Contact: Send complete ms with a cover letter. "Online submissions only. No attachments." Include estimated word count, 25-30 word bio and list of publications. Responds in 2 months. Sample copy and guidelines free online. Reviews novels, short story collections and nonfiction books of interest to writers. Contact the publisher.

Payment/Terms: Acquires one-time rights. Sponsors contest: information on website.

Advice: "I look for originality. A creative approach to the theme catches my attention. Be original. Read the magazine. Sloppy mechanics are sickening. Write the best you can without using four-letter words."

☑ ◿ ☗ **GUIDEPOSTS FOR KIDS,** P.O. Box 638, Chesterton IN 46304. E-mail: rtolin@guideposts.org. Website:www.gp4k.com (for children, includes sample stories, games, interactives). **Contact:** Rosanne Tolin, managing editor. Editor-in-Chief: Mary Lou Carney. "Value-centered bimonthly for kids 6-11 years old. Not preachy, concerned with contemporary issues." E-zine. Estab. 1998. Circ. 36,000 unique visitors/month.

● The magazine publishes many new writers but is primarily a market for writers who have already been published. *Guideposts for Kids* received Awards of Excellence from the Ed Press Association and also has received from SCBWI the Angel Awards.

Needs: Children's/juvenile: fantasy, historical (general), humor, mystery/suspense, holidays. "No 'adult as hero' or 'I-prayed-I-got' stories." Receives 200 unsolicited mss/month. Accepts 1-2 mss/issue; 6-10 mss/year. **Publishes 1-2 new writers/year.** Published work by Beverly Patt and Lisa Harkrader. Length: 600-1,400 words; 1,300 words preferred. Publishes short shorts. Also publishes small amount of poetry. Sometimes comments on rejected mss; "only what shows promise."

How to Contact: Send complete ms with cover letter. Include estimated word count, Social Security number, phone number and SASE. Responds in 2 months. Send SASE for reply, return of ms or send disposable copy of ms. Accepts ms by e-mail and fax. Accepts simultaneous submissions. Sample copy for $3.25. Guidelines for #10 SASE.

Payment/Terms: Pays $150-300. Pays on acceptance for electronic and non-exclusive print rights.

Advice: "We're looking for the good stuff. Fast-paced, well-crafted stories aimed at kids 8-12 years of age. Stories should reflect strong traditional values. Don't preach. This is not a Sunday School handout, but a good solid piece of fiction that reflects traditional values and morality. Build your story around a solid principle and let the reader gain insight by inference. Don't let adults solve problems. While adults can appear in stories, they can't give the characters life's answers. Don't make your kid protagonist grateful and awed by sage, adult advice. Be original. We want a good mix of fiction—contemporary, historical, fantasy, sci-fi, mystery—centered around things that interest and concern kids. A kid reader should be able to identify with the characters strongly enough to think. '*I know just how he feels!*' Create a plot with believable characters. Here's how it works: the story must tell what happens when someone the reader likes (character) reaches an important goal (climax) by overcoming obstacles (conflict). Let kids be kids. Your dialogue (and use plenty of it!) should reflect how the kids sound, think and feel. Avoid slang, but listen to how real kids talk before you try and write for them. Give your characters feelings and actions suitable for the 4th to 6th grader."

☑ $ ▢ ◿ **GWN ONLINE,** (formerly Gotta Write Network), Maren Publications, 515 E. Thacker, Hoffman Estates IL 60194-1957. E-mail: netera@aol.com or GWNLitmag@aol.com. Website: members.aol.com/gwnlitmag/. **Contact:** Denise Fleischer, editor. Magazine: 8½×11; 48-84 pages; saddle-stapled ordinary paper; matte card or lighter weight cover stock; illustrations. Magazine "serves as an open forum to discuss new markets, successes and difficulties. Gives beginning writers their first break into print and promotionally supports established professional novelists." Now accepting fiction for GWN's website. Distributed through the US, Canada and England. Semiannual. Estab. 1988. Circ. 200-300.

● In addition to publishing fiction, *GWN Online* includes articles on writing techniques, small press market news, writers' seminar reviews, and features a "Behind the Scenes" section in which qualified writers can conduct e-mail interviews with small press editors and established writers. Those recently interviewed have included Literal Hatte's editors, romance author Jen Holing, *Writer's Digest* editor Melanie Rigney, authors Beverly Connor, R. Barri Flowers and J.G. Passarella.

Needs: Adventure, contemporary, fantasy, historical, humor/satire, literary, mainstream, prose poem, romance (gothic), science fiction (hard science, soft/sociological). "Currently seeking work with a clear-cut message or a twist at the very end. All genres accepted with the exception of excessive violence, sexual overtones or obscenity." Receives 75-150 unsolicited mss per month. Accepts 1-6 mss per issue; up to 20 mss a year. Publishes mss 6-12 months after acceptance. Length: 10 pages maximum for short stories. Also publishes poetry.

How to Contact: Send complete ms with cover letter. Include "who you are, genre, previous publications and focused area of writing." Responds in 4 months (later during publication months). SASE ("no SASE, no response"). Responds on fax submissions within days. Responds by fax. Accepts electronic (e-mail) submissions but no attached mail. Sample copy for $6. Guidelines for SASE.

Payment/Terms: Pays $10 or 2 contributor's copies. Acquires first North American serial rights.

Advice: "If I still think about the direction of the story after I've read it, I know it's good. Organize your thoughts on the plot and character development (qualities, emotions) before enduring ten drafts. Make your characters come alive by giving them a personality and a background, and then give them a little freedom. Let them take you through the story."

N **⊘** **THE HORSETHIEF'S JOURNAL, Celebrating the Literature of the New West**, Cayuse Press, P.O. Box 66003, Burien WA 98166-0003. E-mail: editor-thj@usa.com. Website: www.cayuse-press.com (includes submission guidelines, deadlines, current and archived issues, tools and tips for writers and a poetry forum). **Contact:** Barbara Benepe, editor-in-chief. Electronic literary journal. "*The Horsethief's Journal* is a triannual online literary journal showcasing the best in contemporary poetry, short fiction and memoir for the general reader. We prefer fiction that illuminates the human condition and complements the memoir and poetry we publish. Our audience spans all ages." Estab. 1998.
Needs: Adventure, ethnic/multicultural (general), historical, literary, mainstream, mystery/suspense, regional (western US), thriller/espionage, translations, cross-genre fiction. No erotica, horror, occult, children's, young adult, sappy romance. Receives 30 unsolicited mss/month. Accepts 2-5 mss/issue; 6-15/year. Publishes ms 1-3 months after acceptance. **Publishes 3 new writers/year.** Recently published work by Paul Tylor and Mary Chandler. Length: 200-3,000 words; average length: 1,500 words. Publishes short shorts. Length: 300 words. Also publishes literary essays and poetry. Sometimes comments on rejected ms.
How to Contact: Send complete ms with a cover letter by e-mail only; no attachments. Include estimated word count, 100-200 word bio and list of publications. Responds in 2 months to mss. Inquire about simultaneous and reprint submissions. Accepts multiple submissions. Guidelines available on website. Reviews novels, short story collections and nonfiction books of interest to writers. Send books to editor.
Payment/Terms: Acquires one-time rights.
Advice: "We're looking for stories with an original slant. No cliched plots, characters or themes. Polish. Polish. Polish. Poor diction, grammar errors—bad mechanics in general—will get you a rejection. Read the magazine. Be original."

⊘ **IN POSSE REVIEW ON WEB DEL SOL**. E-mail: submissions@webdelsol.com. Website: www.webdelsol.com. **Contact:** Rachel Callaghan, editor. Poetry Editor: Ilya Kaminsky. E-zine specializing in literary fiction, poetry, and creative nonfiction. "The best of literary fiction, creative nonfiction and poetry from, well, whoever writes it—we welcome all serious writers; especially those who can demonstrate fresh new style and a slightly skewed point of view. *IPR* is interested in looking for non-PC work concerning ethnic issues. See website for details." Quarterly or Triannual.
Needs: Adventure, erotica, ethnic/multicultural, experimental, family saga, fantasy, feminist, gay, historical, horror (literary), humor/satire, lesbian, literary, mystery/suspense, science fiction, western (literary). Accepts 10 mss/issue; 90 mss/year. Publishes 3 months after acceptance. **Publishes 10 new writers/year.** Length: 3,500 words; average length: 1,500 words. Publishes short shorts. Average length: 500 words. Also publishes literary essays, poetry and book reviews. Sometimes comments on rejected mss.
How to Contact: Cut and paste ms into e-mail. Include estimated word count, brief bio and list of publications. Responds in 3 months to mss. Accepts multiple submissions but limit is 2 short stories. Guidelines on website.
Payment/Terms: Acquires electronic rights for 120 days. Sends galleys to author by e-mail.
Advice: "We have very eclectic tastes. Whatever turns us on at that moment. Different, surprising, cutting edge, intriguing, but well-written is best. A manuscript that stands out is one we would consider printing out. Make sure you have a complete story, not slice of life or good start. Wait after writing and re-read. Use spelling and grammar checkers."

⊘ **INTERTEXT**. E-mail: editors@intertext.com. Submissions to: submissions@intertext.com. Website: www.intertext.com. **Contact:** Jason Snell, editor. Electronic zine. "Our readers are computer literate (because we're online only) and appreciate entertaining fiction. They're usually accepting of different styles and genres—from mainstream to historical to science fiction to fantasy to horror to mystery—because we don't limit ourselves to one genre. They just want to read a story that makes them think or transports them to an interesting new place."
Needs: "Well-written fiction from any genre or setting." Especially looking for intelligent science fiction. No "exploitative sex or violence. We will print stories with explicit sex or violence, but not if it serves no purpose other than titillation." No pornography, fan fiction, novels or by-the-book swords and sorcery. **Publishes 16 new writers/year.** Published work by Jim Cowon, Richard Kadrey, Levi Asher, Marcus Eubanks and Ellen Brenner.
How to Contact: Electronic submissions only. Stories should be in ASCII, HTML, or Microsoft Word formats. Full guidelines available on website.
Advice: "Have a clear writing style—the most clever story we've seen in months still won't make it if it's written badly. Try to make our readers think in a way they haven't before, or take them to a place they've never thought about before. And don't be afraid to mix genres—our readers have come to appreciate stories that aren't easily labeled as being part of one genre or another."

☑ ⬛ **MARGIN: Exploring Modern Magical Realism**, 9407 Capstan Dr. NE, Bainbridge Island WA 98110-4624. E-mail: msellma@attglobal.net. Website: www.magical-realism.com (includes novel excerpts, short stories, links, reading lists, special features, reviews, essays, creation nonfiction, articles). **Contact:** Tamara Kaye Sellman, editor. Electronic anthology specializing in magical realism. "*Margin* seeks to publish high-quality works of magical realism." Perpetual, always accessible. Estab. 2000. Circ. 1,500 unique visitors a month.

• *Margin* has received the Arete "Wave of a Site" award.

Needs: Ethnic/multicultural, experimental, fantasy (magical realism), feminist, gay, historical, horror (supernatural), lesbian, mainstream, psychic/supernatural/occult, regional, science fiction (only if it bridges with magical realism), translations (query first). Receives 100 mss/month. Publishes ms within 6 months after acceptance. **Publishes new writers.** Recently published work by Joe Benevento, Jim Bertolino and Mary Overton. Length: 3,500 words. Publishes short shorts. Also publishes literary essays and literary criticism. Sometimes comments on rejected mss.

How to Contact: Send complete ms with cover letter. Query first on translated work. Accepts submissions by e-mail. We prefer e-mail but accept surface mail subs too. No attachments. Include brief bio, list of publications, list of 10 recommended works of magical realism, the author 100-word definition of magical realism. Responds in 6 months to queries and mss. Send SASE for return of ms or send a disposable copy of ms and #10 SASE for reply only. Accepts simultaneous submissions and previously published work. Sample copy free on website. Guidelines for SASE, e-mail or website. Reviews novels, short story collections, and nonfiction books.

Payment/Terms: Funds distributed to contributors as they are acquired. Rights negotiable.

Advice: "Technical strength, unique, engaging style, well-developed and inventive story. Manuscript must be magical realism. Do not send more than one submission at a time. You will not get a fair reading if you do. Always enclose SASE. Do not inquire before 3 months. Send us your 'A' list, no works-in-progress."

TIMOTHY McSWEENEY'S INTERNET TENDENCY, 394A Ninth St., Brooklyn NY 11215. E-mail: printsubmissions@mcsweeneys.net or websubmissions@mcsweeneys.net. Website: www.mcsweeneys.net. **Contact:** Dave Eggers, Sean Wilsey, Todd Pruzen, Lawrence Weschler, Diane Vadino and Kevin Shay, editors. "*Timothy McSweeney's Internet Tendency* is an offshoot of *Timothy McSweeney's Quarterly Concern*, a journal created by nervous people in relative obscurity, and published four times a year." Visit the website for guidelines for submission to the print edition.

Needs: Literary.

How to Contact: Submit the first 300 words of ms via e-mail, to the "print submissions" or "web submissions" address. Include a "brief and sober" bio and cover letter. Attach the entire ms to the e-mail submission, if possible as an Microsoft Word file. Attachments in BinHex form cannot be read. If your piece is under 1,000 words, paste the entire submission into the e-mail. "Stories submitted without the author's phone number cannot be considered." Responds in up to 4 months to mss. "Please be patient." Sometimes comments on rejected ms. SASE for editor comments.

Payment/Terms: Pays contributor copies for stories published in the print edition.

Advice: "Do not submit your written work to both the print submissions address and the web submissions address, as seemingly hundreds of writers have been doing lately. If you submit a piece of writing intended for the magazine to the web submissions address, you will confuse us, and if you confuse us, we will accidently delete your work without reading it, and then we will laugh and never give it another moment's thought, and sleep the carefree sleep of young children. This is very, very serious."

⬛ ◎ **MERCURY BOOKS, Where Words Have Wings!**, Cayuse Press, P.O. Box 66003, Burien WA 98166-0003. E-mail: publisher@mercurybooks.webtol.com. Website: www.mercurybooks.webtol.com/ (includes guidelines, deadlines and all previous issues, as well as an author chat room and other features). **Contact:** Barbara Benepe, publisher. Online magazine. "Each issue is devoted entirely to the works of one author." Currently publish two collections/year. Estab. 2001.

Needs: Literary. "We seek to publish author's collection of short fiction or poetry, or a mix of fiction and poetry. We will consider new or unpublished authors. The work must be outstanding and the author must be willing to work with our editorial staff."

How to Contact: We accept collections only during the months of June and July. Please visit website for our detailed checklist for submissions and please follow them carefully. Collections chosen for publication will be announced in early 2003 and will be published later in the year. You must include your address, phone and e-mail address so we can contact you. We will consider previously published material if you own the copyright and provide complete documentation. Ideally, we prefer a mix of new material with previously published work. We seek to become the first publisher of a writer's collected works and provide an attractive format for presentation. Guidelines on website.

Payment/Terms: Receives continuous promotion of author's work. Acquire one-time or first-electronic rights.

Advice: "Be original. Read and follow the guidelines. Please include complete documentation with any previously published work."

☑ **MILKWOOD REVIEW, an interdisciplinary journal of literature and the other arts**. Website: www.geocities.com/milkwoodreview (includes complete publication). **Contact:** Joel and Susan Atefat Peckham, co-founding editors. E-zine specializing in literature and the other arts. "The *Milkwood Review* is an interdisciplinary journal specializing in short fiction, poetry, creative nonfiction, and hypertext. Because the journal is published on the web, we seek to create an environment for the work that makes use of the internet's multimedia capacities. All work, for example, is published with real-audio excerpts of passages read by the author. We are also very open to experimental presentation. *Milkwood* is not designed to compete with print journals but to provide an alternative avenue of publication for authors whose work may benefit from a multimedia presentation." Estab. 2000.

Needs: Ethnic/multicultural, experimental, family saga, feminist, historical, humor/satire, literary, hypertext. Accepts mss 3-5/issue. Publishes when all required materials are submitted. Publishes short shorts. Also publishes literary essays, literary criticism, and poetry. Sometimes comments on rejected mss.

How to Contact: Send complete ms with cover letter. Accepts submissions by e-mail or disk (word perfect only). Include brief bio and list of publications. Responds in 2 weeks to queries; 2 months to mss. Send disposable copy of ms and #10 SASE for reply only. Accepts simultaneous submissions, previously published work and multiple submissions. Reviews novels, short story, and nonfiction books. Send review copies to Joel and Susan Atefat Peckham.

Payment/Terms: Acquires first North American serial rights and electronic rights. Sometimes sends galleys to authors.

Advice: "Looking for a strong narrative drive and a lyric pulse. Someone who understands the musical qualities of the language. Avoid fuzzy abstractions. Be persistant and respond to criticism if given. We wouldn't give suggestions if we weren't interested in the work."

☑ **moonbomb press**. E-mail: paul@moonbomb.com. Website: www.moonbomb.com. **Contact:** Paul C. Choi, editor. Electronic zine. "We are contemporary, urban, irreverent, ethnic, random."

Needs: Short stories, poetry, short plays, any fictional format, autobiographical non-fiction, fictional journalism. No children's fiction. Wants more fictional realism and essays. "The main thing we seek in any piece of writing is a clear, identifiable voice. If this voice is also unique, we are even more pleased." **Publishes 2 new writers/year.** Recently published work by Eve Pearlman and Sheryl Ridenour.

How to Contact: Electronic submissions only.

Advice: "Be bold. Do not try to be what you are not. Anything so contrived is obviously so. Content and structure are important, but the voice, the heart behind the writing is even more essential."

☐ **NEW WRITING, A Literary Magazine for New Writers**, P.O. Box 1812, Amherst NY 14226-7812. (716)834-1067. E-mail: 1812@newwriting.com. Website: www.newwriting.com. **Contact:** Sam Meade, editor. Electronic magazine; illustrations; photos. "We publish work that is deserving." Annually. Estab. 1994.

Needs: Work by new writers: action, experimental, horror, humor/satire, literary, mainstream/contemporary, romance, translations, westerns. **Publishes 20 new writers/year.** Recently published work by Rob Roberge and Dom Leone. Length: open. Publishes short shorts. Often comments on rejected mss. Sponsors an annual award.

How to Contact: Send complete ms with a cover letter. "When sending e-mail do not send attached files." Include *brief* list of publications and *short* cover letter. Responds in 2 months. Send SASE for return of ms. Accepts simultaneous submissions. Reviews novels and short story collections.

Payment/Terms: Acquires one-time rights.

Advice: "Don't send first copies of *any* story. Always read over, and rewrite!" Avoid "stories with characters who are writers, stories that start with the character waking, and death and dying stories—we get too many of them."

NEWS OF THE BRAVE NEW WORLD, 114 Britt Court, Chapel Hill NC 27514. Fax: (919)962-2388. E-mail: olaf@indy95.chem.unc.edu. Website: http://indy95.chem.unc.edu. **Contact:** Olaf Kohlmann, editor. Electronic zine. "We serve as a platform for fresh, new authors in need of an outlet for their creative work without the usual rip-off practices, Therefore, this magazine is free of charge for readers and writers. It is published in two languages, i.e. English and German, with different material in each section."

Needs: Erotica, humor, short stories, poems, essays, reviews and novels (no excerpts, only complete works). Want more "dark and/or intelligent humor, erotic (not porn) and everything that offers surprises. No badly written fiction, extremely conservative writings, copycats of bestseller authors, predictable and boring stuff. We believe in a sparse layout to focus attention to the written word. There is no specific theme, because we do not want to tell the contributors what they have to write about." Publishes 20-50 new writers/year. Recently published work by Will Clark, Derek Kittle, Olaf Kohlmann, Surajit Basu, Alfred G. Lapitino, Jane Tyson Clement, Heidi Boehmecke, Marjana Gaponenko, Tillmann Seliger and Anant Kumar.

How to Contact: Accepts queries/mss by e-mail. "Send as e-mail attachments, Word 6.0 documents or Text-only files. No Macintosh please. We cannot read it."

Advice: "Read your submissions at least twice. Correct spelling and grammar mistakes. We publish your work as it is submitted, and part of our philosophy is not to edit anything. It is certainly embarrassing for the author and the publisher as well, if a work contains many mistakes."

NUVEIN ONLINE, (626)401-3466. Fax: (626)401-3460. E-mail: ediaz@nuvein.com. Website: www.nuvein.c om. **Editor:** Enrique Diaz. Electronic zine. "We are open to short works of fiction which explore topics divergent from the mainstream. Especially welcome are stories with a point of view opposite traditional and stereotypical views of minorities, including women and gays. Our philosophy is to provide a forum for voices rarely heard in other publications."

- Nuvein Online has been awarded the Visionary Media Award.

Needs: Short fiction, serials, graphic e-novels and poetry. Wants more "experimental, cyberfiction, serialized fiction, ethnic, as well as pieces dealing with the exploration of sexuality." **Publishes 10 new writers/year.** Recently published work by Ronald L. Boerem, Enrique Diaz, Mia Lawrence and Scott Essman.

How to Contact: Send queries/mss by e-mail, post or fax.

Advice: "Read over each submission before sending it, and if you, as the writer, find the piece irresistible, e-mail it to us immediately!"

N **THE ORACULAR TREE, A Transformational E-zine**, The Oracular Tree, 4A-385 Fairway Rd. S, Suite #123, Kitchener, Ontario N2C 2N9 Canada. (519)895-1947. E-mail: editor@oraculartree.com. Website: www.oraculartree.com (includes archive of essays, articles, stories, poems which serve to offer alternatives to the endings of our current cultural stories and myths). **Contact:** Jeff Beardwood, editor. E-zine specializing in transformation. "We believe the stories we tell ourselves and each other predict the outcome of our lives, and that we can affect gradual societal transformation by changing the endings to some of our most deeply rooted cultural stories. The genre is not as important as the message and the high quality of the writing. We accept stories, poems, articles and essays which will reach open minded reders around the world. *The Oracular Tree* offers a forum for those who see a need for chance; who want to add their voices to a growing search for alternatives." Monthly newsletter; weekly postings each Friday to the website. Estab. 1997. Circ. 15,000 hit/month.

Needs: Feminist, literary, New Age. "We'll look at any genre that is well-written and can examine a new cultural paradigm. No tired dogma, no greeting card poetry, please." Receives 10-12 unsolicited mss/month. Accepts 25-50 mss/year. Publishes ms 3 weeks after acceptance. **Publishes 20-30 new writers/year.** Recently published work by Dr. Deborah Anapol, Judy Rebick, Janet Buck and David Barnes. Publishes short shorts. Average length: 800 words. Also publishes literary essays and poetry. Often comments on rejected mss.

How to Contact: Send complete ms with a cover letter. Accepts submissions by e-mail (submit in plain text or rich text format). Responds in 2 weeks to queries; 2 months to mss. Accepts simultaneous, previously published and multiple submissions. Sample copy and guidelines on website.

Payment/Terms: Author retains copyright; one-time archived posting. Not copyrighted.

Advice: "The underlying idea must be clearly expressed. The language should be appropriate to the tale, using creative license and an awareness of rhythm. We look for a juxtaposition of ideas that creates resonance in the mind and heart of the reader. Write from your honest voice. Trust your writing to unfold."

$ **PAINTED BRIDE QUARTERLY**, Painted Bride Art Center, 230 Vine St., Philadelphia PA 19106. (215)925-9914. Website: www.webdelsol/pbq. **Contact:** Kathy Volk-Miller, fiction editor. Literary magazine: 6×9; 96-100 pages; illustrations; photos. Quarterly. Estab. 1973. Circ. 1,000.

- *Painted Bride Quarterly* is now a quarterly online magazine with an annual anthology.

Needs: Contemporary, ethnic, experimental, feminist, gay, lesbian, literary, prose poem and translations. **Published new writers within the last year.** Recently published work by Lisa Borders, Jeannie Tietja, Kevin Miller, Mark LaMonda and Jennifer Moses. Length: 5,000 words maximum; average length: 3,000 words. Publishes short shorts. Also publishes literary essays, literary criticism, poetry. Occasionally critiques rejected mss.

How to Contact: Send complete ms. Responds in 6 months. SASE. Sample copy for $6. Reviews novels and short story collections. Send books to editor.

Payment/Terms: Pays $5/accepted piece and 1 contributor's copy, 1 year free subscription; 50% off additional copies. Acquires first North American serial rights.

Advice: Looks for "freshness of idea incorporated with high-quality writing. We receive an awful lot of nicely written work with worn-out plots. We want quality in whatever—we hold experimental work to as strict standards as anything else. Many of our readers write fiction; most of them enjoy a good reading. We hope to be an outlet for quality. A good story gives, first, enjoyment to the reader. We've seen a good many of them lately, and we've published the best of them."

✦ ☑ ◯ **PAPERPLATES, a magazine for fifty readers**, Perkolator Kommunikation, 19 Kenwood Ave., Toronto, Ontario M6C 2R8 Canada. (416)651-2551. Fax: (416)651-2910. E-mail: magazine@paperplates.org. Website: www.paperplates.org. **Contact:** Bethany Gibson, fiction editor. Electronic magazine. Published 2-3 times/year. Estab. 1990.

● *Paperplates* is now published entirely online.

Needs: Condensed/excerpted novel, ethnic/multicultural, feminist, gay, lesbian, literary, mainstream/contemporary, translations. "No science fiction, fantasy or horror." Receives 2-3 unsolicited mss/week. Accepts 2-3 mss/issue; 6-9 mss/year. Publishes ms 6-8 months after acceptance. Published work by Celia Lottridge, C.J. Lockett, Deirdre Kessler and Marvyne Jenoff. Length: 1,500-3,500 words; average length: 3,000 words. Publishes short shorts. Also publishes literary essays, literary criticism and poetry.

How to Contact: Send complete ms with a cover letter. Responds in 6 weeks to queries; 3 months to mss. Send SASE for reply, return of ms or send a disposable copy of ms. Accepts simultaneous submissions and electronic submissions. Guidelines for #10 SASE.

Payment/Terms: Pays 1 contributor's copy. Pays on publication for first North American serial rights.

N ◎ **PARADOXISM**, University of New Mexico, 200 College Rd., Gallup NM 87301. Fax: (505)863-7532. E-mail: smarand@unm.edu. Website: www.gallup.unm.edu/~smarandache/lit.htm. Online magazine. **Contact:** Dr. Florentin Smarandache. "*Paradoxism* is an avant-garde movement based on excessive use of antinomies, antitheses, contradictions, paradoxes in the literary creations set up by the editor in the 1980s." Annual. Estab. 1990.

Needs: Experimental, literary. "No traditional fiction." Receives 5 unsolicited mss/month. Publishes short shorts. Also publishes literary essays, literary criticism and poetry. Sometimes comments on rejected mss.

How to Contact: Accepts simultaneous submissions. Guidelines on website.

Payment/Terms: Pays subscription. Pays on publication. Not copyrighted.

Advice: "We look for work that refers to the paradoxism or is written in this paradoxist style."

◯ **THE PAUMANOK REVIEW**. E-mail: paumanok@etext.org. Website: www.etext.org/Fiction/Paumanok (includes full text of magazine, guidelines, archives and publishing information). **Contact:** Katherine Arline, editor. Online magazine. "*TPR* is dedicated to publishing and promoting the best in world art and literature. The audience is international, well-educated and looking for insight and entertainment from talented new and established voices." Quarterly. Estab. 2000. Circ. Thousands of unique visitors/issue; more than 50 countries.

Needs: Experimental, historical, humor/satire, literary, mainstream. Receives 100 unsolicited mss/month. Accepts 6-8 mss/issue; 24-32 mss/year. Publishes ms 6 weeks after acceptance. Agented fiction 1%. **Publishes 4 new writers/year.** Recently published work by Elisha Porat, Maryanne Stahl, Gaither Stewart and Allegra Wong. Length: 1,500-6,000 words; average length: 3,000 words. Publishes short shorts. Average length: 800 words. Also publishes literary essays, art, music and poetry. Always comments on rejected mss.

How to Contact: Send complete ms with a cover letter. Accepts submissions by e-mail. Include estimated word count, brief bio, list of publications and where you discovered *The Paumanok Review*. Responds in 1 week to queries; 1 month to mss. Accepts simultaneous submissions and previously published work. Sample copy and guidelines online.

Payment/Terms: Free classified ads for the life of the magazine. Acquires one-time and anthology rights. Sends galleys to author.

Advice: "*TPR* was created to bridge the gap between highly specialized e-zines and affluent mega-zines closed to new writers. *TPR* is the ideal place for a writer's first electronic submission since the process closely follows print publishing's methods. Though this is an English-language publication, it is not U.S. or U.K.-centric. Please submit accordingly."

N ◯ **PBW**, 513 N. Central Ave., Fairborn OH 45324. (937)878-5184. E-mail: rianca@aol.com. **Contact:** Richard Freeman, editor. Electronic disk zine: 700 pages; illustrations. "*PBW* is an experimental floppy disk that 'prints' strange and 'unpublishable' in an above-ground-sense writing." Quarterly electronic zine. Featuring avant-garde fiction and poetry. Estab. 1988.

Needs: Erotica, experimental, gay, lesbian, literary. No "conventional fiction of any kind." Receives 3 unsolicited mss/month. Accepts 40 mss/issue; 160 mss/year. Publishes ms within 3 months after acceptance. **Publishes**

10-15 new writers/year. Published work by Dave Castleman, Marie Markoe and Henry Hardee. Length: open. Publishes short shorts and novels in chapters. Publishes literary essays, literary criticisms and poetry. Always comments on rejected mss.

How to Contact: Send complete ms with a cover letter. Accepts queries by e-mail. "Manuscripts are only taken if sent on disk." Responds in 2 weeks. Send SASE for reply, return of ms or send a disposable copy of ms. Accepts simultaneous, reprint and electronic (Mac or modem) submissions. Sample copy for $2. Reviews novels and short story collections.

Payment/Terms: Pays 1 contributor's copy. All rights revert back to author. Not copyrighted.

PEGASUS ONLINE, the Fantasy and Science Fiction Ezine. E-mail: editors@pegasusonline.com. Website: www.pegasusonline.com. **Contact:** Scott F. Marlowe, editor. Electronic zine. "*Pegasus Online* focuses upon the genres of science and fantasy fiction. We look for original work which inspires and moves the reader, writing which may cause him or her to think, and maybe even allow them to pause for a moment to consider the how's and why's of those things around us."

Needs: Fantasy, science fiction. "More specifically, fantasy is to be of the pure fantastic type: dragons, goblins, magic and everything else you can expect from something not of this world. Science fiction can or cannot be of the 'hard' variety." No "excessive profanity or needless gore." **Publishes 16 new writers/year.**

How to Contact: Electronic submissions only. Send mss by e-mail to submissions@pegasusonline.com.

Advice: "Tell a complete tale with strong characters and a plot which draws the reader in from the very first sentence to the very last. The key to good fiction writing is presenting readers with characters they can identify with at some level. Your characters certainly can be larger than life, but they should not be all-powerful. Also, be careful with grammar and sentence structure. We get too many submissions which have good plot lines, but are rejected because of poor English skills. The end-all is this: we as humans read because we want to escape from reality for a short time. Make us feel like we've entered your world and make us want to see your characters succeed (or not, depending on your plot's angle), and you've done your job and made us happy at the same time."

N $ Y PERIDOT BOOKS, Tri-Annual Online Magazine of SF, Fantasy & Horror, Peridot Consulting, Inc., 1225 Liberty Bell Dr., Cherry Hill NJ 08003. (856)354-0786. E-mail: editor@peridotbooks.com. Website: www.peridotbooks.com. **Contact:** Ty Drago, editor. Online magazine specializing in science fiction fantasy and horror. "We are an e-zine by writers for writers. Our articles focus on the art, craft and business of writing. Our links and editorial policy all focus on the needs of fiction authors." Triannual. Estab. 1998.

● Peridot Books won the Page One Award for Literary Contribution.

Needs: Fantasy (space fantasy, sword and sorcery, sociological), horror (dark fantasy, futuristic, supernatural), science fiction (hard science/technological, soft/sociological). "No media tie-ins (Star Trek, Star Wars, etc., or space opera, vampires)." Receives 150 unsolicited mss/month. Accepts 8 mss/issue; 24 mss/year. Publishes ms 2 months after acceptance. Agented fiction 5%. **Publishes 10 new writers/year.** Recently published work by Brenden Connell, E.K. Rivera, Katherine Irving and David Oven. Length: 1,500-7,500 words; average length: 4,500 words. Also publishes literary essays and literary criticism. Often comments on rejected mss.

How to Contact: Send complete ms with a cover letter, electronic only. Accepts submissions by e-mail. Include estimated word count, brief bio, list of publications and name and e-mail address in the body of the story. Responds in 6 weeks to mss. Accepts simultaneous, previously published and multiple submissions. Guidelines on website.

Payment/Terms: Pays 5¢/word. Pays on publication for one-time and electronic rights.

Advice: "Give us something original, preferably with a twist. Avoid gratuitous sex or violence. Funny always scores points. Be clever, imaginative, but be able to tell a story with proper mood and characterization. Put your name and e-mail address in the body of the story. Read the site and get a feel for it before submitting."

$ PIF. (360)493-0596. E-mail: editor@pifmagazine.com. Website: http://pifmagazine.com. **Contact:** Jen Bergmark, managing editor. Fiction Editor: Colette Sartor (fiction@pifmagazine.com). Electronic magazine (pifmagazine.com): circ. 100,000. Monthly. Estab. 1995.

Needs: Literary, experimental, very short ("micro") fiction. No genre fiction. Receives 200-300 mss/month. Accepts 1-2 mss/electronic issue. Publishes 1-4 months after acceptance. Reads year round. Length: 4,000 words maximum. Recently published work by Julia Slavin, Brad Bryant, Richard Madelin. **Publishes several new writers/year.** Also publishes poetry, book reviews, essays and interviews.

How to Contact: Electronic submissions only. Online submissions form and guidelines at http://pifmagazine. com/submit/. Responds in 8-10 weeks. Accepts simultaneous submissions. Sometimes comments on rejected mss.

Payment/Terms: Pays $50-200. Pays on publication.

N̄ THE PINK CHAMELEON, The Pink Chameleon. E-mail: dpfreda@juno.com. Website: www.geocities. com/thepinkchameleon/index.html. **Contact:** Mrs. Dorothy Paula Freda, editor/publisher. Family oriented electronic magazine. Illustrations. Annual. Estab. Online 2000; print 1985-1999.

Needs: Adventure, children's/juvenile (adventure, animal, easy-to-read, fantasy, historical, mystery, preschool, series, sports, all ages), experimental, family saga, fantasy (space fantasy, sword and sorcery), humor/satire, literary, mainstream, mystery (amateur sleuth, cozy, police procedural, private eye/hardboiled), psychic/supernatural/occult, religious (children's religious, general, inspirational, religious fantasy, religious mystery/suspense, religious thriller, religious romance), romance (contemporary, futuristic/time travel, gothic, historical, regency period, romantic suspense), science fiction (hard science/technological, soft/sociological), thriller/espionage, western (frontier saga, traditional), young adult/teen (adventure, easy-to-read, fantasy/science fiction, historical). "No violence for the sake of violence." Receives 50 unsolicited mss/month. Publishes ms within in the year after acceptance. **Publishes 50% new writers/year.** Recently published work by Deanne F. Purcell, James W. Collins and Darlene Palenik. Length: 500-2,500 words; average length: 2,000. Publishes short shorts. Average length: 500 words. Also publishes literary essays and poetry. Always comments on rejected mss.

How to Contact: E-mail submissions with short biography. Accepts mss only by e-mail. No attachments, send work in the body of the e-mail. Include estimated word count and brief bio with submission. Responds in 1 month. Accepts multiple and previously published submissions. Guidelines send e-mail or on website.

Payment/Terms: Acquires one-time rights for 1 year but will return rights earlier upon request.

Advice: "Simple, honest, evocative emotion; upbeat submissions that give hope for the future; well-paced plots; stories, poetry, articles, essays that speak from the heart. Read guidelines carefully. Use a good, but not ostentatious opening hook. Stories should have a beginning, middle and end that make the reader feel the story was worth his or her time. This also applies to articles and essays. In the latter two, wrap your comments and conclusions in a neatly packaged paragraph. Turnoffs include violence, bad language used as padding and to sensationalize. Simple, genuine and sensitive work does not need to shock with vulgarity to be interesting and enjoyable."

⊕ THE PLAZA, A Space for Global Human Relations, U-Kan Inc., Yoyogi 2-32-1, Shibuya-ku, Tokyo 151-0053, Japan. Tel: +81-(3)-3379-3881. Fax: +81-(3)-3379-3882. E-mail: plaza@u-kan.co.jp. Website: u-kan.co.jp (includes contribution guide, contents of the current and back issues, representative works by *The Plaza* writers). **Contact:** Leo Shunji Nishida, publisher/fiction editor. "*The Plaza* is an intercultural and bilingual magazine (English and Japanese). Our focus is the 'essence of being human.' Some works are published in both Japanese and English (translations by our staff if necessary). The most important criteria is artistic level. We look for works that reflect simply 'being human.' Stories on intercultural (not international) relations are desired. *The Plaza* is devoted to offering a spiritual *Plaza* where people around the world can share their creative work. We introduce contemporary writers and artists as our generation's contribution to the continuing human heritage." Quarterly. Online publication which is freely available to all readers on the Internet.

Needs: Length: less than 2,500 words (longer stories may be recommended for serial publication). Wants to see more fiction "of not human beings, but being human. Of not international, but intercultural. Of not social, but human relationships." No political themes: religious evangelism; social commentary. Publishes about 2 stories/ issue. **Publishes 3 new writers/year.** Recently published work by Richard A. Bunch, Eleanor Lohse and Daniel Lazar.

How to Contact: Send complete ms with cover letter. Accepts queries/mss by e-mail and fax.

Advice: "The most important consideration is that which makes the writer motivated to write. If it is not moral but human, or if it is neither a wide knowledge nor a large computer-like memory, but rather a deep thinking like the quietness in the forest, it is acceptable. While the traditional culture of reading of some thousands of years may be destined to be extinct under the marvellous progress of civilization, *The Plaza* intends to present contemporary works as our global human heritage to readers of forthcoming generations."

✓ THE PROSE MENAGERIE. E-mail: caras@reporters.net. Website: www.geocities.com/Soho/Studios/ 5116/index.html. **Contact:** Cara Swann, editor. E-zine. "*The Prose Menagerie* is a mixture of interesting prose, essays, and articles as well as fiction (short stories/novellas/poetry)."

Needs: Literary. No erotica, science fiction, children's, horror. Wants more "meaningful themes." **Publishes 15-20 new writers/year.** Recently published work by Allen Woodman, John K. Trammell and Zalman Velvel.

How to Contact: Send queries/mss by e-mail. Send in body of e-mail and/or attached as plain ASCII text file only. No MS Word files accepted. Accepts multiple submissions.

Payment/Terms: "Since *The Prose Menagerie* is only available online, the writer maintains copyright; and while there is no payment, there is wide exposure for new and unknown writers, eagerly promoted along with those who do have name recognition."

Advice: "Submit a piece of writing that has meaning, whether it is poetry, fiction or articles. Also open to those who wish to present ideas for regular columns and book reviews."

$ ☑ ☐ SCIFI.COM, USA Networks, 48 Eighth Ave., PMB 405, New York NY 10014. (212)989-3742. E-mail: datlow@www.scifi.com. Website: www.scifi.com (includes all fiction, guidelines, edit info). **Contact:** Ellen Datlow, fiction editor. E-zine specializing in science fiction. "Largest and widest ranging science fiction site on the web. Affiliated with the Sci Fi Channel, Science Fiction Weekly, news, reviews, comics, movies, and interviews." Weekly. Estab. 2000. Circ.50,000/day.

• Linda Nagata's novella *Goddess*, first published on *Scifi.com*, was the first exclusively net-published piece of fiction to ever win the Nebula Award from the Science Fiction & Fantasy Writers of America.

Needs: Fantasy (urban fantasy), science fiction (hard science/technological, soft/sociological). "No space opera, sword and sorcery, poetry or high fantasy." Receives 100 unsolicited mss/month. Accepts 1 mss/issue; 35 mss/ year. Publishes ms within 6 months after acceptance. Agented fiction 2%. Recently published work by James Blaylock, Linda Nagata and Bruce Sterling. Length: 1,500-20,000 words; average length: 7,500 words. Sometimes comments on rejected mss.

How to Contact: Send complete ms with cover letter. Include estimated word count and list of publications. Responds in 2 months to mss. Send SASE for return of ms or send a disposable copy of ms and #10 SASE for reply only. Guidelines for SASE or on website.

Payment/Terms: Pays 20¢/word up to $3,500. Pays on acceptance for first, electronic and anthology rights.

Advice: "We look for crisp, evocative writing, interesting characters, good storytelling. Check out the kinds of fiction we publish if you can. If you read one, then you know what I want."

☑ ☐ SEED CAKE, 16966 129th Ave. SE, Renton WA 98058. E-mail: seedcake@hotmail.com. Website: www.seedcake.com (includes digital chapbooks published through the website, writer's guidelines, etc.). **Contact:** Lisa Purdy, editor. Literary e-zine. "Each issue is a self-contained file and includes a cover with the contents arranged as an A and B side like old 78 or 45 records." Estab. 1997. Circ. 5,000.

Needs: Comics/graphic novels, experimental, feminist, gay, humor satire, literary, short story collections. "We do not want to see genre fiction or fiction that can be easily classified. Receives 20 unsolicited mss/month. Accepts 2 mss/issue, 10 mss/year. Published ms 1 month after acceptance. **Publishes 3 new writers/year.** Recently published work by Willie Smith, Diana George and Leonard Chang. Length: 6,000 words average. No minimums or maximums. Also publishes literary essays. Often comments on rejected ms.

How to Contact: "We accept only e-mail submissions." Include bio. Responds in 1 week to queries, 1 month to mss. Accepts simultaneous, multiple and reprint submissions. Sample copy and guidelines available free on website. Reviews novels, short story collections or nonfiction books of interest to writers. Send books to Matt Briggs at the above address.

Payment/Terms: Pays free subscription to the magazine. Acquires one-time rights and the right to reprint story "if we ever do an anthology." Send prepublication galleys to author.

Advice: "We look for writing with a distinctive voice or subject matter that can be arranged into a pair of short stories."

❀ ☑ SHADOW VOICES. E-mail: phantomlady@geocities.com. Website: www.geocities.com/Athens/ Styx/1713/index.html. **Contact:** Vida Janulaitis, editor. Electronic zine. "If you speak of the unknown and reach into the darkness of your soul, share your deepest thoughts. Send me your poetry and short stories."

Needs: "Well written fiction or poetry that reveals your inner thoughts. No pornography, or racist material that may inspire someone to do harm to any form of life or property." Wants more fiction that "allows the writer to reveal a different side of life and put those feelings into words." The best writing grabs your attention from the beginnings and surprises you in the end. Recently published work by Taylor Graham, Rich Logsdon and Vida Janulaitis. Publishes new and established writers.

How to Contact: Accepts queries/mss by e-mail. "Each and every submission should be sent on a separate e-mail, no file attachments please. At the top of each page place 'the title of the work,' your real name, complete e-mail address and a short bio. Please indicate submission in the e-mail subject line."

Advice: "Please edit your work carefully. I will assume poetic license. Most of all, write what's inside of you and be sincere about it. Everyone has a unique style, make yours stand out."

☑ ☐ SNREVIEW: Starry Night Review—A Literary E-Zine, 197 Fairchild Ave, Fairfield CT 06432-4856. (203)366-5991. Fax: (203)336-4793. E-mail: SNReviewezine@aol.com. Website: members.aol.com/jconln 1221/snreview.htm. **Contact:** Joseph Conlin, editor. E-zine specializing in literary short stories, essays and poetry. "The *SNReview* searches for material that not only has strong characters and plot but also a devotion to imagery." Quarterly. Estab. 1999.

Needs: "We only want literary and mainstream." Receives 10 mss/month. Accepts 5 mss/issue; 20 mss/year. Publishes ms up to 6 months after acceptance. **Publishes 20 new writers/year.** Recently published work by E. Lindsey Balkan, Marie Griffin and Jonathan Lerner. Word length: 4,000 words average; 1,500 words minimum; 7,000 words maximum. Also publishes literary essays, literary criticism and poetry.

How to Contact: Send complete ms with a cover letter via e-mail only. Include 100 word bio and a list of publications. Responds in 1 month. Accepts simultaneous and reprint submissions. Sample copy and guidelines free on website.

Payment/Terms: Acquires first rights. Sends prepublication webpages to the author.

N STAGGER. E-mail: staggerpress@yahoo.com. Website: http://staggerpress.homestead.com/. Online Magazine. "We are looking for poetry, proses, essays, rants, basically anything that moves you and subsequently moves us. Estab. 1997.

Needs: Literary. "Not only do we like 'sudden fiction', but we find lean, economical prose to be the greater challenge. Anyone can barrage a reader with unlimited verbiage but it takes a true marksman to hit us between the eyes with the first shot." Length: 2,000 words or less.

How to Contact: E-mail complete text in body of message. Attached files will be deleted unread. "Write 'submission' in the subject line of your post, and include your name (no handles, please), e-mail address and phone number." Deadline for Spring issue is February 15; Summer issue, May 15; Fall issue, August 15; Winter issue, November 15. Responds in 1 month. Sample copy free online.

Payment/Terms: "By submitting to us, you give us permission to use and archive your work, but you retain the right to rescind that permission at any time. Say the word and your work comes down immediately. We'd much rather lose some writing and keep our friends than the other way around."

N STEEL POINT QUARTERLY, An Online Journal of Poetry and Prose, Crosstown Studios, P.O. Box 5463, Harrisburg PA 17110-0465. E-mail: point@onesteel.net. Website: www.steelpoint.net. **Contact:** Deborah Ryder, editor-in-chief. Literary e-zine specializing in poetry and prose. Illustrations; photos. Quarterly. Estab. 2000.

Needs: "We are interested in most well-crafted writing though there are some genres we do not want. No children's/juvenile, graphic, new age, psychic/supernatural/occult, religious or romance." Publishes 3 mss/issue; 12-16 mss/year. Publishes ms up to 8 months after acceptance. Length: 500-2,000 words; average length: 1,200 words. Publishes short shorts. Average length: 600 words.

How to Contact: Send complete mss pasted in body of e-mail. Accepts mss only by e-mail. No attachments. Include estimated word count, brief bio about 5 lines, and 3 most recent list of publications with submission. Responds in 3 weeks to queries; 3 months to mss. Accepts simultaneous submissions. Guidelines on website.

Payment/Terms: No payment, other than a link in your web page. Acquires first North American serial rights for 3 months and one-time print rights. Sends prepublication galleys for our author's approval prior to publication in the form of a web page e-mail attachment. It is necessary to provide valid contact e-mail address with your submission.

N $ STICKMAN REVIEW, Stickman Review, 2890 N. Fairview Dr., Flagstaff AZ 86004. (928)913-0869. E-mail: editors@stickmanreview.com. Website: www.stickmanreview.com. **Contact:** Anthony Brown, Darrin English, editors. Online journal specializing in literary fiction. "Stickman Review considers previously unpublished fiction of literary quality. We welcome all stories whose first purpose is literary. We consider all mainstream and experimental literary fiction. We are very unlikely to publish genre fiction unless the story transcends the typical requirements of the genre. Semiannual. Estab. 2001.

Needs: Erotica, ethnic/multicultural, experimental, feminist, gay, humor/satire, lesbian, literary. "Preferably no romance, religious or inspirational fiction." Accepts 5-10 mss/issue, 10-20/year. Publishes ms 3 months after acceptance. Length: 250-10,000 words; average length 3,000 words. Publishes short shorts. Average length 750 words. Also publishes literary essays and poetry. Sometimes critiques rejected mss.

How to Contact: Submit electronically to fiction@stickmanreview.com. Responds in 1 month to queries; 2 months to mss. Accepts simultaneous and multiple submissions. Guidelines on website.

Payment/Terms: Pays $20. Pays on acceptance for all rights. Publication is not copyrighted.

Advice: "To see the kinds of stories we publish, read what the best literary magazines are publishing today. We seek literary fiction, first and foremost. Avoid sending us stories that fall under a specific genre."

N ☪ A TASTE FOR FLESH, 1 Massey Square #1217, East York, Ontario M4C 5L4 Canada. (416)699-6471. E-mail: theswan@geocities.com. Website: www.geocities.com/Athens/Troy/1541. **Contact:** Andrew R. Crow, editor. Electronic zine. Publishes "horror poetry, fiction and ranting and raving for adult audiences. It's a place for those with a predilection for pain, poetry and the dark side of life."

Needs: Horror. No romance, westerns. "Want more psychological horror." **Publishes over 20 new writers/ year.** Recently published work by Brian Knight, Robert James Berry, Scott C. Holstad, Andrew R. Crow and Holly Day.

How to Contact: Send queries/mss by e-mail (plain text in e-mail or WordPerfect attachments).

Advice: "Read the masters of horror first. Make me squirm."

N ☑ **THE 13TH WARRIOR REVIEW**, Asterius Press, P.O. Box 5122, Seabrook NJ 08302-3511. E-mail: theeditor@asteriuspress.com. Website: www.asteriuspress.com (includes guidelines, interviews, articles, etc.). **Contact:** John C. Erianne, publisher/editor. Online magazine. Triannual. Estab. 2000.

Needs: Erotica, experimental, humor/satire, literary, mainstream. Receives 200 unsolicited mss/month. Accepts 4-5 mss/issue; 10-15 mss/year. Publishes ms 6 months after acceptance. **Publishes 1-2 new writers/year.** Recently published work by George Lynn, Ehren Biving and D. Olsen. Length: 300-3,000 words; average length: 1,500 words. Publishes short shorts. Average length: 250 words. Also publishes literary essays, literary criticism and poetry. Sometimes comments on rejected mss.

How to Contact: Send complete ms with a cover letter. Accepts submissions by e-mail. Include estimated word count, brief bio and address/e-mail. Responds in 1 week to queries; 3 weeks to mss. Send SASE (or IRC) for return of ms or send a disposable copy of ms and #10 SASE for reply only. Accepts simultaneous submissions. Guidelines on website. Reviews novels, short story collections and nonfiction books of interest to writers. Send review copies to Asterius Press.

Payment/Terms: Acquires first and electronic rights.

☑ **$** ☑ ☑ **TWILIGHT SHOWCASE**, 1436 Fifth St., Waynesboro VA 22980. (540)949-4294. E-mail: gconn@rica.net. Website: www.twilightshowcase.com. **Contact:** Gary W. Conner, editor. Electronic zine. "We're interested in growing various subgenres of fantasy, those mainly being horror, dark fantasy and speculative fiction. We like a nice mix of writers you've read within these genres and writers you've never heard of." Quarterly.

● Twilight Showcase ranked #30 on *Writer's Digest*'s Top 50 Places to Get Published Online.

Needs: Fantasy (dark), horror, speculative fiction. No vampire fiction. Wants to see more character-driven fiction. **Publishes 4-5 new writers/year.** Recently published work by Diana Price, John B. Rosenman and Mark West.

How to Contact: Prefers queries/mss by e-mail. "Submissions should be carefully edited and e-mailed to strangeconcepts@rica.net. They may be sent in the body of the e-mail, in MSWord or .rtf formats.

Payment/Terms: Pays 3¢/word. Pays on publication.

Advice: "We enjoy concise writing and original plots with well-rounded characters. We want stories that have a beginning, middle and an end. Read the magazine. Won't cost you a thing. Web fiction is flourishing, as it gives any number of new writers an opportunity to make themselves heard. I have read so many incredible stories on the internet that I am actually a fan of people I've never seen in print. There are some great e-zines out there."

N ◯ ☑ **VERGE MAGAZINE, vergemag.com**, VERGE Communications, LLC, 5505 Connecticut Ave., NW #241, Washington DC 20015-2601. (562)773-9664. E-mail: info@vergemag.com. Website: www.vergemag. com. **Contact:** Rie Sheridan, senior fiction editor. Online and ezine specializing in visual, literary and performance arts as well as regular music and film columns: illustrations; photos. "*Verge* is an arts magazine showcasing visual, literary and performance art forms. Writer's guidelines are available online. All past issues are archived. We accept prose and poetry submissions as well as feature article queries. Profiles of artists are presented under Featured Artists. We are always looking for quality writers to submit work." Monthly. Estab. 2000. Circ. 150,000-200,000 visitors/month.

● *Verge* won a *Writer's Digest* Zine award for Best Art and Design.

Needs: "All categories would be considered for publication. Nothing directly offensive and/or prejudiced." List of upcoming themes available online. Receives 3-10 unsolicited mss/month. Publishes ms 1 month after acceptance. Recently published work by Wynelda Anne Shelton and Daniel Veiez. Length: 100-1,500 words. Publishes short shorts. Average length: 100-300 words. Also publishes literary essays and poetry. Always comments on rejected mss.

How to Contact: Send complete ms with a cover letter. Accepts submissions by e-mail and disk. Include estimated word count and brief bio. Responds in 2 weeks to queries; 1 month to mss. Send SASE (or IRC) for return of ms or send a disposable copy of ms and #10 SASE for reply only. Accepts simultaneous, previously published and multiple submissions. Guidelines on website. Reviews novels, short story collections and nonfiction books of interest to writers. Send review copies to Rie Sheridan.

Payment/Terms: Contests and awards vary from month to month and by department.

Advice: "Our editors read for content, voice, style, etc. and evaluate it based on needs of the current issue. Some stories will be included because of the writing excellence as well, depending on the editor's recommendations. Read as much as you can. Generate your formulas carefully. Research anything and everything. Fiction draws me in a lot more when it is wrapped in truth."

◯ **VOIDING THE VOID**™, 8 Henderson Place, New York NY 10028. E-mail: mail@vvoid.com. or EELIPP @aol.com. Website: www.voidingthevoid.com. **Contact:** E.E. Lippincott, editor-in-chief. Electronic zine and hard copy specializing in personal world views: 8½ × 11; 8 pages; mock newsprint hard copy. "A small reader specializing in individuals' fictional and nonfictional views of the world around them." Monthly. Estab. 1997. Circ. 2,000 both in US and UK.

Needs: All categories. "We will consider anything the potential contributor feels is appropriate to the theme 'tangibility.' All fiction genres OK." Publishes holiday issues; submit at least 3 months prior to holiday. Receives 100 unsolicited mss/month. Accepts 5-10 mss/issue; 120 mss/year. Publishes ms immediately to 1 year after acceptance. Recently published work by Erik Seims, Craig Coleman, R. Ambardar, T. Liam Vederman and Jenny Wu. Length: no length restrictions. Publishes short shorts. Also publishes literary essays, literary criticism, poetry. Always comments on rejected ms.

How to Contact: Send complete ms with a cover letter; send electronic submissions via website or direct e-mail. Include estimated word count. Responds in 2 weeks to queries; 3 months to mss. Send SASE for reply or return of ms. Accepts simultaneous and reprint (with date and place indicated) submissions. Guidelines for #10 SASE. Reviews novels and short story collections

Payment/Terms: Pays 4 contributor's copies. Acquires one-time rights. Individual issues not copyrighted.

Advice: "*Voiding the Void* is not about the 'writing' or the 'art' so much as it is about the human being behind it all."

VQ ONLINE, 8009 18th Lane SE, Lacey WA 98053. (360)455-4607. E-mail: jmtanaka@webtv.net. Website: http://community.webtv.net/JM/TANAKA/VQ. **Contact:** Janet Tanaka, editor. "VQ Online readers are professional and amateur volcanologists and other volcanophiles. It is not a journal, but an interesting ezine that features fiction, poetry, nonfiction articles, book and movie reviews, and announcements of interest to volcano scientists." Updated 4 times/year.

Needs: Short stories or serialized novellas. Nothing pornographic. "Must have volcanoes as a central subject, not just window dressing." **Publishes 15-20 new writers/year.** Recently published work by Susan Mauer, Bill West and Wendall Duffield.

How to Contact: Accepts queries by e-mail and disk (if convertible to ASCII).

Payment/Terms: Pays in contributor's copies.

Advice: "Material must be scientifically accurate."

WEB DEL SOL, E-mail: submissions@webdelsol.com. Website: www.webdelsol.com. **Contact:** Rachel Callaghan, editor. Electronic magazine. "The goal of *Web Del Sol* is to use the medium of the Internet to bring the finest in contemporary literary arts to a larger audience. To that end, *WDS* not only webpublishes collections of work by accomplished writers and poets, but hosts other literary arts publications on the WWW such as *Del Sol Review, North American Review, Zyzzyva, 5-Trope, Global City Review, The Literary Review* and *The Prose Poem.*

● *Web Del Sol* ranked #10 on *Writer's Digest*'s Fiction 50 list of top markets for fiction writers.

Needs: "*WDS* publishes work considered to be literary in nature, i.e., non-genre fiction. *WDS* also publishes poetry, prose poetry, essays and experimental types of writing." Publishes short shorts. **Publishes 30-40 new writers/year.** Recently published work by Robert Olen Butler, Forrest Gander, Xue Di, Michael Buceja, Martine Billen and Roldey Wilson. "Currently, *WDS* published Featured Writer/Poet websites, approximately 15 per year at this time; but hopes to increase that number substantially in the coming year. *WDS* also occasionally publishes individual works and plans to do more of these also."

How to Contact: "Submissions by e-mail from September through November and from January through March only. Submissions must contain some brief bio, list of prior publications (if any), and a short work or prortion of that work, neither to exceed 1,000 words. Editors will contact if the balance of work is required."

Advice: "*WDS* wants fiction that is absolutely cutting edge, unique and/or at a minimum, accomplished with a crisp style and concerning subjects not usually considered the objects of literary scrutiny. Read works in such publications as *Conjunctions* (www.conjunctions.com) and *North American Review* (webdelsol.com/NorthAmRe view/NAR) to get an idea what we are looking for."

WILMINGTON BLUES. E-mail: editor@wilmingtonblues.com. Website: www.wilmingtonblues.com. **Editor:** Trace Ramsey. Electronic zine.

Needs: Humor/satire, literary. Receives 60-80 unsolicited mss/month. Publishes ms 1 month after acceptance. **Publishes as many new writers as possible.** Recently published work by Alex Stolis and Steve Gibbs. Length: 250-10,000 words; average length: 2,500 words. Publishes short shorts. Length: 250 words. Also publishes essays, poetry. Often comments on rejected mss.

 A BULLET INTRODUCES COMMENTS by the editor of *Novel & Short Story Writer's Market* indicating special information about the listing.

How to Contact: Electronic submissions only. "Please submit work as a text attachment to an e-mail." Include estimated word count, bio, e-mail address. Responds in 2 weeks to queries; 1 month to mss. Accepts simultaneous submissions.

Payment/Terms: Acquires one-time rights.

Advice: "If your work has something to offer, it will be published. We offer comments on work that isn't accepted, and we encourage resubmissions!"

☑ ◑ ♈ ZUZU'S PETALS QUARTERLY, P.O. Box 4853, Ithaca NY 14852. (607)387-6916. E-mail: info@zuzu.com. Website: zuzu.come. **Contact:** T. Dunn, editor. Internet magazine. "Arouse the senses; stimulate the mind." Estab. 1992.

 • *Zuzu's Petals Quarterly* ranked #50 on *Writer's Digest*'s Fiction 50 list of top markets.

Needs: Ethnic/multicultural, feminist, gay, humor/satire, lesbian, literary, regional. No "romance, sci-fi, the banal, TV style plotting." Receives 110 unsolicited mss/month. Accepts 1-3 mss/issue; 4-12 mss/year. Publishes ms 4-6 months after acceptance. Agented fiction 10%. Published work by Norah Labiner, Vincent Zandri and LuAnn Jacobs. Length: 1,000-6,000 words. Publishes short shorts. Also publishes hypertext fiction (flexible length). Length: 350 words. Also publishes literary essays, literary criticism and poetry. Sometimes comments on rejected mss.

How to Contact: Send complete ms with a cover letter. Include estimated word count and list of publications. Responds in 2 weeks to queries; 2 weeks to 2 months to mss. Send SASE (or IRC) for reply, return of ms or send a disposable copy of ms. Accepts simultaneous and electronic submissions. Back issue for $5. Guidelines free. Reviews novels and short story collections. Send to Doug DuCap, Reviewer.

Advice: Looks for "strong plotting and a sense of vision. Original situations and true to life reactions."

Consumer Magazines

In this section of *Novel & Short Story Writer's Market* are consumer magazines with circulations of more than 10,000. Many have circulations in the hundreds of thousands or millions. While much has been made over the shrinking consumer magazine market for fiction, new markets are opening. Both United Air Lines inflight magazine *Hemispheres* and *Seventeen* magazine have placed new emphasis on publishing fiction. And among the oldest magazines listed here are ones not only familiar to us, but also to our parents, grandparents and even great-grandparents: *The Atlantic Monthly* (1857); *The New Yorker* (1925); *Capper's* (1879); *Esquire* (1933); and *Jack and Jill* (1938).

Consumer periodicals make excellent markets for fiction in terms of exposure, prestige and payment. Because these magazines are well-known, however, competition is great. Even the largest consumer publications buy only one or two stories an issue, yet thousands of writers submit to these popular magazines.

Despite the odds, it is possible for talented new writers to break into print in the magazines listed here. Your keys to breaking into these markets are careful research, professional presentation and, of course, top-quality fiction.

TYPES OF CONSUMER MAGAZINES

In this section you will find a number of popular publications, some for a broad-based, general-interest readership and others for large but select groups of readers—children, teenagers, women, men and seniors. There are also religious and church-affiliated magazines, publications devoted to the interests of particular cultures and outlooks, and top markets for genre fiction.

SELECTING THE RIGHT MARKET

Unlike smaller journals and publications, most of the magazines listed here are available at newsstands and bookstores. Many can also be found in the library, and guidelines and sample copies are almost always available by mail. Start your search by reviewing the listings, then familiarize yourself with the fiction included in the magazines that interest you.

Don't make the mistake of thinking that just because you are familiar with a magazine, their fiction is the same today as when you first saw it. Nothing could be further from the truth—consumer magazines, no matter how well established, are constantly revising their fiction needs as they strive to expand their audience base.

In a magazine that uses only one or two stories an issue, take a look at the nonfiction articles and features as well. These can give you a better idea of the audience for the publication and clues to the type of fiction that might appeal to them.

If you write genre fiction, check out the specific sections for lists of magazines publishing in that genre (mystery, page 91; romance, page 105; science fiction/fantasy & horror, page 121). For other types of fiction look in the Category Index beginning on page 618. There you will find a list of markets that say they are looking for a particular subject.

FURTHERING YOUR SEARCH

See The "Quick Start" Guide to Publishing Your Fiction (page 2) for information about the material common to all listings in this book. In this section in particular, pay close attention to the number of submissions a magazine receives in a given period and how many they publish in the same period. This will give you a clear picture of how stiff your competition can be.

While many of the magazines listed here publish one or two pieces of fiction in each issue, some also publish special fiction issues once or twice a year. We have indicated this in the listing information. We also note if the magazine is open to novel excerpts as well as short fiction and we advise novelists to query first before submitting long work.

The Business of Fiction Writing, beginning on page 70, covers the basics of submitting your work. Professional presentation is a must for all markets listed. Editors at consumer magazines are especially busy, and anything you can do to make your manuscript easy to read and accessible will help your chances of being published. Most magazines want to see complete manuscripts, but watch for publications in this section that require a query first.

As in the previous section, we've included our own comments in many of the listings, set off by a bullet (●). Whenever possible, we list the publication's recent awards and honors. We've also included any special information we feel will help you in determining whether a particular publication interests you.

The maple leaf symbol (🍁) identifies our Canadian listings. You will also find some English-speaking markets from around the world. These foreign magazines are denoted with 🌐 at the beginning of the listings. Remember to use International Reply Coupons rather than stamps when you want a reply from a country other than your own.

For More Information

For more on consumer magazines, see issues of *Writer's Digest* (by F&W Publications) and other industry trade publications available in larger libraries.

For news about some of the genre publications listed here and information about a particular field, there are a number of magazines devoted to genre topics, including *The Mystery Review*, *Locus* (for science fiction); *Science Fiction Chronicle*; and *Romance Writers' Report* (available to members of Romance Writers of America). Addresses for these and other industry magazines can be found in the Publications of Interest section of this book.

N **$** 🖾 **A & U, America's AIDS Magazine**, A & U, Inc., 25 Monroe St., Suite 205, Albany NY 12210. (518)426-9010. Fax: (518)436-5354. Email: mailbox@aumag.org. **Contact:** Chael Needle, managing editor. Magazine: 8⅛ × 10⅛; 48-72 pages; coated paper; coating u/v cover; illustrations; photos. Monthly. Estab. 1991. Circ. 200,000.
Needs: HIV/AIDS. Receives 5-10 unsolicited mss/month. Accepts 0-1 mss/issue; 9 mss/year. Publishes ms 3-5 months after acceptance. **Publishes 1-2 new writers/year.** Recently published work by Rachel S. Thomas-Medwid, Joe Rudy, Barbara Deming, Sarah Schulman, Lee Varon, Paul Lisicki, Felice Picano. Length: 900-2,000 words; average length: 1,200 words. Also publishes literary essays, literary criticism and poetry.
How to Contact: Send complete ms with cover letter. Include estimated word count, brief bio and list of publications. Responds in 1 month to queries; 6 months to mss. Send SASE for return of ms or disposable copy of ms and #10 SASE for reply only. Accepts simultaneous and multiple submissions. Sample copy free. Guidelines for SASE. Reviews novels, short story collections and nonfiction books of interest.
Payment/Terms: Pays $90-200 and 3 contributor's copies; additional copies $3.95. Pays on publication for first North American serial rights. Sends galleys to author.
Advice: "Fiction addressing the HIV/AIDS pandemic in a honest, non-sensationalistic, original way. Characters who have HIV/AIDS, going through day-to-day experiences. We are looking for shorter pieces to match space requirements."

✓ ⭐ **$** 🖾 **AFRICAN VOICES, A Soulful Collection of Art and Literature**, African Voices Communications, Inc., 270 W. 96th St., New York NY 10025. (212)865-2982. Fax: (212)316-3335. E-mail: africanvoices@aol.com. Website: www.africanvoices.com. **Contact:** Carolyn A. Butts, publisher/editor. Managing Editor: Layding Kaliba. Fiction Editor: Kim Horne. Book Review Editor: Debbie Officer. Magazine: 52 pages; illustrations; photos. "*AV* publishes enlightening and entertaining literature on the varied lifestyles of people of color." Quarterly. Estab. 1993. Circ. 20,000.

Needs: African-American: children's/juvenile (10-12 years), condensed/excerpted novel, erotica, ethnic/multi-cultural, gay, historical (general), horror, humor/satire, literary, mystery/suspense, psychic/supernatural/occult, religious/inspirational, science fiction, young adult/teen (adventure, romance). List of upcoming themes available for SASE. Publishes special fiction issue. Receives 20-50 unsolicited mss/month. Accepts 20 mss/issue. Publishes ms 3-6 months after acceptance. Agented fiction 5%. **Publishes 30 new writers/year.** Published work by Junot Díaz, Michel Marriott and Carol Dixon. Length: 500-3,000 words; average length: 2,000 words. Occasionally publishes short shorts. Also publishes literary essays and poetry.

How to Contact: Query with clips of published work. Include short bio. Accepts submissions by e-mail and on disk. Responds in 3 months to queries and mss. Send SASE for return of ms. Accepts simultaneous, reprint and electronic submissions. Sample copy for $5 and 9×12 SASE. Guidelines free. Subscriptions are $12 for 1 year. Reviews novels and short story collections. Send books to Book Editor.

Payment/Terms: Pays $25 maximum and 5 contributor's copies. Pays on publication for first North American serial rights.

Advice: "A manuscript stands out if it is neatly typed with a well-written and interesting story line or plot. Originality encouraged. We are interested in more horror, erotic and drama pieces. *AV* wants to highlight the diversity in our culture. Stories must touch the humanity in us all."

■ $⬙ AIM MAGAZINE, P.O. Box 1174, Maywood IL 60153. (773)874-6184. Fax: (206)543-2746. Editor: Myron Apilado, EdD. **Contact:** Mark Boone, fiction editor. Magazine: 8½×11; 48 pages; slick paper; photos and illustrations. Publishes material "to purge racism from the human bloodstream through the written word—that is the purpose of *Aim Magazine*." Quarterly. Estab. 1973. Circ. 10,000.
  • *Aim* sponsors an annual short story contest.

Needs: Open. No "religious" mss. Published special fiction issue last year; plans another. Receives 25 unsolicited mss/month. Buys 15 mss/issue; 60 mss/year. **Publishes 40 new writers/year.** Published work by Christina Touregny, Thomas Lee Harris, Michael Williams and Jake Halpern. Length: 800-1,000 words average. Publishes short shorts. Sometimes comments on rejected mss.

How to Contact: Send complete ms. Include SASE with cover letter and author's photograph. Accepts simultaneous submissions. Responds in 1 month. Sample copy for $4 with SAE (9×12) and $1.80 postage. Guidelines for #10 SASE.

Payment/Terms: Pays $15-25. Pays on publication for first rights.

Advice: "Search for those who are making unselfish contributions to their community and write about them. Write about your own experiences. Be familiar with the background of your characters." Known for "stories with social significance, proving that people from different ethnic, racial backgrounds are more alike than they are different."

$⬙ ⬙ AMERICAN GIRL, Pleasant Company Publications, Box 620986, Middleton WI 53562-0986. (608)836-4848. E-mail: readermail.ag.pleasantco.com. Website: www.americangirl.com. Editor: Kristi Thom. **Contact:** Magazine Department Assistant. Magazine: 8½×11; 52 pages; illustrations; photos. "Four-color bimonthly magazine for girls age 8-12. Our mission is to celebrate girls, yesterday and today. We publish fiction up to 2,300 words and the protagonist is a girl between 8-12. We want thoughtfully developed children's literature with good characters and plots." Estab. 1991. Circ. 700,000.
  • *American Girl* won the 2000 and 1999 Parent's Choice Gold Award. Pleasant Company is known for its series of books featuring girls from different periods of American history.

Needs: Children's/juvenile (girls 8-12 years): "contemporary, realistic fiction, adventure, historical, problem stories." No romance, science fiction, fantasy. Receives 100 unsolicited mss/month. Accepts 1 ms/year. Length: 2,300 words maximum. Publishes short shorts. Also publishes literary essays and poetry (if age appropriate). **Publishes 2-3 new writers year.** Recently published work by Kay Thompson, Mavis Jukes and Susan Shreve.

How to Contact: Query with published samples. Include bio (1 paragraph). Send SASE for reply, return of ms or send a disposable copy of ms. Accepts simultaneous submissions. Send SASE for guidelines. Sample copy for $3.95 plus $1.93 postage.

Payment/Terms: Pays in cash; amount negotiable. Pays on acceptance for first North American serial rights. Sends galleys to author.

Advice: "We're looking for excellent character development within an interesting plot."

⬙ $⬙ THE ANNALS OF ST. ANNE DE BEAUPRÉ, Redemptorist Fathers, P.O. Box 1000, St. Anne de Beaupré, Quebec G0A 3C0 Canada. (418)827-4538. Fax: (418)827-4530. **Contact:** Father Roch Achard, C.Ss.R., editor. Magazine: 8×11; 32 pages; glossy paper; photos. "Our aim is to promote devotion to St. Anne and Catholic family values." Monthly. Estab. 1878. Circ. 50,000.

Needs: Religious/inspirational. "We only wish to see something inspirational, educational, objective, uplifting. Reporting rather than analysis is simply not remarkable." Receives 50-60 unsolicited mss/month. Published work by Beverly Sheresh, Eugene Miller and Aubrey Haines. Publishes short stories. Length: 1,500 maximum. Always comments on rejected ms.

How to Contact: Send complete, typed, double spaced ms with a cover letter. Include estimated word count. Responds in 1 month. Send SASE for reply or return of ms. No simultaneous submissions. Free sample copy and guidelines.

Payment/Terms: Pays 3-4¢/word on acceptance and 3 contributor's copies on publication for first North American rights. "No reprints."

☑ $⌀ ART TIMES, Commentary and Resources for the Fine and Performing Arts, P.O. Box 730, Mt. Marion NY 12456. Phone/fax: (845)246-6944. **Contact:** Raymond J. Steiner, editor. Magazine: 12×15; 24 pages; Jet paper and cover; illustrations; photos. "Arts magazine covering the disciplines for an over-40, affluent, arts-conscious and literate audience." Monthly. Estab. 1984. Circ. 23,000.

Needs: Adventure, contemporary, ethnic, fantasy, feminist, gay, historical, humor/satire, lesbian, literary, mainstream and science fiction. "We seek quality literary pieces. Nothing violent, sexist, erotic, juvenile, racist, romantic, political, etc." Receives 30-50 mss/month. Accepts 1 ms/issue; 11 mss/year. Publishes ms within 48-60 months of acceptance. Publishes 1-5 new writers/year. Length: 1,500 words maximum. Publishes short shorts.

How to Contact: Send complete ms with cover letter. Accepts simultaneous submissions. Responds in 6 months. SASE. Sample copy for $1.75, 9×12 SAE and 3 first-class stamps. Guidelines for #10 SASE.

Payment/Terms: Pays $25, free one-year subscription to magazine and 6 contributor's copies. Pays on publication for first North American serial rights.

Advice: "Competition is greater (more submissions received), but keep trying. We print new as well as published writers."

★ $⌀ ♥ ASIMOV'S SCIENCE FICTION, 475 Park Ave. S., Floor 11, New York NY 10016-6901. (212)686-7188. Fax: (212)686-7414. E-mail: asimovs@dellmagazines.com. Website: www.asimovs.com (includes guidelines, names of editors, short fiction, interviews with authors, editorials, and more). **Contact:** Gardner Dozois, editor. Executive Editor: Sheila Williams. Magazine: 5¼×8¼ (trim size); 144 pages; 30 lb. newspaper; 70 lb. to 8 pt. C1S cover stock; illustrations; rarely photos. Magazine consists of science fiction and fantasy stories for adults and young adults. Publishes "the best short science fiction available." Estab. 1977. Circ. 50,000. 11 issues/year (one double issue).

• Named for a science fiction "legend," *Asimov's* regularly receives Hugo and Nebula Awards. Editor Gardner Dozois has received several awards for editing including Hugos and those from *Locus* and *Science Fiction Chronicle* magazines.

Needs: Science fiction (hard science, soft sociological), fantasy. No horror or psychic/supernatural. Receives approximately 800 unsolicited fiction mss each month. Accepts 10 mss/issue. Publishes ms 6-12 months after acceptance. Agented fiction 10%. **Publishes 6 new writers/year.** Published work by Robert Silverberg, Connie Willis and Greg Egan. Length: up to 20,000 words. Publishes short shorts. Comments on rejected mss "when there is time."

How to Contact: Send complete ms with SASE. Responds in 3 months. Guidelines for #10 SASE. Sample copy for $5 and 9×12 SASE. Reviews novels and short story collections. Send books to Book Reviewer.

Payment/Terms: Pays 6-8¢/word for stories up to 7,500 words; 5¢/word for stories over 12,500; $450 for stories between those limits. Pays on acceptance for first World English serial rights plus specified foreign rights, as explained in contract. Very rarely buys reprints. Sends galleys to author.

Advice: "We are looking for character stories rather than those emphasizing technology or science. New writers will do best with a story under 10,000 words. Every new science fiction or fantasy film seems to 'inspire' writers—and this is not a desirable trend. Be sure to be familiar with our magazine and the type of story we like; workshops and lots of practice help. Try to stay away from trite, cliched themes. Start in the middle of the action, starting as close to the end of the story as you possibly can. We like stories that extrapolate from up-to-date scientific research, but don't forget that we've been publishing clone stories for decades. Ideas must be fresh."

☑ $ THE ATLANTIC MONTHLY, 77 N. Washington St., Boston MA 02114. (617)854-7749. Fax: (617)854-7877. E-mail: mcurtis@theatlantic.com. Editor: Michael Kelly. **Contact:** C. Michael Curtis, senior editor. Managing Editor: Cullen Murphy. General magazine for an educated readership with broad cultural interests. Monthly. Estab. 1857. Circ. 500,000.

• *The Atlantic Monthly* ranked #1 on the *Writer's Digest*'s "Fiction 50" list of top markets for fiction writers.

Needs: Literary and contemporary. "Seeks fiction that is clear, tightly written with strong sense of 'story' and well-defined characters." Accepts 15-18 stories/year. Receives 1,000 unsolicited fiction mss each month. **Publishes 3-4 new writers/year.** Recently published work by Mary Gordon, Donald Hall and Roxana Robinson. Preferred length: 2,000-6,000 words.

How to Contact: Send cover letter and complete ms with SASE. Accepts submissions on disk. Accepts multiple submissions. Responds in 2 months or less to mss.

Payment/Terms: Pays $3,000/story. Pays on acceptance for first North American serial rights.

Advice: When making first contact, "cover letters are sometimes helpful, particularly if they cite prior publications or involvement in writing programs. Common mistakes: melodrama, inconclusiveness, lack of development, unpersuasive characters and/or dialogue."

☑ $⊘ THE BEAR DELUXE MAGAZINE, Orlo, 2516 NW 29th, P.O. Box 10342, Portland OR 97296. (503)242-1047. Fax: (503)243-2645. E-mail: bear@orlo.org. Website: www.orlo.org (includes writing guidelines). **Contact:** Thomas L. Webb, editor. Magazine: 11×14; 60 pages; newsprint paper; Kraft paper cover; illustrations; photos. *"The Bear Deluxe* has an environmental focus, combining all forms and styles. Fiction should have environmental thread to it and should be engaging to a cross-section of audiences. The more street-level, the better." Triannual. Estab. 1993. Circ. 19,000.

- *The Bear Deluxe* has received a publishing grant from the Oregon Council for the Humanities.

Needs: Environmentally focused: humor/satire, literary, science fiction. "We would like to see more nontraditional forms." No childrens or horror. List of upcoming themes available for SASE. Receives 20-30 unsolicited mss/month. Accepts 2-3 mss/issue; 8-12 mss/year. Publishes ms 6 months after acceptance. **Publishes 10 new writers/year.** Recently published work by Peter Houlahan, John Reed and Scott Svatos. Length: 900-4,000 words; average length: 2,500 words. Publishes short shorts. Also publishes literary essays, literary criticism, poetry, reviews, opinion, investigative journalism, interviews and creative nonfiction. Sometimes comments on rejected mss.

How to Contact: Send complete ms with a cover letter and clips. Include estimated word count, 10 to 15-word bio, list of publications. Accepts queries/mss by e-mail (mss by permission only). Responds in 3 months to queries; 6 months to mss. Send a disposable copy of mss. Accepts simultaneous and electronic (disk is best, then e-mail) submissions. Sample copy for $3. Guidelines for #10 SASE. Reviews novels and short story collections.

Payment/Terms: Pays free subscription to the magazine, contributor's copies and 5¢ per published word; additional copies for postage. Acquires first or one-time rights. Not copyrighted.

Advice: "Keep sending work. Write actively and focus on the connections of man, nature, etc., not just flowery descriptions. Urban and suburban environments are grist for the mill as well. Have not seen enough quality humorous and ironic writing. Interview and artist profile ideas needed. Juxtaposition of place welcome. Action and hands-on great. Not all that interested in environmental ranting and simple 'walks through the park.' Make it powerful, yet accessible to a wide audience."

☑ $⊘ BOMB MAGAZINE, New Art Publications, 594 Broadway, Suite 905, New York NY 10012. (212)431-3943. Fax: (212)431-5880. E-mail: suzan@bombsite.com. Website: www.bombsite.com. Editor-in-Chief: Betsy Sussler. **Contact:** Suzan Sherman, associate editor. Magazine: 11×14; 104 pages; 70 lb. glossy cover; illustrations; photos. Publishes "work which is unconventional and contains an edge, whether it be in style or subject matter." Quarterly. Estab. 1981.

Needs: Contemporary, experimental, novel excerpts. No genre: romance, science fiction, horror, western. Upcoming theme: "The Americas," featuring work by artists and writers from Central and South America (no unsolicited mss for theme issue, please). Receives 50 unsolicited mss/week. Accepts 6 mss/issue; 24 mss/year. Publishes ms 3-6 months after acceptance. Agented fiction 70%. **Publishes 2-3 new writers/year.** Recently published work by Melanie Rae Thon, Carole Maso, Molly McQuade and Mary Jo Bang. Length: 10-12 pages average. Publishes interviews.

How to Contact: Send complete ms up to 25 pages in length with cover letter. Responds in 4 months to mss. SASE. Accepts multiple submissions. Sample copy for $4.50 with $1.67 postage.

Payment/Terms: Pays $100 and contributor's copies. Pays on publication for first or one-time rights. Sends galleys to author.

Advice: "We are committed to publishing new work that commercial publishers often deem too dangerous or difficult. The problem is, a lot of young writers confuse difficult with dreadful. Read the magazine before you even think of submitting something."

$⊘ ☒ BOSTON REVIEW A political and literary forum, 30 Wadsworth St., E53-407, MIT, Cambridge MA 02139. (617)253-3642. Fax: (617)252-1549. E-mail: bostonreview@mit.edu. Website: www-polisci.mit.edu/bostonreview/ (includes full issue 1 month after publication, poetry and fiction links page, guidelines and contests guidelines, bookstore listing and subscription info). Managing Editor: Jeff Decker. **Contact:** Jodi Daynard, fiction editor. A bimonthly magazine "providing a forum of ideas in politics, literature and culture. Essays, reviews, poetry and fiction are published in every issue. Audience is well educated and interested in under recognized writers." Magazine: 10¾ × 14¾; 56 pages; newsprint. Estab. 1975. Circ. 30,000.

• *Boston Review* is the recipient of a Pushcart Prize in poetry.

Needs: Contemporary, ethnic, experimental, literary, prose poem, regional, translations. No romance, erotica, genre fiction. Receives 150 unsolicited fiction mss/month. Buys 4-6 mss/year. Publishes ms an average of 4 months after acceptance. Published work by David Mamet, Rhoda Stamell, Jacob Appel, Elisha Porat and Diane Williams. Length: 4,000 words maximum; average length: 2,000 words. Occasionally comments on rejected ms.

How to Contact: Send complete ms with cover letter and SASE. "You can almost always tell professional writers by the very thought-out way they present themselves in cover letters. But even a beginning writer should find some link between the work (its style, subject, etc.) and the publication—some reason why the editor should consider publishing it." No queries or manuscripts by e-mail. Responds in 4 months. Accepts simultaneous submissions (if noted). Sample copy for $4.50. Reviews novels and short story collections. Send books to Matthew Howard, managing editor.

Payment/Terms: Pays $50-100 and 5 contributor's copies. Pays after publication for first rights.

Advice: "I'm looking for stories that are emotionally and intellectually substantive and also interesting on the level of language. Things that are shocking, dark, lewd, comic, or even insane are fine so long as the fiction is *controlled* and purposeful in a masterly way. Subtlety, delicacy and lyricism are attractive too. Work tirelessly to make the work truly polished before you send it out. Make sure you know the publication you're submitting—don't send blind."

☑ $ ⊚ **BOWHUNTER MAGAZINE, The Number One Bowhunting Magazine**, Primedia Special Interest Publications, 6405 Flank Dr., Harrisburg PA 17112. (717)657-9555. Fax: (717)657-9552. E-mail: bowhunter@cowles.com. Website: www.bowhunter.com/ (includes writer's guidelines). Founder/Editor-in-Chief: M.R. James. Associate Publisher/Managing Editor: Jeffrey S. Waring. **Contact:** Dwight Schuh, editor. Magazine: 8 × 10½; 150 pages; 75 lb. glossy paper; 150 lb. glossy cover stock; illustrations; photos. "We are a special interest publication for people who hunt with the bow and arrow. We publish hunting adventure and how-to stories. Our audience is predominantly male, 30-50, middle income." Bimonthly. Circ. 180,000.

• Themes included in most fiction considered for *Bowhunter* are pro-conservation as well as pro-hunting.

Needs: Bowhunting, outdoor adventure. "Writers must expect a very limited market. We buy only one or two fiction pieces a year. Writers must know the market—bowhunting—and let that be the theme of their work. No 'me and my dog' types of stories; no stories by people who have obviously never held a bow in their hands." Receives 25 unsolicited fiction mss/month. Accepts 30 mss/year. Publishes ms 3 months to 2 years after acceptance. **Publishes 3-4 new writers/year.** Recently published work by John "Maggie" McGee, Troy Bungay and Marcy Buchanan. Length: 500-2,000 words; average length: 1,500 words. Publishes short shorts. Length: 500 words. Sometimes comments on rejected mss and recommends other markets.

How to Contact: Query first or send complete ms with cover letter. Accepts mss by e-mail, fax and disk. Responds in 2 weeks to queries; 1 month to mss. Sample copy for $2 and 8½ × 11 SAE with appropriate postage. Guidelines for #10 SASE.

Payment/Terms: Pays $100-350. Pays on acceptance for first worldwide serial rights.

Advice: "We have a resident humorist who supplies us with most of the 'fiction' we need. But if a story comes through the door which captures the essence of bowhunting and we feel it will reach out to our readers, we will buy it. Despite our macho outdoor magazine status, we are a bunch of English majors who love to read. You can't bull your way around real outdoor people—they can spot a phony at 20 paces. If you've never camped out under the stars and listened to an elk bugle and try to relate that experience without really experiencing it, someone's going to know. We are very specialized; we don't want stories about shooting apples off people's heads or of Cupid's arrow finding its mark. James Dickey's *Deliverance* used bowhunting metaphorically, very effectively . . . while we don't expect that type of writing from everyone, that's the kind of feeling that characterizes a good piece of outdoor fiction."

$ ◻ **BOYS' LIFE, For All Boys**, Boy Scouts of America, Magazine Division, Box 152079, 1325 W. Walnut Hill Lane, Irving TX 75015-2079. (972)580-2355. Website: www.boyslife.org. **Contact:** Rich Haddaway, associate editor. Magazine: 8 × 11; 68 pages; slick cover stock; illustrations; photos. "*Boys' Life* covers Boy Scout activities and general interest subjects for ages 8 to 18, Boy Scouts, Cub Scouts and others of that age group." Monthly. Estab. 1911. Circ. 1,300,000.

Needs: Adventure, humor/satire, mystery/suspense (young adult), science fiction, sports, western (young adult), young adult. "We publish short stories aimed at a young adult audience and frequently written from the viewpoint of a 10- to 16-year-old boy protagonist." Receives approximately 150 unsolicited mss/month. Accepts 12-18 mss/year. **Publishes 1 new writer/year.** Recently published work by Gary Paulsen, G. Clifton Wisler, Iain Lawrence and William Ken Krueger. Length: 500-1,500 words; average length: 1,200 words. "Very rarely" comments on rejected ms.

How to Contact: Send complete ms with SASE. "We'd much rather see manuscripts than queries." Responds in 2 months. For sample copy "check your local library." Guidelines for SASE.

Payment/Terms: Pays $750 and up ("depending on length and writer's experience with us"). Pays on acceptance for one-time rights.

Advice: "*Boys' Life* writers understand the readers. They treat them as intelligent human beings with a thirst for knowledge and entertainment. We tend to use some of the same authors repeatedly because their characters, themes, etc., develop a following among our readers. Read at least a year's worth of the magazine. You will get a feeling for what our readers are interested in and what kind of fiction we buy."

✓ $ ◑ ◎ **BUGLE, Elk Country and the Hunt**, Rocky Mountain Elk Foundation, P.O. Box 8249, Missoula MT 59807-8249. (406)523-3481. Fax: (406)523-4550. E-mail: dburgess@rmef.org. Website: www.rmef .org/ (includes writer's guidelines, names of editors and excerpts). Editor: Dan Crockett. **Contact:** Don Burgess, hunting/human interest editor. Assistant Editor: Lee Cromrich. Magazine: 8½×11; 114-172 pages; 55 lb. Escanaba paper; 80 lb. sterling cover; b&w, 4-color illustrations; photos. "The Rocky Mountain Elk Foundation is a nonprofit conservation organization established in 1984 to help conserve critical habitat for elk and other wildlife. *BUGLE* specializes in research, stories (fiction and nonfiction), art and photography pertaining to the world of elk and elk hunting." Bimonthly. Estab. 1984.

Needs: Elk-related adventure, children's/juvenile, historical, human interest, natural history, conservation. "We would like to see more humor. No formula outdoor or how-to writing. No stories of disrespect to wildlife." Upcoming theme: "Bowhunting." Receives 10-15 unsolicited mss/month. Accepts 5 mss/issue; 18-20 mss/year. Publishes ms 6 months after acceptance. **Publishes 12 new writers/year.** Recently published work by Wayne van Zwoll. Length: 1,500-5,000 words; 2,500 words preferred. Publishes short shorts. Also publishes literary essays and poetry.

How to Contact: Query first or send complete ms with a cover letter. Accepts queries/mss by e-mail, fax and disk (ms by permission only). Accepts multiple submissions. Include estimated word count and bio (100 words). Responds in 1 month to queries; 3 months to ms. Send SASE for reply, return of ms or send a disposable copy of ms. Sample copy for $5. Guidelines free.

Payment/Terms: Pays 20¢/word maximum. Pays on acceptance for one-time rights.

Advice: "We accept fiction and nonfiction stories about elk that show originality, and respect for the animal and its habitat."

$ ☑ **CALLIOPE, World History for Young People**, Cobblestone Publishing, Co., 30 Grove St., Suite C, Peterborough NH 02740. Fax: (603)924-7380. E-mail: cfbakeriii@meganet.net. Website: www.cobblestone pub.com. Managing Editor: Lou Waryncia. **Contact:** Rosalie Baker, editor. Magazine. "*Calliope* covers world history (east/west) and lively, original approaches to the subject are the primary concerns of the editors in choosing material. For 8-14 year olds." Monthly except June, July, August. Estab. 1990. Circ. 11,000.

● Cobblestone Publishing also publishes the children's magazines *Appleseeds, Footsteps, Odyssey, Cobblestone* and *Faces*, some listed in this section. *Calliope* has received the Ed Press Golden Lamp and One-Theme Issue awards.

Needs: Material must fit upcoming theme; write for themes and deadlines. Childrens/juvenile (8-14 years). "Authentic historical and biographical fiction, adventure, retold legends, etc. relating to the theme." Send SASE for guidelines and theme list. Published after theme deadline. Published work by Duane Damon and Amita V. Sarin. Publishes 5-10 new writers/year. Length: 800 words maximum. Publishes short shorts.

How to Contact: Query first or query with clips of published work (if new to *Calliope*). Include a brief cover letter stating estimated word count and 1-page outline explaining information to be presented, extensive bibliography of materials used. Responds in several months (if interested, response 5 months before publication date). Send SASE (or IRC) for reply (writers may send a stamped reply postcard to find out if query has been received). Sample copy for $4.95, 7½×10½ SAE and $2 postage. Guidelines for #10 SAE and 1 first-class stamp or on website.

Payment/Terms: Pays 20-25¢/word. Pays on publication for all rights.

Tips: "We primarily publish historical nonfiction. Fiction should be retold legends or folktales related to appropriate themes."

✓ $ ◑ ☑ **CAMPUS LIFE MAGAZINE**, Christianity Today, Inc., 465 Gundersen Dr., Carol Stream IL 60188. (630)260-6200. Fax: (630)260-0114. E-mail: CLmag@campuslife.net. Website: www.campuslife.net/ (includes writer's guidelines, names of editors, excerpts, and fiction not included in print edition). **Contact:** Amber Penney, assistant editor. Managing Editor: Christopher Lutes. Magazine: 8¼×11¼; 100 pages; 4-color and b&w illustrations; 4-color and b&w photos. "Teen magazine with a Christian point of view." Articles "vary from serious to humorous to current trends and issues, for teen readers." Bimonthly. Estab. 1942. Circ. 100,000.

● *Campus Life* regularly receives awards from the Evangelical Press Association.

Needs: "All fiction submissions must be contemporary, reflecting the teen experience in the new millennium. We are a Christian magazine but are *not* interested in sappy, formulaic, sentimentally religious stories. We *are* interested in well-crafted stories that portray life realistically, stories high school and college youth relate to. Writing must reflect a Christian world view. If you don't understand our market and style, don't submit." Accepts 5 mss/year. Reading and response time slower in summer. **Publishes 3-4 new writers/year.** Length: 1,000-2,000 words average, "possibly longer."

How to Contact: Query with short synopsis of work, published samples and SASE. Accepts queries by e-mail, fax and disk. Responds in 6 weeks to queries. Sample copy for $3 and 9½×11 envelope.

Payment/Terms: Pays "generally" 15-20¢/word and 2 contributor's copies. Pays on acceptance for one-time rights.

Advice: "We print finely-crafted fiction that carries a contemporary teen (older teen) theme. First person fiction often works best. Ask us for sample copy with fiction story. We want experienced fiction writers who have something to say to young people without getting propagandistic."

$⊘ CAPPER'S, Ogden Publications, Inc. 1503 S.W. 42nd St., Topeka KS 66609-1265. (785)274-4346. Fax: (785)274-4305. E-mail: cappers@kspress.com. Website: www.cappers.com (includes sample items from publication and subscription information). **Contact:** Ann Crahan, editor. Magazine: 36-56 pages; newsprint paper and cover stock; photos. A "clean, uplifting and nonsensational newspaper for families, from children to grandparents." Biweekly. Estab. 1879. Circ. 250,000.

● *Capper's* is interested in longer works of fiction, 7,000 words or more. They would like to see more stories with older characters.

Needs: Serialized novels suitable for family reading. "We accept novel-length stories for serialization. No fiction containing violence, sexual references or obscenity. We would like to see more western romance, pioneer stories." Receives 2-3 unsolicited fiction mss each month. Accepts 4-6 stories/year. Recently published work by C.J. Sargent and Mona Exinger. Published new writers within the last year. Length: 7,000-40,000 words.

How to Contact: Send complete ms with SASE. Cover letter and/or synopsis helpful. Responds in 8 months on ms. Sample copy for $2.

Payment/Terms: Pays $75-300 for one-time serialization and contributor's copies (1-2 copies as needed for copyright). Pays on acceptance for second serial (reprint) rights and one-time rights.

Advice: "Since we publish in serialization, be sure your manuscript is suitable for that format. Each segment needs to be compelling enough so the reader remembers it and is anxious to read the next installment. Please proofread and edit carefully. We've seen major characters change names partway through the manuscript."

✓ ◎ CELESTIAL PRODUCTS, (formerly Contact Advertising), Box 3431, Ft. Pierce FL 34948. (561)464-6047. E-mail: nietzche@cadv.com. Website: www.cadv.com (includes short fiction club information). **Contact:** Herman Nietzche, editor. Magazines and newspapers "specializing in alternative lifestyles." Publications vary in size, 56-80 pages. "Group of 26 erotica, soft core publications for swingers, single males, married males, gay males, transgendered and bisexual persons." Bimonthly, quarterly and monthly. Estab. 1975. Circ. combined is 2,000,000.

● This is a group of regional publications with explicit sexual content, graphic personal ads, etc. Not for the easily offended.

Needs: Erotica, fantasy, swinger, fetish, gay, lesbian. Receives 8-10 unsolicited mss/month. Accepts 1-2 mss/issue; 40-50 mss/year. Publishes ms 1-3 months after acceptance. **Publishes 3-6 new writers/year.** Length: 2,000-3,500 words. Sometimes comments on rejected mss.

How to Contact: Query first, query with clips of published work or send complete ms with cover letter. SASE. Accepts submissions by e-mail and on disk. Accepts simultaneous, multiple and reprint submissions. Sample copy for $7. Guidelines with SASE.

Payment/Terms: First submission, free subscription to magazine; subsequent submissions $25 on publication for all rights or first rights; all receive 3 contributor's copies.

Advice: "Know your grammar! Content must be of an adult nature but well within guidelines of the law. Fantasy, unusual sexual encounters, swinging stories or editorials of a sexual bent are acceptable. Read Henry Miller!"

⚏ ✓ $⊘ �ய CHICKADEE, Owl Communications, 49 Front St. E, 2nd Floor, Toronto, Ontario M5E 1B3 Canada. (416)340-2700. Fax: (416)340-9769. E-mail: owl@owlkids.com. Website: www.owlkids.com. **Contact:** Hilary Bain, editor. Magazine: 8½×11¾; 36 pages; glossy paper and cover stock; illustrations; photos. "*Chickadee* is created to give children aged 6-9 a lively, fun-filled look at the world around them. Each issue has a mix of activities, puzzles, games and stories." Published 10 times/year. Estab. 1979. Circ. 80,000.

● *Chickadee* has won several awards including the Ed Press Golden Lamp Honor award and the Parents' Choice Golden Seal and Silver Seal awards.

Needs: Juvenile. No religious material. Accepts 1 ms/issue; 10 mss/year. **Published new writers within the last year.** Length: 600-700 words.

How to Contact: Send complete ms and cover letter with $1 or IRC to cover postage and handling (must be international postal coupon). Accepts simultaneous submissions. Responds in 2 months. Sample copy for $4.50. Guidelines for SAE and IRC.

Payment/Terms: Pays $25-350 (Canadian) and 3 contributor's copies. Pays on acceptance for all rights. Occasionally buys reprints.

Advice: "Read back issues to see what types of fiction we publish. Common mistakes include loose, rambling, and boring prose; stories that lack a clear beginning, middle and end; unbelievable characters; and overwriting."

☑ $ ⦸ **CHILDREN'S DIGEST**, Children's Better Health Institute, P.O. Box 567, 1100 Waterway Blvd., Indianapolis IN 46206. (317)634-1100. **Contact:** Penny Rasdall, managing editor. Magazine: 7 × 10⅛; 36 pages; reflective and preseparated illustrations; color and b&w photos. Magazine with special emphasis on health, nutrition, exercise and safety for preteens.

- Other magazines published by Children's Better Health Institute and listed in this book are *Children's Playmate*, *Humpty Dumpty*, *Jack and Jill* and *Turtle*.

Needs: "Realistic stories, short plays, adventure and mysteries. Humorous stories are highly desirable. We especially need stories that *subtly* encourage readers to develop better health or safety habits. Stories should not exceed 1,500 words." Receives 40-50 unsolicited fiction mss each month. Published work by Judith Josephson, Pat McCarthy and Sharen Liddell; published new writers within the last year.

How to Contact: Currently not accepting unsolicited mss or art. Sample copy for $1.75. Guidelines for SASE.

Payment/Terms: Pays 12¢/word minimum with up to 10 contributor's copies on publication for all rights.

Advice: "We try to present our health-related material in a positive—not a negative—light, and we try to incorporate humor and a light approach wherever possible without minimizing the seriousness of what we are saying. Fiction stories that deal with a health theme need not have health as the primary subject but should include it in some way in the course of events. Most rejected health-related manuscripts are too preachy or they lack substance. Children's magazines are not training grounds where authors learn to write 'real' material for 'real' readers. Because our readers frequently have limited attention spans, it is very important that we offer them well-written stories."

$ ⊚ **CHILDREN'S PLAYMATE**, Children's Better Health Institute, P.O. Box 567, 1100 Waterway Blvd., Indianapolis IN 46206. (317)636-8881. **Contact:** Terry Harshman, editor. Magazine: 7½ × 10; 48 pages; preseparated and reflective art; b&w and color illustrations. Juvenile magazine for children ages 6-8 years. Published 8 times/year.

- *Children's Digest*, *Humpty Dumpty*, *Jack and Jill* and *Turtle* magazines are also published by Children's Better Health Institute and listed in this book.

Needs: Juvenile with special emphasis on health, nutrition, safety and exercise. "Our present needs are for short, rebus stories only." No adult or adolescent fiction. Receives approximately 150 unsolicited fiction mss each month. **Published new writers within the last year.** Recently published work by Valeri Gorbachev. Length: 300-700 words.

How to Contact: Send complete ms with SASE. Indicate word count on material and date sent. Responds in 3 months. Sample copy for $1.75. Writer's guidelines for SASE.

Payment/Terms: Pays up to 17¢/word and 10 contributor's copies. Pays on publication for *all* rights.

Advice: "Study past issues of the magazine—be aware of vocabulary limitations of the readers."

☑ $ ▢ ⊚ **CITYCYCLE MOTORCYCLE NEWS**, Motormag Corp., P.O. Box 808, Nyack NY 10960-0808. (845)353-MOTO. Fax: (845)353-5240. E-mail: bigcheese@motorcyclenews.cc. Website: www.motorcyclenews.cc (includes short fiction, interviews with authors). **Contact:** Mark Kalan, editor. Magazine: tabloid; 64 pages; newsprint; illustrations; photos. Monthly magazine about motorcyling. Estab. 1990. Circ. 50,000.

Needs: "Anything about motorcycles." No "sexual fantasy." Accepts 10 mss/year. Publishes ms 2-6 months after acceptance. Length: 750-2,000 words average. Publishes short shorts. Also publishes literary essays, literary criticism and poetry. Sometimes comments on rejected mss.

How to Contact: Query with clips of published work. Responds in 1 month to queries. Send SASE for reply. Accepts reprints. Sample copy for $3 and 9 × 12 SAE. Guidelines for #10 SASE. Reviews novels and short story collections. Send books to editor.

Payment/Terms: Pays up to $150. Pays on publication for one-time rights.

Advice: "Articles, stories and poetry can be about any subject, fiction or non-fiction, as long as the subject pertains to motorcycles or the world of motorcycling. Examples would include fiction or non-fiction stories about traveling cross-country on a motorcycle, biker lifestyle or perspective, motorcycling/biker humor, etc. Stories should reflect the love of riding motorcycles and the experience of what riding is like. Romance is fine. Science fiction is fine as long as it will interest our mostly male audience."

✔ $ ◙ **CLUBHOUSE, Focus on the Family,** 8605 Explorer Dr., Colorado Springs CO 80920. (719)531-3400. **Contact:** Suzanne Hadley, assistant editor. Editor: Jesse Florea. Magazine: 8×11; 24 pages; illustrations; photos. Publishes literature for kids aged 8-12. "Stories must have moral lesson included. *Clubhouse* readers are 8- to 12-year-old boys and girls who desire to know more about God and the Bible. Their parents (who typically pay for the membership) want wholesome, educational material with Scriptual or moral insight. The kids want excitement, adventure, action, humor or mystery. Your job as a writer is to please both the parent and child with each article." Monthly. Estab. 1987. Circ. 115,000.

Needs: Children's/juvenile (8-12 years), religious/inspirational. No science fiction. Receives 150 unsolicited ms/month. Accepts 1 ms/issue. Agented fiction 15%. **Publishes 8 new writers/year.** Published work by Sigmund Brower and Nancy Rue. Length: 500-1,200 words average.

How to Contact: Send complete ms with cover letter. Include estimated word count, bio and list of publications. Responds in 6 weeks. Send SASE for reply, return of ms or send a disposable copy of ms. Sample copy for $1.50. Guidelines free.

Payment/Terms: Pays $250 maximum for first-time contributor and 5 contributor's copies; additional copies available. Pays on acceptance for first North American serial rights.

Advice: Looks for "humor with a point, historical fiction featuring great Christians or Christians who lived during great times; contemporary, exotic settings; holiday material (Christmas, Thanksgiving, Easter, President's Day); parables; fantasy (avoid graphic descriptions of evil creatures and sorcery); mystery stories; choose-your-own adventure stories and westerns. No contemporary, middle-class family settings (we already have authors who can meet these needs) or stories dealing with boy-girl relationships."

☐ ◪ $ ◩ **COBBLESTONE, Discover American History**, 30 Grove St., Suite C, Peterborough NH 03458. (603)924-7209. Fax: (603)924-7380. Website: www.cobblestonepub.com. **Contact:** Meg Chorlian, editor. Magazine. "Historical accuracy and lively, original approaches to the subject are primary concerns of the editors in choosing material. For 8-14 year olds." Monthly (except June, July and August). Estab. 1979. Circ. 33,000.

• Cobblestone Press also publishes *Calliope* and *Faces* as well as *Odyssey* (science magazine), *Footsteps* (African American magazine) and *Appleseeds* (for 7-9 year olds). *Cobblestone* has received Ed Press and Parent's Choice awards.

Needs: Material must fit upcoming theme; write for theme list and deadlines. Childrens/juvenile (8-14 years). "Authentic historical and biographical fiction, adventure, retold legends, etc., relating to the theme." Upcoming themes available for SASE. Published after theme deadline. Length: 800 words maximum. Publishes short shorts. Also publishes poetry.

How to Contact: Query first or query with clips of published work (if new to *Cobblestone*). Include estimated word count. "Include detailed outline explaining the information to be presented in the article and bibliography of material used." Responds in several months. If interested, responds to queries 5 months before publication date. Send SASE (or IRC) for reply or send self-addressed postcard to find out if query was received. Accepts electronic submissions (disk, Microsoft Word or MS-DOS). Sample copy for $4.95, 7½×10½ SAE and $2 postage. Guidelines for #10 SAE and 1 first-class stamp or on website.

Payment/Terms: Pays 20-25¢/word. Pays on publication for all rights.

Advice: Writers may send $8.95 plus $3 shipping for *Cobblestone*'s catalog for a listing of subjects covered in back issues.

$ ◉ **COUNTRY WOMAN,** Reiman Publications, 5400 South 60th St., Greendale WI 53129. (414)423-0100. Editor: Ann Kaiser. **Contact:** Kathleen Pohl, executive editor. Magazine: 8½×11; 68 pages; excellent quality paper; excellent cover stock; illustrations and photographs. "Stories should have a rural theme and be of specific interest to women who live on a farm or ranch, or in a small town or country home, and/or are simply interested in country-oriented topics." Bimonthly. Estab. 1971.

Needs: Fiction must be upbeat, heartwarming and focus on a country woman as central character. "Many of our stories and articles are written by our readers!" Published work by Edna Norrell, Millie Thomas Kearney and Rita Peterson. **Published new writers within last year.** Publishes 1 fiction story/issue. Length: 1,000 words.

How to Contact: Send $2 and SASE for sample copy and writer's guidelines. All manuscripts should be sent to Kathy Pohl, Executive Editor. Responds in 3 months. Include cover letter and SASE. Accepts simultaneous and reprint submissions.

Payment/Terms: Pays $90-125 for fiction. Pays on acceptance for one-time rights.

Advice: "Read the magazine to get to know our audience. Send us country-to-the-core fiction, not yuppie-country stories—our readers know the difference! Very traditional fiction—with a definite beginning, middle and end, some kind of conflict/resolution, etc. We do not want to see contemporary avant-garde fiction—nothing dealing with divorce, drugs, etc., or general societal malaise of the '90s."

◯ ◎ ☒ **CREATIVE KIDS**, Prufrock Press, P.O. Box 8813, Waco TX 76714-8813. (254)756-3337. Fax: (254)756-3339. E-mail: creative_kids@prufrock.com. Website: www.prufrock.com (includes catalog, submission guidelines and information about our staff). **Contact:** Libby Lindsey, editor. Magazine: 7×10½; 36 pages; illustrations; photos. Material by children for children. Published 4 times/year. Estab. 1980. Circ: 45,000.

• *Creative Kids* featuring work by children has won Ed Press and Parents' Choice Gold and Silver Awards.

Needs: "We publish work by children ages 8-14." Publishes short stories, essays, games, puzzles, poems, opinion pieces and letters. Accepts 3-4 mss/issue; 12-16 mss/year. Publishes ms up to 2 years after acceptance. **Published new writers within the last year.** No novels.

How to Contact: Send complete ms with cover letter; include name, age, birthday, home address, school name and address, grade, statement of originality signed by teacher or parent. Must include SASE for response. Do not query. Responds in 1 month to mss. SASE. Sample copy for $3. Guidelines for SASE.

Payment/Terms: Pays 1 contributor's copy. Acquires all rights.

Advice: "*Creative Kids* is designed to entertain, stimulate and challenge the creativity of children ages 8 to 14, encouraging their abilities and helping them to explore their ideas, opinions and world. Your work reflects you. Make it neat, have it proofread and follow ALL guidelines."

$ ◻ ☒ **CRICKET MAGAZINE**, Carus Publishing Company, P.O. Box 300, Peru IL 61354. (815)224-6656. **Contact:** Marianne Carus, editor-in-chief. Magazine: 8×10; 64 pages; illustrations; photos. Magazine for children, ages 9-14. Monthly. Estab. 1973. Circ. 71,000.

• *Cricket* has received a Parents Choice Award, and awards from Ed Press. Carus Corporation also publishes *Spider, the Magazine for Children, Ladybug, the Magazine for Young Children, Babybug*, and *Cicada*.

Needs: Adventure, contemporary, ethnic, fantasy, historic fiction, folk and fairytales, humorous, juvenile, mystery, science fiction and translations. No adult articles. All issues have different "mini-themes." Receives approximately 1,100 unsolicited fiction mss each month. Publishes ms 6-24 months or longer after acceptance. Accepts 180 mss/year. Agented fiction 1-2%. **Published new writers within the last year.** Published work by Peter Dickinson, Mary Stolz and Jane Yolen. Length: 500-2,000 words.

How to Contact: Do not query first. Send complete ms with SASE. List previous publications. Responds in 3 months to mss. Sample copy for $5. Guidelines for SASE.

Payment/Terms: Pays up to 25¢/word and 2 contributor's copies; $2 charge for extras. Pays on publication for first rights. Sends edited mss for approval. Buys reprints.

Advice: "Do not write *down* to children. Write about well-researched subjects you are familiar with and interested in, or about something that concerns you deeply. Children *need* fiction and fantasy. Carefully study several issues of *Cricket* before you submit your manuscript." Sponsors contests for readers of all ages.

$ ◻ **CRUSADER MAGAZINE**, Calvinist Cadet Corps, Box 7259, Grand Rapids MI 49510-7259. (616)241-5616. **Contact:** G. Richard Broene, editor. Magazine: 8½×11; 24 pages; illustrations; photos. Magazine "for boys (ages 9-14) who are members of the Calvinist Cadet Corps. *Crusader* publishes stories and articles that have to do with the interests and concerns of boys, teaching Christian values subtly." 7 issues/year. Estab. 1958. Circ. 12,000.

Needs: Adventure, comics, juvenile, religious/inspirational, spiritual and sports. No fantasy, science fiction, fashion, horror or erotica. List of upcoming themes available for SASE. Receives 60 unsolicited fiction mss/ month. Buys 3 mss/issue; 18 mss/year. Publishes ms 4-11 months after acceptance. Published work by Sigmund Brouwer, Douglas DeVries and Betty Lou Mell. Publishes 0-3 new writers/year. Length: 800-1,500 words; average length: 1,200 words. Publishes short shorts.

How to Contact: Send complete ms and SASE with cover letter including theme of story. Responds in 3 months. Accepts simultaneous, multiple and previously published submissions. Sample copy with a 9×12 SAE and 4 first-class stamps. Guidelines for #10 SASE.

Payment/Terms: Pays 4-6¢/word and 1 contributor's copy. Pays on acceptance for one-time rights. Buys reprints.

Advice: "On a cover sheet, list the point your story is trying to make. Our magazine has a theme for each issue, and we try to fit the fiction to the theme. All fiction should be about a young boy's interests—sports, outdoor activities, problems—with an emphasis on a Christian perspective. No simple moralisms. Avoid simplistic answers to complicated problems."

$ ◎ **DIALOGUE, A World of Ideas for Visually Impaired People of All Ages**, Blindskills Inc., P.O. Box 5181, Salem OR 97304-0181. (800)860-4224. (503)581-4224. Fax: (503)581-0178. E-mail: blindskl@telepo rt.com. Website: www.blindskills.com. **Contact:** Carol McCarl, editor/publisher. Magazine: 9×11; 130 pages; matte stock. Publishes information of general interest to visually impaired. Quarterly. Estab. 1961. Circ. 10,000.

Needs: Adventure, contemporary, fantasy, humor/satire, literary, mainstream, mystery/suspense, romance, science fiction, senior citizen/retirement. No erotica, religion, confessional, controversial, political or experimental.

Receives approximately 10 unsolicited fiction mss. Accepts 2 mss/issue, 10 mss/year. Publishes ms an average of 1 year after acceptance. Published work by Joseph Orth, Patrick Quinn and Deanna Noriega. Published new writers within the last year. Length: 800-1,200 words; average length: 1,000 words. Publishes short shorts. Occasionally comments on rejected mss. Sometimes recommends other markets. "We primarily feature blind or visually impaired (legally blind) authors."

How to Contact: Query first or send complete ms with SASE. Also send statement of visual disability. "Should be in large print." Responds in 2 weeks to queries; 6 weeks to mss. No fax or e-mail submissions. Accepts electronic submissions on disk; IBM and compatible; Word Perfect 5.1 or 6.0 preferred; also cassette tape or Braille. Sample copy for #10 SAE with 1 first-class stamp. Guidelines free.

Payment/Terms: Pays $15-30 and contributor's copy. Pays on publication.

Advice: "Authors should be blind or visually impaired. We prefer contemporary problem stories in which the protagonist solves his or her own problem. We are looking for strongly-plotted stories with definite beginnings, climaxes and endings. Characters may be blind, sighted or visually in-between. Because we want to encourage any writer who shows promise, we may return a story for revision when necessary."

✓ $⊘ **DISCOVERIES,** WordAction Publishing Company, 6401 The Paseo, Kansas City MO 64131-1213. (816)333-7000 ext. 2728. Fax: (816)333-4439. E-mail: khendrixson@nazarene.org. **Contact:** Kathy Hendrixson, editorial assistant. Story paper: 8½×11; 4 pages; illustrations. "Committed to reinforce the Bible concept taught in Sunday School curriculum, for ages 8-10 (grades 3-4)." Weekly.

Needs: Religious stories, puzzles, Bible trivia, 100-200 words. "Avoid fantasy, science fiction, personification of animals and cultural references that are distinctly American. Nothing preachy. No unrealistic dialogue." List of upcoming themes available for SASE. Accepts 1 story, 1 Bible trivia, and 1 puzzle/issue. Publishes ms 1-2 years after acceptance. **Publishes 5-7 new writers/year.** Story length: 500 words.

How to Contact: Send complete ms with cover letter and SASE. Accepts ms by e-mail, fax and disk. Accepts multiple submissions. Send SASE for sample copy and guidelines.

Payment/Terms: Pays 5¢/word. Pays on acceptance or on publication for multiple rights.

Advice: "Stories should vividly portray definite Christian emphasis or character building values, without being preachy."

✓ $⊘ **DISCOVERY TRAILS,** Gospel Publishing House, 1445 N. Boonville Ave., Springfield MO 65802-1894. (417)862-2781. Fax: (417)862-6059. E-mail: discoverytrails@gph.org. Website: www.radiantlife.org. **Contact:** Sinda S. Zinn, editor. Magazine: 8×10; 4 pages; coated offset paper; art illustrations; photos. "A Sunday school take-home paper of articles and fictional stories that apply Christian principles to everyday living for 10- to 12-year-old children." Weekly. Estab. 1954. Circ. 20,000.

Needs: Contemporary, juvenile, religious/inspirational, spiritual, sports. Adventure and mystery stories and serials are welcome. No Biblical fiction, Halloween, Easter "bunny," Santa Claus or science fiction. Accepts 2 mss/issue. **Published new writers within the last year.** Recently published work by Ellen Javernick, Carolyn Short and Theresa Bubulka. Length: 800-1,000 words. Publishes short shorts.

How to Contact: Send complete ms with SASE. Accepts submissions by e-mail. Responds in 6 weeks. Free sample copy and guidelines with SASE.

Payment/Terms: Pays 7-10¢/word and 3 contributor's copies. Pays on acceptance.

Advice: "Know the age level and direct stories or articles relevant to that age group. Since junior-age children (grades 5 and 6) enjoy action, fiction provides a vehicle for communicating moral/spiritual principles in a dramatic framework. Fiction, if well done, can be a powerful tool for relating Christian principles. It must, however, be realistic and believable in its development. Make your children be children, not overly mature for their age. We would like more serial stories. Write for contemporary children, using setting and background that includes various ethnic groups."

✓ $◒ ♆ **ESQUIRE, The Magazine for Men,** Hearst Corp., 250 W. 55th St., New York NY 10019. (212)649-4020. Fax: (212)977-3158. Website: www.esquire.com. Editor: David Granger. **Contact:** Adrienne Miller, literary editor. Magazine. Monthly. Estab. 1933. Circ. 750,000. General readership is college educated and sophisticated, between ages 30 and 45.

READ "THE BUSINESS OF FICTION WRITING" section for information on manuscript preparation, mailing tips, rights and more.

● *Esquire* is well-respected for its fiction and has received several National Magazine Awards. Work published in *Esquire* has been selected for inclusion in the *Best American Short Stories* and *O. Henry* anthologies.

Needs: No "pornography, science fiction or 'true romance' stories." Publishes special fiction issue in July. Receives over 10,000 unsolicited mss/year. Rarely accepts unsolicited fiction. Recently published work by Russell Banks and Tim O'Brien.

How to Contact: Send complete ms with cover letter or submit through an agent. Accepts simultaneous and multiple submissions. Guidelines for SASE.

Payment/Terms: Pays in cash on acceptance, amount undisclosed. Publishes ms an average of 2-6 months after acceptance.

Advice: "Submit one story at a time. Worry a little less about publication, a little more about the work itself."

$ ⬛ ◎ EVANGEL, Light & Life Communications, P.O. Box 535002, Indianapolis IN 46253-5002. (317)244-3660. **Contact:** Julie Innes, editor. Sunday school take-home paper for distribution to adults who attend church. Fiction involves people coping with everyday crises, making decisions that show spiritual growth. Magazine: 5½ × 8½; 8 pages; 2- and 4-color illustrations; color and b&w photos. Weekly. Estab. 1897. Circ. 22,000.

Needs: Religious/inspirational. "No fiction without any semblance of Christian message or where the message clobbers the reader." Receives approximately 300 unsolicited fiction mss/month. Accepts 3-4 mss/issue, 156-200 mss/year. **Publishes 90 new writers/year.** Published work by Karen Leet and Dennis Hensley. Length: 250-1,200 words.

How to Contact: Send complete ms with SASE. Responds in 2 months. Accepts submissions by e-mail and disk (WordPerfect); send hard copy with disk. Accepts multiple submissions. Sample copy and writer's guidelines with #10 SASE.

Payment/Terms: Pays 4¢/word and 2 contributor's copies. Pays on publication.

Advice: "Choose a contemporary situation or conflict and create a good mix for the characters (not all-good or all-bad heroes and villains). Don't spell out everything in detail; let the reader fill in some blanks in the story. Keep him guessing." Rejects mss because of "unbelievable characters and predictable events in the story."

$ FACES, People, Places and Cultures, A Cobblestone Publication, Cobblestone Publishing, Co., 30 Grove St., Suite C, Peterborough NH 03458. (603)924-7209. Fax: (603)924-7380. E-mail: faces@cobblestonepub .com. Website: www.cobblestonepub.com. Editor: Elizabeth Crooker. **Contact:** Lou Waryncia, managing editor. Magazine. *Faces* is a magazine about people and places in the world for 8 to 14-year-olds. Estab. 1984. Circ. 15,000. Monthly, except June, July and August.

● Cobblestone also publishes *Cobblestone* and *Calliope*, listed in this section.

Needs: All material must relate to theme; send for theme list. Children's/juvenile (8-14 years), "retold legends, folk tales, stories from around the world, etc., relating to the theme." Length: 800 words preferred. Publishes short shorts.

How to Contact: Query first or query with clips of published work. Themes posted on website. Send query 6-9 months prior to theme issue publication date. Include estimated word count and bio (2-3 lines). Responds 4 months before publication date. Send SASE for reply. Sample copy for $4.95, 7½ × 10½ SAE and $2 postage. Guidelines for SASE.

Payment/Terms: Pays 20-25¢/word. Pays on publication for all rights.

$ ⬛ ◎ FIRST HAND, Experiences for Loving Men, First Hand Ltd., Box 1314, Teaneck NJ 07666. (201)836-9177. Fax: (201)836-5055. E-mail: firsthand3@aol.com. **Contact:** Don Dooley, editor. Magazine: digest size; 130 pages; illustrations. "Half of the magazine is made up of our readers' own gay sexual experiences. Rest is fiction and columns devoted to health, travel, books, etc." Monthly. Estab. 1980. Circ. 60,000.

Needs: Erotica, gay. "Should be written in first person." No science fiction or fantasy. Erotica should detail experiences based in reality. Receives 75-100 unsolicited mss/month. Accepts 6 mss/issue; 72 mss/year. Publishes ms 9-18 months after acceptance. Length: 2,000-3,750 words; 3,000 words preferred. Sometimes comments on rejected mss.

How to Contact: Send complete ms with cover letter. Include name, address, telephone and Social Security number and "advise on use of pseudonym if any. Also whether selling all rights or first North American rights." No simultaneous submissions. Responds in 2 months. SASE. Sample copy for $5. Guidelines for #10 SASE.

Payment/Terms: Pays $100-150 on publication for all rights or first North American serial rights.

Advice: "Avoid the hackneyed situations. Be original. We like strong plots."

$ ⬛ THE FRIEND MAGAZINE, The Church of Jesus Christ of Latter-day Saints, 50 E. North Temple, 24th Floor, Salt Lake City UT 84150-3226. (801)240-2210. **Contact:** Vivian Paulsen, editor. Magazine: 8½ × 10½; 50 pages; 40 lb. coated paper; 70 lb. coated cover stock; illustrations; photos. Publishes for 3- to 11-year-olds. Monthly. Estab. 1971. Circ. 275,000.

Needs: Children's/juvenile: adventure, ethnic, some historical, humor, mainstream, religious/inspirational, nature. Length: 1,000 words maximum. Publishes short shorts. Length: 250 words.

How to Contact: Send complete ms. "No query letters please." Responds in 2 months. SASE. Sample copy for $1.50 with 9½×11 SAE and four 34¢ stamps.

Payment/Terms: Pays 10-13¢/word. Pays on acceptance for all rights.

Advice: "The *Friend* is particularly interested in stories with substance for tiny tots. Stories should focus on character-building qualities and should be wholesome without moralizing or preaching. Boys and girls resolving conflicts is a theme of particular merit. Since the magazine is circulated worldwide, the *Friend* is interested in stories and articles with universal settings, conflicts and characters. Other suggestions include rebus, picture, holiday, sports, and photo stories, or manuscripts that portray various cultures. Very short pieces (up to 250 words) are desired for younger readers and preschool children. Appropriate humor is a constant need."

☑ $ ◻ **GOLF JOURNAL,** United States Golf Assoc., Golf House, P.O. Box 708, Far Hills NJ 07931-0708. (908)470-5016. Fax: (908)781-1112. E-mail: golfjournal@usga.org. Website: www.usga.org (includes excerpts from publication). **Contact:** Catherine Wolf, managing editor. Editor: Brett Avery. Magazine: 48-56 pages; self cover stock; illustrations; photos. "The magazine's subject is golf—its history, lore, rules, equipment and general information. The focus is on amateur golf and those things applying to the millions of American golfers. Our audience is generally professional, highly literate and knowledgeable; they read *Golf Journal* because of an interest in the game, its traditions, and its noncommercial aspects." Published 9 times/year. Estab. 1948. Circ. 750,000.

Needs: Poignant or humorous essays and short stories. "Golf jokes will not be used." Accepts 6 mss/year. Recently published work by Don Marquis and J.G. Nursall. Length: 1,000-2,000 words.

How to Contact: Send complete ms with SASE. Responds in 2 months to mss. Sample copy for SASE.

Payment/Terms: Pays $500-1,500 and 5 contributor's copies. Pays on acceptance.

Advice: "Know your subject (golf); familiarize yourself first with the publication." Rejects mss because "fiction usually does not often serve the function of *Golf Journal*, which, as the official magazine of the United States Golf Association, deals chiefly with the history, lore and rules of golf."

$ **GOOD HOUSEKEEPING,** 959 Eighth Ave., New York NY 10019. **Contact:** Fiction Editor. "It is now our policy that all submissions of unsolicited fiction received in our offices will be read and, if found to be unsuitable for us, destroyed by recycling. If you wish to introduce your work to us, you will be submitting material that will not be critiqued or returned. The odds are long that we will contact you to inquire about publishing your submission or to invite you to correspond with us directly, so please be sure before you take the time and expense to submit it that it is our type of material."

Advice: "We welcome short fiction submissions (1,000-3,000 words). We look for stories with strong emotional interest—stories revolving around, for example, courtship, romance, marriage, family, friendships, personal growth, coming of age. The best way to gauge whether your story might be appropriate for us is to read the fiction in several of our recent issues. (We are sorry but we cannot furnish sample copies of the magazine.) We prefer double-spaced, typewritten (or keyboarded) manuscripts, accompanied by a short cover letter listing any previous writing credits. (We're sorry, but no e-mailed or faxed submissions will be accepted.) Make sure that your name and address appear on the manuscript and that you retain a copy for yourself."

☑ $ ◻ **GRIT, American Life & Traditions,** Ogden Publications, Inc., 1503 S.W. 42nd St., Topeka KS 66609-1265. (785)274-4300. Fax: (785)274-4305. E-mail: grit@cjnetworks.com. Website: www.grit.com (includes cover story from current issue plus titles of other features and book and products store). **Contact:** Peggy Mooney, fiction editor. Note on envelope: Attn: Fiction Department. Tabloid: 50 pages; 30 lb. newsprint; illustrations; photos. "*Grit* is a 'good news' publication and has been since 1882. Fiction should be 1,200 words or more and interesting, inspiring, perhaps compelling in nature. Audience is *conservative*; readers tend to be 40+ from smaller towns, rural areas who love to read." Biweekly. Estab. 1882. Circ. 200,000.

● *Grit* is considered one of the leading family-oriented publications.

Needs: Adventure, nostalgia, condensed novelette, mainstream/contemporary (conservative), mystery/suspense, light religious/inspirational, romance (contemporary, historical), science fiction, westerns (frontier, traditional). "No sex, violence, drugs, obscene words, abuse, alcohol, or negative diatribes." Upcoming themes: "Gardening" (January/February); "Love & Romance (February); "Presenting the Harvest" (June); "Health Issue" (September); "Home for the Holidays" (November); "Christmas Theme" (December); special storytellers issue (5-6 mss needed; submit in June). Buys 1 mss/issue; 30 mss/year. **Publishes 20-25 new writers/year.** Recently published work by John Floyd, Dede Hammond, Genevieve White and Don White. Length: 1,200 words minimum; 4,000-6,000 words maximum for serials; average length: 1,500 words. Also publishes poetry.

How To Contact: Send complete ms with cover letter. Include estimated word count, brief bio, Social Security number, list of publications with submission. Send SASE for return of ms. No simultaneous submissions. Sample copy for $4 postage/appropriate SASE. No e-mail submissions. Accepts fax submissions.

Payment/Terms: Pays up to 22¢/word. Purchases first North American serial or one-time rights.
Advice: Looks for "well-written, fast-paced adventures, lessons of life, wholesome stories with heart. Especially need serials with cliffhangers. Prefer western, historical with romantic interest and mysteries."

N $ © ⊻ HADASSAH MAGAZINE, 50 W. 58th St., New York NY 10019. E-mail: hadamag@aol.com. Executive Editor: Alan M. Tigay. **Contact:** Zelda Shluker, managing editor. Jewish general interest magazine: 8½ × 11; 48-70 pages; coated and uncoated paper; slick, medium weight coated cover; drawings and cartoons; photos. Primarily concerned with Israel, the American Jewish community, Jewish communities around the world, Jewish women's issues and American current affairs. Monthly except combined June/July and August/September issues. Circ. 300,000.
• *Hadassah* has been nominated for a National Magazine Award and has received numerous Rockower Awards for Excellence in Jewish Journalism.
Needs: Ethnic (Jewish). Receives 20-25 unsolicited fiction mss each month. Published fiction by Joanne Greenberg, Anita Desai and Lori Ubell. Published new writers within the last year. Length: 1,500-2,000 words.
How to Contact: Query first with writing samples to Leah Funkelshteyh. Responds in 4 months to mss. "Not interested in multiple submissions or previously published articles." Must submit appropriate size SASE.
Payment/Terms: Pays $500 minimum on acceptance for first North American serial rights.
Advice: "Stories on a Jewish theme should be neither self-hating nor schmaltzy."

$ © HARPER'S MAGAZINE, 666 Broadway, 11th Floor, New York NY 10012. (212)420-5720. Website: www.harpers.org (includes submission guidelines). **Editor:** Lewis H. Lapham. Magazine: 8 × 10¾; 80 pages; illustrations. Magazine for well-educated, widely read and socially concerned readers, college-aged and older, those active in political and community affairs. Monthly. Circ. 218,000.
Needs: Contemporary and humor. Stories on contemporary life and its problems. Receives 600 unsolicited fiction mss/year. Accepts 12 mss/year. Recently published work by David Guterson, David Foster Wallace, Johnathan Franzen, Steven Millhauser, Lisa Roney, Rick Moody and Steven Dixon. Published new writers within the last year. First published David Foster Wallace. Length: 3,000-5,000 words.
How to Contact: Query to managing editor, or through agent. Responds in 6 weeks to queries.
Payment/Terms: Pays $1,000-2,000. Pays on acceptance for rights, which vary on each author materials and length. Sends galleys to author.

✓ $ HEMISPHERES, The Magazine of United Airlines, Pace Communications, 1301 Carolina St., Greensboro NC 27401. (336)378-6065. Fax: (336)275-2864. Website: www.hemispheresmagazine.com (includes mastheads, archived travel articles, information about Faux Faulkner and Imitation Hemingway contests). **Contact:** Lisa Fann, fiction editor and Shelby Bateman, senior editor. Magazine: 8 × 10; 190 pages; 45 lb. paper; 120 lb. West Vaco cover; illustrations; photos. "*Hemispheres* is an inflight magazine that interprets 'inflight' to be a mode of delivery rather than an editorial genre. As such, Hemispheres' task is to engage, intrigue and entertain its primary readers—an international, culturally diverse group of affluent, educated professionals and executives who frequently travel for business and pleasure on United Airlines. The magazine offers a global perspective and a focus on topics that cross borders as often as the people reading the magazine. That places our emphasis on ideas, concepts, and culture rather than products. We present that perspective in a fresh, artful and sophisticated graphic environment." Monthly. Estab. 1992. Circ. 500,000.
Needs: Ethnic/multicultural, historical, humor/satire, literary, mainstream, mystery/suspense, regional. Receives 30-40 unsolicited ms/month. Publishes 1 ms/issue; 12 mss/year. Publishes ms 4-6 months after acceptance. **Publishes 1 new writer/year.** Published work by Ray Bradbury, Caroline Koeppel, Robert Olen Butler, Frederick Waterman. Length: 1,000-3,500 words.
How to Contact: Send complete ms with cover letter. Include estimated word count, brief bio and list of publications. Responds in 2 months to queries and mss. Send disposable copy of ms and SASE for reply. Accepts multiple submissions. Sample copy for $7.50. Guidelines for SASE.
Payment/Terms: Varies by author. Pays by the word and in contributor's copies; additional copies $7.50. Buys first world rights. Sometimes sends galleys to author. Sponsors the Faux Faulkner and Imitation Hemingway competitions. Details on website.
Advice: "In our information-saturated, hyperlinked age, fiction is often viewed as a bit superfluous. It doesn't solve whatever problem we have this second, and so is often relegated to a position of entertainment—something enjoyable to be fit in around the more important aspects of life. But good fiction has much longer lasting value—it should entertain, certainly, but it should also cause us to reconsider, to look at things from another perspective, to mull over what's really important. It should encourage us to explore with new eyes the mysteries of life."

✓ $ © HIGHLIGHTS FOR CHILDREN, 803 Church St., Honesdale PA 18431-1895. (570)253-1080. Website: www.highlights.com/ (includes editorial guidelines, contact information and excerpts). Editor: Christine

French Clark. **Contact:** Marileta Robinson, senior editor. Magazine: 8½×11; 42 pages; uncoated paper; coated cover stock; illustrations; photos. Monthly. Circ. 2.8 million. Highlights publishes "general interest for children between the ages of 2 and 12. Our philosophy is 'fun with a purpose.' "

• *Highlights* is very supportive of writers. The magazine sponsors a contest and a workshop each year at Chautauqua (New York). Several authors published in *Highlights* have received SCBWI Magazine Merit Awards.

Needs: Juvenile (ages 2-12). Unusual stories appealing to both girls and boys; stories with good characterization, strong emotional appeal, vivid, full of action. "Need stories that begin with action rather than description, have strong plot, believable setting, suspense from start to finish." Length: 400-900 words for older readers; 100-400 for younger readers. No war, crime or violence. Receives 600-800 unsolicited fiction mss/month. Accepts 6-7 mss/issue. Also publishes rebus (picture) stories of 125 words or under for the 3- to 7-year-old child. **Publishes 30 new writers/year.** Recently published work by Eileen Spinelli, Toby Speed, Marilyn Kratz and Ruskin Bond. Comments on rejected mss occasionally, "especially when editors see possibilities in story."

How to Contact: Send complete ms with SASE and include a rough word count and cover letter "with any previous acceptances by our magazine; any other published work anywhere." Accepts multiple submissions. Responds in 2 months. Guidelines with SASE.

Payment/Terms: Pays $125 and up. Pays on acceptance for all rights. Sends galleys to author.

Advice: "We accept a story on its merit whether written by an unpublished or an experienced writer. Mss are rejected because of poor writing, lack of plot, trite or worn-out plot, or poor characterization. Children *like* stories and learn about life from stories. Children learn to become lifelong fiction readers by enjoying stories. Feel passion for your subject. Create vivid images. Write a child-centered story; leave adults in the background."

☑ $🖉 🖵 **ALFRED HITCHCOCK'S MYSTERY MAGAZINE,** Dell Magazines, 475 Park Ave. S., New York NY 10016. (212)686-7188. Website: www.themysteryplace.com (includes guidelines, stories, subscription forms and logic puzzles). **Contact:** Cathleen Jordan, editor. Mystery fiction magazine: 5¼×8⅜; 144 pages; 28 lb. newsprint paper; 60 lb. machine-/coated cover stock; illustrations; photos. Published 11 times/year, including 1 double issue. Estab. 1956.

• Stories published in *Alfred Hitchcock's Mystery Magazine* have won Edgar Awards for "Best Mystery Story of the Year," Shamus Awards for "Best Private Eye Story of the Year" and Robert L. Fish Awards for "Best First Mystery Short Story of the Year."

Needs: Mystery and detection (amateur sleuth, private eye, police procedural, suspense, etc.). No sensationalism. Number of mss/issue varies with length of mss. Length: up to 14,000 words. Recently published work by Joyce Carol Oates, Jeremiah Healy, Kathy Lynn Emerson and Joseph Hensen.

How to Contact: Send complete ms and SASE. Responds in 2 months. Guidelines for SASE. Sample issue for $5.

Payment/Terms: Pays 8¢/word. Pays on acceptance.

🅽 $🖉 ◎ **HORIZONS, The Magazine of Presbyterian Women**, 100 Witherspoon St., Louisville KY 40202-1396. (502)569-5688. Fax: (502)569-8085. E-mail: sdunne@ctr.pcusa.org. Website: www.pcusa.org/horizons/ (includes writer's guidelines, themes and deadlines, excerpts and staff contacts). **Contact:** Sharon Dunne, assistant editor. Magazine: 8×11; 40 pages; illustrations; photos. Magazine owned and operated by Presbyterian Women offering "information and inspiration for Presbyterian women by addressing current issues facing the church and the world." Bimonthly. Estab. 1988. Circ. 25,000.

Needs: Ethnic/multicultural, feminist, historical, humor/satire, literary, mainstream/contemporary, religious/inspirational, senior citizen/retirement, translations. "No sex/violence or romance." List of upcoming themes available for SASE. Receives 50 unsolicited mss/month. Accepts 1 ms/issue. Publishes ms 4 months after acceptance. **Publishes 10 new writers/year.** Recently published work by Charlotte Johnstone. Length: 800-1,200 words. Publishes short shorts. Length: 500 words. Also publishes literary essays, fiction and poetry. Sometimes comments on rejected mss.

How to Contact: Send complete ms with cover letter. Include estimated word count and Social Security number. Responds in 1 week to queries; 2 weeks to mss. SASE or send a disposable copy of ms. Accepts mss by e-mail, fax and disk. Accepts simultaneous and multiple submissions. Sample copy for 9×12 SAE. Guidelines for #10 SASE. Reviews novels and short story collections. Send books to Leah Bradley.

Payment/Terms: Pays $50/page and 2 contributor's copies on publication for all rights; additional copies for $2.50.

Advice: "We are most interested in stories or articles that focus on current issues—family life, the mission of the church, and the challenges of culture and society—from the perspective of women committed to Christ."

$🖉 **HUMPTY DUMPTY'S MAGAZINE,** Children's Better Health Institute, Box 567, 1100 Waterway Blvd., Indianapolis IN 46206. (317)636-8881. Fax: (317)684-8094. Website: www.humptydumptymag.org. **Con-**

tact: Nancy S. Axelrad, editor. Magazine: 7⅝×10⅛; 36 pages; 35 lb. paper; coated cover; illustrations; some photos. Children's magazine "seeking to encourage children, ages 4-6, in healthy lifestyle habits, especially good nutrition and fitness." Publishes 8 issues/year.

• The Children's Better Health Institute also publishes *Children's Digest, Children's Playmate, Jack and Jill* and *Turtle,* also listed in this section.

Needs: Juvenile health-related material. No inanimate talking objects, animal stories and science fiction. Wants more "health and fitness stories with a positive slant." Rhyming stories should flow easily with no contrived rhymes. Receives 100-200 unsolicited mss/month. Accepts 2-3 mss/issue. **Publishes 1-2 unpublished writers/ year.** Length: 300 words maximum.

How to Contact: Send complete ms with SASE. No queries. Responds in 3 months. Sample copy for $1.75. Editorial guidelines for SASE. Accepts multiple submissions.

Payment/Terms: Pays up to 22¢/word for stories plus 10 contributor's copies. Pays on publication for all rights. (One-time book rights returned when requested for specific publication.)

Advice: "In contemporary stories, characters should be up-to-date, with realistic dialogue. We're looking for health-related stories with unusual twists or surprise endings. We want to avoid stories and poems that 'preach.' We try to present the health material in a positive way, utilizing a light humorous approach wherever possible." Most rejected mss "are too wordy or not age appropriate."

$ ◎ HUSTLER BUSTY BEAUTIES, HG Publications, Inc., 8484 Wilshire Blvd., Suite 900, Beverly Hills CA 90211. (323)651-5400. **Contact:** N. Morgen Hagen, editor. Magazine: 8×11; 100 pages; 60 lb. paper; 80 lb. cover; illustrations; photos. "Adult entertainment and reading centered around large-breasted women for an over-18 audience, mostly male." Published 13 times/year. Estab. 1988. Circ. 150,000.

Needs: Adventure, erotica, fantasy, mystery/suspense. All must have erotic theme. Receives 25 unsolicited fiction mss/month. Accepts 1 ms/issue; 6-12 mss/year. Publishes mss 3-6 months after acceptance. Published work by Mike Dillon and H.H. Morris. Length: 1,000-2,000 words; 1,600 words preferred.

How to Contact: Query first. Then send complete ms with cover letter. Responds in 2 weeks to queries; 1 month to mss. SASE. Sample copy for $5. Guidelines free.

Payment/Terms: Pays $350-500 (fiction) and $50 (erotic letters). Pays on publication for all rights.

Advice: Looks for "1. plausible plot, well-defined characters, literary ingenuity; 2. hot sex scenes; 3. readable, coherent, grammatically sound prose."

☑ $ ◻ ◎ ☒ IN TOUCH FOR MEN, 13122 Saticoy St., North Hollywood CA 91605-3402. (818)764-2288. Fax: (800)637-0101. E-mail: info@intouchformen.com. Website: www.intouchformen.com (includes a retrospective of all back issues, hyperfiction, magazine and video sales sections, and other things of interest to our readers). **Contact:** Michael Jimenez, editor. Magazine: 8×10¾; 100 pages; glossy paper; coated cover; illustrations; photos. "*In Touch* is a gay adult publication which focuses on youth and takes a lighthearted approach to sexuality. We publish erotic fiction which portrays a positive view of homosexuality. We also publish two other magazines, *Indulge* and *Blackmale.*" Monthly. Estab. 1973. Circ. 70,000.

• *In Touch For Men* has had eleven stories published in *Fiction 3: Best Gay Erotica* in 2000.

Needs: Confession, gay erotica, romance (contemporary, historical). All characters must be over 18 years old. Stories must have an explicit erotic content. No heterosexual or internalized homophobic fiction. Accepts 7 mss/ month; 80 mss/year. Publishes ms 6 months after acceptance. **Publishes 20 new writers/year.** Recently published work by Barry Alexander, L.M. Ross, Roddy Martin and Derek Adams. Length: up to 3,500 words maximum; average length: 2,500 words. Sometimes comments on rejected mss and recommends other markets.

How to Contact: Send complete ms with cover letter, name, address and Social Security number. Accepts queries and mss by e-mail and fax (mss by permission only). Responds in 2 weeks to queries; 2 months to mss. SASE. Accepts simultaneous, multiple and reprint submissions, if from local publication. Accepts disk submissions (call before sending by modem). Sample copy for $6.95. Guidelines free. Reviews novels and short story collections.

Payment/Terms: Pays $25-75 (except on rare occasions for a longer piece). Pays on publication for one-time rights.

Advice: Publishes "primarily erotic material geared toward gay men. We sometimes run nonfiction or features about gay issues. I personally prefer (and accept) manuscripts that are not only erotic/hardcore, but show a developed story, plot and a concise ending (as opposed to just sexual vignettes that basically lead nowhere). If it has a little romance, too, that's even better. Emphasis still on the erotic, though. We now only use 'safe sex' depictions in fiction, hoping that it will prompt people to act responsibly. We have a new interest in experimental fiction as long as it does not violate the standards of the homoerotic genre. All fiction must conform to the basic rules of the genre. Beyond that, we look for inventive use of language, unique content, exciting themes and, on occasion, experimental structures or subversive issues. If you're writing for a genre, know that genre, but don't be afraid to twist things around just enough to stand out from the crowd. Our website is becoming increasingly important to us. We have our eyes open for interesting hyperfiction because we want people to keep returning to our site, hoping that they might subscribe to the magazine."

INDIAN LIFE MAGAZINE, Indian Life Ministries, P.O. Box 3765, RPO, Redwood Centre, Station B, Winnipeg, Manitoba R2W 3R6 Canada. (204)661-9333 or (800)665-9275 in Canada only. Fax: (204)661-3982. E-mail: jim.editor@indianlife.org. Website: www.indianlife.org. **Contact:** Jim Uttley, editor. Newspaper: 11×17 Tabloid; 24 pages; newsprint paper and cover stock; illustrations; full cover; photos. A nondenominational Christian newspaper written and read mostly by Native Americans. Bimonthly. Estab. 1979. Circ. 32,000.

● *Indian Life Magazine* has won several awards for "Higher Goals in Christian Journalism" and "Excellence" from the Evangelical Press Association. The magazine also won awards from the Native American Press Association.

Needs: Contemporary stories of Native Americans in everyday life. Ethnic (Indian), historical (general), juvenile, religious/inspirational, young adult/teen, native testimonies, Bible teaching articles. No erotic or stories of Native American spirituality. Upcoming themes: "TV and its effect on Native culture" and "Domestic Abuse." **Publishes 4 new writers/year.** Recently published work by Crying Wind and Helen Lieschid. Length: 1,000-1,200 words average.

How to Contact: Query letter preferred. Accepts submissions by e-mail, fax and disk. Accepts simultaneous submissions. Responds in 1 month to queries. Sample copy and guidelines for $2.50 and 8½×11 SAE.

Advice: "Keep it simple with an Indian viewpoint at about a ninth grade reading level. Read story out loud. Have someone else read it to you. If it doesn't come across smoothly and naturally, it needs work."

INSIDE, The Magazine of the Jewish Exponent, Jewish Federation, 2100 Arch St., Philadelphia PA 19103. (215)832-0797. (215)832-0745. E-mail: mledger@insidemagazine.com. **Editor-in-Chief:** Robert Leiter. Magazine: 88-144 pages; glossy paper; illustrations; photos. Aimed at middle- and upper-middle-class audience, Jewish-oriented articles and fiction. Quarterly. Estab. 1980. Circ. 60,000.

Needs: Contemporary, ethnic, humor/satire, literary and translations. No erotica. Receives approximately 10 unsolicited fiction mss/month. Buys 1-2 mss/year. Recently published work by Jennifer Moses. Published new writers within the last year. Length: 1,200-2,000 words; average length: 1,500 words. Occasionally comments on rejected mss.

How to Contact: Query first with clips of published work. Responds in 3 months to queries. SASE. Accepts simultaneous submissions. Sample copy for $5 and 9×12 SAE. Guidelines for SASE.

Payment/Terms: Pays $350. Pays on acceptance for first rights. Sometimes buys reprints. Sends galleys to author.

Advice: "Originality is what we're looking for. We're a longshot for fiction right now, but if something is outrageously good we'll publish it."

IRELAND'S OWN, 1 North Main St., Wexford, Ireland. **Contact:** Gerry Breen and Phil Murphy, editors. Weekly. Circ. 50,000. Publishes 2 stories/issue. "*Ireland's Own* is a homey family-oriented weekly magazine with a strong emphasis on the traditional values of Irish society. Short stories must be written in a straightforward nonexperimental manner with an Irish orientation." Length: 1,800-2,000 words. Pays £40-50 on publication. "Study and know the magazine's requirements, orientation and target market. Guidelines and copies sent out on request."

JACK AND JILL, The Children's Better Health Institute, P.O. Box 567, 1100 Waterway Blvd., Indianapolis IN 46206. (317)636-8881. **Contact:** Daniel Lee, editor. Children's magazine of articles, stories and activities, many with a health, safety, exercise or nutritional-oriented theme, ages 7-10 years. Monthly except January/February, April/May, July/August, October/November. Estab. 1938. Circ. 360,000.

● The Children's Better Health Institute also publishes *Children's Digest, Children's Playmate, Humpty Dumpty* and *Turtle*, listed in this section.

Needs: Science fiction, mystery, sports, adventure, historical fiction and humor. Health-related stories with a subtle lesson. Published new writers within the last year. Buys 30-35 mss/year. Length: 500-800 words.

How to Contact: Send complete ms with SASE. Responds in 3 months to mss. Sample copy for $1.75. Guidelines for SASE.

Payment/Terms: Pays up to 20¢/word on publication for all rights.

Advice: "Try to present health material in a positive—not a negative—light. Use humor and a light approach wherever possible without minimizing the seriousness of the subject. We need more humor and adventure stories."

N **$** ⊘ **KIDZ CHAT**®, 8121 Hamilton Ave., Cincinnati OH 45231-2396. (513)931-4050. **Editor:** Elaina Meyers. Magazine (Sunday school take-home paper): 5⅜ × 8⅜; 8 pages; Choctaw matte 45 lb. paper. "*Kidz Chat*® correlates with Standard Publishing's Middler Sunday school curriculum. Features tie into the theme of the Sunday school lesson each week." Weekly. Estab. 1999. Circ. 55,000.
 • *Kidz Chat*® is not accepting any unsolicited items at this time.

A 🔳 **LADIES' HOME JOURNAL**, Published by Meredith Corporation, 125 Park Ave., 20th Floor, New York NY 10017. (212)557-6600. Editor-in-Chief: Myrna Blyth. **Contact:** Shana Aborn, books/fiction editor. Managing Editor: Carolyn Noyes. Magazine: 190 pages; 34-38 lb. coated paper; 65 lb. coated cover; illustrations; photos.
 • *Ladies' Home Journal* has won several awards for journalism.
Needs: Book mss and short stories, *accepted only through an agent*. Return of unsolicited material cannot be guaranteed. Published work by Fay Weldon, Anita Shreve, Jane Shapiro and Anne Rivers Siddons. Length: approximately 2,000-2,500 words.
How to Contact: Send complete ms with cover letter (credits). Accepts simultaneous submissions. Publishes ms 4-12 months after acceptance.
Payment/Terms: Acquires First North American rights.
Advice: "Our readers like stories, especially those that have emotional impact. Stories about relationships between people—husband/wife—mother/son—seem to be subjects that can be explored effectively in short stories. Our readers' mail and surveys attest to this fact: Readers enjoy our fiction and are most keenly tuned to stories dealing with children. Fiction today is stronger than ever. Beginners can be optimistic; if they have talent, I do believe that talent will be discovered. It is best to read the magazine before submitting."

🌐 ✅ **$** **THE LADY**, 39-40 Bedford St., Strand, London WC2E 9ER England. Phone: (0207)379 4717. Fax: (0207)836 4620. **Contact:** Arline Usden, editor. Magazine. Weekly. Estab. 1885. Circ. 42,000. "A magazine for women over forty."
Needs: Family saga, feminist, historical, literary, mainstream, mystery/suspense (cozy), regional, romance (contemporary, gothic, historical, Regency, romantic suspense). "Looking for uplifting stories with a twist in the tale." Buys 1 ms/issue. **Publishes dozens of unpublished writers/year.** Recently published work by Rosemary Trollope and John Mortimer. Length: 2,000 words. Also publishes poetry.
How to Contact: Send complete ms with cover letter. Include estimated word count. Responds in 3 months to mss. SASE. Accepts multiple submissions.
Payment/Terms: Pays variable rate and 1 contributor's copy. Buys first British serial rights.

$ ⊘ ◎ 🔳 **LADYBUG**, Cricket Magazine Group, P.O. Box 300, Peru IL 61354. (815)224-6656. **Contact:** Marianne Carus, editor-in-chief. Editor: Paula Morrow. Magazine: 8 × 10; 36 pages plus 4-page pullout section; illustrations. "*Ladybug* publishes original stories and poems by the world's best children's authors. For young children, ages 2-6." Monthly. Estab. 1990. Circ. 125,000.
 • *Ladybug* has received the Parents Choice Award; the Golden Lamp Honor Award and the Golden Lamp Award from Ed Press, and Magazine Merit awards from the Society of Children's Book Writers and Illustrators.
Needs: Fantasy (children's), folk tales, humor, juvenile, picture stories, preschool, read-out-loud stories and realistic fiction. Length: 300-750 words preferred.
How to Contact: Send complete ms with cover letter. Include word count on ms (do not count title). Responds in 3 months. SASE. Accepts reprints are. Guidelines for #10 SASE or on website. Sample copy for $5. For guidelines *and* sample send 9 × 12 SAE (no stamps required) and $5.
Payment/Terms: Pays 25¢/word (less for reprints). Pays on publication for first publication rights or second serial (reprint) rights. For recurring features, pays flat fee and copyright becomes property of Cricket Magazine Group.
Advice: Looks for "well-written stories for preschoolers: age-appropriate, not condescending. We look for rich, evocative language and sense of joy or wonder."

$ ⬜ ◎ 🔳 **LIGUORIAN,** "A Leading Catholic Magazine," Liguori Publications, 1 Liguori Dr., Liguori MO 63057-9999. (800)464-2555. Fax: (800)325-9526. E-mail: aweinert@liguori.org. Website: www.ligouri.org (*Liguorian* magazine is part of Liguori Publications website. It includes condensed articles from present issue, writer's guidelines and subscription information.) **Contact:** Fr. Allan Weinert, CSSR, editor-in-chief. Magazine: 5 × 8½; 64 pages; b&w illustrations; photos. "*Liguorian* is a general interest magazine firmly committed to orthodox Catholic Christianity. Our effort is to inform and inspire, making spirituality accessible to our readers and assisting them in those matters most important to them—their families, their work, their own personal growth—as they live out their life in an ever-changing world." Monthly. Estab. 1913. Circ. 330,000.

• *Liguorian* received Catholic Press Association awards for 2001 including Third Place: Best Short Story ("Spinoza's Socks," by Mary Beth Leymaster).

Needs: Religious/inspirational, young adult and senior citizen/retirement (with moral Christian thrust), spiritual. "Stories submitted to *Liguorian* must have as their goal the lifting up of the reader to a higher Christian view of values and goals. We are not interested in contemporary works that lack purpose or are of questionable moral value." Receives approximately 25 unsolicited fiction mss/month. Accepts 12 mss/year. **Publishes 8-10 new writers/year.** Published work by Darlene Takarsh, Mary Beth Teymaster and Maeve Mullen Ellis. Length: 1,500-2,000 words preferred. Also publishes short shorts. Occasionally comments on rejected mss "if we feel the author is capable of giving us something we need even though this story did not suit us."

How to Contact: Send complete ms with SASE. Accepts disk submissions compatible with IBM, using a WordPerfect 5.1 program; prefers hard copy with disk submission. Accepts submissions by e-mail and fax. Responds in 3 months to mss. Sample copy and guidelines for #10 SASE.

Payment/Terms: Pays 10-12¢/word and 5 contributor's copies. Pays on acceptance for all rights. Offers 50% kill fee for assigned mss not published.

Advice: "First read several issues containing short stories. We look for originality and creative input in each story we read. Since most editors must wade through mounds of manuscripts each month, consideration for the editor requires that the market be studied, the manuscript be carefully presented and polished before submitting. Our publication uses only one story a month. Compare this with the 25 or more we receive over the transom each month. Also, many fiction mss are written without a specific goal or thrust, i.e., an interesting incident that goes nowhere is *not a story*. We believe fiction is a highly effective mode for transmitting the Christian message and also provides a good balance in an unusually heavy issue."

$ ⃠ ◎ LIVE, Assemblies of God, 1445 N. Boonville, Springfield MO 65802-1894. (417)862-2781. Fax: (417)862-6059. E-mail: rl-live@gph.org. Website: www.radiantlife.org (includes writer's guidelines, names of editors, short fiction and non-fiction and devotionals). **Contact:** Paul W. Smith, editor. "A take-home story paper distributed weekly in young adult/adult Sunday school classes. *Live* is a story paper primarily. Stories in both fiction and narrative style are welcome. Poems, first-person anecdotes and humor are used as fillers. The purpose of *Live* is to present in short story form realistic characters who utilize biblical principles. We hope to challenge readers to take risks for God and to resolve their problems scripturally." Weekly. Circ. 90,000.

Needs: Religious/inspirational prose, poem and spiritual. "Inner city, ethnic, racial settings." No controversial stories about such subjects as feminism, war or capital punishment. Accepts 2 mss/issue. **Publishes 75-100 new writers/year.** Recently published work by Carrie Darlington, Chris Williams, Melodie Wright and Dorothy B. Kidney. Length: 500-1,700 words.

How to Contact: Send complete ms. Accepts disk submissions. Accepts queries and submissions by e-mail and fax. Social Security number and word count must be included. Accepts simultaneous submissions. Responds in 6 weeks. Sample copy and guidelines for SASE.

Payment/Terms: Pays 10¢/word (first rights); 7¢/word (second rights). Pays on acceptance.

Advice: "Study our publication and write good, inspirational true to life or fiction stories that will encourage people to become all they can be as Christians. Stories should go somewhere! Action, not just thought—life; interaction, not just insights. Heroes and heroines, suspense and conflict. Avoid simplistic, pietistic conclusions, preachy, critical or moralizing. We don't accept science or Bible fiction. Stories should be encouraging, challenging, humorous. Even problem-centered stories should be upbeat." Reserves the right to change titles, abbreviate length and clarify flashbacks for publication.

Ⓝ $ ◎ ☯ LIVING LIGHT NEWS, Living Light Ministries, #200, 5306-89 St., Edmonton, Alberta T6E 5P9. (780)468-6397. Fax: (780)468-6872. E-mail: shine@livinglightnews.org. Website: www.livinglightnews.org (includes sample articles from current issues, archives of past articles, writer's guidelines and mission statement). **Contact:** Jeff Caporale. Newspaper: 11×17; 36 pages; newsprint; electrobrite cover; illustrations; photos. "Our publication is an evangelical Christian newspaper sharing the good news of Jesus Christ in a fresh and contemporary way for non-Christians. We only publish Christmas-related fiction in our special Christmas issue." Bimonthly. Estab. 1995. Circ. 22,000. Member, Evangelical Press Association.

• Received 1996 and 2000 Award of Excellence winner; 1998 and 1999 Award of Merit winner.

MARKET CONDITIONS are constantly changing! If you're still using this book and it is 2003 or later, buy the newest edition of *Novel & Short Story Writer's Market* at your favorite bookstore or order from Writer's Digest Books by calling 1-800-289-0963.

Needs: Religious (inspirational), Christmas fiction focusing on the true meaning of Christmas. Christmas deadline is November 1st. Receives 3-4 unsolicited mss/month. Accepts 5 mss/year. Published 2-6 months after acceptance. **Publishes 2-6 new writers/year.** Length: 400-1,800 words; average length: 700 words. Publishes short shorts. Average length: 700 words. Always comments on rejected mss.
How to Contact: Send complete ms with cover letter. Accepts mss by e-mail and disk. Include estimated word count, brief bio and list of publications with submissions. Responds in 1 month to queries; 2 months to mss. Send SASE (or IRC) in Canadian postage for return of ms or disposable copy of ms and #10 SASE for reply only. Accepts simultaneous, multiple and previously published submissions. Sample copy free with SASE (9 × 13; $2.50 in Canadian postage). Guidelines for SASE, e-mail or on website.
Payment/Terms: Pays 8¢ (US)/word and 2 contributor's copies; additional copies: $2.50. Pays on publication for first, first North American serial, one-time, electronic, second and reprint rights.
Advice: "We are looking for lively, humorous, inviting or heart-warming Christmas-related fiction that focuses on the non-materialistic side of Christmas or shares God's love and grace with others. Try to write with pizzazz. We get many bland submissions. Do not be afraid to use humor and have fun."

☑ $⌂ ▼ MAGAZINE OF FANTASY & SCIENCE FICTION, P.O. Box 3447, Hoboken NJ 07030-1605. Phone/fax: (201)876-2551. E-mail: gordonfsf@aol.com. Website: www.sfsmag.com or www.sfsite.com/fsf (includes writer's guidelines, letter column, subscription information, nonfiction features, current issue, information on back issues and links). **Contact:** Gordon Van Gelder, editor. Magazine: illustrations on cover only. Publishes science fiction and fantasy. "We aspire to publish science fiction and fantasy of the highest entertainment quality. Our readers are age 13 and up." Monthly. Estab. 1949. Circ. 50,000.
● *Magazine of Fantasy and Science Fiction* has won numerous Nebula awards and ranks #4 on the *Writer's Digest* Fiction 50 list of top markets for fiction writers.
Needs: Fantasy and science fiction. "We're always looking for more science fiction." Receives 500-700 unsolicited fiction submissions/month. Buys 8 fiction mss/issue ("on average"); 100-120 mss/year. Time between acceptance and publication varies; up to 3 years. **Publishes 6-10 new writers/year.** Published work by Ray Bradbury, Ursula K. Le Guin, Joyce Carol Oates and Robert Sheckley. Length: 25,000 words maximum. Publishes short shorts. Comments on rejected ms, "if quality warrants it." Sometimes recommends other markets.
How to Contact: Send complete ms with cover letter. Responds in 1 month to queries; 2 months to mss. SASE (or IRC). Sample copy for $5. Guidelines for SASE.
Payment/Terms: Pays 5-8¢/word. Pays on acceptance for first North American serial rights; foreign, option on anthology if requested.
Terms: Pays on acceptance for first North American serial rights; foreign, option on anthology if requested.
Advice: "Our only real criterion for selecting fiction is how strongly it affects us when we read it. The manuscripts that stand out most are the ones that are prepared properly. Read a copy of the magazine first."

$⌂ ▼ MATURE LIVING, Lifeway Christian Resources of the Southern Baptist Convention, MSN 140, 127 Ninth Ave. North, Nashville TN 37234-0140. (615)251-2191. Fax: (615)251-5008. E-mail: matureliving@bssb.com. **Editor:** Al Shackleford. Magazine: 8½ × 11; 52 pages; non-glare paper; slick cover stock; full color illustrations; photos. "Our magazine is Christian in content and the material required is what would appeal to 55 and over age group: inspirational, informational, nostalgic, humorous. Our magazine is distributed mainly through churches (especially Southern Baptist churches) that buy the magazine in bulk and distribute it to members in this age group." Monthly. Estab. 1977. Circ. 360,000.
● *Mature Living* received the gold award in the 1998 National Mature Media Awards.
Needs: Humor, religious/inspirational and senior citizen/retirement. Avoid all types of pornography, drugs, liquor, horror, science fiction and stories demeaning to the elderly. Receives 10 mss/month. Buys 1-2 mss/issue. Publishes ms an average of 1 year after acceptance. Published work by Burndean N. Sheffy, Pearl E. Trigg, Joyce M. Sixberry; published new writers within the last year. Length: 800-1,200 words; prefers 1,000.
How to Contact: Send complete ms with SASE. "No queries please." Include estimated word count and Social Security number. Responds in 2 months. Sample copy for $1. Guidelines for SASE.
Payment/Terms: Pays $75 on acceptance; 3 contributor's copies. $1 charge for extras. First rights if requested.
Advice: Mss are rejected because they are too long or subject matter unsuitable. "Our readers seem to enjoy an occasional short piece of fiction. It must be believable, however, and present senior adults in a favorable light."

$⌂ ◎ MATURE YEARS, United Methodist Publishing House, 201 Eighth Ave. S., Nashville TN 37202. (615)749-6292. Fax: (615)749-6512. E-mail: matureyears@4mpublishing.org. **Contact:** Marvin W. Cropsey, editor. Magazine: 8½ × 11; 112 pages; illustrations; photos. Magazine "helps persons in and nearing retirement to appropriate the resources of the Christian faith as they seek to face the problems and opportunities related to aging." Quarterly. Estab. 1953.
Needs: Humor, intergenerational relationships, nostalgia, older adult issues, religious/inspirational, spiritual (for older adults). "We don't want anything poking fun at old age, saccharine stories or anything not for older adults.

Must show older adults (age 55 plus) in a positive manner." Accepts 1 ms/issue, 4 mss/year. Publishes ms 1 year after acceptance. Published work by Ann S. Gray, Betty Z. Walker and Vickie Elaine Legg. **Published new writers within the last year.** Length: 1,000-1,800 words.

How to Contact: Send complete ms with SASE and Social Security number. Accepts mss by e-mail (preferred). No simultaneous submissions. Responds in 2 months. Sample copy for 10½×11 SAE and $5.

Payment/Terms: Pays 6¢/word. Pays on acceptance.

Advice: "Practice writing dialogue! Listen to people talk; take notes; master dialogue writing! Not easy, but well worth it! Most inquiry letters are far too long. If you can't sell me an idea in a brief paragraph, you're not going to sell the reader on reading your finished article or story."

$ ⚫️ MESSENGER OF THE SACRED HEART, Apostleship of Prayer, 661 Greenwood Ave., Toronto, Ontario M4J 4B3 Canada. (416)466-1195. **Contact:** Rev. F.J. Power, S.J. and Alfred DeManche, editors. Magazine: 7×10; 32 pages; coated paper; self-cover; illustrations; photos. Magazine for "Canadian and U.S. Catholics interested in developing a life of prayer and spirituality; stresses the great value of our ordinary actions and lives." Monthly. Estab. 1891. Circ. 14,000.

Needs: Religious/inspirational. Stories about people, adventure, heroism, humor, drama. No poetry. Accepts 1 ms/issue. Length: 750-1,500 words. Recommends other markets.

How to Contact: Send complete ms with SAE. Rarely buys reprints. Responds in 1 month. Sample copy for $1.50 (Canadian).

Payment/Terms: Pays 6¢/word and 3 contributor's copies. Pays on acceptance for first North American serial rights.

Advice: "Develop a story that sustains interest to the end. Do not preach, but use plot and characters to convey the message or theme. Aim to move the heart as well as the mind. If you can, add a light touch or a sense of humor to the story. Your ending should have impact, leaving a moral or faith message for the reader."

$ ⚫️ ◎ MONTANA SENIOR NEWS, Barrett-Whitman Co., Box 3363, Great Falls MT 59403. (406)761-0305. Fax: (406)761-8358. E-mail: montsrnews@imt.net. **Contact:** Jack Love, editor. Tabloid: 11×17; 60-80 pages; newsprint paper and cover; illustrations; photos. Publishes "everything of interest to seniors, except most day-to-day political items like Social Security and topics covered in the daily news. Personal profiles of seniors, their lives, times and reminiscences." Bimonthly. Estab. 1984. Circ. 28,000.

Needs: Historical, senior citizen/retirement, western (historical or contemporary). No fiction "unrelated to experiences to which seniors can relate." Buys 1 or fewer mss/issue; 4-5 mss/year. Length: 500-800 words preferred. Publishes short stories. Length: 500-800 words.

How to Contact: Send complete ms with cover letter and phone number. Only responds to selected mss. Accepts simultaneous and reprint submissions. Accepts queries by e-mail. Sample copy for 9×12 SAE and $3 postage and handling.

Payment/Terms: Pays 5¢/word. Pays on publication for first rights or one-time rights.

☑ $ ◎ NA'AMAT WOMAN, Magazine of NA'AMAT USA, The Women's Labor Zionist Organization of America, 350 Fifth Ave., Suite 4700, New York NY 10118-3903. (212)563-5222. **Contact:** Judith A. Sokoloff, editor. "Magazine covering a wide variety of subjects of interest to the Jewish community—including political and social issues, arts, profiles; many articles about Israel; and women's issues. Fiction must have a Jewish theme. Readers are the American Jewish community." Published 4 times/year. Estab. 1926. Circ. 20,000.

Needs: Contemporary, ethnic, literary. Receives 10 unsolicited fiction mss/month. Accepts 3-5 fiction mss/year. Length: 1,500-3,000 words. Also buys nonfiction.

How to Contact: Query first or send complete ms with SASE. Responds in 3 months to mss. Free sample copy for 9×11½ SAE and $1.20 postage.

Payment/Terms: Pays 10¢/word and 2 contributor's copies. Pays on publication for first North American serial rights; assignments on work-for-hire basis.

Advice: "No maudlin nostalgia or romance; no hackneyed Jewish humor and no poetry."

N 🌐 $ ◎ NEW IMPACT, AnSer House of Marlow UK, Courtyard Offices, 3 High St., Marlow, Buckinghamshire SL7 3QR England. (44)01628 481581. Fax: (44)01628 475570. E-mail: info@anserhouse.co.uk. Website: www.anserhouse.co.uk (a leading forum for diversity issues from a minority perspective). **Contact:** Zulf Ali. Magazine: 60 pages; photos. "*AnSer House of Marlow UK* is the leading establishment in the United Kingdom for encouraging and developing good diversity practice. It publicly enhances diversity as opposed to the pejorative 'equal opportunity' because it assumes everyone is equal as a base. Our main mission is to raise the profile, value and achievements of visible culturally diverse communities in the UK; to advance the cause and practice of true diversity in British society; to encourage those with influence to value personal difference, and to work in partnership with the White majority to increase cultural understanding and mutual respect." Bimonthly. Estab. 1993. Circ. 10,000.

Needs: Ethnic/multicultural, fantasy. "No romance, mono-cultural, horror, science fiction or religious." Receives 15-30 unsolicited mss/month. Accepts 1 ms/issue; 6 mss/year. Publishes ms 4 months after acceptance. **Publishes 3 new writers/year.** Recently published work by Jesse Quinones, R.A. Bolden and Jeannete Dean. Length: 1,200-1,600 words; average length: 1,400 words. Publishes short shorts. Average length: 1,400 words. Also publishes poetry.

How to Contact: Send complete ms with a cover letter. Accepts submissions by e-mail. Include brief bio. Responds in 1 month to mss. Send SASE. Accepts simultaneous and multiple submissions. Sample copy free with SASE (A4 and $5 postage). Guidelines for SASE.

Payment/Terms: Pays $40-60 "only after second submission is published." Pays on publication for first rights.

Advice: "We select short stories according to individual appeal. Keep submissions between 1,200 and 1,400 words; possibly reflect personal or life experience; be appealing to diverse audience; not relating to romance, religious or horror themes."

$ ☑ NEW MYSTERY, The Best New Mystery Stories, 101 W. 23rd St., PH-1, New York NY 10011-7703. (212)353-1582. E-mail: editorial@newmystery.com. Website: www.NewMystery.com (includes book and film reviews, short shorts and investigative journalism). **Contact:** editor. Magazine: 8½×11; 96 pages; illustrations; photos. "Mystery, suspense and crime." Quarterly. Estab. 1990. Circ. 90,000.

● Fiction published in *New Mystery* has been nominated for Edgar, Blaggard, Shamus, Macavity and Anthony awards for best short story of the year. Response time for this magazine seems to be slower in summer months. The mystery included here is varied and realistic.

Needs: Mystery/suspense (cozy to hardboiled). No horror or romance. Wants more suspense and espionage. Plans special annual anthology. Receives 350 unsolicited mss/month. Buys 6-10 ms/issue. Agented fiction 50%. **Publishes 1 new writer/issue.** Published work by Stuart Kaminsky and Andrew Greeley. Length: 3,000-5,000 words preferred. Also buys short book reviews 500-3,000 words. Sometimes comments on rejected mss.

How to Contact: *New Mystery charges a $7 fee for purchase of a contributor's packet, which includes guidelines and 2 sample copies.* Send complete ms with cover letter. "We cannot be responsible for unsolicited manuscripts." Responds in 1 month to ms. SASE. Sample copy for $5, 9×12 SAE and 4 first-class stamps.

Payment/Terms: Pays $25-1,000. Pays on publication for negotiated rights.

Advice: Stories should have "believable characters in trouble; sympathetic lead; visual language." Sponsors "Annual First Story Contest."

$ ☑ THE NEW YORKER, The New Yorker, Inc., 4 Times Square, New York NY 10036. **Contact:** Fiction Department. A quality magazine of interesting, well-written stories, articles, essays and poems for a literate audience. Weekly. Estab. 1925. Circ. 750,000.

How to Contact: Send complete ms with SASE. Responds in 3 months to mss. Publishes 1 ms/issue.

Payment/Terms: Varies. Pays on acceptance.

Advice: "Be lively, original, not overly literary. Write what you want to write, not what you think the editor would like. Send poetry to Poetry Department."

$ ☑ ◎ NUGGET, Dugent Corp., 2201 W. Sample Rd., Building Q, Suite 4A, Pompano Beach FL 33073. (954)917-5820. **Contact:** Christopher James, editor-in-chief. A newsstand magazine designed to have erotic appeal for a fetish-oriented audience. Published 13 times a year. Estab. 1956. Circ. 100,000.

Needs: Offbeat, fetish-oriented material encompassing a variety of subjects (B&D, TV, TS, spanking, amputeeism, golden showers, infantalism, catfighting, etc.). Most of fiction includes several sex scenes. No fiction that concerns children or religious subjects. Accepts 2 mss/issue. Agented fiction 5%. Length: 2,000-3,500 words.

How to Contact: Send complete ms with SASE. Responds in 1 month. Sample copy for $5. Guidelines for legal-sized SASE.

Payment/Terms: Pays minimum $200 and 1 contributor's copy. Pays on publication for first rights.

Advice: "Keep in mind the nature of the publication, which is fetish erotica. Subject matter can vary, but we prefer fetish themes."

$ ODYSSEY, Adventures in Science, Cobblestone Publishing, Inc., 30 Grove St., Suite C, Peterborough NH 03458. (603)924-7209. **Contact:** Elizabeth E. Lindstrom, senior editor. Magazine. "Scientific accuracy, original approaches to the subject are primary concerns of the editors in choosing material. For 10-16 year olds." Monthly (except July and August). Estab. 1991. Circ. 30,000.

Needs: Material must match theme; send for theme list and deadlines. Children's/juvenile (10-16 years), "authentic historical and biographical fiction, science fiction, retold legends, etc., relating to theme." List of upcoming themes available for SASE. Length: 750-1,000 words.

How to Contact: Query first or query with clips of published work (if new to *Odyssey*). "Include estimated word count and a detailed 1-page outline explaining the information to be presented; an extensive bibliography of materials authors plan to use." Responds in several months. Send SASE for reply or send stamped postcard to find out if ms has been received. Sample copy for $4.50, 9×12 SAE and $1.05 postage. Guidelines for SASE.
Payment/Terms: Pays 20-25¢/word. Pays on publication for all rights.
Advice: "We also include in-depth nonfiction, plays and biographies."

N **$** **⊘** **ON THE LINE,** Mennonite Publishing House, 616 Walnut Ave., Scottdale PA 15683-1999. (724)887-8500. Website: www.mph.org (includes guidelines and general information). **Editor:** Mary Clemens Meyer. Magazine: 7×10; 28 pages; illustrations; some photos. "A Christian magazine with the goal of helping children grow in their understanding and appreciation of God, the created world, themselves and other people." For children ages 9-14. Weekly. Estab. 1970. Circ. 5,500.
Needs: Problem-solving stories with Christian values for older children and young teens (9-14 years). No fantasy or fictionalized Bible stories. Wants more mystery and humorous. Receives 50-100 unsolicited mss/ month. Accepts 52 mss/year. Recently published work by Judy Stoner, Karen L. Rempel-Arthur, Sandra Smith and Danielle Hammelef. **Publishes 10-20 new writers/year.** Length: 800-1,500 words.
How to Contact: Send complete ms noting whether author is offering first-time or reprint rights. Responds in 1 month. SASE. Accepts simultaneous and previously published work. Free sample copy and guidelines.
Payment/Terms: Pays on acceptance for one-time rights.
Advice: "We believe in the power of story to entertain, inspire and challenge the reader to new growth. Know children and their thoughts, feelings and interests. Be realistic with characters and events in the fiction. Stories do not need to be true, but need to *feel* true. We look for easy readibility, realistic kids and grownups, humor, fun characters and plot movement without excessive description. Watch kids, interact with kids, listen to kids. It will show up in your writing."

✓ **$** **⊘** **◎** **OPTIONS, The *Bi*-Monthly,** AJA Publishing, Box 170, Irvington NY 10533. (914)591-2011. E-mail: dianaeditr@aol.com. Website: www.youngandtight.com/men (includes short fiction). **Contact:** Diana Sheridan, associate editor. Magazine: digest-sized; 114 pages; newsprint paper; glossy cover stock; illustrations; photos. Sexually explicit magazine for and about bisexuals. "Please read our Advice subhead." 10 issues/year. Estab. 1982. Circ. 100,000.
Needs: Erotica, bisexual, gay, lesbian. "First person as-if-true experiences." Accepts 6 unsolicited fiction mss/ issue. "Very little" of fiction is agented. **Published new writers within the last year.** Length: 2,000-3,000 words. Sometimes comments on rejected mss.
How to Contact: Send complete ms with or without cover letter. Responds in 3 weeks. SASE. Accepts ms e-mail and disk. Sample copy for $2.95 and 6×9 SAE with 5 first-class stamps. Guidelines for SASE. Accepts multiple submissions, "but discouraged."
Payment/Terms: Pays $100 for mss that arrive in readable electronic format; $80 for hardcopy only mss. Pays on publication for all rights. Will reassign book rights on request.
Advice: "Read a copy of *Options* carefully and look at our spec sheet before writing anything for us. That's not new advice, but to judge from some of what we get in the mail, it's necessary to repeat. We only buy two bi/ lesbian pieces per issue; need is greater for bi/gay male mss. Though we're a bi rather than gay magazine, the emphasis is on same-sex relationships. If the readers want to read about a male/female couple, they'll buy another magazine. Gay male stories sent to *Options* will also be considered for publication in *Beau*, or one of our other gay male magazines. Must get into the hot action by 1,000 words into the story. (Sooner is fine too!) *Most important:* We *only* publish male/male stories that feature 'safe sex' practices unless the story is clearly something that took place pre-AIDS."

$ **♡** **PLAYBOY MAGAZINE,** 680 N. Lake Shore Dr., Chicago IL 60611. (312)751-8000. **Contact:** Fiction Editor. Monthly magazine. "As the world's largest general-interest lifestyle magazine for men, *Playboy* spans the spectrum of contemporary men's passions. From hard-hitting investigative journalism to light-hearted humor, the latest in fashion and personal technology to the cutting edge of the popular culture, *Playboy* is and always has been both guidebook and dream book for generations of American men . . . the definitive source of information and ideas for over 10 million readers each month. In addition, *Playboy*'s 'Interview' and '20 Questions' present profiles of politicians, athletes and today's hottest personalities." Estab. 1953, Circ. 3,283,000.
How to Contact: Query first. "Fiction manuscripts must be no longer than 7,500 words for acceptance." Send SASE for guidelines.
Advice: "*Playboy* does not consider poetry, plays, story outlines or novel-length manuscripts."

$ **⊘** **▼** **POCKETS, Devotional Magazine for Children,** The Upper Room, 1908 Grand Ave., Box 340004, Nashville TN 37203-0004. (615)340-7333. Fax: (615)340-7267. E-mail: pockets@upperroom.org. Web-site: www.upperroom.org/pockets (includes themes, guidelines and contest guidelines). **Editor:** Janet R. Knight.

Contact: Lynn W. Gilliam, associate editor. Editorial Assistant: Patricia McIntyre. Magazine: 7×9; 48 pages; 50 lb. white econowrite paper; 80 lb. white coated, heavy cover stock; color and 2-color illustrations; some photos. Magazine for children ages 6-12. "The magazine offers stories, activities, prayers, poems—geared to giving children a better understanding of themselves as children of God." Published monthly except for January. Estab. 1981. Estimated circ. 99,000.

● *Pockets* has received honors from the Educational Press Association of America. The magazine's fiction tends to feature children dealing with real-life situations "from a faith perspective." *Pockets* ranked #15 on the *Writer's Digest* Fiction 50 list of top markets for fiction writers.

Needs: Adventure, contemporary, ethnic, historical (general), juvenile, religious/inspirational and suspense/mystery. No fantasy, science fiction, talking animals. "All submissions should address the broad theme of the magazine. Each issue is built around one theme with material which can be used by children in a variety of ways. Scripture stories, fiction, poetry, prayers, art, graphics, puzzles and activities are all included. Submissions do not need to be overtly religious. They should help children experience a Christian lifestyle that is not always a neatly-wrapped moral package, but is open to the continuing revelation of God's will. Seasonal material, both secular and liturgical, is desired. No violence, horror, sexual and racial stereotyping or fiction containing heavy moralizing." No dying grandparents (or with Alzheimer's). Receives approximately 200 unsolicited fiction mss/month. Accepts 4-5 mss/issue; 44-60 mss/year. **Publishes 15 new writers/year.** Length: 600-1,600 words; average length: 1,200 words.

How to Contact: Send complete ms with SASE. Accepts previously published submissions. Accepts multiple submissions. Responds in 1 month to mss. Publishes ms 1 year to 18 months after acceptance. Sample copy free with SAE and 4 first-class stamps. Guidelines and themes for SASE. "Strongly advise sending for themes or checking website before submitting."

Payment/Terms: Pays 14¢/word and 2-5 contributor's copies. Pays on acceptance for first North American serial rights.

Advice: "Listen to children as they talk with each other. Please send for a sample copy as well as guidelines and themes. Many manuscripts we receive are simply inappropriate. Each issue is theme-related. Please send for list of themes. New themes published in December of each year. Include SASE." Sponsors annual fiction writing contest. Deadline: Aug. 15. Send for guidelines. $1,000 award and publication.

☑ ⊘ PORTLAND MAGAZINE, Maine's City Magazine,, 578 Congress St., Portland ME 04101. (207)775-4339. Fax: (207)775-2334. E-mail: editor@portlandmonthly.com. Website: www.portlandmagazine .com. **Contact:** Colin Sargent, editor. Magazine: 56 pages; 60 lb. paper; 100 lb. cover stock; illustrations; photos. "City lifestyle magazine—fiction style, business, real estate, controversy, fashion, cuisine, interviews and art relating to the Maine area." Monthly. Estab. 1986. Circ. 100,000.

Needs: Contemporary, historical, literary. Receives 20 unsolicited fiction mss/month. Accepts 1 mss/issue; 10 mss/year. Publishes short shorts. **Publishes 50 new writers/year.** Recently published work by C.D.B Bryan and Sebastian Junger. Length: 3 double-spaced typed pages.

How to Contact: Query first. "Fiction below 700 words, please." Send complete ms with cover letter. Responds in 6 months. SASE. Accepts submissions by e-mail.

Payment/Terms: Pays on publication for first North American serial rights.

Advice: "We publish ambitious short fiction featuring everyone from Frederick Barthelme to newly discovered fiction by Edna St. Vincent Millay."

$ ⊘ PURPOSE, Mennonite Publishing House, 616 Walnut Ave., Scottdale PA 15683-1999. (724)887-8500. Fax: (724)887-3111. E-mail: horsch@mph.org. Website: www.mph.org (includes information about products, editors' names, guidelines). **Contact:** James E. Horsch, editor. Magazine: 5⅜×8⅜; 8 pages; illustrations; photos. "Magazine focuses on Christian discipleship—how to be a faithful Christian in the midst of everyday life situations. Uses personal story form to present models and examples to encourage Christians in living a life of faithful discipleship." Weekly. Estab. 1968. Circ. 11,500.

Needs: Historical, religious/inspirational. No militaristic/narrow patriotism or racism. Receives 100 unsolicited mss/month. Accepts 3 mss/issue; 140 mss/year. **Publishes 15 new writers/year.** Recently published work by Susan Miller Balzer, Karen O'Conner and David Faust. Length: 750 words maximum; average length: 500 words. Occasionally comments on rejected mss.

How to Contact: Send complete ms only. Responds in 2 months. Accepts simultaneous and multiple submissions as well as previously published work. Sample copy for 6×9 SAE and 2 first-class stamps. Guidelines free with sample copy only.

Payment/Terms: Pays up to 5¢/word for stories and 2 contributor's copies. Pays on acceptance for one-time rights.

Advice: Many stories are "situational—how to respond to dilemmas. Looking for first-person storylines. Write crisp, action moving, personal style, focused upon an individual, a group of people, or an organization. The story form is an excellent literary device to use in exploring discipleship issues. There are many issues to explore. Each writer brings a unique solution. The first two paragraphs are crucial in establishing the mood/issue to be resolved in the story. Work hard on developing these."

☑ $ ⊘ ☑ **ELLERY QUEEN'S MYSTERY MAGAZINE**, Dell Magazines, 475 Park Ave. S., New York NY 10016. (212)686-7188. Fax: (212)686-7414. E-mail: elleryqueen@dellmagazines.com. Website: www.themy steryplace.com (includes writer's guidelines, short fiction, book reviews and magazine's history and awards). **Contact:** Janet Hutchings, editor. Magazine: 5⅜×8½; 144 pages with special 240-page combined September/ October issue. Magazine for lovers of mystery fiction. Published 11 times/year. Estab. 1941. Circ. 500,000 readers.

● This publication ranked #3 on the *Writer's Digest* Fiction 50 list of top markets for fiction writers. *EQMM* has won numerous awards and sponsors its own award for best stories of the year, nominated by its readership.

Needs: "We accept only mystery, crime, suspense and detective fiction." No explicit sex or violence. Wants more classical whodunits. Receives approximately 400 unsolicited fiction mss each month. Accepts 10-15 mss/ issue. Publishes ms 6-12 months after acceptance. Agented fiction 50%. **Publishes 10 new writers/year.** Recently published work by Jeffrey Deaver and Joyce Carol Oates. Length: 3,000-10,000 words. Publishes minute mysteries of 250 words; novellas of 20,000 words from established authors. Critiques rejected mss "only when a story might be a possibility for us if revised." Sometimes recommends other markets.

How to Contact: Send complete ms with SASE. Cover letter should include publishing credits and brief biographical sketch. Accepts simultaneous and multiple submissions. Responds in 3 months to mss. Guidelines with SASE. Sample copy for $5.

Payment/Terms: Pays 5¢/word and up. Pays on acceptance for first North American serial rights. Occasionally buys reprints.

Advice: "We have a Department of First Stories and usually publish at least one first story an issue—i.e., the author's first published fiction. We select stories that are fresh and of the kind our readers have expressed a liking for. In writing a detective story, you must play fair with the reader, providing clues and necessary information. Otherwise you have a better chance of publishing if you avoid writing to formula."

$ ⊘ **RADIANCE, The Magazine for Large Women**, Box 30246, Oakland CA 94604. (510)482-0680. Website: www.radiancemagazine.com. Editor: Alice Ansfield. **Contact:** Alice Ansfield and Catherine Taylor, fiction editors. Magazine: 8½×11; 64 pages; glossy/coated paper; 70 lb. cover stock; illustrations; photos. "Theme is to encourage women to live fully now, whatever their body size. To stop waiting to live or feel good about themselves until they lose weight." Quarterly. Estab. 1984. Circ. 17,000. Readership: 80,000.

Needs: Adventure, contemporary, erotica, ethnic, fantasy, feminist, historical, humor/satire, mainstream, mystery/suspense, prose poem, science fiction, spiritual, sports, young adult/teen. "Want fiction to have a larger-bodied character; living in a positive, upbeat way. Our goal is to empower women." Receives 150 mss/month. Accepts 40 mss/year. Publishes ms within 1-2 years of acceptance. Published work by Marla Zarrow, Sallie Tisdale and Mary Kay Blakely. Publishes 15 new writers/year. Length: 1,000-5,000 words; average length: 2,000 words. Publishes short shorts. Sometimes comments on rejected mss.

How to Contact: Query with clips of published work and send complete ms with cover letter. Responds in 4 months. SASE. Accepts reprint submissions. Sample copy for $5. Guidelines for #10 SASE. Reviews novels and short story collections "with at least one large-size heroine."

Payment/Terms: Pays $35-100 and contributor's copies on publication for one-time rights. Sends galleys to the author if requested.

Advice: "Read our magazine before sending anything to us. Know what our philosophy and points of view are before sending a manuscript. Look around your community for inspiring, successful and unique large women doing things worth writing about. At this time, prefer fiction having to do with a larger woman (man, child). *Radiance* is one of the leading resources in the size-acceptance movement. Each issue profiles dynamic large women from all walks of life, along with articles on health, media, fashion and politics. Our audience is the 30 million American women who wear a size 16 or over. Feminist, emotionally-supportive, quarterly magazine."

$ ⊘ ☑ **RANGER RICK MAGAZINE**, National Wildlife Federation, 8925 Leesburg Pike, Vienna VA 22184. (703)790-4000. Editor: Gerald Bishop. **Contact:** Deborah Churchman, fiction editor. Magazine: 8×10; 40 pages; glossy paper; 60 lb. cover stock; illustrations; photos. "*Ranger Rick* emphasizes conservation and the enjoyment of nature through full-color photos and art, fiction and nonfiction articles, games and puzzles, and special columns. Our audience ranges in ages from 7-12, with the greatest number in the 7 and up. We aim for a fourth grade reading level. They read for fun and information." Monthly. Estab. 1967. Circ. 650,000.

● *Ranger Rick* has won several Ed Press awards. The editors say the magazine has had a backlog of stories recently, yet they would like to see more *good* mystery and science fiction stories (with nature themes).

Needs: Adventure, fantasy, humor, mystery (amateur sleuth), science fiction and sports. "Interesting stories for kids focusing directly on nature or related subjects. Fiction that carries a conservation message is always needed, as are adventure stories involving kids with nature or the outdoors. Moralistic 'lessons' taught children by parents or teachers are not accepted. Human qualities are attributed to animals only in our regular feature, 'Adventures of Ranger Rick.' " Receives about 150-200 unsolicited fiction mss each month. Accepts about 6 mss/year. Published fiction by Leslie Dendy. Length: 900 words maximum. Comments on rejected mss "when there is time."

How to Contact: Query with sample lead and any clips of published work with SASE. May consider simultaneous submissions. Very rarely buys reprints. Responds in 3 months to queries and mss. Publishes ms 8 months to 1 year after acceptance, but sometimes longer. Sample copy for $2. Guidelines for legal-sized SASE.

Payment/Terms: Pays $600 maximum/full-length ms. Pays on acceptance for all rights. Sends galleys to author.

Advice: "For our magazine, the writer needs to understand kids and that aspect of nature he or she is writing about—a difficult combination! Manuscripts are rejected because they are contrived and/or condescending—often overwritten. Some manuscripts are anthropomorphic, others are above our readers' level. We find that fiction stories help children understand the natural world and the environmental problems it faces. Beginning writers have a chance equal to that of established authors *provided* the quality is there. Would love to see more science fiction and fantasy, as well as mysteries."

REDBOOK, The Hearst Corporation, 224 W. 57th St., New York NY 10019. (212)649-2000. **Contact:** Fiction Editor. Magazine: 8 × 10¾; 150-250 pages; 34 lb. paper; 70 lb. cover; illustrations; photos. "*Redbook*'s readership consists of American women, ages 25-44. Most are well-educated, married, have children and also work outside the home." Monthly. Estab. 1903. Circ. 3,200,000.

Needs: Query. *Redbook* was not accepting unsolicited mss at the time of publication.

N $ THE REPORTER, WOMEN'S AMERICAN ORT, Women's American ORT, 315 Park Ave. S., New York NY 10010-3677. (212)505-7700. Fax: (212)674-3057. E-mail: editor@waort.org. Website: www.waort.org/ (includes excerpts and writer's guidelines). **Contact:** Marlene Heller, editor. Magazine: 8¼ × 10½; glossy; photographs. "Jewish women's issues; education, for membership." Quarterly. Estab. 1966. Circ. 60,000.

Needs: Condensed/excerpted novel, ethnic, feminist, humor/satire and literary. Receives 8 unsolicited mss/month. Buys 3 mss/year. Publishes ms 3 months after acceptance. **Publishes 4 new writers/year.** Length: 1,850 words. Possibly publishes short shorts.

How to Contact: Send complete ms with cover letter. Include Social Security number. Responds in 3 weeks. SASE. Sample copy for SASE and 3 first-class stamps. Accepts e-mail submissions. Accepts multiple submissions.

Payment/Terms: Varies. Starts at $200.

Terms: Pays within 60 days of publication for first North American serial rights.

Advice: "Fiction should be thought-provoking and have at least peripheral Jewish content. No Holocaust stories, please!"

$ ST. ANTHONY MESSENGER, 1615 Republic St., Cincinnati OH 45210-1298. (513)241-5615. Fax: (513)241-0399. E-mail: stanthony@americancatholic.org. Website: www.AmericanCatholic.org (includes Saint of the day, selected articles, product information). **Contact:** Father Jack Wintz, O.F.M., O.F.M., editor. Magazine: 8 × 10¾; 60 pages; illustrations; photos. "*St. Anthony Messenger* is a Catholic family magazine which aims to help its readers lead more fully human and Christian lives. We publish articles which report on a changing church and world, opinion pieces written from the perspective of Christian faith and values, personality profiles, and fiction which entertains and informs." Monthly. Estab. 1893. Circ. 340,000.

● This is a leading Catholic magazine, but has won awards for both religious and secular journalism and writing from the Catholic Press Association, the International Association of Business Communicators, the Society of Professional Journalists and the Cincinnati Editors Association.

Needs: Contemporary, religious/inspirational, romance, senior citizen/retirement and spiritual. "We do not want mawkishly sentimental or preachy fiction. Stories are most often rejected for poor plotting and characterization; bad dialogue—listen to how people talk; inadequate motivation. Many stories say nothing, are 'happenings' rather than stories." No fetal journals, no rewritten Bible stories. Receives 70-80 unsolicited fiction mss/month. Accepts 1 ms/issue; 12 mss/year. Publishes ms up to 1 year after acceptance. **Publishes 3 new writers/year.** Recently published work by Geraldine Marshall Gutfreund, John Salustri, Beth Dotson, Miriam Pollikatsikis and Joseph Pici. Length: 2,000-3,000 words. Comments on rejected mss "when there is time." Sometimes recommends other markets.

How to Contact: Send complete ms with SASE. Queries should usually come by regular mail, but will also accept them by e-mail and fax. Responds in 2 months. Sample copy and guidelines available. Reviews novels and short story collections. Send books to Barbara Beckwith, book review editor.

Payment/Terms: Pays 16¢/word maximum and 2 contributor's copies; $1 charge for extras. Pays on acceptance for first serial rights.

Advice: "We publish one story a month and we get up to 1,000 a year. Too many offer simplistic 'solutions' or answers. Pay attention to endings. Easy, simplistic, deus ex machina endings don't work. People have to feel characters in the stories are real and have a reason to care about them and what happens to them. Fiction entertains but can also convey a point and sound values."

☒ ☑ $ SATURDAY NIGHT, Saturday Night Magazine Ltd., 300-1450 Don Mills Rd., Don Mills, Ontario M3B 2X7 Canada. (416)386-2789. Fax: (416)386-2779. E-mail: editorial@saturdaynight.ca. Website: www.saturdaynight.ca/ (includes writer's guidelines, excerpts and web exclusives). Editor: Dianna Symonds. **Contact:** Lisa Rundle, assistant to the editor. Weekly magazine. Readership is urban concentrated. Well-educated, with a high disposable income. Average age is 43. Estab. 1887. Circ. 440,000.

Needs: Publishes contracted novel excerpts. **Publishes 10 new writers/year.** Recently published work by Margaret Atwood and John Le Carré.

How to Contact: Submit seasonal material 3-4 months in advance. Accepts mss by e-mail and fax. Accepts simultaneous and multiple submissions. Sample copy for $3.50. Writer's guidelines free.

Payment/Terms: Pays on receipt of a publishable ms. Buys first North American serial rights.

$ ☑ SEEK®, Standard Publishing, 8121 Hamilton Ave., Cincinnati OH 45231-2396. (513)931-4050. Fax: (513)931-4050. E-mail: ewilmoth@standardpub.com. Website: www.standardpub.com. **Contact:** Eileen H. Wilmoth, editor. Magazine: 5½×8½; 8 pages; newsprint paper; art and photos in each issue. "Inspirational stories of faith-in-action for Christian young adults; a Sunday School take-home paper." Weekly. Estab. 1970. Circ. 40,000.

Needs: Religious/inspirational. Accepts 150 mss/year. Publishes ms an average of 1 year after acceptance. **Publishes 20-30 new writers/year.** Length: 500-1,200 words.

How to Contact: Send complete ms with SASE. Accepts queries by mail, fax or e-mail. Accepts multiple submissions. Buys reprints. Responds in 3 months. Free sample copy and guidelines.

Payment/Terms: Pays 5¢/word on acceptance.

Advice: "Write a credible story with Christian slant—no preachments; avoid overworked themes such as joy in suffering, generation gaps, etc. Most manuscripts are rejected by us because of irrelevant topic or message, unrealistic story, or poor character and/or plot development. We use fiction stories that are believable."

☑ $ ☑ SEVENTEEN, Primedia Consumer Magazines, 850 Third Ave., New York NY 10022-6258. (212)407-9850. Fax: (212)407-9899. Website: www.seventeen.com. **Contact:** Darcy Jacobs, fiction editor. Magazine: 8½×11; 125-400 pages; 40 lb. coated paper; 80 lb. coated cover stock; illustrations; photos. A general interest magazine with fashion; beauty care; pertinent topics such as current issues, attitudes, experiences and concerns of teenagers. Monthly. Estab. 1944. Circ. 2.5 million.

● *Seventeen* sponsors an annual fiction contest for writers age 13-21.

Needs: High-quality literary fiction. No science fiction, action/adventure or pornography. Receives 200 unsolicited fiction mss/month. Accepts 6-9 mss/year. Agented fiction 50%. **Publishes 3 new writers/year.** Recently published work by Thisbe Nissen, Meg Cabot and David Schickler. Length: approximately 750-3,000 words.

How to Contact: Send complete ms with SASE and cover letter with relevant credits. Responds in 3 months to mss. Guidelines for submissions with SASE.

Payment/Terms: Pays $500-2,500 on acceptance for one-time rights.

Advice: "Respect the intelligence and sophistication of teenagers. *Seventeen* remains open to the surprise of new voices. Our commitment to publishing the work of new writers remains strong; we continue to read every submission we receive. We believe that good fiction can move the reader toward thoughtful examination of her own life as well as the lives of others—providing her ultimately with a fuller appreciation of what it means to be human. While stories that focus on female teenage experience continue to be of interest, the less obvious possibilities are equally welcome. We encourage writers to submit literary short stories concerning subjects that may not be immediately identifiable as 'teenage,' with narrative styles that are experimental and challenging. Too often, unsolicited submissions possess voices and themes condescending and unsophisticated. Also, writers hesitate to send stories to *Seventeen* that they think too risqué or sophisticated. Good writing holds the imaginable and then some, and if it doesn't find its home here, we're always grateful for the introduction to a writer's work. We're more inclined to publish cutting edge fiction than simple, young adult fiction."

☑ $ ☑ ☒ SHINE BRIGHTLY, (formerly *Touch*), GEMS (Girls Everywhere Meeting the Savior) Girls' Clubs, Box 7259, Grand Rapids MI 49510. (616)241-5616. Fax: (616)241-5558. E-mail: sara@gemsgc.org. Website: www.gospelcom.net/gems. Editor: Jan Boone. **Contact:** Sara Lynne Hilton, managing editor. Magazine:

8½ × 11; 24 pages; 50 lb. paper; 50 lb. cover stock; illustrations; photos. "Our purpose is to lead girls into a living relationship with Jesus Christ and to help them see how God is at work in their lives and the world around them. Puzzles, poetry, crafts, stories, articles, and club input for girls ages 9-14." Monthly. Circ. 16,000.

● *Touch* has received awards for fiction and illustration from the Evangelical Press Association.

Needs: Adventure, ethnic, juvenile and religious/inspirational. Write for upcoming themes. Each year has an overall theme and each month has a theme to fit with yearly themes. Receives 50 unsolicited fiction mss/month. Buys 3 mss/issue; 30 mss/year. **Published new writers within the last year.** Published work by A.J. Schut. Length: 400-1,000 words; average length: 800 words.

How to Contact: Send complete ms with 8 × 10 SASE. Cover letter with short description of the manuscript. Responds in 2 months. Accepts simultaneous and previously published submissions. Sample copy for 8 × 10 SASE. Free guidelines.

Payment/Terms: Pays 3-5¢/word. Pays on publication for simultaneous, first or second serial rights.

Advice: "Try new and refreshing approaches. The fluffy fiction with Polyanna endings. We want stories dealing with real issues facing girls today. The one-parent, new girl at school is a bit overdone in our market. We have been dealing with issues like AIDS, abuse, drugs, and family relationships in our stories—more awareness-type articles."

SOJOURNER, The Women's Forum, 42 Seaverns Ave., Jamaica Plain MA 02130. (617)524-0415. E-mail: info@sojourner.org. Website: www.sojourner.org. **Contact:** Amy Pett, editor. Magazine: 11 × 17; 48 pages; newsprint; illustrations; photos. "Feminist journal publishing interviews, nonfiction features, news, viewpoints, poetry, reviews (music, cinema, books) and fiction for women." Published monthly. Estab. 1975. Circ. 45,000.

Needs: "Writing on race, sex, class and queerness." Experimental, fantasy, feminist, lesbian, humor/satire, literary, prose poem and women's. Query for upcoming themes. Receives 20 unsolicited fiction mss/month. Accepts 10 mss/year. Agented fiction 10%. Published work by Ruth Ann Lonardelli and Janie Adams. Published new writers within the last year. Length: 1,000-4,000 words; average length: 2,500 words.

How to Contact: Send complete ms with SASE and cover letter with description of previous publications; current works. Accepts simultaneous submissions. Responds in 8 months. Publishes ms an average of 6 months after acceptance. Sample copy for $3 with 10 × 13 SASE. Guidelines for SASE.

Payment/Terms: Pays subscription to magazine and 2 contributor's copies, $15 for first rights. No extra charge up to 5 contributor's copies; $1 charge each thereafter.

Advice: "Pay attention to appearance of manuscript! Very difficult to wade through sloppily presented fiction, however good. Do write a cover letter. If not cute, it can't hurt and may help. Mention previous publication(s)."

SPIDER, The Magazine for Children, Carus Publishing Co./Cricket Magazine Group, P.O. Box 300, Peru IL 61354. (800)588-8585. Website: www.spidermag.com. **Contact:** Marianne Carus, editor-in-chief. Assistant Editor: Heather Delabre. Magazine: 8 × 10; 33 pages; illustrations; photos. "*Spider* publishes high-quality literature for beginning readers, mostly children ages 6 to 9." Monthly. Estab. 1994. Circ. 76,000.

● Carus Publishing also publishes *Cricket, Ladybug, Babybug* and *Cicada.*

Needs: Children's/juvenile (6-9 years), fantasy (children's fantasy), humor and folk tales. "No religious, didactic, or violent stories, or anything that talks down to children." Accepts 4 mss/issue. Publishes ms 2-3 years after acceptance. Agented fiction 2%. Published work by Lissa Rovetch, Ursula K. LeGuin and Eric Kimmel. Length: 300-1,000 words; average length: 775 words. Also publishes poetry. Often comments on rejected ms.

How to Contact: Send complete ms with a cover letter. Include exact word count. Responds in 3 months. Send SASE for return of ms. Accepts simultaneous and reprint submissions. Sample copy for $5. Guidelines for #10 SASE.

Payment/Terms: Pays 25¢/word and 2 contributor's copies; additional copies $2. Pays on publication for first rights or one-time rights.

Advice: "Read back issues of *Spider.*" Looks for "quality writing, good characterization, lively style, humor."

STANDARD, Nazarene International Headquarters, 6401 The Paseo, Kansas City MO 64131. (816)333-7000. Fax: (816)333-4439. E-mail: ssm@nazarene.org. Website: www.nazarene.org. **Contact:** Everett Leadingham, editor. Magazine: 8½ × 11; 8 pages; illustrations; photos. Inspirational reading for adults. Weekly. Estab. 1936. Circ. 165,000.

● *Standard* ranked #40 on the *Writer's Digest* Fiction 50 list of top markets for fiction writers.

INTERESTED IN A PARTICULAR GENRE? Check our sections for: **Mystery/Suspense**, page 91; **Romance**, page 105; **Science Fiction & Fantasy**, page 121.

Needs: "Looking for stories that show Christianity in action." Publishes ms 14-18 months after acceptance. **Published new writers within the last year.** Length: 500-1,200 words.

How to Contact: Send complete ms with name, address and phone number. Responds in 3 months to mss. SASE. Accepts simultaneous submissions but will pay only reprint rates. Sample copy and guidelines for SAE and 2 first-class stamps.

Payment/Terms: Pays 3½¢/word; 2¢/word (reprint). Pays on acceptance. Pays contributor's copies on publication.

☑ $◪ STORY FRIENDS, Mennonite Publishing House, 616 Walnut Ave., Scottdale PA 15683-1999. (724)887-8500. Fax: (724)887-3111. E-mail: rstutz@mph.org. Website: www.mph.org. **Contact:** Rose Mary Stutzman, editor; Susan Reith, assistant editor. A magazine which portrays Jesus as a friend and helper. Nonfiction and fiction for children 4-9 years of age. Monthly.

● The Mennonite Publishing House also published *On the Line*, *Purpose* and *With* magazines.

Needs: Juvenile. Stories of everyday experiences at home, in church, in school or at play, which provide models of Christian values. "Wants to see more fiction set in African-American, Latino or Hispanic settings. No stories about children and their grandparents or children and their elderly neighbors. I have more than enough." **Publishes 10-12 new writers/year.** Published work by Virginia Kroll and Lisa Harkrader. Length: 300-800 words.

How to Contact: Send complete ms with SASE. Seasonal or holiday material should be submitted 6 months in advance. Buys reprints. Free sample copy with SASE.

Payment/Terms: Pays 3-5¢/word. Pays on acceptance for one-time rights. Not copyrighted.

Advice: "I am buying more 500-word stories since we switched to a new format. It is important to include relationships, patterns of forgiveness, respect, honesty, trust and caring. Prefer exciting yet plausible short stories which offer varied settings, introduce children to wide ranges of friends and demonstrate joys, fears, temptations and successes of the readers. Read good children's literature, the classics, the Newberry winner and the Caldecott winners. Respect children you know and allow their resourcefulness and character to have a voice in your writing."

$◪ THE SUN, The Sun Publishing Company, Inc., 107 N. Roberson St., Chapel Hill NC 27516. (919)942-5282. Fax: (919)932-3101. Website: www.thesunmagazine.org (includes guidelines, staff list and order forms). **Contact:** Sy Safransky, editor. Magazine: 8½ × 11; 48 pages; offset paper; glossy cover stock; photos. "While we tend to favor personal writing, we're open to just about anything—even experimental writing, if it doesn't make us feel stupid. Surprise us; we often don't know what we'll like until we read it." Monthly. Estab. 1974. Circ. 50,000.

● *The Sun* ranked #36 on the *Writer's Digest* Fiction 50 list of top markets for fiction writers.

Needs: Open to all fiction. Receives approximately 500 unsolicited fiction mss each month. Accepts 2 ms/issue. **Publishes 4-6 new writers/year.** Published work by Poe Ballantine, Sybil Smith and Gillian Kendall. Length: 7,000 words maximum. Also publishes poetry.

How to Contact: Send complete ms with SASE. Responds in 3 months. Publishes ms an average of 6-12 months after acceptance. Sample copy for $5

Payment/Terms: Pays up to $500, 2 contributor's copies, and a complimentary one-year subscription. Pays on publication for one-time rights. Publishes reprints.

Tips: "We favor honest, personal writing with an intimate point of view."

Ⓝ $◪ ◎ SWANK MAGAZINE, Swank Publication, 210 Route 4 East, Suite 401, Paramus NJ 07652. Fax: (201)843-8636. **Contact:** Paul Gambino, editor. Magazine: 8½ × 11; 116 pages; 20 lb. paper; 60 lb. coated stock; illustrations; photos. "Men's sophisticated format. Sexually-oriented material. Our readers are after erotic material." Published 13 times a year. Estab. 1952. Circ. 350,000.

Needs: High-caliber erotica. "Fiction always has an erotic or other male-oriented theme; also eligible would be mystery or suspense with a very erotic scene. Also would like to see more humor. Writers should try to avoid the clichés of the genre." Receives approximately 80 unsolicited fiction mss each month. Accepts 1 ms/issue, 18 mss/year. **Published new writers within the last year.** Length: 1,500-2,750 words.

How to Contact: Send complete ms with SASE and cover letter, list previous publishing credits. Accepts electronic submissions. Responds in 3 weeks to mss. Sample copy for $5.95 with SASE.

Payment/Terms: Pays $300-500. Buys first North American serial rights. Offers 25% kill fee for assigned ms not published.

Advice: "Research the men's magazine market." Mss are rejected because of "typical, overly simple storylines and poor execution. We're looking for interesting stories—whether erotic in theme or not—that break the mold of the usual men's magazine fiction. We're not only just considering strict erotica. Mystery, adventure, etc. with erotica passages will be considered."

$ 🗗 **'TEEN MAGAZINE**, Petersen Publishing Co., 6420 Wilshire Blvd., Los Angeles CA 90048-5515. (213)782-2955. Fax: (213)782-2660. Website: www.teenmag.com. **Contact:** Tommi Lewis, editor. Magazine: 100-150 pages; 34 lb. paper; 60 lb. cover; illustrations; photos. "The magazine contains fashion, beauty and features for the young teenage girl. The median age of our readers is 16. Our success stems from our dealing with relevant issues teens face." Monthly. Estab. 1957. Circ. 1.1 million.

Needs: Adventure, humor, mystery, romance and young adult. Every story, whether romance, mystery, humor, etc., must be aimed at teenage girls. The protagonist should be a teenage girl. Subject matter should be appropriate for the average 15-year-old reader. No experimental, science fiction, fantasy or horror. Buys 1 ms/issue; 12 mss/ year. Generally publishes ms 3-5 months after acceptance. Length: 2,500-4,000 words. Publishes short shorts.

How to Contact: Send complete ms and short cover letter with SASE. Responds in 10 weeks to mss. Sample copy for $2.50. Guidelines for SASE.

Payment/Terms: Pays $500. Pays on acceptance for all rights.

Advice: "Try to find themes that suit the modern teen. We need innovative ways of looking at the age-old problems of young love, parental pressures, making friends, being left out, etc. Subject matter and vocabulary should be appropriate for an average 16-year-old reader. *'TEEN* would prefer to have romance balanced with a plot, re: a girl's inner development and search for self. Handwritten mss will not be read."

N 🗗 **TEEN VOICES, Because you're more than just a pretty face**, Women Express, Inc., 515 Washington St., Floor 6, Boston MA 02111-1759. (617)426-5505. Fax: (617)426-5577. E-mail: womenexpress@teenvoices.com. Website: www.teenvoices.com. **Contact:** Submissions Director. Magazine: 8⅜×10⅞; 48-64 pages; 50 lb. gloss; cover 70 lb. gloss with UV coat; illustrations; photos. "*Teen Voices* is an interactive, educational forum that challenges media images of women and serves as a vehicle of change, improving young women's social and economic status. *Teen Voices* is written by, for and about young women. Also provides a vehicle for mutual support between teens and adult women." Quarterly. Estab. 1990. Circ. 75,000. Member, Independent Press Association.

Needs: Adventure, children's/juvenile, comic/graphic novels, ethnic (general), experimental, family saga, fantasy, feminist, gay, humor/satire, lesbian, literary, mainstream, military/war, mystery/suspense, regional, religious, young adult/teen (easy-to-read). "*Teen Voices* only publishes submissions written by and for teen girls, ages 12-19. We will not publish anything written by a boy or an adult. Upcoming themes available online. Receives 1,000 unsolicited mss/month. Accepts 40 mss/issue; 160 mss/year. Published 4-5 months after acceptance. **Publishes 175 new writers/year.** Average length: 500 words. Publishes short shorts. Average length: 500 words. Also publishes literary essays and poetry. Sometimes comments on rejected mss.

How to Contact: Send complete ms with cover letter. Accepts mss by e-mail and fax. Include brief bio with submissions. Responds in 3 weeks. Send disposable copy of ms and #10 SASE for reply only. Accepts simultaneous, multiple and previously published submissions. Sample copy for $5. Guidelines for SASE, e-mail, fax, or on website.

Payment/Terms: Pays 5 contributor's copies; additional copies: $5. Acquires all rights.

Advice: "We try to publish as many teen girls as possible, especially those who don't normally have the opportunities and encouragement to write and be published. We also focus on issues that are not usually addressed in typical teen magazines, such as activism, teen pregnancy, cultural harmony, social justice, feminism, and empowerment. Write about what makes you think, what makes you angry, what makes you cry and what makes you laugh. Issues that are important to you, as a teen girl, are important to us at Teen Voices."

☑ $ 🗗 **TROIKA MAGAZINE, Wit, Wisdom, and Wherewithal**, Lone Tout Publications, Inc., P.O. Box 1006, Weston CT 06883. (203)319-0873. Fax: (203)319-0755. E-mail: submit@troikamagazine.com. Website: www.troikamagazine.com. **Contact:** Celia Meadow, editor. Magazine: 8⅛×10⅝; 100 pages; 45 lb. Expression paper; 100 lb. Warren cover; illustrations; photos. "Our general interest magazine is geared toward an audience aged 30-50 looking to balance a lifestyle of family, community and personal success." Quarterly. Estab. 1994. Circ. 100,000.

Needs: Humor/satire, literary, mainstream/contemporary. No genre, experimental or children's. List of upcoming themes available for SASE. Receives 200 unsolicited mss/month. Accepts 2-5 mss/issue; 8-20 mss/year. Publishes ms 3-6 months after acceptance. **Publishes 40-50 new writers/year.** Recently published work by Daniel Etessani, J.P. Maney and Olivia Goldsmith. Length: 2,000-3,000 words. Also publishes literary essays and literary criticism. Sometimes comments on rejected ms.

How to Contact: Send complete ms with a cover letter giving address, phone/fax number and e-mail address. Accepts queries/mss by e-mail. Include estimated word count, brief bio, SASE and list of publications with submission. Responds in 3 months. Send SASE for reply to query. Send a disposable copy of ms. Accepts simultaneous and electronic submissions. Sample copy for $5. Guidelines for #10 SASE, also at troikamagazine.com.

Payment/Terms: Pays $250 maximum. Pays on publication for first North American serial rights.

Tips: "What makes a manuscript stand out? An authentic voice, an original story, a strong narrative, a delight in language, a sharp eye for detail, a keen intelligence. But proper grammar and spelling don't hurt either."

☑ $ ⬭ **TURTLE MAGAZINE FOR PRESCHOOL KIDS,** Children's Better Health Institute, Benjamin Franklin Literary & Medical Society, Inc., Box 567, 1100 Waterway Blvd., Indianapolis IN 46206-0567. (317)636-8881. Fax: (317)684-8094. Website: www.turtlemag.com. **Contact:** Terry Harshman, editor. Magazine of picture stories and articles for preschool children 2-5 years old.

● The Children's Better Health Institute also publishes *Children's Digest, Children's Playmate, Jack and Jill* and *Humpty Dumpty,* also listed in this section.

Needs: Juvenile (preschool). Special emphasis on health, nutrition, exercise and safety. Also has need for "very simple science experiments, and simple food activities." Receives approximately 100 unsolicited fiction mss/month. **Publishes 16-20 new writers/year.** Recently published work by Eileen Spinelli, Valeri Gorbachev and Timothy LaBelle. Length: 100-300 words.

How to Contact: Send complete ms with SASE. No queries. Responds in 10 weeks. Send SASE for Editorial Guidelines. Accepts multiple submissions. Sample copy for $1.75.

Payment/Terms: Pays up to 22¢/word (approximate); varies for poetry and activities; includes 10 complimentary copies of issue in which work appears. Pays on publication for all rights.

Advice: "Become familiar with recent issues of the magazine and have a thorough understanding of the preschool child. You'll find we are catering more to our youngest readers, so think simply. Also, avoid being too heavy-handed with health-related material. First and foremost, health features should be fun! Because we have developed our own turtle character ('PokeyToes'), we are not interested in fiction stories featuring other turtles."

☑ $ ⬭ ◎ **WITH: The Magazine for Radical Christian Youth,** Faith & Life Resources, Box 347, Newton KS 67114-0347. (316)283-5100. Fax: (316)283-0454. E-mail: deliag@gcmc.org. Website: www.withonline.org/ (includes excerpts). **Contact:** Carol Duerksen, editor. Editorial Assistant: Delia Graber. Magazine: 8½×11; 32 pages; 60 lb. coated paper and cover; illustrations; photos. "Our purpose is to help teenagers understand the issues that impact them and to help them make choices that reflect Mennonite-Anabaptist understandings of living by the Spirit of Christ. We publish all types of material—fiction, nonfiction, teen personal experience, etc." Published 6 times/year. Estab. 1968. Circ. 6,100.

Needs: Contemporary, ethnic, humor/satire, mainstream, religious, young adult/teen (15-18 years). "We accept issue-oriented pieces as well as religious pieces. No religious fiction that gives 'pat' answers to serious situations." Would like to see more humor. List of upcoming themes available for SASE. Receives about 50 unsolicited mss/month. Accepts 1-2 mss/issue; 10-12 mss/year. Publishes ms up to 1 year after acceptance. **Publishes 1-3 new writers/year.** Recently published work by Steven James. Length: 400-2,000 words; 1,500 words preferred.

How to Contact: Send complete ms with cover letter, include short summary of author's credits and what rights they are selling. Responds in 2 months to mss. SASE. Accepts mss by e-mail and fax. Accepts simultaneous, multiple and reprint submissions. Sample copy for 9×12 SAE and $1.21 postage. Guidelines for #10 SASE.

Payment/Terms: Pays 4¢/word for reprints; 6¢/word for simultaneous rights (one-time rights to an unpublished story); 6-10¢/word for assigned stories (first rights). Supplies contributor's copies; charge for extras.

Advice: "Each story should make a single point that our readers will find helpful through applying it in their own lives. Request our theme list and detailed guidelines (enclose SASE). All our stories are theme-related, so writing to our themes greatly improves your odds."

Ⓝ ⊕ $ **WOMAN'S DAY,** 54-58 Park St., Sydney NSW 2000 Australia. Phone: 9282 8000. Fax: 9267 4360. E-mail: womansday@acp.com.au. **Contact:** Julie Redlich, fiction editor. Weekly. "Magazine for women of all ages (and the men in their lives enjoy it too)."

Needs: "*Woman's Day* looks for two types of short stories: first for Five Minute Fiction page around 650-850 words long; longer short stories, between 2,500 and 3,000 words in length, are used less frequently." **Publishes 25-30 new writers/year.** Recently published work by Jackie Collins, Fay Thompson and Isolde Martyn.

How to Contact: "Manuscripts should be typed with double spacing and sufficient margins on either side of the text for notes and editing. They should be sent to the Fiction Editor with SAE and IRC. We accept unsolicited manuscripts, but must point out that we receive around 100 of these in the fiction department each week, and obviously, are limited in the number we can accept." Accepts mss by e-mail and fax. Accepts multiple submissions.

Payment/Terms: Payment is usually about $300 (Australian) for the Five Minute Fiction, from $350 for longer stories. *Woman's Day* purchases the first Australian and New Zealand rights. After publication, these revert to the author.

Advice: "Study the market and submit manuscripts suitable for that publication."

■ $□ **WOMAN'S WORLD MAGAZINE, The Woman's Weekly**, 270 Sylvan Ave., Englewood Cliffs NJ 07632. E-mail: dearww@aol.com. **Fiction Editor:** Johnene Granger. Magazine; 9½×11; 54 pages. "We publish short romances and mini-mysteries for all women, ages 18-68." Weekly. Estab. 1980. Circ. 1.5 million.

Needs: Romance (contemporary), mystery. "We buy contemporary romances of 1,500 words. Stories must revolve around a compelling, true-to-life relationship dilemma; may feature a male or female protagonist, and may be written in either the first or third person. We are *not* interested in stories of life-or-death, or fluffy, fly-away style romances. No explicit sex or historic, foreign or science fiction settings. When we say romance, what we really mean is relationship, whether it's just beginning or is about to celebrate its 50th anniversary." Receives 2,500 unsolicited mss/month. Accepts 2 mss/issue; 104 mss/year. Publishes mss 2-3 months after acceptance. Published work by Linda S. Reilly, Linda Yellin and Tim Myers. Length: romances—1,500 words; mysteries—1,000 words.

How to Contact: Send complete ms, "double spaced and typed in number 12 font." Cover letter not necessary. Include name, address, phone number and fax on first page of mss. *No queries*. Responds in 8 months. SASE. Guidelines free.

Payment/Terms: Romances—$1,000, mysteries—$500. Pays on acceptance for first North American serial rights only.

Advice: "Familiarize yourself totally with our format and style. Read at least a year's worth of *Woman's World* fiction. Analyze and dissect it. Regarding romances, scrutinize them not only for content but tone, mood and sensibility."

▦ ◑ **WONDER TIME**, WordAction Publications, 6401 The Paseo, Kansas City MO 64131-1213. (816)333-7000. **Contact:** Pamela Smits, editor. Magazine: 8¼×11; 4 pages; self cover; color illustrations. Hand-out story paper published through WordAction Publications; stories follow outline of Sunday School lessons for 6-8 year-olds. Weekly. Circ. 45,000.

Needs: Religious/inspirational. Wants "family time activities and ideas." Stories must have first- to second-grade readability. Receives 50-75 unsolicited fiction mss/month. Accepts 1 ms/issue. **Publishes 20 new writers/ year.** Length: 100 words.

How to Contact: Send complete ms with SASE. Responds in 6 weeks. Sample copy and curriculum guide with SASE.

Payment/Terms: Pays on acceptance for all rights.

Advice: "Basic themes reappear regularly. Please write for a theme list. Ask for guidelines, sample copies, theme list before submitting."

⊕ ▼ **THE WORLD OF ENGLISH**, P.O. Box 1504, Beijing China. **Contact:** Yu-Lun Chen, chief editor. Monthly. Circ. 300,000.

• *The World of English* was named among the 100 Key National Social Periodicals for 2000-2001.

Needs: "We welcome contributions of short and pithy articles that would cater to the interest of our reading public, new and knowledgeable writings on technological finds, especially interesting stories and novels, etc."

How to Contact: Accepts mss by e-mail or fax.

Payment/Terms: "As our currency is regrettably inconvertible, we send copies of our magazines as the compensation for contributions."

Advice: "Aside from literary works, we put our emphasis on the provision of articles that cover various fields in order to help readers expand their vocabulary rapidly and enhance their reading level effectively, and concurrently to raise their level in writing. Another motive is to render assistance to those who, while learning English, are able also to enrich their knowledge and enlarge their field of vision."

$ ◑ ▼ **YANKEE MAGAZINE**, Yankee Publishing Inc., P.O. Box 520, Dublin NH 03444. (603)563-8111. Fax: (603)563-8252. E-mail: queries@yankeepub.com. **Editor: Jim Collins. Contact:** Editorial Assistant. Magazine: 6×9; 176 pages; glossy paper; 4-color glossy cover stock; illustrations; color photos. "Entertaining and informative New England regional on current issues, people, history, antiques and crafts for general reading audience." Published 10 times/year. Estab. 1935. Circ. 500,000.

• *Yankee* ranked #12 in the *Writer's Digest* Fiction 50 list of top markets for fiction writers.

Needs: Literary. Fiction is to be set in New England or compatible with the area. No religious/inspirational, formula fiction or stereotypical dialect, novels or novellas. Accepts 3-4 mss/year. Published work by Andre Dubus, H. L. Mountzoures and Fred Bonnie. Published new writers within the last year. Length: 2,500 words. Publishes short shorts.

How to Contact: Send complete ms with SASE and previous publications. "Cover letters are important if they provide relevant information: previous publications or awards; special courses taken; special references (e.g. 'William Shakespeare suggested I send this to you . . . .')" Accepts simultaneous submissions, "within reason." Responds in 2 months.

Payment/Terms: Pays $1,000. Pays on acceptance; rights negotiable. Makes "no changes without author consent." Supplies contributor copies; sends galleys to authors.

Advice: "Read previous ten stories in *Yankee* for style and content. Fiction must be realistic and reflect life as it is—complexities and ambiguities inherent. Our fiction adds to the 'complete menu'—the magazine includes many categories—humor, profiles, straight journalism, essays, etc. Listen to the advice of any editor who takes the time to write a personal letter. Go to workshops; get advice and other readings before sending story out cold."

✓ $ ⊘ ◎ **YOUNG SALVATIONIST**, The Salvation Army, P.O. Box 269, 615 Slaters Lane, Alexandria VA 22313. (703)684-5500. Fax: (703)684-5539. E-mail: ys@usn.salvationarmy.org. Website: www.warcry.com (includes selected articles, writer's guidelines and discussion forums). **Contact:** Lt. Col. Marlene Chase, editor-in-chief. Magazine: 8×11; 24 pages; illustrations; photos. Christian emphasis articles for youth members of The Salvation Army. 10 issues/year. Estab. 1984. Circ. 50,000.

Needs: Religious/inspirational, young adult/teen. No historical. Would like to see "contemporary, real-life stories that don't preach or talk down to readers." Receives 60 unsolicited mss/month. Buys 9-10 ms/issue; 90-100 mss/year. Publishes ms 3-4 months after acceptance. **Publishes 5 new writers/year.** Published work by Teresa Cleary and Betty Steele Everett. Length: 600-1,200 words; 1,000 words preferred. Publishes short shorts. Sometimes comments on rejected mss and recommends other markets.

How to Contact: Send complete ms. Accepts queries/mss by fax and e-mail. Responds in 2 weeks to queries; 1 month to mss. SASE. Accepts simultaneous and reprint submissions. Sample copy for 9×12 SAE and 3 first-class stamps. Guidelines and theme list for #10 SASE.

Payment/Terms: Pays 10-15¢/word for all rights, first rights, first North American serial rights and one-time rights; 10¢/word for reprint rights. Pays on acceptance.

Advice: "Don't write about your high school experience. Write about teens now. Know the magazine, its readers and its mission."

FOR EXPLANATIONS OF THESE SYMBOLS,
SEE THE INSIDE FRONT AND BACK COVERS OF THIS BOOK.

Book Publishers

In this section, you will find many of the "big-name" book publishers. Many of these publishers remain tough markets for new writers or for those whose work might be considered literary or experimental. Indeed, some only accept work from established authors, and then often only through an author's agent. Although having your novel published by one of the big commercial publishers listed in this section is difficult, it is not impossible. The trade magazine *Publishers Weekly* regularly features interviews with writers whose first novels are being released by top publishers. Many editors at large publishing houses find great satisfaction in publishing a writer's first novel.

Also listed here are "small presses" publishing four or more titles annually. Included among them are small and mid-size independent presses, university presses and other nonprofit publishers. Introducing new writers to the reading public has become an increasingly more important role of these smaller presses at a time when the large conglomerates are taking less chances on unknown writers. Many of the successful small presses listed in this section have built their reputations and their businesses in this way and have become known for publishing prize-winning fiction.

These smaller presses also tend to keep books in print longer than larger houses. And, since small presses publish a smaller number of books, each title is equally important to the publisher, and each is promoted in much the same way and with the same commitment. Editors also stay at small presses longer because they have more of a stake in the business—often they own the business. Many smaller book publishers are writers themselves and know first-hand the importance of a close editor-author or publisher-author relationship.

At the end of this section, we've included information on a number of "micropresses," small presses publishing three or fewer books per year.

TYPES OF BOOK PUBLISHERS

Large or small, the publishers in this section publish books "for the trade." That is, unlike textbook, technical or scholarly publishers, trade publishers publish books to be sold to the general consumer through bookstores, chain stores, or other retail outlets. Within the trade book field, however, there are a number of different types of books.

The easiest way to categorize books is by their physical appearance and the way they are marketed. Hardcover books are the more expensive editions of a book, sold through bookstores and carrying a price tag of around $20 and up. Trade paperbacks are soft-bound books, also sold mostly in bookstores, but they carry a more modest price tag of usually around $10 to $20. Today a lot of fiction is published in this form because it means a lower financial risk than hardcover.

Mass market paperbacks are another animal altogether. These are the smaller "pocket-size" books available at bookstores, grocery stores, drug stores, chain retail outlets, etc. Much genre or category fiction is published in this format. This area of the publishing industry is very open to the work of talented new writers who write in specific genres such as science fiction, romance and mystery.

At one time publishers could be easily identified and grouped by the type of books they do. Today, however, the lines between hardcover and paperback books are blurred. Many publishers known for publishing hardcover books also publish trade paperbacks and have paperback imprints. This enables them to offer established authors (and a very few lucky newcomers) hard-soft deals in which their book comes out in both versions. Thanks to the mergers of the past decade, too, the same company may own several hardcover and paperback subsidiaries and imprints, even though their editorial focuses may remain separate.

CHOOSING A BOOK PUBLISHER

In addition to checking the bookstores and libraries for books by publishers that interest you, you may want to refer to the Category Index at the back of this book to find publishers divided by specific subject categories. If you write genre fiction, check our new genre sections for lists of book publishers: (mystery, page 91; romance, page 105; science fiction/fantasy & horror, page 121). The subjects listed in the Indexes are general. Read individual listings to find which subcategories interest a publisher. For example, you will find several romance publishers listed in the For Romance Writers Section, but read the listings to find which type of romance is considered—gothic, contemporary, Regency or futuristic. See How to Use This Book to Publish Your Fiction for more on how to refine your list of potential markets.

The icons appearing before the names of the publishers will also help you in selecting a publisher. These codes are especially important in this section, because many of the publishing houses listed here require writers to submit through an agent. A ☑ icon identifies those that mostly publish established and agented authors, while a ☐ points to publishers most open to new writers. See the inside front and back covers of this book for a complete list and explanations of symbols used in this book.

IN THE LISTINGS

As with other sections in this book, we identify new listings with a 🅽 symbol. In this section, most with this symbol are not new publishers, but instead are established publishers who decided to list this year in the hope of finding promising new writers.

In addition to the 🅽 symbol indicating new listings, we include other symbols to help you in narrowing your search. English-speaking foreign markets are denoted by a 🌐 . The maple leaf symbol 🍁 identifies Canadian presses. If you are not a Canadian writer, but are interested in a Canadian press, check the listing carefully. Many small presses in Canada receive grants and other funds from their provincial or national government and are, therefore, restricted to publishing Canadian authors.

We continue to include editorial comments set off by a bullet (●) within listings. This is where we include information about any special requirements or circumstances that will help you know even more about the publisher's needs and policies. The 🏆 symbol identifies publishers who have recently received honors or awards for their books. And the 🅰 symbol indicates that a publisher accepts agented submissions only.

Each listing includes a summary of the editorial mission of the house, an overarching principle that ties together what they publish. Under the heading **Contact**: we list one or more editors, often with their specific area of expertise.

Book editors asked us again this year to emphasize the importance of paying close attention to the Needs and How to Contact subheads of listings for book publishers. Unlike magazine editors who want to see complete manuscripts of short stories, most of the book publishers listed here ask that writers send a query letter with an outline and/or synopsis and several chapters of their novel. The Business of Fiction Writing, beginning on page 70 of this book, outlines how to prepare work to submit directly to a publisher.

There are no subsidy book publishers listed in *Novel & Short Story Writer's Market*. By subsidy, we mean any arrangement in which the writer is expected to pay all or part of the cost of producing, distributing and marketing his book. We feel a writer should not be asked to share in any cost of turning his manuscript into a book. All the book publishers listed here told us that they *do not charge writers* for publishing their work. *If any of the publishers listed here ask you to pay any part of publishing or marketing your manuscript, please let us know.*

A NOTE ABOUT AGENTS

Many publishers are willing to look at unsolicited submissions, but most feel having an agent is to the writer's best advantage. In this section more than any other, you'll find a number of publishers who prefer submissions from agents. That's why we've included a section of agents open to submissions from fiction writers (page 139).

For listings of more agents and additional information on how to approach and deal with them, see the 2002 *Guide to Literary Agents*, published by Writer's Digest Books. Be wary of those who charge large sums of money for reading a manuscript. Reading fees do not guarantee representation. Think of an agent as a potential business partner and feel free to ask tough questions about his or her credentials, experience and business practices.

For More Information

Check out issues of *Publishers Weekly* for publishing industry trade news in the U.S. and around the world or *Quill & Quire* for book publishing news in the Canadian book industry.

For more small presses see the *International Directory of Little Magazines and Small Presses* published by Dustbooks (P.O. Box 100, Paradise CA 95967). To keep up with changes in the industry throughout the year, check issues of two small press trade publications: *Small Press Review* (also published by Dustbooks) and *Independent Publisher* (Jenkins Group, Inc., 121 E. Front St., Traverse City MI 49684).

ABSEY & CO., INC., 23011 Northcrest Dr., Spring TX 77389. (281)257-2340. Fax: (281)251-4676. E-mail: abseyandco@aol.com. Website: www.absey.com (includes authors, titles and descriptions, contact information). **Contact:** Edward E. Wilson, publisher. "We are interested in book-length fiction of literary merit with a firm intended audience." Publishes hardcover and paperback originals. Averages 6-10 titles/year. **Published 3-5 new writers within the last year.**
Needs: Juvenile, mainstream/contemporary, short story collections. Also publishes poetry. Published *Where I'm From*, by George Ella Lyon; and *Dragonfly*, by Alice McLerran.
How to Contact: Accepts unsolicited mss. Send query letter. Send SASE or IRC for return of ms. Does not accept e-mail submissions. Responds in 3 months to queries; 9 months to mss.
Terms: Pays royalties of 8-15% on wholesale price. Publishes ms 1 year after acceptance. Writer's guidelines for #10 SASE.
Advice: "Since we are a small, new press looking for good manuscripts with a firm intended audience, we tend to work closely and attentively with our authors. Many established authors who have been with the large New York houses have come to us to publish their work because we work closely with them."

ACADEMY CHICAGO PUBLISHERS, 363 W. Erie St., Chicago IL 60610. (312)751-7300. Website: www.academychicago.com (submission guidelines, catalog, press history). **Contact:** Anita Miller, senior editor. Estab. 1975. Midsize independent publisher. "In addition to publishing reprints of neglected classics, Academy Chicago publishes original trade fiction and nonfiction" in paperback and hardback.
 • *Cutter's Island*, by Vincent Panella placed in both the Foreward Magazine's Book of the Year contest and the 2000 Independent Publishers Awards.
Needs: Biography, history, academic and anthologies. Only the most unusual mysteries, no private-eyes or thrillers. No explicit sex or violence. Serious fiction, no romance/adventure. "We will consider historical fiction that is well researched. No science fiction/fantasy, no religious/inspirational, no how-to, no cookbooks. In general, we are very conscious of women's roles. We publish very few children's books." Recently published *The Sweep of the Second Hand*, by Dean Monti (first fiction); *Cutter's Island: Caesar in Captivity*, by Vincent Panella (first fiction, historical); *Death and Strudel*, by Dorothy and Sidney Rosen (mystery).
How to Contact: Does not accept unsolicited mss. Query with first three consecutive chapters, triple spaced. Include cover letter briefly describing the content of your work. Send SASE or IRC for return of ms. "Manuscripts without envelopes will be discarded. *Mailers* are a *must*."
Terms: Pays royalties of 5-10% on net; no advance. Publishes ms 18 months after acceptance. Sends galleys to author.

Advice: "At the moment we are swamped with manuscripts and anything under consideration can be under consideration for months."

ACE SCIENCE FICTION, Berkley Publishing Group, Imprint of Penguin Putnam Inc., 375 Hudson St., New York NY 10014. (212)366-2000. **Contact:** Susan Allison, editor-in-chief; Anne Sowards, assistant editor. Estab. 1948. Publishes paperback originals and reprints and 6-10 hardcovers per year. Number of titles: 6/month. Buys 85-95% agented fiction.

Needs: Science fiction and fantasy. No other genre accepted. No short stories. Published *Forever Peace*, by Joe Haldeman; *Neuromancer*, by William Gibson; *King Kelson's Bride*, by Katherine Kurtz.

How to Contact: Accepts unsolicited mss. Query with outline/synopsis and 3 sample chapters. Send SASE. No simultaneous submissions. Responds in 2 months minimum to mss. "Queries answered immediately if SASE enclosed." Publishes ms an average of 18 months after acceptance.

Terms: Standard for the field. Sends galleys to author.

Advice: "Good science fiction and fantasy are almost always written by people who have read and loved a lot of it. We are looking for knowledgeable science or magic, as well as sympathetic characters with recognizable motivation. We are looking for solid, well-plotted science fiction: good action adventure, well-researched hard science with good characterization and books that emphasize characterization without sacrificing plot. In fantasy we are looking for all types of work, from high fantasy to sword and sorcery." Submit fantasy and science fiction to Anne Sowards.

ADVENTURE BOOK PUBLISHERS, Durksen Enterprises Ltd., 3545-32 Ave. NE, #712, Calgary, Alberta T1Y 6M6 Canada. Phone/fax: (403)285-6844. E-mail: adventure@puzzlesbyshar.com. Website: www.puzzlesbyshar.com/adventurebooks/ (includes e-book sales with secure ordering, basic instructions for queries, FAQs, who and where we are, how we publish and all about e-books, including browsing samples). **Contact:** S. Durksen, editor. Estab. 1998. "Small, independent. e-books and some print versions (trade edition style). We are unique in that we are beginning to supply 'physical' e-books to bookstores." Publishes e-books (download and disk versions). **Published 20 new writers within the last year.** Plans 40 first novels in 2001. Averages 50 total titles, 45 fiction titles/year.

Needs: Adventure, children's/juvenile, fantasy (space fantasy, sword and sorcery), historical (general), humor/satire, military/war, mystery/suspense (amateur sleuth, cozy, police procedural, private eye/hardboiled), romance (contemporary, historical, romantic suspense), science fiction (hard science/technological, soft/sociological), thriller/espionage, western (frontier saga, traditional), young adult/teen (adventure, fantasy/science fiction, mystery/suspense, problem novels, romance, series, sports, western). Recently published *Wolfe's Pack*, by Robert M. Blacketer (adventure/military); *The Triumph Mine*, by AJ Lee (fiction); and *Blood Drops Through Time*, by Christine Westendorp (historical fiction/fantasy).

How to Contact: Does not accept unsolicited mss; returns mss "if adequate international postage and envelopes are provided." Query via e-mail with 1-2 page synopsis. Include estimated word count and brief bio. Responds in 3 weeks to queries; up to 6 months to mss. Accepts ms submissions "only by invitation and in accordance with guidelines given to those invited." Always comments on rejected mss.

Terms: Pays royalties of 20%. Does not send galleys to author. Publishes ms 7-10 months after acceptance. Writer's guidelines on website.

Advice: "Good stories can be told without excessive sex and violence graphically detailed for shock value only. We do not consider works of a pornographic, illegal or harmful nature. Preference is given to mainstream manuscripts as opposed to topics with time or issue limitations. Please take the time to proofread with a critical eye before submitting."

ADVOCACY PRESS, Box 236, Santa Barbara CA 93102-0236. (805)962-2728. Fax: (805)963-3508. E-mail: advpress@impulse.net. Website: www.advocacypress.com (includes book catalog, order form, mission statement). **Contact:** Curriculum Specialist. Estab. 1983. "We promote gender equity and positive self-esteem through our programs and publications." Small publisher. Publishes hardcover and paperback originals. Books: perfect or Smyth-sewn binding; illustrations. Average print order: 5,000-10,000. First novel print order: 5,000-10,000. Averages 3-5 total titles, 2 children's fiction titles/year. Promotes titles through catalogs, distributors, tradeshows, individuals, schools and bookstores.

● Advocacy Press books have won the Ben Franklin Award and the Friends of American Writers Award. The press also received the Eleanor Roosevelt Research and Development Award from the American Association of University Women for its significant contribution to equitable education.

Needs: Juvenile. Wants only gender equity/positive esteem messages to boys and girls—picture books; self-esteem issues. Published *Minou*, by Mindy Bingham (picture book); *Kylie's Song*, by Patty Sheehan (picture book); *Nature's Wonderful World in Rhyme*, by William Sheehan.

How to Contact: Accepts unsolicited mss. Submit complete manuscript with SASE for return. Accepts queries by e-mail and fax. Responds in 3 months to queries. Accepts simultaneous submissions.

Terms: Pays royalties of 5-10%. Book catalog for SASE.
Advice: Wants "stories for children that give messages of self-sufficiency/self esteem. Please review some of our publications *before* you submit to us. For layout and writing guidelines, we recommend that you read *The Children's Book: How to Write It, How to Sell It* by Ellen Roberts, Writers Digest Books. *Because of our limited focus, most of our titles have been written inhouse.*"

ALASKA NATIVE LANGUAGE CENTER, University of Alaska, P.O. Box 757680, Fairbanks AK 99775-7680. (907)474-7874. **Contact:** Tom Alton, editor. Estab. 1972. Small education publisher limited to books in and about Alaska native languages. Generally nonfiction. Publishes hardcover and paperback originals. Books: 60 lb. book paper; offset printing; perfect binding; photos, line art illustrations. Average print order: 500-1,000 copies. Averages 6-8 total titles/year.
Needs: Ethnic. Publishes original fiction only in native language and English by Alaska native writers. Published *A Practical Grammar of the Central Alaskan Yup'ik Eskimo Language*, by Steven A. Jacobson; *One Must Arrive With a Story to Tell*, by the Elders of Tununak, Alaska.
How to Contact: Does not accept unsolicited mss. Accepts electronic submissions via ASCII for modem transmissions or Macintosh compatible files on 3.5 disk.
Terms: Does not pay. Sends galleys to author.

ALGONQUIN BOOKS OF CHAPEL HILL, Subsidiary of Workman Publishing, P.O. Box 2225, Chapel Hill NC 27515-2225. Website: www.algonquin.com (includes catalog, submission guidelines, articles by authors, author's tour schedules). Averages 24 total titles/year.
Imprint(s): Front Porch Paperbacks.
 • Algonquin Books is not accepting unsolicited mss or queries at this time.

ALYSON PUBLICATIONS, INC., 6922 Hollywood Blvd., Suite 1000, Los Angeles CA 90028. (323)860-6065. Fax: (323)467-6805. Website: www.alyson.com (includes guidelines, calls for submissions, synopses of books and mission statement). **Contact:** Scott Brassart and Angela Brown, fiction editors. Estab. 1979. Medium-sized publisher specializing in lesbian- and gay-related material. Publishes paperback originals, reprints and some hardcover. Books: paper and printing varies; trade paper, perfect-bound. Average print order: 8,000. First novel print order: 6,000. **Published new writers within the last year.** Plans 50 total titles, 25 fiction titles/year.
Imprint(s): Alyson Wonderland, Advocate Books.
 • In addition to adult titles, Alyson Publications has been known for its line of young adult and children's books.
Needs: "We are interested in all categories; *all* materials must be geared toward lesbian and/or gay readers. No poetry." Recently published *Silk Road*, by Jane Summer; *Trailblazing*, by Eric Anderson; and *The New York Years*, by Felice Picano. Publishes anthologies. Authors may submit to them directly.
How to Contact: Query first with SASE. Responds in up to 3 months.

ANNICK PRESS LTD., 15 Patricia Ave., Willowdale, Ontario M2M 1H9 Canada. (416)221-4802. Publisher of children's books. Publishes hardcover and paperback originals. Books: offset paper; full-color offset printing; perfect and library bound; full-color illustrations. Average print order: 9,000. First novel print order: 7,000. Plans 18 first picture books this year. Averages approximately 25 titles each year, both fiction and nonfiction. Average first picture book print order 2,000 cloth, 12,000 paper copies. Distributes titles through Firefly Books Ltd.
Needs: Children's books only.
How to Contact: "Annick Press publishes only work by Canadian citizens or residents." Does not accept unsolicited mss. Query with SASE. Free book catalog. Occasionally critiques rejected mss.
Terms: No terms disclosed.

ARCADE PUBLISHING, 141 Fifth Ave., New York NY 10010. (212)475-2633. Fax: (212)353-8148. President, Editor-in-Chief: Richard Seaver. **Contact:** Richard Seaver, Jeannette Seaver, Cal Barksdale and Webster Younce. Estab. 1988. Independent publisher. Publishes hardcover originals and paperback reprints.

READ "THE BUSINESS OF FICTION WRITING" section for information on manuscript preparation, mailing tips, rights and more.

Books: 50-55 lb. paper; notch, perfect-bound; illustrations. Average print order: 10,000. First novel print order: 3,500-7,500. **Published new writers within the last year.** Averages 40 total titles, 12-15 fiction titles/year. Distributes titles through Time Warner Trade Publishing.

Needs: Literary, mainstream/contemporary, mystery/suspense, translations. No romance, science fiction, young adult. Published *Trying to Save Piggy Sneed*, by John Irving; *Europa*, by Tim Parks; *Dreams of My Russian Summers*, by Andrei Makine; *The Brush-Off*, by Shane Maloney; and *The Queen's Bastard*, by Robin Maxwell.

How to Contact: Does not accept unsolicited mss. Submit through an agent only. Agented fiction 100%. Responds in 2 weeks to queries; 4 months to mss.

Terms: Pays negotiable advances and royalties and 10 author's copies. Writer's guidelines and book catalog for SASE.

☑ ⊘ **ARCHWAY PAPERBACKS**, Imprint of Pocket Books for Young Readers, 1230 Avenue of the Americas, New York NY 10020. (800)223-2348. Website: www.simonsayskids.com. **Contact**: Patricia MacDonald, vice president/editorial director. Published by Pocket Books. Publishes paperback originals and reprints. **Published new writers within the last year.**

Imprint(s): Minstrel Books (ages 7-12); and Archway (ages 12 and up).

Needs: Young adult: horror, mystery, suspense/adventure, thrillers. Young readers (80 pages and up): adventure, animals, humor, family, fantasy, friends, mystery, school, etc. No picture books. Published *Fear Street: The New Boy*, by R.L. Stine; and *Aliens Ate My Homework*, by Bruce Coville.

How to Contact: Not accepting unsolicited mss.

Payment/Terms: Pays royalties of 6-8%. Publishes ms 2 years after acceptance.

☀ ☑ ⊘ ◎ **ARSENAL PULP PRESS**, 103-1014 Homer St., Vancouver, British Columbia V6B 2W9 Canada. (604)687-4233. Fax: (604)669-8250. E-mail: contact@arsenalpulp.com. Website: www.arsenalpulp.com (includes guidelines, ordering information, book catalog and publicity information). **Contact**: Linda Field, editor. Literary press. Publishes paperback originals. Average print order: 1,500-3,500. First novel print order: 1,500. **Published new writers within the last year.** Averages 12-15 total writers, 2 fiction writers/year. Distributes titles through Whitecap Books (Canada) and LPC Group/In Book (U.S.). Promotes titles through reviews, excerpts and print advertising.

• Arsenal Pulp Press has received 3 Alcuin Society Awards for Excellence in Book Design.

Needs: Ethnic/multicultural (general), feminist, gay, lesbian, literary, short story collections. No genre fiction, i.e. westerns, romance, horror, mystery, etc. Recently published *Flat*, by Mark Macdonald (fiction); and *Hot & Bothered 3*, by Karen X. Tulchinsky, editor (anthology, lesbian erotic fiction).

How to Contact: Accepts unsolicited mss. Query with cover letter, outline/synopsis and 2 sample chapters. Include list of publishing credits. Send SASE for return of ms or send disposable copy of ms and SASE for reply only. Agented fiction 10%. Responds in 1 month to queries; 4 months to mss. Accepts simultaneous submissions. Sometimes comments on rejected mss.

Terms: Pays royalties of 10%. Negotiable advance. Sends galleys to author. Publishes ms 1 year after acceptance. Writer's guidelines and book catalog free for 9 × 11 SASE.

Advice: "We very rarely publish American writers."

☑ ⊘ ◎ **ARTE PUBLICO PRESS**, University of Houston, 4800 Calhoun, Houston TX 77204-2174. (713)743-2841. Fax: (713)743-2847. Website: www.arte.uh.edu. **Contact**: Dr. Nicolás Kanellos, publisher. Estab. 1979. "Small press devoted to the publication of contemporary U.S.-Hispanic literature. Mostly trade paper; publishes 4-6 clothbound books/year. Publishes fiction and belles lettres." Publishes 36 paperback originals and occasionally reprints. Average print order 2,000-5,000. First novel print order 2,500-5,000.

Imprint(s): Piñata Books featuring children's and young adult literature by U.S.-Hispanic authors.

• Arte Publico Press is the oldest and largest publisher of Hispanic literature for children and adults in the United States.

Needs: Mainstream, contemporary, ethnic, literary, written by US-Hispanic authors. Published *Project Death*, by Richard Bertematti (novel/mystery); *A Perfect Silence*, by Alba Ambert; *Song of the Hummingbird*, by Graciela Limón; and *Little Havana Blues: A Cuban-American Literature Anthology*.

How to Contact: Accepts unsolicited mss. Query with outline/synopsis and sample chapters or complete ms with cover letter. Agented fiction 1%. Responds in 1 month to queries; 4 months to mss. Sometimes comments on rejected mss.

Terms: Pays royalties of 10% on wholesale price. Average advance: $1,000-3,000. Provides 20 author's copies; 40% discount on subsequent copies. Sends galleys to author. Publishes ms minimum 2 years after acceptance. Guidelines for SASE; book catalog free on request.

Advice: "Include cover letter in which you 'sell' your book—why should we publish the book, who will want to read it, why does it matter, etc."

☑ ◎ ⊘ ⊠ **ATHENEUM BOOKS FOR YOUNG READERS**, Simon & Schuster, 1230 Avenue of the Americas, New York NY 10022. (212)698-2715. Website: www.simonsayskids.com. **Contact**: Caitlyn Dlouhy, senior editor; Anne Schwartz, editorial director, Anne Schwartz Books. Second largest imprint of large publisher/corporation. Publishes hardcover originals. Books: illustrations for picture books, some illustrated short novels. Average print order: 6,000-7,500. First novel print order: 5,000. Averages 70 total titles, 25 middle grade and YA fiction titles/year.

- Books published by Atheneum Books for Children have received the Newbery Medal (*The View From Saturday*, by E.L. Konigsburg) and the Christopher Award (*The Gold Coin*, by Alma Flor Ada, illustrated by Neal Waldman).

Needs: Juvenile (adventure, animal, contemporary, fantasy, historical, sports, preschool/picture book), young adult/teen (fantasy/science fiction, historical, mystery, problem novels, sports, spy/adventure). No "paperback romance type" fiction. Published *The Century That Was*, by Giblin; *Horace and Morris But Mostly Dolores*, by Howe; and *Doodle Dandies*, by Lewis.

How to Contact: Does not accept unsolicited mss. Send query letter. Send SASE or IRC for return of the ms. Agented fiction 40%. Responds in 6 weeks to queries. Accepts simultaneous submissions "if we are so informed and author is unpublished."

Terms: Pays royalties of 10%. Average advance: $3,000. "Along with advance and royalties, authors receive ten free copies of their book and can purchase more at a special discount." Sends galleys to author. Writer's guidelines for #10 SASE.

Advice: "We have few specific needs except for books that are fresh, interesting, and well written. Again, fad topics are dangerous, as are works you haven't polished to the best of your ability. (The competition is fierce.) Other things we don't need at this time are safety pamphlets, ABC books, coloring books and board books. In writing picture books texts, avoid the copy and 'cutesy', such as stories about characters with alliterative names. Query letter for all submissions. We do not accept unsolicited manuscripts."

◙ **AVALON BOOKS**, Imprint of Thomas Bouregy Company, Inc., 160 Madison Ave., New York NY 10016. (212)598-0222. E-mail: editorial@avalonbooks.com. Website: www.avalonbooks.com. **Contact:** Erin Cartwright, senior editor; Mira Son, assistant editor. Publishes hardcover originals. **Published new writers within the last year.** Averages 60 titles/year. Distributes titles through Baker & Taylor, libraries, Barnes&Noble.com and Amazon.com. Promotes titles through *Library Journal*, Booklist and local papers.

Needs: "Avalon Books publishes wholesome romances, mysteries, westerns. Intended for family reading, our books are read by adults as well as teenagers and their characters are all adults. There is no graphic sex in any of our novels. Currently, we publish 10 books bimonthly: two contemporary romances, two historical romances, two career romances, two mysteries and two westerns. All westerns are historical." Published *A Golden Trail of Murder*, by John Paxson (mystery); *Renovating Love*, by Mary Leask (romance); *Shannon US Marshall*, by Charles Friend (western); and *Brooklyn Ballerina*, by Zelda Benjamin (career romance).

How to Contact: Does not accept unsolicited mss. Query with the first 3 chapters and a brief synopsis (2-3 pages). "We'll contact you if we're interested." Send SASE (ms size) or IRC for return of ms. Responds in about 4 months. "Send SASE for a copy of our writer's guidelines or visit our website www.avalonbooks.com."

Terms: The first half of the advance is paid upon signing of the contract; the second within 30 days after publication. Usually publishes ms within 6-8 months.

◙ **AVON BOOKS**, Imprint of HarperCollins, Children's Books Group, HarperCollins Publishers, 10 E. 53 St., New York NY 10022. (212)207-7000. Website: www.harpercollins.com. **Contact:** Michael Morrison, publisher. Estab. 1941. Large hardcover and paperback publisher. Publishes hardcover and paperback originals and reprints. Averages more than 400 titles a year.

Imprint(s): Avon, Avon EOS.

Needs: Literary fiction and nonfiction, health, history, mystery, science fiction, romance, young adult, pop culture.

How to Contact: Does not accept unsolicited mss. Send query letters only. SASE to insure response.

Terms: Vary.

◙ **AVON EOS,** Imprint of Avon Books, 1350 Avenue of the Americas, New York NY 10019. (212)261-6821. Fax: (212)261-6895. **Acquisitions:** Jennifer Brehl, executive editor. Diana Gill, associate editor. Imprint estab. 1998. Science fiction and fantasy imprint for serious readers. Imprint of major general trade publisher. Publishes trade hardcover, trade paperback (original and reprint), mass market paperback (original and reprint). Published new writers within the last year. Publishes 48 total titles/year, all fiction.

Needs: Fantasy, science fiction. Recently published *Ends of Days*, by Dennis Danvers; *Krondor: The Betrayal*, by Raymond E. Feist; and *Singer From the Sea*, by Sheri S. Tepper.

How to Contact: Send query with outline/synopsis and 3 sample chapters. Do not send full ms. Include estimated word count, bio and list of publishing credits. Send SASE for reply. Agented fiction 99%. Responds in 1 month to queries. Accepts simultaneous submissions.

Terms: Pays negotiable advance. Sends galleys to author.

Advice: "Get an agent."

☑ 🖉 🅐 **BALLANTINE BOOKS**, The Ballantine Publishing Group, A Division of Random House, Inc., 1540 Broadway, New York NY 10036. Fax: (212)792-8442. Website: www.randomhouse.com/BB (includes a complete catalog, author interviews, author chat opportunities, reading guides and topical newsletters). **Contact**: Joe Blades, executive editor (suspense, mystery); Peter Borland, editorial director (commercial and literary); Tracy Brown, senior editor (commercial and literary); Allison Dickens, assistant editor (commercial, literary, women's); Anita Diggs, senior editor (literary, commercial, mystery, romance); Elisabeth Dyssegaard, executive editor; Charlotte Herscher, associate editor (historical and contemporary romance); Linda Morrow, editorial director (suspense, women's fiction, crime); Leona Nevler (literary, thrillers, women's commercial, mystery); Maureen O'Neal, editorial director (women's quality commercial, Southern fiction); Patricia Peters, assistant editor (commercial, literary, mysteries); Dan Smetanka, senior editor (literary, story collections); Anika Streitfeld, assistant editor (literary); Shauna Summers, senior editor (romance women's, thrillers, suspense).

How to Contact: Does not accept unsolicited proposals or mss. Agented proposals and mss only.

Advice: "Writers should obtain representation by a literary agent."

☑ 🅐 ☷ **BANTAM, DOUBLEDAY, DELL/DELACORTE, KNOPF AND CROWN BOOKS FOR YOUNG READERS**, Random House Children's Books, A Division of Random House, Inc., 1540 Broadway, New York NY 10036. (212)782-9000 or (800)200-3552. Fax: (212)782-9452. Website: www.randomhouse.com/ kids. Vice President/Publisher: Beverly Horowitz. **Contact:** Michelle Poplof, editorial director. Publishes 300 titles/year.

● *Bud, Not Buddy*, by Christopher Paul Curtis won the Newbery Medal and the Coretta Scott King Award.

Imprint(s): Delacorte Books for Young Readers, Doubleday Books for Young Readers; Laurel Leaf; Skylark; Starfire; Yearling Books.

Needs: Fiction, nonfiction, humor, mystery, adventure, historical, picture books, chapter books, middle-grade, young adult. Recently published *Bud, Not Buddy*, by Christopher Paul Curtis; *White Fox*, by Gary Paulsen; and *Ties That Bind, Ties That Break*, by Lensey Namiska.

How to Contact: Agented fiction only. Can submit to Delacorte Contest for a First Young Adult Novel or Marguerite de Angeli Contest for contemporary or historical fiction set in North America for readers age 7-10. Send SASE for contest guidelines. Responds in up to 4 months. Accepts simultaneous submissions but must be indicated as such.

🏆 🖉 ◎ **BEACH HOLME PUBLISHERS LTD.**, 226-2040 W. 12th Ave., Vancouver, British Columbia V6J 2G2 Canada. (604)733-4868. Fax: (604)733-4860. E-mail: bhp@beachholme.bc.ca. Website: www.beachhol me.bc.ca (includes guidelines, reviews, authors, excerpts, titles, ordering information). **Contact:** Michael Carroll, publisher; Trisha Telep, publicity and marketing coordinator. Estab. 1971. Publishes trade paperback originals. Averages 14 titles/year. "Accepting only Canadian submissions." **Published 6 new writers within the last year.** Titles distributed through General Distribution (Canada) and Stockpole Distribution (US).

Imprints: Sandcastle Press (YA novels), Porcepic Books (literary fiction), Prospect Books (literary nonfiction).

Needs: Adult literary fiction from authors published in Canadian literary magazines. Young adult (Canada historical/regional). "Interested in excellent quality, imaginative writing." Recently published *Tending the Remnant Damage*, by Sheila Peters (short fiction); *Ondine's Curse*, by Steven Manners (literary); *Cold Clear Morning*, by Lesley Choyce.

How to Contact: Query with outline and two chapters. Responds in 4 months.

Terms: Pays royalties of 10% on retail price. Average advance: $500. Publishes ms 1 year after acceptance. Writer's guidelines free.

Advice: "Make sure the manuscript is well written. We see so many that only the unique and excellent can't be put down. Prior publication is a must. This doesn't necessarily mean book-length manuscripts, but a writer should try to publish his or her short fiction."

🖉 **FREDERIC C. BEIL, PUBLISHER, INC.**, 609 Whitaker St., Savannah GA 31401. E-mail: beilbook@beil .com. Website: www.beil.com. **Contact**: Frederic C. Beil III, president; Mary Ann Bowman, editor. Estab. 1983. "Our objectives are (1) to offer to the reading public carefully selected texts of lasting value; (2) to adhere to high standards in the choice of materials and in bookmarking craftsmanship; (3) to produce books that exemplify good taste in format and design; and (4) to maintain the lowest cost consistent with quality." General trade publisher. Publishes hardcover originals and reprints. Books: acid-free paper; letterpress and offset printing; Smyth-sewn, hardcover binding; illustrations. Average print order: 3,000. First novel print order: 3,000. Averages 14 total titles, 4 fiction titles/year.

Imprint(s): The Sandstone Press, Hypermedia, Inc.

Needs: Historical, biography, literary, regional, short story collections, translations. Published *The Dry Well*, by Marlin Barton (fiction); *Joseph Jefferson*, by Arthur Bloom (biography); and *Goya, Are You With Me Now?*, by H.E. Francis (fiction).

How to Contact: Does not accept unsolicited mss. Send query letter. Responds in 1 week to queries.

Terms: Payment "all negotiable." Sends galleys to author. Book catalog free on request.

Advice: "Write about what you love."

THE BERKLEY PUBLISHING GROUP, Imprint of Penguin Putnam Inc., 375 Hudson St., New York NY 10014. (212)366-2000. **Contact:** Tom Colgan, senior editor (history, business, suspense/thriller, mystery, adventure); Gail Fortune, senior editor (women's fiction, romance, mystery); Martha Busko, associate editor (mystery, literary fiction, narrative nonfiction, suspense/thriller); Kimberly Waltemyer, editor (adult western, romance, mystery); Christine Zika, senior editor (women's fiction, romance, mystery, health, New Age); Allison McCabe, senior editor (women's fiction, literary fiction, narrative nonfiction, suspense/thriller, romance). Large commercial category line. Publishes paperback originals, trade paperbacks and hardcover and paperback reprints. Books: paperbound printing; perfect binding. Average print order: "depends on position in list." Averages 800 total titles.

Imprint(s): Berkley, Jove, Boulevard, Ace Science Fiction.

Needs: Adventure, historical, literary, mystery, romance, spiritual, suspense, western, young adult. No occult fiction. Published works by Tom Clancy and Patricia Cornwell.

How to Contact: *Strongly* recommends agented material. Queries answered if SASE enclosed. Accepts simultaneous submissions.

Terms: Pays royalties of 4-10%. Provides 10 author's copies. Publishes ms 2 years after acceptance. Writer's guidelines and book catalog not available.

Advice: "Aspiring novelists should keep abreast of the current trends in publishing by reading *The New York Times* Bestseller Lists, trade magazines for their desired genre and *Publishers Weekly*."

BETHANY HOUSE PUBLISHERS, 11400 Hampshire Ave. S., Minneapolis MN 55438. (612)829-2500. Fax: (952)829-2768. Website: www.bethanyhouse.com. Publisher: Gary Johnson. **Contact:** Sharon Madison, ms review editor; David Horton, senior editor (adult fiction); Barbara Lilland, senior editor (adult fiction); Rochelle Gloege, senior editor (children and youth). Estab. 1956. "The purpose of Bethany House Publisher's publishing program is to relate biblical truth to all areas of life—whether in the framework of a well-told story, of a challenging book for spiritual growth, or of a Bible reference work." Publishes hardcover and trade paperback originals and mass market paperback reprints. Averages 120-150 total titles/year.

Needs: Adult historical fiction, teen/young adult, children's fiction series (age 8-12) and Bethany Backyard (age 6-12). New interest in contemporary fiction. Recently published *The Crossroad*, by Beverly Lewis (fiction).

How to Contact: Does not accept unsolicited fiction. First send SASE or visit website for guidelines. Responds in 3 months. Accepts simultaneous submissions.

Terms: Pays negotiable royalty on wholesale price. Offers negotiable advance. Publishes ms 1 year after acceptance. Writer's guidelines free or on website. Book catalog for 9×12 SAE with 5 first-class stamps.

BIRCH BROOK PRESS, P.O. Box 81, Delhi NY 13753. Fax: (607)746-7453. E-mail: birchbrkpr@prodigy. net. Website: www.birchbrookpress.com. **Contact:** Tom Tolnay, publisher. Estab. 1982. Small publisher of popular culture and literary titles in handcrafted letterpress editions. Specializes in fiction anthologies with specific theme, and an occasional novella. "Not a good market for full-length novels." Books: 80 lb. vellum paper; letterpress printing; wood engraving illustrations. Average print order: 500-1,000. Averages 4-6 total titles, 2-3 fiction titles/year. Distributes titles through Ingram, Baker and Taylor, Barnes&Noble.com Amazon.com. Promotes titles through catalogs, direct mail and group ads.

Imprint(s): Birch Brook Press, Persephone Press and Birch Brook Impressions.

Needs: Literary. "We make specific calls for fiction when we are doing an anthology." Plans to publish literary-quality anthology of mysterious short stories on loneliness and another containing short fiction relating to fly fishing. Published *Magic & Madness in the Library*, edited by Eric Graeber (fiction collection); *Kilimanjaro Burning*, by John Robinson (novella); *Fateful Choices*, edited by Marshall Brooks and Stephanie Greave; and *A Punk in Gallows, America*, by P.W. Fox.

How to Contact: Prefers samples with query letter. Must include SASE. Responds in up to 6 weeks to queries; up to 4 months to mss. Accepts simultaneous submissions. Sometimes comments on rejected mss.

Terms: Pays modest flat fee on anthologies. Writers guidelines and catalog for SASE.

Advice: "Write well on subjects of interest to BBP such as outdoors, fly fishing, baseball, music, literate mysteries, cultural history."

☑ 🖋 ◎ **BJU PRESS**, 1700 Wade Hampton Blvd., Greenville SC 29614-0001. (864)242-5100, ext. 4350. E-mail: jb@bjup.com. Website: www.bjup.com. **Contact:** Nancy Lohr, manuscript editor (juvenile fiction). Estab. 1974. "Small independent publisher of excellent, trustworthy novels, information books, audio tapes and ancillary materials for readers pre-school through high school. We desire to develop in our children a love for and understanding of the written word, ultimately helping them love and understand God's word." Publishes paperback originals and reprints. Books: 50 lb. white paper; Webb lithography printing; perfect-bound binding. Average print order: 5,000. First novel print order: 5,000. **Published new writers within the last year.** Averages 12 total titles, 10 fiction titles/year. Distributes titles through Spring Arbor and Appalachian. Promotes titles through CBA Marketplace.

Needs: Children's/juvenile (adventure, animal, easy-to-read, historical, mystery, series, sports), young adults (adventure, historical, mystery/suspense, series, sports, western). "Our fiction is all based on a moral and Christian word-view." Recently published *Susannah and the Secret Coins*, by Elaine Schulte (historical young adult fiction); *Arby Jenkins Meets His Match*, by Sharon Hambrick (contemporary young adult); *Over the Divide*, by Catherine Farnes (young adult fiction).

How to Contact: Accepts unsolicited mss. Query with outline and 5 sample chapters or submit complete ms with cover letter. Include estimated word count, short bio, Social Security number and list of publishing credits. Send SASE or IRC for return of ms or send disposable copy of ms and SASE for reply only. Responds in 1 month to queries; 3 months to mss. Accepts simultaneous and disk submissions (IBM compatible).

Terms: Pays royalties. Sends final ms to author. Publishes ms 12-18 months after acceptance. Writer's guidelines and book catalog free. "Check our webpage for guidelines."

Advice: "Study the publisher's guidelines. Make sure your work is suitable or you waste time for you and the publisher."

☑ 🖋 ◐ **BLACK HERON PRESS**, P.O. Box 95676, Seattle WA 98145. Website: www.blackheronpress.com. **Contact:** Jerry Gold, publisher. Estab. 1984. Two-person operation; no immediate plans to expand. "We're known for literary fiction. We've done several Vietnam War titles and several surrealistic fictions." Publishes paperback and hardback originals. Average print order: 2,000; first novel print order: 1,500. Averages 4 fiction titles/year. Distributes titles nationally through Midpoint Trade Books.

● Four books published by Black Heron Press have won awards from King County Arts Commission. This press received Bumbershoot Most Significant Contribution to Literature in 1996. "One author won the American Book Award."

Needs: Adventure, contemporary, experimental, humor/satire, literary, science fiction. Vietnam war novel—literary. "We don't want to see fiction written for the mass market. If it sells to the mass market, fine, but we don't see ourselves as a commercial press." Published *The Bathhouse*, by Farnoosh Moshiri (mainstream); *Moses in Sinai*, by Simone Zelitch (mainstream); and *The Master of Fate*, by Gonzalo Munevar (mainstream).

How to Contact: Query with first 50 pages only. Responds in 3 months to queries. Accepts simultaneous submissions.

Terms: Pays standard royalty rates. No advance.

Advice: "A query letter should tell me: 1) number of words; 2) number of pages; 3) if ms is available on disk; 4) if parts of novel have been published; 5) if so, where? And at least scan some of our books in a bookstore or library. Most submissions we get have come to the wrong press."

☑ ◐ ◎ **JOHN F. BLAIR, PUBLISHER**, 1406 Plaza Dr., Winston-Salem NC 27103. (336)768-1374. Fax: (336)768-9194. Website: www.blairpub.com. **Contact:** Carolyn Sakowski, president. Estab. 1954. Small independent publisher. Publishes hardcover and paperback originals. Books: Acid-free paper; offset printing; illustrations. Average print order: 5,000. "Among our 17-20 books, we do one novel a year."

Needs: Prefers regional material dealing with southeastern U.S. No confessions or erotica. "Our editorial focus concentrates mostly on nonfiction." Published *Freedom's Altar*, by Charles Price; *Caveat*, by Laura Kalpakian; and *Something Blue*, by Jean Spaugh.

How to Contact: Accepts unsolicited mss. Send query letter or submit complete ms with cover letter (prefers query). Send SASE or IRC for return of ms. Accepts simultaneous submissions. Responds in 1 month. Complete guidelines available on website.

Terms: Negotiable. Publishes ms 1-2 years after acceptance. Book catalog for free.

Advice: "We are primarily interested in nonfiction titles. Most of our titles have a tie-in with North Carolina or the southeastern United States. Please enclose a cover letter and outline with the manuscript. We prefer to review queries before we are sent complete manuscripts. Queries should include an approximate word count."

N 🔘 **BLUE JEAN PRESS**, Blue Jean Media, Inc., 1115 East Main St., Box 60, Rochester NY 14609. (716)288-6980. Fax: (716)288-3417. Email: info@bluejeanpress.com. Website: www.bluejeanpress.com (includes names of editors, writer's guidelines, direct link to order books directly from publisher). **Contact:** Sherry S. Handel, publisher/editor-in-chief (young adult/teen and feminist). Estab. 2001. "Blue Jean Press is devoted to empowering girls and young women to create their own media. Blue Jean Press is seeking short story fiction submissions for and by women for new collective series." Publishes trade paperback originals. Books: 50# text; offset printing, 60# cover (perfect); illustrations; some photos. **Published 20 new writers within the last year.** Distributes titles by advertising, Blue Jean Online websites, Partner cross promotions and book tours.
Needs: Feminist, young adult/teen. We do not publish novels, and only publish short story collections 700-2,000 words. Anthology material is selected by a teen editorial board, comprised of young women editors. Recently published *Blue Jean: What Young Women are Thinking, Saying, and Doing* (anthology compilation, one chapter is fiction only). Publishes *Blue Jean: What Young Women are Thinking, Saying, and Doing* series II.
How to Contact: Accepts unsolicited mss. Submit complete ms with cover letter. Accepts queries by e-mail. Include estimated word count, brief bio and list of publishing credits. Send disposable copy of ms and SASE for reply only. Responds in 2 months. Accepts simultaneous submissions. Sometimes comments on rejected mss.
Terms: Pays in 2 author's copy. "Self-publisher that publishes collective works. Arrangement varies by author." Writer's guidelines on website; book catalogs not available.
Advice: "We will be publishing more fiction, as we publish fiction in the print magazine (*Blue Jean Magazine*), online and in our collective works book publishing division. Young women are seeking outlets for publication of their creative works. Blue Jean Media supports new authors and artists by providing a worldwide audience to showcase their creative talents. Therefore, we encourage new teen authors to submit their short stories for publication consideration. We do not publish previously published works that have appeared in other books and magazines. However, we will consider short stories that have been published in newspapers and online."

🔘 🚫 **THE BLUE SKY PRESS**, Imprint of Scholastic Inc., 555 Broadway, New York NY 10012. (212)343-6100. Website: www.scholastic.com. **Contact** The editors. Blue Sky Press publishes primarily juvenile picture books. Publishes hardcover originals. Averages 15 titles/year.
● Because of a long backlog of books, the Blue Sky Press is not accepting unsolicited submissions.
Needs: Juvenile: adventure, fantasy, historical, humor, mainstream/contemporary, picture books, multicultural, folktales. Published *Bluish*, by Virginia Hamilton (novel); *No, David!*, by David Shannon (picture book); and *To Every Thing There is a Season*, by Leo and Diane Dillon (multicultural/historical).
How to Contact: Agented fiction 25%. Responds in 6 months to queries from previously published authors.
Terms: Pays 10% royalty on wholesale price, between authors and illustrators. Publishes ms 2½ years after acceptance.

🍁 ⭕ 🔘 🏆 **BOREALIS PRESS**, 110 Bloomingdale St., Ottawa, Ontario K2C 4A4 Canada. Fax: (613)829-7783. E-mail: borealis@istar.ca. Website: www.borealispress.com (includes names of editors, authors, all Borealis Press and Tecumseh Press books in print in 2000). **Contact**: Frank Tierney, editor; Glenn Clever, editor. Estab. 1970. "Publishes Canadiana, especially early works that have gone out of print, but also novels of today and shorter fiction for young readers." Publishes hardcover and paperback originals and reprints. Books: standard book-quality paper; offset printing; perfect and cloth binding. Average print order: 1,000. Buys juvenile mss with b&w illustrations. **Published new writers within in the last year.** Averages 10 total titles/year. Promotes titles through website, catalogue distribution, fliers for titles, ads in media.
Imprint(s): *Journal of Canadian Poetry*, Tecumseh Press Ltd., Canadian Critical Editions Series.
● Borealis Press has a "New Canadian Drama," with 7 books in print. The series won Ontario Arts Council and Canada Council grants.
Needs: Contemporary, literary, juvenile, young adult. "Must have a Canadian content or author; query first." Recently published *Blue: Little Cat Come Home to Stay*, by Donna Richards (young adult); *An Answer for Pierre*, by Gretel Fisher (novel); *The Love of Women*, Jennifer McVaugh (comic novel).
How to Contact: Send query letter. Send SASE (Canadian postage) or IRC. Accepts queries by e-mail, fax. No simultaneous submissions. Responds in 2 weeks to queries; 4 months to mss. Publishes ms 1-2 years after acceptance.
Terms: Pays royalties of 10% and 3 free author's copies. No advance. Sends galleys to author. Publishes ms 18 months after acceptance. Free book catalog with SASE.
Advice: "Have your work professionally edited. Our greatest challenge is finding good authors, i.e., those who submit innovative and original material."

⭕ 🔘 **BOYDS MILLS PRESS**, Subsidiary of *Highlights for Children*, 815 Church St., Honesdale PA 18431. (800)490-5111. Website: www.boydsmillspress.com (includes names of editors, author information, book information and reviews). **Contact**: Larry Rosler, editorial director. Estab. 1990. "Independent publisher of quality books for children of all ages." Publishes hardcover. Books: Coated paper; offset printing; case binding; 4-color illustrations. Average print order: varies. **Published 2 new writers within the last year.** Plans 4 fiction titles/ year. Distributes titles through independent sales reps and via order line directly from Boyds Mills Press. Promotes titles through sales and professional conferences, sales reps, reviews.

Needs: Juvenile, young adult (adventure, animal, contemporary, ethnic, historical, humor, mystery, sports). Recently published *Sharks! Strange and Wonderful*, by Laurence Pringle; *Groover's Heart*, by Carole Crowe; and *Storm Coming!*, by Audrey B. Baird.

How to Contact: Accepts unsolicited mss. Query with first 3 chapters and synopsis. Responds in 1 month. Accepts simultaneous submissions.

Terms: Pays standard rates. Sends pre-publication galleys to author. Time between acceptance and publication depends on "what season it is scheduled for." Writer's guidelines for #10 SASE.

Advice: "Read through our recently-published titles and review our catalogue. If your book is too different from what we publish, then it may not fit our list. Feel free to query us if you're not sure."

○ BRANDEN BOOKS, Subsidiary of Branden Press, P.O. Box 812 094, Wellesley MA 02482. (781)235-3634. Fax: (781)790-1056. E-mail: branden@branden.com. Website: www.branden.com. **Contact**: Adolph Caso, editor. Estab. 1967. Publishes hardcover and paperback originals and reprints. Books: 55-60 lb. acid-free paper; case- or perfect-bound; illustrations. Average print order: 5,000. Averages 15 total titles, 5 fiction titles/year.

Imprint(s): I.P.L., Dante University Press, Four Seas, Branden Publishing Co.

Needs: Ethnic, historical, literary, military/war, short story collections and translations. Looking for "contemporary, fast pace, modern society." No porno, experimental or horror. Published *I, Morgain*, by Harry Robin; *The Bell Keeper*, by Marilyn Seguin; and *The Straw Obelisk*, by Adolph Caso.

How to Contact: Does not accept unsolicited mss. Query *only* with SASE. Responds in 1 week to queries, with either "we cannot use" or "send entire manuscript."

Terms: Pays royalties of 5-10% minimum. Advance negotiable. Provides 10 author's copies. Sends galleys to author. Publishes ms "several months" after acceptance.

Advice: "Publishing more fiction because of demand. *Do not make phone, fax or e-mail inquiries.* Do not oversubmit; single submissions only; do not procrastinate if contract is offered. Our audience is a well-read general public, professionals, college students, and some high school students. We like books by or about women."

○ Ⓐ BROADWAY BOOKS, The Doubleday Broadway Publishing Group, A Division of Random House, Inc. 1540 Broadway, New York NY 10036. (212)354-6500. Website: www.broadwaybooks.com. **Contact:** Gerald Howard, publisher/editor-in-chief. Broadway publishes general interest nonfiction and fiction for adults. Publishes hardcover and trade paperback originals and reprints.

Needs: Commercial literary fiction. Published *Freedomland*, by Richard Price.

How to Contact: Accepts agented fiction only.

▣ ○ ◎ ▽ BROKEN JAW PRESS, Box 596, Stn. A, Fredericton, New Brunswick E3B 5A6 Canada. Phone/fax: (506)454-5127. E-mail: jblades@nbnet.nb.ca. Website: www.brokenjaw.com. **Contact**: Joe Blades, publisher. "We are a small, mostly literary, Canadian publishing house. We accept only Canadian authors." Publishes Canadian-authored trade paperback originals and reprints. **Published 1 new writer within the last year.** Averages 10-15 titles/year, plus *New Muse of Contempt* magazine. Distributes titles through General Distribution Services Ltd. (Toronto, Vancouver and Buffalo). E-books distributed through www.PublishingOnline.com.

• *What Was Always Hers*, by Uma Parameswaran won the 2000 Canadian Authors Association Jubilee Award for Short Stories.

Imprint(s): Book Rat, SpareTime Editions, Dead Sea Physh Products, Maritimes Arts Projects Productions, Broken Jaw Press eBooks.

Needs: Literary. Published *Rum River*, by Raymond Fraser; *Herbarium of Souls*, by Vladimir Tasic; and *Reader Be Thou Also Ready*, by Robert James (first novel).

How to Contact: Not currently accepting unsolicited book mss or queries. Only accepting mss or queries pertaining to the contest for first book for unpublished fiction writers (New Muse Award). For details visit website.

Terms: Pays royalties of 10% on retail price. Average advance: $0-100. Publishes ms 1 year after acceptance. Writer's guidelines for #10 SASE (Canadian postage or IRC or visit website). Book catalog for 9 × 12 SAE with 2 first-class Canadian stamps or IRC or visit website.

▣ ◎ CAITLIN PRESS, INC., P.O. Box 2387 Station B, Prince George, British Columbia V2N 2S6 Canada. (250)964-4953. Fax: (250)964-4970. E-mail: caitlin_press@telus.net. Website: www.caitlin-press.com (includes writer's guidelines, catalogue, what's new, author tours, interviews, author bios, about US order info). **Contact**: Cynthia Wilson. Estab. 1977. "We publish books about the British Columbia interior or by people from the interior." Publishes trade paperback and soft cover originals. Averages 6-7 titles/year. Distributes titles directly from publisher and through general distribution and Harbour Publishing. Promotes titles through *BC Book World*, *Candian Books in Print* and website.

Needs: Adventure, historical, humor, mainstream/contemporary, short story collections, young adult.

How to Contact: Accepts unsolicited mss. Send query letter with SASE. Responds in 3 months to queries. Accepts simultaneous submissions.

Terms: Pays royalties of 15% on wholesale price. Publishes ms 18 months after acceptance.

Advice: "Our area of interest is British Columbia and Northern Canada. Submitted manuscripts should reflect our interest area."

CANADIAN INSTITUTE OF UKRAINIAN STUDIES PRESS, CIUS Toronto Publications Office, University of Toronto, 1 Spadina Crescent, Room 109, Toronto, Ontario M5S 235 Canada. (416)978-6934. Fax: (416)978-2672. E-mail: cius@chass.utoronto.ca. Website: www.utoronto.ca/cius. **Contact**: Roman Senkus, director or publications; Marko Stech, managing director. Estab. 1976. "We publish scholarship about Ukraine and Ukrainians in Canada." Publishes hardcover and trade paperback originals and reprints. Publishes 5-10 titles/year.

Needs: Ukrainian literary works. "We do not publish fiction except for use as college textbooks." Recently published *History of Ukraine-Rus'* Volume VII, by Mykhailo Hrushevsky; *From Nationalism to Universalism*, by Vladimir Jabotinsky; *On Sunday Morning She Gathered Herbs*, by Olha Kobylianska.

How to Contact: Query or submit complete ms. Accepts queries by fax or e-mail. Responds in 1 month to queries, 3 months to mss.

Terms: Nonauthor-subsidy publishes 20-30% of books. Pays 0-2% royalty on retail price. Publishes ms 2 years after acceptance. Writer's guidelines and book catalog free.

Advice: "We are a scholarly press and do not normally pay our authors. Our audience consists of university students and teachers and the general public interested in Ukrainian and Ukrainian-Canadian affairs."

CANDLEWICK PRESS, Subsidiary of Walker Books Ltd. (London), 2067 Massachusetts Ave., Cambridge MA 02140. (617)661-3330. Fax: (617)661-0565. E-mail: bigbear@candlewick.com. Website: www.candlewick.com (catalog, guidelines, author interviews). **Contact:** Karen Lotz, president and publisher; Liz Bicknell, editorial director/associate publisher; Joan Powers, editorial director (novelty); Mary Lee Donovan, executive editor (nonfiction/fiction); Amy Ehrlich, editor at large (picture books); Kara LaReau, editor (fiction/poetry); Yolanda Leroy (editor fiction/nonfiction); Sarah Ketchersid, editor; Deborah Wayshak, associate editor (fiction); Jamie Michalak, associate editor (fiction); Cynthia Platt, associate editor (fiction/nonfiction); Erin Postl, assistant editor (fiction). Candlewick Press publishes high-quality illustrated children's books for ages infant through young adult. "We are a truly child-centered publisher." Estab. 1991. Publishes hardcover originals, trade paperback originals and reprints. Publishes 200 titles/year.

● *Because of Winn-Dixie*, by Kate DiCamillo, was a Newbery Honor book for 2001.

Needs: Juvenile. Recently published *Because of Winn-Dixie*, by Kate DiCamillo; and *A Poke in the 'I'*, edited by Paul Janeczko, illustrated by Chris Raschka.

How to Contact: For novels: Query first with synopsis and 2 sample chapters to the attention of Manuscripts Editor. Send SASE or IRC for reply. For picture books: Submit complete ms to the attention of Manuscripts Editor. Send SASE or IRC for return of ms. Responds in 3 months. Accepts simultaneous submissions, if so noted.

Terms: Pays royalties of 10% on retail price. Advance varies. Publishes ms 3 years after acceptance for illustrated books, 1 year for others.

CAROLRHODA BOOKS, INC., Division of the Lerner Publishing Group, 241 First Ave. N., Minneapolis MN 55401. (612)332-3344. Fax: (612)332-7615. Website: www.lernerbooks.com. **Contact:** Rebecca Poole, submissions editor. Estab. 1969. Carolrhoda Books seeks creative K-6 children's nonfiction and historical fiction with unique and well-developed ideas and angles. Publishes hardcover originals. Averages 50-60 titles/year.

Needs: Juvenile, historical, picture books, multicultural, fiction for beginning readers. "We continue to add fiction for middle grades and 1-2 picture books per year. Not looking for folktales or anthropomorphic animal stories." Published *The War*, by Anais Vaugelade; *Little Wolf's Haunted Hill for Small Horrors*, by Ian Whybrow. Carolrhoda does not publish alphabet books, puzzle books, song books, textbooks, workbooks, religious subject matter or plays.

How to Contact: "Submissions are accepted in the months of March and October only. Submissions received in any other month will be returned unopened." Query with SASE or send complete ms for picture books. Send SASE or IRC for return of ms. Responds in 6 months. Accepts simultaneous submissions.

Terms: Pays royalty on wholesale price, makes outright purchase or negotiates payments of advance against royalty. Advance varies. Publishes ms 18 months after acceptance. Writer's guidelines and book catalog for 9 × 12 SASE with $3 in postage. No phone calls.

Advice: "Our audience consists of children ages four to eleven. We publish very few picture books. We prefer manuscripts that can fit into one of our series. Spend time developing your idea in a unique way or from a unique angle; avoid trite, hackneyed plots and ideas."

☑ ☻ Ⓐ **CARROLL & GRAF PUBLISHERS, INC.**, Avalon Publishing Group, 161 William St., New York NY 10038-2607. (646)375-2570. Fax: (646)375-2571. Website: www.avalonpub.com. **Contact**: Herman Graf, publisher; Philip Turner, executive editor; Tina Pohlman, senior editor. Estab. 1983. Publishes hardcover and trade paperback originals. Averages 120 total titles, 50 fiction titles/year.
Needs: Contemporary, science fiction, literary, mainstream and mystery/suspense. No romance. Recently published *Book of Cain*, by Herb Chapman; and *According to Queeny*, by Beryl Bainbridge.
How to Contact: Does not accept unsolicited mss. *Agented submissions only.* Query first or submit outline/synopsis and sample chapters. Send SASE or IRC for reply. Responds in 2 weeks. Occasionally comments on rejected mss.
Terms: Pays royalties of 6-15%. Advance negotiable. Sends galleys to author. Publishes ms up to 18 months after acceptance. Free book catalog on request.

◎ ⃠ Ⓐ **CARTWHEEL BOOKS**, Imprint of Scholastic, Inc., 555 Broadway, New York NY 10012. (212)343-6100. Fax: (212)343-4444. Website: www.scholastic.com. Vice President/Editorial Director: Bernette Ford. **Contact:** Grace Maccarone, executive editor; Sonia Black, editor; Jane Gerver, executive editor; Sonali Fry, editor. Estab. 1991. "Cartwheel Books publishes innovative books for children, ages 3-9. We are looking for 'novelties' that are books first, play objects second. Even without its gimmick, a Cartwheel Book should stand alone as a valid piece of children's literature." Publishes hardcover originals. Averages 85-100 titles/year.
Needs: Children's/juvenile (fantasy, humor, juvenile, mystery, picture books, science fiction). "The subject should have mass market appeal for very young children. Humor can be helpful, but not necessary. Mistakes writers make are a reading level that is too difficult, a topic of no interest or too narrow, or manuscripts that are too long." Published *Little Bill (series)*, by Bill Cosby (picture book); *Dinofours* (series), by Steve Metzger (picture book); and *The Haunted House*, by Fiona Conboy (3-D puzzle storybook).
How to Contact: *Agented submissions or previously published authors only.* Responds in 2 months to queries; 6 months to mss. Accepts simultaneous submissions.
Terms: Pays royalty on retail price. Offers advance. Publishes ms 2 years after acceptance. Book catalog for 9×12 SAE. Writer's guidelines free.
Advice: Audience is young children, ages 3-9. "Know what types of books the publisher does. Some manuscripts that don't work for one house may be perfect for another. Check out bookstores or catalogs to see where your writing would 'fit' best."

☑ ☻ ◎ **CHARLESBRIDGE PUBLISHING,** 85 Main St., Watertown MA 02472-2535. (617)926-0329. Fax: (617)926-5720. E-mail: schooleditorial@charlesbridge.com. Website: www.charlesbridge.com (includes writer's guidelines, names of editors, authors, titles, chat lines). **Contact:** Elena Dworkin Wright, vice president school division. Estab. 1980. **Published 1 new writer within the last year.** Publishes school programs and hardcover and trade paperback originals. Averages 20 titles/year. Distributes titles through schools, bookstores, book clubs, sales reps, catalogs, direct mail offers, distributors and international conventions. Promotes titles through catalogs, sales reps, trade shows, conventions and author presentations.
Needs: Math concepts in nonrhyming story. Recently published *Sir Cumference and the Great Knight of Angleland*, by Cindy Neuschwander (a math adventure picture book). Also seeking picture books about current topics on astronomy.
How to Contact: Responds in 2 months. Submit complete ms.
Terms: Publishes ms 1 year after acceptance.
Advice: "We look for stories with enough science, problem solving, or historical context to interest parents and teachers as well as the humor to interest kids."

☒ ◎ **CIRCLET PRESS,** 1770 Massachusetts Ave., #278, Cambridge MA 02140. (617)864-0492 (noon-4p.m. EST). Fax: (617)864-0663, call before faxing. E-mail: circlet-info@circlet.com. Website: www.circlet.com/ (includes previews of upcoming books, catalog of complete books in print, links to authors' web pages and other publishers). **Contact:** Cecilia Tan, publisher. Estab. 1992. Small, independent specialty book publisher. "We are the only book publisher specializing in science fiction and fantasy of an erotic nature." Publishes paperback originals. Books: perfect binding; illustrations sometimes. Average print order: 2,500. **Published 50 new writers within the last year.** Averages 6-8 anthologies/year. Distributes titles through the LPC Group in the US/Canada, Turnaround UK in the UK and Bulldog Books in Australia. Promotes titles through reviews in book trade and general media, mentions in *Publishers Weekly, Bookselling This Week* and regional radio/TV.
● "Our titles were finalists in the Independent Publisher Awards in both science fiction and fantasy."
Imprints: The Ultra Violet Library (non-erotic lesbian/gay fantasy and science fiction).

Needs: "We publish only short stories of erotic science fiction/fantasy, of all persuasions (gay, straight, bi, feminist, lesbian, etc.). No horror! No exploitative sex, murder or rape. No degradation." No novels. All books are anthologies of short stories. Recently published *Nymph*, by Francesca Lia Block; *Sextopia*, edited by Cecilia Tan (science fiction erotica).

How to Contact: Accepts unsolicited mss between April 15 and August 31. Accepts queries (no mss) by e-mail. "Any manuscript sent other than this time period will be returned unread or discarded." Submit complete short story with cover letter. Include estimated word count, 50-100 word bio, list of publishing credits. Send SASE for reply, return of ms or send a disposable copy of ms. Agented fiction 5%. Responds in up to 18 months. Accepts simultaneous submissions. Always comments on rejected mss.

Terms: Pays ½¢/word minimum for 1-time anthology rights only, plus 2 copies; author is free to sell other rights. Sends galleys to author. Publishes ms 1-24 months after acceptance. Writer's guidelines for #10 SASE; book catalog for #10 SAE and 2 first-class stamps.

Advice: "Read what we publish, learn to use lyrical but concise language to portray sex positively. Make sex and erotic interaction integral to your plot. Stay away from genre stereotypes. Use depth of character, internal monologue and psychological introspection to draw me in."

CLARION BOOKS, Imprint of Houghton Mifflin Company, 215 Park Ave. S., New York NY 10003. Website: www.houghtonmifflinbook.com. **Contact:** Dinah Stevenson, editorial director; Michele Coppola, editor; Jennifer B. Greene, editor; Julie Strauss-Gabel, associate editor. Estab. 1965. "Clarion is a strong presence in the fiction market for young readers. We are highly selective in the areas of historical and contemporary fiction. We publish chapter books for children ages 7-10 and middle grade novels for ages 9-14, as well as picture books and nonfiction." Publishes hardcover originals. Averages 50 titles/year.

How to Contact: "Please submit entire manuscript for novels (no queries, please). Send to only *one* Clarion editor."

N ☑ COMMUTERS LIBRARY, Sound Room Publishers, P.O. Box 3168, Falls Church VA 22043. (703)790-8250. Fax: (703)790-8234. E-mail: commlib@bellatlantic.com. Website: www.commuterslibrary.com. **Contact:** Joe Langenfeld, editor. Estab. 1991. "Small publisher of audiobooks (many classics) with plans to publish new works of fiction and nonfiction, primarily novellas." Publishes audiobooks. Plans 5-10 first novellas in 2002. Averages 80 total titles, 70 fiction titles/year.
   ● Audio Best of the year for six years.

Imprint(s): Commuters Library, Joe Langenfeld (fiction and nonfiction).

Needs: Adventure, children's/juvenile, family saga, fantasy, historical, horror, humor/satire, literary, mainstream, military/war, mystery/suspense, New Age/mystic, western, young adult/teen. "Novellas—popular genres."

How to Contact: Accepts unsolicited mss. Query with outline/synopsis and 1 sample chapter. Accepts e-mail and fax queries. Include estimated word count with submission. Agented fiction: 0%. Responds in 1 month to queries; 3 months to mss. Considers simultaneous submissions and disk submissions (word Perfect); no electronic submissions.

Terms: Pays royalties of 5-10%. Average advance: $200-1,000. Does not send galleys to author. Writer's guidelines for SASE. Time between acceptance and publication is up to 1 year.

Advice: "Audio books are growing in popularity. Authors should consider going directly to audio for special works. Give us good writing 15,000 to 18,000 words in length."

☐ ☑ COMPASS POINT MYSTERIES/TORY CORNER EDITIONS, The Quincannon Publishing Group, P.O. Box 8100, Glen Ridge NJ 07028. Phone/fax: (973)669-8367. E-mail: editors@Quincannon.bizland. com. Website: www.Quincannon.bizland.com (includes everything necessary—contacts, writers' etiquette and guidelines, catalogue, sales channels). **Contact:** Holly Benedict, editor (mystery fiction); Alan Quincannon, editor (miscellaneous fiction). Estab. 1990. "Compass Point Mysteries specializes in regional mystery novels made unique by involving some element of a region's history (the setting and time-frame or the mystery's origin). If at all possible, we like to tie each of these novels to a regional museum where they can be sold with some degree of exclusivity. From time to time Tory Corner Editions considers fiction which is set at a particular historic site but whose subject matter may fall outside the parameters of the mystery genre." Publishes paperback originals and reprints (on very rare occasions if they meet the specified criteria). Books: trade paperbacks; perfect binding. Average print order: 500; first novel print order: 500. Averages 3 total titles, 1-2 fiction titles/year. "We seek to place our novels almost exclusively in the gift shops of the regional museums they feature and schedule periodic booksignings at those locales. Our novels are also offered through Internet booksellers and local independent bookstores."

Needs: Mystery/suspense (amateur sleuth, cozy, psychic/supernatural), regional (mysteries). Recently published *Wind of Time* (romantic mystery) and *Wicked is the Wind* (cozy mystery), both by John Dandola; and *Echoes from the Castle Walls*, by John Hays Hammond, Jr. (collection of mystery/horror stories).

How to Contact: Does not accept unsolicited mss. Send query letter (not by e-mail); no agented submissions. Include estimated word count and brief bio; also "a letter of intent from the museum director and/or museum board of directors of the featured historic site stating that the manuscript has been read and approved and that, if published, the title will be stocked by the museum gift shop." Responds in 6 weeks to queries; up to 9 months to mss. Always comments on rejected mss.

Terms: "Books are published in runs of 500 and reprinted as supplies necessitate. Authors are paid a flat fee per run. Fees vary as to the cover price of each book." Sends galleys to author. Publishes ms 1 year after acceptance. Writer's guidelines and book catalog on website.

Advice: "Unfortunately, we are finding that many would-be authors consider that once they have created a plot and a premise and their computers have made their submissions look pretty, editors can be relied upon to anonymously rewrite their manuscripts. Editors are only a part of the guiding process and storytelling requires an awareness of succinctness and pacing, a mastery of language and grammar, and a willingness to polish and restructure. Our mystery novels should first tell a good interesting story which just happens to be a mystery, and they should usually not run more than 224 typeset pages. Besides using an historic site as a locale, our fiction must be well-written; it will be judged first and foremost on that merit. Please also bear in mind that an affiliation with a specific museum does not guarantee acceptance of any manuscript."

CONTEXT BOOKS, 368 Broadway, Suite 314, New York NY 10013. (212)233-4880. Fax: (212)964-1810. E-mail: info@contextbooks.com. Website: www.contextbooks.com. **Contact:** Beau Friedlander. Estab. 1999. Books: offset printing; cloth/paper binding; illustrations. Average print order 20,000. Average first novel print order: 10,000. Plans 1 first novel in 2002. Averages 8 total titles, 6 fiction titles/year. Member, ABA. Titles distributed through Publisher's Group West. Promotes titles on a "book by book basis."
  • Context Books has received an Independent Publishers Prize, NBCC nomination, QPBC New Vision and *L.A. Times* Book Prize.

Needs: Comics/graphic ethnic/multicultural, experimental, feminist, historical, horror (supernatural, futuristic), literary, mainstream, military/war, short story collections. Publishes the *Esquire Fiction Anthology*. Recently published *After Dachau*, by David Quinn (fiction); *Assorted Fire Events*, by David Means (short stories); *Mind the Doors*, by Zinovy Zinik (Russian literature).

How to Contact: Sometimes accepts unsolicited mss. Does not return unsolicited mss. Submit complete ms with cover letter. No queries by e-mail, fax or phone. Agented fiction: 99.9%. Responds in 4 months to queries and mss. Considers simultaneous submissions and submissions on disk; no electronic submissions.

Terms: Pays royalties of 7½-15%. Pays advance and author's copies. Time between acceptance and publication is 1 year. Writer's guidelines for SASE. Book catalogs for 9 × 12 SASE.

Advice: "Tell me who you are in three sentences; tell me what the work accomplishes in the same."

COTEAU BOOKS, Thunder Creek Publishing Co-operative Ltd., 401-2206 Dewdney Ave., Regina, Saskatchewan S4R 1H3 Canada. (306)777-0170. Fax: (306)522-5152. E-mail: coteau@coteaubooks.com. Website: www.coteaubooks.com. **Contact:** Barbara Sapergia, acquisitions editor. Estab. 1975. "Coteau Books publishes the finest Canadian fiction, poetry drama and children's literature, with an emphasis on western writers." Independent publisher. Publishes paperback originals. Books: #2 offset or 60 lb. hi-bulk paper; offset printing; perfect bound; 4-color illustrations. Average print order: 1,500-3,000; first novel print order: approx. 1,500. **Published new writers within the last year.** Averages 18 total titles, 6-8 fiction titles/year. Distributes titles through General Distribution Services.
  • Books published by Coteau Books have received awards including the City of Edmonton Book Prize for *Banjo Lessons*, Jubilee Fiction Award for *In the Misleading Absence of Light*, and the Danuta Gleed Literary Award for *The Progress of an Object in Motion*.

Needs: Novels, short fiction, middle years and young adult fiction. No science fiction. No children's picture books. Publishes Canadian authors only.

How to Contact: *Canadian writers only.* Accepts unsolicited mss. Submit complete ms with cover letter and résumé to Acquisitions Editor. Accepts queries by e-mail. Send SASE or IRC for return of ms. Responds in 3 months to queries and mss. Sometimes comments on rejected mss.

Terms: "We're a co-operative and receive subsidies from the Canadian, provincial and local governments. We do not accept payments from authors to publish their works." Sends galleys to author. Publishes ms 1-2 years after acceptance. Book catalog for 8½ × 11 SASE.

MARKET CONDITIONS are constantly changing! If you're still using this book and it is 2003 or later, buy the newest edition of *Novel & Short Story Writer's Market* at your favorite bookstore or order from Writer's Digest Books by calling 1-800-289-0963.

Advice: "We publish short-story collections, novels, drama, nonfiction and poetry collections, as well as literary interviews and children's books. This is part of our mandate. The work speaks for itself! Be bold. Be creative. Be persistent!"

N ⊕ ◻ ⊘ CRESCENT MOON, Box 393, Maidstone, Kent ME14 5XU United Kingdom. E-mail: jrobin son@crescentmoon.org.uk. Website: www.crescentmoon.org.uk. Subsidiaries: Joe's Press, *Passion Magazine, Pagan America.* **Contact:** J. Robinson, director. Estab. 1988. Small independent publisher. Publishes hardcover and paperback originals. Published new writers within the last year. Plans 1-2 first novels in 1999. Averages 25 total titles, 1-2 fiction titles/year. Sometimes comments on rejected ms.

Needs: Erotica, experimental, feminist, gay, lesbian, literary, New Age/mystic/spiritual, short story collections, translations. Plans anthology. Send short stories to editor.

How to Contact: Accepts unsolicited mss. Query with outline/synopsis and 2 sample chapters. Include estimated word count, list of publishing credits. Send SASE (IRCs) for reply, return of ms or send a disposable copy of ms. Agented fiction 10%. Responds in 1 month to queries; 4 months to mss. Accepts simultaneous submissions.

Terms: Negotiable. Sends galleys to author. Publishes ms 12-18 months after acceptance. Writer's guidelines for SASE (2 IRCs); Book catalog for SASE (2 IRCs).

Advice: "We publish a small amount of fiction, and mainly in *Pagan Magazine* and *Passion Magazine.*"

✓ ⊘ ◎ ⚇ CROSSWAY BOOKS, Division of Good News Publishers, 1300 Crescent, Wheaton IL 60187-5800. Fax: (630)682-4785. Website: www.Crosswaybooks.org. **Contact:** Jill Carter. Estab. 1938. " 'Making a difference in people's lives for Christ' as its maxim, Crossway Books lists titles written from an evangelical Christian perspective." Midsize independent evangelical religious publisher. Publishes paperback originals. Average print order 5,000-10,000 copies. Averages 85 total titles, 5 fiction titles/year. Distributes titles through Christian bookstores and catalogs. Promotes titles through magazine ads, catalogues.

- *King of the Stable*, by Melody Carlson received the "Gold Medallion" award from the Evangelical Christian Publishers Association.

Needs: Contemporary, adventure, historical, literary, religious/inspirational, young adult. "All fiction published by Crossway Books must be written from the perspective of evangelical Christianity. It must understand and view the world through a Christian worldview." No sentimental, didactic, "inspirational" religious fiction, romance, heavy-handed allegorical or derivative fantasy. Recently published *Freedom's Shadow*, by Marlo Schalesky (historical); *The Senator's Other Daughter*, by Stephen Bly (western/historical); *Picture Rock*, by Stephen Bly (western/historical).

How to Contact: Does not accept unsolicited mss. Query with synopsis and sample chapters only. Does not accept queries by fax or e-mail. Responds in 2 months to queries. Publishes ms 1-2 years after acceptance.

Terms: Pays royalties. Negotiates advance. Writer's guidelines for SASE; book catalog for 9×12 SAE and 7 first-class stamps.

Advice: "We feel called to publish fiction in the following categories: Christian realism, historical fiction, intrigue, western fiction and children's fiction. All fiction should include explicit Christian content, artfully woven into the plot, and must be consistent with our statements of vision, purpose and commitment. Crossway can successfully publish and market *quality* Christian novelists. Also read John Gardner's *On Moral Fiction*. We require a minimum word count of 25,000 words."

◎ CROWN BOOKS FOR YOUNG READERS, Bantam, Doubleday, Dell/Delacorte, Knopf and Crown Books for Young Readers, Random House Children's Books, A Division of Random House, Inc., 1540 Broadway, New York NY 10036. (212)782-9000 or (800)200-3552. Website: www.randomhouse.com/kids.

- See listing for Bantam, Doubleday, Dell/Delacorte, Knopf and Crown Books for Young Readers, page 414.

◻ DAN RIVER PRESS, Conservatory of American Letters, P.O. Box 298, Thomaston ME 04861-0298. Phone/fax: (207)354-0998. E-mail: cal@americanletters.org. Website: www.americanletters.org (includes guidelines, editors, book catalog). **Contact:** Richard S. Danbury, fiction editor. Estab. 1977. "Small press publisher of fiction and biographies owned by a non-profit foundation." Publishes hardcover and paperback originals. Books: paperback; offset printing; perfect and cloth binding; illustrations. Average print order: 500; first novel print order: 500-1,000. Averages 2-3 total titles, 2-3 fiction titles/year. Promotes titles through the author's sphere of influence. Distributes titles by mail order to libraries and bookstores.

Needs: Family saga, fantasy (space fantasy, sword and sorcery), historical (general), horror (dark fantasy, futuristic, psychological, supernatural), humor/satire, literary, mainstream, mystery/suspense (amateur sleuth, police procedural, private eye/hardboiled), New Age/mystic, psychic/supernatural, regional, religious (general religious, inspirational, religious mystery/suspense, religious thriller, religious romance), romance (contemporary, futuristic/time travel, gothic, historical, romantic suspense), science fiction (hard science/technological, soft/sociological), short story collections, thriller/espionage, western (frontier saga, traditional), outdoors/fishing. Publishes poetry and fiction anthology (submission guidelines to *Dan River Anthology* on the Web). Recently published *Dan River Anthology 2002*, by R.S. Danbury III, editor (poetry and short stories); and *Wytopitloc: Tales of a Deer Hunter*, by Ed Rau Jr. (hunting stories).

How to Contact: Accepts unsolicited mss. Submit synopsis with cover letter. Include estimated word count, brief bio, Social Security number and list of publishing credits. Send SASE or IRC for return of ms or send disposable copy and SASE for reply only. Responds in 1 month to queries; 2 months to mss. Accepts simultaneous submissions.

Terms: Pays royalties of 10-15%. Average advance: $250. Pays 1 author's copy. Sends galleys to author. Publishes ms 8-12 months after acceptance. Writer's guidelines on website; book catalog for 6×9 SAE and 55¢ postage or on website.

Advice: "Spend some time developing a following."

✓ JOHN DANIEL AND COMPANY, PUBLISHERS, P.O. Box 21922, Santa Barbara CA 93121. (805)962-1780. Fax: (805)962-8835. E-mail: dand@danielpublishing.com. Website: www.danielpublishing.com. **Contact:** John Daniel, publisher. Estab. 1980. "We publish small books, usually in small editions, but we do so with pride." Publishes hardbound and paperback originals. Publishes poetry, fiction, nonfiction. Average print order: 2,000. Averages 4 total titles/year. Distributes through SCB Distributors. Promotes through direct mail, reviews.

Needs: Publishes poetry, fiction and nonfiction; specializes in belles lettres, literary memoir. Recently published *Seas Outside the Reef*, by Rosalind Brackenburg (novel); *A Hole in the Water*, by Mae Briskin (novel); *On Her Way Home*, by Harriet Rochlin (novel).

How to Contact: Accepts unsolicited mss. Responds in 2 months. Accepts simultaneous submissions.

Terms: Pays royalties of 10% of net receipts. No advance.

Advice: "Write for the joy of writing. That's as good as it gets."

Ⓝ ◗ DANTE UNIVERSITY OF AMERICA PRESS, INC., P.O. Box 812158, Wellesley MA 02482. (781)790-1056. E-mail: danteu@danteuniversity.org. Website: www.danteuniversity.org. **Contact:** Adolph Caso, president. "The Dante University Press exists to bring quality, educational books pertaining to our Italian heritage as well as the historical and political studies of America. Profits from the sale of these publications benefit the Foundation, bringing Dante University closer to a reality." Estab. 1975. Publishes hardcover and trade paperback originals and reprints. Publishes 5 titles/year. Average print order for a first book is 3,000.

Needs: Translations from Italian and Latin. Recently published *Marconi My Beloved*, by C. Marconi; *Unpaid Ballads*, by A. Mirini; and *Italian Poetry*, by Ridinger/Renello.

How to Contact: Query first with SASE. Agented fiction 50%. Responds in 2 months.

Terms: Pays royalty. Negotiable advance. Publishes ms 10 months after acceptance.

◗ ◎ MAY DAVENPORT, PUBLISHERS, 26313 Purissima Rd., Los Altos Hills CA 94022. (650)947-1275. Fax: (650)947-1373. E-mail: mdbooks@earthlink.net. Website: www.maydavenportpublishers.com (includes catalog, author information). **Contact:** May Davenport, editor/publisher. Estab. 1976. "We prefer books which can be *used* in high schools as supplementary readings in English or creative writing courses. Reading skills have to be taught, and novels by humorous authors can be more pleasant to read than Hawthorne's or Melville's novels, war novels, or novels about past generations. Humor has a place in literature." Publishes hardcover and trade paperback originals. Averages 4 titles/year. Distributes titles through direct mail order.

Imprint(s): md Books (nonfiction and fiction).

Needs: Humor, literary. "We want to focus on novels junior and senior high school teachers can share with their reluctant readers in their classrooms." Recently published *Surviving Sarah*, by Dinah Leigh (novel); *Significant Footsteps*, by Ashley E. Grange (novel).

How to Contact: Query with SASE. Responds in 1 month.

Terms: Pays royalties of 15% on retail price. No advance. Publishes ms 1 year after acceptance. Book catalog and writer's guidelines for #10 SASE.

Advice: "Just write humorous fictional novels about today's generation with youthful, admirable, believable characters to make young readers laugh. TV-oriented youth need role models in literature, and how a writer uses descriptive adjectives and similes enlightens youngsters who are so used to music, animation, special effects with stories."

◖ DAW BOOKS, INC., Distributed by Penguin Putnam Inc., 375 Hudson St., 3rd Floor, New York NY 10014-3658. (212)366-2096. Fax: (212)366-2090. E-mail: daw@penguinputnam.com. Website: www.dawbooks.com. Publishers: Elizabeth Wollheim and Sheila Gilbert. **Contact:** Peter Stampfel, submissions editor. Estab. 1971. Publishes hardcover and paperback originals and reprints. Averages 60-80 titles/year.

Needs: "We are interested in science fiction and fantasy novels. We need science fiction more than fantasy right now, but we're still looking for both. We like character-driven books with attractive characters. We're not looking for horror novels, but we are looking for mainstream suspense thrillers. We accept both agented and unagented manuscripts. Long books are absolutely not a problem. We are not seeking collections of short stories or ideas for anthologies." Recently published *Mountains of Black Glass*, by Tad Williams (science fiction).

How to Contact: First send query letter with SASE or IRC for reply. Simultaneous submissions "returned unread at once unless prior arrangements are made by agent." Responds in 6 weeks "or longer if a second reading is required."

Terms: Pays in royalties with an advance negotiable on a book-by-book basis. Sends galleys to author. Book catalog free.

Advice: "We strongly encourage new writers. Research your publishers and submit only appropriate work."

☑ ◎ **DEL REY BOOKS**, The Ballantine Publishing Group, A Division of Random House, Inc., 1540 Broadway, New York NY 10036. (212)782-8449. E-mail: Delray@randomhouse.com. Website: www.randomhouse.com/delrey/ (includes writers guidelines, names of editors, a writers workshop where you can get your work critiqued, an online newsletter with updates, author interviews and contests). **Contact:** Shelly Shapiro, senior editor; Steve Saffel, senior editor; Christopher Evans, associate editor; Chris Schluep, assistant editor. Estab. 1977. "In terms of mass market, we basically created the field of fantasy bestsellers. Not that it didn't exist before, but we put the mass into mass market." Publishes hardcover originals and paperback originals and reprints. Plans 6-7 first novels in 2001. Averages 70 fiction titles/year.

Needs: Fantasy ("should have the practice of magic as an essential element of the plot"), alternate history ("novels that take major historical events, such as the Civil War, and bend history in a new direction sometimes through science fiction and fantasy devices"), science fiction ("well-plotted novels with good characterization, exotic locales, and detailed alien cultures"). Recently published *Darwin's Radio*, by Greg Bear; *The Great War: Walk in Hell*, by Harry Turtledove; *The Skies of Peru*, by Anne McCaffrey; *Perdido Street Station*, by China Mieville.

How to Contact: Does not accept unsolicited mss. Sometimes comments on rejected mss.

Terms: Pays royalty on retail price. "Advance is competitive." Publishes ms 1 year after acceptance. Sends galleys to author.

Advice: Has been publishing "more fiction and hardcovers, because the market is there for them. Read a lot of science fiction and fantasy, such as works by Anne McCaffrey, David Eddings, Larry Niven, Arthur C. Clarke, Terry Brooks, Frederik Pohl, Barbara Hambly. When writing, pay particular attention to plotting (and a satisfactory conclusion) and characters (sympathetic and well-rounded) because those are what readers look for."

◖ **DELACORTE PRESS**, The Bantam Dell Publishing Group, A Division of Random House, Inc., 1540 Broadway, New York NY 10036. Website: www.bantamdell.com.

◖ **DELACORTE BOOKS FOR YOUNG READERS**, Bantam, Doubleday, Dell/Delacorte, Knopf and Crown Books for Young Readers, Random House Children's Books, 1540 Broadway, New York NY 10036. (212)782-9000 or (800)200-3552. Website: www.randomhouse.com/kids.

• See listing for Bantam, Doubleday, Dell/Delacorte, Knopf and Crown Books for Young Readers, page 414.

DELL, The Bantam Dell Publishing Group, A Division of Random House, Inc., 1540 Broadway, New York NY 10036. Website: www.bantamdell.com.

☑ ◎ Ⓐ **DIAL BOOKS FOR YOUNG READERS**, Children's Division of Penguin Putnam Inc., 345 Hudson St., 3rd Floor, New York NY 10014-3657. (212)366-2800. Website: www.penguinputnam.com. President/Publisher: Nancy Paulsen. Editorial Director: Lauri Hornik. **Contact:** Submissions Editor. Estab. 1961. Trade children's book publisher, "looking for picture book mss and novels." Publishes hardcover originals. Averages 50 titles/year, mainly fiction.

Imprint(s): Easy-to-Read Books.

Needs: Adventure, fantasy, juvenile, picture books, young adult. Especially looking for "lively and well-written novels for middle grade and young adult children involving a convincing plot and believable characters. The subject or theme should not already be overworked in previously published books. The approach must not be demeaning to any minority group, nor should the roles of female characters (or others) be stereotyped, though we don't think books should be didactic. No topics inappropriate for juvenile, young adults and middle grade audiences. No plays." Recently published *Asteroid Impact*, by Doug Henderson; *A Year Down Yonder*, by Richard Parl; and *The Missing Mitten Mystery*, by Steven Kellog.

How to Contact: Does not accept unsolicited mss. Send query letter with SASE. Occasionally comments on rejected ms.

Terms: Pays advance against royalties. "We will send a catalog to anyone who sends 4 first-class stamps with a self-addressed, 9×12 envelope."

◖ DISKUS PUBLISHING, P.O. Box 43, Albany IN 47320. E-mail: books@diskuspublishing.com. Website: www.diskuspublishing.com (includes writer's guidelines, names of editors, book catalog, interviews with authors, About Us, submission status log, About Our Authors). **Contact:** Marilyn Nesbitt, editor-in-chief; Joyce McLaughlin, inspirational and children's editor; Holly Janey, submissions editor. Estab. 1997. Publishes paperback originals and e-books. **Published 10 new writers within the last year.** Averages 60 total titles, 50 fiction titles/year. Member, AEP, PMA.

- *The Best Laid Plans*, by Leta Nolan Childers was the #1 bestselling e-book of 1999. *Paper Roses* was a winner of The Rising Star Contest for Historical Fiction. *Eye of the Beholder* was a finalist (inspirational genre) in the Eppie Awards.

Needs: Adventure, children's/juvenile, ethnic/multicultural (general), family saga, fantasy (space fantasy), historical, horror, humor/satire, literary, mainstream, military/war, mystery/suspense, psychic/supernatural, religious, romance, science fiction, short story collections, thriller/espionage, western, young adult/teen. Recently published *The Best Laid Plans*, by Leta Nolan Childers (romance); *Brazen*, by Lori Foster (adventure/romance); and *A Change of Destiny*, by Marilynn Mansfield (science fiction/futuristic).

How to Contact: Accepts unsolicited mss. No queries; complete ms only. Include estimated word count, brief bio, list of publishing credits and genre. Send SASE or IRC for return of ms or send disposable copy of ms and SASE for reply only. Agented fiction 5%. Accepts simultaneous submissions and submissions on disk plus print out of synopsis and first chapter. Sometimes comments on rejected mss.

Terms: Pays royalties of 40%. Sends galleys to author. Publishes ms 6-8 months after acceptance. Writer's guidelines free for #10 SASE. Book catalog available for #10 SASE or online.

◖◣ DOUBLEDAY ADULT TRADE, The Doubleday Broadway Publishing Group, A Division of Random House, Inc., 1540 Broadway., New York NY 10036. (212)782-9000. Fax: (212)782-9700. Website: www.doubleday.com. **Contact:** William Thomas, vice president/editor-in-chief. Estab. 1897. Publishes hardcover and paperback originals and paperback reprints. Averages 200 titles/year.

Imprint(s): Currency; Nan A. Talese; Religious Division; Image; Anchor Books.

Needs: Adventure, confession, ethnic, experimental, feminist, gay/lesbian, historical, humor, literary, mainstream/contemporary, religious, short story collections, suspense. Recently published *The Street Lawyer*, by John Grisham.

Terms: "Doubleday is not able to consider unsolicited queries, proposals or manuscripts unless submitted through a bona fide literary agent." Pays in royalties; offers advance. Publishes ms 1 year after acceptance.

◎ DOUBLEDAY BOOKS FOR YOUNG READERS, Bantam, Doubleday, Dell/Delacorte, Knopf and Crown Books for Young Readers, Random House Children's Books, A Division of Random House, Inc., 1540 Broadway, New York NY 10036. (212)782-9000 or (800)200-3552. Website: www.randomhouse.com/kids.

- See listing for Bantam, Doubleday, Dell/Delacorte, Knopf and Crown Books for Young Readers, page 414.

✿◯◣ DOUBLEDAY CANADA, Random House of Canada, A Division of Random House, Inc., 1 Toronto St., Suite 300, Toronto, Ontario M5C 2V6 Canada. Website: www.randomhouse.ca. Publishes hardcover and paperback originals. Averages 50 total titles/year.

Imprint(s): Seal Books (mass market publisher).

How to Contact: Does not accept unsolicited mss. Agented fiction only.

✓◯◎ DUFOUR EDITIONS, P.O. Box 7, Chester Springs PA 19425-0007. (610)458-5005. Fax: (610)458-7103. E-mail: info@dufoureditions.com. Website: www.dufoureditions.com. **Contact:** Thomas Lavoie, associate publisher. Estab. 1940s. Small independent publisher, tending toward literary fiction. Publishes hardcover and paperback originals and reprints. Averages 6-7 total titles, 1-2 fiction titles/year. Promotes titles through catalogs, reviews, direct mail, sales reps, Book Expo and wholesalers.

Needs: Literary, short story collections, translations. Published *Tideland*, by Mitch Cullin; *The Case of the Pederast's Wife*, by Clare Elfman; *Lost Love in Constantinople*, by Milorad Pavic.

How to Contact: Send query letter only. Accepts queries by fax or e-mail. Include estimated word count, bio and list of publishing credits. Include SASE for reply. Responds in 3 weeks to queries; 3 months to mss.

◣ THOMAS DUNNE BOOKS, Imprint of St. Martin's Press, 175 Fifth Ave., New York NY 10010. (212)674-5151. **Contact:** Tom Dunne. Publishes wide range of fiction and nonfiction. Publishes hardcover originals, trade paperback originals and reprints. Averages 90 titles/year.

Needs: Mainstream/contemporary, mystery/suspense, "women's" fiction, thrillers. Recently published *Winter Solstice*, by Rosamunde Pilcher; and *Marines of Autumn*, by James Brady.

How to Contact: "Thomas Dunne Books does not accept any manuscripts, proposals or queries unless solicited by a legitimate literary agent first."

Terms: Pays royalties of 10-15% on retail price for hardcover, 7½% for paperback. Advance varies with project. Publishes ms 1 year after acceptance. Book catalog and writer's guidelines free.

☑ ◑ ☑ Ⓐ **DUTTON**, Imprint of Penguin Putnam Inc., 375 Hudson St., New York NY 10014. (212)366-2000. Website: www.penguinputnam.com. President: Clare Ferraro. Estab. 1852. Publishes hardcover originals. **Published new writers within the last year.**
Needs: Adventure, historical, literary, mainstream/contemporary, mystery, short story collections, suspense. Recently published *The Darwin Awards*, by Wendy Northcutt (humor); *Girl with a Pearl Earring*, by Tracy Chevalier (fiction); and *Bubbles Unbound*, by Sarah Strohmeyer (mystery).
How to Contact: Agented mss only. Accepts simultaneous submissions. Responds in 6 months.
Terms: Pays royalties and author's copies; offers advance. Sends galleys to author. Publishes ms 12-18 months after acceptance. Book catalog for SASE.
Advice: "Write the complete manuscript and submit it to an agent or agents. They will know exactly which editor will be interested in a project."

☑ ◐ **DUTTON CHILDREN'S BOOKS**, Imprint of Children's Division, Penguin Putnam Inc., 345 Hudson St., New York NY 10014. (212)414-3700. Website: www.penguinputnam.com. **Contact:** Lucia Monfried, associate publisher and editor-in-chief (picture books, easy-to-read, fiction); Stephanie Owens Lurie, president and publisher (picture books and fiction); Donna Brooks, editorial director; Susan Van Metre, senior editor (picture books and middle grade fiction); Tamar Mays, executive editor (novelty, picture books, fiction); Meredith Mundy Wasinger, editor (picture books, fiction, nonfiction). Estab. 1852. Dutton Children's Books publishes fiction and nonfiction for readers ranging from preschoolers to young adults on a variety of subjects. Publishes hardcover originals. Averages 100 titles/year.
Needs: Dutton Children's Books has a complete publishing program that includes picture books; easy-to-read books; and fiction for all ages, from "first-chapter" books to young adult readers. Recently published *Sun Bread*, by Elsa Kleven (picture book); *Food Rules*, by Bill Haduch (nonfiction); and *Dial a Ghost*, by Eve Ibbotson.
How to Contact: Does not accept unsolicited mss. Send query with SASE.
Terms: Offers advance. Pays royalty on retail price.

◯ ◎ **E.M. PRESS, INC.,** P.O. Box 336, Warrenton VA 20188. Phone/fax: (540)349-9958 (call first for fax). E-mail: empress2@erols.com. Website: www.empressinc.com. President: Beth A. Miller. **Contact**: Montana Umbel, assistant publisher. Estab. 1991. "A small press devoted to publishing quality work that might otherwise go unpublished." Publishes paperback and hardcover originals. Books: 50 lb. text paper; offset printing; perfect binding; illustrations. Average print order: 1,200-5,000. Averages 4 total titles, fiction, poetry and nonfiction, each year. Distributes titles through wholesalers and direct sales. Promotes titles through radio and TV, Interview Report, direct mailings and Ingram's catalogs.
Needs: "We're emphasizing nonfiction and a children's line, though we still consider 'marketable' fiction." Recently published *Looking for Pa*, by Geraldine Lee Susi (young reader) and *Moving the Nest, A Mid-Life Guide to Relocating*, by Bernard and Rhoda Faller.
How to Contact: Accepts unsolicited mss. Submit outline/synopsis and sample chapters or complete ms with cover letter. Include estimated word count. Send SASE or IRC for return of ms or send disposable copy of the ms and SASE for reply only. Agented fiction 10%. Responds in 3 months to queries; 3 months to mss. Accepts simultaneous submissions.
Terms: Amount of royalties and advances varies. Sends galleys to author. Publishes ms 18 months after acceptance. Writer's guidelines for SASE.
Advice: Publishing "less fiction, more regional work, though we look for fiction that will do well in secondary rights sales."

Ⓝ ◐ ◎ **EAKIN PRESS**, P.O. Box 90159, Austin TX 78709-0159. (512)288-1771. Fax: (512)288-1813. E-mail: eakinpub@sig.net. Website: www.eakinpress.com. **Contact:** Edwin M. Eakin, editorial director; Virginia Messer, publisher. Estab. 1978. Eakin specializes in Texana and Western Americana for juveniles.
Imprint(s): Nortex.
Needs: Juvenile. Specifically needs historical fiction for school market, juveniles set in Southwest for Southwest grade schoolers. Published *Inside Russia*, by Inez Jeffry.
How to Contact: Prefers queries, but accepts unsolicited mss. Send SASE for guidelines. Agented fiction 5%. Accepts simultaneous submissions. Responds in 3 months to queries.

insider report

Alexandra Styron: living her literary legacy

Most literary debuts are relatively quiet affairs. But when your father has a Pulitzer and your mother is an accomplished poet, a low-key entrance into the publishing world isn't very likely.

Thus, it's with an enviable flair, usually reserved for the most established writers, that Alexandra Styron marked the publication of her first book, a novel titled *All the Finest Girls* (Little, Brown & Co., June 2001). But as the 34-year-old emerges from the shadowing achievements of parents William—author of *Sophie's Choice*, *The Confessions of Nat Turner* and *Darkness Visible*—and Rose Styron, she acknowledges the attention for what it is: a hook that may pull in more publicity and readers, and an open invitation for critical comparison to one of the most esteemed writers of the past century.

"I feel very much aware of the weight of my parents' legacy," she says. "I recognize that more eyes will be on me because of it. And more eyes will be on me from potentially a more critical point of view because of it. And that's a big obstacle to climb.

"But, to be completely frank, I am not unconscious of the fact that it also gives me an advantage, and I hope I don't take that for granted."

Despite the substantial benefits that come with being a legacy to the literary inner circle, Styron's road to publication was filled with the same pressures that haunt so many other new writers.

At the age of 28, after spending a few years pursuing acting—she had bit parts in *French Exit* and *Last Summer in the Hamptons*—Styron says she "backed into being a writer." Though it was a profession—and lifestyle—she had "steadfastly avoided" after watching her father's arduous battles, Styron says she found the creative freedom in writing that she had longed for in acting. And so, armed with an imbued sense of passion and the shell of an idea, she enrolled in a creative writing program at Columbia University—a two-year tenure that guided her through the first half of her novel.

"I certainly didn't have even the outline of a full story when I started graduate school," she says. "I knew that it began with a girl going to an island in the Caribbean to attend the funeral of her nanny. And I knew that the process, the journey to the island, would include a journey back through her own history"—and a journey through Styron's history as well.

Though she weaves in universal coming-of-age themes like acceptance, forgiveness and the acknowledgement of one's future, the book is a blend of fiction and autobiographical fragments—a combination Styron says is necessary to produce strong fiction.

"I don't think you could find a fiction writer who could write a work of fiction of any value that wasn't autobiographical in some way," she says. "The feelings and the sensations that the characters have and express—for me at least—come from a deeply autobiographical place."

All the Finest Girls chronicles 32-year-old Addy Abraham's journey of self-discovery as she confronts her past—including a childhood riddled with heated parental disputes that only strengthened young Addy's relationship with her now-deceased nanny. The book also explores how such an intense bond between a child and an additional caregiver can create a lasting familial transformation—a subject with which Styron is quite familiar.

Though she stresses that little of the actual story is based on fact, the author says her own closeness to her childhood nanny—which she also explores in an essay in the May issue of *Real Simple*—"very much informed the writing of that part of the book."

While weaving emotional bits of her life into her fiction was difficult, it was only a small part of the writing process. Spending six months on her first 16 pages, Styron worked to create a trajectory for the rest of the narrative. And though she knew the direction in which she wanted her story to progress, she still had to contend with self-doubt, an age-old impasse that held constant as the days she spent honing her tale turned into weeks, and into months, and into years.

"I spent four years writing this book," she says. "That's four years of having people I'd meet say, 'And what do you do?' and having to look them in the eye and say, 'I'm a writer. I'm writing a novel.' And when someone asks, 'Who's publishing it?' and you have to say, 'Well, I haven't sold it yet,' it's very hard to continue to do it and to believe in yourself when you feel certain there's no reason someone else should believe in you."

Indeed, four years is a long time to spend alone inside a story no one else has validated. That's 1,460 days of dedication to a project that "has every possibility of complete failure." And it's during these uncertain times when the inner courage of a writer matters most.

"I think too many people rush out with a work that's half done because they want people to pat them on the back and make them feel it's OK," she says. "The great challenge is to trust yourself and stick with it by yourself for yourself until you've done all you can do." Getting it done, in Styron's case, meant balancing a Caribbean dialect, flashbacks and intermittent snippets of italicized dialogue meant to express "dialogue that was essential in the ear of a little girl, though not officially recognized as the main focus." In addition to such technique-oriented challenges, Styron also struggled to stay motivated and faithful to the project because, as she puts it, "Writing fiction is so hard when nobody is waiting for you to finish."

Though no one may be waiting when those final words are written—and rewritten—perhaps there's an even greater reward to be found in the completion of a dream, if, as Styron proves, there first exists the courage of pursuit.

"I certainly had a lot of dark moments. . . . I think the greatest challenge, for me at least, was working through those anxieties and apprehensions and just making the leap of faith that it was going to be OK and that when it was done, it might even be good."
—*Kelly Nickell*

This article originally appeared in Writer's Digest *magazine. It is used here by permission.*

Terms: Pays royalties; no advance. Sends galleys to author. Publishes ms 18 months years after acceptance. Writers guidelines for #10 SASE. Book catalog for $1.25.
Advice: "Juvenile fiction only with strong Southwest theme. We receive around 1,200 queries or unsolicited mss a year."

THE ECCO PRESS, Imprint of HarperCollins General Books Group, HarperCollins Publishers, 10 E. 53rd St., New York NY 10022. (212)207-7000. Website: www.harpercollins.com. **Contact**: Daniel Halpern, editor-in-chief. Estab. 1970. Publishes hardcover and paperback originals and reprints. Books: acid-free paper; offset printing; Smythe-sewn binding; occasional illustrations. First novel print order: 3,000 copies. Averages 60 total titles, 20 fiction titles/year.

Needs: "We can publish possibly one or two original novels a year." Literary, short story collections. No science fiction, romantic novels, western (cowboy) or historical novels. Recently published *Blonde*, by Joyce Carrol Oates; *Pitching Around Fidel*, by S.L. Price.

How to Contact: Does not accept unsolicited mss.

Terms: Pays royalties. Advance is negotiable. Publishes ms 1 year after acceptance. Writer's guidelines for SASE; book catalog free on request.

Advice: "We are always interested in first novels and feel it's important they be brought to the attention of the reading public."

[N] [symbols] ECW PRESS, 2120 Queen St. E., Suite 200, Toronto, Ontario M4E 1E2 Canada. (416)694-3348 Fax: (416)698-9906. E-mail: ecw@sympatico.ca. Website: www.ecwpress.com. Estab. 1979. **Contact:** Jack David, publisher.

Needs: Literary. Receives 1,000 mss/year; publishes 8-12 books/year.

How to Contact: "Rarely" accepts unsolicited mss. Submit sample chapter, 15-25 pages double-spaced with SASE and IRC with sufficient postage. Include cover letter, brief bio, and publication history. Responds in between two weeks and four months. "We hope for the former and apologize for the latter."

Advice: "We are idiosyncratically picky about the kind of fiction we can stomach. We dabble almost exclusively in Canadian-authored fiction, unless you're Don DeLillo or Martin Amis . . . well, you get the idea."

[symbols] LES ÉDITIONS DU VERMILLON, 305 St. Patrick St., Ottawa, Ontario K1N 5K4 Canada. (613)241-4032. Fax: (613)241-3109. E-mail: editver@magi.com. Website: www.francoculture.ca/edition/vermillon (includes book catalog). **Contact:** Jacques Flamand, editorial director. Publishes trade paperback originals. **Published new writers within the last year.** Averages 15 books/year. Distributes titles through Prologue in Canada. Promotes titles through advertising, book fairs and media.

● *Lithochronos*, poetry by Andrée Christensen and Jacques Flamand was awarded the Prix Trillium 2000, and *Toronto, je t'aime*, novel by Didier Leclair, the Prix Trillium 2001.

Needs: Juvenile, literary, religious, short story collections, young adult. Recently published *Le chien de Shibuya*, by J.-Fr. Somain (adventure, youth); *La Vie L'Écriture*, by Gabrielle Poulin (essay); and *Le dernier vol du Petit Prince/The Last Flight of the Little Prince*, by Jean-Pierre de Villers (bilingual fiction).

How to Contact: Query with SASE or IRC for reply. Responds in 6 months to mss.

Terms: Pays royalties of 10%. Offers no advance. Publishes ms 18 months after acceptance. Book catalog free.

[symbols] ÉDITIONS LA LIBERTÉ INC., 3020 Chemin Ste-Foy, Ste-Foy, Quebec G1X 3V6 Canada. Phone/fax: (418)658-3763. **Contact:** Nathalie Roy, director of operations. Publishes trade paperback originals. **Published 1 new writer within the last year.** Averages 4-5 titles/year.

Needs: Historical, juvenile, literary, mainstream/contemporary, short story collections, young adult. Published *L'espace Montauban/Le Dernier Roman Scout*, by Jean Désy.

How to Contact: Accepts only mss written in French. Query with synopsis. Accepts simultaneous submissions.

Terms: Pays royalties of 10% on retail price. Publishes ms 4 months after acceptance. Book catalog free.

[symbols] WM. B. EERDMANS PUBLISHING CO., 255 Jefferson Ave. SE, Grand Rapids MI 49503-4570. (800)253-7521. Fax: (616)459-6540. Website: www.eerdmans.com. **Contact:** Jon Pott, editor-in-chief, fiction editor (adult fiction); Judy Zylstra, fiction editor (children); Gwen Penning, assistant to the editor-in-chief (adult fiction). Estab. 1911. "Although Eerdmans publishes some regional books and other nonreligious titles, it is essentially a religious publisher whose titles range from the academic to the semi-popular. Our children's fiction is meant to help a child explore life in God's world and to foster a child's exploration of her or his faith. We are a midsize independent publisher. We publish the occasional adult novel, and these tend to engage deep spiritual issues from a Christian perspective." Publishes hardcover and paperback originals and reprints. **Published 1 new writer within the last year.** Averages 140 total titles, 6-8 fiction titles (mostly for children)/year.

Imprint(s): Eerdmans Books for Young Readers.

● Wm. B. Eerdmans Publishing Co.'s titles have won awards from the American Library Association and The American Bookseller's Association.

Needs: Religious (children's, general, fantasy). Published *At Break of Day*, by Nikki Grimes (children's); *The Goodbye Boat*, by Mary Joslin (children's); and *A Traitor Among Us*, by Elizabeth Van Steenwyk (middle reader).

How to Contact: Accepts unsolicited mss. Query with outline/synopsis and 2 sample chapters. Include 150-to 200-word bio and list of publishing credits. Send either SASE for return of ms or send disposable copy of ms and SASE for reply only. Agented fiction 25%. Responds in 1 month to queries; 3 months to mss. Accepts simultaneous submissions, "if notified." Sometimes comments on rejected ms.

Terms: Pays royalties of 7% minimum. Average advance: negotiable. Sends galleys to author. Publishes ms 12-18 months after acceptance. Writer's guidelines and book catalog free.

Advice: "Our readers are educated and fairly sophisticated, and we are looking for novels with literary merit."

N **▼** **⊘** **EMPYREAL PRESS,** P.O. Box 1746, Place Du Parc, Montreal, Quebec H2W 2R7 Canada. Website: http://skarwood.com. **Contact:** Colleen B. McCool. "Our mission is the publishing of literature which doesn't fit into any standard 'mold'—writing which is experimental yet grounded in discipline, imagination." Publishes trade paperback originals. Publishes 50% previously unpublished writers/year. Publishes 1-4 titles/ year.

• Empyreal Press is not currently accepting unsolicited manuscripts "due to extremely limited resources."
How to Contact: No unsolicited mss.
Terms: Book catalog for #10 SASE.
Advice: "Seriously consider self-publication: for instance, Roddy Doyle's *The Commitments* was published by the author himself. Talk about a success. Small and large presses, Empyreal included, are overloaded, some with waiting lists up to 5 years long. By publishing one's own work, one maintains full control, especially if the work is a commercial success."

⦸ **Ⓐ** **M. EVANS & CO., INC.,** 216 E. 49th St., New York NY 10017. (212)688-2810. Fax: (212)486-4544. E-mail: editorial@mevans.com. Website: www.mevans.com (includes book catalog). **Contact:** Editor. Estab. 1960. Publishes hardcover and trade paper nonfiction and a small fiction list. Averages 30-40 titles/year.
Needs: "Small general trade publisher specializing in nonfiction titles on health, nutrition, diet, cookbooks, parenting, popular psychology."
How to Contact: Does not accept unsolicited mss. Agented fiction: 100%. Accepts simultaneous submissions.
Terms: Pays in royalties and offers advance; amounts vary. Sends galleys to author. Publishes ms 6-12 months after acceptance.

N **♥** **FAITH KIDS**®, Imprint of Cook Communications Ministries, 4050 Lee Vance View, Colorado Springs CO 80918. (719)536-3271. Fax: (719)536-3269. Website: www.cookministries.com. **Contact:** Heather Gemmen, senior editor. "Faith Kids Books publishes works of children's inspirational titles, ages 1-12, with a clear 'God print' or value to influence children's spiritual growth." Publishes hardcover and trade paperback originals. Publishes 40 titles/year.
Needs: "Toddler, picture books, devotionals, Bible storybooks, for an age range of 1-12. We're particularly interested in materials for beginning readers." We are not accepting juvenile fiction at this time. Recently published The Heaven and Mirth series by Mike Thaler.
How to Contact: "Faith Kids is accepting unsolicited manuscripts at this time." Queries from previously published authors preferred. Query with SASE. Responds in 4 months to queries. Accepts simultaneous submissions, if so noted.
Terms: Pays variable royalty on retail price. Offers advance. Publishes ms 2 years after acceptance. Writer's guidelines for #10 SASE. Book catalog on request.

Ⓐ **FARRAR, STRAUS & GIROUX**, 19 Union Square W., New York NY 10003. (212)741-6900. Fax: (212)633-2427. Estab. 1946. Averages 120 titles/year.
Imprint(s): Hill & Wang, North Point Press and Farrar, Straus & Giroux Books for Young Readers, Sunburst Books.
Terms: Offers advance. Pays variable royalties. Publishes ms 18 months after acceptance.

Ⓐ **FARRAR, STRAUS & GIROUX PAPERBACKS**, 19 Union Square W., New York NY 10003. (212)741-6900. Fax: (212)633-2427. FSG Paperbacks emphasizes literary nonfiction and fiction, as well as poetry. Publishes trade paperback originals and reprints. Averages 70 total titles/year.
Needs: Literary. Mostly reprints of classic authors. Recently published *Enemies: A Love Story*, by Seamus Heaney; and *The Magic Barrel*, by Isaac Bashevis Singer (fiction).
How to Contact: No unsolicited ms.

✓ **◐** **◎** **▼** **FARRAR, STRAUS & GIROUX/BOOKS FOR YOUNG READERS**, 19 Union Square W., New York NY 10003. (212)741-6900. **Contact**: Wesley Adams, senior editor (children's); Beverly Reingold, executive editor (children's); Robert Mayes, editor (children's). Estab. 1946. "We publish original and well-written material for all ages." **Published new writers within the last year.** Averages 70 total titles/year.
• *Joey Pigza Loses Control*, by Jack Gantos, won a Newbery Honor Medal. *Everything on a Waffle*, by Polly Horvath, was awarded a *Boston Globe*/Horn Book Honor.
Imprints: Frances Foster Books, edited by Frances Foster (children's); Melanie Kroupa Books, edited by Melanie Kroupa (children's).
Needs: Children's picture books, juvenile novels, nonfiction. Published *Holes*, by Louis Sacher; *The Trolls*, by Polly Horvath; and *Tribute to Another Dead Rock Star*, by Randy Powell.

How to Contact: Query with outline/synopsis and 3 sample chapters. Include brief bio, list of publishing credits with submission. Agented fiction 25%. No electronic submissions. Responds in 3 months to queries; 3 months to mss.

Terms: Pays royalties; offers advance. Publishes ms 18-24 months after acceptance. Book catalog with 9 × 12 SASE and $1.87 postage.

Advice: "Study our list to avoid sending something inappropriate. Send query letters for long manuscripts; don't ask for editorial advice (just not possible, unfortunately); and send SASEs!"

☑ ⊘ Ⓐ **FAWCETT**, The Ballantine Publishing Group, A Division of Random House, Inc., 1540 Broadway, New York NY 10036. Estab. 1955. Major publisher of mystery mass market and trade paperbacks. Publishes paperback originals and reprints. **Contact:** Joe Blades, executive editor (suspense, mystery); Peter Borland, editorial director (commercial, literary); Tracy Brown, senior editor (commercial, literary); Allison Dickens, assistant editor (commercial, literary, women's); Anita Diggs, senior editor (literary, commercial, mystery, romance); Elisabeth Dyssegaard, executive editor; Charlotte Herscher, associate editor (historical and contemporary romance); Linda Morrow, editorial director (suspense, women's crime); Leona Nevler (literary, thriller, women's commercial, mystery); Maureen O'Neal, editorial director (women's quality commercial, Southern fiction); Patricia Peters, assistant editor (commercial, literary, mystery); Dan Smetanka, senior editor (literary, story collections); Anika Streitfeld, assistant editor (literary); Shauna Summers, senior editor (romance, women's, thrillers, suspense).

Needs: Mysteries.

How to Contact: Agented material only. Unsolicited mss will be promptly returned unopened.

☑ **FC2**, Dept. of English, FSU, Tallahassee FL 32306-1580. (850)644-2260. E-mail: fc2@english.fsu.edu. Website: http://FC2.org (includes guidelines, backlist, press history, reviews and interviews). **Contact:** R.M. Berry, publisher (fiction); Jeffrey DeShell, publisher. Estab. 1974. Publisher of innovative fiction. Publishes hardcover and paperback originals. Books: perfect/Smyth binding; illustrations. Average print order: 2,200. First novel print order: 2,200. **Published new writers within the last year.** Plans 2 first novels, 4 novels total; 1 first story collection this year. Averages 6 total titles, 6 fiction titles each year. Often comments on rejected mss. Titles distributed through Northwestern U.P.

Needs: Formally innovative, experimental, modernist/postmodern, avant-garde, anarchist, feminist, gay, minority, cyberpunk. Published *Book of Lazarus*, by Richard Grossman; *Is It Sexual Harassment Yet?*, by Cris Mazza; *Liberty's Excess*, by Lidia Yuknavitch; *Aunt Rachel's Fur*, by Raymond Federman.

How to Contact: Accepts unsolicited mss. Query first with outline/synopsis. Include 1-page bio, list of publishing credits. SASE with ms. Agented fiction 5%. Responds in 3 weeks to queries; 4 months to mss. Accepts simultaneous submissions. Send queries to: FC2, Unit for Contemporary Literature, Illinois State University, 109 Fairchild Hall, Normal IL 61790-4241.

Terms: Pays royalties of 7½%. Sends galleys to author. Publishes ms 1 year after acceptance.

Advice: "Be familiar with our list."

☑ ◎ **THE FEMINIST PRESS AT THE CITY UNIVERSITY OF NEW YORK**, 365 Fifth Ave., New York NY 10016. Website: www.feministpress.org (includes writer's guidelines, online catalog, teacher's resources). **Contact:** Jean Casella, publisher. Estab. 1970. "Nonprofit, tax-exempt, education and publishing organization interested in changing the curriculum, the classroom and consciousness." Publishes hardcover and paperback reprints. "We use an acid-free paper, perfect-bind our books, four color covers; and some cloth for library sales if the book has been out of print for some time; we shoot from the original text when possible. We always include a scholarly and literary afterword, since we are introducing a text to a new audience. Average print run: 2,500." Publishes no original fiction; exceptions are anthologies and international works. Averages 10-15 total titles, 4-8 fiction titles/year (reprints of feminist classics only). Distributes titles through Consortium Book Sales and Distribution. Promotes titles through author tours, advertising, exhibits and conferences.

Needs: Contemporary, ethnic, feminist, gay, lesbian, literary, regional, science fiction, translations, women's. Published *Apples From the Desert*, by Savyon Liebrecht (short stories, translation); *Confessions of Madame Psyche*, by Dorothy Bryant (novel); and *Mulberry and Peach*, by Hualing Nen (novel, translation).

How to Contact: Accepts unsolicited mss. Query with outline/synopsis and 1 sample chapter. Accepts queries by fax. Send SASE. Responds in 1 month to queries; 3 months to mss. Accepts simultaneous submissions.

Terms: Pays royalties of 10% on net sales. Average advance: $100. Pays 10 author's copies. Sends galleys to author. Book catalog free.

◻ ☑ **FORGE BOOKS**, Tom Doherty Associates, LLC, 175 5th Ave., New York NY 10010. (212)388-0100. Fax: (212)388-0191. Website: www.tor.com (includes FAQ, writer's guidelines, info on authors and upcoming books, first chapter of selected books, list of award winners). **Contact:** Melissa Ann Singer, senior editor (general fiction, mysteries, thriller); Patrick Nielsen Hayden, senior editor (science fiction, fantasy). Estab. 1980. "Forge imprint specializes in thrillers, historicals, and mysteries. Tor imprint focuses on science fiction, fantasy and horror." Publishes hardcover and paperback originals. **Published new writers within the last year.** Averages 130 total titles, 129 fiction titles/year.

Imprint(s): Forge, Tor, Orb.

• Recently won the Locus Award and the Western Writers of America Award for best publisher.

Needs: Historical, horror, mainstream/contemporary, mystery/suspense (amateur sleuth, police procedural, private eye/hardboiled), thriller/espionage, western (frontier saga, traditional), science fiction, fantasy.

How to Contact: Accepts unsolicited mss. Query with outline/synopsis and first 3 sample chapters. Include estimated word count, bio and list of publishing credits. SASE for reply. Agented fiction 95%. Responds in 4 months to proposals. Sometimes comments on rejected mss.

Terms: Pays royalties. Sends galleys to author. Publishes ms 12-18 months after acceptance.

Advice: "The writing mechanics must be outstanding for a new author to break into today's market."

✔ 🏆 ◑ **FOUR WALLS EIGHT WINDOWS**, 39 W. 14th St., #503, New York NY 10011. (212)206-8965. E-mail: edit@4w8w.com. Website: www.4w8w.com (includes complete catalog, featured books and ordering information). **Contact:** John Oakes, publisher. Estab. 1987. "We are a small independent publisher." Publishes hardcover and paperback originals and paperback reprints. Books: quality paper; paper or cloth binding; illustrations sometimes. Average print order: 3,000-7,000. First novel print order: 3,000-5,000. **Published new writers within the last year.** Averages 30 total titles; approximately 9 fiction titles/year. Distributes titles through Publishers Group West, the largest independent distributor in the country. Promotes titles through author tours, bound galleys, select advertising, postcard mailing, etc.

• Four Walls Eight Windows' books have received mention from the *New York Times* as "Notable Books of the Year" and have been nominated for *L.A. Times* fiction and nonfiction prizes. Won Special Citation, Philip K. Dick Award for Paul DiFilippo's *Lost Pages*. Won 1999 National Book Critics Circle Nonfiction Finalist for Jean-Paul Kauffmann's *Black Room at Longwood*.

Needs: Nonfiction. Published *The Angle Quickest for Flight*, by Steven Kotler (novel); *Extremities*, by Kathe Koja (stories); *Beast of the Heartland*, by Lucius Shepard (stories).

How to Contact: Does not accept unsolicited submissions. "Query letter accompanied by sample chapter, outline and SASE is best. Useful to know if writer has published elsewhere, and if so, where." Accepts electronic queries but *not* submissions. Agented fiction 50%. Responds in 2 months. Accepts simultaneous submissions. No electronic submissions.

Terms: Pays standard royalties. Average advance: varies. Sends galleys to author. Publishes ms 1-2 years after acceptance. Book catalog free on request.

Advice: "Please read our catalog and/or our website to be sure your work would be compatible with our list."

✔ ◑ ◎ 🏆 **FRONT STREET BOOKS**, 20 Battery Park Ave., #403, Asheville NC 28801. (828)236-3097. Fax: (828)236-3098. E-mail: contactus@frontstreetbooks.com. Website: www.frontstreetbooks.com (includes writer's guidelines, names of editors, book catalog, interviews with authors, first chapters of some books). **Contact:** Stephen Roxburgh, president and publisher; Joy Neaves, editor. Estab. 1994. "Small independent publisher of high-quality picture books and literature for children and young adults." Publishes hardcover originals. Distributes titles through PGW. Titles promoted on Internet, through sales conferences, and catalog.

• *Many Stones*, by Carolyn Coman, was a Printz Honor book and an NBA finalist.

Needs: Children's/juvenile (adventure, animal, fantasy, historical, mystery, preschool/picture book, sports), young adult/teen (adventure, fantasy/science fiction, historical, mystery/suspense, problem novels, sports). Recently published *Myrtle of Willendorf*, by Rebecca O'Connell (young adult fiction); *Many Stones*, by Carolyn Coman (young adult fiction); *Cut*, by Patricia McCormick (first fiction, young adult fiction); *Letters from Vinnie*, by Maureen Sappéy (young adult fiction); and *A Day, A Dog*, by Gabrielle Vincent (picture book).

How to Contact: Accepts unsolicited mss. Query with outline/synopsis and a few sample chapters or submit complete ms with cover letter. Accepts queries by e-mail. Include short bio and list of publishing credits. Send SASE for reply, return of ms or send disposable copy of ms. Agented fiction 10%. Responds in 2 weeks to queries; 3 months to mss. Accepts simultaneous submissions. No electronic submissions.

Terms: Pays royalties. Offers negotiable advance.

CHECK THE CATEGORY INDEXES, located at the back of the book, for publishers interested in specific fiction subjects.

[N] [icons] GAY SUNSHINE PRESS AND LEYLAND PUBLICATIONS, P.O. Box 410690, San Francisco CA 94141. Fax: (415)626-1802. Website: www.gaysunshine.com. **Contact:** Winston Leyland, editor. Estab. 1970. Midsize independent press. Publishes hardcover and paperback originals. Books: natural paper; perfect-bound; illustrations. Average print order: 5,000-10,000.

● Gay Sunshine Press has received a Lambda Book Award for *Gay Roots* (volume 1), named "Best Book by a Gay or Lesbian Press," and received grants from the National Endowment for the Arts.

Needs: Literary, experimental, translations—all gay male material only. "We desire fiction on gay themes of *high* literary quality and prefer writers who have already had work published in literary magazines. We also publish erotica—short stories and novels." Published *Partings at Dawn: An Anthology of Japanese Gay Literature from the 12th to the 20th Centuries*; and *Out of the Blue: Russia's Hidden Gay Literature—An Anthology.*

How to Contact: "Do not send an unsolicited manuscript." Query with SASE. Responds in 3 weeks to queries; 2 months to mss. Send $1 for catalog.

Terms: Negotiates terms with author. Sends galleys to author. Pays royalties or by outright purchase.

Advice: "We continue to be interested in receiving queries from authors who have book-length manuscripts of high literary quality. We feel it is important that an author know exactly what to expect from our press (promotion, distribution, etc.) before a contract is signed. Before submitting a query or manuscript to a particular press, obtain critical feedback on your manuscript from knowledgeable people. If you alienate a publisher by submitting a manuscript shoddily prepared/typed, or one needing very extensive rewriting, or one which is not in the area of the publisher's specialty, you will surely not get a second chance with that press."

[icons] LAURA GERINGER BOOKS, Imprint of HarperCollins Children's Books Group, HarperCollins Publishers, 1350 Avenue of the Americas, New York NY 10019. (212)261-6500. Website: www.harpercollins.c om. **Contact:** Laura Geringer, senior vice president/publisher. "We look for books that are out of the ordinary, authors who have their own definite take, and artists that add a sense of humor to the text." Publishes hardcover originals. **Published new writers within the last year.** Averages 15-20 titles/year.

Needs: Adventure, fantasy, historical, humor, literary, young adult. Recently published *Regular Guy*, by Sarah Weeks; and *Throwing Smoke*, by Bruce Brooks.

How to Contact: Accepts unsolicited mss. Submit complete ms with cover letter. Send SASE or IRC for return of ms. Agented fiction 75%. Responds in 4 months to queries.

Terms: Pays royalties of 10-12½% on retail price. Advance varies. Publishes ms 6-12 months after acceptance for novels. Writer's guidelines for #10 SASE. Book catalog for 8×10 SAE with 3 first-class stamps.

Advice: "A mistake writers often make is failing to research the type of books an imprint publishes, therefore sending inappropriate material."

[icons] GOOSE LANE EDITIONS, 469 King St., Fredericton, New Brunswick E3B 1E5 Canada. (506)450-4251. Fax: (506)459-4991. **Contact:** Laurel Boone, editorial director. Estab. 1957. Publishes hardcover and paperback originals and occasional reprints. Books: some illustrations. Average print order: 3,000. First novel print order: 1,500. Averages 14 total titles, 4-5 fiction titles/year. Distributes titles through General Distribution Services. Promotes titles through Literary Press Group (Canada).

● Goose Lane author Lynn Coady was a finalist for the Governor General's Award for fiction for *Strange Heaven*. Luther Corhern's *Salmon Camp Chronicles* was a finalist for the Stephen Leacock Medal for Humour.

Needs: Contemporary, historical, literary, short story collections. "Not suitable for mainstream or mass market submissions. No genres, i.e.: modern and historical adventure, crime, modern and historical romance, science fiction, fantasy, westerns, confessional works (fictional and autobiographical), and thrillers and other mystery books." Recently published *Overnight Sensation*, by Colleen Curran; *Sisters of Grass*, by Theresa Kishkan; *The Time of Her Life*, by David Helwig.

How to Contact: Considers unsolicited mss. Submit outline/synopsis and 30-50 page sample. Send SASE "with Canadian stamps, International Reply Coupons, cash, check or money order. No U.S. stamps please." Responds in 6 months.

Terms: Pays royalties of 8-12%. Average advance: $100-200, negotiable. Sends galleys to author. Writers guidelines for SAE and IRC or Canadian stamps.

Advice: "We do not consider submissions from outside Canada."

[icons] GRAYWOLF PRESS, 2402 University Ave., Suite 203, St. Paul MN 55114. (651)641-0077. Fax: (651)641-0036. E-mail: wolves@graywolfpress.com. Website: www.graywolfpress.org (includes writers' guidelines, catalog, author bios, news). Director: Fiona McCrae. **Contact:** Anne Czarniecki, executive editor; Katie Dublinski, editor. Estab. 1974. "Graywolf Press is an independent, nonprofit publisher dedicated to the creation and promotion of thoughtful and imaginative contemporary literature essential to a vital and diverse culture." Growing small literary press, nonprofit corporation. Publishes trade cloth and paperback originals. Books: acid-free quality paper; offset printing; hardcover and soft binding; illustrations occasionally. Average print order:

3,000-10,000. First novel print order: 2,000-6,000. Averages 14-16 total titles, 4-6 fiction titles/year. Distributes titles nationally through Consortium Book Sales and Distribution. "We have an in house marketing staff and an advertising budget for all books we publish."

Needs: Literary, and short story collections. Literary fiction; no genre books (romance, western, science fiction, suspense). Published *War Memorials*, by Clint McCown; *Loverboy*, by Victoria Redel; *The Ghost of Bridgetown*, by Debra Spark.

How to Contact: Query with SASE. "Please do not fax or e-mail queries or submissions." Agented fiction: 50%. Responds in 3 months. Accepts simultaneous submissions.

Terms: Pays royalties on retail price; negotiates advance and number of author's copies. Sends galleys to author. Publishes ms 18 months after acceptance. Guidelines for #10 SASE; book catalog free.

Advice: "Please review the catalog and submission guidelines before submitting your work. We rarely publish collections or novels by authors who have not published work previously in literary journals or magazines."

N **O** **GREEN BEAN PRESS**, P.O. Box 237, New York NY 10013. (718)302-1955. Fax: (718)302-1955. E-mail: gbpress@earthlink.net. Website: www.greenbeanpress.com (includes guidelines, catalog, links, excerpts and special offers). **Contact:** Ian Griffin, editor. Estab. 1993. "Small independent press dedicated to publishing gritty, unique, distinctive authors." Publishes paperback originals. Books: acid-free paper; perfect bound. Average print order: 600; first novel print order: 500. **Published 3 new writers within the last year.** Averages 15 total titles, 5 fiction titles/year. Titles distributed through Ingram, promotion through print ads, author signings and redings, direct mail and e-mail.

Needs: Humor/satire, literary, mystery (private eye/hardboiled), short story collections. Recently published *One Last Chance*, by Brent McKnight (short story); *Do Not Look Directly Into Me*, by Daniel Crocker (short story); *Wing-Ding at Uncle Tug's*, by Jeff Grimshaw (humor/short story).

How to Contact: Does not accept unsolicited mss; any unsolicited mss will be returned. Send query letter or query with outline/synopsis and 2-4 sample chapters. Accepts e-mail queries. Include brief bio with submission. Agented fiction: 10%. Responds in 2 weeks to queries; 2 months to mss. No simultaneous, electronic or disk submissions.

Terms: Pays royalties of 10-15%. Sends galleys to author. Time between acceptance and publication is 6-12 months. Writer's guidelines for SASE or on website. Book catalogs free upon request, on website.

Advice: "As a result of corporate publishers' 'bestseller only' mentality, there are more and more high-quality authors out there looking for presses they can have closer, more personal relationships with. This is a great opportunity for small independent presses. Let your work speak for itself. If you feel the need to send a letter explaining every little thing about your manuscript, then the manuscript's not doing its job."

O **O** **GREENWILLOW BOOKS,** Imprint of HarperCollins Publishers, 1350 Avenue of the Americas, New York NY 10019. (212)261-6500. Website: www.harperchildrens.com. **Contact:** Fiction Editor. Estab. 1974. "Greenwillow Books publishes quality hardcover books for children." Publishes hardcover originals and reprints. **Published new writers within the last year.** Averages 50-60 titles/year.

Needs: Juvenile: picture books, humor, fantasy, literary, mystery. For novels submit synopsis and sample chapters. Include SASE for reply and return on ms. Recently published *The Queen of Attolia*, by Megan Whalen Turner; *Bo & Mzzz Mad*, by Sid Fleischman; *Whale Talk*, by Chris Crutcher; *Year of the Griffen*, by Diana Wynne Jones.

How to Contact: Agented fiction 70%. Responds in 3 months to mss. Accepts simultaneous submissions.

Terms: Pays royalties of 10% on wholesale price for first-time authors. Average advance varies. Publishes ms 2 years after acceptance. Writer's guidelines for #10 SASE; book catalog available for $2.30 and 9×12 SASE.

A **GROVE/ATLANTIC, INC.**, 841 Broadway, New York NY 10003. (212)614-7850. Fax: (212)614-7886. "Grove/Atlantic publishes serious nonfiction and literary fiction." Publishes hardcover originals, trade paperback originals and reprints. Averages 60-70 titles/year.

Imprint(s): Grove Press (Estab. 1952), Atlantic Monthly Press (Estab. 1917).

Needs: Experimental, literary. Published *Four Blondes*, by Candace Bushnell (Atlantic Monthly); and *How the Dead Live*, by Will Self (Grove Press).

How to Contact: Does not accept unsolicited mss. Agented submissions only. Accepts simultaneous submissions.

Terms: Pays royalties of 7½-15% on retail price. Advance varies considerably. Publishes ms 1 year after acceptance. Book catalog free.

O **GRYPHON BOOKS**, P.O. Box 209, Brooklyn NY 11228. (718)646-6126 (after 6 pm EST). Website: www.gryphonbooks.com. **Contact:** Gary Lovisi, owner/editor. Estab. 1983. Publishes paperback originals and trade paperback reprints. Books: bond paper; offset printing; perfect binding. Average print order: 500-1,000. **Published new writers within the last year.** Averages 10-15 total titles, 12 fiction titles/year.

Imprint(s): Gryphon Books, Gryphon Doubles, Gryphon SF Rediscovery Series.

Needs: Mystery/suspense (private eye/hardboiled, crime), science fiction (hard science/technological, soft/socio-logical). No supernatural, horror, romance or westerns. Published *The Dreaming Detective*, by Ralph Vaughn (mystery-fantasy-horror); *The Woman in the Dugout*, by Gary Lovisi and T. Arnone (baseball novel); and *A Mate for Murder*, by Bruno Fischer (hardboiled pulp). Publishes Gryphon Double novel series.

How to Contact: "I am not looking for novels now; *will only see a 1-page synopsis with SASE.*" Include estimated word count, 50-word bio, short list of publishing credits, "how you heard about us." Do not send ms. Agented fiction 5-10%. Responds in 1 month to queries; 2 months to mss. Accepts simultaneous and electronic submissions (with hard copy—disk in ASCII). Often comments on rejected mss.

Terms: For magazines, $5-45 on publication plus 2 contributor's copies; for novels/collections payment varies and is much more. Sends galleys to author. Publishes ms 1-3 years after acceptance. Writers guidelines and book catalog for SASE.

Advice: "I am looking for better and better writing, more cutting-edge material with *impact*! Keep it lean and focused."

GUERNICA EDITIONS, Box 117, Station P, Toronto, Ontario M5S 2S6 Canada. (416)658-9888. Fax: (416)657-8885. E-mail: guernicaeditions@cs.com. Website: www.guernicaeditions.com. **Contact:** Antonio D'Alfonso, fiction editor (novel and short story). "Guernica Editions is a small press that produces works of fiction and nonfiction on the viability of pluriculturalism." Publishes paperback originals and reprints. Books: various paper; offset printing; perfect binding. Average print order: 1,500; first novel print order: 1,500. **Published 6 new writers within the last year.** Averages 25 total titles, 18-20 fiction titles/year. Distributes titles through professional distributors.

• Two titles by Guernica Editions have won American Book Awards.

Imprint(s): Prose Series, Antonio D'Alfonso, editor, all; Picas Series, Antonio D'Alfonso, editor, reprints.

Needs: Erotica, literary, translations. "We are open to all styles, but especially shorter pieces." Publishes anthology of Arab women writers/Italian women writers. Recently published *The Blue Whale*, by Stanislao Niero; *A Father's Revenge*, by Pan Bouyoucas; and *Moncton Mantra*, by Gérald Leblanc.

How to Contact: Accepts unsolicited mss. Send query letter. Include estimated word count, brief bio and list of publishing credits. Send IRC for return of ms. Responds in weeks to queries; months to mss.

Terms: Pays royalties of 10%. Average advance: $500-1,000. Sends galleys to author. Publishes ms 12 months after acceptance. Book catalogs for $5 and on website.

Advice: "Know what publishers do, and send your works only to publisher whose writers you've read and enjoyed."

ROBERT HALE LIMITED, Clerkenwell House, 45/47 Clerkenwell Green, London EC1R 0HT England. Fax: 020-7490-4958. **Contact:** Fiction Editor. Publishes hardcover and trade paperback originals and hardcover reprints. **Published approximately 50 new writers within the last year.**

Imprint(s): J.A. Allen; Caroline Burt, editor (horse books nonfiction); Nag Press (Horological and gemmological nonfiction).

Needs: Historical (not U.S. history), mainstream and western. Length: 40,000-150,000 words. Recently published *Greenwich*, by Harold Fast (mainstream); *The Judas Judge*, by Michael McGarrity (crime); and *The Savage Lord Griffin*, by Joan Smith (regency romance).

How to Contact: Query with synopsis and 2 sample chapters. Acceptes queries by fax.

Advice: "Write well and have a strong plot!"

HAMPTON ROADS PUBLISHING COMPANY, INC., 134 Burgess Ln., Charlottesville VA 22902. (804)296-2772. Fax: (804)296-5096. E-mail: editorial@hrpub.com. Website: www.hrpub.com (includes writer's guidelines, authors, titles, synopsis of books, message board, guest book). **Contact:** Rebecca Williamson, managing editor. Estab. 1989. Publishes and distributes hardcover and paperback originals on subjects including metaphysics, health, complementary medicine, visionary fiction and other related topics. "We work as a team to produce the best books we are capable of producing which will impact, uplift and contribute to positive change in the world. We publish what defies or doesn't quite fit the usual genres. We are noted for visionary fiction." Average print order: 3,000-5,000. **Published 6 new writers within the last year.** Averages 60 total titles/year, 5-6 fiction titles/year. Distributes titles through distributors. Promotes titles through advertising, representatives, author signings and radio-TV interviews with authors.

Needs: Literary, New Age/mystic/spiritual, psychic/supernatural/occult. Looking for "visionary fiction, past-life fiction, based on actual memories." Recently published *Rogue Messiahs*, by Colin Wilson; *Spirit Matters*, by Michael Lerner; and *The Authenticator*, by William M. Valtos.

How to Contact: Does not accept unsolicited mss. Query with synopsis, chapter-by-chapter outline and 2 sample chapters. Accepts queries by e-mail and fax. Send SASE or IRC for return of ms or send disposable copy of ms and SASE for reply only (preferred). Agented fiction 5%. Responds in 1 month to queries; up to 5 months to mss. Accepts simultaneous submissions.

Terms: Pays in royalties; advance is negotiable. Sends galleys to author.

Advice: "Send us something new and different. Be patient. We take the time to give each submission the attention it deserves."

[A] [Y] HARCOURT INC., 525 B St., Suite 1900, San Diego CA 92101. (619)231-6616. Fax: (619)699-6777. Publisher: Louise Phelan. **Contact:** Jeannette Larson, senior editor (general fiction); Allyn Johnston, editorial director of Harcourt Brace Children's Books; Elizabeth Van Doren, editorial director of Gulliver Books; Paula Wiseman, editorial director of Silver Whistle. Publishes hardcover originals and paperback reprints. **Published "very few" new writers within the last year.** Averages 150 titles/year.

Imprint(s): Harcourt Trade Children's Books, Gulliver Books, Red Wagon Books and Silver Whistle.

● Books published by Harcourt Trade Publishers have received numerous awards including the Caldecott and Newbery medals and selections as the American Library Association's "Best Books for Young Adults." Note that the publisher only accepts manuscripts through an agent. Unagented writers may query only.

Needs: Nonfiction for all ages, picture books for very young children, historical, mystery. Published *To Market, To Market*, by Ann Miranda; *Antarctic Antics*, by Judy Sierra; *Armageddon Summer*, by Bruce Coville and Jane Yolen; *Count On Me*, by Alice Provensen.

How to Contact: Does not accept unsolicited mss. Submit through agent only.

Terms: Terms vary according to individual books; pays on royalty basis. Book catalog for 9×12 SASE.

Advice: "Read as much current fiction as you can; familiarize yourself with the type of fiction published by a particular house; interact with young people to obtain a realistic picture of their concerns, interests and speech patterns."

[■] [/] [◎] HARLEQUIN ENTERPRISES, LTD., 225 Duncan Mill Rd., Don Mills, Ontario M3B 3K9 Canada. (416)445-5860. Website: www.eHarlequin.com (includes product listings, guidelines, author information, a full range of related information). Chairman and CEO: Brian E. Hickey. President: Donna Hayes. Vice President Editorial: Isabel Swift. **Contact:** Randall Toye, editorial director (Harlequin, Gold Eagle, Worldwide Library); Tara Gavin, editorial director (Silhouette, Steeple Hill, Red Dress Ink); Diane Moggy, editorial director (MIRA). Estab. 1949. Publishes paperback originals and reprints. Books: Newsprint paper; web printing; perfect-bound. **Published new writers within the last year.** Averages 700 total titles/year. Distributes titles through retail market, direct mail market and overseas through operating companies. Promotes titles through trade and consumer advertising: print, radio, TV.

Imprint(s): Harlequin, Silhouette, MIRA, Gold Eagle, Worldwide Mysteries, Steeple Hill, Red Dress Ink.

Needs: Romance, heroic adventure, mystery/suspense (romantic suspense *only*). Will accept nothing that is not related to the desired categories.

How to Contact: Send query letter or query with outline and first 50 pages (2 or 3 chapters) or submit through agent with SASE (Canadian). Does not accept simultaneous or electronic submissions. Responds in 6 weeks to queries; 2 months to mss.

Terms: Offers royalties, advance. Must return advance if book is not completed or is unacceptable. Sends galleys to author. Publishes ms 1 year after acceptance. Guidelines available.

Advice: "The quickest route to success is to follow directions for submissions: Query first. We encourage first novelists. Before sending a manuscript, read as many current Harlequin titles as you can. It's very important to know the genre and the series most appropriate for your submission." Submissions for Harlequin Romance and Harlequin Presents should go to: Mills & Boon Limited Eton House, 18-24 Paradise Road, Richmond, Surrey TW9 1SR United Kingdom, Attn: Karin Stoecker; Superromances: Paula Eykelhof, senior editor, (Don Mills address); Temptation: Birgit Davis-Todd, senior editor (Don Mills address). Intrigue: Denise O'Sullivan, associate senior editor, Harlequin Books, 6th Floor, 300 E. 42 Street, New York, NY 10017. Silhouette and Steeple Hill submissions should also be sent to the New York office, attention Tara Gavin. Red Dress Ink submissions should be sent to the New York office, attention Margaret Marbury. MIRA submissions to Dianne Moggy, editorial director (Don Mills address); Gold Eagle and Worldwide Mysteries submissions to Feroze Mohammed, senior editor (Don Mills address). "The relationship between the novelist and editor is regarded highly and treated with professionalism."

[N] [⊕] [/] HARLEQUIN MILLS & BOON LTD., Subsidiary of Harlequin Enterprises Ltd., Eton House, 18-24 Paradise Rd., Richmond, Surrey TW9 1SR United Kingdom. (44)0208-288-2800. Website: www.millsandb oon.co.uk (includes forthcoming titles and author profiles). **Contact:** K. Stoecker, editorial director; Tessa Shapcott, senior editor (Harlequin Presents®); Samantha Bell, senior editor (Harlequin Romance®); Linda Fildew, editor (Mills & Boon Historicals); Sheila Hodgson, editor (Mills & Boon Medicals). Estab. 1908-1909. "World's largest publisher of brand name category romance; books are available for translation into more than 20 languages and distributed in more than 100 international markets." Publishes paperback originals. Published new writers within the last year. Plans 3-4 first novels this year.

Imprint(s): Harlequin, Silhouette, MIRA, Mills & Boon.

Needs: Romance (contemporary, historical, regency period, medical). Publishes Christmas anthologies. Publishes Harlequin Romance, Harlequin Presents (historical romance, medical romance in the UK).

How to Contact: Accepts unsolicited mss; returns unsolicited mss, if return postage included. Query with first 3 chapters and synopsis. Send SASE for reply, return of ms. Responds in up to 5 month to mss. No simultaneous submissions. Often comments on rejected mss.

Terms: Advance against royalty. Sends galleys to author. Publishes ms up to 2 years after acceptance. Writer's guidelines free.

Advice: "Study a wide selection of our current paperbacks to gain an understanding of our requirements—then write from the heart."

⬛⬛ HARPERCOLLINS CANADA LTD., 55 Avenue Rd., Suite 2900, Toronto, Ontario M5R 3L2 Canada. (416)975-9334. Fax: (416)975-5223. Website: www.harpercanada.com.
● HarperCollins Canada is not accepting unsolicited material at this time.

⊘ Ⓐ HARPERCOLLINS PUBLISHERS, 10 E. 53rd St., New York NY 10022. (212)207-7000. Website: www.harpercollins.com. "HarperCollins, one of the largest English language publishers in the world, is a broad-based publisher with strengths in academic, business and professional, children's, educational, general interest, and religious and spiritual books, as well as multimedia titles." Publishes hardcover and paperback originals and paperback reprints. Trade publishes 120-150 titles/year.

Imprint(s): Harper Adult Trade; Harper Audio, Harper Business, HarperLibros, HarperPaperbacks, HarperPerennial, Harper Children's Books, HarperSan Francisco, Regan Books, Cliff Street Books, HarperEntertainment, HarperResource, HarperVoyager, Ecco Press, Zondervan Publishing House.

Needs: Adventure, fantasy, gothic, historical, mystery, science fiction, suspense, western, literary. "We look for a strong story line and exceptional literary talent." Published *The Tennis Partner*, by Abraham Verghese; *The Professor and the Madman*, by Simon Winchester; *I Know This Much Is True*, by Wally Lamb; *The Antelope Wife*, by Louise Erdrich; *Cloudsplitter*, by Russell Banks; and *The Soul of Sex*, by Thomas Moore.

How to Contact: *No unsolicited queries or mss.* Agented submissions only. Responds in 6 weeks to solicited queries.

Terms: Pays standard royalties. Advance negotiable.

Advice: "We do not accept any unsolicited material."

⊕ ◎ HARPERCOLLINS PUBLISHERS (NEW ZEALAND) LIMITED, P.O. Box 1, Auckland, New Zealand. Website: www.harpercollins.co.nz. **Contact**: Ian Watt, publisher. Averages 8-10 fiction titles/year (25-30 nonfiction).

Imprint(s): Flamingo, HarperCollins, Voyager.

Needs: Adult fiction: Flamingo and HarperCollins imprints (40,000+ words); Junior fiction: 8-11 years (15-20,000 words).

How to Contact: Full ms preferred.

Terms: Pays royalties. "Write and ask for guidelines."

Advice: "It helps if the author and story have New Zealand connections/content."

⊘ Ⓐ HARPERPERENNIAL, Imprint of HarperCollins Publishers, 10 E. 53rd St., New York NY 10022. (212)207-7000. Website: www.harpercollins.com. **Acquisitions:** Susan Weinberg, senior vice president/publisher. Estab. 1963. "HarperPerennial publishes a broad range of adult fiction and nonfiction paperbacks." Publishes trade paperback originals and reprints. Publishes 100 titles/year.

Needs: Ethnic, feminist, literary. "Don't send us novels—go through hardcover." Published *Lying On the Couch*, by Irwin D. Yalom (psycho-thriller novel); *American Pie*, by Michael Lee West (novel); and *Bird Girl and the Man Who Followed the Sun*, by Velma Wallis (fiction/native American studies).

How to Contact: Agented submissions only.

Terms: Pays 5-7½% royalty. Advance varies. Publishes ms 6 months after acceptance. Book catalog free.

Advice: Audience is general reader—high school, college. "Call and get the name of an editor and they will look at it. Usually an editor is listed in a book's acknowledgments. You should address your submission to an editor or else it will probably be returned."

◎ **HARPERTORCH**, (formerly HarperPaperbacks), Division of HarperCollins Publishers, 10 E. 53rd St., New York NY 10022. (212)207-7000. Fax: (212)207-7901. Publisher: Michael Morrison. **Contact**: Jennifer Hershey, editorial director. Publishes paperback originals and reprints. **Published new writers within the last year.**

Needs: Mainstream/contemporary, mystery/suspense, romance (contemporary, historical, romantic suspense), thriller/espionage.

How to Contact: Does not accept unsolicited mss. Query by letter or through agent. Send SASE or IRC for reply.

Terms: Pays advance and royalties.

☑ ◎ **HARVEST HOUSE PUBLISHERS**, 990 Owen Loop N, Eugene OR 97402. (541)343-0123. Editorial Managing Director: LaRae Weikert. Vice President of Editorial: Carolyn McCready. **Contact:** Acquisitions. Estab. 1974. "The foundation of our publishing program is to publish books that 'help the hurts of people' and nurture spiritual growth." Midsize independent publisher. Publishes hardcover and paperback originals and reprints. Books: 40 lb. ground wood paper; offset printing; perfect binding. Average print order: 10,000. First novel print order: 10,000-15,000. Average 120 total titles, 7 fiction titles/year.

How to Contact: Does not accept unsolicited mss. Recommends using Evangelical Christian Publishers Association website (www.ecpa.org) or the Writer's Edge.

◎ **HAWK PUBLISHING GROUP**, 6420 S. Richmond Ave., Tulsa OK 74136-1619. (918)492-3677. Fax: (918)492-2120. E-mail: wb@hawkpub.com. Website: www.hawkpub.com (includes writer's guidelines, book catalog, forthcoming titles, author information). Estab. 1999. Independent publisher of general trade/commercial books, fiction and nonfiction. Publishes hardcover and paperback originals. **Published 4 new writers within the last year.** Plans 2 first novels in 2002. Averages 8 total titles, 4 fiction titles/year. Member, PMA, SPAN. Distributes titles through Biblio/NBN.

Needs: Recently published *Family Correspondence*, by Teresa Miller (literary); and *Dark Within*, by John Wooley.

How to Contact: Accepts unsolicited mss. Query with outline/synopsis and sample chapters. Include brief bio and list of publishing credits. Send disposable copy of ms. Agented fiction 60%. Accepts simultaneous submissions. "No replies unless interested."

Terms: Terms vary. Sends galleys to author.

Advice: "Send us something different and really, really good."

◎ ♟ **HELICON NINE EDITIONS**, Subsidiary of Midwest Center for the Literary Arts, Inc., P.O. Box 22412, Kansas City MO 64111-2820. (816)753-1016. E-mail: helicon9@aol.com. Website: www.heliconnine. com (includes general information about title, book and author, ording information for books). **Contact**: Gloria Vando Hickok. Estab. 1990. Small press publishing poetry, fiction, creative nonfiction and anthologies. Publishes paperback originals. Books: 60 lb. paper; offset printing; perfect-bound; 4-color cover. Average print order: 1,000-5,000. **Published one new writer within the last year.** Averages 4 total titles, 2-4 fiction titles/year. Also publishes one-story chapbooks called *feuillets*, which come with envelope, 250 print run. Distributes titles through Baker & Taylor, The Booksource, Brodart, Ingrams, Follett (library acquisitions), Midwest Library Service, all major distributors and booksellers. Promotes titles through reviews, readings, radio and television interviews.

● Helicon Nine Editions has received the Society of Midland Authors Prize as well as grants rom the Kansas Arts Commission, the Missouri Arts Council and the National Endowment for the Arts. *Diasporadic*, by Patty Seyburn received the Notable Book Award, and Amy Tan selected "Africans" from Shiela Kohler's *One Girl* for *Best American Short Stories*.

How to Contact: Currently not accepting unsolicited mss or query letters.

Terms: Pays royalties, advance and author's copies. "Individual arrangement with author." Sends galleys to author. Publishes ms 6-12 months after acceptance.

Advice: "We accept short story collections. We welcome new writers and first books. Submit a clean, readable copy in a folder or box—paginated with title and name on each page. Also, do not pre-design book, i.e., no illustrations. We'd like to see books that will be read 50-100 years from now."

🌐 ◎ **HODDER & STOUGHTON/HEADLINE**, Hodder Headline, 338 Euston Rd., London NW1 3BH England. Phone: (020)7873 6000. Fax: (020)7873 6024. **Contact:** Mrs. Betty Schwartz, submissions editor, Hodder & Stoughton (adult fiction, nonfiction); Caroline Stofer, submissions editor, Headline (adult fiction). "Big commercial, general book publishers of general fiction/nonfiction, thrillers, romance, sagas, contemporary original, literary, crime." Publishes hardcover and paperback originals and paperback reprints. **Published 5 new writers within the last year.**

Imprint(s): Coronet, Sceptre, Flame, Hodder & Stoughton, NEL, LIR (Headline, Review, Feature).

Needs: Family saga, historical (general), literary, mainstream, mystery/suspense (amateur sleuth, cozy, police procedural, private eye/hardboiled), romance (contemporary, romantic suspense), thriller/espionage.

How to Contact: Accepts unsolicited mss. Query with outline/synopsis and first sample chapter. Accepts queries by e-mail. Include estimated word count and brief bio. Send disposable copy of ms and SASE for reply only. Responds in 2 weeks minimum to queries; 1 month to mss. Accepts simultaneous submissions.

Terms: Writer's guidelines for SASE. Book catalogs for flat A4 SASE.

Advice: "Minimum 80,000 words. For popular fiction titles (i.e. thrillers) we require around 120,000 words. Send cover letter, short synopsis (1-2 pages) and first sample chapter, typewritten, double-spaced. Writing should be of good quality, and commercial. No single short stories."

☑ 🌓 ◎ 🌱 **HOLIDAY HOUSE, INC.,** 425 Madison, New York NY 10017. (212)688-0085. Fax: (212)421-6134. Editor-in-Chief: Regina Griffin. **Contact:** Suzanne Reinoehl, associate editor. Estab. 1935. "Holiday House has a commitment to publishing first-time authors and illustrators." Independent publisher of children's books, picture books, nonfiction and novels for young readers. Publishes hardcover originals and paperback reprints. **Published new writers within the last year.** Averages approximately 50 hardcovers and 15 paperbacks/year.

 • *The Wright Brothers: How They Invented the Airplane* by Russell Freedman and published by Holiday House was a Newbery Honor Book.

Needs: Children's books only: literary, contemporary, Judaica and holiday, adventure, humor and animal stories for young readers. Recently published *A Child's Calendar*, by John Updike, illustrated by Trina Schart Hyman; *The Jar of Fools*, by Eric A. Kimmel, illustrated by Mordicai Gerstern; *The Blues of Flats Brown*, by Walter Dean Myers, illustrated by Nina Laden. "We're not in a position to be too encouraging, as our list is tight, but we're always open to good writing."

How to Contact: "We ask for query letters only with SASE. We do not accept simultaneous submissions. No phone calls, please."

Terms: Royalties, advance are flexible, depending upon whether the book is illustrated. Publishes ms 1-3 years after acceptance.

Advice: "Please submit only one project at a time."

🌓 ◎ **HENRY HOLT & COMPANY BOOKS FOR YOUNG READERS**, Imprint of Henry Holt & Co., Inc., 115 W. 18th St., New York NY 10011. (212)886-9200. Fax: (212)645-5832. Website: www.henryholt.com/byr/. **Contact:** Laura Godwin, associate publisher (picture books, chapter books, middle grade); Nina Ignatowicz, senior editor (picture books, chapter books); Christy Ottaviano, executive editor (picture books, chapter books, middle grade fiction); Reka Simonsen, editor (picture books, chapter books, middle grade). Estab. 1866 (Holt). Henry Holt Books for Young Readers publishes excellent books of all kinds (fiction, nonfiction, illustrated) for all ages, from the very young to the young adult. Publishes hardcover originals. Averages 70-80 titles/year.

Imprint(s): Edge Books (Marc Aronson, senior editor, "a high caliber young adult fiction imprint"); Red Feather Books ("covers a range between early chapter and younger middle grade readers"); Owlet Paperbacks.

Needs: Juvenile: adventure, animal, contemporary, fantasy, history, humor, multicultural, religion, sports, suspense/mystery. Picture books: animal, concept, history, humor, multicultural, religion, sports. Young adult: contemporary, fantasy, history, multicultural, nature/environment, problem novels, sports. Published *The Road to Home*, by Mary Jane Auch (middle grade fiction); *Where Once There Was a Wood*, by Denise Fleming (picture book paperbacks); and *Ola's Wake*, by B.J. Stone (middle grade fiction).

How to Contact: Accepts unsolicited mss. Query with outline/synopsis or submit complete ms with cover letter. Include estimated word count, brief bio and list of publishing credits. Send SASE or IRC for return of ms. Responds in 4 months to queries and mss. No longer accepts multiple or simultaneous submissions.

Terms: Pays royalty and advance. Publishes ms 18 months after acceptance. Book catalog and writer's guidelines upon request with SASE or visit website.

🌑 🅰 **HENRY HOLT & COMPANY**, 115 W. 18th St., 6th Floor, New York NY 10011. (212)886-9200. **Contact:** Sara Bershtel, associate publisher (Metropolitan Books, literary fiction); Jennifer Barth, executive editor (adult literary fiction). Publishes hardcover and paperback originals and reprints.

Imprint(s): John Macrae Books; Metropolitan Books; Henry Holt & Company Books for Young Readers.

How to Contact: Accepts queries; no unsolicited mss. Agented fiction 95%.

☑ 🌑 ◎ 🌱 **HOUGHTON MIFFLIN BOOKS FOR CHILDREN,** Imprint of Houghton Mifflin Company, 222 Berkeley St., Boston MA 02116-3764. (617)351-5000. Fax: (617)351-1111. E-mail: children's_books@hmco.com. Website: www.houghtonmifflinbooks.com. (includes titles, job postings, etc.) **Contact:** Hannah Rodgers, submissions coordinator; Margaret Raymo, senior editor; Amy Flynn, editor; Dinah Stevenson (New York City); W. Lorraine (Walter Lorraine Books). "Houghton Mifflin gives shape to ideas that educate, inform, and above all, delight." Publishes hardcover and trade paperback originals and reprints. **Published 12 new writers within the last year.** Averages approximately 60 titles/year. Promotes titles through author visits, advertising, reviews.

Imprint(s): Clarion Books, New York City, Walter Lorraine Books.
• Houghton Mifflin Books for Children received the Caldecott Award in 1999 for *Snowflake Bentley*.
Needs: Adventure, ethnic, historical, humor, juvenile (early readers), literary, mystery, picture books, suspense, young adult, board books. Recently published *Gathering Blue*, by Lois Lowry; *The Circuit*, by Francisco Jimenez; and *When I Was Older*, by Garret Freymann-Weyr.
How to Contact: Submit complete ms with appropriate-sized SASE. Responds in 3 months. Accepts simultaneous submissions. No mss or proposals by e-mail, fax or disk.
Terms: Pays royalties of 5-10% on retail price. Average advance: dependent on many factors. Publishes ms 18 months after acceptance. Writer's guidelines for #10 SASE; book catalog for 9×12 SASE with 3 first-class stamps.

☑ Ⓐ **HOUGHTON MIFFLIN COMPANY**, 222 Berkeley St., Boston MA 02116. (617)351-5000. Fax: (617)351-1202. Website: www.hmco.com. **Contact:** Submissions Editor. Estab. 1832. Publishes hardcover and paperback originals and paperback reprints. **Published new writers within the last year.** Averages 100 total titles, 50 fiction titles/year.
Needs: Literary. "We are not a mass market publisher. Study the current list." Recently published *Columbus Slaughters Braves*, by Mark Friedman; *The Dying Animal*, by Phillip Roth; and *Hotel Honolulu*, by Paul Theroux.
How to Contact: Does not accept unsolicited mss. Accepts agented submissions only.
Terms: Pays royalties of 10-15%. Average advance: varies. Publishes ms 1-2 years after acceptance.

☑ ♣ ⊘ ◎ ☘ **HOUSE OF ANANSI PRESS**, Stoddart Publishing, 895 Don Mills Rd., 400-2 Park Centre, Toronto, Ontario M3C 1W3 Canada. (416)445-3333. Fax: (416)445-5967. E-mail: info@anansi.ca. Website: www.anansi.ca (includes submission guidelines, book catalog, names of editors, news, awards info, order form). **Contact:** Martha Sharpe, publisher, editor; Adrienne Leahey, editor. Estab. 1967. "House of Anansi Press finds and publishes innovative literary works of fiction, nonfiction and poetry by Canadian writers. Anansi acquired a reputation early on for its editors' ability to spot talented writers who push the boundaries and challenge the expectations of the literary community." Publishes hardcover and paperback originals and paperback reprints. Books: perfect binding. **Published 2 new writers within the last year.** Averages 10-15 total titles, 2-5 fiction titles/year. Member, ACP, LPG, OBPO. Distributes titles through General Distribution Services.
• Anansi Press received the Giller Prize (shortlist) for 1999.
Needs: Ethnic/multicultural (general), experimental, feminist, gay, literary, short story collections, translations. "All books must be by Canadians or Canadian landed immigrants." Recently published *19 Knives*, by Mark Anthony Jarman (short stories); *This All Happened*, by Michael Winter (literary novel); and *Am I Disturbing You?*, by Anne Hébert (novel in translation). Publishes the CBC Massey Lectures Series.
How to Contact: Accepts unsolicited mss. Query with outline/synopsis and 2 sample chapters. Accepts queries by regular mail only. Include brief bio and list of publishing credits. Send SASE or IRC for return of ms OR send disposable copy of ms and SASE for reply only. Agented fiction 60%. Responds in 6 months to queries and mss. Accepts simultaneous submissions. Sometimes comments on rejected mss.
Terms: Pays royalties of 8-12%. Average advance. Sends first proofs only to author. Publishes ms 6-12 months after acceptance. Writer's guidelines on website. Book catalogs free or on website.
Advice: "Read and submit your work to literary journals and magazines. Attend or participate in literary events—readings, festivals, book clubs. Visit our website, see the kinds of books we publish, think about whether we're the right publisher for your work."

Ⓝ **HOWELLS HOUSE**, P.O. Box 9546, Washington DC 20016-9546. (202)333-2182. **Contact:** W.D. Howells, publisher. Estab. 1988. "Our interests are institutions and institutional change." Publishes hardcover and trade paperback originals and reprints. Publishes 4 titles/year; each imprint publishes 2-3 titles/year.
Imprint(s): The Compass Press, Whalesback Books.
Needs: Historical, literary, mainstream/contemporary.
How to Contact: Query first. Responds in 2 months to proposals.
Terms: Pays 15% net royalty or makes outright purchase. May offer advance. Publishes ms 8 months after ms development completed.

Ⓝ ♣ ◎ **HUMANITAS**, 990 Croissant Picard, Brossard, Quebec J4W 1S5 Canada. Phone/fax: (450)466-9737. E-mail: humanitas@cyberglobe.net. **Contact:** Constantin Stoiciu, director. Publishes hardcover originals. Publishes, on average, 15 new writers/year. Publishes 20 titles/year. Distributes titles through Quebec-Livres.
• Humanitas publishes novels in French only.
Needs: Fantasy, romance, short story collections. Recently published *Enigmes de la seduction politique*, by Andrei Stoiciu (nonfiction); *Les yeux de la comtesse*, by Marie Desjardins (biography); and *Sang mêlé*, by Irina Egli (fiction).
How to Contact: Query first. Accepts queries by fax. No e-mail queries. Accepts simultaneous submissions.

Terms: Pays 10-12% royalty on wholesale price. Publishes ms 2 months after acceptance. Writer's guidelines and book catalog free on request.

◐ ♥ **IMAJINN BOOKS**, ImaJinn, P.O. Box 162, Hickory Corners MI 49060-0162. (616)671-4633. Fax: (616)671-4535. E-mail: imajinn@worldnet.att.net. Website: www.imajinnbooks.com (includes book list, writer's guidelines, author pictures and bios, contests, ImaJinn book news, tips for writers, author questions/answers from readers, etc.). **Contact:** Linda J. Kichline, editor. Estab. 1998. "ImaJinn Books is a small independent publishing house that specializes in romances with story lines involving ghosts, psychics or psychic phenomena, witches, vampires, werewolves, angels, reincarnation, time travel, space travel, the future, and any other form of 'other worldly' or 'new-age' type story line. Occasionally, ImaJinn Books will publish a straight fantasy or general fiction novel that falls into the above categories and has romantic elements in it, but is not a traditional romance. We also intend to publish a science fiction young adult series beginning in 2001." Publishes paperback originals and reprints. Books: 60 lb. text stock paper; camera ready and disk to film printing; perfect binding; illustrations occasionally but rare. Average print order: 2,500; first novel print order: 1,000. **Published 2 new writers within the last year.** Averages 12-24 total titles, 12-24 fiction titles/year. Member, SPAN and PMA. Distributes titles through Baker & Taylor, Ingram Books, Amazon.com, BN.com and imajinnbooks.com. Promotes titles through advertising review magazines.
   • ImaJinn Books has won the Reviewers International Organization (RIO) 1999 Dorothy Parker Award for Best Fantasy. Two titles were nominated for the PEARL (Paranormal Excellence in Romantic Literature) Award and one book cover was nominated for best paranormal cover of the year.
Needs: Children's/juvenile (fantasy), fantasy (romance), horror (romance), New Age/mystic, psychic/supernatural, romance (futuristic/time travel), science fiction (romance), young adult/teen (fantasy/science fiction). "We look for specific story lines based on what the readers are asking for and what story lines in which we're short. We post our current needs on our website." Recently published *Dreamsinger*, by J.A. Ferguson (fantasy romance); *Midnight Enchantment*, by Nancy Gideon (vampire romance); and *Time of the Wolf*, by Julie D'Arcy (fantasy).
How to Contact: Does not accept or return unsolicited mss. Send query letter. Accepts queries by e-mail. Include estimated word count, brief bio and list of publishing credits. Send disposable copy of ms and SASE for reply only. Agented fiction 20%. Responds in 3 months to queries; 6 months to mss. Often comments on rejected mss.
Terms: Pays royalties of 10%. Sends galleys to author. Publishes ms up to 2 years after acceptance. Writer's guidelines free for #10 SASE and 33¢ postage. Book catalogs free.
Advice: "Carefully read the author guidelines, and read books published by ImaJinn Books."

◪ **INSOMNIAC PRESS**, 192 Spadina Ave., #403, Toronto, Ontario M5T 2C2 Canada. (416)504-6270. Fax: (416)504-9313. E-mail: mike@insomniacpress.com. Website: www.insomniacpress.com (includes writer's guidelines, author tour info, book descriptions). Estab. 1992. "Midsize independent publisher with a mandate to produce edgy experimental fiction." Publishes paperback originals. First novel print order: 3,000. **Published 15 new writers within the last year.** Plans 4 first novels in 2002. Averages 20 total titles, 5 fiction titles/year.
Needs: Experimental, gay, lesbian, literary, mainstream, mystery/suspense. Recently published *Pray For Us Sinners*, by Patrick Taylor (novel).
How to Contact: Accepts unsolicited mss. Send query by e-mail. Include estimated word count, brief bio and list of publishing credits. Send SASE or IRC for return of ms or send disposable copy of ms and SASE for reply only. Agented fiction 5%. Responds in 2 weeks to queries; 2 months to mss. Accepts simultaneous submissions. Sometimes comments on rejected ms.
Terms: Pays royalties of 10%. Advance is negotiable. Sends galleys to author. Publishes ms 8 months after acceptance. Writer's guidelines free on website.
Tips: "Visit our website, read our writer's guidelines."

◎ ◓ **INTERLINK PUBLISHING GROUP, INC.**, 46 Crosby St., Northampton MA 01060-1804. Fax: (413)582-7057. E-mail: interpg@aol.com. **Contact:** Michel Moushabeck, publisher; Pam Thompson, fiction editor. Contemporary fiction in translation published under Emerging Voices: New International Fiction. Estab. 1987. "Midsize independent publisher specializing in world travel, world literature, world history and politics." Publishes hardcover and paperback originals. Books: 55 lb. Warren Sebago Cream white paper; web offset printing; perfect binding. Average print order: 5,000. First novel print order: 5,000. **Published new writers within the last year.** Averages 30 total titles, 2-4 fiction titles/year. Distributes titles through distributors such as Baker & Taylor. Promotes titles through book mailings to extensive, specialized lists of editors and reviewers, authors read at bookstores and special events across the country.
Imprint(s): Interlink Books, Olive Branch Press and Crocodile Books USA.
Needs: "Adult translated fiction from around the world." Published *House of the Winds*, by Mia Yun (first novel); *The Gardens of Light*, by Amin Maalouf (novel translated from French); and *War in the Land of Egypt*, by Yusef Al-Qaid (novel translated from Arabic). Publishes the International Folk Tales series.

How to Contact: Does not accept unsolicited mss. Submit query letter and brief sample only. No queries by e-mail or fax. Send SASE. Responds within 6 weeks to queries.

Terms: Pays royalties of 6-7%. Sends galleys to author. Publishes ms 1-1½ years after acceptance.

Advice: "Our Emerging Voices Series is designed to bring to North American readers the once-unheard voices of writers who have achieved wide acclaim at home, but were not recognized beyond the borders of their native lands. We are also looking for folktale collections (for adults) from around the world that fit in our International Folk Tale Series."

N ◪ ◎ ITALICA PRESS, 595 Main St., #605, New York NY 10044. (212)935-4230. Fax: (212)838-7812. E-mail: italica@idt.net. Website: www.italica.com (includes authors, titles). **Contact:** Eileen Gardiner and Ronald G. Musto, publishers. Estab. 1985. Small independent publisher of Italian fiction in translation. Publishes paperback originals. Books: 50-60 lb. natural paper; offset printing; Smythe-sewn binding; illustrations. Average print order: 1,500. "First time translators published. We would like to see translations of Italian writers well-known in Italy who are not yet translated for an American audience." Publishes 6 total titles each year; 2 fiction titles. Distributes titles through direct mail. Promotes titles through catalogs and website.

Needs: Translations of 20th Century Italian fiction. Published *Eruptions*, by Monica Sarsini; *The Great Bear*, by Ginevra Bompiani; and *Sparrow*, by Giovanni Verga.

How to Contact: Accepts unsolicited mss. Query first. Accepts queries by e-mail and fax. Responds in 3 weeks to queries; 2 months to mss. Accepts simultaneous submissions. Electronic submissions via Macintosh disk. Sometimes critiques rejected mss.

Terms: Pays in royalties of 5-15% and 10 author's copies. Sends pre-publication galleys to author. Publishes ms 1 year after acceptance. Book catalog free on request.

Advice: "Remember we publish *only* fiction that has been previously published in Italian. A *brief* call saves a lot of postage. 90% of the proposals we receive are completely off base—but we are very interested in things that are right on target. Please send return postage if you want your manuscript back."

☑ ◪ KAEDEN BOOKS, P.O. Box 16190, Rocky River OH 44116-0190. (440)356-0030. Fax: (440)356-5081. E-mail: jbackus@kaeden.com. Website: www.kaeden.com (includes samples of books, reviews and titles). **Contact:** Kathleen Urmston, fiction editor (children's grades 2-6); Karen Evans, fiction editor (children's K-3). Estab. 1990. "Children's book publisher for education K-6 market: reading stories, science, math and social studies materials, also poetry." Publishes paperback originals. Books: offset printing; saddle binding; illustrations. Average print order: 5,000. First novel print order: 5,000. **Published 6 new writers within the last year.** Plans 2 first juvenile novels in 2002. Averages 8-16 total titles/year.

Needs: Fiction: adventure, children's/juvenile (adventure, animal, historical, mystery, series, sports), ethnic/multicultural, fantasy, historical (general), humor/satire, mystery/suspense (amateur sleuth), science fiction (soft/sociological), short story collections, thriller/espionage. Nonfiction: all subjects.

How to Contact: Accepts unsolicited mss. Query with outline/synopsis. Include 1-page bio and list of publishing credits. Send a disposable copy of ms and SASE for reply only. Responds only "if interested."

Terms: Negotiable, either royalties or flat fee by individual arrangement with author depending on book. No advance. Publishes ms 6-24 months after acceptance.

Advice: "Our line is expanding with particular interest in fiction/nonfiction for grades two to six. Material must be suitable for use in the public school classroom, be multicultural and be high interest with appropriate word usage and a positive tone for the respective grade."

N ◪ ◎ KAYA PRODUCTION, 373 Broadway, Suite E-2, New York NY 10013. (212)343-9503. Fax: (212)343-8291. E-mail: kaya@kaya.com. Website: www.kaya.com. **Contact:** Sunyoung Lee, editor. "Kaya is a small independent press dedicated to the publication of innovative literature from the Asian diaspora." Publishes hardcover originals and trade paperback originals and reprints.

Needs: "Kaya publishes Asian, Asian-American and Asian diasporic materials. We are looking for innovative writers with a commitment to quality literature."

How to Contact: Submit synopsis and 2-4 sample chapters with SASE. Responds in 6 months to mss. Accepts simultaneous submissions.

Terms: Guidelines available at website. Book catalog free.

Advice: Audience is people interested in a high standard of literature and who are interested in breaking down easy approaches to multicultural literature.

◪ Ⓐ KENSINGTON PUBLISHING CORP., 850 Third Ave., 16th Floor, New York NY 10022. (212)407-1500. Fax: (212)935-0699. Editor-in-Chief: Paul Dinas. **Contact:** Kate Duffy, editorial director; John Scognamiglio, editorial director; Ann LaFarge, executive editor; Karen Thomas, executive editor (Dafina Books); Elaine

Sparber, senior editor (Twins Streams health books); Amy Garvey, consulting editor (romance); Hilary Sares, consulting editor (romance). Full service trade commercial publisher, all formats. Averages over 500 total titles/year.

Imprint(s): Kensington Books; Zebra Books; Pinnacle Books; Dafina Books; Twin Streams Books; Citadel Books; Brava Books; Encanto Books; Precious Gems; BET Books.

Needs: "Romance (contemporary, historical, regency, erotica), mysteries, true crime, westerns, multicultural women's fiction, mainstream women's commercial fiction, gay and lesbian fiction and nonfiction, thrillers, romantic suspense, biographies, humor, paranormal, self-help, alternative health, pop culture nonfiction. No science fiction/fantasy, experimental fiction, business texts or children's titles."

How to Contact: Does not accept unsolicited mss. Agented submissions only.

Terms: Pays industry standard royalties and advances.

N ☘ ◎ KIDS CAN PRESS, 29 Birch Ave., Toronto, Ontario M4V 1E2 Canada. (416)925-5437. Fax: (416)960-5437. Website: www.nelvana.com/kidscanpress/KidsCanPress_3/kcp/f_home.htm. **Contact:** Acquisitions editor. "Our company's goal is to offer books that entertain, inform and delight the most important audience in the world—young readers."

Needs: Picture books, young adult.

How to Contact: Query by mail with outline and SASE. "Include SAE large enough to hold your material and sufficient IRCs for return. If you do not want your material recycled, please indicate this in the cover letter. Please specify the genre of the work-picture book or novel-in the front of the envelope. No simultaneous submissions. No fax, disk or e-mail submissions. Do not include artwork."

▼ ◎ ALLEN A. KNOLL, PUBLISHERS, 200A W. Victoria St., Suite 3, Santa Barbara CA 93101-3627. Fax: (805)966-6657. E-mail: bookinfo@knollpublishers.com. Website: www.knollpublishers.com (includes book catalog, interviews with authors, special news items). **Contact:** Fiction Editor. Estab. 1990. Small independent publisher. "We publish books for intelligent people who read for fun." Publishes hardcover originals. Books: offset printing; sewn binding. Member, PMA, SPAN, ABA. Distributes titles through Ingram, Baker & Taylor, Brodart. Promotes titles through advertising in specialty publications, direct mail, prepublication reviews and advertising.

• *Today's Librarian* named Theodore Roosevelt Gardner II's *He's Back* 'Best Overall Fiction.'

Needs: Published *He's Back*, by Theodore Roosevelt Gardner II (fiction); *What Now, King Lear?*, by Alistair Boyle (mystery); *Too Rich and Too Thin*, by David Champion (courtroom drama). Publishes A Bomber Hanson Mystery (courtroom drama series) and A Gil Yates Private Investigator Novel (P.I. series).

How to Contact: Does not accept unsolicited mss. Book catalog free.

◖ ALFRED A. KNOPF, The Knopf Publishing Group, A Division of Random House, Inc., 299 Park Ave., New York NY 10171. (212)751-2600. Website: www.aaknopf.com. **Contact:** Senior Editor. Estab. 1915. Book-length fiction of literary merit by known and unknown writers. Publishes hardcover originals. Averages 200 titles/year. **Published new writers in the last year.** Also publishes nonfiction.

Needs: Publishes book-length fiction of literary merit by known or unknown writers. Length: 40,000-150,000. Recently published *Gertrude and Claudius*, by John Updike.

How to Contact: Does not accept unsolicited mss. Query with outline or synopsis. Send SASE or IRC for reply. Agented fiction 90%. Responds within 3 months to mss.

Terms: Pays royalties of 10-15%; offers advance. Must return advance if book is not completed or is unacceptable. Publishes ms 1 year after acceptance.

◎ Ⓐ ALFRED A. KNOPF BOOKS FOR YOUNG READERS, A Division of Random House, Inc., 1540 Broadway, New York NY 10036. (212)782-5623. Website: www.randomhouse.com/kids. **Contact:** Crown/Editorial Department. Publishes 60 total titles/year.

Needs: Juvenile, literary, picture books, young adult.

How to Contact: *Accepts agented submissions only.* Accepts simultaneous submissions.

Terms: Pays in royalties of 4-10% Offers advance. Publishes ms 1-2 years after acceptance.

◖ Ⓐ LAUREL BOOKS, Imprint of Dell Publishing, Division of Bantam Doubleday Dell, 1540 Broadway, New York NY 10036. (212)354-6500. **Acquisitions:** Maggie Crawford, editorial director. Publishes trade paperback originals, mostly light, humorous material and books on pop culture. Publishes 4 titles/year.

Needs: Literary.

How to Contact: Agented submissions only.

Terms: Pays 7½-12½% royalty on retail price. Advance varies. Publishes ms 1 year after acceptance. Book catalog for 9×12 SAE and 3 first class stamps.

☑ ◎ **LEE & LOW BOOKS**, 95 Madison Ave., New York NY 10016. (212)779-4400. Fax: (212)683-1894. Website: www.leeandlow.com. **Contact:** Louise May, executive editor. Estab. 1991. "Our goals are to meet a growing need for books that address children of color, and to present literature that all children can identify with. We only consider multicultural children's picture books. Of special interest are stories set in contemporary America." Publishes hardcover originals—picture books only. Averages 12-15 total titles/year.

Needs: Children's/juvenile (historical, multicultural, preschool/picture book for children ages 2-10). "We do not consider folktales, fairy tales or animal stories." Published *The Secret to Freedom*, by Marcia Vaughan; *Love to Mama: A Tribute to Mothers*, edited by Pat Mora.

How to Contact: Accepts unsolicited mss. Send complete ms with cover letter or through an agent. Send SASE for return of ms or send a disposable ms and SASE for reply only. Agented fiction 30%. Responds in 5 months. Accepts simultaneous submissions. Sometimes comments on rejected mss.

Terms: Pays royalties. Offers advance. Sends galleys to author. Writer's guidelines for #10 SASE or on website. Book catalog for SASE with $1.43 postage.

Advice: "Writers should familiarize themselves with the styles and formats of recently published children's books. Lee & Low Books is a multicultural children's book publisher. We would like to see more contemporary stories set in the U.S. Animal stories and folktales are not considered at this time."

◎ **LERNER PUBLICATIONS COMPANY**, 241 First Ave. N., Minneapolis MN 55401. (612)332-3344. Fax: (612)332-7615. Website: www.lernerbooks.com. **Contact:** Jennifer Zimian, submissions editor. Estab. 1959. "Midsize independent *children's* publisher." Publishes hardcover originals and paperback reprints. Books: Offset printing; reinforced library binding; perfect binding. Average print order: 5,000. First novel print order: 5,000. Averages 150-175 total titles, 1-2 fiction titles/year.

Needs: Young adult: general, problem novels, sports, adventure, mystery (young adult). Looking for "well-written middle grade and young adult. No *adult fiction* or single short stories."

How to Contact: "Submissions are accepted in the months of March and October only. Work received in any other month will be returned unopened." Accepts unsolicited mss. Query first or submit outline/synopsis and 2 sample chapters. Responds in up to 6 months. Accepts simultaneous submissions.

Terms: Pays royalties. Offers advance. Provides author's copies. Sends galleys to author. Publishes ms 12-18 months after acceptance. Writer's guidelines for #10 SASE. Book catalog for 9×12 SAE with $3.20 postage.

◎ **ARTHUR A. LEVINE BOOKS**, Imprint of Scholastic Inc., 555 Broadway, New York NY 10012. (212)343-6100. **Contact:** Arthur A. Levine, publisher. "Arthur A. Levine Books is looking for distinctive literature, for whatever's extraordinary." Averages 14 titles/year.

Needs: Juvenile fiction: picture books, novels. Published *When She Was Good*, by Norma Fox Mazer and *Beautiful Warrior*, by Emily Arnold McCully.

How to Contact: Query only. Send SASE. "We are willing to work with first-time authors, with or without agent."

Terms: Pays variable royalty on retail price. Advance varies. Book catalog available for 9×12 SASE.

◎ ▼ **LIONHEARTED PUBLISHING, INC.**, P.O. Box 618, Zephyr Cove NV 89448-0618. (775)588-1388. Fax: (775)588-1386. E-mail: admin@LionHearted.com. Website: www.LionHearted.com (includes writer's guidelines, authors, interviews, titles, articles and writing tips for authors). **Contact:** Historical or Contemporary Acquisitions Editor. Estab. 1994. "Multiple award-winning, independent publisher of single title, mass market paperback, romance novels." Publishes paperback originals. Books: mass market paperback; perfect binding. Also expanded romance into e-book formats. Publishers, on average, 12 new writers/year. Averages 12-72 fiction titles/year. Distributes titles through Ingram, Barnes & Noble, Baker & Taylor, Amazon and Internet website. Promotes titles through trade romance reader magazines, website and Internet.

> ● *P.S. I've Taken a Lover*, by Patricia Lucas White won the National Reviewer's Choice Award for Best Book of the Year. *The Alliance*, by Patricia Waddell was a nominee for Best Electronic Book of the Year by *Romantic Times*. *My Captain Jack*, by Diane Drew was an EPPIE Award finalist.

Needs: Romance (contemporary, futuristic/time travel, historical, regency period, romantic suspense; over 65,000 words only). Recently published *Lord Darver's Match*, by Susanne Marie Knight (Regency time travel); *In the Buff*, by Carol Givner (contemporary romance); *Heart of the Diamond*, by Carrie Brock (Regency romance).

How to Contact: Accepts unsolicited mss. Query with outline/synopsis and 3 sample chapters. Accepts queries by e-mail. Include estimated word count, list of publishing credits, cover letter and 1 paragraph story summary

---

 A BULLET INTRODUCES COMMENTS by the editor of *Novel & Short Story Writer's Market* indicating special information about the listing.

in cover or query letter. Send SASE or IRC for return of ms or send disposable copy of ms and SASE for reply only. Agented fiction: less than 10%. Responds in 1 month to queries; 3 months to mss. No simultaneous submissions. Always comments on rejected mss.

Terms: Pays royalties of 10% maximum on paperbacks; 30% on electronic books. Average advance: $1,000. Sends galleys to author. Publishes ms 18-24 months after acceptance. Writer's guidelines free for #10 SASE; book catalog for SASE.

Advice: "If you are not an avid reader of romance, don't attempt to write romance, and don't waste your time or an editor's by submitting to a publisher of romance. Read a few of our single title releases (they are a bit different) before submitting your romance novel."

⊘ LITTLE, BROWN AND COMPANY, 1271 Avenue of the Americas, New York NY 10020. (212)522-8700. Website: www.twbookmark.com. **Contact:** Editorial Department. Estab. 1837. "The general editorial philosophy for all divisions continues to be broad and flexible, with high quality and the promise of commercial success always the first considerations." Medium-size house. Publishes adult and juvenile hardcover and paperback originals. Averages 100 total adult titles/year. Number of fiction titles varies.

Imprint(s): Little, Brown; Back Bay; Bulfinch Press.
● Children's submissions: Submissions Editor, Children's Books, at Boston address. Bulfinch submissions: Submissions Editor, Bulfinch Press, at Boston address. Include SASE.

Needs: Literary, mainstream/contemporary. No science fiction. Published *When the Wind Blows*, by James Patterson; *Angels Flight*, by Michael Connelly; and *The Pilot's Wife*, by Anita Shreve.

How to Contact: Unable to consider unsolicited materials by mail, but encourages submissions to iPublish.com (online publishing company).

Terms: "We publish on a royalty basis, with advance."

☑ ◖ ◉ Ⓐ LITTLE, BROWN AND COMPANY CHILDREN'S BOOKS, Trade Division; Children's Books, 3 Center Plaza, Boston MA 02108. (617)227-0730. Website: www.littlebrown.com. **Contact:** Leila Little. Estab. 1837. Publishes hardcover originals and trade paperback reprints. Averages 60-70 total titles/year. Books: 70 lb. paper; sheet-fed printing; illustrations. Sometimes buys juvenile mss with illustrations "if by professional artist." **Published "a few" new writers within the last year.** Distributes titles through sales representatives. Promotes titles through author tours, book signings, posters, press kits, magazine and newspapers and Beacon Hill Bookbay.

Imprint(s): Megan Tingley Books (Megan S. Tingley, executive editor).

Needs: Children's/juvenile: adventure, ethnic, historical, humor, mystery, picture books, science fiction, suspense.

How to Contact: Submit through agent only.

Terms: Pays on royalty basis. Offers negotiable advance. Sends galleys to author. Publishes ms 1-2 years after acceptance.

Advice: "We are looking for trade books with bookstore appeal. We are especially looking for young children's (ages 3-5) picture books. New authors should be aware of what is currently being published. We recommend they spend time at the local library and bookstore familiarizing themselves with new publications." Known for "humorous middle grade fiction with lots of kid appeal. Literary, multi-layered young adult fiction with distinctive characters and complex plots."

◖ ◉ LITTLE SIMON, Imprint of Simon & Schuster Children's Publishing Division, 1230 Avenue of the Americas, New York NY 10022. (212)698-7200. Website: www.simonsays.com. **Contact:** Submissions Editor. "Our goal is to provide fresh material in an innovative format for pre-school age. Our books are often, if not exclusively, illustrator driven." Averages 65 total titles/year. This imprint publishes novelty books only (pop-ups, lift-the-flaps board books, etc.).

How to Contact: Does not accept unsolicited mss. Query for more information. Responds in 8 months. Accepts simultaneous submissions.

Terms: Negotiable.

☑ LOST HORSE PRESS, 105 Lost Horse Lane, Sandpoint ID 83864. (208)255-4410. Fax: (208)255-1650. E-mail: losthorsepress@mindspring.com. **Contact:** Christine Holbert, editor of novels, novellas. Estab. 1998. Publishes hardcover and paperback originals and reprints. Books: 60-70 lb. natural paper; offset printing; b&w illustration. Average print order: 1,000-2,500. First novel print order: 1,000. **Published 2 new writers within the last year.** Plans 2 first novels in 2001. Averages 4 total titles, 2 fiction titles/year.

Needs: Erotica, ethnic/multicultural, experimental, feminist, gay, historical, humor/satire, lesbian, literary, regional (Pacific NW), short story collections, translations. Recently published *Tales of a Dalai Lama*, by Pierre Delattre (literary fiction); *Love*, by Valerie Martin (short stories); *Sailing Away*, by Richard Morgan (short stories).

How to Contact: Accepts unsolicited mss. Submit complete ms with cover letter. Accepts queries by e-mail. Include brief bio and list of publishing credits. Send SASE or IRC for return of ms or send disposable copy of ms and SASE for reply only. Responds in 3 months to queries and mss. Accepts submissions on disk. Sometimes comments on rejected mss.

Terms: Pays royalties of 10% and 20 author's copies. Sends galleys to author. Publishes ms 1-2 years after acceptance. Writer's guidelines for SASE; book catalog free.

✓ ▼ ❧ ◑ **LTDBOOKS,** 200 N. Service Rd. West, Unit 1, Suite 301, Oakville, Ontario L6M 2Y1 Canada. Phone/fax: (905)847-6060. E-mail: publisher@ltdbooks.com. Website: www.ltdbooks.com. **Contact:** Dee Lloyd, Terry Sheils, editors. Estab. 1999. "LTDBooks, an energetic presence in the rapidly expanding e-book market, is a multi-genre, royalty-paying fiction publisher specializing in high quality stories with strong characters and great ideas." Publishes electronic books on disk or by download. Books: 3½″ floppy disk with cover and jewel case, or as a download. **Published 14 new writers within the last year.** Averages 36 total titles, 36 fiction titles/ year. Member, Electronic Publishers Association. Distributes titles through the Internet, Barnes&Noble.com and Powells.

• *Butterfly House*, by T.K. Sheils, won 2001 EPPIE for horror and the 2001 IPPY for horror. *Ties That Blind*, by Dee Lloyd, won the 2000 EPPIE for contemporary romance. *Wintertide*, by Megan Sybil Baker, won the 2001 EPPIE for fantasy.

Needs: Adventure, fantasy (space fantasy, sword and sorcery), historical (general), horror (dark fantasy, futuristic, psychological, supernatural), literary, mainstream, mystery/suspense (amateur sleuth, cozy, police procedural, private eye/hardboiled), romance (contemporary, futuristic/time travel, gothic, historical, regency period, romantic suspense), science fiction (hard science/technological, soft/sociological), thriller/espionage, western, young adult/ teen (adventure, fantasy/science fiction, historical, horror, mystery/suspense, problem novels, romance, series, sports, western). Recently published *Rat*, by Edward Keyes (follow up to *The French Connection*); *Last Flight of the Arrow*, by Daniel Wyatt. "Our new trade paperback program started June 2001."

How to Contact: Accepts unsolicited mss. Query with synopsis and 3 sample chapters. Prefers queries by e-mail. Include estimated word count, brief bio and list of publishing credits. Send disposable copy of ms and SASE for reply only. Responds in 2 weeks to queries; 6 weeks to mss. Accepts simultaneous submissions, electronic submissions and disk. Always comments on rejected mss.

Terms: Pays royalties of 30%. Sends galleys to author. Publishes ms 6-9 months after acceptance. Writer's guidelines on website.

Advice: "We publish only fiction. Many of our books are electronic (as download or on disk) with ongoing additions to our new trade paperback program."

◎ **MAGE PUBLISHERS,** 1032 29th St. NW, Washington DC 20007. (202)342-1642. Fax: (202)342-9269. E-mail: info@mage.com. Website: www.mage.com. **Contact:** Amin Sepehri, assistant to publisher. Estab. 1985. "Small independent publisher." Publishes hardcover originals. Averages 4 total titles, 1 fiction title/year.

Needs: **"We publish only books on Iran and Persia and translations of Iranian fiction writers."** Ethnic (Iran) fiction. Published *My Uncle Napoleon*, by Iraj Pezeshkzad; *King of the Benighted*, by M. Irani; and *Sutra and Other Stories*, by Simin Daneshvar.

How to Contact: Does not accept unsolicited mss. Send query letter with SASE or IRC. Responds in 3 months to queries. Accepts simultaneous and electronic submissions.

Terms: Pays royalties. Publishes ms 1 year after acceptance. Writer's guidelines on web.

Advice: "If it isn't related to Persia/Iran, don't waste our time or yours."

◎ **MAJESTIC BOOKS,** P.O. Box 19097, Johnston RI 02919-0097. E-mail: majesticbk@aol.com. **Contact:** Cindy MacDonald, publisher. "Majestic Books is a small press. We publish young writers under the age of 18 in an anthology filled with poems and short stories." Publishes paperback originals. Books: 60 lb. white paper; offset printing; perfect binding. Average print order: 300. **Published new writers within the last year.** Averages 3 total titles, 3 fiction titles/year. Distribution and promotion of titles is conducted through mail orders.

• "Three-Tenths," a short story by John Repku Fentiman, was awarded the Scholastic Gold Key Award.

Needs: Adventure, family saga, fantasy, mainstream, mystery/suspense, psychic/supernatural, romance, science fiction (soft/sociological), thriller/espionage, western, young adult/teen. Recently published *Tribute to Talent*; *Mysteries, Monsters, Memories and More VIII* (short story contest anthology); *Dare to Dream* (anthology); *Reach for the Stars* (anthology), all by various authors.

How to Contact: Accepts unsolicited mss. Submit complete ms with cover letter. Include estimated word count and age (under 18). Send SASE or IRC for return of ms or send disposable copy of ms and SASE for reply only. Responds in 2 weeks to mss. Accepts simultaneous and electronic submissions.

Terms: Pays royalties of 10% on sales relating directly to authors inclusion. Publishes ms 1 year after acceptance. Writer's guidelines for SASE.

Tips: "Our press only publishes talented young writers under the age of 18. Please include age with all submissions and keep stories under 2,000 words. Originality is a must."

MARCH STREET PRESS, 3413 Wilshire, Greensboro NC 27408-2923. Phone/fax: (336)282-9754. E-mail: rbixby@aol.com. Website: http://users.aol.com/marchst (includes writer's guidelines; names of editors, authors, titles; free websites, business directory, library of books and past issues). **Contact:** Robert Bixby, editor/publisher. Estab. 1988. Publishes paperback originals. Books: vellum paper; photocopy; saddle-stitch binding. Averages 4-6 total titles, 1 or fewer fiction titles/year.
Needs: Literary. Short story collections. Published *Road to Alaska*, by Ray Miller; *Placing Ourselves Among the Living*, by Curtis Smith; *The John-Paul Story*, by Eric Torgersen.
How to Contact: *"Accepts unsolicited mss if $20 reading fee enclosed."* Submit complete ms with a cover letter and reading fee. Send SASE for return of ms or send a disposable copy of ms. Responds in 1 week to queries; 6 months to mss. Accepts simultaneous submissions. Sometimes comments on a rejected ms.
Terms: Pays royalty of 15%. Provides 10 author's copies. Sends galleys to author. Publishes ms 6-12 months after acceptance. Writer's guidelines for #10 SASE or on website. Obtaining guidelines prior to submission is highly recommended.

McBOOKS PRESS, 120 W. State St., Ithaca NY 14850. (607)272-2114. Fax: (607)273-6068. E-mail: mcbooks@mcbooks.com. Website: www.McBooks.com (includes some guidelines, staff names, book catalog). **Contact:** S.K. List, editorial director. Estab. 1980. "Small independent publisher; specializes in historical nautical fiction, American publisher of Alexander Kent's Richard Bolitho series, Dudley Pope's Ramage novels." Publishes paperback reprints "mostly." Averages 19 total titles, 17 fiction titles/year. Distributes titles through LPC Group.
Needs: Historical (nautical). Recently published *Ramage and the Rebels*, by Dudley Pope (nautical fiction); *The Wicked Trade*, by Jan Needle (nautical fiction); and *Second to None*, by Alexander Kent (Douglas Reeman) (nautical fiction). Publishes the continuing Bolitho and Ramage series.
How to Contact: Accepts unsolicited mss. Query with outline/synopsis and 1-2 sample chapters. Accepts queries by e-mail. Include list of publishing credits. Send SASE or IRC for return of ms. Mostly agented fiction. Responds in 3 months to queries. Accepts simultaneous submissions.

MARGARET K. McELDERRY BOOKS, Imprint of the Simon & Schuster Children's Publishing Division, 1230 Sixth Ave., New York NY 10020. (212)698-2761. **Contact:** Emma D. Dryden, editorial director. Estab. 1971. Publishes hardcover originals. Books: high quality paper; offset printing; three-piece and POB bindings; illustrations. Average print order: 10,000. First novel print order: 6,000. **Published new writers within the last year.** Averages 30 total titles/year.
• Books published by Margaret K. McElderry Books have received numerous awards including the Newbery and the Caldecott Awards.
Needs: All categories (fiction and nonfiction) for juvenile and young adult: adventure, contemporary, early chapter books, fantasy, poetry, literary and picture books. "We will consider any category. Results depend on the quality of the imagination, the artwork and the writing." Recently published *Firefighters A to Z*, by Chris L. DeMarest (picture book); *The Year of Miss Agnes*, by Kirkpatrick Hill (middle grade fiction); and *24 Hours*, by Margaret Mahy (young adult).
How to Contact: Send query letter.
Terms: Pays in royalties; offers advance. Publishes ms 18-36 months after acceptance.
Advice: "Imaginative writing of high quality is always in demand; also picture books that are original and unusual. Keep in mind that McElderry Books is a very small imprint, so we are very selective about the books we will undertake for publication. We try not to publish any 'trend' books. Be familiar with our list and with what is being published this year by all publishing houses."

MIGHTYBOOK, Guardian Press, 10924 Grant Rd., #225, Houston TX 77070. (281)955-9855. Fax: (281)469-6466. E-mail: reaves@houston.rr.com. Website: www.mightybook.com. **Contact:** Richard Eaves, acquisitions director. Estab. 1991. "Small independent publisher of electronic, read aloud picture books, books on audio cassette/cd, and print-on-demand books. Much of our marketing and sales are done on the Internet." Publishes hardcover and paperback originals. Books: matte paper; offset/litho printing; perfect binding. **Published 5 new writers within the last year.** Averages 6 total titles, 4 fiction titles/year.
Needs: Children's/juvenile, young adult/teen. Very short children's picture books (100-200 words). Recently published *Furello*, by Harriett Fabrick (juvenile adventure); *Sabbath Queen*, by Myra Lichtman-Fields (children's); and *Cloud Over My Head*, by Kana Levinski (children's).

How to Contact: Accepts unsolicited mss. Submit complete ms with cover letter. Accepts queries by e-mail and phone. Include estimated word count and brief bio. Send disposable ms and SASE for reply only. Agented fiction 5%. Responds in 6 weeks to queries and mss. Accepts simultaneous submissions, electronic submissions and submissions by disk.

Terms: Pays royalties of 20% gross. No advance. Publishes ms 3-6 months after acceptance. Writer's guidelines and book catalog on website.

Tips: "Write really good, very short stories for children."

✔️ 🌐 🔲 **MILKWEED EDITIONS**, 1011 Washington Ave. S., Suite 300, Minneapolis MN 55415. (612)332-3192. Fax: (612)215-2550. E-mail: editor@milkweed.org. Website: www.milkweed.org (includes writer's guidelines, mission statement, catalog, poem of day, excerpts from titles). **Contact**: Emilie Buchwald, publisher; Elisabeth Fitz, first reader. Estab. 1980. Nonprofit publisher. Publishes hardcover and paperback originals and paperback reprints. Books: book text quality—acid-free paper; offset printing; perfect or hardcover binding. Average print order: 4,000. First novel print order depends on book. **Published new writers within the last year.** Averages 15 total titles/year. Number of fiction titles "depends on manuscripts." Distributes titles through Publisher's Group West. Each book has its own marketing plan involving print ads, tours, conferences, etc.

● Milkweed Editions books have received numerous awards, including Finalist, *LMP* Individual Achievement Award for Editor Emilie Buchwald, awards from the American Library Association, several *New York Times* Notables, and several Pushcarts, and was named Favorite Publisher 2001 by *Minnesota Women's Press*. Carol Bly was awarded the 2001 Minnesota Humanities Prize for Literature for her entire body of work. *The $66 Summer*, by John Armistead, was named one of the New York Public Library's Best Books for Teenagers in 2001. *PU-239 & Other Russian Fantasies*, by Ken Kalfus was awarded a 2001 Pushcart Prize. V.M. Caldwell's *The Ocean Within* was nominated in 2001 for the Young Hoosiers Book Award.

Needs: For adult readers: literary fiction, nonfiction, poetry, essays; for children (ages 8-12): literary novels. Translations welcome for both audiences. No legends or folktales for children. No romance, mysteries, science fiction. Recently published *Falling Dark*, by Tim Tharp (first fiction, novel); *The Tree of Red Stars*, by Tessa Bridal (novel); and *Hell's Bottom, Colorado*, by Laura Pritchett (first fiction, short stories).

How to Contact: Send for guidelines first, then submit complete ms. Responds in 6 months. Accepts simultaneous submissions.

Terms: Pays royalties of 7½% on list price. Advance varies. Sends galleys to author. Publishes ms 1-2 years after acceptance. Book catalog for $1.50 postage. "Send for guidelines. Must enclose SASE."

Advice: "Read good contemporary literary fiction, find your own voice, and persist. Familiarize yourself with our list before submitting."

✔️ 🅐 **WILLIAM MORROW**, HarperCollins Publishers, 10 E. 53rd St., New York NY 10022. (212)207-7000. Fax: (212)207-7145. **Contact**: Acquisitions Editor. Estab. 1926. Approximately one fourth of books published are fiction.

Needs: "Morrow accepts only the highest quality submissions" in adult fiction.

How to Contact: Does not accept unsolicited mss or queries. *Submit through agent.*

Terms: Pays royalties; offers advance. Sends galleys to author. Publishes ms 2 years after acceptance. Free book catalog.

✔️ 🌐 🅐 🔲 **MULTNOMAH PUBLISHERS, INC.**, P.O. Box 1720, Sisters OR 97759. (541)549-1144. Fax: (541)549-8048. E-mail: editorial@multnomahbooks.com. Website: www.multnomahbooks.com. **Contact**: Editorial Dept. Estab. 1987. Midsize independent publisher of evangelical fiction and nonfiction. Publishes paperback originals. Books: perfect binding. Average print order: 12,000. Averages 100 total titles.

● Multnomah Books has received several Gold Medallion Book Awards from the Evangelical Christian Publishers Association.

Imprint(s): Multnomah Books ("Christian living and popular theology books"); Multnomah Fiction ("well-crafted fiction that uses truth to change lives"); Multnomah Gift ("substantive topics with beautiful, lyrical writing").

Needs: Literary, mystery/suspense, religious/inspirational issue or thesis fiction. Published *Home to Harmony*, by Philip Gulley (short stories/inspirational); *Margaret's Peace*, by Linda Hall (suspense); and *A Gathering of Finches*, by Jane Kirkpatrick (historical novel).

How to Contact: Multnomah is currently not accepting unsolicited mss, proposals or queries. Queries accepted through agents and at writers' conferences in which a Multnomah representative is present.

Terms: Pays royalties. Provides 100 author's copies. Sends galleys to author. Publishes ms 1-2 years after acceptance. Writer's guidelines for SASE or on website.

Advice: "Looking for clean, moral, uplifting fiction. We're particularly interested in contemporary women's fiction, historical fiction, superior romance, mystery/suspense and thesis fiction."

⊕ ◎ **MY WEEKLY STORY COLLECTION,** D.C. Thomson and Co., Ltd., 22 Meadowside, Dundee DD19QJ, Scotland. **Contact:** Mrs. D. Hunter, fiction editor. "Cheap paperback story library with full-colour cover. Material should not be violent, controversial or sexually explicit." Averages 48 romantic novels/year. Distributes titles through national retail outlets. Promotes titles through display cards in retail outlets and in-house magazine adverts.

Needs: Contemporary and historical novels. Length: approximately 30,000 words.

How to Contact: Query with outline/synopsis and 3 opening chapters.

Terms: Writers are paid on acceptance. Writers guidelines available on request.

Advice: "Avoid too many colloquialisms/Americanisms. Stories can be set anywhere but local colour not too 'local' as to be alien."

✓ ◎ ◎ Ⓐ **THE MYSTERIOUS PRESS,** Crime and mystery fiction imprint for Warner Books, 1271 Avenue of the Americas, New York NY 10020. (212)522-7200. Fax: (212)522-7990. Website: www.twbookmark. com. (includes authors, titles, guidelines, bulletin board, tour info, contests). **Contact:** Sara Ann Freed, editor-in-chief. Estab. 1976. Publishes hardcover and paperback originals, trade and paperback reprints. Books: hardcover (some Smythe-sewn) and paperback binding; illustrations rarely. First novel print order: 10,000 copies. **Published new writers within the last year.** Averages 36-45 total titles/year.

Needs: Mystery/suspense. Recently published *Bad News*, by Donald Westlake; and *The Red Room*, by Nicci French.

How to Contact: Submit through an agent only.

Terms: Pays royalties of 10% minimum. Average advance: negotiable. Sends galleys to author. Buys hard and softcover rights. Publishes ms 1 year after acceptance.

Advice: "Write a strong and memorable novel, and with the help of a good literary agent, you'll find the right publishing house. Don't despair if your manuscript is rejected by several houses. All publishing houses are looking for new and exciting crime novels, but it may not be at the time your novel is submitted. Hang in there, keep the faith—and good luck."

○ ◎ **THE NAIAD PRESS, INC.,** P.O. Box 10543, Tallahassee FL 32302. (850)539-5965. Fax: (850)539-9731. E-mail: naiadpress@aol.com. Website: www.naiadpress.com (includes complete and detailed catalog, order capacity). **Contact:** Barbara Grier, editorial director. Estab. 1973. "Oldest and largest lesbian publishing company. We are scrupulously honest and we keep our books in print for the most part." Books: 50 lb. offset paper; sheet-fed offset; perfect-bound. Average print order: 12,000. First novel print order: 12,000. Averages 34 total titles/year. Distributes titles through distributors, direct sales to stores and individuals and over the Web. Promotes titles through a first class mailing to over 26,000 lesbians monthly; 2,300 bookstores on mailing list.

● The Naiad Press is one of the most successful and well-known lesbian publishers. They have also produced eight of their books on audio cassette.

Needs: Lesbian fiction, all genres. Published *She Walks in Beauty*, by Nicole Conn (romance); *Substitute for Love*, by Karin Kallmaker (romance); *Out of Sight*, by Claire McNab (mystery).

How to Contact: Does not accept unsolicited mss. Query with outline/synopsis. Include estimated word count and 2-sentence bio. Send SASE or IRC for reply. Responds in 3 weeks to queries; 3 months to mss.

Terms: Pays royalties of 15% using a standard recovery contract. Occasionally pays royalties of 7½% against cover price. "Seldom gives advances and has never seen a first novel worthy of one. Believes authors are investments in their own and the company's future—that the best author is the author who produces a book every 12-18 months forever and knows that there is a *home* for that book." Publishes ms 1-2 years after acceptance. Book catalog for legal-sized SASE and $1.50 postage and handling.

Advice: "We publish lesbian fiction primarily and prefer honest work (i.e., positive, upbeat lesbian characters). Lesbian content must be accurate . . . a lot of earlier lesbian novels were less than honest. No breast beating or complaining. Our fiction titles are becoming increasingly *genre* fiction, which we encourage. Original fiction in paperback is our main field, and its popularity increases. We publish books BY, FOR AND ABOUT lesbians. We are not interested in books that are unrealistic. You know and we know what the real world of lesbian interest is like. Don't even try to fool us. Short, well-written books do best. Authors who want to succeed and will work to do so have the best shot."

◎ **THE NAUTICAL & AVIATION PUBLISHING CO. OF AMERICA INC.,** 1250 Fairmont Ave., Mt. Pleasant SC 29464. (843)856-0561. Fax: (843)856-3164. President: Jan Snouck-Hurgronje. **Contact:** Heather Parker, editor. Estab. 1979. Small publisher interested in quality military and naval history and literature. Publishes hardcover originals and reprints. Averages 10 total titles, 1-4 fiction titles/year.

Needs: Revolutionary War, War of 1812, Civil War, WWI and II, Persian Gulf and Marine Corps. history. Looks for "novels with a strong military history orientation." Recently published *The Black Flower*, by Howard Bahn; *Lieutenant Christopher and Normandy*, by VADM William P. Mack; and *The General*, by C.S. Forester (all military fiction).

How to Contact: Accepts unsolicited mss. Send query letter or query with cover letter and 2 chapters or brief synopsis. SASE necessary for return of mss. Agented fiction "miniscule." Responds in 3 weeks to queries and mss. Accepts simultaneous submissions. Sometimes comments on rejected mss.
Terms: Pays royalties of 10-12% on selling price. After acceptance publishes ms "as quickly as possible—next season." Book catalog free on request.
Advice: Publishing more fiction. Encourages first novelists. "We're interested in good writing—first novel or last novel. Keep it historical, put characters in a historical context. Professionalism counts. Know your subject. *Convince us.*"

◐◎▧ **NAVAL INSTITUTE PRESS** Imprint of U.S. Naval Institute, 291 Wood Rd., Annapolis MD 21402-5034. Fax: (410)295-1084. E-mail: esecunda@usni.org. Website: www.nip.org (includes book catalog, author guidelines, staff list, and occasional chat room event with authors). Press Director: Ronald Chambers.
Contact: Paul Wilderson, executive editor; Tom Cutler, senior acquisitions editor; Eric Mills, acquisitions editor. Estab. 1873. "Best known for introducing Tom Clancy's and Stephen Coonts' first novels. We've been publishing books for 125 years (but do very little fiction) to advance knowledge of the naval and maritime services." First novel print order: 2,500. Averages 80 titles/year. Distributes titles through wholesalers such as Ingram and Baker & Taylor.
• E.H. Simmons' *Dog Company Six* has won the ALA's Bill Boyd Award, the Alfred Thayer Mahan Award and the Samuel Eliot Marison Award.
Imprint(s): Bluejacket Books (paperback reprints).
Needs: Limited fiction on military and naval themes. Recently published *Dog Company Six*, by Edwin P. Simmons (Korean War novel); and *Punk's War*, by Ward Carroll (first novel).
How to Contact: Send query letter only.
Terms: Pays royalties of 5-10% on net sales. Publishes ms 1 year after acceptance. Writer's guidelines for #10 SASE; book catalog free for 9×12 SASE.

◐ **THOMAS NELSON PUBLISHERS**, Nelson Publishing Group, Box 141000, Nashville TN 37214-1000. Estab. 1798. **Contact:** Acquisitions Editor. "Largest Christian book publishers." Publishes hardcover and paperback originals. Averages 70 total titles/year.
Imprint(s): Janet Thoma Books; Oliver Nelson Books.
Needs: Seeking successfully published commercial fiction authors who write for adults from a Christian perspective. Published *Kingdom Come*, by Larry Burkett and T. Davis Bunn; *Dakota Moon* series, by Stephanie Grace Whitson (romance); and *Empty Coffin*, by Robert Wise (mystery/suspense).
How to Contact: Corporate office does not accept unsolicited mss. "No phone queries."
Terms: Pays royalty on net sales with rates negotiated for each project. Publishes ms 1-2 years after acceptance.
Advice: "We are a conservative publishing house and want material which is conservative in morals and in nature."

Ⓝ◯◐ **NESHUI PUBLISHING**, Midenpress, 45 Aberdeen, St. Louis MO 63105. (314)644-4941. E-mail: neshui62@hotmail.com. Website: www.neshui.com. **Contact:** B. Hodge, editor (literature); Kenneth Allen, editor (literature). Estab. 1995. Midsize press. Publishes paperback originals and paperback reprints. Books: 50 lb. paper; perfect binding. Average first novel print order: 500. **Published new writers within the last year.** Plans 10 first novels in 2002. Averages 10 total titles, 10 fiction titles/year. Distributes titles through Ingram.
Needs: Comics, experimental, fantasy (space fantasy, sword and sorcery), gay, historical, horror (dark fantasy, futuristic, psychological, supernatural), humor/satire, lesbian, literary, mainstream, military/war, mystery/suspense, religious, thriller, romance, science fiction, short story collections, thriller/espionage, translations, westerns. "We would like to publish lit." Publishes the *Swimming in Ground* anthology, translated by Hungry Poets. Recently published *Humberg*, by Mark Hickey (mystery); *Breakfast Anytime*, by Spacey Thompson (mystery); *Fou*, by Victor Fleming (fiction).
How to Contact: Accepts unsolicited mss. Send query letter Accepts queries by e-mail. Include brief bio and a list of publishing credits with submission. Send disposable copy of the ms and SASE for reply only. Agented fiction: 10%. Responds in 6 weeks to qeries; in 6 months to mss. Considers simultaneous submissions as well as submissions by e-mail or on disk. Sometimes comments on rejected mss.
Terms: Pays royalties of 10-12%. Sends galleys to author. Time between acceptance and publication is 6-12 months. Writer's guidelines for SASE. Book catalogs free upon request.

◐Ⓐ **NEW AMERICAN LIBRARY (NAL)**, Division of Penguin Putnam Inc., 375 Hudson St., New York NY 10014. (212)366-2000. Fax: (212)366-2889. **Contact:** Carolyn Nichols, executive director, NAL editorial (fiction, nonfiction); Ellen Edwards, executive editor (commercial women's fiction); Laura Anne Gilman, executive editor (science fiction/fantasy/horror); Audrey LeFehr, executive editor (contemporary and historical romance, multicultural fiction); Hilary Ross, associate executive editor (Regency, romance); Doug Grad, senior editor (thrillers, historical and military fiction/nonfiction); Dan Slater, senior editor (westerns, thrillers, commercial fiction, media tie-ins); Marie Timell, senior editor (New Age, inspirational); Genny Ostertag, editor (mystery, women's fiction); Cecilia Oh, associate editor (Regency, romance, inspirational). Estab. 1948. Publishes hardcover and paperback originals and paperback reprints. **Published new writers within the last year.**

Imprint(s): Signet, Onyx, Signet Classic, ROC, NAL Accent.

Needs: "All kinds of commercial fiction, including mainstream, historical, Regency, New Age, western, thriller, science fiction, fantasy. Full length novels and collections." Recently published *On Secret Service*, by John Jakes; *False Pretenses*, by Catherine Coulter; *Suspicion of Betrayal*, by Barbara Parker; and *The Quiet Game*, by Greg Iles.

How to Contact: Agented mss only. Queries accepted with SASE. "State type of book and past publishing projects." Simultaneous submissions OK. Responds in 3 months.

Terms: Pays in royalties and author's copies; offers advance. Send galleys to authors. Publishes ms 18 months after acceptance. Book catalog for SASE.

Advice: "Write the complete manuscript and submit it to an agent or agents."

◙ NEW HOPE BOOKS, INC., P.O. Box 38, New Hope PA 18938. (888)741-BOOK. Fax: (215)244-0935. E-mail: NewHopeBks@aol.com. Website: www.NewHopeBooks.net (includes book catalogue, featured authors, submission guidelines, contact information). **Contact:** Barbara Taylor, publisher; Tamara Hayes, assistant editor. Estab. 1999. "We are a small but quickly growing press that savors zippy, mainstream page turners, which readily adapt to feature film." Publishes hardcover and paperback originals and reprints. **Published 1 new writer within the last year.** Averages 6 total titles, 6 fiction titles/year.

Needs: Adventure, literary, mainstream, mystery/suspense, thriller/espionage. "Plot-driven fiction only that tugs on the heartstrings." Recently published *The Boardwalkers* (murder mystery); and *A Run to Hell* (crime/espionage), both by Frederick Schofield.

How to Contact: Does not accept unsolicited mss. Query with outline/synopsis and 1 sample chapter. Include estimated word count. Send SASE or IRC for return of ms OR send disposable copy of ms and SASE for reply only. "Almost all of our fiction is agented." Responds in 1 month to queries; 6 weeks to mss. Accepts simultaneous submissions.

Terms: Pays royalty. Offers negotiable advance. Sends galleys to author. Publishes ms 1 year after acceptance. Writer's guidelines free for #10 SASE; book catalog on website.

Advice: "Current industry trends heavily favor our approach. Submissions must perfectly fit our guidelines for consideration."

◙ ◎ NEW VICTORIA PUBLISHERS, P.O. Box 27, Norwich VT 05055-0027. Phone/fax: (802)649-5297. E-mail: newvic@aol.com. Website: www.NewVictoria.com (includes list of titles). **Contact:** Claudia Lamperti, editor; ReBecca Béguin, editor. Estab. 1976. "Publish mostly lesbian fiction—strong female protagonists. Most well known for Stoner McTavish mystery series." Small, three-person operation. Publishes trade paperback originals. Averages 4-6 titles/year. Distributes titles through LPC Group (Chicago), Airlift (London) and Bulldog Books (Sydney, Australia). Promotes titles "mostly through lesbian feminist media."

• *Mommy Deadest*, by Jean Maray, won the Lambda Literary Award for Mystery.

Needs: Lesbian/feminist: adventure, fantasy, historical, humor, mystery (amateur sleuth), romance. Looking for "strong feminist characters, also strong plot and action. We will consider most anything if it is well written and appeals to a lesbian/feminist audience; mostly mysteries." Publishes anthologies or special editions. Published *Killing at the Cat*, by Carlene Miller (mystery); *Queer Japan*, by Barbara Summerhawk (anthology); *Skin to Skin*, by Martha Miller (erotic short fiction); *Talk Show*, by Melissa Hartman (novel); *Flight From Chador*, by Sigrid Brunel (adventure); and *Do Drums Beat There*, by Doe Tabor (novel),

How to Contact: Accepts unsolicited mss. Query with outline/synopsis and sample chapters. Accepts queries by e-mail, fax. Send SASE or IRC for reply. Responds in 2 weeks to queries; 1 month to mss.

Terms: Pays royalties of 10%. Publishes ms 1 year after acceptance. Writer's guidelines for SASE; book catalog free.

Advice: "We are especially interested in lesbian or feminist mysteries, ideally with a character or characters who can evolve through a series of books. Mysteries should involve a complex plot, accurate legal and police procedural detail, and protagonists with full emotional lives. Pay attention to plot and character development. Read guidelines carefully."

SENDING TO A COUNTRY other than your own? Be sure to send International Reply Coupons (IRC) instead of stamps for replies or return of your manuscript.

NEWEST PUBLISHERS LTD., 201, 8540-109 St., Edmonton, Alberta T6G 1E6 Canada. (780)432-9427. Fax: (780)433-3179. E-mail: info@newestpress.com. Website: www.newestpress.com (includes guidelines and catalog). **Contact:** Ruth Linka, general manager. Estab. 1977. Publishes trade paperback originals. **Published new writers within the last year.** Averages 12 total titles/year, fiction and nonfiction. Distributes titles through General Distribution Services. Promotes titles through book launches, media interviews, review copy mailings and touring.

Imprints: Prairie Play Series (drama), Writer as Critic (literary criticisim).

• Newest Publishers won the Gabrielle Roy Prize for best critical writing on Canadian Literature. *Vanilla*, by Candas Jane Dorsey, won the Howard O'Hayen Award for Short Fiction.

Needs: Literary. "Our press is interested in western Canadian writing." Published *Man Who Beat the Man*, by F.B. Andre (first fiction, short stories); *I'm Frankie Sterne*, by Dave Margoshes (novel); *Tips of the Halo*, by R.F. Darian (first fiction, mystery). Publishes the Nunatak New Fiction Series.

How to Contact: Accepts unsolicited mss. Accepts queries by e-mail, but not by fax. SASE necessary for return of ms. Responds in 2 months to queries; 6 months to mss.

Terms: Pays royalties of 10% minimum. Sends galleys to author. Publishes ms within 18 months after acceptance. Book catalog for 9×12 SASE.

Advice: *"We publish western Canadian writers only or books about western Canada. We are looking for excellent quality and originality."*

NORTH-SOUTH BOOKS, affiliate of Nord-Sud Verlag AG, 1123 Broadway, Suite 800, New York NY 10010. (212)706-4545. Website: www.northsouth.com. **Contact:** Julie Amper. Estab. 1985. "The aim of North-South is to build bridges—bridges between authors and artists from different countries and between readers of all ages. We believe children should be exposed to as wide a range of artistic styles as possible with universal themes." **Published new writers within the last year.** Averages 100 titles/year.

• North-South Books is the publisher of the international bestseller, *The Rainbow Fish*.

Needs: Picture books, easy-to-read. "We are currently accepting only picture books; all other books are selected by our German office." Published *The Rainbow Fish & the Big Blue Whale*, by Marcus Pfister (picture); *The Other Side of the Bridge*, Wolfram Hänel (easy-to-read); and *A Mouse in the House*, by G. Wagener.

How to Contact: Agented fiction only. Query. Does not respond unless interested. All unsolicited mss returned unopened. Returns submissions accompanied by SASE.

Terms: Pays royalty on retail price. Publishes ms 2 years after acceptance.

W.W. NORTON & COMPANY, INC., 500 Fifth Ave., New York NY 10110. (212)354-5500. Fax: (212)869-0856. Website: www.wwnorton.com. **Contact:** Starling Lawrence, editor-in-chief; Robert Weil, executive editor; Edwin Barber; Jill Bialosky; Carol Houck-Smith; Alane Mason. Estab. 1924. Midsize independent publisher of trade books and college textbooks. Publishes literary fiction. Publishes hardcover and paperback originals and reprints.

• *Ship Fever*, by Andrea Barrett, published by W.W. Norton & Company, Inc., won the National Book Award.

Needs: High-quality literary fiction. No occult, science fiction, religious, gothic, romances, experimental, confession, erotica, psychic/supernatural, fantasy, horror, juvenile or young adult. Published *Ship Fever*, by Andrea Barrett; *Oyster*, by Jannette Turner Hospital; and *Power*, by Linda Hogan.

How to Contact: Does not accept unsolicited mss. Send query letter to "Editorial Department" listing credentials and briefly describing ms. Send SASE or IRC for reply. Accepts simultaneous submissions. Responds in 10 weeks. Packaging and postage must be enclosed to ensure safe return of materials. Occasionally comments on rejected mss.

OAK TREE PRESS, Barker Thomas Group Inc., 915 W. Foothill Blvd., #411, Claremont CA 91711. (909)615-8400. Fax: (909)624-3930. E-mail: oaktreepub@aol.com. Website: www.oaktreebooks.com. **Contact:** Billie Johnson, publisher (mysteries and mainstream). Estab. 1998. "Small independent publisher with a philosophy of author advocacy. Welcomes first-time authors and sponsors annual mystery contest which publishes the winning entry." Publishes hardcover and paperback originals and paperback reprints. Books: perfect binding. **Published 4 new writers within the 1st year.** Averages 10 total titles, 8 fiction titles/year. Member, SPAN, SPAWN. "We do our own distribution." Promotes through website, conferences, PR.

Imprint(s): Oak Tree Press, Dark Oak Mysteries (mysteries); Timeless Love (romance).

Needs: Humor/satire, mystery/suspense (amateur sleuth, cozy, police procedural, private eye/hardboiled), romance (contemporary, futuristic/time travel, romantic suspense), Recently published *Tulsa Time*, by Letha Albright (mystery); *An Affinity for Murder*, by Anne White (mystery); *Callie & the Dealer & a Dog Named Jake*, by Wendy Howell Mills (mystery).

insider report

Jody Shields: The case history of a writer

Jody Shield's story of first publication is the kind of Cinderella story most novelists dream about: "I already had an agent. But since I hadn't written a novel before, there was no way someone was going to buy it unless it was finished," says Shields, author of *The Fig Eater* (Little, Brown & Co., March 2000).

"In October, my agent said, 'Well, we have to get it in before Thanksgiving, because no money will be around, people will be on vacation, it's the holidays. This is the deadline.' So I sped through it, got it done on a Tuesday. I gave it to her Wednesday, and she made copies. On Thursday, she called people and said she was sending them a manuscript and wanted bids on it the next week. On Friday, the UPS man came and she sent out I think about 10 copies to different editors.

Jody Shields

"Monday morning at 10:15 we got our first offer, which was in the six figures, and she turned it down," Shields continues. "She said 'we're going to do better than that.' At this point I was broke, but I thought well, OK. And she was right. So many people wanted the book that we ended up auctioning it off the next week and sending out more copies. It was a wonderful dream come true. So people should be encouraged—these things do happen."

But despite the dizzying speed of the sale, Shields is the first to admit there's nothing easy about writing a bestseller. No secret trick to make the process go a little smoother. No magic formula to follow that makes the words flow effortlessly from mind to paper. Shields spent more than a year writing that first novel. And the effort certainly paid off; the book was nominated for the Edgar Allan Poe Award and optioned by Miramax.

"I didn't do anything else while I wrote this," she says. "I stopped answering the telephone and wrote about 12 hours a day. It was hard. You get up and think 'Oh my God, how can I write again today, it's so awful. I only got one page done. I hate it.' But I was running out of money, so that was a big motivator."

Making her task a bit more difficult was the fact that Shields was writing an historical fiction novel based on one of Sigmund Freud's most famous and well-documented patients, Dora. Freud used the case to publish his theory on female hysteria and its association with sexual repression.

The book proved to be quite a leap from Shields' two previous nonfiction fashion books (both now out of print), and though she had written a few screenplays—none of which was produced—there was nothing in her past that guaranteed she'd find success as a novelist. But it was a risk Shields says she willing take—and one that clearly paid off.

Set in 1910 Vienna, *The Fig Eater* delves deep into the mysterious murder of the 18-year-

Photo by Brigitte LaCombe

old Dora. And while the skeleton of the book—the central families and their relationships—is based on Freud's case history of Dora, the two ensuing murder investigations, one led by the fictional Inspector (whose first name is never given) and the other by his Hungarian wife, Erszebet, come from the imagination of Shields. "I think D.M. Thomas' *The White Hotel* set the precedent for me," she says. "I took the case history and sort of speculated on what provoked the murder. Another person could take the same outline and write a completely different story. You feed it your own particular case history.

"It's funny, but after you write historical fiction, you can kind of see the author's footprints in ways that you weren't aware of until you've tried it yourself."

And Shields insists all the historical customs in the book are true, including the wide array of superstitions and folklore adopted by Erszebet. Originally seen as a secondary character, Shields says Erszebet's presence in the book—and ultimate impact on the story at large—was shaped mainly by material she found while researching the time period.

"As I started researching Hungarian superstitions, I became so interested in that, that Erszebet's character grew and grew, because the information was so fascinating. She's a scary person."

But as Erszebet's presence grew, that of the titular fruit decreased. While Shields continued to use the fig as a central tie throughout the novel, the story's botanical slant was decidedly lessened. Shields admits that some readers may be disappointed by the "erotic" object's decreased presence, but she says the book's focus simply shifted as the story progressed. "I'm sure this happens to other writers, but as you research something and other facts come to light, it changes the direction of your book.

"I know some people sort of coughed about that," she says. "Some people really wanted to know what happened to the fig, so I actually put it in the last scene, but it just seemed so fake that I took it out again. That last scene is so intense, that you can't have one of the characters pop up and say, 'Well, where's the fig?' "

As for the murder investigation itself, Shields turned elsewhere for motivation—and found it in the most auspicious of places. Instrumental in *The Fig Eater*'s direction and tone was *Sytem der Kriminalistick*, a criminology book written by Hans Gross and published in 1904—a book Shields came across at a flea market. Written in a form that closely mirrored Freud's own technique of psychoanalytical detachment, the book was a perfect match for Shields' subject matter. "I just happened to find that book while I was toying with the idea of writing the Dora case history as a novel. And when I discovered that it was published at exactly the same time, it seemed like fate."

Fate indeed. The book contributed greatly to character development, with the Inspector adopting much of its ideology as his own and often quoting the book. The criminology book's endless information created only one problem for Shields: deciding what to use.

"I had to find just the right excerpts, put them at just the right places," she says. "But I thought that (Gross) was just an amazing writer. His work is so succinct and intelligent. And he's writing pre-Freud, which is astonishing." Shields drew on her previous experience as a contributing editor for *Vogue* and *House and Garden* and as a design editor for *The New York Times Magazine* to establish the story's third-person point of view. Having written for magazines for most of her career, writing in the first person would have been "completely unnatural." Third-person point of view also allowed Shields to create a sense of distance between readers and the story, a distance she says parallels the tone of Freud's original work.

"If you read Freud's case history, the language is not sensationalistic at all," she says. "And when I wrote the book, I tried to make it as restrained and minimal as I could, which sort of mirrors the case history language. As a writing style, the case histories are sort of overlooked as an interesting way of describing an intense emotional experience."

And as she prepares to write her next novel, Shields certainly will draw on the lessons she learned the first time around. "I guess I had the assumption before I wrote the novel that it was easier for people other than me, which isn't true.

"So, I guess you just have to accept the fact that it's difficult. It's just part of the package. It's torture for everyone, I guess. But even if it was torture, probably people would lie and tell you the opposite because you want to hear a writer say it's really easy."

—*Kelly Nickell*

This article originally appeared in Writer's Digest *magazine, and is used here by permission.*

How to Contact: Does not accept or return unsolicited mss. Send query letter. Accepts queries by e-mail and fax. Include estimated word count and brief bio with submission. Agented fiction: 1%. Responds in 1-2 weeks to queries; 1-2 months to mss. Accepts simultaneous submissions, electronic submissions. Sometimes comments on rejected mss.
Terms: Pays royalties of 10-20%. Advance is negotiable. Sends galleys to author. Publishes ms 9-18 months after acceptance. Writer's guidelines for SASE. Book catalogs for SASE.
Advice: "Understand the business and be eager and enthusiastic about participating in the marketing and promotion of the title."

☑ ⊘ **ORCHARD BOOKS**, An imprint of Scholastic Inc., 95 Madison Ave., New York NY 10016. (212)951-2600. Fax: (212)213-6435. Website: www.scholastic.com. **Contact:** Karen Nagel (*No Phone Calls*). Orchard specializes in children's illustrated and picture books. Publishes hardcover originals. **Published new writers within the last year.**
Needs: Picture books, young adult, middle reader, board book, novelty and some nonfiction. Recently published *Eli's Night-Light*, by Liz Rosenberg and illustrated by Joanna Yardley; and *Flora's Blanket*, by Debi Gliori.
How to Contact: Currently not accepting queries or unsolicited mss.
Terms: Pays royalties of 7½-10% on retail price. Advance varies. Publishes ms 1 year after acceptance.
Advice: "Go to a bookstore and read several Orchard Books to get an idea of what we publish. Write what you feel. It's worth finding the right publishing match."

☑ 🌐 ◎ **ORIENT PAPERBACKS,** A Division of Vision Books Pvt Ltd., Madarsa Rd., Kashmere Gate, Delhi 110 006 India. Phone: +91-11-386-2201 or +91-11-386-2267. Fax: +91-11-386-2935. E-mail: orientpbk @vsnl.com. **Contact:** Sudhir Malhotra, editor. Averages 10-15 novels or story collections/year. "We are one of the largest paperback publishers in S.E. Asia and publish English fiction by authors from this part of the world."
Needs: Length: 40,000 words minimum.
How to Contact: Send cover letter, brief summary, 1 sample chapter and author's bio data. "We send writers' guidelines on accepting a proposal."
Terms: Pays royalty on copies sold.

☑ 🌐 **PETER OWEN PUBLISHERS**, 73 Kenway Rd., London SW5 ORE England. Phone: 44+ 020 7373 5628. Fax: 44+ 020 7373 6760. E-mail: admin@peterowen.com. Website: www.peterowen.com (includes complete backlists, book catalog plus ordering information). **Contact**: Antonia Owen, editorial director/fiction editor. "Independent publishing house now 50 years old. Publish fiction from around the world, from Russia to Japan. Publishers of Shusaku Endo, Paul and Jane Bowles, Hermann Hesse, Octavio Paz, Colette, etc." Averages 15 fiction titles/year. Titles distributed through Central Books, London, and Dufour Editions, USA.
Needs: Does not accept short stories, only excerpts from novels of normal length. Recently published *Hermes in Paris*, by Peter Vansittart (literary fiction); *Doubting Thomas*, by Atle Naess (translated literary fiction); *Lying*, by Wendy Perriam (fiction).
How to Contact: Query by post or e-mail with synopsis and/or sample chapter or submit through agent (preferred). Send SASE (or IRC).

Terms: Pays standard royalty. Average advance. Book catalog for SASE, SAE with IRC or on website.
Advice: "Be concise. It would help greatly if author was familiar with the list. U.K. bookselling, especially since end of net book agreement, is making new fiction very hard to sell; it is also hard to get fiction reviewed. At the moment we are publishing less fiction than nonfiction."

RICHARD C. OWEN PUBLISHERS INC., P.O. Box 585, Katonah NY 10536. Fax: (914)232-3903. Website: www.rcowen.com (includes guidelines, book-of-the-month sample book, teacher development). **Contact:** Janice Boland, director of children's books. "We believe children become enthusiastic, independent, life-long readers when supported and guided by skillful teachers who choose books with real and lasting value. The professional development work we do and the books we publish support these beliefs." Publishes hardcover and paperback originals. **Published 15 previously unpublished writers within the last year.** Distributes titles to schools via mail order. Promotes titles through website, database mailing, reputation, catalog, brochures and appropriate publications—magazines, etc.
Needs: Picture books. "Brief, strong story line, real characters, natural language, exciting—child-appealing stories with a twist. No lists, alphabet or counting books." Also seeking mss for new anthologies of short, snappy stories for 7-8-year-old children (2nd grade). Subjects include humor, careers, mysteries, science fiction, folktales, women, fashion trends, sports, music, myths, journalism, history, inventions, planets, architecture, plays, adventure, technology, vehicles. Recently published *Sea Lights*, by R. Hugh Rice (nonfiction); *Autumn on My Street*, by Lisa Brokie Cook (fiction).
How to Contact: Send for ms guidelines, then submit full ms with SASE. No fax or e-mail queries. Responds in 1 month to queries; 2 months to mss. Accepts simultaneous submissions, if so noted.
Terms: Pays royalties of 5% on wholesale price; Books for Young Learners Anthologies and picture storybooks: flat fee for all rights. Publishes ms 3 years after acceptance. Writer's guidelines for SASE with 52¢ postage.
Advice: "We don't respond to queries. Send entire ms. Write clear strong stories with memorable characters and end with a big wind up finish. Write for today's children—about real things that interest them. Read books that your public library features in their children's room to acquaint yourself with the best modern children's literature."

OWL BOOKS, Imprint of Henry Holt & Co., Inc., 115 W. 18th St., New York NY 10011. (212)886-9200. Fax: (212)633-0748. **Contact:** Jennifer Barth, senior editor; Tom Bissell, associate editor. Estab. 1996.
Needs: Literary mainstream/contemporary. Published *White Boy Shuffle*, by Paul Beatty and *The Debt to Pleasure*, by John Lanchester.
How to Contact: Holt does not accept unagented submissions.
Terms: Pays royalties of 6-7½% on retail price. Advance varies. Publishes ms 1 year after acceptance.

PANTHEON BOOKS, The Knopf Publishing Group, A Division of Random House, Inc., 299 Park Ave., New York NY 10171. (212)751-2600. Fax: (212)572-6030. Website: www.pantheonbooks.com. Editorial Director: Dan Frank. Senior Editors: Deborah Garrison, Shelley Wagner. Executive Editor: Erroll McDonald. **Contact:** Editorial Department. Estab. 1942. "Small but well-established imprint of well-known large house." Publishes hardcover and trade paperback originals and trade paperback reprints. Averages 75 total titles, about 25 fiction titles/year.
Needs: Quality fiction and nonfiction. Published *Crooked Little Heart*, by Anne Lamott.
How to Contact: Does not accept unsolicited mss. Query with cover letter and sample material. Send SASE or IRC for return.
Payment/Terms: Pays royalties; offers advance.

PAPIER-MACHE PRESS, 40 Commerce Park, Milford CT 06460. (203)877-8573. Estab. 1984. "Small women's press." Publishes anthologies, novels. Books: 60-70 lb. offset paper; perfect-bound or casebound. Average print order: 25,000.
Needs: Not publishing new titles at this time. Published *At Our Core: Women Writing About Power*, by Sandra Martz (anthology); and *Generation to Generation*, by Sandra Martz and Shirley Coe (anthology).

PASSEGGIATA PRESS, INC., 222 W. B St., Pueblo CO 81003-3404. (719)544-1038. Fax: (719)544-7911. E-mail: passegpress@cs.com. **Contact:** Donald Herdeck, publisher/editor-in-chief. Estab. 1973. "We search for books that will make clear the complexity and value of non-Western literature and culture." Small independent publisher with expanding list. Publishes hardcover and paperback originals and reprints. Books: library binding; illustrations. Average print order: 1,000-1,500. First novel print order: 1,000. Averages 15 total titles, 6-8 fiction titles each year. **Publishes 2-3 new writers/year.**
• Passeggiata, formerly Three Continents Press, has published three authors awarded the Nobel Prize in Literature.

Needs: "We publish original fiction only by writers from Africa, the Caribbean, the Middle East, Asia and the Pacific. No fiction by writers from North America or Western Europe." Recently published *Not Yet African*, by Kevin Gordon; and *Ghost Songs*, by Kathryn Abdul-Baki.

How to Contact: Query with outline/synopsis and sample pages with SASE. Accepts queries by fax and e-mail. State "origins (non-Western), education and previous publications." Responds in 1 week to queries; 1 month to mss. Accepts simultaneous submissions. Occasionally critiques ("a few sentences") rejected mss.

Terms: "Send inquiry letter first and ms only if so requested by us. We are not a subsidy publisher, but do a few specialized titles a year with grants. In those cases we accept institutional subventions. Foundation or institution receives 20-30 copies of book and at times royalty on first printing. We pay royalties twice yearly (against advance) as a percentage of net paid receipts." Royalties of 5% minimum; 10% maximum. Offers negotiable advance, $300 average. Provides 10 author's copies. Sends galleys to author. Free flyers available; inquiry letter first and ms only if so requested by us.

Advice: "Submit professional work (within our parameters of interest) with well worked-over language and clean manuscripts prepared to exacting standards."

PEACHTREE PUBLISHERS, LTD., 1700 Chattahoochee Ave., Atlanta GA 30318. (404)876-8761. Fax: (404)875-2578. Website: www.peachtree-online.com (includes writer's guidelines, current catalog of titles, upcoming promotional events, behind-the-scenes look at creating a book). President: Margaret Quinlin. **Contact:** Helen Harriss, fiction editors. Estab. 1977. Small, independent publisher specializing in general interest publications, particularly of Southern origin. Publishes hardcover and paperback originals and hardcover reprints. First novel print run 3,000. **Published 2 new writers within the last year.** Averages 18-20 total titles, 1-2 fiction titles/year. Promotes titles through review copies to appropriate publications, press kits and book signings at local bookstores.

Imprint(s): Freestone and Peachtree Jr.

Needs: Young adult and juvenile fiction. "Absolutely no adult fiction! We are seeking YA and juvenile works including mystery and historical fiction, of high literary merit."

How to Contact: Accepts unsolicited mss. Query, submit outline/synopsis and 3 chapters, or submit complete ms with SASE. Responds in 6 months to queries; 6 months to mss. Accepts simultaneous submissions. Do not fax or e-mail queries, manuscripts or submissions

Terms: Pays in royalties. Sends galleys to author. Free writer's guidelines. Publishes ms 2 years after acceptance. Book catalog for 5 first-class stamps.

Advice: "We encourage original efforts in first novels."

PELICAN PUBLISHING COMPANY, Box 3110, Gretna LA 70054-3110. (504)368-1175. Website: www.pelicanpub.com (includes writer's guidelines, featured book, index of Pelican books). **Contact:** Nina Kooij, editor-in-chief. Estab. 1926. "We seek writers on the cutting edge of ideas. We believe ideas have consequences. One of the consequences is that they lead to a bestselling book." Publishes hardcover and paperback originals and reprints. Books: hardcover and paperback binding; illustrations sometimes. Buys juvenile mss with illustrations. Distributes titles internationally through distributors, bookstores, libraries. Promotes titles at reading and book conventions, in trade magazines, in radio interviews, print reviews and TV interviews.

● *The Warlord's Puzzle*, by Virginia Walton Pilegard was #2 on *Independent Bookseller*'s Book Sense 76 list. *Dictionary of Literary Biography* lists *Unforgotten*, by D.J. Meador as "one of the best of 1999."

Needs: Juvenile fiction, especially with a regional and/or historical focus. No young adult fiction, contemporary fiction or fiction containing graphic language, violence or sex. Also no "psychological" novels. Recently published *The Loki Project*, by Benjamin King (adult historical fiction); and *The Warlord's Puzzle*, by Virginia Walton Pilegard (children's fairytale).

How to Contact: Does not accept unsolicited mss. Send query letter. May submit outline/synopsis and 2 sample chapters with SASE. "Not responsible if writer's only copy is sent." Responds in 1 month to queries; 3 months to mss. Comments on rejected mss "infrequently."

Terms: Pays royalties of 10% and 10 contributor's copies; advance considered. Sends galleys to author. Publishes ms 9-18 months after acceptance. Catalog of titles and writer's guidelines for SASE.

Advice: "Research the market carefully. Request our catalog to see if your work is consistent with our list. For ages 8 and up, story must be planned in chapters that will fill at least 90 double-spaced manuscript pages. Topic for ages 8-12 must be Louisiana related and historical. We look for stories that illuminate a particular place and time in history and that are clean entertainment. The only original adult work we might consider is historical fiction, preferably Civil War (not romance). Please don't send three or more chapters unless solicited. Follow our guidelines listed under 'How to Contact.' "

PERFECTION LEARNING CORP., 10520 New York Ave., Des Moines IA 50322-3775. (515)278-0133. Fax: (515)278-2980. E-mail: sthies@plconline.com. Website: www.perfectionlearning.com (includes writer's guidelines, names of editors, book catalog). **Contact:** Sue Thies, editorial director. "We are an educational publisher of hi/lo fiction and nonfiction with teacher support material." **Published 10 new writers within the last year.** Publishes 50-75 total titles/year, fiction and nonfiction. Distributes titles through sales reps, direct mail and online catalog. Promotes titles through educational conferences, journals and catalogs.

Imprint(s): Cover-to-Cover; Sue Thies, editorial director (all genres).

Needs: Hi/lo mss in all genres. Readability of ms should be at least two grade levels below interest level. "Please do not submit mss with fewer than 4,000 words or more than 30,000 words." Published *Tall Shadow*, by Bonnie Highsmith Taylor (Native American); *The Rattlesnack Necklace*, by Linda Baxter (historical fiction); and *Tales of Mark Twain*, by Peg Hall (retold short stories).

How to Contact: Accepts unsolicited mss. Query with outline/synopsis and 3-4 sample chapters or submit complete ms with a cover letter. Accepts queries by e-mail and fax. Include 1-page bio, estimated word count and list of publishing credits. Send SASE or IRC for return of ms or send a disposable copy of ms and SASE for reply only. Responds in 3 months. Accepts simultaneous submissions.

Terms: Publishes ms 6-8 months after acceptance. Writer's guidelines on website; book catalog for 9×12 SASE with $2.31 postage.

Advice: "We are an educational publisher. Check with educators to find out their needs, their students' needs and what's popular."

PHILOMEL BOOKS, Imprint of the Children's Division of Penguin Putnam Inc., 345 Hudson St., New York NY 10014. (212)414-3610. **Contact**: Patricia Lee Gauch, editorial director; Michael Green, senior editor. Estab. 1980. "A high-quality oriented imprint focused on stimulating picture books, middle-grade novels, and young adult novels." Publishes hardcover originals. Averages 25 total titles, 5-7 novels/year.

Needs: Adventure, ethnic, family saga, fantasy, historical, juvenile (5-9 years), literary, preschool/picture book, regional, short story collections, translations, western (young adult), young adult/teen (10-18 years). Looking for "story-driven novels with a strong cultural voice but which speak universally." No "generic, mass-market oriented fiction." Published *The Long Patrol*, by Brian Jacques; *I Am Morgan LeFay*, by Nancy Springer; and *Betty Doll*, by Patricia Palacco.

How to Contact: No unsolicited mss. Query first or submit outline/synopsis and first 3 chapters. Send SASE or IRC for return of ms. Agented fiction 40%. Responds in 10 weeks to queries; up to 4 months to mss. Accepts simultaneous submissions. Sometimes comments on rejected ms.

Terms: Pays royalties, negotiable advance and author's copies. Sends galleys to author. Publishes ms anywhere from 1-2 years after acceptance. Writer's guidelines for #10 SASE. Book catalog for 9×12 SASE.

Advice: "We are not a mass-market publisher and do not publish short stories independently. In addition, we do just a few novels a year."

PHONY LID PUBLICATIONS, P.O. Box 29066, Los Angeles CA 90029-0066. E-mail: phonylid@m indspring. Website: www.fyuocuk.com (includes information on Phony Lid Publications, *Vagabond Magazine*, excerpts from the magazine, guidelines and available titles). **Contact**: K. Vaughn Dessaint, fiction editor; Jesse Hopkins (contemporary subcultures). Estab. 1998. "Publisher of aggressive, gut-instinct short fiction with a focus on post punk, urban gore and the female experience." Publishes paperback originals. Books: glossy cover, standard inside; doutech printing; perfect/flat binding; illustrations. Average print order: 300-500. **Published more than 30 new writers within the last year.** Plans 1-3 first novels this year. Averages 20 total titles, 10 fiction titles/year. Distributes titles through Amazon.com, Last Gasp, The Book House, direct mail order, Internet sales. Promotes titles through readings, reviews, direct mail marketing, etc.

Imprints: Pick Pocket Books, Louis Baudrey (short aggressive fiction); The Meat League, S.A. Griffin (poetry).

Needs: Experimental, humor, satire, literary. "We are looking for short novels 100-200 pages, aggressive, post-punk, urban gore. We read everything but prefer a literary bent on the pulp genre." Recently published *The Bus*, by Steve Abee (personal history); *Sleeveless*, by Joi Brozek (fiction noir); and *Minden Row*, by Marie Kazacia (travel fiction).

How to Contact: Accepts unsolicited mss. Submit complete ms with cover letter. Accepts queries by e-mail. Include estimated word count and 1 paragraph bio. Send SASE for reply, return of ms or send a disposable copy of ms. Responds in 2 weeks to queries; 2 months to mss. Accepts simultaneous submissions. Always comments on rejected mss.

Terms: Pays in author's copies (25% of print order). Sends galleys to author. Publishes ms 2-4 months after acceptance. Writer's guidelines for SAE and 2 IRCs. Book catalog free.

Advice: "We publish more fiction in our magazine *Vagabond* because we are finally receiving the type of material we want to use. In this process, we are coming in contact with writers that have novels or short story collections that fit our criteria. The principle trend we have noticed is that the type of fiction that is selling is not the type of work that is being published by the literary journals. We focus on works that entertain, present them with illustrations and pursue larger works from these writers. As the popularity of the magazine grows so does the market for collections and novels that we wish to publish. Don't try to be another Charles Bukowski or Jack Kerouac. Find a voice through these writers. Recognize that it's not the themes that appeal to us, but the honest approach to subjects that entertain and challenge the reader."

PICADOR USA, St. Martin's Press, 175 Fifth Ave., New York NY 10010. **Contact:** Frances Coady, publisher (literary fiction); Joshua Kenall, associate editor (literary fiction); Melanie Fleishman, associate publisher (literary fiction). Estab. 1994. "We publish high-quality literary fiction and nonfiction. We are open to a broad range of subjects, well written by authoritative authors." Publishes hardcover originals and trade paperback originals and reprints. Titles distributed through Von Holtzbrinck Publishers. Titles promoted through national print advertising and bookstore coop.

• *The Amazing Adventures of Kavalier & Clay*, by Michael Chabon, won the Pulitzer Prize for fiction; *In America*, by Susan Sontag, won the National Book Award. Jame Crace's *Being Dead* won the National Book Critics Circle Award.

Needs: Literary. Recently published *No One Thinks of Greenland*, by John Griesmer (first novel, literary); *Summerland*, by Malcolm Knox (first novel, literary fiction); *Half a Heart*, Rosellen Brown (literary fiction).
How to Contact: Does not accept unsolicited mss. Query only with SASE, by e-mail, or by fax. Publishes few unagented writers. Responds in 2 months to queries. Accepts simultaneous submissions.
Terms: Pays royalties of 7½-12½% on retail price. Advance varies. Publishes ms 18 months after acceptance. Writer's guidelines for #10 SASE. Book catalog for 9 × 12 SASE and $2.60 postage.

PINEAPPLE PRESS, P.O. Box 3899, Sarasota FL 34230-3899. (800)746-3275. Fax: (941)351-9988. E-mail: info@pineapplepress.com. Website: www.pineapplepress.com (includes searchable database of titles, news events, featured books, company profile, and option to request a hard copy of catalog). **Contact**: June Cussen, executive editor. Estab. 1982. Small independent trade publisher. Publishes hardcover and paperback originals. Books: quality paper; offset printing; Smyth-sewn or perfect-bound; illustrations occasionally. **Published new writers within the last year.** Averages 20 total titles/year. Distributes titles through Pineapple, Ingram and Baker & Taylor. Promotes titles through reviews, advertising in print media, direct mail, author signings and the World Wide Web.

Needs: Historical, literary, mainstream, regional (most fiction is set in Florida). Recently published *Antonia's Island*, by Nick Maginnis (novel).
How to Contact: No unsolicited mss. Query with outline, brief synopsis and sample chapters. Send SASE or IRC for reply. Responds in 3 months. Accepts simultaneous submissions.
Terms: Pays royalties of 6½-15% on net price. Advance is not usually offered. "Basically, it is an individual agreement with each author depending on the book." Sends galleys to author. Publishes ms 18 months after acceptance. Book catalog for 9 × 12 SAE with $1.24 postage.
Advice: "Quality first novels will be published, though we usually only do one or two novels per year. We regard the author/editor relationship as a trusting relationship with communication open both ways. Learn all you can about the publishing process and about how to promote your book once it is published. A query on a novel without a brief sample seems useless."

PIPPIN PRESS, 229 E. 85th Street, Gracie Station Box 1347, New York NY 10028. (212)288-4920. Fax: (732)225-1562. **Contact**: Barbara Francis, publisher; Joyce Segal, senior editor. Estab. 1987. "Small, independent children's book company, formed by the former editor-in-chief of Prentice Hall's juvenile book division." Publishes hardcover originals. Books: 135-150 GSM offset-semi-matte paper (for picture books); offset, sheet-fed printing; Smythe-sewn binding; full color, black and white line illustrations and half tone, b&w and full color illustrations. Averages 5-6 titles/year.

Needs: Juvenile only for ages 4-12. "I am interested in humorous novels for children of about 7-12. Also interested in autobiographical novels for 8-12 year olds and selected historical fiction and idiosyncratic nonfiction for the same age group. Less interested in picture books at this time."
How to Contact: Does not accept unsolicited mss. Send query letter with SASE or IRC for reply. Responds in 3 weeks to queries. Accepts simultaneous submissions. Sometimes comments on rejected mss.
Terms: Pays royalties. Sends galleys to author. Publication time after ms is accepted "depends on the amount of revision required, type of illustration, etc." Writer's guidelines for #10 SASE.

PLEASANT COMPANY PUBLICATIONS, Subsidiary of Pleasant Company, 8400 Fairway Place, Middleton WI 53528. (608)836-4848. Fax: (608)836-1999. Website: www.americangirl.com (includes writer's guidelines, names of editors, press releases, e-store including book list). **Contact:** Erin Falligant, submissions editor; Andrea Weiss, senior editor (contemporary fiction); Peg Ross, editor (history mysteries). Estab. 1986. Midsize independent publisher. "Moving in new directions, and committed to high quality in all we do. Pleasant

Company has specialized in historical fiction and contemporary nonfiction for girls 7-12 and is now actively seeking strong authors for middle-grade contemporary fiction, historical fiction and fantasy for all ages." Publishes hardcover and paperback originals. Averages 30-40 total titles, 30 fiction titles/year.

● *The Night Flyers*, by Elizabeth McDavid Jones won the 2000 Edgar Allan Poe Award for Best Children's Mystery. *Speak*, by Laurie Halse Anderson is a 2000 Printz Honor Book (ALA).

Imprints: The American Girls Collection and American Girls Library.

Needs: Children's/juvenile (historical, mystery, contemporary for girls 8-12). "Contemporary fiction submissions should capture the spirit of contemporary American girls and also illuminate the ways in which their lives are personally touched by issues and concerns affecting America today. We are looking for thoughtfully developed characters and plots, and a discernible sense of place." Stories must feature an American girl, aged 10-13; reading level 4th-6th grade. No first-romance stories. Recently published *The Night Flyer*, by Elizabeth McDavid Jones (historical fiction); *Smoke Screen*, by Amy Goldman Koss (contemporary fiction); and *The Secret Voice of Gina Zhang*, by Dori Jones Yang (contemporary fiction).

How to Contact: Accepts unsolicited mss. Query with outline/synopsis and 3 sample chapters for hisotircal fiction. Submit complete ms with cover letter for contemporary fiction. Include list of publishing credits. "Tell us why the story is right for us." Send SASE or IRC for return of ms or send disposable copy of ms and SASE for reply only. Agented fiction 5%. Responds in up to 4 months to queries; 4 months to mss. Accepts simultaneous submissions.

Payment/Terms: Advance against royalties. Publishes ms 3-12 months after acceptance. Writer's guidelines for SASE.

Advice: For historical fiction "your story *must* have a girl protagonist age 8-12. No early reader. Our readers are girls 10-12, along with parents and educators. We want to see character development and strong plotting."

A POCKET BOOKS, Imprint of Simon & Schuster, 1230 Avenue of the Americas, New York NY 10020. (212)698-7000. Website: www.simonandschuster.com. **Contact:** Tracy Behar, vice president/editorial director. "Pocket Books publishes general interest nonfiction and adult fiction." Publishes paperback originals and reprints, mass market and trade paperbacks and hardcovers. **Published new writers within the last year.** Averages 250 titles/year.

Needs: Mysteries, romance, Star Trek® novels, thriller/psychological suspense, westerns.

How to Contact: Agented fiction only. Does not accept unsolicited mss. Send query letter with SASE or IRC for reply. Responds in 1 month.

Terms: Pays royalties of 6-8% on retail price. Publishes ms 2 years after acceptance. Writer's guidelines for #10 SASE; book catalog free.

PRAIRIE JOURNAL PRESS, Prairie Journal Trust, P.O. Box 61203, Brentwood Postal Services, Calgary, Alberta T2L 2K6 Canada. E-mail: prairiejournal@yahoo.com. Website: www.geocities.com/prairiejournal/ (includes guidelines, subscription information and home page). **Contact:** Anne Burke, literary editor. Estab. 1983. Small-press, noncommercial literary publisher. Publishes paperback originals. Books: bond paper; offset printing; stapled binding; b&w line drawings. **Published new writers within the last year.** Averages 2 total titles or anthologies/year. Distributes titles by mail and in bookstores and libraries (public and university). Promotes titles through direct mail, reviews and in journals.

● Prairie Journal Press authors have been nominated for The Journey Prize in fiction.

Needs: Literary, short stories. No romance, horror, pulp, erotica, magazine type, children's, adventure, formula, western. Published *Prairie Journal Fiction, Prairie Journal Fiction II* (anthologies of short stories); *Solstice* (short fiction on the theme of aging); and *Prairie Journal Prose*. "Our new series *Prairie Annals* is 8½×11, stapled, soft cover, full color art."

How to Contact: Accepts unsolicited mss. Query first and send Canadian postage or IRCs and $8 for sample copy, then submit 1-2 stories with SAE and IRCs (sorry, no US stamps). Responds in 6 months or sooner. Occasionally comments on rejected mss if requested.

Terms: Pays 1 author's copy; honorarium depends on grant/award provided by the government or private/corporate donations. Sends galleys to author. Book catalog free on request to institutions; SAE with IRC for individuals. "No U.S. stamps!"

Advice: "We wish we had the means to promote more new writers. We look for something different each time and try not to repeat types of stories if possible. We receive fiction of very high quality. Short fiction is preferable although excerpts from novels are considered if they stand alone on their own merit."

PRESIDIO PRESS, 505B San Marin Dr., Suite 160, Novato CA 94945. (415)898-1081, ext. 125. Fax: (415)898-0383. **Contact:** E.J. McCarthy, editor-in-chief. Estab. 1976. Small independent general trade—specialist in military. Publishes hardcover originals. Publishes an average of 2 works of fiction per list. **Published new writers within the past year. Averages 24 new titles/year.**

Needs: Historical with military background, war, thriller/espionage. Published *Synbat*, by Bob Mayer; *Proud Legions*, by John Antal; and *A Murder of Crows*, by Steve Shepard.

How to Contact: Accepts unsolicited mss. Send query letter with SASE or IRC for reply. Responds in 2 weeks to queries; 3 months to mss. Accepts simultaneous submissions. Comments on rejected ms.

Terms: Pays royalties of 15% of net minimum. Average advance: $1,000. Sends edited manuscripts and page proofs to author. Publishes ms 12-18 months after acceptance. Book catalog and guidelines for 9 × 12 SASE with $1.30 postage.

Advice: "Think twice before entering any highly competitive genre; don't imitate; do your best. Have faith in your writing and don't let the market disappoint or discourage you."

PUFFIN BOOKS, Imprint of Penguin Putnam Inc., 345 Hudson St., New York NY 10014-3657. (212)414-2000. Website: www.penguinputnam.com. **Contact:** Sharyn November, senior editor; Kristin Gilson, executive editor. "Puffin Books publishes high-end trade paperbacks and paperback reprints for preschool children, beginning and middle readers, and young adults." Publishes trade paperback originals and reprints. Averages 175-200 titles/year.

Needs: Picture books, young adult novels, middle grade and easy-to-read grades 1-3. "We publish mostly paperback reprints. We do few original titles." Published *A Gift for Mama*, by Esther Hautzig (Puffin chapter book).

How to Contact: Does not accept unsolicited mss. Send query letter with SASE or IRC for reply. Responds in 3 months to mss. Accepts simultaneous submissions, if so noted.

Terms: Royalty and advance vary. Publishes ms 1 year after acceptance. Book catalog for 9 × 12 SASE with 7 first-class stamps; send request to Marketing Department.

Advice: "Our audience ranges from little children 'first books' to young adult (ages 14-16). An original idea has the best luck."

G.P. PUTNAM'S SONS, Imprint of Penguin Putnam Inc., 375 Hudson St., New York NY 10014. (212)366-2000. Fax: (212)366-2666. Website: www.penguinputnam.com. **Contact**: Acquisitions Editor. Publishes hardcover and trade paperback originals. Published new writers within the last year.

Imprint(s): Putnam, Riverhead, Jeremy P. Tarcher.

Needs: Adventure, literary, mainstream/contemporary, mystery/suspense, women's. Recently published *Rainbow Six*, by Tom Clancy (adventure).

How to Contact: Does not accept unsolicited mss. Prefers agented submissions. Responds in 6 months to queries. Accepts simultaneous submissions.

Payment/Terms: Pays variable royalties on retail price. Advance varies.

QUARTET BOOKS LIMITED, 27 Goodge Street, London W1P1FD England. Fax: 0171 637 1866. E-mail: quartetbooks@easynet.co.uk. **Contact:** Stella Kane, publishing director. Publishes "cutting-edge, avant-garde literary fiction." **Published new writers within the last year.** Averages 30 novels/year. Distributes titles through Plymbridge Distribution Services. Promotes titles through trade advertising mostly.

Needs: "Contemporary literary fiction including translations, popular culture, biographies, music, history and politics. *No* romantic fiction, science fiction or poetry." Recently published *Resentment*, by Gary Indiana (literary-black comic); *As Good As It Gets*, by Simon Nolan (edgy, Brit-lit); and *The Romance Reader*, by Pearl Abraham (rites of passage-literary).

How to Contact: Query with brief synopsis and sample chapters. Accepts unsolicited queries by e-mail and fax.

Terms: Pays advance—half on signature, half on delivery or publication.

QUIXOTE PRESS, 1854 345th Ave., Wever IA 52658. (800)571-2665 or (319)372-7480. Fax: (319)372-7485. E-mail: maddmack@interl.net. **Contact:** Bruce Carlson, president. Quixote Press specializes in humorous regional folklore and special interest cookbooks. Publishes trade paperback originals and reprints. **Published mostly new writers within the last year.**

Needs: Adventure, ethnic, experimental, humor, short story collections, children's. Published *Eating Ohio*, by Rus Pishnery (short stories about Ohio); *Lil' Red Book of Fishing Tips*, by Tom Whitecloud (fishing tales); and *How to Talk Hoosier*, by Netha Bell (humor).

How to Contact: Query with synopsis and SASE. Responds in 2 months. Accepts simultaneous submissions.

Terms: Pays royalties of 10% on wholesale price. No advance. Publishes ms 1 year after acceptance. Writer's guidelines and book catalog for #10 SASE.

Advice: "Carefully consider marketing considerations. Audience is women in gift shops, on farm site direct retail outlets. Contact us at *idea* stage, not complete ms. stage. Be receptive to design input by us."

☑ ◎ ∅ 🅐 **RANDOM HOUSE BOOKS FOR YOUNG READERS**, Random House Children's Books, A Division of Random House, Inc., 201 E. 50th St., New York NY 10022. (212)751-2600. Fax: (212)940-7685. Website: www.randomhouse.com/kids. Vice President/Publisher: Kate Klimo. **Contact:** Naomi Kleinberg, senior editor (picturebacks); Mallory Loehr, senior editor (Stepping Stones); Heidi Kilgras, editor (Step into Reading).
Needs: Humor, juvenile, mystery, early picture/board books, picture books, chapter books, middle-grade, young adult. Published the works of Dr. Seuss, P.D. Eastman and the Berenstain Bears; *The Story of Babar*; the Step into Reading beginning readers series; the Junie B. Jones series; the Magic Tree House series; *The Protector of the Small Quartet*, by Tamora Pierce; and *The Phantom Tollbooth*, by Norman Juster.
How to Contact: Agented fiction only. No unsolicited mss. Responds in up to 4 months. Accepts simultaneous submissions but must be indicated as such.
Advice: (for all imprints) "We look for original, unique stories. Do something that hasn't been done before."

∅ ◎ **RANDOM HOUSE CHILDREN'S BOOKS**, 1540 Broadway, New York NY 10036. (212)782-9000 or (800)200-3552. Website: www.randomhouse.com/kids. **Contact**: Craig W. Virden, president/publisher. Vice President/Associate Publisher: Kevin Jones.
• See listings for Bantam, Doubleday, Dell/Delacorte, Knopf and Crown Books for Young Readers and Random House Books for Young Readers.

☑ ∅ 🅐 **RANDOM HOUSE, INC.**, 201 E. 50th St., New York NY 10022. (212)751-2600. Website: www.randomhouse.com. Estab. 1925. Publishes hardcover and paperback originals. Averages 120 total titles/year.
Needs: Adventure, contemporary, experimental, fantasy, historical, horror, humor, literary, mainstream, short story collections, mystery/suspense. "We publish fiction of the highest standards." Authors include James Michener, Robert Ludlum, Mary Gordon, Norman Mailer.
How to Contact: Does not accept queries or unsolicited mss. *Agented materials only.*
Terms: Payment as per standard minimum book contracts.

🍁 ☑ ∅ ◎ 🅥 **RED DEER PRESS**, MacKimmie Library Tower, Room 813, 2500 University Dr., NW, Calgary, Alberta T2N 1N4 Canada. (403)220-4334. Fax: (403)210-8191. E-mail: rdp@ucalgary.ca. Website: www.reddeerpress.com. **Contact**: Dennis Johnson, managing editor; Aritha van Herk, fiction editor. Estab. 1975. Publishes adult and young adult hardcover and paperback originals "focusing on books by, about, or of interest to Western Canadians." Books: offset paper; offset printing; hardcover/perfect-bound. Average print order: 5,000. First novel print order: 2,500. Averages 14-16 total titles, 2 fiction titles/year. Distributes titles in Canada, the US, the UK, Australia and New Zealand.
Imprint(s): Roundup Books (edited by Ted Stone), Inprints (fiction reprint series, edited by Aritha van Herk).
• Red Deer Press has received numerous honors and awards from the Book Publishers Association of Alberta, Canadian Children's Book Centre, the Governor General of Canada and the Writers Guild of Alberta. *A Fine Daughter*, by Catherine Simmons Niven received the Georges Bugnet Award for Best Novel.
Needs: Contemporary, experimental, literary, young adult. No romance or horror. Published anthologies under Roundup Books imprint focusing on stories/poetry of the Canadian and American West. Published *Great Stories of the Sea*, edited by Norman Ravvin (anthology); *A Fine Daughter*, by Catherine Simmons Niven (novel); *Great Stories from the Prairies* (anthology); *The Kappa Child*, by Hiromi Goto (novel).
How to Contact: *Canadian authors only.* Does not accept unsolicited mss in children's and young adult genres. Query first or submit outline/synopsis and 2 sample chapters. Send SASE or IRC. Responds in 6 months to queries and mss. Accepts simultaneous submissions. Final mss must be submitted on Mac disk in MS Word.
Terms: Pays royalties of 8-10%. Advance is negotiable. Sends galleys to author. Publishes ms 1 year after acceptance. Book catalog for 9 × 12 SASE.
Advice: "We're very interested in literary and experimental fiction from Canadian writers with a proven track record (either published books or widely published in established magazines or journals) and for manuscripts with regional themes and/or a distinctive voice. We publish Canadian authors exclusively."

☑ ♥ **REVELL PUBLISHING**, Subsidiary of Baker Book House, P.O. Box 6287, Grand Rapids MI 49516-6287. (616)676-9185. Fax: (616)676-9573. E-mail: lhdupont@bakerbooks.com or petersen@bakerbooks.com. Website: www.bakerbooks.com. **Contact**: Sheila Ingram, assistant to the editorial director; Jane Campbell, editorial director (Chosen Books). Estab. 1870. Midsize publisher. "Revell publishes to the heart (rather than to the head). For 125 years, Revell has been publishing evangelical books for personal enrichment and spiritual growth of general Christian readers." Publishes hardcover, trade paperback and mass market originals and reprints. Average print order: 7,500. **Published new writers within the last year.** Averages 60 total titles, 8 fiction titles/year.
Imprint(s): Spire Books.

Needs: Religious/inspirational (general). Published *Triumph of the Soul*, by Michael R. Joens (contemporary); *Daughter of Joy*, by Kathleen Morgan (historical); and *Blue Mist on the Danube*, by Doris Eliane Fell (contemporary).

How to Contact: Query with outline/synopsis. Include estimated word count, bio and list of publishing credits. Send SASE or IRC for return of ms or send disposable copy of ms and SASE for reply only. Agented fiction 20%. Responds in 3 weeks to queries; 2 weeks to mss. Accepts simultaneous submissions. Sometimes comments on rejected mss.

Terms: Pays royalties. Sends galleys to author. Publishes ms 1 year after acceptance. Writer's guidelines for SASE.

☑ ◯ **RISING TIDE PRESS**, P.O. Box 30457, Tucson AZ 85751-0457. (520)888-1140. Fax: (520)888-1123. E-mail: milestonepress@earthlink.net. Website: www.risingtidepress.com (includes book catalog, writer's guidelines, about our authors, annual award information, monthly specials). **Contact:** Debra S. Tobin and Brenda J. Kazen. Estab. 1988. "Independent women's press, publishing lesbian and feminist nonfiction and fiction." Publishes paperback trade originals. Books: 60 lb. vellum paper; sheet fed and/or web printing; perfect-bound. Average print order: 5,000. First novel print order: 3,000. **Published 4-5 new writers within the last year.** Averages 12 total titles/year. Distributes titles through Ingram, Bookpeople, Baker & Taylor, Alamo Square, Marginal (Canada), Turnaround (UK) and Banyon Tree (Pacific Basin). Promotes titles through magazines, journals, newspapers, *PW*, Lambda Book Report, distributor's catalogs, special publications and Internet.

Needs: Lesbian adventure, contemporary, erotica, fantasy, feminist, romance, science fiction, suspense/mystery, western. Looking for romance and mystery. Recently published *One Summer Night*, by Gerri Hall (first novel, romance); *Taking Risks*, by Judith McDaniel (poetry); and *Deadly Butterfly*, by Diane Davidson (mystery). Seeking "coming out stories" and stories about growing up in a gay household for anthologies.

How to Contact: Accepts unsolicited mss. Query with 1-page outline/synopsis and SASE. Responds in 3 months to mss.

Terms: Pays 10% royalties. Publishes ms 6-18 months after acceptance. Writer's guidelines for #10 SASE.

Advice: "Outline your story to give it boundaries and structure. Find creative ways to introduce your characters and begin the story in the middle of some action and dialogue. Our greatest challenge is finding quality manuscripts that are well plotted and not predictable, with well-developed, memorable characters."

◐ ◎ **ROC**, Imprint of New American Library, A Division of Penguin Putnam, Inc., 375 Hudson St., New York NY 10014. (212)366-2000. Website: www.penguinputnam.com. **Contact:** Laura Anne Gilman, executive editor; Jennifer Heddle, assistant editor. "Roc tries to strike a balance between fantasy and science fiction. We're looking for books that are a good read, that people will want to pick up time and time again." Publishes mass market, trade and hardcover originals. Averages 36 total titles/year.

Needs: Fantasy, horror, science fiction. Recently published *Queen of the Darkness*, by Anne Bishop; and *On the Oceans of Eternity*, by S.M. Stirling.

How to Contact: Discourages unsolicited mss. Query with synopsis and 1-2 sample chapters. Send SASE or IRC for reply. Responds in 3 month to queries. Accepts simultaneous submissions.

Terms: Pays royalty. Advance negotiable.

⊘ Ⓐ **ST. MARTIN'S PRESS**, 175 Fifth Ave., New York NY 10010. Estab. 1952. General interest publisher of both fiction and nonfiction. Publishes hardcover and paperback trade and mass market originals. Averages 1,500 total titles/year.

Imprint(s): Bedford Books; Buzz Books; Thomas Dunne Books; Forge; Minotaur; Picador USA; Stonewall Inn Editions; TOR Books; Thomas Dunne, Picador USA, Stonewall, Minotaur and Griffin.

Needs: General fiction: fantasy, historical, horror, literary, mainstream, mystery, science fiction, suspense, thriller, western (contemporary).

Terms: Pays royalty. Offers advance.

◯ **SALVO PRESS**, P.O. Box 9095, Bend OR 97708. Phone/fax: (541)330-8746. E-mail: salvopress@hotmail.com. Website: www.salvopress.com (includes book catalog, writer's guidelines, author pages, sample chapters, author tours and links). **Contact:** Scott Schmidt, publisher (mystery, suspense, thriller & espionage). Estab. 1998. "We are a small press specializing in mystery, suspense, espionage and thriller fiction. We plan on expanding into science fiction and literary fiction. Our press publishes in hardcover and trade paperback and e-book format." Publishes paperback originals and e-books. Books: 5½×8½ or 6×9 paper; offset printing; perfect binding. Average print order: 2,000; first novel print order: 1,500. "Also, Print on Demand." **Published 3 new writers within the last year.** Averages 6 fiction titles/year. Distributes titles through Seven Hills Book Distributors.

Needs: Adventure, literary, mystery/suspense (amateur sleuth, police procedural, private eye/hardboiled), science fiction (hard science/technological), thriller/espionage. Recently published *Hypershot*, by Trevor Scott (mystery/thriller); *Dog Walker*, by Heath Kizzier (first fiction, thriller); and *Kafka's Fedora*, by A.J. Adler (mainstream).

How to Contact: Does not accept unsolicited mss. Send query letter. Accepts queries by e-mail; no queries by fax. Include estimated word count, brief bio, list of publishing credits "and something to intrigue me so I ask for more." Send SASE or IRC for return of ms or send disposable copy of ms and SASE for reply only. Agented fiction 15%. Responds in 3 weeks to queries; 1 month to mss. Accepts simultaneous and electronic submissions. Sometimes comments on rejected mss.
Terms: Pays royalties of 10-15%. No advance. Sends galleys to author. Publishes ms 9 months after acceptance. Writer's guidelines and book catalogs can be found on website.

SANS SOLEIL, Expanded Media Ed., P.O. Box 190136, Bonn 53037 Germany. Phone: 228-22-9583. Fax: 228-21-9507. E-mail: pociao@t-online.de. Website: www.sansoleil.de (includes presentation of books and CD's, reviews). **Contact:** Pociao (female fiction, biography, letters, etc.). Estab. 1997. "Independent publisher. We publish preferably female writing or texts about outstanding women, biography, letters. Second part of our business is music. Also audio poetry, spoken word, etc. Again, reserved to women." Publishes paperback originals. Average print order: 1,000. First novel print order: 1,000. Averages 2 total titles, 1 fiction titles/year.
Needs: Lesbian, literary. Spoken word audio material is welcome. Recently published *Last Words*, by William S. Burroughs (journals); *Gonza Magilla*, by Jane Bowles (letters); and *Clarice Lispector*, by Ana Miranda (fiction).
How to Contact: Accepts unsolicited mss. Query with outline/synopsis and 2 sample chapters. No query by fax or e-mail. Include estimated word count and brief bio. Send disposable copy of ms and SASE for reply only. Agented fiction 50%. Accepts simultaneous submissions.
Terms: Pays royalties of 10%. Advance is negotiable. Sends galleys to author upon request. Book catalogs available on website.

SARABANDE BOOKS, INC., 2234 Dundee Rd., Suite 200, Louisville KY 40205-1845. Fax: (502)458-4065. E-mail: sarabandek@aol.com. Website: www.SarabandeBooks.org (includes authors, forthcoming titles, backlist, writer's guidelines, names of editors, author interviews and excerpts from their work and ordering and contest information). **Contact:** Sarah Gorham, editor-in-chief; Kirby Gann, fiction editor. Estab. 1994. "Small literary press publishing poetry and short fiction." Publishes hardcover and paperback originals. **Published new writers within the last year.** Averages 8 total titles, 4-5 fiction titles/year. Distributes titles through Consortium Book Sales & Distribution. Promotes titles through advertising in national magazines, sales reps, brochures, newsletters, postcards, catalogs, press release mailings, sales conferences, book fairs, author tours and reviews.

● Books published by Sarabande Books have received the following awards: 1997/98 Society of Midland Authors Award and 1997 Carl Sandburg Award—Sharon Solwitz, *Blood & Milk*; 1997 Poetry Center Book Award and First Annual Levis Reading Prize—Belle Waring, *Dark Blonde*; GLEA New Writers Award—Becky Hagenston, *A Gram of Mars*.

Needs: Short story collections, 300 pages maximum (or collections of novellas, or single novellas of 150 pages). "Short fiction *only*. We do not publish full-length novels." Published *Mr. Dalloway*, by Robin Lippincott (novella); *A Gram of Mars*, by Becky Hagenston (short stories); and *The Baby Can Sing and Other Stories*, by Judith Slater.
How to Contact: Submit in September only. Query with outline/synopsis and 1 sample story or 10-page sample. Include 1 page bio, listing of publishing credits. Send SASE or IRC for reply. Responds in 3 months to queries; 6 months to mss. Accepts simultaneous submissions.
Terms: Pays in royalties, author's copies. Sends galleys to author. Writer's guidelines available (for contest only) for #10 SASE. Book catalog available.
Advice: "Make sure you're not writing in a vacuum, that you've read and are conscious of your competition in contemporary literature. Have someone read your manuscript, checking it for ordering, coherence. Better a lean, consistently strong manuscript than one that is long and uneven. Old fashioned as it sounds, we like a story to have good narrative, or at least we like to be engaged, to find ourselves turning the pages with real interest."

SCHOLASTIC CANADA LTD., 175 Hillmount Rd., Markham, Ontario L6C 1Z7 Canada. (905)887-7323. Fax: (905)887-3643. Website: www.scholastic.ca. **Contact:** Editors. Publishes hardcover and trade paperback originals. Averages 30 titles/year.
Imprint(s): North Winds Press; Les Éditions Scholastic (contact Sylvie Andrews, French editor).
Needs: Children's/juvenile, young adult. Published *In My Enemy's House*, by Carol Matas (juvenile novel).
How to Contact: *Accepts agented submissions only.*
Terms: Pays royalties of 5-10% on retail price. Average advance: $1,000-5,000 (Canadian). Publishes ms 1 year after acceptance. Book catalog for 8½×11 SAE with 2 first-class stamps (IRC or Canadian stamps only).

SCHOLASTIC INC., 555 Broadway, New York NY 10012-3999. (212)343-6100. Website: www.scholastic.com (includes general information about Scholastic). **Contact:** Jean Feiwel, senior vice president/publisher, Book Group Scholastic Inc. Estab. 1920. Publishes books for children ages 4-young adult. "We are proud of the many fine, innovative materials we have created—such as classroom magazines, book clubs, book fairs, and our new literacy and technology programs. But we are most proud of our reputation as 'The Most Trusted Name in Learning.' " Publishes juvenile hardcover picture books, novels and nonfiction. Distributes titles through Scholastic Book Clubs, Scholastic Book Fairs, bookstores and other retailers.

Imprint(s): Blue Sky Press (contact: Bonnie Verberg, editorial director); Cartwheel Books (contact: Bernette Ford, editorial director); Arthur A. Levine Books (contact: Arthur A. Levine, editorial director); Mariposa (Spanish language contact: Susana Pasternac, editorial director); Scholastic Press (contact: Elizabeth Szabla); Scholastic Trade Paperbacks (contact: Craig Walker, editorial director; Maria Weisbin, assistant to Craig Walker); Scholastic Reference (contact: Kenneth Wright, editorial director).

● Scholastic published *Out of the Dust*, by Karen Hesse, winner of the Newbery Medal.

Needs: Hardcover—open to all subjects suitable for children. Paperback—family stories, mysteries, school, friendships for ages 8-12, 35,000 words. Young adult fiction, romance, family and mystery for ages 12-15, 40,000-45,000 words for average-to-good readers. Published *Her Stories: African American Folktales, Fairy Tales and True Tales*, by Virginia Hamilton, illustrated by Leo and Diane Dillon; and *Pigs in the Middle of the Road*, by Lynn Plourde.

How to Contact: Does not accept unsolicited manuscripts. Submissions (agented) may be made to the Editorial Director. Responds in 6 months.

Terms: Pays advance and royalty on retail price. Writer's guidelines for #10 SASE.

Advice: "Be current, topical and get an agent for your work."

SCHOLASTIC PRESS, Imprint of Scholastic Inc., 555 Broadway, New York NY 10012. (212)343-6100. Fax: (212)343-4713. Website: www.scholastic.com (includes information for teachers, parents and children, games/contests and information for children as well as book and author information—no guidelines online). **Contact:** Elizabeth Szabla, editorial director (picture books, middle grade, young adult); Dianne Hess, executive editor (picture books, middle grade, young adult); Tracy Mack, executive editor (picture books, middle grade, young adult); Lauren Thompson, senior editor (picture books); Jennifer Braunstein, assistant editor (picture books, middle grade and young adult novels). Publishes hardcover originals. **Published new writers within the last year.** Promotes titles through trade and library channels.

Needs: Juvenile, picture books. Recently published *Witness*, by Karen Hesse; *Belle Teal*, by Ann M. Martin; *The Dinosaurs of Waterhouse Hawkins*, by Barbara Kerley, illustrated by Brian Selznick; and *Silly Little Goose*, by Nancy Tafuri.

How to Contact: Does not accept unsolicited mss. Agented submissions only. Responds in 6 months to submissions from SCBWI members and previously-published authors.

Terms: Pays royalty on retail price. Royalty and advance vary. Publishes ms 18 months after acceptance.

Advice: "Be a big reader of juvenile literature before you write and submit!"

SCRIBNER, An imprint of Simon & Schuster, 1230 Avenue of the Americas, New York NY 10020. (212)698-7000. Publishes hardcover originals. Averages 70-75 total titles/year.

Imprint(s): Rawson Associates; Lisa Drew Books.

Needs: Literary, mystery/suspense. Recently published *Dreamcatcher*, by Stephen King; *The Constant Gardener*, by John Le Carré; and *Fatal Voyage*, by Kathy Reichs.

How to Contact: *Agented fiction only.* Responds in 3 months to queries. Accepts simultaneous submissions.

Terms: Pays royalties of 7½-15%. Advance varies. Publishes ms 9 months after acceptance.

SEAL PRESS, 3131 Western Ave., Suite 410, Seattle WA 98121-1041. Fax: (206)285-9410. E-mail: sealpress@sealpress.com. Website: www.sealpress.com. **Contact**: Faith Conlon, editor/publisher; Leslie Miller, senior editor; Anne Matthews, managing editor. Estab. 1976. "Midsize independent feminist book publisher interested in original, lively, radical, empowering and culturally diverse books by women." Publishes trade paperback originals. Books: 55 lb. natural paper; Cameron Belt, Web or offset printing; perfect binding; illustrations occasionally. Averages 18 total titles/year. Titles distributed by Publishers Group West.

● Lambda Literary Award given to *Valencia*, by Michelle Tea. *Bruised Hibiscus*, by Elizabeth Nunez, received the American Book Award. *Navigating the Darwin Straits*, by Edith Forbes, was a Book Sense Pick.

Imprint(s): Adventura (womens travel, outdoor adventure); Live Girls (pop culture/feminist).

Needs: Feminist, gay/lesbian, literary, multicultural. Recently published *Valencia*, by Michelle Tea (fiction); *Navigating the Darwin Straits*, by Edith Forbes (fiction); and *Bruised Hibiscus*, by Elizabeth Nunez (fiction).

How to Contact: Does not accept unsolicited mss. Query with outline/synopsis and 2 sample chapters. Does not accept e-mail queries. Send SASE for reply. Responds in 2 months to queries.

Terms: Pays royalties of 7-8% on retail price. Average advance: $500-2,000. Publishes ms 18 months after acceptance. Writer's guidelines and book catalog available online.

◑ ▼ **SECOND CHANCE PRESS; THE PERMANENT PRESS,** 4170 Noyac Rd., Sag Harbor NY 11963. (631)725-1101. Fax: (631)725-8215. E-mail: shepard@thepermanentpress.com. Website: www.theperman entpress.com (includes titles, authors, descriptions of backlist and frontlist titles and an order form). **Contact**: Judith and Martin Shepard, publishers. Estab. 1977. Mid-size, independent publisher of literary fiction. Publishes hardcover originals and trade paperbacks. Average print order: 1,500-2,000. First novel print order: 1,500-2,000. **Published new writers within the last year.** Averages 12 fiction titles/year. Distributes titles through Ingram, Baker & Taylor and Brodart. Promotes titles through reviews.

  • Received a Literary Marketplace Award for Editorial Excellence and a Small Press Book Award for Best Gay/Lesbian Title for Elise D'Haene's *Licking Our Wounds*.

Needs: Contemporary, erotica, ethnic/multicultural, experimental, family saga, literary, mainstream. "We like novels with a unique point of view and a high quality of writing." No genre novels. Recently published *Whompy-jawed*, by Mitch Cullen (literary fiction); *Manifesto for the Dead*, by Domenic Stansberry (mystery); and *Blood-lines*, by Bruce Ducker (literary fiction).

How to Contact: Does not accept unsolicited mss. Query with outline and no more than 2 chapters. No queries by e-mail or fax. Send SASE or IRC for reply. Agented fiction 35%. Responds in 6 weeks to queries; 6 months to mss. Accepts simultaneous submissions.

Terms: Pays royalties of 10-20%. Average advance: $1,000. Sends galleys to author. Book catalog for $3.

Advice: "We are looking for good books, be they tenth novels or first ones, it makes little difference. The fiction is more important than the track record. Send us the beginning of the story, it's impossible to judge something that begins on page 302. Also, no outlines and very short synopsis—let the writing present itself."

◑ ◎ ▣ **SERENDIPITY SYSTEMS,** P.O. Box 140, San Simeon CA 93452. (805)927-5259. E-mail: bookware@thegrid.net. Website: www.s-e-r-e-n-d-i-p-i-t-y.com (includes guidelines, sample books, writer's manuscript help, catalog). **Contact**: John Galuszka, publisher. Estab. 1985. "Electronic publishing for IBM-PC compatible systems." Publishes "electronic editions originals and reprints." Books on disk. **Published new writers within the last year.** Averages 36 total titles, 15 fiction titles/year (either publish or distribute).

Imprint(s): Books-on-Disks™ and Bookware™.

Needs: "Works of fiction which use, or have the potential to use, hypertext, multimedia or other computer-enhanced features. We cannot use on-paper manuscripts." No romance, religion, New Age, children's, young adult, occult. "We only publish book-length works, not individual short stories." Recently published *The Blue-Eyed Muse*, by John Peter (novel).

How to Contact: Query by e-mail. Submit complete ms with cover letter and SASE. *IBM-PC compatible disk required.* ASCII files required unless the work is hypertext or multimedia. Send SASE or IRC for return of ms or send disposable copy of ms and SASE for reply only. Responds in 2 weeks to queries; 1 month to mss. Often comments on rejected mss.

Terms: Pays royalties of 25%. Publishes ms 2 months after acceptance. Writer's guidelines on website.

Advice: "We are interested in seeing multimedia works suitable for Internet distribution. Would like to see: more works of serious literature—novels, short stories, plays, etc. Would like to not see: right wing adventure fantasies from 'Tom Clancy' wanna-be's."

🅽 ◑ ◎ **SEVEN BUFFALOES PRESS,** Box 249, Big Timber MT 59011. **Contact**: Art Coelho, editor/publisher. Estab. 1975. Publishes paperback originals. Averages 4-5 total titles each year.

Needs: Contemporary, short story collections, "rural, American Hobo, Okies, Native-American, Southern Appalachia, Arkansas and the Ozarks. Wants farm- and ranch-based stories." Published *Rig Nine*, by William Rintoul (collection of oilfield short stories).

How to Contact: Query first with SASE. Responds in 1 month. Sample copy $7 postpaid.

Terms: Pays royalties of 10% minimum; 15% on second edition or in author's copies (10% of edition). No advance. Writer's guidelines and book catalog for SASE.

Advice: "There's too much influence from TV and Hollywood, media writing I call it. We need to get back to the people, to those who built and are still building this nation with sweat, blood and brains. More people are into it for the money, instead of for the good writing that is still to be cranked out by isolated writers. Remember, I was a writer for ten years before I became a publisher."

✔ ◎ **SEVEN STORIES PRESS,** 140 Watts St., New York NY 10013. (212)226-8760. Fax: (212)226-1411. E-mail: info@sevenstories.com. Website: www.sevenstories.com. **Contact**: Daniel Simon, Michael Manckin, Greg Ruggiero, Violaine Huysman, fiction editors. Estab. 1995. "Publishers of a distinguished list of authors in fine literature, journalism, contemporary culture and alternative health." Publishes hardcover and paperback originals and paperback reprints. Average print order: 5,000. **Published new writers within the last year.** Averages 20 total titles, 10 fiction titles/year.

Needs: Literary. Plans anthologies. Ongoing series of short story collections from other cultures (e.g., *Contemporary Fiction from Central America; from Vietnam*, etc.) Recently published *The Free Thinkers*, by Layle Silbert (novel); *Algerian White*, by Assia Djebar; and *Borrowed Hearts*, by Rick DeMarinis (short stories).

How to Contact: Query with outline/synopsis and 1 sample chapter. Include list of publishing credits. Send SASE or IRC for reply. Agented fiction 60%. Responds in 1 month to queries; 4 months to mss. Accepts simultaneous submissions. Sometimes comments on rejected mss.

Payment/Terms: Pays standard royalty; offers advance. Sends galleys to author. Publishes ms 1-2 years after acceptance. Free guidelines and book catalog.

Advice: "Writers should only send us their work after they have read some of the books we publish and find our editorial vision in sync with theirs."

N ⊕ A SEVERN HOUSE PUBLISHERS, 9-15 High St., Sutton, Surrey SM1 1DF United Kingdom. (0181)770-3930. Fax: (0181)770-3850. **Contact**: Tom Jordan, editorial director. Publishes hardcover and trade paperback originals and reprints. Publishes 120 titles/year.

Needs: Adventure, fantasy, historical, horror, mainstream/contemporary, mystery/suspense, romance, science fiction, short story collections. Published *Future Scrolls*, by Fern Michaels (historical romance); *The Hampton Passion*, by Julie Ellis (romance); *Looking-Glass Justice*, by Jeffrey Ashford (crime and mystery); and *Cold Tactics*, by Ted Allbeury (thriller).

How to Contact: *Agented submissions only.* Submit synopsis and 3 sample chapters. Responds in 3 months to proposals.

Terms: Pays 7½-15% royalty on retail price. Offers $750-5,000 advance. Accepts simultaneous submissions. Book catalog free.

◯ ◎ ▼ SILHOUETTE BOOKS, Harlequin Enterprises, 300 E. 42nd St., 6th Floor, New York NY 10017. (212)682-6080. Fax: (212)682-4539. Website: www.eHarlequin.com (includes guidelines, features regarding romance, book catalog, author interviews and features of interest to women). **Contact:** Mary-Theresa Hussey, senior editor (Silhouette Romance); Joan Marlow Golan, senior editor (Silhouette Desire); Karen Taylor Richman, senior editor (Silhouette Special Editions); Leslie Wainger, executive senior editor (Silhouette Intimate Moments); Tracy Farrell, senior editor/editorial coordinator (Harlequin Historicals). Estab. 1979. International publisher of category romance. Publishes paperback originals. **Published 10-20 new writers within the last year.** Averages 350-400 fiction titles/year.

Imprint(s): Silhouette Romance (contemporary adult romances, 53,000-58,000 words), Silhouette Special Edition (contemporary adult romances, 55,000-60,000 words), Silhouette Desire (contemporary adult romances, 80,000 words), Silhouette Intimate Moments (contemporary adult romance, 80,000 words), Harlequin Historicals (adult historical romances, 95,000-105,000).

• Titles by Silhouette Books have received numerous awards from *Romantic Times*, the Rita Award from Romance Writers of America and best selling awards from national bookstores.

Needs: Romance (contemporary, futuristic/time travel, historical, romantic suspense). Published *Callaghan's Bride*, by Diana Palmer (SR); *Rio: Man of Destiny*, by Cait London (SD); and *The Perfect Neighbor*, by Nora Roberts (SSE).

How to Contact: Does not accept unsolicited mss. Query with brief synopsis. Accepts queries by fax. Include estimated word count, brief bio and list of published credits. Send SASE or IRC for return of ms. Responds in 3 months to queries and mss. Sometimes comments on rejected mss.

Terms: Pays in royalties; offers advance (negotiated on an individual basis). Must return advance if book is not completed or is unacceptable. Sends galleys to author. Publishes ms 3 years after acceptance. Writer's guidelines for SASE.

Advice: "Study the market. Category Romance is a dynamic, ever-changing market with a readership who expect quality, imagination and a love of the genre from their writers."

✓ ⊘ ◎ SILVER DAGGER MYSTERIES, The Overmountain Press, P.O. Box 1261, Johnson City TN 37605. (423)926-2691. Fax: (423)232-1252. E-mail: bethw@overmtn.com. Website: www.silverdaggermysteries.com (includes submission guidelines, book catalog, author bios, links, touring schedules, newsletter). **Contact:** Alex Foster, acquisitions editor (mystery). Estab. 1999. "Small imprint of a larger company. We publish Southern mysteries. Our house is unique in that we are a consortium of authors who communicate and work together to promote each other." Publishes hardcover and paperback originals and reprints. Books: 60 lb. offset paper;

INTERESTED IN A PARTICULAR GENRE? Check our sections for: **Mystery/Suspense**, page 91; **Romance**, page 105; **Science Fiction & Fantasy**, page 121.

perfect/case binding. Average print order: 2,000-5,000; first novel print order: 2,000. **Published 3 new writers within the last year.** Averages 15 fiction titles/year. Member, PAS. Distributes titles through direct mail, Ingram, Baker & Taylor, Partners, trade shows.

- Julie Wray Herman was nominated for the Agatha Award for *Three Dirty Women & the Garden of Death.*

Needs: Mystery/suspense (amateur sleuth, cozy, police procedural, private eye/hardboiled), young adult/teen (mystery/suspense). Publishes *Magnolias & Mayhem*, an anthology of Southern short mysteries. Submissions "closed—editor solicits prior to contract signing." Recently published *The Ambush of My Name*, by Jeffrey Marks (mystery); *Closer Than the Bones*, by Dean James (mystery); and *Three Dirty Women & the Bitter Brew*, by Julie Wray Herman (mystery).

How to Contact: Does not accept or return unsolicited mss. Query with outline/synopsis and first 3 chapters. Does not accept queries by fax or e-mail. Include estimated word count, brief bio and list of publishing credits. Send SASE or IRC for return of ms. Agented fiction 30%. Responds in 1 month to queries; 3 months to mss.

Terms: Pays royalties of 15%. Sends galleys to author. Publishes ms 1 year after acceptance. Writer's guidelines and book catalogs on website.

Advice: "We are very author friendly from editing to promotion. Make sure your book is 'Southern' or set in the South before taking the time to submit."

☑ ◎ ⊘ ♈ **SIMON & SCHUSTER BOOKS FOR YOUNG READERS,** Subsidiary of Simon & Schuster Children's Publishing Division, 1230 Avenue of the Americas, New York NY 10020. (212)698-7000. Website: www.simonsayskids.com. **Contact:** Stephen Geck, vice president/associate publisher; David Gale, editorial director; Kevin Lewis, senior editor; Jessica Schulte, editor; Amy Hampton-Knight, associate editor. "We're looking for complex, challenging YA novels and middle-grade fiction with a fresh, unique slant." Publishes hardcover originals. **Published 3 new writers within the last year.** Averages 80 total titles, 20 fiction titles/year. Promotes titles through trade magazines, conventions and catalog.

- Books from Simon & Schuster Books for Young Readers have received the following awards: 2000 Michael L. Printz Honor Award for *Hard Love.* 1999 Coretta Scott King Author Award and ALA Best Book for Young Adults for *Heaven* by Angela Johnson.

Needs: Children's/juvenile, young adult/teen (adventure, historical, mystery, contemporary fiction). No problem novels. No anthropomorphic characters. Publishes anthologies; editor solicits from established writers. Recently published *The School Story*, by Andrew Clements (middle-grade fiction); *Fever 1793*, by Laurie Anderson (young adult fiction); and *Love & Sex*, by Michael Cart, editor (young adult fiction).

How to Contact: *Does not accept unsolicited mss.* Send query letter and SASE. Agented fiction 90%. Responds in 2 months to queries. Accepts simultaneous submissions.

Terms: Pays royalties. Offers negotiable advance. Sends galleys to author. Publishes ms within 2 years of acceptance. Writer's guidelines for #10 SASE. Book catalog available in libraries.

Advice: "Study our catalog and read books we have published to get an idea of our list. The fiction market is crowded and writers need a strong, fresh, original voice to stand out."

◑ ◎ ♈ **GIBBS SMITH, PUBLISHER/PEREGRINE SMITH**, P.O. Box 667, Layton UT 84041. (801)544-9800. Fax: (801)544-5582. E-mail: info@gibbs-smith.com. Website: www.gibbs~smith.com/. **Contact**: Gail Yngve, editor (poetry); Suzanne Taylor, senior editor; Madge Baird, editorial director (western, humor). Estab. 1969. Small independent press. "We publish books that make a difference." Publishes hardcover and paperback originals and reprints. Averages 40-60 total titles, 1-2 fiction titles/year.

- Gibbs Smith is the recipient of a Western Writers Association Fiction Award. Publishes the winner of the Peregrine Smith Poetry Contest (accepts entries only in April).

Needs: Only short works oriented to gift market. Publishes *The Peregrine Reader*, a series of anthologies based upon a variety of themes. Recently published *A Strong Man*, by Carol Lynn Pearson.

How to Contact: Send query letter or short gift book ms directly to the editor. Send SASE or IRC for return of the ms. Responds in 1 month to queries; 4 months to mss. Accepts simultaneous submissions. Sometimes comments on rejected mss.

Terms: Pays royalty depending on the book. Provides 10 author's copies. Sends galleys to author. Publishes ms 1-2 years after acceptance. Writer's guidelines and book catalog for #10 SASE and $2.13 in postage.

☑ ♈ ◑ **SOHO PRESS**, 853 Broadway, New York NY 10003. (212)260-1900. E-mail: sohojj@aol.com. Website: www.sohopress.com. **Contact**: Juris Jurjevics and Laura M.C. Hruska, editors. Publishes hardcover originals and trade paperback reprints. **Published 7-10 new writers within the last year.** Averages 40 titles/year. Distributes titles through Farrar, Straus & Giroux. Promotes titles through readings, tours, print ads, reviews, interviews, advance reading copies, postcards and brochures.

- *Death of a Red Heroine*, by Qiu Xialong, was an Edgar Award Nominee for Best First Novel in 2000.

Imprint(s): Soho Crime, edited by Laura Hruska and Juris Jurjevics (mystery); Hera, edited by Laura Hruska (historical fiction).

Needs: Ethnic, literary, mystery (procedural), suspense. "We do novels that are the very best of their kind." Recently published *Senseless*, by Stona Fitch; *The Gravity of Sunlight*, by Rosa Shand; and *Death of a Red Heroine*, by Qiu Xialong.

How to Contact: Query with SASE or IRC. Responds in 1 month to queries; 6 weeks to mss. Accepts simultaneous submissions.

Terms: Pays escalating royalties of 10-12.5-15% on retail price. For trade paperbacks pays 7½%. Offers advance. Publishes ms 10 months after acceptance. Book catalog for SASE plus $1.

Advice: Greatest challenge is "introducing brand new, untested writers. We do not care if they are agented or not. Half the books we publish come directly from authors. We look for a distinctive writing style, strong writing skills and compelling plots. We are not interested in trite expression of mass market formulae."

SOUTHERN METHODIST UNIVERSITY PRESS, P.O. Box 750415, Dallas TX 75275-0415. (214)768-1433 (acquisitions). Fax: (214)768-1428. **Contact:** Kathryn M. Lang, senior editor. Estab. 1936. "Small university press publishing in areas of film/theater, Southwest life and letters, religion/medical ethics and contemporary fiction." Publishes hardcover and paperback originals and reprints. Books: acid-free paper; perfect-bound; some illustrations. Average print order: 2,000. **Published 2 new writers within the last year.** Averages 10-12 total titles, 3-4 fiction titles/year. Distributes titles through Texas A&M University Press Consortium. Promotes titles through writers' publications.

Needs: Literary novels and story collections. "We are always willing to look at 'serious' or 'literary' fiction." No "mass market, science fiction, formula, thriller, romance." Recently published *Bombshell*, by Liza Wieland (novel); *In the Country of the Young*, by Daniel Stern (short stories).

How to Contact: Accepts unsolicited mss. Query with outline/synopsis and 3 sample chapters. Send SASE or IRC for return of ms. Responds in 3 weeks to queries; up to 1 year on mss. Sometimes comments on rejected mss.

Terms: Pays royalties of 10% net, negotiable small advance, 10 author's copies. Publishes ms 1 year after acceptance. Book catalog free.

Advice: "We view encouraging first time authors as part of the mission of a university press. Send query describing the project and your own background. Research the press before you submit—don't send us the kinds of things we don't publish." Looks for "quality fiction from new or established writers."

SPECTRA BOOKS, Subsidiary of Random House, Inc., 1540 Broadway, New York NY 10036. (212)782-8771. Fax: (212)782-9523. Website: www.bantamdell.com. **Contact:** Anne Lesley Groell, senior editor; Michael Shohl, editor. Estab. 1985. Large science fiction, fantasy and speculative fiction line. Publishes hardcover originals, paperback originals and trade paperbacks. Averages 60 fiction titles/year.

● Many Bantam Spectra Books have received Hugos and Nebulas.

Needs: Fantasy, literary, science fiction. Needs include novels that attempt to broaden the traditional range of science fiction and fantasy. Strong emphasis on characterization. Especially well written traditional science fiction and fantasy will be considered. No fiction that doesn't have at least some element of speculation or the fantastic. Published *Storm of Swords*, by George R. Martin (medieval fantasy); *Ship of Destiny*, by Robin Hobb (nautical fantasy); and *Antarctica*, by Stanley Robinson (science fiction).

How to Contact: Query with 3 chapters and a short (no more than 3 pages double-spaced) synopsis. Send SASE or IRC for return of ms. Agented fiction 90%. Responds in 6 months. Accepts simultaneous submissions if noted.

Terms: Pays in royalties; negotiable advance. Sends galleys to author. Writer's guidelines for #10 SASE.

Advice: "Please follow our guidelines carefully and type neatly."

SPINSTERS INK, P.O. Box 22005, Denver CO 80222. (303)761-5552. Fax: (303)761-5284. E-mail: spinster@spinstersink.com. Website: www.spinsters-ink.com (includes online catalog, writer's guidelines, staff list, chat rooms, excerpts from books, discussion forums). **Contact:** Sharon Silvas. Estab. 1978. Moderate-size women's publishing company growing steadily. "We are committed to publishing works by women writing from the periphery: fat women, Jewish women, lesbians, poor women, rural women, women of color, etc." Publishes paperback originals and reprints. Books: 55 lb. acid-free natural paper; photo offset printing; perfect-bound; illustrations when appropriate. Average print order: 5,000. **Published new writers within the last year.** Distributes titles through Words Distributing and all wholesalers. Promotes titles through Women's Review of Books, Feminist Bookstore News, *Lesbian Review of Books*, *Colorado Woman News*, regional advertising, author interviews and reviews.

● Spinsters Ink won a the 2000 PMA Benjamin Franklin Award for *Maid Order Catalog*.

Needs: Feminist, lesbian. Wants "full-length quality fiction—thoroughly revised novels which display deep characterization, theme and style. We *only* consider books by women. No books by men, or books with sexist, racist or ageist content." Published *Voices of the Soft-bellied Warrior*, by Mary Saracino (memoir); *Look Me in the Eye: Women, Aging, and Ageism*, by Barbara Macdonald and Cynthia Rich (feminist); *Murder She Wrote*, by Val McDermid (and the Lindsay Gordon series). Publishes anthologies. Writers may submit directly.

How to Contact: Send query letter or submit outline/synopsis and 2-5 sample chapters (not to exceed 50 pages) with SASE. Responds in 1 month to queries; 3 months to mss. Accepts simultaneous submissions. Prefers hard copy submission. Occasionally comments on rejected mss.

Terms: Pays royalties of 7-10%, plus 10 author's copies; unlimited extra copies at 40% discount. Publishes ms 18 months after acceptance. Free book catalog.

Advice: "In the past, lesbian fiction has been largely 'escape fiction' with sex and romance as the only required ingredients; however, we encourage more complex work that treats the lesbian lifestyle with the honesty it deserves. Look at our catalog and mission statement. Does your book fit our criteria?"

STARBURST PUBLISHERS, P.O. Box 4123, Lancaster PA 17604. (717)293-0939. Fax: (717)293-1945. E-mail: starburst@starburstpublishers.com. Website: www.starburstpublishers.com (includes writer's guidelines, authors, titles, editorial information, catalog, rights, distribution, etc.). **Contact:** David A. Robie, editorial director. Estab. 1982. Midsize independent press specializing in inspirational and self-help books. Publishes trade paperback and hardcover originals and trade paperback reprints. **Published new writers within the last year.** Averages 10-15 total titles/year. Distributes titles through all major distributors and sales reps. Promotes titles through print, radio, and major distributors.

Needs: Religious/inspirational: Adventure, contemporary, fantasy, historical, horror, military/war, psychic/supernatural/occult, romance (contemporary, historical), spiritual, suspense/mystery, western. Wants "inspirational material." Published *The Fragile Thread*, by Aliske Webb; and *The Miracle of the Sacred Scroll*, by Johan Christian.

How to Contact: Does not accept unsolicited mss. Query with outline/synopsis and 3 sample chapters. Accepts queries by e-mail. Include bio. Send SASE or IRC for return of ms. Agented fiction less than 25%. Responds in 1 month to queries; 2 months to manuscripts. Accepts electronic submissions via disk and modem, "but also wants clean double-spaced typewritten or computer printout manuscript."

Terms: Pays royalties of 6-16%. "Individual arrangement with writer depending on the manuscript as well as writer's experience as a published author." Publishes ms up to one year after acceptance. Writer's guidelines for #10 SASE. Book catalog for 9×12 SAE and 4 first-class stamps.

Advice: "50% of our line goes into the inspirational marketplace; 50% into the general marketplace. We are one of the few publishers that has direct sales representation into both the inspirational and general marketplace."

STONE BRIDGE PRESS, P.O. Box 8208, Berkeley CA 94707. (510)524-8732. Fax: (510)524-8711. E-mail: sbp@stonebridge.com. Website: www.stonebridge.com (includes complete catalog, contact information, related features, submission guidelines and excerpts). **Contact:** Peter Goodman, publisher. Estab. 1989. "Independent press focusing on books about Japan in English (business, language, culture, literature, animation)." Publishes paperback originals and reprints. Books: 60-70 lb. offset paper; web and sheet paper; perfect-bound; some illustrations. Averages 6 total titles/year. Distributes titles through Consortium. Promotes titles through Internet announcements, special-interest magazines and niche tie-ins to associations.

Imprint(s): Rock Spring Collection of Japanese Literature, edited by Peter Goodman.

● Stone Bridge Press received a Japan-U.S. Friendship Prize for *Life in the Cul-de-Sac*, by Senji Kuroi.

Needs: Japan-themed. No poetry. "Primarily looking at material relating to Japan. Mostly translations, but we'd like to see samples of work dealing with the expatriate experience." Also Asian- and Japanese-American. Recently published *Life in the Cul-de-Sac*, by Senji Kuroi and *Evening Clouds*, by Junzo Shono.

How to Contact: Accepts unsolicited mss. Query with 1-page cover letter, outline/synopsis and 3 sample chapters. Accepts queries by e-mail and fax. Send SASE or IRC for return of the ms. Agented fiction 25%. Responds in 1 month to queries; up to 8 months to mss. Accepts simultaneous submissions. Sometimes comments on rejected ms.

Terms: Pays royalties, offers negotiable advance. Publishes ms 18-24 months after acceptance. Catalog for 1 first-class stamp.

Advice: "As we focus on Japan-related material there is no point in approaching us unless you are very familiar with Japan. We'd especially like to see submissions dealing with the expatriate experience. Please, absolutely no commercial fiction."

STONEWALL INN, Imprint of St. Martin's Press, 175 Fifth Ave., New York NY 10010-7848. (212)674-5151. Website: www.stonewallinn.com (includes guidelines, book excerpts, catalog, author interviews, editorials). **Contact:** Keith Kahla, general editor. "Stonewall Inn is the only gay and lesbian focused imprint at a major house . . . and is more inclusive of gay men than most small presses." Publishes trade paperback originals and reprints. Averages 20-23 titles/year. **Published new writers within the last year.**

Needs: Gay, lesbian, literary, mystery. Recently published *The Coming Storm*, by Paul Russell; and *The Struggle for Happiness*, by Ruthann Robson.

How to Contact: Query with SASE; no fax or e-mail queries. Responds in 6 months to queries. Accepts simultaneous submissions.

Terms: Pays standard royalty on retail price. Average advance: $5,000 (for first-time authors). Publishes ms 1 year after acceptance.

Advice: "Anybody who has any question about what a gay novel is should go out and read half a dozen. For example, there are hundreds of 'coming out' novels in print."

SUNSTONE PRESS, P.O. Box 2321, Santa Fe NM 87504-2321. (505)988-4418. **Contact:** James C. Smith, Jr. Estab. 1971. Midsize publisher. Publishes hardcover and paperback originals. First novel print order: 2,000. **Published new writers within the last year.** Averages 16 total titles, 2-3 fiction titles/year.
- Sunstone Press published *Ninez*, by Virginia Nylander Ebinger which received the Southwest Book Award from the Border Regional Library Association.

Needs: Western. "We have a Southwestern theme emphasis. Sometimes buy juvenile mss with illustrations." No science fiction, romance or occult. Published *Apache: The Long Ride Home*, by Grant Gall (Indian/Western); *Sorrel*, by Rita Cleary; and *To Die in Dinetah*, by John Truitt.

How to Contact: Accepts unsolicited mss. Query first or submit outline/synopsis and 2 sample chapters with SASE. Responds in 2 weeks. Accepts simultaneous submissions.

Terms: Pays royalties of 10% maximum and 10 author's copies. Publishes ms 9-12 months after acceptance.

NAN A. TALESE, The Doubleday Broadway Publishing Group, A Division of Random House, Inc., 1540 Broadway, New York NY 10036. (212)782-8918. Fax: (212)782-9261. Website: www.nanatalese.com. **Contact:** Nan A. Talese, editorial director. "Nan A. Talese publishes nonfiction with a powerful guiding narrative and relevance to larger cultural trends and interests, and literary fiction of the highest quality." Publishes hardcover originals. Averages 15 titles/year.

Needs: Literary. Looking for "well written narratives with a compelling story line, good characterization, and use of language. We like stories with an edge." Published *The Blind Assassin*, by Margaret Atwood (novel); *Desire of Everlasting Hills*, by Thomas Cahill; *Amsterdam*, by Ian McEwan; and *Great Shame*, by Thomas Keneally.

How to Contact: Agented fiction only. Responds in 1 week to queries; 2 weeks to proposals and mss. Accepts simultaneous submissions.

Terms: Pays royalty on retail price, varies. Advance varies. Publishes ms 1 year after acceptance.

Advice: "We're interested in literary narrative, fiction and nonfiction—we do not publish genre fiction. Our readers are highly literate people interested in good story-telling, intellectual and psychologically significant. We want well-written material."

TIDEWATER PUBLISHERS, Imprint of Cornell Maritime Press, Inc., P.O. Box 456, Centreville MD 21617-0456. (410)758-1075. Fax: (410)758-6849. E-mail: cornell@crosslink.net. **Contact:** Charlotte Kurst, managing editor. Estab. 1938. "Tidewater Publishers issues adult nonfiction works related to the Chesapeake Bay area, Delmarva or Maryland in general. The only fiction we handle is juvenile and must have a regional focus." Publishes hardcover and paperback originals. **Published new writers within the last year.** Averages 7-9 titles/year.

Needs: Regional juvenile fiction only. Recently published *Chesapeake ABC*, by Priscilla Cummings and illustrated by David Aiken; and *Finding Birds in the Chesapeake Marsh*, by Zora Aiken and illustrated by David Aiken.

How to Contact: Query or submit outline/synopsis and sample chapters. Responds in 2 months.

Terms: Pays royalties of 7½-15% on retail price. Publishes ms 1 year after acceptance. Book catalog for 10×13 SAE with 5 first-class stamps.

Advice: "Our audience is made up of readers interested in works that are specific to the Chesapeake Bay and Delmarva Peninsula area."

TOR BOOKS, Tom Doherty Associates, 175 Fifth Ave., New York NY 10010. (212)388-0100. Fax: (212)388-0191. E-mail: inquiries@tor.com. Website: www.tor.com. **Contact:** Patrick Nielsen Hayden, senior editor. Estab. 1980. Publishes hardcover and paperback originals, plus some paperback reprints. Books: 5 point Dombook paper; offset printing; Bursel and perfect binding; few illustrations. Averages 200 total titles/year, mostly fiction. Some nonfiction titles.

Imprint(s): Forge Books.

Needs: Fantasy, mainstream, science fiction, historical, adventure and horror. Published *The Path of Daggers*, by Robert Jordan; *1916*, by Morgan Llywelyn; *The Predators*, by Harold Robbins; and *Ender's Shadow*, by Orson Scott Card.

How to Contact: Agented mss preferred. Agented fiction 90%. No simultaneous submissions. Address manuscripts to "Editorial," *not* to the Managing Editor's office. Responds in 4 months to queries; 6 months to proposals.

Terms: Pays in royalties and advance. Writer must return advance if book is not completed or is unacceptable. Sends galleys to author. Publishes ms 1-2 years after acceptance. Free book catalog on request.

TYNDALE HOUSE PUBLISHERS INC., 351 Executive Dr., Carol Stream IL 60188. (608)668-8300. Website: www.tyndale.com. **Contact**: Linda Washington, fiction acquisitions assistant. Estab. 1962. Privately owned religious press. Publishes hardcover and paperback originals. First novel print order: 7,500-15,000. Averages 150 total titles, 25-30 fiction titles/year. **Published new writers within the last year.** Distributes titles through catalog houses, rackers and distributors. Promotes titles through print ads in trade publications, radio, point of sale materials and catalogs.

Imprint(s): Heart Quest; Anne Goldsmith, fiction editor (inspirational romance), Jan Stob, fiction editor (genre and mainstream inspirational fiction), and Virginia Williams, editor (inspirational children's fiction).

 • Three books published by Tyndale House have received the Gold Medallion Book Award. They include *The Last Sin Eater*, by Francine Rivers; *The Sword of Truth*, by Gilbert Morris; and *A Rose Remembered*, by Michael Phillips.

Needs: Religious (children's, general, inspirational, mystery/suspense, thriller, romance). "We primarily publish Christian historical romances, with occasional contemporary, suspense or standalones." Recently published *Left Behind*, by Tim LaHaye and Jerry Jenkins (general/inspirational); *Hope*, by Lori Copeland (inspirational romance); and the *Left Behind—Kids* series, by Tim LaHaye and Jerry Jenkins (children's religious).

How to Contact: Does not accept unsolicited mss. Queries with outline/synopsis and 3 sample chapters. Include estimated word count, brief bio and list of publishing credits. Send SASE or IRC for return of ms or send disposable copy of ms and SASE for reply only. Agented fiction 20%. Responds in 3 months to queries and mss. Accepts simultaneous submissions. Never comments on rejected mss.

Terms: Advance negotiable. Sends galleys to authors. Publishes ms 9 months after acceptance. Writer's guidelines for 9×12 SAE and $2.40 for postage or visit website.

Advice: "We are a religious publishing house with a primarily evangelical Christian market. We are looking for spiritual themes and content within established genres."

TYRO PUBLISHING, 194 Carlbert St., Sault Ste. Marie Ontario P6A 5E1 Canada. (705)253-6402. E-mail: tyro@sympatico.ca. **Contact:** Lorelee Gordon, editor. Estab. 1984. "We are a small press. Currently we publish only talking books on CD-ROM." Average print order: 200. First novel print order: 200. **Published 4 new writers within the last year.** Averages 8 total titles, 2 fiction titles/year.

Needs: Recently published *A Saga of Sable Island*, by Helen Hodgson (historical).

How to Contact: Accepts unsolicited mss only by e-mail. Query with outline/synopsis and 3 sample chapters only by e-mail. Accepts queries by e-mail. Include estimated word count and brief bio. Agented fiction 2%. Accepts electronic submissions. Responds in 2 weeks to queries; 1 month to mss. Often comments on rejected mss.

Terms: Pays royalties of 15%. Normally checks are sent every three months as books are sold. Sends galleys to author. Publishes ms 6 months after acceptance. Writer's guidelines and book catalog available by e-mail only.

UCLA AMERICAN INDIAN STUDIES CENTER, UCLA, 3220 Campbell Hall, Box 951548, Los Angeles CA 90095-1548. (310)825-7315. Fax: (310)206-7060. E-mail: aiscpubs@ucla.edu. Website: www.sscnet.ucla.edu/esplaisc/index.html (contains descriptions of books published, submission guidelines, excerpts from books). **Contact:** Duane Champagne, editor-in-chief. Estab. 1979. "Nonprofit publications unit at UCLA devoted to scholarship by and/or about Indian people; we produce numerous books, bibliographies, monographs, as well as the internationally recognized quarterly *American Indian Culture and Research Journal*, which contains academic articles, commentary, literature and book reviews." Publishes paperback originals and paperback reprints. Books: 60 lb. paper; perfect bound; b&w illustrations. **Published 1 new writer within the last year.** Averages 4 total titles, 2-3 fiction titles/year. Member, SPD, bookpeople.

Needs: Native American, literary. Published *Comeuppance at Kicking Horse Casino*, by Charles Brashear (short stories).

How to Contact: Accepts unsolicited mss. Submit complete ms with cover letter. Accepts queries by e-mail. Include estimated word count and brief bio with submission. Send disposable copy of the ms plus SASE for reply only. Agented fiction: 0%. Responds in 3 months to queries; in 3 months 2 mss. No simultaneous submissions, electronic submissions or submissions on disk. Sometimes comments on rejected mss.

Terms: Pays on royalties. Sends galleys to author. Publishes ms 8-12 months after acceptance. Writer's guidelines for SASE. Book catalogs free and on website.

UNITY HOUSE, (formerly Unity Books), Unity School of Christianity, 1901 NW Blue Parkway, Unity Village MO 64065-0001. (816)524-3550 ext. 3190. Fax: (816)251-3552. E-mail: ~books@unityworldhq.org. Website: www.unityworldhq.org. **Contact**: Michael Maday, editor; Raymond Teague, associate editor. "We are a bridge between traditional Christianity and New Age spirituality. Unity School of Christianity is based on metaphysical Christian principles, spiritual values and the healing power of prayer as a resource for daily living." Publishes hardcover and trade paperback originals and reprints. **Published 9 new writers within the last year.** Averages 18 titles/year.
Needs: Spiritual, inspirational, metaphysical.
How to Contact: Query with synopsis and sample chapter. Responds in 1 month to queries; 2 months to mss.
Terms: Pays royalties of 10-15% royalty on net receipts. Publishes ms 13 months after acceptance of final ms. Writer's guidelines and book catalog free.

UNIVERSITY OF GEORGIA PRESS, 330 Research Dr., Athens GA 30602-4901. (706)369-6130. Fax: (706)369-6131. E-mail: books@ugapress.uga.edu. Website: www.uga.edu/ugapress (includes guidelines, catalog, contact information and mission statement). Estab. 1938. University of Georgia Press is a midsized press that publishes fiction *only* through the Flannery O'Connor Award for Short Fiction competition. Publishes 85 titles/year.
Needs: Published *Break Any Woman Down*, by Dana Johnson and *The Necessary Grace to Fall*, by Gina Ochsner, both recent award winners.
How to Contact: Guidelines available on website or for SASE.
Terms: Standard publishing contract. Publishes ms 1 year after competition judging. Competition guidelines for #10 SASE. Book catalog free.

UNIVERSITY OF NEBRASKA PRESS, 234 N. Eighth St., P.O. Box 880255, Lincoln NE 68588-0255. (402)472-3581. Fax: (402)472-0308. E-mail: pressmail@unl.edu. Website: http://nebraskapress.unl.edu. **Contact**: Daniel Ross, director. Estab. 1941. "The University of Nebraska Press seeks to encourage, develop, publish and disseminate research, literature and the publishing arts. The Press maintains scholarly standards and fosters innovations guided by referred evaluations." Publishes hardcover and paperback originals and reprints. **Published new writers within the last year.**
Needs: Accepts fiction translations but no original fiction. Also welcomes creative nonfiction.
How to Contact: Query first with outline/synopsis, 1 sample chapter and introduction. Responds in 4 months.
Terms: Pays graduated royalty on original books. Occasional advance. Writer's guidelines and book catalog for 9×12 SAE with 5 first-class stamps.

UNIVERSITY OF TEXAS PRESS, P.O. Box 7819, Austin TX 78713-7819. Fax: (512)232-7178. E-mail: utpress@uts.cc.utexas.edu. Website: www.utexas.edu/utpress/. **Contact:** Theresa May, assistant director/editor-in-chief (social sciences, Latin American studies); James Burr, acquisitions editor (humanities, classics); Bill Bishel, acquisitions editor (sciences, Texana). Estab. 1950. **Publishes 50% previously unpublished writers/year.** Publishes 85 titles/year. Average print order for a first book is 1,000.
Needs: Latin American and Middle Eastern fiction only in translation. Published *Whatever Happened to Dulce Veiga?*, by Caio Fernando Abreu (novel).
How to Contact: Query or submit outline and 2 sample chapters. Responds in up to 3 months.
Terms: Pays royalty usually based on net income. Offers advance occasionally. Publishes ms 18 months after acceptance. Writer's guidelines and book catalog free.
Advice: "It's difficult to make a manuscript over 400 double-spaced pages into a feasible book. Authors should take special care to edit out extraneous material. Looks for sharply focused, in-depth treatments of important topics."

VIKING, Imprint of Penguin Putnam Inc., 375 Hudson St., New York NY 10014. (212)366-2000. Publisher: Clare Ferraro. **Contact:** Acquisitions Editor. Publishes a mix of academic and popular fiction and nonfiction. Publishes hardcover and trade paperback originals.
Needs: Literary, mainstream/contemporary, mystery, suspense. Published *A Day Late and A Dollar Short*, by Terry McMillan; *A Common Life*, by Jan Karon; and *In the Heart of the Sea*, by Nathaniel Philbrick.
How to Contact: Agented fiction only. Responds in up to 6 months to queries. Accepts simultaneous submissions.
Terms: Pays royalties of 10-15% on retail price. Advance negotiable. Publishes ms 1 year after acceptance.
Advice: "Looking for writers who can deliver a book a year (or faster) of consistent quality."

VIKING CHILDREN'S BOOKS, Imprint of the Children's Division of Penguin Putnam Inc., 375 Hudson St., New York NY 10014-3657. (212)366-2000. Website: www.penguinputnam.com (includes online catalog of all imprints, feature articles and interviews, young readers site, order information, education and teacher's resources). "Viking Children's Books publishes the highest quality trade books for children including fiction, nonfiction, and novelty books for pre-schoolers through young adults." Publishes hardcover originals. **Published new writers within the last year.** Publishes 80 books/year. Promotes titles through press kits, institutional ads.

Needs: Juvenile, young adult. Recently published *Someone Like You*, by Sarah Dessen (novel); *Joseph Had a Little Overcoat*, by Simms Taback (picture book); *See You Later, Gladiator*, by Jon Scieszka (chapter book).

How to Contact: Accepts unsolicited mss. for picture books and novels, submit entire ms. Responds in 4 months to queries. SASE mandatory for return of materials.

Terms: Pays royalties 5-10% on retail price. Advance negotiable. Publishes ms 12-18 months after acceptance.

Advice: No "cartoony" or mass-market submissions for picture books.

☑ Ⓐ VINTAGE ANCHOR PUBLISHING, The Knopf Publishing Group, A Division of Random House, Inc., 299 Park Ave., New York NY 10171. Website: www.randomhouse.com. Vice President: LuAnn Walther. Editor-in-Chief: Martin Asher. **Contact:** Submissions Editor. Publishes trade paperback originals and reprints. **Published new writers within the last year.**

Needs: Literary, mainstream/contemporary, short story collections. Published *Snow Falling on Cedars*, by Guterson (contemporary); and *Martin Dressler*, by Millhauser (literary).

How to Contact: Agented submissions only. Query with synopsis and 2-3 sample chapters. Responds in 6 months to queries. Accepts simultaneous submissions. No submissions by fax or e-mail.

Terms: Pays 4-8% royalty on retail price. Offers advance of $2,500 and up. Publishes ms 1 year after acceptance.

☑ 🌐 Ⓞ VISION BOOKS PVT LTD., Madarsa Rd., Kashmere Gate, Delhi 110006 India. (+91)11 3862267 or (+91)11 3862201. Fax: (+91)11 3862935. E-mail: orientpbk@vsnl.com. **Contact:** Sudhir Malhotra, fiction editor. Publishes 25 titles/year.

Needs: "We are a large multilingual publishing house publishing fiction and other trade books."

How to Contact: "A brief synopsis should be submitted initially. Subsequently, upon hearing from the editor, a typescript may be sent."

Terms: Pays royalties.

Ⓞ ◎ VISTA PUBLISHING, INC., 422 Morris Ave., Suite One, Long Branch NJ 07740-5901. (732)229-6500. Fax: (732)229-9647. E-mail: czagury@vistapubl.com. Website: www.vistapubl.com (includes titles, authors, editors, pricing and ordering information). **Contact:** Carolyn Zagury, president. Estab. 1991. "Small, independent press, owned by women and specializing in fiction by nurses and allied health professional authors." Publishes paperback originals. **Published 3 new writers within the last year.** Plans 3 first novels in 2001. Averages 12 total titles, 6 fiction titles/year. Distributes titles through catalogs, wholesalers, distributors, exhibits, website, trade shows, book clubs and bookstores. Promotes titles through author signings, press releases, author speakings, author interviews, exhibits, website, direct mail and book reviews.

Needs: Adventure, humor/satire, mystery/suspense, romance, short story collections. Published *Never Be a Witness*, by Nancy Lamoureux (mystery); *Error in Judgement*, by Gary Birken (medical mystery); *The Golden Gate Park Murder*, by Pamela Hausman Hasting (murder mystery).

How to Contact: Accepts unsolicited mss. Query with complete ms. Accepts queries by e-mail but not by fax. Include bio. Send SASE or IRC for reply, return of ms or send disposable copy of ms and SASE for reply only. Responds in 2 months to mss. Accepts simultaneous submissions. Comments on rejected mss.

Terms: Pays royalties. Sends galleys to author. Publishes ms 2 years after acceptance. Writer's guidelines and book catalog for SASE.

Advice: "We prefer to read full mss. Authors should be nurses or allied health professionals."

🆕 ◓ VIVISPHERE PUBLISHING, Net Pub Corporation, 2 Neptune Rd., Poughkeepsie NY 12601. (845)463-1100. Fax: (845)463-0018. Website: www.vivisphere.com (includes book covers, author info, interviews, author readings, author appearances). **Contact:** Teal Hutton. Estab. 1995. "Small independent publisher offering historical, nature, and other nonfiction, spiritual—and a wide range of fiction including mysteries and science fiction." Publishes paperback originals and paperback reprints. Books: 60 lb. paper; soft cover binding; illustrations. **Published 10 new writers within the last year.** Plans 10-12 first novels in 2002. Averages 50 total titles, 30 fiction titles/year. Distributes titles through Baker & Taylor.

Imprint(s): Moon Dragon, Katrina Drake (fantasy/horror); Unifont, Alois Budrys (science fiction); Saddlehorn, Vivian Allison (western).

Needs: Adventure, ethnic/multicultural, fantasy, feminist, gay, historical, horror, lesbian, literary, mainstream, military/war, mystery/suspense, New Age/mystic, psychic/supernatural, religious, romance, science fiction, western. Recently published *Infinite Darkness/Infinite Light*, by Margaret Doner (metaphysical romance); *The Condor Tales*, by Jacques Condor (Native American Horror); *Dancing Suns*, by Karen Daniels (science fiction).

How to Contact: Accepts unsolicited mss. Query with outline/synopsis and 3 sample chapters. Accepts queries by e-mail. Include brief bio and a list of publishing credits with submission. Send disposable copy of the ms plus SASE for reply only. Agented fiction: 50%. Responds in 3 months to queries; 3 months to mss. Considers simultaneous, electronic and disk submissions. Sometimes comments on rejected mss.

Terms: Pays royalties of 10-15% and 25 author's copies. Send galleys to author. Time between acceptance and publication is 3-12 months. Writer's guidelines for SASE, on website. Book catalogs free upon request.

Advice: "Read *Self-Editing for Fiction Writers*, by Renni Browne—then, if you still don't see need for a new draft, submit query and chapters."

⊘ WALKER AND COMPANY, 435 Hudson St., New York NY 10014. Fax: (212)727-0984. Publisher: George Gibson. Editors: Jacqueline Johnson, Michael Seidman. Juvenile Publisher: Emily Easton. Juvenile Editor: Tim Travaglini. **Contact:** submissions editor or submissions editor-juvenile. Estab. 1959. Midsize independent publisher with plans to expand. Publishes hardcover and trade paperback originals. Average first novel print order: 2,500-3,500. Number of titles: 70/year.

Needs: Nonfiction, sophisticated, quality mystery (amateur sleuth, cozy, private eye, police procedural), and children's and young adult nonfiction. Published *The Killing of Monday Brown*, by Sandra West Prowell; *Galileo's Daughter*, by Dave Sobel; *Murder in the Place of Anubis*, by Lynda S. Robinson; and *Who In Hell Is Wanda Fuca*, by G.M. Ford.

How to Contact: *Does not accept unsolicited mss.* Submit outline and chapters as preliminary. Query letter should include "a concise description of the story line, including its outcome, word length of story (we prefer 70,000 words), writing experience, publishing credits, particular expertise on this subject and in this genre. Common mistakes: Sounding unprofessional (i.e. too chatty, too braggardly). Forgetting SASE." Agented fiction 50%. Notify if multiple or simultaneous submissions. Responds in 3 months to queries. Publishes ms an average of 1 year after acceptance. Occasionally comments on rejected mss.

Terms: Negotiable (usually advance against royalty). Must return advance if book is not completed or is unacceptable.

Advice: "As for mysteries, we are open to all types, including suspense novels and offbeat books that maintain a 'play fair' puzzle. We are always looking for well-written western novels that are offbeat and strong on characterization. Character development is most important in all Walker fiction. We expect the author to be expert in the categories, to know the background and foundations of the genre. To realize that just because some subgenre is hot it doesn't mean that that is the area to mine—after all, if everyone is doing female p.i.s, doesn't it make more sense to do something that isn't crowded, something that might serve to balance a list, rather than make it top heavy? Finally, don't tell us why your book is going to be a success; instead, show me that you can write and write well. It is your writing, and not your hype that interests us."

◎ ⊘ Ⓐ ♈ WARNER ASPECT, Imprint of Warner Books, 1271 Avenue of the Americas, New York NY 10020. Fax: (212)522-7990. Website: www.twbookmark.com (includes each month's new titles, advice from writers, previous titles and interviews with authors, "hot news," contests). **Contact:** Betsy Mitchell, editor-in-chief. "We're looking for 'epic' stories in both fantasy and science fiction." Publishes hardcover, trade paperback, mass market paperback originals and mass market paperback reprints. **Published 2 new writers within the last year.** Distributes titles through nationwide sales force.

• Warner Aspect published *Parable of the Talents*, by Octavia E. Butler, winner of the Nebula Award for best novel.

Needs: Fantasy, science fiction. Published *The Naked God*, by Peter F. Hamilton (science fiction); and *A Cavern of Black Ice*, by J.V. Jones (fantasy).

How to Contact: Agented fiction only. Responds in 10 weeks to mss.

Terms: Pays royalty on retail price. Average advance: $5,000 and up. Publishes ms 14 months after acceptance.

Advice: "Think epic! Our favorite stories are big-screen science fiction and fantasy, with plenty of characters and subplots. Sample our existing titles—we're a fairly new list and pretty strongly focused." Mistake writers often make is "hoping against hope that being unagented won't make a difference. We simply don't have the staff to look at unagented projects."

⊘ Ⓐ WARNER BOOKS, Time & Life Building, 1271 Avenue of the Americas, New York NY 10020. (212)522-7200. Website: www.twbookmark.com. Publishes hardcover, trade paperback, mass market paperback originals, reprints and e-books. Warner publishes general interest fiction. Averages 350 total titles/year.

Imprint(s): Mysterious Press, Warner Aspect, Walk Worthy; iPublish.

Needs: Fantasy, mainstream, mystery/suspense, romance, science fiction, thriller. Recently published *First Counsel*, by Brad Meltzer; *Standoff*, by Sandra Brown; and *The Rescue*, by Nicholas Sparks.

How to Contact: Accepts agented submissions *only*.

☑ ☒ **WHITE PINE PRESS**, P.O. Box 236, Buffalo NY 14201. Phone/fax: (716)627-4665. E-mail: wpine@whitepine.org. Website: www.whitepine.org (includes book catalog). **Contact:** Elaine LaMattina, editor (all fiction). Estab. 1973. Small, not-for-profit literary publisher. Publishes paperback originals. Books: text paper; offset printing; perfect binding. Average print order: 1,500. First novel print order: 1,500. Averages 8 total titles, 4 fiction titles/year. Distributes titles through Consortium Book Sales.

• *Stories for a Winter's Night*, by Maurice Kenny won the Stepping Stone Award.

Needs: Ethnic/multicultural, feminist, literary, short story collections, translations. Recently published *Empire Settings*, by David Schmahmann (first fiction, novel); *Some Wine for Remembrance*, by Edmund Keeley (novel); and *River of Sorrows*, by Libertad Demitropoulos (novel in translation). Publishes the New American Fiction series.

How to Contact: Accepts unsolicited mss. Send query letter. "We do not accept queries via e-mail or fax." Include estimated word count and list of publishing credits. Send SASE or IRC for return of ms or send disposable copy of ms and SASE for reply only. Agented fiction 1%. Responds in 1 month to queries; 6 months to mss. Accepts simultaneous submissions. Sometimes comments on rejected mss.

Terms: Pays 100 author's copies. Sends galleys to author. Publishes ms 1-2 years after acceptance. Writer's guidelines free for SASE.

Advice: "Send query letter first detailing project. Stick to our guidelines. Don't telephone to see if we received it. We're interested in what's good, not what's trendy."

☑ ◎ **WILSHIRE BOOK CO.**, 12015 Sherman Rd., North Hollywood CA 91605-3781. (818)765-8579. Fax: (818)765-2922. E-mail: mpowers@mpowers.com. Website: www.mpowers.com (includes types of books published). **Contact:** Melvin Powers, publisher; Marcia Powers, senior editor (adult fables). Estab. 1947. "You are not only what you are today, but also what you choose to become tomorrow." Looking for adult fables that teach principles of psychological growth. Publishes trade paperback originals and reprints. **Published 7 new writers within the last year.** Averages 15 titles/year. Distributes titles through wholesalers, bookstores and mail order. Promotes titles through author interviews on radio and television.

Needs: Allegories that teach principles of psychological/spiritual growth or offer guidance in living. Min. 30,000 words. Published *The Princess Who Believed in Fairy Tales*, by Marcia Grad; *The Knight in Rusty Armor*, by Robert Fisher. Allegories only. No standard novels or short stories.

How to Contact: Accepts unsolicited mss. Query with synopsis, 3 sample chapters and SASE or submit complete ms with cover letter. Accepts queries by e-mail. Responds in 2 months.

Terms: Pays standard royalty. Publishes ms 6 months after acceptance.

Advice: "We are vitally interested in all new material we receive. Just as you hopefully submit your manuscript for publication, we hopefully read every one submitted, searching for those that we believe will be successful in the marketplace. Writing and publishing must be a team effort. We need you to write what we can sell. We suggest that you read the successful books mentioned above or others that are similar: *Greatest Salesman in the World*, *Illusions*, *Way of the Peaceful Warrior*, *Celestine Prophecy*. Analyze them to discover what elements make them winners. Duplicate those elements in your own style, using a creative new approach and fresh material, and you will have written a book we can successfully market."

☑ ☑ ☒ **WINDSTORM CREATIVE LIMITED**, (formerly Pride and Imprints), 7419 Ebbert Drive SE, Port Orchard WA 98367. Website: www.arabyfair.com. **Contact:** Ms. Cris Newport, senior editor. Estab. 1989. Publishes paperback originals and reprints. **Published new writers within the last year.** Averages 50 total titles/year.

• Chosen as the "Best Example of an Independent Publisher" by BookWatch (Midwest Book Review).

Needs: Contemporary, fantasy, gay/lesbian/bisexual, historical, science fiction, young adult. No children's books, horror, "bestseller" fiction, spy or espionage novels, "thrillers," any work which describes childhood sexual abuse or in which this theme figures prominently. Recently published *Bones Become Flowers*, by Jess Mowry (contemporary fiction); *Annabel and I*, by Chris Anne Wolfe (lesbian fiction); *Journey of a Thousand Miles*, by Peter Kasting (gay fiction); *Puzzle from the Past*, by Mike and Janet Golio (young adult).

How to Contact: Does not accept unsolicited mss. Query with cover letter and 1-page synopsis which details the major plot developments. "Visit website for detailed submission instructions." Responds in 6 months to mss.

Terms: Pays royalties of 10-15% on wholesale price. Publishes ms 1-2 years after acceptance. Guidelines online only.

Advice: "Read our books before you even query us."

☑ ◎ **WIZARDS OF THE WEST COAST**, (formerly TSR, Inc.), Wizards of the Coast, P.O. Box 707, Renton WA 98057-0707. (425)226-6500. Website: www.wizards.com. Executive Editor: Mary Kirchoff. Vice President: Mary Kirchoff. Editorial Director: Peter ARcher. **Contact**: Novel Submissions Editor. Estab. 1974. "We publish shared-world fiction set in the worlds of Dungeons & Dragons, Magic: The Gathering, and Legend of the Five Rings." Wizards of the Coast publishes games as well, including the Dungeons & Dragons® role-playing game. Books: standard paperbacks; offset printing; perfect binding; b&w (usually) illustrations. Average first novel print order: 75,000. Averages 50-60 fiction titles/year. Distributes titles through St. Martin's Press.

Imprint(s): Dragonlance® Books; Forgotten Realms® Books; Magic: The Gathering® Books; Legend of the Five Rings Novels.

Needs: Fantasy, science fiction, short story collections. Recently published *Dragons of a Lost Star*, by Margaret Weis and Tracy Hickman (fantasy); *Servant of the Shard*, by R.A. Salvatore (fantasy); and *Apocalypse*, by J. Robert King (fantasy). "We currently publish only work-for-hire novels set in our trademarked worlds. No violent or gory fantasy or science fiction."

How to Contact: Request guidelines first, then query with outline/synopsis and 3 sample chapters. Agented fiction 65%. Responds in 4 months 2 queries. Accepts simultaneous submissions.

Terms: Pays royalties of 4-8% on retail price. Average advance: $4,000-6,000. Publishes ms 1 year after acceptance. Writer's guidelines for #10 SASE.

THE WOMEN'S PRESS, 34 Great Sutton St., London EC1V 0LQ England. Website: www.the-womens-press.com. **Contact:** Kirsty Dunseath, Charlotte Cole and Essie Cousins, fiction editors. Publishes approximately 50 titles/year.

Needs: "Women's fiction, written by women. Centered on women. Theme can be anything—all themes may be women's concern—but we look for political/feminist awareness, originality, wit, fiction of ideas. Includes literary fiction, crime, and teenage list *Livewire*."

Terms: Writers receive royalty, including advance.

Advice: Writers should ask themselves, "Is this a manuscript which would interest a feminist/political press? Is it double-spaced, or one side of the paper only? Have I enclosed return postage?"

THE WONDERLAND PRESS, INC., 160 Fifth Avenue, Suite 625, New York NY 10010. (212)989-2550. E-mail: litraryagt@aol.com. **Contact:** John Campbell. Estab. 1985. Member, American Book Producers Association. Represents 32 clients. Specializes in high-quality nonfiction, illustrated, reference, how-to and entertainment books. "We welcome submissions from new authors, but proposals must be unique, of high commercial interest and well written." Currently handles: 90% nonfiction books; 10% novels.

- The Wonderland Press is also a book packager and "in a very strong position to nurture strong proposals all the way from concept through bound books."

Represents: Interested in reviewing nonfiction books, novels. Considers these nonfiction areas: art/architecture/design; biography/autobiography; enthnic/cultural interests; health/medicine; history; how-to; humor; interior design/decorating; language/literature/criticism; photography; popular culture; psychology; self-help/personal improvement. Considers these fiction areas: action/adventure; literary; picture book; thriller.

How to Contact: Send outline/proposal with SASE. Responds in 3-5 days to queries; 2 weeks to mss.

Needs: Does not want to receive poetry, memoir, children's or category fiction. Recently published *Body Knots*, by Howard Schatz (Rizzoli); and *Nude Body Nude*, by Howard Schatz (HarperCollins).

Terms: Agent receives 15% commission on domestic sales. Offers written contract. 30-90 days notice must be given to terminate contract. Offers criticism service, included in 15% commission. Charges for photocopying, long-distance telephone, overnight express-mail, messengering.

Tips: "Follow your talent. Write with passion. Know your market. Submit work in final form; if you feel a need to apologize for its mistakes, typos, or incompleteness, then it is not ready to be seen. We want to see your best work."

WORLDWIDE LIBRARY, Division of Harlequin Books, 225 Duncan Mill Rd., Don Mills, Ontario M3B 3K9 Canada. (416)445-5860. **Contact:** Feroze Mohammed, senior editor/editorial coordinator. Estab. 1979. Large commercial category line. Publishes paperback originals and reprints. Averages 72 fiction titles/year. "Mystery program is reprint; no originals please."

Imprint(s): Worldwide Mystery; Gold Eagle Books.

Needs: "Action-adventure series and future fiction."

How to Contact: Query with outline/synopsis/series concept or overview and sample chapters. Send SAE with International Reply Coupons or money order. Responds in 10 weeks to queries. Accepts simultaneous submissions.

Terms: Advance and sometimes royalties; copyright buyout. Publishes ms 1-2 years after acceptance.

Advice: "Publishing fiction in very selective areas."

YORK PRESS LTD., 152 Boardwalk Dr., Toronto, Ontario M4L 3X4 Canada. (416)690-3788. Fax: (416)690-3797. E-mail: yorkpress@sympatico.ca. Website: www3.sympatico.ca/yorkpress. **Contact:** Dr. S. Elk-

hadem, general manager/editor. Estab. 1975. "We publish scholarly books and creative writing of an experimental nature." Publishes trade paperback originals. **Published new writers within the last year.** Averages 10 titles/year.
Needs: "Fiction of an experimental nature by well-established writers." Published *The Moonhare*, by Kirk Hampton (experimental novel).
How to Contact: Query first. Responds in 2 months.
Terms: Pays royalties of 10-20% royalty on wholesale price. Publishes ms 6 months after acceptance.

🖤 🃏 **ZOLAND BOOKS, INC.,** 384 Huron Ave., Cambridge MA 02138. (617)864-6252. Fax: (617)661-4998. E-mail: info@zolandbooks.com. Website: www.zolandbooks.com. **Contact**: Roland Pease, publisher/editor. Estab. 1987. "We are a literary press, publishing poetry, fiction, nonfiction, photography, and other titles of literary interest." Publishes hardcover and paperback originals and reprints. Books: acid-free paper; sewn binding; some with illustrations. Average print order: 2,000-5,000. **Published 1-2 new writers within the last year.** Averages 14 total titles/year. Distributes titles through Consortium Book Sales and Distribution. Promotes titles through catalog, publicity, advertisements, direct mail.
   ● Awards include: Hemingway/PEN Award, Kafka Prize for Women's Fiction, National Book Award finalist, *New York Times* Notable Book, *Publishers Weekly* Best Book of the Year.
Needs: Contemporary, feminist, literary, African-American interest, short story collections. Recently published *Children of the Pithiviers*, by Sheila Kohler; *To Repel Ghosts*, by Kevin Young; and *In the Pond*, by Ha Jin.
How to Contact: Accepts unsolicited mss. Query first, then send complete ms with cover letter and SASE. Responds in 3 months to queries.
Terms: Pays royalties of 5-8%. Average advance: $1,500; negotiable (also pays author's copies). Sends galleys to author. Publishes ms 1-2 years after acceptance. Book catalog for 6×9 SAE and 2 first-class stamps.
Advice: "Be original."

🖤 📷 **ZONDERVAN**, Imprint of HarperCollins Publishers, 5300 Patterson SE, Grand Rapids MI 49530. (616)698-6900. E-mail: zondervan@zph.com. Website: www.zondervan.com. **Contact**: Manuscript Review Editor. Estab. 1931. "Our mission is to be the leading Christian communication company meeting the needs of people with resources that glorify Jesus Christ and promote biblical principles." Large evangelical Christian publishing house. Publishes hardcover and paperback originals and reprints. First novel print order: 5,000. **Published new writers in the last year.** Averages 150 total titles, 15-20 fiction titles/year.
Needs: Adult fiction, (mainstream, biblical), "Inklings-style" fiction of high literary quality. Christian relevance necessary in all cases. Will *not* consider collections of short stories. Recently published *Jacob's Way*, by Gilbert Morris; *The Prodigy*, by Alton Gansky; and *Times and Seasons*, by Terri Blackstock and Bev Lattaye.
How to Contact: Accepts unsolicited mss but prefers queries with outline and 2 sample chapters. *Write for writer's guidelines first.* Include #10 SASE. Responds in 2 months to queries; 4 months to mss.
Terms: "Standard contract provides for a percentage of the net price received by publisher for each copy sold."
Advice: "Almost no unsolicited fiction is published. Send plot outline and one or two sample chapters. Editors will *not* read entire manuscripts. Your sample chapters will make or break you."

MICROPRESSES

The very small presses listed here are owned or operated by one to three people, often friends or family members. Some are cooperatives of writers and most of these presses started out publishing their staff members' books or books by their friends. Even the most successful of these presses are unable to afford the six-figure advances, lavish promotional budgets and huge press runs possible in the large, commercial houses. These presses can easily be swamped with submissions, but writers published by them are usually treated as "one of the family."

🃏 **ACME PRESS**, P.O. Box 1702, Westminster MD 21158. (410)848-7577. **Contact**: Ms. E.G. Johnston, managing editor. Estab. 1991. "We operate on a part-time basis and publish 1-2 novels/year." Publishes hardcover and paperback originals. **Published new writers within the last year.** Averages 1-2 fiction titles/year.
Needs: Humor/satire. "We publish only humor novels, so we don't want to see anything that's not funny." Published *She-Crab Soup*, by Dawn Langley Simmons (fictional memoir/humor); *Biting the Wall*, by J. M. Johnston (humor/mystery); *Hearts of Gold*, by James Magorian (humor/mystery); and *Super Fan*, by Lyn A. Sherwood (comic/sports).
How to Contact: Accepts unsolicited mss. Query with outline/synopsis and first 50 pages or submit complete ms with cover letter. Include estimated word count. Send SASE for reply, return of ms or send a disposable copy of ms. Agented fiction 25%. Responds in 2 weeks to queries; 6 weeks to mss. Accepts simultaneous submissions. Always comments on rejected mss.

Terms: Pays 25 author's copies and 50% of profits. Sends galleys to author. Publishes ms 1 year after acceptance. Writer's guidelines and book catalog for #10 SASE.

 **AGELESS PRESS**, P.O. Box 5915, Sarasota FL 34277-5915. Phone/fax: (941)952-0576. E-mail: iris hope@home.com. Website: http://members.home.net/irishope/ageless.htm (includes contest winners, articles, book excerpts). **Contact:** Iris Forrest, editor. Estab. 1992. Independent publisher. Publishes paperback originals. Books: acid-free paper; notched perfect binding; no illustrations. Average print order: 5,000. First novel print order: 5,000. **Published new writers within the last year.** Averages 1 title/year.

Needs: Experimental, fantasy, humor/satire, literary, mainstream/contemporary, mystery/suspense, New Age/mystic/spiritual, science fiction, short story collections, thriller/espionage. Looking for material "based on personal computer experiences." Stories selected by editor. Published *Computer Legends, Lies & Lore*, by various (anthology); and *Computer Tales of Fact & Fantasy*, by various (anthology).

How to Contact: Does not accept unsolicited mss. Send query letter. Accepts queries by e-mail and fax. Send SASE or IRC for return of ms or send a disposable copy of ms and SASE for reply only. Responds in 1 week. Accepts simultaneous submissions, electronic (disk, 5¼ or 3.5 IBM) submissions in ASCII format. Sometimes comments on rejected mss.

Terms: Average advance: negotiable. Publishes ms 6-12 months after acceptance.

ANVIL PRESS, P.O. Box 3008, MPO, Vancouver, British Columbia V6B 3X5 Canada; or Lee Building, #204-A, 175 E. Broadway, Vancouver, British Columbia V5T 1W2 Canada. (604)876-8710. Fax: (604)879-2667. E-mail: subter@portal.ca. Website: www.anvilpress.com (includes writer's guidelines, names of editors, book catalog, sample of magazine, contest info). **Contact:** Brian Kaufman, managing editor. Estab. 1988. "1½-person operation with volunteer editorial board. Anvil Press publishes contemporary fiction, poetry and drama, giving voice to up-and-coming Canadian writers, exploring all literary genres, discovering, nurturing and promoting new Canadian literary talent." Publishes paperback originals. Books: offset or web printing; perfect-bound. Average print order: 1,000-1,500. First novel print order: 1,000. **Published new writers within the last year.** Plans 4 first novels in 2002. Averages 4-5 fiction titles/year.

● Anvil Press titles have been nominated for the Journey Prize, the BC Book Prize and the City of Vancouver Prize. *White Lung*, by Grant Buday, was nominated for the City of Vancouver Book Prize. *Skin*, by Bonnie Bowman, won the inaugural ReLit award.

Needs: Experimental, contemporary modern, literary, short story collections. Recently published *The Door is Open: Memoir of a Soup Kitchen Volunteer*, by Bart Campbell (nonfiction); *The Inanimate World*, by Robert Strandquist (fiction); and *Red Mango-a blues*, by Charles Tidler (drama).

How to Contact: Canadian writers only (with the exception of 3 Day Novel Writing Contest). Accepts unsolicited mss. Send query letter or query with outline/synopsis and 1-2 sample chapters. Include estimated word count and bio. Send SASE or IRC for return of ms or send a disposable copy of ms and SASE for reply only. Responds in 4 months to queries; up to 6 months to mss. Accepts simultaneous submissions (please note in query letter that manuscript is a simultaneous submission).

Terms: Pays royalties of 15% (of final sales). Average advance: $400. Sends galleys to author. Publishes ms within contract year. Book catalog for 9×12 SASE and 2 first-class stamps.

Advice: "We are only interested in writing that is progressive in some way—form, content. We want contemporary fiction from serious writers who intend to be around for awhile and be a name people will know in years to come. Read back titles, look through our catalog before submitting."

AVID PRESS, LLC, 5470 Red Fox Dr., Brighton MI 48114-9079. Website: www.avidpress.com. **Contact:** Colleen Gleason Shulte or Kate Gleason, publishers. "Avid Press is a royalty-paying publisher of fiction and non-fiction, electronic and print books. Avid Press is dedicated to building and maintaining a reputation as an author-friendly publisher. It is important that our authors are pleased and proud to be associated with Avid Press." Publishes e-books and paperback originals and reprints.

Imprints: VIM (young adult titles)

FOR EXPLANATIONS OF THESE SYMBOLS,
SEE THE INSIDE FRONT AND BACK COVERS OF THIS BOOK.

Needs: Romance (historical, contemporary, humorous, paranormal, gothic, suspense/mystery), thriller suspense, mystery, young adult. No science fiction, children's, general nonfiction, short stories, poetry. Recently published *Hunter's Song*, by Natalie Damschroder (romance); *When the Lilacs Bloom*, by Linda Colwell (romance); and *Electronic Publishing: The Definitive Guide*, by Karen Weisner (nonfiction instructional).

How to Contact: Query with synopsis and one sample chapter (send as e-mail attachment). Accepts queries by e-mail at subs@avidpress.com. Include brief author bio.

Terms: Pays royalty. Guidelines on website or for SASE.

Advice: "There are no 'rules' for being published by Avid Press; instead, we are looking for manuscripts that are written from the heart-books the author would want to read-not books that follow a specific guideline or formula. We are looking for entertaining stories and compelling characters."

◐ **A** **BANCROFT PRESS**, P.O. Box 65360, Baltimore MD 21209. (410)358-0658. Fax: (410)764-1967. E-mail: bruceb@bancroftpress.com. Website: www.bancroftpress.com (includes booklist, guidelines and mission statement). **Contact:** Bruce Bortz, editor. Estab. 1991. "Small independent press publishing literary and commercial fiction, often by journalists." Publishes hardcover and paperback originals. First novel print order: 5,000-7,500. **Published 2 new writers within the last year.** Averages 4-6 total titles, 2-4 fiction titles/year.
- *The Re-Appearance of Sam Webber*, by Scott Fuqua is an ALEX Award winner.

Needs: Ethnic/multicultural (general), family saga, feminist, gay, glitz, historical, humor/satire, lesbian, literary, mainstream, military/war, mystery/suspense (amateur sleuth, cozy, police procedural, private eye/hardboiled), New Age/mystic, regional, science fiction (hard science/technological, soft/sociological), thriller/espionage, translations, western (frontier saga, traditional), young adult/teen (historical, problem novels, series). Published *Those Who Trespass*, by Bill O'Reilly (thriller); *The Re-Appearance of Sam Webber*, by Scott Fuqua (literary); and *Malicious Intent*, by Mike Walker (Hollywood).

How to Contact: Accepts unsolicited mss. Query with outline/synopsis and 3 sample chapters. Accepts queries by e-mail and fax. Include bio and list of publishing credits. Send SASE for reply, return of ms or send a disposable copy of ms. Agented fiction 100%. Responds in 6 months. Accepts simultaneous submissions. Sometimes comments on rejected mss.

Terms: Pays royalties of 6-8%. Average advance: $750. Sends galleys to author. Publishes ms 18 months after acceptance.

Advice: "Be patient, send a sample, know your book's audience."

N ◎ **BARDSONG PRESS**, P.O.Box 775396, Steamboat Springs CO 80477. (970)870-1401. Fax: (970)879-2657. E-mail: celts@bardsongpress.com. Website: www.bardsongpress.com (includes book catalog, writers guidelines, contest guidelines information and articles promoting our subjects of interest). **Contact:** Ann Gilpin, editor (Celtic history/historical fiction). Estab. 1997. "Small independent press which specializes in historical novels and poetry with Celtic themes." Publishes hardcover originals and paperback reprints. Averages 1-2 total titles/year. Member, PMA, SPAN, CIPA.

Needs: Historical (Celtic). Recently published *In the Shadow of Dragons*, by Kathleen Cunningham Guler (historical fiction). Publishes the Macsen's Treasure Series.

How to Contact: Does not accept unsolicited mss; will return if SASE provided. Query with outline/synopsis. Accepts e-mail queries. Include a brief bio and a list of publishing credits with submission. Writers should send SASE or IRC for return of the ms. Agented fiction: 50%. Responds to queries in 2 months; to mss in 4 months. Considers simultaneous and disk submissions. No e-mail submissions. Sometimes comments on rejected mss.

Terms: Payment varies. Sends galleys to author. Time between acceptance and publication is 18 months. Writer's guidelines for SASE or on website. Book catalogs on website or available for SASE (envelope size: 6×9; postage or IRCs' 55¢).

Advice: "We are looking for work that reflects the ageless culture, history, symbolism, mythology and spirituality that belongs to Celtic heritage. Settings can range from ancient times to early twentieth century and include the earliest European territories, the current nations of Wales, Scotland, Ireland, Cornwall, Isle of Man, Brittany and Galicia, as well as lands involved in the Celtic Diaspora."

⊘ **BENEATH THE UNDERGROUND**, 132 Woodycrest Dr., East Hartford CT 06118. (860)569-3101. E-mail: vfrazer@home.com. **Contact:** Vernon Frazer, editor. Estab. 1998. One-person operation specializing in cutting-edge poetry and fiction. Publishes paperback originals. Books: 60 lb. paper; offset printing; perfect binding. Average print order: 300. First novel print order: 500. Averages 2 total titles, 1 fiction title/year. Distributes titles through Ingram Book Company and Baker & Taylor.

Needs: Experimental, literary, short story collections, avant-pop, magic realism. Recently published *Stay Tuned to This Channel*, by Vernon Frazer (avant-pop).

How to Contact: Does not accept unsolicited mss. Self-publisher.

Advice: "Start your own press. Preserve your independence."

BILINGUAL PRESS/EDITORIAL BILINGÜE, Hispanic Research Center, Arizona State University, Tempe AZ 85287-2702. (480)965-3867. **Contact:** Gary Keller, editor. Estab. 1973. "University affiliated." Publishes hardcover and paperback originals and reprints. Books: 60 lb. acid-free paper; single sheet or web press printing; case-bound and perfect-bound; illustrations sometimes. Average print order: 4,000 copies (1,000 case-bound, 3,000 soft cover). **Published new writers within the last year.** Averages 8 total titles, 5 fiction titles/year.

Needs: Ethnic, literary, short story collections, translations. "We are always on the lookout for Chicano, Puerto Rican, Cuban-American or other U.S.-Hispanic themes with strong and serious literary qualities and distinctive and intellectually important themes. We have been receiving a lot of fiction set in Latin America (usually Mexico or Central America) where the main character is either an ingenue to the culture or a spy, adventurer or mercenary. We don't publish this sort of 'Look, I'm in an exotic land' type of thing. Also, novels about the Aztecs or other pre-Columbians are very iffy." Recently published *Barefoot Hear: Stories of a Migrant Child*, by Elva Treviño Hart (memoir); and *The Pearl of the Antilles*, by Andrea O'Reilly Herrera (novel).

How to Contact: Does not accept unsolicited mss. Send query letter with SASE or IRC for reply. Responds in 3 weeks to queries; 2 months to mss. Accepts simultaneous submissions. Sometimes comments on rejected mss.

Terms: Pays royalties of 10%. Average advance: $500. Provides 10 author's copies. Sends galleys to author. Publishes ms 1 year after acceptance. Writer's guidelines available. Book catalog free.

Advice: "Writers should take the utmost care in assuring that their manuscripts are clean, grammatically impeccable, and have perfect spelling. This is true not only of the English but the Spanish as well. All accent marks need to be in place as well as other diacritical marks. When these are missing it's an immediate first indication that the author does not really know Hispanic culture and is not equipped to write about it. We are interested in publishing creative literature that treats the U.S.-Hispanic experience in a distinctive, creative, revealing way. The kinds of books that we publish we keep in print for a very long time irrespective of sales. We are busy establishing and preserving a U.S.-Hispanic canon of creative literature."

BIRCH BROOK PRESS, P.O. Box 81, Delhi NY 13753. Email: birchbrkpr@prodigy.net. Website: www.birchbrookpress.com (includes listings of recent titles, info about our antique letterpress methods of books, and comments by media). **Contact:** Tom Tolnay, publisher. "BBP's books are unusual in that we publish/print them in letterpress antique style edtitions, printed from metal type cast and printed in our own shop." Books: 70-80 lb. Mohawk vellum; antique letterpress; illustrations. Averages 2-4 fiction titles/year. Member, Small Press Center of American Poets Academy.

Needs: Literary, regional (Adirondacks), translation (literary only), special interest (fly-fishing, baseball). Recently published Ray Bradbury, Warren Carrier and Frank Fagan.

How to Contact: Query with sample. Send SASE (or IRC) for return of ms or disposable copy of ms and #10 SASE for reply only. Agented fiction 5%. Responds in 6 weeks to queries; 2 months to mss. Accepts simultaneous submissions if indicated. Typed mss only. Sometimes comments on rejected mss.

Terms: Payment varies according to project and 1 author's copy. Writer's guidelines for SASE.

Advice: "We look for the best quality we can find, in areas of our special interests: literary fiction, fly-fishing, baseball, the outdoors, books about books. Mostly BBP specializes in anthologies of short works by various authors."

BOOKS FOR ALL TIMES, INC., Box 2, Alexandria VA 22313. Website: www.bfat.com. **Contact:** Joe David, publisher/editor. Estab. 1981. One-man operation. Publishes paperback originals. Will be testing print-on-demand. Has published 3 fiction titles to date.

Needs: Contemporary, literary, short story collections. "No novels at the moment; hopeful, though, of publishing a collection of quality short stories. No popular fiction or material easily published by the major or minor houses specializing in mindless entertainment. Only interested in stories of the Victor Hugo or Sinclair Lewis quality."

How to Contact: Send query letter with SASE. Responds in 1 month to queries. Occasionally comments on rejected mss.

Terms: Pays negotiable advance. "Publishing/payment arrangement will depend on plans for the book." Book catalog free with SASE.

Advice: Interested in "controversial, honest stories which satisfy the reader's curiosity to know. Read Victor Hugo, Fyodor Dostoyevsky and Sinclair Lewis for an example."

BOSON BOOKS, C&M Online Media, Inc., 3905 Meadow Field Lane, Raleigh NC 27606. (919)233-8164. Fax: (919)233-8578. E-mail: cm@cmonline.com. Website: www.cmonline.com. (All books may be purchased through the website. It is a sales site). **Contact:** Acquisitions Editor. Estab. 1994. "We are an online book company with distribution at our website and through ten separate distributors such as CyberRead.com, powells.com, ebooks.com, mobipocket.com and barnesandnoble.com. Publishes online originals and reprints. **Published 6 new writers within the last year.** Plans 15 first novels in 2002. Averages 12 total titles, 9 fiction titles/year. Member, Association of Online Publishers.

Needs: "The quality of the writing is our only consideration." Publishes ongoing series of Holocaust narratives by eyewitnesses.

How to Contact: Does not accept or return unsolicited mss. Query with synopsis and 2 sample chapters. Accepts queries by e-mail. Electronic submissions only.

Terms: Pays royalties of 25%. Sends galleys to author. Writer's guidelines and book catalog on website.

Advice: "We want to see only excellence in writing."

CALYX BOOKS, P.O. Box B, Corvallis OR 97339-0539. (503)753-9384. Fax: (541)753-0515. E-mail: calyx@proaxis.com. **Contact:** M. Donnelly, director; Micki Reaman, managing editor. Estab. 1986. "Calyx exists to publish women's literary and artistic work and is committed to publishing the works of all women, including women of color, older women, lesbians, working-class women, and other voices that need to be heard." Publishes hardcover and paperback originals. Books: offset printing; paper and cloth binding. Average print order: 4,000-10,000 copies. First novel print order: 4,000-5,000. **Published 1 new writer within the last year.** Averages 3 total titles/year. Distributes titles through Consortium Book Sales and Distribution. Promotes titles through author reading tours, print advertising (trade and individuals), galley and review copy mailings, presence at trade shows, etc.

• Past anthologies include *Forbidden Stitch: An Asian American Women's Anthology*; *Women and Aging*; *Present Tense: Writing and Art by Young Women*; and *A Line of Cutting Women*.

Needs: Contemporary, ethnic, experimental, feminist, lesbian, literary, short story collections, translations. Published *Into the Forest*, by Jean Hegland (women's literature); *Undertow*, by Amy Schutzer (lesbian literature); and *The End of the Class Wars*, by Catherine Brady (short stories).

How to Contact: Send SASE for submission guidelines. Accepts requests by e-mail.

Terms: Pays royalties of 10% minimum, author's copies (depends on grant/award money). Average advance: $200-500. Sends galleys to author. Publishes ms 2 years after acceptance. Writer's guidelines for #10 SASE. Book catalog free on request.

Advice: "We are closed for book submissions until further notice."

CAROLINA WREN PRESS, INC./LOLLIPOP POWER BOOKS, 120 Morris St., Durham NC 27701. (919)560-2738. Fax: (919)560-2759. E-mail: carolinawrenpress@compuserve.com. Website: www.carolinawren press.org. **Contact:** Cherryl Floyd-Miller and Sonja Stone, editors (Carolina Wren Press, contest specific)l Jaqueline Ogburn, editor (Lollipop Power Books, non-stereotypical children's literature). Estab. 1976. "Small, one person, part-time, nonprofit. We depend on grants to operate. We cater to new writers who have been historically under-represented, especially women, people of color, minorities, etc." Publishes paperback originals. Books: 6×9 paper; typeset; various bindings; illustrations. Average print order: 1,500. First novel print order: 1,500. **Published 1 new writer within the last year.** Averages 2 total titles, 1 fiction title/year. Member, SPD. Distributes titles through Amazon.com, Barnes & Noble, Borders, Ingram and Baker & Taylor.

Needs: Children's/juvenile (non-stereotypical), ethnic/multicultural, experimental (poetry), feminist, gay, lesbian, literary, short story collections. Recently published *Letters Lost & Found*, by Elaine Goolsly; *Succory*, by Andrea Selch; and *Gold Indigoes*, by George Elliott Clarke.

How to Contact: Does not accept unsolicited mss; will return if supplied with postage. Send query letter. Accepts queries by e-mail, fax and phone. Include brief bio. Send SASE or IRC for return of ms. Agented fiction "only one of 40" submissions. Responds in 3 months to queries; 6 months to mss.

Terms: Pays in author's copies (10% of print run) and 50% off list price for additional copies. Sends galleys to author. Publishes ms 6 months after acceptance.

Advice: "Please do not submit unless in response to advertised call on specific topic. Workshop your manuscript before submitting."

CATBIRD PRESS, 16 Windsor Rd., North Haven CT 06473-3015. E-mail: catbird@pipeline.com. Website: www.catbirdpress.com (includes writer's guidelines, full book catalog, reviews and excerpts). **Contact:** Robert Wechsler. Estab. 1987. "Catbird is only looking for writers who are deeply interested in prose style and have a great deal of knowledge of stylistic alternatives. We are not interested in plot-and-character-oriented naturalistic fiction, or any sort of genre fiction, but in more creative and imaginative approaches to reality. Most of our fiction has a comic (although often darkly comic)vision, but is not comic in the sense of wacky characters, plots, and writing, or satirical attacks on contemporary society as a whole." Publishes hardcover and paperback originals. Books: acid-free paper; offset printing; some illustrations. Average print order, 2,500. Average first novel print order 2,000.

Needs: Literary translations. Recently published *All His Sons*, by Frederic Raphael (literary); *Labor Day*, by Floyd Kemske (literary); *Living Parallel*, by Alexander Kliment (literary).

How to Contact: Accepts unsolicited mss. Query with outline/synopsis and 1 sample chapter. Include estimated word count, brief bio, and list of publishing credits. Agented fiction: 20%. Responds to queries in 1 week; to mss in 1 month. Considers simultaneous submissions; no electronic or disk submissions. Rarely comments on rejected mss.

Terms: Pays royalties of 7-10%. Average advance is $2,000. Provides author's copies. Sends galleys to author. Time between acceptance and publication varies widely, from 6-24 months. Writer's guidelines for SASE, on website; book catalogs free upon request.

Advice: "Because more first-rate writers are being dropped by big houses, the quality of what we see has gone up and we look for more quality in the work of new authors."

✓ ◎ **CAVE BOOKS**, 756 Harvard Ave., St. Louis MO 63130. (314)862-7646. E-mail: rawatson@artsci.wustl.edu. Website: www.cavebooks.com. **Contact:** Richard Watson, editor. Estab. 1985. Small press devoted to books on caves, karst and speleology. Fiction: novels about cave exploration only. Publishes hardcover and paperback originals and reprints. Books: acid free paper; offset printing. Average print order: 1,500. **Published 2 new writers within the last year.** Averages 4 total titles, 0.2 fiction titles/year.

Needs: Adventure, caves, karst, speleology. Recently published *Emergence*, by Marian McConnell (novel).

How to Contact: Accepts unsolicited mss. Send query letter. Accepts queries by e-mail. Send SASE or IRC for return of ms or send disposable copy of ms and SASE for reply only. Responds in 2 weeks to queries; 2 months to mss. Accepts simultaneous submissions. Sometimes comments on rejected mss.

Terms: Pays royalties of 10%. Sends galleys to author. Publishes ms 18 months after acceptance.

Advice: "In the last three years we have received only three novels about caves, and we have published one of them. We get dozens of inappropriate submissions."

🌐 **CHRISTCHURCH PUBLISHERS LTD.**, 2 Caversham St., London SW3 4AH United Kingdom. Fax: 0044 171 351 4995. **Contact:** James Hughes, fiction editor. Averages 25 fiction titles/year. Length: 30,000 words minimum.

Needs: "Miscellaneous fiction, also poetry. More 'literary' style of fiction, but also thrillers, crime fiction etc."

How to Contact: Query with synopsis ("*brief* synopsis favored"), or letter.

Terms: Pays royalties and advance. "We have contacts and agents worldwide."

[N] ⚓ **CONFLUENCE PRESS INC.**, 500 Eighth Ave., Lewis-Clark State College, Lewiston ID 83501. (208)792-2336. **Contact:** James R. Hepworth, fiction editor. Estab. 1976. Small trade publisher. Publishes hardcover and paperback originals and reprints. Books: 60 lb. paper; photo offset printing; Smyth-sewn binding. Average print order: 1,500-5,000 copies. Published new writers within the last year. Averages 3-5 total titles each year. Distributes titles through Midpoint Trade Books.

Imprint(s): James R. Hepworth Books and Blue Moon Press.

● Books published by Confluence Press have received The Idaho Book Award, Western States Book Awards and awards from the Pacific Northwest Booksellers Association.

Needs: Contemporary, literary, mainstream, short story collections, translations. "Our needs favor serious fiction, 1 fiction collection a year, with preference going to work set in the contemporary western United States." Published *Cheerleaders From Gomorrah*, by John Rember; and *Gifts and Other Stories*, by Charlotte Holmes

How to Contact: Query first. SASE for query and ms. Agented fiction 50%. Responds in 2 months to queries and mss. Accepts simultaneous submissions. *Critiques rejected mss for $25/hour.*

Terms: Pays royalties of 10%. Advance is negotiable. Provides 10 author's copies; payment depends on grant/award money. Sends galleys to author. Book catalog for 6×9 SASE.

Advice: "We are very interested in seeing first novels from promising writers who wish to break into serious print. We are also particularly keen to publish the best short story writers we can find. We are also interested in finding volume editors for our American authors series. Prospective editors should send proposals."

✓ ◯ ◎ ⚓ **CROSS-CULTURAL COMMUNICATIONS**, 239 Wynsum Ave., Merrick NY 11566-4725. (516)868-5635. Fax: (516)379-1901. E-mail: cccpoetry@aol.com. **Contact:** Stanley H. Barkan, editorial director. Estab. 1971. "Small/alternative literary arts publisher focusing on the traditionally neglected languages and cultures in bilingual and multimedia format." Publishes chapbooks, magazines, anthologies, novels, audio cassettes (talking books) and video cassettes (video books, video mags); hardcover and paperback originals. Publishes new women writers series, Holocaust series, Israeli writers series, Dutch writers series, Asian-, African- and Italian-American heritage writers series, Polish writers series, Armenian writers series, Native American writers series, Latin American writers series.

● Authors published by this press have received international awards including Nat Scammacca, who won the National Poetry Prize of Italy and Gabriel Preil, who won the Bialik Prize of Israel.

Needs: Contemporary, literary, experimental, ethnic, humor/satire, juvenile and young adult folktales, and translations. "Main interests: bilingual short stories and children's folktales, parts of novels of authors of other cultures, translations; some American fiction. No fiction that is not directed toward other cultures. For an annual anthology of authors writing in other languages (primarily), we will be seeking very short stories with original-language copy (other than Latin, script should be print quality 10/12) on good paper. Title: *Cross-Cultural Review Anthology: International Fiction 1*. We expect to extend our *CCR* series to include 10 fiction issues: *Five Contemporary* (Dutch, Swedish, Yiddish, Norwegian, Danish, Sicilian, Greek, Israeli, etc.) *Fiction Writers.*" Published *Sicilian Origin of the Odyssey*, by L.G. Pocock (bilingual English-Italian translation by Nat Scammacca); *Sikano L'Americano!* and *Bye Bye America*, by Nat Scammacca; and *Milkrun*, by Robert J. Gress.

How to Contact: Accepts unsolicited mss. Query with SAE with $1 postage to include book catalog. "Note: Original language ms should accompany translations." Accepts simultaneous submissions. Responds in 1 month.

Terms: Pays "sometimes" 10-25% in royalties and "occasionally" by outright purchase, in author's copies—"10% of run for chapbook series," and "by arrangement for other publications." No advance.

Advice: "Write because you want to or you must; satisfy yourself. If you've done the best you can, then you've succeeded. You will find a publisher and an audience eventually. Generally, we have a greater interest in nonfiction, novels and translations. Short stories and excerpts from novels written in one of the traditional neglected languages are preferred—with the original version (i.e., bilingual). Our kinderbook series will soon be in production with a similar bilingual emphasis, especially for folktales, fairy tales, and fables."

DARKTALES PUBLICATIONS, P.O. Box 675, Grandview MO 64030. Phone/fax: (816)965-0514. E-mail: dave@darktales.com. Website: www.darktales.com (includes an entire Web community for horror writers and fans—horror discussion listserve, webring, chatroom, fiction bulletin boards, book catalog, and more). **Contact:** David Nordhaus, CFO/editor (extreme, horror); Keith Herber, editor (horror, "Lovecraftian"). Estab. 1998. Small independent publisher. "Our publishing focus is on horror, from extreme to esoteric. We hope to add some truly wonderful new titles to the body of horror. What makes us unique is that so many of the authors we are working with are new names to the horror scene. We hope to make them succeed, or at least help them on their way." Publishes paperback originals. Books: trade paper; Perma-bound. Average print order: 200-500. **Published 8 new writers within the last year.** Plans 5 first novels in 2002. Plans 15 total titles, all fiction, this year. Member, Horror Writers Association. Distributes titles through Ingram, Diamond Books and others. Promotes titles through print, radio and Internet ads.

● Seven nominations for Bram Stoker Awards, one nomination for Great Lakes Book Awards. Also, the press won the 'Excellence in Publishing' award for 2000 from *Jobs in Hell*.

Needs: Erotic horror, horror (dark fantasy, futuristic, psychological, supernatural, extreme). "We are also considering concepts for dark fantasy/horror role-playing game companions or originals." Publishes *The Asylum* horror anthology series; writers may submit to Victor Heck, editor (see website for details). Recently published *Dial Your Dreams*, by Robert Weinberg (horror); *Cold Comfort*, by Nancy Kilpatrick; and *Six Inch Spikes*, by Edo Van Belkom (erotic horror).

How to Contact: Does not accept unsolicited mss. Query with outline/synopsis and 2-3 sample chapters. Accepts queries by e-mail. Include estimated word count, brief bio and list of publishing credits. Send a disposable copy of ms and SASE for reply only. Agented fiction 20%. Responds in 1 month to queries; 4 months to mss. Accepts simultaneous and electronic submissions and disk. Often comments on rejected mss.

Terms: Pays royalties of 6-8%. Average advance: $100. Sends galleys to author as an electronic typeset version in PDF format. Publishes ms within 2 years of acceptance. Writer's guidelines and book catalog on website.

Advice: "We are the first horror independent press to effectively integrate print-on-demand technology, thus enabling us to publish more books with lower risk than traditional offset publishers. Plus our book quality is second to none. Please follow our submission guidelines. Always query first. We publish only horror and dark erotica. Anything else and we won't be interested."

THE DESIGN IMAGE GROUP INC., 231 S. Frontage Rd., Suite 17, Burr Ridge IL 60527. (630)789-8991. Fax: (630)789-9013. E-mail: dig@designimagegroup.com. Website: www.designimagegroup.com (includes book catalog and links). **Contact:** Editorial Committee. Estab. 1998. "Horror and mystery fiction micropublisher distributing exclusively through normal trade channels." Publishes paperback originals. Books: offset paper; offset printing; perfect binding. Average print order: 3,000. First novel print order: 3,000. **Published 1 new writer within the last year.** Averages 3-6 total titles, 3-6 fiction titles/year. Member, HWA, MWA, PMA. Distributes titles through Ingram, Baker & Taylor and Brodart.

Needs: Horror, supernatural. Looking for "traditional supernatural horror fiction." Publishes horror anthology. Guidelines announced in writers' and genre publications in advance. Recently published *The Big Switch*, by Jack Bludis (first fiction, novel); *Martyrs*, by Edo van Belkom (horror); and *Doomed to Repeat It*, by P.G.L. Goldberg (first fiction, horror).

How to Contact: Accepts unsolicited mss. Send query letter or query with synopsis and 3 sample chapters. Send SASE or IRC for return of ms or send a disposable copy of the ms and SASE for reply only. Agented fiction 15%. Responds in 4 months to queries and mss. Accepts simultaneous submissions. Often comments on rejected mss.

Terms: Pays royalties of 10-15% against advance or 30% royalty without advance on wholesale price, not cover. Sends galleys to author. Publishes ms 3-6 months after acceptance. Writer's guidelines for SASE. Book catalog for 9×12 SASE or see website.

Advice: "We publish traditional supernatural horror (vampires, ghosts, werewolves, witches, etc.) and neo-noir dark mysteries. Please send for writers guidelines, they're quite specific and helpful."

✓ ⃠ ◎ DOWN THERE PRESS, Subsidiary of Open Enterprises Cooperative, Inc., 938 Howard St., #101, San Francisco CA 94103. Fax: (415)974-8989. E-mail: downtherepress@excite.com. Website: www.goodvibes.com/dtp/dtp.html (includes titles, author bios, excerpts, guidelines, calls for submissions). **Contact:** Leigh Davidson, managing editor. Estab. 1975. Small independent press with part-time staff; part of a large worker-owned cooperative. Publishes paperback originals. Books: Web offset printing; perfect binding; some illustrations. Average print order: 5,000. First novel print order: 3,000-5,000. **Published new writers within the last year.** Averages 1-2 total titles, 1 fiction title each year. Member, Publishers Marketing Association and Northern California Book Publicity and Marketing Association.

Imprint(s): Yes Press, Red Alder Books and Passion Press.

Needs: Erotica, feminist. Published *Herotica 6*, edited by Marcy Sheiner (anthology); *Sex Spoken Here: Erotic Reading Circle Stories*, edited by Carol Queen and Jack Davis (anthology); and *Sex Toy Tales*, edited by A. Semans and Cathy Winks.

How to Contact: Accepts unsolicited mss. Submit partial ms with cover letter, synopsis and table of contents (short stories for anthologies only). Accepts queries and correspondence by fax. Include estimated word count. Send SASE or IRC for return of ms or send disposable copy of ms and SASE for reply only. Responds in up to 9 months to mss. Accepts simultaneous submissions. Sometimes comments on rejected mss.

Terms: Pays royalties and author's copies. Sends galleys to author. Publishes ms 18 months after acceptance. Writer's guidelines and book catalog for #10 SASE.

Ⓝ ❧ ⃠ ◎ DREAMCATCHER PUBLISHING INC., One Market Square, Suite 306 Dockside, St. John, New Brunswick E2L 4Z6 Canada. (506)632-4008. Fax: (506)632-4009. E-mail: dcpub@fundy.net. Website: www.dreamcatcher.nb.ca. **Contact:** Yvonne Wilson, editor-in-chief (trade books: novels, occasional collections of short stories); Joan Allison (children's). Estab. 1998. "Dreamcatcher Publishing Inc. is small, independent and literary. We look for, but are not limited to, the work of writers from eastern Canada." Publishes paperback originals. Books: comutell coated paper; web printing; perfect binding; illustrations by artists with BFA. Average print order: 2-3,000; first novel print order: 1,000. **Published 2 new writers within the last year.** Plans 1-2 first novels in 2002. Averages 4 total titles, 3 fiction titles/year. Distributes titles through General Distributing (Toronto).

Needs: Adventure, children's/juvenile, humor/satire, literary, mainstream, regional (Atlantic Canada), romance (contemporary), science fiction (soft/sociological), short story collections, young adult/teen (adventure, fantasy/science fiction, mystery/suspense, problem novels). Recently published *Red Dragon Square*, by Yvonne Wilson (literary); *The Making of Harry Cossaboom*, by Jerrod Edson (black humor); and *Are You There Moriarty*, by Bea Beveridge (children).

How to Contact: Send query letter. Accepts queries by e-mail, fax and phone. Include estimated word count, brief bio and list of publishing credits. Send SASE or IRC for return of ms; or disposable copy of ms and SASE for reply only. Responds in 2 weeks to queries; 2 months to mss. Often critiques or comments on rejected mss.

Terms: Pays royalties of 7-12%. Sends galleys to author. Publishes ms 1-2 years after acceptance. Writer's guidelines on website. Book catalogs on website.

Advice: "Be businesslike. Phone first, but not till you have a well prepared manuscript ready to show us. Our interests in fiction are eclectic, but we may say no. Never ask if we will look at an unfinished manuscript to see if it is worth finishing. Spelling and punctuation count."

Ⓝ ❧ ◎ EDGE SCIENCE FICTION & FANTASY PUBLISHING, P.O. Box 1714, Calgary, Alberta T2P 2L7 Canada. (403)254-0160. Fax: (403)254-0456. E-mail: editor@edgewebsite.com. Website: www.edgewebsite.com (includes writer's guidelines, author bios, company background, books available, sales/order pages). **Contact:** Jackie Arnold, editor (science fiction/fantasy). Estab. 1996. "We are a small independent publisher of science fiction and fantasy novels in hard cover or trade paperback format. We produce high-quality books with lots of attention to detail and lots of marketing effort." Publishes hardcover originals and trade paperback originals. Books: natural offset paper; offset/web printing; HC/perfect binding; b&w illustration only. Average print order: 2,000-3,000. First novel print order: 2,000. Plans 2 first novels in 2002. Averages 4-6 total titles. Member of Books Publishers Association of Alberta (BPAA), Independent Publishers Association of Canada (IPAC), Publisher's Marketing Association (PMA).

Imprints: Edge, Alien Vistas, Riverbend.

Needs: Fantasy (space fantasy, sword and sorcery), science fiction (hard science/technological, soft/sociological). Recently published *The Black Chalice*, by Marie Jakober (fantasy); and *Lysicarian: The Song of the Wind*, by Janice A. Callum (fantasy).

How to Contact: Accepts unsolicited mss. Query with outline/synopsis and 3 sample chapters. Include estimated word count and list of publishing credits. Send SASE (Canadian postage please) or IRC for rereturn of the ms; disposable copy of the ms plus SASE for reply only. Responds in 2 months to queries; 4 months to mss. Accepts simultaneous submissions. Rarely comments on rejected mss.

Responds in 3 months to queries, 5 months to mss. Accepts simultaneous submissions.

Terms: Pays royalties of 8-10%. Average advance: negotiable. Sends galleys to author. Publishes ms 2-3 years after acceptance. Writer's guidelines for SASE and on website.

Advice: "Send us your best polished manuscript. Use proper manuscript format. Take the time to get a critique from someone who can offer you useful advice before you submit. Join a critique group or writing group (check online if there are no local ones)."

FP HENDRIKS PUBLISHING LTD., 4806-53 St., Stettler, Alberta T0C 2L2 Canada. Phone/fax: (403)742-6483. E-mail: editor@fphendriks.com. Website: www.fphendriks.com. **Contact:** Faye Boer, managing editor. Estab. 1994. "Small independent publisher. Will begin publishing fiction in fall 2000. Noted for personal contact with authors." Publishes paperback originals. **Published 2 new writers within the last year.** Averages 2-4 total titles, 1-2 fiction titles/year. Member, Book Publishers Association of Alberta. Distributes titles through Fitzhenry & Whiteside. Distributes titles through catalogs, sales reps and distributor catalog.

• *From Your Child's Teacher* won the 1999 *Parent's Guide* Honor Award.

Needs: Young adult/teen (adventure, easy-to-read, fantasy/science fiction, historical, horror, mystery/suspense, romance, sports, western). Needs "young adult fiction in most genres."

How to Contact: Accepts unsolicited mss. Query with outline/synopsis and 2-3 sample chapters. Accepts queries by e-mail. Include estimated word count, brief bio and list of publishing credits. Send SASE or IRC for return of ms or send disposable copy of ms and SASE for reply only. Responds in 4 months to queries; up to 6 months to mss. Accepts simultaneous submissions, electronic submissions and disk (depending on format).

Terms: Pays royalties of 10%. Sends galleys to author. Publishes ms 1 year after acceptance. Writer's guidelines free for 3×8 SAE and 47¢ postage (Canadian) or IRC or visit website. Book catalog for 9×12 SAE and $1.55 postage (Canadian).

Advice: "Attend always to audience."

GASLIGHT PUBLICATIONS, Empire Publishing Services, P.O. Box 1344, Studio City CA 91614-0344. (818)784-8918. **Contact:** Simon Waters, fiction editor (Sherlock Holmes only). Estab. 1960. Publishes hardcover and paperback originals and reprints. Books: paper varies; offset printing; binding varies; illustrations. Average print order: 5,000. First novel print order: 5,000. **Published 1 new writer within the last year.** Averages 4-12 total titles, 2-4 fiction titles/year. Promotes titles through sales reps, trade, library, etc.

Needs: Sherlock Holmes only. Recently published *On the Scent with Sherlock Holmes*, by Walter Shepherd; *Sherlock Holmes, The Complete Bagel Street Saga*, by Robert L. Fish; and *Subcutaneously, My Dear Watson*, by Jack Tracy (all Sherlock Holmes). Publishes the Sherlock Holmes Mysteries series.

How to Contact: Accepts unsolicited mss. Send query letter. Include estimated word count, brief bio and list of publishing credits. Send SASE or IRC for return of ms or send disposable copy of the ms and SASE for reply only. Agented fiction 10%. Responds in 2 weeks to queries; up to 1 year to mss.

Terms: Pays royaltiesof 8-10%. (Royalty and advances dependant on the material.) Sends prepublication galleys to author. Publishes ms 1-6 months after acceptance. Writer's guidelines for SASE. Book catalog for 9×12 SAE and $2 postage.

Advice: "Please send only Sherlock Holmes material. Other stuff just wastes time and money."

THE GLENCANNON PRESS, P.O. Box 633, Benicia CA 94510. (707)745-3933. Fax: (707)747-0311. E-mail: captjaff@pacbell.net. Website: www.glencannon.com (includes book catalog). **Contact:** Bill Harris (maritime, maritime children's). Estab. 1993. "We publish quality books about ships and the sea." Publishes hardcover and paperback originals and hardcover reprints. Books: Smyth; perfect binding; illustrations. Average print order: 1,000. First novel print order: 750. **Published 1 new writer within the last year.** Averages 4-5 total titles, 1 fiction title/year. Member, PMA. Distributes titles through Ingram and Baker & Taylor. Promotes titles through direct mail, magazine advertising and word of mouth.

Imprint(s): Palo Alto Books (any except maritime); Glencannon Press (merchant marine); Bill Harris, editor.

Needs: Adventure, children's/juvenile (adventure, fantasy, historical, mystery, preschool/picture book), ethnic/multicultural (general), historical (maritime), humor/satire, mainstream, military/war, mystery/suspense, thriller/espionage, western (frontier saga, traditional maritime), young adult/teen (adventure, historical, mystery/suspense, western). Currently emphasizing children's maritime, any age. Recently published *White Hats*, by Floyd Beaver (navy short stories); and *Holy Glencannon*, by Guy Gilpatric (merchant marine short stories).

How to Contact: Accepts unsolicited mss. Submit complete ms with cover letter. Include brief bio and list of publishing credits. Send SASE or IRC for return of ms OR send disposable copy of ms and SASE for reply only. Responds in 1 month to queries; 2 months to mss. Accepts simultaneous submissions. Often comments on rejected mss.

Terms: Pays royalties of 10-20%. "Usually author receives $1-2 per copy for each book sold." Sends galleys to author. Publishes ms 6-24 months after acceptance. Book catalog free and on website.

Advice: "Write a good story in a compelling style."

✓ ◎ **GOTHIC CHAPBOOK SERIES**, Gothic Press, 1701 Lobdell Ave., No. 32, Baton Rouge LA 70806-8242. (225)925-2917. E-mail: gwriter602@aol.com. Website: www.gothicpress.com (includes information, history, links, forums and catalog). **Contact:** Gary W. Crawford, editor (horror, fiction, poetry and scholarship). Estab. 1979. "One person operation on a part-time basis. Publishes horror fiction, poetry, and scholarship and criticism." Publishes paperback originals. Books: printing or photocopying. Average print order: 150-200. Averages 1-2 total titles and fiction titles/year. Distributes titles through direct mail and book dealers.

Needs: Horror (dark fantasy, psychological, supernatural). Need novellas and short stories. Gothic Press is not always an open market. Query first before submitting anything.

How to Contact: Accepts unsolicited mss. Send query letter. Accepts queries by e-mail or phone. Include estimated word count, brief bio and list of publishing credits. Send SASE or IRC for return of ms or send disposable copy of ms and SASE for reply only. Responds in 2 weeks to queries; 4 weeks to mss. Sometimes comments on rejected ms. Pays royalties of 10%. Sends galleys to author. Writer's guidelines send SASE.

Tips: "Know gothic and horror literature well."

✓ ◑ **GREYCORE PRESS**, 2646 New Prospect Rd., Pine Bush NY 12566. (845)744-5081. Fax: (845)744-8081. Website: www.greycore.com (includes catalog, upcoming titles and contact informtion). **Contact:** Polly Lindenbaum, editor. Estab. 1999. Small independent publisher of quality fiction and nonfiction titles. Publishes hardcover originals. Books: cloth binding. Average print order: 2,000. First novel print order: 2,000. **Published 3 new writers within the last year.** Averages 3 total titles, 2 fiction titles/year. Member, Dustbooks. Distributes titles through Seven Hills.

Needs: Literary, mainstream, short story collections. Recently published *The Secret Keepers*, by Julie Mars; *Conjuring Maud*, by Philip Danze; and *The Queen of Hearts: Tales of Middle Age Passion*, by Millie Crace-Brown.

How to Contact: Does not accept unsolicited mss. Send query letter. Accepts queries by e-mail and fax. Include estimated word count and list of publishing credits. Send SASE or IRC for return of ms. Responds in weeks to queries; in months to mss. Accepts simultaneous submissions. Sometimes comments on rejected mss.

Terms: Pays royalties of 50% after production costs. Sends galleys to author. Publishes ms 18 months after acceptance.

Advice: "We prefer to get cover letters that include author credentials and the ways in which writers are willing to help publicize their work. We are very small and can't keep up with the number of manuscripts we receive. Our preference is to receive a cover letter, synopsis and the author's credentials via snail mail. We will read e-mail queries too of course, but as e-mails tend to get lost in the shuffle, our preference is snail mail, with SASE."

⊕ ✓ **HEMKUNT PRESS**, Hemkunt Publishers (P) Ltd., A-78 Naraina Industrial Area Phase-I, New Delhi India 110028. Phone: +91-11-579-5079. Fax: +91-11-611-3705. E-mail: hemkunt1@vsnl.com. Website: www.hemkuntpublishers.com (includes company profile, book jackets, prices, ISBN, brief summary). **Contact**: Arvinder Singh, director. "We specialize in children's fiction and storybooks as well as novels and short stories." Distributes titles through direct sales, direct mailings and distributors and short stories.

Needs: "We would be interested in novels and short stories, preferably by authors with a published work. Unpublished work can also be considered. Would like to have distribution rights for US, Canada and UK besides India. Charges fee depending on author profile, ms and marketability." Recently published *More Tales of Birbal & Akbar*, by Sanjana Singh.

How to Contact: Send a cover letter, brief summary, 3 sample chapters (first, last and one other chapter). Accepts queries by e-mail and fax.

Terms: Catalog on request.

Advice: "Send interesting short stories and novels pertaining to the global point of view."

◑ **HOLLOW EARTH PUBLISHING**, P.O. Box 1355, Boston MA 02205-1355. (617)249-0161. E-mail: hep2@hotmail.com. **Contact**: Helian Grimes, editor/publisher. Estab. 1983. "Small independent publisher." Publishes hardcover and paperback originals and reprints and e-books. Books: acid-free paper; offset printing; Smythe binding.

Needs: Comics/graphic novels, fantasy (sword and sorcery), feminist, gay, lesbian, literary, New Age/mystic/ spiritual, translations. Looking for "computers, Internet, Norse mythology, magic." Publishes various computer application series.

How to Contact: Does not accept unsolicited mss. Contact by e-mail only. Include estimated word count, 1-2 page bio and list of publishing credits. Agented fiction 90%. Responds in 2 months. Accepts submissions on disk.

Terms: Pays in royalties. Sends galleys to author. Publishes ms 6 months after acceptance.

Advice: Looking for "less fiction, more computer information."

◐ ◎ ▼ **ILLUMINATION PUBLISHING CO.**, P.O. Box 1865, Bellevue WA 98009-1865. (425)644-7185. Fax: (425)644-9274. E-mail: liteinfo@illumin.com. Website: www.illumin.com (includes guidelines, names of editors, book catalog and reviews). **Contact:** Ruth Thompson, editorial director. Estab. 1987. "Illumination Arts is a small publishing company publishing high quality, uplifting and inspirational children's picture books that create transformation." Publishes hardcover originals. Averages 3-4 children's picture books/year. Distributes titles through Ingram, New Leaf, De Vorss, Book People, Quality, Baker & Taylor, Koen Pacific and bookstores. Promotes titles through direct mailings, website, book shows, flyers and posters, catalogs. Publisher arranges author and illustrator signings but expects authors/illustrators to actively promote. Enters many book award events. Member, Book Publishers of the Northwest.

● Illumination Publishing's *The Little Wizard* was selected a Best Children's Book 2001 by The Coalition of Visionary Retailers. *The Right Touch* was a winner of the 1999 Ben Franklin Award (parenting).

Needs: Children's/juvenile (adventure, inspirational, preschool/picture books). Recently published *Little Square-head*, by Peggy O'Neill (children's picture book); *What If*, by Regina Williams (children's picture books); and *Cassandra's Angel*, by Gina Otto (children's picture book).

How to Contact: Accepts unsolicited mss. Query first or submit complete ms with cover letter. Include estimated word count and list of publishing credits. Send SASE or IRC for return of ms. Responds in 3 weeks to queries; 2 months to mss. Accepts simultaneous submissions. Often comments on rejected mss.

Terms: Pays royalties. Sends galleys to author. Publishes ms 18 months-2 years after acceptance. Writer's guidelines for SASE and on website.

Advice: "Submit full manuscripts, neatly typed without grammatical or spelling errors. Expect to be edited many times. Be patient. We are very *painstaking*. Read and follow the guidelines posted on our website."

◐ ◎ **IVY LEAGUE PRESS, INC.**, P.O. Box 3326, San Ramon CA 94583-8326. (925)736-0601 or 800-IVY-PRESS. Fax: (925)736-0602 or (888)IVY-PRESS. E-mail: ivyleaguepress@worldnet.att.net. **Contact:** Maria Thomas, editor. Publishes hardcover and paperback originals. Specializes in medical thrillers. Books: perfect binding. First novel print order: 5,000. Averages 2 total titles, 1-2 fiction titles/year. Distributes titles through Baker & Taylor and Ingram. Promotes titles through TV, radio and print.

Needs: Mystery/suspense(medical). Published *Allergy Shots*, by Litman.

How to Contact: Accepts unsolicited mss. Query with outline/synopsis. Include estimated word count, bio and list of publishing credits. Send SASE or IRC for return of the ms or send disposable copy of ms and SASE for reply only. Responds in 2 months to queries. Accepts electronic submissions. Always comments on rejected mss.

Terms: Royalties vary. Sends galleys to author.

Advice: "If you tell a terrific story of medical suspense, one which is hard to put down, we may publish it."

❧ ✓ ○ ◎ **JESPERSON PRESS LTD.**, 39 James Lane, St. John's, Newfoundland A1E 3H3 Canada. (709)753-0633. **Contact:** Russ Thomas, vice president. Midsize independent publisher. Publishes hardcover and paperback originals. Averages 3-4 total titles, 1-2 fiction titles/year.

Needs: Solid contemporary fiction by Newfoundland authors about Newfoundland, preferably novel-length or short story collection. Not interested in young adult, childrens' or poetry of any kind.

How to Contact: Does not accept unsolicited mss. Query with synopsis and SASE (Canadian postage or IRCs, please) only. Responds in 6 months or less. Sometimes comments on rejected mss.

Terms: Pays negotiable royalties. Sends galleys to author. Book catalog free.

[N] ◐ ▼ **ALLEN A. KNOLL, PUBLISHERS**, 200A W. Victoria St., Suite 3, Santa Barbara CA 93101-3627. (805)564-3377. Fax: (804)966-6657. E-mail: bookinfo@knollpublishers.com. Website: www.knollpublishers.com (book catalog, excerpts, interviews with authors, reading guides). Estab. 1990. "Small independent publisher, a few titles a year. Specializes in 'books for intelligent people who read for fun.'" Publishes hardcover originals. Books: offset printing; sewn binding. Titles distributed through Ingram, Baker & Taylor.

● Best Overall Fiction Book (*He's Back*) 2000 voted by *Today's Librarian*.

Needs: Recently published *What Now, King Lear?*, by Alistair Boyle (mystery); *Too Rich and Too Thin*, by David Champion (mystery); *He's Back*, by Theodore Roosevelt Gardner II (fiction/literature). Publishes the Gil Yates private investigator and Bomber Hanson Mystery series.

How to Contact: Does not accept unsolicited mss; will return mss if SASE provided.

Terms: Payment varies. Sends galleys to author. Writer's guidelines not available; book catalogs free upon request or on website.

✓ ◓ ▼ **LEAPFROG PRESS**, P.O. Box 1495, 95 Commercial St., Wellfleet MA 02667-1495. (508)349-1925. Fax: (508)349-1180. E-mail: leapfrog@c4.net. Website: www.leapfrogpress.com (includes description of press, mission statement, writer's guidelines, e-mail link, description of books, sample chapters, link to distributor, cover designs). **Contact:** David Witkowsky, acquisitions editor. Estab. 1996. "We search for beautifully written literary titles and endeavor to market them aggressively to national trade and library accounts." Publishes hardcover and paperback originals and paperback reprints. Books: acid-free paper; sewn binding. Average print order: 5,000. First novel print order: 4,000 (average). Averages 4 total titles, 3-4 fiction titles/year. Distributes titles through Consortium Book Sales and Distribution, St. Paul, MN. Promotes titles through all national review media, bookstore readings, author tours, website, radio shows, chain store promotions, advertisements. Member, Publishers Marketing Association, Bookbuilders of Boston and PEN.

● Leapfrog Press titles have been nominated for the American Library Association—Best of the Year Award and the National Book Critics Circle Award and have been finalists for the Firecracker Alternative Press Book of the Year award, New York Public Library Best of the Teenage List 2000 award and the Benjamin Franklin Award. Ruthann Robson's *Masks* was awarded *Library Journal's* Best of the Year.

Needs: "Genres often blur; we're interested in good writing. We'd love to see memoirs as well as fiction that comments on the world through the lens of personal, political or family experience." Recently published *The War at Home*, by Nora Eisenberg; *Burnt Umber*, by Sheldon Greene; and *Shadows and Elephants*, by Edward Hower.

How to Contact: Query with brief description of book and 2-4 sample chapters (40 pages). Accepts queries by e-mail. Send SASE or IRC for return of ms or send disposable copy of ms and SASE for reply only. Responds in 3 months to queries; 6 months to mss. No simultaneous submissions. "Please see website for information. Do not call the office." Sometimes comments on rejected mss.

Terms: Pays royalties of 4-8%. Offers negotiable advance. Provides negotiable number of author's copies. Sends galleys to author. Publishes ms 1-2 years after acceptance.

Advice: "Because editors have so little time, you had best send them your very best work. Editors don't have a lot of time to line edit. They love to work with you but they do not want to rewrite your book for you. In fact, if you send good material that is poorly written, they may wonder if you actually can do the revisions necessary. So don't be impatient. Send your novel only when you feel it is as good as you can make it . . . and that means knowing what's out there in the market; knowing how to create characters and a dynamite beginning and a plot that doesn't meander all over the place because you don't know where the story is going. Learn your craft."

N: LOST PROPHET PRESS, P.O. Box 583377, Minneapolis MN 55458-3377. (612)209-6689. E-mail: Revjones@Thincoyote.com. Website: http://www.thincoyote.com. **Contact:** Christopher Jones, editor. Estab. 1992. "We are a small, independent publisher of 1-3 books of short stories and poetry per year." **Published 3 new writers within the last year.** Plans 3 first novels in 2002. Averages 3 total titles, 1-3 fiction titles/year. Member, Table of Sin.

Needs: Comics/graphic novels, experimental, horror, literary, psychic/supernatural, short story collections, translations. Plans an anthology in the next year. Recently published *Grinder*, by E. Dick Jr.; and *Very Angry Essays*, by Dan Hutnyak (both short story collections).

How to Contact: Accepts unsolicited mss. Submit complete ms with cover letter. Include brief bio, Send either SASE or IRC for return of ms or send disposable copy of ms and SASE for reply only. Responds in 2 weeks to queries; 2 months to mss. Accepts simultaneous submissions. Sometimes critiques or comments on rejected mss.

Terms: Pays in author's copies (¼ run). Publishes ms 6 months after acceptance. Writer's guidelines for SASE, on website.

Advice: "We are primarily interested in short- and flash-fiction, but will consider longer works. We tend to favor the efforts of scofflaws, muleskinners, seers, witch doctors, maniacs, alchemists, giant-slayers and their ilk."

N: ⊕ THE LUTTERWORTH PRESS, P.O. Box 60, Cambridge CB1 2NT England. Fax: +44(0)1223 366951. E-mail: publishing@lutterworth.com. Website: lutterworth.com (includes catalogs, company résumé, order forms, selection of books with extra details). **Contact:** Adrian Brink, fiction editor. "Two hundred-year-old small press publishing wide range of adult nonfiction, religious and children's books."

Imprint(s): Acorn Editions.

Needs: The only fiction we publish is for children: picture books (with text from 0-10,000 words), educational, young novels, story collections. Also nonfiction as well as religious children's books." Recently published *Whoever You Are*, by S.S. Overeu (children's stores).

How to Contact: Send synopsis and sample chapter. Unsolicited queries/correspondence by e-mail and fax OK. "Send IRCs. English language is universal, i.e., mid-Atlantic English."
Terms: Pays royalty.

MID-LIST PRESS, Jackson, Hart & Leslie, Inc., 4324-12th Ave. S., Minneapolis MN 55407-3218. (612)822-3733. Fax: (612)823-8387. E-mail: guide@midlist.org. Website: www.midlist.org (includes writer's guidelines, history and mission, book catalog, ordering information and news). Associate Publisher: Marianne Nora. **Contact:** Lane Stiles, senior editor. Estab. 1989. "We are a nonprofit literary press dedicated to the survival of the mid-list, those quality titles that are being neglected by the larger commercial houses. Our focus is on first-time writers, and we are probably best known for the Mid-List Press First Series Awards." Publishes hardcover and paperback originals and reprints. Books: acid-free paper; offset printing; perfect or Smyth-sewn binding. Average print order: 2,000. **Published 2 new writers within the last year.** Plans 1 first novel in 2002. Averages 3 fiction titles/year. Distributes titles through Small Press Distribution, Ingram, Baker & Taylor, Midwest Library Service, Brodart, Follett, Bookmen and Emery Pratt. Promotes titles through publicity, direct mail, catalogs, author's events and reviews and awards.
Needs: General fiction. No children's/juvenile, romance, young adult, religious. Recently published *Plan Z, by Leslie Kove*, by Betsy Robinson (first fiction, novel); *Leaving the Neighborhood*, by Lucy Ferriss (first fiction, short fiction); and *Quick Bright Thing*, by Ron Wallace (first fiction, short fiction). Publishes First Series Award for the Novel and First Series Award for Short Fiction. *There is a $20 reading fee for a First Series Award but no charge for publication.*
How to Contact: Accepts unsolicited mss. Send query letter first. Send disposable copy of the ms and SASE for reply only. Agented fiction less than 10%. Responds in 3 weeks to queries; 3 months to mss. Accepts simultaneous submissions.
Terms: Pays royalty of 40-50% of profits. Average advance: $1,000. Sends galleys to author. Publishes ms 6-12 months after acceptance. Writer's guidelines for #10 SASE or visit website.
Advice: "Write first for guidelines or visit our website before submitting a query, proposal or manuscript. And take the time to read some of the titles we've published."

MILKWEEDS FOR YOUNG READERS, Imprint of Milkweed Editions, 1011 Washington Ave. S., Suite 300, Minneapolis MN 55415-1246. (612)332-3192. Fax: (612)215-2550. **Contact:** Emilie Buchwald, publisher; Elisabeth Fitz, first reader. Estab. 1984. "Milkweeds for Young Readers are works that embody humane values and contribute to cultural understanding." Publishes hardcover and trade paperback originals. **Published new writers within the last year.** Averages 3 total titles/year. Distributes titles through Publishers Group West. Promotes titles individually through print advertising, website and author tours.
   ● *PU-239 & Other Russian Fantasies*, by Ken Kalfus, won the Pushcart Prize. *The $66 Summer*, by John Armistead, was one of New York Public Library's 'Best Books for Teenage Readers' in 2001. *The Ocean Within*, by V.M. Caldwell, was nominated for the 'Young Hoosier Book Award' in 2001.
Needs: For ages 8-12: adventure, animal, fantasy, historical, juvenile and mainstream/contemporary. Recently published *Tides*, by V.M. Caldwell (middle-grade novel); *The $66 Summer*, by John Armistead; *Parents Wanted*, by George Harrar; *My Lord Bag of Rice*, by Carol Bly (short stories); and *Falling Dark*, by Tim Tharp (novel).
How to Contact: Submit complete ms with cover letter. Agented fiction 30%. Responds in up to 6 months to mss. Accepts simultaneous submissions.
Terms: Pays royalty of 7½% on retail price. Advance varies. Publishes ms 1 year after acceptance. Writer's guidelines for #10 SASE. Book catalog for $1.50.
Advice: "Familiarize yourself with our books before submitting. You need not have a long list of credentials—excellent work speaks for itself."

MOON MOUNTAIN PUBLISHING, 80 Peachtree Rd., N. Kingstown RI 02852-1933. (401)884-6703. Fax: (401)884-7076. E-mail: hello@moonmountainpub.com. Website: www.moonmountainpub.com (includes catalog, guidelines, contact info, news, children's activities, business-to-business custom publishing). **Contact:** Cathy Monroe, president (juvenile); Robert Holtzman, vice president (juvenile). Estab. 1999. "Small publisher of beautifully illustrated children's picture books that delight, occasionally inspire." Publishes hardcover originals. Books: non-acid paper; offset, 4-color printing. Average print order: 4,000. First novel print order: 4,000. **Published 1 new writer within the last year.** Averages 5 total titles, 5 fiction titles/year. Member, PMA, IPNE. Distributes titles through Words Distributing Co. and all major wholesalers.

VISIT THE WRITER'S MARKET WEBSITE at www.writersmarket.com for hot new markets, daily market updates, writers' guidelines and much more.

Needs: Children's/juvenile (adventure, animal, easy-to-read, fantasy, historical, preschool/picture book). Recently published *Hello Willow*, by Kimberly Poulton; *Hamlet and the Magnificient Sandcastle*, by Brian Lies; and *Petronella*, by Jay Williams.

How to Contact: Accepts unsolicited mss. Submit complete ms with cover letter. Accepts queries by e-mail. Include estimated word count. Send SASE or IRC for return of ms or send disposable copy of ms and SASE for reply only. Responds in 1 month to queries; 3 months to mss. Accepts simultaneous submissions.

Terms: Pays royalty and advance. Sends galleys to author. Publishes ms 1-2 years after acceptance. Writer's guidelines for SASE or on website. Book catalog on website.

Advice: "Let us see positive, not preachy, stories with an element of whimsy or fantasy and definitely some fun."

☑ ◎ MOUNTAIN STATE PRESS, 2300 MacCorkle Ave. SE, Charleston WV 25304-1099. (304)357-4767. Fax: (304)357-4715. E-mail: msp1@newwave.net. Website: www.mountainstatepress.com. **Contact**: Lisa Contreras, fiction editor. Estab. 1978. "A small nonprofit press run by a board of 13 members who volunteer their time. We specialize in books about West Virginia or by authors from West Virginia. We strive to give a voice to Appalachia." Publishes paperback originals and reprints. **Published new writers within the last year.** Plans 2-3 first novels in 2001. Averages 3 total titles, 1-2 fiction titles/year. Distributes titles through bookstores, distributors, gift shops and individual sales (Amazon.com and Barnes & Noble online carry our titles). Promotes titles through newspapers, radio, TV (local author series), mailings and book signings.

Needs: Family saga, historical (West Virginia), military/war, New Age/mystic/spiritual, religious. Currently compiling an anthology of West Virginia authors. Recently published *Homesick for the Hills*, by Alyce Faye Bragg (memoirs, humor); *The Well Ain't Dry Yet*, by Belinda Anderson (short story collection); and *Under the Shade of the Trees: Thomas (Stonewall) Jackson's Life at Jackson's Mill*, by Dennis Norman (historical).

How to Contact: Accepts unsolicited mss. Query with outline/synopsis and 3 sample chapters or submit complete ms with cover letter. Accepts queries by e-mail and fax. Include estimated word count and bio. Send SASE or IRC for return of ms or send disposable copy of ms with SASE for reply only. Responds in up to 6 months to mss. Accepts electronic submissions. Often comments on rejected mss.

Terms: Pays royalties.

Advice: "Topic of West Virginia is the best choice for our press. Send your manuscript in and it will be read and reviewed by the members of the Board of Mountain State Press. We give helpful suggestions and critique the writing."

[N] ◐ NEW CANAAN PUBLISHING COMPANY INC., P.O. Box 752, New Canaan CT 06840. (203)966-3408. Fax: (203)966-3408. E-mail: djm@newcanaanpublishing.com. Website: www.newcanaanpublishing.com (includes catalog, writer's guidelines, contests, help wanted, author bios, etc.). **Contact:** Kathy Mittelstadt, editor (children's/young adult); David Mittelstadt, editor (Christian content). Estab. 1995. "We are a small independent publisher of works for children and Christian content." Publishes hardcover and paperback originals. **Published 2 new writers within the last year.** Plans 1 first novels in 2002. Averages 3-4 total titles, 2-3 fiction titles/year. Member, Publishers Marketing Association. Distributes titles through Faithworks Division of National Book Network.

Needs: Children's/juvenile (historical, mystery, series), religious (children's, general, religious mystery, religious thriller), young adult/teen (adventure, historical, mystery/suspense). Recently published *Journey to the Edge of Nowhere*, by Janet Baird (children's/historical fiction); and *Rainbows and Other Promises*, by Laurie Sunwood (childrens). Publishes a children's adventure series.

How to Contact: Accepts unsolicited mss. Send query with outline/synopsis and 3 sample chapters. Submit complete ms with cover letter. Include estimated word count, brief bio and list of publishing credits. Send disposable copy of ms. Responds in 4-6 months to queries; 4-6 months to mss. Accepts simultaneous submissions, submissions and disk.

Terms: Pays royalties of 8%. Publishes ms 6-12 months after acceptance. Writer's guidelines for SASE.

Advice: "Please be patient, we are small."

◎ ▼ NEW RIVERS PRESS, 420 N. Fifth St., Suite 1180, Minneapolis MN 55401-1384. Fax: (612)339-9047. E-mail: contact@newriverspress.org. Website: www.newriverspress.org (includes guidelines, authors, all books—current and backlist, history, mission, ordering information, excerpts and events calendar). **Contact:** Eric Braun, editor. Estab. 1968. "Our mission is to publish the best writing by new writers—those at the beginnings of their careers. We publish mostly short fiction but are interested in novels as well. Many houses work with authors of note—New Rivers Press discovers those authors." Distributes titles through Consortium Book Sales and Distribution. "All books get at least 2 ads in prominent journals. We go to several conventions and book shows, do thorough direct mail campaigns and work with Consortium to promote in the most efficient ways we can."

- Honors for New Rivers Press titles include Book-of-the-Month Club Alternate Selection and finalists for Minnesota Book Awards and Foreword Book of the Year.

Needs: Contemporary, experimental, literary, translations. "No popular fantasy/romance. Nothing pious, polemical (unless other very good redeeming qualities). We are interested in only quality literature and always have been (though our concentration in the past has been poetry)." Recently published *Tilting the Continent: Southeast Asian American Writing*, edited by Shirley Geok-Lin Lim and Cheng Lol Chua; *Alone with the Owl*, by Alan Davis (short fiction); *The Record Player*, by Winifred Moranville (short fiction); *The Pact*, by Walter J. Roers (novel); and *Woman Lake*, by Richard Broderick.

How to Contact: "At this time we cannot accept unsolicited submissions. You must submit through the Minnesota Voices Project, open to residents of Minnesota, or the Headwaters Literary Contest, open to residents of the United States." (See Contests & Awards).

Terms: Minnesota Voices Project Series pays authors $1,000. Publishes ms 2 years after acceptance. Guidelines for SASE. Book catalog free.

Advice: "We read for quality, which experience has taught can be very eclectic and can come sometimes from out of nowhere. We are interested in publishing short fiction (as well as poetry and translations) because it is and has been a great indigenous American form and is almost completely ignored by the commercial houses. Find a *real* subject, something that belongs to you and not what you think or surmise that you should be doing by current standards and fads."

◎ ▼ **OUR CHILD PRESS**, P.O. Box 74, Wayne PA 19087-0074. (610)964-0606. Fax: (610)964-0938. E-mail: ocp98@aol.com. Website: www.ourchildpress.com. **Contact:** Carol Hallenbeck, CEO. Estab. 1984. Publishes hardcover and paperback originals and reprints.

- Received the Ben Franklin Award for *Don't Call Me Marda*, by Sheila Welch.

Needs: Especially interested in books on adoption or learning disabilities. Recently published *Things Little Kids Need to Know*, by Susan Uhlig.

How to Contact: Does not accept unsolicited mss. Send query letter. Responds in 2 weeks to queries; 2 months to mss. Accepts simultaneous submissions. Sometimes comments on rejected mss.

Terms: Pays royalties of 5% minimum. Publishes ms up to 6 months after acceptance. Book catalog free.

✓ ⊘ ◉ **PAPYRUS PUBLISHERS & LETTERBOX SERVICE**, P.O. Box 27383, Las Vegas NV 89126-1383. (702)256-3838. Website: www.booksbyletterbox.com. Managing Editor: Anthony Wade. Public Relations and Publicity: Erica Neubauer. **Contact:** Geoffrey Hutchison-Cleaves, editor-in-chief; Jessie Rosé, fiction editor. Estab. London 1946; USA 1982. Mid-size independent press. Publishes hardcover originals. Books: audio. Average print order 2,500. Averages 3 total titles/year. Promotes titles through mail, individual author fliers, author tours.

Imprint(s): Letterbox Service; Difficult Subjects Made Easy.

How to Contact: "Not accepting right now. Fully stocked."

Advice: "Don't send it, unless you have polished and polished and polished. Absolutely no established author sends off a piece that has just been 'written' once. That is the first draft of many!"

N ⊕ **DAVID PHILIP PUBLISHERS**, P.O. Box 23408, Claremont 7735 South Africa. Fax: (21)6743358. E-mail: russell.martin@dpp.co.za.

Needs: "Fiction with Southern African concern or focus. Progressive, often suitable for school or university prescription, literary, serious."

How to Contact: Send synopsis and 1 sample chapter.

Terms: Pays royalties. Write for guidelines.

Advice: "Familiarize yourself with list of publisher to which you wish to submit work."

✓ ⊘ ◎ ▼ **PIANO PRESS**, P.O. Box 85, Del Mar CA 92014-0085. (858)481-5650. Fax: (858)755-1104. E-mail: pianopress@aol.com. Website: www.pianopress.com (includes company description, product line, ordering information and writer's guidelines). **Contact:** Elizabeth C. Axford, M.A., editor (short stories/picture books). Estab. 1999. "Piano Press is an independent publisher. We publish books, songbooks and CDs on music-related topics, as well as some poetry." Books: medium weight paper; mimeo/offset printing; comb, saddle stitched or perfect bound; music manuscripts as illustrations. Average print order: 1,000-5,000. Averages 1-10 total titles, 3 fiction titles/year. Member, PMA, ASCAP, NARAS and MIC. Distributes titles through wholesale distribution, Baker & Taylor, The Orchard.

- Honored by San Diego Local authors in 1999 and 2000.

Needs: Children's/juvenile (preschool/picture book, music related), ethnic/multicultural (music), short story collections. "Looking for short stories on music-related topics only. Also short stories and/or essays for our annual anthology, *The Art of Music—A Collection of Writings.*" Writers may submit and/or enter annual contest. See Contests & Awards. Recently published *Merry Christmas, Happy Hanukkah—A Multilingual Songbook & CD.*

How to Contact: Accepts unsolicited mss. Send query letter. Accepts queries by e-mail. Include estimated word count, brief bio, list of publishing credits and music background. Send SASE or IRC for return of ms or send disposable copy of ms and SASE for reply only. Responds in 2 months to queries; 6 months to mss. Accepts simultaneous and electronic submissions. Sometimes comments on rejected mss.

Terms: Pays author's copies or royalties. Pay depends on grants/awards. Sends galleys to author. Publishes ms 6-18 months after acceptance. Writer's guidelines and book catalog free for #10 SAE and first-class postage.

Advice: "We feel there is a need for more original writings on music-related topics. Work should be complete, original, fresh and legible. Typewritten manuscripts only, please."

PIG IRON PRESS, 26 N. Phelps, Box 237, Youngstown OH 44501-0237. (330)747-6932. Fax: (330)747-0599. **Acquisitons:** Jim Villani, editor/publisher. Small independent publisher. Publishes hardcover originals, paperback originals and reprints. Books: 60 lb. offset paper; offset lithography; paper/casebound; illustration on cover only. Average print order: 1,000. First novel print order: 800. Averages 2 total titles, 1 fiction title/year.

Needs: Adventure, experimental, science fiction, short story collections. Published *The Harvest*, by Judith Hemschemeyer (social realism).

How to Contact: Not accepting unsolicited mss at this time.

Terms: Sends galleys to author. Book catalog for SASE.

PIPERS' ASH LTD., Church Rd., Christian Malford, Chippenham, Wiltshire SN15 4BW United Kingdom. Phone: 01249 720563. Fax: 0870 0568916. E-mail: pipersash@supamasu.com. Website: www.supamasu.com (includes catalog and guidelines). **Contact:** Manuscript Evaluation Desk. Estab. 1976. "Small press publisher. Considers all submitted manuscripts fairly—without bias or favor." This company is run by book-lovers, not by accountants. Publishes hardcover and paperback originals and reprints. **Published 12 new writers within the last year.** Averages 12 fiction titles/year. Distributes and promotes titles through direct mail and the Internet.

Needs: Adventure, children's/juvenile (adventure), literary, romance (contemporary, romantic suspense), science fiction (hard science/technological, soft/sociological), short story collections, translations, western (frontier saga, traditional), young adult/teen (adventure, fantasy/science fiction). Currently emphasizing stage plays. Planning anthologies: short stories, science fiction, poetry. "Authors are invited to submit collections of short stories and poetry for consideration for our ongoing programs." Recently published *Jessica A.*, by Phyllis Wyatt (war-time romance); *Recitable Rhymes*, by Alan Millard (poetry); *Tales from Thailand* (travel adventure).

How to Contact: Accepts unsolicited mss. Query with synopsis and first chapter. Accepts queries by e-mail, fax and phone. Include estimated word count. Send SASE or IRC for return of ms or send disposable copy of ms and SASE for reply only. Responds in 1 week to queries; up to 3 months to mss. Accepts electronic submissions and disk. Always comments on rejected mss.

Terms: Pays royalties of 10% and 5 author's copies. No advance. Sends galleys to author. Publishes ms 2 months after acceptance. Writer's guidelines on website. Book catalog A5 SASE and on website.

Advice: "Study the market! Check your selected publisher's catalogue."

PLEASURE BOAT STUDIO, 8630 NE Wardwell Rd., Bainbridge Island WA 98110. (206)842-9772. Fax: (206)842-9773. E-mail: pleasboat@aol.com. Website: www.pbstudio.com (includes sample works, writer's guidelines, company philosophy, authors and titles). **Contact:** Jack Estes, fiction editors. Estab. 1996. "We publish high-quality literary (not mainstream) fiction in original or in translation." Publishes paperback originals. Books: 55 lb. paper; perfect binding. Average print order: 1,500. First novel print order: 1,000. **Published 7 new writers within the last year.** Distributes titles through readings, reviews, mailings, book shows. Averages 4-5 total titles; 3 fiction titles/year. Distributes titles through readings, reviews, mailings, book shows.

Needs: Ethnic/multicultural, feminist, gay, historical, humor/satire, literary, regional, short story collections, translations. Recently published *Pronoun Music*, by Richard Cohen; *The Eighth Day of the Week*, by Alfred Kessler (novel); and *If You Were with Me . . .*, by Ken Harvey (short story collection).

How to Contact: Query with outline/synopsis and 1-2 sample chapters. Prefers queries by e-mail. Include estimated word count, 1-page bio and list of publishing credits. Send SASE or IRC for return of ms. Responds in up to 3 months to queries. Accepts simultaneous submissions.

Terms: Pays royalty of 10%. Provides 25 author's copies. "Payment by individual arrangement." Sends galleys to author. Publishes ms 1-2 years after acceptance.

Advice: "Send query only, not complete manuscript, and don't get discouraged."

PONDER PUBLISHING INC., P.O. Box 23037, RPO McGillivray, Winnipeg, Manitoba R3T 5S3 Canada. (204)269-2985. Fax: (204)888-7159. E-mail: service@ponderpublishing.com. Website: www.ponderpub

lishing.com (includes title information, distribution information, book excerpts, reader survey, website survey, romance/relationship column, writing contest information, editorial staff, contact information). **Contact:** Mary Barton, senior editor (romance); Pamela Walford, assistant editor (romance). Estab. 1996. "Small, independent publisher. Our submissions team is always on the lookout for diamonds in the rough, writers with a unique voice. We feel we've taken the best of formula romance and mainstream romance and combined them into a short, fast-paced, entertaining read." Publishes paperback originals. Books: groundwork paper; mass market format printing; perfect binding. Average print order: 5,000-15,000. First novel print order: 3,000-5,000. **Published 1 new writer within the last year.** Plans 2 first novels in 2002. Averages 2 total titles, 2 fiction titles/year. Member, Small Publishers Association of North America. Distributes titles through four major American and one Canadian distributor. Promotes titles through advertising, the Internet, trade shows and newsletter.

Needs: Romance (contemporary, futuristic/time travel, romantic suspense). "We are looking for a variety of voices and styles, anything unique, for our Ponder Romance line. We like light, highly entertaining story lines that are as enjoyable as the romance." Recently published *Oh Susannah*, by Selena Mindous; *Autumn's Eve*, by Jordanna Boston; and *Sand Pirates*, by Ellis Hoff (all romance). Upcoming 2002 releases, *Reluctant Roulette* (romance), by Ellis Hoff and *Can't Buy Me Love* (first fiction, romance), by Amy Lillard.

How to Contact: Accepts unsolicited mss. Query with outline/synopsis and 3 sample chapters. Include estimated word count, brief bio and list of publishing credits. Send IRC for return of ms or send disposable copy of ms and IRC for reply only. Responds in 3 months to queries; 5 months to mss. Accepts simultaneous submissions. Often comments on rejected mss.

Terms: "Contracts are confidential and negotiable. We pay signing bonuses (as opposed to advances) in addition to royalties." Does not send galleys to author. Publishes ms 1-3 years after acceptance. Writer's guidelines and book catalog for SASE and $1 postage (Canadian).

Advice: "Read our books. They are unique to the genre in a way that the writer's guidelines cannot fully convey. Ponder romances go right down the middle between category and mainstream romance."

THE PRAIRIE PUBLISHING COMPANY, 115 Garrioch Ave., Winnipeg, Manitoba R3J 2T2 Canada. (204)837-7499. **Contact:** Ralph Watkins, publisher. Estab. 1969. Buys juvenile mss with illustrations. Books: 60 lb. high-bulk paper; offset printing; perfect-bound; line-drawings. Average print order: 2,000. First novel print order: 2,000. **Published new writers within the last year.**

Needs: Open. Published *The Homeplace* (historical novel); *My Name is Marie Anne Gaboury* (first French-Canadian woman in the Northwest); and *The Tale of Jonathan Thimblemouse*.

How to Contact: Does not accept unsolicited mss. Send query letter with SASE or IRC. Responds in 1 month to queries; 6 weeks to mss. Publishes ms 4-6 months after acceptance.

Terms: Pays royalties of 10%. No advance. Book catalog free.

Advice: "We work on a manuscript with the intensity of a Max Perkins. A clean, well-prepared manuscript can go a long way toward making an editor's job easier. On the other hand, the author should not attempt to anticipate the format of the book, which is a decision for the publisher to make. In order to succeed in today's market, the story must be tight, well written and to the point. Do not be discouraged by rejections."

PUBLISHERS SYNDICATION, INTERNATIONAL, P.O. Box 6218, Charlottesville VA 22906-6218. Fax: (804)964-0096. Website: www.Publisherssyndication.com. **Contact:** A. Samuels. Estab. 1979.

Needs: Adventure, mystery/suspense (amateur sleuth, police procedural), thriller/espionage, western (frontier saga).

How to Contact: Accepts unsolicited mss. Submit complete ms with cover letter. Include estimated word count. Send SASE or IRC for return of ms. Responds in 1 month.

Terms: Pays royalties of .05-2%. Advance is negotiable. Writer's guidelines for SASE.

Advice: "The type of manuscript we are looking for is devoid of references which might offend. Remember you are writing for a general audience."

PUCKERBRUSH PRESS, 76 Main St., Orono ME 04473. (207)866-4868. **Contact:** Constance Hunting (fiction). Estab. 1971. "Small independent trade publisher, unique because of editorial independent stance." Publishes paperback originals and paperback reprints. Books: perfect-bound, illustrations. Average print order 500. Average first novel print order 500. Averages 2-3 total titles, 1-2 fiction titles/year. Titles distributed through Amazon.com, Baker & Taylor, Barnes & Noble.

Needs: Literary. Recently published *The Crow on the Spruce*, by C. Hall (Maine fiction); *Night-Sea Journey*, by M. Alpert (poetry).

How to Contact: Accepts unsolicited mss. Submit complete ms with cover letter. Accepts phone queries. Include a brief bio and a list of publishing credits with your submissions. Agented fiction: 0%. Responds to queries in 2 weeks; to mss in 2 months. Often comments on rejected mss. Sometimes charges for critiques; "$50 per hour for thorough critique." Pays in royalties of 10-15%. Sometimes sends galleys to author. Writer's guidelines for SASE; book catalog for large SASE and 34¢ postage.

Advice: "Be true to your vision, not to fashion."

☑ ◐ **PUDDING HOUSE PUBLICATIONS**, 60 N. Main St., Johnstown OH 43031. (740)967-6060. E-mail: pudding@johnstown.net. Website: www.puddinghouse.com (includes staff, departments, photos, guidelines, books for direct and wholesale purchase, publications list, writing games, poem of the month, Unitarian Universalist poets page, calls, etc.). **Contact:** Jennifer Bosveld, editor (short short stories only). Estab. 1979. "Small independent publisher seeking outrageously fresh short short stories." Publishes paperback originals. Books, chapbooks, broadsites: paper varies; side stapled; b&w illustrations. **Published new writers within the last year.** Promotes titles through direct mail, conference exhibits, readings, workshops.
Needs: Experimental, literary, the writing experience, liberal/alternative politics or spirituality, new approaches. Recently published *In the City of Mystery*, by Alan Ziegler (short short stories); and *Karmic 4-Star Buckaroo*, by John Bennett (short short stories).
How to Contact: Accepts unsolicited mss. Submit complete ms with cover letter and ample SASE. Include short bio and list of publishing credits. Send SASE for return of ms. Responds immediately unless traveling. No simultaneous submissions. Sometimes comments on rejected mss for various fee, if close.
Terms: Pays in author's copies. Sends galleys to author for chapbooks. Publishes ms 2-24 months after acceptance. Writer's guidelines free for SASE. Publication list available.
Advice: "Be new!"

◐ ▼ **RED SAGE PUBLISHING, INC.**, P.O. Box 4844, Seminole FL 33775-4844. Phone/fax: (727)391-3847. E-mail: alekendall@aol.com. Website: www.redsagepub.com (includes authors and guidelines). **Contact:** Alexandria Kendall, editor (romance erotica). Estab. 1995. Publishes "romance erotica or ultra-sensual romance novellas written by romance writers. Red Sage is the leader in the publishing industry for erotic romance." Publishes paperback originals. Books: perfect binding. **Published 4 new writers within the last year.** Averages 1 total title, 1 fiction title/year. Distributes titles through Baker & Taylor, Amazon, Barnes & Noble, Borders and independent bookstores as well as mail order. Promotes titles through national trade publication advertising, author interviews and book signings.
● Red Sage Publishing received the Fallot Literary Award for Fiction.
Imprint(s): The *Secrets* Collections (romance, ultra-sensual), edited by Alexandria Kendall.
Needs: Romance (ultra-sensual) novellas for *The Secrets Collections: The Best in Women's Sensual Fiction* anthology. Length: 20,000-30,000 words. Writers may submit to anthology editor. Recently published *Insatiable*, by Chevon Gael; and *Strictly Business*, by Shannon Hollis.
How to Contact: Accepts unsolicited mss. Query with outline/synopsis and 10 sample pages. Include estimated word count and list of publishing credits if applicable. Send SASE or IRC for return of ms. Responds in 3 months. Sometimes comments on rejected ms.
Terms: Pays advance and royalty. Sends galleys to author. Publishes ms 1-2 years after acceptance. Writer's guidelines for SASE.
Advice: "Know your reader."

⊕ ◎ **RENDITIONS**, Research Centre for Translation, Institute of Chinese Studies, Chinese University of Hong Kong, Shatin, New Territories, Hong Kong. Phone: 852-26097399. Fax: 852-26035110. E-mail: renditions @cuhk.edu.hk. Website: www.renditions.org (includes sections about Research Centre for Translation, the Chinese University of Hong Kong, *Renditions* magazines, Renditions Paperbacks, Renditions Books, forthcoming, ordering information and related sites). **Contact:** Dr. Eva Hung, editor. Academic specialist publisher. Averages 2 fiction titles/year. Distributes titles through local and overseas distributors and electronically via homepage and Amazon.com. Promotes titles through homepage, exchange ads with *China Now* and *China Review International* and paid ads in *Feminist Bookstore News* and *Journal of Asian Studies* of AAS.
Needs: Will only consider English translations of Chinese fiction, prose, drama and poetry. Fiction published either in semiannual journal (*Renditions*) or in the Renditions Paperback series. Recently published *Hong Kong Stories: Old Themes New Voices*, by Eva Hung, editor; and *Traces of Love and Other Stories*, by Eileen Chang; and *City Women: Contemporary Taiwan Women Writers*, edited by Eva Hung.
How to Contact: For fiction over 5,000 words in translation, sample is required. Sample length: 1,000-2,000 words. Send sample chapter. "Submit only works in our specialized area. Two copies of translation accompanied by two copies of original Chinese text." Accepts fax and e-mail requests for information and guidelines.
Terms: Pays royalties for paperback series; honorarium for publication in *Renditions*.

▼ ◐ ◎ ▼ **RONSDALE PRESS**, 3350 W. 21 Ave., Vancouver, British Columbia V6S 1G7 Canada. (604)738-4688. Fax: (604)731-4548. E-mail: ronhatch@pinc.com. Website: www.ronsdalepress.com (includes guidelines, catalog, events). **Contact:** Ronald B. Hatch, president/editor; Veronica Hatch, editor (YA historical). Estab. 1988. Ronsdale Press is "dedicated to publishing books that give Canadians new insights into themselves and their country." Publishes paperback originals. Books: 60 lb. paper; photo offset printing; perfect binding.

Average print order: 1,500. First novel print order: 1,500. **Published new writers within the last year.** Averages 3 fiction titles/year. Distributes titles through General Distribution. Promotes titles through ads in BC Bookworld and Globe & Mail, and interviews on radio.

- Ronsdale author, Janice MacDonald won the Our Choice Award for *The Ghoul's Night Out. Eyewitness,* by Margaret Thompson was chosen as a B.C. Millennium Book.

Needs: Literary. Published *The City in the Egg,* by Michel Trembly (novel); *Tangled in Time,* by Lynne Fairbridge (children's); and *Daruma Days,* by Terry Watada (short stories).

How to Contact: *Canadian authors only.* Accepts unsolicited mss. Submit outline/synopsis and at least first 100 pages. Accepts queries/correspondence by e-mail. Send SASE or IRC for return of ms. Short story collections must have some previous magazine publication. Responds in 2 weeks to queries; 2 months to mss. Sometimes comments on rejected mss.

Terms: Pays royalties of 10%. Provides author's copies. Sends galleys to author. Publishes ms 6 months after acceptance.

Advice: "We publish both fiction and poetry. Authors *must* be Canadian. We look for writing that shows the author has read widely in contemporary and earlier literature. Ronsdale, like other literary presses, is not interested in mass-market or pulp materials."

◯ JAMES RUSSELL PUBLISHING, 780 Diogenes Dr., Reno NV 89512-1336. E-mail: scrnplay@powernet. net. Website: www.powernet.net/~scrnplay (includes sample query letter, guidelines, advice for writers, catalog). **Contact:** James Russell, publisher. Estab. 2000. "We are a new small publisher in the novel market. We publish Christian novels." Publishes paperback originals and e-books. Books: white 50 lb. paper; web and sheet printing; perfect binding 6×9, 140 pages. Averages 7 total titles/year. Member, PMA. Distributes titles through Ingram, Garoners and Baker & Taylor. Promotes titles through websites, distributors' catalogs, PMA, marketing and print ads.

Needs: Adventure, historical (1800s western), literary, regional (Nevada, California), religious (general religious, inspirational), western (frontier saga), young adult/teen (adventure, western). Recently published *Walking with the Lord,* by James Russell.

How to Contact: Does not accept or return unsolicited mss. Send query letter. Accepts queries by e-mail. Include estimated word or page count. Send disposable copy of ms and SASE for reply only. Responds in 3 weeks to queries; 1 month to mss. Accepts simultaneous submissions. Often comments on rejected mss.

Terms: Pays royalties of 10-15%. Sends galleys to author. Publishes ms 3 months after acceptance. Writer's guidelines for #10 SASE.

Advice: "Employ a proofreader/editor prior to submission. We need manuscripts ready for publishing. Visit our website for advice, guidelines and a free query letter sample. Tell us why your book is better than others on the market. Who do you feel will buy your book? Send query letter only. Keep query to one page. Include SASE. Do not call, use e-mail or postal letter to follow up."

N ◯ ◎ THE SAVANT GARDE WORKSHOP, a privately-owned affiliate of The Savant Garde Institute, Ltd., P.O. Box 1650, Sag Harbor NY 11963-0060. Phone/fax: (516)725-1414. Website: www.savantgarde.o rg. **Acquisitions**: Vilna Jorgen II, publisher; Charles Collins, editor, literary futurist; Artemis Smith, editor, multimedia, philosophy, long poems. Estab. 1953. "Literary multiple-media publisher." Publishes hardcover and paperback originals and reprints. First novel print order: 1,000. Promotes archived titles through listing in R.R. Bowker, barnesandnoble.com, Borders.com, savantgarde.org, dustbooks, amazon.com, Baker & Taylor, word-of-mouth in world literary circles and academic/scientific associations and conferences.

- Be sure to look at this publishers' guidelines and webpage. Works could best be described as avant-garde/post modern, experimental.

Needs: Contemporary, futuristic, humanist, literary, philosophical. "We are open to the best, whatever it is." No "mediocrity or pot boilers." Published *01 or a Machine Called SKEETS,* by Artemis Smith (avant-garde). Series include "On-Demand Desktop Collectors' Editions," "Artists' Limited Editions," "Monographs of The Savant Garde Institute."

How to Contact: Do not send unsolicited mss. Query first by e-mail, include outline, URL, and complete verifiable vita. Responds in 6 weeks to queries ("during academic year"); 2 months to invited mss. Sometimes comments on rejected mss.

Terms: Average advance: $500, honorarium (depends on grant/award money). Terms set by individual arrangement with author depending on the book and previous professional experience. Sends galleys to author. Publishes ms 18 months after final acceptance. Writer's guidelines on website.

Advice: "We are looking for extremely rare offerings. We are not interested in the usual commercial submissions. Convince us you are a real artist, not a hacker." Would like to see more "thinking for the 21st Century of Nobel Prize calibre. We're expanding into multimedia, web and E-Book co-publishing and seek multitalented authors who can produce and perform their own multimedia work for web release. We are overbought, understaffed and underfunded—don't expect a quick reply or fast publication date."

SIGNAL CREST, Tiptoe Literary Service, 434 Sixth St., #206, Raymond WA 98577-1804. (360)942-4596. E-mail: anne@willapabay.org. Website: www.willapabay.org/~anne (includes publishing, product and general information and links). **Contact:** Anne Grimm-Richardson, editor. Estab. 1985. "One-person operation, in-house publishing and syndication." Publishes paperback originals and reprints. Books: 20 lb. paper; photocopy printing; coil bound; pen and ink illustrations. Averages 6 total titles, 3 fiction titles/year.
Needs: Children's/juvenile (adventure, fantasy, read aloud), feminist, science fiction (hard science/technological, soft/sociological), young adult/teen (amateur radio). Currently emphasizing feminist/family, fantasy/science fiction/amateur radio short stories. Planning domestic violence anthology. Editor will select stories.
How to Contact: Does not accept or return unsolicited mss. Send query letter by e-mail. Include 100-word summary. Send disposable copy of ms and SASE for reply only. Responds in 1 month to queries; 3 months to mss. Sometimes comments on rejected mss.
Terms: No payment (or by negotiation). Self-publisher. Book catalogs on website.
Advice: "Look into publishing your own work—keep the profits from your own work."

SNOWAPPLE PRESS, P.O. Box 66024, Heritage Postal Outlet, Edmonton, Alberta T6J 6T4 Canada. (780)437-0191. **Contact:** Vanna Tessier, editor. Estab. 1991. "We focus on topics that are interesting, unusual and controversial." Small independent literary press. Publishes hardcover and paperback originals. Books: non-acid paper; offset printing; perfect binding; illustrations. Average print order: 500. First novel print order: 500. Plans 1 first novel in 2002. Averages 3-4 total titles, 1-2 fiction titles/year. Distributes titles through bookseller and library wholesalers. Promotes titles through press releases and reviews.
Needs: Adventure, children's/juvenile (adventure, fantasy, mystery), experimental, historical, literary, mainstream/contemporary, short story collections, translations, young adult/teen (adventure, mystery/suspense). Published *Thistle Creek*, by Vanna Tessier (short stories); *The Last Waltz of Chopin*, by Gilberto Finzi, translated by Vanna Tessier (novel).
How to Contact: Does not accept unsolicited mss. Query with 1-page cover letter. Include estimated word count, 300-word bio and list of publishing credits. Send SASE with sufficient IRCs. Responds in 1 month to queries; 3 months to mss. Accepts simultaneous submissions.
Terms: Pays honorarium; provides 10-25 author's copies. Sends galleys to author. Publishes ms 12-18 months after acceptance.
Advice: "Query first with proper SASE and IRCs to obtain guidelines."

SWEET LADY MOON PRESS, P.O. Box 1076, Georgetown KY 40324. (502)868-6573. Fax: (502)868-6566. E-mail: troyteegarden@worldradio.org. **Contact:** Troy Teegarden, editor. Estab. 1995. "Small press: fiction under 3,500 words in literary magazine *Stovepipe*; chapbooks maximum 60 pages, 8½ × 5½." Publishes paperback originals. Books: offset printing; stapled binding; illustrations. Average print order: 250. **Published 30 new writers within the last year.** Averages 4 total titles, 2 fiction titles/year. Distributes titles through the Internet, catalog, stores and mail order.
Needs: Comics/graphic novels, experimental, humor/satire, literary, short story collections. Recently published *Why I Hate Reading Books*, by Mike Francis; and *Twenty Shots*, by J. Todd Dockery.
How to Contact: Accepts unsolicited mss. Accepts queries by e-mail. Include estimated word count and brief bio. Send SASE or IRC for return of ms or send disposable copy of ms and SASE for reply only. Responds in 1 month to queries and mss. Accepts simultaneous submissions. Sometimes comments on rejected mss.
Terms: Pays author's copies. Sends galleys to author. Publishes ms 3-6 months after acceptance. Writer's guidelines and book catalog for SASE.
Advice: "We publish who we like. Read our current authors."

TATTERSALL PUBLISHING, P.O. Box 308194, Denton TX 76203-8194. (940)565-0804. Fax: (940)320-8604. E-mail: cwood@tattersallpub.com. Website: www.tattersallpub.com (current and backlist titles, works in progress, ordering, FAQ, writer's guidelines, links). **Contact:** Cheryl Wolfe, associate editor (fantasy, science fiction, mystery/suspense, historical, humor/satire). Estab. 1994. "Tattersall publishing began in 1994 as a self-publishing venture and has grown into a thriving small independent publisher with national distribution." Publishes hardcover originals and paperback originals. Books: 70 lb. paper; offset printing; perfect or smyth-sewn binding. Average print order: 1,000; first novel print order: 1,000. **Published 2 new writers within the last year.** Averages 3 total titles, 2 fiction titles/year. Distributes titles through major trade wholesalers plus Hervey's Booklink.
   ● *The Mendelian Threshold*, by Robert Humphrey was a finalist for *Foreword Magazine*'s 2000 Book of the Year.
Needs: Fantasy (contemporary supernatural), historical (no family sagas), humor/satire, mystery/suspense (amateur sleuth, cozy), and science fiction (soft/sociological). Recently published *The Mendelian Threshold*, by Robert Humphrey (sociological science fiction); *Longhorns & Short Tales*, by Newcomb/Balmer (humor); *Rockhand Lizzie*, by Gerald Stone (historical).

How to Contact: Does not accept unsolicited mss. Query with outline/synopsis and 2-3 sample chapters (up to 50 pages). Accepts queries by e-mail and fax. Include estimated word count with submission. Often comments on rejected mss.

Terms: Pays royalties of 10%. Provides 50 author's copies. Sends galleys to author. Writer's guidelines on website; book catalogs free upon request.

Advice: "I'm publishing less fiction but am open to considering exciting new things. I generally publish in paperback due to up-front costs, but will place an extraordinary book in hardcover. E-publishing and books on CD-ROM are the latest thing, but until there's an industry standard, we'll continue to produce books the old-fashioned way. Content-wise, it's a world of specialization, even in fiction. Find the niche market you like and write for it. Try the 'big guys' first, and use whatever feedback you get to improve your ms. (Who knows, they might buy it for real money!) Then impress me with your professionalism—follow the guidelines I've chosen and pretend you're applying for the best job of your life. Spelling and grammar and punctuation are **important**— the English language has rules that make our communication effective. (You can break rules for effect. But *know* them before you break them!)"

THISTLEDOWN PRESS, 633 Main St., Saskatoon, Saskatchewan S7H 0J8 Canada. (306)244-1722. Fax: (306)244-1762. E-mail: tdpress@home.com. Website: www.thistledown.sk.ca (includes guidelines, catalog, teaching materials). Editor-in-Chief: Patrick O'Rourke. **Contact:** Jesse Stothers, editor. Estab. 1975. Publishes paperback originals—literary fiction, young adult fiction, poetry. Books: quality stock paper; offset printing; perfect-bound; occasional illustrations. Average print order 1,500-2,000. First novel print order: 1,000-1,500. **Published new writers within the last year.** Averages 12 total titles, 6-7 fiction titles/year. Distributes titles through General Distribution Services. Promotes titles through intensive school promotions, online, advertising, special offers.
- Thistledown's *Prisoner in a Red-Rose Chain*, by Jeffrey Moore won the Commonwealth Writers Prize for Best New Book.

Needs: Literary, experimental, short story collections, novels.

How to Contact: Does not accept unsolicited mss. Query first with SASE or IRC for reply. Accepts queries by e-mail and fax. "We *only* want to see Canadian-authored submissions. We will *not* consider multiple submissions." Accepts photocopied submissions. Responds in 2 months to queries. Publishes anthologies. "Stories are nominated." Published *Japanese Baseball & Other Stories*, by W.P. Kinsella (short fiction); *Ariadne's Dream*, by Tess Fragoulis (novel); *A Traveller Came By: Stories About Dying*, by Seán Virgo (short fiction). Also publishes The Mayer Mystery Series (mystery novels for young adults) and The New Leaf Series (first books for poetry and fiction—Saskatchewan residents only).

Terms: Pays standard royalty on retail price. Publishes ms 1-2 years after acceptance. Writer's guidelines and book catalog for #10 SASE.

Advice: "We are primarily looking for quality writing that is original and innovative in its perspective and/or use of language. Thistledown would like to receive queries first before submission—perhaps with novel outline, some indication of previous publications, periodicals your work has appeared in. *We publish Canadian authors only.* We are continuing to publish more fiction and are looking for new fiction writers to add to our list. New Leaf Editions line is first books of poetry or fiction by emerging Saskatchewan authors. Familiarize yourself with some of our books before submitting a query or manuscript to the press."

TURNSTONE PRESS, 607-100 Arthur St., Winnipeg, Manitoba R3B 1H3 Canada. (204)947-1555. Fax: (204)942-1555. E-mail: editor@turnstonepress.mb.ca. Website: www.TurnstonePress.com (includes submission guidelines, new titles, selected backlist, excerpts and author tour information). **Contact:** Manuela Dias, editor. Estab. 1976. "Turnstone Press is a literary press that publishes Canadian writers with an emphasis on writers from, and writing on, the Canadian west." Focuses on eclectic new writing, prairie writers, travel writing and regional mysteries. Books: offset paper; perfect-bound. First novel print order: 1,500. **Published 5 new writers within the last year.** Averages 12-15 total titles/year. Distributes titles through General Distribution Services (Canada and US). Promotes titles through Canadian national and local print media and select US print advertising.
- *Summer of My Amazing Luck*, by Miriam Toews was nominated for the Stephen Leacock Award for Humor. Wayne Tefs, author of *Moon Lake*, won the Margaret Laurence Award for Fiction. *In the Hands of the Living God*, by Lillian Bouzane was longlisted for the Dublin IMPAC Literary Prize. *Sticks and Stones*, by Eileen Coughlan was shortlisted for the Arthur Ellis Award.

TO RECEIVE REGULAR TIPS AND UPDATES about writing and Writer's Digest publications via e-mail, send an e-mail with "SUBSCRIBE NEWSLETTER" in the body of the message to newsletter-request@writersdigest.com

Imprints: Ravenstone.

Needs: Literary, regional (Western Canada), mystery, gothic, noir. "We will be doing only 4-5 fiction titles a year. Interested in new work exploring new narrative/fiction forms, travel/adventure/nature writing of a literary nature and writing that pushes the boundaries of genre." Recently published *This Place Called Absence*, by Linda Kwa (novel); and *Choke Hold*, by Todd Babiak (comic novel).

How to Contact: *Canadian authors only.* Accepts unsolicited mss. Query with 20-40 sample pages. Include list of publication credits. Send SASE or IRC for return of ms. Responds in 2 months to queries; up to 4 months to mss. Accepts simultaneous submissions if notified.

Terms: Pays royalties of 10% and 10 author's copies. Average advance: $500. Publishes ms 1 year after acceptance. Sends galleys to author. Book catalog free with SASE.

Advice: "As a Canadian literary press, we have a mandate to publish Canadian writers only. Do some homework before submitting work to make sure your subject matter/genre/writing style falls within the publishers area of interest."

☑ Ⓐ ULTRAMARINE PUBLISHING CO., INC., Box 303, Hastings-on-the-Hudson NY 10706. (914)478-1339. Fax: (914)478-1365. **Contact:** Christopher P. Stephens, publisher. Estab. 1973. Small publisher. "We have 200 titles in print. We also distribute for authors where a major publisher has dropped a title." Averages 15 total titles, 12 fiction titles/year.

Needs: Experimental, fantasy, mainstream, science fiction, short story collections. No romance, westerns, mysteries.

How to Contact: Does not accept unsolicited mss. Agented fiction 90%. Occasionally comments on rejected mss.

Terms: Pays royalties of 10% minimum; advance is negotiable. Publishes ms an average of 8 months after acceptance. Free book catalog.

Ⓝ ☑ UNIVERSITY OF MISSOURI PRESS, 2910 LeMone Blvd., Columbia MO 65201-8227. (573)882-7641. Fax: (573)884-4498. Website: www.system.missouri.edu.upress (includes authors, titles, book descriptions). **Contact:** Clair Willcox, editor. Estab. 1958. "Mid-size university press." Publishes paperback originals and reprints (short story collections only). Published new writers within the last year. Averages 65 total titles, 4 short story collections each year. Distributes titles through direct mail, bookstores, sales reps.

● The University of Missouri Press is a member of the Association of American University Presses.

Needs: Short story collections. No children's fiction. Recently published *My Favorite Lies*, by Ruth Hamel (short story collection); *Boys Keep Being Born*, by Joan Frank (short story collection); *No Visible Means of Support*, by Dabney Stuart (short story collection).

How to Contact: Query first. Submit cover letter and sample story or two by mail only. Include bio/publishing credits. SASE for reply. Responds in 2 weeks to queries; 3 months to mss. Accepts simultaneous submissions. Sometimes comments on rejected ms.

Terms: Pays royalties of 6%. Sends galleys to author. Publishes ms 1-1½ years after acceptance. Book catalogs are free.

☑ ☑ Ⓒ Ⓨ UNIVERSITY OF NEVADA PRESS, MS 166, Reno NV 89557-0076. (775)784-6573. Fax: (775)784-6200. E-mail: rlatimer@equinox.unr.edu. Director: Ronald E. Latimer. **Contact:** Sandy Crooms, assistant director. Estab. 1961. "Small university press. Publishes fiction that focuses primarily on the American West." Publishes paperback originals and paperback reprints. Books: acid-free paper. Averages 25 total titles, 2 fiction titles/year. Member, AAUP.

● *Straight White Male*, by Gerald Haslam won the WESTAF Award for Fiction in 2000 and *Foreword Magazine*'s second place winner for Book of the Year.

Needs: Ethnic/multicultural (general), family saga, historical (American West), humor/satire, mystery/suspense (U.S. West), regional (U.S. West). Published *Wild Indians & Other Creatures*, by Adrian Louis (short stories); *Gunning for Ito*, by H. Lee Barnes (short stories); and *The Blossom Festival*, by Lawrence Coates (novel). "We have series in Basque Studies, Gambling Studies, history and humanities, ethnonationalism, Western literature."

How to Contact: Accepts unsolicited mss. Query with outline/synopsis and 2-4 sample chapters. Accepts queries by e-mail and fax. Include estimated word count, 1-2 page bio and list of publishing credits. Send SASE or IRC for return of ms or send disposable copy of ms and SASE for reply only. Agented fiction 20%. Responds in 3 weeks to queries; 4 months to mss. Sometimes comments on rejected mss.

Terms: Pays royalties; negotiated on a book-by-book basis. Sends galleys to author. Publishes ms up to 2 years after acceptance. Writer's guidelines for #10 SASE.

Advice: "We are not interested in genre fiction."

◆◎ VÉHICULE PRESS, Box 125, Place du Parc Station, Montreal, Quebec H2W 2M9 Canada. **Contact:** Simon Dardick, publisher/editor. Estab. 1973. Small publisher of scholarly, literary and cultural books. Publishes hardcover and paperback originals. Books: good quality paper; offset printing; perfect and cloth binding; illustrations. Average print order: 1,000-3,000. Averages 15 total titles/year.
Imprint(s): Signal Editions (poetry).
Needs: Feminist, literary, regional, short story collections, translations—"*by Canadian residents only.*" No romance or formula writing. Published *Rembrandt's Model*, by Yeshim Ternar; and *Ice in Dark Water*, by David Manicom.
How to Contact: Send query letter or query with sample chapters. Send SASE or IRC for reply ("no U.S. stamps, please"). Responds in 3 months to mss.
Terms: Pays in royalties of 10-12%. "Depends on press run and sales. Translators of fiction can receive Canada Council funding, which publisher applies for." Sends galleys to author. Book catalog for 9×12 SASE.
Advice: "Quality in almost any style is acceptable. We believe in the editing process."

◎ W.W. PUBLICATIONS, 4108 Menton, Flint MI 48507. **Contact**: Philip Helms, editor. Estab. 1967. One-man operation on part-time basis. Publishes paperback originals and reprints. Books: typing paper; offset printing; staple-bound; black ink illustrations. Average print order: 500. First novel print order: 500. Averages 1 fiction title/year.
Imprint(s): *Minas Tirith Evening Star.*
Needs: Fantasy, science fiction. "Specializes in Tolkien-related or middle-earth." Published *The Adventures of Fungo Hafwirse*, by Philip W. Helms and David L. Dettman.
How to Contact: Accepts unsolicited mss. Submit complete ms with SASE. Responds in 1 month. "Submit hardy copy by mail only. No phone inquiries, no fax and no e-mail. No exceptions." Occasionally comments on rejected mss.
Terms: Individual arrangement with author depending on book, etc.; provides 5 author's copies.
Advice: "We are publishing more fiction and more paperbacks. The author/editor relationship: a friend and helper."

◯ ◎ WAVERLY HOUSE PUBLISHING, P.O. Box 1053, Glenside PA 19038. (215)884-5873. E-mail: info@natsel.com. Website: www.natsel.com (includes book catalog and interviews with authors). **Contact**: Nora Wright, publisher. Estab. 1997. 'Small independent publisher publishing works of high entertainment value which also convey a message of social significance to the African-American community." Publishes hardcover and paperback originals. Books: offset printing; casebound with perfect binding. Average print order: 2,000. First novel print order: 2,000. **Published 1 new writer within the last year.** Averages 2-3 total titles, 2-3 fiction titles/year. Distributes titles through Cultured Plus, Ingram and Baker & Taylor. Promotes titles through advertisement in African-American literary journals and the use of publicity consultant. Member, SPAN.
Needs: Ethnic/multicultural (specific culture, African-American). Recently published *Damaged!*, by Bernadette Y. Connor (novel); and *The Rest of Our Lives*, by Dawn Connelly-Craig.
How to Contact: Does not accept unsolicited mss. Send query letter. Include estimated word count and 50-word bio. Send SASE or IRC for return of ms or send disposable copy of ms and SASE for reply only. Responds in 1 month to queries; 2 months to mss.
Terms: Pays royalties of 6% minimum. Sends galleys to author. Publishes ms 9-18 months after acceptance.

☑ ◎ WOODLEY MEMORIAL PRESS, English Dept., Washburn University, Topeka KS 66621. (785)234-1032. E-mail: zzlaws@washburn.edu.Website: www.washburn.edu/reference/woodley-press (includes writer's guidelines, editors, authors, titles). **Contact**: Robert N. Lawson, editor. Estab. 1980. "Woodley Memorial Press is a small, nonprofit press which publishes book-length poetry and fiction collections by Kansas writers only; by 'Kansas writers' we mean writers who reside in Kansas or have a Kansas connection." Publishes paperback originals. Averages 2 titles/year.
Needs: Contemporary, experimental, literary, mainstream, short story collection. Published *Gathering Reunion*, by David Tangeman (stories and poetry); *The Monday, Wednesday, Friday Girl*, by Stuart Levine (short stories); and *Rudolph, Encouraged by His Therapist*, by Eugene Bales (satiric stories).
How to Contact: Kansas authors should query before sending ms. Accepts unsolicited mss. Submit complete ms with cover letter. Accepts queries by e-mail. Responds in 2 weeks to queries; 2 months to mss. Usually comments on rejected ms.
Terms: "Terms are individually arranged with author after acceptance of manuscript." Publishes ms about 1 year after acceptance. Writer's guidelines on website.
Advice: "We only publish one work of fiction a year, on average, and definitely want it to be by a Kansas author. We are more likely to do a collection of short stories by a single author."

WRITERS DIRECT, Imprint of Titlewaves Publishing, Book Division of H&S Publishing, 1351 Kuhio Highway, Kapaa HI 96746. (808)822-7449. Fax: (808)822-2312. E-mail: rs@hshawaii.com. Website: www.bestpl acesonearth.com (includes book catalog). **Contact**: Rob Sanford, editor. Estab. 1985. "Small independent publishing house founded and run by published authors." Publishes hardcover and paperback originals and reprints. Books: recycled paper; digital printing; perfect binding; illustrations. **Published 4 new writers within the last year.** Averages more than 6 total titles, 2 fiction titles/year.

Needs: Adventure, children's/juvenile, humor satire, literary, mainstream, New Age/mystic, psychic/supernatural, regional (Hawaii), religious (children's religious, inspirational, religious mystery/suspense, religious thriller), science fiction, thriller/espionage.

How to Contact: Accepts unsolicited mss. Query with outline/synopsis and 3 sample chapters. Include estimated word count, 1-page bio, list of publishing credits, why author wrote book, marketing plan. Send SASE for return of ms or send disposable copy of ms and SASE for reply only. Responds in 1 month to queries; 3 months to mss. Accepts simultaneous submissions. Sometimes comments on rejected mss.

Terms: Pays royalties of 15-35%. Sometimes sends galleys to author. Book catalog for legal-size SASE.

Advice: "Do what you do best and enjoy most. Your writing is an outcome of the above."

Contests & Awards

In addition to honors and, quite often, cash prizes, contests and awards programs offer writers the opportunity to be judged on the basis of quality alone without the outside factors that sometimes influence publishing decisions. New writers who win contests may be published for the first time, while more experienced writers may gain public recognition of an entire body of work.

Listed here are contests for almost every type of fiction writing. Some focus on form, such as short stories, novels or novellas, while others feature writing on particular themes or topics. Still others are prestigious prizes or awards for work that must be nominated, such as the Pulitzer Prize in Fiction. Chances are no matter what type of fiction you write, there is a contest or award program that may interest you.

SELECTING AND SUBMITTING TO A CONTEST

Use the same care in submitting to contests as you would sending your manuscript to a publication or book publisher. Deadlines are very important, and where possible, we've included this information. At times contest deadlines were only approximate at our press deadline, so be sure to write or call for complete information.

Follow the rules to the letter. If, for instance, contest rules require your name on a cover sheet only, you will be disqualified if you ignore this and put your name on every page. Find out how many copies to send. If you don't send the correct amount, by the time you are contacted to send more, it may be past the submission deadline. An increasing number of contests invite writers to query by e-mail, and many post contest information on their websites. Check listings for e-mail and website addresses.

One note of caution: Beware of contests that charge entry fees that are disproportionate to the amount of the prize. Contests offering a $10 prize, but charging $7 in entry fees, are a waste of your time and money.

If you are interested in a contest or award that requires your publisher to nominate your work, it's acceptable to make your interest known. Be sure to leave the publisher plenty of time, however, to make the nomination deadline.

AIM MAGAZINE'S SHORT STORY CONTEST, AIM Magazine, P.O. Box 1174, Maywood IL 60153. (708)344-4414. Website: www.aimmagazine.org. **Contact:** Ruth Apilado, associate editor. This annual award is for short stories that embodies our goals of furthering the brotherhood of man by way of the written word. Award: $100 and publications. Competition receives 20 submissions per category. Judge: Staff members. No entry fee. Guidelines available anytime. Accepts inquiries by e-mail and phone. Entries should be unpublished. Contest open to everyone. Length: 4,000 word or less. Winners are announced in the autumn issue and notified by mail on Sept 1. For list of winners send SASE.

ALABAMA STATE COUNCIL ON THE ARTS INDIVIDUAL ARTIST FELLOWSHIP, 201 Monroe St., Montgomery AL 36130-1800. (205)242-4076, ext. 224. Fax: (334)240-3269. E-mail: randy@arts.state.al.us. Website: www.arts.state.al.us. **Contact:** Randy Shoults, Literature program manager. "To recognize the achievements and potential of Alabama writers." Annual. Competition receives 25 submissions annually. Judge: independent peer panel. No entry fee. Guidelines available January 2002. For guidelines, fax, e-mail, visit website. Accepts inquiries by fax, e-mail and phone. Deadline March 1, 2002. "Two copies of the following should be submitted: a resume and a list of published works with reviews, if available. A minimum of ten pages of poetry or prose, but no more than twenty pages. Please label each page with title, artist's name and date. If published, indicate where and the date of publication." Winners announced in June and notified by mail. For list of winners, send SASE, fax, e-mail, or visit website.

✓ ◎ **ALASKA STATE COUNCIL ON THE ARTS CAREER OPPORTUNITY GRANT AWARD**, Alaska State Council on the Arts, 411 West 4th Ave., Suite 1E, Anchorage AK 99501-2343. (907)269-6610. Fax:

(907)269-6601. E-mail: info@aksca.org. Website: www.aksca.org. **Contact:** Director. Grants help artists take advantage of impending, concrete opportunities that will significantly advance their work or careers. Professional artists working in the literary arts who are requesting support for unique, short-term opportunities are eligible. Awards up to $1,000. Deadline: applications must be received by the first of the month preceding the proposed activity. Alaskan residents only. Guidelines available on website. Accepts inquiries by fax, phone and e-mail.

▦ ◎ THE ALLEGHENY REVIEW LITERARY AWARDS, *The Allegheny Review,* Allegheny College, Box 32, Meadville PA 16335. (814)332-6553. E-mail: review@alleghey.edu. Website: www.review.allegheny. edu. **Contact:** Beata M. Gomulak, senior editor. "The purpose is to foster an appreciation of quality undergraduate literature." Annual competition for short stories. Award: $150 and guaranteed publication. Competition receives 50 submissions for fiction; 150-200 for poetry. Entries are judged by the editorial staff and semi-finalists are then reviewed by a published author (Penelope Pelicone in 2001) who picks the winners. $5 entry fee. Guidelines available now. For guidelines, send SASE, e-mail or visit website. Accepts inquiries by e-mail and phone. Entries should be previously unpublished. Contest only open to currently enrolled undergraduate students. "Revise, revise, revise! We're always in need of quality literature." Winners announced April of year of publication.

☑ ◻ SHERWOOD ANDERSON SHORT FICTION AWARD, *Mid-American Review,* Dept. of English, Bowling Green State University, Bowling Green OH 43403. (419)372-2725. Fax: (419)372-6805. E-mail: MidAmReview@hotmail.com. Website: www.bgsu.edu/midamericanreview. **Contact:** Michael Czyzniejewski, fiction editor. Annual. "Contest is open to all writers. It is judged by a well-known writer, e.g., Peter Ho Davies or Melanie Rae Thon. Editors choose the top five entries, then the winner is selected by judge and guaranteed publication in the spring issue of *Mid-American Review,* plus $500. All entrants receive a copy of the issue in which the winners are printed." Competition receives 100-200 submissions. $10 fee per story. Guidelines available in November for SASE, by e-mail or on website. Deadline: October 1. Unpublished material. Winners announced in Spring issue and notified before end of year by phone or mail. For list of winners, send SASE, e-mail or visit website. "Everyone who is interested in our contest should be sure to follow our guidelines, firstly, and then mail us your best story. Anyone can win the contest—anyone who enters."

SHERWOOD ANDERSON WRITER'S GRANT, Sherwood Anderson Foundation, 216 College Rd., Richmond VA 23229. (804)282-8008. Fax: (804)287-6052. E-mail: mspear@richmond.edu. Website: www.richmond. edu/~journalm/comp.html. **Contact:** Michael M. Spear, foundation co-president. Award to "encourage and support developing writers." Annual award for short stories and chapters of novels. Award: range $5,000 to $10,000. Entries are judged by a committee established by the foundation. No entry fee. Guidelines available on website. Accepts inquiries by e-mail. Deadline April 1, 2002. Published or previously unpublished entries. "The contest is open to all struggling writers in the United States." No word length specifications. "Send in your best, most vivid prose that clearly shows talent." Winners announced in mid-summer each year and notified by phone. For list of winners visit website.

ANNUAL FICTION CONTEST, Women In The Arts, P.O. Box 2907, Decatur IL 62524. (217)872-0811. **Contact:** Vice President. Annual competition for essays, fiction, fiction for children, plays, rhymed poetry, unrhymed poetry. Award: $15-30. Competition receives 25-30 submissions. Judges: professional writers. Entry fee $2 per submission. Unlimited entries. Guidelines available for #10 SASE. No entries returned. Do not submit drawings for any category. Double-space prose. Entries must be typed on 8½×11 white paper and must be titled. Do not put your name on any page of the manuscript. Do put your name, address, telephone number, e-mail and titles of your entries on a cover sheet. Submit one cover sheet and one check, with all entries mailed flat in one envelope. Do not staple. All entries will be subject to blind judging. Entries that do not comply with the rules may be disqualified. Deadline: November 1 annually. Published or previously unpublished submissions. Open to anyone. Entries must be original work of the author. Entries must be titled. No entries published by WITA; author retains rights. Word length: essay, up to 1,500 words; fiction, up to 1,500 words; fiction for children, up to 1,500 words (do not submit drawings); play, one act only; rhymed poetry, up to 32 lines; unrhymed poetry, up to 32 lines. Winners will be notified by March 15.

ANNUAL JUVENILE-FICTION CONTEST, Women In The Arts, P.O. Box 2907, Decatur IL 62524. (217)872-0811. **Contact:** Vice President. Annual competition for essays, fiction, fiction for children, plays,

---

MARKET CONDITIONS are constantly changing! If you're still using this book and it is 2003 or later, buy the newest edition of *Novel & Short Story Writer's Market* at your favorite bookstore or order from Writer's Digest Books by calling 1-800-289-0963.

rhymed poetry, unrhymed poetry. Award: $15-30. Competition receives 30-40 submissions. Judges: professional writers. Entry fee $2 per submission. Unlimited entries. Guidelines available for #10 SASE. Deadline: November 1 annually. Published or previously unpublished submissions. Open to anyone. "Entries must be original work of the author." Word length: 1,500 words maximum for fiction, essay, fiction for children; one act for plays; up to 32 lines for poetry. "Entrants must send for our contest rules and follow the specific format requirements." Winners notified by March 15.

N ◯ ANTHOLOGY ANNUAL CONTEST, P.O. Box 4411, Mesa AZ 85211-4411. (480)461-8200. E-mail: info@anthologymagazine.com. Website: www.anthologymagazine.com. **Contact:** Sharon Skinner, contest coordinator. Annual competition for short stories. Awards: 1st Prize $150, *Anthology* t-shirt, 1-year subscription; 2nd Prize, $20 gift certificate to website, *Anthology* t-shirt, 1-year subscription; 3rd Prize, $10 gift certificate to website, *Anthology* t-shirt, 1-year subscription. All prize-winning stories are published in January/February of following year. Judge: panel of local writers and *Anthology* staff. Entry fee $5/short story. Maximum number of entries: 5/writer. "All stories submitted to contest are eligible to be printed in upcoming issues of *Anthology*, regardless of finish, unless author specifies otherwise. We ask for one-time rights. All copyrights are held by their original owner." Guidelines available in January for SASE. Deadline: August 31, 2002. Any subject, any genre. Word length: 1,000-6,000 words. Winners announced in January 2003 and notified by mail. SASE for a list of winners.

✓ ANTIETAM REVIEW LITERARY AWARD, *Antietam Review*, 41 S. Potomac St., Hagerstown MD 21740. Phone/fax: (301)791-3132. **Contact:** Winnie Wagaman, managing editor. Annual award to encourage and give recognition to excellence in short fiction. Open only to writers from Maryland, Pennsylvania, Virginia, West Virginia, Washington DC and Delaware. "We consider only previously unpublished work. We read manuscripts between June 1 and September 1." Award: $100 for the story; the story is printed in the magazine with citation as winner of Literary Contest. Competition receives 100 submissions. "We consider all fiction mss sent to *Antietam Review* Literary Contest as entries for inclusion in each issue. We look for well-crafted, serious literary prose fiction under 5,000 words." $10 fee for each story submitted. Guidelines available for #10 SASE. Accepts inquiries by phone. Deadline: September 1. Winners announced in October and notified by phone and mail in October.

✓ ◯ ◎ ARIZONA COMMISSION ON THE ARTS CREATIVE WRITING FELLOWSHIPS, 417 W. Roosevelt St., Phoenix AZ 85003-1326. (602)229-8226. Fax: (602)256-0282. E-mail: pmorris@ArizonaArts. org. Website: www.ArizonaArts.org. **Contact:** Paul Morris, public information and literature director. Fellowships awarded in alternate years to fiction writers and poets. Award: $5,000-7,500. Competition receives 120-150 submissions. Judges: Out-of-state writers/editors. Guidelines available for SASE. Accepts inquiries by fax and e-mail. Deadline: September 13. Arizona resident poets and writers over 18 years of age only. Winners announced by March 2001 and notified in writing. List of winners available for SASE.

✓ ARROWHEAD REGIONAL ARTS COUNCIL INDIVIDUAL ARTIST CAREER DEVELOPMENT GRANT, Arrowhead Regional Arts Council, 101 W. Second St. Suite 204, Duluth MN 55802-2086. (218)722-0952 or (800)569-8134. Fax: (218)722-4459. E-mail: aracouncil@aol.com. Website: www.members.aol .com/aracouncil. **Contact:** Robert DeArmond, executive director. Award to "provide financial support to regional artists wishing to take advantage of impending, concrete opportunities that will advance their work or careers. Applicants must live in the seven-county region of Northeastern Minnesota." Award is granted 3 times a year. Competition open to short stories, novels, story collections and translations. Award: up to $1,000. Competition receives 15-20 submissions per category. Judge: ARAC Board. No entry fee. Guidelines now available. For guidelines send SASE, fax, e-mail or phone. Accepts inquiries by mail, fax, e-mail and phone. Deadline April 16, 2002. Entries should be unpublished. Winners announced June 20, 2002 and notified by mail. List of winners available by phone.

✓ THE ART OF MUSIC ANNUAL WRITING CONTEST, Piano Press, P.O. Box 85, Del Mar CA 92014-0085. (858)481-5650. Fax: (858)755-1104. E-mail: eaxford@aol.com. Website: www.pianopress.com. **Contact:** Elizabeth C. Axford. "Piano Press is looking for children's songs for beginning piano songbooks, poems, short stories, music-related topics only." Award: First, second, and third prizes in each of 3 age-groups. Prizes include cash and publication in the annual anthology *The Art of Music-A Collection of Writings*. Judge: Panel of published writers. Entry fee $20/story, essay or poem. Guidelines available after September. Guidelines for SASE or e-mail. Deadline: June 30. Contest open to all writers. Poems may be of any length and in any style, single-spaced and typed; essays should be bo longer than five double-spaced, typewritten pages. "Make sure all work is fresh and original. Music related topics only." Winners announced on September 1 and notified by mail. For list of winners send SASE.

N ◐ ◎ ARTIST TRUST ARTIST FELLOWSHIPS; GAP GRANTS, Artist Trust, 1402 Third Ave., Suite 404, Seattle WA 98101-2118. (206)467-8734. Fax: (206)467-9633. E-mail: info@artisttrust.org. **Contact:** Heather Dwyer, program director. Artist Trust has 3 grant programs for generative artists in Washington State; the GAP and Fellowships. The GAP (Grants for Artist's Projects) is an annual award of up to $1,400 for a project proposal. The program is open to artists in all disciplines. The Fellowship grant is an award of $6,000 in unrestricted funding. Fellowships for Craft, Media, Literature and Music are awarded in 2001, and Fellowships for Dance, Design, Theater and Visual Art will be awarded in 2002. Competition receives 600 (GAP) submissions; 500 (Fellowship). Judges: Fellowship—Peer panel of 3 professional artists and arts professionals in each discipline; GAP—Interdisciplinary peer panel of 5 artists and arts professionals. Guidelines available in December for GAP grants and in April for Fellowship; send SASE. Accepts inquiries by fax and e-mail. Deadline: late February (GAP), mid-June (Fellowship). Winners announced December (Fellowship), May (GAP) and notified by mail. List of winners available by mail.

N ARTISTS GRANTS, Massachusetts Cultural Council, 10 St. James Ave., Boston MA 02116-3803. (617)727-3668. Fax: (617)727-0044. E-mail: mcc@art.state.ma.us. Website: www.massculturalcouncil.org. **Contact:** Stella Aguirre McGregor, department manager of artists. "To provide direct support to writers in recognition of exceptional work." Biannual competition for fiction. Award: $12,500 for grants and $1,000 for finalists. Competition receive 395 submissions. "Independent peer panels review applications. The panels are composed of artists and arts professionals, primarily from out of state. The review process is anonymous." No entry fee. Guidelines available October 2001. For guidelines visit website. Accepts inquiries by fax, e-mail and phone. Entries should be unpublished or previously published. Contest open to 18 years or older, legal resident of Massachusetts for the last two years and at time of award. This excludes students in directly related degree programs, grant recipients within the last three years. "Send in your best work and follow guidelines." Winners announced June 2002 and notified by mail. For list of winners visit website or mailed to applicants.

N ARTS & LETTERS FICTION PRIZE, Arts & Letters Journal of Contemporary Culture, Campus Box 89, Georgia College and State University, Milledgeville GA 31061-0490. (478)445-1289. E-mail: al@gcsu.edu. Website: www.al.gcsu.edu. **Contact:** Kellie Wells, fiction editor. "To publish short fiction of exceptional quality in our fall issue each year." Annual competition for short stories. Award: $1,000 for winners in fiction (short story), poetry, and drama (one-act play). Competition receive 250-300 submissions. Judges: initial screening by editors; 2001 final judges: Peter Ho Davies (fiction), E. Ethelbert Miller (poetry), Lanford Wilson (drama). $15 fee per entry. Guidelines available Fall 2001. Guidelines for SASE, e-mail and on website. Accepts inquiries by e-mail and phone. Deadline: Jan. 1-April 30, 2002 (postmark deadline). Entries should be unpublished. Contest open to all. Length: 25 pages, double-spaced. "Read the journal." Winners announced late July 2002 and notified by mail, phone and e-mail in June 2002. For list of winners send SASE or visit website.

◐ ◎ ASF TRANSLATION PRIZE, American-Scandinavian Foundation, 58 Park Ave., New York NY 10016. (212)879-9779. Fax: (212)249-3444. E-mail: agyongy@amscan.org. Website: www.amscan.org. **Contact:** Publishing office. Estab. 1980. "To encourage the translation and publication of the best of contemporary Scandinavian poetry and fiction and to make it available to a wider American audience." Annual competition for poetry, drama, literary prose and fiction translations. Award: $2,000, a bronze medallion and publication in *Scandinavian Review*. Competition receives 20-30 submissions. Competition rules and entry forms available with SASE and by fax. Accepts inquiries by fax, phone and e-mail. Deadline: June 3, 2002. Submissions must have been previously published in the original Scandinavian language. No previously published translated material. Original authors should have been born within past 200 years. Winners announced in Autumn 2002 and notified by mail. List of winners available for SASE. "Select a choice literary work by an important Scandinavian author, which has not yet been translated into English."

✓ ◯ ◎ THE ISAAC ASIMOV AWARD, International Association for the Fantastic in the Arts and *Asimov*'s magazine, School of Mass Communications, U. of South Florida, 4202 E. Fowler, Tampa FL 33620. (813)974-6792. Fax: (813)974-2592. E-mail: rwilber@chuma.cas.usf.edu. **Contact:** Rick Wilber, administrator. "The award honors the legacy of one of science fiction's most distinguished authors through an award aimed at undergraduate writers." Annual award for short stories. Award: $500 and consideration for publication in *Asimov's*. Winner receives all-expenses paid trip to Ft. Lauderdale, Florida, to attend conference on the Fantastic in mid-March where award is given. Competition receives 100-200 submissions. Judges: *Asimov's* editors. Entry fee: $10 for up to 3 submissions. Guidelines available for SASE. Accepts inquiries by fax and e-mail. Deadline: December 15. Unpublished submissions. Full-time college undergraduates only. Winners announced in February and notified by telephone. List of winners available in March for SASE.

✿ ◐ ◎ ASTED/GRAND PRIX DE LITTERATURE JEUNESSE DU QUEBEC-ALVINE-BE-LISLE, Association pour l'avancement des sciences et des techniques de la documentation, 3414 Avenue du Parc,

Bureau 202, Montreal, Quebec H2X 2H5 Canada. (514)281-5012. Fax: (514)281-8219. E-mail: info@asted.org. Website: www.asted.org. **Contact:** Micheline Patton, president. "Prize granted for the best work in youth literature edited in French in the Quebec Province. Authors and editors can participate in the contest." Annual competition for fiction and nonfiction for children and young adults. Award: $500. Deadline: June 1. Contest entry limited to editors of books published during the preceding year. French translations of other languages are not accepted.

☑ ◑ ◎ THE ATHENAEUM LITERARY AWARD, The Athenaeum of Philadelphia, 219 S. Sixth St., Philadelphia PA 19106-3794. (215)925-2688. Fax: (215)925-3755. E-mail: erose@PhilaAthenaeum.org. Website: www.PhilaAthenaeum.org. **Contact:** Ellen L. Rose, circulation librarian. Annual award to recognize and encourage outstanding literary achievement in Philadelphia and its vicinity. Award: A certificate bearing the name of the award, the seal of the Athenaeum, the title of the book, the name of the author and the year. Competition receives 8-10 submissions. Judged by committee appointed by Board of Directors. Guidelines available for SASE, by fax, by e-mail and on website. Accepts inquiries by fax, e-mail and phone. Deadline: December. Submissions must have been published during the preceding year. Nominations shall be made in writing to the Literary Award Committee by the author, the publisher or a member of the Athenaeum, accompanied by a copy of the book. The Athenaeum Literary Award is granted for a work of general literature, not exclusively for fiction. Juvenile fiction is not included. Winners announced spring 2003 and notified by mail. List of winners available on website.

☑ ◯ AWP AWARD SERIES IN POETRY, CREATIVE NONFICTION AND SHORT FICTION, AWP/Thomas Dunne Books Novel Award, The Associated Writing Programs, Mail Stop 1E3, George Mason University, Fairfax VA 22030. (703)993-4301. Fax: (703)993-4302. E-mail: awp@gmu.edu. Website: http://awpwriter.org. **Contact:** Katherine Perry. Annual award. The AWP Award Series was established in cooperation with several university presses in order to publish and make fine fiction, nonfiction, and poetry available to a wide audience. The competition is open to all authors writing in English. Awards: $2,000 plus publication for short story collection; $10,000 advance plus publication by Thomas Dunne Books for novel, an imprint of St. Martin's Press. In addition, AWP tries to place mss of finalists with participating presses. Competition receives 700 novel and 400 short fiction submissions. Novels are judged by editors at Thomas Dunne Books. Short fiction is judged by a leading author in the field (2002—Frederick Busch). Entry fee $20 nonmembers, $10 AWP members. Contest/award rules and guidelines available in late summer 2001for business-size SASE or visit our website. No phone calls please. Mss must be postmarked between January 1-February 28. Only book-length mss in the novel and short story collections are eligible (60,000 word minimum for novels; 150-300 pages for story collections). Open to all authors writing in English regardless of nationality or residence. Manuscripts previously published in their entirety, including self-publishing, are not eligible. No mss returned. Winners announced in August and notified by phone. Send SASE for list of winners or visit website.

☑ ◯ ◎ AWP INTRO JOURNALS PROJECT, Mail Stop 1E3, George Mason University, Fairfax VA 22030. E-mail: awp@gmu.edu. Website: www.awpwriter.org. **Contact:** Katherine Perry. "This is a prize for students in AWP member university creative writing programs only. Authors are nominated by the head of the creative writing department. Each school may nominate no more than one work of nonfiction, one work of short fiction and three poems." Annual competition for short stories, nonfiction and poetry. Award: $50 plus publication in participating journal. 2001 journals included *Puerto del Sol, Quarterly West, Mid-American Review, Willow Springs, Bellingham Review, Shenandoah, The Journal, Five Points* and *Hayden's Ferry Review*. Judges: AWP. Guidelines available in Fall 2001 for SASE or on website. Accepts inquiries by e-mail and phone. Deadline: December 1, 2001. Unpublished submissions only. Winners announced Spring 2002 and notified by mail in late spring/early summer. A list of winners will be available for SASE or on website.

☑ AWP PRAGUE SUMMER SEMINARS FELLOWSHIP, Associated Writing Programs, MS 1E3, George Mason University, Fairfax VA 22030. E-mail: awp@gmu.edu. Website: http://awpwriter.org. **Contact:** Katherine Perry, editor. Award to "grant fellowships to promising writers so they can attend the Prague Summer Seminars." Annual award for short stories, poetry, creative nonfiction or novel excerpts. Award: tuition to summer seminars (but not transportation). Competition receives 150-200 submissions per category. Judge: published writers in each field. $5 entry fee. 2002 guidelines available in Fall 2001; send SASE or visit website. Accepts inquiries by e-mail and phone. Deadline: December 2002. Entries should be previously unpublished. Contest open to "any writer writing in English who has yet to publish a first book. Length: 20 pages maximum. Winners announced Spring 2003 and notified by phone. A list of winners will be available for SASE and on website.

⃞N⃞ BAKELESS LITERARY PUBLICATION PRIZES, Bread Loaf Writers' Conference Middlebury College, Middlebury College, Middlebury VT 05753. (802)443-2018. E-mail: bakeless@middlebury.edu. Website: www.middlebury.edu/~blwc. **Contact:** Ian Pounds, contest coordinator. "To promote new writers' careers." Annual competition for novels and story collections. Award: publication by Houghton Mifflin, some advanced money, full fellowship to attend Bread Loaf Writers' Conference. Submit as many entries as you want. Judges:

Ursula Hegi (fiction). $10 fee per entry. Guidelines for SASE and e-mail. Accepts inquiries by e-mail and phone. Deadline: November 15, 2002. Entries should be unpublished. "Contest open to writers writing in English." Length: 450 words. "Be certain the work is as close to being done as possible." Winners notified by mail with SASE. For list of winners visit website.

N ☐ EMILY CLARK BALCH AWARDS, *The Virginia Quarterly Review*, One West Range, Box 400223, Charlottesville VA 22904-4223. **Contact:** Staige D. Blackford. Annual award "to recognize distinguished short fiction by American writers." For stories published in *The Virginia Quarterly Review* during the calendar year. Award: $500.

N ☐ BARRINGTON AREA ARTS COUNCIL/WHETSTONE PRIZES, Box 1266, Barrington IL 60010-1266. (847)382-5626. Fax: (847)382-3685. E-mail: BAACouncil@aol.com. **Contact:** Lani Ori, Charles White, Dale Griffith, Christopher Sweet. Annual competition "to encourage and reward works of literary excellence." Awards: The Whetstone Prize, usually $500 to a single author for best fiction, nonfiction or poetry selected for publication in *Whetstone* (an annual literary journal); The John Patrick McGrath Award, $250 to a single author, for fiction. Competition receives hundreds of entries; all submissions to *Whetstone* are eligible. Judges: co-editors of *Whetstone*. Guidelines available by mail. Deadline: open until publication; "we read all year." Unpublished submissions. Length: prose up to 25 pages; poetry, 3-5 poems. Sample copies with guidelines $5 postpaid. Winners announced in April and notified by letter. List of winners available in January for SASE. Winners announced in front of *Whetstone* as well as press releases, etc.

☐ BEACON STREET REVIEW EDITOR'S CHOICE AWARD, Beacon Street Review, Emerson College, 100 Beacon St., Boston MA 02116. (617)824-8750. E-mail: beaconstreetreveiw@hotmail.com. **Contact:** Prose or Poetry Editor. Award to "recognize highest degree of creative talent and a true seriousness of effort." Annual award for short stories, nonfiction or poetry. Award: $75. Judge: an establshed local author. No entry fee. For guidelines send SASE. Deadline October 4, 2001. Entries should be previously unpublished. Contest open to all writers. Length: 4,000 words maximum for prose entries or 5 poems.

☐ GEORGE BENNETT FELLOWSHIP, Phillips Exeter Academy, 20 Main St., Exeter NH 03833-2460. Website: www.exeter.edu. **Contact:** Charles Pratt, coordinator, selection committee. "To provide time and freedom from monetary concerns to a person contemplating or pursuing a career as a professional writer. The committee favors applicants who have not yet published a book-length work with a major publisher." Annual award of writing residency. Award: A stipend ($6,000 at present), plus room and board for academic year. Competition receives approximately 130 submissions. Judges are a committee of the English department. Entry fee $5. Application form and guidelines for SASE, or obtain from the Academy website: www.exeter.edu. Deadline: December 1. Winners announced in March and notified by letter or phone. List of winners available in March. All entrants will receive an announcement of the winner. "Stay within a few pages of the limit (we won't read more anyway). Trust us to recognize that what you are sending is a work in progress (you have the chance to talk about that in your statement). Hope, but don't expect anything. If you don't win, some well-known writers have been in your shoes—at least as many as have won the Fellowship."

BERTELSMANN'S WORLD OF EXPRESSIONS SCHOLARSHIP PROGRAM, Bertelsmann USA, 1540 Broadway, New York NY 10036. (212)930-4520. Fax: (212)930-4783. E-mail: bwoesp@bmge.com. Website: www.worldofexpression.org. **Contact:** Melanie Fallon-Houska, director. Annual competition for short stories and poems. Award: $500-10,000, 68 awards total. Competition receives 2,000 submissions per category. Judges: various city officials, executives, authors, editors. Guidelines available October 1 for SASE, fax or e-mail. Deadline: February 1. Winners announced mid-May and notified by mail and phone. For list of winners, send SASE, fax, e-mail or visit website. All the winners must be public New York City high school seniors. Word length: 2,500 words or less.

✓ ◯ ◎ "BEST OF OHIO WRITERS" CONTEST, *Ohio Writer Magazine*, P.O. Box 91801, Cleveland OH 44101. (216)421-0403. Fax: (216)791-1727. E-mail: pwlgc@msn.com. **Contact:** Gail and Stephen Bellamy, editors. Award "to encourage and promote the work of writers in Ohio." Annual competition for short stories. Awards: $150 (1st Prize), $50 (2nd Prize). Competition receives 200 submissions. Judges: "a selected panel of prominent Ohio writers." $10 entry fee; includes subscription to *Ohio Writer*. Guidelines available after January 1 for SASE, fax or e-mail. Accepts inquiries by e-mail and phone. Deadline: July 31. Unpublished submissions. Ohio writers only. Length: 2,500 words. "No cliché plots; we're looking for fresh, unpublished voices." Winners announced November 1 and notified by mail. List of winners available November 1 for SASE or e-mail.

◢ IRMA S. AND JAMES H. BLACK CHILDREN'S BOOK AWARD, Bank Street College, 610 W. 112th St., New York NY 10025-1898. (212)875-4450. Fax: (212)875-4558. E-mail: lindag@bnkst.edu. Website: http://

streetcat.bnkst.edu/html/isb.html. **Contact:** Linda Greengrass, award director. Annual award "to honor the young children's book published in the preceding year judged the most outstanding in text as well as in art. Book must be published the year preceding the May award." Award: Press function at Harvard Club, a scroll and seals by Maurice Sendak for attaching to award book's run. Judges: adult children's literature experts and children 6-10 years old. No entry fee. Guidelines available by SASE, fax, e-mail, or on website. Accepts inquiries by phone, fax and e-mail. Deadline: December 15. Expects to receive about 150 fiction entries for 2002 competition. "Write to address above. Usually publishers submit books they want considered, but individuals can too. No entries are returned." Winners notified by phone in April and announced in May. A list of winners will be available on website.

N BLAGGARD AWARD FOR BEST SHORT STORY OF THE YEAR, (formerly Best First New Mystery Award), *New Mystery Magazine*, 101 W. 23rd St., New York NY 10011. (212)353-1582. Fax: (212)353-3495. Website: www.NewMystery.com. **Contact:** Miss Linda Wong. Award to "find the best new mystery, crime or suspense writer, and promote high standards in the short story form. For writers who have never been paid for their fiction writing." Annual award for short stories. Award: publication in *New Mystery Magazine*. Competition receives approximately 3,000 submissions. Judges: editorial panel of veteran mystery writers. No entry fee. No guidelines available. Deadline: July 4. Unpublished submissions. Word length: 3,000-5,000 words. "Please mark ms 'First Mystery Award.' Study back issues of *New Mystery* for style." Sample copy: $7 plus 9×12 SAE with $1.24 postage. Winners announced in May annually.

BOARDMAN TASKER PRIZE, 14 Pine Lodge, Dairyground Rd., Bramhall, Stockport, Cheshire SK7 2HS United Kingdom. Phone/fax: 0161 439 4624. Website: www.boardmantaskr.com. **Contact:** Mrs. Dorothy Boardman. "To reward a book which has made an outstanding contribution to mountain literature. A memorial to Peter Boardman and Joe Tasker, who disappeared on Everest in 1982." Award: £2,000. Competition receives 20 submissions. Judges: A panel of 3 judges elected by trustees. Guidelines for SASE and on website. Deadline: August 1. Limited to works published or distributed in the UK for the first time between November 1 and October 31. Publisher's entry only. "May be fiction, nonfiction, poetry or drama. Not an anthology. Subject must be concerned with a mountain environment. Previous winners have been books on expeditions, climbing experiences; a biography of a mountaineer; novels." Winners announced in November and notified by mail. A list of winners available on website.

N BOOK PUBLISHERS OF TEXAS AWARD, The Texas Institute of Letters, Center for the Study of the Southwest, Flowers Hall 327, Southwest Texas State University, San Marcos TX 78666. (512)245-2232. Fax: (512)245-7462. E-mail: mb13@swt.edu. Website: www.english.swet.edu/css/TIL/index. **Contact:** Mark Busby, secretary. "Award to honor the best book written for children or young people that was published the year prior to that in which the award is given." Annual competition for children's literature. Award: $50. Competition receives approximately 40 submissions. Judges: Committee selected by TIL. Guidelines available after June for SASE. Accepts inquiries by e-mail and fax. Deadline: January 8, 2002. Previously published submissions from January 1 through December 31 of the year prior to the award. "To be eligible, the writer must have been born in Texas or have lived in the state for two years at some time, or the subject matter of the work must be associated with Texas." Winners announced April 15, 2002 and notified by phone. List of winners available on website.

BOOKER PRIZE FOR FICTION, Booktrust, Book House, 45 East Hill, London SW18 2QZ England. Phone: 020 8516 2973 or 020 8516 2972. Fax: 020 8516 2978. E-mail: susy@booktrust.org.uk or tarryn@booktrust.org.uk. Website: www.booktrust.org.uk or www.thebookerprize.com. **Contact:** Susy Behr, prizes manager; Tarryn McKay, prizes administrator. Award to the best novel of the year. Annual competition for novels. Award: £20,000. Each of the short listed authors receive £1,000. Guidelines available for SASE, fax, e-mail or website. Judges: five judges appointed by the Booker Management Committee. Deadline: July. Announcement of winners October/November. Publisher will be notified. Only published submissions eligible; must be a full length novel written in English by a citizen of the Commonwealth or Republic of Ireland. List of winners available for SASE, by fax, e-mail or website.

BOSTON GLOBE-HORN BOOK AWARDS, *Horn Book Magazine, Inc.*, 56 Roland St., Suite 200, Boston MA 02129. (617)628-0225. Fax: (617)628-0882. E-mail: info@hbook.com. Website: www.hbook.com. **Contact:** Anne Quirk, marketing director. Annual award. "To honor excellence in children's fiction or poetry, picture and nonfiction books published within the US." Award: $500 and engraved silver bowl first prize in each category; engraved silver plate for the 2 honor books in each category. Competition receives 1,000 submissions. No entry fee. Guidelines available after January 15 for SASE, fax, e-mail, or on website. Accepts inquiries by fax and e-mail. Entry forms or rules for SASE. Deadline: May 15. "Children's and young adult books published in the U.S. between June 1, 2001-May 31, 2002 can be submitted by publishers." Winners announced in July and notified by phone. List of winners available in July on website, for SASE, by fax and by e-mail.

N ● BOSTON REVIEW SHORT STORY CONTEST, *Boston Review*, E53-407, MIT, Cambridge MA 02139. (617)253-3642. E-mail: review@mit.edu. Website: http://bostonreview.mit.edu. **Contact:** Rob Mitchell. Annual award for short stories. Award: $1,000. Processing fee $15. Deadline: September 1. Unpublished submissions. Competition receives 500 entries. No restrictions on subject matter. Guidelines available in September 2001 for SASE, by e-mail or on website. Accepts inquiries by e-mail. Word length: 4,000 words. Winning entry published in December issue. All entrants receive a 1-year subscription to the *Boston Review* beginning with the December issue. Stories not returned. Winners announced December 1 and notified by mail.

N BOULEVARD SHORT FICTION CONTEST FOR EMERGING WRITERS, *Boulevard Magazine*, PMB 332, 4579 Laclede Ave., St. Louis MO 63108. (314)361-2986. E-mail: ballyman@hotmail.com. Website: www.richardburgin.com. **Contact:** Richard Burgin, editor. Annual competition for short stories. Award: $1,500. Competition receives 2 submissions per category. Judges: *Boulevard*'s editors. $15 fee per entry which includes a year's subscription to *Boulevard*. Guidelines available January 2002 for SASE or e-mail. Accepts inquiries by e-mail. Deadline: December 15, 2002. Entries should be unpublished. Open to: "Writers who have not yet published a book of fiction, poetry or creative nonfiction with a nationally distributed press are welcome." Length: 7,500 words. "Be familiar with *Boulevard Magazine*." Winners announced in the Spring Issue of *Boulevard Magazine* and notified by mail or phone in February/March.

N ● ◎ BRAZOS BOOKSTORE (HOUSTON) AWARD (SINGLE SHORT STORY), The Texas Institute of Letters, Center for the Study of the Southwest, Flowes Hall 327, Southwest Texas State University, San Marcos TX 78666. (512)245-2232. Fax: (512)245-7462. E-mail: mb13@swt.edu. Website: www.english.swt. edu/css/TIL/index. **Contact:** Mark Busby, secretary. Award to "honor the writer of the best short story published for the first time during the calendar year before the award is given." Annual competition for short stories. Award: $750. Competition receives approximately 40-50 submissions. Judges: panel selected by TIL Council. Guidelines for SASE. Accepts inquiries by e-mail. Deadline: January 14. Previously published submissions. Entries must have appeared in print between January 1 and December 31 of the year prior to the award. "Award available to writers who, at some time, have lived in Texas at least two years consecutively or whose work has a significant Texas theme. Entries must be sent directly to the three judges. Their names and addresses are available from the TIL office. Include SASE. Winners announced April 15 and notified by phone."

THE BRIAR CLIFF REVIEW POETRY & FICTION COMPETITION, *The Briar Cliff Review*, Briar Cliff College, 3303 Rebecca St., Sioux City IA 51104-0100. (712)279-5321. Fax: (712)279-5410. E-mail: currans@briar-cliff.edu. Website: www.briar-cliff.edu/bcreview. **Contact:** Tricia Currans-Sheehan, editor. Award "to reward good writers and showcase quality writing." Annual award for short stories and poetry. Award: $200 and publication in spring issue. Competition receives 100-125 submissions. Judges: editors. "All entries are read by at least 3 editors." $10 entry fee. Guidelines for SASE. Deadline: submissions between August 1 and November 1. Previously unpublished submissions. Word length: 5,000 words maximum. "Send us your best work. We want stories with a plot." Winners announced December or January and notified by letter. List of winners available for SASE sent with submission.

ARCH & BRUCE BROWN FOUNDATION, The Arch & Bruce Brown Foundation, PMB 503, 31855 Date Palm Drive #3, Cathedral City CA 92234. E-mail: archwrite@aol.com. Website: www.aabbfoundation.org. **Contact:** Arch Brown, president. Contest for "gay-positive works based on history." Annual contest; type of contest changes each year: short story (2001); playwrighting (2002); novel (2003). Award: $1,000 (not limited to a single winner). No entry fee. For guidelines, send SASE or visit website. Deadline: November 30, 2002. Entries should be unpublished. Contest open to all writers. Winners announced Spring 2003 and notified by mail April 1, 2003. For list of winners send SASE or visit website.

✓ ○ ◎ BUSH ARTIST FELLOWS PROGRAM, (formerly Bush Artist Fellowships), Bush Foundation, E-900 First Nat'l Bank Building, 332 Minnesota St., St. Paul MN 55101-1387. (651)227-5222. Fax: (651)297-6485. E-mail: kpolley@bushfound.org. Website: www.bushfoundation.org. **Contact:** Kathi Polley, program assistant. Award to "provide artists with significant financial support that enables them to further their work and their contribution to their communities. Fellows may decide to take time for solitary work or reflection, engage in collaborative or community projects, or embark on travel or research." Annual grant. Award: $40,000 for 12-18 months. Competition receives 200-300 submissions. Literature (fiction, creative nonfiction, poetry) offered every other year. Next offered 2003 BAF. Applications available August 2002. Accepts inquiries by fax and e-mail. Deadline: October 2002. Must meet certain publication requirements. Judges: a panel of artists and arts professionals who reside outside of Minnesota, South Dakota, North Dakota or Wisconsin. Applicants must be at least 25 years old, and Minnesota, South Dakota, North Dakota or Western Wisconsin residents. Students not eligible. Winners announced in Spring 2003 and notified by letter. List of winners available in May and sent to all applicants.

BYLINE SHORT FICTION & POETRY AWARDS, P.O. Box 130596, Edmond OK 73013-0001. Phone/fax: (405)348-5591. E-mail: bylinemp@aol.com. Website: www.bylinemag.com. **Contact:** Marcia Preston, executive editor/publisher. "To encourage our subscribers in striving for high quality writing." Annual awards for short stories and poetry. Award: $250 in each category. Competition receives approximately 200 submissions in each category. Judges are published writers not on the *ByLine* staff. Entry fee $5 for stories; $3 for poems. Guidelines available for SASE. Accepts inquiries by e-mail and phone. Postmark deadline: November 1. "Judges look for quality writing, well-drawn characters, significant themes. Entries should be unpublished and not have won money in any previous contest. Winners notified by mail and phone in January and announced in February issue, accompanied by photo and short bio. For list of winners, send SASE, read magazine or visit website. Open to subscribers only."

CALIFORNIA BOOK AWARDS, The Commonwealth Club of California, 595 Market St., San Francisco CA 94105. (415)597-4846. Fax: (415)597-6729. E-mail: bookawards@commonwealth.org. Website: www.commonwealthclub.org. **Contact:** Barbara Lane, book award manager. Annual competition for novels and story collections. Award: $2,000 (1st Prize); $300 (2nd Prize). Competition receives 100 submissions. Judges: panel of jurors. Guidelines available in July 2001 by e-mail, on website or for SASE. Accepts inquiries by fax and e-mail. Deadline: December 28. Previously published submissions that appeared in print between January 1 and December 30. "Writers must have been legal residents of California when manuscript was accepted for publication. Enter as early as possible—supply three copies of book." Winners notified in June by phone, mail or through publisher and announced in summer. List of winners available for SASE or on website.

JOHN W. CAMPBELL MEMORIAL AWARD FOR THE BEST SCIENCE-FICTION NOVEL OF THE YEAR; THEODORE STURGEON MEMORIAL AWARD FOR THE BEST SCIENCE FICTION SHORT FICTION, Center for the Study of Science Fiction, English Dept., University of Kansas, Lawrence KS 66045. (785)864-3380. Fax: (785)864-4298. E-mail: jgunn@ukans.edu. Website: http://falcon.cc.ukans.edu/~sfcenter/. **Contact:** James Gunn, professor and director. "To honor the best novel and short science fiction of the year." Annual competition for short stories and novels. Award: Certificate. "Winners' names are engraved on a trophy." Campbell Award receives approximately 200 submissions. Judges: 2 separate juries. Accepts inquiries by e-mail and fax. Deadline: December 31. For previously published submissions. "Ordinarily publishers should submit work, but authors have done so when publishers would not. Send for list of jurors." Entrants for the Sturgeon Award are selected by nomination only. Winners announced in July. List of winners available for SASE.

CANADA COUNCIL GOVERNOR GENERAL'S LITERARY AWARDS, Canada Council for the Arts, 350 Albert St., P.O. Box 1047, Ottawa, Ontario K1P 5V8 Canada. (613)566-4414, ext. 5576. E-mail: josiane.polidori@canadacouncil.ca. **Contact:** Writing and Publishing Section. "Awards of $10,000 each are given annually to the best English-language and best French-language Canadian work in each of seven categories: children's literature (text) and children's literature (illustration), drama, fiction, poetry, nonfiction and translation." Canadian authors, illustrators and translators only. Books must be submitted by publishers (4 copies must be sent to the Canada Council) and accompanied by a Publisher's Submissions Form, available from the Writing and Publishing Section. Self-published books are not eligible.

THE CAPRICORN AWARD, The Writer's Voice, 5 W. 63rd St., New York NY 10023. (212)875-4124. Fax: (212)875-4184. E-mail: wswritersvoice@gmcanyc.org. Website: www.yoncanyc.org. **Contact:** David Andrews, literary manager. Annual competition for novels or story collections. Award: $1,000, plus featured reading. Entry fee $15. Deadline: December 31. Applicants may submit excerpts of work that have been previously published,

FOR EXPLANATIONS OF THESE SYMBOLS,
SEE THE INSIDE FRONT AND BACK COVERS OF THIS BOOK.

however, complete work cannot have been previously published elsewhere. Submit first 150 pgs. of novel/story collection. Guidelines/entry form for SASE, e-mail or on website. Accepts inquiries by e-mail. Winners announced mid-summer and notified by mail, phone.

☑ ◘ CAPTIVATING BEGINNINGS CONTEST, *Lynx Eye*, 542 Mitchell Dr., Los Osos CA 93402. (805)528-8146. Fax: (805)528-7876. E-mail: pamccully@aol.com. **Contact:** Pam McCully, co-editor. Annual award for stories "with engrossing beginnings, stories that will enthrall and absorb readers." Award: $100 plus publication, 1st Prize; $10 each for 4 honorable mentions plus publication. Competition receives 600-700 submissions. Judges: *Lynx Eye* editors. Entry fee $5/story. Guidelines available for SASE or by e-mail. Accepts inquiries by e-mail and phone. Unpublished submissions. Length: 7,500 words or less. "The stories will be judged on the first 500 words." Guidelines available year round for SASE. Accepts inquiries by e-mail and phone. Deadline: January 31. Winners announced March 15 and notified by mail. List of winners available March 31 for SASE.

Ⓝ ◎ CELTIC VOICE WRITING CONTEST, Bardsong Press, P.O. Box 775396, Steamboat Springs CO 80477-5396. (970)870-1401. Fax: (970)879-2657. E-mail: celts@bardsongpress.com. Website: www.bardsong press.com. **Contact:** Ann Gilpin, editor. Annual competition for short stories. Award: cash awards for category winners; publication for winners and honorable mentions. Judges: selected guest judges. $10 fee per entry. Guidelines available January 1, 2002 for SASE, e-mail or on website. Accepts inquiries by e-mail. Deadline: September 30, 2002. Entries should be unpublished. Open to all writers. "We are looking for work that reflects the ageless culture, history, symbolism, mythology and spirituality that belongs to Celtic heritage. Following the guidelines specifications closely will give the greatest chance to do well in the competition. Let your imagination soar freely." Winners announced in January 2003 and notified by mail or e-mail. List of winners available for SASE.

◑ THE CHELSEA AWARDS, P.O. Box 773, Cooper Station, New York NY 10276-0773. E-mail: rafoerster @aol.com. *Mail entries to*: Chelsea Awards, %Richard Foerster, Editor, P.O. Box 1040, York Beach ME 03910-1040. Annual competition for short stories. Award: $1,000 and publication in *Chelsea* (all entries are considered for publication). Competition receives 300 submissions. Judges: the editors. Entry fee $10 (for which entrants also receive a subscription). Guidelines available for SASE. Deadline: June 15. Unpublished submissions. Absolutely no simultaneous submissions. Manuscripts may not exceed 30 typed pages or about 7,500 words. The stories must not be under consideration elsewhere or scheduled for book publication within 8 months of the competition deadline. Include separate cover sheet; no name on ms. Mss will not be returned; include SASE for notification of results. Winners announced August 15 and notified by telephone. List of winners available August 20 for SASE.

Ⓝ CHICAGO LITERARY AWARDS, *Another Chicago Magazine*, 3709 N. Henmore, Chicago IL 60613-2901. E-mail: editors@anotherchicagomag.com. Website: www.anotherchicagomag.com. **Contact:** Editor. "To award excellence in fiction and poetry writing." Annual competition for short stories and poetry. Award: $1,000 and publication in *Another Chicago Magazine*. Competition receives 400 submissions. Judge: Diane Wakoski (poetry). $10/story; length: 6,500; $10/set of 3 poems; length: 300 lines total. Checks payable to Left Field Press. No previously published work eligible; if work is under consideration elsewhere, *ACM* must be notified and work must be withdrawn upon acceptance elsewhere. "No names on mss; include cover page with name, address, titles, word count for fiction and line count for poetry. No mss returned." Winners announced April 1, 2002. Include SASE for notification of winners; SAS postcard for acknowledgement of entry. No certified mail please.

Ⓝ ◘ ◎ CHICANO/LATINO LITERARY CONTEST, Dept. of Spanish & Portuguese, University of California-Irvine, Irvine CA 92697-5275. (949)824-5443. Fax: (949)824-2803. E-mail: CLLP@uci.edu. Website: www.humanities.hnet.uci.edu/spanishandportuguese/contest.html. **Contact:** Barbara Caldwell, coordinator. Annual award for different genre each year; novels (2003), short stories (2004), poetry (2005) and drama (2006). Award: Usually $1,000. Guidelines available in January 2002 for SASE or on website. Deadline: June 1. Accepts inquiries by fax and e-mail. Unpublished submissions. Winners notified by letter in October. A list of winners will be available on website.

⊕ ◑ THE CHILDREN'S BOOK AWARD, Federation of Children's Book Groups, The Old Malt House, Aldbourne, Marlborough, Wilts SN8 2DW England. Award to "promote good quality books for children." Annual award for short stories, novels, story collections and translations. Award: "Portfolio of children's writing and drawings and a magnificent trophy of silver and oak." Judges: Thousands of children from all over the United Kingdom. Guidelines for SASE or SAE and IRC. Deadline: December 31. Published and previously unpublished submissions (first publication in UK). "The book should be suitable for children."

☑ ⊙ **CHILDREN'S WRITERS FICTION CONTEST**, Stepping Stones, P.O. Box 8863, Springfield MO 65801-8863. (417)863-7369. Fax: (417)864-4745. E-mail: verwil@alumni.pace.edu. **Contact:** V.R. Williams, coordinator. Award to "promote writing for children by encouraging children's writers and giving them an opportunity to submit their work in competition." Annual competition for short stories and translations. Award: $260 and/or publication in *Hodge Podge*. Competition receives 160 submissions. "Judged by Goodin, Williams, Goodwin and/or associates. Entries are judged for clarity, grammar, punctuation, imagery, content and suitability for children." Entry fee $8. Guidelines available for SASE, fax, website or e-mail. Accepts inquiries by fax, phone, and e-mail. Deadline: July 31. Previously unpublished submissions. Word length: 2,000 words. "Work submitted on colored paper, book format is not acceptable. Stories should have believable characters." Winners announced in September and notified by mail. List of winners for SASE or fax. "To avoid disqualification of entry, contestants must follow guidelines. If possible, the child should be the main character in the story. Stories about animals or inanimate objects should have a purpose. Children should enjoy the story, but also learn from it."

☑ **THE CHRISTOPHER AWARDS,** The Christophers, 12 E. 48th St., New York NY 10017-1091. (212)759-4050. Fax: (212)838-5073. E-mail: awads_coordinator@christophers.org. Website: www.christophers.org. **Contact:** Judith Trojan, program manager. Annual award "to encourage creative people to continue to produce works which affirm the highest values of the human spirit in adult and children's books." Published submissions only. Award: Bronze medallion. "Award judged by a grassroots panel and a final panel of experts. Juvenile works are 'children tested.' " No entry forms or submission fees. "Potential winners are nominated and reviewed throughout the year by panels of media professionals, members of the Christopher staff and by specially supervised children's reading groups. Friends of The Christophers are also encouraged to nominate titles." For guidelines send 6x9 SASE or fax. Accepts inquiries accepted by fax, e-mail and phone. Two deadlines: June 1 and November 1 every year. Books may be submitted any time in between as well. Winners announced in January and notified by mail and phone late January. List of winners available for SASE, by fax or visit website. Example of book award: *I Love You, Blue Kangaroo!*, by Emma Chicester Clark (children's book category 2000).

◯ **CNW/FFWA FLORIDA STATE WRITING COMPETITION,** Florida Freelance Writers Association, P.O. Box A, North Stratford NH 03590. (603)922-8338. Fax: (603)922-8339. E-mail: danakcnw@ncia.net. Website: www.writers-editors.com. **Contact:** Dana K. Cassell, executive director. Award "to recognize publishable writing." Annual competition for short stories and novels. Awards: $100 (first place), $75 (second place), $50 (third place). Competition receives 50-100 submissions in short story/novel division. Total 400-500 in all divisions. Judges: published authors, teachers, editors. Entry fee ($5-20) varies with membership status. Guidelines available for SASE or on website. Deadline: March 15. Previously unpublished submissions. Winners will be notified by mail by May 31. For list of winners, send SASE or visit website.

Ⓝ ⊙ **COLORADO BOOK AWARDS**, Colorado Center for the Book, 2123 Downing St., Denver CO 80205. (303)839-8320. Fax: (303)839-8319. Website: www.ColoradoBook.org. **Contact:** Chris Citron, executive director. "To celebrate the excellence of Colorado writers." Annual competition for novels. Award: $350, plaque and speaking appearances. Competition receives 190 submissions. Judges: 5 judges in each of the ten categories. $40 fee per entry. Guidelines for SASE or fax. Accepts inquiries by fax. Deadline: January 15, 2002. Entries should be published in preceding year. Contest open to Colorado residents. Winners announced Fall of each year and notified by mail. For list of winners send SASE or fax.

CONNECTICUT COMMISSION ON THE ARTS ARTIST FELLOWSHIPS, One Financial Plaza, Hartford CT 06103-2601. (860)566-4770. Fax: (860)566-6462. E-mail: kdemeo@csunet.ctstateu.edu. Website: www.ctarts.org/artfellow.htm (to download application from website). **Contact:** Linda Dente, program manager. "To support the creation of new work by creative artists *living in Connecticut*." Biennial competition for the creation or completion of new works in literature, i.e., short stories, novels, story collections, poetry and playwriting. Awards: $5,000 and $2,500. Competition receives 50-75 submissions. Judges: Peer professionals (writers, editors). Guidelines available in June by e-mail or on website. Accepts inquiries by phone and e-mail. Deadline: September 18. Writers may send either previously published or unpublished submissions—up to 25 pages of material. Connecticut residents only. "Write to please yourself. If you win, that's a bonus." Winners announced in January and notified by mail. For list of winners, send SASE.

☘ ◻ ⊙ **CONSEIL DE LA VIE FRANCAISE EN AMÉRIQUE/PRIX CHAMPLAIN**, Conseil de la vie Française en Amérique, Maison de la Francophonie 39, rue Dalhousie, Quebec G1K 8R8 Canada. (418)646-9117. Fax: (418)644-7670. E-mail: cvfa@cvfa.ca. Website: www.cvfa.ca. Prix Champlain estab. 1957. Annual award to encourage literary work in novel or short story in French by Francophiles living outside Quebec, in the US or Canada. "There is no restriction as to the subject matter. If the author lives in Quebec, the subject matter must be related to French-speaking people living outside of Quebec." Award: $1,500 in Canadian currency. The prize will be given alternately; one year for fiction, the next for nonfiction. Next fiction award in 1999. 3 different judges each year. Guidelines for SASE or IRC or on website at www.cvfa.ca/PrixBoursesOrdre/Prix_Champlain/prix_champlain.html. Deadline: December 31. For previously published or contracted submissions, published no more than 3 years prior to award. Author must furnish 4 examples of work, curriculum vitae, address and phone number.

☑ ◯ **THE CRUCIBLE POETRY AND FICTION COMPETITION**, *Crucible*, Barton College, College Station, Wilson NC 27893. (252)399-6456. E-mail: tgrimes@barton.edu. **Contact:** Terrence L. Grimes, editor. Annual competition for short stories. Award: $150 (1st Prize); $100 (2nd Prize) and publication in *Crucible*. Judges: in-house editorial board. Guidelines available in January for SASE. Deadline: April. "The best time to submit is December through April." Unpublished submissions only. Fiction should be 8,000 words or less.

◎ **DANA AWARD IN SHORT FICTION**, 7207 Townsend Forest Court, Browns Summit NC 27214-9634. (336)656-7009. E-mail: danaawards@pipeline.com. Website: http://danaawards.home.pipeline.com. **Contact:** Mary Elizabeth Parker, chair. Award "to reward work that has been previously unrecognized in the area of fiction. All genres, including literary/mainstream, and speculative fiction. No work for or by persons under 16. "Let authors be aware work must meet standards of literary complexity and excellence. Character development, excellence of style are as important as the plot line." Award: $1,000. Competition receives 300 submissions annually. Entry fee $10/short story. Make checks payable to Dana Awards. Guidelines for SASE, by e-mail or on website. Accepts inquiries by e-mail and phone. Unpublished submissions, not under contract to any publisher. "See 'What We're Looking For' on our website for submission tips." Word length: No longer than 10,000 words, 3,000 word average preferred. Postmark deadline: October 31. Winners announced March 2003 and notified by phone, then by letter or e-mail. Send SASE with submissions to receive competition results letter.

DANA AWARD IN THE NOVEL, 7207 Townsend Forest Court, Browns Summit NC 27214-9634. (336)656-7009. E-mail: danaawards@pipeline.com. Website: http://danaawards.home.pipeline.com. **Contact:** Mary Elizabeth Parker, chair. Award to "reward work that has not yet been recognized, since we know from firsthand experience how tough the literary market is." Annual competition for novels. Award: $1,000. Competition receives 300-400 submissions annually. Judges: nationally-published novelists. $20 fee for each submission. Guidelines for SASE, e-mail or on website by March. "See website under 'What We're Looking For' for submission tips." Accepts inquiries by e-mail. Postmark deadline October 31. Unpublished submissions and not under contract to be published. Novelists should submit first 50 pages only of a novel either completed or in progress. No novels for or by children/young adults. In-progress submissions should be as polished as possible. Multiple submissions accepted, but each must include a separate $20 entry fee. Make checks payable to Dana Awards. Winners announced March-April and notified by phone, mail, or e-mail. List of winners available late spring for SASE, e-mail, or on website. Send SASE for winners and finalists results letter along with submissions.

☑ ◯ **MARGUERITE DE ANGELI PRIZE**, Delacorte Press Books for Young Readers, 1540 Broadway, New York NY 10036. (212)782-8633. Fax: (212)782-9452. Website: www.randomhouse.com. "To encourage the writing of fiction for middle grade readers (either contemporary or historical) in the same spirit as the works of Marguerite de Angeli." Open to US and Canadian writers. Annual competition for first novels for middle-grade readers (ages 7-10). Award: One BDD hardcover and paperback book contract, with $1,500 cash prize and $3,500 advance against royalties. Competition receives 350 submissions. Judges: Editors of Delacorte Press Books for Young Readers. Send SASE, fax, or visit website for guidelines; available in August. Deadline: Submissions must be postmarked by June 30. Previously unpublished (middle-grade) fiction. Length: 40-144 pages. Winners announced by October 31 and notified by phone. List of winners available by SASE or on website.

DEAD METAPHOR PRESS CHAPBOOK CONTEST, Dead Metaphor Press, P.O. Box 2076, Boulder CO 80306-2076. **Contact:** Richard Wilmarth. Award to "promote quality writing." Annual competition for short stories. Award: 10% of the press run plus discounted copies. Books assigned ISBN numbers and distributed by Small Press Distribution. Sample chapbook: $6. Competition receives 250-300 submissions. Judge: Richard Wilmarth. Entry fee $12. Guidelines available for SASE. Deadline: October 31. Maximum length: 24 pages. Winners announced at end of summer and notified by mail. For list of winners, send SASE.

⊕ ☑ **DEBUT DAGGER**, Crime Writers' Association, % website. E-mail: judith.cutler@virgin.net. Website: www.thecwa.co.uk. Competition to stimulate new crime writing. Annual competition for first 3,000 words of novel and 500 word outline. Award: £250 cash, silver pin and free tickets for prize ceremony. Entry fee: £10. Guidelines available April/May 2002 on website. Deadline: Mid-August. Entries should be unpublished. Contest open to anyone who has not had a novel published in any genre. Winners announced October 2002 and notified by phone.

◯ ◎ **DELAWARE DIVISION OF THE ARTS**, 820 N. French St., Wilmington DE 19801. (302)577-8284. Fax: (302)577-6561. E-mail: kpleasanton@state.de.us. Website: www.artsdel.org **Contact:** Kristin Pleasanton, coordinator. "To help further careers of emerging and established professional artists." Annual awards for Delaware residents only. Awards: $10,000 for masters, $5,000 for established professionals; $2,000 for emerging professionals. Competition receives 100 submissions. Judges are out-of-state professionals in each division. Entry forms or rules available after January 1 for SASE. Accepts inquiries by fax and e-mail. Deadline: August 1. Winners announced in December and notified by mail.

N DOBIE/PAISANO FELLOWSHIPS, Texas Institute of Letters, Center for the Study of the Southwest, Flowers Hall 327, Southwest Texas State University, San Marcos TX 78666. (512)245-2232. Fax: (512)245-7462. E-mail: mb13@swt.edu. Website: www.english.swt.edu/css/TIL/index. **Contact:** Mark Busby, secretary. Award to "honor the achievement and promise of two writers." Annual competition for fiction, poetry or nonfiction. Award: $1,200/month for six months and rent-free stay at Paisano ranch southwest of Austin, TX. Judges: committee from Texas Institute of Letters and the University of Texas. Guidelines available June for SASE. Accepts inquiries by e-mail and fax. Deadline: January 14, 2001. "To be eligible, a writer must have been born in Texas or have lived in the state for at least two consecutive years at some point. The winners usually have notable publishing credits behind them in addition to promising work that is under way." Winners announced April 15, 2002. List of winners available on website.

◯ **JACK DYER FICTION PRIZE**, *Crab Orchard Review*, English Dept., Southern Illinois University, Carbondale IL 62901-4503. (618)453-6833. Website: www.siu.edu/~crborchd. **Contact:** Jon Tribble, managing editor. Award to "reward and publish exceptional fiction." Annual competition for short stories. Award: $1,000 and publication. Competition receives approximately 200 submissions. Judges: pre-screened by *Crab Orchard* staff; winner chosen by outside judge. Entry fee $10; year's subscription included. Guidelines available after January for SASE or on website. Deadline March 15. Previously unpublished submissions. Word length: 6,000. "Please note that no stories will be returned." Winners announced by August 15 and notified by phone or mail. List of winners available for SASE or on website.

◯ **EATON LITERARY ASSOCIATES' LITERARY AWARDS PROGRAM**, Eaton Literary Associates, P.O. Box 49795, Sarasota FL 34230-6795. (941)366-6589. Fax: (941)365-4679. E-mail: eatonlit@aol.com. Website: www.eatonliterary.com. **Contact:** Richard Lawrence, vice president. Biannual award for short stories and novels. Award: $2,500 for best book-length ms, $500 for best short story. Competition receives approx. 2,000 submissions annually. Judges are 2 staff members in conjunction with an independent agency. Guidelines for SASE, fax, e-mail or on website. Accepts inquiries by fax, phone and e-mail. Deadline: March 31 for short stories; August 31 for book-length mss. Winners announced in April and September and notified by mail. For list of winners, send SASE, fax, e-mail or on website.

✔ ◐ **VIRGINIA FAULKNER AWARD FOR EXCELLENCE IN WRITING**, *Prairie Schooner*, 201 Andrews Hall, University of Nebraska, Lincoln NE 68588-0334. (402)472-0911. Fax: (402)472-9771. E-mail: eflanagan2@unl.edu. Website: www.unl.edu/schooner/psmain.htm. **Contact:** Hilda Raz, editor. "An award for writing published in *Prairie Schooner* in the previous year." Annual competition for short stories, novel excerpts and translations. Award: $1,000. Judges: Editorial Board. Guidelines for SASE or on website. Accepts inquiries by fax and e-mail. "We only read mss from September through May." Work must have been published in *Prairie Schooner* in the previous year. Winners announced in spring issue and notified by mail in February or March. List of winners will be published in spring *Prairie Schooner*.

✔ ◯ **WILLIAM FAULKNER CREATIVE WRITING COMPETITION**, The Pirate's Alley Faulkner Society Inc., 624 Pirate's Alley, New Orleans LA 70116-3254. (504)586-1612. Fax: (504)522-9725. E-mail: faulkhouse@aol.com. Website: www.wordsandmusic.org. **Contact:** R. James, contest director. "To encourage publisher interest in writers with potential." Annual competition for short stories, novels, novellas, personal essays and poetry. Award: $7,500 for novel, $2,500 for novella, $2,000 for Novel-in-Progress; $1,500 for short story, $1,000 personal essay, $750 poetry and gold medals, plus trip to New Orleans for presentation. Competition receives 1,500-1,800 submissions. Judges: professional writers, academics. $25 fee for each poem, essay, short story; $30 for novella and novel-in-progress; $35 for novel. Guidelines for SASE or on website. Accepts inquiries by e-mail. Deadline: April 1. Unpublished submissions. Word length: for novels, over 50,000; for novellas, under 50,000; for novels-in-progress, outline and first 50 pages; for short stories, under 20,000. All entries must be accompanied by official entry form which is provided with guidelines. Winners announced September 1 and notified by mail. List of winners available for SASE or on website.

✔ ◎ **FAUX FAULKNER CONTEST**, *Hemispheres* Magazine, *Faulkner Newsletter* of Yoknapatawpha Press and University of Mississippi, P.O. Box 248, Oxford MS 38655. (601)234-0909. E-mail: faulkner@waterval ley.net. Website: www.watervalley.net/yoknapatawphapress/index.htm or www.hemispheresmagazine.com. Award "to honor William Faulkner by imitating his style, themes and subject matter in a short parody." Annual competition for a 500-word (2-pages) parody. Award: 2 round-trip tickets to Memphis, plus complimentary registration and lodging for the annual Faulkner and Yoknapatawpha Conference at the University of Mississippi. Competition receives approximately 200-300 submissions. Past judges have included George Plimpton, Tom Wicker, John Berendt and Arthur Schlesinger, Jr. (judges rotate every year or so—well-known authors). Guidelines for SASE. Deadline: March 1. Previously unpublished submissions. Winners announced July 1 and notified May 1. Contestants grant publication rights and the right to release entries to other media and to the sponsors.

N ⬤ ◎ ROBERT L. FISH MEMORIAL AWARD, Mystery Writers of America, Inc., 17 E. 47th St., 6th Floor, New York NY 10017. E-mail: mwa_org@earthlink.net. Website: www.mysterywriters.org. Estab. 1984. Annual award "to encourage new writers in the mystery/detective/suspense short story—and, subsequently, larger work in the genre." Award: $500 and plaque. Judges: The MWA committee for best short story of the year in the mystery genre. Deadline: November 30. Submissions must be published the year prior to the award. Looking for "a story with a crime that is central to the plot that is well written and distinctive." Guidelines and application available for SASE, e-mail or on website.

🌐 ☑ FISH SHORT STORY PRIZE, Fish Publishing, Durrus, Bantry, Co. Cork, Ireland. Phone: (00)353-27-61246. E-mail: info@fishpublishing.com. Website: www.fishpublishing.com. **Contact:** Clem Cairns, editor. Award to "discover, encourage, and publish new literary talent." Annual competition for short stories. Award: First prize $1,200 and publication; second prize one week residence at Anam Cara Writers Retreat, Ireland and publication. Competition receives 1,200 submissions per category. Judge: Entries are shortlisted to approximately 100. These are sent to independent judges, who are well-known writers. "Top 18 stories will be published in an anthology." $12 entry fee. Guidelines available in July. Accepts inquiries by e-mail and phone. For guidelines, send SASE, e-mail or visit website. Deadline: November 30, 2001. Entries should *not* be previously published. Contest open to everybody. Length: 5,000 words or fewer. "Send your most finished, polished work." Don't be afraid of originality. Winners announced March 17 and notified in February. For list of winners send SASE, e-mail, or visit website.

⬤ DOROTHY CANFIELD FISHER AWARD, Vermont Dept. of Libraries, 109 State St., Montpelier VT 05609-0601. (802)828-3261. Fax: (802)828-2199. E-mail: ggreene@dol.state.vt.us. Website: www.dol.state.vt.us. **Contact:** Grace Greene, children's services consultant. Estab. 1957. Annual award. "To encourage Vermont schoolchildren to become enthusiastic and discriminating readers and to honor the memory of one of Vermont's most distinguished and beloved literary figures." Award: Illuminated scroll. Publishers send the committee review copies of books to consider. Only books of the current publishing year can be considered for next year's master list. Master list of titles is drawn up in March each year. Children vote each year in the spring and the award is given before the school year ends. Submissions must be "written by living American authors, be suitable for children in grades 4-8, and have literary merit. Can be nonfiction also." Accepts inquiries by e-mail. Deadline: December 1. Winners announced in April and notified by mail and phone. Call, write or e-mail for list of winners.

N F. SCOTT FITZGERALD SHORT STORY CONTEST, F. Scott Fitzgerald Literary Conference, Inc., City Hall, 111 Maryland Ave., Rockville MD 20850. (301)309-9461. Fax: (301)294-8073. **Contact:** Marilyn Mullan, administrative assistant. "The purpose is to support and encourage the current and next generation of great writers." Annual competition for short stories. Award: $1,000 first place; $200 runners-up. Competition receives 300 submissions. "The Writer's Center does prejudging. Finalists will be selected by Patricia Griffith. $25 fee per entry. Guidelines available April 2002 for SASE, fax, visit website or call. Accepts inquiries by phone. Deadline: Mid-July 2002 (see guidelines for exact date). Entries should be unpublished. Contest open to residents of Maryland, Virginia or Washington D.C. Length: 3,000 words. "Follow guidelines completely. All writing styles are welcome. The emphasis is not on style, but on the quality of the writing." Winners announced at the F. Scott Fitzgerald Conference in October and notified by mail mid-late September. For list of winners send SASE, fax or visit website.

FLORIDA FIRST COAST WRITERS' FESTIVAL NOVEL, SHORT FICTION & POETRY AWARDS, Writers' Festival & Florida Community College at Jacksonville, FCCJ North Campus, 4501 Capper Rd., Jacksonville FL 32218-4499. (904)766-6559. Fax: (904)766-6654. E-mail: hdenson@fccj.org. Website: www.fccj.org/

 A BULLET INTRODUCES COMMENTS by the editor of *Novel & Short Story Writer's Market* indicating special information about the listing.

wf/. **Contact:** Howard Denson and Brian Hale, festival contest directors. Conference and contest "to create a healthy writing environment, honor writers of merit, select some stories for *The State Street Review* (a literary magazine) and find a novel manuscript to recommend to New York publishers for 'serious consideration.' " Annual competition for short stories and novels. Competition receives 65 novel, 150-250 short fiction and 300-600 poetry submissions. Judges: university faculty and freelance and professional writers. Entry fees $30 (novels), $10 (short fiction), $5 (poetry). Guidelines available in the fall for SASE. Accepts inquiries by fax and e-mail. Deadlines: December 1 for novels; January 2 for poetry and short fiction. Unpublished submissions. Word length: none for novel; short fiction, 6,000 words; poetry, 30 lines. Winners announced at the Florida First Coast Writers' Festival held in May.

◖**FLORIDA STATE WRITING COMPETITION,** Florida Freelance Writers Association, P.O. Box A, North Stratford NH 03590-0167. (603)922-8338. Fax: (603)922-8339. E-mail: danakcnw@ncia.net. Website: www.writers-editors.com. **Contact:** Dana K. Cassell, executive director. "To offer additional opportunities for writers to earn income and recognition from their writing efforts." Annual competition for short stories and novels. Award: varies from $50-100. Competition receives approximately 100 short stories; 50 novels; total 400-500 entries in all categories. Judges: authors, editors and teachers. Entry fee from $5-20. Guidelines for SASE. Deadline: March 15. Unpublished submissions. Categories include short story and novel chapter. "Guidelines are revised each year and subject to change. New guidelines are available in summer of each year." Accepts inquiries by fax and e-mail. Winners announced May 31 and notified by mail. List of winners available for SASE marked "winners" and on website.

◖**FOOD, RECIPES, WINES & SUCH CONTEST,** Creative With Words Publications, P.O. Box 223226, Carmel CA 93922. (831)655-8627. E-mail: cwwpub@usa.net. Website: members.tripod.com/CreativeWith Words. **Contact:** Brigitta Geltrich, editor and publisher. 25th Anniversary award. Competition for short stories, poetry and recipes. Award: $25 (1st Prize); $10 (2nd Prize); $5 (3rd Prize); $1 (4rd-13th Prizes); small gift (3 honorable mentions). "We will close the competition when 300 manuscripts from 300 individual writers have been received." Judges: CWW editors and readers. Guidelines for SASE. Accepts inquiries by e-mail with e-mail return address. Submit only previously unpublished submissions. Word length: 800 words or less. "Recipes must be tried and approved; stories/poetry must be original (the old told in a new exciting way); guidelines must be followed." Winners announced one month after contest closes and notified by mail and e-mail. List of winners available on website.

▨ ◉ ◎ **THE JOSETTE FRANK AWARD,** Children's Book Committee at Bank St. College, 610 W. 112th St., New York NY 10025-1895. (212)875-4540. Fax: (212)875-4759. E-mail: bookcom@bnkst.edu. Website: www.bankstreet.edu/bookcom. **Contact:** Alice B. Belgray, committee chair. Annual award "to honor a book, or books, of outstanding literary merit in which children or young people deal in a positive and realistic way with difficulties in their world and grow emotionally and morally." Only books sent by publishers for review are considered. Books must have been published within current calendar year. Award: Certificate and cash prize. Competition receives approximately 2,000 submissions. Accepts inquiries by e-mail and fax. Deadline: November. Winners announced in March and notified through their publishers and by mail.

🌐 ✔ ◒ ◎ **MILES FRANKLIN LITERARY AWARD,** Arts Management Pty. Ltd., Station House, Rawson Place, 790 George St., Sydney NSW 2000 Australia. Phone: 61-2-9212 5066. Fax: 61-2-9211 7762. E-mail: claudia@artsmanagement.com.au. **Contact:** Claudia Crosariol, associate director. Award "for the advancement, improvement and betterment of Australian literature." Annual award for novels. Award: AUS $28,000 (in 2001), to the author "of the novel which is of the highest literary merit for the year and which presents Australian life in any of its phases." Competition receives 60 submissions. Judges: Peter Rose, Dagmar Schmidmaier, Professor Elizabeth Webby, Hilary McPhee and Father Ed Campion (in 2001). Guidelines available; send SASE, fax or e-mail. Accepts inquiries by fax, phone and e-mail. Previously published submissions. "The novel must have been published in the year prior to competition entry and must present Australian life in any of its phases." Winners announced May/June and notified by phone. List of winners for SASE.

▨ ◒ ◎ **SOUERETTE DIEHL FRASER AWARD,** The Texas Institute of Letters, Center for the Study of the Southwest, Flowers Hall 327, Southwest Texas State University San Marcos TX 78666. (512)245-2232. Fax: (512)245-7462. E-mail: mb13@swt..edu. Website: www.english.swt.edu/css/TIL/index. **Contact:** Mark Busby, secretary. "To recognize the best literary translation of a book into English, the translation published between January 1 and December 30 of the year prior to the award's announcement in the spring." Annual competition for translations. Award: $1,000. Judges: committee of three. Guidelines available June 2000 for SASE. Accepts inquiries by fax and e-mail. Deadline: January 8, 2002. "Award available to translators who were born in Texas or who have lived in the state at some time for two consecutive years." Winners announced in April 15, 2002 and notified by phone or mail. List of winners available on website.

☑ **FRENCH BREAD AWARDS**, *Pacific Coast Journal*, P.O. Box 56, Carlsbad CA 92018-0056. E-mail: paccoastj@frenchbreadpublications.com. Website: www.frenchbreadpublications.com. **Contact:** Stillson Graham, editor. Award with the goal of "finding the best fiction and poetry out there." Annual competition for short stories and poetry. Award: $50 (1st Prize), $25 (2nd Prize). Competition receives approximately 50 submissions. Judges: Editorial staff of *Pacific Coast Journal*. $6 fee per entry. Guidelines for SASE, e-mail or on website. Accepts inquiries by e-mail. Deadline: September 1. Unpublished submissions. Length: 4,000 words. "Manuscripts will not be returned. Send SASE for winners' list. All entrants will receive issue in which first place winners are published." Winners announced in December and notified by mail and/or e-mail. List of winners available for SASE, e-mail or on website.

THE FUNNY PAPER COMPETITION, F/J Writers Service, P.O. Box 22557, Kansas City MO 64113-0557. E-mail: felix22557@aol.com. Website: http://www.angelfire.com/biz/funnypaper. **Contact:** Editor. Award to "provide readership, help, and the opportunity to write for money to budding authors of all ages." Competition for short stories, fillers, jokes, poems, cartoons held 4 times/year. Award: $5-100. Competition receives 50-300 submissions per category. Judge: editors and selected assistants. No entry fee. Guidelines in every issue. For guidelines, send SASE or visit website. Accepts inquiries by e-mail. No deadline (unused entries are held for next contest). Entries should be unpublished, or published only if we are advised where and when. Contest open to all writers. Length: 1,000 words maximum. Winners announced in each issue and notified by mail on publication.

☒ **THE JOHN GARDNER MEMORIAL PRIZE FOR FICTION**, *Harpur Palate*, English Dept., Binghamton University, Box 6000, Binghamton NY 13902-6000. E-mail: moebius-77@hotmail.com (for contest queries only). **Contact:** Fiction Editor, *Harpur Palate*. John Gardner—novelist, poet, translator, dramatist, and teacher—helped found the creative writing program at Binghamton University. In honor of his dedication to the development of writers, *Harpur Palate* is pleased to announce The First Annual John Gardner Memorial Prize for Fiction. Annual award. Award: $500 and publication in *Harpur Palate*. $10/story. Entries should be previously unpublished. "Stories may be in any genre but should not exceed 8,000 words. Don't sacrifice character for plot or plot for character. Stories that have the best chance of winning take risks with genre and style. Please include your name and contact information in the cover letter *only*." All entrants receive a copy of the issue with the winning story. Make sure your entry fee is paid by a check (drawn on U.S. bank) or money order.

☑ **THE JANE GESKE AWARD**, *Prairie Schooner*, 201 Andrews Hall, P.O. Box 880034, Lincoln NE 68588-0334. (402)472-0911. Fax: (402)472-9771. E-mail: eflangan2@unl.edu. Website: www.unl.edu/schooner/psmain. htm. **Contact:** Hilda Raz, editor-in-chief or Erin Flanagan, managing editor. Annual award "to honor work published the previous year in Prairie Schooner including fiction, essays, and poetry. Award: $200. Competition is judged by the editorial staff of *Prairie Schooner*. No entry fee. For guidelines send SASE or visit website. "Only work published in *Prairie Schooner* in the previous year is considered." Work is nominated by the editorial staff. Winners announced in the spring issue and notified in February or March by mail.

◯ **GLIMMER TRAIN'S FALL SHORT-STORY AWARD FOR NEW WRITERS**, Glimmer Train Press, Inc., 710 SW Madison St., Suite 504, Portland OR 97205-2900. (503)221-0836. Fax: (503)221-0837. Website: www.glimmertrain.com (includes writers' guidelines and a Q&A section for writers). **Contact:** Linda Swanson-Davies, fiction editor. Contest offered for any writer whose fiction hasn't appeared in a nationally-distributed publication with a circulation over 5,000. "We want to read your original, unpublished short (1,200-8,000 words) story." $12 reading fee. Make your submissions online (www.glimmertrain.com) by September 30. Winners will be notified and top 25 places will be posted by January 2. Winner receives $1,200, publication in *Glimmer Train Stories* and 20 copies of that issue. First/second runners-up receive $500/$300, respectively, and consideration for publication. All applicants receive a copy of the issue in which winning entry is published and runners-up announced."

◯ **GLIMMER TRAIN'S FICTION OPEN**, Glimmer Train Press, Inc., 710 SW Madison St., Suite 504, Portland OR 97205-2900. (503)221-0836. Fax: (503)221-0837. Website: www.glimmertrain.com (includes writers' guidelines and a Q&A section for writers). **Contact:** Linda Swanson-Davies, contest director. Contest for short story, open to all writers. Award: First place $2,000, publication in *Glimmer Train Stories* (circ. 13,000) and 20 copies of that issue. First/second runners-up receive $1,000/$600 respectively and consideration for publication. "We want to read your original, unpublished short story. No theme or word count limitations. $15 reading fee. Make your submissions online (www.glimmertrain.com) by June 30. Winners will be notified and top 25 places will be posted by October 15."

◯ **GLIMMER TRAIN'S SPRING SHORT-STORY AWARD FOR NEW WRITERS**, Glimmer Train Press, Inc., 710 SW Madison St., Suite 504, Portland OR 97205-2900. (503)221-0836. Fax: (503)221-0837.

Website: www.glimmertrain.com (includes writers' guidelines and a Q&A section for writers). **Contact:** Linda Swanson-Davies, contest director. Contest offered for any writer whose fiction hasn't appeared in a nationally-distributed publication with a circulation over 5,000. "We want to read your original, unpublished short (1,200-8,000 words) story. $12 reading fee. Make your submissions online (www.glimmertrain.com) by March 31. Winners will be notified and top 25 places will be posted by July 1. Winner receives $1,200, publication in *Glimmer Train Stories* and 20 copies of that issue. First/second runners-up receive $500/$300, respectively, and consideration for publication. All applicants receive a copy of the issue in which winning entry is published and runners-up announced."

N ❧ ◎ GOD USES INK ANNUAL CHRISTIAN WRITERS' CONTEST, *Faith Today*, M.I.P. Box 3745, Markham, Ontario L3R 0Y4 Canada. (905)479-5885. Fax (905)479-4742. E-mail: ft@efc-canada.com. Website: www.faithtoday.ca. **Contact:** Carol Lowes, contest director. Award "to encourage Canadian Christian writers in the pursuit of excellence in the craft of print communication." Annual competition for short stories, articles, non-fiction books and novels. Awards: from $150-$250. Entry fee $25/book, $15/article. Maximum 3 entries/person. Competition receives 6 short story and 13 novel submissions. Total of 12 or more judges. Two independent judges hired for each category. Guidelines available for SASE/IRC or on website. Accepts inquiries by fax or e-mail. Published submissions. Published entries must have appeared in print between January 1, 2000 and December 31, 2001. Canadian Christian writers only. Writers may submit their own fiction or publisher may nominate the writer's work. "Read entry guidelines and form carefully. Winners announced June (at our writers' conference in Guelph)" and notified after June by phone. List of winners available after June 20.

N ◖ GOLD MEDALLION BOOK AWARDS, Evangelical Christian Publishers Association, 1969 East Broadway Rd. #2, Tempe AZ 85282. (480)966-3998. Fax: (480)966-1944. E-mail: jmeegan@ecpa.org. Website: www.ecpa.org. **Contact:** Doug Ross, president. Award to "recognize quality/encourage excellence." Annual competition for 20 categories including fiction. Award: Gold Medallion plaque. Competition receives approximately 44 submissions in the fiction category. Judges: "Two rounds of judges—first round primarily Christian bookstore owners, managers and book buyers; second round primarily editors, book reviewers, industry leaders and selected Christian bookstore leaders. First round will determine five finalists in each of the 20 categories. Second round judges the finalists in each category." Entry fee of $300 for non-members. Guidelines available October 1, 2001. Accepts inquiries by fax and e-mail. Deadline: December 1. Previously published submissions appearing during the calendar year preceding the year in which the award are to be presented. Entries must be submitted by the publisher. Winners announced in July 2002 at the Annual Gold Medallion Book Awards Banquet. List of winners available by contacting the ECPA offices.

◖ GREAT AMERICAN BOOK AWARDS, Great American Book Project, 417 N. Sangamon St., Chicago IL 60622. (312)491-0300. Fax: (312) 491-8091. E-mail: greatamericanbk@aol.com. **Contact:** Caroline Francis Carney, director. Award to "discover American authors of exceptional talent whose work equals or surpasses the finest of American's past and future." Annual competition for book-length prose. Ten finalists selected. Award: Grand Prize $3,000 and a meeting with a book editor; $750 honorable mention for an author 30 years or younger whose "strong voice exhibits the next generation's literary promise." Competition receives 600+ submissions. Judges: jury of authors, literary experts, academics. Entry fee $30. Guidelines available May 2002 for SASE. Deadline: December 31. Previously unpublished submissions. "Story must have an American setting, authors must have an exceptional narrative voice and the recommended length is between 45,000-300,000 words." Finalists announced on or by April 1, 2003 and notified by phone. For list of winners send SASE or visit website.

◖ THE GREAT BLUE BEACON SHORT-SHORT STORY CONTEST, *The Great Blue Beacon: The Newsletter for Writers of All Genres and Skill Levels*, 1425 Patriot Dr., Melbourne FL 32940-6881. (321)253-5869. E-mail: ajircc@juno.com. **Contact:** A.J. Byers, editor/publisher. Award to "recognize outstanding short-short story." Annual award for short-short stories. Award: $50 (1st prize); $25 (2nd prize); $10 (3rd prize), plus publication of winning entry in *The Great Blue Beacon*. Judges: outside panel of judges. Entry fee $5 ($4 for subscribers). Guidelines available periodically when announced. For guidelines send SASE or e-mail. Accepts inquiries by e-mail. Deadline: TBA. Entries should be previously unpublished. Open to all writers. Length: 1,000 words or fewer. Winners announced two months after contest deadline. Winners notified by SASE or e-mail. List of winners available for SASE or by e-mail.

◖ ◎ GREAT LAKES BOOK AWARDS, Great Lakes Booksellers Awards, 208 Franklin St., Grand Haven MI 49417. (616)847-2460. Fax: (616)842-0051. E-mail: glba@books~glba.org. Website: www.books~glba.org. Award to "recognize and reward excellence in the writing and publishing of books that capture the spirit and enhance awareness of the region." Annual competition for fiction, children's and nonfiction. Award: $500 plus bookstore promotion. Competition receives approximately 90 submissions. Five judges each category. No entry fee. Guidelines available. Deadline: May 31, 2002. Writer must be nominated by members of the GLBA. Winners announced August 2002.

☑ **GREAT LAKES COLLEGES ASSOCIATION NEW WRITERS AWARD**, Great Lakes Colleges Association Inc., 535 W. William, Suite 301, Ann Arbor MI 48103. (734)761-4833. Fax: (734)761-3939. E-mail: newwriters@glca.org. Annual award. Winners are invited to tour the GLCA colleges. An honorarium of at least $300 will be guaranteed the author by each of the GLCA member colleges they visit. Receives 30-40 entries in each category annually. Judges: Professors from member colleges. No entry fee. Guidelines available after November 1. Accepts inquiries by fax and e-mail. Deadline: February 28. First publication in fiction or poetry. Writer must be nominated by publisher. Four copies of the book should be sent to: Director, New Writers Award. Winners announced in May. Letters go to publishers who have submitted.

☑ ◐ **GREAT PLAINS STORYTELLING & POETRY READING CONTEST**, P.O. Box 492, Anita IA 50020-0492. Phone/fax: (712)762-4363. E-mail: bobeverhart@yahoo.com. Website: www.oldtimemusic.big step.com. **Contact:** Robert Everhart, director. Estab. 1976. Annual award "to provide an outlet for writers to present not only their works but also to provide a large audience for their presentation *live* by the writer. Attendance at the event, which takes place annually in Avoca, Iowa, is *required*." Awards: $50 (1st Prize); $25 (2nd Prize); $15 (3rd Prize); $10 (4th Prize); $5 (5th Prize). $5 entry fee. Entry forms available at contest only. Guidelines available in August of 2002 by SASE or e-mail. Deadline: August 26, 2002. Contest takes place over Labor Day Weekend. Previously published or unpublished submissions.

☑ **THE JUDY & A.C. GREENE LITERARY FESTIVAL CONTEST**, The Living Room Theatre of Salado, P.O. Box 1023, Salado TX 76571-1023. (254)947-3104. E-mail: rcarver@vvm.com. **Contact:** Dr. Raymond Carver, director/producer. "The purpose of the festival is development of unpublished works by Texas writers. The Festival seeks unpublished literary works which may be adapted by staff of the Living Room Theatre for dramatic performance with two to five actors using scripts and lecture stands but no other theatrical elements." Annual competition for short stories, novels, story collections. Award: 1st prize $1,500; 3 finalists $250 each. Competition receives about 50 submissions per category. Judge: contest/festival staff. $20 entry fee. Guidelines available in August. For guidelines, send SASE, e-mail or visit website. Accepts inquiries by e-mail or phone. Deadline March 31. Entries must be unpublished. Contest open to Texas residents or former residents. Length: 30-60 minutes reading aloud time. "No poems or discursive writing." Finalists announced in May and notified by mail or e-mail. List of winners available on website. "30-60 minutes performance time material will be read aloud by 2-4 performers at festival. Emphasize dialog, plot, character. Short stories and plays will be adapted to readers theatre format."

◯ **THE GREENSBORO REVIEW LITERARY AWARDS**, English Dept., 134 McIver Bldg., UNC-Greensboro, P.O. Box 26170, Greensboro NC 27402-6170. (336)334-5459. E-mail: jlclark@uncg.edu. Website: www.un cg.edu/eng/mfa. **Contact:** Jim Clark, editor. Annual award. Award: $250. Competition receives 1,000 submissions. Guidelines for SASE or on website. Accepts inquiries by e-mail. Deadline: September 15. Unpublished submissions. "All manuscripts meeting literary award guidelines will be considered for cash award as well as for publication in *The Greensboro Review*." Winners notified by mail, phone or e-mail. List of winners published in the Spring issue of *The Greensboro Review*.

▓ **GULF COAST POETRY AND SHORT FICTION AWARDS**, Gulf Coast: a Journal of Literature and Fine Art, University of Houston, Dept. of English, Houston TX 77204-3012. (713)743-3223. Fax: (713)743-3215. E-mail: gulfcoast@gulfcoast.uh.edu. Website: www.gulfcoast.uh.edu. **Contact:** Pablo Peschlera, managing editor. "To showcase excellent contemporary writing that pays attention to craft and language." Annual competition for short stories. Award: $300-500. Competition receives 100 submissions. $15 fee per entry. Guidelines available October 2001 for SASE or visit website. Accepts inquiries by phone. Deadline: February 15, 2002. Entries should be unpublished. Contest open to all. Length: 6,000. "Provide a short cover letter and enter what you consider to be your best work." Winners notified by mail or phone in May 2002. For list of winners send SASE.

◐ **DRUE HEINZ LITERATURE PRIZE**, University of Pittsburgh Press, 3347 Forbes Ave., Pittsburgh PA 15261. (412)383-2456. Fax: (412)383-2466. E-mail: press@pitt.edu. Website: www.pitt.edu/~press. Annual award "to support the writer of short fiction at a time when the economics of commercial publishing make it more and more difficult for the serious literary artist working in the short story and novella to find publication." Award: $10,000 and publication by the University of Pittsburgh Press. "It is imperative that entrants request complete rules of the competition by sending an SASE before submitting a manuscript." Submissions will be received only during the months of May and June. Postmark deadline: June 30. Manuscripts must be unpublished in book form. The award is open to writers who have published a book-length collection of fiction or a minimum of three short stories or novellas in commercial magazines or literary journals of national distribution. Winners announced in February and notified by phone or mail. List of winners available for SASE sent with manuscript.

☑ ◑ **ERNEST HEMINGWAY FOUNDATION/PEN AWARD FOR FIRST FICTION**, PEN New England, P.O. Box 400725, North Cambridge MA 02140. (617)499-9550. Fax: (617)353-7134. E-mail: awards@ pen-ne.org. Website: www.pen-ne.org. **Contact:** Mary Louise Sullivan, awards coordinator. Annual award "to give beginning writers recognition and encouragement and to stimulate interest in first books of fiction among publishers and readers." Receives 130 submissions. Award: $7,500. Novels or short story collections must have been published during calendar year under consideration. Entry form or rules for SASE, e-mail or on website after September. Deadline: December 15. "The Ernest Hemingway Foundation/PEN Award For First Fiction is given to an American author of the best first-published book-length work of fiction published by an established publishing house in the US each calendar year." Winners will be announced in March. List of winners available by e-mail or on website.

◐ **LORIAN HEMINGWAY SHORT STORY COMPETITION**, P.O. Box 993, Key West FL 33041-0993. (305)294-0320. Fax: (305)292-3653. E-mail: calico2419@aol.com. Website: www.shortstorycompetition.com. **Contact:** Carol Shaughnessy, co-director. Award to "encourage literary excellence and the efforts of writers who have not yet had major-market success." Annual competition for short stories. Awards: $1,000 (1st Prize); $500 (2nd Prize); $500 (3rd Prize); honorable mentions. Competition receives approximately 850 submissions. Judges: A panel of writers, editors and literary scholars selected by novelist Lorian Hemingway. Entry fee $10 for each story postmarked by May 1, 2002; $15 for each story postmarked between May 1 and May 15, 2002. Guidelines available January 15 by e-mail, phone, on website or for SASE. Accepts inquiries by SASE, fax, e-mail or visit website. Deadline: May 1-15, 2002. Unpublished submissions. "Open to all writers whose fiction has not appeared in a nationally distributed publication with a circulation of 5,000 or more." Word length: 3,000 words maximum. "We look for excellence, pure and simple—no genre restrictions, no theme restrictions—we seek a writer's voice that cannot be ignored." Winners announced at the end of July during Hemingway Days Festival and notified by phone prior to announcement. For list of winners, e-mail, visit website. "All entrants will receive a letter from Lorian Hemingway and a list of winners by October 1."

☑ ◐ ◎ **HIGHLIGHTS FOR CHILDREN**, 803 Church St., Honesdale PA 18431. (570)253-1080. Website: www.highlights.com. **Contact:** Marileta Robinson, senior editor. Award "to honor quality stories (previously unpublished) for young readers." Three $1,000 awards. Competition receives 1,500 submissions. Judges: *Highlights* editors. Guidelines available July 2001 for SASE or on website. Deadline February 28, 2002. Length: 500 words maximum for beginning readers (to age 8) and 900 words for more advanced readers (ages 9 to 12). No minimum word length. No entry form necessary. To be submitted between January 1 and February 28 to "Fiction Contest" at address above. "No violence, crime or derogatory humor. Obtain a copy of the guidelines, since the theme changes each year." Nonwinning entries returned in June if SASE is included with ms. Winners announced in June and notified by phone or letter. List of winners will be sent with returned mss. "All other submissions will be considered for purchase by Highlights."

☑ ◑ **THE ALFRED HODDER FELLOWSHIP**, The Council of the Humanities, Princeton University, Joseph Henry House, Princeton NJ 08544-5264. E-mail: humcounc.princeton.edu. Website: www.princeton.edu/ ~humcounc. **Contact:** Cass Garner, department manager. "This fellowship is awarded for the pursuit of independent work in the humanities. The recipient is usually a writer or scholar in the early stages of his or her career, a person 'with more than ordinary learning' and with 'much more than ordinary intellectual and literary gifts.' " Traditionally, the Hodder Fellow has been a humanist outside of academia. Candidates for the Ph.D. are not eligible. Award: $46,500. The Hodder Fellow spends an academic year in residence at Princeton working independently. Competition receives 300 submissions. Judges: Princeton Committee on Humanistic Studies. Guidelines available by July 15 for SASE. Deadline: November 1. Winners are announced and notified in February. A list of winners will be available on website. Applicants must submit a résumé, a sample of previous work (10 page maximum, not returnable), and a project proposal of 2 to 3 pages. Letters of recommendation are not required.

MARKET CONDITIONS are constantly changing! If you're still using this book and it is 2003 or later, buy the newest edition of *Novel & Short Story Writer's Market* at your favorite bookstore or order from Writer's Digest Books by calling 1-800-289-0963.

PEARL HOGREFE FELLOWSHIP, The Pearl Hogrefe Fund and Department of English, 203 Ross Hall, Iowa State University, Ames IA 50011. (515)294-2477. Fax: (515)294-6814. E-mail: englgrad@iastate.edu. Website: www.engl.iastate.edu. **Contact:** Kathleen Hickok, graduate studies coordinator. "To provide new Iowa State University M.A. students with writing time." Annual competition for manuscript sample of 25 pages, any genre. Award: $1,000/month for 9 months and full payment of tuition and fees. Competition receives 60-75 submissions. Judges: the creative writing staff at Iowa State University. Guidelines available by e-mail. Accepts inquiries by fax, e-mail, phone. Deadline: February 1. Either published or unpublished submissions. "No restrictions, except the applicant cannot hold or expect to receive a masters in English or creative writing during the current year." Winners announced and notified by phone on April 1.

THE WINIFRED HOLTBY MEMORIAL PRIZE, The Royal Society of Literature, Somerset House, Strand, London WC2R 1LA United Kingdom. E-mail: info@rslit.org. Website: http://www.rslit.org. **Contact:** Julia Abel Smith. Award for "regional fiction, i.e., fiction with a strong sense of a particular place." Annual competition for novels. Award: £1,000. Competition receives 60 submissions per category. Judge: 3 judges, who are as yet unchosen. No entry fee. For guidelines, send fax, e-mail, website or call. Accepts inquiries by fax, e-mail, phone. Deadline December 15, 2001. Entries should be previously published. Contest open to citizens of the Commonwealth who may enter and only publishers can submit books. Publishers must nominate work. Winners are announced June 2003 and notified by phone in May. List of winners available by fax or e-mail.

HONOLULU MAGAZINE FICTION CONTEST, *Honolulu* Magazine, 36 Merchant St., Honolulu HI 96813. (808)524-7400. **Contact:** A. Kam Napier, managing editor. "We do not accept fiction except during our annual contest, at which time we welcome it." Annual award for short stories. Award: $1,000 and publication in the April issue of *Honolulu* Magazine. Competition receives approximately 400 submissions. Judges: editorial staff of *Honolulu* magazine. Rules for SASE. Deadline: early December. "Stories must have a Hawaii theme, setting and/or characters. Author should enclose name and address in separate small envelope. Do not put name on story."

L. RON HUBBARD'S WRITERS OF THE FUTURE CONTEST, P.O. Box 1630, Los Angeles CA 90078. (323)466-3310. Website: www.writersofthefuture.com. **Contact:** Contest Administrator. Estab. 1984. Quarterly. Foremost competition for new and amateur writers of unpublished short stories or novelettes (under 17,000 words) of science fiction or fantasy. Awards $1,000, $750, $500 in quarterly prizes, $4,000 annual Grand Prize. Judged by panel of professional authors. No entry fee. Entrants retain all rights. Guidelines available for #10 SASE. Deadlines March 31, June 30, September 30, and December 31. Winners contacted quarterly.

INDIANA REVIEW FICTION PRIZE, *Indiana Review*, Ballantine Hall 465, 1020 E. Kirkwood Ave., Bloomington IN 47405-7103. (812)855-3439. Fax: (812)855-4253. E-mail: inreview@indiana.edu. Website: www.indiana.edu/~inreview/ir.html. **Contact:** Shannon Gibney, editor. Annual. Contest for fiction in any style and on any subject. Award: $1,000, publication in the *Indiana Review* and contributor's copies (1st place). Each entrant will receive the prize issue. Competition receives over 500 submissions. Judges: *Indiana Review* staff and outside judges. Guidelines available in December for SASE. Accepts inquiries by fax, e-mail or phone. Deadline: October 28, 2002. All entries considered for publication. Cover letter must include name, address, phone number, and title of story. Entrant's name should appear only in the cover letter, as all entries will be considered anonymously. Manuscripts will not be returned. No previously published works, or works forthcoming elsewhere, are eligible. Simultaneous submissions acceptable, but in event of entrant withdraw, contest fee will not be refunded. Length: 40 pages maximum, double spaced. Winners announced by December 2002 and notified by mail. For list of winners, send SASE. "We look for a command of language and structure, as well as a facility with compelling and unusual subject matter. It's a good idea to obtain copies of issues featuring past winners to get a more concrete idea of what we are looking for."

INDIVIDUAL ARTIST FELLOWSHIP, Nebraska Arts Council, 3838 Davenport, Omaha NE 68131-2329. (402)421-3627. Fax: (402)595-2334. E-mail: swise@nebraskaartscouncil.org. Website: www.nebraskaartscouncil.org. **Contact:** Suzanne Wise, program manager. Award to "recognize outstanding achievement by Nebraska writers." Competition every third year for short stories and novels. Award: $5,000 Distinguished Achievement; $1,000-2,000 Merit Awards. Competition receives 70-80 submissions per category. Judges: panel of 3. Next deadline for literature: November 15, 2002. Published or previously unpublished submissions. Nebraska residents only. Length: 50 pages.

INDIVIDUAL ARTIST FELLOWSHIP, Louisiana Division of the Arts, P.O. Box 44247, Baton Rouge LA 70804-4247. (225)342-8180. Fax: (225)342-8173. E-mail: arts@crt.state.la.us. Website: www.crt.state.la.us/arts.org. **Contact:** Dee Hamilton, director, performing and literary arts program. "Recognition of excellence." Annual competition for short stories, novels, poetry and or nonfiction. Award: $5,000. Competition receives 6-

10 submissions. "Peer panel reviews process through a blind review of samples of work only. Only finalists application packets are studied in full." For Guidelines fax, visit website or call. Accepts inquiries by fax, e-mail or phone. Deadline: September 1, 2001. Entries should be unpublished or previously published. "Students enrolled in arts-related degree or certificate granting program at grant deadline are ineligible to apply." Contest open to professional writers who are legal resident in Louisiana. Length: 30 pages of text (duplex 15 sheets of paper with copy on front and back sides of the page). "Present yourself professionally by submitting as complete and correct application as possible. Refrain from wordiness and colloquialism in the application. Save flowery language for sample. Always submit recent work. Address evaluation criteria. Winners notified by mail, phone in December 2001. For list of winners send SASE, fax, e-mail or visit website.

N INDIVIDUAL ARTIST FELLOWSHIP PROGRAM, Florida Department of State, Division of Cultural Affairs, The Capitol, Tallahassee FL 32399-0250. (904)487-2980. **Contact:** Valerie Ohlsson, arts administrator. Annual competition for $5,000 fellowship award. Judges: A peer review panel. Guidelines available. Deadline: January. Published or previously unpublished submissions. Residents of Florida only; in fiction, short story, poetry and children's literature. Word length: up to 30 pages.

N INDIVIDUAL ARTIST FELLOWSHIP/MINI FELLOWSHIP, Kansas City Commission, 700 SW Jackson St., Suite 1004, Topeka KS 66603-3761. (785)296-3335. Fax: (785)296-4989. E-mail: kac@arts.state.ks. us. Website: www.arts.state.ks.us. **Contact:** Jean Denney, program consultant II. "To celebrate the excellence in arts." Annual competition for short stories and novels. Award: $5,000 (fellowship); $500 (mini-fellowship). Competition receives 40-50 fellowship submissions; 10-15 mini-fellowship submissions (fiction, poetry, playwriting). Judges: panel of writers, editors, educators and publishers from Kansas. For guidelines fax, e-mail, visit website or call. Accepts inquiries by fax, e-mail or phone. Deadline: October 17, 2001. Entries should be unpublished or previously published year. Contest open to Kansas residents. Full-time students are ineligible. Length: 20 pages/mss format. "Follow guidelines for application explicitly." Winners announced in February each year and notified by mail or phone. For list of winners fax or e-mail.

IOWA SCHOOL OF LETTERS AWARD FOR SHORT FICTION, THE JOHN SIMMONS SHORT FICTION AWARD, Iowa Writers' Workshop, 102 Dey House, 507 N. Clinton St., Iowa City IA 52242-1000. Annual awards for short story collections. To encourage writers of short fiction. Award: publication of winning collections by University of Iowa Press the following fall. Entries must be at least 150 pages, typewritten, and submitted between August 1 and September 30. Stamped, self-addressed return packaging must accompany manuscript. Rules for SASE. Iowa Writer's Workshop does initial screening of entries; finalists (about 6) sent to outside judge for final selection. "A different well-known writer is chosen each year as judge. Any writer who has not previously published a volume of prose fiction is eligible to enter the competition for these prizes. Revised manuscripts which have been previously entered may be resubmitted."

THE IOWA SHORT FICTION AWARD, University of Iowa Press, 100 Kuhl House, Iowa City IA 52242-1000. (319)335-2000. Fax: (319)335-2055. Website: http://www.uiowa.edu/~uipress. **Contact:** Holly Carver, director. Award to "give exposure to promising writers who have not yet published a book of prose." Annual competition for story collections. Award: Publication only under Press's standard contract. Competition receives 300-400 mss. Judge: "Senior Iowa Writers' Workshop members screen manuscripts; published fiction author of note makes final two selections." No entry fee. For guidelines, send SASE or visit website. Accepts inquiries by fax, phone. Deadline: Entries accepted during August and September. "Individual stories can have been previously published (as in journals) but never in *book* form." Stories in English. Length: "at least 150 word-processed, double-spaced pages; 8-10 stories on average for manuscript." Winners announced January following competition and notified by phone in January.

JOSEPH HENRY JACKSON AWARD, Intersection for the Arts/The San Francisco Foundation, 446 Valencia St., San Francisco CA 94103-3415. (415)626-2787. Fax: (415)626-1636. E-mail: info@theintersection.o rg. Website: www.theintersection.org. **Contact:** Kevin B. Chen, program director. Award "to encourage young, unpublished writers." Annual award for short stories, novels and story collections. Award: $2,000 and certificate. Competition receives 150-200 submissions. Entry form and rules available in mid-October for SASE. Deadline: January 31. Unpublished submissions only. Applicant must be resident of northern California or Nevada for 3 consecutive years immediately prior to the deadline date. Age of applicant must be 20 through 35. Work cannot exceed 100 double-spaced, typed pages. "Submit a serious, ambitious portion of a book-length manuscript." Winners announced June 15 and notified by mail. "Winners will be announced in letter mailed to all applicants."

✓ JAPANOPHILE SHORT STORY CONTEST, *Japanophile*, P.O. Box 7977, Ann Arbor MI 48107-7977. (734)930-1553. Fax: (734)930-9968. E-mail: jpnhand@japanophile.com. Website: www.japano phile.com. **Contact:** Susan Aitken, editor. Estab. 1974. Annual award "to encourage quality writing on Japan-

America understanding." Award: $100 plus possible publication. Competition receives 200 submissions. Entry fee: $5. Send $4 for sample copy of magazine. Guidelines available by August for SASE, e-mail or on website. Accepts inquiries by fax and e-mail. Deadline: December 31. Prefers unpublished submissions. Stories should involve Japanese and non-Japanese characters, maximum 5,000 words. Winners notified in March and notified by mail. List of winners available in March for SASE.

☒ ◐ ◎ JESSE JONES AWARD FOR FICTION (BOOK), The Texas Institute of Letters, Center for the Study of the Southwest, Flowers Hall 327, Southwest Texas State University, San Marcos TX 78666. (512)245-2232. Fax: (512)245-7462. E-mail: mb12@swt.edu. Website: www.english.swt.edu/css/TIL/index. **Contact:** Mark Busby, secretary. "To honor the writer of the best novel or collection of short fiction published during the calendar year before the award is given." Annual award for novels or story collections. Award: $6,000. Competition receives 30-40 entries per year. Judges: Panel selected by TIL Council. Guidelines available in July 2001 for SASE. Accepts inquiries by fax and e-mail. Deadline: January 8, 2002. Previously published fiction, which must have appeared in print between January 1 and December 31 of the prior year. "Award available to writers who, at some time, have lived in Texas at least two years consecutively or whose work has a significant Texas theme." Winners announced April 15, 2002 and notified by phone or mail. List of winners available on website.

☑ ◐ JAMES JONES FIRST NOVEL FELLOWSHIP, Wilkes University, Wilkes-Barre PA 18766. (570)408-4530. Fax: (570)408-7829. E-mail: english@wilkes.edu. Website: http://wilkes.edu. **Contact:** J. Michael Lennon, English department professor. Award to "honor the spirit of unblinking honesty, determination, and insight into modern culture exemplified by the late James Jones, author of *From Here to Eternity* and other prose narrations of distinction," by encouraging the work of an American writer who has not published a book-length work of fiction. Annual award for unpublished novel, novella, or collection of related short stories in progress. Award: $5,000. Receives approximately 600 applications. Application fee: $15 payable to Wilkes University. Guidelines available after June 1, 2001 by fax, by e-mail or for SASE. Accepts inquiries by e-mail and fax. Deadline: Postmark March 1. Unpublished submissions. Award is open to American writers. Word length: 50 double-spaced pages and a two-page thematic outline. "Name, address, telephone number on title page only." Winners announced October and notified by phone.

KATHA: INDIAN AMERICAN FICTION CONTEST, *India Currents* Magazine, P.O. Box 21285, San Jose CA 95148. (408)274-6966. Fax: (408)274-2733. E-mail: editor@indiacurrents.com. Website: www.indiacurrents. com. **Contact:** Vandana Kumar, managing editor. Award "to encourage creative writing which has as its focus India, Indian culture, Indian-Americans and America's views of India." Annual competition for short stories. Awards: $300 (1st Prize), $200 (2nd Prize), $100 (3rd Prize), 2 honorable mentions. Competition received 50 submissions last year. Judges: "A distinguished panel of Indian-American authors. Guidelines for SASE, e-mail, or on website. Accepts inquiries by e-mail and phone. Deadline: December 31. Unpublished submissions only. Length: 3,000 words maximum. Winners announced on April 1 and notified by mail. For list of winners, send SASE. "Write about something you have experienced personally or do extensive research, so that you can write knowledgebly."

☒ ◯ ◐ EZRA JACK KEATS/KERLAN COLLECTION MEMORIAL FELLOWSHIP, University of Minnesota, 113 Andersen Library, 222-21st Ave. S., Minneapolis MN 55455. (612)624-4576. Fax: (612)625-5525. E-mail: clrc@tc.umn.edu. Website: http://special.lib.umn.edu/clrc/. Award to provide "travel expenses to a talented writer and/or illustrator of children's books who wishes to use the Kerlan Collection for the furtherance of his or her artistic development." Annual competition for books of children's literature. Award: $1,500. Competition receives approximately 10 submissions. Judges: panel of non-Kerlan Collection staff; area professionals, educators, etc. Guidelines available after November for 55¢ SASE. Accepts inquiries by fax, phone and e-mail. Deadline: early May. Accepts unpublished and previously published submissions. Winners announced mid June and notified by phone and letter. List of winners available for SASE.

☑ ◐ THE LAWRENCE FOUNDATION AWARD, *Prairie Schooner*, 201 Andrews Hall, P.O. Box 880334, Lincoln NE 68588-0334. (402)472-0911. Fax: (402)472-9771. E-mail: eflanagan2@unl.edu. Website: www.unl.edu/schooner/psmain.htm. **Contact:** Hilda Raz, editor-in-chief or Erin Flanagan, managing editor. Award "to honor and recognize the best short story published in *Prairie Schooner* in the past year." Annual competition for short stories. Award: $1,000. Judge: The editorial staff of *Prairie Schooner*. No entry fee. For guidelines send SASE or visit website. "Only work published in *Prairie Schooner* in the previous year is considered." Work is nominated by editorial staff. Winners announced in the Spring issue and notified by mail in February or March.

N ◯ LAWRENCE FOUNDATION PRIZE, *Michigan Quarterly Review*, 3032 Rackham Bldg., Ann Arbor MI 48109-1070. (734)764-9265. E-mail: mgr@umich.edu. Website: www.umich.edu/~mgr. **Contact:** Doris Knight, administrative assistant. "An annual cash prize awarded to the author of the best short story published in *Michigan Quarterly Review* each year." Annual competition for short stories. Award: $1,000. Competition receives approximately 500 submissions. "Stories must already be published in *MQR*; this is not a competition in which manuscripts are read outside of the normal submission process." Guidelines available for SASE or on website. Accepts inquiries by e-mail and phone. Deadline: September. Winners announced in December and notified by phone or mail.

☑ URSULA K. LE GUIN PRIZE FOR IMAGINATIVE FICTION, *Rosebud*, P.O. Box 459, Cambridge WI 53523. (608)423-4750. E-mail: JrodClark@smallbytes.net. Website: www.rsbd.net. **Contact:** Roderick Clark, publisher or John Lehman, associate publisher. This biennual competition is to select the very best imaginative short story entered. Award: $1,000 and publication in *Rosebud*. Competition receives 200-250 entries per category. Judge: a panel of 2-3 pre-judges and Ursula K. Le Guin is final judge. Entry fee is $10. Guidelines available in the fall on website or for SASE. Deadline: September 31, 2003. Entries should be previously unpublished. Contest open to anyone. Winners announced in mid-spring of each year and notified by mail, phone, or e-mail. For list of winners send SASE.

N ◎ LEAGUE OF UTAH WRITERS CONTEST, League of Utah Writers, 4621 W. Harman Dr., West Valley City UT 84120-3752. Phone/fax: (801)964-0861. E-mail: crofts@numucom.com. Website: http://luwrite.tr ipod.com. **Contact:** Dorthy Crofts, membership chair. "The annual LUW Contest has been held since 1935 to give Utah writers an opportunity to get their works read and critiqued. It also encourages writers to keep writing in an effort to get published." Annual competition for short stories and novels. Award: Twenty-five categories, cash award of $30/$20/$10 ; children's book category, $50/$25/$15; full length book category $100/$50/$25; published writers category. Competition receives 10-100 submissions/category. Judges: professional judges who are paid for their services. Entry fee $4, short story; $10, full length book. Guidelines available January 2000 for SASE. Accepts inquiries by fax, e-mail and phone. Deadline: June 15, 2002. Both published and previously unpublished submissions. Published submissions much have appeared in print between June 2001 and June 2002. "For the first time since 1935, the LUW Contest was opened up to writers from the 10 western states. No specific genre, although we do have separate categories for speculative fiction, children's and teen's besides our full length book category on any subject." Word length: 1,500 words maximum, short short story; 3,000 words maximum, short story; 6,000 words maximum, speculative fiction; 75,000 word maximum, full length book; 3,500 words maximum children's story; 3,500 words maximum, teen story; 5,000 words maximum, Agnes Burke Short Story. "Read the contest rules and guidelines—don't skim over them. Rules chance and are revised from year to year. Don't forget to enclose your entry fee when mailing your entries." Winners will be announced at the Annual Writers Round-up in September. List of winners available at Round-up or for SASE.

☑ LITERAL LATTÉ FICTION AWARD, *Literal Latté*, 61 E. 8th St., Suite 240, New York NY 10003. (212)260-5532. E-mail: litlatte@aol.com. Website: www.literal-latte.com. **Contact:** Edward Estlin, contributing editor. Award to "provide talented writers with three essential tools for continued success: money, publication and recognition." Annual competition for short stories. Award: $1,000 (1st Prize); $200 (2nd Prize); $100 (3rd Prize); up to 7 honorable mentions. Competition receives 400-600 submissions. Judges: the editors. Entry fee $10 ($15 includes subscription) for each story submitted. Guidelines available for SASE, by e-mail or on website. Accepts inquiries by e-mail. Deadline: mid-January. Previously unpublished submissions. Open to new and established writers worldwide. Word length: 6,000 words maximum. "The First Prize Story in the First Annual *Literal Latté* Fiction Awards has been honored with a Pushcart Prize." Winners notified by phone. List of winners available in late April for SASE or by e-mail.

☑ LITERALLY HORSES POETRY/SHORT STORY CONTEST, *Literally Horses*, 201 Cherry Hill St., Kalamazoo MI 49006-4221. (616)345-5915. **Contact:** Laurie A. Cerny, publisher. Award to "promote/recognize horse/western lifestyle related poetry and short stories." Annual competition for short stories and poetry. Award: $100 first place short story; $75 first place poetry; honorable mention prizes in each category. "Anticipate at least 100 entries." Judge: a panel of judges—including *Literally Horses* publisher. $9.95 entry fee covers 3 poems or one short story (includes a 1-year subscription). Guidelines available fall 2001. For guidelines, send SASE. Deadline: July 30, 2002. Entries can be previously published. Contest open to anyone. Length: 3,500 words. "Make sure the topic has something to do with horses; racing, driving, riding, showing, backyard horse, etc. Also, cowboy/western lifestyle theme oriented is OK. Something different. Inspirational." Winners announced Fall 2002. For list of winners send SASE.

☑ ◯ LONG FICTION CONTEST INTERNATIONAL, White Eagle Coffee Store Press, P.O. Box 383, Fox River Grove IL 60021-0383. (847)639-9200. E-mail: wecspress@aol.com. Website: http://members.aol.com/

wecpress. **Contact:** Frank E. Smith, publisher. To promote and support the long story form. Annual award for short stories. "Entries accepted from anywhere in the world; story must be written in English." Winning story receives A.E. Coppard Award—publication as chapbook plus $500, 25 contributor's copies; 40 additional copies sent to book publishers/agents and 10 press kits. Entry fee $15 US, ($10 for second story in same envelope). Must be in US funds. Competition receives 200 entries. Guidelines available in April by SASE, e-mail or website. Accepts inquiries by e-mail. Deadline: December 15. Accepts previously unpublished submissions, but previous publication of small parts with acknowledgements is OK. Simultaneous submissions OK. No limits on style or subject matter. Length: 8,000-14,000 words (30-50 pages double spaced) single story; may have multiparts or be a self-contained novel segment. Send cover with title, name, address, phone; second title page with title only. Submissions are not returned; they are recycled. "Previous winners include Adria Bernardi, Doug Hornig, Christy Sheffield Sanford, Eleanor Swanson, Gregory J. Wolos and Joe Hill. SASE for most current information." Winners announced March 30 and notified by phone. List of winners available March 30 for SASE or on website. "Write with richness and depth."

N ☐ ◎ THE LONGMEADOW JOURNAL LITERARY COMPETITION, c/o Robert and Rita Morton, 6750 Longmeadow Ave, Lincolnwood IL 60710. (312)726-9789. Fax: (312)726-9772. **Contact:** Robert and Rita Morton. Award to "stimulate the young to write." Annual competition for short stories. Award: $175 (1st Prize); $100 (2nd Prize); 5 prizes of $50. Competition receives 700 submissions. Judges: Robert and Rita Morton. Guidelines for SASE or fax. Accepts inquiries by fax. Award for "short story writers between the ages of 10-19." Word length: 3,000 words or less. Winners notified by June 15, 2002.

✓ ◉ LOS ANGELES TIMES BOOK PRIZES, *L.A. Times*, 202 W. First St., Los Angeles CA 90012. (213)237-5775. Fax: (213)237-4609. E-mail: tom.crouch@latimes.com. Website: www.latimes.com/bookprizes. **Contact:** Tom Crouch, administrative coordinator. Annual award. For books published between January 1 and December 31. Award: $1,000 cash prize in each of the following categories: fiction, first fiction (the Art Seidenbaum Award), young adult fiction and mystery/thriller. In addition, the Robert Kirsch Award recognizes the body of work by a writer living in and/or writing on the American West. Entry is by nomination of juries—no external nominations or submissions are accepted. Juries appointed by the *L.A. Times*. No entry fee. "Works must have their first U.S. publication during the calendar year." Writers must be nominated by committee members. "The Times provides air fare and lodging in Los Angeles for the winning authors to attend the awards ceremony held in April as part of the *Los Angeles Times* Festival of Books."

✓ THE HUGH J. LUKE AWARD, *Prairie Schooner*, 201 Andrews Hall, P.O. Box 880334, Lincoln NE 68588-0334. (402)472-0911. Fax: (402)472-9771. E-mail: eflanagan2@unl.edu. Website: www.unl.edu/schooner/psmain.htm. **Contact:** Hilda Raz, editor-in-chief or Erin Flanagan, managing editor. Award "an annual cash prize to honor work published in the previous year in *Prairie Schooner*, including essays, fiction and poetry." Award: $250. Judge: Competition is judged by the editorial staff of *Prairie Schooner*. No entry fee. For guidelines, send SASE or visit website. "Only work published in *Prairie Schooner* in the previous year is considered." Work is nominated by the editorial staff. Winners announced in the Spring issue and notified by mail in February or March.

N ☐ ◎ MAGGIE AWARD. Website: www.georgiaromancewriters.org. "To encourage and instruct unpublished writers in the romance genre." Award: Silver pendant (1st place), certificates (2nd-4th). 5 categories—short contemporary romance, long contemporary romance, historical romance, single title contemporary, paranormal/fantasy. Competition receives about 300 submissions. Judges: Published romance authors for first round, acquiring editors for second. Entry fee $25 for GRW members, $30 non-members. Guidelines available on website after March. Deadline is on or about June 1. Unpublished submissions. Entrants must be members of Romance Writers of America. Entries consist of 35 pages including synopsis. Winners notified by phone and mail and announced at Moonlight and Magnolias conference late September or mid-October.

⊕ ✓ MAIL ON SUNDAY/JOHN LLEWELLYN RHYS PRIZE, % Booktrust, Book House, 45 East Hill, London, SW18 2QZ England. Phone: 020-856-2973/2. Fax: 020-8516-2978. E-mail: susy@booktrust.org.uk

FOR EXPLANATIONS OF THESE SYMBOLS,
SEE THE INSIDE FRONT AND BACK COVERS OF THIS BOOK.

or tarryn@booktrust.org.uk. Website: www.booktrust.org.uk. **Contact:** Susy Behr, prizes manager or Tarryn McKay, prizes administrator. "The prize was set up by Jane Oliver, the widow of John Lewellyn Rhys, a young writer killed in action in World War II. It is awarded to a writer under the age of 35 and brings to light new and exciting talent." Annual award for short stories, novels, non-fiction and poetry. $500 to shortlist authors and $5,000 to winner. Number of submissions. No entry fee. "For 2002 guidelines either request direct from Booktrust, or ask publisher to contact us by SASE, fax, e-mail or website." Accepts inquiries by fax, e-mail, phone and post. Deadline end of June/July. Entries should be published during year preceding award. Open to any author who is a British or Commonwealth citizen. Writers may submit their own fiction only if it is published. Publishers will be notified of winners by September. List of winners should be in the papers, or contact us for a press release by SASE, fax, e-mail or website.

✔ ◯ **THE MASTERS AWARD**, Titan Press, P.O. Box 17897, Encino CA 91416-7897. Website: www.titanp ress.info. "One yearly Grand Prize of $1,000; and four quarterly awards of 'Honorable Mention' each in either 1) fiction; 2) poetry and song lyrics; 3) nonfiction." Judges: 3 literary professional, TBA. $15 entry fee. Awards are given on March 15, June 15, September 15 and December 15. Any submission received prior to an award date is eligible for the subsequent award. Submissions accepted throughout the year. Fiction and nonfiction must be no more than 20 pages (5,000 words); poetry no more than 150 lines. All entries must be in the English language. #10 SASE required for guidelines. "Be persistant, be consistent, be professional."

ℕ **MARY McCARTHY PRIZE IN SHORT FICTION**, Sarabande Books, P.O. Box 4456, Louisville KY 40204. (502)458-4028. Fax: (502)458-4065. E-mail: sarabandeb@aol.com. Website: www.sarabandebooks.org. **Contact:** Kirby Gann, managing editor. "To publish an outstanding collection of stories and/or novellas, oe a short novel (less than 300 pages)." Annual competition for story collections and novella/novella collections. "The Mary McCarthy Prize in Short Fiction includes a $2,000 cash award, publication of a collection of stories, novellas, or a short novel, and a standard royalty contract." Compedition receives 800-1,000 submissions per contest. Each year this contest is judged by a well-established writer. Past judges include Amy Hempel, Barry Hannah, and Rosellen Brown. Judge in 2002: Chris Offut. $20 entry fee. Guidelines currently available. Deadline February 15, 2002. "The collections themselves must be unpublished, but published individual stories are okay." Contest open to any writer of English (no translations) who is a citizen of the US. Length: 150-300 pages. "Read past contest winners to see the quality of writing we seek: *Head*, by William Tester; *The Baby Can Sing*, by Judith Slater; *A Gram of Mars*, by Becky Hagenston. Keep in mind that our final judge changes each year." Winners announced June 2002 and notified by mail or phone in May or June. For list of winners, send SASE.

◯ **THE JOHN H. McGINNIS MEMORIAL AWARD**, *Southwest Review*, P.O. Box 750374, 307 Fondren Library West, Southern Methodist University, Dallas TX 75275-0374. (214)768-1037. **Contact:** Elizabeth Mills, senior editor. Annual awards (fiction and nonfiction). Stories or essays must have been published in the *Southwest Review* prior to the announcement of the award. Awards: $1,000. Pieces are not submitted directly for the award but for publication in the magazine.

◓ **MID-LIST PRESS FIRST SERIES AWARD FOR SHORT FICTION**, Mid-List Press, 4324-12th Ave. South, Minneapolis MN 55407-3218. (612)822-3733. Fax: (612)823-8387. E-mail: guide@midlist.org. Website: www.midlist.org. **Contact:** Lane Stiles, senior editor. To encourage and nurture short fiction writers who have never published a collection of fiction. Annual competition for fiction collections. Award: $1,000 advance and publication. Competition receives 300 submissions. Judges: manuscript readers and the editors of Mid-List Press. $20 entry fee. Guidelines available in February for SASE or on website. Deadline: July 1. Previously published or unpublished submissions. Word length: 50,000 words minimum. "Application forms and guidelines are available for a #10 SASE or visit our website." Winners announced in January and notified by phone and mail in January. For a list of winners, send SASE or visit website.

◯ **MID-LIST PRESS FIRST SERIES AWARD FOR THE NOVEL**, Mid-List Press, 4324-12th Ave. South, Minneapolis MN 55407-3218. (612)822-3733. Fax: (612)823-8387. E-mail: guide@midlist.org. Website: www.m idlist.org. **Contact:** Lane Stiles, senior editor. To encourage and nurture first-time novelists. Annual competition for novels. Award: $1,000 advance and publication. Competition receives approximately 500 submissions. Judges: manuscript readers and the editors of Mid-List Press. $20 entry fee. Guidelines available in July for SASE or on website. Deadline: February 1. Unpublished submissions. Word length: minimum 50,000 words. "Application forms and guidelines are available for a #10 SASE, or visit our website." Winners announced in July and notified by phone and mail. Winners' list published in *Poets & Writers* and *AWP Chronicle*; also available by SASE, e-mail or on website.

✔ ◓ **MILKWEED EDITIONS NATIONAL FICTION PRIZE**, Milkweed Editions, 1011 Washington Ave. S., Suite 300, Minneapolis MN 55415-1246. (612)332-3192. Fax: (612)215-2550. E-mail: editor@milkweed

.org. Website: www.milkweed.org. **Contact:** Elisabeth Fitz, first reader. Annual award for a novel, a short story collection, one or more novellas, or a combination of short stories and novellas. Award: $7,500 cash advance as part of any royalties agreed upon at the time of acceptance. Contest receives 3-5000 submissions per category. Judged by Milkweed Editions. Guidelines available for SASE or check website. Accepts inquiries by e-mail and phone. Deadline: "Rolling—but 2002 winner chosen by October 2001." "Please look at previous winners: *Hell's Bottom, Colorado*, by Laura Pritchett; *The Empress of One*, by Faith Sullivan; *Falling Dark*, by Tim Tharp; *Montana 1948*, by Larry Watson; and *Aquaboogie*, by Susan Straight—this is the caliber of fiction we are searching for. Catalog available for $1.50 postage, if people need a sense of our list." Winners are notified by phone and announced in November. See catalog for winners.

N **◎ MILTON CENTER FELLOWSHIP,** The Milton Center, MN 2nd, Newman University, 3100 McCormick, Wichita KS 67213. (316)942-4291, ext. 326. Fax: (316)942-4483. E-mail: miltonc@newmanu.edu. **Contact:** Essie Sappenfield, program director. Award to "help new writers of Christian commitment complete first book-length manuscript." Annual competition for fiction or poetry. Competition receives 20 submissions. Judges: Milton Center staff. Entry fee $15. Guidelines for SASE. Deadline: March 15. Submit novel or book of stories: proposal and 3 chapters; poetry: 12-15 poems and proposal.

✓ **◎ MINNESOTA STATE ARTS BOARD/ARTIST ASSISTANCE FELLOWSHIP,** Park Square Court, 400 Sibley St., Suite 200, St. Paul MN 55101-1928. (612)215-1600. Fax: (612)215-1602. E-mail: msab@arts.state.mn.us. Website: www.arts.state.mn.us. **Contact:** Amy Frimpong, artist assistance program officer. "To provide support and recognition to Minnesota's outstanding literary artists." Annual award for fiction writers, creative nonfiction writers and poets. Award: up to $8,000. Competition receives approximately 150 submissions/year. Deadline: October. Previously published or unpublished submissions. Application guidelines available in mid-June by e-mail, phone or on website. Accepts inquiries by phone, fax and e-mail. A list of winners available by e-mail and on website. *Minnesota residents only.*

N **MISSISSIPPI REVIEW PRIZE,** University of Southern Mississippi/Mississippi Review, P.O. Box 5144 USM, Hattiesburg MS 39406-5144. (601)266-4321. Fax: (601)266-5757. E-mail: rief@netdoor.com. Website: http://orca.otr.usm.edu/mrw. **Contact:** Rie Fortenberry, managing editor. Annual award to "reward excellence in new fiction and poetry and to find new writers who are just beginning their careers." Award: $1,000 plus publication for the winning story and poem; publication for all runners-up. Prize issues $5 for contributor. Entry fee $15/story. No manuscripts returned. Guidelines available for SASE, e-mail or on website. Accepts inquiries by e-mail or phone. Deadline: May 31. Previously unpublished submissions. List of winners and runners-up for SASE.

THE MISSOURI REVIEW EDITORS' PRIZE CONTEST, 1507 Hillcrest Hall, Columbia MO 65211. (573)882-4474. Fax: (573)884-4671. Website: www.missourireview.org. **Contact:** Hoa Ngo, managing editor. Annual competition for short stories, poetry and essays. Award: $2,100 for fiction and poetry, $1,500 for essay and publication in *The Missouri Review*. Competition receives more than 1,200 submissions. Judges: *The Missouri Review* editors. $15 entry fee (checks payable to *The Missouri Review*). Each fee entitles entrant to a one-year subscription to *The Missouri Review*, an extension of a current subscription, or a gift subscription. Guidelines available June for SASE. Deadline: October 15. Outside of envelope should be marked "Fiction," "Essay," or "Poetry." Enclose an index card with author's name, address, and telephone number in the left corner and, for fiction and essay entries only, the work's title in the center. Entries must be previously unpublished and will not be returned. Page length restrictions: 25 typed, double-spaced, for fiction and essays, 10 for poetry. Winners announced in January and notified by phone and mail. List of winners available for SASE. "Send fully realized work with a distinctive voice, style and subject."

MONEY FOR WOMEN, Money for Women/Barbara Deming Memorial Fund, Inc., Box 630125, Bronx NY 10463. **Contact:** Susan Pliner, administrator. "Small grants to individual feminists in the arts." Biannual competition. Award: $500-1,500. Competition receives approximately 150 submissions. Judges: Board of Directors. Guidelines and required application available for SASE. Deadline: December 31, June 30. Limited to US and Canadian citizens. Word length: 25 pages. May submit own fiction. "Only for feminists in the arts." Winners announced five months after deadline and notified by mail.

✓ **MOONLIGHT & MAGNOLIA FICTION WRITING CONTEST: SF, F, H, Genre Writing Program,** P.O. Box 180489, Richland MS 39218-0489. (601)825-7263. E-mail: hoover59@aol.com. **Contact:** K. Mark Hoover, contest administrator. This annual award is for short stories that recognizes and encourage new and unpublished writers throughout the south while rewarding excellence in genre writing. Award: $250 (1st prize); $100 (2nd prize); $50 (3rd prize); top ten finalist receive certificates suitable for framing. Entries must be in competition format. Judges: This year Richard Parks; changes annually. Entry fees $7.50/story; $2.50/

additional entry. Guidelines available for SASE or by e-mail. Accepts inquiries by e-mail. Deadline: December 15, 2002. Open to unpublished writers and those who have not published more than 2 stories in a nationally-distributed publication with a circulation over 5,000. Length: 10,000 words. "We are open to multiple submissions but please send only your best work. Southern writers are encouraged to participate, but the contest is world-wide. Regional contestants will not be given preference during judging." Winners will be announced January 31, 2003 and notified by mail, phone, or e-mail. For list of winners send SASE or by e-mail.

MYSTERY MAYHEM CONTEST, *Mystery Time*/Hutton Publications, P.O. Box 2907, Decatur IL 62524. **Contact:** Linda Hutton, editor. Award "to encourage writers to have fun writing a mystery spoof." Annual competition for short stories. Award: $10 cash and publication in *Mystery Time*. Competition receives approximately 100 submissions. Judge: Linda Hutton, editor of *Mystery Time*. No entry fee. Guidelines for SASE. Deadline: September 15 annually. Unpublished submissions. Word length: Must be one sentence of any length. "One entry per person, of one sentence which can be any length, which is the opening of a mystery spoof. Must include SASE. Entry form not required. Handwritten envelope and/or entries will be discarded. Flyer of previous years' winners available for $1 plus #10 SASE." Winners announced in October in *Mystery Time Anthology* Autumn issue.

THE NATIONAL CHAPTER OF CANADA IODE VIOLET DOWNEY BOOK AWARD, The National Chapter of Canada IODE, 254-40 Orchard View Blvd., Toronto, Ontario M4R 1B9 Canada. (416)487-4416. Fax: (416)487-4417. Website: www.iodecanada.com. **Contact:** Sandra Connery, chair, book award committee. "The award is given to a Canadian author for an English language book suitable for children 13 years of age and under, published in Canada during the previous calendar year. Fairy tales, anthologies and books adapted from another source are not eligible." Annual competition for novels, children's literature. Award: $3,000. Competition receives 100-120 submissions. Judges: A six-member panel of judges including four National IODE officers and two non-members who are recognized specialists in the field of children's literature. Guidelines for SASE. Accepts inquiries by fax and phone. Deadline: December 31. Previously published January 1, 2001 and December 31, 2001. "The book must have been written by a Canadian citizen and must have been published in Canada during the calendar year." Word length: Must have at least 500 words of text preferably with Canadian content. Winner announced in May and notified by phone.

NATIONAL WRITERS ASSOCIATION ANNUAL NOVEL WRITING CONTEST, National Writers Association, 3140 Peoria St., PMB 295, Aurora CO 80014. (303)841-0246. Fax: (303)841-2607. **Contact:** Sandy Whelchel, director. Annual award to "recognize and reward outstanding ability and to increase the opportunity for publication." Award: $500 (1st Prize); $300 (2nd Prize); $100 (3rd Prize). Award judged by editors and agents. $35 entry fee. Judges' evaluation sheets sent to each entry with SASE. Contest rules and entry forms available with SASE. Opens December 1. Deadline: April 1. Unpublished submissions, any genre or category. Length: 20,000-100,000 words.

NATIONAL WRITERS ASSOCIATION ANNUAL SHORT STORY CONTEST, National Writers Association, 3140 S. Peoria #295, Aurora CO 80014-3155. (303)841-0246. Fax: (303)841-2607. E-mail: sandywrter@aol.com. Website: www.nationalwriters.com. **Contact:** Sandy Whelchel, executive director. Annual award to encourage and recognize writing by freelancers in the short story field. Award: $200 (1st Prize); $100 (2nd Prize); $50 (3rd Prize). Competition receives 200 submissions for short story category. Opens April 1. Entry fee $15. Guidelines available in January for SASE, fax, e-mail, or on website. All entries must be postmarked by July 1. Accepts inquiries by fax, phone and e-mail. Evaluation sheets sent to each entrant if SASE provided. Unpublished submissions. Length: No more than 5,000 words. Winners announced at the NWAF Summer Conference in June and notified by phone or e-mail. List of winners published in *Authorship* or on website.

THE NEBRASKA REVIEW AWARD IN FICTION, The Nebraska Review, University of Nebraska at Omaha, Omaha NE 68182-0324. (402)554-3159. E-mail: jreed@unomaha.edu. **Contact:** James Reed, managing editor. Award to "recognize short fiction of the highest possible quality." Annual competition for short fiction. Award: publication plus $500. Competition receives 400-500 submissions. Judges: staff. $15 entry fee for each story submitted. Guidelines for SASE. Accepts inquiries by e-mail, phone. Deadline: November 30. Previously unpublished submissions. Length: 5,000 words. Winners announced March 15 and notified by phone, e-mail and/or mail in February. List of winners for SASE.

NEUSTADT INTERNATIONAL PRIZE FOR LITERATURE, *World Literature Today*, 110 Monnet Hall, University of Oklahoma, Norman OK 73019-4033. **Contact:** Robert Con Davis-Undiano, director. Biennial award to recognize distinguished and continuing achievement in fiction, poetry or drama. Awards: $40,000, an eagle feather cast in silver, an award certificate, and a special issue of *WLT* devoted to the laureate. "We are looking for outstanding accomplishment in world literature. The Neustadt Prize is not open to application.

Nominations are made only by members of the international jury, which changes for each award. Jury meetings are held in the fall of even-numbered years. Unsolicited manuscripts, whether published or unpublished, cannot be considered."

N ☐ ◎ NEVADA ARTS COUNCIL ARTISTS' FELLOWSHIPS, 716 N. Carson St., Carson City NV 89701. (702)687-6680. Fax: (702)687-6688. Website: http://dmla.clan.lib.nv.us. **Contact:** Fran Morrow, artists' services coordinator. Award "to honor individual artists and their artistic achievements to support artists' efforts in advancing their careers." Annual competition for fiction, nonfiction, poetry, playwriting. Award: $5,000 ($4,500 immediately, $500 after public service event completed). Competition receives approximately 100 submissions. Judges: Peer panels of professional artists. Guidelines available by e-mail, on website or by calling, no SASE required. Deadline: April 19, 2002. "Only available to Nevada residents." Word length: 25 pages prose and plays, 10 pages poetry. Winners announced June and notified by mail and phone. Entrants receive list of winners. "Inquire about jackpot grants for Nevada residents' projects, up to $1,000."

N NEW CENTURY WRITERS AWARD, New Century Writer LLC, 32 Alfred St., Suite B, New Haven CT 06512-3927. (203)469-8824. Fax: (203)468-0333. E-mail: newcenturywriter@yahoo.com. Website: www.newcenturywriter.org. **Contact:** Jason J. Marchi, executive director. "To discover and encourage emerging writers of fiction, screenplays and stage plays, and to provide cash awards, sponsor writing fellowships, and connect writers to agents, producer in the film industry, and editors in the publishing industry. Also to educate via the quarterly educational newsletter, *The Anvil*." Annual competition for short stories, novels, screenplays, stage plays and TV scripts. Prizes: $3,000; $1,000; $500; and four $100. Also, character/plot development software for selected finalists and one *Zoetrope* Short Story Writer's Fellowship worth $5,000 to finalist who is not in the top ten. Competition receives 750 submissions. Judged initially by published writers, editors, produced film makers, and other film industry professionals. $30 fee per entry (screenplay, stage play, novel excerpt); $30 for first three short stories; $10 for additional short stories. Guidelines available July 15, 2001 for SASE, fax, e-mail or visit website. Accepts inquiries by mail only. Deadline: January 31st, sometimes extended. Entries should be published and small circulation for previously unpublished. "All genres accepted. We have a diverse group of alliance companies with different tastes." Contest open to all writers and in all countries. "Submit your best writing. Take the time to go over your work again and make your characters strong, make your technical errors minimal. Avoid clichéd situations and stereotypical characters. You do not have to be Hemingway, just tell a good, solid story." Winners notified by mail in June/July. For list of winners visit website or will mail list to those without web access.

☑ ☐ NEW ENGLAND WRITERS SHORT, SHORT FICTION CONTEST, New England Writers, P.O. Box 483, Windsor VT 05089-0483. (802)674-2315. Fax: (802)674-5503. E-mail: newvtpoet@aol.com. Website: http://hometown.aol.com/newvtpoet/myhomepage/index.html. **Contact:** Frank Anthony, president. Competition for publication in annual *Anthology of New England Writers*. Annual competition for short stories. Marjory Bartlett Sangor Award: $300. Competition receives 150 submissions. 2002 poetry judge: Yusef Komunyakaa. 2002 fiction judge: TBA. $6 entry fee; 2 or more entries $5 each. Guidelines available for SASE. Inquiries by e-mail, phone or fax OK. Deadline: June 15 postmark. Unpublished submissions. Length: 1,000 words maximum. "We want well-crafted stories written for an audience with high standards." Winners announced at annual N.E.W. conference in July. Winners notified by mail or phone right after conference. List of winners available for SASE.

N ◖ ◎ NEW HAMPSHIRE STATE COUNCIL ON THE ARTS INDIVIDUAL ARTIST FELLOWSHIP, 40 N. Main St., Concord NH 03301-4974. (603)271-2789. Website: www.state.nh.us/nharts. **Contact:** Audrey V. Sylvester, artist services coordinator. Fellowship "recognizes artistic excellence and professional commitment of professional artists in literature who are legal/permanent residents of the state of New Hampshire. Individual artists fellowships are being reviewed as part of the council's five year plan. Please visit our website for current information."

N ☐ ◎ NEW JERSEY STATE COUNCIL ON THE ARTS PROSE FELLOWSHIP, P.O. Box 306, Trenton NJ 08625. (609)292-6130. Annual grants for writers of short stories, novels, story collections. Past awards have ranged from $5,000-12,000. 1999 awards averaged $6,285. Judges: Peer panel. Guidelines for SASE. Deadline: mid-July. For either previously published or unpublished submissions. "Previously published work must be submitted as a manuscript." Applicants must be New Jersey residents. Submit copies of short fiction, short stories or prose not exceeding 15 pages and no less than 10 pages. For novels in progress, a one-page synopsis and sample chapter should be submitted.

N ☐ NEW LETTERS LITERARY AWARD, UMKC, 5101 Rockhill Rd., Kansas City MO 64110-2499. (816)235-1168. Fax: (816)235-2611. E-mail: buckm@umkc.edu. **Contact:** Mary Ellen Buck, awards coordinator.

Award to "discover and reward unpublished work by new and established writers." Annual competition for short stories. Award: $1,000 and publication. Competition receives 400-600 entries/year. Entry fee $10. Guidelines available in September for SASE, by e-mail, fax and website. Accepts inquiries by fax, phone and e-mail. Deadline: May 18. Submissions must be unpublished. Length requirement: 5,000 words or less. Winners notified by personal letter in September. List of winners available for SASE.

☑ **NEW MILLENNIUM WRITING AWARDS**, P.O. Box 2463, Knoxville TN 37901-2463. (423)428-0389. Fax: (865)428-2302. E-mail: DonWilliams7@att.net. Website: www.mach2.com/books or www.WritingAwards. com. **Contact:** Don Williams, editor. Award "to promote literary excellence in contemporary fiction." Annual competition for short stories. Award: $1,000 and publication in *New Millennium Writings*. Competition receives approximately 1,000 submissions. Judges: Novelists and short story writers. Competition receives 50 entries/year. Entry fee: $15. Guidelines available year round for SASE and on website. Accepts inquiries by e-mail. Deadline: mid-June. Unpublished submissions. Length: 1,000-6,000 words. "Provide a bold, yet organic opening line, sustain the voice and mood throughout, tell an entertaining and vital story with a strong ending. *New Millennium Writings* is a forward-looking periodical for writers and lovers of good reading. It is filled with outstanding poetry, fiction, essays and other speculations on subjects both topical and timeless about life in our astonishing times. Our pages brim with prize-winning essays, humor, full-page illustrations, writing advice, poetry from writers at all stages of their careers. First timers find their works displayed alongside well-known writers as well as profiles and interviews with famous authors such as John Updike, Sharyn McCrumb, Lee Smith, Howard Nemerov, Norman Mailer, Madison Smartt Bell, William Kennedy, David Hunter, Cormac McCarthy, Shelby Foote and more!" Winners announced October and March and notified by mail and phone. All entrants will receive a list of winners, plus a copy of the journal. Send letter-sized SASE with entry for list.

☑ ◎ **JOHN NEWBERY AWARD**, American Library Association (ALA) Awards and Citations Program, Association for Library Service to Children, 50 E. Huron St., Chicago IL 60611. (312)280-2163. Fax: (312)944-7671. E-mail: alsc@ala.org. Website: www.ala.org/alsc. **Contact:** Executive Director. Annual award. Only books for children published in the US during the preceding year are eligible. Award: Medal. Entry restricted to US citizens-residents. Guidelines available February 1. Accepts inquiries by fax and e-mail. Deadline: December. Winners announced in January and notified by phone. List of winners available in February on website.

▒N▒ ☑ ◎ **THE NOMA AWARD FOR PUBLISHING IN AFRICA**, P.O. Box 128, Witney, Oxon 0X8 5XU United Kingdom. (44)1993-775235. Fax: (44)1993-709265. E-mail: maryljay@aol.com. **Contact:** Mary Jay. Sponsored by Kodansha Ltd. Award "to encourage publication of works by African writers and scholars in Africa, instead of abroad as is still too often the case at present." Annual competition for a new book in any of these categories: Scholarly or academic; books for children; literature and creative writing, including fiction, drama and poetry. Award: $10,000. Competition receives approximately 140 submissions. Judges: A committee of African scholars and book experts and representatives of the international book community. Chairman: Walter Bgoya. Guidelines for SASE. Deadline: February 28. Previously published submissions. Submissions are through publishers only. Maximum number of entries per publisher is 3. Winners announced October and notified through publishers. List of winners available for SASE.

▒N▒ ◎ **NORTH CAROLINA ARTS COUNCIL FELLOWSHIP**, 221 E. Lane St., Raleigh NC 27699-4632. (919)715-1519. **Contact:** Deborah McGill, literature director. Grants program "to encourage the continued achievements of North Carolina's writers of fiction, poetry, literary nonfiction and literary translation." Biannual awards: Up to $8,000 each. Council receives approximately 300 submissions. Judges are a panel of editors and published writers from outside the state. Writers must be over 18 years old, not currently enrolled in degree-granting program, and must have been a resident of North Carolina for 1 full year as of the application deadline. Deadline: November 1, 2002.

▒N▒ ◎ **NORTH CAROLINA ARTS COUNCIL WRITERS' RESIDENCIES**, 221 E. Lane St., Raleigh NC 27699-4632. (919)715-1519. Fax: (919)733-4834. E-mail: debbie.mcgill@ncmail.net. Website: www.ncarts. org. **Contact:** Deborah McGill, literature director. Award "to recognize and encourage North Carolina's finest creative writers. Every year we offer a two-month residency for one writer at the LaNapoule Art Foundation in southern France, a three-month residency for one writer at Headlands Center for the Arts (California), and a one-month residency for one writer at Vermont Studio Center." Judges: Panels of writers and editors convened by the residency centers. Guidelines available after March 1 by phone or mail. Accepts inquiries by fax and e-mail. Deadline: early June. Writers must be over 18 years old, not currently enrolled in degree-granting program on undergraduate or graduate level and *must have been a resident of North Carolina for 1 full year as of application deadline*. Winners announced in the Fall and notified by phone. List of winners available by phone, mail or on website.

N ⊕ ◯ NORWEGIAN LITERATURE ABROAD GRANT (NORLA), Bygdoy Allè 21, 0262 Oslo Norway. +47 2212 2540. Fax: +47 2212 2544. E-mail: firmapost@norla.no. **Contact:** Kristin Brudevoll, manager. Award to "help Norwegian fiction to be published outside Scandinavia and ensure that the translator will be paid for his/her work." Annual compensation for translations, 50-60% of the translation's cost. Judges: an advisory (literary) board of 5 persons. Accepts inquiries by fax, e-mail, phone. Deadline: December 15. Previously published submissions. "Application form can be obtained from NORLA. Foreign (non-Scandanavian) publishers may apply for the award."

N ☒ NOVELLA PRIZE, *The Malahat Review*, University of Victoria, P.O. Box 1700 Stn CSC, Victoria, British Columbia V8W 2Y2 Canada. (250)721-8524. Fax: (250)472-5051. E-mail: malahat@uvic.ca. Website: www.web.uvic.ca/malahat. **Contact:** Marlene Cookshaw, editor. Purpose: "To promote the writings of novellas." Biannual competition for novellas. Prizes: $500 plus payment for publication at our regular rate of $30/magazine page. Competition receives 100-150 submissions. Judges: editorial board and select judges. Entry fee: $30 in Canada; $40 Canadian; includes one year subscription. Guidelines available for SASE or visit website. Accepts inquiries by e-mail or phone. Deadline: March 1, 2002. Entries should be unpublished. Contest open to all writers. Length: 30,000 words. Winners notified by mail 2-3 months after deadline.

☑ NTPWA ANNUAL POETRY & FICTION CONTEST, North Texas Professional Writers' Association, P.O. Box 563, Bedford TX 76095-0563. (817)428-2822. Fax: (817)428-2181. E-mail: through website. Website: www.ntpwa.org. **Contact:** Elaine Lanmon. Award "to recognize and encourage previously unpublished writers." Annual competition for short stories, novels and poetry. Fiction awards: $75 (1st Prize), $35 (2nd Prize). Poetry awards: $75 (1st Prize), $35 (2nd Prize). Judges: Published writers. Entry fee: $5 fiction, $5/2 poems. Guidelines for SASE. Accepts inquiries by e-mail. Deadline: May 31, 2002. Unpublished submissions. Length: 20 pages (fiction); 30 lines (each poem). Winners announced July 31, 2002. List of winners available for SASE. "Chapbooks of winner's work available for $5 each."

☑ ◯ THE FLANNERY O'CONNOR AWARD FOR SHORT FICTION, The University of Georgia Press, 330 Research Dr., Athens GA 30602-4901. (706)369-6135. Fax: (706)369-6131. E-mail: emontjoy@ugapress.uga.edu. Website: www.uga.edu/ugapress. **Contact:** Emily Montjoy, award coordinator. Annual award "to recognize outstanding collections of short fiction. Published and unpublished authors are welcome." Award: $1,000 and publication by the University of Georgia Press. Competition receives 330 submissions. Guidelines for SASE, fax, e-mail or on website. Accepts inquiries by fax, e-mail, phone. Deadline: April 1-May 31. "Manuscripts cannot be accepted at any other time." $15 entry fee. Ms will not be returned. Winners announced in November and notified by mail. List of winners for SASE, fax, e-mail or on website.

☑ ◯ FRANK O'CONNOR FICTION AWARD, *descant*, Dept. of English, Texas Christian University, Box 297270, Fort Worth TX 76129. (817)257-6537. Fax: (817)257-6239. E-mail: descant@tcu.edu. Website: www.eng.tcu.edu/usefulsites/descant.htm#subm. **Contact:** David Kuhne, editor. Estab. 1979 with *descant*; earlier awarded through *Quartet*. Annual award to honor the best published fiction in *descant* for its current volume. Award: $500 prize. Competition receives 500-1,000 submissions. Judge: *descant* fiction editors. No entry fee. Guidelines available for SASE or on website. Deadline April 1, 2002. Winners announced August 2002 and notified by phone in July. A list of winners will be available for SASE. "About 12 to 15 stories are published annually in *descant*. Winning story is selected from this group."

N ◎ OKLAHOMA BOOK AWARD, Oklahoma Center for the Book, 200 NE 18th, Oklahoma City OK 73105-3298. (405)681-8871. Fax: (405)525-7804. E-mail: gcarlile@oltn.odl.state.ok.us. Website: www.odl.state.ok.us/OCB. **Contact:** Glenda Carlile, executive director. Award to "recognize Oklahoma authors or books written about Oklahoma in the pervious year." Annual competition for novels and story collections. Award: Medal. Competition receives 25-30 submissions for fiction and nonfiction. Judges: a panel of 5 judges for each of 5 categories (fiction, nonfiction, children/young adult, poetry and design/illustration). Guidelines available mid-July for SASE, fax, e-mail or website. Accepts inquiries by fax, e-mail and phone. Deadline: January 8. Previously published submissions appearing between January 1 and December of the previous year. "Writers much live or have lived in Oklahoma or book must have an Oklahoma theme. Entry forms available after August 1. Mail entry along with 6 copies of book." Winners announced at book award ceremony March 9. Call for list of winners available March 13.

N THE OMAHA PRIZE, The Backwaters Press, 3502 N. 52nd Street, Omaha NE 68104-3506. (402)451-4052. E-mail: gkosm62735@aol.com. Website: www.thebackwaterspress.homestead.com. **Contact:** Greg Kosmicki, editor. "To find the best possible novel and publish it in order to help further authors' careers." Annual competition for novels. Award: $1,000 and publication, 10 copies to winner, distribution and promotion by The Back Water Press. Competition receives 300-500 submissions. Judge: Jonis Agee. $20 per entry fee. Guidelines for SASE, e-mail or visit website. Deadline: December 4, 2002. Entries should be unpublished. Contest open to all who write in English. Length: 250-500 pages; typed; double-spaced. "Send your best work." Winners notified by phone 6 months after deadline. For list of winners send SASE, e-mail or visit website.

☑ ◯ **ORANGE BLOSSOM FICTION CONTEST**, *The Oak*, 1530 Seventh St., Rock Island IL 61201. (309)788-3980. **Contact:** Betty Chezum Mowery, editor. "To build up circulation of publication and give new authors a chance for competition and publication along with seasoned writers." Award: Subscription to *The Oak*. Competition receives approximately 75 submissions. Judges: published authors. Entry fee six 34¢ stamps. Guidelines available in December for SASE. Word length: 500 words maximum. "May be on any subject, but avoid gore and killing of humans or animals." Deadline: April 1. Winners announced mid-April and notified by mail. "Material is judged on content and tightness of writing as well as word lengths, since there is a 500-word limit."

🌐 ☑ **ORANGE PRIZE IN FICTION**, Orange pcs, %Booktrust, Book House, 45 East Hill, London SW18 2QZ England. (020)8516-2973/2. Fax: (020)8516-2978. E-mail: susy@booktrust.org.uk or tarryn@booktrust.org.uk. Website: www.orangeprize.com or http://booktrust.org.uk. **Contact:** Susy Behr, prizes manager or Tarryn McKay, prizes administrator. "This award was set up to find and reward the very best in women's fiction writing." Annual competition for novels only. Award: £30,000 and a "Bessie" statue to the winner. Number of entries varies. Judges have not been confirmed for 2002. No entry fee. Guidelines available by SASE, fax, e-mail or website. Authors should "either request direct from Booktrust, or ask their publisher to contact us." Accepts inquiries by fax, e-mail, phone and post. Entries should be previously published novels by women, all nationalities. Must be published in the UK by a UK publisher. Length: open. Publishers will be notified of winning entry. Winner should be announced in the papers "or contact us for press release." Shortlist announced in March; winner announced in June. List of winners available by fax, e-mail or website.

☑ ◎ **DOBIE PAISANO FELLOWSHIPS**, Dobie House, 702 E. Dean Keeton St., Austin TX 78705. (512)471-8542. Fax: (512)471-9997. E-mail: aslate@mail.utexas.edu. Website: www.utexas.edu/ogs/Paisano. **Contact:** Audrey N. Slate, director. Annual fellowships for creative writing (includes short stories, novels and story collections). Award: 6 months residence at ranch; $2,000 monthly living stipend. Competition receives approximately 100 submissions. Judges: faculty of University of Texas and members of Texas Institute of Letters. $10 entry fee. Application and guidelines available after July 1, 2001 by fax, e-mail and on website. Accepts inquiries by fax, e-mail and phone. "Open to writers with a Texas connection—native Texans, people who have lived in Texas at least two years, or writers with published work on Texas and Southwest." Deadline: January 25. Winners announced in May and notified by telephone followed by mail. A list of winners will be available on website.

☑ **THE PATERSON FICTION PRIZE**, The Poetry Center at Passaic County Community College, One College Boulevard, Paterson NJ 07505-1179. (973)684-6555. Fax: (973)523-6085. E-mail: m.gillan@pccc.cc.nj.us. Website: www.pccc.cc.nj.us/poetry. **Contact:** Maria Mazziotti Gillan, director. Award to "encourage recognition of high-quality writing." Annual competition for books of short stories and novels. Award: $1,000. Competition expects 500 submissions this year. Judge: A different one every year. Guidelines available for SASE or on website. Deadline: March 15, 2002. Winners announced in July and notified by mail. For list of winners, send SASE or visit website.

◯ **PEARL SHORT STORY PRIZE**, *Pearl* Magazine, 3030 E. Second St., Long Beach CA 90803-5163. Phone/fax: (562)434-4523. E-mail: mjohn5150@aol.com. Website: www.pearlmag.com. **Contact:** Marilyn Johnson, fiction editor. Award to "provide a larger forum and help widen publishing opportunities for fiction writers in the small press; and to help support the continuing publication of *Pearl*." Annual competition for short stories. Award: $250, publication in *Pearl* and 10 copies. Competition receives approximately 100 submissions. Judges: Editors of *Pearl* (Marilyn Johnson, Joan Jobe Smith, Barbara Hauk). $10 entry fee per story. Includes copy of magazine featuring winning story. Guidelines for SASE or visit website. Accepts inquiries by e-mail or fax. Deadline: May 15. Unpublished submissions. Length: 4,000 words maximum. Include a brief biographical note and SASE for reply or return of manuscript. Accepts simultaneous submissions, but asks to be notified if story is accepted elsewhere. All submissions are considered for publication in *Pearl*. "Although we are open to all types of fiction, we look most favorably upon coherent, well-crafted narratives, containing interesting, believable characters and meaningful situations." Winners announced and notified by mail in August. List of winners available for SASE, fax, e-mail or on website.

Ⓝ ◯ ◎ **JUDITH SIEGEL PEARSON AWARD**, Wayne State University, Detroit MI 48202. (313)577-2450. **Contact:** Robert Burgoyne, Chair, English Dept. Competition "to honor writing about women." Annual award. Short stories up to 20 pages considered every third year (poetry and drama/nonfiction in alternate years).

Fiction: 2000. Award: Up to $400. Competition receives up to 50 submissions/year. Judge: Submissions are internally screened; then a noted writer does final reading. Guidelines available in October 2001 for SASE. Deadline: March 1, 2002. Winners announced mid-April and notified by mail. List of winners mailed to all entrants.

○ **WILLIAM PEDEN PRIZE IN FICTION**, *The Missouri Review*, 1507 Hillcrest Hall, University of Missouri, Columbia MO 65211. (573)882-4474. Website: www.missourireview.org. **Contact:** Speer Morgan, Evelyn Somers, Hoa Ngo, editors. Annual award "to honor the best short story published in *The Missouri Review* each year." Submissions are to be previously published in the volume year for which the prize is awarded. Award: $1,000. No application process; all fiction published in *The Missouri Review* is automatically entered.

◐ ◎ **PEN CENTER USA WEST LITERARY AWARD IN FICTION**, PEN Center USA West, 672 S. LaFayette Park Place, #41, Los Angeles CA 90057. (213)365-8500. Fax: (213)365-9616. E-mail: pen@pen-usa-west.org. Website: www.pen-usa-west.org. **Contact:** Eric Chow, awards coordinator. To recognize fiction writers who live in the western United States. Annual competition for published novels and story collections. Award: $1,000, plaque, and honored at a ceremony in Los Angeles. Competition receives 125 submissions. Judges: panel of writers, booksellers, editors. $20 fee for each book submitted. Guidelines available in August for SASE, fax, e-mail or on website. Accepts inquiries by fax, phone and e-mail. Deadline: December 31. Books published between January 1 and December 31. Open only to writers living west of the Mississippi. All entries must include 4 non-returnable copies of each submission and a completed entry form. Winners announced in May and notified by phone and mail. List of winners available for SASE or on website.

☑ ◎ **PEN NEW ENGLAND/L.L. WINSHIP AWARD**, P.O. Box 400725, N. Cambridge MA 02140. (617)499-9550. Fax: (617)353-7134. E-mail: awards@pen-ne.org. Website: www.pen-ne.org. **Contact:** Mary L. Sullivan, coordinator. Award to "acknowledge and praise a work of (published 2001) fiction, nonfiction or poetry with a New England topic and setting and/or by an author whose main residence is New England." Annual competition for novels and poetry. Award: $2,500. Competition receives 150 submissions. Five judges. Guidelines available in September for SASE. Accepts inquiries by fax, e-mail and website. Deadline: December 1. Previously published submissions that appeared between January 1 and December 31 of the preceeding year. Winners announced mid-March and notified through publisher or PEN-NE Executive Board member. List of winners available in April by fax or phone.

◐ ◎ **PEN/BOOK-OF-THE-MONTH CLUB TRANSLATION PRIZE**, PEN American Center, 568 Broadway, New York NY 10012. (212)334-1660. E-mail: jm@pen.org. **Contact:** John Morrone, awards coordinator. Award "to recognize the art of the literary translator." Annual competition for translations. Award: $3,000. Deadline: December 15. Previously published submissions within the calendar year. "Translators may be of any nationality, but book must have been published in the US and must be a book-length literary translation." Books may be submitted by publishers, agents or translators. No application form. Send three copies. "Early submissions are strongly recommended."

◑ ◎ **THE PEN/FAULKNER AWARD FOR FICTION**, c/o The Folger Shakespeare Library, 201 E. Capitol St. SE, Washington DC 20003. (202)675-0345. Fax: (202)608-1719. E-mail: delaney@folger.edu. Website: www.folger.edu. **Contact:** Janice Delaney, PEN/Faulkner Foundation Executive Director. Annual award. "To award the most distinguished book-length work of fiction published by an American writer." Award: $15,000 for winner; $5,000 for nominees. Judges: Three writers chosen by the Trustees of the Award. Deadline: October 31. Published submissions only. Writers and publishers submit four copies of eligible titles published the current year. No juvenile. Authors must be American citizens.

◑ ◎ **PEN/NORMA KLEIN AWARD**, PEN American Center, 568 Broadway, New York NY 10012. (212)334-1660. E-mail: jm@pen.org. Award Director: John Morrone. "Established in 1990 in memory of the late PEN member and distinguished children's book author, the triennial prize recognizes an emerging voice of literary merit among American writers of children's fiction. Candidates for the award are new authors whose books (for elementary school to young adult readers) demonstrate the adventuresome and innovative spirit that characterizes the best children's literature and Norma Klein's own work (but need not resemble her novels stylistically)." Award: $3,000. Judges: a panel of three distinguished children's authors. Guidelines for SASE. Previously published submissions. Writer must be nominated by other authors or editors of children's books. Next award: 2002.

◎ **PEW FELLOWSHIP IN THE ARTS, The University of the Arts**, 230 S. Broad St., Suite 1003, Philadelphia PA 19102. (215)875-2285. Fax: (215)875-2276. E-mail: pewarts@mindspring.com. Website: www.pewarts.org. **Contact:** Melissa Franklin, director. Program Assistant: Christine Miller. "The Pew Fellowships in the Arts provides financial support directly to artists so that they may have the opportunity to dedicate themselves wholly to the development of their artwork for up to two years. A goal of the Pew Fellowships in the Arts is to provide such support at a critical juncture in an artist's career, when a concentration on artistic development and exploration is most likely to contribute to personal and professional growth." Annual fellowship is awarded in three of 12 fields. The 2002 awards will be in poetry, performance art, and sculpture. Award: up to 12 $50,000 fellowships/year. Competition receives 100-200 submissions per category. Judges: a panel of artists and arts professionals. Application and guidelines available in late August for SASE and on website. Accepts inquiries by SASE, fax, e-mail, phone, website. Limited to 2 year or longer residents of Bucks, Chester, Delaware, Montgomery or Philadelphia counties who are 25 years of age or older. No students. Winners announced June 2002 and notified by mail. List of winners will be mailed to entrants.

☑ **MARY ANN PFENNINGER LITERARY AWARD**, GEM Literary, 4717 Poe Rd., Medina OH 44256-9745. (330)725-8807. E-mail: gemlit@earthlink.net. Website: www.gembooks.com. **Contact:** Darla Pfenninger, agent. Award to "honor unpublished authors in memory of the founder of the company and an author." Annual award for novels or story collections. Award: literary representation and cash awards for top three winners, as well as certificates for top ten. Competition receives 100 submissions. Judge: local and company readers give point values. Readers are assigned by genre; synopsis required. $20 entry fee plus return postage. Guidelines available July 2001 for SASE, e-mail or visit website. Accepts inquiries by e-mail. Deadline June 30, 2002. Entries should be unpublished but will accept self-published, or e-books. Contest open to anyone over the age of 18. Winners announced in August 28, 2002 and notified by mail or webpage. For list of winners send SASE, e-mail, or visit website. Submit "thought-provoking stories with unique characters, well written, with a sense of humor."

◐ ◎ **JAMES D. PHELAN AWARD**, Intersection for the Arts/The San Francisco Foundation, 446 Valencia St., San Francisco CA 94103-3415. (415)626-2787. Fax: (415)626-1636. E-mail: info@theintersection.org. Website: www.theintersection.org. **Contact:** Kevin B. Chen, program director. Annual award "to author of an unpublished work-in-progress of fiction (novel or short story), nonfictional prose, poetry or drama." Award: $2,000 and certificate. Competition receives more than 160 submissions. All submissions are read by three initial readers (change from year to year) who forward ten submissions each on to three judges (change from year to year). Judges are established Bay Area writers with extensive publishing and teaching histories. Rules and entry forms available after October 15 for SASE. Deadline: January 31. Unpublished submissions. Applicant must have been born in the state of California, but need not be a current resident; must be 20-35 years old. Winners announced June 15 and notified by letter.

◐ **POCKETS FICTION WRITING CONTEST**, *Pockets Magazine*, Upper Room Publications, P.O. Box 340004, Nashville TN 37203-0004. (615)340-7333. Fax: (615)340-7267. (Do not send submissions via fax.) E-mail: pockets@upperroom.org. Website: www.upperroom.org/pockets. **Contact:** Patricia McIntyre, editorial assistant. The purpose of the contest is to "find new freelance writers for the magazine." Annual competition for short stories. Award: $1,000 and publication. Competition receives 600 submissions. Judged by *Pockets* staff and staff of other Upper Room publications. Guidelines available for #10 SASE or on website. Accepts inquiries by e-mail and fax. No entry fee or entry form required. Submissions must be postmarked between March 1 and August 15. Deadline August 15, 2001. Former winners may not enter. Unpublished submissions. Word length: 1,000-1,600 words. "No historical fiction or fantasy." Winner announced November 1 and notified by mail. "Send SASE with 4 first-class stamps to request guidelines and a past issue."

Ⓝ ◐ ◎ **EDGAR ALLAN POE AWARDS**, Mystery Writers of America, Inc., 17 E. 47th St., Sixth Floor, New York NY 10017. (212)888-8171. Fax: (212)888-8107. E-mail: mwa-org@earthlink.net. Website: www.mysterywriters.org. **Contact:** Mary Beth Becker, executive director. Annual awards to enhance the prestige of the mystery. For mystery works published or produced during the calendar year. Award: Bust of Poe. Awards for best mystery novel, best first novel by an American author, best softcover original novel, best short story, best critical/biographical work, best fact crime, best young adult, best juvenile novel, best play, best screenplay, best television feature and best episode in a series. Contact above address or check website for specifics. Deadline: November 30. Winners announced in February.

Ⓝ ◎ **MARY RUFFIN POOLE AWARD FOR BEST WORK OF FICTION**, North Carolina Literary and Historical Association, 4610 Mail Service Center, Raleigh NC 27699-4610. (919)733-9375. Fax: (919)733-8807. E-mail: michael.hill@ncmail.net. **Contact:** Michael Hall, awards coordinator. "Presented annually to best first published book-length work of fiction." Annual competition for novels and story collections. Award: $1,000 and an engraved plate. Competition receives 5-10 submissions per award category. Judge: three judge panel.

Guidelines available July 1, 2001 for SASE, fax, e-mail or call. Deadline: July 15, 2002. Entries should be previously published (3 copies). Contest open to residents of North Carolina, minimum residency of 3 years. Winners notified by mail in October. For list of winners send SASE, fax or e-mail.

☑ ○ **KATHERINE ANNE PORTER PRIZE FOR FICTION**, *Nimrod International Journal of Prose and Poetry*, University of Tulsa, 600 S. College, Tulsa OK 74104-3189. (918)631-3080. Fax: (918)631-3033. E-mail: nimrod@utulsa.edu. Website: www.utulsa.edu/NIMROD. **Contact:** Francine Ringold, editor-in-chief. "To award promising writers and to increase the quality of manuscripts submitted to *Nimrod*." Annual award for short stories. Award: $2,000 (1st Prize), $1,000 (2nd Prize) plus publication and two contributors copies. Competiton receives approximately 500 entries/year. Judge varies each year. Past judges: Ron Carlson, Anita Shreve, Mark Doty, Gordon Lish, George Garrett, Toby Olson, John Leonard and Gladys Swan. $20 entry fee. Guidelines available after January for #10 SASE or by e-mail. Accepts inquiries by e-mail or by phone. Deadline: April 30. Previously unpublished manuscripts. Length: 7,500 words maximum. "Must be typed, double-spaced. Our contest is judged anonymously, so we ask that writers take their names off of their manuscripts. Include a cover sheet containing your name, full address, phone and the title of your work. Include a SASE for notification of the results. We encourage writers to read *Nimrod* before submission to discern whether or not their work is compatible with the style of our journal. Single issues are $10 (book rate postage included)." Winners announced in July and notified by mail. List of winners available for SASE with entry.

🅽 **POTOMAC REVIEW FIFTH ANNUAL SHORT STORY CONTEST**, P.O. Box 11437, Washington DC 20008. (301)934-1412. Fax: (301)753-1648. E-mail: elilu@juno.com. Website: www.meral.com/potomac. **Contact:** Eli Flam, editor. Annual competition for short stories. Award: $500 and publication for each winner in the fall 2002 issue. Competition receives more than 50 submissions. Judge: A top, independent writer. "No fee per se but submittor asked take $18 year's subscription." Guidelines will be in the fall-winter 2002 issue, website, or send SASE for guidelines or order sample copy ($5 ppd). Deadline: January-March 31. Previously unpublished submissions. There are no limitations of style or provenance. Word length: up to 3,000 words. Winners announced by summer via SASE. "We see stories that get at 'the concealed' side of life."

☑ **PRAIRIE SCHOONER READERS' CHOICE AWARDS**, *Prairie Schooner*, 201 Andrews Hall, P.O. Box 880334, Lincoln NE 68588-0334. (402)472-0911. Fax: (402)472-9771. E-mail: eflanagan2@unl.edu. Website: www.unl.edu/schooner/psmain.htm. **Contact:** Hilda Raz, editor-in-chief or Erin Flanagan, managing editor. Awards to "honor work published the previous year in *Prairie Schooner*, including poetry, essays and fiction." Award: $250 each. "We usually award 6-12 of these." Judge: the editorial staff of *Prairie Schooner*. No entry fee. For guidelines, send SASE or visit website. "Only work published in *Prairie Schooner* in the previous year is considered." Work is nominated by the editorial staff. Winners announced in the Spring issue and notified by mail in February or March.

🅽 ◐ ◎ **THE PRESIDIO LA BAHIA AWARD**, The Sons of the Republic of Texas, 1717 8th St., Bay City TX 77414. (979)245-6644. Fax: (979)244-3819. E-mail: srttexas@srttexas.org. Website: www.srttexas.org. **Contact:** Janet Hick, administrative assistant. "To promote suitable preservation of relics, appropriate dissemination of data, and research into our Texas heritage, with particular attention to the Spanish Colonial period." Annual competition for novels. Award: "A total of $2,000 is available annually for winning participants, with a minimum first place prize of $1,200 for the best published book. At its discretion, the SRT may award a second place book prize or a prize for the best published paper, article published in a periodical or project of a nonliterary nature." Judges: recognized authorities on Texas history. Guidelines available in June for SASE, by fax, e-mail or on website. Accepts inquiries by mail, fax and e-mail. Entries will be accepted from June 1 to September 30. Previously published submissions and completed projects. Competition is open to any person interested in the Spanish Colonial influence on Texas culture. Winners announced December and notified by phone and mail. List of winners available for SASE.

🌐 **MATHEW PRICHARD AWARD FOR SHORT STORY WRITING**, SAMWAW (South and Mid Wales Association of Writers), 6 Lias Cottages Porthcawl, Bridgend CF36 3RD South Wales. 01656-786531 **Contact:** Jean Barraclough, organiser. Award to "encourage writers." Annual award for short stories. Award: £2,000. Competition receives 350-400 submissions per category. Judges: two writers who are secondary adjudicators and a famous writer who is the final adjudicator, not named yet £4 entry fee ($3 for SAMWAW members). Guidelines available August 2001. For guidelines, send SASE. Accepts inquiries by phone. Deadline: February 28, 2002. Entries should be unpublished. Contest open to all. Length: 2,500 words or fewer. Winners are announced in mid-May 2002 and notified by mail, phone before mid-May. For list of winners send SASE.

▨ ◎ PRISM: Futuristic, Fantasy and Paranormal Sub-Genre Chapter of Romance Writers of America. E-mail: michelehauf@uswest.net. Website: www.ffp-romance.com. **Contact:** Cyndee Somerville, secretary. Award to "recognize excellence in paranormal romances and paranormals with a strong romantic theme." Annual award for novels. Award: "PRISM award for 1st place in 5 novel categories as well as novellas and short stories, certificates for 2nd and 3rd place in each category." Competition receives approximately 50 submissions. Judges: "Entries judged on a scale of 1-10 in 3 categories (FF&P elements, writing & style, emotional impact); judged by published authors and readers." Entry fee $30. Guidelines available late 2001/early 2002 at website or by e-mail. Previously published submissions that appeared between January 2001-December 2001. "Books must be romances with paranormal elements (i.e., futuristic/fantasy, time travel, or paranormal), or be paranormals with strong romance theme. We accept both print and e-book entries. Romance must be central to the story, but the story much contain paranormal elements." Winner announced July 2002 and notified by mail or e-mail and on website.

◪ ○ PRISM INTERNATIONAL SHORT FICTION CONTEST, *Prism International*, Dept. of Creative Writing, University of British Columbia, Buchanan E462-1866 Main Mall, Vancouver, British Columbia V6T 1Z1 Canada. (604)822-2514. Fax: (604)822-3616. E-mail: prism@interchange.ubc.ca. Website: www.arts.ubc.ca/prism. **Contact:** Director. Award: $2,000; five $200 runner-up prizes. Competition receives 650 submissions. Deadline: January 31. Entry fee $22 plus $5 reading fee for each story; 1 year subscription included. Guidelines available May for SASE, fax, e-mail, or visit website. Accepts inquiries by fax, phone and e-mail. Winners announced in June and notified in May by phone or e-mail. List of winners available in June for SASE, e-mail or on website. "Read a fiction contest issue of *PRISM International* to see what editors are looking for. The fiction contest issue comes out each summer in July or August."

◖ ◎ PULITZER PRIZE IN FICTION, Columbia University, 709 Journalism Bldg., Mail Code 3865, New York NY 10027-6902. (212)854-3841. Fax: (212)854-3342. E-mail: pulitzer@www.pulitzer.org. Website: www.pulitzer.org. **Contact:** Professor Seymour Topping, administrator. Annual award for distinguished short stories, novels and story collections *first* published in US in book form during the year by an American author, preferably dealing with American life. Award: $7,500 and certificate. Competition receives about 200 submissions. Guidelines and entry forms available in May 2001 for SASE or request by phone, fax, e-mail or on website. Accepts inquiries by fax, phone and e-mail. Deadline: Books published between January 1 and June 30 must be submitted by July 1. Books published between July 1 and October 31 must be submitted by November 1; books published between November 1 and December 31 must be submitted in galleys or page proofs by November 1. Submit 4 copies of the book, entry form, biography and photo of author and $50 handling fee. Open to American authors. Winners announced April 8 and notified by telegram. A list of winners will be available for SASE, fax, e-mail or on website.

PUSHCART PRIZE, Pushcart Press, P.O. Box 380, Wainscott NY 11975. (516)324-9300. **Contact:** Bill Henderson, president. Annual award "to publish and recognize the best of small press literary work." Previously published submissions, short stories, poetry or essays on any subject. Must have been published during the current calendar year. Award: Publication in *Pushcart Prize: Best of the Small Presses*. Deadline: December 1. Nomination by small press publishers/editors only.

○ QUINCY WRITERS GUILD ANNUAL CREATIVE WRITING CONTEST, P.O. Box 433, Quincy IL 62306-0433. (217)885-3327. E-mail: chillebr@adams.net. Website: www.quincylibrary.org/guild.htm. **Contact:** Carol Hillebrenner, treasurer. "A contest to promote new writing." Annual competition for short stories, nonfiction, poetry. Awards: Cash for 1st, 2nd, 3rd Place entries; certificates for honorable mention. Competition receives approximately 150 submissions. Judges: Writing professionals not affiliated with Quincy Writers Guild. Entry fee $4 (fiction and nonfiction, each entry); $2 (poetry each entry). "Guidelines are very important." Guidelines available after July 2001 for SASE, by e-mail or on website. Accepts inquiries by e-mail or post. Deadline: April 1, 2002. Unpublished submissions. Word length: fiction and nonfiction, 2,000 words; poetry, 3 pages maximum, any style. No entry form is required. Entries accepted after January 1. Winners announced June 2002 and at July annual meeting and notified by mail in late June. List of winners available after July 2002 for SASE or by e-mail.

DAVID RAFFELOCK AWARD FOR PUBLISHING EXCELLENCE, National Writers Assn., 3140 S. Peoria #295, Aurora CO 80014. (303)841-0246. Fax: (303)841-2607. E-mail: sandywrter@aol.com. Website: http://www.nationalwriters.com. **Contact:** Sandy Whelchel, executive director. Award to "assist published authors in marketing their works and promoting them." Annual award for novels, story collections. Award: $5,000 value promotional tour and services of a publicist. Judges: publishers and agents. $100 entry fee. Guidelines available. For guidelines, send SASE, e-mail or visit website. Accepts inquiries by fax, e-mail, phone. Deadline

May 1 annually. Entries should be previously published. Contest open to anyone with a published book in the English language. Winners are announced in June at the NWAF Conference and notified by mail or phone. For list of winners send SASE or visit website.

SIR WALTER RALEIGH AWARD, North Carolina Literary and Historical Association, 4611 Mail Service Center, Raleigh NC 27699-4610. (919)733-9375. **Contact:** Michael Hill, awards coordinator. "To promote among the people of North Carolina an interest in their own literature." Annual award for novels. Award: Statue of Sir Walter Raleigh. Competition receives 8-12 submissions. Judges: University English and history professors. Guidelines available in August for SASE. Accepts inquiries by fax. Deadline: July 15, 2002. Book must be an original work published during the 12 months ending June 30 of the year for which the award is given. Writer must be a legal or physical resident of North Carolina for the three years preceding the close of the contest period. Authors or publishers may submit 3 copies of their book to the above address. Winners announced October and notified by mail. List of winners available for SASE.

THE REA AWARD FOR THE SHORT STORY, Dungannon Foundation, 53 W. Church Hill Rd., Washington CT 06794. (860)868-9455. **Contact:** Elizabeth Rea, president. Annual award "sponsored by the Dungannon Foundation, the Rea Award was established in 1986 by Michael M. Rea to honor a living U.S. or Canadian writer who has made a significant contribution to the short story form. Award cannot be applied for. The recipient is nominated and selected by a jury annually." Award: $30,000. Judges: 3 jurors. Award announced in spring annually.

REAL WRITERS SHORT STORY COMPETITION, Real Writers Support and Appraisal Services for Aspiring Writers, P.O. Box 170, Chesterfield, Derbyshire, S40 1FE United Kingdom. (+44)01246-238492. Fax: (+44)01246-238492. E-mail: realwrtrs@aol.com. Website: www.turtledesign.com/RealWriters/. **Contact:** Lynne Patrick, coordinator. Award to "provide a regular outlet for short fiction." Annual competition for short stories. Award: One prize of £2,500 ($3,500); other cash prizes decided on merit; sponsored prizes of weekend breaks, writers' workshop places and magazine subscriptions—these change annually. "We publish a winners' anthology, and runners-up are considered for publication in a leading magazine for writers." Competition receives 1,100 submissions per category. Judge: Winners selected for a shortlist by a well-known writer or personality with a writing connection. Lesley Claister, Anjéle Lambert, Jane Mays and Colin Baker are past judges. Shortlist chosen by an experienced panel. £5 or $10 plus critique fee/entry. Guidelines available May 2001. For guidelines, send SASE, fax, e-mail, visit website or call. Accepts inquiries by fax, e-mail, phone. Deadline September 30, 2002. Entries should be unpublished. Contest open to anyone as long as the work entered is unpublished. Length: 5,000 words. Winners are announced January 2002 and notified by mail. For list of winners send SASE.

REGIONAL BOOK AWARDS, Mountains & Plains Booksellers Association, 19 Old Town Square, Suite 238, Ft. Collins CO 80524. (970)484-5856. Fax: (970)407-1479. E-mail: lknudsen@mountainsplains.org. Website: www.mountainsplains.org. **Contact:** Lisa Knudsen, director. Purpose: "to honor outstanding books set in the Mountains and Plains regions." Annual competition for one children's book and three adult books in fiction, non-fiction and poetry/art. Award: $500 and framed copy of Regional Book Awards Poster. "There are two panels of judges, one for adult books and one for children's. Each panel consists of 3-5 persons selected by the Awards Committee." Guidelines available for SASE, fax, e-mail, visit website or call. Deadline: November 1, 2001. Entries should be previously published. The book must be published for the first time within the year under consideration, November 1 through October 31. Contest open to all; "however, should relate to our region." Winners announced January 2002 and notified by phone December 2001. For list of winners visit website.

LOUISE E. REYNOLDS MEMORIAL FICTION AWARD, the new renaissance, 26 Heath Rd., #11, Arlington MA 02474-3645. (781)646-0118. **Contact:** Louise T. Reynolds, editor-in-chief. Purpose: "Honor *tnr*'s founding manager Louise E. Reynolds. To recognize *tnr*'s reward, writers. Also to promote quality writing of fiction in independent literary magazines." Award is after publication of a three issue volume of *tnr*. Award is for short stories and translations. Award: $500; $250; $125; one $50 honorable mention. Competition receives 40-60 submissions January-June; 25-40 during September-October. Judges: are independent and are new each volume presentation. "We usually approach writers and critics who are familiar with *tnr*." $16.50 per entry fee after August 31. Guidelines available after July 15, 2001 for SASE or e-mail. Deadline: Jan. 2-June 30; Sept. 1-

VISIT THE WRITER'S MARKET WEBSITE at www.writersmarket.com for hot new markets, daily market updates, writers' guidelines and much more.

Oct. 31. Accepts inquiries by e-mail. Entries should be unpublished. "All work must have been published in a three issue volume of *tnr*; all entries are considered for possible publication in trn." Contest open to all serious, quality or literary fiction. Length: 36 pages; double-spaced. "Read, read, read. Short fiction and long stories, not only those of the immediate present but also collective of fiction from the twentieth century. Know what's been done, how well it's been, and by whom. Have your own vision. Read an issue of *tnr*." Winners notified by mail within 1 month of publication. For list of winners send SASE or e-mail.

◐ ◎ **HAROLD U. RIBALOW PRIZE**, *Hadassah Magazine*, 50 W. 58th St., New York NY 10019. (212)688-0227. Fax: (212)446-9521. E-mail: hadamag@aol.com. **Contact:** Alan M. Tigay, executive editor. Estab. 1983. Annual award "for a book of fiction on a Jewish theme. Harold U. Ribalow was a noted writer and editor who devoted his time to the discovery and encouragement of young Jewish writers." Book should have been published the year preceding the award. Award: $1,000 and excerpt of book in *Hadassah Magazine*. Deadline is April of the year following publication.

▩ ◯ ◐ ◎ **SUMMERFIELD G. ROBERTS AWARD**, The Sons of the Republic of Texas, 1717 8th St., Bay City TX 77414. (409)245-6644. Fax: (979)244-3819. E-mail: srttexas@srttexas.org. Website: www.srttexas. org. **Contact:** Janet Hickl, administrative assistant. "Given for the best book or manuscript of biography, essay, fiction, nonfiction, novel, poetry or short story that describes or represents the Republic of Texas, 1836-1846." Annual award of $2,500. Competition receives 10-20 submissions. Competition is judged by a panel comprised of winners of the last three years' competitions. Guidelines available after June for SASE, by fax, e-mail or on website. Accepts inquiries by fax and e-mail. Deadline January 15. "The manuscripts must be written or published during the calendar year for which the award is given. Entries are to be submitted in quintuplicate and will not be returned." Winners announced March and notified by mail or phone. List of winners available for SASE.

ROTTEN ROMANCE, Hutton Publications, P.O. Box 2907, Decatur IL 62524. **Contact:** Linda Hutton, editor. Award to "have fun writing a spoof of genre fiction." Annual competition for short stories. Award: $10 and publication. Competition receives 100 submissions. Judge: Linda Hutton, editor. Guidelines available for SASE. Deadline: Valentine's Day annually. Previously unpublished submissions. Open to anyone. Word length: no more than 1 sentence, any length. "An entry form is available, but not required. Handwritten envelopes and/or entries will be discarded; all material must be typed. SASE required with entry. Tickle your sense of humor and ally it with your best writing. Study paperback romances to get a feel for the genre." Winners announced March 1 and notified by mail.

▩ **MARJORY BARTLETT SANGER AWARD/NEW ENGLAND WRITERS SHORT FICTION CONTEST**, The Anthology of New England Writers, 151 Main St., Box 483, Windsor VT 0508-0483. (802)674-2315. E-mail: newvtpoet@aol.com. Website: www.hometown.aol.com/newvtpoet/myhomepage/index.html. **Contact:** Dr. Frank Anthony or Susan C. Anthony, co-directors. "To discover individual writing of integrity and timelessness." Annual competition for short stories. Award: $300; three to five $30 honorable mentions. Judge: Ernest Hebert (2001). $6 one fiction entry fee; $5 two or more entries. Guidelines for SASE, e-mail, visit website or call. Deadline: June 15. Entries should be unpublished. Contest open to all writers. Length: 1,000 words. "Send your best work." Winners notified by mail or phone in July after conference. For list of winners send SASE.

✔ **THE SCARS/CC&D EDITOR'S CHOICE AWARDS**, Scars Publications and Design/Children, Churches & Daddies Magazine, 829 Brian Court, Gurnee IL 60031-3155. E-mail: ccandd96@aol.com. Website: http://scars.tv. **Contact:** Janet Kuypers, editor/publisher. Award to "showcase good writing in an annual book." Annual competition for short stories. Award: publication of story/essay and one copy of book. $11 entry fee. For guidelines, visit website. Accepts inquiries by e-mail. Deadline November. Entries may be unpublished or previously published. Contest open to anyone. Length: "We appreciate shorter works. Shorter stories, more vivid and more real storylines in writing have a good chance." Winners announced at book publication, online and notified by mail when book is printed. For list of winners send SASE or e-mail.

◯ ◎ **SCIENCE FICTION WRITERS OF EARTH (SFWoE) SHORT STORY CONTEST**, Science Fiction Writers of Earth, P.O. Box 121293, Fort Worth TX 76121-1293. (817)451-8674. E-mail: sfwoe@flash.net. Website: www.flash.net/~sfwoe. **Contact:** Gilbert Gordon Reis, SFWoE administrator. Purpose "to promote the art of science fiction/fantasy short story writing." Annual award for short stories. Award: $200 (1st Prize); $100 (2nd Prize); $50 (3rd Prize). First place story is published by *Altair—Magazine of Speculative Fiction*. *Altair* also pays 1¢/word to the author of the winning story on publication. "If *Altair* is unable to publish the winning story, SFWoE will place the story on their website for 180 days and pay the author $75 in addition to the $200 prize money." Competition receives approximately 200 submissions/year. Judge: Author Edward Bryant. Entry fee $5 for first entry; $2 for additional entries. Guidelines available after November for SASE, e-mail, or print from website. Accepts inquiries by e-mail and phone. Deadline: October 30. Submissions must be unpublished or must not have received payment for a published piece of fiction. Stories should be science fiction or fantasy, 2,000-7,500 words. "Visit our website and read in our online newsletter what the judge looks for in a good story. Contestants enjoy international competition." Winners announced January 31 and notified by phone and e-mail, mail. "Each contestant is mailed the contest results, judge's report, and a listing of the top ten contestants." Send separate SASE for complete list of the contest stories and contestants (or print from website).

○ ◎ **SEVENTEEN MAGAZINE FICTION CONTEST**, *Seventeen Magazine*, 850 Third Ave., New York NY 10022-6258. (212)407-9700. Fax: (212)407-9899. Website: www.seventeen.com. **Contact:** Attn: Writer's Guidelines. Awarded to "honor best short fiction by a young writer." Competition receives 5,000 submissions. Guidelines for SASE. Rules published in the November issue. Contest for 13-21 year olds. Deadline: April 30. Submissions judged by a panel of outside readers, former winners and *Seventeen*'s editors. Cash awarded to winners. First-place story published in the December or January issue. Winners announced in late 2002 and notified by phone or mail. List of winners available in an early issue in year 2003 with SASE.

◐ ◎ **SFWA NEBULA® AWARDS**, Science-Fiction and Fantasy Writers of America, Inc., 532 La Guardia Place #632, New York NY 10012-1428. President: Michael Capobianco. Annual awards for previously published short stories, novels, novellas, novelettes. Science fiction/fantasy only. "No submissions; nominees upon recommendation of members only." Deadline: December 31. "Works are nominated throughout the year by active members of the SFWA."

☑ **FRANCES SHAW FELLOWSHIP FOR OLDER WOMEN WRITERS**, The Ragdale Foundation, 1260 N. Green Bay Rd., Lake Forest IL 60045-1106. (847)234-1063. Fax: (847)234-1075. E-mail: ragdaleevents @aol.com. Website: www.ragdale.org. **Contact:** Sylvia Brown, director of programming and marketing. Award to "nurture and support older women writers who are just beginning to write seriously." Annual competition for short stories, novels and poetry. Award: 2 months free residency at Ragdale, plus domestic travel. Competition receives 150 submissions. Judges: a panel of four anonymous women writers. Guidelines available for SASE. Accepts inquiries by fax or e-mail. Deadline: February 1. Previously unpublished submissions. Females over 55. Length: 20 pages/12 short poems. "Make your letter of application interesting, covering your desire to write and the reasons you have been thwarted to this point." Winners announced in April and notified by phone.

Ⓝ ◑ ◎ **SHORT AND SWEET CONTEST**, Perry Terrell Publishing, M.A. Green Shopping Center, Inc., Metairie Bank Bldg., 7809 Airline Hwy., Suite 215-A, Metairie LA 70003-6439. (504)737-7781. **Contact:** Perry Terrell, editor. "The purpose is to inspire and encourage creativity in humor. (My personal purpose is to see who has a sense of humor and who doesn't.)" Monthly competition, 1 to 2 months after deadline, for short stories. Award: $5. Receives 15 to 47/month. Judges: Perry Terrell. Entry fee 50¢/entry. Guidelines for SASE or by e-mail. Send SASE for details.

Ⓝ **SHORT FICTION COMPETITION**, *Inkwell Magazine* and Manhattanville College, 2900 Purchase St., Purchase NY 10577. (914)323-7239. Fax: (914)694-3488. E-mail: inkwell@mville.edu. **Contact:** Melissa Lugo, editor. "To reward excellence in short fiction writing." Every other year competition for short stories. Award: $1,500; two $50 honorable mentions; publication of the writing entries and the finalist in Inkwell. Competition receives 800 submissions. Judge: Alice Elliot Dark (2001). Contests are officiated by distinguished short fiction writers. $15 per entry fee. Guidelines available in the Spring of 2002. Deadline: September 30, 2002. Entries should be unpublished. Contest open to previously unpublished writers. "The beginning must immediately draw the reader in and that tension must be sustained throughout. The ending must be organic to the story, original and emotionally powerful. The characters must be colorful, quirky and complex. The language must be fresh and concise. It should include a strong imagery and symbolism." Winners announced Spring of 2003. Winners notified by phone in March 2003. For list of winners send SASE.

✿ ☑ ○ **SHORT GRAIN CONTEST**, Box 1154, Regina, Saskatchewan S4P 3B4 Canada. (306)244-2828. Fax: (306)244-0255. E-mail: grain.mag@sk.sympatico.ca. Website: www.skwriter.com/grain. ("E-mail entries not accepted.") **Contact:** Jennifer Still, business administrator. Annual competition for postcard stories, prose poems, dramatic monologues and creative non-fiction. Awards: 3 prizes of $500 in each category. Competition receives approximately 900 submissions. Judges: Canadian writers with national and international reputations. Query first. Entry fee $22 for 2 entries in one category (includes one-year subscription); each additional entry in any category $5. US and International entries in US dollars. US writers add $4 US postage. International writers add $6 US postage. Guidelines available by fax, e-mail, on website, for SASE or SAE and IRC. Deadline: January 31. Unpublished submissions. Contest entries must be either an original postcard story (a work of narrative fiction written in 500 words or less) or a prose poem (a lyric poem written as a prose paragraph or paragraphs in 500 words or less), a dramatic monologue (a self-contained speech given by a single character in

500 words or less) or creative nonfiction (a creative, nonfiction prose piece in 5,000 words or less). Winners announced April and notified by phone, e-mail and mail. List of winners available for SASE by e-mail, fax, on website.

◪ **SIDE SHOW 8TH SHORT STORY CONTEST**, Somersault Press, P.O. Box 1428, El Cerrito CA 94530-1428. E-mail: jisom@atdial.net. **Contact:** Shelley Anderson, editor. Award "to attract quality writers for our 300-odd page paperback fiction anthology." Awards: $200 (1st Prize); $100 (2nd Prize); $75 (3rd Prize); $5/ printed page paid to all accepted writers (on publication). Competition receives 1,000 submissions. Judges: The editors of *Side Show*. $10 entry fee; year's subscription included. Leaflet available but no guidelines or restrictions on length, subject or style. For leaflet, send SASE or e-mail. Accepts inquiries by e-mail. Sample copy for $10 plus $2 postage. Multiple submissions (in same mailing envelope) encouraged (only one entry fee required for each writer). Will critique if requested. "No deadline. Book published when we accept 20-25 stories." Winners announced when book published and notified before book is printed. "A story from *Side Show* was selected for inclusion in *Pushcart Prize XVIII: Best of the Small Presses*."

◎ **SKIPPING STONES HONOR AWARDS**, P.O. Box 3939, Eugene OR 97403-0939. (541)342-4956. Fax: (541)342-4956. E-mail: skipping@efn.org. Website: www.efn.org/~skipping. **Contact:** Arun N. Toké, executive editor. Award to "promote multicultural and/or nature awareness through creative writings for children and teens." Annual competition for short stories, novels, story collection, poetry and nonfiction. Award: honor certificates; seals; reviews; press release/publicity. Competition receives 125 submissions. Judges: "A multicultural committee of readers, reviewers and editors." $50 entry fee ($25 for small/low income publishers/self-publishers). Guidelines for SASE or e-mail. Accepts inquiries by e-mail, fax and phone. Deadline: January 15, 2002. Previously published submissions that appeared in print between January 2000 and January 2002. Writer may submit own work or can be nominated by publisher, authors or illustrators. "We seek authentic, exceptional, child/youth friendly books that promote intercultural/international/intergenerational harmony and understanding through creative ways. Writings that come out of your own experiences/cultural understanding seem to have an edge." Winners announced April 2002 and notified through press release, personal notifications and by publishing reviews of winning titles. List of winners available for SASE, e-mail or on website.

☑ **THE BERNICE SLOTE AWARD**, *Prairie Schooner*, 201 Andrews Hall, P.O. Box 880334, Lincoln NE 68588-0334. (402)472-0911. Fax: (402)472-9771. E-mail: eflanagan2@unl.edu. Website: www.unl.edu/schooner/ psmain.htm. **Contact:** Hilda Raz, editor-in-chief or Erin Flanagan, managing editor. Award to "recognize the best work by a beginning writer published in *Prairie Schooner* in the previous year, including stories, essays and poetry." Award: $500. Judge: Competition is judged by the editorial staff of *Prairie Schooner*. No entry fee. For guidelines, send SASE, or visit website. "Only work published in *Prairie Schooner* in the previous year will be considered." Work is nominated by the editorial staff. Winners announced in the Spring issue and notified by mail in February or March.

☑ **SMOKY MOUNTAIN VALENTINE CONTEST**, Smoky Mountain Romance Writers, 521 Woodland Dr., Clinton TN 37716-3422. (865)457-4571. Fax: (865)463-6797. E-mail: LKL77@aol.com. Website: http:// www.smrw.org. **Contact:** Katie Lovette, contest coordinator. Award to "encourage all authors, published or unpublished, by rewarding their creativity in the romance genre." Annual competition for novels. Award: Heart pendant and certificate. Competition receives 75-100 submissions. Judge: First round judges are experienced critiquers and published authors; final round judges are multi-published authors. $10 entry fee. Guidelines available June. For guidelines, send SASE, e-mail, fax or visit website. Accepts inquiries by fax, e-mail, phone. Deadline first Saturday in December. Entries should be unpublished. Contest open to writers unpublished in book-length in past five years. Length: submit one scene (5 pages maximum) and a one page set-up. "Follow guidelines closely. Know the romance market." Winners announced February 14, 2002 and notified by phone and e-mail. For list of winners send SASE, e-mail or visit website.

◻ ◎ **KAY SNOW CONTEST**, Willamette Writers, 9045 SW Barbur Blvd., Suite 5-A, Portland OR 97219-4027. (503)452-1592. Fax: (503)452-0372. E-mail: wilwrite@teleport.com. Website: www.willamettewriters. com. **Contact:** Bill Johnson, office manager. Award "to create a showcase for writers of all fields of literature." Annual competition for short stories; also poetry (structured and nonstructured), nonfiction, juvenile and student writers and screenwriters. Award: $300 (1st Prize) in each category, second and third prizes, honorable mentions. Competition receives approximately 160 submissions. $500 Liam Cullen Memorial Award for best overall entry to the contest. Judges: nationally recognized writers and teachers. $15 entry fee, nonmembers; $10, members; students free. Guidelines for #10 SASE, fax, e-mail or website. Accepts inquiries by fax, phone and e-mail. Deadline: May 15 postmark. Unpublished submissions. 1 poem with maximum 5 double-spaced pages per entry fee. Winners announced August and notified by mail and phone. List of winners available for SASE. Prize winners will be honored at the two-day August Willamette Writers Conference. Press releases will be sent to local and national media announcing the winners, and excerpts from winning entries may appear in our newsletter.

SOCIETY FOR THE STUDY OF THE SHORT STORY/SHORT STORY CONTEST, 1817 Marengo St., New Orleans LA 70115. (504)894-0389. Fax: (504)894-0388. E-mail: shrtsti@aol.com. Website: www.s hortstorysociety.com. **Contact:** Dale Hrebik, assistant to the president. "To recognize and award achievement in the short story." Competition every two years for short stories. Award: $500 and publication in *Short Story*. Competition receives 100 submissions. Judges: panel of experts, final decision by short story writer. Janette Turner Hospital (2001). $15 per entry fee. Guidelines for SASE, e-mail or visit website. Deadline: Post marked by March 13, 2002. Entries should be unpublished. Winners announced at the International Conference on the Short Story in English in July 2002 and notified by phone or e-mail in June 2002. For list of winners e-mail or visit website.

SOCIETY OF CHILDREN'S BOOK WRITERS AND ILLUSTRATORS GOLDEN KITE AWARDS, Society of Children's Book Writers and Illustrators, 8271 Beverly Blvd., Los Angeles CA 90048. (323)782-1010. **Contact:** Mercedes Coats, chair. Annual award. "To recognize outstanding works of fiction, nonfiction and picture illustration for children by members of the Society of Children's Book Writers and Illustrators and published in the award year." Published submissions should be submitted from January to December of publication year. Deadline: December 15. Rules for SASE. Award: Statuette and plaque. Looking for quality material for children. Individual "must be member of the SCBWI to submit books."

SOCIETY OF CHILDREN'S BOOK WRITERS AND ILLUSTRATORS WORK-IN-PROGRESS GRANTS, 8271 Beverly Blvd., Los Angeles CA 90048. (323)782-1010. **Contact:** SCBWI. Annual grant for any genre or contemporary novel for young people; also nonfiction research grant and grant for work whose author has never been published. Award: $1,500 (1st Prize), $500 (2nd Prize). Work-in-progress. Competition receives approximately 180 submissions. Judges: Members of children's book field—editors, authors, etc. Guidelines for SASE. Deadline: February 1-May 1. Unpublished submissions. Applicants must be SCBWI members.

SOUTH DAKOTA ARTS COUNCIL, 800 Governors Dr., Pierre SD 57501-2294. (605)773-3131. **Contact:** Dennis Holub, executive director. "Individual Artist Grants are planned for the fiscal year 2002 through 2003—Artist Mentorship Grant (up to $3,000) and Artists Collaboration Grant (up to $6,000)." Guidelines available. Deadline: March 1. Grants are open only to residents of South Dakota.

THE SOUTHERN REVIEW/LOUISIANA STATE UNIVERSITY SHORT FICTION AWARD, *The Southern Review*, 43 Allen Hall, Louisiana State University, Baton Rouge LA 70803-5005. (225)578-5108. Fax: (225)578-5098. E-mail: mgriffi@lsu.edu. Website: www.lsu.edu/guests/wwwtsm. **Contact:** Michael Griffith, associate editor. Annual award "to recognize the best first collection of short stories by an American writer published in the United States during the past year." Award: $500, possible campus reading. Competition receives 40-60 submissions. Judges: committee of editors and faculty members. Guidelines available for SASE. Accepts inquiries by fax and e-mail. Deadline: January 31. Two copies to be submitted by publisher or author. Winner announced summer and notified by mail or phone.

WALLACE E. STEGNER FELLOWSHIP, Creative Writing Program, Stanford University, Stanford CA 94305-2087. (650)725-1208. Fax: (650)723-3679. E-mail: gay-pierce@forsythe.stanford.edu. Website: www.stanford.edu/dept/english/cw. **Contact:** Gay Pierce, program administrator. Annual award for short stories, novels, poetry and story collections. Five fellowships in fiction ($20,000 stipend plus required tuition of approximately $6,000). Competition receives 700 submissions. $40 entry fee. Guidelines available in July for SASE, by e-mail and on website. Accepts inquiries by phone and e-mail. Deadline: December 1. For unpublished or previously published fiction writers. Residency required. Word length: 9,000 words or 40 pages. Winners announced April and notified by telephone in mid-March. List of winners will be on website.

SUB-TERRAIN ANNUAL SHORT STORY CONTEST, *sub-TERRAIN Magazine*, P.O. Box 3008, Vancouver, British Columbia V6B 3X5 Canada. (604)876-8710. Fax: (604)879-2667. E-mail: subter@porta l.ca. Website: www.anvilpress.com. **Contact:** Brian Kaufman, managing editor. Award "to inspire writers to get down to it and struggle with a form that is condensed and difficult. To encourage clean, powerful writing." Annual award for short stories. Award: $500 and publication. Runners-up also receive publication. Competition receives 150-200 submissions. Judges: An editorial collective. Entry fee $15 for one story, $5 extra for each additional story (includes 3-issue subscription). Guidelines available in November for SASE. "Contest kicks off in November." Deadline: May 15. Unpublished submissions. Length: 2,000 words maximum. Winners announced in July issue and notified by phone call and press release. "We are looking for fiction that has MOTION, that goes the distance in fewer words. Also, originality and a strong sense of voice are two main elements we look for."

⬤ **TALL GRASS WRITERS GUILD LITERARY ANTHOLOGY/CONTEST**, Outrider Press, 937 Patricia, Crete IL 60417-1375. (708)672-6630 or (800)933-4680 (code 03). Fax: (708)672-5820. E-mail: outriderpr@ aol.com. Website: www.OutriderPr.com. **Contact:** Whitney Scott, senior editor. 2002 competition to collect diverse writings by authors of all ages and backgrounds on the theme of food: "Take Two, They're Small." Open to poetry, short stories and creative nonfiction on food and food-related topics, such as diet and weight. Award: publication in anthology; free copy to all published contributors. $1,000 in cash prizes. Competition receives 400-600 submissions. Judges: Mark Richard Zubro (prose), Pamela Miller (poetry). Entry fee $16; $12 for members. Guidelines and entry form available for SASE, by fax, e-mail and on website. Accepts inquiries by e-mail. Deadline: February 28, 2002. Unpublished and published submissions. Word length: 2,500 words or less. Maximum 2 entries per person. Include SASE. Winners announced in July. "Must include e-mail address and SASE for response."

N SYDNEY TAYLOR MANUSCRIPT COMPETITION, Association of Jewish Libraries, 315 Maitland Ave., Teaneck NJ 07666. (201)862-0312. Fax: (201)862-0362. E-mail: rkglasser@aol.com. Website: www.jewish libraries.org. Award to "deepen the understanding of Judaism for all children by helping to launch new writers of children's Jewish fiction." Annual competition for novels. Award: $1,000. Competition receives 25 submissions. Judges: 5 children's librarians. Guidelines for #10 SASE. Accepts inquiries by fax and e-mail. Deadline: December 1. Previously unpublished submissions. "Children's fiction for readers 8-11 years with universal appeal and Jewish content. Writer must not have a previously published book." Word length: 64 page minimum-200 page maximum, double-spaced. Winners announced May 1 and notified by phone or mail. List of winners available on website.

N ◎ TEDDY BOOK AWARD, Writers League of Texas, 1501 W. 5th St., Suite E-2, Austin TX 78703-5155. (512)499-8914. Fax: (512)499-0441. E-mail: awl@writersleague.org. Website: www.writersleague.org. **Contact:** Jim Bob McMillan, executive director. "To honor an outstanding book for children published by a member of the Writers' League of Texas." Annual competition for novels. Award: $1,000. Competition receives 25-50 submissions. $10 per entry fee. Guidelines available December 2001; send SASE, fax, e-mail, visit website or call. Deadline: June 30, 2002. Accepts inquiries by fax, e-mail or phone. Entries should be previously published children's book by Writers' League of Texas member. Winners announced September 2002 and notified at ceremony. For list of winners send SASE.

TEXAS INSTITUTE OF LETTERS ANNUAL AWARD, Texas Institute of Letters, Center for the Study of the Southwest, Southwest Texas State University, San Marcos TX 78666. (512)245-2232. Fax: (512)245-7462. E-mail: mb13@swt.edu. Website: www.English.swt.edu/css/TIL/rules.htm. **Contact:** Dr. Mark Busby, secretary. Award to recognize writers of Texas literature. Annual competition for short stories and novels. Award: The Book Publishers of Texas Award for the best book published for children or young people ($500) and the Fred Whitehead Award for the best design of a trade book ($750), The Brazos Bookstore Short Story Award for best short story given in memory of Bill Shearer ($750), and the Natalie Ornish Poetry Award for the best book of poetry ($1,000). Judge: committees to be set up. No entry fee. Guidelines available by July, 2001 on website. Accepts inquiries by fax, e-mail and phone. Deadline January 8, 2002. Entries should be previously published. "Each entry should be accompanied by a statement of the entrant's eligibility: birth in Texas or 2 years consecutive residence in the state at some time. A work whose subject matter substantially concerns Texas is also eligible." For list of winners, send e-mail.

N THOUGHT MAGAZINE WRITER'S CONTEST, *Thought Magazine*, P.O. Box 117098, Burlingame CA 94011-7098. E-mail: ThoughtMagazine@yahoo.com. Website: www.geocities.com/ThoughtMagazine. **Contact:** Kevin J. Feeney, publisher. "To recognize and publish quality writing in the areas of short fiction, poetry, and short nonfiction and to identify and give exposure to writers who have not yet been published in a national magazine." Award: 1st prize-$75 plus publication in *Thought Magazine*; 2nd prize-$50 plus publication in *Thought Magazine*. "All submissions are considered for publication in *Thought Magazine*." Competition receives 100 submissions per category. "Entries are judged by the editors and a panel of judges consisting of published writers and academics." $5 entry fee/story or essay or 3 poems. Accepts inquiries by e-mail. Deadlines: April 15 and August 15. Entries should be unpublished. Contest open to all writers. Length: fiction maximum of 3,000 words. Poetry maximum of 100 lines. Include name, address, phone number and/or e-mail. "We are not interested in extreme violence or pornography. May be helpful to review a back issue available for $6." Winners announced 1 month after deadlines and notified by phone or e-mail. List of winners available with SASE.

N THREE OAKS PRIZE FOR FICTION, Story Line Press, Three Oaks Farm, P.O. Box 1240, Ashland OR 97520-0055. (541)512-8792. Fax: (541)512-8793. E-mail: mail@storylinepress.com. Website: www.storyline press.com. **Contact:** Three Oaks Competition. Annual prize for novels and story collections. "The winner receives $1,500 cash sponsored by Bloomsbury Books of Ashland, Oregon, and publication of the winning entry by Story Line Press. Judge: Robert McDowell, publisher. $25 entry fee. Guidelines available for SASE, e-mail or on website. Deadline April 30, 2002. Entries should be unpublished, "except if published in literary journals or anthologies." Length: "Although there is no minimum or maximum requirements for length, the page count must be reasonable." Winners announced 6-8 weeks after deadline and notified by phone. "A press release announcing the winner along with a letter from the publisher is sent to all entrants who supply an SASE for contest results. If for some reason the contestant does not receive this, they may contact us by phone, fax, e-mail or mail."

✔ ◐ THURBER HOUSE RESIDENCIES, The Thurber House, 77 Jefferson Ave., Columbus OH 43215-3840. (614)464-1032. Fax: (614)228-7445. E-mail: thhouse@thurberhouse.org. Website: www.thurberhouse.org. **Contact:** Trish Houston, residency director. "Four writers/year are chosen as writers-in-residence, one for each quarter." Award for writers of novels and story collections. Award: $6,000 stipend and housing for a quarter in the furnished third-floor apartment of James Thurber's boyhood home. Competition receives over 50 submissions. Judges: Residencies Advisory panel. Guidelines available in August for SASE. To apply, send letter of interest and curriculum vitae. Deadline: December 15. "The James Thurber Writer-in-Residence will teach a two-week, graduate level intensive workshop/seminar in the Creative Writing Program at The Ohio State University; participate in a writing residency with a community agency; and offer a public reading in this newly redesigned residency. Candidates should have national visibility in poetry, fiction, or creative nonfiction, substantial book publications, and teaching experience." Winners announced in April and notified by mail. List of winners available in May for SASE.

✔ ◑ THE THURBER PRIZE FOR AMERICAN HUMOR, The Thurber House, 77 Jefferson Ave., Columbus OH 43215-3840. (614)464-1032. Fax: (614)228-7445. E-mail: thhouse@thurberhouse.org. Website: www .thurberhouse.org. Award "to give the nation's highest recognition of the art of humor writing." Biennial competition for books of humor. Award: $5,000; Thurber statuette. Up to 3 Honor Awards may also be conferred. Judges: Well-known members of the national arts community. Entry fee $25/title. 2003 competition guidelines available in January for SASE. Deadline: April 1, 2003. Published submissions or accepted for publication in US for first time. No reprints or paperback editions of previously published books. Word length: no requirement. Primarily pictorial works such as cartoon collections are not considered. Work must be nominated by publisher. Winners announced in October 2003 and notified by mail in August. A list of winners available on website.

▰ TICKLED BY THUNDER ANNUAL FICTION CONTEST, Tickled By Thunder, 14076-86A Ave., Surrey, British Columbia V3W 0V9 Canada. (604)591-6095. E-mail: thunder@istar.ca. Website: home.istar.ca/ ~thunder. **Contact:** Larry Lindner, editor. "To encourage new writers." Annual competition for short stories. Award: 50% of all fees, $150 minimum (Canadian), 1 year's (4-issue) subscription plus publication. Competition receives approximately 30 submissions. Judges: The editor and other writers. Entry fee $10 (Canadian) per entry (free for subscribers but more than one story requires $5 per entry). Guidelines available for SASE, e-mail, website. Accepts inquiries by e-mail. Deadline: February 15. Unpublished submissions. Word length: 2,000 words or less. Winners announced in May and notified by mail. List of winners available for SASE.

✔ JOHN TIGGES WRITING CONTEST, Loras College, 1450 Alta Vista, Dubuque IA 72004-0708. (563)588-7139. Fax: (563)588-4962. E-mail: lcrosset@loras.edu. Website: www.loras.edu/conted. **Contact:** Linda Crossett, director of continuing education. This annual award encourages and recognizes writers. Prizes given for fiction, nonfiction, and poetry. Awards: $100 and publication in *Julien's Journal*, Dubuque area magazine (1st prize, fiction prize); $50 (2nd prize); and $25 (3rd prize). Poetry and nonfiction receive same monetary awards. First place in both are published in Dubuque *Telegraph Herald*. Receives 25-30 fiction entries, 20-25 nonfiction entries, and 50-60 poetry entries. Judges are either faculty or graduates of Loras College English Department. Entry fee: $5/entry. Guidelines available February 1, 2002 for SASE, fax, e-mail, or phone. Accepts inquiries by fax, e-mail, or phone. Deadline: April 8, 2002. Entries should be unpublished. Length: 1,500 words. Winners announced at the Sinipee Writer's Workshop, April 27, 2002 and notified by mail, first week in May. For list of winners send SASE or e-mail.

N ◐ ◎ TOWSON UNIVERSITY PRIZE FOR LITERATURE, College of Liberal Arts, Towson University, Towson MD 21252-0001. (410)704-2128. Fax: (410)704-6392. E-mail: bleetch@towson.edu. **Contact:** Beverly Leetchy, dean, College of Liberal Arts. Annual award for novels or short story collections, previously published. Award: $1,500. Competition receives 5-10 submissions. Requirements: Must be a Maryland resident.

Guidelines available spring 2001 for SASE. Accepts inquiries by fax and e-mail. Deadline: June 15, 2002. Winners announced December 2002 and notified by letter. List of winners available by calling or writing Sue Ann Nordhoff-Klaus.

☑ ◯ **TROUBADOUR'S SHORT STORY CONTEST**, Troubadour's Writers Group, P.O. Box 138, Woodstock IL 60098-0138. E-mail: ghstwnl@aol.com. Website: http://home2owc.net/~mason/troubadours.html. **Contact:** Carla Fortier, contest coordinator. Contest "for those who enjoy writing competitions and/or appreciate feedback from judges." Annual competition for short stories. Award: $75 (1st prize); $50 (2nd prize); $25 (3rd prize); each entry is given a written critique, which is returned to the author with SASE; winners are offered the opportunity to have the their stories published in *The Lantern*. Competition receives 100 submissions. Judges: published authors. $5 entry fee per story; multiple entries OK if each is accompanied by $5 fee. Guidelines available for SASE, by e-mail or on website. Accepts inquiries by e-mail. Deadline: postmarked March 1. Unpublished submissions. Length: 1,500 words maximum. "Follow the format guidelines and enter a complete story with a beginning, middle and end. No poetry, vignettes, personal reminiscences or essays." Judges look for "a well-conceived storyline that revolves around characters in conflict with themselves or others. Writing should grab reader's attention and display a vitality of language and style through a balanced use of dialogue and narrative." Winners announced before July and notified by mail. For list of winners, visit website or send SASE.

Ⓝ ◑ ◎ **STEVEN TURNER AWARD,** The Texas Institute of Letters, Center for the Study of the Southwest, Flowers Hall 327, Southwest Texas State University, San Marcos TX 78666. (512)245-2232. Fax: (512)245-7462. E-mail: mb13@swt.edu. Website: www.english.swt.edu/css/TIL/index. **Contact:** Mark Busby, secretary. "To honor the best first book of fiction published by a writer who was born in Texas or who has lived in the state for two years at some time, or whose work concerns the state." Annual award for novels and story collections. Award: $1,000. Judges: Committee. Guidelines available in July for SASE. Accepts inquiries by e-mail. Deadline: January 14. Previously published submissions appearing in print between January 1 and December 31. Winners announced in April and notified by phone. List of winners available on website.

☑ ◔ ◎ **MARK TWAIN AWARD**, Missouri Association of School Librarians, 3912 Manorwood Dr., St. Louis MO 63125. Phone/fax: (314)416-0462. E-mail: masl@i1.net. Website: www.maslonline.org. **Contact:** Pam Thomeczek. Estab. 1970. Annual award to introduce children to the best of current literature for children and to stimulate reading. Award: A bronze bust of Mark Twain, created by Barbara Shanklin, a Missouri sculptor. A committee selects pre-list of the books nominated for the award; statewide reader/selectors review and rate the books, and then children throughout the state vote to choose a winner from the final list. Books must be published two years prior to nomination for the award list. Publishers may send books they wish to nominate for the list to the committee members. 1) Books should be of interest to children in grades 4 through 8; 2) written by an author living in the US; 3) of literary value which may enrich children's personal lives. Accepts inquiries by fax and e-mail. Winners announced in May and notified in April by phone. List of winners available.

VERY SHORT FICTION SUMMER AWARD, *Glimmer Train Stories*, 710 SW Madison St., Suite 504, Portland OR 97205. (503)221-0836. Fax: (503)221-0837. Website: www.glimmertrain.com (includes writers' guidelines and Q&A section for writers). **Contact:** Linda Swanson-Davies, editor. Annual award offered to encourage the art of the very short story. "We want to read your original, unpublished, very short story (2,000 words or less). $10 reading fee. Make your submissions online (www.glimmertrain.com) by July 31. Winners will be notified and Top 25 places will be posted by November 1." Awards: $1,200 and publication in *Glimmer Train Stories* (1st Place); $500 (2nd Place); $300 (3rd Place).

VERY SHORT FICTION WINTER AWARD, *Glimmer Train Stories*, 710 SW Madison St., Suite 504, Portland OR 97205. (503)221-0836. Fax: (503)221-0837. Website: www.glimmertrain.com (includes writer's guidelines and a Q&A section for writers). **Contact:** Linda Swanson-Davies, editor. Award offered to encourage the art of the very short story. "We want to read your original, unpublished, very short story (2,000 words or less). $10 reading fee. Make your submissions online (www.glimmertrain.com) by January 31. Winners will be notified and Top 25 places will be posted by May 1." Awards: $1,200 and publication in *Glimmer Train Stories* (1st Place); $500 (2nd Place); $300 (3rd Place).

Ⓝ ◎ **VIOLET CROWN AUDIOBOOK AWARDS**, Writers' League of Texas & Earful of Books, 1501 W. 5th St., Austin TX 78703-5155. (512)499-8989. Fax: (504)894-0388. E-mail: awl@writersleague.org. Website: www.writersleague.org. **Contact:** Jim Bob McMillan, executive director. "To honor two outstanding published audiobooks with a Texas connection. The intent of the award is to recognize, encourage and sustain talented writers." Annual competition for novels. Award: $1,000 (fiction, nonfiction). $10 per entry fee. Guidelines available December 2001; SASE, fax, e-mail, visit website or call. Deadline: June 30, 2002. Accepts inquiries by fax, e-mail or phone. Entries should be previously published. Contest open to writers with a Texas connection. Winners announced September 2002 and notified at ceremony. For list of winners send SASE.

VIOLET CROWN BOOK AWARD, Writers' League of Texas, 1501 W. Fifth St., Suite E-2, Austin TX 78703-5155. (512)499-8914. Fax: (512)499-0441. E-mail: awl@writersleague.org. Website: www. writersleague.org. **Contact:** Jim Bob McMillan, executive director. Award "to recognize the best books published by Writers' League members over the period July 1 to June 30 in fiction, nonfiction and poetry categories." Award: Three $1,000 cash awards and trophies. Competition receives approximately 100 submissions. Judges: A panel of judges who are not affiliated with the Writers' League or Barnes & Noble. Entry fee $10. Guidelines after January for SASE, fax, e-mail or website. Accepts inquiries by fax, e-mail or phone. Deadline: June 30. "Entrants must be Writers' League members. League members reside all over the U.S. and some foreign countries. Persons may join the League when they send in entries." Publisher may also submit entry in writer's name. Winners announced September 2002 and notified by phone and mail. List of winners available for SASE. "Awards are co-sponsored by Barnes & Noble Booksellers. Special citations are presented to finalists."

WALDEN FELLOWSHIP, Coordinated by: Extended Campus Programs, Southern Oregon University, 1250 Siskiyou Blvd., Ashland OR 97520-5038. (541)552-6901. Fax: (541)552-6047. E-mail: friendly@so u.edu. Website: www.sou.edu/ecparts/walden. **Contact:** Brooke Friendly, arts coordinator. Award "to give Oregon writers the opportunity to pursue their work at a quiet, beautiful farm in southern Oregon." Annual competition for all types of writing. Award: 3-6 week residencies. Competition receives approximately 30 submissions. Judges: Committee judges selected by the sponsor. Guidelines for SASE and on website. Accepts inquiries by fax and e-mail. Deadline: End of November. Oregon writers only. Word length: maximum 30 pages prose, 8-10 poems. Winners announced in January and notified by mail. List of winners available for SASE and on website.

EDWARD LEWIS WALLANT MEMORIAL BOOK AWARD, 3 Brighton Rd., West Hartford CT 06117. Sponsored by Dr. and Mrs. Irving Waltman. **Contact:** Mrs. Irving Waltman. Annual award. Memorial to Edward Lewis Wallant offering incentive and encouragement to beginning writers, for books published the year before the award is conferred in the spring. Award: $500 plus award certificate. Judges: A panel of 3 literary critics. Books may be submitted for consideration to Dr. Sanford Pinsker, Department of English, Franklin & Marshall College, P.O. Box 3003, Lancaster PA 17604-3003. Deadline: December 31. "Looking for creative work of fiction by an American which has significance for the American Jew. The novel (or collection of short stories) should preferably bear a kinship to the writing of Wallant. The award will seek out the writer who has not yet achieved literary prominence." Winners announced January-February and notified by phone.

WESTERN HERITAGE AWARDS, National Cowboy and Western Heritage Museum, 1700 NE 63rd St., Oklahoma City OK 73111-7997. (405)478-6404. Fax: (405)478-4714. **Contact:** M.J. Van Deuenter, director of publications. Annual award "to honor outstanding quality in fiction, nonfiction and art literature." Submissions are to have been published during the previous calendar year. Award: The Wrangler, a replica of a C.M. Russell Bronze. Competition receives 350 submissions. Entry fee $35. Guidelines available by SASE, fax or e-mail. Entry forms and rules available October 1 for SASE. Accepts inquiries by fax and e-mail. Deadline: November 30. Looking for "stories that best capture the spirit of the West. Submit five actual copies of the work." Winners announced March 1 and notified by letter. List of winners available by SASE, fax or e-mail. "All work must be published by a legitimate, professional publishing company. Self published works are disqualified and the entry fee is not returned. Entries should have a broad appeal to those interested in the West, western history and the western lifestyle."

WESTERN WRITERS OF AMERICA CONTEST, 386 Highway 124 W, Damascus AR 72039-9242. E-mail: carlj@mail.uca.edu. Website: www.westernwriters.org/roundup.html. **Contact:** W.C. Jameson, awards administrator. Award to "honor western and frontier fiction and nonfiction." Annual competition for short stories, novels, children's fiction and scripts. Guidelines available for SASE, by e-mail and on website. Deadline: December 31. Published submissions during the previous year. Only work "which is set in the territory west of the Mississippi River or on the early frontier." Send for complete guidelines and entry forms.

WHITING WRITERS' AWARDS, Mrs. Giles Whiting Foundation, 1133 Avenue of the Americas, New York NY 10036-6710. **Contact:** Barbara K. Bristol, director, writer's program. Annual award for writers of fiction, poetry, nonfiction and plays with an emphasis on emerging writers. Award: $35,000 (10 awards). Candidates are submitted by appointed nominators and chosen for awards by an appointed selection committee. Direct applications and informal nominations not accepted by the foundation. List of winners available October 30 by request.

☑ **LAURA INGALLS WILDER AWARD**, American Library Association/Association for Library Service to Children, 50 E. Huron St., Chicago IL 60611. **Contact:** Malore Brown, executive director. Award offered every 2 years; next year 2003. "To honor a significant body of work for children, for illustration, fiction or nonfiction." Award: Bronze medal. Authors must be nominated by ALSC members. Guidelines available for SASE, fax, e-mail and on website. Winners announced January 27, 2003 and notified by phone.

ℕ PHOEBE WINTER FICTION PRIZE, (formerly Renee Sagive Fiction Prize), *Phoebe*, MSN 2D6 George Mason University, 4400 University Dr., Fairfax VA 22030-4444. (703)993-2915. E-mail: phoebe@gmu.edu. Website: www.gmu.edu/pubs/phoebe. **Contact:** Emily Tuszynska, editor. Award to "find and publish new and exciting fiction." Annual competition for short stories. Award: $1,000 and publication. Competition receives 300 submissions. Judges: Known fiction writers. Entry fee $10 for each story submitted. Guidelines available after July for SASE or on website. Deadline: December 1. Previously unpublished submissions. Word length: maximum of 25 pages. "Guidelines only (no submissions) may be requested by e-mail." Winners announced in fall and notified by mail. List of winners available. All entrants receive fall issue with published winners. "Phoebe encourages experimental writing."

☑ ◑ ◎ **WISCONSIN INSTITUTE FOR CREATIVE WRITING FELLOWSHIP**, University of Wisconsin—Creative Writing, English Department, 600 N. Park St., Madison WI 53706. Website: http://creativewritingwisc.edu. Competition "to provide time, space and an intellectual community for writers working on first books." Six annual awards for short stories, novels and story collections. Awards: $25,000/9-month appointment. Competition receives 500 submissions. Judges: English Department faculty. Guidelines available for SASE; write to Ron Kuka or check website. Deadline: February. Published or unpublished submissions. Applicants must have received an M.F.A. or comparable graduate degree in creative writing and not yet published a book. Limit 1 story up to 30 pages in length. No name on writing sample. Two letters of recommendation and vita or resume required.

☑ ◯ **TOBIAS WOLFF AWARD FOR FICTION**, Mail Stop 9053, Western Washington University, Bellingham WA 98225. E-mail: bhreview@cc.wwv.edu. Website: www.wwv.edu/~bhreview. **Contact:** Fiction Editor. Annual competition for novel excerpts and short stories. Award: $1,000 (1st Prize); $300 (2nd Prize); $200 (3rd Prize). Judge: Laura Kalpakian. Entry fee $15 for the first entry, $10/story or chapter thereafter. Guidelines available August 2001 on website or for SASE. Deadline: December 1-March 15. Unpublished submissions. Length: 8,000 words or less per story or chapter. Winner announced July. List of winners available for SASE.

☑ **DAVID T.K. WONG FELLOWSHIP**, University of East Anglia, School of English & American Studies, Norwich, Norfolk NR4 7TJ United Kingdom. Phone: (00)44 1603 592810. Fax: (00)44 1603 507728. E-mail: v.striker@uea.ac.uk. Website: www.uea.ac.uk/eas/Fellowships/wong/WongFell.htm. **Contact:** Val Striker, fellowship administrator. Annual fellowship for short stories, novels and story collections. Award £25,000 (pounds sterling) and residence at the University of East Anglia. Competition receives 120 submissions per category. Judge: by international panel nominated by various institutions including UEA's Professor of Creative Writing, biographer and Poet Laureate, Andrew Motion. £5 sterling/entry. Guidelines are currently available. For guidelines, fax, e-mail, visit website or call. Accepts inquiries by fax, e-mail, phone. Deadline October 31. Entries should be unpublished. "The Fellow will be someone of exceptional talent who plans to write in English about life in the Far East." Length: 5,000 words or fewer. Winners are announced in late March/early April 2003 and notified by mail or e-mail.

☑ **WORLD FANTASY AWARDS**, World Fantasy Awards Association, P.O. Box 43, Mukilteo WA 98275-0043. E-mail: sfexessec@aol.com. Website: www.worldfantasy.org. **Contact:** Peter Dennis Pautz, president. Award to "recognize excellence in fantasy literature worldwide." Annual competition for short stories, novels, story collections, anthologies, novellas and life achievement. Award: Bust of HP Lovecraft. Judge: Panel. Guidelines available for SASE. Deadline: June 30. Published submissions from previous calendar year. Word length: 10,000-40,000 novella; 10,000 short story. "All fantasy is eligible, from supernatural horror to Tolkienesque to sword and sorcery to the occult, and beyond." Winners announced November 1. List of winners available November 1.

☑ **WORLD WIDE WRITERS AWARD**, Writers International Ltd., P.O. Box 3229, Bournemouth BH1 12S United Kingdom. Phone/fax: (44)1202 589828. E-mail: writintl@globalnet.co.uk. Website: www.worldwidewriters.com. **Contact:** Zena O'Toole, editorial assistant. Award "to encourage the art of short story writing." Awards annual and bimonthly prizes (six times a year) for short stories. Annual Prizes: (Best Short Story of the Year): £3,000 ($5,000) (1st Prize); £625 ($1,000) (2nd and 3rd Prize). Prizes per issue: £625 ($1,000) (1st Prize); £315 ($500) (2nd Prize); £200 ($200) (3rd Prize). Competition receives approximately 200 submissions per month. Judge: Panel provides a short list to the editor. £6 ($10) entry fee. Guidelines available. For guidelines, send

SASE, e-mail or visit website. Accepts inquiries by e-mail. Entries should be unpublished. Contest open to anyone. Length: 2,000-5,000 words. "Read *World Wide Writers*." Winners announced in every issue of *World Wide Writers* and notified by mail within 3 months. For list of winners, send SASE.

✓ WORLD'S BEST SHORT SHORT STORY CONTEST, English Department Writing Program, Florida State University, Tallahassee FL 32306-1580. (850)644-2640. E-mail: sundog@english.fsu.edu. Website: www.en glish.fsu.edu/sundog. **Contact:** Todd Pierce, editor. Annual award for short-short stories, unpublished, under 300 words. Prizewinning story gets $300 and a crate of Florida oranges; winner and finalists are published in *SunDog: The Southeast Review*. Competition receives approx. 5,000 submissions. Entry fee $1. Guidelines on website. Deadline: April 15. Open to all. Length: 300 words maximum. Winners are announced on July 15 and notified by mail between July 1.

✿ ✓ WRITE YOUR HEART OUT™, Ponder Publishing Inc., P.O. Box 23037, RPO McGillivray, Winnipeg, Manitoba R3T 5S3 Canada. (204)269-2985. Fax: (204)888-7159. E-mail: service@ponderpublishing.com. Website: www.ponderpublishing.com. **Contact:** Pamela Walford, assistant editor. "We are looking for potential Ponder Romances, and we felt the contest would be incentive for writers to pen something specifically for us since the mss do no have to be in a complete state." Awards: $500 cdn (grand prize); $100 cdn (2nd prize); and 10 consolation prizes (detailed critiques). Receives 100 entries per category. "Judged by our entire submissions team. Assistant Submissions Editors, Sr. Submission Editor, and Assistant & Sr. Editors. Entry fee: $10 U.S. & international; $15 Canadian. Guidelines now available for SASE, e-mail or visit website. Accepts inquiries by fax and e-mail. Deadline: April 30, 2002 (midnight). Entries must be unpublished. Open to anyone with romance mss. Length: First 3 chapters and 2 page synopsis. "Read our Ponder Romances. They are unique to the romance market." Winners announced September 1, 2002 and notified by phone before September 1, 2002. For list of winners visit website or include $1 extra with entry fee.

◖ WRITER'S DIGEST ANNUAL WRITING COMPETITION, (Short Story Division), *Writer's Digest*, 1507 Dana Ave., Cincinnati OH 45207. (513)531-2690, ext. 328. E-mail: competitions@fwpubs.com. Website: www.writersdigest.com. **Contact:** Terri Boes or Promotion Assistant. Grand Prize $1,500 cash and your choice of a trip to New York City to meet with editors and agents or a trip to the 2003 Maui Writer's Conference. Other awards include cash, reference books and certificates of recognition. Names of grand prize winner and top 100 winners are announced in the November issue of *Writer's Digest*. Top entries published in booklet ($6). Send SASE to *WD* Annual Writing Competition for rules and entry form, or see January through May issues of *Writer's Digest*. Deadline: May 15. Entry fee $12 per manuscript. All entries must be original, unpublished and not previously submitted to a *Writer's Digest* contest. No acknowledgment will be made of receipt of mss nor will mss be returned. Three of the ten writing categories target short fiction: mainstream/literary, genre and children's fiction.

WRITER'S DIGEST NATIONAL SELF-PUBLISHED BOOK AWARDS, *Writer's Digest*, 1507 Dana Ave., Cincinnati OH 45207. (513)531-2690, ext. 328. E-mail: competitions@fwpubs.com. Website: www.writersd igest.com. **Contact:** Terri Boes or Promotion Assistant. Award to "recognize and promote excellence in self-published books." Annual competition with nine categories: mainstream/literary fiction; genre fiction, nonfiction, inspirational (spiritual, New Age), life stories, children's and young adult books, reference books, poetry and cookbooks. Grand prize: $1,500 plus an ad in *Publishers Weekly* and promotion in *Writer's Digest*. Category winners receive $500 and promotion in *Writer's Digest*. Entry fee $100 for first entry; $50 for each additional entry. Guidelines available for SASE. Deadline: December 16. Published submissions. Author must pay full cost and book must have been published in year of contest or two years prior.

⦿ WRITERS' FILM PROJECT, The Chesterfield Film Co., 1158 26th St., PMB 544, Santa Monica CA 90403. (213)683-3977. E-mail: info@chesterfield-co.com. Website: www.chesterfield-co.com. **Contact:** Ed Rugoff, administrator. Award "provides up to 5 (20,000) dollar yearly stipends to promote and foster talented screenwriters, fiction writers and playwrights." Annual competition for short stories, novels and screenplays. Award: 5 $20,000 awards sponsored by Paramount Pictures. Judges: Mentors, panel of judges. Entry fee $39.50

TO RECEIVE REGULAR TIPS AND UPDATES about writing and Writer's Digest publications via e-mail, send an e-mail with "SUBSCRIBE NEWSLETTER" in the body of the message to newsletter-request@writersdigest.com.

US dollars for each story submitted. Guidelines available in January 2002 for SASE or on website. Deadline: June 1, 2002. Published or previously unpublished submissions. "Program open to all age groups, race, religion, educational level etc. Past winners have ranged in age from early 20's to late 50's."

☑ ◯ **WRITERS' JOURNAL ANNUAL FICTION CONTEST**, Val-Tech Media, P.O. Box 394, Perham MN 56573-0394. (218)346-7921. Fax: (218)346-7924. E-mail: writersjournal@lakesplus.com. Website: www.writersjournal.com. **Contact:** Leon Ogroske, publisher/managing editor. Award: $50 (1st Place); $25 (2nd Place); $15 (3rd Place). Publishes prize winners and selected honorable mentions. Competition receives approximately 250 submissions/year. Entry fee $5 each. Unpublished submissions. Entry forms or rules available for SASE. Deadline: January 30 annually. Maximum length is 2,000 words. "Writer's name must not appear on submission. A separate cover sheet must include: name of contest, title and writer's name, address, and telephone number (e-mail address if available)." Winners announced and notified June 30 by mail. A list of winners is published in July/August issue and posted on website.

☑ ◯ **WRITERS' JOURNAL ROMANCE CONTEST**, Val-Tech Media, P.O. Box 394, Perham MN 56573-0394. (218)346-7921. Fax: (218)346-7924. E-mail: writersjournal@lakesplus.com. Website: www.writersjournal.com. **Contact:** Leon Ogroske, editor. Award: $50 (1st Prize); $25 (2nd Prize); $15 (3rd Prize); publishes prize winers plus honorable mentions. Competition receives 350 submissions. Entry fee $5/entry. Guidelines available for SASE (4 entries/person). Deadline: July 30, annually. Unpublished submissions. Word length: 2,000 words maximum. Winners announced in February and notified by mail and winners list published in *Writers' Journal Magazine* and on website. "Enclose #10 SASE for winner's list."

☑ ◯ **THE WRITERS' WORKSHOP INTERNATIONAL FICTION CONTEST,** The Writers' Workshop, 387 Beaucatcher Rd., Asheville NC 28805. Phone/fax: (828)254-8111. **Contact:** Karen Ackerson, executive director. Annual awards for fiction. Awards: $350 (1st Prize); $250 (2nd Prize); $100 (3rd Prize). Competition receives approximately 200 submissions. Past judges have been Peter Matthiessen, Kurt Vonnegut, E.L. Doctorow. Entry fee $18/$15 members. Guidelines for SASE. Unpublished submissions. Length: 10,000 words typed, double-spaced pages per story. Multiple submissions are accepted. Winners announced 4-6 weeks after submission and notified by mail or phone.

◼ ⊕ **WRITESPOT AUTUMN 2002 SHORT STORY COMPETITION**, WriteSpot Publishers International, P.O. Box 221, The Gap Queensland 4061 Australia. Phone: (07)3300-1948. E-mail: frontdesk@writersspot.com. Website: www.writersspot.com. **Contact:** The Coordinator. "The competition is to allow writers a creative outlet. It is also used as a source for stories to be included in upcoming anthologies." Two competitions are held annually. Competition for short stories. Award: $750.; $250; $100; $50; Encouragement Award $50 value (for entrants under 18); publication also offered on up to 12 selected stories. Competition receives 100+ submissions. Judges: six members of the Publications Committee. $8 single entry fee; $12 two entries; $5 three or more entries. Guidelines are available now and will appear on website one month prior to the opening of the competition; send SASE, e-mail, visit website or call. Accepts inquiries by e-mail and phone. Accepts inquiries by fax, e-mail or phone. Deadline: May 31, 2002. Entries should be previously published. Contest open to all ages and locations. Length: 5,000 words. "Work may be of any theme and should display flair and originality." Winners announced June 14, 2002. Winners notified by phone and e-mail. List of winners send SASE, e-mail or visit website.

◼ ⊕ **WRITESPOT SPRING SHORT STORY COMPETITION**, WriteSpot Publishers International, P.O. Box 221, The Gap Queensland 4061 Australia. Phone: (07)3300-1948. E-mail: frontdesk@writersspot.com. Website: www.writersspot.com. **Contact:** The Coordinator. "The competition is to allow writers a creative outlet. It is also used as a source for stories to be included in upcoming anthologies." Two competitions are held annually. Competition for short stories. Award: $750.; $250; $100; $50; Encouragement Award $50 value (for entrants under 18); publication also offered on up to 12 selected stories. Competition receives 100+ submissions. Judges: six members of the Publications Committee. $8 single entry fee; $12 two entries; $5 three or more entries. Guidelines are available now and will appear on website one month prior to the opening of the competition; send SASE, e-mail, visit website or call. Accepts inquiries by e-mail and phone. Accepts inquiries by fax, e-mail or phone. Deadline: November 15, 2002. Entries should be previously published. Contest open to all ages and locations. Length: 5,000 words. "Work may be of any theme and should display flair and originality." Winners announced December 6, 2002. Winners notified by phone and e-mail. List of winners send SASE, e-mail or visit website.

◼ ◎ **YOUNG TEXAS WRITERS AWARDS**, Writers' League of Texas, 1501 W. Fifth St., Suite E-2, Austin TX 78703-5155. (512)499-8914. Fax: (512)499-0441. E-mail: awl@writersleague.org. Website: www.writersleague.org. **Contact:** Jim Bob McMillan, executive director. Award to "recognize outstanding young writing talent enrolled in grades 9-12 in Texas schools." Annual competition for short stories (other categories: essays, poetry, journalism). Awards: 12 cash awards ($50 to $150). Competition receives more than 300 submissions. Judges: Experienced writers. Entry fee $5 (one time fee for multiple entries). Fee may be waived. Guidelines for SASE, fax, e-mail, website. Accepts inquiries by fax, e-mail and phone. Deadline: January 31. Entrants must be Texas resident. Word length: requirements specified on guidelines for each category. Winning entries are published in special anthology. Winners announced in May and notified by mail and phone. List of winners available for SASE.

ZOETROPE SHORT STORY CONTEST, Zoetrope: All Story, 1350 Avenue of the Americas, 24th Floor, New York NY 10019. (212)696-5720. Fax: (212)696-5845. Website: www.all-story.com. **Contact:** Adrienne Brodeur, editor-in-chief. Annual competition for short stories. Award: $1,000 (1st Prize); $500 (2nd Prize); $250 (3rd Prize). 2001 judge: Robert Olen Butler. Entry fee $10. Guidelines available on website. Unpublished submissions. Word length: 5,000 words maximum. "Please mark envelope clearly 'short fiction contest.'" Winners notified in December. A list of winners will be posted on website and printed in February issue.

Resources

Conferences & Workshops

Why are conferences so popular? Writers and conference directors alike tell us it's because writing can be such a lonely business—at conferences writers have the opportunity to meet (and commiserate) with fellow writers, as well as meet and network with publishers, editors and agents. Conferences and workshops provide some of the best opportunities for writers to make publishing contacts and pick up valuable information on the business, as well as the craft, of writing.

The bulk of the listings in this section are for conferences. Most conferences last from one day to one week and offer a combination of workshop-type writing sessions, panel discussions and a variety of guest speakers. Topics may include all aspects of writing from fiction to poetry to scriptwriting, or they may focus on a specific area such as those sponsored by the Romance Writers of America for writers specializing in romance or the SCBWI conferences on writing for children's books.

Workshops, however, tend to run longer—usually one to two weeks. Designed to operate like writing classes, most require writers to be prepared to work on and discuss their work-in-progress while attending. An important benefit of workshops is the opportunity they provide writers for an intensive critique of their work, often by professional writing teachers and established writers.

Each of the listings here includes information on the specific focus of an event as well as planned panels, guest speakers and workshop topics. It is important to note, however, some conference directors were still in the planning stages for 2002 when we contacted them. If it was not possible to include 2002 dates, fees or topics, we have provided information from 2001 so you can get an idea of what to expect. For the most current information, it's best to send a self-addressed, stamped envelope to the director in question about three months before the date(s) listed.

FINDING A CONFERENCE

Many writers try to make it to at least one conference a year, but cost and location count as much as subject matter or other considerations when determining which conference to attend. There are conferences in almost every state and province and even some in Europe open to North Americans.

To make it easier for you to find a conference close to home—or to find one in an exotic locale to fit into your vacation plans—we've divided this section into geographic regions. The conferences appear in alphabetical order under the appropriate regional heading.

Note that conferences appear under the regional heading according to where they will be held, which is sometimes different than the address given as the place to register or send for information. The regions are as follows:

Northeast (pages 554-559): Connecticut, Maine, Massachusetts, New Hampshire, New York, Rhode Island, Vermont

Midatlantic (pages 559-562): Washington DC, Delaware, Maryland, New Jersey, Pennsylvania

Midsouth (pages 562-564): North Carolina, South Carolina, Tennessee, Virginia, West Virginia

LEARNING AND NETWORKING

Besides learning from workshop leaders and panelists in formal sessions, writers at conferences also benefit from conversations with other attendees. Writers on all levels enjoy sharing insights. Often, a conversation over lunch can reveal a new market for your work or let you know which editors are most receptive to the work of new writers. You can find out about recent editor changes and about specific agents. A casual chat could lead to a new contact or resource in your area.

Many editors and agents make visiting conferences a part of their regular search for new writers. A cover letter or query that starts with "I met you at the Green Mountain Writers Conference," or "I found your talk on your company's new romance line at the Moonlight and Magnolias Writer's Conference most interesting . . ." may give you a small leg up on the competition.

While a few writers have been successful in selling their manuscripts at a conference, the availability of editors and agents does not usually mean these folks will have the time there to read your novel or six best short stories (unless, of course, you've scheduled an individual meeting with them ahead of time). While editors and agents are glad to meet writers and discuss work in general terms, usually they don't have the time (or energy) to give an extensive critique during a conference. In other words, use the conference as a way to make a first, brief contact.

SELECTING A CONFERENCE

Besides the obvious considerations of time, place and cost, choose your conference based on your writing goals. If, for example, your goal is to improve the quality of your writing, it will be more helpful to you to choose a hands-on craft workshop rather than a conference offering a series of panels on marketing and promotion. If, on the other hand, you are a science fiction novelist who would like to meet your fans, try one of the many science fiction conferences or "cons" held throughout the country and the world.

Look for panelists and workshop instructors whose work you admire and who seem to be writing in your general area. Check for specific panels or discussions of topics relevant to what you are writing now. Think about the size—would you feel more comfortable with a small workshop of eight people or a large group of 100 or more attendees?

If your funds are limited, start by looking for conferences close to home, but you may want to explore those that offer contests with cash prizes—and a chance to recoup your expenses. A few conferences and workshops also offer scholarships, but the competition is stiff and writers interested in these should find out the requirements early. Finally, students may want to look for conferences and workshops that offer college credit. You will find these options included in the listings here. Again, send a self-addressed, stamped envelope for the most current details.

Northeast (CT, MA, ME, NH, NY, RI, VT)

THE BLUE MOUNTAIN CENTER, Blue Mountain Lake, New York NY 12812-0109. (518)352-7391. **Contact:** Harriet Barlow, director. Residencies for established writers. "Provides a peaceful environment where residents may work free from distractions and demands of normal daily life." Residencies awarded for 1 month between June 19 and November 1 (approx.). For more information, send SASE for brochure.
To Apply: Send for brochure. Application deadline: February 1.

BREAD LOAF WRITERS' CONFERENCE, Middlebury College, Middlebury VT 05753. (802)443-5286. Fax: (802)443-2087. E-mail: blwc@mail.middlebury.edu. **Contact:** Noreen Cargill, administrative coordinator. Estab. 1926. Annual. Conference held in late August. Conference duration: 11 days. Average attendance: 230. For fiction, nonfiction and poetry. Held at the summer campus in Ripton, Vermont (belongs to Middlebury College).
Costs: $1,798 (includes room/board).
Accommodations: Accommodations are at Ripton. Onsite accommodations $626.
Additional Information: Conference information available January 2001. Accepts inquiries by fax and e-mail.

N: THE FOUNDATIONS OF CREATIVITY® WRITING WORKSHOP, The Elizabeth Ayres Center for Creative Writing, P.O. Box 8235 Ridgeway Station, Stamford CT 06905. (212)689-4692 or (800)510-1049. E-mail: mail@CreativeWritingCenter.com. Website: www.CreativeWritingCenter.com. Owner/Director: Elizabeth Ayres. Estab. 1990. Conference held 10 times/year. Workshops begin every 7 weeks, 1 time/week for 6 weeks. Average attendance: 10. "The purpose of the workshop is to help fledgling writers conquer their fear of the blank page; develop imaginative tools; capitalize on the strengths of their natural voice and style; develop confidence; and interact with other writers in a stimulating, supportive atmosphere." Writers' Retreats also offered 3-5 times/year in weekend and week-long formats. Average attendance: 15. "Retreats provide an opportunity for extended writing time in a tranquil setting with like-minded companions."
Costs: $285 (2001); retreats vary from $350-700 depending on duration.
Additional Information: Workshop brochures and guidelines free. Inquiries by mail, phone, e-mail.

GOTHAM WRITERS' WORKSHOP, WritingClasses.com (online division), 1841 Broadway, Suite 809, New York NY 10023-7603. (212)974-8377. Fax: (212)307-6325. E-mail: office@write.org. Website: www.WritingClasses.com. **Contact:** Dana Miller, director of student affairs. Estab. 1993. "Classes are held throughout the year. There are four terms, beginning in January, April, June/July, September/October in 2002." Workshop duration: 10-week, 1-day, and online courses offered. Average attendance: approximately 1,000 students per term, 4,000 students per year. Offers craft-oriented creative writing courses in fiction writing, screenwriting, nonfiction writing, memoir writing, novel writing, children's book writing, playwriting, poetry, songwriting, mystery writing, sketch comedy and business writing. Also, Gotham Writers' Workshop offers a teen program and private instruction. Site: Classes are held at various schools in New York City as well as online at www.WritingClasses.com. View a sample online class on the website.
Costs: Ten-week and online courses—$415 (includes $20 registration fee); one-day courses—$165 (includes $20 registration fee). These fees are before any discounts. For information regarding our discounts, please contact us for a catalog. Meals and lodging not included.
Additional Information: "Participants do not need to submit workshop material prior to their first class." Sponsors a contest for a free 10-week online creative writing course (value = $415) offered each term. Students should fill out a form online at www.WritingClasses.com to participate in the contest. The winner is randomly selected. For brochure send e-mail, visit website, call or fax. Accepts inquiries by SASE, e-mail, phone, fax. Agents and editors participate in some workshops.

GREEN MOUNTAIN WRITERS CONFERENCE, 47 Hazel Street, Rutland VT 05701. (802)775-5326. E-mail: ommar@stanford.edu. Website: www.vermontwriters.com. **Contact:** Yvonne Daley, director. Estab. 1999. Annual. Conference to be held July 30-Aug. 3, 2001. Average attendance: 40. "Focus is to teach and celebrate writing across the genres. We have workshops in fiction, creative non-fiction, memoir, poetry, magazine writing, opinion writing, and travel writing." Conference held at an old dance pavillion on a 5-acre site on a remote pond in Tinmouth, VT. Features: Place in story—The Importance of Environment; creating character through description, dialogue, action, reaction, and thought; The collision of real events and imagination. Panelists, lecturers have included Grace Paley, Chris Bohjalian, David Budbill, and many more.
Costs: In 2001 cost was $375 (including lunch, snacks, beverages).
Accommodations: Transportation can be had at cost from area airports. Offers list of area hotels and lodging.
Additional Information: Participants mss can be read and commented on upon at a cost. Sponsors contests. Requirements: Free tuition, no lodging ($500); reading cost fee: $15. Essays plus 3 poems or 10 pages of fiction/non-fiction. Essays should say why the writer wants to attend our conference. Length: 1,000 words. Brochures

available February, 2001 or on website before then. Brochures for SASE, e-mail, website or call. Accepts inquiries by SASE, e-mail, phone. Editors participate in conferences. "We aim to create a community of writers who support one another and serve as audience/mentors for one another. Participants often continue to correspond and share work after conferences."

HOFSTRA UNIVERSITY SUMMER WRITERS' CONFERENCE, 250 Hofstra University, UCCE, Hempstead NY 11549. (516)463-5016. Fax: (516)463-4833. E-mail: uccelibarts@hofstra.edu. Website: www.hofstra.edu (under "Academics/Continuing Education"). **Contact:** Kenneth Henwood, director, Liberal Arts Studies. Estab. 1972. Annual (every summer, starting week after July 4). Conference to be held July 8-19, 2002. Average attendance: 65. Conference offers workshops in fiction, nonfiction, poetry, juvenile fiction, stage/screenwriting and, on occasion, one other genre such as detective fiction or science fiction. Workshops in prose and poetry for high school student writers are also offered. Site is the university campus, a suburban setting, 25 miles from NYC. Guest speakers are not yet known. "We have had the likes of Oscar Hijuelos, Robert Olen Butler, Hilma and Meg Wolitzer, Budd Schulberg and Cynthia Ozick."
Costs: Non-credit: approximately $410 per workshop or $630 for two workshops. Credit: Approximately $1,100/workshop (2 credits) undergraduate and graduate; $2,100 (4 credits) undergraduate and graduate. "Continental breakfast and lunch are provided daily. Tuition also includes cost of the banquet."
Accommodations: Free bus operates between Hempstead Train Station and campus for those commuting from NYC. Dormitory rooms are available for approximately $350 for the 2 week conference.
Additional Information: "All workshops include critiquing. Each participant is given one-on-one time of ½ hour with workshop leader. We submit work to the Shaw Guides Contest and other Writer's Conferences and Retreats contests when appropriate." Conference information available March 2000. Accepts inquiries by fax, e-mail.

IL CHIOSTRO, 241 W. 97th St., #13N, New York NY 10025. (800)990-3506. Fax: (212)666-3506. E-mail: ilchiostro@hotmail.com. Website: www.ilchiostro.com. **Contacts:** Michael Mele, Linda Mironti. Estab. 1995. Annual conference held June, 2001. Conference duration: three 1-week sessions. Average attendance: 10 students/week. Conference focuses on fiction writing and poetry. Location: characteristic Tuscan estate farmhouse on a Chianti vinyard and also grove—"Very scenic and inspiring." Panel subjects in past workshops have included sensory stimulation and building characters.
Costs: 2001 fees: $1,000/week, included: 2 meals/day, shared double room, transfers from Siena.
Accommodations: Will pick-up conferees upon arrival at Siena station. "One grant is awarded each year. Requirements: cultural diversity and financial need." Conference information is available January 1, 2001. For brochure send SASE, e-mail, visit website or call. Accepts inquiries by SASE, e-mail, phone, fax. Editors participate in conference.

IWWG MEET THE AGENTS AND EDITORS: THE BIG APPLE WORKSHOPS, ℅ International Women's Writing Guild, P.O. Box 810, Gracie Station, New York NY 10028-0082. (212)737-7536. Fax: (212)737-9469. E-mail: iwwg@iwwg.com. Website: www.iwwg.com. **Contact:** Hannelore Hahn, executive director. Estab. 1976. Biannual. Workshops held second weekend in April, and the second weekend in October. Average attendance: 200. Workshops to promote creative writing and professional success. Site: Private meeting space of the City Athletic Club, mid-town New York City. Saturday: One day workshop. Sunday morning: open house/meet the authors and panel discussion with eight recently published authors. Sunday afternoon: open house/meet the agents, independent presses and editors.
Costs: $130 for the weekend.
Accommodations: Information on transportation arrangements and overnight accommodations made available.
Additional Information: For workshop information send SASE. Accepts inquires by fax, e-mail.

KEY WEST LITERARY SEMINAR, 4 Portside Lane, Searsport ME 04974. (888)293-9291. E-mail: keywest@mint.net. Website: www.keywestliteraryseminar.org. **Contact:** Miles Frieden, executive director. Estab. 1981. Annual. Spirit of Place: American Literary Landscapes January 10-20, 2002. Workshop duration: 7 days. Average attendance: 400.
Costs: $400 plus tax.
Accommodations: Provides list of area hotels or lodging options.
Additional Information: For brochure send e-mail, visit website or call. Accepts inquiries by e-mail, phone. Agents and editors participate in conference.

SARAH LAWRENCE COLLEGE SUMMER SEMINAR FOR WRITERS, Office of Graduate Studies, 1 Mead Way, Bronxville NY 10708. (914)395-2373. Fax: (914)395-2664. E-mail: wallace@mail.sld.edu. Website: www.slc.edu. **Contact:** Jennifer Wallace, assistant Director, Graduate Writing Program. Annual. Conference held June for 1 week. Average attendance: 100. The Sarah Lawrence College Summer Seminar provides published and unpublished writers with the opportunity to explore their subject matter and deepen their craft. Our faculty of acclaimed poets, fiction and nonfiction writers meet with seminar participants daily in small, intensive workshops and individual conferences. So that participants and faculty can engage one another accross workshops and genres, faculty offer lectures, readings and panel discussions. Workshops embrace a noncompetitive, supportive model designed to help participants discover their strengths as well as areas for further development and exploration. The week-long community of writers formed by the Seminar enables participants to find new directions, produce new work and engage new ideas in the company of people devoted to the calling and craft of writing. Students will have access to the facilities at Sarah Lawrence College, including a state of the art computer center, a pool, squash courts, indoor running track and the Sarah Lawrence College Library. There are several locations on campus for participants to find the privacy to write, as well as places to gather. A focal point is the Ruth Leff Siegel Center, where meals are served and participants meet for coffee and talk throughout the week. Workshops are noncompetitive environments in which students are encouraged to take risks, generate new work and reflect on work completed before the program. The emphasis is one each writer's effort to discover voice, explore subject matter and engage craft elements necessary to bring the writer's vision to fruition. Workshops are limited to 10 participants. Each participant is given ample opportunity to present work for discussion. Conferences are a unique aspect of the Seminar Week. Workshop members meet individually with their teachers for in-depth discussions. Conferences are held as single hour sessions or 2 half hour sessions, depending on the workshop and genre. Previous conference faculty members have included Ann Beard, Mary La Chapelle, Wesley Brown and Valerie Martin.

Costs: Tuition: $700; accomodations: $180; meal plan: $175; swimming pool: $10/day. If you are a currently enrolled graduate or undergraduate student, you may earn one hour of graduate or undergraduate credit through the Summer Seminar at an additional cost. For those wishing to stay on campus, private air-conditioned dormitory rooms with shared baths are available for the length of the seminar. A meal plan is also available consisting of 3 meals daily and lunch and dinner on June 20 for students who choose to stay on campus as well as commuters.

Additional Information: In addition to the application form, include a brief biographical sketch and a ms. Your name should be on each page of your ms and on your biographical sketch. A $25 registration fee is required. Make checks out to Sarah Lawrence College. Acceptance letters and registration materials will be mailed by May 31. All fees must be received by June 10. The ms should total no more than 20 pages. A limited number of partial scholarships are available. Indicate that you would like to be considered on your application and attach a letter to Susan Guma, Director of Graduate Studies, describing need. This letter should be separate from your biographical sketch. Brochures or guidelines available in February. For brochure, writers should e-mail, call, fax. Accepts inquiries by SASE, e-mail, phone, fax.

☑ THE MACDOWELL COLONY, 100 High St., Peterborough NH 03458. (603)924-3886. Fax: (603)924-9142. Website: www.macdowellcolony.org. **Contact:** Admissions Coordinator. Estab. 1907. Open to writers, composers, visual artists, film/video artists, interdisciplinary artists and architects. Includes main building, library, 3 residence halls and 32 individual studios on over 450 mostly wooded acres, 1 mile from center of small town in southern New Hampshire. Available up to 8 weeks year-round. Provisions for the writer include meals, private sleeping room, individual secluded studio. Accommodates variable number of writers, 10 to 20 at a time.

Costs: Artists are asked to contribute toward the cost of their residency according to their financial resources. "The MacDowell Colony is pleased to offer grants up to $1,000 for writers in need of financial assistance during a residency at MacDowell. At the present time, only artists reviewed and accepted by the literature panel are eligible for this grant."

To Apply: Application forms available. Application deadline: January 15 for summer (May-August), April 15 for fall/winter (September-December), September 15 for winter/spring (January-April). Writing sample required. For novel, send a chapter or section. For short stories, send 2-3. Send 6 copies. Brochure/guidelines available; SASE appreciated.

☑ MANHATTANVILLE COLLEGE SUMMER WRITERS' WEEK, School of Graduate and Professional Studies, 2900 Purchase St., Purchase NY 10577-2131. (914)694-3425. Fax: (914)694-3488. E-mail: gps@mville. edu. Website: www.manhattanville.edu. **Contact:** Ruth Dowd, R.S.C.J., dean, School of Graduate and Professional Studies. Estab. 1982. Annual. Conference held June 25-29, 2001. Average attendance: 110. Workshops include children's literature, journal writing, creative nonfiction, personal essay, poetry, screenwriting, fiction, travel writing and short fiction. The Conference is designed not only for writers but for teachers of writing. Students do intensive work in the genre of their choice. Manhattanville is a suburban campus 30 miles from New York City. The campus centers around Reid Castle, the administration building, the former home of Whitelaw Reid. Workshops are conducted in Reid Castle. A major author is featured as guest lecturer during the Conference. Past speakers have included such authors as Toni Morrison, Andy Bienen, Gail Godwin, Richard Peck and poet Mark Doty.

Costs: Conference cost was $560 in 2001 plus $30 fee.

Accommodations: Students may rent rooms in the college residence halls. More luxurious accommodations are available at neighboring hotels. In the summer of 1999 the cost of renting a room in the residence halls was $40 per night.

Additional Information: Conference information available March 15, 2002. For brochure send e-mail, visit website, call or fax. Accepts inquiries by SASE, e-mail, fax, phone.

■ NEW ENGLAND WRITERS CONFERENCE, P.O. Box 483, 151 Main St., Windsor VT 05089-0483. (802)674-2315. Fax: (802)674-3503. E-mail: newvtpoet@aol.com. Website: http://hometown.aol.com/newvt-poet/myhomepage/profile.html. **Contact:** Dr. Frank or Susan Anthony, co-directors. Estab. 1986. Annual. Conference held third Sunday in July. Conference duration: 1 day. Average attendance: 150. The purpose is "to bring an affordable literary conference to any writers who can get there, and to expose them to emerging excellence in the craft. Site: The Grace Outreach Building, 1 mile south of the Dartmouth campus, Hanover NH. Offers panel and seminars by prominent authors, agents, editors or publishers; open readings, contest awards and book sales/signings.

Costs: $15 (includes lunch). No pre-registration required.

Accommodations: Provides a list of area hotels or lodging options.

Additional Information: Sponsors poetry and fiction contests as part of conference (award announced at conference). Conference information available in May. For brochure send SASE or visit website. Accepts inquiries by SASE, e-mail, phone.

ODYSSEY, 20 Levesque Lane, Mont Vernon NH 03057-1420. Phone/fax: (603)673-6234. E-mail: jcavelos@sff. net. Website: www.sff.net/odyssey. **Contact:** Jeanne Cavelos, director. Estab. 1995. Annual. Workshop to be held June 10 to July 19, 2002. Attendance limited to 20. "A workshop for fantasy, science fiction and horror writers that combines an intensive learning and writing experience with in-depth feedback on students' manuscripts. The only workshop to combine the overall guidance and in-depth feedback of a single instructor with the varied perspectives of guest lecturers and the only such workshop run by an editor." Conference held at Southern New Hampshire University in Manchester, New Hampshire. Previous guest lecturers included: Harlan Ellison, Ben Bova, Dan Simmons, Jane Yolen, Elizabeth Hand, Craig Shaw Gardner, Terry Brooks, Patricia McKillip and John Crowley.

Costs: In 2001: $1,200 tuition, $367 housing (double room), $25 application fee, $350 food (approximate), $55 processing fee to receive college credit.

Accommodations: "Workshop students stay at Southern New Hampshire University townhouses and eat at college."

Additional Information: Students must apply and include a writing sample. Students' works are critiqued throughout the 6 weeks. Workshop information available in October. For brochure/guidelines send SASE, e-mail, visit website, call or fax. Accepts inquiries by SASE, e-mail, fax, phone.

▣ PERSPECTIVES IN CHILDREN'S LITERATURE, University of Massachusetts, Amherst MA 01003-3035. (413)545-1116 or (413)545-4325. E-mail: childlit@educ.umass.edu. Website: www.unix.oit.umass.edu/~childlit. **Contact:** Jane Pierce, coordinator. Estab. 1970. Annual. Conference duration: 8:30-4:00 p.m. Average attendance: 300-500. Conference is for teachers, librarians, writers, illustrators, parents, and students. Location: Isenberg School of Management classroom building. Previous presenters have included Julius Lester, Gail Carson Levine, Jane Dyer, Liza Ketchem, Jane Yolen, Rich Michelson, and more.

Costs: $55, general admission; $50, students.

Additional Information: Conference Information is available by January: send SASE, e-mail, visit website or call. Accepts inquiries by SASE, e-mail, phone. Agents and/or editors participate in conference.

ROBERT QUACKENBUSH'S CHILDREN'S BOOK WRITING & ILLUSTRATING WORKSHOPS, 460 E. 79th St., New York NY 10021-1443. (212)744-3822. Fax: (212)861-2761. E-mail: rqstudios@aol.com. Website: www.rquackenbush.com. **Contact:** Robert Quackenbush, director. Estab. 1982. Annual. Workshop held July 8-12, 2001. Average attendance: limited to 10. Workshops to promote writing and illustrating books for children. Held at the Manhattan studio of Robert Quackenbush, author and illustrator of over 170 books for young readers. "Focus is generally on picture books, easy-to-read and early chapter books. All classes led by Robert Quackenbush."

Costs: $650 tuition covers all costs of the workshop, but does not include housing and meals. A $100 nonrefundable deposit is required with the $550 balance due two weeks prior to attendance. 10% discount for all who enroll by June 15, 2002.

Accommodations: A list of recommended hotels and restaurants is sent upon receipt of deposit.

Additional Information: Class is for beginners and professionals. Critiques during workshop. Private consultations also available at an hourly rate. "Programs suited to your needs; individualized schedules can be designed.

Write or phone to discuss your goals and you will receive a prompt reply." Conference information available July 2001. For brochure send SASE, e-mail, visit website, call or fax. Accepts inquiries by fax, e-mail, phone, SASE.

N "REMEMBER THE MAGIC" IWWG ANNUAL SUMMER CONFERENCE, International Women's Writing Guild, P.O. Box 810, Gracie Station, New York NY 10028-0082. (212)737-7536. Fax: (212)737-9469. E-mail: dirhahn@aol.com. Website: www.iwwg.com. **Contact:** Hannelore Hahn. Estab. 1978. Annual. Conference held August 10-17 2001. Duration of conference 1 week. Average attendance: 500. The conference features 70 workshops held every day on every aspect of writing and the arts. Saratoga Springs, 30 minutes from Albany NY and 4 hours from New York City, is blessed with every type of recreation. The town itself is a Victorian paradise, offering gingerbread houses and antique shops galore. Famous for its mineral springs, conference attendees may take baths at Spa Park. Conference attendees may also avail themselves of the famous Saratoga racing season, offering "race breakfasts" at 7:00 a.m. as well as ballet and music performances scheduled at the Saratoga Arts Festival. Workshop topics at previous conferences have included Promoting Your Book; Self-Publishing; The Art of Fiction Writing and One-Act Playwriting.
Costs: $900 for 7 days, inclusive of meals and lodging.
Accommodations: Accommodations in modern, air-conditioned and non-air-conditioned dormitories—single and/or double occupancy. Equipped with spacious desks and window seats for gazing out onto nature. Meals served cafeteria-style with choice of dishes. Variety of fresh fruits, vegetables and salads have been found plentiful . . . even by vegetarians. Conference information is available in January. For brochure send SASE, e-mail, visit website or fax. Accepts inquiries by SASE, e-mail, phone or fax. "The conference is for women only."

N SCBWI/HOFSTRA CHILDREN'S LITERATURE CONFERENCE, Hofstra University, University College of Continuing Education, Republic Hall, Hempstead NY 11549. (516)463-5016. **Contact:** Connie C. Epstein, Adrienne Betz and Kenneth Henwood, co-organizers. Estab. 1985. Annual. Conference to be held April 20, 2002. Average attendance: 200. Conference to encourage good writing for children. "Purpose is to bring together various professional groups—writers, illustrators, librarians, teachers—who are interested in writing for children. Each year we organize the program around a theme. Last year it was Finding Your Voice." The conference takes place at the Student Center Building of Hofstra University, located in Hempstead, Long Island. "We have two general sessions, an editorial panel and five break-out groups held in rooms in the Center or nearby classrooms." Previous agents/speakers have included: Paula Danziger and Anne M. Martin and a panel of children's book editors who critique randomly selected first-manuscript pages submitted by registrants. Special interest groups are offered in picture books, nonfiction and submission procedures with others in fiction.
Cost: $70 (previous year) for SCBWI members; $78 for nonmembers. Lunch included.

STATE OF MAINE WRITERS' CONFERENCE, 18 Hill Rd., Belmont MA 02478. (617)489-1548. **Contact:** June Knowles and Mary Pitts, co-chairs. Estab. 1941. Annual. Conference held in August. Conference duration: 4 days. Average attendance: 40. "We try to present a balanced as well as eclectic conference. There is quite a bit of time and attention given to poetry but we also have children's literature, travel, novels/fiction and other issues of interest to writers. Our speakers are publishers, editors, illustrators and other professionals. Our concentration is, by intention, a general view of writing to publish. We are located in Ocean Park, a small seashore village 14 miles south of Portland. Ours is a summer assembly center with many buildings from the Victorian Age. The conference meets in Porter Hall, one of the assembly buildings which is listed on the National Register of Historic Places. Within recent years our guest list has included Lewis Turco, Amy MacDonald, Jeffrey Aronson, Wesley McNair, John N. Cole, Betsy Sholl, Denis Ledoux, John Tagliabue, Roy Fairfield, Oscar Greene and many others. We usually have about 10 guest presenters a year."
Costs: $90-100 includes the conference banquet. There is a reduced fee, $45, for students ages 21 and under. The fee does not include housing or meals which must be arranged separately by the conferees.
Accommodations: An accommodations list is available. "We are in a summer resort area and motels, guest houses and restaurants abound."
Additional Information: "We have a list of about nine contests on various genres. The prizes, all modest, are awarded at the end of the conference and only to those who are registered." Send SASE for program guide and contest announcements.

WESLEYAN WRITERS CONFERENCE, Wesleyan University, Middletown CT 06459. (860)685-3604. Fax: (860)685-2441. E-mail: agreene@wesleyan.edu. Website: www.wesleyan.edu/writing/conferen.html. **Contact:** Anne Greene, director. Estab. 1956. Annual. Conference held the last week in June. Average attendance: 100. For fiction techniques, novel, short story, poetry, screenwriting, nonfiction, literary journalism, memoir. The conference is held on the campus of Wesleyan University, in the hills overlooking the Connecticut River. Meals and lodging are provided on campus. Features readings of new fiction, guest lectures on a range of topics including publishing and daily seminars. "Both new and experienced writers are welcome."

Costs: In 2001, day rate $725 (including meals); boarding students' rate $845 (including meals and room for 5 nights).

Accommodations: "Participants can fly to Hartford or take Amtrak to Meriden, CT. We are happy to help participants make travel arrangements." Overnight participants stay on campus.

Additional Information: Manuscript critiques are available as part of the program but are not required. Participants may attend seminars in several different genres. Scholarships and teaching fellowships are available, including the Jakobson awards for new writers and the Jon Davidoff Scholarships for journalists. Accepts inquiries by e-mail, fax.

N WILDBRANCH WORKSHOP, Sterling College, Craftsbury Common VT 05827. (800)648-3591. Fax: (802)586-2596. E-mail: wldbrnch@sterlingcollege.edu. **Contact:** David Brown, director. Estab. 1987. Annual. Conference held June 2002. Conference duration: 1 week. Average attendance: 20-25. Conference focuses on outdoor, natural history and environmental writing in fiction as well as nonfiction. Site: Sterling College. Faculty members are Diana Kappel-Smith, Gale Lawrence and Joel Vance.

Costs: In 2001: tuition was $675 and room and board was $200. Arranges transportation from airport. Overnight accommodations available; $200 for on-campus room and board.

Additional Information: Prior to arrival, submit a brief description of writing background and goals. Conference information available in early winter, 2002. For brochure send SASE, e-mail, call or fax. Accepts inquiries by SASE, e-mail, phone and fax. Editors participate in conference.

☑ THE WRITER'S VOICE OF THE WEST SIDE YMCA, 5 West 63rd St., New York NY 10023. (212)875-4124. (212) 875-4184. E-mail: wswritersvoice@ymcanyc.org. **Contact:** Fanon Howell, associate director. Estab. 1981. Workshop held four times/year (summer, spring, winter and fall). Workshop duration: 1-10 weeks, two hours one night/week. Average attendance: 15. Workshop on "fiction, poetry, writing for performance, non-fiction, multi-genre, playwriting and writing for children." Workshop held at the Westside YMCA.

Costs: $325/workshop.

Additional Information: Sponsors several contests including awards for poetry, fiction and non-fiction and a literary magazine. For workshop brochures/guidelines send SASE, e-mail, visit website, call or fax. Accepts inquiries by SASE, e-mail, fax, phone. "The Writer's Voice of the Westside Y is the largest non-academic literary arts center in the U.S."

☑ YADDO, Box 395, Saratoga Springs NY 12866-0395. (518)587-0746. Fax: (518)584-1312. E-mail: yaddo@yaddo.org. Website: www.yaddo.org. **Contact:** Admissions Committee. Estab. 1926. "Those qualified for invitations to Yaddo are highly qualified writers, visual artists, composers, choreographers, performance artists and film and video artists who are working at the professional level in their fields. Artists who wish to work collaboratively are encouraged to apply. An abiding principle at Yaddo is that applications for residencies are judged on the quality of the artists' work and professional promise." Provisions include room, board and studio space. No stipends are offered. Site includes four small lakes, a rose garden, woodland. Two seasons: large season is mid-May-August; small season is October-May (stays from 2 weeks to 2 months; average stay is 5 weeks). Accommodates approximately 16 writers in large season.

Costs: No fee is charged; residency includes room, board and studio space. Limited travel expenses are available to artists accepted for residencies at Yaddo.

To Apply: Filing fee is $20 (checks to Corporation of Yaddo). Two letters of recommendation are requested. Applications are considerd by the Admissions Committee and invitations are issued by April (deadline: January 15) and September (deadline: August 1). Conference information available for SASE (55¢ postage), by e-mail, fax or phone and on website. Accepts inquiries by e-mail, fax, SASE, phone.

Midatlantic (DC, DE, MD, NJ, PA)

N BALTIMORE WRITERS ALLIANCE CONFERENCE, P.O. Box 410, Riderwood MD 21139-0410. (410)377-5265. Fax: (410)377-4325. E-mail: hdiehl@bcpl.net. Website: www.baltimorewriters.org. **Contact:** Barbara Diehl. Estab. 1993. Annual. Conference held in November. Conference duration: 1 day. Average attendance: 150-200. Conference focuses on "many areas of writing and getting published." Site: Towson University. Panels featured in the 2001 conference include short fiction, romance novel, general fiction. Donna Boctig, Mary Joe Putney and Allegra Bennett participated as speakers.

Costs: $75, includes food.

Accommodations: Provides a list of area hotels or lodging options "if asked."

Additional Information: Conference information is available August/September. For brochure send SASE, e-mail, visit website or call. Accepts inquiries by e-mail and phone. Agents and editors participate in conference.

N BOOKTOWNS OF EUROPE WRITERS WORKSHOPS, P.O. Box 1626, West Chester PA 19380. (610)486-6687. Fax: (610)486-0204. E-mail: info@booktownwriters.com. Website: www.booktownwriters. com/. **Contact:** Lenore M. Scallan, workshops coordinator. Estab. 1995. 3-4 per year. Conferences due to be held July 14-20, 2002, France; July 21-27, 2002, Germany; July 28-August 3, 2002, The Netherlands; August 5-10, 2002, Norway; December 8-14, 2002, Ireland. Average attendance: under 12 per site. "Booktowns of Europe focuses on the book-length project. We remove writers from daily distractions, provide a learning vacation atmosphere in the small villages and towns of western Europe, offer intensive support for all fiction and non-fiction topics: autobiography, biography, business, history, romance, sci-fi, self help, sports, etc. (no poetry, erotica or script-writing)." Site: offer 5-6 sites/year throughout Europe. Panels planned for next conference include two daily sessions - a morning writing assignment related to the location, and an afternoon session reviewing the morning session's results. Lenore M. Scallan and Bruce Mowday are scheduled to participate as faculty members. **Costs:** $1,600 for entire package, including transportation between transfer city and workshop site; full tuition; all course materials; one half-hour private conference with workshop leader; six nights accommodation with daily breakfast and dinner; one afternoon/evening excursion.
Accommodations: All accommodations are comfortable, two-star European, double occupancy, first-come first-served. 10% discount for full-time students (with university ID) and seniors, plus group discounts for groups of six or more. Accommodations are limited.
Additional Information: A 10-page sample chapter, excerpt and/or full treatment for the book project with a $25 fee may be submitted 60 days prior to workshop for a technical and potential marketing evaluation. The submission will be returned with a marked copy and one-page evaluation sheet at the start of the workshop program. Conference information for SASE. "The workshop environment, while intense, offers plenty of private time opportunity for participants to write. They also have free time to explore the unique distinctions of each site. One additional option: a free-ranging post-dinnertime evening discussion in which town 'locals' often take part. Attendance is not required, but these open discussions often become the most memorable parts of the workshop experience.

THE COLLEGE OF NEW JERSEY WRITERS' CONFERENCE, English Dept., The College of New Jersey, P.O. Box 7718, Ewing NJ 08628-0718. (609)771-3254. Fax: (609)637-5112. E-mail: write@tcnj.edu. **Contact:** Jean Hollander, director. Estab. 1980. Annual. Conference will be held April 18, 2002. Conference duration: 9 a.m. to 10:30 p.m. Average attendance: 600-1,000. "Conference concentrates on fiction (the largest number of participants), poetry, children's literature, play and screenwriting, magazine and newspaper journalism, overcoming writer's block, nonfiction books. Conference is held at the student center at the college in two auditoriums and workshop rooms; also Kendall Theatre on campus." The focus is on various genres: romance, detective, mystery, TV writing, etc. Topics have included "How to Get Happily Published," "How to Get an Agent" and "Earning a Living as a Writer." The conference usually presents twenty or so authors, plus two featured speakers, who have included Arthur Miller, Saul Bellow, Toni Morrison, Joyce Carol Oates, Erica Jong, Alice Walker, Joseph Heller, John Updike, Anna Quindlen, etc.
Costs: General registration $45, plus $10 for each workshop. Lower rates for students.
Additional Information: Conference information available for SASE. Accepts inquiries by SASE, e-mail, fax, phone.

MID-ATLANTIC MYSTERY BOOK FAIR & CONVENTION, Detecto Mysterioso Books at Society Hill Playhouse, 507 S. Eighth St., Philadelphia PA 19147. (215)923-0211. Fax: (923)923-1789. E-mail: shp@erols.c om. Website: www.erols.com/SHP. **Contact:** Deen Kogan, chairperson. Estab. 1991. Annual. Convention held September 27-29, 2002. Average attendance: 450-500. Focus is on mystery, suspense, thriller, true crime novels. "An examination of the genre from many points of view." The convention is held at the Wyndham Franklin Plaza, located in the historic area of Philadelphia. Previous speakers included Lawrence Block, Jeremiah Healy, Michael Connelly, Paul Levine, Eileen Dreyer, Earl Emerson, Wendy Hornsby, S.J. Rozan, George Pelecanos.
Costs: $135 registration fee.
Accommodations: Attendees must make their own transportation arrangements. Special room rate available at convention hotel.
Additional Information: "The Bookroom is a focal point of the convention. Twenty-five specialty dealers are expected to exhibit and collectables range from hot-off-the-press bestsellers to 1930's pulp; from fine editions to reading copies. Conference information available by mail or telephone after September 30, 2001. Accepts inquiries by e-mail, fax, provide address."

CAN'T FIND A CONFERENCE? Conferences are listed by region. Check the introduction to this section for a list of regional categories.

MONTROSE CHRISTIAN WRITER'S CONFERENCE, 5 Locust St., Montrose Bible Conference, Montrose PA 18801-1112. (570)278-1001 or (800)598-5030. Fax: (570)278-3061. E-mail: mbc@montrosebible.org. Website: www.montrosebible.org. **Contact:** Donna Kosik, MBC Secretary/Registrar. Estab. 1990. Annual. Conference held in July, 2002. Average attendance: 75. "We try to meet a cross-section of writing needs, for beginners and advanced, covering fiction, poetry and writing for children. It is small enough to allow personal interaction between conferences and faculty. We meet in the beautiful village of Montrose, Pennsylvania, situated in the mountains. The Bible Conference provides hotel/motel-like accommodations and good food. The main sessions are held in the chapel with rooms available for other classes. Fiction writing has been taught each year."
Costs: In 2001 registration (tuition) was $120.
Accommodations: Will meet planes in Binghamton NY and Scranton PA; will meet bus in Great Bend PA. Information on overnight accommodations is available. On-site accommodations: room and board $170-255/conference; $38-$57/day including food.
Additional Information: "Writers can send work ahead and have it critiqued for $25." The attendees are usually church related. The writing has a Christian emphasis." Conference information available March 2002. For brochure send SASE, visit website, e-mail, call or fax. Accepts inquiries by SASE, e-mail, fax, phone.

N WILLIAM PATERSON UNIVERSITY SPRING WRITER'S CONFERENCE, English Dept., Atrium 232, 300 Pompton Rd., Wayne NJ 07470. (973)720-3067. Fax: (973)720-2189. E-mail: parrasj@wpunj.edu. Website: www.wpunj.edu/cohss/english/writer's_conference/Writer'sconference.html. **Contact:** Dr. John Parras. Annual. Conference held April 2002. Conference duration: 1 day. Average attendance: 100-150. Several hands-on workshops are offered in many genres of creative writing, critical writing and literature. Includes reading by nationally recognized author. Site: William Paterson University campus. Past faculty has included Yusef Komunyakaa, Joyce Carol Oates, Susan Sontag and Jimmy Santiago Braca.
Costs: $35 (2001) includes 2 workshops, primary reading, meals.
Accommodations: Conference information is available. For brochure send SASE, e-mail, visit website, call or fax. Accepts inquiries by SASE, e-mail, phone and fax. Agents and editors participate in conference.

PENNWRITERS CONFERENCE, RR #2, Box 241, Middlebury Center PA 16935. (717)871-0599. (717)871-6104. E-mail: elizwrite8@aol.com. Website: www.pennwriters.org. **Contact:** Elizabeth Darrach. Estab. 1987. Annual. Conference held May 18-20, 2001. Average attendance: 120. "We encompass all genres and will be aiming for workshops to cover many areas, including fiction (long and short), nonfiction, etc." Workshop held at the Holiday Inn Grantville. Theme for 2001 was "A Way with Words." Speakers included Leonard Bishop, *Writer's Digest* columnist Amanda Lynch, Valerie Maimont and motivational speaker Bill Foster.
Costs: 2000 fees: $125 for members.
Accommodations: Special rate of $82/night if reservation is made by April 20.
Additional Information: Sponsors contest: published authors judge fiction in 2 categories, short stories and Great Beginnings (novels). For conference information send SASE. Accepts inquiries by fax and e-mail. "Agent/editor appointments are available on a first-come, first serve basis."

✓ WASHINGTON INDEPENDENT WRITERS (WIW) SPRING WRITERS CONFERENCE, 733 15th St. NW, Suite 220, Washington DC 20005-2112. (202)347-4973. Fax: (202)628-0298. E-mail: info@washwriter.org. Website: www.washwriter.org. **Contact:** Melissa Herman, executive director. Estab. 1975. Annual. Conference held May 14-15. Conference duration: Friday evening and Saturday. Average attendance: 250. "Gives participants a chance to hear from and talk with dozens of experts on book and magazine publishing as well as meet one-on-one with literary agents." National Press Club as conference site. Past keynote speakers include Erica Jong, Diane Rehm, Kitty Kelley, Lawrence Block, John Barth.
Costs: $135 members; $175 nonmembers; $210 membership and conference.
Additional Information: Conference information available for SASE in February. Accepts inquiries by fax, e-mail.

WINTER POETRY & PROSE GETAWAY IN CAPE MAY, 18 North Richards Ave., Ventnor NJ 08406-2136. (609)823-5076. E-mail: wintergetaway@hotmail.com. Website: www.wintergetaway.com. **Contact:** Peter E. Murphy, founder/director. Estab. 1994. Annual. Workshop held January 12-15, 2001. Average attendance: 150. "Open to all writers, beginners and experienced over the age of 18. Prose workshops meet all day Saturday and Sunday and on Monday morning. Participants choose one workshop from among the following choices: short story (beginning and advanced), memoir, novel, drama, poetry, photography, story telling and pottery. Classes are small so each person receives individual attention for the new writing or work-in-progress that they are focusing on. The workshops are held at the Grand Hotel on the oceanfront in historic Cape May, New Jersey." 2002 speakers include Michael Steinberg, Terese Svoboda, Stephen Dunn, Donna Perry, Mimi Schwartz, Robbie Clipper Sethi, and Richard Weems.

Costs: Cost for 2002 is $395 which includes breakfast and lunch for three days, all workshop session and evening activities, and a double room. Dinners are not included. Participants may choose a single room at an additional cost. Some workshops require additional material fees. Commuters who make their own arrangements are welcome. A $25 early bird discount is available if full payment is made by November 15.

Accommodations: "Participants stay in comfortable rooms, most with an ocean view, perfect for thawing out the muse. Hotel facilities include a pool, sauna and a whirlpool, as well as a lounge and disco for late evening dancing."

Additional Information: "Individual critiques may be available to prose writers at an additional cost. Work in progress should be sent ahead of time." For conference information (after September 15) send e-mail, visit website or call. Accepts inquiries by SASE, e-mail, phone. "The Winter Getaway is known for its challenging and supportive workshops that encourage imaginative risk-taking and promote freedom and transformation in the participants' writing."

WRITING FOR PUBLICATION, Villanova University, Villanova PA 19085-1099. (610)519-4618. Fax: (610)519-4623. E-mail: ray.heitzmann@villanova.edu. **Contact:** Wm. Ray Heitzmann, director. Estab. 1975. Annual. Conference dates vary, held in spring. Average attendance: 15-20 (seminar style). Conference covers marketing one's manuscript (fiction, nonfiction, book, article, etc.); strong emphasis on marketing. Conference held in a seminar room at Villanova University (easy access, parking, etc.). Panels include "Advanced Writing for Publication," "Part-time Writing," "Working With Editors." Panelists include Ray Heitzman, and others.

Costs: $430 (graduate credit); $100 (non-credit) plus $10 registration fee.

Accommodations: List of motels/hotels available, but most people live in area and commute. Special arrangements made on an individual basis.

Additional Information: Critiques available. Voluntary submission of manuscripts. Conference information available in late Fall. Brochures available for SASE, e-mail, fax or phone. Accepts inquiries by SASE, e-mail, phone, fax. "Workshop graduates have been very successful." Emphasis: Non-fiction.

Midsouth (NC, SC, TN, VA, WV)

AMERICAN CHRISTIAN WRITERS CONFERENCES, P.O. Box 110390, Nashville TN 37222. (800)21-WRITE. Fax: (615)834-7736. E-mail: regaforder@aol.com. Website: www.ACWriters.com (includes schedule). **Contact:** Reg Forder, director. Estab. 1981. Annual. Conference duration: 2 days. Average attendance: 100. To promote all forms of Christian writing. Conferences held throughout the year in over 2 dozen cities. Usually located at a major hotel chain like Holiday Inn.

Costs: Approximately $169 plus meals and accommodation.

Accommodations: Special rates available at host hotel.

Additional Information: Conference information available for SASE, e-mail, phone or fax. Accepts inquiries by fax, e-mail, phone, SASE.

ASSOCIATED WRITING PROGRAMS ANNUAL CONFERENCE, Tallwood House, MS 1E3 GMU, Fairfax VA 22030. (703)993-4301. Fax: (703)993-4302. E-mail: awp@gmu.edu. Website: www.awpwriter. org. Estab. 1992. Annual. Conference held March 6-9, 2002, and February 28-March 1, 2003. Average attendance: 2,000. Conference focuses on fiction; poetry; pedagogy of creative writing; information for readers, writers, editors, etc. Site: New Orleans LA in 2002, and Baltimore MD in 2003. Ernest Gaines and Rita Dove are scheduled to participate as faculty members.

Costs: $130 for AWP members, $155 for nonmembers. Airline discount.

Accommodations: Offers overnight accommodations.

Additional Information: Participants must submit workshop material by May 31 of previous Spring. Conference information is available on website. Brochure available by e-mail request. Accepts inquiries by SASE, e-mail, phone, fax. Agents and editors participate in conference.

BLUE RIDGE MOUNTAIN CHRISTIAN WRITERS CONFERENCE, P.O. Box 128, Ridgecrest NC 28770. (828)669-3596. Fax: (828)669-4843. E-mail: rhawkin@lifeway.com. Website: www.ridgecresetconferenc es.com. **Contact:** Robin Hawkins, event planning coordinator. Estab. 1999. Annual. Conference held April 7-11, 2002. Average attendance: 200. All areas of Christian writing, specializing in scriptwriting. Site: LifeWay Ridgecrest Conference Center. 2001 theme based upon Philippians 1:6. 2001 speakers included Dr. Ted Baehr, Janet Thoma, and Ken Wales.

Costs: Tuition, accommodations, and 12 meals, $444-592. Off-campus rate is $309.

Accommodations: LifeWay Ridgecrest Conference Center.

Additional Information: Sponsors contests in published and unpublished categories for poetry and lyrics, articles and short stories, novels and novellas, and scripts. Award includes trophy and $100 scholarship toward next year's conference. Contest entry fee: $10/entry. For brochure, send e-mail, call, or fax. Accepts inquiries by e-mail, phone, fax. Agents participate in conference. "Our conference is continuing to grow. We have received much positive feedback along with many reports of writers being published due to what they have learned and experienced at this event."

N **WINSTON GROOM LITERARY CONFERENCE**, P.O. Box 338, Cashiers NC 28717. (828)743-2411. Fax: (828)743-5991. E-mail: info@highhamptoninn.com. Website: www.highhamptoninn.com. **Contact:** Agnus Crisp. Estab. 1994. Annual. May 31-June 2, 2002. Average attendance: 100. 2001 panel included Winston Groom, Kaye Gibbons, Dominick Dunne, John Logue, and Peter Maas.
Costs: To be determined.
Accommodations: Offers overnight accommodations with onsite facilities.
Additional Information: For brochure send e-mail, visit website, call, fax. Accepts inquiries by e-mail, phone, fax. Agents and editors participate in conference.

N **HIGHLAND SUMMER CONFERENCE**, Box 7014, Radford University, Radford VA 24142-7014. (540)831-5366. Fax: (540)831-5004. E-mail: jasbury@radford.edu. Website: www.radford.edu/~arsc. Chair, Appalachian Studies Program: Dr. Grace Toney Edwards. **Contact:** Jo Ann Asbury, assistant to director. Estab. 1978. Annual. Conference held first 2 weeks of June 2002. Conference duration: 12 days. Average attendance: 25. Three hours graduate or undergraduate credit. "The HSC features one (two weeks) or two (one week each) guest leaders each year. As a rule, our leaders are well-known writers who have connections, either thematic, or personal, or both, to the Appalachian region. The genre(s) of emphasis depends upon the workshop leader(s). In the past we have had as guest lecturers Nikki Giovanni, Sharyn McCrumb, Gurney Norman, Denise Giardinia, George Ella Lyon, Jim Wayne Miller, Wilma Dykeman and Robert Morgan. The Highland Summer Conference is held at Radford University, a school of about 9,000 students. Radford is in the Blue Ridge Mountains of southwest Virginia about 45 miles south of Roanoke, VA."
Costs: "The cost is based on current Radford tuition for 3 credit hours plus an additional conference fee. On-campus meals and housing are available at additional cost. In 2001 conference tuition was $369 for instate undergraduates, $477 for graduate students."
Accommodations: "We do not have special rate arrangements with local hotels. We do offer accommodations on the Radford University Campus in a recently refurbished residence hall. (In 2001 cost was $17-26 per night.)"
Additional Information: "Conference leaders typically critique work done during the two-week conference, but do not ask to have any writing submitted prior to the conference beginning." Conference information available after February, 2001 for SASE. Accepts inquiries by e-mail, fax.

✓ **NORTH CAROLINA WRITERS' NETWORK FALL CONFERENCE**, P.O. Box 954, Carrboro NC 27510-0954. (919)967-9540. Fax: (919)929-0535. E-mail: mail@ncwriters.org. Website: www.ncwriters.org. **Contact:** Shannon Woolfe, program and services director, NCWN. Estab. 1985. Annual. Average attendance: 450. "The conference is a weekend full of workshops, panels, readings and discussion groups. It endeavors to serve writers of all levels of skill from beginning, to emerging, to established. We try to have *all* genres represented. In the past we have had novelists, poets, journalists, editors, children's writers, young adult writers, storytellers, playwrights, screenwriters, etc. We take the conference to a different location in North Carolina each year in order to best serve our entire state. We hold the conference at a conference center with hotel rooms available."
Costs: "Conference cost is approximately $175 and includes two meals."
Accommodations: "Special conference hotel rates are obtained, but the individual makes his/her own reservations."
Additional Information: Conference information available September 1, 2002. For brochure send SASE with 2 first-class stamps, e-mail, visit website, fax or phone. Accepts inquiries by SASE, phone, fax, e-mail.

✓ **SEWANEE WRITERS' CONFERENCE**, 310 St. Luke's Hall, Sewanee TN 37383-1000. (931)598-1141. E-mail: cpeters@sewanee.edu. Website: www.sewaneewriters.org. **Contact:** Cheri B. Peters, creative writing programs manager. Estab. 1990. Annual. Conference held July 16-28, 2002. Average attendance: 110. "We offer genre-based workshops in fiction, poetry, and playwriting, and a full schedule of readings, craft lectures, panel discussions, talks, Q&A sessions, and the like. The Sewanee Writers' Conference uses the facilities of the University of the South. Physically, the University is a collection of ivy-covered Gothic-style buildings, located on the Cumberland Plateau in mid-Tennessee. We allow invited editors, publishers, and agents to structure their own presentations, but there is always opportunity for questions from the audience." The 2001 faculty included Tony Earley, Daisy Foote, Debora Greger, Barry Hannah, Robert Hass, John Hollander, Romulus Linney, Margot Livesey, William Logan, Alison Lurie, Alice McDermott, Eric McGraw, Tim O'Brien and Padgett Powell.
Costs: Full conference fee (tuition, board, and basic room) is $1,205; a single room costs an additional $50.

Accommodations: Complimentary chartered bus service is available, on a limited basis, on the first and last days of the conference. Participants are housed in University dormitory rooms. Motel or B&B housing is available but not abundantly so. Dormitory housing costs are included in the full conference fee.

Additional Information: "We offer each participant (excluding auditors) the opportunity for a private manuscript conference with a member of the faculty. These manuscripts are due one month before the conference begins." Conference information available after February. For brochure send address and phone number, e-mail, visit website or call. "The conference has available a limited number of fellowships and scholarships; these are awarded on a competitive basis." Accepts inquiries by website, e-mail, phone, regular mail (send address and phone number).

☑ VIRGINIA FESTIVAL OF THE BOOK, 145 Ednam Dr., Charlottesville VA 22903. (434)924-6890. Fax: (434)296-4714. E-mail: vabook@virginia.edu. Website: www.vabook.org. **Contact:** Nancy Damon, programs director. Estab. 1995. Annual. Festival held March 20-24, 2001. Average attendance: 15,700. Festival held to celebrate books and promote reading and literacy. Held throughout the Charlottesville/Albemarle area.

Costs: $30 fee for luncheon and $30 fee for reception. "All other programs free and open to the public."

Accommodations: Overnight accommodations can be found on the web at www.travelingamerica.com.

Additional Information: "Authors must 'apply' to the festival to be included on a panel." Conference information is available on the website, e-mail, fax or phone. For brochure visit website. Accepts inquiries by e-mail, fax, phone. Agents and editors participate in conference. "The festival is a five-day event featuring authors, illustrators and publishing professionals. The featured authors are invited or write and inquire to participate. All attendees welcome."

░N░ WILDACRE WRITERS WORKSHOP, 233 S. Elm St., Greensboro NC 27401-2602. (800)635-2049. Fax: (336)273-4044. E-mail: judihill@aol.com. Website: www.Wildacres.com. **Contact:** Judith Hill, director. Estab. 1985. Annual. Workshop held first week in July. Workshop duration: 1 week. Average attendance: 110. Workshop focuses on novel, short story, poetry, creative nonfiction. Site: Beautiful retreat center on top of a mountain in the Blue Ridge Mountains of North Carolina. Panels planned for next workshop include 2 novel classes; 2 short story classes; 1 mystery/suspense class. Past faculty has included Gail Adam, Janice Eidus, John Dufresne and Clint McCown.

Costs: $480 (everything is included: workshop, manuscript critique, double room, all meals).

Accommodations: Vans available, $50 round trip.

Additional Information: "New people must submit a writing sample to be accepted. Those attending send their manuscript one month prior to arrival." Workshop information is available mid-January. For brochure send e-mail or visit website. Accepts inquiries by e-mail and phone. Agents and editors participate in conference.

Southeast (AL, AR, FL, GA, LA, MS, PR [Puerto Rico])

☑ ALABAMA WRITERS' CONCLAVE, P.O. Box 230787, Montgomery AL 36123-0787. (334)244-8920. Fax: (334)215-0811. E-mail: poettennis@aol.com. **Contact:** Donna Jean Tennis, editor. Estab. 1923. Annual. Conference held for three days, the first week in August. 2002 conference dates are August 1-3. Average attendance: 75-100. Conference to promote "all phases" of writing. Held at the Ramsay Conference Center (University of Montevallo). "We attempt to contain all workshops under this roof."

Costs: Fees for 3 days are $45 for members; $55 for nonmembers (which includes membership). Lower rates for 1- or 2-day attendance. Meals and awards banquet additional cost.

Accommodations: Accommodations available on campus. $18 for single, $36 for double.

Additional Information: "We have 'name' speakers and workshops with members helping members. We offer open mike readings every evening. We sponsor a contest each year with a published book of winners." Conference brochures/guidelines available for SASE and on website after March 2002. Accepts inquiries by SASE, e-mail. Membership dues are $15 and include a quarterly newsletter. Membership information from Donna Jean Tennis at above address.

░N░ ATLANTIC CENTER FOR THE ARTS, 1414 Art Center Ave., New Smyrna Beach FL 32168. (386)427-6975. Fax: (386)427-5669. E-mail: program@atlanticcenterforthearts.org. Website: www.atlanticcenterforthearts. org. **Contact:** Rachel Ward, program coordinator. Estab. 1977. Rotating calendar. Conference duration: 3 weeks. Average attendance: 20. "All formats—the development of work in progress in a collaborative environment with other disciplines." Writing residencies with Spalding Gray, Jeffery Frank, Anne Waldman and Ishmael Reed.

Costs: Meals and lodging provided at no cost to accepted associates.

Accommodations: Offers overnight accommodations. Basic hotel/dorm facility private room & bath at no cost.

Additional Information: Variable application materials and deadlines. Conference information is available September 2001: e-mail, visit website, or call. Accepts inquiries by e-mail or phone.

N. HARRIETTE AUSTIN WRITERS CONFERENCE, G-9 Aderhold, University of Georgia, Athens GA 30602-7101. (706)542-3876. Fax: (706)542-0360. E-mail: hawc@coe.uga.edu. Website: www.coe.uga.edu/torra nce/hawc. **Contact:** Dr. Charles Connor, program director. Estab. 1994. Annual. Conference held July 19-20, 2002. Conference duration: 5:00 p.m. Friday, July 19 to 9:00 p.m. Saturday, July 20. Average attendance: 400. "The purpose of the conference is to provide a supportive environment in which writers can meet with professionals from the publishing industry to learn about the craft of writing, becoming published and the life of a writer. Workshops focus on all aspects of writing skills and the publishing world. Attendees receive professional advice on getting published, manuscript critiques and personal consultation, and information from experts in specialized topics, such as, forensic science, criminal investigation and the law. Areas of focus include a wide range of fiction (mainstream, children, young adult, women's fiction, historical, mystery, thriller, crime, etc.), and nonfiction (historical, essays, memoirs, how-to, etc.)." Site: "The conference is held at the Georgia Center for Continuing Education on the University of Georgia campus in Athens, Georgia. The Georgia Center is a modern conference facility containing within it a 400 bed hotel, restaurant, coffee shop, gift shop, theatre, auditorium, meeting rooms, banquet facilities and comprehensive support services." 2001 panels include In the Face of Terrible Odds, Still We Write; Finding the Story in Your Story; Writing Across Genres; Developing the Story Idea in Science Fiction; What is Southern, Anyway?; Characters That Get Noticed; Breaking into Hollywood's Asylum; Building Your Characters and Revealing Their Substance; What Writers Can Write About Other People; How to Write the Juvenile Mystery; Bugs as Forensic Evidence; Forensic Artist Techniques & Demonstration; Forensic Anthropology: From the Field to the Courtroom; The 21st Century Writer: The Pursuit of Excellence and the Perfect Marketing Plan; The Original Idea: The Foundation for Successfully Writing and Marketing Your Novel; Research and Writing: Knowing What You Write About. Panelists included Tom Dupree (executive editor, HarperEntertainment); Toni Weisskopf (executive editor, Baen Books); Miriam Goderich (vice president at Jane Dystel Literary Management); Doris Booth (editor-in-chief, Authorlink.com and Authorlink Press); Lyn Deardorff (associate editor, Peachtree Publishers); Tina Andreadis (assistant director of publicity for Warner Books); Jessica Faust (co-founder of Bookends LLC); Jeff Kleinman (literary agent with Graybill & English); Tracey Adams (literary agent at McIntosh & Otis); Ron Pitkin (president of Cumberland House Publishing); Judy Long (editor-in-chief of Hill Street Press); Don O'Briant (book editor for the Atlanta Journal-Constitution); and authors Terry Kay, Stephen Michand, Less Standiford, Andrea Campbell, Diana Palmer and more.

Costs: 2001 conference fees: pre-registration by July 6, $155; registration after July 6, $165; Friday dinner (optional), $20; Saturday breakfast (optional), $10; Saturday dinner (optional), $20.

Accommodations: Airport shuttle service is available every 2 hours between the conference center in Athens and Hartsfield International Airport in Atlanta. Offers overnight accommodations at the Georgia Center Hotel. 2001 rates for single occupancy range from $62-69; double occupancy from $74-81.

Additional Information: "Manuscript evaluations and a one-on-one meeting with an editor, agent or writing instructor are available. Submit a two-page manuscript synopsis and up to fifteen double-spaced, typed sample pages. Must be received no later than four weeks prior to the conference. The number of manuscripts that can be accepted is limited, so submit early. No more than two evaluations per participant will be accepted, please. Label your manuscript as to genre or type and specify your preferred evaluator. (We cannot guarantee your first choice). A fee of $30 is charged for each evaluation. Make check payable to HAWC Manuscript Evaluations, and mail two copies of writing sample directly to Dr. Charles Connor." Sponsors contest in cooperation with Authorlink.com. Full details about the competition can be found on the Authorlink website at www.authorlink. com/. Conference information is available by May 2002. For brochure send SASE, e-mail, visit website, call or fax. Accepts inquiries by SASE, e-mail, phone and fax. Agents and editors participate in conference. "The goal of the Harriette Austin Writers Conference is to bring writers, agents, editors and special experts together in a supportive environment for a productive and memorable experience. We make every effort to extend the best in professionalism and Southern hospitality. Our reputation is best expressed by those who have been here and those who choose to come back again and again. Come visit us in Georgia."

✓ FLORIDA FIRST COAST WRITERS' FESTIVAL, 9911 Old Baymeadows Rd., FCCJ Deerwood Center, Jacksonville FL 32256-8117. (904)997-2726. Fax: (904)997-2727. E-mail: kclower@fccj.org. Website: www.f ccj.org/wf/. **Contact:** Kathleen Clower, conference coordinator. Estab. 1985. Annual. Festival held May 16-18, 2002. Average attendance: 300-350. All areas: mainstream plus genre. Held at Sea Turtle Inn on Atlantic Beach.

Costs: "Early bird special $175 for 2 days (including lunch and banquet) or $150 for 2 days (including lunch) or $75 for each day; pre-conference workshops extra."

Accommodations: Sea Turtle Inn, (904)249-7402 or (800)874-6000, has a special festival rate.

Additional Information: Sponsors contests for short fiction, poetry and novels. Novel judges are David Poyer and Lenore Hart. Entry fees: $30, novels; $10, short fiction; $5, poetry. Deadline: November 1 for novels, short fiction, poems. Conference information available March 2001. For brochures/guidelines visit website, e-mail, fax, call. Accepts inquiries by e-mail, phone, fax. E-mail contest inquiries to hdenson@fccj.org.

N: FLORIDA SUNCOAST WRITERS' CONFERENCE, University of South Florida, Division of Lifelong Learning, 4202 E. Fowler Ave., MHH116, Tampa FL 33620-6756. (813)974-2403. Fax: (813)974-5732. E-mail: mglakis@admin.usf.edu. Website: www.conted.usf.edu/flcenter.htm. **Contact:** Martha Lakis, conference coordinator. Estab. 1970. Annual. Held February 7-9, 2002. Conference duration: 3 days. Average attendance: 350-400. Conference covers poetry, short story, novel and nonfiction, including science fiction, detective, travel writing, drama, TV scripts, photojournalism and juvenile. "This is a working writers' conference, targeting categories and mechanics of writing and being published. Designated one of the 'Top 10 Workshops/Conferences for Writers' by *Writer's Digest*." Features panels with agents and editors. Guest speakers have included Lady P.D. James, William Styron, David Guterson, John Updike, Joyce Carol Oates, Wally Lamb, Frank McCourt and Francine Prose.
Costs: Call for verification.
Accommodations: Special rates available at area hotels. "All information is contained in our brochure."
Additional Information: Participants may submit work for critiquing. Extra fee charged for this service. Conference information available in October; request by e-mail, fax, phone. Accepts inquiries by e-mail, fax, phone.

HEMINGWAY DAYS WRITER'S WORKSHOP AND CONFERENCE, P.O. Box 4045, Key West FL 33041-4045. (305)294-4440. Fax: (305)292-3653. E-mail: calico2419@aol.com. Director of Workshop: Dr. James Plath. Festival Director: Carol Shaughnessy. Estab. 1989. Annual. Conference held July. Conference duration: 3½ days. Average attendance: 60-100. "We deliberately keep it small so that there is a greater opportunity for participants to interact with presenting writers. The Hemingway Days Writer's Workshop and Conference focuses on fiction, poetry and Ernest Hemingway and his work. The workshop and conference is but one event in a week-long festival which honors Ernest Hemingway. The first evening features a reception and presentation of the Conch Republic Prize for Literature to a writer whose life's work epitomizes the creative spirit of Key West. Then, one day focuses on the writing of fiction, one day on the writing of poetry, and one day on Ernest Hemingway's life and work. We are offering more hands-on directed writing sessions than ever before, and combine them with our traditionally-offered presentations and after-sunset readings by critically-acclaimed writers. Most years, we also offer the opportunity for participants to have their own work critiqued. Traditionally, the Workshop & Conference is held at a resort in Key West's historic Old Town section. Directed writing exercises take place at a variety of locations in the Old Town area such as gardens and historic sites, while after-sunset readings will take place at an open-air atrium or restaurant."
Costs: $120 (1998); included all panels, directed writing exercises, attendance at all literary receptions and after-sunset readings.
Accommodations: Material available upon request.
Additional Information: Brochures/guidelines are available for SASE. "The conference/workshop is unique in that it combines studies in craft with studies in literature, and serious literary-minded events to celebrate Hemingway the writer with a week-long festival celebrating 'papa' the myth."

✓ HOW TO BE PUBLISHED WORKSHOPS, P.O. Box 100031, Birmingham AL 35210-3006. (205)907-0140. E-mail: mike@writing2sell.com. Website: www.writing2sell.com. **Contact:** Michael Garrett. Estab. 1986. Workshops are offered continuously year-round at various locations. Workshop duration: 1 session. Average attendance: 10-15. Workshop to "move writers of category fiction closer to publication." Workshop held at college campuses and universities. Themes include "Marketing," "Idea Development" and manuscript critique.
Costs: $49-79.
Additional Information: "Special critique is offered, but advance submission is not required." Workshop information available on website. Accepts inquiries by e-mail.

MOONLIGHT AND MAGNOLIAS WRITER'S CONFERENCE, 999 Flower's Crossing, Lawrenceville GA 30044. E-mail: info@georgiaromancewriters.org. Website: www.georgiaromancewriters.org. Estab. 1982. **Contact:** Anna DeStefano. Annual. 2001 Conference held October 12-14 in Atlanta. Average attendance: 300. "Conference focuses on writing of women's fiction with emphasis on romance. Includes agents and editors from major publishing houses. Workshops have included: beginning writer track, general interest topics, and professional issues for the published author, plus sessions for writing for children, young adult, inspirational, multicultural and Regency. Speakers have included experts in law enforcement, screenwriting and research. Literacy raffle and advertised speaker and GRW member autographing open to the public. Published authors make up 25-30% of attendees." Brochure available for SASE in June.

Costs: Secure conference rate of $84 for single/double/triple/quad, "ask for the Moonlight and Magnolias Block." Conference: non GRW members $160; $145 for GRW members.

Additional Information: Maggie Awards for excellence are presented to unpublished writers. The Maggie Award for published writers is limited to Region 3 members of Romance Writers of America. Proposals per guidelines must be submitted in early June. Please check with president for new dates. Published authors judge first round, category editors judge finals. Guidelines available for SASE in spring.

N. NATCHEZ LITERARY AND CINEMA CELEBRATION, P.O. Box 1307, Natchez MS 39121-1307. (601)446-1208. Fax: (601)446-1214. E-mail: carolyn.smith@colin.cc.ms.us. Website: www.colin.cc.ms.us/NL CC. **Contact:** Carolyn Vance Smith, co-chairman. Estab. 1990. Annual. Conference held February 27-March 3, 2002. Average attendance: 3,000. Conference focuses on "all literature, including film scripts." Site: 500-seat auditorium, 1,200 seat auditorium, various sizes of break-out rooms. Theme will be "Creativity in the South: A Living Legacy." Novelist Greg Iles is to speak and scholars will speak on Welty, Faulkner, others and their creativity in many areas of writing. Speakers will include Greg Iles, Bruce Boyd Raeburn, Lewis Norton, Clifton Taulbert, Judi Betts, Tom Thurman and many others.

Costs: "About $100, including a meal, receptions, book signings, workshops. Lectures/panel discussions are free."

Accommodations: "Groups can ask for special assistance. Usually they can be accommodated." Offers overnight accommodations. Low-cost dormitory space is about $20 per night; low-cost rooms in area hotels is about $50 per night.

Additional Information: "Participants need to read selected materials prior to attending writing workshops. Thus, pre-enrollment is necessary." Conference information is available in the Fall 2001. For brochure send SASE, e-mail, visit website, call or fax. Accepts inquiries by SASE, e-mail, phone and fax. Agents and editors participate in conference.

SCBWI SOUTHERN BREEZE FALL CONFERENCE, "Writing and Illustrating for Kids," P.O. Box 26282, Birmingham AL 35260. E-mail: joanbroerman@home.com. Website: http://members.home.net/southernb reeze/. **Contact:** Joan Broerman, regional advisor. Estab. 1992. Annual. Conference held in October. One-day Saturday conference. Average attendance: 125. "All Southern Breeze SCBWI conferences are geared to the production and support of quality children's literature." Keynote speaker will be Lin Oliver, executive director and founding member of SCBWI; luncheon speaker will be Atlanta-published Gail Karwaski.

Costs: About $60 for SCBWI members, $75 for non-members, plus lunch (about $6). Individual critiques are available for additional fees.

Accommodations: "We have a room block with a conference rate. The conference is held at a nearby school If we can get an airline discount, we publish this in our newsletter and on our webpage."

Additional Information: "The fall conference offers 30 workshops on craft and the business of writing, including a basic workshop for those new to the children's field." Manuscript critiques are offered; manuscripts must be sent by deadline. Conference information is included in the Southern Breeze newsletter, mailed in September. Brochure is available for SASE, by e-mail or visit website for details. Accepts inquiries by SASE or e-mail. Agents and editors attend/participate in conference.

SCBWI SOUTHERN BREEZE SPRING CONFERENCE, "Springmingle'02," P.O. Box 26282, Birmingham AL 35260. E-mail: joanbroerman@home.com. Website: http://members.home.net/southernbreeze/. **Contact:** Joan Broerman, regional advisor. Estab. 1992. Annual. Conference held in February. Conference duration is 3 days. Expected attendance: 100. "All Southern Breeze SCBWI conferences are geared to the production and support of quality children's literature." Event is held "in a hotel in one of the 3 states which compose our region: Alabama, Georgia or Mississippi." Springmingle'02 speakers will be Larry Dane Brimner (author); Karen Stormer Brooks (illustrator); and editors Paula Morrow (Carus Group), Alison Keehn (Barefoot Books), Wendy Lamb (Random House).

Costs: "About $100; SCBWI non-members pay $10-15 more. Sometimes 1 or 2 meals are included."

Accommodations: "We have a room block with a conference rate in the hotel conference site. Individuals make their own reservcations. If we can get an airline discount, we publish this in our newsletter and on our webpage."

Additional Information: There will be ms critiques available this year for an additional fee. Sometimes individual manuscript consulttions are offered; manuscripts must be sent ahead of time. Conference information is included in the Southern Breeze newsletter, mailed in January. Brochure is available for SASE, by e-mail or visit website for details. Accepts inquiries by SASE, e-mail. Agents and editors participate in conference.

SCBWI/FLORIDA ANNUAL FALL CONFERENCE, 2158 Portland Ave., Wellington FL 33414. E-mail: barcafer@aol.com. **Contact:** Barbara Casey, Florida regional advisor. Estab. 1985. Annual. Conference duration: one-half day. Average attendance: 70. Conference to promote "all aspects of writing and illustrating for children. Time and location to be announced."

Costs: $50 for SCBWI members, $55 for non-SCBWI members. Ms and art evaluations, $30.
Accommodations: Special conference rates at Airport Hilton, West Palm Beach, Florida.
Additional Information: Accepts inquiries by e-mail.

N SLEUTH FEST, SW 93rd Ave., Cooper City FL 33328. (954)262-8209. E-mail: LindaBell002@aol.com.
Website: www.mwa-florida.org. **Contact:** Iris Zerba, registration. Estab. 1990. Annual. Conference held March
15-17, 2002. Average attendance: 240. This is "a conference for working mystery writers with emphasis on the
craft of writing, forensics and police procedure, as well as contact with top editors and agents and other writers."
Site: "Convention Hotel in 2001 (and probably 2002) at the Fort Lauderdale Airport Hilton, with tennis, swim-
ming, free parking, shuttle access to beaches, shopping and dining in Fort Lauderdale." 2001 panels included
The Basics—how to write a proposal, get an agent, etc.; Building Suspense; Organizing Your Novel; Police
Interviewing Techniques. Guest speakers include Daniel Keyes (*Flowers for Algernon*); Les Standiford (*Black
Mountain*); Barbara Parker (*Suspicion of Betrayal*); Harlan Coben; Elaine Uets (*Doc in the Box*); police and legal
experts, editors and agents.
Costs: $169 (early registration); $189, includes keynote lunch, welcome cocktail party Saturday and Sunday
breakfast.
Accommodations: Hotel has shuttle from Lauderdale airport. Offers overnight accommodations provided by
the Fort Lauderdale Hilton; special conference rate $118 (2001).
Additional Information: Conference information is available August 2001. For brochure send SASE, e-mail
or visit website. Accepts inquiries by SASE and e-mail. Agents and editors participate in conference. "Editor
appointment is included in the cost of registration. Appointments available on a first come, first served basis."

N SOUTHEASTERN WRITERS ASSOCIATION, P.O. Box 774, Hinesville GA 31310-0774. (912)876-
3118. E-mail: rube774@clds.net. Website: www.southeasternwriters.com. **Contact:** Harry Rubin, treasurer. Estab.
1975. Annual. Conference held June 18-24, 2002. Average attendance: 75 (limited to 100). Conference offers
classes in short fiction, juvenile writing, nonfiction, etc. Site: Epworth-by-the-Sea, St. Simons Island, GA. Most
classes are related to fiction writing.
Costs: 2001 costs: $250 early bird registration, $290 after April 15. $70 daily tuition.
Accommodations: Offers overnight accommodations. 2001 rate was $520 for the week, including motel-type
room and board (3 meals/day).
Additional Information: Sponsors contests for humor, Southern regional literary fiction, limericks, fiction,
short fiction/poetry/essay of 1,200 words maximum about the holiday season. Judged by the instructors. Conference information will be available March 2002. For brochure send SASE, e-mail, visit website, call. Accepts
inquiries for SASE, e-mail, phone. Agents and editors participate in conference.

N TENNESSEE WILLIAMS/NEW ORLEANS LITERARY FESTIVAL, 938 Lafayette St., Suite 300,
New Orleans LA 70113. (504)581-1144. Fax: (504)523-3680. E-mail: info@tennesseewilliams.net. Website:
www.tennesseewilliams.net. **Contact:** LouAnn Morehouse, executive director. Estab. 1987. Annual. Conference
held March 20-24, 2002. Average attendance: "8,000 audience seats filled." Conference focuses on "all aspects
of the literary arts including editing, publishing, and the artistic process. Other humanities areas are also featured,
including theater and music." Site: "The festival is based at historic Le Petit Theatre du Vieux Carré and continues
at other sites throughout the French Quarter." In 2001, a few panels included Writing and Publishing the Short
Story, Character in Fiction, Writing Historical Fiction, Jazz in Literature, The Holocaust in Politics and Memory,
and The Vieux Carré circa 1930. Several speakers from 2001 conference are Philip Caputo, Michael Cunningham,
Anne Jackson, Eli Wallach, Dakin Williams, Jane Isay, Adrienne Miller, Wally Lamb.
Costs: "Ticket prices range from $5 for a single event to $45 for special event. Master classes are $35 per class.
Theatre events are sold separately and range from $10-21."
Accommodations: "Host hotel is the Omni Royal Orleans."
Additional Information: "In conjunction with the University of New Orleans we sponsor a one-act play
competition. Entries are accepted from September 1 through December 15, 2001. There is a $15 fee which must
be submitted with the application form. There is a $1,000 cash prize and a staged reading at the 2002 festival,
as well as a full production of the work at the 2003 festival." Conference information is available in late January.
For brochure send e-mail. Accepts inquiries by e-mail and phone. Agents and editors participate in conference.

⊕ WRITE IT OUT, P.O. Box 704, Sarasota FL 34230-0704. (941)359-3824. Fax: (941)359-3931. E-mail:
rmillerwio@aol.com. Website: www.writeitout.com. **Contact:** Ronni Miller, director. Estab. 1997. Workshops
held 2-3 times/year in March, June, July and August, 2002. Duration: 5-10 days. Average attendance: 4-10.
Workshops on "fiction, travel writing, poetry, memoirs." Workshops held across the United States as well as in
Italy in a Tuscan villa, in Bermuda at a hotel or in Cape Cod at an inn. Theme: "Landscape—Horizon." Past
speakers included Arturo Vivante, novelist.

Costs: 2002 fees: Italy $1,595; Bermuda $495; Cape Cod $420. Price includes tuition, room and board in Italy, all other locations just tuition. Airfare not included.

Additional Information: "Critiques on work are given at the workshops." Conference information available year round. For brochures/guidelines e-mail, fax, phone or visit website. Accepts inquiries by fax, phone, e-mail. Workshops have "small groups, option to spend time writing and not attend classes with personal appointments made with instructors for feedback."

WRITING STRATEGIES FOR THE CHRISTIAN MARKET, 2712 S. Peninsula Dr., Daytona Beach FL 32118-5706. (904)322-1111. Fax: (904)322-1111*9. E-mail: romy14@juno.com. Website: www.amyfound.org. **Contact:** Rosemary Upton. Estab. 1991. Independent studies with manual. Includes Basics I, Marketing II, Business III, Building the Novel. Critique by mail with SASE. Question and answer session via e-mail or U.S. mail. Critique shop included once a month, except summer (July and August). Instructors include Rosemary Upton, novelist; Kistler London, editor.

Costs: $30 for manual and ongoing support.

Additional Information: "Designed for correspondence students as well as the classroom experience, the courses are economical and include all materials, as well as the evaluation of assignments." Those who have taken Writing Strategies instruction are able to attend an on-going monthly critiqueshop where their peers critique their work. Manual provided. For brochures/guidelines/newsletter send SASE, e-mail, fax or call. Accepts inquiries by fax, e-mail. Independent study by mail only offered at this time.

☑ WRITING TODAY—BIRMINGHAM-SOUTHERN COLLEGE, Box 549003, Birmingham AL 35254-9765. (205)226-4921. Fax: (205)226-3072. E-mail: dcwilson@bsc.edu. Website: www.bsc.edu. **Contact:** Annie Green, director of special events; Dee Wilson, assistant director of special events. Estab. 1978. Annual. Conference held April 12-13, 2002. Average attendance: 400-500. "Writing Today provides a quality event that is far more affordable than other conferences its size and quality. The conference presents writers, editors, agents and other literary professionals from around the country to conduct workshops on a variety of literary styles and topics tailored to meet the needs of writers of every stage of development. The conference is sponsored by Birmingham-Southern College and is held on the campus in classrooms and lecture halls." Previous speakers have included Eudora Welty, Edward Albee, James Dickey, Erskine Caldwell, Ray Bradbury, Pat Conroy, John Barth, Ernest Gaines and Galway Kinnell.

Costs: $120 for both days. This includes lunches, reception and morning coffee and rolls.

Accommodations: Attendees must arrange own transportation. Local hotels and motels offer special rates, but participants must make their own reservations.

Additional Information: "We usually offer a critique for interested writers. We have had poetry and short story critiques. There is an additional charge for these critiques." Conference brochures and registration forms available in March 2002 for SASE, e-mail or on website. Accepts inquiries by SASE, e-mail or fax. Sponsors the Hackney Literary Competition Awards for poetry, short story and novels. Guidelines available for SASE.

Midwest (IL, IN, KY, MI, OH)

ANTIOCH WRITERS' WORKSHOP, P.O. Box 494, Yellow Springs OH 45387. E-mail: info@antiochwriter sworkshop.com. Website: www.antiochwritersworkshop.com. Estab. 1984. Annual. Conference held from August 5-12. Average attendance: 80. Workshop concentration: poetry, nonfiction and fiction. Workshop located on Antioch College campus in the village of Yellow Springs. Speakers have included Sue Grafton, Imogene Bolls, George Ella Lyon, Herbert Martin, John Jakes, Virginia Hamilton and Natalie Goldberg.

Costs: Tuition is $485—lower for local and repeat—plus meals.

Accommodations: "We pick up attendees free at the airport." Accommodations made at dorms and area hotels. Cost is $16-26/night (for dorms).

Additional Information: Offers mss critique sessions. Conference information are available after March 2000.

⚏ CINCINNATI SHORT STORY WORKSHOP, 11029 Corona Rd., Cincinnati OH 45240-3615. (513)825-3760. E-mail: dorothygoepel@hotmail.com. Website: http://writing.shawguides.com/CincinnatiShortSt oryWorkshop/. **Contact:** Dorothy Goepel, workshop organizer. Estab. 2000. Annual. Workshop held June 1-2, 2002. Workshop duration: 1 weekend. Average attendance: 14. Workshop focuses on the short story—discussions and helpful critiques of each participant's short story. Site: A Cincinnati-area hotel with conference room. "The workshop focuses on guiding writers in the development of a powerful short story. *Atlantic Monthly* senior editor C. Michael Curtis leads the workshop. Mr. Curtis edits virtually all fiction appearing in the magazine and screens most of *The Atlantic*'s unsolicited stories, which number some 12,000 manuscripts yearly."

Costs: $175-200 (fee does not include meals or lodging).

Additional Information: Registrants are asked to mail a short story of no more than 20 double-spaced pages to each participant and to Mr. Curtis at least one month prior to the workshop. Accepts inquiries by e-mail and phone. "Sign up early to reserve a spot. Once the workshop is filled, names will go on a waiting list."

THE COLUMBUS WRITERS CONFERENCE, P.O. Box 20548, Columbus OH 43220. (614)451-3075. Fax: (614)451-0174. E-mail: AngelaPL28@aol.com. Website: www.creativevista.com. **Contact:** Angela Palazzolo, director. Estab. 1993. Annual. Conference held in September. Average attendance: more than 200. "The conference covers a variety of fiction and nonfiction topics presented by writers, editors and literary agents. Writing topics have included novel, short story, children's, young adult, poetry, historical fiction, science fiction, fantasy, humor, mystery, playwriting, screenwriting, magazine writing, travel, humor, cookbook, technical, queries, book proposals and freelance writing. Other topics have included finding and working with an agent, targeting markets, time management, obtaining grants, sparking creativity and networking." Speakers have included Lee K. Abbott, Rita Rosenkrantz and Mark D. Ryan as well as many other professionals in the writing field.
Costs: Early registration fee for Friday afternoon sessions is $60; otherwise fee is $75. Full conference early registration fee is $169 (Friday afternoon sessions, dinner, after-dinner program and Saturday program); otherwise fee is $189. Early registration for the Saturday program (includes continental breakfast, lunch, and afternoon refreshments) is $134; otherwise fee is $154.
Additional Information: Call, write, e-mail or send fax to obtain a conference brochure, available mid-summer.

CHARLENE FARIS SEMINARS FOR BEGINNERS, 610 W. Poplar St. #4, Zionsville IN 46077-1220. Phone/fax: (317)873-0738. **Contact:** Charlene Faris. Estab. 1985. Held 2 or 3 times/year in various locations in spring, summer and fall. Conference duration: 2 days. Average attendence: 10. Concentration on all areas of publishing and writing, particularly marketing and working with editors. Locations have included Phoenix, Los Angeles and Indianapolis.
Costs: $200, 2 days; $100, one day.
Accommodations: Information on overnight accommodations available.
Additional Information: Conference brochures and registration forms available September 1, 2001; request information by e-mail or phone. Accepts inquiries by SASE, e-mail, phone.

KENTUCKY WOMEN WRITERS CONFERENCE, % The Carnegie Center, 251 W. Second St., Lexington KY 40507-1135. (859)254-4175. Fax: (859)281-1151. E-mail: kywwc@hotmail.com Website: www.carnegieliter acy.org. **Contact:** Jan Isenhour, director. Estab. 1979. Annual spring conference. Conference held March 28-30, 2002. Average attendance: 100-150. "Conference is a gathering to foster feminist creativity highlighting readings, panel discussions, workshops, performances and films. Features all genres including memoir, poetry, fiction, nonfiction, and feminist theory. This is the longest running writers' conference celebrating the work of women." Site: "Located in historic Gratz Park in downtown Lexington, The Carnegie Center for Literacy and Learning is in walking distance of all facilities. This center for community literacy was dedicated by Barbara Bush on September 11, 1992 and hailed as unique with programs for all ages and abilities; reading, writing, and literacy-related workshops; presentations; after school tutoring; visiting poets, writers, storytellers and artists." 2002 conference theme is "Moving the Borders." 2001 conference featured Pat Mora, Nancy Mairs, Linda Scott deRosier, Crystal Wilkinson, Maud Casey, Janice Eidus, Kelly Notman Ellis and Elizabeth Nunez.
Costs: $100-150 (TBA) for entire conference (meals and lodging not included).
Accommodations: There are hotels within walking distance of conference site. Contact Lexington Visitor & Convention Bureau, (800)848-1224.
Additional Information: Sponsors a contest as part of conference. Conference information is available January 2002. For brochure e-mail or visit website. Accepts inquiries by e-mail. Agents and editors participate in conference.

KENYON REVIEW WRITERS WORKSHOP, The Kenyon Review, Kenyon College, Gambier OH 43022. (740)427-5207. Fax: (740)427-5417. E-mail: kenyonreview@kenyon.edu. Website: www.kenyonreview.org. **Contact:** David Lynn, director. Estab. 1990. Annual. Workshop held late June through early July. Workshop duration: 9 days. Average attendance: 40-50. Participants apply in poetry, fiction or creative nonfiction, and then participate in intensive daily workshops which focus on the generation and revision of significant new work. The conference takes place on the campus of Kenyon College in the rural village of Gambier, Ohio. Students have access to college computing and recreational facilities, and are housed in campus housing. 2001 faculty: Fiction—Keith Banner and Sharon Dilworth; Poetry—Linda Gregerson and Janet McAdams; Nonfiction—Rebecca McClanahan.
Costs: $1,450 including room and board.
Accommodations: The workshop operates a shuttle from Gambier to the airport in Columbus, Ohio. Offers overnight accommodations. Students are housed in Kenyon College student housing. The cost is covered in the tuition.

Additional Information: Application includes a writing sample. Admission decisions are made on a rolling basis beginning Februrary 1. Workshop information is available November 1. For brochure send e-mail, visit website, call, fax. Accepts inquiries by SASE, e-mail, phone, fax.

N: MAGNA CUM MURDER CRIME FICTION CONFERENCE, Ball State University, Muncie IN 47306. (765)285-8975. Fax: (765)747-9566. E-mail: kennisonk@aol.com. Website: www.magnacummurder.com. **Contact:** Kathryn Kennison, director. Estab. 1994. Annual. Conference held from October 25-27, 2002. Average attendance: 350. "The main focus is the crime fiction novel, but attention is also paid to short stories, true crime." Site: the Radisson Hotel Roberts and the Horizon Convention Center directly across the street. Past workshops have included plotting, characterization, getting published, historical, and ethics.
Costs: $175 includes reception, continental breakfast and boxed lunch, banquet.
Accommodations: Offers list of area hotels or lodging options.
Additional Information: Conference information available: e-mail, visit website, call, or fax. Accepts inquiries by e-mail, phone, or fax. Agents and/or editors participate in conference.

MAUMEE VALLEY FREELANCE WRITERS' CONFERENCE, Lourdes College, 6832 Convent Blvd., Sylvania OH 43560. (419)824-3707. Fax: (419)824-3510. E-mail: gburke@lourdes.edu. Website: www.lourdes.e du. **Contact:** Gloria Burke, conference coordinator. Estab. 1997. Annual. Conference held March 16, 2002. Average attendance: 50. "The purpose is to provide a venue for freelance writers in a variety of genres. For example, in 2001, we offered breakout sessions including writing query letters, science writing, writing online, travel writing, getting published locally and breaking into the national market. This is a small Franciscan facility located in Sylvania OH, 10 miles from Toledo OH. Buildings are of Spanish style architecture, many adorned with large, exquisite tile murals. Many inside hallways are decorated with statues, paintings, tiles, and unusual designs imported from Italy and Spain. This year's conference will be held in the Franciscan Center and Mother Adelaide Hall on the Lourdes College Campus." Keynote speaker for the 2002 conference will be Barbara Kuroff, Editorial Director of Writer's Digest Market Books.
Costs: $69/person including lunch.
Additional Information: Conference information is available in January. For brochure send SASE, e-mail, visit website, call, fax. Accepts inquiries by SASE, e-mail, phone, fax. Agents and editors participate in conference. "Evaluations show that this is a well planned, well organized conference. Every effort has been made to reach freelance writers in the Maumee Valley and Southeastern Michigan areas. We have had anywhere from 38-65 people in attendance; as the conference coordinator, it is my goal to reach for the 100+ mark—hopefully, in 2002."

✓ MIDLAND WRITERS CONFERENCE, Grace A. Dow Memorial Library, 1710 W. St. Andrews, Midland MI 48640-2698. (989)837-3435. Fax: (989)837-3468. E-mail: ajarvis@midland-mi.org. Website: www.midl and-mi.org/gracedowlibrary. **Contact:** Ann C. Jarvis, conference coordinator. Estab. 1980. Annual. Conference held June 8, 2002. Average attendance: 100. "The Conference is composed of a well-known keynote speaker and workshops on a variety of subjects including poetry, children's writing, freelancing, agents, etc. The attendees are both published and unpublished authors. The Conference is held at the Grace A. Dow Memorial Library in the auditorium and conference rooms. Keynoters in the past have included Dave Barry, Pat Conroy, Kurt Vonnegut, Peggy Noonan, Roger Ebert."
Costs: Adult—$50 before May 26, $60 after May 27; students, senior citizens and handicapped—$40 before May 26, $50 after May 26. A box lunch is available. Costs are approximate until plans for upcoming conference are finalized.
Accommodations: A list of area hotels is available.
Additional Information: Conference brochures/guidelines available April/May 2002. Call, e-mail or write to be put on mailing list. Accepts inquiries by e-mail, fax, phone.

MIDWEST WRITERS' CONFERENCE, 6000 Frank Ave. NW, Canton OH 44720-7599. (216)499-9600. Fax: (330)494-6121. E-mail: Druhe@Stark.Kent.Edu. Conference Director: Debbie Ruhe. Estab. 1968. Annual. Conference held in early October. Conference duration: 2 days. Average attendance: 350. "The conference provides an atmosphere in which aspiring writers can meet with and learn from experienced and established writers through lectures, workshops, competitive contest, personal interviews and informal group discussions. The areas of concentration include fiction, nonfiction, juvenile literature and poetry. The Midwest Writers' Conference is held on Kent State University Stark Campus in Canton, Ohio. This two-day conference is held in Main Hall, a four-story building and wheel chair accessible."
Costs: $125 includes Friday workshops, keynote address, Saturday workshops, box luncheon and manuscript entry fee (limited to two submissions); $70 for contest only (includes two manuscripts) (2001 prices).

Accommodations: Arrangements are made with a local hotel which is near Kent Stark and offers a special reduced rate for conference attendees. Conferees must make their own reservations 3 weeks before the conference to be guaranteed this special conference rate.

Additional Information: Each manuscript entered in the contest will receive a critique. If the manuscript is selected for final judging, it will receive an additional critique from the final judge. Conference attendees are not required to submit manuscripts to the writing contest. Manuscript deadline is early August. For contest: A maximum of 1 entry for each category is permitted. Entries must be typed on 8½ × 11 paper, double-spaced. A separate page must accompany each entry bearing the author's name, address, phone, category and title of the work. Entries are not to exceed 3,000 words in length. Work must be original, unpublished and not a winner in any contest at the time of entry. Conference brochures and guidelines are available for SASE. Accepts inquiries by e-mail, fax.

N MIDWEST WRITERS WORKSHOP, Dept. of Journalism, Ball State University, Muncie IN 47306. (765)285-5587. Fax: (765)285-5997. E-mail: info@midwestwriters.org. Website: www.midwestwriters.org. **Contact:** Earl L. Conn. Estab. 1974. Annual. Workshop to be held July 25-27, 2002. Average attendance: 900. Conference held at New Alumni Center, Ball State University.

Costs: In 2001, cost was $195 including opening reception, hospitality room and closing banquet.

Accommodations: Special hotel rates offered.

Additional Information: Critiques available. Conference brochures/guidelines are available for SASE.

N MISSISSIPPI VALLEY WRITERS CONFERENCE, 3403 45th St., Moline IL 61265. (309)762-8985. E-mail: kimseuss@aol.com. **Contact:** David R. Collins, conference founder/director. Estab. 1973. Annual. Conference held June 3-7, 2002. Average attendance: 80. "Conference for all areas of writing for publication." Conference held at Augustana College, a liberal arts school along the Mississippi River. 2000 workshop leaders will be bj elsner, Mel Boring, Max Collins, Dick Stahl, H.E. Francis, Bess Pierce, Karl Largent, Roald Tweet and Rich Johnson.

Costs: $25 for registration; $50 for 1 workshop; $90 for two; plus $40 for each additional workshops; $25 to audit.

Accommodations: On-campus facitilites available. Accommodations are available at Erickson Hall on the Augustana College campus. Cost for 6 nights is $100; cost for 15 meals is $100.

Additional Information: Conferees may submit mss to workshop leaders for personal conferences during the week. Cash awards are given at the end of the conference week by workshop leaders based on mss submitted. Conference brochures/guidelines are available for SASE. "Conference is open to the beginner as well as the polished professional—all are welcome."

OAKLAND UNIVERSITY WRITERS' CONFERENCE, 221 Varner Hall, Rochester MI 48309-4401. (248)370-3125. Fax: (248)370-4280. E-mail: gjboddy@oakland.edu. Website: www.oakland.edu/contin-ed/ writersconf/. **Contact:** Gloria J. Boddy, program director. Estab. 1961. Annual. Conference held in October 2002. Average attendance: 400. Held at Oakland University: Oakland Center: Vandenburg Hall and O'Dowd Hall. Each annual conference covers all aspects and types of writing in 36 concurrent workshops on Saturday. Major writers from various genres are speakers for the Saturday conference. Individual critiques and hands-on writing workshops are conducted Friday. Areas: poetry, articles, fiction, short stories, playwriting, nonfiction, young adult, children's literature. Keynote speaker in 2000: Patricia Polacco.

Costs: 2000: Conference registration: $85; lunch, $15; individual ms, $58; writing workshop, $48.

Accommodations: List is available.

Additional Information: Conference information available after August 2001. For brochures/guidelines send SASE, visit website, e-mail, fax, call. Accepts inquiries by e-mail, fax, phone, SASE.

OF DARK & STORMY NIGHTS, Mystery Writers of America—Midwest Chapter, P.O. Box 1944, Muncie IN 47308-1944. (765)288-7402. E-mail: spurgeonmwa@juno.com. **Contact:** W.W. Spurgeon, director. Estab. 1982. Annual. Workshop held June 8, 2002. Average attendance: 200. Dedicated to "writing *mystery* fiction and crime-related nonfiction. Workshops and panels presented on techniques of mystery writing from ideas to revision, marketing, investigative techniques and more, by published writers, law enforcement experts and publishing professionals." Site is Holiday Inn, Rolling Meadows IL (suburban Chicago).

Costs: $135 for MWA members; $165 for non-members; $50 extra for ms critique.

Accommodations: Easily accessible by car or train (from Chicago) Holiday Inn, Rolling Meadows $89 per night plus tax; free airport bus (Chicago O'Hare) and previously arranged rides from train.

Additional Information: "We accept manuscripts for critique (first 30 pages maximum); $50 cost. Writers meet with critics during workshop for one-on-one discussions." Conference information available January 1, 2002. For brochures/guidelines send SASE, e-mail, call. Accepts inquiries by SASE, phone, e-mail. Postal address required for response.

☑ GARY PROVOST'S WRITERS RETREAT WORKSHOP, % Write It/Sell It, 2507 S. Boston Place, Tulsa OK 74114. E-mail: wrwwisi@aol.com. Website: www.writersretreatworkshop.com. **Contact:** Gail Provost Stockwell, director. Executive Director: Lance Stockwell. Estab. 1987. Workshop held May 24-June 2, 2002. Average attendance: 30. Focus on fiction and narrative nonfiction books in progress. All genres. Site: Marydale Retreat Center in Erlanger, KY (just south of Cincinnati, OH). "The Writers Retreat Workshop is an intensive learning experience for small groups of serious-minded writers. Founded by the late Gary Provost, one of the country's leading writing instructors and his wife Gail, an award-winning author, the WRW is a challenging and enriching adventure. The goal of the WRW core staff and visiting agents/editors/authors is for students to leave with a solid understanding of the marketplace as well as the craft of writing a novel. In the heart of a supportive and spirited community of fellow writers, students learn Gary Provost's course and make remarkable leaps in their writing, editing and marketing skills."

Costs: $1,695 for 10 days which includes all tuition, food and lodging (discount for past participants), consultations and course materials. The Marydale Retreat Center is 5 miles from the Cincinnati airport and offers shuttle services.

Additional Information: Participants are selected based upon the appropriateness of this program for the applicant's specific writing project. Participants are asked to submit a brief overview and synopsis before the workshop and are given assignments and feedback during the 10-day workshop. Workshop information available by mid-November 2001. For brochures/guidelines call 1-800-642-2494, e-mail or visit website. Accepts inquiries by e-mail, phone, SASE.

North Central (IA, MN, NE, ND, SD, WI)

PETER DAVIDSON'S WRITER'S SEMINAR, 982 S. Emerald Hills Dr., P.O. Box 497, Arnolds Park IA 51331-0497. (712)332-9329. Fax: (712)362-8363. **Contact:** Peter Davidson, seminar presenter. Estab. 1985. Seminars held about 30 times annually, in various sites. Offered year round. Seminars last 1 day, usually 9 a.m.-4 p.m. Average attendance: 35. "All writing areas including books of fiction and nonfiction, children's works, short stories, magazine articles, poetry, songs, scripts, religious works, personal experiences and romance fiction. All seminars are sponsored by community colleges or colleges across the U.S. Covers many topics including developing your idea, writing the manuscript, copyrighting, and marketing your work. The information is very practical—participants will be able to put into practice the principles discussed. The seminar is fast-paced and should be a lot of fun for participants."

Costs: Each sponsoring college sets own fees, ranging from $42-59, depending on location, etc.

Accommodations: "Participants make their own arrangements. Usually, no special arrangements are available."

Additional Information: "Participants are encouraged to bring their ideas and/or manuscripts for a short, informal evaluation by seminar presenter, Peter Davidson." Conference brochures/guidelines are available for SASE. No inquiries by fax or e-mail. "On even-numbered years, usually present seminars in Colorado, Wyoming, Nebraska, Kansas, Iowa, Minnesota and South Dakota. On odd-numbered years, usually present seminars in Illinois, Iowa, Minnesota, Arkansas, Missouri, South Dakota, Nebraska and Tennessee."

⚞N⚟ INTERNATIONAL MUSIC CAMP CREATIVE WRITING WORKSHOP, 1725 11th St. SW, Minot ND 58701. Phone/fax: (701)838-8472. E-mail: info@internationalmusiccamp.com. Website: www.internationalm usiccamp.com. **Contact:** Joseph T. Alme, camp director. Estab. 1956. Annual. Conference held June 23-29, 2002. Average attendance: 15. "The workshop offers students the opportunity to refine their skills in thinking, composing and writing in an environment that is conducive to positive reinforcement. In addition to writing poems, essays, and stories, individuals are encouraged to work on their own area of interest with conferencing and feedback from the course instructor." Site: International Peace Garden on the border between the US and Canada. "Similar to a University Campus, several dormitories, classrooms, lecture halls and cafeteria provide the perfect site for such a workshop. The beautiful and picturesque International Peace Garden provide additional inspiration to creative thinking." Professor Joseph Ringen from Minot State University is the instructor.

**FOR EXPLANATIONS OF THESE SYMBOLS,
SEE THE INSIDE FRONT AND BACK COVERS OF THIS BOOK.**

Costs: The cost including meals and housing is $200.

Accommodations: Airline and depot shuttles are available upon request. Housing is included in the $200 fee.

Additional Information: Conference information is available in October 2002. For brochure visit website, call or fax. Accepts inquiries by e-mail, phone and fax. Agents and editors participate in conference.

IOWA SUMMER WRITING FESTIVAL, 116 International Center, University of Iowa, Iowa City IA 52242-1802. (319)335-2534. E-mail: peggy-houston@uiowa.edu; amy-margolis@uiowa.edu. Website: www.edu/~iswfest. Directors: Peggy Houston, Amy Margolis. Estab. 1987. Annual. Festival held in June and July. Workshops are one week or a weekend. Average attendance: limited to 12/class—over 1,500 participants throughout the summer. "We offer courses in most areas of writing: novel, short story, essay, poetry, playwriting, screenwriting, humor, travel, writing for children, memoir, women's writing, romance and mystery." Site is the University of Iowa campus. Guest speakers are undetermined at this time. Readers and instructors have included Lee K. Abbott, Susan Power, Joy Harjo, Gish Jen, Abraham Verghese, Robert Olen Butler, Ethan Canin, Clark Blaise, Gerald Stern, Donald Justice, Michael Dennis Browne, Marvin Bell, Hope Edelman.

Costs: $400/week; $175, weekend workshop (1999 rates). Discounts available for early registration. Housing and meals are separate.

Accommodations: "We offer participants a choice of accommodations: dormitory, $27/night; Iowa House, $65/night; Holiday Inn, $70/night (rates subject to changes)."

Additional Information: Conference information available in February. Accepts inquiries by fax, e-mail.

☑ SINIPEE WRITERS' WORKSHOP, Continuing Education Loras College, Dubuque IA 52004-0708. (563)588-7139. Fax: (563)588-4962. E-mail: lcrosset@loras.edu. Website: www.loras.edu. **Contact:** Linda Crossett, director continuing education. Estab. 1985. Annual. Workshop held April 27, 2002. Average attendance: 40-50. The conference provides general information for writers on how to get published. There are several speakers at each workshop, usually someone for fiction, poetry, nonfiction and either a publisher, editor or agent. The conference is held in the Alumni Campus Center on the Loras College campus. The Campus Center is handicapped accessible. Speakers for 2002 are Jim Schaeffer (photo journalist); Connie Meester (poet); Catherine Struck (e-publisher); Bill Goldberg (freelance writer).

Costs: $60 ($65 at the door); $30 ($32.50 at door) for senior citizens and students.

Accommodations: Provides a list of area hotels or lodging options.

Additional Information: No prior submissions required. Sponsors a contest as part of workshop. Requirements: $5 entry fee/$15 additional fee for written critique. Poetry must not exceed 40 lines and short fiction and nonfiction entries must be 1,500 words or less. Style and subject are open and work by aspiring writers as well as seasoned professionals is welcome. Contest judges are faculty in the Loras College English Department who teach creative writing, or graduates of the creative writing program. Workshop information is available February 1, 2002. For brochure send e-mail, call, fax. Accepts inquiries by SASE, e-mail, phone, fax. Agents and editors participate in conference.

UNIVERSITY OF NORTH DAKOTA WRITERS CONFERENCE, Box 7209 UND, Grand Forks ND 58202-7209. (701)777-2768. Fax: (701)777-2373. E-mail: James_McKenzie@UND.nodak.edu. Website: www. UND.edu/culture/WC. **Contact:** James McKenzie, director. Estab. 1969. Annual. Conference held March 19-23, 2001. Average attendance: 800/day. Covers all genres, focused around a specific theme. The conference is a regional cultural and intellectual festival that puts nationally known writers in intimate and large audience contact with other writers and the student, academic and general public. Almost all events take place in the campus memorial union which has a variety of small rooms and a 1,500 seat main hall. Ursula Hegi will be writer in residence in 2002. Fiction writers at the 2001 conference were Kent Haruf, Joy Williams, Peter Carey.

Costs: Free, open to the public.

Accommodations: Offers overnight accommodations. "Campus residence halls are available at very good prices." Also provides a list of area hotels or lodging options.

Additional Information: Conference information is available January 31, 2001. For brochure send SASE, e-mail, visit website, call, fax. Accepts inquiries by SASE, e-mail, phone, fax.

⚑ WISCONSIN REGIONAL WRITER'S ASSOCIATION CONFERENCES, 510 W. Sunset Ave., Appleton WI 54911-1139. (920)734-3724. E-mail: wrwa@lakeside.net. Website: www.inkwells.net/wrwa. **Contact:** Donna Potrykus, vice president. Estab. 1948. Annual. Conferences held in May and September "are dedicated to self-improvement through speakers, workshops, and presentations. Topics and speakers vary with each event." Average attendance: 100-150. "We honor all genres of writing. Spring conference is a one-day event featuring the Jade Ring Banquet and awards for six genre categories." Keynote speaker at the 2001 Fall conference was Ellen Kort, Wisconsin's first poet laureate. Spring 2002 conference site will be the Holiday Inn, Manitowoc, WI. Agents and editors participate in each conference.

Costs: $40-75.

Accommodations: Provides a list of area hotels or lodging options. "We negotiate special rates at each facility. A block of rooms is set aside for a specific time period."

Additional Information: Award winners receive a certificate and a cash prize. First place winners of the Jade Ring contest receive a jade ring. Must be a member to enter contests. For brochure, call, write, e-mail or visit website.

South Central (CO, KS, MO, NM, OK, TX)

N AGENTS! AGENTS! AGENTS . . . & EDITORS TOO!, 1501 W. Fifth St., Suite E-2, Austin TX 78703-5155. (512)499-8914. Fax: (512)499-0441. E-mail: awl@writersleague.org. Website: www.writersleague.org. **Contact:** Jim Bob McMillan, executive director. Estab. 1994. Annual. Conference held July 2002. Conference duration: 3 days. Average attendance: 220. The conference's purpose is to help writers "learn about the business of writing, and get the most up-to-date information about the writing industry." Site: Austin, Texas. 2001 topics included Agents & Editors: The Current Market for Fiction, The Current Market for Nonfiction; Exploring Audiobooks; Realistic Dialogue; Electronic Publishing; Genre Panels; Small Press; The Author-Editor Relationship; Writing Treatments That Sell; Taking Care of Business Matters for Writers; Ways to Market Your Writing; The Agony and Ecstasy of Self-Publishing. Agents in 2001: Ken Atchity, Sheree Bykofsky, Mary Evans, Felicia Eth, Michael Larsen, Elizabet McHugh, Elizabeth Pomada, Nancy Stender, Andrew Whelchel. Editors in 2001: Tim Bent, Karen V. Haas, Kati Hesford, Ron Martirano. Authors in 2001: Carolyn Banks, Mary Willis, Rick Riordan, Russ Hall, Suzy Spencer, Lana Castle, Kyung Kim, Darlene Marwitz, Cynthia Leal Massey, Evelyn Palfrey, Karen Stolz, Mary Powell, Jim Gramon, Wendy Wheeler, Elizabeth Moon, Don Webb, Lawrence Person, Jim Sanderson, Mindy Reed, Joe O'Connell, Laurie Drummond, Karin Marie.

Costs: In 2001, $185 members; $245 nonmembers; $50 optional workshops.

Accommodations: Hotel offers special conference rate.

Additional Information: "The Writers' League of Texas sponsors a manuscript contest in conjunction with the annual agents and editors conference. For guidelines, please SASE or send an e-mail. Entry fee for 2001 was $20. All manuscripts receive two written critiques. Finalists receive an additional written critique from a published author. Winners will be announced at the agents conference in July. There are no monetary prizes nor is there any offer for publication. Deadline for entry is approximately three months prior to conference." Conference information is available December 2001. For brochure send SASE, e-mail, visit website, call or fax. Accepts inquiries by SASE, e-mail, phone and fax. "As a bonus for attending the conference, participants will be offered a ten-minute consult with the agent or editor of their choice. For those that desire a consult, early registration is encouraged."

✓ ART AND SOUL, P.O. Box 97404, Baylor University, Waco TX 76798-7404. (254)710-4805 or 6879. Fax: (254)710-3894. E-mail: Rel_Lit@baylor.edu. Website: www.baylor.edu/~Rel_lit. **Contact:** Greg Garrett, director. Estab. 2000. Annual. Conference held March 14-17, 2002. Average attendance: 200-400. Areas of focus include fiction, poetry, spiritual autobiography, humor, creative nonfiction, screenwriting, songwriting, religion and creativity. Sessions take place in auditoriums, conference rooms, and classrooms on the historic campus of Baylor University in Waco, Texas. 2001 panels, workshops, and master classes included humor, fiction and autobiography, creativity and spirituality, agent representation and submission and publication. Bret Lott, Robert Olen Butler and Elizabeth Dewberry are scheduled to participate in the 2002 conference.

Costs: Tuition costs range from $60 for student registration to $120 for regular registration. One meal is included.

Accommodations: Offers shuttle service to hotels from campus, plus discounts on airfare and car rental. No overnight accommodations. List of area hotels/lodging options provided.

Additional Information: Registrants requesting an individual ms consultation should contact the conference to check on availability. Conference information is available fall 2001. For brochure send SASE, e-mail, visit website, phone, fax. Accepts inquiries by SASE, e-mail, phone, fax. Agents and editors participate in conference.

N BLACK WRITERS REUNION AND CONFERENCE, P.O. Box 700065, Dallas TX 75370-0065. E-mail: bwrc@blackwriters.org. Website: www.blackwriters.org/conference. **Contact:** Tia Shabazz, conference chairperson. Estab. 2000. Annual. Conference held August 22-25, 2002 at Manhattan Beach, Los Angeles, CA. Conference duration: 3 days. Average attendance: 250-300. Conference focuses on the craft of writing, publishing, poetry and the genres of romance, Christian fiction, fiction, television, playwriting, screenwriting. Site: "Touring conference; held in a different city and state each year." 2001 workshops included What's Wrong with My Manuscript; Dialogue; Point of View; Plot and Characterization; How to Get Published; Writing for Television; Writing the Sequel; Writing Outside the Box; Ideas, Theme and Premise; Writing Christian Fiction; Starting Your Writing Career; Editing; Self-Publishing; E-Publishing; Writer's Journey; How to Turn a Novel into a Film; Publicity; Marketing Strategies; Profitable Writing; Playwriting; The Power of Packaging; Building Better Interview Skills; Literary Legalities. 2001 panelists include Jewell Parker Rhodes, Donna Hill, Tananarive Due,

Rochelle Alers, Brenda Jackson, Steven Barnes, Robert Fleming, Gwynne Forster, Angela Benson, Sandra Kitt, Tonya Marie Evans, Deirdre Savoy, Carol Taylor, Donna Williams, Ta'Shia Asanti, Mack Smith, Sara Freeman Smith, Margie Walker.

Costs: In 2001, full conference $165-205. Includes reception, banquet dinner, brunch and admission to all workshops and Gold Pen Awards Banquet.

Accommodations: Offers overnight accommodations. Negotiated rate of $89/night at the hosting Manhattan Beach Marriott.

Additional Information: Sponsors an essay contest (500 words) for high school and college students. Essays are judged by committee. Also sponsors novella ms contest. For brochure visit website. Accepts inquiries by e-mail. Agents and editors participate in conference.

☑ CAT WRITERS ASSOCIATION WRITERS CONFERENCE, 22841 Orchid Creek Lane, Lake Forest CA 92630. (949)454-1368. Fax: (949)454-0134. E-mail: kthornton@home.com. Website: www.catwriters.org. **Contact:** Kim Thornton, president. Estab. 1994. Annual. Conference held November 16-18, 2001 in Houston, TX. Average attendance: 100-120. The conference provides basic to advanced information on how to get published, research sources, market work (nonfiction and fiction); offers networking opportunities between writers, editors, publishers, broadcasters, illustrators; and celebrates good writing that has a focus on cats. The conference is held in a new city each year, typically in conjunction with the Cat Fanciers Association International Cat Show. 16 seminars are held in a hotel conference facility. A major book-signing event is held in the cat show hall, typically a large convention center. 2000 conference included writing for children panel; understanding 'net rights; book editors' panel; working with a publicist; magazine editors' panel; media training; and a fiction authors' panel. 2000 included authors Peter Mandel, Shirley Rousseau Murphy, Ann Whitehead Nagola and Suzanne Liurance; and agents Meredith Bernstein and Lucy Lourien.

Costs: Cost for 2000 conference was $65 for CWA members; $88 for nonmembers. (Included all seminars; reception; book signing event; night cocktail reception/awards banquet; Sunday morning breakfast and members meeting; press pass into the cat show hall.)

Accommodations: Hosting hotel offers reduced rate for conference attendees. Will also provide a list of area Houston hotels or lodging options. Hotels ran about $95/night for the 2001 event.

Additional Information: Sponsors a contest. "Work must have been published in contest year July-June; cost is $10/entry for members, $15/entry for nonmembers; more than 30 categories; contest judged by professional CWA members. Conference information available June/July 2001. For brochure send SASE, visit website. Accepts inquiries by SASE, e-mail. Agents and editors participate in conference. "We make available one-on-one appointments with editors/agents for writers to 'pitch' their projects. Also, the Dog Writers Association is a sponsor of the seminars, so those who attend have an interest in both cat and dog topics. All seminars are applicable to all writing disciplines and not restricted to cat writing."

Ⓝ COLORADO GOLD CONFERENCE, The Embassy Suites, Denver South, 10250 E. Costilla Ave., Englewood CO. (303)331-2608. E-mail: mmpoole@hotmail.com. Website: www.rmfw.org. **Contact:** Monica Poole, conference coordinator. Estab. 1983. Annual. Conference held September 6-8, 2002. Average attendance: 300-350. Conference focuses on commercial fiction writing. Site: The Embassy Suites, Denver South. Panels planned for next conference covers every aspect of novel length fiction from the basics of the writing craft to promoting a book in print. "We have published authors addressing a variety of craft topics as well as professionals speaking on topics of interest to writers in every genre. A full list of faculty/panels/guest speakers/editors and agents can be found by requesting a brochure via e-mail or hotline number or by visiting the web at www.rmfw.org/."

Costs: Registration before July 20, $149; after July 20, $169.

Accommodations: "Please send an e-mail to inquire about any transportation needs. Discounted suites at the Embassy are $82/night. Reservations must be made before August 24, 2001. Call (800)654-4810 and indicate that you will be attending the Colorado Gold Conference. $82 in the single/double rate."

Additional Information: "The is an opportunity to read to editors and agents during a Friday workshop. There is a $20 fee and slots are on a first come, first served basis. Participation in the Friday workshop does require an early submission of material to the workshop coordinator. Full details are in the registration brochure. Participants may—at no cost—sign up for one on one meetings with editors and agents. Again, details are in the brochure. Complete details are found on our website. The finalists are judged by an editor or agent seeking manuscripts in the contestant's category—mainstream, mystery, romance and science fiction/fantasy." Conference information is available. For brochure send e-mail, visit website or call. Accepts inquiries by SASE, e-mail and phone. Agents and editors participate in conference.

☑ COLORADO MOUNTAIN WRITERS' WORKSHOP, P.O. Box 85394, Tucson AZ 85754. (520)206-9479. E-mail: mfiles@pimacc.pima.edu. Website: www.sheilabender.com. **Contact:** Meg Files, director. Estab.

1999. Annual. Conference to be held June 24-28, 2002. Average attendance: 30. Focuses on fiction, poetry, and personal essay. Conference is held on the campus of Colorado Mountain College, Steamboat Springs, Colorado. Features personal writing. Faculty includes Meg Files, Sheila Bender, and Jack Heffron.
Costs: $300.
Accommodations: Offers overnight lodging in on-site dormitory $308 (6 nights, also meals).
Additional Information: Brochures available November, 2001 for SASE, e-mail, website, fax or call. Accepts inquiries for SASE, e-mail, fax, phone. Editors participates in conferences. The conference is designed to lift writers, novice or experienced, to the next level. It offers writers isolation, intimacy, and inspiration. Daily activities include craft talks, small group workshops, readings, and ms consultations, as well as writing time.

☑ FLATIRONS BLUNT INSTRUMENT MYSTERY WORKSHOP, % FBI-UII, P.O. Box 19486, Boulder CO 80308-2486. Website: www.crosswinds.net/~rmcsinc. **Contact:** Barbara Steiner. Estab. 1996. Annual. Conference held June 22, 2002. Average attendance: 70. Conference for "mystery writers and readers." Conference held in "two very large auditorium size rooms at the local Elks club." 2001 speakers included Sujata Massey, Nancy Pickard, Rex Burns, Margaret Coel, Julie Kaewert and Barbara Steiner.
Costs: 2001 fees: $65 (included continental breakfast and buffet lunch).
Additional Information: "Limited critiquing is available from published authors on a first come basis." Conference information available January 2002. For brochure/guidelines send SASE, visit website. "It is the only genre specific mystery workshop in the Rocky Mountain area. The scenery is fabulous. The conference is sponsored by the Rocky Mountain Chapter of Sisters in Crime."

Ⓝ FORT BEND WRITERS GUILD WORKSHOP, 12523 Folkcrest Way, Stafford TX 77477-3529. (281)498-5025. E-mail: rapdunit@aol.com. Website: http://fortbendwritersguild.tripod.com. **Contact:** Roger Paulding. Estab. 1997. Biannual. Workshop held March 16, 2002, August 10, 2002. Average attendance: 75. Workshop focuses on fiction (novels) and screenwriting. Site: Holiday Inn.
Costs: $50 (including buffet lunch).
Additional Information: Sponsors a contest. Submit for novel competition—first 10 pages plus one page synopsis, entry fee $10; screenplay—treatment of 5-7 pages plus 3-5 pages of opening, total entry 10 pages, $10 each; short story—10 pages complete, $10 each. "Judges are published novelists." For brochure send SASE or e-mail. Accepts inquiries by SASE and e-mail.

Ⓝ GLORIETA CHRISTIAN WRITERS' CONFERENCE, Glorieta Conference Center, P.O. Box 8, Glorieta NM 87535-0008. (800)797-4222. Fax: (505)757-6149. E-mail: bdaniel@lifeway.com. Website: www.lifeway. org/Glorieta. **Contact:** Brian Daniel, events director. Estab. 1997. Annual. Conference held October 15-19, 2002. Average attendance: 250. Conference focuses on "beginners, professionals, fiction, poetry, screenwriting, writing for children, drama, magazine writing, nonfiction books." Site: "Conference center with hotels and dining hall with buffet-style meals." Plans "continuing course for fiction writers and numerous one-hour workshops" for 2002 conference. 2001 speakers included Liz Curtis Higgs and T. Davis Bunn.
Costs: $500-600, depending on housing preference. Includes tuition, hotel room and 12 meals.
Additional Information: Sponsors a contest with entries judged by published authors and editors. Guidelines available upon request. Conference information is available in Spring 2002. For brochure send e-mail, visit website, call or fax. Accepts inquiries by e-mail, phone and fax. Agents and editors participate in conference.

Ⓝ GREENVILLE CHRISTIAN WRITER'S CONFERENCE, P.O Box 8942, Greenville TX 75404-8942. (903)450-4944. E-mail: info@tuppence.org. Website: www.gcwg.org. **Contact:** James H. Pence, conference director. Estab. 1998. Annual. Conference held from October 25-26, 2002. Average attendance: 50. "Christian fiction, non-fiction, magazine articles, greeting cards, e-publishing." Site: Ridgecrest Baptist Church in Greenville, Texas. Panels planned for next conference include writing fiction that sells. Guest speakers for 2000 included Reg Grant, novelist, emmy winning producer; Becky Freeman, bestselling Christian author; Jim Pence, novelist, The Osmosis Project 2003, Tyndale House, author of How to Do Everything with HTML.
Costs: $125 includes Saturday lunch.
Accommodations: Offers list of area hotels and lodging options.
Additional Information: Conference information available January 2002; send SASE, e-mail, visit website, or call. Accepts inquiries by SASE, e-mail, or phone. "The Greenville Christian Writers' Conference is a small conference where both new and experienced writers can interact with published authors. We have informative workshops, opportunities for personal consultations and a pre-conference seminar on novel writing."

☑ NATIONAL WRITERS ASSOCIATION FOUNDATION CONFERENCE, 3140 S. Peoria, Suite 295, Aurora CO 80014. (303)841-0246. Fax: (303)841-2607. E-mail: sandywriter@aol.com. Website: www. nationalwriters.com. **Contact:** Sandy Whelchel, executive director. Estab. 1926. Annual. Conference held June 7-9, 2002, in Denver, CO. Average attendance: 200-300. Conference focuses on general writing and marketing.

Costs: $200 (approx.).

Additional Information: Awards for previous contests will be presented at the conference. Conference information available annually in December. For brochures/guidelines send SASE, visit website, e-mail, fax, or call. Accepts inquiries by SASE, e-mail, fax, phone.

NIMROD ANNUAL WRITERS' WORKSHOP, (formerly Oklahoma Writer's Workshop), *Nimrod*, University of Tulsa, 600 S. College, Tulsa OK 74104. (918)631-3080. Fax: (918)631-3033. E-mail: nimrod@utulsa.edu. Website: www.utulsa.edu/nimrod. **Contact:** Francine Ringold, PhD, editor-in-chief. Estab. 1978. Workshop held annually in October. Workshop duration: 1 day. Average attendance: 100-150. Workshop in fiction and poetry. "Prize winners (Nimrod/Hardman Prizes) conduct workshops as do contest judges. Past judges: Rosellen Brown, Stanley Kunitz, Toby Olson, Lucille Clifton, W.S. Merwin, Ron Carlson, Mark Doty, Anita Shreve and Francine Prose."

Costs: Approximately $30-40. Lunch provided.

Additional Information: *Nimrod International Journal* sponsors *Nimrod*/Hardman Literary Awards: The Kathe rine Anne Porter Prize for fiction and The Pablo Neruda Prize for poetry. Poetry and fiction prizes: $2,000 each and publication (1st prize); $1,000 each and publication (2nd prize). Deadline: must be postmarked no later than April 20. Guidelines for SASE.

☑ OKLAHOMA WRITERS FEDERATION CONFERENCE, 8416 Huckleberry, Edmond OK 73034. (405)348-0276. Fax: (405)282-7230. E-mail: DBouziden@worldnet.att.net. Website: www.owfi.net. **Contact:** Deborah Bouziden, president, or Lou Mansfield, treasurer. Estab. 1968. Annual. Conference held the first weekend of May every year. Average attendance: 250-300. Conference covers all genres, fiction, poetry, nonfiction. Site: "Our conference is held at the Embassy Suites Hotel. It has 6 floors. Everything, all meetings are contained within the hotel."

Costs: Full conference, $100; one day only, $50; authors' banquet, $30; awards banquet, $30 (2000 fees).

Accommodations: The hotel provides a shuttle to and from airport. Embassy Suites room rates have been $79. Guests of the hotel get free buffet breakfast.

Additional Information: "The annual OWFI contest is open only to paid-up members. It features competitions for cash prizes in 28 unpublished ms categories and awards 4 trophies for the best books published during the previous calendar year. A $20 entry fee entitles participants to enter as many categories as they want, but they may enter no single category more than once. Since the contest's purpose is to encourage writers to produce professionally acceptable mss, the contest rules are very explicit, and contestants must follow them closely. Categories include mainstream novel; contemporary romance novel; historical romance novel; mystery/suspense novel; Western novel; science fiction/fantasy/horror novel; nonfiction book; picture book; middle reader book; and young adult book." For brochures/guidelines send SASE, e-mail, visit website, call. Accepts inquiries by SASE, e-mail, phone. Agents and editors participate in conference.

ROCKY MOUNTAIN BOOK FESTIVAL, 2123 Downing St., Denver CO 80205. (303)839-8320. Fax: (303)839-8319. E-mail: ccftb@compuserve.com. Website: www.coloradobook.org. **Contact:** Christiane Citron, executive director. Estab. 1991. Annual. Festival held in March. Average attendance: 10,000. Festival promotes published work from all genres. Held at Denver Merchandise Mart. Offers a wide variety of panels. Approximately 200 authors are scheduled to speak at the next festival. "Please submit a copy of book, bio and publicity material for consideration."

Costs: $4 (adult); $2 (child).

Additional Information: Brochures/guidelines available. Accepts inquiries by e-mail, fax.

ROCKY MOUNTAIN CHILDREN'S BOOK FESTIVAL, 2123 Downing St., Denver CO 80205-5210. (303)839-8320. Fax: (303)839-8319. E-mail: ccftb@compuserve.com. Website: www.coloradobook.org. **Contact:** Christiane Citron, executive director. Estab. 1996. Annual festival held in March as part of the Rocky Mountain Book Festival. Festival duration: 2 days. Average attendance: 10,000. Festival promotes published work for and about children/families. It is solely for children's authors and illustrators—open to the public. Held at Denver Merchandise Mart. Approximately 100 authors speak annually. Past authors include Ann M. Martin, Sharon Creech, Nikki Grimes, T.A. Barron, Laura Numeroff, Jean Craighead George and Jane Yolen.

Costs: $2 children, $4 adults.

Accommodations: "Information on accommodations available."

Additional Information: Send SASE for brochure/guidelines. Accepts inquiries by fax, e-mail.

ROMANCE WRITERS OF AMERICA NATIONAL CONFERENCE, 3707 FM 1960 West, Suite 555, Houston TX 77068. (281)440-6885, ext. 27. Fax: (281)440-7510. E-mail: info@rwanational.com. Website: www. rwanational.com. Executive Director: Allison Kelley. **Contact:** Jane Detloff, office manager. Estab. 1981. Annual.

Conference held July 17-20, 2002. Average attendance: 1,500. Over 100 workshops on writing, researching and the business side of being a working writer. Publishing professionals attend and accept appointments. Keynote speaker is renowned romance writer. Conference will be held in Denver, Colorado in 2002.
Costs: $300.
Additional Information: Annual RITA awards are presented for romance authors. Annual Golden Heart awards are presented for unpublished writers. Conference brochures/guidelines are available for SASE in May 2001. Accepts inquiries by SASE, e-mail, fax, phone.

SCBWI INSIDE THE CHILDREN'S BOOK BIZ CONFERENCE, Wyndham Garden Hotel, 8051 LBJ Freeway, Dallas TX 75251-8051. Website: http://star-telegram.com/homes/SCBWI. **Contact:** Vickie Perez, conference publication relations. Estab. 1983. Annual. One-day conference held in September, usually the 4th Saturday. Average attendance: 200. Conference focusing on children's fiction and nonfiction, from picture books to young adult, with illustrator interests as well. Sponsored by the NC/NE Texas Chapter of the Society of Children's Book Writers and Illustrators (SCBWI). The 2000 faculty included Connie Epstein, Publisher's Corner/*SCBWI Bulletin*; Stephen Geck, vice president and assciate publisher, Simon & Schuster Books for Young Readers; Wendy Loggia, senior editor, Random House Children's Books; George Nicholson, senior agent, Sterling Lord Literistic; David Saylor, vice president and creative director, Scholastic; Phoebe Yeh, editorial director, Harper-Collins Children's Books. Speakers give inside information on the current trends.
Costs: In 2000 Early Bird registration fee was $75 for national SCBWI members, $80 for non-members. Late registration fee was $85 for national SCBWI members, $90 for non-members. Cost includes lunch.
Accommodations: Wyndham Garden Hotel, easily accessible off LBJ Freeway in Dallas, TX. Offers food, lodging and spacious conference room. 2000 room rates were $69 double/single, $79 triple, $89 quad (price includes breakfast buffet for two).
Additional Information: "We always have 'Pitch to the Pros' 15-minute consultations with speakers on a first registered, first scheduled basis." There is also an illustrator's table for displays and an author autographs table for published SCBWI members. Conference brochure is available in July by e-mail, phone or visit website. Accepts inquiries by SASE, e-mail, phone. Agents and editors attend/participate in this conference.

N: SHORT COURSE ON PROFESSIONAL WRITING, University of Oklahoma, Journalism, 860 Van Vleet Oval, Norman OK 73019-0270. (405)325-4171. Fax: (405)325-7565. E-mail: jmadisondavis@ou.edu. Estab. 1938. Annual conference held the second weekend in June. Average attendance: 200. Conference focuses on writing for publication—all paying markets.
Costs: $230.
Accomodations: Provides special rates.
Additional Information: "Critiques are optional, but we provide them. Manuscripts must be submitted ahead of time." Brochures available in March for SASE. Accepts inquiries by fax, e-mail. "We have sixty years of success with editors, agents and authors. Many successful writers were 'discovered' at the Short Course."

N: SOUTHWEST LITERARY CENTER/RECURSOS DE SANTA FE, 826 Camino de Monte Rey, Santa Fe NM 87505. (505)988-5992. Fax: (505)989-8608. E-mail: litcenter@recursos.org. **Contact:** Literary Center Director. Estab. 1984. Annual. Conference duration: 5 days. Average attendance: 50 people. "We have done conferences on fiction, poetry and two conferences on themes, writing women's lives and writing yourself—autobiography. We will continue to focus on voices, autobiography, poetry and fiction." Site: "Very pleasant but simple. Two blocks from Santa Fe Plaza. Meals are included. People have enjoyed this facility." 2001 faculty included Mickey Pearlman, Jean Gould, Wendy Lichtman, Phillip Lopate, Rob Simbeck, Michael Steinberg.
Costs: $675 (conference, no residence); $925 (conference and residence—double occupancy); $1125 (conference, residence and single room).
Additional Information: "Participants must submit a manuscript of no more than 10 double-spaced typed pages from the work they wish to focus on during the conference. A $35 non-refundable reading fee must be included. There is not deadline, however, workshop space is limited and a spot is reserved on a first-come, first-served basis upon payment of the full Website." For brochure send e-mail, visit website, call or fax. Accepts inquiries by e-mail, phone and fax. Agents and editors participate in conference.

SOUTHWEST WRITERS CONFERENCE, 8200 Mountain Rd. NE, Suite 106, Albuquerque NM 87110-7835. (505)265-9485. Fax: (505)265-9483. E-mail: swriters@aol.com. Website: www.southwestwriters.org. **Contact:** Stephanie Dooley, conference chair. Estab. 1983. Annual. Conference held in September. Average attendance: about 400. "Conference concentrates on all areas of writing and includes preconference sessions, appointments and networking." Workshops and speakers include writers and editors of all genres for all levels from beginners to advanced. 2001 keynote speaker: Catherine Ryan Hyde, author of *Pay It Forward*.
Costs: $195-260 (members), $255-320 (nonmembers); includes conference sessions and 2 luncheons.

Accommodations: Usually have official airline and discount rates. Special conference rates are available at hotel. A list of other area hotels and motels is available.

Additional Information: Sponsors a contest judged by authors, editors and agents from New York, Los Angeles, etc., and from major publishing houses. Eighteen categories. Deadline: May 1. Entry fee is $29 (members) or $39 (nonmembers). Conference information available in April 2001. For brochures/guidelines send SASE, visit website, e-mail, fax, call. Accepts inquiries by SASE, e-mail, fax, phone. "An appointment (10 minutes, one-on-one) may be set up at the conference with editor or agent of your choice on a first-registered/first-served basis."

N **SPRING AND FALL WORKSHOPS AND CLASSES**, 1501 W. Fifth St., Suite E-2, Austin TX 78703-5155. (512)499-8914. Fax: (512)499-0441. E-mail: awl@writersleague.org. Website: www.writersleague.org. **Contact:** Jim Bob McMillan, executive director. Biannual. Workshop held in March, April, May, September, October, and November. Workshops held Saturday mornings; classes held one evening/week and lasts 2-8 weeks. Average attendance: 20 for workshops; 12 for classes. "Classes and workshops provide practical advice and guidance on various aspects of fiction, creative nonfiction and screenwriting." Site: Writers' League of Texas resource center. "There are two multipurpose classrooms, a library, three offices and a copy center." Some classes are by e-mail. "Topics for workshops and classes have included E-Publishing; Creative Nonfiction; Screenwriting Basics; Novel in Progress; Basics of Short Fiction; Technique; Writing Scenes; Journaling; Manuscript Feedback; Essays; and Newspaper Columns." Instructors include: Marion Winik, Emily Vander Veer, Susan Rogers Cooper, Bonnie Orr, Jan Epton Seale, Susan Wade, Ana McDonald, Lila Guzman, Laurie Lynn Drummond, Darryl Wimberly, Patricia Wynn, Sara Stiffler, Joan Neubauer, Michael Morgan, Graham Shelby, John Pipkin, Mindy Reed and Ann McCutchan.

Costs: Workshops $50; Classes $5-225.

Additional Information: Conference information is available in January 2002 and August 2002. For brochure send SASE, e-mail, visit website, call or fax. Accepts inquiries by SASE, e-mail, phone and fax.

✓ **SPRING MUSE MAGIC RETREAT**, (formerly Fall Inspiration Retreat 2000), P.O. Box 272, Tinnie NM 88351. Telephone/fax: (505)653-4437. E-mail: mysticsprings@magicplace.com. Website: www.guardians.nativeland.com. **Contact:** Deborah Vanderleelie, director. Estab. 1999. Annual. Workshop held in May. Average attendance: 20-30. "Conference sessions cover poetry, fiction, nonfiction and journaling. Workshops are geared towards achieving deeper levels of creativity for all writers." Site: A guest ranch featuring large casitas (homes) fully equipped. Catering is also available. All homes and cabins have decks and grills. The ranch is surrounded by national forest and is nestled in the pines of The Capitan Mountains. 2000 sessions covered meditation writing, journaling and creative expression. Also included "Circle of Souls" discussion forum where all attendees shared on-site writing.

Costs: $295-395; also offers couples packages for $495 (2000 rates). Fee covered 2 nights' lodging, meals and all workshops.

Accommodations: Offers overnight accommodations, included in price of conference. If staying more nights than are included in conference package, room rental is $59-89/night.

Additional Information: Conference information is available on website only. Accepts inquiries by e-mail, phone. Editors participate in conference.

✓ **STEAMBOAT SPRINGS WRITERS GROUP**, P.O. Box 774284, Steamboat Springs CO 80477. (970)879-8079. E-mail: MsHFreiberger@cs.com. **Contact:** Harriet Freiberger, director. Estab. 1982. Annual. Conference held July 2001. Conference duration: 1 day. Average attendance: 30. "Our conference emphasizes instruction within the seminar format. Novices and polished professionals benefit from the individual attention and the camaraderie which can be established within small groups. A pleasurable and memorable learning experience is guaranteed by the relaxed and friendly atmosphere of the old train depot. Registration is limited." Steamboat Arts Council sponsors the group at the restored train depot.

Costs: $35 before June 1, $45 after. Fee covers all conference activities, including lunch. Lodging available at Steamboat Resorts. Optional dinner and activities during evening preceding conference.

Additional Information: Available April 2001. Accepts inquiries by e-mail, phone, mail.

N **TEXAS CHRISTIAN WRITERS' CONFERENCE**, First Baptist Church, Houston TX 77024-2199. (713)686-7209. E-mail: martharexrogers@aol.com. **Contact:** Martha Rogers. Estab. 1990. Annual. Conference held August 3, 2002. Conference duration: 1 day. Average attendance: 60-65. "Focus is on all genres." Site: First Baptist Church fellowship center and classrooms. Panels planned for 2001 conference book proposal, 2002 creating character plate, point of view. Cecil Murphey, DiAnn Mills, Dennis Hensley and Dinella Kimura are scheduled to participate.

Costs: $60 members of IWA, $70 non-members, discounts for seniors and couples, meal at noon, continental breakfast, and breaks.

Accommodations: Offers list of area hotels or lodging options.

Additional Information: Open conference for all interested writers. Sponsors a contest for short fiction; categories include articles, devotionals, poetry, short story, book proposals, drama. Fees: $8 member, $10 non-member. Conference information available send SASE or e-mail. Accepts inquiries by SASE or e-mail. Agents participate in conference.

N MARK TWAIN CREATIVE WRITING WORKSHOPS, University House, 5101 Rockhill Rd., Kansas City MO 64110-2499. (816)235-1168. Fax: (816)235-2611. E-mail: buckm@umkc.edu. Website: www.umkc.edu/newsletters. **Contact:** Mary Ellen Buck, administration associate. Estab. 1990. Annual. Conference held in March 21, 2002, June 2002. Conference duration: 3 weeks. Average attendance: 40. "Focus is on fiction, poetry, and literary nonfiction." Site: University of Missouri-Kansas City Campus. Panels planned for next conference include the full range of craft essentials. Professor James McKinley and Robert Stewart are scheduled to participate.

Costs: Fees for regular credit and non-credit courses.

Accommodations: Offers list of area hotels or lodging options.

Additional Information: Submit workshop six poems/one short story prior to arrival. Conference information is available March 2002: send SASE, e-mail, or visit website. Accepts inquiries by SASE, e-mail, phone, or fax. Editors participate in conference.

UNIVERSITY OF NEW MEXICO'S TAOS SUMMER WRITERS CONFERENCE, Dept. of English, Humanities 255, University of New Mexico, Albuquerque NM 87131-1106. (505)277-6248. Fax: (505)277-2950. E-mail: taosconf@unm.edu. Website: www.unm.edu/~taosconf. **Contact:** Sharon Oard Warner, director. Estab. 1999. Annual. Conference held July 13-19, 2002 (weekend workshops July 13-14, week-long workshop July 14-19). Average attendance: 150. Conference offers both weekend and week-long workshops for beginning and experienced writers. Workshop size is a maximum of 12, which allows for both group support and individual attention. We offer workshops in novel writing, short story writing, screenwriting, poetry, creative nonfiction, travel writing, and in special topics, such as historical fiction and revision. Workshops and readings are all held at the Sagebrush Inn Conference Center, part of the Sagebrush Inn, an historic hotel and Taos landmark since 1929.

Costs: Week-long workshop tuition is $475, includes a Sunday evening Mexican buffet dinner, a Friday evening barbecue, and evening museum tour. A weekend workshop tuition is $225.

Accommodations: We offer a discounted car rental rate through the Sagebrush Inn. Offers overnight accommodations. Participants may choose to stay at either the Sagebrush Inn or the adjacent Comfort Suites. Conference participants receive special discounted rates $59-99 per night. Room rates at both hotels include a full hot breakfast.

Additional Information: "Participants do not submit mss in advance. Instead, they bring copies to distribute at the first meeting of the workshop." Sponsors contest. "We offer four merit-based scholarships to participants and one D. H. Lawrence Fellowship. Scholarship awards are based on submissions of poetry and fiction." They provide tuition remission; transportation and lodging not provided. To apply, participants submit 10 pages of poetry or fiction along with registration and deposit. Applicants should be registered for the conference. The Fellowship is for emerging writers with one book in print or press, provides tuition remission and the cost of lodging. Brochures available late January-early February 2001. For brochures send e-mail, visit website, call or fax. Accepts inquiries by SASE, e-mail, phone, fax. "The conference offers a balance of special events and free time. If participants take a morning workshop, they'll have afternoons free, and vice versa. We've also included several outings, including a tour of the Harwood Arts Center and a visit to historic D. H. Lawrence Ranch outside Taos."

N UNIVERSITY OF THE NATIONS SCHOOL OF WRITING AND WRITERS WORKSHOPS, YWAM Woodcrest, P.O. Box 1380, Lindale TX 75771-1380. (903)882-WOOD [9663]. Fax: (903)882-1161. E-mail: info@ywamwoodcrest.com. Website: www.ywamwoodcrest.com. **Contact:** Pamela Warren, director of training. Estab. 1983. Annual. Conference held September 26-December 17, 2002. School of Writing lasts 12 weeks, individual workshops last 1 week each. Average attendance: 6-12. Site: "We are located in East Texas about 90 miles east of Dallas. Our campus is on 107 acres of wooded area."

Costs: "Interested parties should double check fees for School of Writing as housing/food costs may vary. 2001 School of Writing costs are $50 registration fee; $2,700 tuition/food/housing plus $50 book fee."

Accommodations: "We can pick up students at Tyler Airport or Mineola Amtrack train station. Otherwise, we can assist in arranging shuttle service from Dallas. Costs vary depending on number of people. Housing is dormitory-style with several students sharing a common room and shower area (one for men, one for women). Married students or families housing will vary and is arranged on an as needed basis."

Additional Information: For brochure send e-mail, visit website or call. Send request. Accepts inquiries by e-mail, phone, fax or send request. Editors participate in conference. "If a student desires credit for a workshop or plans to attend the full School of Writing they must meet University of the Nations prerequisite (usually just the Discipleship Training School). Although we are associated with the *Youth With A Mission* missionary organization we welcome inquiries and attendees from all backgrounds, not just missionaries."

☑ **ROBERT VAUGHAN'S "WRITE ON THE BEACH"**, ATAP Financial Corp., P.O. Box 1092, Addison TX 75001-1092. (972)960-1140. Fax: (972)960-8464. E-mail: jch90@yahoo.com. Website: www.writeonthebeach. com. **Contact:** Jim Harris, director. Estab. 1998. Annual. Conference held February. Average attendance: 23. Focus is on fiction, nonfiction and screenwriting. The retreat is held in very large beach houses near Gulf Shores, Alabama. Each attendee has private room & bath, most with a view of the Gulf. Ratio of writers to staff, is never higher than 3:1, thus affording maximum consultation time. Faculty includes Greg Tobin (editor-in-chief & sr. vp at Ballentine); Pat LoBruto, (sr. editor Bantam); Bob Robison (agent with Robison & Assoc.); Jim Harris (film producer, Paragon Pictures); and Robert Vaughan (author, screenwriter).
Costs: $1,350 for 6 days. Includes all meals and lodging.
Accommodations: Shuttle service is provided by retreat staff.
Additional Information: Brochures available by e-mail, visit website, phone or fax. Accepts inquiries by e-mail, phone, and fax. Agents and editors participate in conference. " 'Write on the Beach' is more of a writer's working retreat than a conference, with writers having virtually unlimited access to staff for consultation and problem solving." Special Session available for published writers and speakers/consultants seeking assistance in completing books to establish them as an expert in their field.

N WINTER WRITERS CONFERENCE, 1501 W. 5th St., Suite E-2, Austin TX 78703-5155. (512)499-8914. Fax: (512)499-0441. E-mail: awl@writersleague.org. Website: writersleague.org. **Contact:** Jim Bob McMillan, executive director. Estab. 1999. Annual. Conference held Winter 2002. Conference duration: 3 days. Average attendance: 125. "The purpose of the conference is to bring writers together to explore the craft of writing. The 2000 conference featured Christopher Vogler and focused on fiction, screenwriting, and creative nonfiction. The 2001 conference featured Lee Gutkind and focused on creative nonfiction." Site: Austin, Texas. Topics for 2000 included Characterization, Point of View, Structure & Narrative, and Movie Genres. In addition to Lee Gutkind, presenters in 2001 included Jim Hornfischer, Joe Nick Patoski, Robert Draper, Laurie Lynn Drummond, Skip Hollandsworth, Arturo Longoria, Lee Martin, Don Graham, and Spike Gillespie.
Costs: 2001 conference was $135 for members. Included lunch on Saturday and a continental breakfast on both Saturday and Sunday.
Additional Information: Conference information is available December 2001. For brochure send SASE, e-mail, visit website, call or fax. Accepts inquiries by SASE, e-mail, phone and fax.

N WOODLAND WRITERS GUILD CONFERENCE AND WRITING COMPETITION, P.O. Box 132451, Spring TX 77393-2451. Website: www.woodlandsonline.com/wwg. **Contact:** Mary Ann Ball. Estab. 1993. Annual. Conference held September 2002. Conference duration: 1 day. Average attendance: 125 people. Site: Community Center. 2001 panels include Tried & True Approaches for Marketing, Setting Selection is a Major Component, What Acquisitions Editors Look for in a Proposal, Becoming a Repeat Author, The Burgeoning Market for Poetic Works, Book Manufacturing, The Psychology of Writing for Publication. Alyysia Gonzalez, Bill Crider, Elaine Moore Lamon, Harry Preston, Margaret Anderson, Rita Mills, Thomas Fensch, Susie Flatan and James Hoggard are scheduled to participate.
Costs: In 2001, $80 nonmembers, includes lunch; $60 members, includes lunch.
Additional Information: Sponsors contest. "All entries must be unpublished by time of the deadline, and the author must not have received monetary compensation for any work in the category entered. Each finalist manuscript will be judged by a published author, professional editor, or agent. Awards will be presented at the conference. Manuscripts must be double-spaced, in Courier New, 12 point size, on 8½×11 white paper with one-inch margins. The page number and title or keyword must appear in the upper right corner of every page except the first. A cover sheet with the manuscript title, author's name, address, phone number, category and word count must be included. This is the only place where the author's name should appear, else the entry will be disqualified without refund." Contest fees are $10/entry. For brochure send SASE, e-mail or visit website. Accepts inquiries by SASE and e-mail. Agents and editors participate in conference.

N WRITER'S RETREATS, 906 Chelsey Lane, Durango CO 81301-3408. (970)247-5327. E-mail: thunder@animas-net. Website: www.manuscriptdevelopment.com. **Contact:** Michael Thunder. Estab. 1998. Duration: 1-2 weeks. Average attendance: 1 individual. Focus is on fiction and screenwriting. Site: Smiley School, Durango, Colorado, "beautiful mountain environment."
Costs: $750 coaching fee. Meals and lodging are dependent on the writer's taste and budget.
Accommodations: Provides a list of area hotels or lodging options.

Additional Information: "These writer's retreats are geared toward vision questing, a project or project development. Usually writers stay one week and receive 10 hours of one-on-one coaching. The rest of their time is spent writing." For brochure send e-mail, visit website or call. Accepts inquiries by SASE, e-mail and phone. Agents and editors participate in conference.

WRITERS WORKSHOP IN SCIENCE FICTION, English Department/University of Kansas, Lawrence KS 66045-2115. (785)864-3380. Fax: (785)864-4298. E-mail: jgunn@ukans.edu. Website: falcon.cc.ukans.edu/~sfcenter/. **Contact:** James Gunn, professor. Estab. 1985. Annual. Average attendance: 15. Conference for writing and marketing science fiction. "Housing is provided and classes meet in university housing on the University of Kansas campus. Workshop sessions operate informally in a lounge." The workshop is "small, informal and aimed at writers on the edge of publication or regular publication." Past guests include: Frederik Pohl, SF writer and former editor and agent; John Ordover, writer and editor; and Kij Johnson and Christopher McKittrick, writers.
Costs: Tuition: $400. Housing and meals are additional.
Accommodations: Several airport shuttle services offer reasonable transportation from the Kansas City International Airport to Lawrence. During past conferences, students were housed in a student dormitory at $12/day double, $22/day single.
Additional Information: "Admission to the workshop is by submission of an acceptable story. Two additional stories should be submitted by the end of June. These three stories are copied and distributed to other participants for critiquing and are the basis for the first week of the workshop; one story is rewritten for the second week." Conference information available December 2000. For brochures/guidelines send SASE, visit website, e-mail, fax, call. Accepts inquiries by SASE, phone, fax, e-mail. "The Writers Workshop in Science Fiction is intended for writers who have just started to sell their work or need that extra bit of understanding or skill to become a published writer."

West (AZ, CA, HI, NV, UT)

N BIG BEAR WRITER'S RETREAT, P.O. Box 1441, Big Bear Lake CA 92315-1441. (909)585-9922. Fax: (909)324-2080. E-mail: duffen@aol.com. **Contact:** Mike Foley, director. Estab. 1995. Biannual. Conference held May 2002. Conference duration: 3 days. Average attendance: 15-25. Site: "A small intimate lodge in Big Bear, California, San Bernardino mountains of Southern California." Themes for 2001 included Chracterization, Writing From the Heart, Encountering the Muse, Sensory Description, Using Myth & Symbol, Writing Through Intuition. Retreat is hosted annually by Mike Foley, editor, Dream Merchant Magazine and Tom Foley, Ph.D., artistic psychologist.
Costs: $499, includes meals and lodging.
Accommodations: Offers overnight accommodations. On-site facilities included in retreat fee.
Additional Information: Prior to arrival, submit a fiction or nonfiction sample, 10 double-spaced pages maximum. Conference information is available March 2002. For brochure send SASE, e-mail, call or fax. Accepts inquiries by SASE, e-mail, phone and fax. Editors participate in conference. "This is unlike the standard writers conference. Participants will live as writers for a weekend. Retreat includes workshop sessions, open writing time and private counseling with retreat hosts. A weekend of focused writing, fun and friendship. This is a small group retreat, known for its individual attention to writers, intimate setting and strong bonding among participants."

N JAMES BONNET'S STORYMAKING: THE MASTER CLASS, P.O. Box 841, Burbank CA 91503-0841. (818)567-0521. Fax: (818)567-0038. E-mail: bonnet@storymaking.com. Website: www.storymaking.com. **Contact:** James Bonnet. Estab. 1990. Conference held April, July, October 2002; January 2003. Conference duration: 2 days. Average attendance: 40. Conference focuses on fiction, mystery and screenwriting. Site: In 2001, Sportsmen's Lodge, Studio City, California. Panels planned for next conference include High Concept, Anatomy of a Great Idea, the Creative Process, Metaphor, The Hook, The Fundamentals of Plot, Structure, Genre, Character, Complications, Crisis, Climax, Conflict, Suspense and more. James Bonnet (author) is scheduled to participate as speaker.
Costs: $300 per weekend.
Accommodations: Provides a list of area hotels or lodging options.

 A BULLET INTRODUCES COMMENTS by the editor of *Novel & Short Story Writer's Market* indicating special information about the listing.

Additional Information: For brochure send SASE, e-mail, visit website, call or fax. Accepts inquiries by SASE, e-mail, phone and fax. "James Bonnet, author of *Stealing Fire From the Gods*, teaches a story structure and storymaking seminar that guides writers from inspiration to final draft."

N CANYONLANDS WHITEWATER WRITERS RIVER TRIP/CANYONLANDS FIELD INSTI-TUTE, P.O. Box 68, Moab UT 84532. (435)259-7750. Fax: (435)259-2335. E-mail: cfiinfo@canyonlandsfieldins t.org. Website: www.canyonlandsfieldinst.org. **Contact:** CFI Registrar. Estab. 1998. Annual. Conference held last week of July. Conference duration: 6 days. Average attendance: 15. "Enjoy three days of instruction and critique as well as private time to do some of your own writing down Westwater Canyon of the Colorado River. You'll also learn about the fascinating geology, ecology and history of this beautiful canyon and run both mild and exciting rapids (class I-III riverstretch)." Site: "This workshop/river trip begins with an evening motel stay and introductory seminar in Grand Junction, Colorado. Our four-day, three-night river trip follows. The program concludes with a dinner, wrap-up and motel stay the last night back in Grand Junction." Past faculty: Scott Russell Sanders.
Costs: $550, $200 deposit. Includes meals, instruction, boating gear and hotel stay.
Additional Information: Brochures available, send SASE, e-mail, visit website, call or fax. Accepts inquiries by SASE, e-mail, phone and fax.

N DESERT WRITERS WORKSHOP/CANYONLANDS FIELD INSTITUTE, P.O. Box 68, Moab UT 84532. (435)259-7750 or (800)860-5262. Fax: (435)259-2335. E-mail: cfiinfo@canyonlandsfieldinst.org. Website: www.canyonlandsfieldinst.org/. **Contact:** Canyonlands Field Institute Registrar. Estab. 1984. Annual. Held first weekend in November. Conference duration: 3 days. Average attendance: 30. Concentrations include fiction, nonfiction, poetry. Site is at a ranch near Moab, Utah. "Theme is oriented towards understanding the vital connection between the natural world and human communities." Faculty panel has included in past years Ann Zwinger, Pam Houston, Linda Hogan, Christopher Merrill, Terry Tempest Williams and Richard Shelton.
Costs: $450 (members of CFI, $510); $150 deposit, which includes meals Friday-Sunday, instruction, field trip, lodging.
Accommodations: At a guest ranch, included in cost.
Additional Information: Brochures are available for SASE. Accepts inquiries by phone, fax, e-mail. "Participants may submit work in advance, but it is not required. Student readings, evaluations and consultations with guest instructors/faculty are part of the workshop. Desert Writers Workshop is supported in part by grants from the Utah Arts Council and National Endowment for the Arts. A partial scholarship is available. College credit is also available for an additional fee."

☑ FOOTHILL WRITERS' CONFERENCE, 12345 El Monte Rd., Los Altos Hills CA 94022-4599. (650)949-7316. Fax: (650)949-7375 (include cover sheet; attn: Wolterbeek). E-mail: wolterbeekkim@fhda.edu. **Contact:** Kim Wolterbeek. Annual. Conference held in June. Conference duration: 6 days. Average attendance: 150-200. Conference includes fiction, nonfiction, poetry, memoir, screenwriting. Held at Foothill College. Previous topics include "Let's Write: In-class exercises for Jumpstarting the Muse"; "Writing the Erotic"; and "Nature Poems: The Power of Place." Past faculty members include Chitia Divakaruni, Lawson Inada and Mary Jane Moffat.
Costs: Approximately $100.
Accommodations: Bus service provided. Offers list of area hotels.
Additional Information: Manuscript to be critiqued may be submitted the first day of workshop. Conference information is available in May. For brochure send SASE or e-mail.

IWWG EARLY SPRING IN CALIFORNIA CONFERENCE, International Women's Writing Guild, P.O. Box 810, Gracie Station, New York NY 10028-0082. (212)737-7536. Fax: (212)737-9469. E-mail: iwwg@iwwg. com. Website: www.IWWG.com. **Contact:** Hannelore Hahn, executive director. Estab. 1982. Annual. Conference held second weekend in March. Average attendance: 80. Conference to promote "creative writing, personal growth and empowerment." Site: Bosch Bahái School, a redwood forest mountain retreat in Santa Cruz, California.
Costs: $345 for weekend program with room and board ($325 for members); $90 per day for commuters ($80 for members), $170 for weekend program without room and board ($150 for members).
Accommodations: Accommodations are all at conference site.
Additional Information: Conference information is available after August. For brochures/guidelines send SASE. Accepts inquiries by e-mail, fax.

☑ LEAGUE OF UTAH WRITERS ROUND-UP, 4621 W. Harman Dr., W.V.C. UT 84120-3752. Phone/fax: (801)964-0861. E-mail: crofts@numucom.com. Website: http://luwrite.tripod.com/. **Contact:** Dorothy Crofts, membership chairman. Estab. 1935. Annual. Conference held in September 2000. Conference duration: 2 days, Friday and Saturday. Average attendance: 200. "The purpose of the conference is to award the winners of our annual contest as well as instruction in all areas of writing. Speakers cover subjects from generating ideas to

writing a novel and working with a publisher. We have something for everyone." Conference held at hotel conference rooms and ballroom facilities with view of lakeside for awards banquet. Dinner at poolside. 2001 themes included Essays, Financial Planning for Writers, Freelance Writing from Home, Writing for Magazines. Past speakers included Peter Steinberg, literary agent; Anne Perry, historical mystery; Jennifer Wingertzahn, Random House children's editor; and Diane Thomas, author.
Costs: 2001 costs: $100 for LUW members ($80 if registered before August 31); $150 for nonmembers (fee includes 4 meals).
Accommodations: Shuttle service is available from Salt Lake International Airport to Salt Lake Airport Hilton. List of hotel/motel accommodations available. Special hotel rate for conference attendees $79.
Additional Information: Opportunity for writers to meet one-on-one with literary agent from New York, 10 pages of their novel will be read and reviewed with writer. Sponsors contests for eight fiction categories, three open to nonmembers of League. Word limits vary from 1,500 to 90,000. Conference brochures/guidelines available for SASE, e-mail, fax, phone and on website after May 2002. Accepts inquiries by fax, e-mail, SASE, phone.

☑ ◎ **MOUNT HERMON CHRISTIAN WRITERS CONFERENCE**, P.O. Box 413, Mount Hermon CA 95041-0413. (831)335-4466. Fax: (831)335-9413. E-mail: slist@mhcamps.org. Website: www.mounthermon.org.
Contact: David R. Talbott, director of adult ministries. Estab. 1970. Annual. Conference held Friday-Tuesday over Palm Sunday weekend, March 22-26, 2002. Average attendance: 400. "We are a broad-ranging conference for all areas of Christian writing, including fiction, children's, poetry, nonfiction, magazines, books, educational curriculum and radio and TV scriptwriting. This is a working, how-to conference, with many workshops within the conference involving on-site writing assignments. The conference is sponsored by and held at the 440-acre Mount Hermon Christian Conference Center near San Jose, California, in the heart of the coastal redwoods. Registrants stay in hotel-style accommodations, and full board is provided as part of conference fees. Meals are taken family style, with faculty joining registrants. The faculty/student ratio is about 1:6 or 7. The bulk of our faculty are editors and publisher representatives from major Christian publishing houses nationwide."
Costs: Registration fees include tuition, conference sessions, resource notebook, refreshment breaks, room and board and vary from $575 (economy) to $850 (deluxe), double occupancy (2001 fees).
Accommodations: Airport shuttles are available from the San Jose International Airport. Housing is not required of registrants, but about 95% of our registrants use Mount Hermon's own housing facilities (hotel-style double-occupancy rooms). Meals with the conference are required and are included in all fees.
Additional Information: Registrants may submit 1 work for critique in advance of the conference, then have personal interviews with critiquers during the conference. No advance work is required however. Conference brochures/guidelines are available in December for SASE or by calling (888)MH-CAMPS. Accepts inquiries by e-mail, fax. "The residential nature of our conference makes this a unique setting for one-on-one interaction with faculty/staff. There is also a decided inspirational flavor to the conference, and general sessions with well-known speakers are a highlight." Brochures/registration forms available in December 2001 on website, by e-mail, fax or phone.

PALM SPRINGS WRITERS CONFERENCE, 2700 N. Cahuenga Blvd., Suite 4204, Los Angeles CA 90068. (213)874-5158. Fax: (213)874-5767. E-mail: valtrain@aol.com. Website: home.earthlink.net/~pswriterconf/.
Contact: Mary Valentine. Estab. 1992. Annual. Conference held April 8-11, 1999. Average attendance: 230. Conference concentration is on the teaching and marketing of publishable fiction and nonfiction. "Conference is held at Marquis Hotel Resort, a first-class resort in the heart of Palm Springs. Classes on all aspects of fiction, short and long; stresses commercial, saleable fiction." Featured speakers/panelists include Catherine Coulter, Ray Bradbury, Tami Hoag, Harlan Ellison, Gerald Petievich, V.C. Andrews (Andrew Neiderman), Dianne Pugh, Arthur Lyons.
Costs: $345-395.
Accommodations: Complimentary hotel shuttle service from Palm Springs Regional Airport. Special hotel rates for Marquis Hotel.
Additional Information: "We offer critiques (half hour) for manuscripts by qualified professional writers (there is a charge), as well as free ten-minute one-on-one with agents and editors." Guidelines available for SASE. Accepts inquiries by fax, e-mail.

☑ **PASADENA WRITERS' FORUM**, P.C.C. Extended Learning Dept., 1570 E. Colorado Blvd., Pasadena CA 91106-2003. (626)585-7608. E-mail: mbrucker@nccf.org. **Contact:** Meredith Brucker, coordinator. Estab. 1954. Annual. Conference held in March of 2002. Average attendance: 200. "For the novice as well as the professional writer in any field of interest: fiction or nonfiction, including scripts, children's, humor and poetry." Conference held on the campus of Pasadena City College. A panel discussion by agents, editors or authors is often featured at the end of the day.
Costs: $100, including box lunch, for one-day conference.

Additional Information: Brochure upon request, no SASE necessary. "Pasadena City College also periodically offers an eight-week class 'Writing for Publication'."

N PIMA WRITERS' WORKSHOP, Pima Community College, 2202 W. Anklam Rd., Tucson AZ 85709-0170. (520)206-6974. Fax: (520)206-6020. E-mail: mfiles@pimacc.pima.edu. **Contact:** Meg Files. Estab. 1988. Annual. Conference held in May. Conference duration 3 days. Average attendance 200. "For anyone interested in writing—beginning or experienced writer. The workshop offers sessions on writing short stories, novels, nonfiction articles and books, children's and juvenile stories, poetry and screenplays." Sessions are held in the Center for the Arts on Pima Community College's West Campus. Past speakers include Michael Blake, Ron Carlson, Gregg Levoy, Nancy Mairs, Linda McCarriston, Jerome Stern, Connie Willis, Larry McMurtry, Barbara Kingsolver and Robert Morgano.
Costs: $65 (can include ms critique). Participants may attend for college credit, in which case fees are $85 for Arizona residents and $215 for out-of-state residents. Meals and accommodations not included.
Accommodations: Information on local accommodations is made available, and special workshop rates are available at a specified motel close to the workshop site (about $60/night).
Additional Information: Participants may have up to 20 pages critiqued by the author of their choice. Mss must be submitted 2 weeks before the workshop. Conference brochure/guidelines available for SASE. Accepts inquiries by e-mail. "The workshop atmosphere is casual, friendly, and supportive, and guest authors are very accessible. Readings, films and panel discussions are offered as well as talks and manuscript sessions."

SAN DIEGO STATE UNIVERSITY WRITERS' CONFERENCE, SDSU College of Extended Studies, 5250 Campanile Drive, San Diego State University, San Diego CA 92182-1920. (619)594-2517. E-mail: xtension @mail.sdsu.edu. Website: www.ces.sdsu.edu. **Contact:** Paula Pierce, coordinator, SWSU extension programs. Estab. 1984. Annual. Conference held on 3rd weekend in January. Conference duration: 2 days. Average attendance: approximately 375. "This conference is held in San Diego, California, at the Doubletree Hotel, Mission Valley. Each year the SDSU Writers Conference offers a variety of workshops for the beginner and the advanced writer. This conference allows the individual writer to choose which workshop best suits his/her needs. In addition to the workshops, editor/agent appointments and office hours are provided so attendees may meet with speakers, editors and agents in small, personal groups to discuss specific questions. A reception is offered Saturday immediately following the workshops where attendees may socialize with the faculty in a relaxed atmosphere. Keynote speaker is to be determined."
Costs: Approximately $280. This includes all conference workshops and office hours, coffee and pastries in the morning, lunch and reception Saturday evening. Editor/agent appointments extra fee.
Accommodations: Doubletree, Mission Valley, (800)222-TREE. Conference rate available for SDSU Writers Conference attendees. Attendees must make their own travel arrangements.
Additional Information: Editor/Agent sessions are private, one-on-one opportunities to meet with editors and agents to discuss your submission. To receive a brochure, e-mail, fax, call or send a postcard to above address. No SASE required.

☑ THE WILLIAM SAROYAN WRITER'S CONFERENCE, P.O. Box 5331, Fresno CA 93755-5331. Phone/fax: (559)224-2516. E-mail: law@pacbell.net. **Contact:** Stephen Mettee, conference chair. Estab. 1991. Annual. Conference held April 5-7, 2002. Conference duration: "Friday noon to Sunday noon." Average attendance: 150. Conference on "how to write and how to get published." The conference is held at Piccadilly Inn which is "close to the airport, other hotels and all workshops in one section of the hotel." 2000 speakers included John Baker, John Kremer, Linda Mead, James Frey, Barbara Kuroff and Andrea Brown.
Costs: 2000 fees: $225 for all workshops (choice of 39), most meals, critique sessions, one-on-ones with agents, editors, etc. Overnight accommodations listed in brochure. On-site accommodations approximately $80/night.
Additional Information: Conference information available February 2002. For brochures/guidelines visit website, e-mail, fax or call. Accepts inquiries by fax, SASE, phone, e-mail. The conference is "small, intimate—easy to talk with agents, editors, etc."

SCBWI/NATIONAL CONFERENCE ON WRITING & ILLUSTRATING FOR CHILDREN, 8271 Beverly Blvd., Los Angeles CA 90048. (323)782-1010. Fax: (323)782-1892. E-mail: scbwi@scbwi.org. Website: www.scbwi.org. **Contact:** Lin Oliver, executive director. Estab. 1972. Annual. Conference held in August. Conference duration: 4 days. Average attendance: 650. Writer and illustrator workshops geared toward all levels. Covers all aspects of children's magazine and book publishing.
Costs: Approximately $375; includes all 4 days and one banquet meal. Does not include hotel room.
Accommodations: Information on overnight accommodations made available.
Additional Information: Manuscript and illustration critiques are available. Brochure/guidelines available for SASE or visit website.

N SOUTHERN CALIFORNIA WRITERS' CONFERENCE, 4406 Park Blvd., Suite E, San Diego CA 92116. (619)282-2983. E-mail: WeWrite@WritersConference.com. Website: www.WritersConference.com. **Contact:** Michael Steven Gregory, executive director. Estab. 1986. Annual. Conference held February 15-18, 2002. Conference duration: 4 days. Average attendance: 250. Conference focuses on facilitating mainstream fiction, nonfiction to market. Emphasis is on reading and critiquing conferees' manuscripts. Site: Holiday Inn Hotel & Suites, located in historic Old Town, San Diego, approximately 2 miles from Sea World. Panels planned for next conference include Fulfilling a Story's Promise; Sustaining Narrative Drive; Writing the Synopsis That Sells; and over 3 dozen workshops with extensive read and critiques, agents' panel and more. Gayle Lynds, Jerry Hannah, Bill Johnson, Mark Clements, Larry Brody and Mary Koski are scheduled to participate.
Costs: $275, which includes all workshops and events, including Saturday evening's banquet. Day rates available.
Accommodations: Hotel lodging discount available to conferees. Shuttle service to San Diego airport. Approximately $118-130/night.
Additional Information: Sponsors contest. 250-word "Topic" competition is announced the opening day of conference. There is no advance submission. Conference information is available September 2001. For brochure send e-mail, visit website, call or fax. Accepts inquiries by SASE, e-mail, phone and fax. Agents and editors participate in conference.

SQUAW VALLEY COMMUNITY OF WRITERS FICTION WORKSHOP, P.O. Box 2352, Olympic Valley CA 96146-2352. (530)274-8551. Fax: (530)274-0986. E-mail: svcw@oro.net. Website: www.squawvalley writers.org. **Contact:** Brett Hall Jones, executive director. Estab. 1969. Annual. Conference held in August. Conference duration is 7 days. Average attendance: 120. "The Fiction Workshop assists talented writers by exploring the art and craft as well as the business of writing." Offerings include daily morning workshops lead by writer-teachers, editors, or agents of the staff, limited to 12-13 participants; seminars; panel discussions of editing and publishinng; craft colloquies; lectures; and staff readings. Themes and panels in 2000 included "Personal History in Fiction," "Narrative Structure," "Roots" and "Anatomy of a Short Story." Past faculty and speakers included Will Allison, Max Byrd, Mark Childress, Carolyn Doty, Jennifer Egan, Molly Giles and Bharati Mukherjee.
Costs: Tuition is $625, which included six dinners. See "Accommodations" below for housing costs.
Accommodations: The Community of Writers rents houses and condominiums in the Valley for participants to live in during the week of the conference. Single room (one participant): $400/week. Double room (twin beds, room shared by conference participant of the same sex): $285/week. Multiple room (bunk beds, room shared with two or more participants of the same sex): $175/week. All rooms subject to availability; early requests are recommended. Can arrange airport shuttle pick-ups for a fee.
Additional Information: Admissions are based on submitted manuscript (unpublished fiction, a couple of stories or novel chapters); requires $25 reading fee. Submit ms to Brett Hall Jones, Squaw Valley Community of Writers Fiction Workshops, 10626 Banner Lava Cap, Nevada City CA 95959. Deadline: May 10, 2002. Notification: June 10. Brochure/guidelines available February, 2002 by phone, e-mail or visit website. Accepts inquiries by SASE, e-mail, phone. Agents and editors attend/participate in conference.

N STEINBECK FESTIVAL, 1 Main St., Salinas CA 93901. (831)796-3833. Fax: (831)796-3828. Website: www.steinbeck.org. Estab. 1980. Annual. Conference held August 1-4, 2002. Average attendance: 1,000 "over 4 day period." Conference focuses on the life and writings of John Steinbeck. Site: National Steinbeck Center, a museum with a permanent, multimedia exhibition about John Steinbeck and changing art and cultural exhibits. Panels planned for the 2002 conference include The Banning of Books, History of Migrant Labor, Steinbeck's Influence on Contemporary Authors, Steinbeck & Tourism, and Steinbeck in the Schools. Guest speakers include Judith Krug, director of the Office for Intellectual Freedom at the American Library Association and Dr. Susan Shillinghaw, director of the Center for Steinbeck Studies at San Jose State University.
Costs: Fees for 2001 were $55 passport (includes admission to all sessions, movies and the museum); $45 bus tours, $10 individual sessions (includes museum admission).
Accommodations: Provides a list of area hotels or lodging options.
Additional Information: Sponsors The John Steinbeck Award for The Short Story. $1,000 First Prize. Must be less that 6,000 words, Deadline: December 1, 2001. $15 reading fee. Conference information is available September 1, 2001. For brochure visit website. Accepts inquiries by SASE and e-mail. Agents and editors participate in conference. "The 22nd Steinbeck Festival will be celebrating the Steinbeck centennial."

VOLCANO WRITERS' RETREAT, P.O. Box 163, Volcano CA 95689-0163. (209)296-7945. E-mail: khexber g@volcano.net. Website: www.volcano.net/~khexberg. **Contact:** Karin Hexberg, director. Estab. 1998. Three times/year. Weekend retreat held in April and October. Duration: 3 days. "Summer Camp" held in August. Duration: 5 days. Average attendance: 20-25 (limited). Retreat for writing "fiction, poetry, essay, memoir." Held at the St. George Hotel. Hotel is 150 years old and located in the most picturesque of all the gold country towns, Volcano.

Squaw Valley Community of Writers emphasizes teaching, not celebrity

When it comes to hiring staff members for the Squaw Valley Community of Writers (SVCW), executive director Brett Jones isn't looking for big-name authors. "We try not to pay any attention to the star-quality of our staff members," she says. "We prefer to invite writer-teachers who have shown themselves to be generous and helpful in workshops."

It's an approach in keeping with the conference's goal—"to assist fledgling writers of obvious talent to become published authors"—and, judging from Squaw's alumni rolls, the conference has more than succeeded. Past participants include such noted authors as Aimee Bender, Michael Chabon, Janet Fitch, Richard Ford, Jay Gummerman, Rhoda Huffey, Louis B. Jones, Kem Nunn, Frederick Reiken, Anne Rice, Alice Sebold, Martin J. Smith and Amy Tan.

To maintain its high teaching standards, Squaw relies on a regular core of staff members, many of whom are past participants themselves. Some attend almost every year (including Max Byrd, Henry Carlisle, Mark Childress, Carolyn Doty, Jay Gummerman, Jim Houston, Lynn Freed, Amy Tan and Al Young) while others come nearly every other year (Richard Ford, Alan Chuese, Susan Trott, Molly Giles). Recent staffers also include Anne Lamott and Robert Stone.

"While new staffers do cycle in, this core really sustains a terrific sense of community," says Lisa Alvarez, co-director of SVCW's Writers Workshops (formerly the Fiction Program).

A sense of community, as the conference's name suggests, is important at Squaw. The annual *Omnium Gatherum & Newsletter* helps attendees keep in touch year round. Rather than dormitories or hotel rooms, participants are housed in private homes that dot the basin of Squaw Valley, a ski resort just north of Lake Tahoe in California's Sierra Nevadas. Staff readings are open to the public. And the conference organizers foster an inclusive and relaxed atmosphere, encouraging plenty of interaction between staff and participants. The result is a conference that, by week's end, radiates the hospitable feel of a family get-together.

Not surprisingly, SVCW is something of a family affair. Executive director Brett Jones is the daughter of Oakley and Barbara Hall. Oakley is the conference's general director, Barbara, its unofficial photographer. Brett's sister, novelist Sands Hall, is the general director's assistant; Brett's husband, novelist Louis B. Jones, is co-director of the Writers Workshops. But the Halls aren't the only family at Squaw; the staff roster often features husband-and-wife teams such as Bharati Mukherjee and Clark Blaise, Michael Chabon and Ayelet Waldman, and Henry and Olga Carlisle.

When Oakley Hall and fellow novelist Blair Fuller founded SVCW in 1970, they hoped to bring attention to West Coast writers who, says Hall, were neglected at the time by New York editors and agents. Today, the conference attracts staff and participants from across the country, though it retains a distinctly Western appeal thanks in part to its stunning mountain landscape. Squaw Valley, site of the 1960 Winter Olympics, is a four-hour drive from the Bay

Area and a one-hour drive from the Reno/Lake Tahoe Airport. The conference facilities are nestled on the valley floor, surrounded by mountains with nearby hiking trails and waterfalls. Brave writers can ride a cable car two thousand feet up to High Camp, a mountaintop recreation club offering swimming, tennis, and ice-skating.

In addition to being perhaps the country's most majestically situated writers' conference, SVCW has also earned a reputation for innovation. Squaw pioneered the use of editors, publishers and agents as workshop leaders (in addition to using writers, who traditionally lead workshops). The conference also employs a unique workshop format in which staff members rotate from workshop to workshop, giving participants exposure to many teachers while allowing each workshop group to become close-knit. It's an arrangement that empowers participants and keeps staff members on their toes. The conference's guidelines advise staff members that workshops are to be participatory, not pedagogical: "Workshop leaders should be aware that by the second half of the week, workshops will have become quite cohesive, with a group intelligence and considerable self-confidence. Unfruitful hassles may result if the leader then seeks to impose his opinions over those of the workshop."

To encourage personalized attention, the workshops are small—no more than 12 or 13 members. In addition to daily workshops, all participants meet with a staff member for a one-on-one conference or take part in an additional craft workshop focusing on a topic such as personal narrative or creative nonfiction. Afternoon and evening programs include craft lectures, panel discussions, staff readings, and open workshops. "It's a full week," says Alvarez, "one that is ideally inspiring and humbling."

The Writers Workshops include 132 participants, 28-32 teaching staff members, and 10-12 guests (editors, agents, and writers who don't stay for the conference's full eight days). SVCW also invites four published alumni to give readings each year.

Admission to the Writers Workshops is competitive, with only 50-60 percent of applicants gaining acceptance. Each applicant must submit a previously unpublished writing sample of 5,000 or fewer words.

"The only thing we really pay attention to is the manuscript," says Jones. "It's important that applicants send their best work." (After they've been accepted, applicants are free to submit different manuscripts for consideration in the workshops or conferences.)

Thanks to a generous scholarship program, Squaw is able to offer financial aid to 40 percent percent of its participants. Of those, 72 percent receive partial scholarships or tuition waivers; 16 percent receive full scholarships, which cover all but $100; and 12 percent receive work scholarships, which require the participant to do office or set-up work.

"Scholarships are awarded primarily on the perceived quality of the manuscript," says Jones, "though we also consider financial need and the distance a participant must travel."

—*Will Allison*

(For information on applications, fees, and deadlines, see the Squaw Valley Community of Writers listing on page 587. In addition to the Writers Workshops, SVCW also hosts the Poetry Program and the Screenwriting Program. To learn more, visit the SVCW website at www.squawvalleywriters.org).

Costs: 2001 fees: weekend: $245-265; summer camp: $370-415 (including lodging and some meals).

Accommodations: Most attendees stay at the site although individuals may make other arrangements.

Additional Information: "Absolutely no critiquing. The purpose of this retreat is to create a non-competitive, non-judgmental, safe atmosphere where we are all free to write the worst stuff in the world." Brochures/guidelines for SASE. Accepts inquiries by e-mail.

☑ **WRANGLING WITH WRITING**, Society of Southwestern Authors, P.O. Box 30355, Tucson AZ 85751. (520)546-9382. E-mail: wporter202@aol.com. Website: www.azstarnet.com/nonprofit/SSA. **Contact:** Penny Porter, director. Estab. 1971. Annual. Conference held third weekend in January. Attendance: limited to 350. Conference "to assist writers in whatever ways we can. We cover all areas." Held at the Holiday Inn with hotel rooms available. Keynote speaker for 2002 conference will be Ray Bradbury. Plus 36 workshops for all genres of writing.

Costs: $235; includes meals.

Accommodations: Holiday Inn Pala Verde in Tucson. Information included in brochure available for SASE.

Additional Information: Critiques given if ms sent ahead. Sponsors short story contest (2,500 words or less) separate from the conference. Deadline May 31. Awards given September 21. Brochures/guidelines available after November for SASE, e-mail, fax, phone call or on website. Accepts inquiries by e-mail, fax, phone, SASE.

☑ **WRITER'S CONSORTIUM**, (formerly Fallbrook Writer's Colony), P.O. Box 976, Fallbrook CA 92088-0976. Phone/fax: (760)451-1669. E-mail: carolroper@writersconsortium.com. Website: www.writersconsortium. com. **Contact:** Carol Roper. Estab. 1995. Ongoing seminars monthly. Seminar duration: 2 days. Average attendance: up to 16. "Writers learn in a peaceful, creative environment unrestrained by the demands of everyday obligation. To write in a compelling way, writers need more than technique, writers need to know themselves. Only then can we write from a compelling sense of truth." Site: "Fallbrook, California is a small, friendly town, famous for its avocados, 50 miles north of San Diego's Lindbergh Field and 90 miles south of Los Angeles. The town boasts respected art galleries, several excellent restaurants, and four championship golf courses nearby. There are nature preserves to enjoy." Panels planned for upcoming workshops include Creativity and Spirituality; Discovering Your Muse; Creative Intuition; Personal Powers; A Return to Innocence. Award-winning writer, Carol Roper facilitates one and two day workshops.

Costs: $90-100/weekend; includes meals. Individual feedback and/or instruction available at $50/hour.

Accommodations: Nearby motels and bed & breakfasts. See website at www.writersconsortium.com.

Additional Information: Unpublished or unproduced writers must submit a 5-page writing sample with registration. For brochure send e-mail, visit website, call. Accepts inquiries by SASE, e-mail, phone.

N WRITING FOR YOUNG READERS WORKSHOP, 348 HCEB, BYU, Provo UT 84602-1532. (801)378-2567. Fax: (801)378-8165. Website: http://ce.byu.edu/cw/writing. **Contact:** Susan Overstreet, coordinator. Estab. 2000. Annual. Workshop held July 15-18, 2002. Average attendance: 1,000. Workshop focuses on fiction for young readers: picture books, chapter books, middle grade novels, YA novels. Also nonfiction for young readers: books and magazines. Site: Conference center at Brigham Young University in the foothills of the Wasatch Mountain range. 2001 faculty included Joan Bauer, Louise Plummer, Carol Lynch Williams, Alane Ferguson, Claudia Mills, Hellen Ketteman and Rick Walton.

Costs: $385, includes final banquet.

Accommodations: Local lodging, airport shuttle. Lodging rates: $60-85/night.

Additional Information: Participants must bring at least one manuscript in progress to the workshop. Sponsors a contest. Daily contests judged by the workshop faculty. Conference information is available April 15, 2002. For brochure visit website, call or fax. Accepts inquiries by e-mail, phone and fax. Editors participate in conference.

Northwest (AK, ID, MT, OR, WA, WY)

CLARION WEST WRITERS' WORKSHOP, 340 15th Ave. E., Suite 350, Seattle WA 98112-5156. (206)322-9083. E-mail: KFISHLER@fishler.com. Website: www.sff.net/clarionwest. **Contact:** Leslie Howle, administrator. Estab. 1983. Annual. Workshop held June 17-July 28, 2001. Average attendance: 17. "Conference to prepare students for professional careers in science fiction and fantasy writing. Held at Seattle Central Community College on Seattle's Capitol Hill, an urban site close to restaurants and cafes, not too far from downtown." Deadline for applications: April 1.

Costs: Workshop: $1,400 ($100 discount if application received by March 1). Dormitory housing: $800, meals not included.

Accommodations: Students are strongly encouraged to stay on-site, in dormitory housing at Seattle University. Cost: $800, meals not included, for 6-week stay.

Additional Information: "This is a critique-based workshop. Students are encouraged to write a story a week; the critique of student material produced at the workshop forms the principal activity of the workshop. Students and instructors critique manuscripts as a group." Conference information available in fall 2001. For brochures/guidelines send SASE, visit website, e-mail or call. Accepts inquiries by e-mail, phone, SASE. Limited scholarships are available, based on financial need. Students must submit 20-30 pages of ms with $25 application fee to qualify for admission. Dormitory and classrooms are handicapped accessible.

FISHTRAP, P.O. Box 38, Enterprise OR 97828. (503)426-3623. E-mail: rich@fishtrap.org.. Website: www.fishtrap.org. **Contact:** Rich Wardschneider, director. Estab. 1988. Conferences held July 8-14 (2 days, plus 4 days of workshops) and February 22-24, 2002. Average attendance: 100-120. "Conferences are built around themes, this summer is 'The Legacy of Vietnam.' " Site: old Methodist Church Camp. 2001 faculty members included Yusef Komunyakaa, Alfredo Vea, Andrew X. Pham, songwriter Laurie Lewis, publisher Michael Wiegers (Copper Canyon).
Costs: Workshop (4 days, 12 classroom hours) $225; Conference (2 days) $180; Food and Lodging $34/day; food only $20/day.
Accommodations: Offers overnight accommodations (see above). Also provides list of area hotels. (Nearby motels $60-100/night).
Additional Information: Five fellowships given annually. Submit 8 pages of poetry or 2,500 words of prose (no name on ms) by February 7. Entries judged by a workshop instructor. Awards announced March 15. Conference information available November 2001 (for February conference) and March 2001 (for July conference). For brochures/guidelines send SASE, e-mail, visit website or call. Accepts inquiries by SASE, e-mail, phone. Agents and editors occasionally participate in conference. "Fishtrap Gatherings are about writing and the West. They are about ideas more than mechanics and logistics of writing/publishing. Workshops are not manuscript reviews, but writing sessions."

N. THE GLEN WORKSHOP, Image, 3307 Third Ave. W., Seattle WA 98119. (206)281-2988. Fax: (206)281-2335. E-mail: glenworkshop@imagejournal.org. Website: www.imagejournal.org. Estab. 1991. Annual. Workshop held August 2002. Workshop duration: 1 week. Average attendance: 100-140. Workshop focuses on "fiction, poetry and spiritual writing, essay, memoir. Run by *Image*, a literary journal with a religious focus. The Glen welcomes writers who practice or grapple with religious faith." Site: TBA for 2002. 2002 conference will feature "presentations and readings by the faculty." 2001 faculty included Erin McGraw (fiction); Scott Cairns (poetry); Kate Daniels (poetry); Emilie Griffin (spiritual writing).
Costs: $500-800, including room and board; $300-375 for commuters (lunches only).
Accommodations: Arrange transporatation by shuttle. (15) Accommodations included in conference cost.
Additional Information: Prior to arrival, participants may need to submit workshop material depending on the teacher. "Usually 10-25 pages." Conference information is available in February, 2002. For brochure send SASE, e-mail, visit website, call or fax. Accepts inquiries by SASE, e-mail, phone and fax. "The tone isn't overtly religious, but that element is part of our purpose and identity."

N. HAYSTACK WRITING PROGRAM, PSU Summer Session, P.O. Box 1491, Portland OR 97207-1491. (503)725-4186. Fax: (503)725-4840. E-mail: herrinm@pdx.edu. Website: www.haystackpdx.edu. **Contact:** Maggie Herrington. Estab. 1968. Annual. Program runs from mid-July through first week of August. Workshop duration varies; one-week and weekend workshops are available throughout the six-week program. Average attendance: 10-15/workshop; total program: 400. "The program features a broad range of writing courses for writers at all skill levels. Classes are held in Cannon Beach, Oregon." Past instructors have included William Stafford, Ursula K. LeGuin, Craig Lesley, Molly Gloss, Mark Medoff, Tom Spanbauer, Sallie Tisdale.
Costs: Approximately $435/course weeklong; $150 (weekend). Does not include room and board.
Accommodations: Attendees make their own transportation arrangements. Various accommodations available including: B&B, motel, hotel, private rooms, camping, etc. A list of specific accommodations is provided.
Additional Information: Free brochure available after March. Accepts inquiries by e-mail and fax. University credit (graduate or undergraduate) is available.

N. JACKSON HOLE WRITERS CONFERENCE, P.O. Box 3972, Laramie WY 82071-3972. Fax: (307)766-3914. E-mail: kguille@uwyo.edu. **Contact:** Keith Guille, coordinator. Estab. 1992. Annual. Conference held from June or July 2002. Conference duration: 4 days. Average attendance: 75. "The Jackson Hole Writers Conference draws a wide range of participants, from beginners to published writers. The conference is directed toward fiction, screenwriting, and creative nonfiction, offering programs relevant to all three disciplines: story structure, narrative thrust, character development, work habits and business techniques. Faculty's goal is to help our writers get published." Site: Tetons and Yellowstone National Park at the Snow King Resort. Deborah Bedford, Jon Billman, John Byrne Cooke, Carolyn Lampman, plus many more are scheduled to participate as faculty members.

Costs: $350 includes mss, meals and functions; $300 without.

Accommodations: Offers list of area hotels and lodging options.

Additional Information: Manuscripts should be 15 pages (20 pages for screenplays); title page with author's name, address, and phone or e-mail; typewritten or laser-printed; double-spaced; identification of submission. Conference information is available February 2002: e-mail, visit website, call, or fax. Accepts inquiries by e-mail, phone, or fax. Agents and editors participate in conference.

[N] NATURE WRITERS RETREAT WITH NORTH CASCADES INSTITUTE, North Cascades Institute, 810 Highway 20, Secro-Woolley WA 98284-9394. (360)856-5700, ext. 209. Fax: (360)859-1934. E-mail: nci@ncascades.org. Website: www.ncascades.org. **Contact:** Deb Martin, registrar. Estab. 1999. Annual. Conference duration: 4 days. Average attendance: 40. "Led by four outstanding authors and poets, the NCI Nature Writers Retreat engages amateur and professional writers alike—lectures, discussions, readings and writing exercises centered on the natural world." Site: The 2001 conference was held at Sun Mountain Lodge, one of Washington's premier resorts. Perched atop 2,000 acres of rolling hills, the lodge is surrounded by breathtaking views of the North Cascades and the Methow Valley. Its accommodations include elegant mountain-top rooms, world class cuisine, outdoor pools and hot tubs. "Nature writing, at its simplest, strives to explore basic principles at work—nature and to convey these in language that introduces readers to the facility and wonder of their own place in the world." Previous faculty has included Tim McNulty and Barbara Kingsolver.

Costs: In 2001: $650/person (triple/quad occupancy); $725/person (double); $895/person (single), includes lodging and meals.

Additional Information: Conference information is available in February. For brochure send e-mail, visit website or call. Accepts inquiries by e-mail and phone. Editors participate in conference.

[N] PORTLAND STATE UNIVERSITY HAYSTACK WRITING PROGRAM, PSU Summer Session, P.O. Box 1491, Portland OR 97207. (503)725-4186. **Contact:** Maggie Herrington. Estab. 1968. Annual. Conference held from mid-July to early August in one-week sessions meeting Monday through Friday; some weekend workshops. Average attendance: 10-15/class. Conference offers a selection of writing courses including fiction, nonfiction, poetry, essay and memoir—taught by well-known writers in small-group sessions. Classes are held in the local school with supplemental activities at the beach, community lecture hall, and other areas of the resort town. University credit available.

Costs: $185 (weekend)-$435 (weeklong). Participants locate their own housing and meals.

Accommodations: Housing costs are $50-400/week. Camping, bed and breakfasts and hotels are available.

[N] SAGEBRUSH WRITERS WORKSHOP, P.O. Box 1255, Big Timber MT 59011-1255. Phone/fax: (406)932-4227. E-mail: sagebrsh@ttc-cmc.net. **Contact:** Gwen Petersen, director. Estab. 1990. Annual. Workshop held March 23-24, 2002. Average attendance: 30-35. "Each year, the workshop has a different focus. For 2002, novel writing and creative nonfiction." Site: Carriage House Ranch bed and breakfast. 2002 faculty members include a journalist, novelist and screenplay writer.

Costs: $190, includes Saturday evening banquet dinner, Sunday lunch, all snack breaks.

Accommodations: Offers shuttle from airport by arrangement with Sagebrush. Provides a list of area hotels and/or lodging options.

Additional Information: "Submissions optional but encouraged—up to 15 pages." Workshop information is available January 2002. For brochure send SASE, e-mail, call or fax. Accepts inquiries by SASE, e-mail, phone and fax. Agents and editors participate in conference.

SITKA CENTER FOR ART AND ECOLOGY, P.O. Box 65, Otis OR 97368. (541)994-5485. Fax: (541)994-8024. E-mail: info@sitkacenter.org. Website: www.sitkacenter.org. **Contact:** Amy Buringrud, associate director. Estab. 1970. Annual workshop program. "We don't have conferences. Our workshop program is open to all levels and is held annually from late May until late March. We also have a residency program from September through May." Average attendance: 10-16/workshop. A variety of workshops in creative processes, including book arts and other media. The Center borders a Nature Conservancy Preserve, the Siuslaw National Experimental Forest and the Salmon River Estuary, located just north of Lincoln City, Oregon.

Costs: "Workshops are generally $50-300; they do not include meals or lodging."

Accommodations: Does not offer overnight accommodations. Provides a list of area hotels or lodging options.

Additional Information: Brochure available in February of each year by SASE, phone, e-mail, fax or visit website. Accepts inquiries by SASE, e-mail, phone, fax.

[N] SITKA SYMPOSIUM ON HUMAN VALUES & THE WRITTEN WORD, P.O. Box 2420, Sitka AK 99835-2420. (907)747-3794. Fax: (907)747-6554. E-mail: island@ak.net. Website: www.islandinstitutealaska. org. **Contact:** Carolyn Servid, director. Estab. 1984. Annual. Conference held in June. Conference duration: 1 week. Average attendance: 60. Conference "to consider the relationship between writing and the ideas of a

selected theme focusing on social and cultural issues." The Symposium is held in downtown Sitka. Many points of visitor interest are within walking distance. The town looks out over surrounding water and mountains. Guest speakers have included Alison Deming, Scott Russell Sanders, Rina Swentzell, Barry Lopez, William Kittredge, Gary Snyder, Margaret Atwood, Terry Tempest Williams, Robert Hass, Richard Nelson and Linda Hogan. **Costs:** $300.
Accommodations: Accommodation rates are listed on Symposium brochure.
Additional Information: Ms critiques (individually with faculty) are available for people submitting work before May 20. Conference brochures/guidelines are available for SASE. Accepts inquiries by e-mail and fax.

WILLAMETTE WRITERS CONFERENCE, 9045 SW Barbur, Suite 5-A, Portland OR 97219-4027. (503)452-1592. Fax: (503)452-0372. E-mail: wilwrite@teleport.com. Website: www.willamettewriters.com. **Contact:** Bill Johnson, office manager. Estab. 1968. Annual. Conference held in August. Average attendance: 400. "Willamette Writers is open to all writers, and we plan our conference accordingly. We offer workshops on all aspects of fiction, nonfiction, marketing, the creative process, etc. Also we invite top notch inspirational speakers for keynote addresses. Recent theme was 'The Writers Way.' We always include at least one agent or editor panel and offer a variety of topics of interest to both fiction and nonfiction writers and screenwriters." Recent editors, agents and film producers in attendance have included: Donald Maass, Donald Maass Literary Agency; Jeff Herman, The Jeff Herman Agency, LLC; Mark Ryan, Web Brand Agency Group; Claire Eddy, Tor/ Forge Books; Rachel Kahan, Crown Publishers; Mira Son, Avalon Books; Frederick Levy, Marty Katz Productions; Julian Fowles, Asparzc-Katz Productions; Christopher Vogler, *The Writer's Journey.*
Costs: Cost for full conference including meals is $210 members; $246 nonmembers.
Accomodations: If necessary, these can be made on an individual basis. Some years special rates are available.
Additional Information: Conference brochures/guidelines are available in May for catalog-size SASE, e-mail, fax, phone or on website. Accepts inquiries by fax, e-mail, phone, SASE.

☑ **WRITE ON THE SOUND WRITERS' CONFERENCE**, 700 Main St., Edmonds WA 98020-3032. (425)771-0228. Fax: (425)771-0253. E-mail: wots@ci.edmonds.wa.us. **Contact:** Frances Chapin, cultural resources coordinator. Sponsored by Edmonds Arts Commission. Estab. 1986. Annual. Conference held October 5-6, 2002. Conference duration: 2 days. Average attendance: 160. "Conference is small—good for networking— and focuses on the craft of writing rather than publishers and editors. Edmonds is a beautiful community on the shores of Puget Sound, just north of Seattle."
Costs: $85 for 2 days, $50 for 1 day (1999); includes registration, morning refreshments and 1 ticket to keynote lecture.
Additional Information: Brochures available August 1, 2002. Accepts inquiries by e-mail, fax.

Canada

▨ **BLOODY WORDS MYSTERY CONFERENCE**, 12 Roundwood Court, Toronto, Ontario M1W 1Z2. Phone/fax: (416)497-5293. E-mail: soles@sff.net. Website: www.bloodywords.com. **Contact:** Caro Soles, chair. Estab. 1999. Annual. Conference held June 7-9, 2002. Average attendance: 300. Focus: Mystery/true crime/ forensics, with Canadian slant. Purpose: To bring readers and writers of the mystery genre together in a Canadian setting. Site: Delta Chelsea Inn, Gerrard St., Toronto. Conference includes a workshop and 2 tracks of panels, one on factual information such as forensics, agents, scene of the crime procedures, etc. and one on fiction, such as "Death in a Cold Climate," "Murder on the Menu," "Elementary My Dear Watson," and a First Novelists Panel. 2001 guests included William Deverell and Loren D. Estleman with Donald Maass as a guest agent and Joan Hall Houey, an experienced writer/editor.
Costs: 2002 fee: $150 (included the banquet and all panels, readings, dealers room and workshop).
Accommodations: Offers hotel shuttle from the airport. Offers block of rooms in hotel; list of optional lodging available. Call Delta Chelsea Inn for special conference rates (1-800-CHELSEA).
Additional Information: Sponsors short mystery story contest—4,000 word limit; judges are experienced editors of anthologies; fee is $5 (entrants must be registered). Conference information is available now. For brochure visit website. Accepts inquiries by e-mail and phone. Agents and editors participate in conference. "This is a conference for both readers and writers of mysteries, the only one of its kind in Canada. For 2002,

we will have a Canadian Guest of Honor Peter Robinson as well as an International Guest from the U.K. We also run 'The Mystery Café,' a chance to get to know 15 authors, hear them read and ask questions (half hour each)."

BOOMING GROUND, Buch E-462, 1866 Main Mall, Creative Writing Program, UBC, Vancouver, British Columbia V6T 121 Canada. (604)822-2469. Fax: (604)822-3616. E-mail: bg@arts.ubc.ca. Website: www.arts.ubc.ca/bg. **Contact:** Andrew Gray, director. Estab. 1998. Annual. Conference held July 6-12, 2002. Average attendance: 70. Conference on "fiction, poetry, non-fiction, drama." Conference held at "Green College, a residential college at the University of Columbia, overlooking the ocean." 2001 panels included "The Writing Life" and "Paths to Publication." 2001 panelists included Martha Sharpe, Gary Geddes, Kerri Sakamoto and Caroline Adderson.
Costs: 2001 fees were $650 (Canadian). Meals and accommodation separate. Some scholarships available.
Accommodations: "Information on overnight accommodations is available and students are encouraged to stay on-site at Green College." On site accommodations: $360 and $397 (Canadian) for 7 nights.
Additional information: "Workshops are based on works-in-progress. Writers must submit manuscript with application for jury selection." Conference information available February 2002. For brochures/guidelines send SASE, visit website, e-mail, fax or call. Accepts inquiries by SASE, phone, fax, e-mail. "Classes are offered for writers at all levels—from early career to mid-career."

THE FESTIVAL OF THE WRITTEN ARTS, Box 2299, Sechelt, British Columbia V0N 3A0 Canada. (800)565-9631 or (604)885-9631. Fax: (604)885-3967. E-mail: written_arts@sunshine.net. Website: www.sunshine.net/rockwood. **Contact:** Gail Bull, festival producer. Estab. 1983. Annual. Festival held August 9-12, 2001. Average attendance: 3,500. To promote "all writing genres." Festival held at the Rockwood Centre. "The Centre overlooks the town of Sechelt on the Sunshine Coast. The lodge around which the Centre was organized was built in 1937 as a destination for holidayers arriving on the old Union Steamship Line; it has been preserved very much as it was in its heyday. A new twelve-bedroom annex was added in 1982, and in 1989 the Festival of the Written Arts constructed a Pavilion for outdoor performances next to the annex. The festival does not have a theme. Instead, it showcases 20 or more Canadian writers in a wide variety of genres each year—the only all Canadian writer's festival."
Costs: $12 per event or $150 for a four-day pass (Canadian funds).
Accommodations: Lists of hotels and bed/breakfast available.
Additional Information: The festival runs contests during the 3½ days of the event. Prizes are books donated by publishers. Festival information available in spring. For brochures visit website, e-mail, fax or call. Accepts inquiries by e-mail, fax.

SAGA SEMINARS, P.O. Box 52188, Garneau Station, Edmonton Alberta T6C 0L4 Canada. (780)988-554 or (888)323-1231. Fax: (780)436-9660. E-mail: info@sagaseminars.com. Website: www.sagasemiars.com. **Contact:** Kerry Mulholland, administrative assistant. Estab. Edmonton: 1996; Santa Fe: 1996. Biannual. One in each location. Conference held from May 4-10, 2002 in Santa Fe, NM; July 15-26 in Edmonton, Alberta. Average attendance: 20 per location. "Workshops are designed for new and experienced women writers of prose, poetry and memoir." Site: Santa Fe (residential) at the Sunrise Springs Inn and Retreat Center. Edmonton: (non-residential) Alumni House on the University of Alberta campus. Eunice Scarfe (Santa Fe, Edmonton) and Di Brandt (Edmonton) scheduled to participate as faculty members.
Costs: Santa Fe (2001): $1,580 includes single accommodations, all meals, and tuition with early payment; $1,340 includes double accommodations, all meals, and tuition with early payment; late registration add $150. Edmonton: $225 includes tuition only for one week long session; $200 includes tuition only for 2 week long sessions.
Accommodations: Offers overnight accommodations for the conference held in Santa Fe. List of area hotels and lodging options available for conference held in Edmonton. Onsite accommodations at Sunrise Springs Inn and Retreat Center, see cost of packages.

SAGE HILL WRITING EXPERIENCE, Box 1731, Saskatoon, Saskatchewan S7K 3S1 Canada. Phone/fax: (306)652-7395. E-mail: sage.hill@sk.sympatico.ca. Website: www.lights.com/sagehill. **Contact:** Steven Ross Smith. Annual. Workshops held in August and November. Workshop duration 10-21 days. Attendance: limited to 36-40. "Sage Hill Writing Experience offers a special working and learning opportunity to writers at different stages of development. Top quality instruction, low instructor-student ratio and the beautiful Sage Hill setting offer conditions ideal for the pursuit of excellence in the arts of fiction, poetry and playwriting." The Sage Hill location features "individual accommodation, in-room writing area, lounges, meeting rooms, healthy meals, walking woods and vistas in several directions." Seven classes are held: Introduction to Writing Fiction & Poetry; Fiction Workshop; Nonfiction Workshop; Writing Young Adult Fiction Workshop; Poetry Workshop; Poetry Colloquium; Fiction Colloquium; Playwriting Lab.

Costs: $675 (Canadian) includes instruction, accommodation, meals and all facilities. Fall Poetry Colloquium: $975.

Accommodations: On-site individual accommodations located at Lumsden 45 kilometers outside Regina. Fall Colloquium is at Muenster, Saskatchewan, 150 kilometers east of Saskatchewan.

Additional Information: For Introduction to Creative Writing: A five-page sample of your writing or a statement of your interest in creative writing; list of courses taken required. For intermediate and colloquium program: A resume of your writing career and a 12-page sample of your work plus 5 pages of published work required. Application deadline is May 1. Guidelines are available after February for SASE, e-mail, fax, phone or on website. Accepts inquiries by SASE, phone, e-mail and fax. Scholarships and bursaries are available.

SUNSHINE COAST FESTIVAL OF THE WRITTEN ARTS, Box 2299, Sechelt, British Columbia V0N 3A0 Canada. (604)885-9631 or (800) 565-9631. Fax: (604)885-3967. E-mail: written_arts@sunshine.net. Website: www.sunshine.net/rockwood. **Contact:** Gail Bull. Estab. 1982. Annual. Festival held August 8-11, 2000. Average attendance: 9,500. Festival "tries to represent all genres." Held in a "500 seat pavilion set in the beautiful Rockwood Gardens in the seaside town of Sechelt, B.C." 1999 speakers included Maragret Atwood, Arthur Black, Andreas Schroeder, Bill Richardson, Anne Petrie and Margo Button.

Costs: Individual events, $12; Festival pass, $175; student discounts. Meals and lodging are not included.

Accommodations: Information on overnight accommodations is available.

Additional information: Conference brochures/guidelines available in May. Accepts inquiries by fax, e-mail, SASE, phone.

SURREY WRITERS' CONFERENCE, (formerly A Writer's W*O*R*L*D), 12870 72nd Ave., Surrey, British Columbia V4P 1G1 Canada. (640)594-2000. Fax: (604)590-2506. E-mail: phoenixmcf@aol.com. **Contact:** Rollie Koop, principal. Estab. 1992. Annual. Conference held in fall. Conference duration: 3 days. Average attendance: 350. Conference for fiction (romance/science fiction/fantasy/mystery—changes focus depending upon speakers and publishers scheduled), nonfiction and poetry. "For everyone from beginner to professional." Conference held at Sheraton Guildford. Guest lecturers included authors Diana Gabaldon, Don McQuinn and Daniel Wood; agents and editors.

Accommodations: On request will provide information on hotels and B&Bs. Conference rate, $90. Attendee must make own arrangements for hotel and transportation.

Additional Information: "A drawing takes place and ten people's manuscripts are critiqued by a bestselling author." Writer's contest entries must be submitted about 1 month early. Length: 1,000 words fiction, nonfiction, poetry, young writers (19 or less). 1st Prize $250, 2nd Prize $125, 3rd Prize $75. Contest is judged by a qualified panel of writers and educators. Write, call or e-mail for additional information.

THE VANCOUVER INTERNATIONAL WRITERS FESTIVAL, 1398 Cartwright St., Vancouver, British Columbia V6H 3R8 Canada. (604)681-6330. Fax: (604)681-8400. E-mail: alee@writersfest.bc.ca. Website: www.writersfest.bc.ca. Estab. 1988. Annual. Held in October. Average attendance: 11,000. "This is a festival for readers and writers. The program of events is diverse and includes readings, panel discussions, seminars. Lots of opportunities to interact with the writers who attend." Held on Granville Island—in the heart of Vancouver. Two professional theaters are used as well as Performance Works (an open space). "We try to avoid specific themes. Programming takes place between February and June each year and is by invitation."

Costs: Tickets are $10-15 (Canadian).

Accommodations: Local tourist info can be provided when necessary and requested.

Additional Information: Festival information available on website. Accepts inquiries by e-mail, fax. "A reminder—this is a festival, a celebration, not a conference or workshop."

THE VICTORIA SCHOOL OF WRITING, Box 8152, Victoria, British Columbia V8W 3R8 Canada. (250)598-5300. E-mail: vicwrite@islandnet.com. Website: www.islandnet.com/vicwrite. **Contact:** Ruth Slavin, director. Conference held from July 14-19, 2002. "Five-day intensive workshop on beautiful Vancouver Island with outstanding author-instructors in fiction, poetry, historical fiction and nonfiction, humour, children's lit."

Cost: $575 (Canadian).

Accommodations: On site.

Additional Information: Workshop brochures available. Accepts inquiries by e-mail and phone.

International

ART WORKSHOPS IN GUATEMALA, 4758 Lyndale Ave. S, Minneapolis MN 55409-2304. (612)825-0747. Fax: (612)825-6637. E-mail: info@artguat.org. Website: www.artguat.org. **Contact:** Liza Fourré, director.

Estab. 1995. Annual. Workshops held year-round. Maximum class size: 10 students per class. Workshop titles include: Fiction Writing: Shaping and Structuring Your Story with Gladys Swan (April 6-15, 2002) and Creative Writing: Developing the Novel with Tessa Bridal (October 25-November 3, 2002).
Costs: $1,725 (includes tuition, air fare to Guatemala from USA, lodging and ground transportation).
Accommodations: All transportation and accommodations included in price of conference.
Additional Information: Conference information available now. For brochure/guidelines visit website, e-mail, fax or call. Accepts inquiries by e-mail, phone, fax.

THE ARVON FOUNDATION LTD. WORKSHOPS, Totleigh Barton Sheepwash, Beaworthy, Devon EX21 5NS United Kingdom. Phone: 00 44 14 09231338. E-mail: t-barton@arvonfoundation.org. Website: www.arvonfoundation.org. **Contact:** Helen Chaloner, national director. Estab. 1968 (workshops). Workshops held April through November at 3 centers. Workshops last 4½ days. Average attendence: 16/workshop. Workshops cover all types of fiction writing. "Totleigh Barton in Devon was the first Arvon centre. Next came Lumb Bank (Hebden Bridge, West Yorkshire HX7 6DF) and now, 12 courses at Moniack Mhor (Moniack, Kirkhill, Inverness IV 5 7PQ)." Totleigh Barton is a thatched manor house. Lumb Bank is an 18th century mill owner's home and Moniack Mhor is a traditional croft house. All are in peaceful, rural settings. In the three houses there are living rooms, reading rooms, rooms for private study, dining rooms and well equipped kitchens."
Costs: In 2002 course fee will be £360 which includes food, tuition and accommodation. For those in need, a limited number of grants and bursaries are available from the Arvon Foundation.
Accommodations: There is sleeping accommodation for up to 16 course members, but only limited single room accommodation (there are 8 bedrooms at Lumb Bank, 12 bedrooms at Moniack Mhor and 13 bedrooms at Totleigh Barton). The adjacent barns at Lumb Bank and Totleigh Barton have been converted into workshop/studio space and there are writing huts in the garden.
Additional Information: Sometimes writers are required to submit work. Check for details. Workshop brochure/guidelines available for SASE.

FEDERWELT AUTORENTREFFEN, Albrechtstrasse 107, Berlin, Germany 12167. Phone: +49(030)79747679. E-mail: redaktion@federwelt.com. Website: www.federwelt.com. **Contact:** Titus Müller. Estab. 1999. Annual. Conference held October 3, 2002. Average attendance: 70 authors. The purpose of the conference is to help "authors get in contact with professionals and learn from them. Each co-source has a focus on 2-3 specific genres." Site: literatur WERKstatt, Berlin—"the 'house of literature,' for Germany's capital." 2001 panels included "How to Write a Crime Thriller," "How to Write Historical Novels," and "How to Work with Literary Agents/Publishing Houses in Germany." Panelists were Horst Sosetzky (crime thrillers), Thomas R.P. Mielke (historical novels) and Michael Gaeb (literary agent).
Costs: 120 DM, includes 2 meals.
Additional Information: Conference information is available in April, 2002. For brochure send SASE, e-mail or visit website. Accepts inquiries by SASE and e-mail. Agents participate in conference.

PARIS WRITERS WORKSHOP/WICE, 20, Bd du Montparnasse, Paris, France 75015. (331)45.66.75.50. Fax: (331)40.65.96.53. E-mail: pww@wice-paris.org. Website: www.wice-paris.org. **Contact:** Rose Burke and Marcia Lebre, directors. Estab. 1987. Annual. Conference held June 30-July 5, 2002. Average attendance: 40-50. "Conference concentrates on fiction, nonfiction, creativity and poetry. Visiting lecturers speak on a variety of issues important to beginning and advanced writers. 2001 lecturers included Harry Clifton, Irish poet and writer, Lauren Davis, Canadian writer and Denis Hirson, South African author. Located in the heart of Paris on the Bd. du Montparnasse, the stomping grounds of such famous American writers as Ernest Hemingway, Henry Miller and F. Scott Fitzgerald. The site consists of 4 classrooms, a resource center/library and private terrace."
Costs: 380 Euros—tuition only.
Additional Information: "Students submit 1 copy of complete ms or work-in-progress which is sent in advance to writer in residence. Each student has a one-on-one consultation with writer in residence concerning ms that was submitted." Conference information available late fall 2001. For brochures/guidelines visit website, e-mail, call or fax. Accepts inquiries by SASE, phone, e-mail, fax. "Workshop attracts many expatriate Americans and other English language students from all over Europe and North America. We can assist with finding a range of hotels, from budget to more luxurious accommodations. We are an intimate workshop with an exciting mix of more experienced, published writers and enthusiastic beginners." 2002 writers in residence are Sharon Olds (poetry), Speer Morgan (fiction), Laurie Stone (nonfiction), Eric Maisel (deepwriting).

PROPRIOCEPTIVE WRITING IN IRELAND, P.O. Box 76, Yarmouth ME 04096. Phone/fax: (207)846-8863. E-mail: ginkeegon@aol.com. Website: www.contemplativewriting.com. **Contact:** Ginny Keegon, director. Estab. 2001. Spring/Fall. Workshop duration: 1 week. Average attendance: 10. "Proprioceptive Writing is a meditative form of writing—we write to candlelight and music under relaxed conditions. Writers and non-writers alike find this writing a clarifying process, unusually effective in enlivening students intellectually and freeing them creatively, opening the floodgates of expression." Site: Anam Cara Artist's & Writers Retreat Center, West Cork, Ireland. Faculty includes Annie Jacobsen, MSW, MA (poet, novelist Jungion psychotherapist) and Ginny Keegon (certified teacher Metcalf-Simon Practice of Proprioceptive Writing).

Costs: $995 includes workshop fees, room and all meals (2001 rate).

Accommodations: Transfer to and from Cork airport to Anam Cara. "Participants stay at traditional (Irish B&B's—a short walk from Anam Cara, our workshop site."

Additional Information: Conference information is available. For brochure send e-mail, visit website, call or fax. Accepts inquiries by SASE, e-mail, phone and fax.

N: THE SPOLETO WRITERS' WORKSHOP, 760 W. End Ave., Suite 3A, New York NY 10025. (212)663-4440. Website: www.spoletoarts.com. **Contact:** C.J. Everett. Estab. 1994. Annual. Workshop held July 21-August 3, 2001. Workshop duration: 2 weeks. Average attendance: 30. "Workshops designed to advance the mastery of writing in one's chosen genre, in a small, select group. Participants will be serious writers, interested in advancing their craft and deepening their sense of the writer's art." Site: Spoleto, Italy. "Participants will write new work based on specific writing assignments or exercises and then will discuss the results and the implications of the exercises for their own work. Each participant will also have one private consultation with one of the three instructors. The writers will be divided into groups that change as the workshop proceeds, so that writers will work with all instructors, and all will produce new work in different genres. In addition to free writing time, there will be evening sessions of readings and discussions of relevant topics such as publications, manuscript preparation, etc. Much emphasis will be placed on each writer's engagements and improvement in his/her craft, on further writing and reading, and on a sense of the writer's vocation. The program also includes optional Italian language classes; a day trip in Umbria for the entire group; attendance at a Master Class in singing and a concert by vocal program participants." 2001 faculty included Rosellen Brown, James Magnuson and Marie Howe.

Costs: $2,350-2,500.

Accommodations: Offers overnight accommodations. Many options for additional lodging.

Additional Information: Conference information is available early Winter 2002. For brochure send SASE, e-mail, visit website, call or fax. Accepts inquiries by SASE, e-mail, phone and fax. Agents participate in conference.

SUMMER IN FRANCE WRITING WORKSHOPS, HCOI, Box 102, Plainview TX 79072. Phone/fax: (806)889-3533. E-mail: bettye@parisamericanacademy.edu. Website: www.parisamericanacademy.edu. **Contact:** Bettye Givens, director. Annual. Conference: 27 days in July. Average attendance: 10-15. For fiction, poetry, nonfiction, drama. The classrooms are in the Val de Grace, 277 Rue St. Jacques in the heart of the Latin Quarter near the Luxeumbourg Gardens in Paris. Guest speakers include Paris poets, professors and editors (lectures in English or through interpreters).

Costs: Costs vary. 2001 cost was $2,950 for shared apartment, no meals except opening and closing dinners. Costs also include literature classes, art history and the writing workshop.

Accommodations: Some accommodations with a French family.

Additional Information: Conference information available. For brochures/guidelines send SASE, e-mail or visit website. Accepts inquiries by SASE, e-mail, fax. "Enroll early. Side trips out of Paris are planned as are poetry readings at the Paris American Academy, Tea and Tattered Pages and Shakespeare & Co."

✓ TŶ NEWYDD WRITER'S CENTRE, Llanystumdwy, Cricieth Gwynedd LL52 OLW, United Kingdom. Phone: 01766-522811. Fax: 01766 523095. E-mail: tynewydd@dial.pipex.com. Website: www.tynewydd.o rg. **Contact:** Sally Baker, director. Estab. 1990. Regular courses held throughout the year. Every course held Monday-Saturday. Average attendance: 14. "To give people the opportunity to work side by side with professional writers, in an informal atmosphere." Site is Tŷ Newydd, large manor house, last home of the prime minister, David Lloyd George. Situated in North Wales, Great Britain—between mountains and sea." Past featured tutors include novelists Beryl Bainbridge and Bernice Rubens.

Costs: £340 for Monday-Saturday (includes full board, tuition).

Accommodations: Transportation from railway stations arranged. Accommodation in Tŷ Newydd (onsite).

Additional Information: Conference information available after January by mail, phone, e-mail, fax or visit website. Accepts inquiries by SASE, e-mail, fax, phone. "We have had several people from U.S. on courses here in the past three years. More and more people come to us from the U.S. often combining a writing course with a tour of Wales."

Organizations

When you write, you write alone. It's just you and the typewriter or computer screen. Yet the writing life does not need to be a lonely one. Joining a writing group or organization can be an important step in your writing career. By meeting other writers, discussing your common problems and sharing ideas, you can enrich your writing and increase your understanding of this sometimes difficult, but rewarding life.

The variety of writers' organizations seems endless—encompassing every type of writing and writer—from small, informal groups that gather regularly at a local coffeehouse for critique sessions to regional groups that hold annual conferences to share technique and marketing tips. National organizations and unions fight for writers' rights and higher payment for freelancers, and international groups monitor the treatment of writers around the world.

In this section you will find state-, province- and regional-based groups. You'll also find national organizations including the National Writers Association. Sisters in Crime and the Western Writers of America are examples of groups devoted to a particular type of writing. Whatever your needs or goals, you're likely to find a group listed here to interest you.

SELECTING A WRITERS' ORGANIZATION

To help you make an informed decision, we've provided information on the scope, membership and goals of the organizations listed on these pages. We asked groups to outline the types of memberships available and the benefits members can expect. Most groups will provide additional information for a self-addressed, stamped envelope, and you may be able to get a sample copy of their newsletter for a modest fee.

Keep in mind joining a writers' organization is a two-way street. When you join an organization, you become a part of it and, in addition to membership fees, most groups need and want your help. If you want to get involved, opportunities can include everything from chairing a committee to writing for the newsletter to helping set up an annual conference. The level of your involvement is up to you, and almost all organizations welcome contributions of time and effort.

Selecting a group to join depends on a number of factors. As a first step, you must determine what you want from membership in a writers' organization. Then send away for more information on the groups that seem to fit your needs. Start, however, by asking yourself:
- Would I like to meet writers in my city? Am I more interested in making contacts with other writers across the country or around the world?
- Am I interested in a group that will critique and give me feedback on work-in-progress?
- Do I want marketing information and tips on dealing with editors?
- Would I like to meet other writers who write the same type of work I do or am I interested in meeting writers from a variety of fields?
- How much time can I devote to meetings and are regular meetings important to me? How much can I afford to pay in dues?
- Would I like to get involved in running the group, working on the group's newsletters, planning a conference?
- Am I interested in a group devoted to writers' rights and treatment or would I rather concentrate on the business of writing?

For More Information

Because they do not usually have the resources or inclination to promote themselves widely, finding a local writers' group is usually a word-of-mouth process. If you would like to start a writers' group in your area, ask your local libraries and bookstores if they sponsor writers' groups.

The Internet is also an excellent resource for finding or establishing a writer's group. Many commercial online services have writers sections and clubs. Websites such as Coffeehouse for Writers (www.coffeehouseforwriters.com) have discussion boards, critique groups and even writing workshops available.

ASHLAND AREA CHRISTIAN WRITERS GUILD, 1552 County Rd. 995, Ashland OH 44805. (419)281-1766. E-mail: apple_b45@yahoo.com. **Contact:** April Boyer, director. Estab. 1999. Number of members: 10. Types of membership: Professional, associate, student. "Ashland Area serves any county, township, or town within comfortable driving distance. Members are asked to respect our purpose and statement. Our purpose is to share any knowledge, experiences, fellowship, support and prayer that we can for one another in pursuing God-honoring or family-friendly markets to publish our products; one that we each believe is a gift from God and a responsibility." Benefits include support and fellowship, occasional speakers at monthly meetings, "Word Warriors" newsletter, e-letter to absentees and supportive affiliates and friends. Dues: "There is no fee, but a donation is encouraged to cover small expenses. Non-attending affiliates who receive the e-letter or newsletters are also encouraged to donate. Any amount is appreciated." Mail, e-mail, phone for more information.

ASSOCIATED WRITING PROGRAMS, Tallwood House, Mail Stop 1E3, George Mason University, Fairfax VA 22030-9736. (703)993-4301. Fax: (703)993-4302. E-mail: awp@gmu.edu. Website: www.awpwriter.org (includes FAQ, membership information/ordering, award series guidelines, links to institutional members, AWP news). **Contact:** Membership Services. Estab. 1967. Number of Members: 5,000 individuals and 324 institutions. Types of Membership: Institutional (universities); graduate students; individual writers; and *Chronicle* subscribers. Open to any person interested in writing; most members are students or faculty of university writing programs (worldwide). Benefits include information on creative writing programs; grants, awards and publishing opportunities for writers; job list for academe and writing-related fields; a job placement service for writers in academe and beyond. AWP holds an annual conference in a different US city every spring; also conducts an annual Award Series in poetry, short story collections, novel and creative nonfiction, in which winner receives $2,000 honorarium and publication by a participating press. AWP acts as agent for finalists in Award Series and tries to place their manuscript with publishers throughout the year. Manuscripts accepted January 1-February 28 only. Novel competition: winner receives publication by St. Martin's Press and $10,000 in royalties. Send SASE for new guidelines. Publishes *The Writer's Chronicle* 6 times/year; 3 times/academic semester. Available to members for free. Nonmembers may order a subscription for $20/year; $27/year Canada; call for overseas rates. Also publishes the *AWP Official Guide to Writing Programs* which lists about 330 creative writing programs in universities across the country and in Canada. *Guide* is updated every 2 years; cost is $25.95, which includes shipping and handling. Dues: $57 for individuals; $37 students (must send copy of ID); additional $62 for full placement service. AWP keeps dossiers on file and sends them to school or organization of person's request. Send SASE for information. Inquiries by fax and e-mail OK.

THE AUTHORS GUILD, 330 W. 42nd St., 29th Floor, New York NY 10036-6902. (212)563-5904. E-mail: staff@authorsguild.org. Website: www.authorsguild.org (includes publishing industry news, business, legal and membership information). Executive Director: Paul Aiken. **Contact:** John McCloskey, membership coordinator. Purpose of organization: membership organization of 8,000 members offers services and informational materials intended to help published authors with the business and legal aspects of their work, including contract problems, copyright matters, freedom of expression and taxation. Maintains staff of attorneys and legal interns to assist members. Group health insurance available. Qualifications for membership: book author published by an established American publisher within 7 years or any author who has had 3 works, fiction or nonfiction, published by a magazine or magazines of general circulation in the last 18 months. Associate membership also available. Annual dues: $90. Different levels of membership include: associate membership with all rights except voting available to an author who has a firm contract offer from an American publisher. Workshops/conferences: "The Guild and the Authors Guild Foundation conduct several symposia each year at which experts provide information, offer advice, and answer questions on subjects of concern to authors. Typical subjects have been the rights of privacy and publicity, libel, wills and estates, taxation, copyright, editors and editing, the art of interviewing, standards of criticism and book reviewing. Transcripts of these symposia are published and circulated to members." The *Authors Guild Bulletin*, a quarterly journal, contains articles on matters of interest to published writers, reports of Guild activities, contract surveys, advice on problem clauses in contracts, transcripts of Guild and League symposia, and information on a variety of professional topics. Subscription included in the cost of the annual dues. Inquiries by mail, e-mail and fax OK.

BLOOMINGTON AREA CHRISTIAN WRITERS, 9576 W. State Rd. 48, Bloomington IN 47404-9737. (812)876-8265. E-mail: katadams55@aol.com. **Contact:** Kathi Adams. Estab. 1994. Number of members: 10. Types of membership: Professional, associate. Open to all. Purpose is to "encourage Christians in their writing, both fiction and nonfiction, and to give useful critique to their work." Benefits include resource sharing-books, tapes, magazines, etc. "Share expenses related to attending writers' conferences. Prayer and emotional support." Inquiries by mail, e-mail, phone.

CANADIAN SOCIETY OF CHILDREN'S AUTHORS, ILLUSTRATORS AND PERFORMERS (CANSCAIP), 35 Spadina Rd., Toronto, Ontario M5R 2S9 Canada. (416)515-1559. Fax: (416)515-7022. E-mail: canscaip@interlog.com. Website: www.interlog.com/~canscaip (includes children's authors, seminar information, art collection—samples [traveling]). **Contact:** Nancy Prasad, executive secretary. Estab. 1977. Number of Members: 1,100. Types of membership: Full professional member and friend (associate member). Open to professional active writers, illustrators and performers in the field of children's culture (full members); beginners and all other interested persons and institutions (friends). International scope, but emphasis on Canada. Benefits include quarterly newsletter, minutes of monthly meetings, marketing opportunities, publicity via our membership directory and our "members available" list, jobs (school visits, readings, workshops, residencies, etc.) through our "members available" list, mutual support through monthly meetings. Sponsors annual workshop, "Packaging Your Imagination," held every fall. Publishes *CANSCAIP News*, quarterly, available to all (free with membership, otherwise $25 Canadian). Dues: professional fees: $60 Canadian/year; friend fees: $25/year; institutional $30/year. "Professionals must have written, illustrated or performed work for children commercially, sufficient to satisfy the membership committee (more details on request)." CANSCAIP National has open meetings from September to June, monthly in Toronto. CANSCAIP West holds bimonthly meetings in Vancouver. Also has a London, Ontario branch. Send SASE for information. Inquiries by fax and e-mail OK.

CINCINNATI WRITER'S PROJECT, College of Mount St. Joseph, 5601 Delhi Rd., Cincinnati OH 45233. (513)244-4200. E-mail: Jeff_Hillard@mail.msj.edu. **Contact:** Jeff Hilliard. Estab. 1988. Organization of Cincinnati area writers. Members receive *Rough Draft*, the CWP monthly newsletter; general membership meeting held the third Thursday of each month. Members also participate in regularly scheduled workshops, critique sessions and readings in fiction, nonfiction, poetry and script/screen writing. Members' books are offered through the CWP book catalog and at other local writers' events. Dues for one year: $25, individual; $35 family. Send SASE for information.

FEDERATION OF BRITISH COLUMBIA WRITERS, #905-626 W. Pender St., Vancouver, British Columbia V6B 1V9 Canada. (604)683-2057. Fax: (604)608-5522. E-mail: fedbcwrt@pinc.com. Website: www.bcwriters.com. **Contact:** Merrill Fearon, executive director. Estab. 1982. Number of Members: 1,000. Types of Membership: regular. "Open to established and emerging writers in any genre, province-wide." Benefits include newsletter, liaison with funding bodies, publications, workshops, readings, literary contests, various retail and educational discounts. Sponsors readings and workshops. Publishes a newsletter 4 times/year, included in membership. Dues: $60 regular. Send SASE for information. Inquiries by fax and e-mail OK.

GARDEN STATE HORROR WRITERS, 18 Embury Ave., Ocean Grove NJ 07756-1375. (609)443-3438. Website: www.dreamwater.org/GSHW. **Contact:** Bob Biederman, president. Estab. 1991. Number of Members: 60. Membership levels: active and associate. Open to "anyone interested in pursuing a career in fiction writing." Scope is national. Benefits include "latest market news, use of library meeting rooms, free copies of guidelines for magazine and book publishers, free in-house critique service in person and by mail and e-mail." Sponsors monthly guest speakers and/or workshops, annual short fiction contest. A free sample of monthly

**FOR EXPLANATIONS OF THESE SYMBOLS,
SEE THE INSIDE FRONT AND BACK COVERS OF THIS BOOK.**

newsletter *The Graveline* is available for SASE. Subscription is included in the cost of any membership. Dues: $35 active; $24 associate/annually. Active members must be 16 years of age. Holds regular monthly meetings. Send SASE for information.

N GREATER CINCINNATI CHRISTIAN WRITERS' FELLOWSHIP, 5499 Yellowstone Dr., Fairfield OH 45014-3868. (513)858-6609. E-mail: wwriter@fuse.net. Website: www.gccwf.com. **Contact:** Wayne Holmes, director. Estab. 1991. Number of members: 20-30. Type of membership: Professional. Open to all. "We are a 'Christian writers' fellowship and specialize in the 'Christian market.' Our purpose is to train men and women with an interest in writing from a Christian perspective in the art of communicating God's Word through articles, books, poetry and other media. We do this through encouraging our members to network, by bringing in guest speakers knowledgeable in the publishing industry, and by helping one another outside of the structured setting." Benefits include newsletter, which gives members an opportunity to see their writing in print. The articles deal with an aspect of the writing life. "Our organization offers fellowship, friendship, learning, and sharing of knowledge." Free membership. E-mail for information.

N INSPIRATIONAL WRITERS ALIVE!, 6038 Greenmont, Houston TX 77092. (713)686-7209. E-mail: martharexrogers@aol.com. **Contact:** Martha Rogers, president, State Board of Directors. Estab. 1990. Number of members: 125 in five chapters. Types of members: Professional, associate, affiliate. No membership restrictions. Purpose is to "promote creative writing to glorify God as a ministry of writers, to aid its members in perfecting their writing skills, and to assist members in finding markets for their work. We have five chapters in Texas: Pasadena/Main, Houston First Baptist, Humble, Amarillo, East Texas/ Jacksonville." Benefits include newsletter, guest speakers, critique groups. Sponsors Open Writing Competition, January 1-May 15. Categories: short story, article, poetry, devotional, book proposal, drama. Dues: $25/year. Inquiries by e-mail.

N INTERNATIONAL ASSOCIATION OF CRIME WRITERS NORTH AMERICAN BRANCH, P.O. Box 8674, New York NY 10116-8674. (212)243-8966. Fax: (212)361-1477. E-mail: mfrisque@igc.org. **Contact:** Mary A. Frisque, executive director, North America. Estab. 1987. Number of members: 265. Type of membership: Professional. "IACW is an organization of professional writers who have formed national branches in order to encourage communication among writers of all nationalities and to promote crime writing as an influential and significant art form." Quarterly newsletter. Offers North American Hammett Prize annually "for the best work of literary excellence in the field of crime writing by a US or Canadian author or permanent resident." Benefits include "opportunities to attend conferences and festivals abroad, sponsored by foreign branches. Dues: $50/ year. Inquiries by SASE or e-mail.

🍁 ✔ MANITOBA WRITERS' GUILD, 206-100 Arthur St., Winnipeg, Manitoba R3B, 1H3 Canada. (204)942-6134 or (888)637-5802. Fax: (204)942-5754. E-mail: mbwriter@escape.ca. Website: www.mbwriter. mb.ca. Number of members: approximately 550. Type of memberships: Regular, student, senior and fixed income. Open to anyone: writers, emerging and established; readers, particularly those interested in Manitoba literature. "Membership is provincial in general, although we have members from across Canada, USA and the world." Benefits include special discounts on programs, goods and services; regular mailings of program notices; and *WordWrap*, published 6 times/year, featuring articles, regular columns, information on current markets and competitions, announcements, and profiles of Manitoba writers. Programs include Mentor/Apprentice program, small resource center (2-staff, small resource library, nonlending); open workshops once a month in fall and winter; annual conference, usually April; online database of Manitoba Authors, www.mbwriter.mb.ca/mapindex; online database of freelance authors and editors called Career Corner. Dues: $50 regular; $25 seniors, students, fixed-income. Send SASE for information.

N THE MYSTERY WRITERS' FORUM, 111 Baywood Avenue, Menlo Park CA 94025-2701. Phone/fax: (650)328-6828. E-mail: mysmaster@zott.com. Website: www.mysterywriters.forum.com. **Contact:** Lauri Hart, administrator. Types of membership: Professional, associate, affiliate, student. Membership open to all. Purpose is to " provide a place for published and aspiring mystery writers to trade information on the technical aspects peculiar to the mystery genre. Volunteer specialists in law enforcement, private investigation, and various forensic specialties can be checked with for advice on technical issues." Website has threaded discussion forum. Benefits include critique opportunites, information on agents and publishers, opportunities for authors, conferences and convention information, support and encouragement from peers. Free membership. Information available by e-mail or on website.

✔ MYSTERY WRITERS OF AMERICA (MWA), 17 E. 47th St., 6th Floor, New York NY 10017. (212)888-8171. Fax: (212)888-8107. E-mail: mwa_org@earthlink.net. Website: www.mysterywriters.org (includes information about the newsletter, awards and membership). **Contact:** Lawrence Block, president. Estab. 1945. Number of Members: 2,600. Type of memberships: Active (professional, published writers of fiction or nonfiction crime/

mystery/suspense); associate (professionals in allied fields, i.e., editor, publisher, critic, news reporter, publicist, librarian, bookseller, etc.); corresponding (writers qualified for active membership who live outside the US); affiliate (writers unpublished in the mystery field and those interested in the genre). Benefits include promotion and protection of writers' rights and interests, including counsel and advice on contracts, MWA courses and workshops, a national office, an annual conference featuring the Edgar Allan Poe Awards, the *MWA Anthology*, a national newsletter, regional conferences, insurance, marketing tools, meetings and research publications. Newsletter, *The Third Degree*, is published 10 times/year for members. Annual dues: $80 for US members; $60 for corresponding members.

☑ **THE NATIONAL LEAGUE OF AMERICAN PEN WOMEN, INC.**, Headquarters: The Pen Arts Building, 1300 17th St., NW, Washington DC 20036-1973. (202)785-1997. Fax: (202)452-6868. E-mail: nlapw1 @juno.com. Website: members.aol.com/penwomen/pen.htm. **Contact:** Dr. Wanda Rider, president. Estab. 1897. Number of Members: 5,000. Types of Membership: Three classifications: Art, Letters, Music. Publication and payment for work is a membership requirement. "Professional to us means our membership is open to women who sell their art, writings, or music compositions. We have over 175 branches in the mainland US plus Hawaii and the Republic of Panama. Some branches have as many as 100 members, some as few as 10 or 12. It is necessary to have 5 members to form a new branch." Benefits include a bimonthly magazine and local and national competitions. "Our facility is The Pen Arts Building. It is a 20-room Victorian mansion. One distinguished resident was President Abraham Lincoln's son, Robert Todd Lincoln, the former Secretary of War and Minister of Great Britain. It has rooms available for Pen Women visiting the D.C. area, and for Board members." In session 3 times a year. There are Branch and State Association competitions, as well as Biennial Convention competitions. Offers a research library of books by members and histories of the organization. Sponsors awards biennially to Pen Women in each classification: Art, Letters, Music, and $1,000 award biennially in even-numbered year to non-Pen Women in each classification for women age 35 and over who wish to pursue special work in art, music or letters field. *The Pen Woman* is the membership magazine, published 6 times a year, free to members, $18 a year for nonmember subscribers. Dues: $40/first year for national organization, $30/year thereafter; from $5-10/year for branch membership and from $1-5 for state association dues. Branches hold regular meetings each month, September through May except in northern states which meet usually March through September (for travel convenience). Send SASE for information. Inquiries via e-mail or fax OK, but SASE preferred.

NATIONAL WRITERS ASSOCIATION, 3140 S. Peoria, #295, Aurora CO 80014. (303)841-0246. Fax: (303)841-2607. Website: www.nationalwriters.com (includes contests, job listings and all other services). **Contact:** Sandy Whelchel, executive director. Estab. 1937. Number of Members: 4,000. Types of Memberships: Regular membership for those without published credits; professional membership for those with published credits. Open to: "Any interested writer, national/international plus we have 16 chapters in various states." Benefits include critiques, marketing advice, editing, literary agency, complaint service, research reports on various aspects of writing, 6 contests, National Writers Press—self-publishing operation, regular newsletter with updates on marketing, bimonthly magazine on writing-related subjects, discounts on supplies, magazines and some services. Sponsors periodic conferences and workshops; short story contest opens April, closes July 1; novel contest opens December, closes April 1. Publishes *Authorship Magazine* (quarterly publication available by subscription $20 to nonmembers). Dues: $65 regular; $85 professional. For professional membership, requirement is equivalent of 3 articles or stories in a national or regional magazine; a book published by a royalty publisher; a play, TV script or movie produced. Chapters hold meetings on a monthly basis. Inquiries by SASE, e-mail and fax OK.

NORTH CAROLINA WRITERS' NETWORK, P.O. Box 954, Carrboro NC 27510-0954. (919)967-9540. Fax: (919)929-0535. E-mail: mail@ncwriters.org. Website: www.ncwriters.org. (includes workshop and competition guidelines, links to other organizations, N.C. Literary Hall of Fame bios and more). **Contact:** Linda W. Hobson, executive director. Estab. 1985. Number of Members: 1,800. Open to: All writers, all levels of skill and friends of literature. Membership is approximately 1,600 in North Carolina and 200 in 33 other states and 5 other countries. Benefits include bimonthly newsletter; reduced rates for competition entry fees; fall and spring conferences, workshops, etc.; use of critiquing service; use of library and resource center; press release and publicity service; information database(s). Sponsors annual Fall Conference for Writers, statewide workshops, Blumenthal Writers & Readers Series, Randall Jarrell/Harperprints Poetry Chapbook Competition. Publishes the 24-page bimonthly *Writers' Network News*, and *North Carolina's Literary Resource Guide*. Subscription included in dues. Dues: $55/year individual, $30/year students enrolled in a degree-granting program, and $40/year seniors 65 + and disabled. Events scheduled throughout the year. Send SASE for information.

☑ **ROMANCE WRITERS OF AMERICA (RWA)**, 3707 FM 1960 West, Suite 555, Houston TX 77068. (281)440-6885. Fax: (281)440-7510. E-mail: info@rwanational.com. Website: www.rwanational.com. **Contact:**

Allison Kelley, executive director. President: Harold Lowry (aka Leigh Greenwood). Estab. 1981. Number of members: over 7,500. Type of Memberships: General and associate. Open to: "Any person actively pursuing a writing career in the romance field." Membership is international. Benefits include annual conference, contests and awards, magazine, forums with publishing representatives, network for published authors, group insurance, regional newsletters and more. Dues: $70/new members; $60/renewal fee. Send SASE for information.

[N] ST. DAVIDS CHRISTIAN WRITERS ASSOCIATION, The Upper Case, Time of Singing, 87 Pines Road East, Hadley PA 16130. (814)382-8667. E-mail: timesing@toolcity.net. Website: www.stdavidswriters.com. **Contact:** Audrey Stallsmith, registrar. Estab. 1957. Number of members: 120. Types of membership: Professional, associate. Open to all. Purpose to "discover, encourage, and train writers, editors, and artists in high professional standards for the Christian and secular market." Benefits include annual week-long conference; poetry and prose contests, awards at conference; learning; critiquing; support for writers. Dues: $12/year. Inquiries by SASE, e-mail (audstall@nauticom.net).

[N] ⊕ THE DOROTHY L. SAYERS SOCIETY, Rose Cottage, Malthouse Lane, Hurstpierpoint, West Sussex BN6 9IY, United Kingdom. Phone: (+44)1273 833444. Fax: (+44)1273 835988. E-mail: jasmine@sayers.org.uk. **Contact:** Christopher Dean, chairman. Estab. 1976. Number of members: 500. Type of membership: Student. Membership open to anyone with an interest in Dorothy Sayers' life-works. Purpose to "promote the study of the life, works, and thoughts of Dorothy Sayers, and to encourage performance of her plays, publication of her works, and to assist researchers." Annual conference in July/August usually in UK, to consider a particular work or aspect of Sayers' life and work. Benefits include access to society archives, advice and help to scholars, bimonthly newsletter. Dues: $28/year. Inquires by SASE, e-mail, fax.

☑ SCIENCE FICTION AND FANTASY WORKSHOP, 1193 S. 1900 East, Salt Lake City UT 84108-1855. (801)582-2090. Fax: (801)650-2168. E-mail: workshop@burgoyne.com. Website: www.burgoyne.com/pages/workshop. **Contact:** Kathleen D. Woodbury, director/newsletter editor. Estab. 1980. Number of members: 300. Types of memberships: "Active" is listed in the membership roster and so is accessible to all other members; "inactive" is not listed in the roster. Open to "anyone, anywhere. Our scope is international although over 96% of our members are in the US." Benefits include "several different critique groups: short stories, novels, articles, screenplays, poetry, etc. We also offer services such as copyediting, working out the numbers in planet building (give us the kind of planet you want and we'll tell you how far it is from the sun, etc.—or tell us what kind of sun you have and we'll tell you what your planet is like), brainstorming story, fragments or cultures or aliens, etc." Publishes *SF and Fantasy Workshop* (monthly), free via e-mail or may be downloaded from above website. Membership is also free in e-mail. See website.

SCIENCE FICTION WRITERS OF EARTH, P.O. Box 121293, Fort Worth TX 76121-1293. (817)451-8674. E-mail: sfwoe@flash.net. Website: www.flash.net/~sfwoe (includes contest rules, entry form, judge's report, contest results, list of writers who entered contest, interviews with the winners, reviews of the top three stories, short bios of the top 10 contestants, newsletter with articles of interest to contestants and writers in general). **Contact:** Gilbert Gordon Reis, SFWoE administrator. Estab. 1980. Number of Members: 150-200. Open to: Unpublished writers of science fiction and fantasy short stories. "We have writers in Europe, Canada, Australia and several other countries, but the majority are from the US. Writers compete in our annual contest. This allows the writer to find out where he/she stands in writing ability. Winners often receive requests for their story from publishers. Many winners have told us that they believe that placing in the top ten of our contest gives them recognition and has assisted in getting their first story published." Dues: One must submit a science fiction or fantasy short story to our annual contest each year to be a member. Cost is $5 for membership and first story. $2 for each additional ms. The nominating committee meets several times a year to select the top ten stories of the annual contest. Author Edward Bryant selects the winners from the top ten stories. Contest deadline is October 30 and the cash awards and results are mailed out on January 31 of the following year. The first place story is published by *Altair*, magazine of speculative fiction, or placed on the SFWoE website. Inquiries by SASE, e-mail (no contest submissions) or from the Internet OK.

SCIENCE-FICTION AND FANTASY WRITERS OF AMERICA, INC., % SFWA Executive Direcotr, P.O. Box 171, Unity ME 04988-0171. E-mail: execdir@sfwa.org. Website: www.sfwa.org/. **Contact:** Michael Capobianco, president. Executive Director: Sharon Lee. Estab. 1965. Number of Members: 1,400. Type of Memberships: Active, associate, affiliate, institutional, estate and junior. Open to: "Professional writers, editors, anthologists, artists in the science fiction/fantasy genres and allied professional individuals and institutions. Our membership is international; we currently have members throughout Europe, Australia, Central and South America, Canada and some in Asia." We produce a variety of journals for our members, annual membership directory and provide a grievance committee, publicity committee, circulating book plan and access to medical/life/disability insurance. We award the SFWA Nebula Awards each year for outstanding achievement in the genre at novel, novella, novelet and short story lengths." Quarterly *SFWA Bulletin* to members; nonmembers may subscribe at $15/4 issues within US/Canada; $18.50 overseas. Bimonthly *SFWA Forum* for active and associate members only. Annual *SFWA Membership Directory* for members; available to professional organizations for $60. Active membership requires professional sale in the US of at least 3 short stories or 1 full-length book. Affiliate membership is open to professionals affiliated with science fiction writing. Associate membership require at least 1 professional sale in the US or other professional sale in the US or other professional involvement in the field respectively. Dues are pro-rated quarterly; info available upon request. Business meetings are held during Annual Nebula Awards weekend and usually during the annual World SF Convention. Send SASE for information.

⟨N⟩ SHORT MYSTERY FICTION SOCIETY. E-mail: gmh222222@aol.com. **Contact:** G. Miki Hayden, president. Estab. 1995. Number of members: 350. "All fans and authors (even editors) welcome." Supports writers of short mystery fiction. "We sponsor the yearly Derringer Awards for best published short stories." Benefits include a daily e-mail digest; subscribe to shortmystery-subscribe@onelist.com. Free membership. Inquiries by e-mail.

SISTERS IN CRIME, Box 442124, Lawrence KS 66044-8933. (785)842-1325. E-mail: sistersincrime@juno.com. Website: www.sistersincrime.org. **Contact:** Beth Wasson, executive secretary. Estab. 1986. Number of Members: 3,200. The original purpose of this organization was to combat discrimination against women in the mystery field. Memberships are open to men as well as women, as long as they are committed to the organization and its goals. Offers membership assistance in networking and publicity.

SOCIETY OF MIDLAND AUTHORS, P.O. Box 10419, Fort Dearborn Station, Chicago IL 60610. Website: www.midlandauthors.com. **Contact:** Richard Lindberg, president. Estab. 1915. Number of Members: 260. Type of memberships: Regular, published authors and performed playwrights; Associate, librarians, editors, etc., others involved in publishing. Open to: Residents or natives of 12 midland states: Illinois, Iowa, Indiana, Michigan, Wisconsin, Nebraska, S. Dakota, N. Dakota, Ohio, Kansas, Missouri and Minnesota. Benefits include newsletter, listing in directory. Sponsors annual awards in 7 categories, with upwards of $300 prizes. Awards dinner in May at Cliff Dwellers Club, 200 S. Michigan Ave., Chicago IL 60603. Publishes newsletter several times/year. Dues: $25/year. Holds "5 program meetings/year, open to public at Cliff Dwellers Club, Chicago, featuring writers, editors, etc. on bookwriting subjects, theatrical subjects etc." Brochures are available for SASE.

WESTERN WRITERS OF AMERICA, Office of the Secretary Treasurer, 1012 Fair St., Franklin TN 37064-2718. Phone/fax: (615)791-1444. E-mail: tncrutch@aol.com. Website: www.westernwriters.org (includes membership information, authors' profiles and magazine articles). **Contact:** James A. Crutchfield, secretary/treasurer. Estab. 1953. Number of Members: 600. Type of Membership: Active, associate, patron. Open to: Professional, published writers who have multiple publications of fiction or nonfiction (usually at least three) about the West. Associate membership open to those with one book, a lesser number of short stories or publications or participation in the field such as editors, agents, reviewers, librarians, television producers, directors (dealing with the West). Patron memberships open to corporations, organizations and individuals with an interest in the West. Scope is international. Benefits: "By way of publications and conventions, members are kept abreast of developments in the field of Western literature and the publishing field, marketing requirements, income tax problems, copyright law, research facilities and techniques, and new publications. At conventions members have the opportunity for one-on-one conferences with editors, publishers and agents." Sponsors an annual four-day conference during fourth week of June featuring panels, lectures and seminars on publishing, writing and research. Includes the Spur Awards to honor authors of the best Western literature of the previous year. Publishes *Roundup Magazine* (6 times/year) for members. Available to nonmembers for $30. Publishes membership directory. Dues: $75 for active membership or associate membership, $250 for patron. For information on Spur Awards, send SASE. Inquiries by fax and e-mail OK.

☑ WILLAMETTE WRITERS, 9045 SW Barbur Blvd., Suite 5A, Portland OR 97219. (503)452-1592. Fax: (503)452-0372. E-mail: wilwrite@teleport.com. Website: www.willamettewriters.com. **Contact:** Bill Johnson, office manager. Estab. 1965. Number of members: 700. "Willamette Writers is a nonprofit, tax exempt corporation staffed by volunteers. Membership is open to both published and aspiring writers. WW provides support, encouragement and interaction for all genres of writers." Open to national membership, but serves primarily the Pacific Northwest. Benefits include a writers' referral service, critique groups, membership discounts, youth programs (4th-12th grades), monthly meetings with guest authors, annual writing contest, community projects, library and research services, as well as networking with other writing groups, office with writing reference and screenplay library. Sponsors annual conference held the second weekend in August; quarterly workshops; annual Kay Snow Writing Contest; and the Distinguished Northwest Writer Award. Publishes *The Willamette Writer* monthly: a 12-page newsletter for members and complimentary subscriptions. Information consists of features, how-to's, mechanics of writing, profile of featured monthly speaker, markets, workshops, conferences and benefits available to writers. Dues: $36/year; includes subscription to newsletter. Meets first Tuesday of each month; board meeting held last Tuesday of each month. Inquiries by SASE, fax and e-mail OK.

N. WORD & PEN CHRISTIAN WRITERS CLUB, American Christian Writers (chapter #3006), 1963 Indian Point Rd., Oshkosh WI 54901-1371. (920)235-0664. E-mail: word_pen@focol.org. Website: www.focol. org/~word_pen. **Contact:** Beth A. Ziarnik, president. Estab. 1985. Number of members: 14. Types of membership: Professional, associate. "We are a nondenominational organization of writers who are Christian and write for Christian and/or secular markets. Our only other requirement is that the manuscripts submitted to our critique groups be free of indecent language and explicit sex, and not hinder the message of Christianity. Our purpose is to help one another develop our God-given abilities and achieve publication." Benefits include: "Monthly meetings which provide education (speakers, workshops, etc.), market and conference news, open forum (to get writing questions answered), accountability (report writing progress including submissions and sales). Monthly critique groups: one for short manuscripts, one for book length manuscripts. We also maintain a club library of books, videos, and cassette tapes on writing. Affiliation with ACW also gives members discounts on writing conferences, courses, and 'The Christian Communicator' " Dues: $20/year. Inquiries by SASE, e-mail, phone, website.

THE WRITER'S CENTER, 4508 Walsh St., Bethesda MD 20815-6006. (301)654-8664. Fax: (301)654-8667. E-mail: postmaster@writer.org. Website: www.writer.org. Executive Director: Jane Fox. **Contact:** Sunil Freeman, assistant director. Estab. 1977. Number of Members: 2,800. Open to: Anyone interested in writing. Scope is regional DC, Maryland, Virginia, West Virginia, Pennsylvania. Benefits include newsletter, discounts in bookstore, workshops, public events, subscriptions to *Poet Lore*, use of equipment and annual small press book fair. Center offers workshops, reading series, equipment, newsletter and limited workspace. Sponsors workshops, conferences, award for narrative poem. Publishes *Writer's Carousel*, bimonthly. Nonmembers can pick it up at the Center. Dues: $40/year. Fees vary with service, see publications. Brochures are available for SASE. Inquiries by e-mail and fax OK.

WRITERS' FEDERATION OF NOVA SCOTIA, 1113 Marginal Rd., Halifax, Nova Scotia B3H 4P7 Canada. (902)423-8116. E-mail: talk@writers.ns.ca. Website: www.writers.ns.ca. **Contact:** Jane Buss, executive director. Estab. 1976. Number of Members: 600. Types of Memberships: General membership, student membership, Nova Scotia Writers' Council membership (professional), Honorary Life Membership. Open to anyone who writes. Provincial scope, with a few members living elsewhere in the country or the world. Benefits include advocacy of all kinds for writers, plus such regular programs as workshops and publications, including directories and a newsletter. Sponsors workshops, 3 book awards, one annual competition for unpublished manuscripts in various categories; a writers-in-the-schools program, a manuscript reading service, reduced photocopying rates. Publishes *Eastword*, 6 issues annually, available by subscription for $35 (Canadian) to nonmembers. Dues: $35/ year (Canadian). Holds an annual general meeting, several board meetings annually, two awards ceremonies. Send SASE or e-mail for information.

WRITERS GUILD OF ALBERTA, Percy Page Centre, 11759 Groat Rd., 3rd Floor, Edmonton, Alberta T5M 3K6 Canada. (780)422-8174. Fax: (780)422-2663. E-mail: wga@oanet.com. Website: www.writersguild.ab. ca. **Contact:** Miki Andrejevic, executive director. Estab. 1980. Number of Members: 750. Membership open to current and past residents of Alberta. Regional (provincial) scope. Benefits include discounts on programs offered; manuscript evaluation service available; bimonthly newsletter; contacts; info on workshops, retreats, readings, etc. Sponsors workshops 2 times/year, retreats 3 times/year, annual conference, annual book awards program (Alberta writers only). Publishes *WestWord* 6 times/year; available for $60/year (Canadian) to nonmembers. Dues: $60/year for regular membership; $20/year senior/students/limited income; $100/year donating membership— charitable receipt issued (Canadian funds). Organized monthly meetings. Send SASE for information.

WRITERS INFORMATION NETWORK, P.O. Box 11337, Bainbridge Island WA 98110. (206)842-9103. Fax: (206)842-0536. E-mail: WritersInfoNetwork@juno.com. Websites: www.bluejaypub.com/win or www.ecpa. org/win. **Contact:** Elaine Wright Colvin, director. Estab. 1980. Number of members: 1,000. Open to: All interested in writing for religious publications/publishers. Scope is national and several foreign countries. Benefits include bimonthly magazine, *The WIN Informer*, market news, advocacy/grievance procedures, professional advice, writers conferences, press cards, author referral, free consultation. Sponsors workshops, conferences throughout the country each year—mailing list and advertised in *The WIN Informer* magazine. Dues: $33 US; $40 foreign/year in US equivalent funds. Holds meetings throughout the Pacific Northwest. Brochures are available for SASE. Inquiries by fax and e-mail OK.

☑ WRITERS' LEAGUE OF TEXAS, (formerly Austin Writer's League), Writers' League of Texas, 1501 W. Fifth, E-2, Austin TX 78703. (512)499-8914. Fax: (512)499-0441. E-mail: awl@writersleague.org. Website: www.writerleague.org. **Contact:** Jim Bob McMillan, executive director. Estab. 1981. Number of Members: 1,600. Types of Memberships: Regular, student/senior citizen, family. Monthly meetings and use of resource center/library is open to the public. "Membership includes both aspiring and professional writers, all ages and all ethnic groups." Job bank is also open to the public. Public also has access to technical assistance. Partial and full scholarships offered for some programs. Of 1,600 members, 800 reside in Austin. Remaining 800 live all over the US and in other countries. Benefits include monthly newsletter, monthly meetings, study groups, resource center/library-checkout privileges, discounts on workshops, seminars, classes, job bank, discounts on books and tapes, participation in awards programs, technical/marketing assistance, copyright forms and information, Writers Helping Writers (mentoring program). Center has 5 rooms plus 2 offices and storage area. Public space includes reception and job bank area; conference/classroom; library; and copy/mail room. Library includes 1,400 titles. Sponsors fall and spring workshops, weekend seminars, informal classes, sponsorships for special events such as readings, production of original plays, media conferences, creative writing programs for children and youth; Violet Crown Book Awards, newsletter writing awards, Young Texas Writers awards, contests for various anthologies. Publishes *Austin Writer* (monthly newsletter), sponsors with Texas Commission on the Arts Texas Literary Touring Program. Administers literature subgranting program for Texas Commission on the Arts. Membership/subscription: $50, $70 family membership. Monthly meetings. Study groups set their own regular meeting schedules. Send SASE for information.

THE WRITERS ROOM, INC., 10 Astor Place, 6th Floor, New York NY 10003-6935. (212)254-6995. Fax: (212)533-6059. E-mail: writersroom@writersroom.org. Website: www.writersroom.org (includes organization's background information and downloadable application). **Contact:** Donna Brodie, executive director. Estab. 1978. Number of Members: 200 fulltime and 40 part-time. Founded in 1978 to provide a "home away from home" for any writer who needs a place to work. Description: Large room with 35 desks separated by partitions, space for 300 writers each quarter; open 24 hours a day year-yound; kitchen, lounge and bathrooms, storage for files and laptops, small reference library; monthly readings. Dues: $110-185 per quarter year, $50 application fee, $60 key deposit. Send SASE for application and background information. Inquiries by SASE, e-mail and fax OK or visit website.

☑ THE WRITERS' WORKSHOP, 387 Beaucatcher Rd., Asheville NC 28805. Phone/fax: (828)254-8111. E-mail: writrwkshp@aol.com. Website: www.writer.org/asheville. **Contact:** Karen Ackerson, executive director. Estab. 1984. Number of Members: 1,250. Types of Memberships: Student/low income $25; family/organization $65; individual $35. Open to all writers. Scope is national and international. Benefits include discounts on workshops, quarterly newsletter, critiquing services through the mail. Center offers reading room, assistance with editing your work. Publishes a newsletter; also available to nonmembers ($20). Offers workshops year-round in NC and the South; 2 retreats a year, 4 readings with nationally awarded authors. Contests and classes for children and teens as well. Advisory board includes Kurt Vonnegut, E.L. Doctorow, Peter Matthiessen, Reynolds Price and John Le Carré. Also sponsors international contests in fiction, memoirs, poetry and creative nonfiction. Brochures are available for SASE.

Publications of Interest

This section features listings for magazines and newsletters that focus on writing or the publishing industry. While many of these are not markets for fiction, they do offer articles, marketing advice or other information valuable to the fiction writer. Several magazines in this section offer actual market listings while others feature reviews of books in the field and news on the industry.

The timeliness factor is a primary reason most writers read periodicals. Changes in publishing happen very quickly and magazines can help you keep up with the latest news. Some magazines listed here, including *Writer's Digest*, cover the entire field of writing, while others such as *The Mystery Review*, *Locus* (science fiction), *Horn Book* (children's) and *Romantic Times* focus on a particular type of writing. You'll also find publications which focus on particular segments of the publishing industry.

Information on some publications for writers can be found in the introductions to other sections in this book. In addition, many of the literary and commercial magazines for writers listed in the markets sections are helpful to the fiction writer. Keep an eye on the newsstand and library shelves for others and let us know if you've found a publication particularly useful.

☑ **BOOK, The Magazine for the Reading Life**, West Egg Communications LLC, 4645 N. Rockwell St., Chicago IL 60625. (800)317-BOOK. Website: www.bookmagazine.com. Editor: Jerome Kramer. **Contact:** Adam Langer. Estab. 1998. Bimonthly. Magazine covering books and reading. Includes book excerpts, essays, interview/profile pieces. Subscription price: $20 US/year (6 issues); $24 Canadian/year; $38 international/year.

🍁 ☑ **CANADIAN WRITER'S JOURNAL**, Box 5180, New Liskeard, Ontario P0J 1P0 Canada. (705)647-5424. Fax: (705)647-8366. E-mail: cwj@ntl.sympatico.ca. Website: http://go.to/cwj. **Contact:** Deborah Ranchuk, editor. Bimonthly. "Mainly short how-to and motivational articles related to all types of writing and of interest to both new and established writers. Fiction is published in limited quantities, and needs are fully supplied through an semiannual short fiction competition." SASE with Canadian postage or IRC for contest rules or visit website. Lists markets for fiction. Sample copies available for $8 ($C for Canadian orders, $US for US orders). Subscription price: $35 US/year ; $67.50 US/2 years; $37.45 Canadian/year; $72.23 Canadian/2 years.

CHILDREN'S BOOK INSIDER, The Newsletter for Children's Writers, 901 Columbia Rd., Fort Collins CO 80525. (800)807-1916. E-mail: mail@write4kids.com. Website: www.write4kids.com. **Contact:** Laura Backes, editor/publisher. Monthly. "Publication is devoted solely to children's book writers and illustrators. 'At Presstime' section gives current market information each month for fiction, nonfiction and illustration submissions to publishers. Other articles include writing and illustration tips for fiction and nonfiction, interviews with published authors and illustrators, features on alternative publishing methods (self-publishing, co-op publishing, etc.), how to submit work to publishers, industry trends. Also publishes books and writing tools for both beginning and experienced children's book writers." E-mail cbi@sendfree.com for free online catalog. Single copy price: $3.25. Subscription price: $29.95/year (US); $34.95/year (Canadian); $42.95 everywhere else. Electronic Edition: $26.95 US (worldwide).

THE HORN BOOK MAGAZINE, The Horn Book, Inc., 56 Roland St., Suite 200, Boston MA 02129. (617)628-0225. Fax: (617)628-0882. E-mail: magazine@hbook.com. Website: www.hbook.com. **Contact:** Roger Sutton, editor-in-chief. Estab. 1924. Bimonthly. Magazine covering children's literature for librarians, booksellers, professors, teachers and students of children's literature. Includes interview/profile pieces on children's book authors and illustrators as well as topics of interest to the children's book world. Sampoly copy available on website (includes original content not found in print edition and writer's guidelines).

☑ **LAMBDA BOOK REPORT**, Lambda Literary Foundation, P.O. Box 73910, Washington DC 20056. (202)682-0952. Fax: (202)682-0955. E-mail: lbreditor@lambdalit.org. **Contact:** Greg Herren, senior editor. Monthly. "This review journal of contemporary gay and lesbian literature appeals to both readers and writers.

Fiction queries published regularly." Lists fiction markets. Reviews novels, short story collections, poetry and nonfiction. Single copy price is $4.95/US. Subscriptions: $29.95/year (US); international rate: $58.95 (US $); Canada/Mexico: $46.95/year (US $).

LOCUS, The Newspaper of the Science Fiction Field, P.O. Box 13305, Oakland CA 94661. (510)339-9198. Fax: (510)339-8144. E-mail: locus@locusmag.com. Website: www.locusmag.com. **Contact:** Charles N. Brown, editor. Monthly. "Professional newsletter of science fiction, fantasy and horror; has news, interviews with authors, book reviews, column on electronic publishing, forthcoming books listings, monthly books-received listings, etc." Lists markets for fiction. Reviews novels or short story collections. Sample copies available. Single copy price: $6.95. Subscriptions: $46/year (2nd class mail) for US; $52 (US)/year (2nd class) for Canada; $52 (US)/year (sea mail) for overseas.

THE MYSTERY REVIEW, A Quarterly Publication for Mystery Readers, P.O. Box 233, Colborne, Ontario K0K 1S0 Canada. (613)475-4440. Fax: (613)475-3400. E-mail: mystrev@reach.net. Website: www.themysteryreview.com. **Contact:** Barbara Davey, editor. Quarterly. "Book reviews, information on new releases, interviews with authors and other people involved in mystery, 'real life' mysteries, out-of-print mysteries, mystery/suspense films, word games and puzzles with a mystery theme." Reviews mystery/suspense novels and short story collections. Single copy price is $6.95 Canadian in Canada/$6.95 US in the United States. Subscriptions: $27/year Canadian (includes GST) in Canada; $25/year US in the US and $32/year US elsewhere (US address for subscriptions: P.O. Box 488, Wellesley Island NY 13640-0488).

NEW WRITER'S MAGAZINE, P.O. Box 5976, Sarasota FL 34277. (941)953-7903. E-mail: newriters@aol.com. Website: www.newriters.com. **Contact:** George J. Haborak, editor. Bimonthly. *"New Writer's Magazine* is a publication for aspiring writers. It features 'how-to' articles, news and interviews with published and recently-published authors. Will use fiction that has a tie-in with the world of the writer." Lists markets for fiction. Reviews novels and short story collections. Send #10 SASE for guidelines. Sample copies available; single copy price is $3. Subscriptions: $15/year, $25/2 years. Canadian $20 (US funds). International $35/year (US funds).

OHIO WRITER, Poets' and Writers' League of Greater Cleveland, P.O. Box 91801, Cleveland OH 44101. (216)421-0403. **Contact:** Gail and Stephen Bellamy, editor. Bimonthly. "Interviews with Ohio writers of fiction, nonfiction and poetry; current fiction markets in Ohio." Reviews novels and short story collections. Sample copies available for $2.50. Subscriptions: $15/year; $40/3 years; $20/year institutional rate.

POETS & WRITERS MAGAZINE, 72 Spring St., New York NY 10012. Fax: (212)226-3963. E-mail: editor@pw.org. Website: www.pw.org. **Contact:** Therese Eiben, editor. Bimonthly. Publishes articles about poetry and fiction writing. "Includes profiles of noted authors and publishing professionals, practical how-to articles, a comprehensive listing of grants and awards for writers and special sections on subjects ranging from small presses to writers conferences." Lists markets for fiction. Sample copies available; single copy price is $7.95. Subscriptions: $19.95/year; $38/2 years. Subscriptions ordered through *Poets & Writers Magazine*, P.O. Box 543, Mount Morris IL 61054; through website or (815)734-1123.

PUBLISHERS WEEKLY. Website: www.publishersweekly.com. **Contact:** Nora Rawlinson, editor-in-chief. Weekly. International news magazine of book publishing and bookselling. "Industry professionals depend on *Publishers Weekly* for in-depth interviews with top authors, publishing industry news, bestseller lists, and early reviews of adult and children's books." Subscriptions: $189/year (US); $239/year US (Canada); $319/year US (all other countries). **For subscriptions only:** P.O. Box 16178, North Hollywood CA 91615-6178. (800)278-2991 (within the US), (818)487-4557 (outside the US). Fax: (818)487-4550.

ROMANCE WRITERS REPORT, Romance Writers of America, 3707 F.M. 1960 W., Suite 555, Houston TX 77068. (281)440-6885. Fax: (281)440-7510. E-mail: info@rwanational.com. **Contact:** Charis Calhoon, editor. Monthly professional journal of Romance Writers of America, Inc. Subscriptions included as part of RWA membership. Includes articles, essays and tips written by established writers, contest and conference information and articles by romance editors. Membership dues: $75/year plus $25 processing fee for new applicants and $15 postage for journal.

ROMANTIC TIMES MAGAZINE, 55 Bergen St., Brooklyn NY 11201. (718)237-1097. Website: www.romantictimes.com. Monthly. Features reviews, news and interviews of interest to the romance reader. Each issue also has special features such as photo tours of authors' houses, interviews with male cover models and articles on romantic pursuits (teas, salons, etc.) and mysteries. Subscriptions: $43/year in US; $66/year in Canada.

☑ **SCIENCE FICTION CHRONICLE**, P.O. Box 2988, Rockford VA 24143. (540)763-2925. Website: www. dnapublications.com/sfc. **Contact:** Warren Lapine, publisher. Monthly. Publishes news, interviews, reviews, poems, nothing about UFOs. "Newsmagazine for professional writers, editors, readers of SF, fantasy, horror." Lists markets for fiction "updated every 6 months." Reviews novels, small press publications, audiotapes and short story collections. Subscriptions: $45 US; $56 Canada; $125 overseas. **For subscriptions:** DNA Publications, Inc., P.O. Box 2988, Radford VA 24143-2988. *Note: As with other listings in this section, this is not a "market"—Do not send mss or artwork.*

SMALL PRESS REVIEW/SMALL MAGAZINE REVIEW, Dustbooks, P.O. Box 100, Paradise CA 95967. (530)877-6110. E-mail: dustbooks@dcsi.net. Website: www.dustbooks.com. **Contact:** Len Fulton, editor. Bimonthly. "Publishes news and reviews about small publishers, books and magazines." Lists markets for fiction and poetry. Reviews novels, short story and poetry collections. Subscription price: $25/year for individuals, $31/ year for institutions.

☑ **WRITER'S CAROUSEL**, The Writer's Center, 4508 Walsh St., Bethesda MD 20815-6006. (301)654-8664. E-mail: postmaster@writers.org. Website: www.writer.org. **Contact:** Allan Lefcowitz, editor. Bimonthly. "*Writer's Carousel* publishes book reviews and articles about writing and the writing scene." Lists fiction markets. Reviews novels and short story collections. Sample copies available. Subscriptions: $30 Writer's Center Membership; also available online to members.

WRITER'S DIGEST, 1507 Dana Ave., Cincinnati OH 45207. (513)531-2222. **Contact:** Melanie Rigney, editor. Monthly. "*Writer's Digest* is a magazine of techniques and markets. We *inspire* the writer to write, *instruct* him or her on how to improve that work, and *direct* him or her toward appropriate markets." Lists markets for fiction, nonfiction, poetry. Single copy price: $5. Subscription price: $19.96.

WRITER'S DIGEST BOOKS–MARKET BOOKS, 1507 Dana Ave., Cincinnati OH 45207. (513)531-2690. Annual. In addition to *Novel & Short Story Writer's Market*, Writer's Digest Books also publishes *Writer's Market*, *Poet's Market*, *Children's Writer's and Illustrator's Market* and the *Guide to Literary Agents*. All include articles and listings of interest to writers. All are available at bookstores, libraries or through the publisher. (Request catalog.)

WRITER'S YEARBOOK, 1507 Dana Ave., Cincinnati OH 45207. (513)531-2690. Annual. "A collection of the best writing *about* writing, with an exclusive survey of the year's 100 top markets for article-length nonfiction." Single copy price: $6.25.

Websites of Interest

The Internet is second only to the imagination as the fiction writer's greatest resource. Since websites appear and disappear from existence almost daily, it's impossible to list everything here. Below are some perennial favorites, still active when this edition of *Novel & Short Story Writer's Market* went to press. Visit these websites to refresh your dedication, discover new markets or stumble across a new technique.

ORGANIZATIONS

Canadian Authors Association: www.islandnet.com/~caa/national.html.

Horror Writers of America: www.horror.org.

Mystery Writers of America: www.mysterywriters.org.

National Writers Union: www.nwu.org.

PEN American Center: www.pen.org.

Romance Writers of America: www.rwanational.org.

Science Fiction and Fantasy Writers of America: www.sfwa.org.

Sisters in Crime: www.sistersincrime.org.

Society of Children's Book Writers and Illustrators: www.scbwi.org.

The Writers Guild of America: www.wga.org.

MARKET LISTINGS

Spicy Green Iguana: www.spicygreeniguana.com.

Writer's Guidelines Database: http://mav.net/guidelines.

Writer's Market: www.writersmarket.com.

The Writer's Place: www.awoc.com.

Writer's Resource: www.writersresource.net.

Writer's Write: www.writerswrite.com.

RESOURCES

Bookwire: www.bookwire.com.

Children's Literature Web Guide: www.ucalgary.ca/~dkbrown/index.html.

Children's Writing Resource Center: www.write4kids.com.

Elements of Style, by William Strunk, Jr.: www.bartleby.com/141/index.html.

Exquisite Corpse—A Journal of Letters and Life: www.corpse.org.

John Hewitt's Writer's Resource Center: www.poewar.com.

Novel Advice: www.noveladvice.com.

Overbooked Genre Fiction: www.overbooked.org/genre.html.

Robin's Nest: www.robinsnest.com.

Romance Central: http://romance-central.com.

RoseDog.com: www.rosedog.com.

Writer's Digest: www.writersdigest.com.

Writer's Toolbox: www.writerstoolbox.com.

Zuzu's Petals Literary Resource: www.zuzu.com.

BUSINESS OF WRITING

Canadian Postal Service: www.canadapost.com.
IRS: www.irs.ustreaas.gov/basic/cover.html.
Publishing Law Center: www.publaw.com.
US Postal Service: www.usps.gov.

◪ Canadian Writers Take Note

While much of the information contained in this section applies to all writers, here are some specifics of interest to Canadian writers:

Postage: When sending an SASE from Canada, you will need an International Reply Coupon. Also be aware, a GST tax is required on postage in Canada and for mail with postage under $5 going to destinations outside the country. Since Canadian postage rates are voted on in January of each year (after we go to press), contact a Canada Post Corporation Customer Service Division, located in most cities in Canada, for the most current rates.

Copyright: For information on copyrighting your work and to obtain forms, write Copyright and Industrial Design, Phase One, Place du Portage, 50 Victoria St., Hull, Quebec K1A 0C9 or call (819)997-1936. Website: www.cipo.gc.ca.

The public lending right: The Public Lending Right Commission has established that eligible Canadian authors are entitled to payments when a book is available through a library. Payments are determined by a sampling of the holdings of a representative number of libraries. To find out more about the program and to learn if you are eligible, write to the Public Lending Right Commission at 350 Albert St., P.O. Box 1047, Ottawa, Ontario K1P 5V8 or call (613)566-4378 for information. Website: www.plr-dpp.ca/. The Commission, which is part of The Canada Council, produces a helpful pamphlet, *How the PLR System Works,* on the program.

Grants available to Canadian writers: Most province art councils or departments of culture provide grants to resident writers. Some of these, as well as contests for Canadian writers, are listed in our Contests and Awards section. For national programs, contact The Canada Council, Writing and Publishing Section, P.O. Box 1047, Ottawa, Ontario K1P 5V8 or call (613)566-4338 for information. Fax: (613)566-4390. Website: www.canadacouncil.ca.

For more information: See the Organizations and Resources section of *Novel & Short Story Writer's Market* for listings of writers' organizations in Canada. Also contact The Writer's Union of Canada, 40 Wellington St. E, 3rd Floor, Toronto, Ontario M5E 1C7; call them at (416)703-8982 or fax them at (416)504-7656. E-mail: twuc@the-wire.com. Website: www.writersunion.ca. This organization provides a wealth of information (as well as strong support) for Canadian writers, including specialized publications on publishing contracts; contract negotiations; the author/editor relationship; author awards, competitions and grants; agents; taxes for writers, libel issues and access to archives in Canada.

Printing & Production Terms Defined

In most of the magazine listings in this book you will find a brief physical description of each publication. This material usually includes the number of pages, type of paper, type of binding and whether or not the magazine uses photographs or illustrations.

Although it is important to look at a copy of the magazine to which you are submitting, these descriptions can give you a general idea of what the publication looks like. This material can provide you with a feel for the magazine's financial resources and prestige. Do not, however, rule out small, simply produced publications as these may be the most receptive to new writers. Watch for publications that have increased their page count or improved their production from year to year. This is a sign the publication is doing well and may be accepting more fiction.

You will notice a wide variety of printing terms used within these descriptions. We explain here some of the more common terms used in our listing descriptions. We do not include explanations of terms such as Mohawk and Karma which are brand names and refer to the paper manufacturer.

PAPER

acid-free: Paper that has a low or no acid content. This type of paper resists deterioration from exposure to the elements. More expensive than many other types of paper, publications done on acid-free paper can last a long time.

bond: Bond paper is often used for stationery and is more transparent than text paper. It can be made of either sulphite (wood) or cotton fiber. Some bonds have a mixture of both wood and cotton (such as "25 percent cotton" paper). This is the type of paper most often used in photocopying or as standard typing paper.

coated/uncoated stock: Coated and uncoated are terms usually used when referring to book or text paper. More opaque than bond, it is the paper most used for offset printing. As the name implies, uncoated paper has no coating. Coated paper is coated with a layer of clay, varnish or other chemicals. It comes in various sheens and surfaces depending on the type of coating, but the most common are dull, matte and gloss.

cover stock: Cover stock is heavier book or text paper used to cover a publication. It comes in a variety of colors and textures and can be coated on one or both sides.

CS1/CS2: Most often used when referring to cover stock, CS1 means paper that is coated only on one side; CS2 is paper coated on both sides.

newsprint: Inexpensive absorbent pulp wood paper often used in newspapers and tabloids.

text: Text paper is similar to book paper (a smooth paper used in offset printing), but it has been given some texture by using rollers or other methods to apply a pattern to the paper.

vellum: Vellum is a text paper that is fairly porous and soft.

Some notes about paper weight and thickness: Often you will see paper thickness described in terms of pounds such as 80 lb. or 60 lb. paper. The weight is determined by figuring how many pounds in a ream of a particular paper (a ream is 500 sheets). This can be confusing, however, because this figure is based on a standard sheet size and standard sheet sizes vary depending on the type of paper used. This information is most helpful when comparing papers of the same type. For example, 80 lb. book paper versus 60 lb. book paper. Since the size of the paper is the same it would follow that 80 lb. paper is the thicker, heavier paper.

Some paper, especially cover stock, is described by the actual thickness of the paper. This is expressed in a system of points. Typical paper thicknesses range from 8 points to 14 points thick.

PRINTING

letterpress: Letterpress printing is printing that uses a raised surface such as type. The type is inked and then pressed against the paper. Unlike offset printing, only a limited number of impressions can be made, as the surface of the type can wear down.

offset: Offset is a printing method in which ink is transferred from an image-bearing plate to a "blanket" and from the blanket to the paper.

sheet-fed offset: Offset printing in which the paper is fed one piece at a time.

web offset: Offset printing in which a roll of paper is printed and then cut apart to make individual sheets.

There are many other printing methods but these are the ones most commonly referred to in our listings.

BINDING

case binding: In case binding, signatures (groups of pages) are stitched together with thread rather than glued together. The stitched pages are then trimmed on three sides and glued into a hardcover or board "case" or cover. Most hardcover books and thicker magazines are done this way.

comb binding: A comb is a plastic spine used to hold pages together with bent tabs that are fed through punched holes in the edge of the paper.

perfect binding: Used for paperback books and heavier magazines, perfect binding involves gathering signatures (groups of pages) into a stack, trimming off the folds so the edge is flat and gluing a cover to that edge.

saddle stitched: Publications in which the pages are stitched together using metal staples. This fairly inexpensive type of binding is usually used with books or magazines that are under 80 pages.

Smythe-sewn: Binding in which the pages are sewn together with thread. Smythe is the name of the most common machine used for this purpose.

spiral binding: A wire spiral that is wound through holes punched in pages is a spiral bind. This is the binding used in spiral notebooks.

Glossary

Advance. Payment by a publisher to an author prior to the publication of a book, to be deducted from the author's future royalties.

All rights. The rights contracted to a publisher permitting a manuscript's use anywhere and in any form, including movie and book club sales, without additional payment to the writer.

Anthology. A collection of selected writings by various authors.

Auction. Publishers sometimes bid against each other for the acquisition of a manuscript that has excellent sales prospects.

Backlist. A publisher's books not published during the current season but still in print.

Book producer/packager. An organization that may develop a book for a publisher based upon the publisher's idea or may plan all elements of a book, from its initial concept to writing and marketing strategies, and then sell the package to a book publisher and/or movie producer.

Cliffhanger. Fictional event in which the reader is left in suspense at the end of a chapter or episode, so that interest in the story's outcome will be sustained.

Clip. Sample, usually from a newspaper or magazine, of a writer's published work.

Cloak-and-dagger. A melodramatic, romantic type of fiction dealing with espionage and intrigue.

Commercial. Publishers whose concern is salability, profit and success with a large readership.

Contemporary. Material dealing with popular current trends, themes or topics.

Contributor's copy. Copy of an issue of a magazine or published book sent to an author whose work is included.

Copublishing. An arrangement in which the author and publisher share costs and profits.

Copyediting. Editing a manuscript for writing style, grammar, punctuation and factual accuracy.

Copyright. The legal right to exclusive publication, sale or distribution of a literary work.

Cover letter. A brief letter sent with a complete manuscript submitted to an editor.

"Cozy" (or "teacup") mystery. Mystery usually set in a small British town, in a bygone era, featuring a somewhat genteel, intellectual protagonist.

Cyberpunk. Type of science fiction, usually concerned with computer networks and human-computer combinations, involving young, sophisticated protagonists.

E-mail. Mail that has been sent electronically using a computer and modem.

E-zine. A magazine that is published electronically, especially on the Internet.

Electronic submission. A submission of material by modem or on computer disk.

Experimental fiction. Fiction that is innovative in subject matter and style; avant-garde, non-formulaic, usually literary material.

Exposition. The portion of the storyline, usually the beginning, where background information about character and setting is related.

Fair use. A provision in the copyright law that says short passages from copyrighted material may be used without infringing on the owner's rights.

Fanzine. A noncommercial, small-circulation magazine usually dealing with fantasy, horror or science-fiction literature and art.

First North American serial rights. The right to publish material in a periodical before it appears in book form, for the first time, in the United States or Canada.

Galleys. The first typeset version of a manuscript that has not yet been divided into pages.

Genre. A formulaic type of fiction such as romance, western or horror.

Gothic. A genre in which the central character is usually a beautiful young woman and the setting an old mansion or castle, involving a handsome hero and real danger, either natural or supernatural.

Graphic novel. An adaptation of a novel into a long comic strip or heavily illustrated story of 40 pages or more, produced in paperback.

Hard-boiled detective novel. Mystery novel featuring a private eye or police detective as the protagonist; usually involves a murder. The emphasis is on the details of the crime.

Horror. A genre stressing fear, death and other aspects of the macabre.

Imprint. Name applied to a publisher's specific line (e.g. Owl, an imprint of Henry Holt).

Interactive fiction. Fiction in book or computer-software format where the reader determines the path the story will take by choosing from several alternatives at the end of each chapter or episode.

International Reply Coupon (IRC). A form purchased at a post office and enclosed with a letter or manuscript to a international publisher, to cover return postage costs.

Juvenile. Fiction intended for children 2-12.

Libel. Written or printed words that defame, malign or damagingly misrepresent a living person.

Literary. The general category of serious, non-formulaic, intelligent fiction, sometimes experimental, that most frequently appears in little magazines.

Literary agent. A person who acts for an author in finding a publisher or arranging contract terms on a literary project.

Mainstream. Traditionally written fiction on subjects or trends that transcend experimental or genre fiction categories.

Malice domestic novel. A traditional mystery novel that is not hard-boiled; emphasis is on the solution. Suspects and victims know one another.

Manuscript. The author's unpublished copy of a work, usually typewritten, used as the basis for typesetting.

Mass market paperback. Softcover book on a popular subject, usually around 4×7, directed to a general audience and sold in drugstores and groceries as well as in bookstores.

Ms(s). Abbreviation for manuscript(s).

Multiple submission. Submission of more than one short story at a time to the same editor. Do not make a multiple submission unless requested.

Narration. The account of events in a story's plot as related by the speaker or the voice of the author.

Narrator. The person who tells the story, either someone involved in the action or the voice of the writer.

New Age. A term including categories such as astrology, psychic phenomena, spiritual healing, UFOs, mysticism and other aspects of the occult.

Nom de plume. French for "pen name"; a pseudonym.

Novella (also novelette). A short novel or long story, approximately 7,000-15,000 words.

#10 envelope. $4 \times 9\frac{1}{2}$ envelope, used for queries and other business letters.

Offprint. Copy of a story taken from a magazine before it is bound.

One-time rights. Permission to publish a story in periodical or book form one time only.

Outline. A summary of a book's contents, often in the form of chapter headings with a few sentences outlining the action of the story under each one; sometimes part of a book proposal.

Payment on acceptance. Payment from the magazine or publishing house as soon as the decision to print a manuscript is made.

Payment on publication. Payment from the publisher after a manuscript is printed.

Pen name. A pseudonym used to conceal a writer's real name.

Periodical. A magazine or journal published at regular intervals.

Plot. The carefully devised series of events through which the characters progress in a work of fiction.

Proofreading. Close reading and correction of a manuscript's typographical errors.

Proofs. A typeset version of a manuscript used for correcting errors and making changes, often a photocopy of the galleys.

Proposal. An offer to write a specific work, usually consisting of an outline of the work and one or two completed chapters.

Protagonist. The principal or leading character in a literary work.

Public domain. Material that either was never copyrighted or whose copyright term has expired.

Pulp magazine. A periodical printed on inexpensive paper, usually containing lurid, sensational stories or articles.

Query. A letter written to an editor to elicit interest in a story the writer wants to submit.

Reader. A person hired by a publisher to read unsolicited manuscripts.

Reading fee. An arbitrary amount of money charged by some agents and publishers to read a submitted manuscript.

Regency romance. A genre romance, usually set in England between 1811-1820.

Remainders. Leftover copies of an out-of-print book, sold by the publisher at a reduced price.

Reporting time. The number of weeks or months it takes an editor to report back on an author's query or manuscript.

Reprint rights. Permission to print an already published work whose rights have been sold to another magazine or book publisher.

Roman à clef. French "novel with a key." A novel that represents actual living or historical characters and events in fictionalized form.

Romance. The genre relating accounts of passionate love and fictional heroic achievements.

Royalties. A percentage of the retail price paid to an author for each copy of the book that is sold.

SAE. Self-addressed envelope.

SASE. Self-addressed stamped envelope.

Science fiction. Genre in which scientific facts and hypotheses form the basis of actions and events.

Second serial (reprint) rights. Permission for the reprinting of a work in another periodical after its first publication in book or magazine form.

Self-publishing. In this arrangement, the author keeps all income derived from the book, but he pays for its manufacturing, production and marketing.

Sequel. A literary work that continues the narrative of a previous, related story or novel.

Serial rights. The rights given by an author to a publisher to print a piece in one or more periodicals.

Serialized novel. A book-length work of fiction published in sequential issues of a periodical.

Setting. The environment and time period during which the action of a story takes place.

Short short story. A condensed piece of fiction, usually under 700 words.

Simultaneous submission. The practice of sending copies of the same manuscript to several editors or publishers at the same time. Some people refuse to consider such submissions.

Slant. A story's particular approach or style, designed to appeal to the readers of a specific magazine.

Slice of life. A presentation of characters in a seemingly mundane situation which offers the reader a flash of illumination about the characters or their situation.

Slush pile. A stack of unsolicited manuscripts in the editorial offices of a publisher.

Social fiction. Fiction written with the purpose of bringing about positive changes in society.

Speculation (or Spec). An editor's agreement to look at an author's manuscript with no promise to purchase.

Speculative fiction (SpecFic). The all-inclusive term for science fiction, fantasy and horror.

Splatterpunk. Type of horror fiction known for its very violent and graphic content.

Subsidiary. An incorporated branch of a company or conglomerate (e.g. Alfred Knopf, Inc., a subsidiary of Random House, Inc.).

Subsidiary rights. All rights other than book publishing rights included in a book contract, such as paperback, book club and movie rights.

Subsidy publisher. A book publisher who charges the author for the cost of typesetting, printing and promoting a book. Also Vanity publisher.

Subterficial fiction. Innovative, challenging, nonconventional fiction in which what seems to be happening is the result of things not so easily perceived.

Suspense. A genre of fiction where the plot's primary function is to build a feeling of anticipation and fear in the reader over its possible outcome.

Synopsis. A brief summary of a story, novel or play. As part of a book proposal, it is a comprehensive summary condensed in a page or page and a half.

Tabloid. Publication printed on paper about half the size of a regular newspaper page (e.g. *The National Enquirer*).

Tearsheet. Page from a magazine containing a published story.

Theme. The dominant or central idea in a literary work; its message, moral or main thread.

Trade paperback. A softbound volume, usually around 5×8, published and designed for the general public, available mainly in bookstores.

Unsolicited manuscript. A story or novel manuscript that an editor did not specifically ask to see.

Vanity publisher. See Subsidy publisher.

Viewpoint. The position or attitude of the first- or third-person narrator or multiple narrators, which determines how a story's action is seen and evaluated.

Western. Genre with a setting in the West, usually between 1860-1890, with a formula plot about cowboys or other aspects of frontier life.

Whodunit. Genre dealing with murder, suspense and the detection of criminals.

Work-for-hire. Work that another party commissions you to do, generally for a flat fee. The creator does not own the copyright and therefore cannot sell any rights.

Young adult. The general classification of books written for readers 12-18.

Zine. Often one- or two-person operations run from the home of the publisher/editor. Themes tend to be specialized, personal, experimental and often controversial.

Category Index

Our Category Index makes it easy for you to identify publishers who are looking for a specific type of fiction. Under each fiction category are magazines and book publishers looking for that kind of fiction. Publishers who are not listed under a fiction category either accept all types of fiction or have not indicated specific subject preferences. Also not appearing here are listings that need very specific types of fiction, e.g., "fiction about fly fishing only." To use this index to find a book publisher for your mainstream novel, for instance, go to the Mainstream/Contemporary section and look under Book Publishers. Finally, read individual listings *carefully* to determine the publishers best suited to your work.

For a listing of agents and the types of fiction they represent, see the Literary Agents Category Index beginning on page 158.

ADVENTURE

Magazines

ALL CATEGORIES OF FICTION
Magazines

CHILDRENS/JUVENILE
Magazines

ETHNIC/MULTICULTURAL
Magazines

EXPERIMENTAL

Magazines

Book Publishers

FAMILY SAGA

Magazines

Book Publishers

FANTASY

Magazines

FEMINIST

Magazines

Book Publishers

GAY

Magazines

Book Publishers

HUMOR/SATIRE
Magazines

Book Publishers

MAINSTREAM/CONTEMPORARY

Magazines

Book Publishers

MILITARY/WAR

Magazines

Book Publishers

MYSTERY/SUSPENSE

Magazines

Book Publishers

NEW AGE/MYSTIC/SPIRITUAL
Magazines

Book Publishers

ONLINE MAGAZINES
Magazines

PSYCHIC/SUPERNATURAL/ OCCULT
Magazines

Book Publishers

REGIONAL
Magazines

RELIGIOUS/INSPIRATIONAL

Novel Writing Workshop: Iron out your plot, create your main characters, develop a dramatic background, and complete the opening scenes and summary of your novel's complete story. Plus, you'll pinpoint potential publishers for your type of book.

NEW! **Getting Started in Writing:** From short fiction and novels to articles and nonfiction books, we'll help you discover where your natural writing talents lie.

Writing & Selling Short Stories: Learn how to create believable characters, write vivid, true-to-life dialogue, fill your scenes with conflict, and keep your readers on the edge of their seats.

Writing & Selling Nonfiction Articles: Master the components for effective article writing and selling. You'll learn how to choose attention-grabbing topics, conduct stirring interviews, write compelling query letters, and slant a single article for a variety of publications.

Writing Your Life Stories: Learn how to weave the important events of your personal or family's history into a heartfelt story. You'll plan a writing strategy, complete a dateline of events, and discover how to combine factual events with narrative flow.

Writer's Digest Criticism Service: Have an experienced, published writer review your manuscripts before you submit them for pay. Whether you write books, articles, short stories or poetry, you'll get professional, objective feedback on what's working well, what needs strengthening, and which markets you should pursue.

The Elements of Effective Writing: Discover how to conquer the pesky grammar and usage problems that hold so many writers back. You'll refresh your basic English composition skills through step-by-step lessons and writing exercises designed to help keep your manuscripts out of the rejection pile.

Marketing Your Nonfiction Book: You'll work with your mentor to create a book proposal that you can send directly to a publisher, develop and refine your book idea, write a chapter-by-chapter outline of your subject, line up your sources and information, write sample chapters, and complete your query letter.

Screenwriting Workshop: Learn to write for the silver screen! Work step by step with a professional screenwriter to craft your script, find out how to research the right agent or producer for your work, and get indispensable information about the Hollywood submission process.

BUSINESS REPLY MAIL
FIRST-CLASS MAIL   PERMIT NO. 17   CINCINNATI OH

POSTAGE WILL BE PAID BY ADDRESSEE

WRITER'S DIGEST SCHOOL
1507 DANA AVE
CINCINNATI OH 45207-9965

ROMANCE

Magazines

Book Publishers

Book Publishers

SENIOR CITIZEN/RETIREMENT

Magazines

SERIALIZED/EXCERPTED NOVEL

Magazines

SHORT STORY COLLECTIONS

Magazines

Book Publishers

Book Publishers

WESTERN

Magazines

Book Publishers

YOUNG ADULT/TEEN

Magazines

Book Publishers

General Index

Markets that appeared in the 2001 edition of *Novel & Short Story Writer's Market* but are not included in this edition are identified by a two-letter code explaining why the market was omitted: **(ED)**—Editorial Decision, **(NS)**—Not Accepting Submissions, **(NR)**—No (or late) Response to Listing Request, **(OB)**—Out of Business, **(RR)**—Removed by Market's Request, **(UC)**—Unable to Contact, **(UF)**—Uncertain Future.